Statements on Auditing Standards (AICPA)—*Concluded*

SAS No.	Date Issued	Title	AU Section[1]
79	1995	Amendment to Statement on Auditing Standards No. 58, Reports on Audited Financial Statements	508
84	1997	Communications Between Predecessor and Successor Auditors	315
85	1997	Management Representations	333
86	1998	Amendment to *Statement on Auditing Standards No. 72*, Letters for Underwriters and Certain Other Requesting Parties	634
87	1998	Restricting the Use of an Auditor's Report	532
88	1999	Service Organizations and Reporting on Consistency	324, 420
89	1999	Audit Adjustments	333
90	1999	Audit Committee Communications	380
91	2000	Federal GAAP Hierarchy	411
92	2000	Auditing Derivative Instruments, Hedging Activities, and Investments in Securities	332
93	2000	Omnibus Statement on Auditing Standards—2000	Various
95	2001	Generally Accepted Auditing Standards	150
97	2002	Amendment to *Statement on Auditing Standards No. 50*, Reports on the Application of Accounting Principles	625
98	2002	Omnibus Statement on Auditing Standards—2002	Various
99	2002	Consideration of Fraud in a Financial Statement Audit	316
100	2002	Interim Financial Information	722
101	2003	Auditing Fair Value Measurements and Disclosures	328
102	2005	Defining Professional Requirements in Statements on Auditing Standards	120
103	2005	Audit Documentation	339
104	2006	Amendment to "Due Professional Care in the Performance of Work" of *Statement on Auditing Standards No. 1*, Codification of Auditing Standards and Procedures	230
105	2006	Amendment to *Statement on Auditing Standards No. 95*, Generally Accepted Auditing Standards	150
106	2006	Audit Evidence	326
107	2006	Audit Risk and Materiality in Conducting an Audit	312
108	2006	Planning and Supervision	311
109	2006	Understanding the Entity and Its Environment and Assessing the Risks of Material Misstatement	314
110	2006	Performing Audit Procedures in Response to Assessed Risks and Evaluating the Audit Evidence Obtained	318
111	2006	Amendment to *Statement on Auditing Standards No. 39*, Audit Sampling	350
112	2006	Communicating Internal Control Related Matters Identified in an Audit	325
113	2006	Omnibus Statement on Auditing Standards—2006	Various
114	2006	The Auditor's Communication With Those Charged With Governance	380

Statements on Standards for Attestation Engagements (AICPA)

SSAE No.	Date Issued	Title	AT Sec.
10	2001	Attest Engagements	101
10	2001	Agreed-Upon Procedures Engagements	201
10	2001	Financial Forecasts and Projections	301
10	2001	Reporting on ProForma Financial Information	401
10	2001	Reporting on an Entity's Internal Control Over Financial Reporting	501
10	2001	Compliance Attestation	601
10	2001	Management's Discussion and Analysis	701
10	2001	Attestation Standards: Revision and Recodification	Various
11	2002	Attest Documentation	Various
12	2002	Amendment to Statement on Standards for Attestation Engagements No. 10, *Attestation Standards: Revision and Recodification*	101
13	2005	Defining Professional Requirements in Statements on Standards for Attestation Engagements	20
14	2006	SSAE Hierarchy	50

Statements on Standards for Accounting and Review Services (AICPA)

SSAR No.	Date Issued	Title	AR Sec.
1	1978	Compilation and Review of Financial Statements	100
2	1979	Reporting on Comparative Financial Statements	200
3	1981	Compilation Reports on Financial Statements Included in Certain Prescribed Forms	300
4	1981	Communications Between Predecessor and Successor Accountants	400
6	1986	Reporting on Personal Financial Statements Included in Written Personal Financial Plans	600
7	1992	Omnibus Statement on Standards for Accounting and Review Services–1992	Various
8	2000	Amendment to Statement on Standards for Accounting and Review Services No. 1, *Compilation and Review of Financial Statements*	100
9	2002	Omnibus Statement on Standards for Accounting and Review Services–2002	Various
10	2004	Performance of Review Engagements	100
11	2004	Standards for Accounting and Review Services	200
12	2005	Omnibus Statement on Standards for Accounting and Review Services–2005	Various
13	2005	Compilation of Specified Elements Accounts, or Items of a Financial Statement	110
14	2005	Compilation of Pro Forma Financial Information	120
15	2007	Elimination of Certain References to Statements on Auditing Standards and Incorporation of Appropriate Guidance Into Statements on Standards for Accounting and Review Services	Various

Auditing &
Assurance Services

Auditing & Assurance Services

Timothy J. Louwers, PhD, CPA, CISA, CIA
Jackson E. Ramsey Centennial Chair in Business
James Madison University

Robert J. Ramsay, PhD, CPA
Arthur Andersen Alumni Professor of
Accounting
The University of Kentucky

David H. Sinason, PhD, CPA, CIA, CFE, CFSA
PricewaterhouseCoopers Professor of
Accountancy
Northern Illinois University

Jerry R. Strawser, PhD, CPA
KPMG Chair of Accounting
Texas A&M University

McGraw-Hill
Irwin

Boston Burr Ridge, IL Dubuque, IA New York San Francisco St. Louis
Bangkok Bogotá Caracas Kuala Lumpur Lisbon London Madrid Mexico City
Milan Montreal New Delhi Santiago Seoul Singapore Sydney Taipei Toronto

The McGraw·Hill Companies

 McGraw-Hill
Irwin

AUDITING & ASSURANCE SERVICES

Published by McGraw-Hill/Irwin, a business unit of The McGraw-Hill Companies, Inc., 1221 Avenue of the Americas, New York, NY, 10020. Copyright © 2008, 2007, 2005 by The McGraw-Hill Companies, Inc. All rights reserved. No part of this publication may be reproduced or distributed in any form or by any means, or stored in a database or retrieval system, without the prior written consent of The McGraw-Hill Companies, Inc., including, but not limited to, in any network or other electronic storage or transmission, or broadcast for distance learning.

Some ancillaries, including electronic and print components, may not be available to customers outside the United States.

This book is printed on acid-free paper.

4 5 6 7 8 9 0 QPD/QPD 0 9

ISBN 978-0-07-337936-4
MHID 0-07-337936-0

Executive editor: *Tim Vertovec*
Developmental editor: *Daryl Horrocks*
Marketing director: *Dan Silverburg*
Senior project manager: *Harvey Yep*
Production supervisor: *Gina Hangos*
Design manager: *Kami Carter*
Project manager: *Suresh Babu*
Cover design: *Kami Carter*
Interior design: *Kami Carter*
Typeface: *10.5/12 Times New Roman*
Compositor: *Aptara, Inc.*
Printer: *Quebecor World Dubuque Inc.*

Library of Congress Cataloging-in-Publication Data
Auditing & assurance services / Timothy J. Louwers, ... [et al.]. —3rd ed.
 p. cm.
 Includes index.
 ISBN-13: 978-0-07-337936-4 (alk. paper)
 ISBN-10: 0-07-337936-0 (alk. paper)
 1. Auditing. I. Louwers, Timothy J. II. Title: Auditing and assurance services.
HF5667.A815 2008
657'.45—dc22

 2007041256

www.mhhe.com

Some people come into our lives and quickly go. Some stay awhile and leave footprints on our hearts and we are never quite the same.

Anonymous

We dedicate this book to the following educators whose footprints we try to follow:

Professor Homer Bates
(University of North Florida)

Professor Lewis C. Buller
(Indiana State University)

Professor Patrick Delaney
(Northern Illinois University)

Professor William Hillison
(Florida State University)

Professor John Ivancevich
(University of Houston)

Professor Jack Robertson
(University of Texas at Austin)

Professor Robert Strawser
(Texas A&M University)

Professor "IBM Jim" Whitney
(The Citadel)

Meet the Authors

Timothy J. Louwers *teaches auditing at James Madison University, where he holds the Jackson E. Ramsey Centennial Chair in Business.*

Professor Louwers received his undergraduate and master's degrees from The Citadel and his Ph.D. from Florida State University. The American Accounting Association (AAA) recognized his doctoral dissertation examining the link between going concern opinions and auditors' loss functions as the 1994 Outstanding Auditing Dissertation. Prior to beginning his academic career, he worked in public accounting with KPMG specializing in financial, governmental, and information systems auditing. He is a Certified Public Accountant (South Carolina), a Certified Internal Auditor, and a Certified Information Systems Auditor.

Professor Louwers' research interests include auditors' reporting decisions and ethical issues in the accounting profession. He has authored or co-authored 10 books and almost 40 articles on a wide range of accounting, auditing, and technology-related topics, including publications in the *Journal of Accounting Research, Accounting Horizons, Behavioral Research in Accounting, Decision Sciences,* the *Journal of Forensic Accounting, Issues in Accounting Education,* the *Journal of Accountancy,* the *CPA Journal,* and *Today's CPA.* Some of his published work has been reprinted in Russian and Chinese. He is a respected lecturer on auditing and technology-related issues, and has received teaching excellence awards from the University of Houston and Louisiana State University. He has appeared on both local and national television news broadcasts, including MSNBC and CNN news programs.

Robert J. Ramsay *is the Arthur Andersen Alumni Professor of Accounting in The Von Allmen School of Accountancy at The University of Kentucky.*

Professor Ramsay completed his Ph.D. at Indiana University in 1991. He teaches auditing and advanced auditing. He has previously taught information systems, advanced managerial accounting, and a seminar on research in judgment and decision-making. His research interests relate to auditor judgment and decision-making.

Professor Ramsay has been active in the American Accounting Association, serving on the Professionalism and Ethics committee, the Notable Contributions to Accounting Literature Award Screening Committee, and the Annual Meeting Committee as auditing section chair. He is also active in the AAA Auditing section where he currently serves on the Auditing Standards committee, and previously served as chairman of the 2003 Mid-Year Meeting, and as a member of the nominations committee. Professor Ramsay worked nine years for Arthur Young & Company serving clients in the restaurant, mining, electronics, and manufacturing sectors. He also worked four years as Vice President, Controller for Chi-Chi's, Inc., a publicly held restaurant company. He currently serves on audit committees for two nonprofit agencies.

David H. Sinason *is the PricewaterhouseCoopers Professor of Accountancy at Northern Illinois University (NIU), and director of the NIU Internal Audit program.*

Professor Sinason received a B.S. in engineering from the University of Illinois; B.B.A. and M.Acc. in Accounting from the University of North Florida; and a Ph.D. in Accounting from Florida State University. He has certifications as a Certified Public Accountant, a Certified Internal Auditor, a Certified Financial Services Auditor, and a Certified Fraud Examiner. Professor Sinason has written articles for over 40 publications, mostly in the areas of assurance services, fraud prevention and detection, and auditor liability.

Professor Sinason has taught in the areas of accounting information systems, auditing and assurance services, and financial accounting. He has received teaching awards at each of the universities where he has taught including the 2002-2003 Department of Accountancy and Northern Illinois University Awards for Excellence in Undergraduate Teaching.

Jerry R. Strawser *is Interim Executive Vice President and Provost at Texas A&M University, and holds the KPMG Chair in Accounting.*

Prior to his current appointment, Professor Strawser served as Dean of Mays Business School at Texas A&M University, interim Dean of the C. T. Bauer College of Business at the University of Houston and Arthur Andersen & Co. Alumni Professor of Accounting.

Professor Strawser has co-authored three textbooks and over 60 journal articles. In addition to his academic experience, Professor Strawser had prior public accounting experience at two Big Five accounting firms. He has also developed and delivered numerous executive development programs to organizations such as Centerpoint Energy, Continental Airlines, ConocoPhillips, Halliburton, KPMG, Minute Maid, PricewaterhouseCoopers, McDermott International, Shell, Southwest Bank of Texas, and the Texas Society of Certified Public Accountants. Professor Strawser is a Certified Public Accountant in the state of Texas and earned his BBA and Ph.D. in Accounting from Texas A&M University. In addition, he currently serves on the Technical Standards Review Committee of the Texas State Board of Public Accountancy.

Brief Contents

Contents

Look Beneath The Surface...

As auditors, we are trained to investigate beyond appearances to determine the underlying facts—in other words, to *look beneath the surface*. The consequences of recent accounting scandals have made this skill even more crucial to the business community. Maintaining a clear perspective, probing for details, and understanding the big picture are indispensable to effective auditing. The author team of Louwers, Ramsay, Sinason, and Strawser has dedicated years of experience in the auditing field to this new edition of *Auditing & Assurance Services,* supplying the necessary investigative tools for future auditors.

Cutting-Edge Coverage

The third edition of *Auditing & Assurance Services* is the most up-to-date auditing text on the market. All chapters and modules in the third edition have been revised to incorporate professional standards through *SAS 114, AS 5,* and the international standards of auditing (ISAs). In addition, all chapters include new problems, Kaplan CPA Review simulations, and comprehensive case questions. Fraud awareness, a thorough understanding of internal controls, and the ability to use technology effectively are the hallmarks of a successful auditor in business today. With *Auditing & Assurance Services,* 3e, students are prepared to take on auditing's latest challenges.

Engage Your Students

An effective accounting textbook integrates real-world scenarios with theoretical discussion. *Auditing & Assurance Services* places the student in the role of decision maker, using situations from companies such as Time Warner, Disney, Hewlett-Packard, and Wal-Mart to illustrate the

> *"The tone of the textbook is in a conversational manner that allows for more student-friendly reading material."*
> —Aretha Hill, *Florida A&M University*

application of auditing concepts. Real-world in EACH chapter are pulled from recent headlines, including infamous accounting scandals at Siemens, HealthSouth, Adelphia Communications Corporation, and WorldCom. The Louwers author team uses a conversational, yet professional, tone—hailed by reviewers as a key strength of the book.

Market-Leading Technology

Auditing in modern business utilizes the latest technology. The author team of *Auditing & Assurance Services* added ACL software to the third edition so students can benefit from the kind of cutting-edge software they'll use the first day on the job. Exercises to accompany ACL are included on the book's Web site, www.mhhe.com/louwers3e. The expanded selection of Kaplan CPA Review audit simulations allows students to go online and complete simula-
tions similar to those on the CPA exam—seamlessly integrating technology with the textbook.

Fraud Awareness

The fraud coverage in *Auditing & Assurance Services* is the most extensive available and is complemented by real-world examples chosen to engage students. The authors use short "Auditing Insights" to provide real-life (and often humorous!) examples of fraud, as well as how auditors contributed to solving the case. Extended discussions of fraud cases at WorldCom, Enron, Freddie Mac, and Sunbeam, just to name a few, give students an inside view of fraud detection. Chapters 3 and 6 cover management and employee fraud, respectively, while Module D focuses on the Certified Fraud Examiner Exam. With the Apollo Shoes Case available online, *Auditing & Assurance Services* is truly the leading auditing textbook for fraud coverage.

CHAPTER THREE

Management Fraud and Audit Risk

Professional Standards References

Compendium Section	Document Reference	Topic
AU 310	SAS 83	"Establishing an Understanding with the Client"
AU 311	SAS 108	"Planning and Supervision"
	ISA 300	"Planning an Audit of Financial Statements"
AU 312	SAS 107	"Audit Risk and Materiality in Conducting an Audit"

Flexible Organization

Auditing & Assurance Services teaches students auditing concepts by emphasizing context and the auditing process. The authors use chapters and modules to achieve this goal:

> "The format allows you to integrate the modules into the chapter material in any format you would find useful."
> —Frank J. Beil, *University of Minnesota*

Chapters	Modules
The first 12 chapters cover the auditing process extensively, with a multitude of cases designed to give students a better understanding of how a best-practice concept developed from real-world situations.	Modules A–H provide instructors with additional material that can be used throughout the course. Topics such as fraud, ethics, sampling, and technology are covered in the modules, which are designed to be taught whenever instructors want to introduce the topic in their course.

Highlights of *Auditing & Assurance Services*, 3e

- Chapter 5 has been extensively updated with more emphasis on additional internal control auditing and reporting requirements of PCAOB *Auditing Standard No. 5 (AS 5)*.
- All chapters and modules have been revised to incorporate professional standards through *SAS 114* and now include international standards of auditing (ISAs).
- All chapters feature new end-of-chapter material, including Kaplan CPA Review simulations. The Kaplan simulations are available on the book's Online Learning Center (OLC), www.mhhe.com/louwers3e.
- A free copy of ACL auditing software is included with each copy of *Auditing & Assurance Services*. Selected chapters also include exercises to be used with the software (available on the book's OLC).
- Two new comprehensive cases on public accounting firm fees and indemnification clauses are included. All cases are now located after Module H.

New to The Third Edition of

Part I: The Contemporary Auditing Environment

CHAPTER 1: Auditing and Assurance Services
- Coverage of ISAs has been added.
- An Auditing Insight has been added for assurance services in the market for baseball cards.
- Assertions have been conformed to new auditing standards.
- GAO engagement examples have been updated.

CHAPTER 2: Professional Standards
- Coverage of the 10 GAAS has been revised to incorporate the most recent editorial and wording changes to these standards (provided by *SAS 113*).
- The most recent (2007) auditors' report for Wal-Mart Stores, Inc. has been included to demonstrate the four standards of reporting.
- Attestation standards have been revised to incorporate the most recent editorial and wording changes to these standards (*SSAE 114*).
- The discussion of the PCAOB's monitoring role has been expanded, including a summary of the findings from the most recent inspection reports for the Big Four firms.

CHAPTER 3: Management Fraud and Audit Risk
- Auditing Insights have been added that discuss illegal acts involving Siemens, fraud at HealthSouth, and additional verdicts for "When CEOs Go Bad."
- A discussion of the risk of material misstatement has been added to the discussion of the audit risk model.
- The exhibit entitled "General Categories of Errors and Frauds" has been expanded to include specific examples of frauds and errors.
- The exhibit listing assertions and related audit procedures has been expanded to include both the PCAOB and new ASB financial statement assertions.
- Although key examples, findings, and implications have been kept, the discussion of the effectiveness of audit procedures has been reduced.
- The discussions of audit procedures and audit programs have been reordered to increase readability and understandability.

Part II: The Financial Statement Audit

CHAPTER 4: Engagement Planning
- The ERM model has been further expanded and explained comparing Wal-Mart's timely response to Hurricane Katrina with FEMA's delayed response.
- The discussion of engagement letters has been expanded to include limited liability caps and indemnification clauses. A mini-case discussing the issue in depth also has been added.
- The discussion of working with internal auditors has been expanded as a result of *AS 5*.

CHAPTER 5: Risk Assessment: Internal Control Evaluation
- Krispy Kreme's management report on the company's numerous internal control deficiencies provides the introduction for the chapter.
- The chapter has an increased focus on assessing the risk of material misstatement (not just control risk).
- Two Auditing Insights for internal controls have been added, highlighting real-world examples of control deficiencies.
- A new discussion of entity-level controls has been added.

- The section discussing additional procedures required for publicly traded companies has been completely rewritten as a result of the issuance of *AS 5*.
- A summary of Moody's report on internal control deficiencies has been added.
- The definitions of significant deficiencies and material weaknesses have been amended and examples of each have been provided.
- A summary of evidence is provided on the question of whether Sarbanes-Oxley is working or not.
- Reports on internal control over financial reporting have been moved from Chapter 12 and expanded for more extensive coverage.
- New *AS 5* questions have been added to end-of-chapter materials.

CHAPTER 6: Employee Fraud and the Audit of Cash
- New ISAs and *AS 5* coverage have been added.
- New Auditing Insights—The Model Employee, Lapping up the Profits, Lack of Separation of Duties, Training to Catch Fraudulent Checks, and Payroll Fraud—have been added.
- All assertions have been conformed to new auditing standards.

Auditing & Assurance Services

CHAPTER 7: Revenue and Collection Cycle

- New ISAs and *AS 5* coverage have been added.
- Auditing Insights for TJ Maxx, PCAOB inspections, and the revenue and collection cycle have been added.
- The risk assessment discussion and assertions have been conformed to new auditing standards.
- The confirmation discussion has been updated for AICPA *Practice Alert 03-1: Audit Confirmations,* June 2007.
- Discussion of required disclosures for the revenue and collection cycle has been added.

CHAPTER 8: Acquisition and Expenditure Cycle

- New ISAs and *AS 5* coverage have been added.
- The risk assessment discussion has been conformed to new standards.
- Discussion has been added for auditing the income tax provision.
- Auditing Insights have been added for H&R Block and PCAOB inspections of the acquisition and expenditure cycle.
- Discussion has been added for the required disclosures for the acquisition and expenditure cycle.
- The payroll cycle has been shortened and moved from Chapter 5.

CHAPTER 9: Production Cycle

- New ISAs and *AS 5* coverage have been added.
- Risk assessment discussion has been conformed to new auditing standards.
- Assertions have been conformed to new auditing standards.
- A new section on the use of technology in taking inventory (using bar codes and RFID) has been added.
- Auditing Insights for lack of separation of duties, stolen inventory sold on eBay, using RFID to combat counterfeit fraud, and PCAOB inspections and the production cycle have been added.
- Analysis of presentation and disclosure of inventory in Boeing Corporation's 2006 annual report has been added.

CHAPTER 10: Finance and Investment Cycle

- New ISAs and *AS 5* coverage have been added.
- Risk assessment discussion has been conformed to new auditing standards.
- Assertions have been conformed to new auditing standards.

- Auditing Insights for watching out for leases, the importance of disclosure, how not disclosing information can hurt, and PCAOB inspections and the investment cycle have been added.

CHAPTER 11: Completing the Audit

- Merck's potential liabilities related to customer use of Vioxx are discussed in the section on auditing contingencies.
- The sample management representation letter has been modified to include matters identified by *AS 5*.
- An Auditing Insight has been added highlighting the recent failure of management representations involving KPMG and Gemstar-TV Guide.
- Other Auditing Insights involving Wal-Mart, PricewaterhouseCoopers, and Cisco Systems have been added.
- The discussion of adjustments has been expanded to include both the rollover method and iron-curtain method (with an example of each).
- The auditors' required communications with individuals charged with governance under *SAS 114* have been included.

CHAPTER 12: Reports on Audited Financial Statements

- Reports on internal control over financial reporting have been moved to Chapter 5 for more extensive coverage.
- The integrated report on the entity's financial statements and internal control over financial reporting has been modified in response to *AS 5*.
- The opening vignette discusses PricewaterhouseCoopers' reporting in the Adelphia Communications case.
- The auditors' standard report has been revised to focus on the PCAOB version.
- Reports issued in various scenarios have been revised to be derived from the same standard auditors' report to allow readers to more clearly see how these matters affect the content of auditors' reports.
- A schematic has been added to illustrate the auditors' various options when a division of responsibility exists.
- A summary table has been included that identifies how the standard report is modified for a variety of reporting issues.

Part III: Other Topics

MODULE A: Other Public Accounting Services

- The coverage of assurance services has been updated (e.g., a new WebTrust report has been included) but is being deemphasized with the profession's renewed focus on auditing engagements.
- Auditing Insights have been added summarizing recent academic research addressing prospective financial information and internal control attestation engagements and the value of "plain paper" financial statements.
- The discussion of reviews and compilations has been revised following recent SSAR issuances.
- A summary of the differences among audits, reviews, and compilations has been added.

MODULE B: Professional Ethics

- This module has been completely reorganized and rewritten. Additionally, interpretations formerly included in an appendix have been incorporated into the body of the text without reducing readability.
- Two Auditing Insights have been added addressing sanctions for wrongdoing, including the PCAOB censuring an accountant and China executing an accountant for committing fraud.
- An Auditing Insight has been added regarding client confidentiality.

MODULE C: Legal Liability

- An opening vignette discussing BDO Seidman's potential liability in the E.S. Bankest case and their decision to fight this case in court has been added.
- A summary of major settlements involving all of the Big Four firms has been included.
- A schematic illustrating the roles and responsibilities of auditors, clients, and third-party users of financial statements has been added to show how legal liability arises.
- The discussion of SEC filing processes and expanded discussion of auditors' liability under the Securities Acts has been greatly reduced.
- A table has been added that summarizes the parties involved, plaintiff proof, type of offense, and auditor defenses for common law liability and liability under the Securities Acts.
- The section that summarizes significant changes in the landscape of auditors' liability has been expanded.

MODULE D: Internal, Governmental, and Fraud Audits

- Two Auditing Insights—Who's Minding Cash and How Hard Did You Study for Your Last Exam?—have been added.

- Coverage of the reliance of Congress on the GAO has been added.
- The governmental audit section for new yellow book standards has been updated.

MODULE E: Overview of Sampling

- The risk assessment discussion has been conformed to new auditing standards.
- A brief discussion of audit sampling has been added so Module E can be used as a stand-alone chapter on sampling.
- This module has been updated for *SAS 111*.
- The results of the study "How Reliable Is Haphazard Sampling?" by Hall, Herron, and Pierce has been incorporated.
- An Auditing Insight for PCAOB inspections and sampling has been added.

MODULE F: Attribute Sampling

- The risk assessment discussion has been conformed to new auditing standards.
- A new section on nonstatistical attribute sampling has been added.

MODULE G: Variables Sampling

- The risk assessment discussion has been conformed to new auditing standards.
- An expanded discussion of dollar unit sampling includes effects of understatements.

MODULE H: Information Systems Auditing

- An opening vignette has been added that discusses weaknesses in Fannie Mae's information technology controls.
- A summary of examples from PCAOB inspection reports has been added.
- Summary tables for categories, examples, and objectives of ITGC, as well as a summary table of the different types of ITAC, have been added.
- Numerous Auditing Insights discussing issues related to information technology controls in business have been added.

Comprehensive Cases:

- Six comprehensive cases are now included: Arthur Andersen, HealthSouth Corporation, KPMG, Parmalat, General Electric, and a case concerning indemnification clauses.

Supplements

For Instructors . . .

INSTRUCTOR'S RESOURCE CD-ROM (ISBN 0073344885)

This all-in-one resource includes essential course supplements such as the EZ Test Bank, Instructor's Manual/Solutions Manual and PowerPoint® presentations. All items are prepared by the text authors.

ONLINE LEARNING CENTER (OLC)
www.mhhe.com/louwers3e

Instructors will find a wealth of material that complements *Auditing & Assurance Services,* including an electronic version of the Solutions Manual, solutions to the Apollo Shoes Case, monthly updates from the authors, sample syllabi, in addition to all of the material available on the Instructor's Resource CD-Rom. A monthly update service, the Updated Auditor, provides references and brief summaries of accounting and business articles appearing in popular and business media. Publications excerpted include *The Wall Street Journal, Forbes, Fortune, BusinessWeek, CFO.com, Auditing: A Journal of Practice and Theory,* and others. Students also can access the Kaplan CPA Review simulations from the Online Learning Center—all of which are fully integrated into the end-of-chapter material in the textbook.

For Students . . .

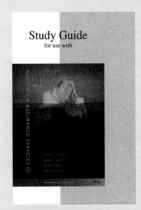

STUDY GUIDE (ISBN 0073344907)

The Study Guide reviews the highlights of *Auditing & Assurance Services* and includes an overview of each chapter in the textbook. Following each chapter summary is a self-assessment section that includes true/false, completion, and multiple choice questions, as well as problems. Solutions to all items in the self-assessment section are included.

ONLINE LEARNING CENTER (OLC)
www.mhhe.com/louwers3e

The OLC for *Auditing & Assurance Services* provides students with the full Apollo Shoes Case, the ONLY stand-alone fraud audit case on the market, Kaplan CPA Review simulations, text updates, multiple choice quizzes, flashcards, and chapter summaries.

Acknowledgments

OUR SINCEREST THANKS . . .

The American Institute of Certified Public Accountants (AICPA) has generously given permission for liberal quotations from official pronouncements and other AICPA publications, all of which lend authoritative sources to the text. In addition, several publishing houses, professional associations, and accounting firms have granted permission to quote and extract from their copyrighted material. Their cooperation is much appreciated because a great amount of significant auditing thought exists in this wide variety of sources.

A special acknowledgment is due the Association for Certified Fraud Examiners (ACFE). The ACFE has been a generous contributor to the fraud auditing material in this text. The authors also acknowledge the valuable inclusion of ACL software in the third edition, which significantly enhances the practical application of the book. A special thanks to Michael K. Shaub for his last-minute, valuable critique of Chapter 5.

Also, the authors are particularly grateful to Jeannie Folk of College of DuPage for her many insightful comments over the past two years. The feedback she contributed while teaching from the second edition has contributed greatly to the clarity and accuracy of the third edition.

We are also sincerely grateful to the following individuals for their participation in the review process for *Auditing & Assurance Services*:

Dawn P. Addington
Central New Mexico Community College

Michael D. Akers
Marquette University

Jeffrey J. Archambault
Marshall University

Jack Armitage
University of Nebraska–Omaha

MaryAnne Atkinson
Central Washington University

LuAnn Bean
Florida Institue of Technology

Frank J. Beil
University of Minnesota

Russell F. Briner
University of Texas at San Antonio

Suzanne M. Busch
California State University–East Bay

Eric Carlsen
Kean University

John Critchett
Madonna University

John E. Delaney
Southwestern Texas University

Tom English
Boise State University

Diana R. Franz
University of Toledo

David Gelb
Seton Hall University

Judith G. Grant
N. Virginia Community College at Annandale

James Hansen
University of Illinois at Chicago

Aretha Hill
Florida A&M University

Steven C. Hunt
Western Illinois University

Bonita K. Peterson Kramer
Montana State University–Bozeman

Joseph M. Larkin
St. Joseph's University

Pamela Legner
College of DuPage

R. D. Licastro
Penn State University at University Park

Maureen Mascha
Marquette University

Dorothy McMullen
Rider University

Bharat Merchant
Baruch College

Eddie Metrejean
Georgia Southern University

Charles Miller
California Polytech University

Perry Moore
Lipscomb University

Vincent Owhoso
Northern Kentucky University

Dwight M. Owsen
Long Island University

Gary Peters
University of Arkansas

Marshall K. Pitman
University of Texas at San Antonio

Kathy Pollock
*Indiana University–Purdue
University Fort Wayne*

Duane Ponko
Indiana University of Pennsylvania

Abdul Qastin
North Carolina A&T State

Hema Rao
SUNY–Oswego

Barbara Reider
University of Montana

John Rigsby
Mississippi State University

Maria Sanchez
Rider University

Bunney L. Schmidt
Utah Valley State College

Carol Shaver
Louisiana Tech University

Duane Smith
Brescia University

Beverly Strachan
Troy University at Montgomery

Iris Stuart
California State University

Christine N. Todd
Colorado State University–Pueblo

Jerry L. Turner
University of Memphis

J. Donald Warren Jr.
Rutgers University

Lin Zheng
Northeastern Illinois University

In addition, we would like to recognize our outstanding staff at McGraw-Hill/Irwin: Editorial Director, Stewart Mattson; Executive Editor, Tim Vertovec; Developmental Editor, Daryl Horrocks; Marketing Director, Dan Silverburg; Project Manager, Harvey Yep; Designer, Kami Carter; Media Producer, Suresh Babu; and Supplement Producer, Christine Vaughan. For their encouragement, assistance, and guidance in the production of this book, we are grateful.

Few understand the enormous commitment of time and energy that it takes to put together a textbook. As authors, we are constantly scanning *The Wall Street Journal* and other new outlets for real-world examples to illustrate theoretical discussions, rereading and rewriting each other's work to make sure that key concepts are understandable, and doublechecking our solutions to end-of-chapter problems. Among the few who do understand the time and energy commitment are our family members (Barbara Louwers; Sue Ramsay; Karen, Matthew, Joshua, and Adam Sinason; and Susan and Meghan Strawser) who uncomplainingly endured endless refrains of "I just need a couple more minutes to finish this section." Words cannot express our gratitude to each of them for their patience and unending support.

Tim Louwers
Bob Ramsay
Dave Sinason
Jerry Strawser

Auditing &
Assurance Services

Auditing and Assurance Services

Professional Standards References

Compendium Section	Document Reference	Topic
AU 110	SAS 1	"Responsibilities and Functions of the Independent Auditor"
	ISA 200	"Objective and General Principles Governing an Audit of Financial Statements"
AU 321	SAS 99	"Consideration of Fraud in a Financial Statement Audit"
	ISA 240	"The Audito"s Responsibility to Consider Fraud in an Audit of Financial Statements"
AU 326	SAS 106	"Audit Evidence"
	ISA 500	"Audit Evidence"
	ISA 501	"Audit Evidence—Additional Considerations for Specific Items"
AU 801	SAS 74	"Compliance Auditing Considerations in Audits of Governmental Entities and Recipients of Governmental Financial Assistance"

If you want to be successful, it's just this simple: Know what you're doing. Love what you're doing. And believe in what you're doing.

Will Rogers, Cowboy Philosopher

Learning Objectives

Your earlier accounting courses helped you learn accounting principles and practices. To be an auditor, however, knowledge of accounting rules is not enough. Not only must you be an excellent financial accountant (to ensure that clients are recording complex transactions correctly), you also must be part business advisor (to help clients establish strong internal control within their organizations), part industry expert (to ensure that you understand the environment in which the organization is operating), and part detective (to determine if clients are trying to fool you or others through fraudulent financial reporting). In other words, auditors are the "superheroes" of the business community, keeping the business world safe for the investing public. Chapter 1 provides an introduction to the auditing and assurance profession.

Your objectives are to be able to:

1. Define *information risk* and explain how auditing and assurance services play a role in reducing this business risk.

2. Define and contrast *auditing, attestation,* and *assurance services.*

3. Describe and define the management assertions embodied in financial statements and explain why auditors use them as a focal point of the audit.

4. Explain some characteristics of professional skepticism.

5. Describe the organization of public accounting firms and identify the various services they offer.

6. Describe the audits and auditors in governmental, internal, and operational auditing.

7. List and explain the requirements for becoming a certified information professional.

USER DEMAND FOR RELIABLE INFORMATION

LEARNING
OBJECTIVE

1. Define *information risk* and explain how auditing and assurance services play a role in reducing this business risk.

Enron, HealthSouth, Parmalat, Tyco, WorldCom, Fannie Mae, Hollinger International—the list of financial accounting frauds that have been uncovered over the past several years has shocked the business community. Investor confidence has been understandably shaken, causing stock prices across all companies and industries to plummet. Financial experts estimate that investors lost approximately $7 *trillion* over a three-year period from the capital markets' high levels of September 2000. Where were the auditors? How could they have missed such high-profile frauds? These questions are not easy to answer. Before we attempt to address these questions, we must first explain the vital role information assurance providers (such as auditors) play in supplying key decision makers (management, investors, and creditors) with useful, understandable, and timely information. When you have a better understanding of why auditing has been so critical in establishing America's capital markets as the strongest in the world, we will explore the issues surrounding the audit failures. As many of you plan to enter the public accounting profession, we hope that you will arm yourself with this knowledge so that you may help avoid similar problems in the future and play a role in restoring public confidence in both the auditing profession and U.S. capital markets.

Information and Information Risk

All businesses make a countless number of decisions each and every day. Decisions to purchase or sell goods or services, lend money, enter into employment agreements, or buy or sell investments depend in large part on the quality of useful information. These decisions affect *business risk,* the chance a company takes that customers will buy from competitors, that product lines will become obsolete, that taxes will increase, that government contracts will be lost, or that employees will go on strike. In other words, **business risk** is *the risk an entity will fail to meet its objectives.* (If the company fails to meet its objectives enough times, the company may ultimately fail.) To minimize these risks and take advantage of other opportunities presented in today's competitive economy, decision makers such as chief executive officers (CEOs) demand timely, relevant, and reliable information. Similarly, investors and creditors demand high-quality information to make educated financial decisions. Information professionals (such as accountants, auditors, and information assurance providers) help satisfy this demand.

Four environmental conditions increase user demand for relevant, reliable information:

1. *Complexity.* Events and transactions in today's economy are numerous and often very complicated. You may have studied derivative securities and hedging activities in other accounting courses, but investors and other decision makers may not have your same level of expertise when dealing with these complex transactions. Further, they are not trained to collect, compile, and summarize the key operating information themselves. They need the services of information professionals to make the information more understandable for their decision process.

2. *Remoteness.* Decision makers are usually separated from current and potential business partners, not only by a lack of expertise, but also by distance and time. Investors may not be able to visit distant locations to check up on their investments. They need to employ full-time information professionals to do the work they cannot do for themselves.

3. *Time-sensitivity.* Today's economic environment requires businesses, investors and other financial information users to make decisions more rapidly then ever before. The ability to promptly obtain high-quality information is essential to businesses that want to remain competitive in our global business environment.

4. *Consequences.* Decisions can involve significant investments of resources. The consequences are so important that reliable information, obtained and verified by information professionals, is an absolute necessity. Enron's aftermath provides a graphic example of how decisions affect individuals' (as well as companies') financial security and well-being. Enron's stock dropped from $90 to $0.90 in little more than a year, leaving employees who had invested their life savings in the company virtually penniless.

AUDITING INSIGHT The Consequences of Fraudulent Financial Information

Houston—Former Enron Corp. Chief Accounting Officer Richard Causey began serving his 5½ year prison term Tuesday for his role in the fraud that destroyed the company. Causey, 46, pleaded guilty to one count of securities fraud in December 2005, less than a month before he was to stand trial alongside former Chief Executive Jeffrey Skilling and company founder Kenneth Lay, both of whom were convicted. Causey was the last of 16 former executives to plead guilty to crimes at Enron, the world's largest

energy trading company before it plunged into bankruptcy in December 2001 as widespread accounting fraud came to light. More than 5,000 jobs and $1 billion in employee pensions vanished virtually overnight when Enron collapsed. Investors are suing to recover more than $30 billion in losses.

Source: "Former Accounting Chief Begins Prison Term for Securities Fraud," *Chicago Tribune*, January 3, 2007.

A further complication in effective decision making is the presence of information risk. **Information risk** is *the probability that the information circulated by a company will be false or misleading.* Decision makers usually obtain their information from companies or organizations with which they want to conduct business, to obtain (or provide) loans, or to buy or sell stock. Since the primary source of information is the target company itself, an incentive exists for that company's management to make their business or service appear to be better than it actually may be. Preparers and issuers of financial information (directors, managers, accountants, and other people employed in a business) might benefit by giving false, misleading, or overly optimistic information. This potential *conflict of interest* between information providers and users has become real often enough to create a natural skepticism on the part of users. Thus, they depend on information professionals to serve as objective intermediaries who will lend some credibility to the information. This "lending of credibility" to information is known as **assurance.** When the assurance is provided for specific assertions made by management (usually about financial information), we often refer to the assurance provided as **attestation.** When the assertions are embodied in a company's financial statements, we refer to the attestation as **auditing.** The following Auditing Insight box indicates how the quality of information can assist both buyers and sellers in today's market.

EXHIBIT 1.1
Professional Sports Authenticators as Third-Party Assurors

AUDITING INSIGHT

Exhibit 1.1 shows two 1976 Topps Mike Schmidt baseball cards. The card on the right was offered on eBay with the seller's representation that the card was in Near Mint/Mint condition. This representation is a standard description and is the equivalent of a grade 8 on a standard 10-point scale used in grading the quality of a trading card. The card was purchased on eBay for $11.55.

Within a week, a second 1976 Topps Mike Schmidt baseball card was sold on eBay. Again, this card was offered with the seller's representation that the card was in Near Mint/Mint condition (card on the left). The only difference was that this card had been sent to Professional Sports Authenticators (PSA), a company that receives and verifies the authenticity and quality

of sports items. Note, they do not buy or sell sports merchandise; they act as an independent third party expressing a professional opinion regarding the merchandise in question. This card sold for $22.53.

The only difference between the two transactions was that the buyers of the card on the right had more information risk inherent in the transaction. Why was the first transaction riskier? What were the buyers' concerns? Were the concerns only from intentional misstatements? How did the grading of the card by PSA reduce these concerns? What are the incentives for PSA to grade the card accurately? How does the business of PSA relate to the profession of auditing?

Review Checkpoints

1.1 What is business risk?

1.2 What conditions increase demand for relevant, reliable information?

1.3 What condition creates a demand for objective outsiders to provide assurance to decision makers?

AUDITING, ATTESTATION, AND ASSURANCE SERVICES

LEARNING OBJECTIVE

2. Define and contrast *auditing, attestation,* and *assurance services.*

Now that you understand why decision makers need independent information professionals to provide assurance on key information, we define further auditing and expand the discussion of attestation and assurance services in this section and explain their roles in today's "information economy."

Definition of Auditing

While assurance services include many areas of information, auditing refers specifically to the certification of financial statements. The most general definition of auditing comes from a committee of the American Accounting Association (AAA)—the organization of accounting professors. The AAA Committee on Basic Auditing Concepts defined **auditing** as follows:

> Auditing is a systematic process of objectively obtaining and evaluating evidence regarding assertions about economic actions and events to ascertain the degree of correspondence between the assertions and established criteria and communicating the results to interested users.[1]

This definition contains several ideas important in a wide variety of audit practices. Auditing is a *systematic process.* It is purposeful and logical and is based on the discipline of a structured approach to decision making. It is not haphazard, unplanned, or unstructured.

The process involves obtaining and evaluating *evidence.* Evidence consists of all influences that ultimately guide auditors' decisions and relates to *assertions about economic actions and events.* When beginning an audit engagement, an independent auditor is provided with financial statements and other disclosures by management and thus obtains management's explicit assertions about economic actions and events (listed assets really exist, recorded revenue transactions really occurred, the list of liabilities is complete, etc.), as well as implied assertions that the statements are fairly presented.

Independent auditors generally begin work with explicit representations from management—financial statement numbers and information disclosed in footnotes—and then set out to obtain evidence to prove or disprove these representations. Other auditors, however, often are not provided with explicit representations. An internal auditor may be assigned to evaluate the cost effectiveness of the company's policy to lease, rather than to purchase, heavy equipment. A governmental auditor may be assigned to determine whether goals of providing equal educational opportunity have been achieved with federal grant funds. Oftentimes, these latter two types of auditors must develop the explicit performance criteria for themselves.

[1] American Accounting Association Committee on Basic Auditing Concepts, *A Statement of Basic Auditing Concepts* (Sarasota, FL: American Accounting Association, 1973).

AUDITING INSIGHT

Although most of the largest accounting firms (collectively referred to as the "Big 4") trace their roots to the turn of the 19th century, auditing in the United States has a rich history. When the Pilgrims had a financial dispute with the English investors who financed their trip, an "auditor" was sent to resolve the difference. George Washington sent his financial records to the comptroller of the Treasury to be audited before he could be reimbursed for expenditures he made during the Revolutionary War. One of the first Congress's actions in 1789 was to set up an auditor to review and certify public accounts. Even the "modern" concept of an audit committee is not so modern; the bylaws of the Potomac Company, formed in 1784 to construct locks on the Potomac River to increase commerce, required that three shareholders annually examine the company's records.

Source: D. Flesher, G. Previts, and W. Samson, "Auditing in the United States: A Historical Perspective," *Abacus* 41 (2005), pp. 21–39.

The purpose of obtaining and evaluating evidence is to ascertain the degree of correspondence between the assertions and established criteria. Auditors will ultimately communicate their findings to interested users. To communicate in an efficient and understandable manner, auditors and users must have a common basis for measuring and describing financial information. This basis is the established criteria essential for effective communication.

Established criteria may be found in a variety of sources. For independent auditors, the criteria largely consist of the generally accepted accounting principles (GAAP). IRS agents rely heavily on criteria specified in the Internal Revenue Code. Governmental auditors may rely on criteria established in legislation or regulatory agency rules. Bank examiners and state insurance board auditors look to definitions and rules of law. Internal and governmental auditors rely a great deal on financial and managerial models of efficiency and economy. All auditors rely to some extent on elusive criteria of general truth and fairness.

Exhibit 1.2 depicts an overview of financial statement auditing.

EXHIBIT 1.2
Overview of Financial Statement Auditing

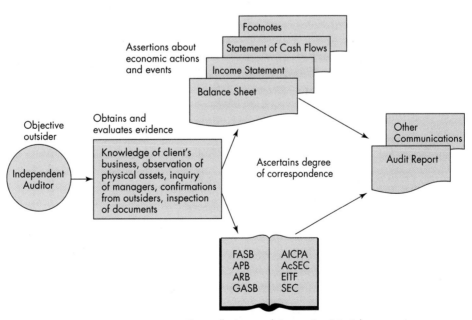

The American Accounting Association definition is broad and general enough to encompass independent (external), internal, and governmental auditing. The more specific viewpoint of external auditors in public accounting practice is reflected in the American Institute of Certified Public Accountants (CPAs) (AICPA) statement of the main objective of a financial statement audit:

> The objective of the ordinary examination of financial statements by the independent auditor is the expression of an opinion on the fairness with which they present, in all material respects, financial position, results of operations, and cash flows in conformity with generally accepted accounting principles. The auditor's report is the medium through which he expresses his opinion or, if circumstances require, disclaims an opinion. In either case, he states whether his examination has been made in accordance with generally accepted auditing standards. (*SAS 1*, AU 110.01)[2]

As your study of auditing continues, you will find that auditors perform many tasks designed to reduce the risk of giving an inappropriate opinion on financial statements. Auditors are careful to work for trustworthy clients, to gather and analyze evidence about the assertions in financial statements, and to take steps to ensure that audit personnel report properly on the financial statements when adverse information is known.

Attestation Engagements

Many people appreciate the value of auditors' attestations to historical financial statements, and they have found other financial information for Certified Public Accountants (CPAs) to *attest*. The all-inclusive definition of an **attest engagement** is

> An engagement in which a practitioner is engaged to issue or does issue a report on subject matter or an assertion about the subject matter that is the responsibility of another party. (*SSAE 10*, AT 101.01)

By comparing the AAA's earlier definition of auditing with the definition of attestation, you can see that the auditing definition is a specific type of attestation engagement. According to the earlier definition, in an audit engagement, an auditor (more specific than a *practitioner*) issues a report on assertions (financial statements) that are the responsibility of management. Other examples of attestation engagements accepted by CPAs (discussed in greater detail in Module A) appear in the following box.

Examples of Attestation Engagements

- **Agreed Upon Procedures Engagements** (AT 201), such as verifying inventory quantities and locations.
- **Examination or Review of Financial Forecasts and Projections** (AT 301), such as analysis of prospective or hypothetical "what if" financial statements for some time period *in the future* (e.g., what would the financial statements look like next year for two companies considering a merger?).
- **Examination or Review of Pro Forma Financial Information** (AT 401), such as retroactively analyzing the effect of a proposed or consummated transaction on the *historical* financial statements

"as if" that transaction had already occurred (e.g., what would the consolidated financial statements look like if two companies merged last year?).

- **Reporting on an Entity's Internal Control over Financial Reporting** (AT 501).
- **Compliance Attestation Engagements** (AT 601), such as ascertaining a client's compliance with debt covenants.
- **Examination of Management's Discussion and Analysis** (AT 701).

[2] The *Statements on Auditing Standards* (*SASs*) and *Statements on Standards for Attestation Engagements* (*SSAEs*) are authoritative AICPA pronouncements on auditing and attestation theory and practice. *Statements on Auditing Procedure* (*SAPs*) numbers 1–54 were codified into *SAS 1* in 1972. Statements on Auditing Standards are issued periodically. You can find the number of the most recent *SAS* or *SSAE* by referring to the AICPA Web site (www.aicpa.org). Throughout this text, *SAS* references are followed by parenthetical section numbers (e.g., AU 110.01), which refer to the *SAS* volumes published by AICPA. *SSAE* references are followed by parenthetical section numbers (e.g., AT 101.01), which refer to the SSAE volumes published by AICPA.

Assurance Services

While *auditing* refers specifically to expressing an opinion on financial statements and *attestation* refers to expressing an opinion on an expanded set of financial information beyond financial statements or a specified element of financial statement information, *assurance services* include many areas of information, including nonfinancial information.

Although the primary focus of our earlier discussion of information risk was in the context of economic decisions, information risk is present whenever a decision must be made when one does not have complete knowledge. The AICPA, the public accounting community's professional association, expanded the profession's traditional focus on accounting information to include all types of information, both financial and nonfinancial. The expanded services are collectively referred to as **assurance services:**

> Assurance services are independent professional services that improve the quality of information, or its context, for decision makers.[3]

The major elements, and boundaries, of the definition are

- *Independence.* CPAs want to preserve their attestation and audit reputations and competitive advantages by preserving integrity and objectivity when performing assurance services.
- *Professional services.* Virtually all work performed by CPAs (accounting, auditing, data management, taxation, management, marketing, finance) is defined as a "professional service" as long as it involves some element of judgment based on education and experience.
- *Improving the quality of information, or its context.* The emphasis is on "information"—CPAs' traditional stock in trade. CPAs can enhance quality by assuring users about the reliability and relevance of information, and these two features are closely related to the familiar credibility-lending products of attestation and audit services. "Context" is relevance in a different light. For assurance services, improving the context of information refers not to the information itself, but to how the information is used in a decision-making context. An example would be providing key information in a database that could be used by management to make important decisions.
- *For decision makers.* They are the "consumers" of assurance services, and they personify the consumer focus of new and different professional work. They may or may not be the "client" that pays the fee, and they may or may not be one of the parties to an assertion or other information. The decision makers are the beneficiaries of the

AUDITING INSIGHT WebTrust

When you buy music compact disks (CDs) online, you take a risk that the company is legitimate, that it will send you the CDs that you ordered on a timely basis, and that you can return a CD if it is defective in any way. You also must be concerned about entering private information such as a credit card number to make payment in a purchase transaction. You can control your risk when you buy online by limiting the amount of your purchase, by dealing only with reputable companies, or by paying through a third party (such as PayPal). An alternative way to control your risk is by making sure independent information professionals (such as CPAs) provide us assurance that the Web site is real, that the company will ship its products on a timely basis, and that the company honors its return policies.

Assurance practitioners developed the WebTrust service to examine commercial Web sites' operations. When the Web site of a business or organization has engaged the service and the practitioners have completed a review of its operations to ensure that they are conducted in accordance with the Web site's stated principles, the business is entitled to display a "WebTrust" icon. A user can click on the icon and read the assurance service report that gives comfort about the security of the transaction.

[3] Report of the Special Committee on Assurance Services (1997), available through the AICPA's Web site (www.aicpa.org).

assurance services. Depending upon the assignment, decision makers may be a very small, targeted group (e.g., managers of a database) or a large targeted group (e.g., potential investors interested in a mutual fund manager's performance).

Examples of Assurance Services

While they are subsets of assurance services, attestation and audit services are highly structured and intended to be useful for large groups of decision makers (e.g., investors, lenders). On the other hand, assurance services other than audit and attestation services tend to be more customized for use by smaller, targeted groups of decision makers. In this sense, nonaudit assurance services bear some resemblance to consulting services. The AICPA conducted surveys and found hundreds of examples of current and potential assurance services. We present a few examples of assurance services to illustrate the variety of services that fall under the assurance service umbrella. Some will look familiar and others may defy imagination. Be aware, however, that the possibilities for assurance services may lie within the expertise of some but not all CPA firms—nobody maintains that all CPA firms will want or be able to provide all the assurance services.

- Internet Web site certification (WebTrust).
- Business risk assessment (Risk Advisory).
- Accounts receivable review and cash enhancement.
- Third-party reimbursement maximization.
- Rental property operations review.
- Customer satisfaction surveys.
- Benchmarking/best practices (Performance View).
- Evaluation of investment management policies.
- Fraud and illegal acts prevention and deterrence.
- Information systems security reviews (SysTrust).
- Internal audit outsourcing.

Attestation and audit services are special types of assurance services, but consulting services are not. In providing consulting services, CPAs use their professional skills and experiences to provide recommendations to a client for outcomes like information system design and operation; in assurance services, the focus is entirely on the information that decision makers use. However, like consulting services, assurance services have a "customer focus," and CPAs develop assurance services that add value for customers (decision makers).

Exhibit 1.3 depicts the relationships among assurance, attestation, and auditing services.

AUDITING INSIGHT Fore!

Wilson Sporting Goods Company is using CPAs to prove that amateur golfers can hit Wilson's Ultra golf ball farther than they can hit competitors' golf balls. Wilson says the CPAs certify that Wilson's Ultra outdistances its competitors by an average of 5.7 yards per drive. While Marlene Baddeloo, the engagement manager for the accounting firm that oversees Wilson's golf ball competitions, concedes "anyone could pace off a golf driving range to see how far a ball goes," she says firm staffers have checked that Wilson employees haven't doctored the results at more than 30 driving ranges. "We also make sure the amateurs participating aren't affiliated with Wilson or its competitors and haven't been paid to participate." Providing assurance on golf ball distance is certainly a unique engagement for a CPA firm, but it sure makes the firm's employees happy. "Our personnel love . . . [to] wear shorts and spend the day out in the air," says Ms. Baddeloo. "I get a lot of volunteers."

Source: Lee Berton, "After This, CPAs May Take Over Instant-Replay Duties for Football," *The Wall Street Journal,* July 9, 1991, p. B1.

EXHIBIT 1.3
The Relationships among Auditing, Attestation, and Assurance Engagements

Although audits are specific types of assurance engagements, and auditors can be described more generally as information assurors, hereafter we will use the term *auditor* instead of *information assuror* because of the specific responsibilities that auditors have under generally accepted auditing standards (GAAS), as well as under regulatory bodies such as the Securities and Exchange Commission (SEC). However, many of the procedures that auditors perform as part of an audit engagement are similar to those performed as part of other information assurance engagements. We will point out these shared procedures when appropriate.

Review Checkpoints

1.4 Define and explain auditing. What would you answer if asked by an anthropology major, "What do auditors do?"

1.5 What is an *attest engagement?*

1.6 What is an *assurance engagement?*

1.7 In what ways are assurance services similar in general to attestation services (including audits of financial statements)?

1.8 What are the four major elements of the broad definition of assurance services?

MANAGEMENT'S ASSERTIONS EMBODIED IN THE FINANCIAL STATEMENTS

LEARNING OBJECTIVE

3. Describe and define the management assertions embodied in financial statements and explain why auditors use them as a focal point of the audit.

From your earlier studies, you know that accounting is the process of recording, classifying, and summarizing into financial statements a company's transactions that create assets, liabilities, equities, revenues, and expenses. It is the means of satisfying users' demands for financial information that arise from the forces of complexity, remoteness, time-sensitivity, and consequences.

Auditing does not include the function of financial report production. The function of **financial reporting** is to provide statements of financial position (balance sheets), results of operations (income statements, statements of shareholders' equity, and statements of comprehensive income), changes in cash flows (statements of cash flows), and accompanying disclosures (footnotes) to outside decision makers who do not have access to management's internal sources of information. A company's accountants, under the direction of its management, perform this function. In fact, auditing standards emphasize that the financial statements are the responsibility of a company's management. Thus, the financial statements contain management's assertions about *transactions and events* that occurred during the period being audited (primarily the income statement, statement of

AUDITING INSIGHT — Sarbanes-Oxley and Management's Responsibility for Financial Reporting

Congress passed the Sarbanes-Oxley Act in 2002 in an attempt to address a number of weaknesses found in corporate financial reporting in the wake of recent accounting scandals. One of its most important provisions (Section 302) states that the key company officials must *certify* the financial statements. Certification means that the company's chief executive officer and chief financial officer must sign a statement indicating

1. They have read the financial statements.
2. They are not aware of any false or misleading statements (or any key omitted disclosures).

3. They believe that the financial statements present an accurate picture of the company's financial condition.

Management must also make assertions regarding the effectiveness of the company's internal controls over financial reporting.

Source: U.S. Congress, *Sarbanes-Oxley Act of 2002*, Pub. L. No. 107-204, 116 Stat. 745 (2002).

shareholders' equity, statement of comprehensive income, and statement of cash flows), assertions about *account balances* at the end of the period (primarily the balance sheet), and assertions about financial statement *presentation and disclosure* (primarily the footnote disclosures).

Auditors use management's assertions when assessing risks by determining the different types of misstatements that could occur and developing audit procedures that are appropriate in the circumstances. Auditors then report to the users that the assertions are reliable by expressing an opinion that the company's presentation of financial position, results of operations, and cash flows are fairly presented in accordance with generally accepted accounting principles. As you study this section, keep in mind this scheme of things.

Exhibit 1.4 provides a list of all of management's assertions and some of the key questions that the audit team must address. Note that column 1 in Exhibit 1.4 denotes the

EXHIBIT 1.4
Management Assertions

| (1) PCAOB Assertions | ASB Assertions | | | (5) |
	(2) Assertions about Events and Transactions	(3) Assertions about Account Balances	(4) Assertions about Presentation and Footnote Disclosures	Key Questions
Existence or occurrence	Occurrence	Existence	Occurrence	Did the recorded sales transactions really occur? Do the assets listed really exist?
Rights and obligations		Rights and obligations	Rights and obligations	Does the company really own the assets? Are related legal responsibilities identified?
Completeness	Completeness Cutoff	Completeness	Completeness	Are the financial statements (including footnotes) complete? Were all transactions recorded?
Valuation or allocation	Accuracy	Accuracy Valuation	Accuracy Valuation	Are the accounts valued correctly? Are expenses allocated to the period(s) benefited?
Presentation and disclosure	Classification		Classification Understandability	Were all transactions recorded in the correct accounts?

traditional management assertions, currently used by the Public Company Accounting Oversight Board (PCAOB)[4] and most CPA firms. Recently, the Auditing Standards Board (ASB)[5] provided an additional classification of management assertions (columns 2 through 4 in Exhibit 1.4). The key questions (column 5) indicate how each of these assertions, both PCAOB and ASB, are utilized when evaluating specific aspects of management's financial statements and disclosures. Each of the assertions is defined and described in detail in the following sections, organized along the lines of the traditional assertions identified in column 1.

Existence or Occurrence (Existence, Occurrence)

Numbers on financial statements are meaningless unless they *faithfully represent* actual transactions, assets, and liabilities of the company. (Note: As a general rule, the *occurrence* transaction relates to events and transactions (as indicated in column 2 of Exhibit 1.4), while the *existence* assertion relates to account balances (as indicated in column 3).) Therefore, auditors must view the balance sheet as management's assertions that reported assets, liabilities, and equities actually exist. To test the existence assertion, auditors count cash and inventory, confirm receivables and insurance policies with customers, and perform other procedures to obtain evidence whether management is in fact correct. Similarly, management asserts that each of the revenue and expense transactions summarized on the income statement or disclosed in the financial statement footnotes really occurred during the period being audited. As an auditor, you must develop audit procedures to ensure that the reported sales transactions really occurred and were not created to fraudulently inflate the company's profits.

AUDITING INSIGHT Q: When Is a Sale of Computer Disk Drives Not a Sale?
A: When They Are Bricks.

Miniscribe was a manufacturer of computer disk drives. When sales did not occur at a sufficient level to support the company's efforts to obtain outside financing, management generated fictitious sales to fraudulently boost the company's net income. After first sending obsolete inventory to customers who never ordered the goods, the company packaged bricks (about the same size and shape as the company's disk drives) in disk drive boxes and shipped them to "customers" that were in fact company-owned warehouses.

Rights and Obligations

The objective related to rights and obligations is to establish that amounts reported as assets of the company represent its property rights and that the amounts reported as liabilities represent its obligations. In simpler terms, the objective is to obtain evidence about *owning* and *owing.* You should be careful about *ownership,* however, because the idea includes assets (rights) for which a company does not actually hold title. For example, an auditor will have a specific objective of obtaining evidence about the amounts capitalized for leased property. Likewise, *owing* includes "accounting liabilities" a company may not yet be legally obligated to pay. For example, specific objectives would include obtaining evidence about the estimated liability for product warranties. The auditor has an obligation to ensure that the details of the company's obligations are disclosed in the footnotes to the financial statements.

[4] The Public Company Accounting Oversight Board (PCAOB) is a division of the Securities and Exchange Commission (SEC) that has been charged with regulating audits of publicly traded companies. The PCAOB is discussed in more detail in Chapter 2.

[5] The Auditing Standards Board (ASB) was established by the profession to issue auditing standards. Standards issued by the ASB apply to audits of all companies. The ASB is discussed in more detail in Chapter 2.

AUDITING INSIGHT ⟩ Is Your Telephone Bill an Asset?

WorldCom leased telephone lines (basically the last segment entering subscribers' homes) from local telephone companies. Rather than record the expiration of the operating leases as an expense, the company capitalized them as assets, resulting in an estimated $11 *billion* fraud. WorldCom management argued that since the leased lines were not fully used to capacity, the expense should be deferred until the lines started to produce revenue (i.e., the matching concept). Moreover, because they controlled the telephone lines as a result of the long-term lease agreements, no one else could use the telephone lines and, therefore, the exclusivity rights should be treated as an asset. (This explanation is analogous to your saying that your monthly phone bill expense is really an asset, because no one else can use your phone number while you use it.) An internal auditor uncovered the fraud and reported her findings to the company's board of directors.

Completeness (Completeness, Cutoff)

Management asserts that all transactions, events, assets, liabilities, and equities that should have been recorded have been recorded. Further, management asserts that all disclosures that should have been discussed in the footnotes have been included. Thus, auditors' specific objectives include obtaining evidence to determine whether, for example, all inventory on hand is included, all inventory on consignment is included, all inventory held on consignment is excluded, all notes payable are reported, all expenses are recorded, and so forth. A verbal or written management representation saying that all transactions are included in the accounts is not considered a sufficient basis for deciding whether the completeness assertion is true. Auditors need to obtain persuasive evidence about completeness.

Cutoff is a special aspect of completeness. **Cutoff** refers to accounting for revenue, expense, and other transactions in the *proper period* (neither postponing some recordings to the next period nor accelerating next-period transactions into the current-year accounts). Simple cutoff errors can occur when (1) a company records late December sales invoices for goods not actually shipped until January; (2) a company records cash receipts through the end of the week (e.g., Friday, January 4) and the last batch for the year should have been processed on December 31; (3) a company fails to record accruals for expenses incurred but not yet paid, thus understating both expenses and liabilities; (4) a company fails to record purchases of materials not yet received and, therefore, not included in the ending inventory, thus understating both inventory and accounts payable; and (5) a company fails to accrue unbilled revenue through the fiscal year-end for customers on a cycle billing system, thus understating both revenue and accounts receivable. In auditor's jargon, the **cutoff date** refers to the client's year-end balance sheet date.

Valuation and Allocation (Accuracy or Valuation)

Management asserts that the transactions and events have been recorded accurately and that account balances have been valued correctly. The audit objective related to valuation and allocation is to determine whether proper values have been assigned to assets, liabilities, and equities. Accuracy refers to the appropriate recording of these items. Auditors obtain evidence about specific valuations and mathematical accuracy by comparing vendors' invoices to inventory prices, obtaining lower-of-cost-or-market data, evaluating collectibility of receivables, recalculating depreciation schedules, and so forth. Many valuation, accuracy, and allocation decisions amount to decisions about the proper application of GAAP.

Presentation and Disclosure (Classification, Understandability)

Management asserts that all transactions and events have been presented correctly and that all relevant information has been disclosed to financial statement users, usually in the footnotes to the financial statements. This assertion embodies several different components.

AUDITING INSIGHT Say What?

Financial analysts generally regarded Enron's financial disclosures in its annual report as incomprehensible. In fact, Enron's management took pride in the fact that no one could figure out what they were doing to generate incredibly high revenues. A 2003 Congressional Joint Committee on Taxation concluded that Enron's tax avoidance schemes (including 692 partnerships in the Cayman Islands) were "so complex that the IRS has been unable to understand them" (*The New York Times*, February 13, 2003). Following is an excerpt from *Enron's 2001 Annual Report* describing some of its business activities:

> Trading Activities. Enron offers price risk management services to wholesale, commercial and industrial customers through a variety of financial and other instruments including forward contracts involving physical delivery, swap agreements, which require payments to (or receipt of payments from) counterparties based on the differential between a fixed and variable price for the commodity, options and other contractual arrangements. Interest rate risks and foreign currency risks associated with the fair value of the commodity portfolio are managed using a variety of financial instruments, including financial futures.

Unfortunately, because of the incomprehensibility of its financial disclosures, no one realized the extreme risks that the company was taking until it was too late. The company, which reported the fifth highest revenues in the United States in 2000, filed for bankruptcy in 2001.

First, disclosures must be relevant (e.g., footnote disclosure of important accounting policies) and reliable.

Second, transactions must be classified in the correct accounts (e.g., proper current and long-term balance sheet classification of liabilities). To test this assertion, auditors perform audit procedures such as analyzing repair and maintenance expenses to ensure that that they should in fact be expensed, rather than capitalized. Similarly, auditors will test from the opposite direction, examining additions to buildings and equipment to ensure that transactions that should have been expensed were not in fact capitalized.

Third, to be useful to decision makers, information must be understandable. *Statement of Financial Accounting Concepts (SFAC) No. 2,* "Qualitative Characteristics of Accounting Information," defines *understandability* as "the quality of information that enables users to perceive its significance." The responsibility levied on auditors is to make sure that the financial statements are "transparent." In other words, investors should be able to understand how the company is doing by reading a company's financial statements and footnotes, and not have to rely on additional financial experts to help them figure out what the fine print is saying. Another way to regard this assertion is to ask whether the disclosures have been written in *plain English*.

Importance of Assertions

Financial statement assertions are important and fairly complicated. The key questions that must be answered become the focal points for audit procedures. In other words, audit procedures are the means to answer the key questions posed by management's assertions. When evidence-gathering procedures are specified, you should be able to relate the evidence produced by each procedure to one or more specific assertions. The secret to writing and reviewing a list of audit procedures is to ask, "Which assertion(s) does this procedure produce evidence about?" Then ask, "Does the list of procedures (the audit program) cover all the assertions?" Exhibit 1.5 illustrates how the assertions relate to the financial statements.

While standard-setting bodies try to neatly categorize transactions, balances, and disclosures by the different assertions, the *real world* is seldom as orderly. For example, while cutoff procedures provide evidence about completeness, they also provide evidence about valuation and existence. Premature recording of sales transactions inflates revenue and/or asset values because the transaction did not *occur* by the income statement date. Similarly, if a cutoff test shows a delay in recording a liability, the liability is not only incomplete, but *undervalued* as well. Thus, errors in financial statements may affect multiple management assertions.

EXHIBIT 1.5 Assertions and Their Relationship to the Financial Statements

STATEMENT OF FINANCIAL CONDITION
APOLLO SHOES INC.
in thousands

As of December 31	2006	2005
Assets		
Cash	$3,245	$3,509
Accounts Receivable (Net of Allowances of $1,263 and 210, respectively) (Note 3)	15,148	2,738
Inventory (Note 4)	15,813	13,823
Prepaid Expenses	951	352
Current Assets	$35,157	$20,422
Property, Plant, and Equipment (Note 5)	1,174	300
Less Accumulated Depreciation	(164)	(31)
	$1,010	$269
Investments (Note 6)	613	613
Other Assets	14	0
Total Assets	$36,794	$21,304
Liabilities and Shareholders' Equity		
Accounts Payable and Accrued Expenses	$4,675	$3,556
Short-Term Liabilities (Note 7)	10,000	0
Current Liabilities	$14,675	3,556
Long-Term Debt (Note 7)	0	0
Total Liabilities	$14,675	3,556
Common Stock	8,105	8,105
Additional Paid-in Capital	7,743	7,743
Retained Earnings	6,271	1,900
Total Shareholders' Equity	$22,119	$17,748
Total Liabilities and Shareholders' Equity	$36,794	$21,304

The accompanying notes are an integral part of the consolidated financial statements.

Existence—Does this cash really exist?

Rights and Obligations—Does the company really own this inventory?

Valuation and Allocation—Are these investments properly valued?

Occurrence—Did these sales transactions really take place?

Completeness—Are all the expenses included? Are they recorded in the correct period?

STATEMENTS OF INCOME
APOLLO SHOES INC.
in thousands (except per share data)

For year ended December 31,	2006	2005
Net Sales (Note 2)	$240,575	$236,299
Cost of Sales	$141,569	$120,880
Gross Profit	$99,006	$115,419
Selling, General and Administrative Expenses	$71,998	$61,949
Interest Expense (Note 7)	$875	0
Other Expense (Income)	($204)	($1,210)
Earnings from Continuing Operations Before Taxes	$26,337	$54,680
Income Tax Expense (Note 10)	$10,271	$21,634
Earnings from Continuing Operations	$16,066	$33,046
Discontinued Operations, Net of tax benefit		($31,301)
Extraordinary Item, Net of tax benefit (Note 11)	($11,695)	
Net Income	$4,371	$1,745
Earnings Per Common Share		
From Continuing Operations	$1.98	$4.08
Other	($1.44)	($3.86)
Net Income	$0.54	$0.22
Weighted shares of common stock outstanding	8,105	8,105

The accompanying notes are an integral part of the consolidated financial statements.

NOTES TO CONSOLIDATED FINANCIAL STATEMENTS
APOLLO SHOES, INC.

1. Summary of Significant Accounting Policies

Business activity The Company develops and markets technologically superior podiatric athletic products under various trademarks, including *SIREN, SPOTLIGHT,* and *SPEAKERSHOE.*

Marketable Securities Investments are valued using the market value method for investments of less than 20%, and by the equity method for investments greater than 20% but less than 50%.

Cash equivalents Cash equivalents are defined as highly liquid investments with original maturities of three months or less at date of purchase.

Inventory valuation Inventories are stated at the lower of First-in, First-out (FIFO) or market.

Property and equipment and depreciation Property and equipment are stated at cost. The Company uses the straight-line method of depreciation for all additions to property, plant and equipment.

Intangibles Intangibles are amortized on the straight-line method over periods benefited.

Net Sales Sales for 2006 and 2005 are presented net of sales returns and allowances of $4.5 million, and $0.9 million, respectively, and net of warranty expenses of $ 1.1 million, and $0.9 million, respectively.

Income taxes Deferred income taxes are provided for the tax effects of timing differences in reporting the results of operations for financial statements and income tax purposes, and relate principally to valuation reserves for accounts receivable and inventory, accelerated depreciation and unearned compensation.

Net income per common share Net income per common share is computed based on the weighted average number of common and common equivalent shares outstanding for the period.

Reclassification Certain amounts have been reclassified to conform to the 2006 presentation.

2. Significant Customers

Approximately 15%, and 11% of sales are to one customer for years ended December 31, 2006 and 2005, respectively.

Presentation and Disclosure—Are these disclosures understandable? Has everything been disclosed that should be?

Review Checkpoints

1.9 What is the difference between auditing and accounting?

1.10 List and briefly explain the Auditing Standards Board's major assertions that can be made in financial statements and auditors' objectives. List some key questions related to each.

1.11 Why are the Auditing Standards Board's assertions important to auditors? Do these assertions differ from those included in PCAOB standards? If so, how are they different?

AUDITING INSIGHT Professional Skepticism

"Doveryai no Proveryai" (Trust, but Verify)
—Ronald Reagan to Soviet Prime Minister Gorbachev during Cold War missile reduction talks.

MANAGEMENT EXPLANATIONS

Explanations received from an entity's management are merely the first step in an engagement process, not the last. Listen to the explanation, and then examine or test it by looking at sufficient competent audit evidence. The familiar phrase "healthy skepticism" should be viewed as a show-me attitude, not a predisposition to accepting unsubstantiated explanations.

DEALING WITH FORMER CO-WORKERS

If a close relationship previously existed between the auditor and a former colleague now employed by a client, the auditor must guard against being too trusting in accepting representations about the client's financial statements. Otherwise, the auditor may rely too heavily on the word of a former associate, overlooking the fact that a common interest no longer exists.

Source: AICPA, *Audit Risk Alert* (1993, 1994).

While these concerns regarding *professional skepticism* were disseminated many years ago, they not only hold true today, but have been emphasized with addition standards and regulation. *SAS 99* requires a heightened level of professional skepticism when dealing with fraud. In addition, PCAOB regulation prohibits auditors from auditing former employers until a sufficient time has passed to ensure no appearance of impropriety.

PROFESSIONAL SKEPTICISM

LEARNING OBJECTIVE

4. Explain some characteristics of professional skepticism.

Professional skepticism is an auditor's tendency *not* to accept management assertions without corroboration, a tendency to ask management to "prove it" (with evidence). The occurrence of errors and fraud in financial reports dictates this basic aspect of professional skepticism: *A potential conflict of interests always exists between the auditors and the management of the enterprise under audit.* This potential conflict arises because management wants to present the company in the best possible light, while auditors must ensure that the information about the company's financial condition is "presented fairly."

Having recognized this potential conflict, auditors must be professional in their relationships with management, not adversarial or confrontational. Nevertheless, knowing that a potential conflict of interests always exists causes auditors to perform procedures to search for errors and frauds that could have a material effect on financial statements. Even though the vast majority of audits do not contain fraud, auditors have responded by performing additional work in all audits because of misdeeds perpetrated by a few people in a few companies.

Persuading a skeptical auditor is not impossible, just somewhat more difficult than persuading a normal person in an everyday context. Skepticism is a manifestation of objectivity—holding no special concern for preconceived conclusions on any side of an issue. Skepticism is not being cynical, hypercritical, or scornful. The properly skeptical auditor asks these questions: (1) What do I need to know? (2) How well do I know it? (3) Does it make sense?

Professional skepticism should lead auditors to appropriate inquiry about every hint of possible fraud. Auditors must gather the evidence needed, uncover all of the implications from the evidence, and then arrive at the most appropriate and supportable conclusion. Time pressure to complete an assurance engagement is no excuse for failing to exercise professional skepticism. Too many auditors have gotten themselves into trouble by accepting a manager's glib explanation and stopping too early in an investigation without seeking facts.

Even so, auditors must be careful. Once an engagement is under way and procedures designed to search for errors and frauds have found none, the engagement team must be willing to accept the apparent fact that there is no evidence that the potential conflict is real.

Still, due professional care requires a disposition to question all material assertions made by management whether oral or written. This attitude must be balanced by an open

mind about the integrity of management. Auditors should neither blindly assume that every management is dishonest nor thoughtlessly assume management to be perfectly honest. The key lies in auditors' attitude toward gathering the evidence necessary to reach reasonable and supportable conclusions.

Review Checkpoint

1.12 Why should auditors act as though there is always a potential conflict of interest between the auditor and the management of the enterprise under audit?

PUBLIC ACCOUNTING

LEARNING OBJECTIVE

5. Describe the organization of public accounting firms and identify the various services they offer.

Many people think of public accounting, financial statement auditing, and information assurance services in terms of the largest international accounting firms. Notwithstanding this perception, the practice of public accounting is conducted in thousands of practice units ranging in size from sole proprietorships (individuals who "hang out the shingle") to the largest international firms with thousands of professionals. Further, many public accounting firms no longer designate themselves as "CPA firms." Many of them describe their businesses and their organizations as "professional services" firms, or some variation on these terms. Exhibit 1.6 shows an organization for a typical public accounting firm. However, some firms differ in their organization. Some have other departments such as small business advisory and forensic accounting. Other firms may be organized by industry (e.g., entertainment, oil and gas, health care, financial institutions) to take advantage of firmwide expertise. Some firms have other names for their staff and management positions.

Assurance Services

Assurance services involve the lending of credibility to information, whether financial or nonfinancial. CPAs have assured vote counts (Academy Awards), dollar amounts of prizes that sweepstakes have claimed to award, accuracy of advertisements, investment performance statistics, and characteristics claimed for computer software programs. While assurance services (separate and distinct from auditing) currently represent a fairly small part of a normal firm's operating revenues, the AICPA has made a considerable effort to sell the public and businesses on these additional services.

EXHIBIT 1.6
CPA Firm Organization

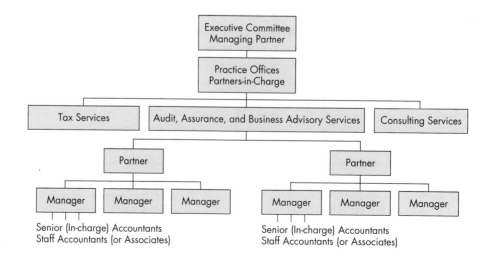

AUDIT INSIGHT — Pushing the Envelopes

On Oscar night, Hollywood's Best Kept Secret Award surely goes to the six-member team of hard-working PricewaterhouseCoopers (PWC) accountants. Charged with counting the ballots and keeping them safely padlocked until the big night, the PWC crew puts in ten 12-hour days in the weeks leading up to the Oscars. They even commit the winners to memory, in case one of the starry-eyed presenters loses the envelope. Here's the behind-the-scenes peek into Hollywood's most sacrosanct ritual:

- 1,700 "person hours" for PWC to count and verify the ballots by hand.
- 420,000 ballots counted by PWC during its 73 years on the job.
- 2,449 winners' envelopes stuffed by the PWC team since 1941.

Source: "Pushing the Envelopes," *BusinessWeek,* February 5, 2007.

Assurance services include audit engagements and attestation engagements. We discuss these services as a component of assurance services that professional service firms offer.

Audit Services

Most of the large, international accounting (Big 4) firms were founded around the turn of the 20th century (late 1800s/early 1900s) during the Industrial Revolution as European financiers sent representatives (individuals whom we now refer to as "auditors") to check up on their investments (mostly railroads) in the United States. As such, the primary focus of their practice has been traditional accounting and auditing services. Audits of traditional financial statements remain the most frequent type of assurance engagement that public companies (and most large and medium nonpublic companies) demand. Exhibit 1.7 shows the auditing (and other assurance services) revenues of the Big 4 accounting firms based on their 2006 annual reports. This level of auditing activity dramatically drops as the size of the public accounting firm decreases. In other words, smaller firms usually provide other nonaudit attestation engagements.

Nonaudit Attestation Engagements

Accounting and review services are "nonaudit" services, performed frequently for medium and small businesses and not-for-profit organizations. Smaller accounting firms

EXHIBIT 1.7 **Revenue for the Big Four CPA Firms**

	Deloitte & Touche[1]	Ernst & Young[2]	KPMG[3]	PricewaterhouseCoopers[4]
Total revenues (in billions)	$20.0	$18.3	$16.9	$21.9
Auditing and assurance services revenues (in billions and as a percent of revenue)	$9.8 49%	$12.1 66%	$8.27 49%	$11.3 52%
Tax revenues (in billions and as a percent of revenue)	$4.3 22%	$4.7 25%	$3.3 19%	$5.0 22%
Consulting and advisory services revenues (in billions and as a percent of revenue)	$6.0 30%	$1.9 10.4%	$5.28 31.2%	$4.3 19.6%

[1]Deloitte.com, Facts and figures.
[2]Ernst and Young Global Review 2006.
[3]KPMG International Annual Review 2006.
[4]PWC.com, Facts and figures.

AUDITING INSIGHT Audit Fees Continue to Grow

Over two-thirds of a sample of 30 Dow Jones Industrial Index companies experienced at least a 40 percent increase in their auditing fees from 2003 to 2004. This represents 65 percent of the total fees received by accounting firms, which is up from 30 percent four years ago. General Electric's audit fee was the largest ($78.2 million of total fees of $102.6 million), while United Technologies' fee increased by the greatest percentage (more than 50 percent). The provisions of Sarbanes-Oxley are largely responsible for this increase.

Source: "Audit Fees Surged in 2004," *CFO.com*, March 28, 2005.

perform a great deal of nonaudit work. For example, CPAs can perform a *compilation,* which consists of preparing financial statements from a client's books and records, without performing any evidence-gathering work. They also can perform a *review,* in which limited evidence-gathering work is performed, but which is narrower in scope than an audit. Although these are the most common attestation engagements, CPAs also can attest to the accuracy of management's discussion and analysis (MD&A) that accompanies the financial statements in an annual report, an entity's internal controls, and hypothetical "what-if" projections relating to mergers or acquisitions.

Tax Services

Local, state, national, and international tax laws are often called "accountant and attorney full-employment acts"! The laws are complex and CPAs perform services of tax planning and tax return preparation in the areas of income, gift, estate, property, and other taxation. A large proportion of the practice in small accounting firms is tax practice. Tax laws change frequently and tax practitioners must spend considerable time in continuing education and self-study to keep current. Exhibit 1.7 shows the tax revenues of the Big 4 accounting firms based on their 2006 annual reports. Smaller professional services firms tend to do more tax consulting engagements and fewer audit engagements.

The role of tax consulting in a professional services firm has been under recent scrutiny. The *Statements on Responsibilities in Tax Practice* specifically state that "A CPA has both the right and responsibility to be an advocate for the client" in arguing tax positions with the IRS [TX 112.04]. Can the CPA be an advocate for the client with respect to tax matters and maintain objectivity with regard to other audit matters? Recent guidance from the Public Company Accounting Oversight Board (PCAOB) prohibits an accounting firm from providing audit services to a public company if the accounting firm provides tax consulting on aggressive interpretations of tax laws or "listed" transactions (those included on the U.S. Treasury Department's list of questionable tax strategies), if contingent fees (i.e., fees depending on a certain outcome) are involved, or if the accounting firm provides tax services for key company executives. In all three cases, the PCAOB argues that auditor independence would be impaired. Providing normal corporate tax return preparation and advice is permissible, as long as the audit committee discusses with the accounting firm the implications of the tax consulting fees on auditor independence and preapproves the relationship in writing.

Consulting Services

Prior to the turn of this century (the 1990s), the largest accounting firms handled a great deal of consulting business. Consulting and management advisory services seemed to present a great new revenue opportunity, and the field appeared to be virtually unlimited. Accounting firms tried to become "one-stop shopping centers" for clients' auditing, taxation, and business advice needs.

AUDITING INSIGHT The Taxman Cometh

There is a fine line between tax avoidance and tax evasion. KPMG, one of the Big 4 accounting firms, fired three partners, including the head of its tax shelter services division, following a criminal investigation by the Department of Justice into the firm's sales of abusive or illegal tax shelters. KPMG reached a $465 million deferred-prosecution agreement with the Department of Justice in 2005 in order to avoid criminal indictment (which would likely force the firm out of business). Yet, 16 former KPMG employees are scheduled to stand trial on criminal issues stemming from the tax shelters. Further, four current and former partners of Ernst & Young are currently charged with tax fraud conspiracy over work on questionable tax shelters.

Sources: "KPMG Ousts Executive, Partners; Steps Tied to Tax-Shelter Scrutiny," *The Wall Street Journal*, April 28, 2005, p. C2: "Four Men, but Not Ernst & Young Are Charged in Tax Shelter Case," *New York Times*, May 31, 2007, Section C, P. 3.

The Securities and Exchange Commission (SEC), the governmental agency charged with investor protection, expressed reservations as to whether the performance of nonaudit services (such as consulting) impaired a CPA firm's ability to conduct an independent audit. The SEC's concern was that the large amount of revenues generated from consulting services might sway the auditor's opinion on the company's financial statements. The CPA firms, on the other hand, argued that the provision of consulting services allowed them a closer look at the client's operations, providing a synergistic, positive effect on the audit.

In response to the spate of corporate frauds, Congress resolved this difference of opinion by passing the Sarbanes-Oxley Act of 2002 (hereafter referred to as *Sarbanes-Oxley*), a broad accounting and corporate governance reform measure. Sarbanes-Oxley prohibits professional service firms from providing any of the following services to a publicly traded audit client: (1) bookkeeping and related services; (2) design or implementation of financial information systems; (3) appraisal or valuation services; (4) actuarial services; (5) internal audit outsourcing; (6) management or human resources services; (7) investment or broker/dealer services; and (8) legal and expert services (unrelated to the audit). Professional service firms may provide general corporate tax return preparation and advice and other nonprohibited services to public audit clients if the company's audit committee has approved them in advance. To briefly summarize these restrictions, Sarbanes-Oxley prohibits professional service firms from performing any client services in which the auditors may find themselves making managerial decisions or auditing their own firm's work.

Although consulting services approached almost 50 percent of a professional service firm's business in the 1990s, firm consulting revenues have fallen to between 10 and 30 percent of the Big 4 firms' total revenues in 2006 (see Exhibit 1.7). This decrease is due to both the divestiture of many firms' consulting practices (partially in response to Sarbanes-Oxley audit client service restrictions) as well as increases in audit revenues as a result of Sarbanes-Oxley's increased audit requirements.

Smaller CPA firms are not required to follow Sarbanes-Oxley guidelines for their non-SEC clients. Often, private businesses regard their CPA firms as business partners that can provide an array of services and a wealth of business information.

Review Checkpoints

1.13 What are some examples of assurance services performed on nonfinancial information?

1.14 What are some of the major areas of public accounting services?

OTHER KINDS OF ENGAGEMENTS AND INFORMATION PROFESSIONALS

LEARNING OBJECTIVE

6. Describe the audits and auditors in governmental, internal, and operational auditing.

The AAA and the AICPA definitions clearly apply to the financial audit practice of independent external auditors who practice auditing in public accounting firms. The word *audit*, however, is used in other contexts to describe broader types of work.

The variety of engagements performed by different kinds of information assurors causes some problems with terminology. In this textbook, *independent auditor, external auditor,* and *CPA* will refer to people doing audit work with public accounting firms. In the internal and governmental contexts discussed below, auditors are identified as *operational auditors, internal auditors,* and *governmental auditors.* Although all of these professionals are information assurors (and many are certified public accountants), the term *CPA* in this book will refer to auditors in public practice.

Internal Auditing

In 1999, the Board of Directors of the Institute of Internal Auditors (IIA) redefined **internal auditing** and stated its objective as follows:

> Internal auditing is an independent, objective assurance and consulting activity that adds value to and improves an organization's operations. It helps an organization accomplish its objectives by bringing a systematic, disciplined approach to evaluate and improve the effectiveness of risk management, control, and governance processes.[6]

Internal auditors are employed by organizations such as banks, hospitals, city governments, and industrial companies or work for CPA firms that provide internal audit services. Internal auditors often perform *operational audits*. **Operational auditing** refers to the study of business operations for the purpose of making recommendations about the efficient and effective use of resources, effective achievement of business objectives, and compliance with company policies. The goal of operational auditing is to help managers discharge their management responsibilities and improve profitability.

Internal auditors also perform audits of financial reports for internal use or limited external distribution (e.g., reports to regulatory agencies), much like external auditors audit financial statements distributed to outside users. Thus, some internal auditing work is similar to the auditing described elsewhere in this textbook. In addition, the services provided by internal auditors include (1) reviews of internal control systems to ensure compliance with company policies, plans, and procedures; (2) compliance with laws and regulations; (3) appraisals of the *economy* and *efficiency* of operations; and (4) reviews of effectiveness in achieving program results in comparison to established objectives and goals.

It should be noted that the AICPA defines operational auditing performed by independent CPA firms as a distinct type of management consulting service whose goal is to help a client improve the use of its capabilities and resources to achieve its objectives. So internal auditors consider operational auditing integral to internal auditing and external auditors define it as a type of assurance service offered by public accounting firms. Providing these types of internal audit services has been a growing business for many large CPA firms. However, both the SEC and the PCAOB prohibit CPA firms from providing these services to publicly traded audit clients.

Governmental Auditing

The U.S. Government Accountability Office (GAO) is an accounting, auditing, and investigating agency of the U.S. Congress, headed by the U.S. comptroller general. In one sense, GAO auditors are the highest level of internal auditors for the federal government. Many states have audit agencies similar to the GAO. These agencies

[6] This definition and other information about internal auditing may be found on the Institute of Internal Auditors' Web site (www.theiia.org).

answer to state legislatures and perform the same types of work described in the following GAO definition. In another sense, GAO and similar state agencies are really external auditors with respect to government agencies they audit because they are organizationally independent.

Many government agencies have their own internal auditors and inspectors general. Well-managed local governments also have internal audit departments. For example, most federal agencies (Department of Defense, Department of Human Resources, Department of the Interior), state agencies (education, welfare, controller), and local governments (cities, counties, tax districts) have internal audit staffs. Governmental and internal auditors have much in common.

The GAO shares with internal auditors the same elements of *expanded-scope* services. The GAO, however, emphasizes the accountability of public officials for the efficient, economical, and effective use of public funds and other resources. The generally accepted government auditing standards (GAGAS) define and describe *expanded-scope* governmental auditing as follows:

> The term "audit" includes both financial and performance audits . . . Financial related audits include determining whether (1) financial information is presented in accordance with established . . . criteria [e.g. GAAP], (2) the entity has adhered to specific financial compliance requirements [with laws and regulations], and (3) the entity's internal control . . . over financial reporting and/or safeguarding assets is suitably designed and implemented to achieve the control objectives . . . Performance audits include economy and efficiency audits and program audits.[7]

In this definition, you can see the attest function applied to financial reports and a compliance audit function applied with respect to laws and regulations. All government organizations, programs, activities, and functions are created by law and are surrounded by regulations that govern the things they can and cannot do. For example, a program established to provide school meals to low-income students must comply with regulations about the eligibility of recipients. A compliance audit of such a program involves a study of schools' policies, procedures, and performance in determining eligibility and handing out meal tickets.

Also in this definition, you see *performance audits* referring to a category that includes two types: (1) economy and efficiency audits and (2) program audits. Governments are concerned about accountability for the appropriate use of taxpayers' resources; performance audits are a means of seeking to improve accountability for the efficient and economical use of resources and the achievement of program goals. In addition, the program audit helps determine if the financial resources being spent are helping the government achieve its stated objectives. Performance audits, like internal auditors' operational audits, involve studies of the management of government organizations, programs, activities, and functions.

Regulatory Auditors

For the sake of clarity, other kinds of auditors deserve separate mention. The U.S. Internal Revenue Service employs auditors. They take the "economic assertions" of taxable income made by taxpayers in tax returns and determine their correspondence with the standards found in the Internal Revenue Code. They also audit for fraud and tax evasion. Their reports can either clear a taxpayer's return or claim that additional taxes are due.

State and federal bank examiners audit banks, savings and loan associations, and other financial institutions for evidence of solvency and compliance with banking and other related laws and regulations. In the 1980s and early 1990s, these examiners made news as a result of the large number of failures of U.S. financial institutions.

[7] The complete Government Auditing Standards can be found on the GAO's Web site (www.gao.gov).

- *Purchase of Degrees from Diploma Mills* (GAO-03-269R).
- *Financial Audit: Independent and Special Council Expenditures for the Six Months Ended September 30, 2006* (GAO-07-531).
- *Battlefield Automation: Army Needs to Update Fielding Plan for First Digitized Corps* (NSIAD-00-167).
- *Information Security: Further Efforts Needed to Address Significant Weaknesses at the Internal Revenue Service* (GAO-07-364).

- *NASA: Issues Surrounding the Transition from the Space Shuttle to the Next Generation of Human Space Flight Systems* (GAO-07-595T).
- *Government Records: Results of a Search for Records Concerning the 1947 Crash Near Roswell, New Mexico* (GAO/NSIAD-95-187).

Review Checkpoints

1.15 What is *operational* auditing? How does the AICPA view operational auditing?

1.16 What are the elements of *expanded-scope* auditing according to the GAO?

1.17 What is *compliance* auditing?

1.18 Name some other types of auditors in addition to external, internal, and governmental auditors.

BECOME CERTIFIED!

LEARNING OBJECTIVE

7. List and explain the requirements for becoming a certified information professional.

If you plan a career in accounting (which we hope you do given that you are reading this book!), certification is the key to a successful career. While being certified as a certified public accountant (CPA) is generally regarded as the highest mark of distinction in the public accounting profession, other certifications may be more applicable to your chosen career aspirations. For example, a certified internal auditor (CIA) certification or certified management accountant (CMA) certification may be equally acceptable for those individuals working with companies to achieve specific goals, both financial and nonfinancial. Other certifications available in the fraud auditing and forensic accounting fields include the certified fraud examiner (CFE) and the certified forensic accountant (CFA) certifications. If you enjoy information systems, key certifications include the certified information systems auditor (CISA) and the certified information systems security professional (CISSP). Regardless of your career choice, a certification adds credibility that will assist you throughout your career.

Education

Education requirements vary across certifying organizations. For the CPA certification, state boards of accountancy, regulatory agencies in each state, set the education requirements for taking the CPA examination and receiving a CPA certificate. Most states presently require 150 semester hours of college education as a condition for sitting for the CPA examination. Other certifications (such as the CIA) allow you to take the exam before you have graduated. In fact, the IIA allows students to take the CIA exam for half price!

In addition to entry-level education requirements, all certifying organizations have regulations about *continuing professional education* (CPE). At present, the AICPA and most states require 120 contact hours (not semester or quarter college hours) over three-year reporting periods with no less than 20 hours in any one year. Once certified, you can obtain CPE hours in a variety of ways: continuing education courses, in-house training, college courses, and private-provider courses. These types of courses range in

length from one hour to two weeks, depending on the subject. Many CPE providers offer courses online.

Examination

The AICPA Board of Examiners administers the Uniform CPA Examination. The 14-hour computer-based examination was revised in 2004. The exam now covers the following subjects:

Topic	Weight
Auditing & Attestation (4.5 hours)	100%
Financial Accounting & Reporting (4 hours)	
Financial statements	80%
Governmental entities	10%
Not-for-profit organizations	10%
Regulation (3 hours)	
Taxation	60%
Law & Professional Responsibilities (all areas other than Business Structure)	40%
Business Environment & Concepts (2.5 hours)	
Business Structure	20%
Financial management	20%
Planning and Measurement (managerial)	25%
Information Technology	25%
Economics	10%

Source: www.gleim.com

Although the Uniform CPA Examination consists mostly of multiple-choice question testlets (24–30 questions each), the Board of Examiners has introduced simulation problems to the exam. Simulations are realistic, 30- to 50-minute case studies in which you will have to apply your accounting and auditing knowledge. A simulation may involve identifying a potential problem, electronically researching the topic using a database of authoritative standards, and reporting your findings. Other simulations may involve using spreadsheet software to compare a company's performance during the current year as opposed to the previous year and identifying potential causes of any identified changes. The exam is kept "TOP SECRET" (and revealing any exam secrets can result in our certifications being revoked), but we have attempted to try to provide our version of simulations in the end-of-chapter materials in subsequent chapters.

General information about the examination can be obtained from the AICPA pamphlet "Information for CPA Candidates." This information is also available online (www.cpa-exam.org). Because qualifications for taking the CPA examination vary from state to state, you should contact your state board of accountancy for an application or more information. You can find your state board of accountancy Web site through the National Association of State Boards of Accountancy (NASBA) Web site (www.nasba.org). Exhibit 1.8 lists the requirements for the most common recognized professional certifications.

Experience

Although not required to *sit* for a professional exam, experience is required to *become certified*. Most states and territories require a person who has attained the education level and passed the CPA examination to have a period of experience working under a practicing CPA before awarding a CPA certificate. Experience requirements vary across states, but the most common system requires two years for holders of bachelor's degrees and one year for holders of master's degrees. A few states require that the experience be obtained in a public accounting firm, but most of them accept experience in other organizations (GAO, internal audit, management accounting, Internal Revenue Service, and the like) as

EXHIBIT 1.8
Certification Requirements

	Certified Public Accountant (CPA)	Certified Information Systems Auditor (CISA)	Certified Internal Auditor (CIA)	Certified Fraud Examiner (CFE)	Certified Management Accountant (CMA)
Education Level	Varies by state. Check with your state board of accountancy	No specific degree requirement	Bachelor's degree or its educational equivalent	Bachelor's degree or its educational equivalent	Bachelor's degree, or pass the CPA examination, or score in the 50th percentile on the GMAT
Experience	Varies by state. Check with your state board of accountancy	5 years of professional IS auditing, control, or security work experience for certification	2 years of internal auditing experience or its equivalent for certification	2 years of professional experience for certification	2 continuous years of professional experience in management accounting and/or financial management
Exam Coverage	1. Auditing and attestation 2. Financial accounting and reporting 3. Regulation 4. Business environment and concepts	1. Information systems (IS) audit process 2. Information technology (IT) governance 3. Systems and infrastructure life cycle management 4. IT service delivery and support 5. Protection of information assets 6. Business continuity and disaster recovery	1. The internal audit activity's role in governance, risk, and control 2. Conducting the internal audit engagement 3. Business analysis and information technology 4. Business management skill	1. Fraudulent transactions 2. Legal elements of fraud 3. Fraud investigation 4. Criminology and ethic	1. Business analysis 2. Management accounting and reporting 3. Strategic management 4. Business applications
Test Length	4 parts, 14 hours	1 part, 4 hours (200 m/c questions)	4 parts (125 m/c questions each), 14 hours	4 parts (125 m/c questions each), 10 hours	12 hours
Passing Score	75%	75%	75%	75%	70%
Test Dates	On demand	June, December	On demand	Self-administered	On demand
Administering Body	American Institute of Certified Public Accountants	Information Systems Audit and Control Association	Institute of Internal Auditors	Association of Certified Fraud Examiners	Institute of Management Accountants
Web site	www.aicpa.org	www.isaca.org	www.theiia.org	www.cfenet.com	www.imanet.org

long as the applicant performs work requiring accounting judgment and is supervised by a competent accountant, preferably a CPA. Other certifying organizations also have experience requirements.

AUDITING INSIGHT Auditors Make a Run for the Border

Efforts are currently underway through the AICPA and NASBA to streamline the reciprocity process so that CPAs can practice across state lines without having to have 50 different licenses. Recently, the concept of *substantial equivalency* was introduced. As long as the licensing (home) state requires (1) 150 hours of education, (2) successful completion of the CPA exam, and (3) one year of experience, a CPA can practice (either in person or electronically) in another substantial equivalency state without having to obtain a license in that state. This arrangement is temporary, however. A CPA who relocates to another state must seek licensing in that state. One KPMG CPA is in trouble for practicing in Texas since 1981 without ever having obtained a Texas license.

Source: "Accounting across State Lines," *AccountingWeb*, August 1, 2005.

State Certificate and License

The AICPA does not issue CPA certificates or licenses to practice. Although the National Association of State Boards of Accountancy (NASBA) and the AICPA are making efforts, national or international CPA certificates do not exist. All states and territories have state accountancy laws and state licensing boards to administer them. After satisfying state requirements for education and experience, successful candidates receive their CPA certificate from their state board of accountancy. At the same time, new CPAs must pay a fee to obtain a state license to practice. Thereafter, state boards of accountancy regulate the behavior of CPAs under their jurisdiction (enforcing state codes of ethics) and supervise the continuing education requirements.

After becoming a CPA licensed in one state, a person can obtain a CPA certificate and license in another state. The process is known as **reciprocity.** CPAs can file the proper application with another state board of accountancy, meet the state's requirements, and obtain another CPA certificate. Many CPAs hold certificates and licenses in several states. From a global perspective, individuals must be licensed in each country. Similar to CPAs in the United States, *Chartered Accountants* (CAs) practice in Canada, Australia, and Great Britain.

Skills Sets and Your Education

The requirements to become certified are rather strenuous, but they may not be enough! Let us take you on a brief tour of the core competencies listed by the AICPA, the Association of Certified Fraud Examiners (ACFE), the Institute of Internal Auditors (IIA), the Institute of Management Accountants (IMA), the Information Systems Audit and Control Association (ISACA), and other guidance-providing groups: history, international culture, psychology, economics, mathematics (calculus and statistics), national and international political science, art, literature, inductive and deductive reasoning, ethics, group dynamic processes, legal-political-social forces impinging on business, finance, capital markets, managing change, history of accounting, regulation, information systems, taxation, and (oh, yes) accounting and auditing. And administrative capability, analytical skills, business knowledge, communication skills (writing and speaking), efficiency, intellectual capability, marketing and selling, model building, people development, capacity for putting client needs first, and more.

We hope you are suitably impressed by this recitation of virtually all of the world's knowledge. You will be very old when you accomplish a fraction of the skills development and education suggested. Now the good news: (1) not everyone needs to be completely knowledgeable in all of these areas upon graduation from college; (2) learning and skill development evolve over a lifetime; and (3) no one expects you to know everything and operate as a "Lone Ranger." Audit teams composed of members specializing in some areas with other members specializing in others seem to work best in practice. We do, however, stress the need to continue your education, even after you leave school. Learning should be a lifelong pursuit, not something that ends when you receive your diploma.

Review Checkpoints

1.19 Why is continuing education required to maintain certification?

1.20 Why do you think experience is required to become certified?

1.21 What are some of the functions of a state board of public accountancy?

1.22 What are some of the limitations to practicing public accounting across state and national boundaries?

Summary

Decision makers need more than just information; they need reliable information. Internet buyers rely on Web site information when purchasing online. Financial analysts and investors depend on financial reports for making stock investment decisions. Suppliers and creditors use financial reports to decide whether to give trade credit and bank loans. Labor organizations use financial reports to help determine a company's ability to pay wages. Government agencies and Congress use financial information in preparing analyses of the economy and in making laws concerning taxes, subsidies, and the like. These various users rely on independent information assurors such as CPAs to reduce information risk. Auditors (and other information assurance providers) assume the social role of certifying (or attesting to) published financial information, thereby offering users the valuable service of assurance that information risk is low.

This chapter begins by defining information risk, and explains how auditing and assurance services play a role in minimizing this risk. The financial statements are explained in terms of the primary assertions management makes in them, and these assertions are identified as the focal points of the auditors' procedural evidence-gathering work. Auditing is practiced in numerous forms by various practice units, including public accounting firms, the Internal Revenue Service, the U.S. Government Accountability Office, internal audit departments in companies, and several other types of regulatory auditors. Fraud examiners, many of whom are internal auditors and inspectors, have found a niche in auditing-related activities.

The public accounting profession recognized that, in today's information economy, information risk exists in areas outside of financial transactions. Assurance services is a broad category of information-enhancement services that build on CPAs' auditing, attestation, accounting, and consulting skills to create products useful to a wide range of decision makers (customers). Many leaders see assurance services as the wave of the future for the business and professionalism of accountants' public practice. While reliable information helps make capital markets efficient and helps people know the consequences of a wide variety of economic decisions, CPAs practicing the assurance function are not the only information professionals at work in the economy. Bank examiners, IRS auditors, state regulatory agency auditors (e.g., auditors in a state's insurance department), internal auditors employed by a company, and federal government agency auditors all practice information assurance in one form or another.

Most auditors aspire to become certified public accountants, which involves successfully completing a rigorous examination, obtaining practical experience, and maintaining competence through continuing professional education. Auditors also obtain credentials as certified internal auditors, certified management accountants, certified information systems auditors, and certified fraud examiners. Each of these fields has large professional organizations that govern the professional standards and quality of practice of its members.

Key Terms

assurance: The *lending of credibility* to information, 4

assurance services: Providing independent professional information, opinion, or report concerning the quality of information, or its context, for decision makers, 7

attest engagement: Providing an opinion on subject matter or an assertion about the subject matter that is the responsibility of another party, 6

attestation: The lending of credibility to assertions made by a third party, 4

auditing: The lending of credibility to financial statements, 4

business risk: The probability an entity will fail to meet its objectives and, ultimately, fail, 2

cutoff (or cutoff date): Refers to a date, normally the client's year-end balance sheet date, around which transactions should be recorded in the proper period (year), 12

financial reporting: Broad-based process of providing statements of financial position (balance sheets), results of operations (income statements, statements of shareholders' equity, and statements of comprehensive income), changes in cash flows (statements of cash flows), and accompanying disclosure notes (footnotes) to outside decision makers who have no internal source of information, 9

information risk: The probability that the information circulated by a company will be false or misleading, 3

internal auditing: An assurance and consulting activity that provides management with information regarding efficient and effective operations; compliance with laws, regulations, policies, and procedures; and other organizational performance issues designed to reduce risk and add value to the organization, 20

operational auditing: The study of business operations for the purpose of making recommendations about the efficient use of resources, effective achievement of business objectives, and compliance with company policies, 20

professional skepticism: An auditor's tendency *not* to believe management's assertions without sufficient corroboration, 15

reciprocity: The process through which CPAs licensed in one state can obtain a CPA certificate and license in another state, 25

Multiple-Choice Questions for Practice and Review

1.23 Which of the following would be considered an assurance engagement?
 a. Giving an opinion on a prize promoter's claims about the amount of sweepstakes prizes awarded in the past.
 b. Giving an opinion on the conformity of the financial statements of a university with generally accepted accounting principles.
 c. Giving an opinion on the fair presentation of a newspaper's circulation data.
 d. Giving assurance about the average drive length achieved by golfers with a client's golf balls.
 e. All of the above.

1.24 It is always a good idea for auditors to begin an audit with the professional skepticism characterized by the assumption that
 a. A potential conflict of interest always exists between the auditor and the management of the enterprise under audit.
 b. In audits of financial statements, the auditor acts exclusively in the capacity of an auditor.
 c. The professional status of the independent auditor imposes commensurate professional obligations.
 d. Financial statements and financial data are verifiable.

1.25 In an attestation engagement, a CPA practitioner is engaged to
 a. Compile a company's financial forecast based on management's assumptions without expressing any form of assurance.
 b. Prepare a written report containing a conclusion about the reliability of a management assertion.
 c. Prepare a tax return using information the CPA has not audited or reviewed.
 d. Give expert testimony in court on particular facts in a corporate income tax controversy.

1.26 A determination of cost savings obtained by outsourcing cafeteria services is most likely to be an objective of

a. Environmental auditing.

b. Financial auditing.

c. Compliance auditing.

d. Operational auditing.

1.27 The primary difference between operational auditing and financial auditing is that in operational auditing

a. The auditor is not concerned with whether the audited activity is generating information in compliance with financial accounting standards.

b. The auditor is seeking to help management use resources in the most effective manner possible.

c. The auditor starts with the financial statements of an activity being audited and works backward to the basic processes involved in producing them.

d. The auditor can use analytical skills and tools that are not necessary in financial auditing.

1.28 According to the AICPA, the objective of an audit of financial statements is

a. An expression of opinion on the fairness with which they present financial position, results of operations, and cash flows in conformity with generally accepted accounting principles.

b. An expression of opinion on the fairness with which they present financial position, results of operations, and cash flows in conformity with accounting standards promulgated by the Financial Accounting Standards Board.

c. An expression of opinion on the fairness with which they present financial position, result of operations, and cash flows in conformity with accounting standards promulgated by the U.S. Securities and Exchange Commission.

d. To obtain systematic and objective evidence about financial assertions and report the results to interested users.

1.29 Bankers who are processing loan applications from companies seeking large loans will probably ask for financial statements audited by an independent CPA because

a. Financial statements are too complex to analyze themselves.

b. They are too far away from company headquarters to perform accounting and auditing themselves.

c. The consequences of making a bad loan are very undesirable.

d. They generally see a potential conflict of interest between company managers who want to get loans and the bank's needs for reliable financial statements.

1.30 The Sarbanes-Oxley Act of 2002 prohibits professional service firms from providing which of the following services to an audit client?

a. Bookkeeping services.

b. Internal audit services.

c. Valuation services.

d. All of the above.

1.31 Independent auditors of financial statements perform audits that reduce and control

a. Business risks faced by investors.

b. Information risk faced by investors.

c. Complexity of financial statements.

d. Timeliness of financial statements.

1.32 The primary objective of compliance auditing is to

a. Give an opinion on financial statements.

b. Develop a basis for a report on internal control.

c. Perform a study of effective and efficient use of resources.

d. Determine whether auditee personnel are following laws, rules, regulations, and policies.

1.33 What requirements are *usually* necessary to become licensed as a certified public accountant?

 a. Successful completion of the Uniform CPA Examination.

 b. Experience in the accounting field.

 c. Education.

 d. All of the above.

1.34 The organization primarily responsible for ensuring that public officials are using public funds efficiently, economically, and effectively is the

 a. Governmental Internal Audit Agency (GIAA).

 b. Central Internal Auditors (CIA).

 c. Securities and Exchange Commission (SEC).

 d. Government Accountability Office (GAO).

1.35 Performance audits usually include (two answers)

 a. Financial audits.

 b. Economy and efficiency audits.

 c. Compliance audits.

 d. Program audits.

1.36 The objective in an auditor's review of credit ratings of a client's customers is to obtain evidence related to management's assertion about

 a. Completeness.

 b. Existence.

 c. Valuation and allocation.

 d. Rights and obligations.

 e. Occurrence.

1.37 Jones, CPA, is planning the audit of Rhonda's Company. Rhonda verbally asserts to Jones that all expenses for the year have been recorded in the accounts. Rhonda's representation in this regard

 a. Is sufficient evidence for Jones to conclude that the completeness assertion is supported for expenses.

 b. Can enable Jones to minimize the work on the gathering of evidence to support Rhonda's completeness assertion.

 c. Should be disregarded because it is not in writing.

 d. Is not considered a sufficient basis for Jones to conclude that all expenses have been recorded.

1.38 The risk to investors that a company's financial statements may be materially misleading is called

 a. Client acceptance risk.

 b. Information risk.

 c. Moral hazard.

 d. Business risk.

1.39 When auditing merchandise inventory at year-end, the auditor performs audit procedures to ensure that all goods purchased before year-end are received before the physical inventory count. This audit procedure provides assurance about which management assertion?

 a. Completeness.

 b. Existence.

 c. Valuation and allocation.

 d. Rights and obligations.

 e. Occurrence.

1.40 When auditing merchandise inventory at year-end, the auditor performs audit procedures to obtain evidence that no goods held on consignment for customers are included in the inventory balance. This audit procedure provides assurance about which management assertion?

a. Completeness.

b. Existence.

c. Valuation and allocation.

d. Rights and obligations.

e. Occurrence.

1.41 When an auditor reviews additions to the equipment (fixed asset) account to make sure that repair and maintenance expenses are not understated, she wants to obtain evidence as to management's assertion regarding

a. Completeness.

b. Existence.

c. Valuation and allocation.

d. Rights and obligations.

e. Occurrence.

1.42 The Sarbanes-Oxley Act of 2002 generally prohibits professional service firms from

a. Acting in a managerial decision-making role for an audit client.

b. Auditing the firm's own work on an audit client.

c. Providing tax consulting to an audit client without audit committee approval.

d. All of the above.

1.43 Reciprocity refers to

a. An auditor's tendency not to believe management's assertions without sufficient corroboration.

b. Providing consulting work for another firm's audit client in exchange for the other firm's providing consulting services to one of your clients.

c. The waiving of certification exam parts for an individual holding an equivalent certification from another professional organization.

d. The granting of a CPA license to a CPA licensed in another state.

1.44 Which of the following best describes the relationship between auditing and attestation engagements?

a. Auditing is a subset of attestation engagements that focuses on the certification of financial statements.

b. Attestation is a subset of auditing that provides lower assurance than that provided by an audit engagement.

c. Auditing is a subset of attestation engagements that focuses on providing clients with advice and decision support.

d. Attestation is a subset of auditing that improves the quality of information, or its context, for decision makers.

1.45 Which of the following *best* describes the focus of the following engagements?

	Auditing Engagement	Attestation Engagement	Assurance Engagement	Consulting Services Engagement
a.	Any information	Financial statements	Advice and decision support	Financial information
b.	Financial information	Advice and decision support	Financial statements	Any information
c.	Advice and decision support	Any information	Financial information	Financial statements
d.	Financial statements	Financial information	Any information	Advice and decision support

1.46 Which of the following is a reason to obtain professional certification?

 a. Certification provides credibility that an individual is technically competent.

 b. Certification often is a necessary condition for advancement and promotion within a professional services firm.

 c. Obtaining certification is often monetarily rewarded by an individual's employer.

 d. All of the above.

Exercises and Problems

1.47 **Audit, Attestation, and Assurance Services.** Following is a list of various professional services. Identify each by its apparent characteristics as "audit engagement," "attestation engagement," or "assurance engagement." Because audits are a subset of attestation engagements, which are a subset of assurance engagements, choose the most specific description. In other words, if you believe the engagement is an audit engagement, select only audit engagement rather than checking all three. Similarly, the choice of "assurance engagement" for an audit, while technically correct, would not be the best choice.

		Audit Engagement	Attestation Engagement	Assurance Engagement
1	Real estate demand studies			
2	Ballot for awards show			✓
3	Utility rate applications		✓	
4	Newspaper circulation audits			✓
5	Third-party reimbursement maximization			✓
6	Annual financial report to stockholders	✓		
7	Rental property operation review			✓
8	Examinations of financial forecasts and projections		✓	
9	Customer satisfaction surveys			✓
10	Compliance with contractual requirements		✓	✓
11	Benchmarking/best practices			✓
12	Evaluation of investment management policies			✓
13	Information systems security reviews			✓
14	Productivity statistics			✓
15	Internal audit strategic review			✓
16	Financial statements submitted to a bank loan officer	✓		

1.48 **Controller as Auditor.** The chairman of the board of Hughes Corporation proposed that the board hire as controller a CPA who had been the manager of the team that conducted Hughes' Corporation's audit engagement. The chairman thought that hiring this person would make the annual audit unnecessary and would consequently result in saving the professional fee paid to the auditors. The chairman proposed to give this new controller a full staff to conduct such investigations of accounting and operating data as necessary. Evaluate this proposal.

1.49 Complete the following chart indicating the corresponding Auditing Standards Board assertions and whether the assertion relates to transactions, balances, or disclosures.

PCAOB Assertion	Corresponding ASB Assertion	Nature of Assertion
Existence or Occurrence		
Rights and Obligations		
Completeness		
Valuation and Allocation		
Presentation and Disclosure		

1.50 **Operational Auditing.** Bigdeal Corporation manufactures paper and paper products and is trying to decide whether to purchase Smalltek Company. Smalltek has developed a process for manufacturing boxes that can replace containers that use fluorocarbons for expelling a liquid product. The price may be as high as $45 million. Bigdeal prefers to buy Smalltek and integrate its products while leaving the Smalltek management in charge of day-to-day operations. A major consideration is the efficiency and effectiveness of Smalltek's operations. Bigdeal wants to obtain a report on the operational efficiency and effectiveness of the Smalltek sales, production, and research and development departments.

Required:

Who can Bigdeal engage to provide and report on this operational audit? Several possibilities exist. Are there any particular advantages or disadvantages in choosing from among them?

1.51 **Auditor as Guarantor.** Your neighbor Loot Starkin invited you to lunch yesterday. Sure enough, it was no "free lunch" because Loot wanted to discuss the annual report of Dodge Corporation. He owns Dodge stock and just received the annual report. Loot says, "Our auditors prepared the audited financial statements and gave an unqualified opinion, so my investment must be safe."

Required:

What misconceptions does Loot Starkin seem to have about the auditor's role with respect to Dodge Corporation?

1.52 **Identification of Audits and Auditors.** Audits may be characterized as (a) financial statement audits, (b) compliance audits, (c) economy and efficiency audits, and (d) program results audits. The work can be done by independent (external) auditors, internal auditors, or governmental auditors (including IRS auditors and federal bank examiners). Following is a list of the purposes or products of various audit engagements:

	Type of Audit	Type of Auditor
1. Analyze proprietary schools' spending to train students for low-demand occupations.		
2. Determine whether an advertising agency's financial statements are fairly presented in conformity with GAAP.		
3. Study the effectiveness of the Department of Defense's expendable launch vehicle program.		
4. Compare costs of municipal garbage pickup services to comparable service subcontracted to a private business.		
5. Investigate financing terms of tax shelter partnerships.		
6. Study a private aircraft manufacturer's test pilot performance in reporting on the results of test flights.		
7. Conduct periodic examinations by the U.S. Comptroller of Currency of a national bank for solvency.		
8. Evaluate the promptness of materials inspection in a manufacturer's receiving department.		
9. Report on the need for the states to consider reporting requirements for chemical use data.		
10. Render a public report on the assumptions and compilation of a revenue forecast by a sports stadium/racetrack complex.		

Required:

For each of the engagements listed, indicate (1) the type of audit (financial statement, compliance, economy and efficiency, or program results) and (2) the type of auditors you would expect to be involved.

1.53 **Financial Assertions and Audit Objectives.** You are engaged to examine the financial statements of Spillane Company for the year ended December 31. Assume that, on November 1, Spillane borrowed $500,000 from Second National Bank to finance plant expansion. The long-term note agreement provided for the annual payment of principal and interest over five years. The existing plant was pledged as security for the loan. Due to the unexpected difficulties in acquiring the building site, the plant expansion did not begin on time. To use the borrowed funds, management decided to invest in stocks and bonds and, on November 16, invested the $500,000 in publicly traded securities.

Required:

Develop specific assertions (audit objectives) related to securities (assets) based on management's five (PCAOB) general assertions.

1.54 **Internet Exercise: Professional Certification.** Each state has unique rules for certification concerning education, work experience, and residency. Visit the Web site for your state board of accountancy and download a list of the requirements for becoming a CPA in your state. Although not all of the state boards of accountancy have Web sites, you can find the Web sites of most states by accessing the National Association of State Boards of Accountancy at its Web site (http://www.nasba.org).

1.55 **Internet Exercise: Professional Certification.** Visit the Web site of the Institute of Internal Auditors (www.theiia.org); the Institute of Management Accountants (www.imanet.org); The Association of Certified Fraud Examiners (www.cfenet.com); or the Information Systems Audit and Control Association (www.isaca.org). Review the information regarding the certifications available. Does the organization explain the benefits of having its certification? What topics are covered on the certification exam? What are the minimum requirements to take the exam? What additional experience is required to receive the certification?

1.56 **Mini-Case: The Market For Audit Services.** Refer to the mini-case "KPMG: How Many Firms?" Shown on page 836 and respond to question 4.

Professional Standards

Professional Standards References

Compendium Section	Document Reference	Topic
	AS 1	"References in Auditors' Reports to the Standards of the Public Company Accounting Oversight Board"
Various*	AS 5	"An Audit of Internal Control over Financial Reporting That Is Integrated with an Audit of Financial Statements"
AU 120	SAS 102	"Defining Professional Requirements in Statements on Auditing Standards"
AU 150	SAS 95	"Generally Accepted Auditing Standards" (amended by SAS 105 and SAS 113)
	ISA 200	"Objective and General Principles Governing an Audit of Financial Information"
AU 161	SAS 25	"The Relationship of GAAS to Quality Control Standards"
	ISA 220	"Quality Control for Audits of Historical Financial Information"
AU 201	SAS 1	"Nature of the General Standards"
AU 210	SAS 1	"Training and Proficiency of the Independent Auditor"
AU 220	SAS 1	"Independence"
AU 230	SAS 104	"Amendment to 'Due Professional Care in the Performance of Work'"
AU 311	SAS 108	"Planning and Supervision"
	ISA 300	"Planning an Audit of Financial Statements"
AU 312	SAS 107	"Audit Risk and Materiality in Conducting an Audit"
	ISA 320	"Audit Materiality"
AU 314	SAS 109	"Understanding the Entity and Its Environment and Assessing the Risks of Material Misstatement"
	ISA 315	"Understanding the Entity and Its Environment and Assessing the Risks of Material Misstatement"
AU 316	SAS 99	"Consideration of Fraud in a Financial Statement Audit"
	ISA 240	"The Auditor's Responsibility to Consider Fraud in an Audit of Financial Statements"
AU 317	SAS 54	"Illegal Acts by Clients"
	ISA 250	"Consideration of Laws and Regulations in an Audit of Financial Statements"
AU 326	SAS 106	"Audit Evidence"
	ISA 500	"Audit Evidence"
	ISA 501	"Audit Evidence—Additional Consideration for Specific Items"
AU 333	SAS 85	"Management Representations"
	ISA 580	"Management Representations"
AU 410	SAS 1	"Adherence to Generally Accepted Accounting Principles"
AU 411	SAS 69	"The Meaning of 'Present Fairly in Conformity with GAAP' in the Independent Auditor's Report" (amended by SAS 91)
AU 420	SAS 1	"Consistency of Application of GAAP"
AU 9420		"Interpretations on Consistent Application of GAAP"
AU 431	SAS 32	"Adequacy of Disclosure in Financial Statements"
AU 504	SAS 26	"Association with Financial Statements"
AU 508	SAS 58	"Reports on Audited Financial Statements"
	ISA 700	"The Independent Auditor's Report on a Complete Set of General Purpose Financial Statements"
AU 530	SAS 1	"Dating of the Independent Auditor's Report" (amended by SAS 103)
AT 50	SSAE 14	"SSAE Hierarchy"

Various**	*SSAE 10*	"Attestation Engagements: Revision and Recodification"
QC 20	*SQCS 2*	"System of Quality Control for a CPA Firm's Accounting and Auditing Practice"
PR 100		"Standards for Performing and Reporting on Peer Reviews"

* *AS 5* amends AU 230, AU 310, AU 312, AU 313, AU 315, AU 316, AU 319, AU 322, AU 325, AU 328, AU 332, AU 333, AU 341, AU 342, AU 380, AU 508, AU 530, AU 543, AU 560, AU 561, AU 711, AU 722, *AS 2,* and *AS 4.*
** *SSAE 10* amends AT 101, AT 201, AT 301, AT 401, AT 501, and AT 601.

> All my growth and development led me to believe that if you really
> do the right thing, and if you play by the rules, and if you've got good
> enough, solid judgment and common sense, that you're going to be
> able to do whatever you want to do with your life . . .
>
> *Barbara Jordan, first African-American woman from the South ever elected to the*
> *U.S. House of Representatives*

Learning Objectives

Chapter 1 gave you a general introduction to professional accounting practice. Chapter 2 explains three sets of interrelated practice standards for audit services offered by auditors and accountants in public practice: generally accepted auditing standards, attestation standards, and quality control standards.

Your objectives are to be able to:

1. Name the various practice standards for internal, governmental, and independent auditors and accounting firms and identify their sources.

2. List the 10 AICPA generally accepted auditing standards (GAAS) and explain how GAAS was or was not followed in specific fact situations.

3. Describe how the audit examination is affected by auditors' responsibility for the general standards and standards of field work.

4. List the standards of reporting and identify how these standards are reflected in the content of the auditors' report.

5. Identify the need for attestation standards and explain how attestation standards differ from generally accepted auditing standards.

6. List and explain the important features of quality control standards for an accounting firm.

PRACTICE STANDARDS

LEARNING OBJECTIVE

1. Name the various practice standards for internal, governmental, and independent auditors and accounting firms and identify their sources.

A profession can be defined as a "vocation requiring knowledge of some department or learning or science" or "any vocation or business."[1] Auditing (and the practice of auditing) certainly qualifies as a profession. One of the unique characteristics of a profession is that a body of knowledge is required to participate in the profession and individuals within the profession owe a duty or responsibility to others as they conduct themselves within the profession. As a result, certain standards and guidelines are necessary to identify (1) what characteristics auditors should possess and (2) what types of activities auditors should and should not engage in while in the practice of the profession of auditing.

Just as highway laws govern interstate highway driving, practice standards serve as general guides to the conduct of auditing and other assurance engagements. Similar to the different "rules of the road" for driving on interstates, on local roads, or in different countries, the accounting and auditing profession has several sets of standards governing the quality of professional work, depending on the type of client. Collectively, the standards are referred to as *practice standards*.

[1] www.dictionary.com.

✳ Know ✳

Client	Public Entities	Private Entities	Governmental Entities	Foreign Entities
Rule-Making Body	Public Company Accounting Oversight Board (PCAOB)	AICPA Auditing Standards Board (ASB)	U.S. Government Accountability Office (GAO)	IFAC International Auditing and Assurance Standards Board (IAASB)
Standards	*Auditing Standards (ASs)*	*Statements on Auditing Standards (SASs)*	*Government Auditing Standards* (The "Yellow Book")	*International Standards on Auditing (ISAs)*
Web Site	www.pcaobus.org	www.aicpa.org	www.gao.gov	www.ifac.org

Provide more guidance on publicly held corp.

For the past 70 years, the American Institute of CPAs (AICPA) has taken the role of primary guidance provider for audits of U.S. private and public entities, most recently through its Auditing Standards Board (ASB). With the passage of the Sarbanes-Oxley Act of 2002, however, Congress removed the responsibility for creating standards for the audits of *publicly traded entities* from the ASB and turned it over to the newly created Public Company Accounting Oversight Board (PCAOB). The PCAOB operates subject to SEC oversight (which means that any rules and standards must ultimately be approved by the SEC before they become effective) and was formed to ensure that audit quality is not compromised and that auditors' performance continues to meet public expectations. The membership of the board consists of five SEC-appointed public members (business executives and investment analysts) and is supported by fees paid by publicly traded entities and their auditors.

With respect to its responsibility to establish rules and standards, the PCAOB declared that the previously created practice standards (standards issued by the ASB and AICPA that were effective as of April 16, 2003) would initially function as the PCAOB's *Interim Auditing Standards* for audits of public entities and would be amended as considered necessary with new *Auditing Standards*. In addition to the responsibility for creating standards for the audits of publicly traded entities, the PCAOB also registers and monitors the work of accounting firms that conduct audits of public entities; these monitoring activities are discussed later in this chapter.

The PCAOB has no jurisdiction, however, over the audits of private entities; therefore, the ASB still has an important role in the standard-setting process. The creation of the PCAOB also has no effect on the rule-making responsibilities for governmental entities, currently handled by the U.S. Government Accountability Office (GAO). Lastly, the new PCAOB rules do not affect audits of entities based outside the United States (unless they want their stock traded on U.S. stock exchanges). Instead, those entities' auditors follow local, usually government-imposed audit guidance.

Having said this, there is another set of auditing standards, known as the *International Standards on Auditing* (*ISAs*), issued by the International Auditing and Assurance Standards Board (IAASB) of the International Federation of Accountants (IFAC). While this text does not directly address international standards, most issues addressed in the international standards are met by following GAAS. Auditors conducting examinations of foreign corporations must undergo training on international standards to ensure that the engagements are conducted with due professional care. As of the end of 2005, over 70 countries around the world have decided to adopt, or announced an intention to adopt, *ISAs* for audits conducted within those countries.[2]

In the international community, accountants and regulators have a great interest in *convergence*—that is, making the standards coordinated, if not uniform, throughout the world. For example, if an accounting firm audits public and private entities throughout the world, that firm may be subject to standards issued by the ASB, PCAOB, and IAASB, among others. The *ISAs* are a first step in this direction. While the *ISAs* are similar to U.S. rules, some differences exist. The AICPA publishes books of standards, and the *ISAs* reproduced in them are accompanied by summaries of the points on which they hold

[2] *International Auditing and Assurance Standards Board Annual Report* (2005), p. 9.

auditors to a higher level of performance or on which they conflict with U.S. GAAS. Other efforts that demonstrate an interest in convergence include the joint project by the ASB and IAASB in developing exposure drafts for the "risk assessment" standards (which eventually became *SASs* 104–111), plans announced by the IFAC to create the Public Interest Oversight Board to be consistent with the public–private partnership of the PCAOB, and the focus of the IAASB's annual report on the importance of convergence. One concern is that, because the PCAOB has the power to regulate foreign accounting firms that audit U.S. clients, it lacks an interest in global convergence compared to its predecessor (the AICPA).[3] However, the PCAOB's 2004 annual report notes that it "considers relevant International Standards on Auditing issued by the IAASB in developing proposals" and notes that registrant firms represent 76 different countries.[4]

In addition to these rules, there are also rule-making bodies for *Statements of Internal Auditing Standards* (the Institute of Internal Auditors) and *Professional Standards and Practices for Certified Fraud Examiners* (the Association of Certified Fraud Examiners). These standards, along with government audit standards (issued primarily by the U.S. GAO), will be discussed in a later module.

As you can see, there are a large number of standards that auditors must follow. To simplify this task, this chapter focuses on three topics: GAAS issued by the ASB and adopted by the PCAOB; attestation standards for accountants performing nonaudit engagements (also issued by the ASB); and quality control standards for accounting firms as a whole (issued by the PCAOB and the AICPA Division for Firms).

Review Checkpoints

2.1 What are the practice standards and who issues them for independent auditors of financial statements? governmental auditors? internal auditors? fraud auditors? auditors in other countries?

GENERALLY ACCEPTED AUDITING STANDARDS (GAAS)

LEARNING OBJECTIVE

2. List the 10 AICPA generally accepted auditing standards (GAAS) and explain how GAAS was or was not followed in specific fact situations.

Unquestionably, the new millennium has not started on a positive note for the accounting profession. However, the accounting community has faced similar crises before and, as a result, become stronger as a profession. On December 9, 1938, a scandal of epic proportions broke at **McKesson & Robbins**, a large pharmaceutical company. The company's president, F. Donald Coster, was arrested for embezzling almost $20 million from the company. Coster gained wealth during prohibition by importing alcohol for the production of hair tonic (although most of the alcohol was instead sold to bootleggers). With McKesson & Robbins, he "bought" and "sold" pharmaceuticals from around the world; in reality, the company's operations were little more than a labyrinth of paperwork. **Price Waterhouse & Co.**, the company's auditors for over 10 years, failed to discover that the company had inflated inventory and receivables through the falsification of supporting documents (including one phony shipment from the United States to Australia by truck!). Auditors merely accepted management's assertions about inventory and receivables balances without verifying their existence. The case resulted in an SEC investigation that found the following:[5]

1. Auditors failed to employ necessary vigilance, inquisitiveness, and analysis of the evidence available (professional skepticism) as would be expected of an auditing professional.

[3] J. Giles, E. Venuti, and R. Jones, "The PCAOB and Convergence of the Global Auditing and Accounting Profession," *The CPA Journal* (September 2004), pp. 36–39.
[4] *PCAOB 2004 Annual Report*, p. 9.
[5] *Accounting Series Release No. 19* (1940).

2. Although auditors are not guarantors and should not be responsible for detecting all fraud, the discovery of gross overstatements in the accounts is a major purpose of an audit.

The accounting profession reacted quite strongly to the scandal. In 1939, the AICPA developed the accounting profession's equivalent of the 10 Commandments. These 10 *generally accepted auditing standards* have been augmented by additional explanations and requirements in *Statements on Auditing Procedures* (1939–72) and in *Statements on Auditing Standards* (1972–present).[6] They remain the basis for the PCAOB's *Auditing Standards*. Taken together, the relevant pronouncements of the AICPA and PCAOB that expanded on these 10 original standards are collectively referred to as **generally accepted auditing standards,** or **GAAS.** GAAS are auditing standards that identify necessary qualifications and characteristics of auditors and guide the conduct of the audit examination.

The 10 basic standards (most recently revised in 2006 by *SAS 113*) are classified as *general standards, standards of field work,* and *standards of reporting* (see Exhibit 2.1).

✳ KNOW ✳

EXHIBIT 2.1 AICPA Generally Accepted Auditing Standards

Stage of Audit Engagement

BASIC for performing an audit

General Standards

Stage of Audit Engagement	
Obtain (or Retain) Engagement	1. The auditor must have adequate technical training and proficiency to perform the audit. 2. The auditor must maintain independence in mental attitude in all matters relating to the audit. 3. The auditor must exercise due professional care in the performance of the audit and the preparation of the report.

Standards of Field Work

Engagement Planning	1. The auditor must adequately plan the work and must properly supervise any assistants.
Risk Assessment	2. The auditor must obtain a sufficient understanding of the entity and its environment, including its internal control, to assess the risk of material misstatement of the financial statements whether due to error or fraud, and to design the nature, timing, and extent of further audit procedures.
Substantive Procedures	3. The auditor must obtain sufficient appropriate audit evidence by performing audit procedures to afford a reasonable basis for an opinion regarding the financial statements under audit.

Standards of Reporting

Reporting	1. The auditor must state in the auditor's report whether the financial statements are presented in accordance with generally accepted accounting principles (GAAP). 2. The auditor must identify in the auditor's report those circumstances in which such principles have not been consistently observed in the current period in relation to the preceding period. 3. When the auditor determines that informative disclosures are not reasonably adequate, the auditor must so state in the auditor's report. 4. The auditor must either express an opinion regarding the financial statements, taken as a whole, or state that an opinion cannot be expressed, in the auditor's report. When the auditor cannot express an overall opinion, the auditor should state the reasons therefor in the auditor's report. In all cases where an auditor's name is associated with financial statements, the auditor should clearly indicate the character of the auditor's work, if any, and the degree of responsibility the auditor is taking, in the auditor's report.

Due professional care must be exercised during all stages of the engagement

[6] *Statements on Auditing Standards (SAS)* are authoritative AICPA pronouncements on auditing theory and practice. *Statements on Auditing Procedure (SAS) Nos.* 1–54 were codified into *SAS 1* in 1972. While the original 10 generally accepted auditing standards have been modified for editorial changes over time (most recently by *SAS 113* in 2006), the basic content has not changed significantly.

In addition to providing guidance on the conduct of an audit, the auditing standards provide a loose overview of the timing of the different phases of an audit engagement. While due professional care must be exercised throughout all stages of the engagement, the general standards discuss the general technical and independence requirements that auditors must consider before accepting an audit engagement. The standards of field work address the next three phases of the audit engagement (planning, risk assessment, and evidence gathering). Each of the four standards of reporting addresses a different aspect of reporting, the last phase of the audit engagement.

The AICPA issues *Statements on Auditing Standards (SASs)* from time to time in a numbered series. Officially they are considered "interpretations" of the 10 basic standards. *SAS 102* notes that, depending upon the wording contained in the standards, these pronouncements may impose *unconditional requirements* on auditors (in which they are expected to fully comply with the provisions of the *SAS*) or *presumptively mandatory requirements* (in which a departure from the provisions of the *SAS* is permitted with appropriate documentation). Generally, auditors who do not follow *SAS* directives can be judged to have performed a deficient audit.

As noted earlier, *SASs* that have not been superseded or amended by the PCAOB's *Auditing Standards* are referred to as *Interim Standards* and are still considered to be applicable to the audits of public entities (i.e., all pronouncements through *SAS 101*, "Auditing Fair Value Measurements and Disclosures"). The auditing standards literature also includes a series of *Interpretations*. Although officially considered less authoritative and less binding than the SASs, auditors still must justify any departures from them. For the most part, interpretations give technical assistance.

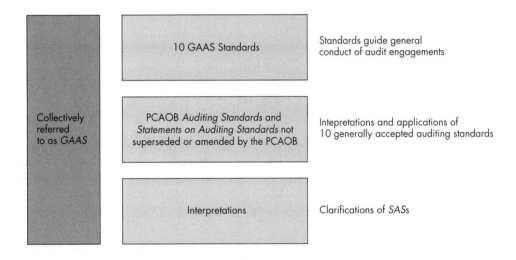

Auditing standards are quite different from *audit procedures*. **Audit procedures** are the particular and specialized actions that auditors take to obtain evidence in a specific audit engagement. **Auditing standards,** on the other hand, are audit quality guides that remain the same through time and for all audits. Procedures may vary, depending on the complexity of an accounting system, on the type of company, or on other situation-specific factors. For example, loans are liabilities for most entities but are assets for financial institutions. Auditors must use different procedures to audit loans depending on the type of client they are auditing. This difference is the reason auditors' reports refer to an audit "conducted in accordance with generally accepted auditing standards" rather than in accordance with audit procedures.

Recall from Chapter 1 the definition of auditing as

. . . a systematic process of objectively obtaining and evaluating evidence regarding assertions about economic actions and events to ascertain the degree of correspondence between the assertions and established criteria and communicating the results to interested users.

Examining the 10 GAAS reveals that these standards closely parallel that definition. The standards of field work require auditors to plan the audit (i.e., conduct the audit using a "systematic process") and to "obtain and evaluate evidence" through understanding the client and its environment and gathering sufficient appropriate evidence. Further, the standards of reporting provide guidance for "communicating the results" of the audit about whether the financial statements are prepared using "established criteria" (GAAP). While the general standards do not appear to be directly related to the definition of auditing, these standards outline the necessary qualifications and characteristics of auditors.

GAAS General Standards

LEARNING
OBJECTIVE

3. Describe how the audit examination is affected by auditors' responsibility for the general standards and standards of field work.

The three general standards of GAAS relate to the personal integrity and professional qualifications of auditors. These issues are normally addressed before a firm accepts a prospective client.

STAGES OF AN AUDIT

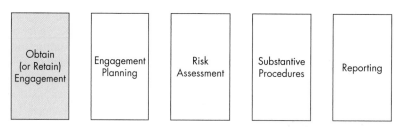

Competence

The auditor must have adequate technical training and proficiency to perform the audit.

The first general standard requires competence—adequate technical training and proficiency. This competence starts with *education* in accounting because auditors hold themselves out as experts in accounting standards, financial reporting, and auditing. *Experience*, another dimension of competence, grows with on-the-job training in developing and applying professional judgment in real-world audit situations. Auditors learn to (1) recognize the underlying assertions being made by the management of a company in each element (account) in the financial statements, (2) decide the evidence that is relevant for supporting or refuting the assertions, (3) select and perform procedures for obtaining the evidence, and (4) evaluate the evidence and decide whether the management assertions correspond to reality and GAAP. Auditors must be thoughtfully prepared to encounter a wide range of judgments on the part of management accountants, varying from true objective judgment to the occasional extreme of deliberate misstatement.

Independence

The auditor must maintain independence in mental attitude in all matters relating to the audit.

The second general standard requires *independence in mental attitude;* auditors are expected to be unbiased and impartial with respect to the financial statements and other information they audit. They are expected to be fair both to the entities and executives who issue financial information and to the outside persons who use it. **Independence in appearance,** on the other hand, relates to others' (particularly financial statement users') perceptions of auditors' independence. For example, while owning a single share of stock in a client would not likely influence auditors' mental attitude (i.e., auditors would be **independent in fact**), it is not likely that third-party users would perceive auditors to be independent (i.e., auditors would not be independent in appearance). The rules relating to independence (as provided by the AICPA Code of Professional Conduct) primarily relate to independence in appearance.

The importance of independence is illustrated by its inclusion as one of the 10 generally accepted auditing standards as well as it serving as the focus of one of the Rules of

AUDITING INSIGHT Independent Auditors?

In an investigation of independence violations at **Pricewater-houseCoopers (PwC)**, an independent consultant disclosed that the accounting firm's personnel had committed over 8,000 violations. A detailed review of the violations revealed the following:

- 45.2 percent were reported by partners who perform services related to audits of financial statements.

- Almost half of the reported violations involved investments in securities, mutual funds, bank accounts, or insurance products associated with a client.

- Almost 32 percent of reported violations involved holdings of a client's stock or stock options.

- Six of 11 partners at the senior management level and each of the 12 regional partners who help administer PwC's independence program reported at least one violation (one reported 38 violations and another reported 34 violations).

The consultant's report, "Report on the Internal Investigation of Independence Issues at PricewaterhouseCoopers, LLP,"

January 6, 2000, available on the SEC Web site (www.sec.gov), concluded, "The combined results of the self-reporting and random tests of those reports indicated that approximately 86.5 percent of PwC partners and 10.5 percent of all other PwC professionals had independence violations." In response to the report, then-SEC Chief Accountant Lynn E. Turner stated, "This report is a sobering reminder that accounting professionals need to renew their commitment to the fundamental principle of auditor independence."

PwC employees noted a number of reasons for the violations, including failure to check their investments against the firm's client list after the merger of PwC's two legacy firms (Price Waterhouse and Coopers & Lybrand). Others suggested that the independence rules were just too complex. Since the disclosure of the violations, PwC has implemented a new proactive monitoring system that requires all partners and managers to report all investments; employees are then notified automatically if there are any independence concerns.

Source: SEC Press Release 2000–4.

Conduct to which accountants are held. In general, two types of relationships that are believed to jeopardize (or compromise) independence are

- *Financial relationships,* such as owning shares of stock in a client or having a loan outstanding to or from a client.
- *Managerial relationships,* such as the ability to act in a decision-making capacity on behalf of a client or providing advice on systems or information that will subsequently be audited.

Clearly, the above relationships would impair perceptions of auditors' independence, but other considerations are necessary. For example, while it seems safe to conclude that an audit team member's spouse should be restricted from the above types of relationships for a client for whom the team member is providing services, could that spouse have these types of relationships with respect to a client served by a distant office of the team member's firm? Could the audit team member's third cousin have the above relationships? Because of situations encountered in practice such as these, several interpretations of the Rules of Conduct related to independence have been promulgated. A full discussion of the Rules of Conduct and interpretations related to independence is provided in Module B of this text. Independence must be zealously guarded because the general public will grant social recognition of professional status to auditors only as long as they are perceived to be independent.

The notion of *individual independence* is more specific in the conduct of each audit engagement. In essence, auditors must not subordinate their judgment to others and must stay away from influences that might bias judgment. Following are three aspects of practical independence:

1. *Programming independence.* Auditors must remain free from interference by client managers who try to restrict, specify, or modify the procedures auditors want to perform, including any attempt to assign personnel to or otherwise control the audit work. Occasionally, client managers try to limit the numbers of auditors permitted in a location.

2. *Investigative independence.* Auditors must have free access to books, records, correspondence, and other evidence. They must have the cooperation of management without any attempt to interpret or screen evidence. Sometimes, client managers refuse auditors' requests for access to necessary information.

3. *Reporting independence.* Auditors must not let any feelings of loyalty to the auditee interfere with their obligation to report fully and fairly. Neither should management be allowed to overrule auditors' judgments on the appropriate content of the auditors' report. Disciplinary actions have been taken against auditors who go to a client management conference with a preliminary estimate for a financial adjustment and emerge after agreeing with management to a smaller adjustment.

Due Professional Care

The auditor must exercise due professional care in the performance of the audit and the preparation of the report.

The exercise of due professional care requires observance of the standards of field work and reporting but adds an additional element of professionalism. Auditors must properly plan and supervise the audit in order to complete the engagement on a timely basis. The hierarchical review process, in which firm auditors continually review each other's work, also contributes to the exercise of due professional care.

The standard for due professional care is the care that would be exercised by reasonable auditors in the same circumstance. Prudent auditors exercise reasonable judgment, are not expected to be omniscient, are presumed to have knowledge special to their profession, are expected to be aware of their own ignorance, and are expected to possess the skills of the profession, whether a beginner or a veteran.

Review Checkpoints

2.2 What is the difference between auditing standards and audit procedures?

2.3 By what standard can a judge determine the quality of due professional care? Explain.

2.4 Distinguish between independence in fact and independence in appearance. Can auditors be independent in fact, yet not be perceived to be independent in appearance?

GAAS Standards of Field Work

The three standards of field work set forth general quality criteria for conducting an audit. Auditors cannot effectively satisfy the general standards requiring due professional care if they have not also satisfied the standards of field work.

Planning and Supervision (SAS 108)

The auditor must adequately plan the work and must properly supervise any assistants.

The professional standards contain several lists of considerations for planning and supervising an audit. They are all concerned with (1) preparing an audit program and supervising the audit work, (2) obtaining knowledge of the client's business, and (3) dealing with differences of opinion among the accounting firm's own personnel.

STAGES OF AN AUDIT

| Obtain (or Retain) Engagement | Engagement Planning | Risk Assessment | Substantive Procedures | Reporting |

AUDITING INSIGHT Too Late

FastTrak Corporation got mad at its auditors because the partner in charge of the engagement would not agree to let management use operating lease accounting treatment for some heavy equipment whose leases met the criteria for capitalization. FastTrak fired the auditors 10 weeks after the company's balance sheet date and then started contacting other accounting firms to restart the audit. However, the auditors' report was due at the SEC in two weeks. Every other accounting firm contacted by FastTrak refused the audit because it could not be planned and performed properly on such short notice with such a tight deadline.

A written audit program is required. An **audit program** is a list of the audit procedures auditors need to perform to gather sufficient appropriate evidence on which to base their opinion on the financial statements. The procedures in an audit program should be stated in enough detail to instruct the assistants about the work to be done. (You will see detailed audit programs later in this textbook.)

An understanding of the client's business and industry is an absolute necessity. This knowledge helps auditors identify areas for special attention (the places where frauds or errors might exist), evaluate the reasonableness of accounting estimates made by management, evaluate management's answers to inquiries, and make judgments about the appropriateness of accounting principle choices. Auditors gain this understanding of a business by conducting interviews with management and other client personnel, through experience with other entities in the same industry, and by reading extensively—AICPA accounting and audit guides, industry publications, other entities' financial statements, business periodicals, and textbooks.

Auditors on an audit team may sometimes disagree among themselves on audit decisions ranging from inclusion or omission of procedures to conclusions about the fair presentation of an account or the whole financial statements. When differences of opinion arise, audit personnel should consult with one another and with experts in the firm to try to resolve the disagreement. If they do not achieve resolution, the accounting firm should have procedures to allow audit team members to document the disagreement and to dissociate themselves from the matter. In this case, the basis for the final audit decision on the matter also should be documented in the audit documentation for later reference.

Timing is important for audit planning. To have time to plan an audit, auditors should be engaged before the client's fiscal year end. The more advance notice auditors can have, the better they are able to provide enough time for planning. The audit team may be able to perform part of the audit at an *interim date*—a date some weeks or months before the fiscal year end—and thereby make the rest of the audit work more efficient. At an *interim date,* auditors can perform preliminary reasonableness tests on the financial statement accounts (commonly referred to as *analytical procedures*), do a preliminary assessment of control risk, and audit some account balances. Advance knowledge of problems can enable auditors to alter the audit program as necessary so that year-end work (performed on and after the fiscal year-end date) can be more efficient. Advance planning for certain types of audit procedures (for example, the observation of physical inventory and the confirmation of accounts receivable) is particularly important.

Engagement planning is discussed in greater detail in Chapter 4. In addition, planning activities related to the audit of various accounts and cycles are discussed in Chapters 6 through 10.

Risk Assessment (SAS 109)

The auditor must obtain a sufficient understanding of the entity and its environment, including its internal control, to assess the risk of material misstatement of the financial statements whether due to error or fraud, and to design the nature, timing, and extent of further audit procedures.

The second standard of field work requires an understanding of the client and its operating environment, including internal controls inherent in the client's accounting information systems that ultimately produce the client's financial statements. **Internal control** may be defined simply as a system's capability to prevent or detect material accounting frauds or errors and provide for their correction on a timely basis. Satisfactory internal control reduces the probability of frauds or errors in the accounts. This understanding provides the foundation for the work auditors do in assessing the **risk of material misstatement,** a combination of **inherent risk** (the probability that a material misstatement, either an error or fraud, will occur) and **control risk** (the probability that a material misstatement, either an error or fraud, will not be prevented or detected on a timely basis by the entity's internal controls).

STAGES OF AN AUDIT

Obtain (or Retain) Engagement	Engagement Planning	Risk Assessment	Substantive Procedures	Reporting

The primary purpose of assessing the risk of material misstatement is to help auditors develop the audit program, which specifies the *nature, timing, and extent of further audit procedures* necessary for gathering sufficient evidence about the account balances that will go into the financial statements. The second standard of field work presumes two necessary relationships: (1) effective internal control reduces the control risk, and auditors thus have a reasonable basis for reducing the necessary effectiveness of further audit procedures; (2) conversely, ineffective internal control increases control risk, and auditors must increase the necessary effectiveness of further audit procedures. Because these audit procedures are used to obtain evidence with respect to the fairness of the account balance (i.e., to "substantiate" the account balance), they are referred to as **substantive procedures.** This relationship is depicted below:

Effective internal control → Lower level of control risk → Reduced effectiveness of substantive procedures

Ineffective internal control → Higher level of control risk → Increased effectiveness of substantiveprocedures

The importance of internal control in the audit examination is evidence by an increase in auditors' responsibility for internal control through the issuance of *Auditing Standard No. 5 (AS 5)* by the PCAOB. Under this standard, auditors are required to evaluate and report on the effectiveness of the entity's internal control over financial reporting. Internal control is discussed in greater detail in Chapter 5; in addition, important elements of internal control related to the audit of various accounts and cycles are discussed in Chapters 6 through 10.

AUDITING INSIGHT Control Lapse Contributes to Duplicate Payments

Allstate Trucking processed insurance claims on damages to shipments in transit on its trucks, paying them from a self-insurance payment reserve. After payment, the claims documents were not marked "paid." Later, the same documents were processed again for duplicate payments to customers who kicked back 50 percent to a dishonest Allstate employee.

Auditors learned that the documents were not marked "paid," concluded that the specific control risk of duplicate payments was high, extended their procedures to include a search for duplicate payments in the damage expense account, found them, and traced the problem to the dishonest employee. Embezzlements of $35,000 per year were stopped.

Review Checkpoints

2.5 What three elements of planning and supervision are considered essential in audit practice?

2.6 Why does the timing of the auditors' appointment matter in the conduct of a financial statement audit?

2.7 For what reasons do auditors obtain an understanding of a client's internal control?

2.8 What is the basic relationship between the effectiveness of the client's internal control and the necessary effectiveness of substantive procedures?

Audit Evidence (SAS 106)

> *The auditor must obtain sufficient appropriate audit evidence by performing audit procedures to afford a reasonable basis for an opinion regarding the financial statements under audit.*

The third standard of field work requires that the audit team collect and evaluate sufficient appropriate evidence to afford a reasonable and logical basis for audit decisions. The ASB defines **evidence** as "all of the information used by auditors in arriving at the conclusions on which the audit opinion is based." Evidence includes the underlying accounting data and all available corroborating information. Examples of evidence include minutes of meetings, confirmations with independent third parties, invoices, analyst reports, and all other information that permits auditors to reach valid, logical conclusions. As noted above, the methods used by auditors to evaluate this evidence are referred to as *substantive procedures.*

STAGES OF AN AUDIT

Obtain (or Retain) Engagement	Engagement Planning	Risk Assessment	Substantive Procedures	Reporting

While the accounting records (journals, ledgers, accounting policy manuals, computer files, and the like) are evidence of the *bookkeeping-accounting process,* they are not sufficient appropriate supporting evidence for the *financial statements*. Evidence corroborating these records must be obtained through auditors' direct personal knowledge, examination of documents, and inquiry of entity personnel. In some cases, evidence the audit team needs may exist only in computerized form. Consequently, the client's data retention policies may require auditors to arrange for some evidence to be retained for review. Alternatively, auditors may need to plan to perform audit procedures at a time when the evidence is still available.

AUDITING INSIGHT Whom Can You Trust?

"The level of fraud and financial deception that took place at **HealthSouth** is a blatant violation of investor trust, and **Ernst & Young** is as outraged as the investing public." In a public statement, the accounting firm asserted that HealthSouth, one of its largest clients, tried to deceive the firm's audit team by creating false documents to support fraudulent journal entries. To support the firm's claim, the statement cited a court hearing in which a former HealthSouth employee testified that "he knew of at least three occasions where company executives prepared false documents specifically to conceal fraud from Ernst."

Source: "Did HealthSouth Auditor Ernst Miss Key Clues to Fraud Risks?" *The Wall Street Journal,* April 10, 2003, pp. C1, C3.

To be considered *appropriate,* evidence must be *reliable, relevant,* and *unbiased.* Evidence may be quantitative or qualitative; it may be objective or subjective; it may be absolutely compelling to a decision or it may only be mildly persuasive. The following hierarchy of *audit evidence quality* will help you understand the relative reliability and persuasiveness of different types of evidence. The hierarchy starts with the strongest form of evidence and proceeds to the weakest.

1. Auditors' *direct, personal knowledge,* obtained through *physical observation* and auditors' own *mathematical computations,* is generally considered the most competent evidence.

2. Documentary evidence obtained directly from external sources (**external evidence**) is generally considered competent. There may be factors, however, that might affect the reliability of evidence received from external sources, including how knowledgeable and objective the source is.

3. Documentary evidence that has originated outside the client's information processing system but that has been received and processed by the client (**external-internal evidence**) is generally considered competent when internal control is strong. To reduce the likelihood for fraud, original documents are preferred to photocopies.

4. **Internal evidence** consisting of documents that are produced, circulated, and finally stored within the client's information system is generally considered low in reliability. However, internal evidence is used extensively when it is produced under satisfactory conditions of internal control. Sometimes, internal evidence is the only type available.

5. **Verbal and written representations** given by the client's officers, directors, owners, and employees are generally considered the least competent evidence. While representations are considered to be a weak form of evidence, GAAS require that auditors obtain written corroboration from the client to emphasize management's responsibility for the fairness of the financial statements. This corroboration (known as **management representations**) addresses the fairness of the entity's financial statements, availability of all financial records and related data, internal control over financial reporting, and other specific representations about the financial statements and accounts.

In most cases, auditors will obtain a combination of different types of evidence to support their conclusions. In fact, finding different sources of corroborating information is advisable. Because management is responsible for the entity's financial statements, inquiry of management personnel is usually the best place to *start* gathering evidence. Inquiry of management is not sufficient, however, and when specifying audit procedures to corroborate management's representations, the best approach is to seek the evidence of the highest reliability. If physical observation and mathematical calculation are not relevant to the account or are impossible or too costly, then move down the hierarchy to obtain the next best evidence available. Having said this, we want to stress that the fact that important evidence is difficult or costly to obtain is not an acceptable reason for failure to obtain it. Auditors, however, may use their professional judgments to determine (i.e., perform a cost-benefit analysis) whether the reliability of the evidence is worth the effort to obtain it.

AUDITING INSIGHT Evidence Gathering: Fooling the Auditors

John S. Jordan, president of **Jordan Concepts, Inc.**, overstated the company's receivables by more than $10 million to provide false collateral for a $24 million loan. How did he fool the auditors? He allegedly planted a listening device in the auditors' workroom! Thus, he had advance knowledge of the documents auditors planned to request. He gave them false documents, including shipping documents, checks, bank statements, and remittance advices printed by a local printer at his request. The scheme unraveled when other officers of the company informed the FBI. Jordan was convicted on charges of conspiracy, bank fraud, mail fraud, and wire fraud.

Observation: A client's use of a hidden listening device is an extreme case, but auditors ought to be careful and suitably skeptical of documents delivered by client personnel.

Source: Association of Certified Fraud Examiners.

While *appropriateness* relates to evidence *quality, sufficiency* relates to evidence *quantity*. The third standard of field work states that auditors should gather enough evidence to support an opinion on the financial statements, but how much evidence is enough? The auditing profession has no official standard, leaving the matter of sufficiency to auditors' *professional judgment*. Note that the standard refers to "sufficient," rather than "absolute," evidence. Auditors do not audit all of an entity's transactions and events. They audit data samples and make audit decisions by inference, in most cases. Although auditors can use statistical sampling to determine sufficiency in a numerical sense (e.g., confidence levels), realistically sufficient evidence can be defined as enough evidence to stand the scrutiny of other auditors (supervisors and reviewers) and outsiders (such as critics, judges, and jurors). The real test of sufficiency is whether you can persuade someone else that your evidential base is strong enough to reach the same conclusions you have reached.

Evidence gathering procedures are discussed in greater detail in Chapter 3. In addition, specific approaches to gathering evidence in the examination of various accounts and cycles are discussed in Chapters 6 through 10.

Review Checkpoints

2.9 Define *audit evidence*.

2.10 How are external, external-internal, and internal documentary evidence generally defined?

2.11 How does the source of evidence affect its reliability?

Standards of Reporting (*SAS 58*)

LEARNING
OBJECTIVE

4. List the standards of reporting and identify how these standards are reflected in the content of the auditors' report.

The ultimate objective of independent auditors—the report on the audit—is guided by the four standards of reporting. These four standards address the content of the auditors' report with respect to generally accepted accounting principles (GAAP), consistency, adequate disclosure, and the degree of responsibility assumed by auditors.

STAGES OF AN AUDIT

| Obtain (or Retain) Engagement | Engagement Planning | Risk Assessment | Substantive Procedures | Reporting |

(handwritten margin notes: "Know readings - signed & dated)")

EXHIBIT 2.2 **Example Auditor's Report**

Report Title	**Report of Independent Registered Public Accounting Firm**
	The Board of Directors and Shareholders,
Addressee	Wal-Mart Stores, Inc.
Introductory Paragraph	We have audited the accompanying consolidated balance sheets of Wal-Mart Stores, Inc. as of January 31, 2007 and 2006, and the related consolidated statements of income, shareholders' equity, and cash flows for each of the three years in the period ended January 31, 2007. These financial statements are the responsibility of the Company's management. Our responsibility is to express an opinion on these financial statements based on our audits.
Scope Paragraph	We conducted our audits in accordance with the standards of the Public Company Accounting Oversight Board (United States). Those standards require that we plan and perform the audit to obtain reasonable assurance about whether the financial statements are free of material misstatement. An audit includes examining, on a test basis, evidence supporting the amounts and disclosures in the financial statements. An audit also includes assessing the accounting principles used and significant estimates made by management, as well as evaluating the overall financial statement presentation. We believe that our audits provide a reasonable basis for our opinion.
Opinion Paragraph	In our opinion, the financial statements referred to above present fairly, in all material respects, the consolidated financial position of Wal-Mart Stores, Inc. at January 31, 2007 and 2006, and the consolidated results of its operations and its cash flows for each of the three years in the period ended January 31, 2007, in conformity with U.S. generally accepted accounting principles.
Internal Control Paragraph	We also have audited, in accordance with the standards of the Public Company Accounting Oversight Board (United States), the effectiveness of Wal-Mart Stores, Inc.'s internal control over financial reporting as of January 31, 2007, based on criteria established in *Internal Control— Integrated Framework* issued by the Committee of Sponsoring Organizations of the Treadway Commission and our report dated March 26, 2007 expressed an unqualified opinion thereon.
	Ernst & Young LLP Rogers, Arkansas March 26, 2007

An example of an auditors' report is shown in Exhibit 2.2, and you should review it in relation to the following discussion.[7] When reading the standards of reporting, you should understand the term *financial statements* to include not only the traditional financial statements but also all footnote disclosures and additional information (e.g., earnings per share calculations) that are integral elements of the basic financial presentation required by GAAP.

Generally Accepted Accounting Principles (GAAP)

> *The auditor must state in the auditor's report whether the financial statements are presented in accordance with generally accepted accounting principles (GAAP).*

The first standard of reporting is a straightforward directive. In the auditors' report, the directive is carried out with the opinion sentence in the third (opinion) paragraph: "In our opinion, the financial statements . . . present fairly, in all material respects, the consolidated financial position . . . and the consolidated results of its operations and its cash flows . . . in conformity with U.S. generally accepted accounting principles."

(handwritten margin notes: "Know Unqualified Qualified Adverse Disclaimer.")

The above report is an example of an **unqualified report,** which expresses an *unqualified opinion* on the company's (in this case, Wal-Mart's) financial statements. "Unqualified" means "good" in the sense that auditors are not calling attention to anything wrong with the financial statements. In other cases, the entity's financial statements (or elements within those financial statements) are materially misstated and do not present the entity's financial

[7] The report shown in Exhibit 2.2 differs slightly from **Ernst & Young's** actual report on **Wal-Mart's** financial statements. Ernst & Young's actual report includes an additional paragraph discussing the adoption of a new accounting principle related to defined benefit pension and postretirement plans. This paragraph is not included in Exhibit 2.2 to allow you to focus on the major paragraphs in the auditors' report. Reporting is discussed in more detail in Chapter 12 of this text.

condition, results of operations, and cash flows in conformity with GAAP; collectively, these situations are known as **departures from GAAP.** In such cases, report modifications are necessary. An **adverse report** is the opposite of an unqualified report; it states that the financial statements *do not present fairly* the financial condition of the entity in conformity with GAAP. A **qualified report** falls somewhere between an unqualified and an adverse report; the auditors' report basically states that *except for* a particular (usually limited) departure from GAAP, the financial statements are fairly stated. A qualified report might also be issued for auditors' inability to follow the requirements of GAAS (a **scope limitation**).

One important phrase in the opinion paragraph is ". . . in all material respects . . ." This phrase reflects the fact that auditors and users do not expect account balances to be accurate to the penny; after all, many entities round their financial statements to the thousands, or even millions, of dollars! Financial statements are considered to be "fairly presented" as long as they are not materially misstated; that is, misstated by an amount large enough to make a difference in users' decisions. For example, Wal-Mart reported net income of $11.2 billion in 2007; clearly, an error of $1,000 would not affect users' decisions, but an error of $750 million might. The choice of report (unqualified, qualified, or adverse) depends on the nature and materiality (significance) of the effect of the GAAP departure.

Finally, note the date on the auditors' report (in the above example, March 26, 2007). The report is dated when all significant procedures have been completed by auditors and auditors have gathered sufficient appropriate evidence (referred to as the **audit completion date**).

Determining the appropriate GAAP in an entity's circumstances is not always an easy matter. Students often think of Financial Accounting Standards Board (FASB) statements on accounting standards as the complete body of GAAP. Not so. GAAP consists of all accounting methods and procedures that have *substantial authoritative support*. FASB (or Federal Accounting Standards Advisory Board [FASAB] for federal entities or Governmental Accounting Standards Board [GASB] for state and local governmental entities) is only one source of such support, albeit the most authoritative. The auditing standard concerning the meaning of present fairly in conformity with GAAP (*SAS 91*) sets forth a hierarchy of authoritative support for various sources of GAAP. Exhibit 2.3 is a summary of the GAAP hierarchy. Higher levels in this exhibit correspond to more authoritative guidance; for example, when researching a technical issue, you should begin with *Statements of Financial Accounting Standards* rather than your intermediate accounting textbook. No, you won't need to memorize this table; it is here so that you can refer back to this hierarchy should the need arise.

Consistency

The auditor must identify in the auditor's report those circumstances in which such principles have not been consistently observed in the current period in relation to the preceding period.

The second standard of reporting deals with the consistent application of GAAP; that is, has the entity changed the accounting principles used to account for and report a particular type of transaction? An official accounting pronouncement (*SFAS 154,* "Accounting Changes and Error Corrections") governs the accounting and disclosure of an entity's change of accounting principles.

Unlike the requirement for reporting on conformity with GAAP in the first standard of reporting, auditors use *implicit* (or *exception-based*) *reporting* for consistency. That is, if no reference is made to consistency, readers can assume that the entity has not changed its accounting principles. However, when an entity has made a change (i.e., an exception occurs), a sentence must be added to the auditors' report to alert users to the fact. This added sentence is the explicit report required when a change has been made.

Adequate Disclosure

When the auditor determines that informative disclosures are not reasonably adequate, the auditor must so state in the auditor's report.

The third standard of reporting is also an *implied* element. This standard requires auditors to use professional judgment to decide whether the financial statements and related

EXHIBIT 2.3 GAAP Hierarchy Summary (*SAS 69, SAS 91*) ✳ KNOW ✳

Authoritative Guidance		Nongovernmental Entities	Federal Governmental Entities	State and Local Governmental Entities
Strongest ⬆	a.	• FASB Statements, Interpretations, and Staff Positions • APB Opinions • AICPA Accounting Research Bulletins	• Federal Accounting Standards Advisory Board (FASAB) Statements and Interpretations • AICPA and FASB pronouncements (if applicable to audits of governmental entities)	• GASB Statements and Interpretations • AICPA and FASB pronouncements (if applicable to audits of state and local governments)
	b.	• FASB Technical Bulletins • AICPA Industry Audit and Accounting Guides • AICPA Statements of Position	• FASAB Technical Bulletins • AICPA Industry Audit and Accounting Guides and AICPA Statements of Position (if applicable to audits of governmental entities)	• GASB Technical Bulletins • AICPA Industry Audit and Accounting Guides and AICPA Statements of Position (if applicable to audits of state and local governments)
	c.	• FASB Emerging Issues Task Force Consensus positions • Practice Bulletins issued by the AICPA Accounting Standards Executive Committee (AcSEC)	• Practice Bulletins issued by the AcSEC (if applicable to audits of governmental entities)	• GASB Emerging Issues Task Force Consensus positions • Practice Bulletins issued by the AcSEC (if applicable to audits of state and local governments)
	d.	• AICPA accounting interpretations • "Qs and As" published by the FASB staff • Industry practices widely recognized and prevalent	• "Qs and As" published by the FASAB staff • Industry practices widely recognized and prevalent	• "Qs and As" published by the GASB staff • Industry practices widely recognized and prevalent
	e.	Other accounting literature: • FASB Concepts Statements • AICPA Issues Papers • International Financial Reporting Standards (issued by International Accounting Standards Board, or IASB) • GASB Statements, Interpretations, and Technical Bulletins • Pronouncements of other professional associations or regulatory agencies • AICPA Technical Practice Aids • Accounting textbooks, handbooks, and articles	Other accounting literature: • FASAB Concepts Statements • Pronouncements referred to in categories (a) through (d) of the hierarchy of nongovernmental entities when not specifically made applicable to federal governmental entities • FASB Concepts Statements • GASB Statements • Interpretations, Technical Bulletins, and Concepts Statements • AICPA Issues Papers • IASB International Financial Reporting Standards • Pronouncements of other professional associations or regulatory agencies • AICPA Technical Practice Aids • Accounting textbooks, handbooks, and articles	Other accounting literature: • GASB Concepts Statements • Pronouncements referred to in categories (a) through (d) of the hierarchy of nongovernmental entities when not specifically made applicable to state and local governments • FASB Concepts Statements • Interpretations, Technical Bulletins, and Concepts Statements • AICPA Issues Papers • IASB International Financial Reporting Standards • Pronouncements of other professional associations or regulatory agencies • AICPA Technical Practice Aids • Accounting textbooks, handbooks, and articles
Weakest ⬇				

disclosures contain all important accounting information required by GAAP. If such disclosures are not provided, the auditors' report should provide them, allowing the users to have all necessary information (either in the financial statements and accompanying disclosures or in the auditors' report) with which to make important decisions. Like consistency in the second standard of reporting, the reporting responsibility for disclosures is *implicit,* or *exception-based reporting.*

When auditors believe some information is necessary for adequate disclosure yet the entity refuses to disclose it, a departure from GAAP exists. A *qualified opinion* is usually prepared, and the reason for the departure (missing disclosure) is described in the auditors' report. Sometimes the missing disclosure is added to the auditors' report itself.

Report Content

> *The auditor must either express an opinion regarding the financial statements, taken as a whole, or state that an opinion cannot be expressed, in the auditor's report. When the auditor cannot express an overall opinion, the auditor should state the reasons therefor in the auditor's report. In all cases where an auditor's name is associated with financial statements, the auditor should clearly indicate the character of the auditor's work, if any, and the degree of responsibility the auditor is taking, in the auditor's report.*

The fourth standard of reporting indicates that the auditors' report should express an opinion (unqualified, qualified, or adverse) or indicate that an opinion cannot be expressed; this latter situation is referred to as a **disclaimer of opinion** (a disclaimer is also required if auditors are not independent). You may ask why an opinion could not be expressed; one reason is if auditors are unable to obtain sufficient evidence regarding the fairness of the entity's financial statements (a pervasive *scope limitation*). In cases when an opinion cannot be expressed, this element of the fourth standard of reporting indicates that the reasons should be provided in the auditors' report.

A second issue addressed by the fourth standard of reporting relates to providing an indication of the work done and responsibilty assumed by auditors. In the report shown in Exhibit 2.2, these responsibilities are summarized in the second (scope) paragraph (the nature of work done) and the last sentence of the first (introductory) paragraph of the report ("Our responsibility is to express an opinion on these financial statements based on our audits."). However, in some cases, auditors may need to deviate from the language shown in Exhibit 2.2. For example, if auditors are not able to perform certain procedures that are considered necessary (a *scope limitation*), descriptions of the work done and procedures performed need to be modified.

In addition to the report on the financial statements, auditors also are required to report on the effectiveness of the entity's internal control over financial reporting; *Auditing Standard No. 5* provides the basis for this report. As shown in Exhibit 2.2, Ernst & Young concluded that Wal-Mart maintained an effective internal control over financial reporting. The reference to Ernst & Young's opinion (and report) on internal control is shown in the fourth paragraph of the report on the financial statements.

Exhibit 2.4 summarizes two important reporting issues, how these issues affect the work done and responsibility assumed by auditors, and the type of opinions issued by auditors. If considered to be significant, these situations require the language in reports

EXHIBIT 2.4 **Reporting Issues and Effect on Auditors' Reports**

Issue	Effect on "Work Done" by the Auditors	Effect on "Responsibilities Assumed" by the Auditors	Type of Opinions Issued
Scope limitation (Departure from GAAS)	Modify language to identify nature of scope limitation	Modify language to identify information for which responsibility is not assumed	Qualified opinion or disclaimer of opinion
Departure from GAAP	No modifications necessary	No modifications necessary	Qualified opinion or adverse opinion

1. *Unqualified:* The financial statements *present fairly*, in all material respects, the financial condition (or the results of operations or cash flows) of the entity in conformity with generally accepted accounting principles.

2. *Qualified: Except for* one (limited) item, the financial statements present fairly, in all material respects, the financial condition (or the results of operations or cash flows) of the entity in conformity with generally accepted accounting principles or the scope of the audit has been limited.

3. *Adverse:* The financial statements *do not present fairly* the financial condition (or the results of operations or cash flows) of the entity in conformity with generally accepted accounting principles.

4. *Disclaimer:* Auditors *do not express an opinion* as to whether the financial statements present fairly the financial condition (or the results of operations or cash flows) of the entity in conformity with generally accepted accounting principles.

such as that shown in Exhibit 2.2 to be modified; these modifications, as well other reporting issues, are discussed in more detail in Chapter 12.

In certain instances, accountants are **associated with financial statements** but did not conduct a GAAS audit. For example, financial statements may be reproduced on an accountant's letterhead or produced by the accountant's computer as part of a bookkeeping service. In such cases, the accountant's report should provide a clear indication of the work done and responsibilty assumed; the reason a report is required is that users may assume an audit has been conducted and the financial statements are fairly presented according to GAAP.

Review Checkpoints

2.12 What is the highest level of authoritative support for GAAP? the lowest level?

2.13 Do auditors take any responsibility for clients' choices of accounting principles?

2.14 What messages are usually implicit in an auditors' standard report?

2.15 What four types of audit opinion statements are identified in this chapter? What is the message of each one?

2.16 Why should public accountants issue a report whenever they are associated with financial statements?

ATTESTATION STANDARDS

LEARNING OBJECTIVE

5. Identify the need for attestation standards and explain how attestation standards differ from generally accepted auditing standards.

An audit is a form of attestation; however, some engagements do not call for the relatively extensive scope and conclusions that result from an audit. **Attestation standards** represent a general set of standards intended to guide attestation work in areas other than audits of financial statements. They were first published in the *1986 Statement on Standards for Attestation Engagements* and significantly revised in 2001. Because assurance services are constantly evolving, there are currently no specific assurance standards. However, because of their similarity to attestation engagements, accountants often rely on attestation standards for guidance in the conduct of assurance engagements. The attestation standards were written long after GAAS and, as you can see in Exhibit 2.5, the ideas are borrowed from the existing GAAS. (The information in Exhibit 2.5 is sequenced to correspond to the ordering of the attestation standards, which differs slightly from that of GAAS).

The major differences between the attestation standards and generally accepted auditing standards lie in the areas of practitioner competence, understanding the entity and its environment, and reporting. With respect to practitioner competence, the GAAS presume knowledge of accounting and require training and proficiency as auditors (meaning auditors of financial statements, since that was the only type of attestation being performed

EXHIBIT 2.5 **Comparison of Attestation and Audit Standards** ✳Know✳

Attestation Standards	Generally Accepted Auditing Standards
General Standards	
1. The *practitioner* must have adequate technical training and proficiency to perform the *attest engagement*.	1. The auditor must have adequate technical training and proficiency to perform the audit.
2. The *practitioner* must have adequate knowledge of the subject matter.	
3. The *practitioner* must have reason to believe that the subject matter is capable of evaluation against criteria that are suitable and available to users.	
4. The *practitioner* must maintain independence in mental attitude in all matters relating to the *engagement*.	2. The auditor must maintain independence in mental attitude in all matters relating to the audit.
5. The *practitioner* must exercise due professional care in the planning and performance of the *engagement* and the preparation of the report.	3. The auditor must exercise due professional care in the performance of the audit and the preparation of the report.
Standards of Field Work	
1. The *practitioner* must adequately plan the work and must properly supervise any assistants.	1. The auditor must adequately plan the work and must properly supervise any assistants.
[Depending upon the subject matter, assessment of the risk of material misstatement may not be required for an attestation engagement.]	2. The auditor must obtain a sufficient understanding of the entity and its environment, including its internal control, to assess the risk of material misstatement of the financial statements, whether due to error or fraud, and to design the nature, timing, and extent of further audit procedures.
2. The *practitioner* must obtain sufficient evidence to provide a reasonable basis for *the conclusion that is expressed in the report*.	3. The auditor must obtain sufficient appropriate audit evidence by performing audit procedures to afford a reasonable basis for an opinion regarding the financial statements under audit.
Standards of Reporting	
1. The *practitioner* must identify the *subject matter* or the assertion being reported on and state the character of the *engagement* in the report.	1. The auditor must either express an opinion regarding the financial statements, taken as a whole, or state that an opinion cannot be expressed, in the auditor's report. When the auditor cannot express an overall opinion, the auditor should state the reasons therefor in the auditor's report. In all cases where an auditor's name is associated with financial statements, the auditor should clearly indicate the character of the auditor's work, if any, and the degree of responsibility the auditor is taking, in the auditor's report.
2. The *practitioner* must state the *practitioner's* conclusion about the *subject matter or the assertion* in relation to *criteria against which the subject matter was evaluated* in the report.	2. The auditor must state in the auditor's report whether the financial statements are presented in accordance with generally accepted accounting principles (GAAP).
	3. The auditor must identify in the auditor's report those circumstances in which such principles have not been consistently observed in the current period in relation to the preceding period.
3. The *practitioner* must state all of the *practitioner's significant reservations about the engagement*, the *subject matter,* and, if applicable, the *assertion* related thereto in the report.	4. When the auditor determines that informative disclosures are not reasonably adequate, the auditor must so state in the auditor's report.
4. The *practitioner* must state in the report that the report is intended solely for the information and use of the *specified parties* under the following circumstances [detail omitted].	

when GAAS were written). On the other hand, the attestation standards are more general, requiring training and proficiency in the "attest function" and knowledge of the "subject matter of the assertions." The *attest function* refers to the ability to recognize the information being asserted, to determine the evidence relevant to the assertions, and to make decisions about the correspondence of the information asserted with suitable criteria. The "knowledge of the subject matter" is not confined to accounting and financial assertions because attestations may cover a wide variety of information.

The attestation standards, unlike GAAS, have no requirement regarding obtaining an understanding of the entity and its environment to assess the risk of material misstatement (unless, of course, the attestation engagement is related to a nonpublic entity's risk of material misstatement). Considerations of the risk of material misstatement are implicit in the task of obtaining sufficient evidence. In any case, some types of attested information may not have an underlying information control system in the same sense as a financial accounting and reporting system. However, it is good practice to evaluate the risk of material misstatement in any engagement in which this assessment is significant to the management assertions being evaluated.

Reporting is different under the two because attestations on nonfinancial information do not depend on generally accepted accounting principles. These are the only criteria for financial statement audits. The attestation standards speak of "criteria against which the subject matter was evaluated" and they leave the door open for attestations on a wide variety of informational assertions.

The AICPA's main objective in publishing the attestation standards was to provide guidance and establish a broad framework for a wide variety of attestation engagements. The relationship between attestation and yet-to-be determined assurance standards remains to be seen. Before the attestation standards were published, accountants used the GAAS guidelines as a point of departure for other attestations. Similarly, accountants now use attestation standards as the point of departure for new assurance opportunities until the ASB publishes specific assurance standards.

Review Checkpoints

2.17 What is the purpose served by the attestation standards?

2.18 What are the major differences between the attestation standards and the generally accepted auditing standards?

STANDARDS FOR ACCOUNTING FIRMS

LEARNING OBJECTIVE

6. List and explain the important features of quality control standards for an accounting firm.

Public accounting firms do business in a competitive environment. They are in business to make a profit, yet they are also in the profession to perform public accounting services in the public/social interest. This duality—profit motive and professional responsibility—creates tensions. Several organizations, including specifically the AICPA, the SEC, and the PCAOB, are very interested in the accounting profession's maintenance of high standards. Toward this end, these organizations work together to provide guidance to firms engaged in the practice of public accounting. The guidance provided by these organizations takes several different forms. The AICPA promulgates *Statements on Quality Control Standards (SQCSs)* that provide firms with guidance on issues such as staff hiring practices and client selection, retention, or withdrawal practices. In addition, accounting firms may become voluntary members of the AICPA Center for Public Company Audit Firms (CPCAF). Membership in the CPCAF brings additional responsibilities, including periodic reviews (referred to as *peer reviews*) of firm quality control practices by another

accounting firm. The SEC provides general oversight, investigates audit failures, and fines accounting firms that have been found to have conducted their engagements negligently. Finally, the PCAOB registers accounting firms that conduct audits of publicly traded entities, establishes rules to govern audit quality, and performs its own inspections of registered accounting firms. These different forms of guidance will be discussed in the following sections.

Elements of Quality Control

Statement on Quality Control Standards No. 2 (*SQCS 2*), "System of Quality Control for a CPA Firm's Accounting and Auditing Practice," describes the following five elements of quality control for an accounting firm:

1. Independence, integrity, and objectivity.
2. Personnel management (hiring, assigning, developing, and promoting personnel).
3. Acceptance and continuance of clients.
4. Engagement performance.
5. Monitoring.

Quality control standards are policies and procedures implemented by firms to improve the quality of their services. For example, firms commonly have policies and procedures that require their personnel to review client listings to verify that they do not have any inappropriate financial or managerial relationships with clients (independence, integrity, and objectivity). In addition, providing continuing education opportunities and guidance related to new accounting and auditing pronouncements (personnel management) is essential in ensuring that the firm's employees maintain currency with respect to their professional knowledge. The objective of implementing and following effective standards of quality control is to ensure that accounting firms' work will be performed at an appropriate level and in conformity with appropriate professional standards (such as GAAS or attestation standards). Viewed another way, quality control standards represent policies and procedures implemented by firms to prevent substandard work (and, potentially, audit failures).

The Monitoring Role of the PCAOB

In addition to the *standard-setting role* previously discussed, one of the primary roles of the PCAOB is to *monitor* firms engaged in the practice of auditing public entities and bring appropriate disciplinary action against member firms. Its goal is to ensure that audit quality is not compromised and that auditors' performance continues to meet public expectations. Soon after it began operations in early 2003, the PCAOB began registering firms providing auditing services to public entities. Firms not registered are not allowed to conduct audits of public entities. Other PCAOB monitoring activities include inspections of registered accounting firms (similar to peer reviews), special investigations, and disciplinary proceedings. (Prior to the creation of the PCAOB, the monitoring function was performed by the SEC Practice Section of the AICPA Division of Firms.)

Sarbanes-Oxley requires the PCAOB to conduct annual inspections of all registered accounting firms that perform audits of more than 100 public entities; firms performing audits of fewer than 100 public entities are subject to inspections every three years. These inspections include a review of a sample of audit engagements conducted by the firm as well as an overall evaluation of the quality control standards implemented by the firm. Copies of the PCAOB's inspection reports can be found (on a firm-by-firm basis) on the PCAOB's Web site. These reports detail deficiencies identified by the PCAOB on the sample audit engagements (the name of the client is not identified); information regarding deficiencies in the firm's quality controls are confidential and not provided and will only be made public if the firm fails to address these deficiencies to the PCAOB's satisfaction within a year following the inspection. A sample of reported deficiencies for audits conducted by Big Four firms in 2005 (which were inspected by the PCAOB in 2006) is

AUDITING INSIGHT Grading the Firms

For the Big Four firms (**Deloitte & Touche, Ernst & Young, KPMG, and PricewaterhouseCoopers**), deficiencies in 47 audit engagements were summarized in the related inspection reports (this is a reduction from 74 audits in 2004). These deficiencies included departures from GAAP that were not identified by auditors and the failure of auditors to gather sufficient appropriate evidence on which to base their conclusions. A sample of areas in which these deficiencies were noted includes

- Revenue recognition (both general and related to specific agreements).
- Unsupported and unreconciled amounts in numerous accounts.
- Classification of lease agreements as operating when they met criteria for classification of capital leases.

- Failure to perform alternative procedures for accounts receivable confirmations not returned by customers.
- Failure to gather sufficient evidence regarding the client's internal controls.
- Incorrectly reporting the gain on the sale of a joint venture as a component of operating income.

In one case, the firm performed more extensive procedures based on the deficiency identified by the PCAOB; these procedures revealed the existence of a material misstatement and resulted in filing restated financial statements for this client. Other responses by the firms indicated that the deficiencies noted by the PCAOB resulted in increased levels of audit documentation.

Source: PCAOB Web site, http://www.pcaob.org/Inspections/Public_Reports/index.aspx.

provided in the Auditing Insight "Grading the Firms." Interestingly, despite the very public nature of these reports, some have criticized the clarity of the findings and timeliness of these reports.[8]

Peer Review

Accounting firms not subject to required inspections by the PCAOB can volunteer to join one or both of the AICPA Division for Firms' Private Companies Practice Section (PCPS) and the Center for Public Company Audit Firms (CPCAF). The Division and its sections form the backbone of the AICPA's "self-regulation" system. Both the PCPS and the CPCAF have peer review committees that review the work and reports of the peer reviewers. A **peer review** is a study of a firm's quality control policies and procedures, followed by a report on the firm's quality of audit practice in accordance with the quality control standards. When a peer review or a quality review is conducted, the reviewers "audit" the accounting firm's statement of policies and procedures designed to ensure compliance with the five elements of quality control. These engagements vary in length and complexity, depending on the size of the accounting firm.

Review Checkpoints

2.19 What is the meaning of quality control as it relates to an accounting firm?

2.20 Consider the following quality control policy and identify the quality control element to which it relates: "Designate individuals as specialists to serve as authoritative resources; provide procedures for resolving differences of opinion between audit personnel and specialists."

2.21 What role does the PCAOB play in connection with the monitoring and regulation of accounting firms?

[8] "Why the Big Four Are Still a Mystery," *CFO.com*, January 29, 2007. In addition, D.R. Hermanson, R.W. Houston, and J.C. Rice, "PCAOB Inspections of Smaller CPA Firms: Initial Evidence from Inspection Reports," *Accounting Horizons*, June 2007, pp. 137–152 summarizes important characteristics of inspection reports issued to firms with 100 or fewer issuer clients.

Summary

Financial statement auditors are most concerned with the 10 GAAS standards because they are the direct guides for the quality of everyday audit practice. The three general standards set requirements for auditors' competence, independence, and due professional care. The three standards of field work set requirements for planning and supervising each audit, obtaining an understanding of the client's environment (including its internal controls), and obtaining sufficient appropriate evidence to serve as a basis for the auditors' opinion. The theory of sufficient, appropriate evidence is introduced with an explanation of the relative strengths of persuasiveness of various types of evidence. The four standards of reporting cover requirements for GAAP, consistency, adequate disclosure, and report content.

While GAAS provide the framework for audit examinations, an audit is only one type of attestation engagement. Attestation standards are the general framework for applying the "attest function" to different scopes of engagements and provide quality guides for general attestation work. Accounting firms implement quality control standards to improve the quality of their audit and accounting practice taken as a whole and ensure that attestation standards and auditing standards are followed faithfully in all aspects of the firm's accounting and auditing practice. The PCAOB, the AICPA's Quality Control Inquiry Committee, and the SEC monitor these aspects of quality control.

Key Terms

adverse report: A report stating that the financial statements are not in conformity with GAAP; the opposite of an unqualified report, 49

associated with financial statements: Circumstances in which an accountant's name is used in connection with the financial statements or an accountant has prepared the statements, even if the accountant's name is not used in any written report, 52

attestation standards: A general set of standards intended to guide attestation work in areas other than audits of financial statements, 52

audit completion date: The date on which auditors have gathered sufficient appropriate evidence on which to base the opinions on the financial statements and internal control over financial reporting, 49

audit procedures: Specialized actions auditors take to obtain evidence in an engagement, 39

audit program: A list of the audit procedures auditors need to perform to gather sufficient appropriate evidence on which to base their opinion on the financial statements, 43

auditing standards: Audit quality guides that remain the same through time and for all audits, 39

control risk: The probability that a material misstatement (error or fraud) will not be prevented or detected on a timely basis by the entity's internal controls, 44

departures from GAAP: Instances in which the entity's financial statements (or elements within those financial statements) are materially misstated and do not present the entity's financial condition, results of operations, and cash flows in conformity with GAAP, 49

disclaimer of opinion: The lowest level of assurance; " no assurance." Auditors explicitly state that they give no opinion and no assurance, thus taking no responsibility for a report on the fair presentation of the financial statements in accordance with GAAP, 51

evidence: The information used by auditors on which to base their opinion on the financial statements, 45

external evidence: Documentary evidence obtained directly from independent external sources, 46

external-internal evidence: Documentary evidence that has originated outside the client's information processing system but that has been received and processed by the client, 46

generally accepted auditing standards (GAAS): Standards that identify necessary qualifications and characteristics of auditors and guide the conduct of the audit examination, 38

independence (in appearance): The extent to which others (particularly third parties) perceive auditors to be independent, 40

independence (in fact): Auditors' mental attitude and impartiality with respect to the client, 40

inherent risk: The probability that a material misstatement (error or fraud) will occur, 44

internal control: An entity's capability to prevent or detect material accounting errors or frauds and provide for their correction on a timely basis, 44

internal evidence: Documents that are produced, circulated, and finally stored within the client's information system, 46

management representations: Written assertions provided by management to auditors on matters such as the fairness of the entity's financial statements, availability of all financial records and related data, internal control over financial reporting, and other specific representations about the financial statements and accounts, 46

peer review: A study of a firm's quality control policies and procedures, followed by a report on the firm's quality of audit practice in accordance with the quality control standards, 56

qualified report: An auditors' report issued when the financial statements contain departures from GAAP or the audit examination was not conducted in accordance with GAAS, 49

quality control standards: Policies and procedures implemented to improve the quality of services provided by accounting firms, 55

risk of material misstatement: The combined probability that a material misstatement (error or fraud) will occur and not be prevented or detected on a timely basis by the entity's internal controls, 44

scope limitation: Situation in which auditors are unable to obtain sufficient evidence regarding the fairness of the entity's financial statements, 49

substantive procedures: Procedures used by auditors to obtain assurance as to the fairness of the entity's financial statements, 44

unqualified report: A "clean" report that makes no mention of accounting or auditing deficiencies. The conclusion of an unqualified report is that the financial statements present the financial condition, results of operations, and cash flows in accordance with GAAP, 48

verbal and written representations: Responses to audit inquiries provided by the client's officers, directors, owners, and employees, 46

Multiple-Choice Questions for Practice and Review

2.22 Which of the following is one of the four standards of reporting included in GAAS?

 a. The auditor must exercise due professional care in the performance of the audit and the preparation of the report.

 b. The auditor must state in the auditor's report whether the financial statements are presented in accordance with GAAP.

 c. The auditor must obtain sufficient appropriate audit evidence by performing audit procedures to afford a reasonable basis for an opinion regarding the financial statements under audit.

 d. The report shall state that GAAS have been followed in the conduct of the audit.

2.23 To exercise due professional care, an accountant should

 a. Take continuing professional education classes.

 b. Report whether the financial statements are in accordance with GAAP.

 c. Gather enough audit evidence to have complete assurance that there is enough support for the accountant's opinion on the financial statements.

 d. Conduct the engagement in accordance with GAAS and ensure that the engagement is completed on a timely basis.

2.24 One of an accounting firm's basic objectives is to provide professional services that conform to professional standards. Reasonable assurance of achieving this objective can be obtained by following

 a. Generally accepted auditing standards (GAAS).

 b. Quality control standards.

 c. Generally accepted accounting practices (GAAP).

 d. International auditing standards.

2.25 After auditors learned of Client Company's failure to record an expense for obsolete inventory, they agreed to a small adjustment to the financial statements because Client's president told them the company would violate its debt agreements if the full amount were recorded. This is an example of a lack of

 a. Auditors' training and proficiency.

 b. Planning and supervision.

 c. Audit investigative independence.

 d. Audit reporting independence.

2.26 The primary purpose for obtaining an understanding of the entity's environment (including its internal control) in a financial statement audit is

 a. To determine the nature, timing, and extent of further audit procedures to be performed.

 b. To make consulting suggestions to the management.

 c. To obtain direct sufficient appropriate audit evidence to afford a reasonable basis for an opinion on the financial statements.

 d. To determine whether the entity has changed any accounting principles.

2.27 Ordinarily, what source of evidence should least affect audit conclusions?

 a. External.

 b. Inquiry of management.

 c. Auditor prepared.

 d. Inquiry of entity legal counsel.

2.28 The most persuasive evidence regarding the existence of newly acquired computer equipment is

 a. Inquiry of management.

 b. Documentation prepared externally.

 c. Observation of auditee's procedures.

 d. Physical observation.

2.29 Which of the following procedures would provide the most reliable audit evidence?

 a. Inquiries of the client's internal audit staff held in private.

 b. Inspection of prenumbered client purchase orders filed in the vouchers payable department.

 c. Inspection of customer sales invoices received from client personnel.

 d. Inspection of bank statements obtained directly from the client's financial institution.

2.30 Breaux & Co., CPAs require that all audit documentation contain the initials of the preparer and the reviewer in the top right-hand corner. This procedure provides evidence of Breaux & Co., CPAs' professional concern regarding which generally accepted auditing standard?

 a. Independence.

 b. Adequate technical training and proficiency.

 c. Adequate planning and supervision.

 d. Gathering sufficient appropriate evidence.

2.31 The attestation standards do not contain a requirement that auditors obtain

 a. Adequate knowledge in the subject matter of the assertions being examined.

 b. An understanding of the auditee's internal controls.

 c. Sufficient evidence for the conclusions expressed in an attestation report.

 d. Independence in mental attitude.

2.32 Auditor Jones is studying an entity's accounting treatment of a series of complicated transactions in exotic financial instruments. She should look for the highest level of authoritative support for proper accounting in

 a. Consensus positions of the FASB Emerging Issues Task Force (EITF).

 b. AICPA industry audit and accounting guides.

 c. FASB statements on accounting standards.

 d. FASB statements on financial accounting concepts.

2.33 The evidence considered most appropriate by auditors is best described as

 a. Internal documents such as sales invoice copies produced under conditions of strong internal control.

 b. Written representations made by the president of the entity.

 c. Documentary evidence obtained directly from independent external sources.

 d. Direct personal knowledge obtained through physical observation and mathematical recalculation.

2.34 Auditors' understanding of the internal control system in an entity contributes information for

 a. Determining whether members of the audit team have the required technical training and proficiency to perform the audit.

 b. Ascertaining the independence in mental attitude of members of the audit team.

 c. Planning the professional development courses the audit staff needs to keep up to date with new auditing standards.

 d. Planning the nature, timing, and extent of further audit procedures on an audit.

2.35 An auditee uses an innovative accounting method to account for an unusual transaction. Which of the following is the most authoritative source for guidance when considering whether the auditee's accounting method is consistent with GAAP?

 a. The FASB Concepts Statements.

 b. A FASB Emerging Issues Task Force Consensus position.

 c. An AICPA Issue Paper.

 d. A best-selling intermediate accounting textbook.

2.36 Which of the following standards is mismatched with its rule-making body?

 a. Public Company Accounting Oversight Board, *Auditing Standards*

 b. Governmental Accounting Standards Board, *Government Auditing Standards*

 c. Auditing Standards Board, *Statements on Auditing Standards*

 d. International Auditing and Assurance Standards Board, *International Standards on Auditing*

2.37 Kramer, CPA consulted with an independent appraiser regarding the valuation of fine art for a not-for-profit museum. Consultation with a specialist in this case would

 a. Be considered proper due professional care.

 b. Be considered a failure to follow GAAS because Kramer should have known how to value fine art before accepting the engagement.

 c. Not be considered a violation of GAAS because GAAS does not apply to not-for-profit entities.

 d. None of the above.

2.38 Vandalay Industries omits a footnote regarding litigation from its financial statements, although it was included in the previous year. Vandalay's auditor, George Costanza, makes no mention of it in the auditors' opinion. Which of the following generally accepted auditing standards have *not been* violated by the omission?

a,c,d WERE ALL VIOLATED.

 a. The auditor must exercise due professional care in the performance of the audit and the preparation of the report.

 b. The auditor must identify in the auditor's report those circumstances in which such principles have not been consistently observed in the current period in relation to the preceding period.

 c. When the auditor determines that informative disclosures are not reasonably adequate, the auditor must so state in the auditor's report.

 d. The auditor must state in the auditor's report whether the financial statements are presented in accordance with generally accepted accounting principles.

2.39 Which of the following is a conceptual difference between attestation standards and generally accepted auditing standards?

 a. The attestation standards provide a framework for the attest function beyond historical financial statements.

 b. The requirement that the practitioner be independent is not required under attestation standards.

 c. The attestation standards do not permit an attestation engagement to examine prospective "what-if" financial statements.

 d. None of the standards of field work are included in the attestation standards.

Exercises, Problems, and Simulations

2.40 **Audit Engagement Independence.** You are meeting with executives of Cooper Cosmetics Corporation to arrange your firm's engagement to audit the corporation's financial statements for the year ending December 31. One executive suggests the audit work be divided among three staff members. One person would examine asset accounts, a second would examine

liability accounts, and the third would examine income and expense accounts to minimize audit time, avoid duplication of staff effort, and curtail interference with entity operations.

Advertising is the corporation's largest expense and the advertising manager suggests that a staff member of your firm, whose uncle owns the advertising agency that handles the corporation's advertising, be assigned to examine the Advertising Expense account because the staff member has a thorough knowledge of the complex contact between Cooper Cosmetics and the advertising agency.

Required:

 a. To what extent should auditors follow the client's suggestions for the conduct of an audit? Discuss.

 b. List and discuss the reasons that audit work should not be assigned solely according to asset, liability, and income and expense categories.

 c. Should the staff member of your accounting firm whose uncle owns the advertising agency be assigned to examine advertising costs? Discuss.

2.41 **Standards of Field Work.** You have accepted the engagement of auditing the financial statements of the C. Reis Company, a small manufacturing firm that has been your client for several years. Because you were busy writing the report for another engagement, you sent a staff accountant to begin the audit, with the suggestion that she start with the accounts receivable. Using the prior-year's audit documentation as a guide, she prepared a trial balance of the accounts, aged them, prepared and mailed positive confirmation requests, examined underlying support for charges and credits, and performed other work she considered necessary to obtain evidence about the validity and collectibility of the receivables. At the conclusion of her work, you reviewed the audit documentation she prepared and found she had carefully followed the prior-year's audit documentation.

Required:

The opinion rendered by auditors states that the audit was made in accordance with generally accepted auditing standards. List the three generally accepted standards of field work. Relate them to this illustration by indicating how they were fulfilled or, if appropriate, how they were not fulfilled.

(AICPA adapted)

2.42 **Time of Appointment and Planning.** Your public accounting practice is located in a city of 15,000 people. Your work, conducted by you and two assistants, consists of compiling clients' monthly statements and preparing income tax returns for individuals from cash data and partnership returns from books and records. You have a few corporate clients; however, service to them is limited to preparation of income tax returns and assistance in year-end closings where bookkeeping is deficient.

One of your corporate clients is a retail hardware store. Your work for this client has been limited to preparing the corporation income tax return from a trial balance submitted by the bookkeeper.

On December 26, you receive from the president of the corporation a letter containing the following request:

> We have made arrangements with First National Bank to borrow $500,000 to finance the purchase of a complete line of appliances. The bank has asked us to furnish our auditors' certified statement as of December 31, which is the closing date of our accounting year. The trial balance of the general ledger should be ready by January 10, which should allow ample time to prepare your report for submission to the bank by January 20. In view of the importance of this certified report to our financing program, we trust you will arrange to comply with the foregoing schedule.

Required:

From a theoretical viewpoint, discuss the difficulties that are caused by such a short-notice audit request.

(AICPA adapted)

2.43 **Standards of Reporting.** CPA Musgrave and his associates audited the financial statements of North Company, a computer equipment retailer. Musgrave conducted the audit in accordance with the general standards and the standards of field work of generally accepted auditing standards and therefore issued a standard report. Then he received an emergency call to fill in as a substitute tenor in his barbershop quartet.

No one else was in the office that Saturday afternoon, so he handed you the completed financial statements and footnotes and said: "Make sure it's OK to issue an unqualified opinion on these statements. The audit documentation is on the table. I'll check with you on Monday morning."

Required:

In general terms, what must you determine in order to issue an unqualified opinion paragraph for Musgrave's signature?

2.44 **GAAS in a Computerized Environment.** The Lovett Corporation uses an IBM mainframe computer system with peripheral optical reader and high-speed laser printer equipment. Transaction information is initially recorded on paper documents (e.g., sales invoices) and then read by the optical reader, which produces a computer file containing the data. These files are processed by a computer program and printed listings, journals, and general ledger balances are produced on the high-speed laser printer.

Required:

Explain how the audit standard requiring "adequate technical training and proficiency" is important for satisfying the general standards and standards of field work in the audit of Lovett Corporation's financial statements.

2.45 **Authoritative Support.** Auditors' reports on financial statements contain an opinion on the conformity of the statements with generally accepted accounting principles (GAAP). An audit decision on GAAP includes the determination of whether an accounting treatment is "generally accepted," and this determination is made by finding the authoritative support for the accounting treatment.

Required:

List in order of priority the sources of authoritative support auditors can consult when faced with a decision about GAAP.

2.46 **Sources of Professional Standards.** Listed here are nine descriptions of professional standards or parts thereof.

a. Definition of a financial statement audit for a private entity.

b. Guidance for reporting on internal control for a public entity.

c. Standards for the practice of internal auditing.

d. Generally accepted government auditing standards.

e. Standards of financial accounting.

f. Auditing standards for public entities.

g. Auditing standards for private entities.

h. Guidance for lending credibility to nonfinancial information.

i. Auditing standards for foreign entities.

Required:

Name the AICPA committee or other authoritative source of each of the professional standards. Choose from these: AICPA Auditing Standards Board (ASB), Institute of Internal Auditors (IIA), Financial Accounting Standards Board (FASB), IFAC International Auditing and Assurance Standards Board (IAASB), Public Company Accounting Oversight Board (PCAOB), U.S. Government Accountability Office (GAO).

2.47 **Auditors' Reports.** Two situations that may result in a modification of the auditors' report are (a) scope limitations and (b) departures from generally accepted accounting principles. For each of these situations, identify how the auditors' report would be modified to reflect the work performed and responsibility assumed by auditors. In addition, indicate what type of opinion(s) could be issued in the circumstances.

2.48 **Association with Financial Statements.** For each of the situations described here, state whether the accountant is or is not associated with the financial statements. What is the consequence of being associated with financial statements?

a. Accountant audits financial statements and his or her name is in the corporate annual report containing them.

b. Accountant prepares the financial schedules in the partnership tax return.

c. Accountant uses the computer to process client-submitted data and delivers financial statement output.

d. Accountant uses the computer to process client-submitted data and delivers a general ledger printout.

e. Accountant lets client copy client-prepared financial statements on the accountant's letterhead.

f. Accountant issues quarterly financial statements and prints the accountant's name in the document.

g. Accountant renders consulting advice about the system to prepare interim financial statements but does not review the statements prior to their release.

2.49 **Investment Performance Attestation.** Nancy Drew is the president of Mystery Capital Management, Inc. Mystery manages $1.2 billion in two mutual funds, one a stock fund and the other a bond fund. Competition for investors' money is fierce and hundreds of money management companies compete by advertising their funds' performance statistics. The U.S. Securities and Exchange Commission has criticized the advertisements for misrepresenting the returns investors can actually earn. In addition to the investment performance statistics, money management firms also advertise the amounts of their fees, usually representing no-load or low-fee arrangements, but they often do not advertise the Rule 12(b) expenses allowed under SEC rules.

Ms. Drew has retained your accounting firm to give an opinion on the fair presentation of Mystery Capital Management's investment performance statistics and expense ratios used in its advertisements. The plan is to present your report in the entity's advertisements.

Required:

For each of the attestation standards, state its applicability in relation to the engagement.

2.50 **Auditing Standards Case Study.** Ray, the owner of a small entity, asked Holmes, CPA, to conduct an audit of the entity's records. Ray told Holmes that the audit was to be completed in time to submit audited financial statements to a bank as part of a loan application. Holmes immediately accepted the engagement and agreed to provide an auditors' report within three weeks. Ray agreed to pay Holmes a fixed fee plus a bonus if the loan was granted.

Holmes hired two accounting students to conduct the audit and spent several hours telling them exactly what to do. Holmes told the students not to spend time reviewing the controls but, instead, to concentrate on proving the mathematical accuracy of the ledger accounts and on summarizing the data in the accounting records that support Ray's financial statements. The students followed Holmes' instructions and, after two weeks, gave Holmes the financial statements, which did not include footnotes. Holmes studied the statements and prepared an unqualified auditors' report. The report, however, did not refer to generally accepted accounting principles or to the fact that Ray had changed to the accounting standard for capitalizing interest.

Required:

Briefly describe each of the generally accepted auditing standards and indicate how the action(s) of Holmes resulted in a failure to comply with each standard.

(AICPA adapted)

2.51 **Generally Accepted Auditing Standards.** In each of the following scenarios, identify which of the 10 generally accepted auditing standards is most applicable. In addition, discuss whatever action(s) (if any) you believe auditors should take with respect to these issues.

a. An entity has changed its method of accounting for inventories from LIFO to FIFO. You agree that the decision to make the change is reasonable and the entity has accounted for and disclosed this change properly in its financial statements.

b. An entity has contacted you about performing their audit engagement. You have not previously served a client in the entity's industry, which has many industry-specific accounting issues that are both technical and complex.

c. An entity has entered into a number of lease agreements. Based on the provisions of *SFAS 13,* you believe that these obligations meet the criteria for being classified as capital leases; however, the entity has elected to treat these leases as operating leases, providing full and complete disclosure of this treatment in the footnotes to the financial statements.

d. Because of a disagreement with its current auditors, an entity has contacted you about conducting its current-year audit. However, because the previous auditors have just recently resigned the engagement, you have some questions as to whether an audit can be completed in time to meet the entity's deadlines for providing audited financial statements to a lender.

e. Based on the effectiveness of the entity's internal control, you have assessed control risk at low levels and decided that a smaller number of customer accounts need to be confirmed.

f. An entity has contacted you about performing their audit engagement. This entity became aware of your firm because the husband of one of your partners is currently serving as the entity's chief financial officer.

g. An entity for whom you provide bookkeeping services has requested that you generate financial statements for them and print these financial statements on your letterhead. They believe that having these statements produced on your letterhead will provide them with additional credibility as they seek financing from potential lenders and investors.

h. One of your clients is currently a potential defendant in several cases because of the damage caused by one of their products. Because this entity does not believe that they are likely to receive an unfavorable outcome from this litigation, they did not disclose the potential litigation in the footnotes accompanying their financial statements.

i. You are performing tests of the client's controls over the processing of revenue transactions to determine whether these controls are operating effectively and can be relied upon to prevent or detect misstatements.

j. One of your supervisors has requested a number of clarifications based on her review of your work on an audit engagement. A subsequent meeting with her has resolved these clarifications and you have both concluded that your work supports the opinion on the client's financial statements.

2.52 **Quality Control Standards.** Each of the following quality control policies and procedures is typical of ones that can be found in accounting firms' quality control documents. Identify each of them with one of the elements of quality control required by the AICPA quality control standards.

a. Review semiannual performance reports with individuals and assess their progress in relation to job performance, future objectives, assignment preferences, and career opportunities.

b. Publish guidelines for review of each auditors' report, including the determination of the adequacy of evidence shown in the audit documentation, the conformity of the report with professional standards, and the review of the report by a partner not otherwise connected with the audit engagement.

c. Maintain or provide access to adequate reference libraries and designated experts by (1) maintaining technical manuals and internal technical newsletters and (2) advising staff personnel of the degree of authority accorded internal experts' opinions and the procedures to be followed for resolving disagreements with experts.

d. Consider the experience and training of the engagement personnel in relation to the complexity or other requirements of the engagement and the extent of supervision to be provided.

e. Review recruiting results annually to determine whether goals and personnel needs are being achieved.

f. Distribute new professional pronouncements (FASB, ASB, IRS, others) and encourage personnel at all levels to join the professional organizations (AICPA, state society of CPAs, others).

g. A special team will review a selection of completed audits for compliance with professional standards, including generally accepted auditing standards, generally accepted accounting principles, and the firm's quality control policies and procedures.

h. Obtain from personnel periodic written representations listing their investments, outside business relationships, and employment of their close relatives.

i. A firm management committee shall annually review client relationships in light of changes in management, directors, ownership, legal counsel, financial condition, litigation status, nature of client's business, and scope of the engagement.

2.53 **Relative Appropriateness of Evidence.** The third generally accepted standard of audit field work requires that auditors obtain sufficient appropriate audit evidence to afford a reasonable basis for an opinion regarding the financial statements under examination. In considering what constitutes sufficient appropriate audit evidence, a distinction should be made between underlying accounting data and all corroborating information available to auditors.

Required:

What presumptions can be made about

a. The relative reliability of evidence obtained from external and internal sources?

b. The role of internal control with respect to internal evidence produced by a client's information processing system?

c. The relative persuasiveness of auditors' observation and recalculation evidence compared to external, external-internal, and internal documentary evidence?

2.54 **Public Company Accounting Oversight Board Inspection Reports (Internet Exercise).** Refer to the Public Company Accounting Oversight Board's (PCAOB's) Web site (www. pcaob.org) and review the information under "Inspections" and select the most current inspection report for one of the Big Four firms (Deloitte & Touche, Ernst & Young, KPMG, and PricewaterhouseCoopers).

Required:

a. What information is contained in the "public" version of the PCAOB's inspection reports?

b. What categories of practices, policies, and procedures are evaluated in the PCAOB's inspection of the firm's quality control system?

c. For the firm you selected, how many practice offices had audits inspected by the PCAOB?

d. For the firm you selected, for how many audits (issuers) did the PCAOB find deficiencies?

e. Identify five deficiencies that were cited in the PCAOB's inspection report. For each deficiency, to which of the 10 generally accepted auditing standards does it most closely relate?

f. Briefly summarize the firm's response (if any) to the PCAOB's inspection report.

2.55 **Kaplan CPA Exam Simulation: Generally Accepted Auditing Standards.**

Required:

Go to the Kaplan Web site link at www.mhhe.com/louwers3e, click on AUD: Kerklaan Enterprises case and the "Communication" tab and complete the assigned task.

2.56 **Kaplan CPA Exam Simulation: GAAP Hierarchy.**

Required:

Go to the Kaplan Web site link at www.mhhe.com/louwers3e, click on AUD: NivotnySchmidt and the "GAAP Hierarchy" tab and complete the assigned task.

Management Fraud and Audit Risk

Professional Standards References

Compendium Section	Document Reference	Topic
AU 311	SAS 108	"Planning and Supervision"
	ISA 300	"Planning an Audit of Financial Statements"
AU 312	SAS 107	"Audit Risk and Materiality in Conducting an Audit"
	ISA 320	"Audit Materiality"
AU 314	SAS 109	"Understanding the Entity and Its Environment and Assessing the Risks of Material Misstatement"
	ISA 315	"Understanding the Entity and Its Environment and Assessing the Risks of Material Misstatement"
AU 316	SAS 99	"Consideration of Fraud in a Financial Statement Audit"
	ISA 240	"The Auditor's Responsibility to Consider Fraud in an Audit of Financial Statements"
AU 317	SAS 54	"Illegal Acts by Clients"
	ISA 250	"Consideration of Laws and Regulations in an Audit of Financial Statements"
AU 318	SAS 110	"Performing Audit Procedures in Response to Assessed Risks and Evaluating the Audit Evidence Obtained"
	ISA 330	"The Auditor's Procedures in Response to Assessed Risks"
AU 326	SAS 106	"Audit Evidence"
	ISA 500	"Audit Evidence"
	ISA 501	"Audit Evidence—Additional Considerations for Specific Items"
AU 329	SAS 56	"Analytical Procedures"
	ISA 520	"Analytical Procedures"
AU 330	SAS 67	"The Confirmation Process"
	ISA 505	"External Confirmations"
AU 331	SAS 1	"Inventories"
AU 334	SAS 45	"Related Parties"
	ISA 550	"Related Parties"
AU 9334		"Interpretations: Related Parties"
AU 336	SAS 73	"Using the Work of a Specialist"
	ISA 620	"Using the Work of an Expert"
AU 339	SAS 103	"Audit Documentation"
	AS 3	"Audit Documentation"
	ISA 230	"Documentation"
AU 342	SAS 57	"Auditing Accounting Estimates"
	ISA 540	"Auditing Accounting Estimates"
AU 9342		"Interpretation: Auditing Accounting Estimates"
AU 380	SAS 114	"The Auditor's Communication with Those Charged with Governance"
	ISA 260	"Communication with Those Charged with Governance"

My actions are inexcusable . . . I'm sorry for the hurt that has been caused by my cowardly behavior.

Scott Sullivan, former WorldCom CFO, at his sentencing

It takes 20 years to build a reputation and five minutes to ruin it. If you think about that, you'll do things differently.

Warren Buffet, billionaire investor

Learning Objectives

This chapter begins with a discussion of fraudulent financial reporting. The identification of the potential for management fraud provides a beginning point for a discussion of some of the risks auditors face when conducting audit engagements. Controlling these risks provides a framework for the conduct of the engagement, culminating in the preparation of the program of procedures used to gather enough evidence to express an opinion on the financial statements or other information in question.

Your objectives are to be able to:

1. Define and explain the differences among several types of fraud, errors, and illegal acts that might occur in an organization.

2. Explain auditors' responsibilities with respect to detecting and reporting fraud.

3. List and explain some conditions that can lead to frauds.

4. Explain auditors' responsibilities with respect to illegal acts.

5. Describe the conceptual audit risk model and explain the meaning and importance of its components in terms of professional judgment and audit planning.

6. Define *materiality* and explain its relationship to the audit risk model.

7. List and describe eight general types of audit procedures for gathering evidence.

8. Describe the content and purpose of audit programs.

INTRODUCTION

Take a step back in time to March 2001. **Enron**, one of the world's largest energy companies, reported revenues that ranked it among the top 10 U.S. companies. The company had doubled its revenues from 1999 to 2000 and company management predicted that it would do so again for the 2001 fiscal year. **Arthur Andersen**, one of the world's five largest professional service firms, provided Enron with auditing and consulting services, earning Andersen a million dollars a week in fees. While the audit team members expressed concerns with respect to some of Enron's aggressive accounting practices in Andersen's planning meeting for Enron's upcoming fiscal year audit, the future appeared strong for both companies. Andersen's planning team projected both increased growth for Enron and increased fees for Andersen.

Fast-forward now nine months. By December 2001, Enron was a shell of its former self. The company had terminated almost its entire workforce, leaving its Houston skyline-dominating complex of buildings dark and empty. Enron's share price had plummeted from $90 in August 2000 to less than a dollar by December 2001, leaving many of its employees who had invested their life savings in the high-flying energy company out of work and virtually penniless. Enron's failure struck an irreparable blow to Andersen's reputation; one by one, its other clients decided to find other auditors rather than be associated with a firm that was now labeled by media as "low quality." Beset with shareholder lawsuits and government-led investigations of its audit practices, the firm struggled to maintain its very existence. After providing auditing services for almost a century to some of America's largest companies, Andersen decided to leave the practice of auditing publicly traded companies by August 31, 2002. Most of the firm's personnel also left the failing firm, attempting to find positions with other professional service organizations that had picked up Andersen's departing clientele. The firm's partnership equity, depleted by litigation and shareholder settlements, had been reduced to almost nothing, leaving brand

new partners with nothing to show for the hundreds of thousands of dollars it took to buy into the firm's partnership. Accounting students with prestigious (and lucrative) offers from Enron and Andersen found themselves scrambling for jobs when their offers were rescinded late in the recruiting season.

How could one of the largest and fastest-growing companies implode within a matter of months? How could one of the oldest and most venerable auditing firms miss the abuses going on at one of its largest clients, resulting in the firm's virtual dissolution? The answers to both of these questions lie in the risks that each company chose to undertake and the failure of both to adequately monitor and control these risks. In this chapter, we will discuss the risks that businesses face and how auditors try to manage and control the risks that they face when auditing clients.

MANAGEMENT FRAUD OVERVIEW

LEARNING OBJECTIVE

1. Define and explain the differences among several types of fraud, errors, and illegal acts that might occur in an organization.

Fraud consists of knowingly making material misrepresentations of fact, with the intent of inducing someone to believe the falsehood and act on it and, thus, suffer a loss or damage. This definition encompasses all means by which people can lie, cheat, steal, and dupe other people. **Management fraud** is deliberate fraud committed by management that injures investors and creditors through materially misleading information. Because management fraud usually takes the form of deceptive financial statements, management fraud is sometime referred to as *fraudulent financial reporting*. The National Commission on Fraudulent Financial Reporting (1987) defined *fraudulent financial reporting* as intentional or reckless conduct, whether by act or omission, that results in materially misleading financial statements.

Exhibit 3.1 shows some acts and devices that are often involved in financial frauds. Notice that these actions may be perpetrated *by* the organization or may be perpetrated *upon* the organization. Collectively, these are known as **white-collar crime**—the misdeeds of people who wear ties to work and steal with a pencil or a computer terminal. White-collar crime produces ink stains instead of bloodstains.

Auditing standards (specifically *SAS 99*) require that auditors specifically assess the risk of material misstatement due to fraud for each engagement. Fraud risk factors relate

**EXHIBIT 3.1
Overview of Types of Frauds**

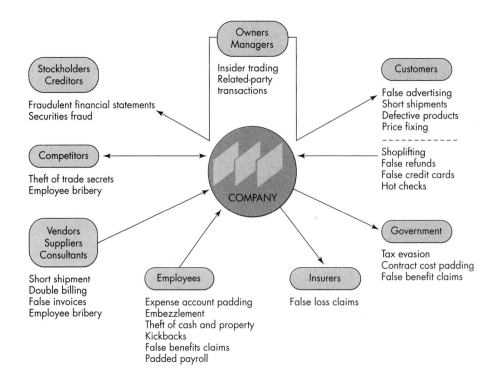

Other Definitions Related to Fraud

Employee fraud is the use of fraudulent means to misappropriate funds or other property from an employer. It usually involves falsifications of some kind: using false documents, lying, exceeding authority, or violating an employer's policies. It consists of three phases: (1) the fraudulent act, (2) the conversion of the funds or property to the fraudster's use, and (3) the cover-up. Employee fraud can be classified as either embezzlement or larceny.

Embezzlement is a type of fraud involving employees or nonemployees wrongfully misappropriating funds or property entrusted to their care, custody, and control, often accompanied by false accounting entries and other forms of lying and cover-up.

Larceny is simple theft; for example, an employee misappropriates an employer's funds or property that has not been entrusted to the custody of the employee.

Defalcation is another name for employee fraud, embezzlement, and larceny. *SAS 99* also calls it "misappropriation of assets."

Errors are unintentional misstatements or omissions of amounts or disclosures in financial statements.

Direct-effect illegal acts are violations of laws or government regulations by the company or its management or employees that produce direct and material effects on dollar amounts in financial statements.

to both misstatements arising from fraudulent financial reporting and misstatements arising from misappropriations of assets (usually as a result of employee theft and the resultant attempt to conceal this theft through erroneous journal entries). Further, auditors should consider these risk factors when determining what audit procedures to perform.

The fraud risk assessment comes first. This risk assessment demands audit skills for noticing the "red flags" (signs of fraud) and deciding whether they are significant for planning subsequent procedures. Thus, performance of fraud-detection procedures depends on (1) the existence of red flags, (2) the auditors' skill in noticing them and assessing the fraud risk, and (3) the auditors' willingness to follow them with fraud-detection procedures.

Although auditing standards concentrate on fraudulent financial reporting, *SAS 99* also requires auditors to pay some attention to employee fraud (*misappropriation of assets*) perpetrated against a client organization, which will be discussed in more detail in Chapter 6. Attention to employee fraud is important because the cover-up can create financial statement misstatements (e.g., overstating inventory to disguise theft of valuable products).

Review Checkpoint

3.1 What are the defining characteristics of (a) white-collar crime, (b) employee fraud, (c) embezzlement, (d) larceny, (e) defalcation, (f) management fraud, (g) errors, and (h) illegal acts?

CONSIDERATION OF FRAUD IN A FINANCIAL STATEMENT AUDIT (*SAS 99*)

LEARNING OBJECTIVE

2. Explain auditors' responsibilities with respect to detecting and reporting fraud.

Many users of audited financial statements generally believe that one of the main objectives of audits is fraud detection. Independent auditors know the issue is very complex and they fear the general view that their work should ferret out all manner of major and minor fraud and misstatement in financial statements. This difference in viewpoints is one of the chronic "expectation gaps" between auditors and users of published financial statements. Independent auditors' responsibilities regarding fraud in financial statements begin with an attitude of professional skepticism:

> The auditor neither assumes that management is dishonest nor assumes unquestioned honesty. In exercising professional skepticism, the auditor should not be satisfied with less than persuasive evidence because of a belief that management is honest. (*SAS 99*, AU 321)

EXHIBIT 3.2
Considering the
Risk of Fraud

Step 1:
Audit Team Discussion ("Brainstorming")

Step 2:
Identify Information Necessary to Assess Fraud Risk Factors

Step 3:
a. Identify and b. Assess Fraud Risk Factors

Step 4:
Respond to Risk Assessment

Step 5:
Evaluate Audit Evidence

Step 6:
Communicate Fraud Matters

Step 7:
Document Fraud Matters

SAS 99 presents an extensive array of audit responsibilities. Basically, the standard requires auditors to understand fraud; assess fraud risks; design audits to provide reasonable assurance of detecting management fraud and employee fraud that could have a material effect on financial statements; and report findings to management, directors, users of financial statements (sometimes), and outside agencies (under certain conditions).

Steps in Considering the Risk of Fraud

Exhibit 3.2 presents the steps involved in the audit team's consideration of the potential for fraud in an audit engagement.

Step 1: Audit Team Discussion ("Brain Storming")

The fraud consideration process presented in Exhibit 3.2 begins with required audit team "brainstorming" sessions in which critical audit areas are discussed. These sessions update audit team members on important aspects of the audit and heighten team members' awareness of the potential for fraud in the engagement. Items typically discussed include previous experiences with the client, how a fraud might be perpetrated and concealed by the client, and procedures that might detect fraud. When studying a business operation, auditors' ability to "think like a crook" and devise ways to steal can help in creating procedures to determine whether fraud has happened. Often, imaginative "extended procedures" can be employed to unearth evidence of fraudulent activity.

A secondary objective of the discussions is to set a proper tone for the engagement. While these "brainstorming" sessions typically begin during the planning phase of the engagements, they should be held on a continuous basis through the conclusion of the engagement.

Many firms have firmwide "fraud specialists" that assist audit teams throughout the process depicted in Exhibit 3.2. If utilized on engagements, the involvement of these individuals during this "brainstorming" session is particularly important, as these specialists are particularly adept at identifying critical audit areas and how these areas influence the risk of misstatement due to fraud.

Step 2: Identify Information Necessary to Assess Fraud Risk Factors

In the second stage, team members gather information necessary to identify key fraud risk factors (*red flags*), indicating an increased potential for fraud occurring. These key fraud indicators can be uncovered as a result of discussions with key members of management, internal auditors, and other employees or through other methods. Comparisons of reported financial statement numbers with estimates developed by the audit team for reasonableness (commonly referred to as *analytical procedures*) have been found to be very useful in identifying unusual relationships among financial statement accounts that merit additional investigation. Another source of information is company discussion boards (such as those found on Yahoo.com) where anonymous "whistleblowers" can post information that management may not wish to disclose to the audit team.

Review Checkpoint

3.2 What are the AICPA auditing standards requirements regarding (a) awareness of fraud, (b) procedural audit work, (c) professional skepticism, and (d) reporting?

3.3 What are the seven steps in the auditor's consideration of fraud?

LEARNING
OBJECTIVE

3. List and explain some conditions that can lead to frauds.

Step 3a: Identify Risk Factors Related to Fraudulent Financial Reporting

Through both fraud and aggressive financial reporting, some companies have caused financial statements to be misleading, usually by (1) overstating revenues and assets,

AUDITING INSIGHT Auditors Fail to Respond to Warning Signs at HealthSouth

After failing to get the auditors' attention through direct e-mail, former **HealthSouth** bookkeeper Michael Vines tried to expose HealthSouth's accounting fraud on Yahoo's bulletin board forum devoted to the company. He wrote, "What I know about the accounting at [HealthSouth] will bring [the company] to its knees . . . what is going on at [HealthSouth], if discovered by the right people will bring change to the accounting department if not the entire company." Although prophetic, his warnings were not heeded by the auditors. They were, however, noticed by HealthSouth security personnel who were able to identify Mr. Vines through his Yahoo ID (which contained some digits from his social security number). What HealthSouth officials intended to do with the information never came to light. One month later, the SEC filed a civil lawsuit alleging "massive accounting fraud," followed quickly by criminal indictments of key executives.

Source: "Ex-Employee Took His Case to Auditors, Then Internet—but Convinced No One," *The Wall Street Journal,* May 20, 2003, pp. A1, A13.

(2) understating expenses and liabilities, and (3) giving disclosures that are misleading or that omit important information.[1] Fraud that affects financial (or other) information and causes financial statements to be materially misleading often arises from the perceived need to "get through a difficult period." The difficult period may be characterized by cash shortage, increased competition, cost overruns, and similar events that cause financial difficulty. Managers usually view these conditions as temporary, believing that getting a new loan, selling stock, or otherwise buying time to recover can overcome them. In the meantime, falsified financial statements are used to "benefit the company." Generally, fraudulent financial statements show financial performance and ratios that are more favorable than current industry experience or than the company's own history. Sometimes the performance meets exactly the earnings targets announced by management months earlier.

On the other hand, there are times when management finds it beneficial to understate assets and revenues and overstate expenses and liabilities. This can be in times when profits are low anyway and management wants to put reserves in a "cookie jar" to be used to increase profits in future years. Understating profits also can be desirable if the company is under scrutiny by governmental bodies, tax authorities, labor, or competitors.

Auditors need to know about the red flags, those telltale signs and indications that have accompanied many frauds. Because of the double-entry bookkeeping system, fraudulent accounting entries always affect at least two accounts and two places in financial statements. Because many frauds involve improper recognition of assets, there is a theory of the "dangling debit," which is an asset amount that can be investigated and found to be false or questionable. Frauds may involve the omission of liabilities, but the matter of finding and investigating the dangling credit is normally very difficult. It "dangles" off the books. Misleading disclosures also present difficulty, mainly because they involve words and messages instead of numbers. Omissions may be difficult to notice, and misleading inferences may be very subtle. Exhibit 3.3 presents some other conditions and circumstances ("fraud risk factors") that have characterized situations in which frauds occurred; these items are the red flags that were discussed earlier.

Step 3b: Assess Fraud Risks

Once risk factors have been identified, the audit team has a better understanding of the potential for fraud. The audit team's next task is to assess the types of fraud risk present (return to Exhibit 3.1 for a graphic illustration of different types of fraud), the likelihood that

[1] A recent academic study (see M. Nelson, J. Elliott, and R. Tarpley, "How Are Earnings Managed? Examples from Auditors," *Accounting Horizons,* November 2002) examined over 500 attempts to manage earnings that were detected by auditors. The majority (over 50 percent) of the attempts involved improper expense reductions, approximately 20 percent involved improper revenue increases, and the remainder involved business combinations and other accounting artifices.

Perpetrator (age at trial)	Company	Verdict	Punishment
Richard Adelson (40)	Impath	Found guilty of conspiracy, securities fraud, and filing false statements with the SEC	Currently serving a 3½-year sentence. Adelson also was fined $1.2 million and ordered to pay $50 million in restitution.
Kim Woo Choong (69)	Daewoo	Found guilty of fraud and embezzlement charges by a South Korean court	Currently serving a 10-year sentence in Korea; forfeited $22 billion in assets.
Conrad Black (62)	Hollinger International Inc.	Found guilty of mail fraud and obstruction of justice.	Currently awaiting sentencing; facing up to 35 years in prison.
Bernie Ebbers (63)	WorldCom	Found guilty on fraud and conspiracy charges related to an $11 billion accounting scandal	Currently serving 25-year sentence in federal prison
Walter Forbes (64)	Cendant	Found guilty of conspiracy to commit securities fraud and two counts of making false statements	Currently serving over 12 years in prison; ordered to pay $3.3 billion in restitution.
Martin Grass (50)	Rite Aid	Pleaded guilty to conspiracy charges	Currently serving 7-year sentence in federal prison.
Cees van der Hoeven (59)	Ahold	Found guilty of committing fraud by a Dutch court	Fined $300,000 and given a 9-month suspended sentence; prosecutors are appealing the leniency of the sentence.
Dennis Kozlowski (59)	Tyco International	Found guilty of stealing $600 million from the company	Currently serving 8-year sentence in New York state prison
Sanjay Kumar (44)	Computer Associates International, Inc. (CA)	Pleaded guilty to obstruction of justice and securities fraud charges related to CA's $3.3 billion accounting scandal	Fined $8 million and sentenced to 12 years in prison.
Ken Lay (64)	Enron	Found guilty of securities fraud and related charges	Suffered a massive coronary and passed away while awaiting sentencing.
John Rigas (80)	Adelphia Communications, Inc.	Found guilty on 18 felony counts of fraud and conspiracy	Currently serving 15-year sentence in federal prison.
Joseph Nacchio (57)	Qwest Communications International, Inc.	Found guilty of 19 counts of insider trading	Currently awaiting sentencing.
Richard Scrushy (52)	HealthSouth	Although 15 other executives were found guilty related to the fraud, Scrushy was acquitted of 36 criminal conspiracy charges related to the fraud; he was later found guilty of other bribery, conspiracy, and mail fraud charges	Currently awaiting sentencing. He also settled civil charges with the SEC for $81 million.
Jeffrey Skilling (52)	Enron	Found guilty of securities fraud and related charges	Currently serving 24-year sentence in prison.
Martha Stewart (63)	Martha Stewart Enterprises	Found guilty of conspiracy and obstruction of justice	Served 5 months in federal prison and 5 months under house arrest.
Sam Waksal (57)	ImClone	Pleaded guilty to insider trading	Currently serving 7-year sentence in federal prison.
Andrew Yao (52)	Student Finance Corp.	Found guilty of two counts of bankruptcy fraud	Currently awaiting sentencing.
Henry Yuen (53)	Gemstar-TV Guide International	Lost a civil trial for his role in fraudulently inflating revenues between 2000 and 2002	Ordered to pay civil fines of $22.3 million, Mr. Yuen is currently "at large."

Sources: "Ebbers Is Sentenced to 25 Years for $11 Billion WorldCom Fraud," *The Wall Street Journal,* July 14, 2005, p. A1; "Daewoo Founder Gets Prison Term," *The Wall Street Journal,* May 31, 2006, p. B9; "Scrushy Is Convicted in Bribery Case," *The Wall Street Journal,* June 30, 2006, p. A3; "Ahold's Ex-CEO, Finance Chief Are Found Guilty in Fraud Case," *The Wall Street Journal,* May 23, 2006, p. B9; "Ex-CEO of Cendant Is Found Guilty in Third Trial," *The Wall Street Journal,* November 1, 2006, p. C3; "Skilling Gets 24 Years in Prison," *The Wall Street Journal,* October 24, 2006, p. C1; "Gemstar's Yuen Said He Destroyed Evidence; Judge: 'A No-Brainer,'" *The Wall Street Journal,* April 25, 2006, p. A1; "Qwest's Nacchio Is Found Guilty in Trading Case," *The Wall Street Journal,* April 20, 2007, p. A1; "Yao Guilty in Fraud Case," *The Wall Street Journal,* March 15, 2007, p. C5; "Press Baron Black Guilty in Fraud Case," *The Wall Street Journal;* July 14, 2007; p. A3.

AUDITING INSIGHT Honey, I Shrunk the Company

The SEC investigated **W. R. Grace & Company** for *underreporting* earnings. Court documents indicate that CFO Brian Smith instructed one of Grace's subsidiaries to report earnings only to the extent of the division's 24 percent growth target. The excess earnings were to be deferred until a "rainy day" by increasing expenses and corresponding reserve accounts (such as the allowance for doubtful accounts). These "cookie jar" reserves could then be decreased in the future, thus increasing income in down periods.

Source: "SEC Claims Profit 'Management,'" *The Wall Street Journal,* April 7, 1999, pp. C1, C20.

fraud has occurred, the magnitude of the fraud risk (usually measured in dollars), and the pervasiveness of the potential for fraud (how widespread the threat is). Part of this assessment includes considering client controls in place to prevent fraud from occurring or detecting fraud once it has occurred.

In addition to the fraud risk assessment based on factors identified, *SAS 99* requires several other fraud risk assessments. First, the audit team must presume that improper revenue recognition is a fraud risk. Another risk is that, despite the existence of controls, management might override the controls through force of authority. Because several major frauds were committed through year-end adjusting entries (such as **WorldCom's** capitalization of telephone line expenses), the audit team must examine journal entries and other adjustments (especially those made close to year end). If any significant unusual accounting entries are identified, the audit team must evaluate the business rationale for the transactions.

EXHIBIT 3.3 Fraud Risk Factors

Management's Characteristics and Influence	Industry Conditions	Operating Characteristics and Financial Stability
• Management has a motivation (bonus compensation, stock options, etc.) to engage in fraudulent reporting.	• Company profits lag the industry.	• A weak internal control environment prevails.
• Management decisions are dominated by an individual or a small group.	• New requirements are passed that could impair stability or profitability.	• The company is not able to generate sufficient cash flows to ensure that it is a going concern.
• Management fails to display an appropriate attitude about internal control and financial reporting.	• The company's market is saturated due to fierce competition.	• There is pressure to obtain capital.
• Managers' attitudes are very aggressive toward financial reporting.	• The company's industry is declining.	• The company operates in a tax haven jurisdiction.
• Managers place too much emphasis on earnings projections.	• The company's industry is changing rapidly.	• The company has many difficult accounting measurement and presentation issues.
• Nonfinancial management participates excessively in the selection of accounting principles or determination of estimates.		• The company has significant transactions or balances that are difficult to audit.
• The company has a high turnover of senior management.		• The company has significant and unusual related-party transactions.
• The company has a known history of violations.		• Company accounting personnel are lax or inexperienced in their duties.
• Managers and employees tend to be evasive when responding to auditors' inquiries.		
• Managers engage in frequent disputes with auditors.		

AUDITING INSIGHT A Man Called "Chainsaw"

"Chainsaw Al" Dunlap is the "poster child" for aggressive, domineering CEOs. He got his nickname for his reputation for firing employees whenever he took the reins of a new company. As CEO of **Sunbeam**, Dunlap presided over the artificial inflation of net income to make the small appliance company more attractive to potential buyers. The fraudulent financial reporting occurred through two primary schemes: (1) a "bill-and-hold" scheme in which customers were billed six months prior to the shipment of goods and (2) premature recording of a restructuring charge that allowed the company to report increased profits in subsequent periods.

Source: "Chainsaw," *BusinessWeek*, October 18, 1999, pp. 128–49.

Accounting estimates are a concern because numerous fraud cases have involved the deliberate manipulation of estimates to increase net income. **Accounting estimates** are approximations of financial statement numbers and are often included in financial statements. Examples include net realizable value of accounts receivable, market (lower than cost) value of inventory, depreciation expense, property and casualty insurance loss reserves, percentage-of-completion contract revenues, pension expense, warranty liabilities, and many more. Management is responsible for making accounting estimates. Auditors are responsible for determining that all appropriate estimates have been made, that they are reasonable, and that they are presented in conformity with GAAP and adequately disclosed.

With respect to auditing accounting estimates (*SAS 57*), auditors are supposed to (1) monitor the differences between management's estimates and the closest reasonable estimates supported by the audit evidence and (2) evaluate the differences taken altogether for indications of a systematic bias. For example, management may estimate an allowance for doubtful accounts to be $50,000 and the auditors may estimate that the allowance could be $40,000 to $55,000. In this case, management's estimate is within the auditors' range of reasonableness. However, the auditors should note that the management estimate leans toward the conservative side (more than the auditors' $40,000 lower estimate, but not much less than the auditors' higher $55,000 estimate). If other estimates exhibit the same conservatism (or aggressiveness) and the effect is material, the auditors will need to evaluate the overall reasonableness of the effect of all estimates taken together.

Step 4: Respond to Assessed Risks

The audit team must next respond to the results of the fraud risk assessments. For example, if the potential for fraud is high, the audit team should include more experienced team members. Other responses include performing more extensive tests, targeting tests toward specific areas, and gathering more effective evidence. Finally, because key financial

AUDITING INSIGHT Things Don't Smell So Good at Waste Management

Associate Director of the SEC's Division of Enforcement Thomas C. Newkirk called it "one of the most egregious accounting frauds we have seen." From 1992 to 1997, **Waste Management's** key executives "engaged in a systematic scheme to falsify and misrepresent Waste Management's financial results . . . in order to enrich themselves, preserve their jobs, and dupe unsuspecting shareholders." Waste Management used the flexibility and discretion inherent in financial estimates in order to fraudulently meet earnings targets. Among the company's more flagrant schemes are these:

- To avoid depreciation expense, company officials assigned inflated salvage values and extended useful lives to the company's garbage trucks and assigned arbitrary salvage values to assets that previously had no salvage value.
- Company officials failed to record expenses for the decreasing value of company landfills as they became filled with waste.

Source: *AccountingWEB*, March 27, 2002.

executives are often CPAs themselves, *SAS 99* also suggests that the team use less predictable audit procedures (commonly referred to as **extended procedures**) such as contract confirmations with customers and "surprise" inventory observations in which management is not told at which company warehouse locations the audit team will show up to watch the client counting inventory.

Step 5: Evaluate Audit Evidence

When collecting corroborating evidence to support the financial statements, the audit team must remain vigilant to the potential for fraud. Discrepancies in the accounting records, conflicting evidence, and missing documentation are all symptomatic of financial statement fraud. When such instances are identified, the audit team must follow up with management to identity the source of the problems. Management's response is a key source of evidence; vague, implausible, or inconsistent responses to inquiries can be a key indicator of the pervasiveness of the fraud. Similarly, problematic or unusual relationships between the audit team and management are often present in financial statement frauds.

The collection of evidence concerning fraud (which can lead to prosecution and court scrutiny) is different from the collection of evidence to support the auditor's opinion. If the auditors do come across questionable documents or other evidence of fraud, they should know how to preserve the chain of custody of evidence. The *chain of custody* is the crucial link of the evidence to the suspect, called the *"relevance" of evidence* by attorneys and judges. If documents are lost, mutilated, coffee stained, or otherwise compromised (so a defense attorney can argue that they were altered to frame the suspect), they lose their effectiveness for the prosecution. Auditors should learn to mark the evidence, writing an identification of the location, condition, date, time, and circumstances as soon as it appears to be a signal of fraud. This marking should be on a separate tag or page; the original document should be put in a protective (plastic) envelope for preservation and locked away for protection and then audit work should proceed with copies of the documents instead of originals. A record should be made of the safekeeping and of all persons who use the original. Any eyewitness observations should be timely recorded in a memorandum or on tape (audio or video) with corroboration of colleagues, if possible. Other features of the chain of custody relate to interviews, interrogations, confessions, documents obtained by subpoena, and other matters, but auditors usually do not conduct these activities.

Step 6: Communicate Fraud Matters

Auditors must always exercise technical and personal care because accusations of fraud are always taken very seriously. For this reason, after preliminary findings indicate fraud possibilities, auditors should enlist the cooperation of management and assist fraud examination professionals when bringing an investigation to a conclusion.

Standards for external auditors contain materiality thresholds related to auditors reporting their knowledge of frauds. Auditors may consider some minor frauds inconsequential, especially when they involve misappropriations of assets by employees at low organizational levels. Auditors should report these to management at least one level above the people involved. The idea is that small matters can be kept in the management family. Having said this, fraud has often been compared to an iceberg: most of it can be hidden from sight. For this reason, auditors should be extremely cautious in deciding whether a fraud is "clearly inconsequential."

On the other hand, frauds involving senior managers are never inconsequential and should be reported (along with any frauds that cause material misstatement in the financial statements) directly to the enity's *audit committee* of its board of directors. All companies with securities traded on the exchanges (e.g., New York, American, NASDAQ) are required to have audit committees. **Audit committees** are composed of independent, outside members of the board of directors (those not involved in the company's day-to-day operations) who can provide a buffer between the audit firm and management. *SAS 114*

sets forth requirements intended to ensure that audit committees are informed about the scope and results of the independent audit.[2] External auditors are required to make oral or written communications about other topics, including the discovery of fraud.

Auditors are normally required to keep client information confidential. However, under AICPA audit standards (specifically, *SAS 99* and *SAS 54*), limited disclosures to outside agencies of frauds and clients' illegal acts are permitted. If the audit firm resigns or is fired, the firm can cite these matters in the letter attached to SEC Form 8-K, which requires explanation of an organization's change of auditors. An ex-auditor may tell the successor auditor about the client when the successor makes the inquiries required by audit standards. Auditors must respond when answering a subpoena issued by a court or other agency with authority. When performing work under GAO-mandated generally accepted government auditing standards (GAGAS), auditors are required to report frauds and illegal acts to the client agency under the audit contract.

Step 7: Document Fraud Matters

The last step involves documenting the fraud consideration process in writing to provide a record of the procedures performed. Items that must be documented include these:

- Discussions of engagement personnel.
- Procedures to identify and assess risk.
- Specific risks identified and audit team responses.
- Explanation of why improper revenue recognition is not a risk.
- Results of procedures regarding management override.
- Other conditions causing auditors to believe that additional procedures are required.
- Communications to management and those charged with governance, such as the audit committee

Although the consideration of fraud is discussed in a number of sequential steps, the evaluation for potential fraud continues throughout the audit. Audit team members must be on the lookout for unusual findings or events and, upon discovery, not simply write them off as isolated occurrences.

Review Checkpoint

3.4 What types of conditions provide opportunities for financial statement fraud?

3.5 Why must care be taken with evidence of fraudulent activity?

AUDITORS' RESPONSIBILITIES FOR ILLEGAL ACTS (*SAS 54*)

LEARNING OBJECTIVE

4. Explain auditors' responsibilities with respect to illegal acts.

A client's illegal acts can cause financial statements to be misstated, and external auditors are advised to be aware of circumstances that could indicate illegal acts. *SAS 54* deals with two types of *illegal acts*: (1) **direct-effect illegal acts** produce direct and material effects on financial statement amounts (e.g., violations of tax laws and government contracting regulations for cost and revenue recognition), and they require the same assurance as errors and frauds; and (2) **indirect-effect illegal acts** refer to violations of laws and

[2] *SAS 114* has broadened communications to include groups that serve in a similar role for private companies and refers to such groups as "those charged with governance." Audit committees serve in this role for public companies.

AUDITING INSIGHT | KPMG Germany Fails to Spot Bribery and Money Laundering at Siemens

German prosecutors are examining **KPMG Germany's** role in the alleged bribery scheme at **Siemens AG**, specifically whether the firm ignored questionable payments on the company's books. Two Siemens executives claim that a junior member of the firm had identified questionable payments, but under pressure from Siemens' CFO, a senior partner in the firm chose to ignore them rather than contact authorities. Despite ongoing police investigations into money laundering, KPMG Germany gave unqualified opinions on Siemens's financial statements and on the adequacy of Siemens's internal controls in the company's 2005 SEC filings.

In December 2006, KPMG withdrew its opinion and began a forensic investigation that identified €420 million ($551.8 million) in suspicious "consulting" transactions spanning seven years. In a written response to questions, the firm denied any wrongdoing and said that it always has fulfilled its annual auditing obligations, that it is cooperating fully with authorities, and that none of its employees have been named as suspects. Confidentiality agreements prevented the firm from answering questions about its audit work.

Source: *The Wall Street Journal*, February 24, 2007, p. B3

regulations that are far removed from financial statement effects (e.g., violations relating to insider securities trading, occupational health and safety, food and drug administration, environmental protection, and equal employment opportunity). The far-removed illegal acts require a general awareness, particularly in matters of contingent liability disclosure, but not routine responsibility for detection and reporting. Indirect-effect illegal acts also can have significant effects on the financial statements because of legal fees and penalties. An audit team who becomes aware of indirect-effect illegal acts must follow up to determine whether they represent a material misstatement.

Following are signs and signals (red flags) of potential illegal acts:

- Unauthorized transactions.
- Government investigations.
- Regulatory reports of violations.
- Payments to consultants, affiliates, or employees for unspecified services.
- Excessive sales commissions and agents' fees.
- Unusually large cash payments.
- Unexplained payments to government officials.
- Failure to file tax returns or to pay duties and fees.

Similar to frauds committed by low-level employees, clients' illegal acts also come under a "clearly inconsequential" materiality threshold. Illegal acts having financial statement effects greater than this threshold should be reported to those charged with governance such as the audit committee and the financial statements should contain adequate disclosures about the organization's illegal acts. External auditors always have the option to withdraw from an engagement if management and directors do not take satisfactory action in the circumstances.

In addition, another reporting obligation was imposed by the Private Securities Litigation Reform Act of 1995 (amending the Securities and Exchange Act of 1934). Under this law (specifically, section 10A), when auditors believe an illegal act that is more than "clearly inconsequential" has or could have occurred, the auditors must inform the organization's board of directors. When the auditors believe the illegal act has a material effect on the financial statements, the board of directors has one business day to inform the U.S. Securities and Exchange Commission (SEC). If the board decides to not inform the SEC, the auditors must (1) within one business day give the SEC the same report they gave the board of directors or (2) resign from the engagement and, within one business day, give the SEC the report. If the auditors do not fulfill this legal obligation, the SEC can impose a civil penalty (e.g., monetary fine) on them. Exhibit 3.4 summarizes audit team responsibilities for detecting and communicating findings with respect to errors, frauds, and illegal acts.

EXHIBIT 3.4
Auditor's Responsibility for Detecting Errors, Fraud, and Illegal Acts

	Responsible for Detection?		Must Communicate Findings?	
	Material	**Immaterial**	**Material**	**Immaterial**
Errors	Yes	No	Yes (audit committee)	No
Fraud	Yes	No	Yes (audit committee)	Yes (by low-level employee, to one level above) (by management-level employee, to audit committee)
Illegal Acts	Yes (Direct Effect)	No	Yes (audit committee)	Yes (one level above)

Review Checkpoints

3.6 How do the standards differ for (a) errors, (b) frauds, (c) direct-effect illegal acts, and (d) indirect-effect illegal acts?

THE AUDIT RISK MODEL

LEARNING OBJECTIVE

5. Describe the conceptual audit risk model and explain the meaning and importance of its components in terms of professional judgment and audit planning.

Information risk is the probability that the information (including financial statements) distributed by an entity will be *materially* false and misleading. Auditors' evidence-gathering and reporting reduce this risk to financial statement users, but auditors themselves face the risk of issuing an incorrect opinion on the financial statements—giving an unqualified audit opinion when unknown material misstatements (whether due to errors, frauds, or direct-effect illegal acts) actually exist in the statements. This overall risk is known as *audit risk*. Auditing standards require auditors to design audits to provide reasonable assurance of detecting material errors and frauds to minimize this risk.

Audit Risk

In an overall sense, **audit risk** is the probability that an audit team will give an inappropriate opinion on financial statements (e.g., giving an unqualified opinion on financial statements that are misleading because of material misstatements the auditors failed to discover). Such a risk always exists, even when audits are well planned and carefully performed. The risk is much greater in poorly planned and carelessly performed audits.

Audit risk is a conceptual *quality criterion* for audit performance. The auditing profession has no official standard for an acceptable level of overall audit risk, except that it should be "acceptably low." However, auditors would be appalled to think that even 1 percent of their audits would be bad. For a large firm with 2,000 audit clients, 1 percent would mean 20 bad audits per year!

Audit risk is most often used in practice with regard to individual balances, assertions, and disclosures. You should keep this context in mind when you study the risk model summary presented at the end of this section. In the overall sense and for an individual account or disclosure, the audit risk cannot be too high (e.g., 50 percent, the flip of a coin) or too low (e.g., zero). Some audit risk, but not too much, is allowable under GAAS. Auditors specify it by professional judgment and firm policy.

EXHIBIT 3.5 **Inherent, Control, and Detection Risk**

Audit risk (see Exhibit 3.5) can be briefly summarized as the risk that (1) a material misstatement occurs (*inherent risk*), (2) it would not be caught by client internal controls (*control risk*), and (3) it would not be detected by the auditor's procedures (*detection risk*). The following sections discuss each of these components in more detail.

Inherent Risk

Inherent risk is the probability that, in the absence of internal controls, material errors or frauds could enter the accounting system used to develop financial statements. You can think of inherent risk as the *susceptibility* of the account to misstatement. Inherent risk is a characteristic of the client's business, the major types of transactions, and the effectiveness of its accountants. Auditors do not create or control inherent risk. They can only try to assess its magnitude.

External auditors' basis for assessing a client's inherent risk is found in their familiarity with the types of misstatements that can occur in any account balance or class of transactions. Clearly, hundreds of innocent errors and not-so-innocent fraud schemes are possible. Instead of trying to learn hundreds of possible errors and frauds, it is better to start with seven general categories of them. In a sense, these seven categories answer the audit question: "What can go wrong?" Exhibit 3.6 shows a typology of the seven categories with some examples.

An assessment of inherent risk can be based on a variety of information. Auditors can know that material misstatements were discovered during the last year's audit, so inherent risk will be considered higher than it would be if last year's audit had shown no material misstatements. Auditors could believe the client's accounting clerks tend to misunderstand GAAP and the entity's own accounting policies, thus suggesting a significant probability of mistakes in transaction processing. The nature of the client's business can produce complicated transactions and calculations generally known to be subject to information processing and accounting treatment error. (For example, real estate, franchising, and oil and gas transactions are frequently complicated and subject to accounting error. Some types of inventories are more difficult than others to count, value, and keep accurately in perpetual records.) The following factors have been suggested as being related to the susceptibility of accounts to misstatement or fraud:

- *Dollar size of the account.* The larger the account balance, the greater the chance of having errors or fraud in the account.
- *Liquidity.* The greater the account's liquidity (ability to be easily converted to cash), the more susceptible the account is to fraud. For example, cash is more susceptible to theft than, say, a building.
- *Volume of transactions.* The greater the volume of transactions, the greater the chance of error or fraud occurring in the transactions.

EXHIBIT 3.6 **General Categories of Errors and Frauds**

	Error Examples	Fraud Examples
1. Invalid transactions are recorded	A computer malfunction causes a sales transaction to be recorded twice	Fictitious sales are recorded and charged to nonexistent customers
2. Valid transactions are omitted from the accounts	Shipments to customers are never recorded because of problems in the company's information processing system	Shipments are made to an employee's friend and purposely never recorded
3. Unauthorized transactions are executed and recorded	A customer's order is not approved for credit yet the goods are shipped, billed, and charged to the customer without requiring payment in advance	Unauthorized purchases are made and shipped to an employee's house
4. Transaction amounts are inaccurate	An employee calculates depreciation incorrectly	A company "short ships" a shipment to a customer and bills the customer for the full amount ordered
5. Transactions are classified in the wrong accounts	Sales to a subsidiary company are recorded as sales to outsiders instead of intercompany sales or the amount is charged to the wrong customer account receivable record	A loan to the company's CEO (not permitted under Sarbanes-Oxley) is classified as an account receivable to conceal the transaction
6. Transaction accounting and posting are incorrect	Sales are posted in total to the accounts receivable control account, but some are not posted to individual customer account records	Capital leases are accounted for as operating leases in order to keep related liabilities off the balance sheet
7. Transactions are recorded in the wrong period	The company fails to record a shipment that was sent by a supplier FOB shipping point in December, but the shipment was not received (or recorded) until January	Shipments made in January (of the next fiscal year) are backdated and recorded as sales in December

- *Complexity of the transactions.* Very complex transactions tend to have a greater percentage of errors than simple transactions.
- *Subjective estimates.* Subjective measurements (e.g., estimating the allowance for doubtful accounts) tend to have more errors and fraud than objective measurements (e.g., counting petty cash).

In addition, auditors should be aware of the effects that economic distress and slow recovery can have on their clients. The following is a list of issues affecting inherent risk assessments arising from an economic downturn:[3]

- Asset valuations should be challenged in considering whether amounts are recoverable and the bases of accounting are appropriate.
- Inappropriate offsetting of assets and liabilities should be carefully evaluated.
- Changes in cost-deferral policies and the reasonableness of amortization periods should be carefully evaluated.
- Allowances for doubtful accounts, in general, and loan-loss allowances for financial institutions, in particular, should be evaluated carefully and thoroughly.
- Compliance with financial covenants and the necessity to obtain waivers from lending institutions to meet current requirements should be carefully reviewed.
- Changes in sales practices or terms that may require a change in accounting should be identified and considered.

[3] AICPA *Practice Alert 01-2,* October 2001.

Control Risk

Control risk is the probability that the client's internal control policies and procedures will *fail* to prevent or detect material misstatements, provided any enter or would have entered the accounting system in the first place. Recall from our discussion of the 10 GAAS in Chapter 2 that one of the major purposes of internal control is to ensure the appropriate processing and recording of transactions (i.e., avoid the general categories of error and fraud shown earlier). Auditors do not create or manage the control risk. They can only evaluate an entity's control system and assess the probability of its failure to prevent or detect material misstatements.

The external auditors' task of control risk assessment starts with learning about an entity's controls designed to prevent, detect, and correct the potential errors and frauds listed earlier. The auditors then observe and test the controls, if necessary, to determine their effectiveness.

Control effectiveness conclusions and risk assessments can be made on a preliminary basis for planning purposes. Auditors often carry over preconceived notions about control risk when they perform the audit on a client year after year. This carryover is known as *anchoring* the control risk assessment (starting with knowledge of last year's conclusions), and it represents (1) a useful continuity of experience with a particular client and (2) a potential pitfall if conditions change for the worse and the audit team fails to acknowledge the deterioration of control.

Control risk should not be assessed so low that auditors place complete reliance on controls and do not perform any other audit work. Conversely, auditors should not disregard the controls and rely solely on other audit procedures to gather sufficient evidence to support their conclusions on the financial statements. The best approach is to rely too heavily neither on the client's internal controls nor on audit procedures to detect errors or frauds in the financial statements.

Detection Risk

Detection risk is the probability that audit procedures will *fail* to detect material misstatements, provided any have entered the accounting system in the first place and not been detected and corrected by the client's internal controls. In contrast to inherent risk and control risk, auditors are responsible for performing the evidence-gathering procedures that manage and establish detection risk. These audit procedures represent the auditors' opportunity to detect material misstatements that can cause financial statements to be misleading.

Later in this chapter, you will study substantive procedures. These are the procedures used to detect material misstatements in dollar amounts and disclosures presented in the financial statements and footnotes. The two categories of *substantive procedures* are (1) audit of the details of transactions and balances and (2) analytical procedures applied to produce circumstantial evidence about dollar amounts in the accounts. Detection risk is realized when procedures in these two categories fail to detect material misstatements.

Risk Model—A Summary

The foregoing components of audit risk can be expressed in a model that assumes that each of the elements is *independent*. Thus, the risks are *multiplied* as follows:

Audit risk (AR) = Inherent risk (IR) × Control risk (CR) × Detection risk (DR)

Auditors want to perform an audit of a particular balance or disclosure well enough to hold the audit risk (AR) to a relatively low level (e.g., 0.05, which means that, on average, 5 percent of audit decisions will be wrong). As such, AR is a *quality criterion* based on professional judgment. All the other risk assessments are estimates based on professional judgment and evidence.

For example, suppose an audit team thought a particular inventory balance was subject to great inherent risk of material misstatement (say, IR = 0.90) and that the client's

internal control was not very effective (say, CR = 0.50). If the audit team wanted to keep audit risk at a low level (say, AR = 0.05), according to the model, this example would produce the following results:

$$AR = IR \times CR \times DR$$

$$0.05 = 0.90 \times 0.50 \times DR$$

Solving for DR: DR = 0.1111 (rounded to 0.11)

You should notice that detection risk (DR) depends on the other risks. DR is derived from the others by solving the risk model equation. It is not an independent judgment. Hence,

$$DR = AR/(IR \times CR)$$

$$DR = 0.11 = 0.05/(0.90 \times 0.50)$$

While detection risk is defined as the risk that the auditors' procedures *fail* to detect material misstatements, it is important that you understand that the application of DR is different. There is not an 11 percent risk of the auditors failing to detect a material misstatement because the auditors have complete control of the procedures that they perform. The auditors can decide to audit everything and reduce detection risk to a negligible amount. Rather, the 11 percent represents *the amount of risk the auditors can allow* and still maintain overall audit risk at 0.05. In other words, the other procedures would need to be so designed that detection risk (DR) did not exceed 0.11 (approximately). Exhibit 3.7 provides a visual display of the steps in the audit risk process.

Because auditors have little control over inherent risk and control risk, the two risks are often combined and referred to as the **risk of material misstatement** (RMM). In Exhibit 3.7, RMM would be.45 [(IR =.90) × (CR =.5) =.45]. Note that there is an inverse relationship between RMM and detection risk. In other words, the greater the risk of material misstatement, the lower the detection risk auditors can allow in order to maintain the level of audit risk with which they feel comfortable.

Based on the allowable detection risk, auditors modify the *nature*, the *timing*, and the *extent* of their audit procedures (see Exhibit 3.8). The *nature* of the procedures refers to audit procedures' overall *effectiveness* at detecting misstatements. While inquiry of management as to whether accounts receivable listed on the balance sheet really exist is an audit procedure, it certainly is not an *effective* one. A much more effective procedure would be to confirm accounts receivable directly with the client's customers. *Timing* refers to when the audit procedures take place. While confirmation of accounts receivable may be performed at an interim period, auditors are expressing an opinion on year-end balances. The closer the procedures are performed to year end (the date of the financial statements), the more effective they are considered because there is less chance of a material misstatement occurring between the interim confirmation date and year end. Finally, *extent* refers to the number of tests performed. Clearly, the more accounts receivable confirmations that are mailed out to customers, the greater the chance of finding errors and fraud.

The practical problem here is knowing whether the audit has been planned and performed well enough to hold the detection risk as low as 0.11. Despite the simplicity of the risk model, it is only a conceptual tool. Auditors have few ways to calculate detection risk,

EXHIBIT 3.7
Audit Risk Process

AUDIT RISK PROCESS

EXHIBIT 3.8
Detection Risk and the Nature, Timing, and Extent of Audit Procedures

	Lower Detection Risk	**Higher Detection Risk**
Nature	More effective tests	Less effective tests
Timing	Testing performed at year-end	Testing can be performed at interim
Extent	More tests	Fewer tests

so the model represents more of a way to think about audit risks than a way to calculate them. However, several accounting firms use this model to calculate risks and the related sample sizes.

The model produces some insights, including these:

1. Auditors cannot rely entirely on an estimate of zero inherent risk to the exclusion of other evidence-gathering procedures. Thus, you *cannot* have the condition

$$AR = IR (= 0) \times CR \times DR = 0$$

2. Auditors cannot place complete reliance on internal controls to the exclusion of other audit procedures. Thus, you cannot have the condition

$$AR = IR \times CR (= 0) \times DR = 0$$

3. Audits would not seem to exhibit due audit care if the level of audit risk was too high, for example:

$$AR = IR (= 0.80) \times CR (= 0.80) \times DR (= 0.50) = 0.32$$

4. Auditors generally should not choose to rely exclusively on evidence produced by substantive procedures. Even if they think inherent risk and control risk are high, auditors should perform some tests of controls to make sure the controls are in place. The concern is that if the controls are so weak as to not detect material misstatements, an audit team would probably not feel comfortable relying solely on substantive procedures. For example, this combination would generally not be considered acceptable:

$$AR = IR (= 1.00) \times CR (= 1.00) \times DR (= 0.05) = 0.05$$

5. We noted earlier that control risk is a function of the client and that auditors only assess control risk. Although this statement is technically true, in practice, auditors make suggestions to improve client controls. By improving client controls, auditors may be able to save audit effort in the future:

$$AR = IR (= 1.00) \times CR (= 0.50) \times DR (= 0.10) = 0.05$$

If the client is able to reduce control risk by half by strengthening internal control in the organization, auditors can allow a greater detection risk, meaning fewer audit procedures need to be performed. Note that the detection risk in this scenario is higher than that in scenario (4).

To this point, the components of the audit risk model have been expressed *quantitatively* (as a number). In practice, most firms use *qualitative* measures of audit risk such as low, moderate, and high. Whether expressed quantitatively or qualitatively, audit theory places control risk on a probability continuum, and the qualitative control risk categories are points with underlying control risk probabilities (Exhibit 3.9).

EXHIBIT 3.9
Qualitative and Quantitative Control Risks

Control Risk Categories (qualitative)	Representative Control Risk Probabilities (quantitative)
Low control risk	0.10–0.45
Moderate control risk	0.40–0.70
Control risk slightly below the maximum	0.60–0.95
Maximum control risk	1.00

EXHIBIT 3.10
Matrix Approach to
Detection Risk
Determination

		CONTROL RISK		
		Low	Moderate	High
INHERENT RISK	Low	High Detection Risk	Moderate to High Detection Risk	Moderate Detection Risk
	Moderate	Moderate to High Detection Risk	Moderate Detection Risk	Low to Moderate Detection Risk
	High	Moderate Detection Risk	Low to Moderate Detection Risk	Low Detection Risk

When risk is measured qualitatively, how do firms multiply words? Rather than multiplying, firms use a matrix approach similar to the one shown in Exhibit 3.10. Auditors find the appropriate detection risk by reading the cell at the intersection of the assessed levels of inherent risk and control risk.

Review Checkpoints

3.7 Define *audit risk*.

3.8 What are the components of audit risk?

3.9 What are some of the effects of bad economic factors that produce risks that auditors should be alert to detect in clients' financial statements?

3.10 What is meant by the terms *nature*, *timing*, and *extent* of audit procedures?

MATERIALITY

LEARNING OBJECTIVE

6. Define *materiality* and explain its relationship to the audit risk model.

You cannot think usefully about audit risk and detection risk without also thinking about the size of misstatements. Audit risk and detection risk go hand in hand with **materiality.** *Information is material if it is likely to influence financial statement users' decisions.* Thus, *material information* is a synonym for *important information*. The emphasis is on the users' point of view, not on accountants' or managers' points of view. However, financial statement users are expected to have a basic knowledge of business activities, a willingness to study financial statements, and a basic understanding of the limitations of an audit (e.g., auditors usually aren't able to examine every transaction, estimates are subject to uncertainties, etc.).

Auditors are limited by the very complex nature of accounting. Financial statement measurements and information in some footnote disclosures are not flawlessly accurate. As recognized in the scope paragraph of the auditor's standard report, the financial statements are a function of the "accounting principles used and significant estimates made by

Auditors use materiality three ways:

1. As a guide to *planning the substantive procedures* (collectively referred to as the *audit program*)—directing attention and audit work to those items or accounts that are important, uncertain, or susceptible to errors or frauds.

2. As a guide to evaluation of the evidence.

3. As a guide for making *decisions about the audit report.* An account such as inventory can be material in an audit context because of its size or its place in the financial statements. Additionally, inventory's importance can result from the potential for misstatement or the effect that a misstatement can have on the financial statements.

management." The choices of depreciation method (straight line versus accelerated), inventory valuation method (e.g., FIFO, LIFO, weighted average cost), or classification of marketable securities (available for sale, trading, or held to maturity) all affect final financial statement numbers. Further, many financial measurements are based on estimates such as the estimated depreciable lives of fixed assets or the estimated amount of uncollectible accounts receivable. Thus, you must think of net income not as the one "true" figure but as one possible measure in a range of potential net income figures allowable under generally accepted accounting principles (GAAP). Because of the range permitted under GAAP, some amount of inaccuracy is permitted in financial statements because (1) unimportant inaccuracies do not affect users' decisions and hence are not material, (2) the cost of finding and correcting small misstatements is too high, and (3) the time taken to find them would delay issuance of financial statements. While accounting numbers are not absolutely accurate, accountants and auditors want to maintain that financial reports are *materially* accurate and do not contain *material* misstatements.

Materiality Judgment Criteria

Many accountants wish that definitive, quantitative materiality guides could be issued, but many fear the rigidity such guides would impose. The best rules of thumb seem to be that anything less than 5 percent is probably not material and anything more than 10 percent probably is material. (A legitimate question, therefore, is 5 percent or 10 percent of *what?*) The SEC, however, cautions auditors about overreliance on certain quantitative benchmarks to assess materiality, noting that "misstatements are not immaterial simply because they fall beneath a numerical threshold."[4] Thus, auditors must examine both *quantitative* and *qualitative* factors when assessing materiality. Some of the more common factors that auditors use in making materiality judgments include the following.

Absolute Size

An amount of potential misstatement can be important regardless of any other considerations. Not many auditors use absolute size alone as a criterion. A given amount, say $50,000, can be appropriate in one case but too large (the local ice cream stand) or too small (Microsoft) in others. Yet some auditors have been known to say: "$1 million (or some other large number) is material, no matter what."

Relative Size

The relation of potential misstatement to a relevant base number is often used (usually with reference to the 5 percent–10 percent rule of thumb). Potential misstatements in income statement accounts usually are related to net income either before or after taxes. If income fluctuates widely, a "normalized" or average income over recent years may be substituted for the current-year net income, or the relation may be to the trend change of income. The base for nonprofit entities may be gross revenue or contributions or a figure important in the statement of cash flows. While many different bases may be used,

[4] SEC *Staff Accounting Bulletin No. 99*, "Materiality," August 12, 1999.

EXHIBIT 3.11
Materiality Table

The larger of Client Total Revenues or Total Assets Is . . .		Planning Materiality Is	+	Factor	×	Excess Over
Over	**But Not Over**					
$0	$30,000	$0	+	0.0593	×	$0
30,000	100,000	1,780	+	0.0312	×	30,000
100,000	300,000	3,960	+	0.0215	×	100,000
300,000	1 million	8,260	+	0.0145	×	300,000
1 million	3 million	18,400	+	0.00995	×	1 million
3 million	10 million	38,300	+	0.00674	×	3 million
10 million	30 million	85,500	+	0.00461	×	10 million
30 million	100 million	178,000	+	0.00312	×	30 million
100 million	300 million	396,000	+	0.00215	×	100 million
300 million	1 billion	826,000	+	0.00145	×	300 million
1 billion	3 billion	1,840,000	+	0.000995	×	1 billion
3 billion	10 billion	3,830,000	+	0.000674	×	3 billion
10 billion	30 billion	8,550,000	+	0.000461	×	10 billion
30 billion	100 billion	17,800,000	+	0.000312	×	30 billion
100 billion	300 billion	39,600,000	+	0.000215	×	100 billion
300 billion	. . .	82,600,000	+	0.000148	×	300 billion

Source: AICPA, *AICPA Audit Sampling Guide* (New York: AICPA, 2001).

auditors most commonly use either total assets or total revenues as the basis for their materiality judgments.

Auditors usually choose one measure of materiality for the entire audit, not separate measures for each of the financial statements. The reason is that all adjusting entries affect at least one balance sheet and one income statement account; what may be immaterial to the balance sheet can be very material to the income statement (or vice versa). A variation of the relative size materiality determination can be found in a materiality table similar to the one shown in Exhibit 3.11. In the table shown, materiality increases as the base grows, but not at the same rate. For example, if a company doubles in size from $200,000 in total assets to $400,000, materiality increases only from $6,110 ($3,960 + [0.0215 × ($200,000 − $100,000)]) to $9,710 ($8,260 + [0.0145 × ($400,000 − $300,000)])—an increase, but not a doubling in size.

Nature of the Item or Issue

An important qualitative factor is the descriptive nature of the item or issue. An illegal payment is important primarily because of its nature as well as because of its absolute or relative amount. Recall that there is no such thing as an immaterial fraud committed by management. Generally, potential errors in the more liquid assets (cash, receivables, and inventory) are considered more important than potential errors in other accounts (such as fixed assets and deferred charges). Materiality may be either qualitative or quantitative.

Circumstances

Auditors' liability is a relevant consideration: Auditors generally place extra emphasis on detection of misstatement in financial statements that will be widely used (publicly held companies) or used by important outsiders (bank loan officers). Troublesome political events in foreign countries also can cause auditors to try to be more accurate with measurements and disclosures. Other circumstances that affect materiality involve amounts that could turn a net loss into a profit or allow a company to meet earnings expectations. In these circumstances, when management can exercise discretion over an accounting treatment, auditors tend to exercise more care and use a more stringent materiality criterion. Finally, matters surrounded by uncertainty about the outcome of future events usually come under more stringent materiality considerations.

AUDITING INSIGHT — Things Add Up at HealthSouth

HealthSouth was able to conceal its $1.4 billion accounting fraud from its auditors Ernst & Young LLP, in part, because it broke it up into smaller pieces. Knowing that the auditors were examining all expenses over $5,000, HealthSouth capitalized approximately $1 billion in expenses with transaction amounts ranging between $500 and $4,999. By capitalizing the transactions (and depreciat-ing them over a long period of time) rather than expensing them in the current year, HealthSouth was able to report significantly higher net income for the current year.

Source: "Ex-Employee Took His Case to Auditors, Then Internet—but Convinced No One," *The Wall Street Journal*, May 20, 2003, pp. A1, A13.

Cumulative Effects

Auditors must evaluate the sum of known or potential misstatements. Considering five different $15,000 misstatements that all increase net income as immaterial is inappropriate when materiality for the income statement is $50,000.

Although we have presented five different factors affecting materiality, decisions about materiality ultimately remain a function of auditors' professional judgment. Many experienced auditors will state that these judgments are among the most difficult they make.

Review Checkpoints

3.11 What is *material information* in accounting and auditing?

3.12 What is planning materiality?

AUDIT PROCEDURES FOR OBTAINING AUDIT EVIDENCE

LEARNING OBJECTIVE

7. List and describe eight general types of audit procedures for gathering evidence.

In the earlier discussion of the audit risk model, we stated that, based on the allowable detection risk, auditors modify the *nature*, the *timing*, and the *extent* of their audit procedures. Auditors use audit procedures for three purposes. First, they use audit procedures to gain an understanding of the client and the risks associated with the client (*risk assessment procedures*). Second, auditors use audit procedures to test the operating effectiveness of client internal control procedures (*tests of controls*). Finally, auditors use audit procedures to produce evidence about management's assertions (i.e., relating to *existence, occurrence, completeness, cutoff, rights and obligations, valuation and allocation, accuracy, classification,* and *understandability*) about amounts and disclosures in a client's financial statements (*substantive procedures*). Exhibit 3.12 shows the relationship among the assertions, the types of evidence available to the auditor, and the procedures most closely related to each.

Auditors use eight general audit procedures to gather evidence: (1) inspection of records and documents (vouching, tracing, scanning), (2) inspection of tangible assets, (3) observation, (4) inquiry, (5) confirmation, (6) recalculation, (7) reperformance, and (8) analytical procedures. One or more of these procedures may be used no matter what account balance, control procedure, class of transactions, or other information is under audit. In the following sections, we discuss these audit procedures in more detail.

1. Inspection of Records and Documents

Much auditing work involves gathering evidence by examining authoritative documents prepared by independent parties and by the client. Such documents can provide evidence regarding many of management's assertions.

EXHIBIT 3.12 Assertions, Evidence, and Audit Procedures

PCAOB Assertions	ASB Assertions	Key Questions	Examples of Evidence Available	Representative Audit Procedures
Existence or occurrence	Existence	Do the assets recorded really exist?	The physical presence of the assets	Inspection of tangible assets
	Occurrence	Did the recorded sales transactions really occur?	Client shipping documents	Inspection of records or documents (vouching)
Completeness	Completeness	Are the financial statements (including footnotes) complete?	Documents prepared by the client	Inspection of records or documents (tracing)
	Cutoff	Were all transactions recorded in the proper period?	Client receiving, shipping reports	Inspection of records or documents (tracing or vouching)
Rights and obligations	Rights and obligations	Does the entity really own the assets? Are related legal responsibilities identified?	Statements by independent parties	Confirmation
Valuation and allocation	Valuation and allocation	Are the accounts valued correctly?	Client-prepared accounts receivable aging schedule	Reperformance
	Accuracy	Were transactions recorded accurately?	Vendor invoices	Inspection of records or documents (tracing or vouching)
Presentation and disclosure	Classification	Were all transactions recorded in the proper accounts?	Comparisons of current-year amounts with those from the prior year	Analytical procedures
	Understandability	Are the presentation and disclosure understandable to users?	Management-prepared financial statements and footnotes	Inquiry

Documents Prepared by Independent Outside Parties

A great deal of documentary evidence is external-internal (i.e., documents initially prepared by an external party but received by the client). The signatures, seals, engraving, or other distinctive artistic attributes of formal authoritative documents make such sources more reliable (less susceptible to alteration) than ordinary documents prepared by outsiders. Some examples of both types of documents are listed here:

Formal Authoritative Documents	Ordinary Documents
1. Bank statements	1. Vendors' invoices
2. Title papers (e.g., automobiles)	2. Customers' purchase orders
3. Insurance policies	3. Loan applications
4. Notes receivable (on unique forms)	4. Notes receivable (on standard bank forms)
5. Securities certificates	5. Insurance policy applications
6. Indenture agreements	6. Simple contracts
7. Elaborate contracts	7. Correspondence

Documents Prepared and Processed by the Client

Documentation of this type is internal evidence. Some of these documents may be quite informal and not very authoritative or reliable. As a general proposition, the reliability of these documents depends on the quality of internal control under which they were produced and processed. Some of the most common of these documents follow:

Internal Documents

1. Sales invoice copies
2. Sales summary reports
3. Cost distribution reports
4. Loan approval memos
5. Budgets and performance reports
6. Documentation of transactions with subsidiary or affiliated companies

7. Shipping documents
8. Receiving reports
9. Requisition slips
10. Purchase orders
11. Credit memoranda
12. Transaction logs
13. Batch control logs (computerized)

Vouching—Examination of Documents

The important point about *vouching* in the examination of documents is the *direction* of the search for audit evidence. In **vouching,** an auditor selects an item of financial information, usually from a journal or ledger, and follows its path back through the processing steps to its origin (i.e., the *source documentation* that supports the item selected). The auditor finds the journal entry or data input list, the sales summary, the sales invoice copy, and the shipping documents, and, finally, the customer's purchase order. Vouching of documents can help auditors decide whether all recorded data are adequately supported (the *existence* and *occurrence* assertions), but vouching does not provide evidence to show whether all events were recorded (the *completeness* assertion). (If the auditors verify amounts, evidence regarding valuation and allocation also may be obtained).

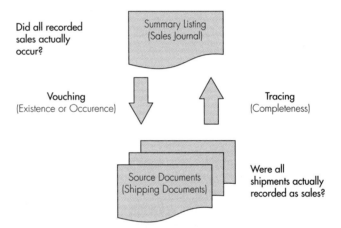

Tracing—Examination of Documents

Tracing in the examination of documents takes the *opposite* direction from vouching. When an auditor performs **tracing,** the auditor selects a basic source document and follows its processing path *forward* to find its final recording in a summary journal or ledger. For example, samples of payroll payments are traced to cost and expense accounts, sales invoices to the sales accounts, cash receipts to the accounts receivable subsidiary accounts, and cash disbursements to the accounts payable subsidiary accounts.

Using tracing, an auditor can decide whether all events were recorded (the *completeness* assertion) and complement the evidence obtained by vouching. (Similar to vouching, if auditors evaluate dollar amounts, tracing also can provide some evidence with respect to valuation and allocation.) However, you must be alert to events that were not captured in the source documents and not entered into the accounting system. For example, the search for unrecorded liabilities for raw materials purchases must include examination of invoices received in the period following the fiscal year end and examination of receiving reports dated near the year end. In practice, the terms *vouch* and *trace* are often used interchangeably. The important concept is the *direction* of the test.

Scanning—Examination of Documents

Scanning is the way auditors exercise their general alertness to unusual items and events in clients' documentation. A typical scanning directive in an audit program is: "Scan the expense accounts for credit entries; vouch any to source documents."

In general, scanning is an "eyes-open" approach of looking for anything unusual. The scanning procedure usually does not produce direct evidence itself, but it can raise questions for which other evidence must be obtained. Scanning can be accomplished on digital records using computerized audit software to select records to be printed out for further audit investigation. Typical items discovered by the scanning effort include debits in revenue accounts, credits in expense accounts, unusually large accounts receivable write-offs, unusually large paychecks, unusually small sales volume in the month following the year end, and large cash deposits just prior to year end. Scanning can contribute some evidence related to the existence of assets and the completeness of accounting records, including the proper cutoff of material transactions.

Scanning is valuable when sampling methods are applied in audit decisions. When a sample is the basis for selecting items for audit, the detection risk of choosing a sample that does not reflect the entire population of items always exists. Such an event may cause a decision error. Auditors subjectively reduce this detection risk by scanning items not selected in the sample and thus guard against decision error.

2. Inspection of Tangible Assets

Physical inspection of tangible assets provides compelling evidence of *existence* and may provide tentative evidence of condition and *valuation*. However, inspection does not necessarily provide evidence that the assets are owned by the entity (*rights*). For example, fixed assets on the client's premises may be leased under operating lease agreements and inventory inspected by auditors may be held on consignment. Inspection of tangible assets includes examining property, plant, and equipment (PP&E), inventory, and securities certificates.

3. Observation

Although inventory observation often refers to the physical inspection of inventory (i.e., tangible assets), *observation* is utilized whenever auditors view the client's physical facilities and personnel on an inspection tour, when they watch personnel carry out accounting and control procedures (such as observing client inventory counts), and when they participate in a surprise payroll distribution. Observation also can produce a general awareness of events in the client's offices. In this sense, observation is commonly used as a test of controls.

4. Inquiry

Inquiry is a procedure that generally involves the collection of oral (but sometimes written) evidence from independent parties and management (commonly referred to as *management representations*). Important inquiries and responses should be documented in writing. Auditors use inquiry procedures during the early office and plant tour and when conferences are conducted. Evidence gathered by formal and informal inquiry generally cannot stand alone as convincing, and auditors must corroborate responses with independent findings based on other procedures. An exception to this general rule is a negative statement where someone volunteers adverse information such as an admission of theft, fraud, or use of an accounting policy that is misleading.

5. Confirmation (*SAS 67*)

Confirmation by direct correspondence with independent parties is a procedure widely used in auditing. It can produce evidence of *existence* and *ownership* and sometimes of *valuation* and *cutoff*. Most transactions involve outside parties and, theoretically, written correspondence could be conducted even on such items as individual paychecks. However, auditors limit their use of confirmation to major transactions and balances about

AUDITING INSIGHT Verbal Inquiry = Interview

Auditors conduct interviews almost every day. Sometimes they seem more like casual conversations than "interviews." Nevertheless, the following guides for the inquiry/interview procedure can help you obtain good information and maintain good relations with client personnel.

1. *Prepare.* Think about the information you want to obtain, the questions to ask, and the best person to interview.

2. *Make an appointment.* Call in advance for a time or at least ask permission to interrupt: "Do you have time to talk with me about [subject]?" Introduce yourself and make enough conversation to warm up the person without wasting time.

3. *Don't ask the questions.* Try to get the person to describe the accounting, the controls, or whatever the subject in his or her own words. You will get more information. Just firing off questions makes the meeting an interrogation. Most auditors find it difficult to think of all of the right questions ahead of time anyway. Do not exhibit a questionnaire or checklist; doing so

makes the interview too mechanical. You can take informal notes to remember the substance of the interview.

4. *Ask questions.* Fill in the gaps in the person's description or explanation by asking prompting questions to elicit additional descriptions and explanations. Start with broad, open-ended questions and use specific questions to obtain more detail.

5. *Listen carefully.* Repeat items you don't completely understand.

6. *Be noncommittal.* Refrain from expressing your own value judgments or criticisms while you talk with the client personnel. Don't reveal any audit-sensitive information.

7. *Close gracefully.* Thank the person for the time and information. Ask permission to return later for "anything I forgot."

8. *Document the interview.* Write a memorandum for the audit documentation. Now you can get out the questionnaire or checklist, complete it, and see whether you overlooked anything important.

which outside parties could be expected to provide information. A selection of confirmation applications includes the following:

- Banks—cash and loan balances.
- Customers—receivables balances.
- Borrowers—note terms and balances.
- Agents—inventory on consignment or in warehouses.
- Lenders—note terms and balances.
- Policyholders—life insurance contracts.
- Vendors—accounts payable balances.
- Registrar—number of shares of stock outstanding.
- Attorneys—litigation in progress.
- Trustees—securities held, terms of agreements.
- Lessors—lease terms.

Confirmations of receivables and payables may take several forms. Two widely used forms are positive and negative confirmations. The *positive confirmation* requests a reply in all cases. The *negative confirmation* requests a reply only if the recipient considers the account balance to be incorrect. Auditors should try to obtain replies from all positive confirmations by sending second and third requests to nonrespondents. If there is no response to positive confirmations, or if the response to either positive or negative confirmations specifies an exception to the client's records, the auditors should investigate with other audit procedures.

6. Recalculation

Auditor recalculation of calculations previously performed by client personnel produces compelling mathematical evidence. A client calculation is either right or wrong. Client calculations performed by computer programs can be recalculated using computer-assisted audit tools (CAATs), with differences printed out for further audit investigation. Mathematical evidence can serve the objectives of *existence* and *valuation* for financial statement amounts that exist principally as calculations, for example, depreciation, interest expense, pension liabilities, actuarial reserves, bad debt reserves, and product

The important general points about confirmations are these:

- Confirmation letters should be printed on the client's letterhead and signed by a client officer. Third parties usually will not release information without client permission.
- Auditors should be very careful that the recipient's address is reliable and not subject to alteration by the client in such a way as to misdirect the confirmation.

- The request should seek information the recipient can supply such as the amount of a balance or the amounts of specified invoices or notes.
- Confirmations should be controlled by the audit firm, not given to client personnel for mailing. Auditing standards require direct communication.
- Responses should be returned directly to the audit firm, not to the client.

guarantee liabilities. Recalculation, in combination with other procedures, also is used to provide evidence of *valuation* for all other financial data.

7. Reperformance

Although similar to recalculation, reperformance is broader in approach. Reperformance can involve any client control procedure such as matching vendor invoices with supporting purchase orders and receiving reports. Reperformance may be done either manually or with the assistance of CAATs. An auditor, for example, can verify that an accounts receivable aging schedule was prepared properly by sorting accounts receivable by due date.

8. Analytical Procedures (*SAS 56*)

Auditors can evaluate financial statement accounts by studying and comparing relationships among financial and nonfinancial data. The methods of study and comparison are known as **analytical procedures.** Auditors are required to use them when

Analytical Procedures	Sources of Information
1. Comparison of current-year account balances to balances of one or more comparable periods	Financial account information for comparable period(s) *Example: Current year's Cost of Goods Sold compared to last year's balance*
2. Comparison of the current-year account balances to anticipated results found in the company's budgets and forecasts	Company budgets and forecasts *Example: Current year's Cost of Goods Sold compared to the company's budgeted amount*
3. Evaluation of the relationships of current-year account balances to other current-year balances for conformity with predictable patterns based on the company's experience	Financial relationships among accounts in the current period *Example: Days' sales in Inventory*
4. Comparison of current-year account balances and financial relationships (e.g., ratios) with similar information for the industry in which the company operates	Industry statistics *Example: Days' sales in Inventory compared to industry averages*
5. Study of the relationships of current-year account balances with relevant nonfinancial information (e.g., physical production statistics)	Nonfinancial information, such as physical production statistics *Example: Days' sales in Inventory compared to unfilled orders*

AUDITING INSIGHT Potholes in the Audit Procedures Road

Performing specified audit procedures might not be enough. The following true stories highlight the need for caution in the conduct of audit procedures.

RECALCULATION

An auditor calculated inventory valuations (quantities × price) thinking the measuring unit was gross (144 units each), when the client had actually recorded counts in dozens (12 units each), thus causing the inventory valuation to be 12 times the proper measure.

INSPECTION OF TANGIBLE ASSETS

While observing the fertilizer tank assets in ranch country, the auditor was fooled when the manager was able to move them to other locations and place new numbers on them. The auditor "observed" the same tanks many times.

OBSERVATION

An audit team visited a building restoration client's job site to verify that the company was actually performing the restoration services. Unbeknownst to the audit team, the client **(ZZZ Best)** had rented the vacant building for the day, put up its "building restoration" signs, and had its employees in hard hats milling around for the audit team's benefit.

CONFIRMATION

An insurance company executive gave the auditor a false address for a marketable securities confirmation, intercepted the confirmation, and then returned it with no exceptions noted. The company falsified $20 million in assets.

INQUIRY

Seeking evidence of the collectibility of accounts receivable, the auditors "audited by conversation" and took the credit manager's word about the collection probabilities on the over-90-day past due accounts. They sought no other evidence.

INSPECTION OF RECORDS AND DOCUMENTS (VOUCHING)

In the HealthSouth audit, auditors requested supporting documentation for an asset purchased for one of the company's Kansas locations. The problem was that it was a fraudulent transaction recorded as an asset to avoid treating the transaction properly as an expense. To conceal the fraud from the auditors, a vice president in the accounting department found a similar purchase invoice for an asset purchased for another location, scanned it into her computer, and then electronically changed the shipping information to match the invoice requested by the auditors.

INSPECTION OF RECORDS AND DOCUMENTS (SCANNING)

The auditors extracted a list of all of the bank's loans over $1,000. They neglected to perform a similar scan for loans with negative balances, a condition that should not occur. The bank had information processing problems that caused many loan balances to be negative, although the trial balance balanced!

planning the audit and when performing the final review of the financial statements before the audit report is issued. Although not required to do so, auditors also use analytical procedures to find evidence about management's assertions at other times during the audit.

Analytical procedures take the following five general forms. Auditors need to be careful to use independent, reliable information for analyses. The sources of information shown for the analytical procedures are very important.

Because analytical procedures can only direct attention to unusual relationships, many auditors consider the evidence they produce to be "soft." Instead, many auditors feel more comfortable with recalculation, observation, confirmation, and inspection of documents that are perceived to produce "hard" evidence. However, you should resist this distinction. Analytical procedures are, in fact, quite effective. Hylas and Ashton collected evidence on procedures used to detect the misstatements requiring financial statement adjustment in a large number of audits.[5] They found that auditors credited analytical procedures for discovery of 27.1 percent of all misstatements. Analytic procedures typically are applied early in the audit, so you should not infer that other types of audit procedures would or would not have detected the same misstatements. Auditors must consider the value of analytical procedures, especially because they are usually less costly than more detailed, document-oriented procedures. An *audit program* (discussed in the next

[5] R. E. Hylas and R. H. Ashton, "Audit Detection of Financial Statement Errors," *Accounting Review,* October 1982, pp. 751–65.

section) consists of several different types of procedures, and analytical procedures deserve a prominent place.

Review Checkpoints

3.13 What is meant by (a) *vouching*, (b) *tracing*, and (c) *scanning*? What is the difference between vouching and tracing?

3.14 List eight basic audit procedures.

3.15 What are the five types of general analytical procedures?

3.16 List five sources of information for analytical procedures.

AUDIT PROGRAMS

LEARNING OBJECTIVE

8. Describe the content and purpose of audit programs.

An **audit program** is a list of the audit procedures the auditors need to perform to gather sufficient appropriate evidence on which to base their opinion on the financial statements. Auditors use two types of audit programs, each with a different objective. An **internal control audit program** contains the specification of procedures for obtaining an understanding of the client's business and internal control and for assessing the inherent risk and the control risk related to the financial account balances and classes of transactions. A **substantive audit program** contains the specification of substantive procedures for gathering direct evidence on management's assertions (i.e., *existence, occurrence, completeness, cutoff, rights and obligations, valuation and allocation, accuracy, classification,* and *understandability*) about amounts and disclosures in the financial statements.

These audit programs are the result of many considerations previously discussed, such as

- Assertions and objectives embodied in the client's financial statements.
- Persuasive strengths of evidence.
- Preliminary risk assessments.
- Preliminary materiality decisions.

Internal Control Program

UNDERSTAND THE BUSINESS, INHERENT RISK, AND CONTROL RISK

- Communicate with predecessor auditors. Study the company's 8-K report regarding audit firm changes.
- Study prior year's audit documentation, AICPA audit and accounting guides, and industry publications concerning the company and its industry.
- Interview management with regard to business and accounting policies.
- Evaluate the competence and independence of the company's internal auditors.
- Determine the need for specialists on the engagement.
- Determine the extent of significant computerized applications in the company's accounting system.

- Obtain the financial statements and make decisions about the planning materiality appropriate in the circumstances.
- Perform preliminary analytical procedures to identify risk areas in the financial statement accounts.
- Assess the inherent risk in general and with respect to particular accounts.
- Obtain an understanding of the company's internal control through interviews, observations, and tests of controls.
- Perform tests of controls.
- Assess the control risk.
- Assess the risk of material misstatement due to fraud.
- Use the control risk assessment to design the nature, timing, and extent of substantive audit procedures.

ACCOUNTS RECEIVABLE

- Obtain an aged trial balance of the receivables. Calculate and analyze the age status of the accounts and the allowance for uncollectible accounts.
- Prepare and send confirmations on a sample of customers' accounts receivable. Analyze the responses.
- Interview the credit manager concerning the past-due accounts. Obtain credit reports and financial statements for independent analysis of overdue accounts.
- Vouch receivables balances to cash received after the confirmation date.
- Study loan agreements and note any pledge of receivables, sales with recourse, or other restrictions or contingencies related to the receivables.
- Study sales contracts for evidence of customers' rights of return or price allowance terms.
- Obtain written representations from the client concerning pledges for collateral, related-party receivables, collectibility, and other matters related to accounts receivable.

In actual field situations, these audit programs are very lengthy. Special program documents may contain separate listings of procedures and questionnaires on the company's internal control environment, internal control procedures, management control, and computerized control. The audit programs contain numerous detailed specifications of procedures that the auditors intend to perform as the work progresses. The following examples abstract elements of audit programs for illustrative purposes.

The technical parts of internal control risk assessment programs are too detailed to cover at this stage. They are explained more fully in subsequent chapters.

The substantive audit program contains brief specifications of procedures for auditing accounts receivable. You can see the elements of general procedures (e.g., confirmation, recalculation, inquiry, examination of documents) and the assertions toward which they are directed. Auditors indicate when they have performed each procedure and where the evidence is documented. Thus, audit programs are used not only for quality control and supervision, but also as documentation that the audit team is following generally accepted auditing standards.

Accounting Cycles

To simplify the audit plan, auditors typically group the accounts into *cycles*. A **cycle** is a set of accounts that go together in an accounting system. Most audit firms recognize four cycles: (1) the revenue and collection cycle, (2) the acquisition and expenditure cycle, (3) the production and conversion cycle, and (4) the finance and investment cycle. Using the revenue and collection cycle as an example, the idea of the cycle organization is to group together accounts (sales, accounts receivable, cash) related to one another by the transactions that normally affect them all. This cycle starts with a sale to a customer, along with recording an account receivable, which is later collected in cash or provided for in an allowance for doubtful accounts.

In Exhibit 3.13A, the Vandalay Industries accounts are rearranged into *cycle* order. You can see that some accounts are in more than one cycle. For example, the cash account is represented in all cycles because (1) cash receipts are involved in cash sales and collections of accounts receivable (revenue and collection cycle), (2) cash receipts are involved in deposit of stock issuance and loan proceeds (finance and investment cycle), (3) cash disbursements are involved in buying inventory and fixed assets and paying for expenses (acquisition and expenditure cycle), and (4) cash disbursements are involved in paying wages and overhead expenses (production cycle).

The substantive audit program approach typically consists of several audit programs, each applicable to a particular account or *cycle*. An alternative approach would be to audit each account group separately (the balance sheet approach); however, most audit firms have found it easier to audit such related accounts with a coordinated set of procedures instead of attacking each account as if it existed alone.

EXHIBIT 3.13A **Vandalay Industries Trial Balance, December 31, 2009**

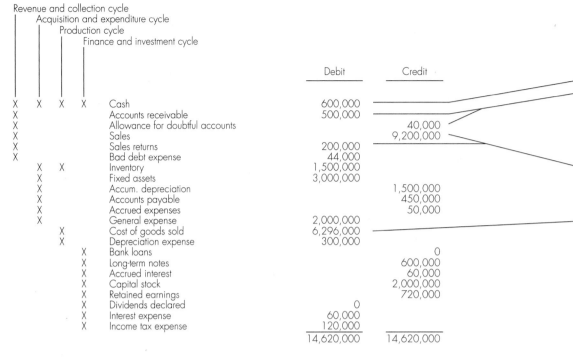

					Debit	Credit
Revenue and collection cycle						
	Acquisition and expenditure cycle					
		Production cycle				
			Finance and investment cycle			
X	X	X	X	Cash	600,000	
X				Accounts receivable	500,000	
X				Allowance for doubtful accounts		40,000
X				Sales		9,200,000
X				Sales returns	200,000	
X				Bad debt expense	44,000	
	X	X		Inventory	1,500,000	
	X			Fixed assets	3,000,000	
	X			Accum. depreciation		1,500,000
	X			Accounts payable		450,000
	X			Accrued expenses		50,000
	X			General expense	2,000,000	
		X		Cost of goods sold	6,296,000	
		X		Depreciation expense	300,000	
			X	Bank loans	0	0
			X	Long-term notes		600,000
			X	Accrued interest		60,000
			X	Capital stock		2,000,000
			X	Retained earnings		720,000
			X	Dividends declared	0	
			X	Interest expense	60,000	
			X	Income tax expense	120,000	
					14,620,000	14,620,000

Review Checkpoints

3.17 What is an audit program? What is its primary purpose?

3.18 Two types of audit programs have been identified. What are they? What is the objective of each?

3.19 What are four of the major "cycles" in an accounting system? What accounts can be identified with each?

Summary

Fraud awareness auditing starts with knowledge of the types of errors, frauds, and illegal acts that can be perpetrated. This chapter is not intended to make you a fraud examiner or fraud auditor; they are the professionals who take assignments to build a case and prosecute a fraud perpetrator after existence of a fraud has already become known. The goal here is to heighten your familiarity with the nature, signs, prevention, detection, and reaction to fraud that can enable you to perform financial statement audits with awareness of fraud possibilities.

Risk assessment is the common language of auditing. *Audit risk* is the likelihood the audit firm could express an incorrect opinion on financial statements that are materially misstated. *Materiality* in this sense is defined as the largest amount of uncorrected dollar misstatement that could exist in published financial statements while the statements would still fairly present the entity's financial position and results of operations in conformity with GAAP. The "audit risk model" decomposes audit risk into three components: *inherent risk*, *control risk*, and *detection risk*. Inherent risk involves the susceptibility of

EXHIBIT 3.13B Vandalay Industries Unaudited Financial Statements

FINANCIAL POSITION

Cash	$ 600,000	Accounts payable	$ 450,000
Accounts receivable	460,000	Accrued expenses	110,000
Inventory	1,500,000	Current debt	200,000
Current Assets	$2,560,000	Current Liabilities	$ 760,000
Fixed assets (net)	$3,000,000	Long-term debt	$ 400,000
Accum. depreciation	(1,500,000)	Capital stock	$2,000,000
Fixed assets (net)	$1,500,000	Retained earnings	900,000
		Total Liabilities	
Total Assets	$4,060,000	and Stockholder Equity	$4,060,000

RESULTS OF OPERATIONS

Sales (net)	$9,000,000
Cost of goods sold	6,296,000
Gross Profit	$2,704,000
General expenses	$2,044,000
Depreciation expense	300,000
Interest expense	60,000
Operating Income Before Taxes	$ 300,000
Income Tax Expense	120,000
Net income	$ 180,000

CASH FLOWS

Operations:	
Net Income	$ 180,000
Depreciation	300,000
Increase in Accounts Receivable	(141,500)
Decrease in Inventory	50,000
Decrease in Accounts Payable	(25,000)
Decrease in Accrued Expenses	(15,000)
Decrease in Accrued Interest	(20,500)
Cash Flow from Operations	$(328,500)
Investing Activities:	
Purchase Fixed Assets	$ 0
Financing Activities:	
Repay Bank Loan	$(275,000)
Repay Notes Payable	(200,000)
Financing Activities	$(475,000)
Increase (Decrease) in Cash	$(146,500)
Beginning Balance	746,500
Ending Balance	$ 600,000

NOTES TO FINANCIAL STATEMENTS
1. Accounting Policies
2. Inventories
3. Plant and Equipment
4. Long-term Debt
5. Stock Options
6. Income Taxes
7. Contingencies
Etc.

accounts to misstatement (assuming that no controls are present). Control risk addresses the effectiveness (or lack thereof) of the controls in preventing or detecting misstatements. Inherent and control risk are often combined and referred to as the *risk of material misstatement*. Detection risk involves the effectiveness of the auditors' procedures in detecting fraud or misstatement. Solving for detection risk in the audit risk model yields guidance for the preparation of the audit program and the nature, timing, and extent of audit procedures to be performed.

Audit programs are lists of audit procedures to be performed and are categorized as "internal control programs" and "substantive audit programs." Audit procedures are intended to enable auditors to conduct the work in accordance with the three AICPA field work standards concerning planning and supervision of the audit, obtaining an understanding of the internal control, and obtaining sufficient competent evidence to serve as a basis for the audit report.

Key Terms

accounting estimates: Approximations of financial statement numbers often included in financial statements, 74

analytical procedures: Reasonableness tests used to gain an understanding of financial statement accounts and relationships, 92

audit committees: A subset of a company's board of directors composed of outside members (those not involved in the day-to-day operations of the company) who can provide a buffer between the audit firm and management, 75

audit program: A list of the audit procedures the auditors need to perform to gather sufficient appropriate evidence on which to base their opinion on the financial statements, 94

audit risk: The probability that an audit firm will give an inappropriate opinion on financial statements (e.g., giving an unqualified opinion on financial statements that are misleading because of material misstatements the auditors failed to discover), 78

control risk: The probability that the client's internal control activities will *fail* to prevent or detect material misstatements, provided any enter or would have entered the accounting system in the first place, 81

cycle: A set of balance sheet and income statement accounts that are related by their common usage in a business process, 95

defalcation: Another name for employee fraud and embezzlement, 69

detection risk: The probability that audit procedures will *fail* to produce evidence of material misstatements, provided any have entered or would have entered the accounting system in the first place and have not been prevented or detected and corrected by the client's control activities, 81

direct-effect illegal acts: Violations of laws or government regulations by the entity or its management or employees that produce direct and material effects on dollar amounts in financial statements, 69, 76

embezzlement: A type of fraud involving employees or nonemployees wrongfully taking money or property entrusted to their care, custody, and control, often accompanied by false accounting entries and other forms of lying and cover-up, 69

employee fraud: The use of fraudulent means to take money or other property from an employer. It consists of three phases: (1) the fraudulent act, (2) the conversion of the money or property to the fraudster's use, and (3) the cover-up, 69

errors: Unintentional misstatements or omissions of amounts or disclosures in financial statements, 69

extended procedures: Audit procedures that are used in response to heightened fraud awareness as the result of identified fraud risks. Extended procedures could include counting petty cash twice on the same day, contract confirmations with customers, and "surprise" inventory observations, 75

fraud: Knowingly making material misrepresentations of fact with the intent of inducing someone to believe the falsehood and act on it and, thus, suffer a loss or damage, 68

indirect-effect illegal acts: Violations of laws and regulations that are far removed from financial statement effects (e.g., violations relating to insider securities trading, occupational health and safety, food and drug administration, environmental protection, and equal employment opportunity), 76

information risk: The probability that the information circulated by an entity will be false or misleading, 78

inherent risk: The probability that, in the absence of internal controls, material errors or frauds could enter the accounting system used to develop financial statements, 79

internal control audit program: The specification of procedures for obtaining an understanding of the client's business and internal control and for assessing the control risk related to the financial account balances, 94

larceny: Simple theft of an employer's property that is not entrusted to an employee's care, custody, or control, 69

management fraud: Deliberate fraud committed by management that injures investors and creditors through materially misleading information, 68

materiality: An amount or event that makes a difference to financial statement users, 84

risk of material misstatement: Combined inherent and control risk; in other words, the likelihood that material misstatements may have entered the accounting system and not been detected and corrected by the client's internal control, 82

substantive audit program: The specification of substantive procedures for gathering direct evidence on management's assertions, 94

tracing: An audit procedure in which the auditor selects a basic source document and follows its processing path *forward* to find its final recording in a summary journal or ledger. In practice, however, the term "tracing" may be used to describe following the path in either direction, 89

vouching: An audit procedure in which an auditor selects an item of financial information, usually from a journal or ledger, and follows its path back through the processing steps to its origin (i.e., the *source documentation* that supports the item selected), 89

white collar crime: Fraud perpetrated by people who work in offices and steal with a pencil or a computer terminal. The contrast is blue-collar crime (violent street crime), 68

Multiple Choice Questions for Practice and Review

3.20 The likelihood that material misstatements may have entered the accounting system and not been detected and corrected by the client's internal control is referred to as
 a. Inherent risk.
 b. Control risk.
 c. Detection risk.
 d. Risk of material misstatement.

3.21 The risk of material misstatements is composed of which audit risk components?
 a. Inherent risk and control risk.
 b. Control risk and detection risk.
 c. Inherent risk and detection risk
 d. Inherent risk, control risk, and detection risk.

3.22 Auditors are not responsible for accounting estimates with respect to
 a. Making the estimates.
 b. Determining the reasonableness of estimates.
 c. Determining that estimates are presented in conformity with GAAP.
 d. Determining that estimates are adequately disclosed in the financial statements.

3.23 AICPA auditing standards do not require auditors of financial statements to
 a. Understand the nature of errors and frauds.
 b. Assess the risk of occurrence of errors and frauds.
 c. Design audits to provide reasonable assurance of detecting errors and frauds.
 d. Report all finding of errors and frauds to police authorities.

3.24 The risk that the auditors' own procedures will lead to the decision that material misstatements do not exist in the financial statements when in fact such misstatements do exist is
 a. Audit risk.
 b. Inherent risk.
 c. Control risk.
 d. Detection risk.

3.25 Auditors are responsible for the quality of the work related to management and control of
 a. Inherent risk.
 b. Business risk.
 c. Control risk.
 d. Detection risk.

3.26 The auditors assessed a combined inherent risk and control risk at 0.50 and said they wanted to achieve a 0.05 risk of failing to express a correct opinion on financial statements that were materially misstated. What detection risk do the auditors plan to use for planning the remainder of the audit work?
 a. 0.20.
 b. 0.10.
 c. 0.75.
 d. 0.00.

3.27 An audit program contains

 a. Specifications of audit standards relevant to the financial statements being audited.

 b. Specifications of procedures the auditors believe appropriate for the financial statements under audit.

 c. Documentation of the assertions under audit, the evidence obtained, and the conclusions reached.

 d. Reconciliation of the account balances in the financial statements with the account balances in the client's general ledger.

3.28 The revenue cycle of a company generally includes which accounts?

 a. Inventory, accounts payable, and general expenses.

 b. Inventory, general expenses, and payroll.

 c. Cash, accounts receivable, and sales.

 d. Cash, notes payable, and capital stock.

3.29 When auditing the existence assertion for an asset, auditors proceed from the

 a. Financial statement amounts back to the potentially unrecorded items.

 b. Potentially unrecorded items forward to the financial statement amounts.

 c. General ledger back to the supporting original transaction documents.

 d. Supporting original transaction documents to the general ledger.

3.30 If tests of controls induce the audit team to change the assessed level of control risk for fixed assets from 0.4 to 1.0, and audit risk (0.05) and inherent risk remain constant, the acceptable level of detection risk is most likely to

 a. Change from 0.1 to 0.04.

 b. Change from 0.2 to 0.3.

 c. Change from 0.25 to 0.1.

 d. Be unchanged.

3.31 When auditors decide to carry out a response to a particular fraud risk in an account balance or class of transactions, they are most likely to

 a. Exercise more professional skepticism.

 b. Carefully avoid conducting interviews with people in the fraud-rich areas.

 c. Perform procedures such as inventory observation and cash counts on a surprise or unannounced basis.

 d. Study more carefully management's selection and application of accounting principles.

3.32 In an audit of a private company, it is acceptable under generally accepted auditing standards for an audit team to

 a. Assess both inherent and control risk at high and achieve an acceptably low audit risk by performing extensive detection work.

 b. Assess control risk at zero and perform a minimum of detection work.

 c. Assess inherent risk at zero and perform a minimum of detection work.

 d. Decide that audit risk can be 40 percent.

3.33 Confirmations of accounts receivable provide evidence primarily about which two assertions?

 a. Completeness and valuation.

 b. Valuation and rights and obligations.

 c. Rights and obligations and existence.

 d. Existence and completeness.

3.34 If sales were overstated by recording a false credit sale at the end of the year, where could you find the false "dangling debit"?

 a. inventory.

 b. cost of goods sold.

 c. bad debt expense.

 d. accounts receivable.

3.35 One of the typical characteristics of management fraud is

 a. Falsification of documents in order to misappropriate funds from an employer.

 b. Victimization of investors through the use of materially misleading financial statements.

 c. Illegal acts committed by management to evade laws and regulations.

 d. Conversion of stolen inventory to cash deposited in a falsified bank account.

3.36 Under the Private Securities Litigation Reform Act, independent auditors are required to

 a. Report in writing all instances of illegal acts to the client's board of directors.

 b. Report to the SEC all instances of illegal acts they believe have a material effect on financial statements if the board of directors does not first report to the SEC.

 c. Report clearly inconsequential illegal acts to the audit committee of the client's board of directors.

 d. Resign from the audit engagement and report the instances of illegal acts to the SEC.

3.37 With respect to the concept of materiality, which one of the following statements is correct?

 a. Materiality depends only on the dollar amount of an item relative to other items in the financial statements.

 b. Materiality depends on the nature of a transaction rather than the dollar amount of the transaction.

 c. Materiality is determined by reference to AICPA guidelines.

 d. Materiality is a matter of professional judgment.

3.38 When evaluating whether accounting estimates made by management are reasonable, the audit team would be most concerned with which of the following?

 a. Key factors that are consistent with prior periods.

 b. Assumptions that are similar to industry guidelines.

 c. Measurements that are objective and not susceptible to bias.

 d. Evidence of a conservative systematic bias.

3.39 Which of the following circumstances would most likely cause an audit team to perform extended procedures?

 a. Supporting documents are produced when requested.

 b. The client made several large adjustments at or near year end.

 c. The company has recently hired a new chief financial officer after the previous one retired.

 d. The company maintains several different petty cash funds.

3.40 An audit committee is

 a. Composed of internal auditors.

 b. Composed of members of the audit team.

 c. Composed of members of a company's board of directors who are not involved in the day-to-day operations of the company.

 d. A committee composed of persons not associating in any way with the client or the board of directors.

3.41 When the audit team becomes aware of an illegal act committed by client personnel, the primary reason that the auditors should obtain a better understanding of the nature of the act is to

 a. Recommend remedial actions to the audit committee.

 b. Evaluate the effect of the illegal act on the financial statements.

 c. Determine whether to contact law enforcement officials.

 d. Determine whether other similar acts could have occurred.

3.42 Which of the following statements best describes the audit team's responsibility for detecting a client's illegal acts?

 a. The responsibility for detecting illegal acts exactly parallels the responsibility for errors and fraud.

 b. The audit team must design tests to detect all material illegal acts that indirectly affect the financial statements.

 c. The audit team must design tests to obtain reasonable assurance that all illegal acts with direct material statement effects are detected.

 d. The audit team must design tests to detect all illegal acts that directly affect the financial statements.

Exercises, Problems, and Simulations

3.43 Risk of Misstatement in Various Accounts. Based on information you have available in Chapter 3:

a. Which accounts are most susceptible to overstatement? To understatement?

b. Why do you think a company could permit asset accounts to be understated?

c. Why do you think a company could permit liability accounts to be overstated?

d. Which direction of misstatement is most likely: income overstatement or income understatement?

3.44 General Audit Procedures and Financial Statement Assertions. The eight general audit procedures produce evidence about the principal management assertions in financial statements. However, some procedures are useful for producing evidence about certain assertions while other procedures are useful for producing evidence about other assertions. The assertion being audited can influence the auditors' choice of procedures.

Required:

Opposite each general audit procedure, write the management assertions most usefully audited by using each procedure.

Audit Procedures	PCAOB Assertions	ASB Assertions
1a. Inspection of records or documents (vouching)		
1b. Inspection of records or documents (tracing)		
1c. Inspection of records or documents (scanning)		
2. Inspection of tangible assets		
3. Observation		
4. Confirmation		
5. Inquiry		
6. Recalculation		
7. Reperformance		
8. Analytical procedures		

3.45 Errors and Frauds. Give an example of an error or fraud that would misstate financial statements to affect the accounts as follows, taking each case independently. (*Note:* "Overstate" means the account has a higher value than would be appropriate under GAAP and "understate" means it has a lower value.)

a. Overstate an asset, understate another asset.

b. Overstate an asset, overstate stockholders' equity.

c. Overstate an asset, overstate revenue.

d. Overstate an asset, understate an expense.

e. Overstate a liability, overstate an expense.

f. Understate an asset, overstate an expense.

g. Understate a liability, understate an expense.

3.46 Audit Simulation: Analysis of Accounting Estimates. Oak Industries, a manufacturer of radio and cable TV equipment and an operator of subscription TV systems, had a multitude of problems. Subscription services in a market area, for which $12 million of cost had been deferred, were being terminated and the customers were not paying on time ($4 million receivables in doubt). The chances are 50–50 that the business will survive another two years.

An electronic part turned out to have defects that needed correction. Warranty expenses are estimated to range from $2 million to $6 million. The inventory of this part ($10 million) is obsolete, but $1 million can be recovered in salvage; or the parts in inventory can be rebuilt at a cost of $2 million (selling price of the inventory on hand would then be $8 million, with 20 percent of the selling price required to market and ship the products, and the normal profit expected is 5 percent of the selling price). If the inventory were scrapped, the company would manufacture a replacement inventory at a cost of $6 million, excluding marketing and shipping costs and normal profit.

The company has defaulted on completion of a military contract and the government is claiming a $2 million refund. Company attorneys think the dispute might be settled for as little as $1 million.

The auditors had previously determined that an overstatement of income before taxes of $7 million would be material to the financial statements. These items were the only ones left for audit decisions about possible adjustment. Management has presented the following analysis for the determination of loss recognition:

Write-off deferred subscription costs	$ 3,000,000
Provide allowance for bad debts	4,000,000
Provide for expected warranty expense	2,000,000
Lower of cost or market inventory write-down	2,000,000
Loss on government contract refund	—
Total write-offs and losses	$11,000,000

Required:

Prepare your own analysis of the amount of adjustment to the financial statements. Assume that none of these estimates have been recorded yet, and give the adjusting entry you would recommend. Give any supplementary explanations you believe necessary to support your recommendation.

3.47 **Audit Risk Model.** Audit risks for particular accounts and disclosures can be conceptualized in the model: Audit risk (AR) = Inherent risk (IR) × Control risk (CR) × Detection risk (DR). Use this model as a framework for considering the following situations and deciding whether the auditor's conclusion is appropriate.

1. Paul, CPA, has participated in the audit of Tordik Cheese Company for five years, first as an assistant accountant and the last two years as the senior accountant. Paul has never seen an accounting adjustment recommended. Paul believes the inherent risk must be zero.

2. Hill, CPA, has just (November 30) completed an exhaustive study and evaluation of the internal controls of Edward Foods, Inc. (fiscal year ending December 31). Hill believes the control risk must be zero because no material errors could possibly slip through the many error-checking procedures and review layers used by Edward.

3. Fields, CPA, is lazy and does not like audit jobs in Philadelphia, anyway. On the audit of Philly Manufacturing Company, Fields decided to use substantive procedures to audit the year-end balances very thoroughly to the extent that his risk of failing to detect material errors and irregularities should be 0.02 or less. Fields gave no thought to inherent risk and conducted only a very limited review of Philly's internal control system.

4. Shad, CPA, is nearing the end of a "dirty" audit of Allnight Protection Company. Allnight's accounting personnel all resigned during the year and were replaced by inexperienced people. The comptroller resigned last month in disgust. The journals and ledgers were a mess because the one computer specialist was hospitalized for three months during the year. "Thankfully," Shad thought, "I've been able to do this audit in less time than last year when everything was operating smoothly."

(AICPA adapted)

3.48 **Audit Procedures.** Auditors frequently refer to the terms *standards* and *procedures. Standards* deal with measures of the quality of performance. *Standards* specifically refer to the generally accepted auditing standards. *Procedures* relate to the acts performed by auditors to gather evidence. *Procedures* specifically refer to the methods or techniques used by auditors in the conduct of the examination.

Required:

List eight different types of procedures auditors can use during an audit of financial statements and give an example of each.

3.49 **Confirmation Procedure.** A CPA accumulates various types of evidence on which to base the opinion on financial statements. Among this evidence are confirmations from third parties.

Required:

a. What is an audit confirmation?

b. What characteristics of the confirmation process and the recipient are important if a CPA is to consider the confirmation evidence competent?

3.50 **Auditing an Accounting Estimate.** Suppose management estimated the market valuation of some obsolete inventory at $99,000; this inventory was recorded at $120,000, which resulted in recognizing a loss of $21,000. The auditors obtained the following information: The inventory in question could be sold for an amount between $78,000 and $92,000. The costs of advertising and shipping could range from $5,000 to $7,000.

Required:

a. Would you propose an audit adjustment to the management estimate? Prepare the appropriate accounting entry.

b. If management's estimate of inventory market (lower than cost) had been $80,000, would you propose an audit adjustment? Prepare the appropriate accounting entry.

3.51 **Risk Assessment.** This question consists of a number of items pertaining to an auditor's risk analysis for a company. Your task is to tell how each item affects overall audit risk—the probability of issuing an unqualified audit report on materially misleading financial statements.

Bond, CPA, is considering audit risk at the financial statement level in planning the audit of Toxic Waste Disposal (TWD) Company's financial statements for the year ended December 31, 2008. TWD is a privately owned company that contracts with municipal governments to remove environmental wastes. Audit risk at the overall financial statement level is influenced by the risk of material misstatements, which may be indicated by a combination of factors related to management, the industry, and the company.

Required:

Based only on the following information, indicate whether each of the following factors (Items 1 through 15) would most likely increase overall audit risk, decrease overall audit risk, or have no effect on overall audit risk. Discuss your reasoning.

Company Profile

1. This was the first year TWD operated at a profit since 2003 because the municipalities received increased federal and state funding for environmental purposes.

2. TWD's board of directors is controlled by Mead, the majority stockholder, who also acts as the chief executive officer.

3. The internal auditor reports to the controller, and the controller reports to Mead.

4. The accounting department has experienced a high rate of turnover of key personnel.

5. TWD's bank has a loan officer who meets regularly with TWD's CEO and controller to monitor TWD's financial performance.

6. TWD's employees are paid biweekly.

7. Bond has audited TWD for five years.

Recent Developments

8. During 2008, TWD changed its method of preparing its financial statements from the cash basis to the accrual basis under generally accepted accounting principles.

9. During 2008, TWD sold one-half of its controlling interest in United Equipment Leasing (UEL) Co. TWD retained significant interest in UEL.

10. During 2008, litigation filed against TWD in 2006 alleging that TWD discharged pollutants into state waterways was dropped by the state. Loss contingency disclosures that TWD included in prior years' financial statements are being removed for the 2008 financial statements.

11. During December 2008, TWD signed a contract to lease disposal equipment from an entity owned by Mead's parents. This related-party transaction is not disclosed in TWD's notes to its 2008 financial statements.

12. During December 2008, TWD completed a barter transaction with a municipality. TWD removed waste from a municipally owned site and acquired title to another contaminated site at below-market price. TWD intends to service this new site in 2009.

13. During December 2008, TWD increased its casualty insurance coverage on several pieces of sophisticated machinery from historical cost to replacement cost.

14. Inquiries about the substantial increase in revenue TWD recorded in the fourth quarter of 2008 disclosed a new policy. TWD guaranteed several municipalities that it would refund the federal and state funding paid to TWD if any municipality fails federal or state site cleanup inspection in 2009.

15. An initial public offering of TWD's stock is planned for late 2009.

3.52 **Potential Audit Procedure Failures.** For each of the general audit procedures of (a) recalculation, (b) observation, (c) confirmation (accounts receivable, securities, or other assets), (d) inquiry, (e) inspection of internal documents, (f) recalculation, (g) reperformance, and (h) analytical procedures, discuss one way the procedure could be misapplied or the auditors could be misled in such a way as to render the work (audit evidence) misleading or irrelevant. Give examples different from the examples in Chapter 3.

3.53 *SAS 99* **Review.** Management fraud (fraudulent financial reporting) is not the expected norm, but it happens from time to time. In the United States, several cases have been widely publicized. They happen when motives and opportunities overwhelm managerial integrity.

 a. What distinguishes management fraud from a defalcation?

 b. What are an auditor's responsibilities under GAAS to detect management fraud?

 c. What are some characteristics of management fraud an audit team should consider to fulfill the responsibilities under GAAS?

 d. What factors might an audit team notice that should heighten the concern about the existence of management fraud?

 e. Under what circumstances might an audit team have a duty to disclose management's frauds to parties other than the company's management and its board of directors?

(AICPA adapted)

3.54 **Internet Exercise: Audit Programs on the Internet.** Auditnet (www.auditnet.org) is a Web site that provides support for practicing internal and external auditors. One of its resources is Auditors Sharing Audit Programs (ASAP), a library of audit programs for a number of different audit areas. If you need an audit program, you can simply visit the site, download a program, and modify it to meet the needs of your client's engagement.

Required:
Access the Auditnet Web site, browse through the programs, and download an audit program that interests you. For the steps listed on the selected audit program, identify which of the general categories of audit procedures (recalculation, observation, confirmation, etc.) is represented by that step.

3.55 **Kaplan CPA Exam Simulation: Inherent Risk.**

Required:
Go to the Kaplan Web site link at www.mhhe.com/louwers3e, click on AUD: Riley and Associates case and the "Communication" tab, and complete your answer.

3.56 **Kaplan CPA Exam Simulation:** *SAS 99* **Fraud Guidelines.**

Required:
Go to the Kaplan Web site link at www.mhhe.com/louwers3e, click on AUD: Harrison Homes case and the "Fraud" tab, and complete your answer.

3.57 **Kaplan CPA Exam Simulation: Financial Statement Assurance.**

Required:
Go to the Kaplan Web site link at www.mhhe.com/louwers3e, click on AUD: Harrison Homes case and the "Assurance" tab, and complete your answer.

3.58 **Kaplan CPA Exam Simulation: Audit Risk.**

Required:
Go to the Kaplan Web site link at www.mhhe.com/louwers3e, click on AUD: Hardi Risk and Independence case and the "Audit Risk" tab, and complete your answer.

3.59 **Kaplan CPA Exam Simulation: Audit Risk.**

Required:
Go to the Kaplan Web site link at www.mhhe.com/louwers3e, click on AUD: Ridge and Associates case and the "Audit Risk" tab, and complete your answer.

3.60 **Kaplan CPA Exam Simulation: Auditor's Consideration of Fraud in a Financial Statement Audit.**

Required:
Go to the Kaplan Web site link at www.mhhe.com/louwers3e, click on AUD: Ridge and Associates case and the "Research" tab, and complete your answer.

3.61 **Kaplan CPA Exam Simulation: Illegal Acts.**

Required:
Go to the Kaplan Web site link at www.mhhe.com/louwers3e, click on AUD: Woodson Flavors International case and the "Communication" tab, and complete your answer.

3.62 **Mini-Case: Red Flags.** Refer to the mini-case "Unhealthy Accounting at HealthSouth" shown on page 833 and respond to Questions 1 and 2.

3.63 **Mini-Case: Red Flags.** Refer to the mini-case "Something Went Sour at Parmalat" shown on page 839 and respond to Question 3.

Engagement Planning

Professional Standards References

Compendium Section	Document Reference	Topic
Various*	AS 5	"An Audit of Internal Control over Financial Reporting Performed in Conjunction with an Audit of Financial Statements"
AU 110	SAS 1	"Responsibilities and Functions of the Independent Auditor"
AU 230	SAS 104	"Amendment to 'Due Professional Care in the Performance of Work'"
AU 311	SAS 108	"Planning and Supervision"
	ISA 300	"Planning and Audit of Financial Statements"
AU 312	SAS 107	"Audit Risk and Materiality in Conducting an Audit"
	ISA 320	"Audit Materiality"
AU 314	SAS 109	"Understanding the Entity and Its Environment and Assessing the Risks of Material Misstatement"
	ISA 315	"Understanding the Entity and Its Environment and Assessing the Risks of Material Misstatement"
AU 315	SAS 84	"Communication between Predecessor and Successor Auditors"
AU 316	SAS 99	"Consideration of Fraud in a Financial Statement Audit"
	ISA 240	"The Auditor's Responsibility to Consider Fraud in an Audit of Financial Statements"
AU 317	SAS 54	"Illegal Acts by Clients"
	ISA 250	"Consideration of Laws and Regulations in an Audit of Financial Statements"
AU 318	SAS 110	"Performing Audit Procedures in Response to Assessed Risks and Evaluating the Audit Evidence Obtained"
	ISA 330	"The Auditor's Procedures in Response to Assessed Risks"
AU 319	SAS 94	"The Effect of Information Technology on the Auditor's Consideration of Internal Control in a Financial Statement Audit"
AU 322	SAS 65	"Auditor's Consideration of Internal Audit Function"
	ISA 610	"Considering the Work of Internal Auditing"
AU 326	SAS 106	"Audit Evidence"
	ISA 500	"Audit Evidence"
	ISA 501	"Audit Evidence—Additional Considerations for Specific Items"
AU 329	SAS 56	"Analytical Procedures"
	ISA 520	"Analytical Procedures"
AU 330	SAS 67	"The Confirmation Process"
	ISA 505	"External Confirmations"
AU 331	SAS 1	"Inventories"
AU 334	SAS 45	"Related Parties"
	ISA 550	"Related Parties"
AU 9334		"Interpretations: Related Parties"
AU 336	SAS 73	"Using the Work of a Specialist"
	ISA 620	"Using the Work of an Expert"
AU 339	SAS 103	"Audit Documentation"
	AS 3	"Audit Documentation"
	ISA 230	"Documentation"
AU 341	SAS 59	"Auditor's Consideration of an Entity's Ability to Continue as a Going Concern"

AU 342	SAS 57	"Auditing Accounting Estimates"
	ISA 540	"Auditing Accounting Estimates"
AU 9342		"Interpretation: Auditing Accounting Estimates"
AU 380	SAS 114	"The Auditor's Communication with Those Charged with Governance"
	ISA 260	"Communications of Audit Matters with Those Charged with Governance"
AU 801	SAS 74	"Compliance Auditing Applicable to Governmental Entities and Recipients of Governmental Financial Assistance"
	ISA 510	"Initial Engagements—Opening Balances"

*AS 5 amends AU 230, AU 310, AU 312, AU 313, AU 315, AU 316, AU 319, AU 322, AU 325, AU 328, AU 332, AU 333, AU 341, AU 342, AU 380, AU 508, AU 530, AU 543, AU 560, AU 561, AU 711, AU 722, AS 3, and AS 4.

> Vision without action is a daydream.
> Action without vision is a nightmare.
>
> *Japanese Proverb*

Learning Objectives

Chapter 4 covers the role of planning in an audit engagement beginning with preengagement arrangements. Other planning topics covered in this chapter include gaining an understanding of the client's business and industry, materiality, analytical procedures, audit documentation, and the role of computer processing in planning and conducting an audit with an emphasis on the use of computer-assisted audit techniques (CAATs) to improve engagement effectiveness and efficiency.

Your objectives are to be able to:

1. List and describe the activities that auditors undertake before beginning an engagement.

2. Identify the procedures and sources of information auditors may use to obtain knowledge of a client's business and industry.

3. Perform analytical procedures to identify potential misstatements.

4. List and discuss matters of planning that auditors should consider for clients who use computerized processing, and describe how a computer can be used as an audit tool.

5. Review audit documentation for proper form and content.

INTRODUCTION

In a planning memo dated February 6, 2001, the **Arthur Andersen** audit team assigned to the **Enron** engagement discussed whether Andersen should remain Enron's auditor. Specifically, the engagement planning team had identified some questionable investment practices and expressed concern that Enron was engaging in "intelligent gambling." Despite these reservations, the Andersen engagement planning team concluded that the firm had the "appropriate people and processes in place to serve Enron and manage our engagement risks." Less than a year later, Enron was in bankruptcy and Andersen was in the midst of a federal investigation that would lead to its ultimate dissolution. What went wrong in Andersen's planning process? Entire books have been written on the shortcomings of Andersen's audit of Enron. This chapter is devoted to engagement planning with attention to the early identification of things that could go wrong in an engagement. In fact, the primary reason for engagement planning is to identify the things that could possibly go wrong and then make sure that the audit team has controls in place to reduce or mitigate those risks. Although controlling engagement risk is the primary reason for engagement planning, this overriding objective is contained in the three basic goals of engagement planning:

1. To obtain (or update) an understanding of important events that have affected the client and its operations.

AUDITING INSIGHT More Accounting Firms Are Dumping Risky Clients

A growing number of high-level executives are suffering from rejection—by their accountants. Hoping to protect themselves, the most prestigious accounting firms are turning more aggressive in dumping audit clients they deem to be high risk. **PricewaterhouseCoopers** "parted ways" with about 50 or 60 public companies in 2003. **Ernst & Young** says it walked away from 200 public and private audit engagements; **Deloitte & Touche,** another 70. To ferret out potential lemons, accounting firms have increased their scrutiny of information that prospective clients sub-

mit about everything from finance to management changes. Accountants are grilling former auditors about management integrity.

Accounting industry officials say the crackdown on potential problem clients is only beginning. All of the largest firms have taken dramatic steps to mitigate risk in their client base. Most are adding "forensic accountants" to their audit teams.

Source: "Accounting Firms Aim to Dispel Cloud of Corporate Fraud," *The Wall Street Journal,* May 27, 2003, p. C1.

2. To identify areas of the engagement that could represent special risks to the firm.
3. To ensure that the engagement can be completed in a timely fashion.

The remainder of this chapter describes the activities that auditors perform to ensure that these goals are met. The focus is on auditors' planning of a financial statement audit, but the planning activities described in this chapter are applicable to most assurance engagements.

PREENGAGEMENT ARRANGEMENTS

LEARNING OBJECTIVE

1. List and describe the activities that auditors undertake before beginning an engagement.

Public accounting firms try to reduce their own business risks by carefully managing their audit engagements. To do so, auditing firms undertake several activities before beginning any engagement. In general, these activities can be called *risk management activities*. Risk in an audit engagement generally refers to the probability that something could go wrong. The flip side of risk management is *quality management,* which was discussed previously under the heading "Quality Control Standards." The topics discussed next can best be understood in the context of risk management and quality management.

Client Selection and Retention

An important element of a public accounting firm's quality control policies and procedures is a system for deciding whether to accept a new client and, on a continuing basis, deciding whether to continue providing services to existing clients. Public accounting firms are not obligated to accept undesirable clients, nor are they obligated to continue to serve clients when relationships deteriorate or when the management comes under a cloud of suspicion.

STAGES OF AN AUDIT

Obtain (or Retain) Engagement | Engagement Planning | Risk Assessment | Substantive Procedures | Reporting

Client acceptance and retention policies and procedures include these:

- Obtaining and reviewing financial information about the prospective client: annual reports, interim statements, registration statements, Form 10-K, and reports to regulatory agencies.

AUDITING INSIGHT Deloitte & Touche Refuses to Ante Up (Go All In?)

Deloitte & Touche recently withdrew as auditor for **WPT Enterprises, Inc.,** the creator of the World Poker Tour, just as the company was starting its new online poker enterprise. The Big Four firm cited additional "audit risks" associated with the new gaming venture that would consume too many resources to adequately audit this client. Not noted in its resignation letter are concerns about the legality of online gaming. It is illegal in the United States, and part of the auditors' responsibilities would include investigating whether any online gambling customers were residing in the United States. Additionally, online gambling requires complex software that involves a general lack of transparency.

Source: "For Audit Firms, All Bets Are Off," *The Wall Street Journal,* July 21, 2005, p. C3.

- Inquiring of the prospective client's bankers, legal counsel, underwriters, analysts, or other persons who do business with the entity for information about the entity and its management.
- For an audit engagement, communicating with the predecessor auditor, if any, for information on management's integrity; on disagreements with management about accounting principles, audit procedures, or similar matters; and the reasons for a change of auditors.
- Considering whether the engagement would require special attention or involve unusual risks.
- Evaluating the public accounting firm's independence with regard to the prospective client.
- Considering the need for special skills (e.g., information system auditing or specialized industry knowledge).

Most large public accounting firms now conduct "background checks" on current and prospective clients and key officers. The firms search for news articles, lawsuits, and bankruptcy court outcomes naming the entity, the chairman of the board, the CEO, the CFO, and other high-ranking officers. The firms also often engage outside search firms (private investigators) to conduct additional searches for information when the prospective clients are financial institutions, companies accused of fraud, companies under SEC or other regulatory investigation, companies that have changed auditors frequently, and companies showing recent losses. These characteristics are "red flags" for the auditors and they intend to be careful to know as much as they can about the companies and their officers. Management integrity (or lack thereof) is the primary reason for accepting (or not accepting) an audit engagement.

Client continuance decisions are similar to acceptance decisions except that the firm will have more firsthand experience with the entity. Retention reviews may be done annually or on occurrence of major events such as changes in management, directors, ownership, legal counsel, financial condition, litigation status, nature of the client's business, or scope of the audit engagement. In general, conditions that would have caused a public accounting firm to reject a prospective client can develop and lead to a decision to discontinue the engagement. For example, a client company could expand and diversify on an international scale so that a small public accounting firm might not have the competence to continue the audit. It is not unusual to see newspaper stories about public accounting firms dropping clients after directors or officers admit to falsification of financial statements or to theft and misuse of corporate assets.

Communication between Predecessor and Successor Auditors (*SAS 84*)

Companies change auditors periodically, sometimes as a result of corporate policy to rotate auditors, sometimes because of fee considerations, and sometimes because of arguments about the scope of the audit or the acceptability of accounting principles. Often,

AUDITING INSIGHT Former Client Failed to Disclose Dispute in 8-K

The accounting firm told the SEC (in the required accountant's letter) that a former client incorrectly reported no disagreements preceding the firm's dismissal as the company's auditor. A disagreement *had* occurred involving the company's wish to capitalize the cost of moving an acquired company's headquarters to another city in the accounting for the acquisition. The accounting firm believed the costs were expenses of the period and were not related to the acquisition.

Note: Another accounting firm, however, agreed with the company's preferred accounting treatment. The company dismissed the former firm and hired the audit firm that agreed with their position.

Source: *Accounting Today.*

these arguments involve auditors' access to necessary evidence, questions of early revenue recognition, or disputes over deferral of expenses and losses. In the past, some auditor changes have occurred for the purpose of procuring new auditors who will agree with management's treatment of a troublesome revenue recognition or expense deferral treatment. Such changes are suspect, and a few of them have turned out to be cases of audit failure on the part of the new auditor. Thus, auditor changes in the context of a disagreement with management are supposed to be of interest to investors.

Whenever a publicly traded company changes auditors, the company must file a *Form 8-K* report with the SEC and disclose that the board of directors approved the change. **Form 8-K,** the "special events report," is required whenever certain significant events occur such as changes in control and legal proceedings. Public companies also must report any disagreements with the former auditors concerning matters of accounting principles, financial statement disclosure, or auditing procedure. At the same time, the former auditor must submit a letter stating whether the auditors agree with the explanation and, if not, provide particulars. These documents are available to the public through the SEC's Electronic Data Gathering, Analysis, and Retrieval system (EDGAR), available on the SEC's Web site (www.sec.gov). The purpose of these public disclosures is to make information available about client–auditor conflicts that could have a bearing on financial presentations and consequent investment decisions. Reported disagreements have included disputes over recoverability of asset cost, revenue recognition timing, expense recognition timing, amounts to be reported as liabilities, and necessity for certain auditing procedures.

The audit firm that has been terminated or voluntarily withdrawn from the engagement (whether the audit has been completed or not) is known as the **predecessor auditor.** The term **successor auditor** refers to any firm considering accepting the engagement.

Auditing a client that has integrity generally results in a problem-free engagement. Conversely, despite conducting an audit in accordance with generally accepted auditing standards, it is difficult for an audit firm to avoid appearing "guilty by association" with a client that lacks integrity. To reduce the risk of accepting a problem client, auditing standards require a successor auditor to initiate contact with and *attempt* to obtain basic information directly from the predecessor regarding issues that reflect directly on the *integrity of management.* Such issues may include

- Disagreements the predecessor could have had with management about accounting principles or audit procedures.
- Communications the predecessor gave the former client about fraud, illegal acts, and internal control recommendations.
- The predecessor's understanding about the reasons for the change of auditors (particularly about the predecessor's termination).

If you read closely, professional standards require only that the successor auditors *attempt* to communicate with the predecessor auditors. The AICPA Code of Professional

Conduct does not permit the predecessor to provide information obtained during the terminated engagement without the explicit consent of the client. Confidentiality remains even when the auditor–client relationship ends. Therefore, auditing standards require the successor auditor to ask that the consent be given to permit the predecessor auditor to speak. If this consent is refused, the refusal should be regarded as a *red flag* and the successor auditor should be cautious about accepting the engagement.

Engagement Letters (*SAS 83*)

Professional standards require auditors to reach a mutual understanding with clients concerning engagement requirements and expectations and to document this understanding, usually in the form of a written letter. When a new client is accepted or when an audit engagement continues from year to year, an **engagement letter** should be prepared. This letter sets forth the understanding with the client, including in particular: (1) the objectives of the engagement, (2) management's responsibilities, (3) the auditors' responsibilities, and (4) any limitations of the engagement. Other matters of understanding such as the ones shown in Exhibit 4.1 also may be included in the letter. For example, the additional internal control considerations required by the Public Company Accounting Oversight Board (PCAOB) in *Auditing Standard 5* are mentioned in the example engagement letter.

In effect, the engagement letter acts as a contract. Thus, it serves as a means for reducing the risk of misunderstandings with the client and as a means of avoiding legal liability for claims that the auditors did not perform the work promised. Also note the indemnification clause toward the end of the engagement letter. More firms are including similar wording to prevent costly litigation. (Often times, litigation settlements are for many more times the amount of the audit fee for the engagement.) Such clauses, however, are not without controversy. The SEC believes that indemnification clauses impair independence because the firm may be tempted to provide substandard services if it is protected from legal liability. The AICPA's Professional Ethics Executive Committee, on the other hand, believes that the indemnification clauses do not impair independence *as long as the audit engagement is conducted in accordance with generally accepted auditing standards.*

Many public accounting firms also have policies about sending a **termination letter** to former clients. Such a letter is a good idea because it provides an opportunity to deal with the subject of future services, in particular: (1) access to audit documentation by successor auditors, (2) reissuance of the auditors' report when required for SEC reporting or comparative financial reporting, and (3) fee arrangements for such future services. The termination letter also may include a report of the auditors' understanding of the circumstances of termination (e.g., disagreements about accounting principles and audit procedures, fees, or other conflicts). These matters can be of great interest to prospective successor auditors who know to ask for a copy of the termination letter.

Staff Assignment

When a new client is obtained, most public accounting firms assign a full-service team to the engagement. For a typical audit engagement, this team usually consists of the audit engagement partner (the person with final responsibility for the audit), the audit manager, an industry specialist, one or more senior audit staff members, computer specialists (if needed), a tax partner, and a second (*concurring*) audit partner.

The **concurring partner,** required for audits of financial statements filed with the Securities and Exchange Commission, reviews the audit team's work in critical audit areas (those areas with the highest potential audit risk). This second partner review provides a level of quality assurance to the engagement. Concurring partners are supposed to have a detached professional point of view because they are not directly responsible for "keeping the client happy." On SEC engagements, the audit engagement partners (as well as the concurring partners) are required to periodically rotate to other clients so that they do not remain in charge of a particular client for more than five years.

EXHIBIT 4.1 **Engagement Letter** — CONTRACT *

October 15, 2008

Dear Mr. Lancaster:

This letter will confirm our understanding of the arrangement for our audit of the financial statements of Apollo Shoes, Inc., for the year ending December 31, 2008.

We will audit the Company's balance sheet at December 31, 2008, and the related statements of income, comprehensive income, stockholders' equity, and cash flows for the year then ended, for the purpose of expressing an opinion on them. We will also audit whether Apollo Shoes, Inc. maintained effective internal control over financial reporting as of December 31, 2008, based on criteria established in Internal Control—Integrated Framework issued by the Committee of Sponsoring Organizations of the Treadway Commission (COSO criteria). Apollo Shoes, Inc.'s management is responsible for these financial statements and for maintaining effective internal control over financial reporting. Management is also responsible for making financial records and related information available for audit and for identifying and ensuring that the company complies with the laws and regulations that apply to its activities. Lastly, management is responsible for adjusting the financial statements to correct material misstatements and for affirming to us in the representation letter that the effects of any uncorrected misstatements aggregated by us during the current engagement and pertaining to the latest period presented are immaterial, both individually and in the aggregate, to the financial statements taken as a whole. Our responsibility is to express an opinion on these financial statements and an opinion on the effectiveness of the company's internal control over financial reporting based on our audits. If, for any reason, we are unable to complete the audit or are unable to form or have not formed an opinion, we may decline to express an opinion or decline to issue a report as a result of the engagement.

We will conduct our audits in accordance with the standards of the Public Company Accounting Oversight Board (United States). Those standards require that we plan and perform the audit to obtain reasonable assurance about whether the financial statements are free of material misstatement and whether effective internal control over financial reporting was maintained in all material respects. Our audit of the financial statements includes examining, on a test basis, evidence supporting the amounts and disclosures in the financial statements, assessing the accounting principles used and significant estimates made by management, and evaluating the overall financial statement presentation. Our audit of internal control over financial reporting includes obtaining an understanding of internal control over financial reporting, testing and evaluating the design and operating effectiveness of internal control, and performing such other procedures as we considered necessary in the circumstances. We believe that our audits provide a reasonable basis for our opinions.

A company's internal control over financial reporting is a process designed to provide reasonable assurance regarding the reliability of financial reporting and the preparation of financial statements for external purposes in accordance with generally accepted accounting principles. A company's internal control over financial reporting includes those policies and procedures that (1) pertain to the maintenance of records that, in reasonable detail, accurately and fairly reflect the transactions and dispositions of the assets of the company; (2) provide reasonable assurance that transactions are recorded as necessary to permit preparation of financial statements in accordance with generally accepted accounting principles, and that receipts and expenditures of the company are being made only in accordance with authorizations of management and directors of the company; and (3) provide reasonable assurance regarding prevention or timely detection of unauthorized acquisition, use, or disposition of the company's assets that could have a material effect on the financial statements.

Because of its inherent limitations, internal control over financial reporting may not prevent or detect misstatements. Also, projections of any evaluation of effectiveness to future periods are subject to the risk that controls may become inadequate because of changes in conditions, or that the degree of compliance with the policies or procedures may deteriorate.

Our fee for these services will be at our regular per diem rates, plus travel and other out-of-pocket costs. Invoices will be rendered on a monthly basis and are payable on presentation.

In the unlikely event that any difference concerning our services should arise that are not resolved by mutual agreement, we both recognize that the matter would be decided most equitably to both parties by a judge hearing the evidence without a jury. Accordingly, we both agree to waive any right to a jury trial in any action, proceeding, or counterclaim arising out of or relating to our services and fees.

If this letter correctly expresses your understanding, please sign the enclosed copy where indicated and return it to us.

Very truly yours,

Smith & Smith, CPAs

APOLLO SHOES, INC.

By _____

Date _____

The assignment of staff depends on the riskiness of the engagement. For new clients, companies with complex transactions, and publicly traded companies, more experienced staff members are typically assigned. No matter the type of engagement, planning meetings should include all team members and focus on potential trouble areas. These planning meetings help to ensure that the engagement is properly planned and that the audit team (especially new) members are properly supervised (the first standard of field work). The meetings also are intended to be "brainstorming sessions" to (1) ensure that all audit team members are informed about potential risks in the engagement and (2) increase team members' awareness for potential fraud.

Time Budget

The timing of the work and the number of hours that each segment of the engagement is expected to take are detailed in a time budget. *Time budgets* are used to maintain control of the audit by identifying problem areas early in the engagement, thereby ensuring that the engagement is completed on a timely basis. Time budgets are usually based on last year's performance for continuing clients while taking changes in the client's business into account. In a first-time audit, the budget may be based on a predecessor auditor's experience or on general experience with similar companies. Extra time also may be assigned to those accounts containing the highest amount of audit risk. A simple time budget for an audit engagement follows.

	Audit Time Budget (hours)	
	Interim	**Year End (final)**
Knowledge of the business	15	
Internal audit familiarization	10	
Internal control evaluation	30	10
Audit program planning	25	
Related-parties investigation	5	15
Client conferences	10	18
Cash	10	15
Accounts receivable	15	5
Inventory	35	20
Accounts payable	5	35
Representation letters		20
Financial statement review		25
Report preparation		12

This time budget is illustrative—actual time budgets are much more detailed. Some specify the expected time by level of staff people on the team (partner, manager, in-charge accountant, staff assistant, specialist). The illustration shows time at *interim* and at *year-end*. **Interim audit work** refers to procedures performed several weeks or months before the balance-sheet date. (Account balances audited during interim are later *rolled forward* at year end.) **Year-end audit work** refers to procedures performed shortly before and after the balance-sheet date. Audit firms typically spread the workload out during the year by scheduling interim audit work so they will have enough time and people available when several audits have year-ends on the same date (December 31 is common). For many audit firms, the auditing "busy season" runs from October through April of the following year. The interim work can consist of both internal control risk assessment work and audit of balances as they exist at the early date.

Everyone who works on the audit reports the time taken to perform procedures for each segment of the audit. These time reports are recorded by budget categories for the purposes of (1) evaluating the efficiency of the audit team members, (2) compiling a record for billing the client, and (3) compiling a record for planning the next audit.

Although the purposes of a time budget are straightforward, time budgets create job pressures. Staff members are under pressure to "meet the budget," and beginning auditors often experience frustration over learning how to do audit work efficiently.

Review Checkpoints

4.1 What sources of information can auditors use in connection with deciding whether to accept a new client?

4.2 Why do predecessor auditors need to obtain the client's consent to give information to successor auditors? What information should successor auditors try to obtain from predecessor auditors?

4.3 What benefits are obtained by having an *engagement letter*? What is a *termination letter*?

4.4 What persons and skills are normally assigned to a "full-service" audit team?

UNDERSTANDING THE CLIENT'S BUSINESS

LEARNING OBJECTIVE

2. Identify the procedures and sources of information auditors may use to obtain knowledge of a client's business and industry.

Knowledge and understanding of the client's business in the context of the client's industry is absolutely essential in an audit. Auditing standards require the audit team to obtain a thorough understanding of the business to plan and perform the audit work.

STAGES OF AN AUDIT

Obtain (or Retain) Engagement	Engagement Planning	Risk Assessment	Substantive Procedures	Reporting

Auditors must understand the broad economic environment in which the client operates, including such things as the effects of national economic policies (e.g., price regulations and import/export restrictions), the geographic location and its economy (northeastern states versus sunbelt states), and developments in taxation and regulatory areas (e.g., telecommunications industry deregulation, approval processes in the drug and chemical industries). Industry characteristics are also important. There is a great deal of difference in the production and marketing activities of banks, insurance companies, mutual funds, supermarkets, hotels, oil and gas industries, agriculture organizations, manufacturers, and so forth. Industry expertise also involves knowledge of the competition and an understanding of the client's market niche. Few auditors are experts in all of these areas. Audit firms typically have people who are expert in one or two industries and rely on them to manage audits in those industries. Indeed, some public accounting firms have reputations for having many audit clients in a particular industry while others have a larger presence in other industries.

Gaining an Understanding of a Client's Business Risk

Given the rapidly changing environment in which today's businesses operate, management, internal auditors, and external auditors must focus on the risks to the entity's operations and ensure controls are in place to eliminate, mitigate, or compensate for those

risks. To address these concerns, the Committee of Sponsoring Organizations (COSO)[1] developed an enterprise risk management framework to facilitate assessing and mitigating business risk. COSO defines **enterprise risk management (ERM)** as

> a process, effected by an entity's board of directors, management and other personnel, applied in strategy setting and across the enterprise, designed to identify potential events that may affect the entity, and manage risks to be within its risk appetite, to provide reasonable assurance regarding the achievement of entity objectives.

The ERM model (Exhibit 4.2) is composed of eight elements: (1) internal environment, (2) objective setting, (3) event identification, (4) risk assessment, (5) risk response, (6) control activities, (7) information and communication, and (8) monitoring.

- *Internal environment* is the "risk consciousness" of the organization and includes the organization's risk management philosophy and "risk appetite," its integrity and ethical values, and the environment in which it operates. The internal environment establishes how the organization responds to risk.

- *Objective setting* is management's responsibility to determine the goals and objectives of the organization. For example, for a retail operation like **Wal-Mart,** an objective is to make sure that the shelves are always stocked. If a customer goes to a Wal-Mart store to purchase a particular item, the store's failure to have the item results in the loss not only of a sale, but also possibly a customer.

- *Event identification* is the identification of conditions and events, either internal or external to the organization, that could adversely affect management's objectives. Many of these are *red flags* that exist in the particular industry, in the organization's management, or in the information-processing systems. Supplier problems, poor weather conditions that can affect the trucks supplying the stores, and information system breakdowns are just several of the events that could adversely affect Wal-Mart's ability to keep its stores' shelves stocked.

- *Risk assessment* is the systematic process for estimating the likelihood of adverse conditions occurring. Risks are assessed in terms of both likelihood and impact. Again using the Wal-Mart example, managers would assess the risk of weather conditions (e.g., hurricane, blizzard) affecting supply or of key suppliers going out of business. As part of this assessment, they also would attempt to determine the financial impact if such an occurrence happened. By combining these risk assessments, they would be able to better prioritize the events and their potential effects on store operations. For example, a week before Hurricane Katrina struck the Gulf Coast in 2005, Wal-Mart's business continuity director was tracking the storm's progress from an emergency command center.

- *Risk response* addresses how the organization will prevent or respond to the adverse conditions if they actually occur. They include management policies and procedures to eliminate, mitigate, or compensate for the risks identified. In Wal-Mart's case, the company has established an excellent logistic system. When items are purchased at each Wal-Mart location, the cash registers, which are electronically linked with the corporate headquarters, track sales and remaining inventory. When inventory levels become low, goods are shipped from centrally located warehouses to prevent shortages from occurring. To control for supplier shortages, Wal-Mart uses suppliers with proven reputations. Other responses include having adequate insurance levels to protect against losses from theft, fire, or natural disaster. Derivative securities could be used to hedge against changes in interest rates or changes in the prices of raw materials.

[1] The Committee of Sponsoring Organizations of the Treadway Commission (COSO) is a private sector initiative established in 1985 composed of five financial professional associations: the Institute of Internal Auditors, the American Institute of Certified Public Accountants, the American Accounting Association, the Institute of Management Accountants, and the Financial Executives Institute. COSO's stated goal is "to improve the quality of financial reporting through a focus on corporate governance, ethical practices, and internal control" (www.coso.org).

EXHIBIT 4.2
Enterprise Risk Management (ERM) Framework

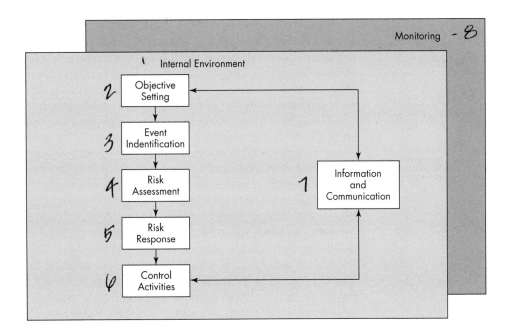

Responding to Hurricane Katrina's progress, Wal-Mart had prepositioned supply truck convoys just outside of the hurricane's path, ready to roll into the affected areas once roads had been cleared. Because of Wal-Mart's preparations, the company was able to supply victims with generators, dry ice, and drinking water within days of the storm. Contrast this response with that of the Federal Emergency Management Agency (FEMA), the government agency charged with aiding victims after natural disasters, which struggled to get supplies to victims even weeks after the storm.

- *Control activities* are policies and procedures to ensure that risk responses are appropriate given the circumstances and environment in which the organization operates.

- *Information and communication* link all components of the ERM. In Wal-Mart's case, its information system is instrumental in providing management with key information so that risks could be minimized or eliminated.

- *Monitoring* includes regular management and supervisory activities over risk management activities.

Risk-Based Auditing (RBA)

Many public accounting firms' audit approaches have paralleled the development of ERM. While organizations employ ERM, auditing firms themselves use a risk-based auditing (RBA) approach that employs a top-down evaluation of the client's risk that goes far beyond the financial statements. For example, audit teams now devote a significant amount of their engagement planning on their clients' business risks (i.e., the risks that the client will fail to achieve its objectives).[2] Firms adopting this approach believe they must learn more about their clients' strategies and processes to understand whether the financial statements are fairly presented.

Under this approach, also known as *strategic systems auditing*,[3] auditors begin by identifying the client's strategy and the processes for developing that strategy. They next examine the core business processes such as product delivery and resource management processes such as human resource management. For each of these key processes (and

[2] W. Lemmon, K. Tatum, and W. Turleym, *Developments in the Audit Methodologies of Large Accounting firms* (London, England: Auditing Practices Board, 2000).

[3] T. Bell, F. Marrs, I. Solomon, and H. Thomas, *Auditing Organizations through a Strategic-Systems Lens* (Montvale, NJ: KPMG, LLP, 1997).

related subprocesses), objectives, inputs, activities, outputs, systems, and transactions are identified. Next, the risks that the processes will not meet their goals and controls related to those risks are assessed. Finally, key performance measures that would indicate that the controls are not working are identified. Such performance indicators can direct auditors to gather evidence to support the audit assertions, much the same way that analytical review procedures direct attention to potential problem areas.

Gaining an understanding of strategies and processes involves gathering evidence in areas generally not addressed by auditors, so auditors could ask production personnel about labor problems or marketing personnel about product quality. Although the process has been criticized by some as more consulting than auditing, it does address factors that auditors could miss by getting lost in the details of a traditional "bottom-up" (focus on individual accounts that compose the financial statements) approach. Business risk auditing also makes auditors much more knowledgeable about their client's business and its environment. We should note that, even when taking this "top-down" approach, the auditor still has to tie procedures to key accounts and assertions.

In RBA, auditors view all activities in the organization first in terms of risks to strategies and objectives and then in terms of management's plans and processes to mitigate the risks. The departure from account-based auditing is subtle. In account-based auditing, auditors first obtain an understanding of controls and assess control risk for particular types of errors and frauds in specific accounts or cycles. In RBA, the auditors obtain an understanding of the client's objectives. Then risks are identified and the auditors determine how *management* plans to mitigate these risks. The three basic ways that management can mitigate a risk are (1) avoid it, (2) control it, and (3) share it.

RBA begins with an auditor's question: "What can prevent management from obtaining its strategies and objectives?" The answer reveals the "risk": the event or action, and its probability, that something could adversely affect the organization. Then the auditing is directed to determining how management plans to mitigate the risk and whether those plans are in place and operating effectively.

An example will help. Consider the cash disbursement activity of a large university that produces 9,000 check payments each month. The amount of potential loss exposure is large, about $50 million each month. The university managers want to safeguard the cash from unauthorized payments. What could go wrong? The list of errors and frauds that can affect cash disbursements is long! One of them is that checks could be produced without official approval. Another is that outsiders could create checks that look like university checks and fool the bank into drawing them on the university account.

So what is the management doing to mitigate this risk of forgery loss? The university can hardly avoid the risk; check payments must be processed. The university can share the risk by purchasing fidelity bonds and other insurance. Is this enough mitigation effort? Maybe it is for some types of operations, but insurance companies usually require an organization to try to avoid loss by having controls. Auditors now get to the study of controls, but it is a very focused study directed to the particular forgery loss risk. The audit question is not the general "Are controls adequate?" but the focused question "Are controls over invalid payments (forgeries) adequate when considered in conjunction with the insurance policies?"

AUDITING INSIGHT "You can observe a lot just by watching."—Yogi Berra

In an audit of a bank branch location, the internal audit team (including one of this textbook's authors) conducting the branch examination requested an important report from one of the branch's clerks. The clerk reached under her desk and pulled the report from a six-month-high pile of unfiled reports. As the audit proceeded, the team found that this haphazard method of doing business was indicative of the business practices of the bank branch as a whole. At the end of the audit, the branch manager was dismissed for inadequate performance.

Suppose these auditors find that one of the prevention controls is a "positive pay" arrangement with the bank. In a positive pay control procedure, the university gives the bank an electronic file listing all checks properly produced by the legitimate university system. The bank compares every university check presented for payment and pays only the checks on the list. This control, in conjunction with other approval procedures, can constitute appropriate mitigation, and the auditors can perform tests of controls to determine whether (1) the production of the positive pay file itself is controlled and (2) any unauthorized or forged checks were paid by the bank despite these controls.

One key question is this: How can you cope with the need to study and evaluate management risk mitigation? Answer: It is not easy! You need to rely on knowledge of marketing, management, production, finance, statistics, business law, economics, taxation, operations research, political science, physical sciences, and other subjects. These are some of the nonaccounting courses you can take in your college curriculum. Such studies are important because they serve as a foundation for organizing your practical experiences and your development of a common sense of business management. You can expect very little to be routine in a study and evaluation of management risk mitigation. Understanding such broad issues in an entity makes financial, governmental, and internal audit assignments exciting challenges.

Inquiry and Observation of Client Personnel

Interviews with the entity's management, directors, and audit committee can bring auditors up to date on changes in the business and the industry. Such inquiries of client personnel have the multiple purposes of building personal working relationships, observing the competence and integrity of client personnel, obtaining a general understanding, and probing gently for problem areas that could harbor financial misstatements. At the same time that inquiries and interviews take place, the audit team can tour the entity's physical facilities. Auditors use this time to look for activities and issues that should be reflected in the accounting records. For example, an auditor could notice a jumbled pile of materials and parts in the warehouse and make a note to check for its inventory condition and valuation. The tour is the time to see entity personnel in their normal workplaces. Later, the auditors will meet these same people in direct evidence-gathering circumstances.

Other early information-gathering activities include (1) reviewing the corporate charter and bylaws or partnership agreement; (2) reviewing contracts, agreements, and legal proceedings; and (3) reading the minutes of the meetings of directors and committees of the board of directors. The minutes provide a history of the company, critical events and transactions, and future company intentions. A company's failure to provide minutes is a significant scope limitation that could result in the audit firm's disclaiming an opinion on the company's financial statements.

Identification of Related Parties (*SAS 45*)

Another purpose of reviewing the board of directors' meeting minutes is to identify key *related parties*. **Related parties** include those individuals or organizations that are closely tied to the auditee, possibly through family ties or investment relationships. Because one

Boards of directors are supposed to monitor the client's business. The minutes of their meetings and the meetings of their committees (e.g., executive committee, finance committee, compensation committee, audit committee) frequently contain information of vital interest to the independent auditors. Some examples follow:

- Amount of dividends declared.
- Elections of officers and authorization of officers' salaries.
- Authorization of stock options and other "perk" compensation.
- Acceptance of contracts, agreements, lawsuit settlements.
- Approval of major purchases of property and investments.
- Discussions of merger and divestiture progress.
- Authorization of financing by stock issuance, long-term debt issuance, and leases.

- Approval to pledge assets as security for debts.
- Discussion of negotiations on bank loans and payment waivers.
- Approval of accounting policies and accounting for estimates and unusual transactions.
- Authorizations of individuals to sign bank checks.

Auditors take notes or make copies of important parts of these minutes and compare them to information in the accounts and disclosures (e.g., compare the amount of dividends declared to the amount paid, compare officers' authorized salaries to amounts paid, compare agreements to pledge assets to proper disclosure in the notes to financial statements).

of the basic assumptions of historical cost accounting is that transactions are valued at prices agreed on by two *objective* parties, *valuation* of related-party transactions is particularly troublesome. For example, audit team members must remember that the economic substance of a particular transaction (and its effect on the financial condition of the entity) could be significantly different from its legal form (e.g., capitalized leases versus operating leases). Auditors strive to identify related-party relationships and transactions during planning to be able to obtain evidence that the financial accounting and disclosure for them are proper. Some methods include reviewing the Board of Directors' meeting minutes, making inquiries of key executives, and reviewing stock ownership records (5 percent ownership in the company is usually used as a good cutoff).

Auditors also should question the persuasiveness (or quality) of the evidence obtained from related parties because the source of the evidence may be biased. Hence, auditors should obtain evidence of the purpose, nature, and extent of related-party transactions and their effect on financial statements, and the evidence should extend beyond inquiry of management.

Review of Prior Audit Documentation

For recurring engagements, specific information about the client is available in the prior year's audit documentation and in the *permanent files*. Audit team members who worked on the audit in prior years are available to convey their understanding of the business, suggest new or altered procedures for subsequent audits, and provide advice for future team members. In addition, auditing research has found that client errors are often repeated one year to the next, so auditors review the prior year's proposed adjustments to identify recurring problem areas. For example, public accounting firms often develop client income tax provisions once the audit is complete; thus, the income tax adjusting entry would show up as an adjustment every year.

An initial audit requires more work than a repeat engagement. If an existing company has been operating for a while but has never been audited, the additional work includes an audit of the beginning balances in the balance-sheet accounts. The starting place for the audited accounting must be established with reliable account balances. Such accounts as inventory, fixed assets, and intangible assets affect the current-year income and cash flow statements. This work may involve going back to examine several years' transactions that make up the balance-sheet accounts.

If the client was previously audited by another (*predecessor*) auditor, the successor auditor must first obtain the client's permission before requesting copies of the predecessor's audit documentation. Although some may think that there could be "bad blood" because the predecessor could have lost a lucrative fee, good business practice dictates that the

AUDITING INSIGHT The Perils of Related-Party Transactions

Although related-party transactions are approved by company boards, some critics charge that such transactions do not pass the "smell test" and should be avoided, especially given recent accounting scandals. One study noted that 40 percent of the S&P 500 companies have business relationships with other companies that are somehow related. For example, **Best Buy** leases two stores, as well as corporate airplanes, from its chairman and founder Richard Schulze. A company spokesperson explained that the store leases were in the best interests of the company; Schulze purchased them when the company was just beginning and short of cash.

In the 1980s, **Phar-Mor** was a large, fast-growing discount retailer. In fact, Sam Walton (founder of **Wal-Mart**) is quoted as saying that Phar-Mor was the only company he feared. His fear was the result of his incapacity to figure out how Phar-Mor was able to report profits while underselling Wal-Mart's prices. The answer was simple: Phar-Mor was "cooking the books." One component of the $1.3 billion fraud involved CEO Mickey Monus's establishment of his own equipment rental stores in areas in which new Phar-Mor stores were opening. The new Phar-Mor stores would then rent equipment from Monus's equipment company. Because of the related-party nature (i.e., transactions were not at arm's length), auditors found it difficult to determine whether Phar-Mor was getting a good deal or was being looted internally by its own CEO.

Enron CFO Andrew Fastow made millions by managing investment partnerships that had significant dealings with Enron. By "selling" appreciated assets to Fastow's LJM partnerships, Enron was able to record profits before the company would normally earn them. The financing vehicles were also instrumental in keeping significant debt off Enron's balance sheet. The problem was that Fastow's millions came at Enron's expense. Although there were safeguards in place to prevent such conflicts of interest, Enron's board of directors waived the rules preventing such transactions. Board members later stated that they had not realized how much Fastow was making from the deals (approximately $45 million). **Arthur Andersen** expressed concern about the related-party transactions but withdrew its reservations when the board signed off on the relationship. The risky partnerships, based on overvalued assets and collateralized with Enron stock, represented one of the primary reasons for Enron's ultimate collapse.

Sources: "Related-Party' Deals Abound at Companies," *The Wall Street Journal*, December 3, 2004, p. C3; "Visionary's Dream Led to Risky Business; Opaque Deals, Accounting Sleight of Hand Built an Energy Giant and Ensured its Demise" *The Washington Post*, July 28, 2002, p. A1.

relationship between the predecessor and successor auditors remain professional. One never knows when the roles could reverse on other engagements and the predecessor becomes the successor.

Study Industry Accounting and Auditing Practices

Numerous sources for obtaining information about the client's industry are available. The AICPA industry accounting and auditing guides are a good place to start. These guides explain the typical transactions and accounts used by various types of businesses and not-for-profit organizations.

Research Sources of Information

A wide variety of records and information are available for business inquiries. Only a few of the hundreds of sources are described briefly here. Many databases and information sources are available on the Internet.

General Business Sources

Most industries have specialized trade magazines and journals. You may not choose to read *Grocer's Spotlight* for pleasure, but magazines of this special type are very valuable for learning and maintaining an industry expertise. In addition, specific information about public companies can be found in registration statements and 10-K reports filed with the SEC. General business magazines and newspapers often contribute insights about an industry, an entity, and individual corporate officers. Many are available, including such leaders as *BusinessWeek, Forbes, Fortune, Harvard Business Review, Barron's,* and *The Wall Street Journal.* Practicing auditors typically read several of these regularly. Additionally, many companies present "company story" information on their Web sites. A visit to the Web site can provide a wealth of information about products, markets, and strategies.

AUDITING INSIGHT Sources of Business and Industry Information

GENERAL INFORMATION

Dun & Bradstreet's *Principal International Businesses*

Standard & Poor's *Register of Corporations, Directors, and Executives*

Value Line Investment Survey

Moody's manuals (various industries)

Standard & Poor's *Corporation Records*

Statistical Abstract of the United States

Dun & Bradstreet's *Key Business Ratios*

COMMUNICATIONS INDUSTRY MEDIA

Broadcasting-Cablecasting Yearbook (annual)

Advertising Age (twice weekly)

Broadcasting (weekly)

Publishers Weekly (weekly)

Variety (weekly)

Source: CPA firm compendium of "Sources of Industry Data."

Business and Asset Identification Sources

Each country and state has a system for registering businesses—corporations, joint ventures, sole proprietorships, partnerships. They keep files on registered "assumed names" (DBA, or "Doing Business As" names). Some businesses can be registered with a state but not a county, or with a county but not a state. All real corporations are chartered by a state, and each state's secretary of state keeps corporate record information such as the date of registration and the initial officers and owners. Crooks often work through a labyrinth of business entities, and you can find all registered entities in these sources. You can find phony vendor companies created by real employees to bilk employers with false billings. Banks, finance companies, and other creditors often file Uniform Commercial Code (UCC) records to record the interest of the creditor in assets used as collateral for a loan so other parties cannot claim interest in the assets (e.g., boats, business equipment, appliances). UCCs are found in county clerks' offices and in a state's office of the secretary of state or commercial department of the state records office. (They are also online in some commercial databases.)

City and county tax assessor-collectors keep files on real property by address and legal description, owner, taxable value, improvements, amount of taxes, and delinquencies. State (and some city) regulatory agencies have directories of liquor licenses and various professionals (e.g., CPAs, dentists, doctors, plumbers, electricians). The U.S. Department of Housing and Urban Development (HUD) has a central index file of appraisers, real estate brokers, and most components of the building industry. The U.S. Department of State has data on companies that apply for import and export licenses. The Federal Aviation Administration maintains files on the chain of ownership of all civil aircraft in the United States. The Securities and Exchange Commission has extensive financial information on about 15,000 registered companies and their properties, principal officers, directors, and owners. Local Better Business Bureaus keep information about criminal rackets, cons, and their operators and can provide information about the business reputation of local businesses. Standard & Poor's *Register of Corporations, Directors, and Executives* lists about 37,000 public and private companies and the names and titles of over 400,000 officials.

Federal and State Revenue Agencies

Ever wonder how revenue agents find tax evaders? One accountant described the following sources of tips for possible big audit findings: Police and Drug Enforcement Agency arrest records point to people who could have illicit unreported income. Real estate sales records can identify people who "forget" to put their sales in a tax return. Auto registrations of expensive cars point to people who have a lot of money to spend, maybe from some unreported income. Comparison of state sales tax returns with income tax revenue amounts can reveal discrepancies (depending on which tax collector is feared more). Agents have used college-town newspaper rental ads to identify people who rent rooms, garage apartments, duplex halves, and the like, but "forget" to report the income.

Materiality and Planning

The major reason for thinking about materiality at the planning stage is to try to fine-tune the audit for effectiveness and efficiency. Thinking about materiality in advance helps to avoid surprises. Suppose, near the end of an audit, the partner decided that individual and aggregate misstatements over $50,000 should be considered material but then realized that the nature, timing, and extent of substantive procedures resulted in an acceptable audit risk only at the $100,000 level! More work should have been done, but now it is very late to do it. Conversely, an audit team could *overaudit*, or perform more audit work than is necessary, thinking in terms of detecting $50,000 in total misstatement, when accuracy to the nearest $100,000 is satisfactory.

To plan the audit of various accounts, auditors need to assign part of the planning materiality to each account. The amount assigned to an account is called the *tolerable misstatement* for that account. The **tolerable misstatement** is the amount by which a particular account may be misstated (error not discovered by auditors), yet still not cause the financial statements taken as a whole to be materially misleading. Thus, tolerable misstatement for each account is based on the overall financial statement materiality.

The extent to which tolerable misstatement is "based on" the overall materiality amount may vary from auditor to auditor. You should not be surprised that there are different methods for assigning overall materiality to tolerable misstatements for accounts. The auditing standards do not even require that the overall materiality judgment be expressed as a dollar amount, much less assigned to individual accounts in dollar amounts. You will find many different thought processes and methods used in practice. For example, when materiality is quantified, some accountants prefer a *bottom-up approach:* judging materiality amounts in each account separately (e.g., $25,000 for accounts receivable, $35,000 for inventory, etc.) and then combining the amounts to see what the overall effect would be. Other accountants prefer a *top-down approach:* judging an overall material amount for the financial statements (e.g., $200,000 would materially misstate an entity's balance sheet) and then allocating it to particular accounts (e.g., receivables, inventory) to help determine the amount of work to be done in each area. There are even variations within the top-down approach:

- One method is to assign tolerable misstatement amounts that exactly add up to materiality.
- A different method assigns tolerable misstatement amounts that add up to twice the overall materiality. The theory is that actual financial misstatements in accounts can be both overstatements and understatements, and the two directions will tend to balance out.
- Another method is to assign tolerable misstatement in amounts such that the square root of the sum of the squared tolerable misstatements is equal to the overall materiality. The theory here is that the different misstatements behave like random errors in a calculation of statistical variance.

The top-down approach is considered theoretically preferable because this method requires the audit team to think first about the financial statements taken as a whole. Then it forces the planning for each account into the context of the financial statements taken as a whole. The top-down approach helps to avoid the problems of "being surprised" when judgments about separate accounts (the bottom-up approach) add up to more than a material amount appropriate for the income statement, balance sheet, or statement of cash flows.

Considering the Work of Internal Auditors (*SAS 65*)

External auditors must obtain an understanding of a client's internal audit department and its work as part of the understanding of the client's internal control. Internal auditors were discussed briefly in Chapter 1 and will be discussed in greater detail in Module D, but here we talk about the working relationship between internal and external auditors. Audit efficiency can be realized when the two groups work together. However, prior to using the

work of internal auditors, external auditors should consider internal auditors' *objectivity* and *competence*:

- *Objectivity.* Internal auditors can never be considered *independent* in the same sense as external auditors because internal auditors are employed and compensated by the client;[4] however, they can (and should) be *objective*. Internal auditors' objectivity is investigated by learning about their organizational status and lines of communication in the company. The theory is that objectivity is enhanced when the internal auditors report directly to the audit committee of the board of directors. Objectivity is questioned when the internal auditors report to divisional management, line managers, or other persons with a stake in the outcome of their findings. Objectivity is especially questioned when managers have some power over the pay or job tenure of the internal auditors. Similarly, objectivity is questioned when individual internal auditors have relatives in audit-sensitive areas or are scheduled to be promoted to positions in the activities under internal audit review.

- *Competence.* Internal auditors' competence is investigated by obtaining evidence about their educational and experience qualifications, their certifications (e.g., CPA, CIA, CISA, etc.) and continuing education status, the department's policies and procedures for work quality and for making personnel assignments, the supervision and review activities, and the quality of reports and audit documentation. This evidence enables the external auditors to evaluate internal auditors' performance.

Favorable conclusions about competence and objectivity enable external auditors to accept the internal auditors' documentation and work on review, assessment, and monitoring of a company's internal control procedures. Internal auditors also can assist (under the supervision of the independent audit team) with performing other parts of the audit, reducing the external auditors' work and avoiding duplication of effort. For example, internal auditors often confirm accounts receivable and conduct observations and make test counts during physical inventory counts. By relying in part on this work, external auditors may be able to reduce the nature, timing, or extent of their own procedures in the same areas. Be careful to note, however, that this utilization of internal auditors' work cannot be a complete substitute for the external auditors' own procedures and evidence related to accounting judgments and material financial statement balances.

The external auditors cannot share responsibility for audit decisions with the internal auditors and must supervise, review, evaluate, and test the work performed by the internal auditors. This requirement applies both to the work of obtaining an understanding of the internal control and the work of using internal auditors' evidence about account balances. In other words, internal auditors should never be delegated tasks that require the external auditors' *professional judgment.* Thus, although internal auditors may investigate accounts receivable confirmation exceptions, they normally would not be involved in assessing the reasonableness of the company's allowance for doubtful accounts. Following is an illustration of how one Big Four firm addresses the use of internal auditors on its engagements. Note that internal auditors' work can be utilized more extensively without reperformance when the account balance involves low judgment and risk and internal auditors are considered to be more competent and objective.

Reliance on Internal Auditors

	Objectivity and Competence	
	Low	**High**
High Judgment/Risk	Auditor should not rely on internal auditors' work	
Low Judgment/Risk	Reperform 50 percent of internal auditor's work	Reperform 30 percent of internal auditor's work

[4] Internal auditors refer to their level of objectivity as "independence." This concept is discussed further in Module D.

Use of Specialists (*SAS 73*)

The understanding of the business can lead to information that indicates the need to employ *specialists* on the audit. **Specialists** are persons skilled in fields other than accounting and auditing—actuaries, appraisers, attorneys, engineers, and geologists—who are not members of the audit team. Auditors are not expected to be expert in all fields of knowledge that can contribute information to the financial statements. When a specialist is engaged, auditors must know about his or her professional qualifications, experience, and reputation. A specialist should be unrelated to the company under audit if possible. Auditors must obtain an understanding of a specialist's methods and assumptions. Provided some additional auditing work is done on the data used by the specialist, auditors may rely on the specialist's work in connection with audit decisions. Normally, specialists are not referred to in the auditor's report unless the specialist's findings (e.g., a difference in an estimate from that of management) cause the auditors' report to be modified (e.g., because of a GAAP departure). In these cases, references to specialists' findings may facilitate understanding the nature of the GAAP departure.

Review Checkpoints

4.5 What are some types of knowledge and understanding about a client's business and industry that an auditor is expected to obtain? What are some of the methods and sources of information for understanding a client's business and industry?

4.6 Where could you find information about (a) real estate valuation, (b) aircraft ownership, (c) assumed (fictitious) business names, and (d) liens on personal property?

4.7 What is the major concern with evidence obtained from related parties?

4.8 What is the primary benefit for auditors' preliminary assessment of materiality as a matter of audit planning?

4.9 What must external auditors do to use the work of internal auditors in the audit of an entity's financial statements?

Preliminary Analytical Procedures (*SAS 56*)

LEARNING
OBJECTIVE

3. Perform analytical procedures to identify potential misstatements.

The auditors' own analyses of the client's financial statements can contribute a significant understanding of the business and how it has operated for the period covered by the financial statements. **Analytical procedures** are *reasonableness tests;* the audit team is comparing its estimates of account balances with those recorded by management. According to auditing standards, *analytical procedures* must be applied in the planning stages of each audit. During this critical point of the engagement, the audit team uses analytical procedures to identify potential problem areas so subsequent audit work can be designed to reduce the risk of missing something important. Analytical procedures during planning also provide an organized approach—a standard starting place—for becoming familiar with the client's business.

The audit team should perform five steps when creating analytical procedures:

1. *Develop an expectation.* A variety of sources can provide evidence for the audit team's expectations of the balance in a particular account:

 • Comparison of current-year account balances to balances for one or more comparable periods (e.g., vertical and horizontal analyses).

 • Comparison of the current-year account balances to anticipated results found in the company's budgets and forecasts.

- Evaluation of the relationships (ratios) of current-year account balances to other current-year balances for conformity with predictable patterns based on the company's experience.
- Comparison of current-year account balances and financial relationships (e.g., ratios) with similar information for the industry in which the company operates.
- Study of the relationships of current-year account balances with relevant nonfinancial information (e.g., physical production statistics).

2. *Define a significant difference.* Basically, the question is, "What percentage (or dollar) difference from your expectation can still be considered reasonable?"
3. *Compare them with the recorded amount.* Many auditors start with comparative financial statements and calculate year-to-year changes in balance-sheet and income-statement accounts (**horizontal analysis**). They next calculate common-size statements (**vertical analysis**) in which financial statement amounts are expressed as percentages of a base such as sales for the income-statement accounts or total assets for the balance-sheet accounts. These initial calculations (see Exhibit 4.3) provide a basis for describing the financial activities for the current year under audit. Although vertical and horizontal analyses are basic beginning analytical procedures, other analytical procedures, including mathematical time series and regression calculations, complicated comparisons of multiyear data, and trend and ratio analyses, can be more complex.
4. *Investigate significant differences.* Auditors typically look for relationships that do not make sense as indicators of problems in the accounts and they use such indicators to plan further audit work. In the planning stage, analytical procedures are used to identify potential problem areas so that subsequent audit work can be designed to reduce the risk of missing something important. The application demonstrated here thus can be described as *attention directing*: pointing out accounts that could contain errors and frauds. The insights derived from *preliminary* analytical procedures do not provide direct evidence about the numbers in the financial statements. Although the insights derived from preliminary analytical procedures provide only limited evidence about the numbers in the financial statements, they do help the audit team identify risks as an aid in planning the audit program.
5. *Document each of the preceding steps.*

For companies that have not undergone any significant changes in operations, one can expect that current-year recorded amounts should be fairly similar to those of the prior year (Step 1). Because changes are not expected, the audit team can identify any changes over 10 percent and $100,000 as deserving additional attention (Step 2). Note that the threshold is *both* 10 percent *and* $100,000 instead of just one trigger or the other. A change in an account balance from $100 to $200 is a 100 percent change, but the change is clearly immaterial. Similarly, an increase in sales from $9.9 million to $10 million meets the $100,000 threshold but does not appear unreasonable in percentage terms. In Step 3, the audit team compares expectations with the recorded balances. Exhibit 4.3 contains financial balances for the prior year (consider them audited) and the current year (consider them unaudited at this stage). Common-size statements (vertical analysis) are shown in parallel columns, and the dollar amount and percentage change (horizontal analysis) are shown in the last two columns.

The investigation of significant differences (Step 4) is probably the most critical step in the analytical procedures process. After generating basic financial data and relationships, the next step is to determine whether the financial changes and relationships actually describe what is going on within the company. According to the current-year unaudited financial statements in Exhibit 4.3, the company increased net income by increasing sales 10 percent, reducing cost of goods sold as a proportion of sales, and controlling other expenses. At least some of the sales growth appears to have been prompted by easier credit (accounts receivable increased by 80 percent) and more service (more equipment in use). The company also appears to have used much of its cash and borrowed more to purchase the equipment, to make its payment on the long-term debt, and to pay

EXHIBIT4.3 Alpha.com, Inc.—Preliminary Analytical Procedures Data

	Prior Year		Current Year		Change	
	Balance	Common Size	Balance	Common Size	Amount	Percent Change
Income						
Sales (net)	$9,000,000	100.00%	$9,900,000	100.00%	$ 900,000	10.00%
Cost of goods sold	6,750,000	75.00	7,200,000	72.73	450,000	6.67
Gross margin	2,250,000	25.00	2,700,000	27.27	450,000	20.00
General expense	1,590,000	17.67	1,734,000	17.52	144,000	9.06
Depreciation	300,000	3.33	300,000	3.03	0	0.00
Operating income	360,000	4.00	666,000	6.46	306,000	85.00
Interest expense	60,000	0.67	40,000	0.40	(20,000)	−33.33
Income taxes (40%)	120,000	1.33	256,000	2.59	136,000	113.33
Net income	$ 180,000	2.00%	$ 370,000	3.74%	$ 190,000	105.56%
Assets						
Cash	$ 600,000	14.78%	$ 200,000	4.12%	($400,000)	−66.67%
Accounts receivable	500,000	12.32	900,000	18.56	400,000	80.00
Allowance for doubtful accounts	(40,000)	−0.99	(50,000)	−1.03	(10,000)	25.00
Inventory	1,500,000	36.95	1,600,000	32.99	100,000	6.67
Total current assets	2,560,000	63.05	2,650,000	54.63	90,000	3.52
Equipment	3,000,000	73.89	4,000,000	82.47	1,000,000	33.33
Accumulated depreciation	(1,500,000)	−36.95	(1,800,000)	−37.11	(300,000)	20.00
Total assets	$4,060,000	100.00%	$4,850,000	100.00%	$ 790,000	19.46%
Liabilities and Equity						
Accounts payable	$ 500,000	12.32%	$ 400,000	8.25%`	($100,000)	−20.00%
Bank loans, 11%	0	0.00	750,000	15.46	750,000	
Accrued interest	60,000	1.48	40,000	0.82	(20,000)	−33.33
Total current liabilities	560,000	13.79	1,190,000	24.53	630,000	112.50
Long-term debt, 10%	600,000	14.78	400,000	8.25	(200,000)	−33.33
Total liabilities	1,160,000	28.57	1,590,000	32.78	430,000	37.07
Capital stock	2,000,000	49.26	2,000,000	41.24	0	0.00
Retained earnings	900,000	22.17	1,260,000	25.98	360,000	40.00
Total liabilities and equity	$4,060,000	100.00%	$4,850,000	100.00%	$ 790,000	19.46%

dividends. Inventory and Cost of Goods Sold, on the other hand, remained fairly constant compared to the previous year, both accounts increasing only 6.7 percent.

The next step is to ask "What could be wrong?" and "What errors and frauds, as well as legitimate explanations, could account for these financial results?" For this explanation, we will limit attention to the Accounts Receivable and Inventory accounts. At this point, some other ratios can help support the analysis. Exhibit 4.4 contains several familiar ratios. (Appendix 4A at the end of this chapter contains these ratios and their formulas.)

- *Question:* Are the accounts receivable collectible? (*Alternative:* Is the allowance for doubtful accounts large enough?) Easier credit can lead to more bad debts. The company has a much larger amount of receivables (Exhibit 4.3), the days' sales in receivables has increased significantly (Exhibit 4.4), the receivables turnover has decreased (Exhibit 4.4), and the allowance for doubtful accounts is smaller in proportion to the receivables (Exhibit 4.4). If the prior year's allowance for bad debts at 8 percent of receivables was appropriate and conditions have not become worse, it could be that the allowance should be closer to $72,000 than $50,000. The auditors should work carefully on the evidence related to accounts receivable valuation.

- *Question:* Could the inventory be overstated? (*Alternative:* Could the cost of the goods sold be understated?) Overstatement of the ending inventory would cause the cost of

EXHIBIT 4.4
Alpha.com, Inc.—
Selected Financial
Ratios

	Prior Year	Current Year	Percent Change
Balance-Sheet Ratios			
Current ratio	4.57	2.23	−51.29%
Days' sales in receivables	18.40	30.91	67.98
Doubtful accounts ratio	0.0800	0.0556	−30.56
Days' sales in inventory	80.00	80.00	0.00
Debt/equity ratio	0.40	0.49	21.93
Operations Ratios			
Receivables turnover	19.57	11.65	−40.47
Inventory turnover	4.50	4.50	0.00
Cost of goods sold/Sales	75.00%	72.73%	−3.03
Gross margin percentage	25.00%	27.27%	9.09
Return on beginning equity	6.62%	12.76%	92.80
Financial Distress Ratios (Altman)			
Working capital/Total assets	0.49	0.30	−38.89
Retained earnings/Total assets	0.22	0.26	17.20
EBIT/Total assets	0.09	0.14	54.87
Market value of equity/Total debt	2.59	1.89	−27.04
Net sales/Total assets	2.22	2.04	−7.92
Discriminant Z-score	4.96	4.35	−12.32

goods sold to be understated. The percentage of cost of goods sold to sales shows a decrease (Exhibits 4.3 and 4.4). If the 75 percent of the prior year represents a more accurate cost of goods sold, then the income before taxes could be overstated by $225,000 (75 percent of $9.9 million minus $7.2 million unaudited cost of goods sold). The days' sales in inventory and the inventory turnover remained the same (Exhibit 4.4), but you could expect them to change in light of the larger volume of sales. Careful work on the physical count and valuation of inventory appears to be needed.

Other questions can be asked and other relationships derived when industry statistics are available. Industry statistics can be obtained from such services as Robert Morris Associates, Dun & Bradstreet, and Standard & Poor's. These statistics include industry averages for important financial benchmarks such as gross profit margin, return on sales, current ratio, debt/net worth, and various others. A comparison with client data can reveal out-of-line statistics, indicating a relatively strong feature of the company, a weak financial position, or possibly an error or misstatement in the client's financial statements. However, care must be taken with industry statistics. A particular company could or could not be well represented by industry averages.

Comparing reported financial results with internal budgets and forecasts also can be useful. If the budget or forecast represents management's estimate of probable future outcomes, planning questions can arise for items that fall short of or exceed the budget. If a company expected to sell 10,000 units of a product sold only 5,000 units, the auditors would want to plan a careful lower-of-cost-or-market study of the inventory of unsold units (*valuation*). If 15,000 were sold, an auditor would want to audit for sales validity (*existence or occurrence*). Budget comparisons can be tricky, however. Some companies use budgets and forecasts as goals rather than as expressions of probable outcomes. Also, meeting the budget with little or no shortfall or excess can result from managers' manipulating the numbers to "meet the budget." Auditors must be careful to know something about an entity's business conditions from sources other than the internal records when analyzing comparisons with budgets and forecasts.

Cash flow analysis enables the auditors to see the crucial information of cash flow from operating, investment, and financing activities. A cash flow deficit from operations can

AUDITING INSIGHT Some Examples of Analytical Procedures

- Auditors noticed large quantities of rolled steel in the company's inventory. Several 60,000-pound rolls were entered in the inventory list. The false entries were detected because the auditor knew the company's forklift trucks had a 20,000-pound lifting capacity.

- Auditors could have compared the total quantity of vegetable oils the company claimed to have inventoried in its tanks to the storage capacity reported in national export statistics. The company's "quantity on hand" amounted to 90 percent of the national supply and greatly exceeded its own tank capacity.

- Last year's audit documentation showed that the company employees had failed to accrue wages payable at the year-end date. A search for the current accrual entry showed it had again been forgotten.

- Auditors developed a complex regression model to estimate the electric utility company's total revenue. They used empirical relations of fuel consumption, meteorological reports of weather conditions, and population census data in the area. The regression model estimated revenue within close range of the reported revenue.

- Auditors for a small regional airline calculated an estimate of airline revenue by multiplying the number of company planes times an estimate of the number of flights made by each plane in a year times the number of seats on each plane times an estimate of the average ticket price. The revenue reported by the airline was significantly higher than the auditors' estimate, meaning that either more than one person was sitting in the same seat at the same time (!) or that the auditors needed to more closely examine recorded revenue transactions. Further investigation discovered that the airline was fraudulently overstating its revenues.

signal financial difficulty. Companies fail when they run out of cash (no surprise) and are unable to pay their debts when they become due. Professional audit standards state that auditors are responsible for letting financial statement users know whether they have substantial doubts as to whether the client will be able to survive into subsequent periods (i.e., whether the company can remain a *going concern*) and cash flow analysis is a good starting place.

Even though particular analytical procedures are not required by audit standards, the *timing of required application* is specified in two instances. Analytical procedures are required (1) at the beginning of an audit—the planning stage application of analytical procedures discussed in this chapter and (2) at the end of an audit when the partners in charge review the overall quality of the work and look for apparent problems. Problems (unexpected relationships) identified at the beginning of the audit may be later corrected by adjusting entries when further substantive procedures are conducted. However, those same adjusting entries can result in other balances becoming unreasonable. The audit team concludes its analytical procedures testing by documenting the team's findings (Step 5).

Review Checkpoints

4.10 What is the purpose of performing preliminary analytical procedures in the audit planning stage?

4.11 What are the five steps involved with the use of preliminary analytical procedures?

4.12 What are some of the ratios that can be used in preliminary analytical procedures?

4.13 When are analytical procedures required and when are they optional?

Planning Memorandum

Auditors usually prepare a **planning memorandum** summarizing the preliminary analytical procedures and the materiality assessment with specific directions about the effect on the audit. This planning memo also usually includes information about each of the following:

1. Investigation or review of the prospective or continuing client relationship.

APOLLO SHOES, INC.
December 31, 2008
Planning Memo (excerpt)

We need to pay particular attention to the audit of physical inventory on hand and the valuation of inventory. In our audit program, we should be careful to provide procedures to (1) interview production managers and inquire about purchase price experience, physical volume of products sold and inventoried, and accounting procedures for transferring costs from inventory to cost of goods sold; (2) schedule our observation of the physical inventory for the year-end date and perform extensive test-counting of quantities on hand selected from the perpetual inventory records; and (3) select a large sample of items for price-testing and lower-of-cost-or-market analysis.

2. Provision of special services or reports and needs for special technical or industry expertise.
3. Staff assignment and timing schedules.
4. Preliminary assessed level of control risk.
5. Significant industry or company risks.
6. Computer system control environment.
7. Utilization of the company's internal auditors.
8. Identification of unusual accounting principles problems.
9. Schedules of work periods, meeting dates with client personnel, and completion dates.

Basically, the memo summarizes all important overall planning information and documents that the audit team is following generally accepted auditing standards. All planning becomes a basis for preparing the **audit program,** which is a list of the audit procedures the auditors need to perform to gather sufficient appropriate evidence on which to base their opinion on the financial statements. Auditing standards require a *written* audit program. The illustrative excerpt from a planning memorandum below connects a tolerable misstatement assignment to a preliminary analytical observation and an audit program procedural plan suggestion.

Review Checkpoints

4.14 What is the purpose of a planning memorandum?

4.15 List some items normally documented in a planning memorandum.

PLANNING IN A COMPUTERIZED ENVIRONMENT

LEARNING OBJECTIVE

4. List and discuss matters of planning that auditors should consider for clients who use computerized processing, and describe how a computer can be used as an audit tool.

Although the term *computerized environment* has a certain mystique, audits performed in clients' complex computerized environments are conceptually the same as audits of less sophisticated systems. To be more specific, even though a client uses computerized processing,

- The definition of auditing is not changed.
- The purposes of auditing are not changed.
- The generally accepted auditing standards are not changed.
- The assertions of management embodied in financial statements are not changed.
- The requirement to gather sufficient appropriate evidence is not changed.
- The independent auditor's report on financial statements is not changed.

AUDITING INSIGHT Extent of Computerized Processing Applications

Transactions Typically Computerized	Transactions Typically Not Computerized
Characteristics	**Characteristics**
Frequent, repetitive, large number	Infrequent, occasional, small number
Examples	**Examples**
Credit sales and billing	Income tax expense and liability
Cash receipts	Bank loan transactions
Accounts receivable charges and credits	Bonds payable transactions
Purchases	Deferred charges and credits
Cash disbursements	Prepaid expenses
Accounts payable charges and credits	Investment purchases and sales
Manufacturing cost accounting	Capital stock sales and repurchases
Inventory accounting	Merger and acquisition transactions
Fixed asset acquisitions and disposals	
Payroll	

Therefore, everything you have learned so far is valid; only the method of recording, processing, and storing accounting data is different. The feature "Extent of Computer Processing Applications" identifies some common applications for computers in business.

Effect of Computerized Processing on Transactions

The method used to process accounting transactions will affect an entity's organizational structure and will influence the procedures and techniques used to accomplish the organization's objectives. The following are characteristics that distinguish computerized processing from manual processing:

- *Unconventional or temporary transaction trails.* An **audit trail** is a chain of evidence provided through coding, cross-references, and documentation connecting account balances and other summary results with the original transaction source documents. Some computerized systems are designed so that a complete transaction trail useful for audit purposes could exist only for a short time or only in computer-readable form. Often the loss of hard-copy documents and reports and the temporary nature of the audit trail require external auditors to alter both the timing and nature of audit procedures.

- *Uniform processing of transactions.* Computerized processing subjects similar transactions to the same processing instructions. Consequently, computerized processing virtually eliminates the occurrence of random errors normally associated with manual processing. Conversely, programming errors (or other similar systematic errors in either the computer hardware or software) will result in all like transactions being processed incorrectly when those transactions are processed under the same conditions.

- *Potential for errors and frauds.* The potential for individuals to gain unauthorized access or alter data without visible evidence, as well as to gain access (direct or indirect) to assets, can be greater in computerized information systems than in manual systems. Employees have more access to information through numerous terminals hooked together in a common computer network. Less human involvement in handling transactions processed by computers can reduce the potential for observing errors and frauds. Errors or fraud made in designing or changing application programs can remain undetected for long periods.

- *Potential for increased management supervision.* Computerized information systems offer management a wide variety of analytical tools to review and supervise the company's operations. The availability of these additional controls can enhance the entire system of internal control and, therefore, reduce control risk. For example, traditional comparisons of actual operating ratios with those budgeted as well as reconciliation of accounts frequently are available for management review on a timelier basis when such information is computerized.

- *Initiation or subsequent execution of transactions by computer.* With automatic transaction initiation, certain transactions can be initiated or executed automatically by a computerized system without human review. Computer-initiated transactions include the generation of invoices, checks, shipping orders, and purchase orders. Without a human-readable document indicating the transaction event, the correctness of automatic transactions is difficult to judge. The authorization of these transactions cannot be documented in the same way as those in a manual accounting system, and management's authorization of these transactions can be implicit in its acceptance of the design of the system. For example, authorization of transactions occurs when certain flags are installed in programs or records (e.g., inventory quantity falling below reorder point). Therefore, authorization is more difficult to trace to the proper person. Control procedures must be designed into the system to ensure the genuineness and reasonableness of automatic transactions and to prevent or detect erroneous transactions.

Review Checkpoints

4.16 What are the general characteristics of transactions that are typically computerized? Typically not computerized?

4.17 Define *audit trail*. How could a computerized system's transaction audit trail in an advanced system differ from one in a simple system or a manual system?

4.18 What are some other important differences between manual and computerized information systems?

Effect of Client Computerized Processing on Audit Planning

Almost all organizations use computers in data processing to some extent. Client automation raises some difficulties (e.g., temporary transaction trails, potential for fraud) perhaps less likely in manual transaction processing. On the positive side, auditors can use the speed and accuracy of their own personal computers (PCs) to increase audit efficiency and effectiveness. Accordingly, when evaluating the effect of a client's computerized processing on an audit of financial statements, auditors should consider such matters as these:

- The extent to which the computer is used in each significant accounting application (e.g., sales and billing, payroll).
- The complexity of the computer operations used by the entity (e.g., batch processing, online processing, outside service centers).
- The organizational structure of the computerized processing activities.
- The availability of data required by the auditor.
- The computer-assisted audit techniques (CAATs) available to increase the efficiency of audit procedures.
- The need for specialized skills.

Extent to Which Computers Are Used

When the client uses computers to process significant accounting applications, the audit team could need computer-related skills to understand the flow of these transactions. The extent of computer use also can affect the nature, timing, and extent of audit procedures.

Complexity of Computerized Operations

When assessing the complexity of computerized information processing, the audit manager should consider his or her training and experience relative to the methods of information processing. A review of the client's computer hardware could show the extent of complexity involved. If the client *outsources* significant accounting applications (e.g., payroll), the auditor could need to coordinate audit procedures with service auditors at the processing center.

Organizational Structure of Computerized Processing

Clients can exhibit great differences in the way their computerized-processing activities are organized. The degree of centralization inherent in the organizational structure can vary. A highly centralized organizational structure generally has all significant computerized processing controlled and supervised at a central location. The control environment, the computer hardware, and the computerized systems can be uniform throughout the company. Auditors can obtain most of the necessary computerized processing information by visiting the central location. At the other extreme, a highly decentralized organizational structure generally allows various departments, divisions, subsidiaries, or geographical locations to develop, control, and supervise computerized processing in an autonomous fashion. In this situation, the computer hardware and the computer systems usually are not uniform throughout the company. Thus, auditors could need to visit many locations to obtain the necessary audit information.

Availability of Data

Computerized systems provide an ability to store, retrieve, and analyze large quantities of data. Input data, certain computer files, and other data the audit team needs might exist for only short periods or only in computer-readable form. In some computerized information systems, hard copy input documents may not exist at all because information is entered directly. For example, electronic signatures have replaced manual signatures on electronic purchase orders sent directly to vendors via electronic data interchange, with the consequence that the auditors are not able to examine a hard-copy signature. The client's data retention policies may require auditors to arrange for some information to be retained for review. Alternatively, auditors might need to plan to perform audit procedures at a time when the information is still available.

In addition, certain information generated by the computerized system for management's internal purposes can be useful in performing analytical procedures. For example, because storage is easy, the client can save larger quantities of operating information (*data warehousing*) such as sales information by month, by product, and by salesperson. Such information can be accessed (*data mining*) for use in analytical procedures to determine whether the revenue amounts are reasonable. Auditors also can drill down to examine individual transactions that compose a general ledger account balance.

Use of Computer-Assisted Audit Techniques (CAATs)

Auditors use personal computers regularly to perform such clerical steps as preparing the working trial balance, posting adjusting entries, grouping accounts that represent one line item on the financial statement into lead schedules, computing comparative financial statements and common ratios for analytical procedures, preparing supporting audit documentation schedules, and producing draft financial statements. Many auditors also use personal computers to assess control risk, perform sophisticated analytical functions on individual accounts, access public and firm databases for analysis of unusual accounting and auditing problems, and utilize decision support software to make complex evaluations.

EXHIBIT 4.5 **Using the Computer as an Audit Tool**

Applications	Goals and Objectives	Software Available
Phase 1: Automating the Audit Process		
Trial balance and audit documentation	Overall audit efficiency	Electronic workpapers developed by auditing firms and vendors
Adjusting and updating financial data	Automation of time-consuming activities	Firm developed or vendor supplied
Time and budget data	Improved control	Firm developed or vendor supplied
Audit program, memorandum, and report generation	Efficiency and increased readability	Word processing
Preparation and consolidation of financial statements preparation	Efficient automation	Firm developed or vendor supplied
Tax return preparation and analysis	Efficient automation	Firm developed or vendor supplied
Phase 2: Basic Auditing Functions		
Spreadsheet analysis audit documentation	Efficiency in common audit documentation	Vendor supplied, firm-developed uses
Analytical procedures evaluation	Improved overall analysis of ratios, fluctuations	Part of automated audit documentation packages
Sampling planning, selection, and evaluation	Evidence collection and evaluation efficiency	Statistical, firm developed.
Text retrieval	Search GAAP and GAAS pronouncements	Public resources (e.g., Compact Disclosure, Lexis-Nexis, FARS, ReSOURCE) or firm developed
Phase 3: Advanced Auditing Functions		
Analytical procedures for specific accounts	Improved auditor analysis	Firm developed
Access to client files on larger computers	Ability to download directly into automated audit documentation software	Vendor supplied or firm developed
Access to firm and public databases	Provide auditor with reference information	Personal computer as a terminal, Internet
Modeling and decision support systems	Improved auditor decisions	Firm-developed decision support systems
Continuous monitoring	Improved audit effectiveness	Firm developed or vendor supplied

Exhibit 4.5 illustrates the different phases a typical public accounting firm or internal audit department can experience when developing expertise in using personal computers as audit tools.

You need to know about CAATs because they are used on most audits in which the client's accounting records are stored in computer files or in a database. The use of CAATs was once reserved for the information system auditor, but the programs have evolved to become much more user friendly to the point that if you understand spreadsheet software, you can use most of the audit-specific functions. The essential advantages of CAATs include

- Original programming is not required. CAATs packages consist of a set of preprogrammed editing, operating, and output subroutines.
- The same software can be used on different clients' computerized systems.
- Training time is short. About one week of intensive training is sufficient to learn how to use a CAATs package.

For the most part, the widely used CAATs packages (such *ACL* and *IDEA*) are very similar. Most have been developed from standard spreadsheet and database applications. The applications, however, have been modified so that auditors can perform common audit tasks at the touch of a button by accessing predeveloped macros.

> ## AUDITING INSIGHT Audit Procedures Performed by CAATs
>
> Computerized accounting applications capture and generate voluminous amounts of data that usually are available only on machine-readable records. CAATs can be used to access the data and organize it into a format useful to the audit team. Audit software can be used to accomplish many different audit procedures.
>
> 1. *Recalculation.* The computer can verify calculations with more speed and accuracy than can be done by hand. The audit software can be used to test the accuracy of client computations and to perform analytical procedures to evaluate the reasonableness of account balances. Examples of this use are to (a) recalculate depreciation expense, (b) recalculate extensions on inventory items, (c) compute file totals, and (d) compare budgeted, standard, and prior-year data with current-year data.
>
> 2. *Confirmation.* Auditors can program statistical or judgmental criteria for selecting customers' accounts receivable, loans, and other receivables for confirmation. The CAATs can be used to print the confirmations and get them ready for mailing. It can do everything except carry them to the post office!
>
> 3. *Document examination* (limited). CAATs can compare audit evidence from other sources to company records efficiently. The audit evidence must be converted to machine-readable form and then can be compared to company records on computer files. Examples are (a) comparing inventory test counts with perpetual records, (b) comparing adjusted audit balances on confirmed accounts receivable to the audit file of the recorded balances, and (c) comparing vendor statement amounts to the company's record of accounts payable.
>
> 4. *Scanning.* Auditors can use CAATs to examine records to determine quality, completeness, consistency, and correctness. This is the computerized version of scanning the records for exceptions to the auditors' criteria. For example, scan (a) accounts receivable balances for amounts over the credit limit, (b) inventory quantities for negative balances or unreasonably large balances, (c) payroll files for terminated employees, or (d) loan files for loans with negative balances.
>
> 5. *Analytical procedures.* CAATs functions can match data in separate files to determine whether comparable information is in agreement. Differences can be printed out for investigation and reconciliation. Examples are comparing (a) payroll details with personnel records, (b) current and prior inventory to details of purchases and sales, (c) paid vouchers to check disbursements, and (d) current- and prior-year fixed asset records to identify dispositions. CAATS also can summarize and sort data in a variety of ways. Examples are (a) preparing general ledger trial balances, (b) sorting inventory items by location to facilitate observations, and (c) summarizing inventory turnover statistics for obsolescence analysis.
>
> 6. *Fraud investigation.* CAATs can be used in a variety of ways to search for fraudulent activities. For example, lists of vendor addresses can be compared to employee address files to see whether employees are paying invoices to companies that they own or operate. Duplicate payments can be found by sorting payments by invoice number and amount paid. Telephone records can be quickly sorted and scanned to ensure that employees are not misusing company telephones.

Notwithstanding the powers of the computer, several general audit procedures are outside its reach. The computer cannot observe and count physical things (inventory, for example), but it can compare auditor-made counts to the computer records. The computer cannot examine external and internal documentation; thus, it cannot vouch accounting output to sources of basic evidence. (An exception would exist in a computerized system that stores the basic source documents on magnetic media.) However, when manual vouching is involved, computer-assisted selection of sample items is quick and easy. Finally, CAATs can never take the place of the auditor's professional judgment (determining the reasonableness of the allowance for doubtful accounts, for example).

Need for Specialized Skills

When planning the engagement, the audit manager could find that certain specialized skills are needed to evaluate the effect of computerized processing on the audit, to understand the flow of transactions, or to design and perform audit procedures. These "information system auditors" are members of the audit team and are called on when the need for their skills arises, just as statistical sampling specialists or SEC specialists are available when their expertise is needed. For example, the audit team could need specialized skills relating to various methods of data processing, programming languages, software packages, or computer-assisted audit techniques. Audit managers and partners should possess sufficient computer knowledge to know when to call on specialists and to understand and supervise their work.

Review Checkpoints

4.19 In addition to the planning matters considered in a manual accounting system, what additional ones should be considered when computerized processing is involved?

4.20 What are computer-assisted audit techniques (CAATs)?

4.21 What are some audit procedures that can be performed using CAATs?

4.22 What advantages are derived from using CAATs to (a) perform recalculations and (b) select samples and print confirmations?

AUDIT DOCUMENTATION (*AS 3, SAS 103*)

LEARNING
OBJECTIVE

5. Review audit
documentation for
proper form and
content.

An engagement is not complete without preparation of proper documentation. PCAOB Auditing Standard 3 (*AS 3*, paragraph 2) defines **audit documentation** as

> the written record of the basis for the auditor's conclusions that provides the support for the auditor's representations, whether those representations are contained in the auditor's report or otherwise.

In other words, audit documentation provides the auditors' record of compliance with generally accepted auditing standards. The documentation (usually in the form of either electronic files or hard copy *workpapers*) should contain support for the decisions regarding planning and performing the audit, procedures performed, evidence obtained, and conclusions reached. Even though the auditors legally own the audit documentation, professional ethics require that the files not be transferred without consent of the client because of the confidential information recorded in them.

Auditors often use the term *workpapers,* but the term is becoming unfashionable. Audit firms rarely use *paper* to document their findings any more; more commonly, firms are using electronic documents. While the auditors' report barely covers a page, audit engagement paper documentation used to fill many binders. Those binders usually ended up in a numbered box in a storage facility with numerous similar boxes containing audit documentation from other engagements, rarely to be seen again. Today, automated audit software allows auditors to create, share, edit, review, correct, approve, and finalize audit documentation without the "paper," thereby reducing the storage space requirements of hard-copy workpapers. In addition to reduced storage costs, auditors' use of electronic documentation can result in improved efficiency because the electronic documents can be easily updated and modified from year to year. Finally, automated audit software can reduce the time spent on numbering, referencing, initialing, dating, and reviewing ("ticking and tying") by automating these tasks through the use of macro programs. These clerical tasks have traditionally consumed large quantities of audit effort that can be directed more productively to more critical aspects of the audit. You already know how to prepare accounting schedules with spreadsheet software and to use word processing software to prepare your class papers. Automated audit software uses these same computer software tools to prepare audit documentation, audit programs, and audit memos. For example, auditors prepare memos using word processing software and financial schedules (such as bank reconciliations and depreciation schedules) using spreadsheet software.

Audit documentation can be classified in three categories: (1) *permanent file,* (2) engagement (audit) administrative files, and (3) engagement (audit) evidence files. The last two categories are often called the *current files* because they relate to the audit of one year.

The Permanent File

The **permanent files** (or **continuing audit files**) contain information of *continuing audit significance* over many years' audits of the same client. The audit team may use this file year

after year, but each year's current audit documentation is stored after the files have served their purpose. Documents of permanent interest and applicability include these:

1. Copies or excerpts of the corporate charter and bylaws, or partnership agreements.
2. Copies or excerpts of continuing contracts, such as leases, bond indentures, and royalty agreements.
3. A history of the company, its products, and its markets.
4. Copies or excerpts of stockholders, directors, and committee minutes on matters of continuing audit significance.
5. Continuing schedules of accounts whose balances are carried forward for several years, such as shareholders' equity, retained earnings, partnership capital, and the like.

Copies of prior years' financial statements and auditors' reports also may be included. Public accounting firms collect articles and other information regarding a client and key personnel throughout the year. This information is often placed in the permanent file to facilitate a review of the client prior to continuing the relationship. Because of the importance of the documents contained and summarized in this one place, the permanent file is a ready source of information for familiarization with the client by new personnel on the engagement.

Audit Administrative Files

Administrative files contain the documentation of the early planning phases of the audit. They usually include the engagement letter, staff assignment notes, conclusions related to understanding the client's business, results of preliminary analytical procedures, initial assessments of audit risks, and the initial assessments of audit materiality. Many public accounting firms follow the practice of summarizing these data in an *engagement planning memorandum*.

Audit planning and administration also include work on the preliminary assessment of control risk and preparation of a written audit program. In general, the following items are usually among the administrative files in each year's current workpaper file:

1. Engagement letter.
2. Staff assignments.
3. Client organization chart.
4. Memoranda of conferences with management.
5. Memoranda of conferences with the directors' audit committee.
6. Preliminary analytical procedure notes.
7. Initial risk assessment notes.
8. Initial materiality assessment notes.
9. Planning memorandum.
10. Audit engagement time budget.
11. Internal control questionnaire and control analyses.
12. Management controls questionnaire.
13. Computer controls questionnaire.
14. Internal control flowcharts.
15. Audit program.

Audit Documentation Files

The current-year audit evidence documentation contains the specific assertions under audit, the record of the procedures performed, the evidence obtained, and the decisions made in the course of the audit (see Exhibit 4.6). Audit documentation should be prepared in sufficient detail to provide a clear understanding of its purpose, source, and the conclusions reached. The audit documentation communicates the quality of the audit, so it must be clear, concise, complete, neat, well indexed, and informative. Each electronic document

EXHIBIT 4.6
Current Audit
Documentation File

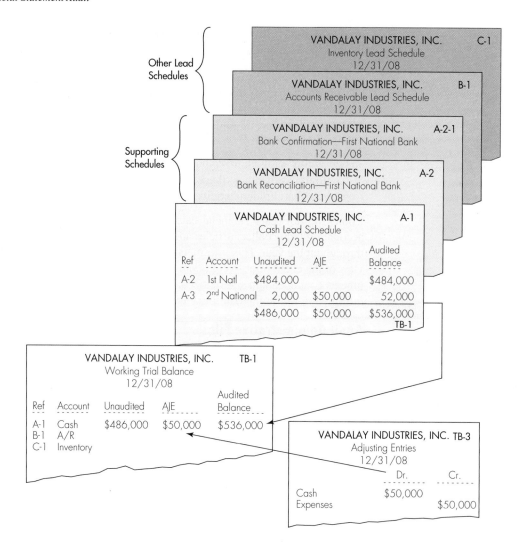

or hard-copy workpaper must be complete in the sense that it can be removed from the audit documentation file and considered on its own, with proper cross-references available to show how the document coordinates with other audit documentation. In other words, the documentation must be sufficient to enable an experienced auditor, having no previous connection with the engagement, to understand (1) the nature, timing, extent, and results of procedures; (2) the conclusions reached with respect to the area covered by the audit documentation, and (3) the audit team member performing the work, the date of work, the audit team member reviewing the work, and the date of review.

The most important facet of the current audit evidence documentation files is the requirement that they show the auditors' conclusions. The documentation must record the management assertions that were audited (book values or qualitative disclosures), the evidence gathered about them, and final conclusions. Professional audit standards require the audit documentation show that (1) the client's accounting records agree or reconcile with the financial statements, (2) the work was adequately planned and supervised, (3) a sufficient understanding of the client's internal control was obtained, and (4) sufficient appropriate audit evidence was obtained as a reasonable basis for an audit opinion. Common sense also dictates that the audit documentation be sufficient to show that the financial statements conform to GAAP and that the disclosures are adequate. The audit documentation also should explain how exceptions, unusual accounting questions, and findings contradictory to the audit team's final conclusions were resolved or treated. In addition, the resolution of any differences among audit team members must be documented. Taken altogether, these features should demonstrate that all auditing standards were observed.

Audit Documentation Arrangement and Indexing

Each public accounting firm has a different method of arranging and indexing audit documentation files. In general, however, the documentation is grouped (or electronically hyperlinked) in order behind the trial balance according to balance-sheet and income-statement captions. Usually, the current assets appear first, followed by fixed assets, other assets, liabilities, equities, income, and expense accounts. A **lead schedule** is a summary of the accounts or components in an account group. For cash, the lead schedule includes all of the company's cash accounts. For inventory, the lead schedule may include inventory amounts by product line, cost of goods sold, and reserves for obsolescence. The amounts on the lead schedule should agree with prior-year numbers, the current-year general ledger amounts, and, after any adjustments, the audited financial statements. The typical arrangement is shown in Exhibit 4.6.

Several audit documentation preparation techniques are quite important for the quality of the finished product. The points explained here are illustrated in Exhibit 4.7.

EXHIBIT 4.7 Illustrative Audit Documentation

Company Name — Initials of auditors and dates of work — Index number

A-2

VANDALAY INDUSTRIES, INC.
BANK RECONCILIATION—FIRST NATIONAL BANK
General Account
(12/31/08)
(Prepared by client)

Prepared *J.D. 1/10/09*
Reviewed *JRA 1/10/09*

Balance per bank statement			506,100	c
Add:				
Deposit in transit as of 12/31/08			51,240	n
			557,340	

Deduct outstanding checks:

Date	No.	Payee		
12/10/07	842	Ace Supply Company	500	⚹
11/31/08	1280	Ace Supply Company	1,800	√
12/15/08	1372	Northwest Lumber Co.	30,760	√
12/28/08	1412	Gibson & Johnson	7,270	X
12/30/08	1417	First National payroll	20,000	√
12/30/08	1418	Ace Supply Company	2,820	√
12/30/08	1419	Windy City Utilities	2,030	√
12/30/08	1420	Howard Hardware Supply	8,160	√
			73,340	

Balance per book

484,000 *f*

A-1

"Tick mark" symbols

Arithmetic footed

Cross-reference to lead schedule

Note: *Obtained cutoff bank statement 1/9/09* A-2-2

f Footed

c Confirmed by bank standard back confirmation A-2-1

n Vouched to cutoff bank statement, deposit recorded by bank on 1/3/09. Vouched to duplicate deposit slip validated 1/03/09.

√ Vouched to paid check cleared with cutoff bank statement.

X Vouched to statement from attorneys. Amount agrees.

⚹ Amount in dispute per controller. Confirmation from supplier claims liability of $5,000. See K-4 recommended adjustment.

Cross-index to other working papers

Explanations of audit work performed

- *Indexing.* Each document (whether electronic or paper) is given an index number, like a book page number, so it can be found, removed, and replaced without loss.
- *Cross-referencing.* Numbers or memoranda related to other documents carry the index of the other documents so the connections can be followed.
- *Heading.* Each document is titled with the name of the company, the balance-sheet date, and a descriptive title of the contents of the document.
- *Signatures and initials.* The auditor who performs the work and the supervisor who reviews it must sign the audit documentation so personnel can be identified.
- *Dates of audit work.* The dates of performance and review are recorded on the documents so reviewers of the documentation can tell when the work was performed.
- *Audit marks and explanations.* Audit marks (or "tick marks") are the auditor's shorthand for abbreviating comments about work performed. Audit marks always must be accompanied by a full explanation of the auditing work. (Notice in Exhibit 4.7 the auditor's confirmation of the disputed account payable liability.) On electronic documents, comments can be hyperlinked so that reviewers can find additional explanations of audit procedures performed.

AS 3 requires that audit documentation, including workpapers and other documents that form the basis of the engagement, be retained for seven years following the conclusion of the engagement (usually the audit report release date). *AS 3* also stresses that audit documentation to be retained include those documenting discussion and subsequent resolution of differences in professional judgment among the audit team members. PCAOB regulations also require that all documentation must be finalized within 45 days of the audit report's release date. With sufficient (documented) justification, auditors may subsequently add, but may not remove, documentation after the 45-day period. While the *AS 3* requirements are only for public companies, most audit firms use the same requirements for their other nonpublic clients.

Review Checkpoints

4.23 What information would you expect to find in (a) a permanent audit file and (b) a current file?

4.24 What is considered the most important content of the auditor's current audit documentation files?

4.25 What audit tasks can be accomplished with (a) word processing software and (b) spreadsheet software?

Summary

Many of the concepts (*materiality, audit risk*) discussed in the previous chapter are part of the *theoretical* foundation for planning and performing audit engagements. This chapter contains the specific set of *practical* planning activities that auditors undertake when beginning an engagement. *Preengagement activities* start with the work of deciding whether to accept a new client and, on an annual basis, deciding whether to continue the engagement for existing clients. Public accounting firms are not obligated to provide audit services to every organization that requests them, and they regularly exercise discretion about the organizations with which they wish to associate. For audit engagements, the investigation may involve the cooperative task of communicating with the former (predecessor) auditors of the organization. Once a client has been accepted, the preengagement work continues with the preparation of an engagement letter; assignment of partners, managers, and staff to the job; and the preparation of a time budget for the engagement.

The activities part of the chapter also covers the important process of *obtaining an understanding* of the client's business and industry, including information-gathering

methods and sources. One of the most important activities is the performance of *preliminary analytical procedures* applied to the client's information. The analytical process includes obtaining the financial data, calculating common-size and comparative financial statements, calculating ratios, describing the company's financial activities, and asking relevant questions. This analysis enables auditors to identify problem areas and signs of potential misstatement in the financial statements. Detecting signs of problems enables the auditors to plan procedures for the audit program to follow up and to determine whether misstatements, errors, or frauds have affected the fair presentation of the financial balances.

Even though computer technology changes the accounting system and the environment in which it operates, technology does not change the basic auditing standards. Qualities of competence, independence, due care, planning, control risk assessment, and sufficient appropriate evidence are not changed. However, the nuances and aspects of achieving them must be tailored to a world of computers. Auditors must consider several factors when planning in an electronic environment. Computer auditing is not something for future consideration; some form of computer analysis is encountered in almost every engagement. Computer-assisted audit techniques (CAATs) improve both engagement effectiveness and efficiency.

The closing topic is a brief preview of audit documentation, with some basic pointers about their form, content, and purpose. At this point, the next step in the audit process is the auditors' study and evaluation of internal control, which serves as the focus of the next chapter.

Key Terms

analytical procedures: Reasonableness tests used to gain an understanding of financial statement accounts and relationships, 125

audit documentation: The written basis for the auditor's conclusions, 136

audit program: A list of the audit procedures the auditors need to perform to gather sufficient appropriate evidence on which to base their opinion on the financial statements, 130

audit trail: The chain of evidence provided through coding, cross-references, and documentation connecting account balances and other summary results with the original transaction source documents, 131

concurring partner: Second audit partner on the audit team, required for audits of financial statements filed with the Securities and Exchange Commission, who reviews the audit team's work in critical audit areas (those areas with the highest potential audit risk), 112

continuing audit files (or permanent files): Audit documentation containing information of *continuing audit significance* for current and past audits of the same client, 136

engagement letter: Letter from the public accounting firm to the management of an engagement client setting forth the terms of the engagement, 112

enterprise risk management (ERM): "A process, effected by an entity's board of directors, management and other personnel, applied in strategy setting and across the enterprise, designed to identify potential events that may affect the entity, and manage risks to be within its risk appetite, to provide reasonable assurance regarding the achievement of entity objectives" (www.COSO.org), 116

Form 8-K: The "special events report" filed with the SEC whenever certain significant corporate events occur such as changes in control, legal proceedings, and changes of auditor, 111

horizontal analysis: Comparative analysis of year-to-year changes in balance-sheet and income-statement accounts, 126

interim audit work: Procedures performed several weeks or months before the balance-sheet date, 114

lead schedule: A summary of the accounts in or components of an account group, 139

permanent files (or continuing audit files): Audit documentation containing information of *continuing audit significance* for current and past audits of the same client, 136

planning memorandum: Document summarizing the preliminary analytical procedures and the materiality assessment with specific directions about the effect on the audit, 129

predecessor auditor: The audit firm that has been terminated or voluntarily withdrawn from an audit engagement (whether the audit has been completed or not), 111

related parties: Those individuals or organizations that are closely tied to the auditee, possibly through family ties or investment relationships, 119

specialists: Persons skilled in fields other than accounting and auditing—actuaries, appraisers, attorneys, engineers, and geologists—who are not members of the audit firm, 125

successor auditor: Any firm considering accepting an audit engagement, 111

termination letter: Documentation provided to former clients dealing with the subject of future services, in particular: (1) access to audit documentation by a successor auditor, (2) reissuance of the auditors' report when required for SEC reporting or comparative financial reporting, and (3) fee arrangements for such future services. The termination letter also can contain a report of the auditor's understanding of the circumstances of termination (e.g., disagreements about accounting principles and audit procedures, fees, or other conflicts), 112

tolerable misstatement: The amount by which a particular account may be misstated (error not discovered by auditors) yet still not cause the financial statements taken as a whole to be materially misleading, 123

vertical analysis: Common-size analysis of financial statement amounts created by expressing amounts as proportions of a common base such as sales for the income-statement accounts or total assets for the balance-sheet accounts, 126

year-end audit work: Procedures performed shortly before and after the balance-sheet date, 114

Multiple Choice Questions for Practice and Review

4.26 Analytical procedures are generally used to produce evidence from

 a. Confirmations mailed directly to the auditors by client customers.

 b. Physical observation of inventories.

 c. Relationships among current financial balances and prior balances, forecasts, and non-financial data.

 d. Detailed examination of external, external-internal, and internal documents.

4.27 Auditors perform analytical procedures in the planning stage of an audit for the purpose of

 a. Deciding the matters to cover in an engagement letter.

 b. Identifying unusual conditions that deserve more auditing effort.

 c. Determining which of the financial statement assertions are the most important for the client's financial statements.

 d. Determining the nature, timing, and extent of audit procedures for auditing the inventory.

4.28 Which of the following relationships between types of analytical procedures and sources of information are most logical?

Type of Analytical Procedure	Source of Information
a. Comparison of current account balances with prior periods	Physical production statistics
b. Comparison of current account balances with expected balances	Company's budgets and forecasts
c. Evaluation of current account balances with relation to predictable historical patterns	Published industry ratios
d. Evaluation of current account balances in relation to nonfinancial information	Company's own comparative financial statements

4.29 Analytical procedures can be used in which of the following ways?

 a. As a means of overall review at the end of an audit.

 b. As "attention-directing" methods when planning an audit at the beginning.

 c. As substantive audit procedures to obtain evidence during an audit.

 d. All of the above.

4.30 Analytical procedures used when planning an audit should concentrate on
 a. Weaknesses in the company's internal control procedures.
 b. Predictability of account balances based on individual transactions.
 c. Management assertions in financial statements.
 d. Accounts and relationships that can represent specific potential problems and risks in the financial statements.

4.31 When successor auditors initiate communications with predecessor auditors, the successors should expect
 a. To take responsibility for obtaining the client's consent for the predecessor to give information about prior audits.
 b. To conduct interviews with the partner and manager in charge of the predecessor audit firm's engagement.
 c. To obtain copies of some or all of the predecessor auditors' audit documentation.
 d. All of the above.

4.32 Generally accepted auditing standards require that auditors always prepare and use
 a. A written planning memorandum explaining the auditors' understanding of the client's business.
 b. Written client consent to discuss audit matters with successor auditors.
 c. A written audit program.
 d. Written time budgets and schedules for performing each audit.

4.33 When planning an audit, which of the following is *not* a factor that affects auditors' decisions about the quantity, type, and content of audit documentation?
 a. The auditors' need to document compliance with generally accepted auditing standards.
 b. The existence of new sales contracts important for the client's business.
 c. The auditors' judgment about their independence with regard to the client.
 d. The auditors' judgments about materiality.

4.34 Audit documentation that shows the detailed evidence and procedures regarding the balance in the accumulated depreciation account for the year under audit will be found in the
 a. Current file evidence audit documentation.
 b. Permanent file audit documentation.
 c. Administrative audit documentation in the current file.
 d. Planning memorandum in the current file.

4.35 An auditor's permanent file audit documentation most likely will contain
 a. Internal control analysis for the current year.
 b. The most recent engagement letter.
 c. Memoranda of conference with management.
 d. Excerpts of the corporate charter and bylaws.

4.36 Which of the following is not a benefit claimed for the practice of determining materiality in the initial planning stage of an audit?
 a. Being able to fine-tune the audit work for effectiveness and efficiency.
 b. Avoiding the problem of doing more work than necessary (overauditing).
 c. Being able to decide early what type of audit opinion to issue.
 d. Avoiding the problem of doing too little work (underauditing).

4.37 Spreadsheet software would be most useful for which of the following audit activities?
 a. Testing internal controls over computerized accounting applications.
 b. Preparing an audit program.
 c. Preparing a comparison of current-year expenses with those from the previous year.
 d. Drafting a planning memorandum.

4.38 Which of the following is an advantage of computer-assisted audit techniques (CAATs)?
 a. The CAATs programs are all written in one computer language.
 b. The software can be used for audits of clients that use differing computer equipment and file formats.
 c. CAATs have reduced the need for the auditor to study input controls for computer-related procedures.
 d. The use of CAATs can be substituted for a relatively large part of the required testing.

4.39 A primary advantage of using CAATs in the audit of an advanced computerized system is that it enables the auditor to

 a. Substantiate the accuracy of data through self-checking digits and hash totals.

 b. Utilize the speed and accuracy of the computer.

 c. Verify the performance of machine operations that leave visible evidence of occurrence.

 d. Gather and store large quantities of supportive audit evidence in machine-readable form.

4.40 When a company that sells its products for a (gross) profit increases its sales by 15 percent and its cost of goods sold by 7 percent, the cost of goods sold ratio will

 a. Increase.

 b. Decrease.

 c. Remain unchanged.

 d. Not be able to be determined with the information provided.

4.41 An audit engagement letter should normally include which of the following matter of agreement between the auditor and the client?

 a. Schedules and analyses to be prepared by the client's employees.

 b. Methods of statistical sampling the auditor will use.

 c. Specification of litigation in progress against the client.

 d. Client representations about availability of all minutes of meetings of the board of directors.

4.42 When auditing Vandalay Jewelry, Costanza, CPA was not familiar with the quality and cut of the company's precious jewel inventory. To address this shortcoming, Costanza hired Benes, an expert in jewel valuation, to assist in the inventory valuation. Should Costanza refer to Benes's work in the audit report?

 a. Yes, the auditors' report should mention the fact that a specialist was used.

 b. The auditors' report should mention the use of the specialist only when the specialist's findings affect the auditors' conclusions.

 c. The use of a specialist need not be mentioned if the auditors decide not to take responsibility for the specialist's findings.

 d. The auditors' report should mention the specialist only if Vandalay agrees with the specialist's findings.

4.43 Which of the following engagement planning procedures would most likely assist the auditor in identifying related-party transactions before the balance-sheet date?

 a. Interviewing internal auditors about their reporting responsibilities.

 b. Reviewing accounting records for recurring transactions occurring near year end.

 c. Inspecting communications with the client's legal counsel regarding recorded contingent liabilities.

 d. Scanning the minutes for significant transactions with members of the board of directors.

4.44 Which of the following communications is most likely to be written before the balance-sheet date?

 a. A report to the audit committee on the results of testing of internal control over cash receipts.

 b. Confirmation letters to vendors confirming the amounts they owe to the client.

 c. An attorney's letter regarding contingent liabilities.

 d. An engagement letter.

4.45 Which of the following procedures would most likely be performed during planning?

 a. Surprise counts of the client's petty cash fund.

 b. Reporting internal control deficiencies to the audit committee.

 c. Performing a search for unrecorded liabilities.

 d. Identifying related parties.

4.46 Prior to accepting a new audit engagement, an public accounting firm should

 a. Attempt to contact the predecessor auditors.

 b. Evaluate the integrity of management.

 c. Assess the firm's resources to ensure that they are sufficient to permit them to accept the engagement.

 d. All of the above.

**Exercises,
Problems, and
Simulations**

4.47 **Analytical Procedures.** Kermit Griffin, an audit manager, had begun preliminary analytical procedures of selected statistics related to the Majestic Hotel. His objective was to obtain an understanding of the hotel's business in order to draft a preliminary audit program. He wanted to see whether he could detect any troublesome areas or questionable accounts that could require special audit attention. Unfortunately, Mr. Griffin caught the flu and was hospitalized. From his sickbed, he sent you the schedule he had prepared (Exhibit 4.47.1). He has asked you to write a memorandum identifying areas of potential misstatements or other matters that the preliminary audit program should cover.

EXHIBIT 4.47.1

AP-6

Prepared by _____
Reviewed by _____

MAJESTIC HOTEL
Preliminary Analytical Procedures
FYE 3/31/09

The Majestic Hotel, East Apple, New Jersey, compiles operating statistics on a calendar-year basis. Hotel statistics, below, were provided by the controller, A. J. Marcello, for 2009. The parallel column contains industry average statistics obtained from the National Hotel Industry Guide.

	Majestic (percent)	Industry (percent)
Sales:		
Rooms	60.4%	63.9%
Food and beverage	35.7	32.2
Other	3.9	3.9
Costs:		
Rooms department	15.2	17.3
Food and beverage	34.0	27.2
Administrative and general	8.0	8.9
Management fee	3.3	1.1
Advertising	2.7	3.2
Real estate taxes	3.5	3.2
Utilities, repairs, maintenance	15.9	13.7
Profit per sales dollar	17.4	25.4
Rooms dept. ratios to room sales dollars:		
Salaries and wages	18.9	15.7
Laundry	1.1	3.7
Other	5.3	7.6
Profit per rooms sales dollar	74.8	73.0
Food/beverage (F/B) ratios to F/B sales dollars:		
Cost of food sold	42.1	37.0
Food gross profit	57.9	63.0
Cost of beverages sold	43.6	29.5
Beverages gross profit	56.4	70.5
Combined gross profit	57.7	64.6
Salaries and wages	39.6	32.8
Music and entertainment	—	2.7
Other	13.4	13.8
Profit per F/B sales dollar	4.7	15.3
Average annual percent of rooms occupied	62.6	68.1
Average room rate per day	$160	$120
Number of rooms available per day	200	148

Required:

Write a memorandum describing Majestic's operating characteristics compared to the "industry average" insofar as you can tell from the statistics. Do these analytical procedures identify any areas that could represent potential misstatements in the audit?

4.48 **Audit Simulation: Preliminary Analytical Procedures.** Alpha.com, Inc. wanted to expand its manufacturing and sales facilities. The company applied for a loan from First Bank, presenting the prior-year audited financial statements and the forecast for the current year shown in Exhibit 4.48.1. (Alpha.com, Inc.'s fiscal year end is December 31.) The bank was impressed with the business prospects and granted a $1,750,000 loan at 8 percent interest to finance working capital and the new facilities that were placed in service July 1 of the current year. Because Alpha.com, Inc. planned to issue stock for permanent financing, the bank made the loan due on December 31 of the following year. Interest is payable each calendar quarter on October 1 of the current year and January 1, April 1, July 1, October 1, and December 31 of the following year.

The auditors' interviews with Alpha.com, Inc. management near the end of the current year produced the following information: The facilities did not cost as much as previously anticipated. However, sales were slow and the company granted more liberal return privilege terms than in the prior year. Officers wanted to generate significant income to impress First Bank and to preserve the company dividend ($120,000 paid in the prior year). The production managers had targeted inventory levels for a 4.0 turnover ratio and were largely successful even though prices of materials and supplies had risen about 2 percent relative to sales dollar volume. The new facilities were depreciated using a 25-year life from the date of opening.

Alpha.com, Inc. has now produced the current-year financial statements (Exhibit 4.48.1, column Current Year) for the auditors' work on the current audit.

EXHIBIT 4.48.1
Alpha.com, Inc.

	Prior Year (Audited)	Forecast	Current Year (Unaudited)
Revenue and Expense:			
Sales (net)	$9,000,000	$9,900,000	$9,720,000
Cost of goods sold	6,296,000	6,926,000	7,000,000
Gross margin	2,704,000	2,974,000	2,720,000
General expense	2,044,000	2,000,000	2,003,000
Depreciation	300,000	334,000	334,000
Operating income	360,000	640,000	383,000
Interest expense	60,000	110,000	75,000
Income taxes (40%)	120,000	212,000	123,200
Net income	180,000	318,000	184,800
Assets:			
Cash	600,000	880,000	690,800
Accounts receivable	500,000	600,000	900,000
Allowance for doubtful accounts	(40,000)	(48,000)	(90,000)
Inventory	1,500,000	1,500,000	1,350,000
Total current assets	2,560,000	2,932,000	2,850,800
Fixed assets	3,000,000	4,700,000	4,500,000
Accum. depreciation	(1,500,000)	(1,834,000)	(1,834,000)
Total assets	$4,060,000	$5,798,000	$5,516,800
Liabilities and Equity:			
Accounts payable	$450,000	$450,000	$330,000
Bank loans, 8%	0	1,750,000	1,750,000
Accrued interest	60,000	40,000	40,000
Accruals and other	50,000	60,000	32,000
Total current liabilities	$560,000	$2,300,000	$2,152,000
Long-term debt, 10%	600,000	400,000	400,000
Total liabilities	$1,160,000	$2,700,000	$2,552,000
Capital stock	2,000,000	2,000,000	2,000,000
Retained earnings	900,000	1,098,000	964,800
Total liabilities and equity	$4,060,000	$5,798,000	$5,516,800

Required:

Perform preliminary analytical procedures on the current-year unaudited financial statements for the purpose of identifying accounts that could contain errors or frauds. Use your knowledge of Alpha.com, Inc. and the forecast in Exhibit 4.48.1. Calculate comparative and common-size financial statements as well as relevant ratios (assume that the market value of

the equity for the company is $3 million). Once your calculations are complete, identify the accounts that could be misstated. (*Note*: This assignment is available in the student section of the textbook Web site in Excel format.)

4.49 **Analytical Procedures: Ratio Relationships.** The following situations represent errors and frauds that could occur in financial statements.

Required:

State how the ratio in question would compare (greater, equal, or less) to what the ratio should have been had the error or fraud not occurred.

a. The company recorded fictitious sales with credits to sales revenue accounts and debits to accounts receivable. Inventory was reduced, and cost of goods sold was increased for the profitable "sales." Is the current ratio greater than, equal to, or less than what it should have been?

b. The company recorded cash disbursements by paying trade accounts payable but held the checks past the year-end date, meaning that the "disbursements" should not have been shown as credits to cash and debits to accounts payable. Is the current ratio greater than, equal to, or less than what it should have been? Consider cases in which the current ratio before the improper "disbursement" recording was (1) greater than 1:1, (2) equal to 1:1, and (3) less than 1:1.

c. The company uses a periodic inventory system for determining the balance-sheet amount of inventory at year end. Very near the year end, merchandise was received, placed in the stockroom, and counted, but the purchase transaction was neither recorded nor paid until the next month. What was the effect of this on inventory, cost of goods sold, gross profit, and net income? How were these ratios affected compared to what they would have been without the error: current ratio (remember three possible cases), gross margin ratio, cost of goods sold ratio, inventory turnover, and receivables turnover?

d. The company is loathe to write off customer accounts receivable even though the financial vice president makes entirely adequate provision for uncollectible amounts in the allowance for bad debts. The gross receivables and the allowance both contain amounts that should have been written off long ago. How are these ratios affected compared to what they would have been if the old receivables had been properly written off: current ratio, days' sales in receivables, doubtful account ratio, receivables turnover, return on beginning equity, working capital/total assets?

e. Since last year, the company has reorganized its lines of business and placed more emphasis on its traditional products while selling off some marginal businesses merged by the previous management. Total assets are 10 percent less than they were last year, but working capital has increased. Retained earnings remained the same because the disposals created no gains, and the net income after taxes is still near zero, the same as last year. Earnings before interest and taxes (EBIT) remained the same, a small positive EBIT. The total market value of the company's equity has not increased, but that is better than the declines of the past several years. Proceeds from the disposals have been used to retire long-term debt. Net sales have decreased 5 percent because the sales' decrease resulting from the disposals has not been overcome by increased sales of the traditional products. Is the discriminant Z-score of the current year higher or lower than the one of the prior year? (See Appendix 4A for the Z-score formula.)

4.50 **Audit Documentation.** The preparation of audit documentation is an integral part of an auditor's examination of financial statements. On a recurring engagement, auditors review the audit programs and audit documentation from the prior audit while planning the current audit to determine their usefulness for the current-year work.

Required:

a. (1) What are the purposes or functions of audit documentation?

(2) What records may be included in audit documentation?

b. What factors affect the auditors' judgment of the type and content of the audit documentation for a particular engagement?

c. To comply with generally accepted auditing standards, auditors include certain evidence in the audit documentation; for example, "evidence that the audit was planned and work of assistants was supervised and reviewed." What other evidence should auditors include in audit documentation to comply with generally accepted auditing standards?

d. How can auditors make the most effective use of the prior year's audit programs in a recurring audit?

(AICPA adapted)

4.51 **Analytical Procedures and Interest Expense.** Weyman Z. Wannamaker is the chief financial officer of Cogburn Company. He prides himself on being able to manage the company's cash resources to maximize the interest expense. Consequently, on the second business day of each month, Weyman pays down or draws cash on Cogburn's revolving line of credit at First National Bank in accordance with his cash requirements forecast.

You are the auditor. You find the information on this line of credit in the following table. You inquired at First National Bank and learned that Cogburn Company's loan agreement specifies payment on the first day of each month for the interest due on the previous month's outstanding balance at the rate of "prime plus 1.5 percent." The bank gave you a report that showed the prime rate of interest was 8.5 percent for the first six months of the year and 8.0 percent for the last six months.

Cogburn Company Notes Payable Balances	
Date	Balance
Jan 1	$150,000
Feb 1	200,000
Apr 1	225,000
May 1	285,000
Jun 1	375,000
Aug 1	430,000
Sep 1	290,000
Oct 1	210,000
Nov 1	172,000
Dec 1	95,000

Required:

a. Prepare an audit estimate of the amount of interest expense you expect to find as the balance of the interest expense account related to these notes payable.

b. Which of the types of analytical procedures did you use to determine this estimate?

c. Suppose that you find that the interest expense account shows expense of $23,650 related to these notes. What could account for this difference?

d. Suppose that you find that the interest expense account shows expense of $24,400 related to these notes. What could account for this difference?

e. Suppose that you find that the interest expense account shows expense of $25,200 related to these notes. What could account for this difference?

4.52 **Appropriateness of Evidence and Related Parties.** Johnson & Company, CPAs, audited Guaranteed Savings & Loan Company. M. Johnson had the assignment of evaluating the collectibility of real estate loans. Johnson was working on two particular loans: (1) a $4 million loan secured by Smith Street Apartments and (2) a $5.5 million construction loan on Baker Street Apartments now being built. The appraisals performed by Guaranteed Appraisal Partners, Inc., showed values in excess of the loan amounts. On inquiry, Mr. Bumpus, the S&L vice president for loan acquisition, stated, "I know the Smith Street loan is good because I myself own 40 percent of the partnership that owns the property and is obligated on the loan."

Johnson then wrote in the audit documentation: (1) the Smith Street loan appears collectible; Mr. Bumpus personally attested to knowledge of the collectibility as a major owner in the partnership obligated on the loan; (2) the Baker Street loan is assumed to be collectible because it is new and construction is still in progress; and (3) the appraised values all exceed the loan amounts.

Required:

a. Do you perceive any problems with related-party involvement in the evidence used by Johnson? Explain.

b. Do you perceive any problems with Johnson's reasoning or the appropriateness of evidence used in that reasoning?

4.53 **Communications between Predecessor and Successor Auditors.** Assume that Smith & Smith, CPAs, audited Apollo Shoes, Inc., last year. Now CEO Larry Lancaster wishes to engage Anderson, Olds, and Watershed, CPAs (AOW) to audit its annual financial statements. Lancaster is generally pleased with the services provided by Smith & Smith, but he

thinks the audit work was too detailed and interfered excessively with normal office routines. AOW has asked Lancaster to inform Smith & Smith of the decision to change auditors, but he does not wish to do so.

Required:

List and discuss the steps AOW should follow with regard to dealing with a predecessor auditor and a new client before accepting the engagement. (*Hint*: Use *SAS 84* and interpretations of the independence rules of conduct for a complete response to this requirement.)

4.54 **Predecessor and Successor Auditors.** The president of Allpurpose Loan Company had a genuine dislike for external auditors. Almost any conflict generated a towering rage. Consequently, the company changed auditors often.

Wells & Ratley, CPAs, was recently hired to audit the 2008 financial statements. W&R succeeded the firm of Canby & Company, which had obtained the audit after Albrecht & Hubbard had been fired. A&H audited the 2007 financial statements and rendered a report that contained an additional paragraph explaining an uncertainty about Allpurpose Loan Company's loan loss reserve. Goodbye A&H! The president then hired Canby & Company to audit the 2008 financial statements, and Art Canby started the work, but before the audit could be completed, Canby was fired and W&R was hired to complete the audit. Canby & Company did not issue an audit report because the audit was not finished.

Required:

Does the Wells & Ratley firm need to initiate communications with Canby & Company? With Albrecht & Hubbard? With both? Explain your response in terms of the purposes of communications between predecessor and successor auditors.

4.55 **Audit Simulation: Client Selection.** You are a CPA in a regional public accounting firm that has 10 offices in three states. Mr. Shine has approached you with a request for an audit. He is president of Hitech Software and Games, Inc., a five-year-old company that has recently grown to $500 million in sales and $200 million in total assets. Mr. Shine is thinking about going public with a $25 million issue of common stock, of which $10 million would be a secondary issue of shares he holds. You are very happy about this opportunity because you know Mr. Shine is the new president of the Symphony Society board and has made quite a civic impression since he came to your medium-size city seven years ago. Hitech is one of the growing employers in the city.

Required:

a. Discuss the sources of information and the types of inquiries that you and the firm's partners may make in connection with accepting Hitech as a new client.

b. Do professional audit standards require any investigation of prospective clients?

c. Suppose Mr. Shine also has told you that 10 years ago his closely held hamburger franchise business went bankrupt, and, on investigation, you learn from its former auditors (your own firm in another city) that Shine played "fast and loose" with franchise-fee income recognition rules and presented such difficulties that your firm resigned from the audit (before the bankruptcy). Do you think the partner in charge of the audit practice should accept Hitech as a new client?

4.56 **Using the Work of Internal Auditors.** North, CPA, is planning an independent audit of the financial statements of General Company. In determining the nature, timing, and extent of the audit procedures, North is considering General's internal audit function, which is staffed by Tyler.

Required:

a. In what ways can the internal auditor's work be relevant to North, the independent auditor?

b. What factors should North consider and what inquiries should North make in deciding whether to use Tyler's internal audit work?

(AICPA adapted)

4.57 **Using the Computer to Discover Intentional Financial Misstatements in Transactions and Account Balances.** AMI International is a large office products company. Headquarters management imposed pressure on operating division managers to meet profit forecasts. The division managers met these profit goals using several accounting manipulations involving the record-keeping system that maintained all transactions and account balances on computer files. Employees who operated the computer accounting system were aware of the

modifications of policy the managers ordered to accomplish the financial statement manipulations. The management and employees carried out these activities:

1. Deferred inventory write-downs for obsolete and damaged goods.
2. Kept open the sales entry system after the quarterly and annual cutoff dates, recording sales of goods shipped after the cutoff dates.
3. Recorded as sales transactions that had been coded as leases of office equipment.
4. Recorded shipments to branch offices as sales.
5. Postponed recording vendors' invoices for parts and services until later, but the actual invoice date was faithfully entered according to accounting policy.

Required:

Describe one or more procedures that could be performed with computer-assisted audit techniques (CAATs) to detect signs of each of these transaction manipulations. Limit your answer to the actual work accomplished by the computer software.

4.58 **Audit Simulation: Horizontal and Vertical Analysis.** *Horizontal analysis* refers to changes of financial statement numbers and ratios across two or more years. *Vertical analysis* refers to financial statement amounts expressed each year as proportions of a base such as sales for the income-statement accounts and total assets for the balance-sheet accounts. Exhibit 4.58.1 contains Retail Company's prior-year (audited) and current-year (unaudited) financial statements, along with amounts and percentages of change from year to year (horizontal analysis) and common-size percentages (vertical analysis). Exhibit 4.58.2 contains selected financial ratios

EXHIBIT 4.58.1
Retail Company

	Prior Year (Audited)		Current Year (Unaudited)		Change	
	Balance	Common Size	Balance	Common Size	Amount	Percent
Assets:						
Cash	$600,000	14.78%	$484,000	9.69%	$(116,000)	−19.33%
Accounts receivable	500,000	12.32	400,000	8.01	(100,000)	−20.00
Allowance doubt. accts.	(40,000)	−0.99	(30,000)	−0.60	10,000	−25.00
Inventory	1,500,000	36.95	1,940,000	38.85	440,000	29.33
Total current assets	2,560,000	63.05	2,794,000	55.95	234,000	9.14
Fixed assets	3,000,000	73.89	4,000,000	80.10	1,000,000	33.33
Accum. Depreciation	(1,500,000)	−36.95	(1,800,000)	−36.04	(300,000)	20.00
Total assets	$4,060,000	100.00%	$4,994,000	100.00%	$934,000	23.00%
Liabilities and equity:						
Accounts payable	$ 450,000	11.08%	$ 600,000	12.01%	$150,000	33.33%
Bank loans, 11%	0	0.00	750,000	15.02	750,000	NA
Accrued interest	50,000	1.23	40,000	0.80	(10,000)	−20.00
Accruals and other	60,000	1.48	10,000	0.20	(50,000)	−83.33
Total current liab.	560,000	13.79	1,400,000	28.03	840,000	150.00
Long-term debt, 10%	500,000	12.32	400,000	8.01	(100,000)	−20.00
Total liabilities	1,060,000	26.11	1,800,000	36.04	740,000	69.81
Capital stock	2,000,000	49.26	2,000,000	40.05	0	0
Retained earnings	1,000,000	24.63	1,194,000	23.91	194,000	19.40
Total liabilities and equity	$4,060,000	100.00%	$4,994,000	100.00%	934,000	23.00%
Statement of operations:						
Sales (net)	$9,000,000	100.00%	$8,100,000	100.00%	$(900,000)	−10.00%
Cost of goods sold	6,296,000	69.96	5,265,000	65.00	(1,031,000)	−16.38
Gross margin	2,704,000	30.04	2,835,000	35.00	131,000	4.84
General expense	2,044,000	22.71	2,005,000	24.75	(39,000)	−1.91
Depreciation	300,000	3.33	300,000	3.70	0	0
Operating income	360,000	4.00	530,000	6.54	170,000	47.22
Interest expense	50,000	0.56	40,000	0.49	(10,000)	−20.00
Income taxes (40%)	124,000	1.38	196,000	2.42	72,000	58.06
Net income	$ 186,000	2.07%	$ 294,000	3.63%	$108,000	58.06%

NA means not applicable.

EXHIBIT 4.58.2
Retail Company

	Prior Year (Audited)	Current Year (Unaudited)	Percent Change
Balance-sheet ratios:			
Current ratio	4.57	2.0	−56.34%
Days' sales in receivables	18.40	16.44	−10.63
Doubtful accounts ratio	0.0800	0.0750	−6.25
Days' sales in inventory	85.77	132.65	54.66
Debt/equity ratio	0.35	0.56	40.89
Operations ratios:			
Receivables turnover	19.57	21.89	11.89
Inventory turnover	4.20	2.71	−35.34
Cost of goods sold/sales	69.96%	65.00%	−7.08
Gross margin %	30.04%	35.00%	16.49
Return on equity	6.61%	9.80%	48.26

based on these financial statements. Analysis of these data can enable auditors to discern relationships that raise questions about misleading financial statements.

Required:

Study the data in Exhibits 4.58.1 and 4.58.2. Write a memorandum identifying and explaining potential problem areas where misstatements in the current year financial statements could exist. Additional information about Retail Company is as follows:

- The new bank loan, obtained on July 1 of the current year, requires maintenance of a 2:1 current ratio.

- Principal of $100,000 plus interest on the 10 percent long-term note obtained several years ago in the original amount of $800,000 is due each January 1.

- The company has never paid dividends on its common stock and has no plans for a dividend.

4.59 **Analysis and Judgment.** As part of your regular year-end audit of a publicly held client, you must estimate the probability of success of its proposed new product line. The client has experienced financial difficulty during the last few years and, in your judgment, a successful introduction of the new product line is necessary for the client to remain a going concern.

Five elements are necessary for the successful introduction of the product: (1) successful labor negotiations before the strike deadline between the construction firms contracted to build the necessary addition to the present plant and the building trades unions, (2) successful defense of patent rights, (3) product approval by the Food and Drug Administration (FDA), (4) successful negotiation of a long-term raw material contract with a foreign supplier, and (5) successful conclusion of distribution contract talks with a large national retail distributor.

In view of the circumstances, you contact experts who have provided your audit firm with reliable estimates in the past. The labor relations expert estimates that there is an 80 percent chance of successfully concluding labor negotiations. Legal counsel advises that there is a 90 percent chance of successfully defending patent rights. The expert on FDA product approvals estimates a 95 percent chance of new product approval. The experts in the remaining two areas estimate the probability of successfully resolving (1) the raw materials contract and (2) the distribution contract talks to be 90 percent in each case. Assume that these estimates are reliable.

Required:

What is your assessment of the probability of successful product introduction? (*Hint:* You can assume that each of the five elements is independent of the others.)

4.60 **Kaplan CPA Exam Simulation: The Effect of Computers on the Audit.**

Required:

Go to the Kaplan Web site link at www.mhhe.com/louwers3e, click on AUD: Kerklaan Enterprises case and the "Research" tab, and complete the assigned task.

KAPLAN
CPA REVIEW

4.61 **Kaplan CPA Exam Simulation: Audit Documentation.**

Required:

Go to the Kaplan Web site link at www.mhhe.com/louwers3e, click on AUD: Amberly Tool and Die case and the "Research" tab, and complete the assigned task.

4.62 **Kaplan CPA Exam Simulation: Planning.**

Required:

a. Go to the Kaplan Web site link at www.mhhe.com/louwers3e, click on AUD: Woodson Flavors International case and the "Engagement Letters" tab, and complete the assigned task.

b. Go to the Kaplan Web site link at www.mhhe.com/louwers3e, click on AUD: Woodson Flavors International case and the "Analytic Procedures" tab, and complete the assigned task.

c. Go to the Kaplan Web site link at www.mhhe.com/louwers3e, click on AUD: Woodson Flavors International case and the "Interpreting Ratios" tab, and complete the assigned task.

d. Go to the Kaplan Web site link at www.mhhe.com/louwers3e, click on AUD: Woodson Flavors International case and the "Audit Considerations" tab, and complete the assigned task.

e. Go to the Kaplan Web site link at www.mhhe.com/louwers3e, click on AUD: Woodson Flavors International case and the "Research" tab, and complete the assigned task.

4.63 **Kaplan CPA Exam Simulation: Planning.**

Required:

a. Go to the Kaplan Web site link at www.mhhe.com/louwers3e, click on the AUD: Fitzgerald Thomas case and the "Audit Assertions" tab, and complete the assigned task.

b. Go to the Kaplan Web site link at www.mhhe.com/louwers3e, click on the AUD: Fitzgerald Thomas case and the "Audit Evidence" tab, and complete the assigned task.

c. Go to the Kaplan Web site link at www.mhhe.com/louwers3e, click on the AUD: Fitzgerald Thomas case and the "Research" tab, and complete the assigned task.

4.64 **Kaplan CPA Exam Simulation: Planning.**

Required:

a. Go to the Kaplan Web site link at www.mhhe.com/louwers3e, click on the AUD: Nivotny-Schmidt case and the "Audit Planning and Materiality" tab, and complete the assigned task.

b. Go to the Kaplan Web site link at www.mhhe.com/louwers3e, click on the AUD: Nivotny-Schmidt case and the "Audit Assertions" tab, and complete the assigned task.

c. Go to the Kaplan Web site link at www.mhhe.com/louwers3e, click on the AUD: Nivotny-Schmidt case and the "Research" tab, and complete the assigned task.

4.65 **Mini-case: Engagement Letters.** Refer to the mini-case "To Indemnify or Not to Indemnify: That is the Question" shown on page 842 and respond to Questions 1 through 3.

4.66 **ACL Case.** ACL Services is the leading global provider of Audit Analytics to financial executives, compliance professionals, and auditors. We are providing you with an opportunity to master this software package before you even begin your professional accounting career. While a demonstration version of the software is included with your textbook, an ACL tutorial and exercises can be found on the textbook Web site (www.mhhe.com/louwers3e). Go to the ACL link at www.mhhe.com/louwers3e and complete the tutorial.

Appendix 4A

Selected Financial Ratios

Balance-Sheet Ratios	Formula*
Current ratio	$\dfrac{\text{Current assets}}{\text{Current liabilities}}$
Days' sales in receivables	$\dfrac{\text{Ending net receivables}}{\text{Credit sales}} \times 360$
Doubtful account ratio	$\dfrac{\text{Allowance for doubtful accounts}}{\text{Ending gross receivables}}$
Days' sales in inventory	$\dfrac{\text{Ending inventory}}{\text{Cost of goods sold}} \times 360$
Debt-to-equity ratio	$\dfrac{\text{Current and long-term debt}}{\text{Stockholder equity}}$

Operations Ratios	
Receivables turnover	$\dfrac{\text{Credit sales}}{\text{Ending net receivables}}$
Inventory turnover	$\dfrac{\text{Cost of goods sold}}{\text{Ending inventory}}$
Cost of goods sold ratio	$\dfrac{\text{Cost of goods sold}}{\text{Net sales}}$
Gross margin ratio	$\dfrac{\text{Net sales} - \text{Cost of goods sold}}{\text{Net sales}}$
Return on beginning equity	$\dfrac{\text{Net income}}{\text{Stockholder equity (beginning)}}$

Financial Distress Ratios (Altman)

The discriminant Z-score is an index of a company's "financial health." The higher the score, the healthier the company. The lower the score, the closer financial failure approaches. The score that predicts financial failure is a matter of dispute. Research suggests that companies with scores above 3.0 never go bankrupt. Generally, companies with scores below 1.0 experience financial difficulty of some kind. The score can be a negative number.

(X_1) Working capital/Total assets	$\dfrac{\text{Current assets} - \text{Current liabilities}}{\text{Total assets}}$
(X_2) Retained earnings/Total assets	$\dfrac{\text{Retained earnings (ending)}}{\text{Total assets}}$
(X_3) Earnings before interest and taxes/Total assets	$\dfrac{\text{Net income} + \text{Interest expense} + \text{Income tax expense}}{\text{Total assets}}$
(X_4) Market value of equity/Total debt	$\dfrac{\text{Market value of common and preferred stock}}{\text{Current liabilities and long-term debt}}$
(X_5) Net sales/Total assets	$\dfrac{\text{Net sales}}{\text{Total assets}}$
Discriminant Z-score (Altman)	$1.2 \times X_1 + 1.4 \times X_2 + 3.3 \times X_3 + 0.6 \times X_4 + 1.0 \times X_5$

*These ratios are shown to be calculated using year end, rather than year-average, numbers for balances such as accounts receivable and inventory. Other accounting and finance reference books could contain formulas using year-average numbers. As long as no dramatic changes have occurred during the year, the year-end numbers can have much audit relevance because they reflect the most current balance data. For comparative purposes, the ratios should be calculated on the same basis for all years being compared.

Risk Assessment: Internal Control Evaluation

Professional Standards References

Compendium Section	Document Reference	Topic
Various*	AS 5	"An Audit of Internal Control over Financial Reporting That Is Integrated with an Audit of Financial Statements"
	AS 4	"Reporting on Whether a Previously Reported Material Weakness Continues to Exist"
AU 110	SAS 1	"Responsibilities and Functions of the Independent Auditor"
AU 150	SAS 95	"Generally Accepted Auditing Standards"
AU 230	SAS 1	"Due Professional Care in the Performance of Work" (amended by SAS 104)
AU 312	SAS 107	"Audit Risk and Materiality in Conducting an Audit"
	ISA 320	"Audit Materiality"
AU 316	SAS 99	"Consideration of Fraud in a Financial Statement Audit"
	ISA 240	"The Auditor's Responsibility to Consider Fraud in an Audit of Financial Statements"
AU 314	SAS 109	"Understanding the Entity and Its Environment and Assessing the Risks of Material Misstatement"
	ISA 315	"Understanding the Entity and Its Environment and Assessing the Risks of Material Misstatement"
AU 322	SAS 65	"The Auditor's Consideration of the Internal Audit Function in an Audit of Financial Statements"
	ISA 610	"Considering the Work of Internal Auditing"
AU 324	SAS 70	"Service Organizations"
AU 325	SAS 112	"Communicating Internal Control Related Matters Identified in an Audit"
AU 326	SAS 106	"Audit Evidence"
	ISA 500	"Audit Evidence"
	ISA 501	"Audit Evidence—Additional Considerations for Specific Items"
AU 380	SAS 114	"The Auditor's Communication with Those Charged with Governance"
	ISA 260	"Communications of Audit Matters with Those Charged with Governance"
AU 801	SAS 74	"Compliance Auditing Applicable to Governmental Entities and Recipients of Governmental Financial Assistance"

*AS 5 amends AU 230, AU 310, AU 312, AU 313, AU 315 AU 316, AU 319, AU 322, AU 325, AU 328, AU 332, AU 333, AU 341, AU 342, AU 380, AU 508, AU 530, AU 543, AU 560, AU 561, AU 711, AU 722, AS 3, and AS 4.

If everything seems under control, you're just not going fast enough.

Mario Andretti, race-car driver

Learning Objectives

Establishing internal control is an important management function. Understanding the elements of control and how to evaluate their effectiveness is an important skill that every accountant should have. Even if you do not go into auditing, you probably will have responsibility for maintaining internal controls at some point in your accounting career. In auditing, internal control evaluation and control risk assessment are essential parts of every engagement. Generally accepted auditing standards (GAAS) emphasize internal control in the *second standard of field work:*

> A sufficient understanding of the entity and its environment, *including its internal control*, is to be obtained to assess the risk of material misstatement of the financial statements whether due to error or fraud and to design the nature, timing, and extent of further audit procedures [emphasis added].

For audits of public companies, *Auditing Standard No. 5 (AS 5)* requires management to assess its internal control and auditors to express an opinion on the effectiveness of the client's internal control as an integrated part of the financial statement audit. This chapter presents a general introduction to the theory and definitions you will find useful for internal control evaluation and control risk assessment. The chapter uses

the payroll cycle to provide specific examples of control procedures and related audit procedures.

Your objectives are to be able to:

1. Distinguish between management's and auditors' responsibilities regarding an entity's internal control.

2. Define and describe *internal control.*

3. Define and describe the five basic components of internal control and specify some of their characteristics.

4. Explain the phases of an evaluation of control and risk assessment and the documentation and extent of audit work required.

5. Describe additional responsibilities for management and auditors of public companies required by Sarbanes-Oxley and *Auditing Standard No. 5.*

6. List the major components of the auditors' report on internal control over financial reporting.

7. Describe situations in which the auditors' report on internal control over financial reporting would be modified.

8. Explain the communication of internal control deficiencies to those charged with governance such as the audit committee and other key management personnel.

9. Explain the limitations of all internal control systems.

INTRODUCTION

By any measure, **BMC Software** (one of the world's largest developers of software solutions) had a great 2005 (its fiscal year-end is March 31). Net income increased from a loss of $26.8 million in 2004 to net income of $75.3 in 2005, with a corresponding increase in earnings per share from a net loss per share of $0.12 to net earnings per share of $0.34. In addition, BMC's stock outperformed the S&P 500, Dow Jones Industrial, and NASDAQ indices. Furthermore, BMC's auditors **(Ernst & Young)** issued an unqualified opinion on the fairness of BMC's financial statements.

However, BMC Software's 10-K did not reveal only good news. Its management issued a report (signed by its chief executive officer and chief financial officer) indicating that three *material weaknesses* in BMC's internal control over financial reporting had been identified; this report concluded that BMC Software did not maintain an effective internal control over financial reporting. What's more, Ernst & Young issued a similar report on BMC's internal control over financial reporting that agreed with BMC's management's assessment of its internal control. Through the first five months of 2005 (the first year of required reporting on internal control), BMC was 1 of 586 companies to report material weaknesses in their internal control over financial reporting.[1]

[1] "Material-Weakness Reports Skyrocket," *CFO.com*, July 18, 2005.

MANAGEMENT VERSUS AUDITORS' RESPONSIBILITY FOR INTERNAL CONTROL: THE SARBANES-OXLEY ACT OF 2002

1. Distinguish between management's and auditors' responsibilities regarding an entity's internal control.

In response to the number of major corporate accounting scandals rocking the financial world (e.g., **Enron**, **WorldCom**, **Xerox**, **KMart**, etc.), on July 30, 2002, Congress passed the most wide-sweeping financial reporting legislation since the 1930s (when it established the Securities and Exchange Commission). The Sarbanes-Oxley Act is intended to strengthen corporate financial reporting by assessing harsher criminal penalties for white-collar crimes, increasing management accountability, and enhancing audit firm independence. The act is very specific about management's responsibility for organizational internal control. In addition to certifying the entity's financial statements (section 302), management also must assess and report on the entity's internal control over financial reporting (section 404). Specifically, the entity's annual report must include the following (see Exhibit 5.1 for an example):

- A statement that management is responsible for establishing and maintaining adequate internal control over financial reporting.
- A statement identifying the framework management uses to evaluate the effectiveness of the entity's internal control.
- A statement providing management's assessment of the effectiveness of the entity's internal control.

Under the new rules, management also must disclose any material weaknesses in internal control. If any material weaknesses exist, management may not be able to conclude that the entity's internal control over financial reporting is effective. Exhibit 5.1 illustrates excerpts from **Krispy Kreme**'s management report on internal control over financial reporting, which identifies numerous material weaknesses in its internal control.

Auditors' Internal Control Responsibilities

The audit team has two primary reasons for conducting an evaluation of an entity's internal control. First, Sarbanes-Oxley requires an audit of the effectiveness of internal control for publicly traded companies. This audit is an integrated part of the financial statement audit. In essence, the audit firm issues two opinions: one on the entity's financial statements and one on the effectiveness of the entity's internal control. The second reason for evaluating an entity's internal control is to assess the risk of material misstatement to give the auditors a basis for planning the audit and determining the *nature, timing,* and *extent* of audit procedures for the substantive audit program. The risk of material misstatement is composed of inherent and control risk. Inherent risk, the susceptibility of an account to misstatement, was discussed in Chapter 3; this chapter focuses on control risk assessment. Recall that **control risk** is the probability that an entity's controls will fail to prevent or detect material misstatements due to errors or frauds that would otherwise have entered the system. To assess control risk, external auditors must evaluate existing control procedures and assess the control risk for the period under audit.

The audit team assesses control risk to comply with the second standard of field work of GAAS. Many auditors express the internal control risk assessment decision with descriptive terminology (e.g., maximum, slightly below maximum, high, moderate, low); some auditors put probability numbers on it (e.g., 100, 50, or 10 percent, but never zero.). If auditors assess control risk as "maximum" or 100 percent (i.e., poor control), they will tend to perform a great deal of substantive procedures with large sample sizes (*extent*), at or near the entity's fiscal year end (*timing*), using procedures designed to obtain high-quality external evidence (*nature*). On the other hand, if auditors assess control risk as "low," usually around 10 to 20 percent (i.e., effective control), they can perform fewer substantive procedures with smaller sample sizes (*extent*), at an interim date before the entity's fiscal year end (*timing*), using a mixture of procedures designed to obtain

EXHIBIT 5.1 Excerpts from Krispy Kreme's Management's Report on Internal Control over Financial Reporting

Our management is responsible for establishing and maintaining adequate internal control over financial reporting . . . Internal control over financial reporting is a process, effected by an entity's board of directors, management and other personnel, designed to provide reasonable assurance regarding the reliability of financial reporting and the preparation of consolidated financial statements for external purposes in accordance with GAAP. Internal control over financial reporting includes those policies and procedures which pertain to the maintenance of records that, in reasonable detail, accurately and fairly reflect the transactions and dispositions of assets; provide reasonable assurance that transactions are recorded as necessary to permit preparation of consolidated financial statements in accordance with GAAP; provide reasonable assurance that receipts and expenditures are being made only in accordance with our and/or our Board of Directors' authorization; and provide reasonable assurance regarding prevention or timely detection of unauthorized acquisition, use or disposition of our assets that could have a material effect on our consolidated financial statements.

Because of its inherent limitations, internal control over financial reporting may not prevent or detect misstatements. Also, projections of any evaluation of the effectiveness of our internal control over financial reporting to future periods are subject to the risk that controls may become inadequate because of changes in conditions, or that the degree of compliance with the policies or procedures may deteriorate.

Management assessed the effectiveness of our internal control over financial reporting as of January 28, 2007, using the criteria established in Internal Control—Integrated Framework issued by the Committee of Sponsoring Organizations of the Treadway Commission ("COSO").

A material weakness is a control deficiency, or combination of control deficiencies, that results in more than a remote likelihood that a material misstatement of the annual or interim consolidated financial statements will not be prevented or detected. As of January 28, 2007, management identified the material weaknesses described below.

We did not maintain an effective control environment based on the criteria established in the COSO framework. The following material weaknesses were identified related to our control environment:

- We did not establish a formal enterprise risk assessment process.
- We did not formalize lines of communication among legal, finance and operations personnel. Specifically, procedures were not designed and in place to ensure sharing of financial information within and across our corporate and divisional offices and other operating facilities such that significant issues are brought to the attention of appropriate level of accounting and financial reporting personnel.
- We did not maintain certain written accounting policies and procedures including those over critical accounting policies.
- We did not have an effective process for monitoring the appropriateness of user access and segregation of duties related to financial applications.

These control environment material weaknesses contributed to the material weaknesses described below.

We did not maintain effective control over our financial closing and reporting processes. Specifically, the following material weaknesses were identified:

- We did not maintain effective controls to ensure that journal entries were reviewed and approved. Specifically, effective controls were not designed and in place to ensure that journal entries were reviewed and approved to ensure the completeness, accuracy and validity of the entries recorded.
- We did not maintain effective controls to ensure the completeness and accuracy of our accounting for equity method franchisees in accordance with GAAP.
- We did not design and maintain effective controls to ensure that accrued expenses, including accruals for legal and professional fees, were complete and accurate in accordance with GAAP.

We did not maintain effective controls over the completeness and accuracy of certain franchisee revenue. Specifically, effective controls were not designed and in place to ensure that revenue was recognized in the proper period for sales of equipment to franchisees in connection with new store openings.

We did not maintain effective controls over the completeness and accuracy of our accounting for lease related assets, liabilities and expenses. Specifically, our controls over the application and monitoring of accounting policies related to lease renewal options, rent escalations, amortization periods for leasehold improvements and lease classification principally affecting property and equipment, accrued rent, capital lease obligations, rent expense and depreciation were ineffective to ensure that such transactions were completely and accurately accounted for in conformity with GAAP.

We did not maintain effective controls over the accuracy and completeness of our property and equipment accounts, including the related depreciation. Specifically, effective controls were not designed and in place to ensure that retired assets were written off in the appropriate period, that appropriate depreciable lives were assigned to capital additions and assets were capitalized in accordance with GAAP.

These control deficiencies contributed to the previously reported restatement of our consolidated financial statements for fiscal 2003 and fiscal 2004 and all quarterly periods in fiscal 2004 and the first three quarters of fiscal 2005. Management has concluded that each of the control deficiencies above could result in a misstatement of account balances or disclosures that would be material to our annual or interim consolidated financial statements that would not be prevented or detected. Accordingly, management has concluded that each of the control deficiencies listed above constitutes a material weakness as of January 28, 2007. Because of these material weaknesses, management has concluded that we did not maintain effective internal control over financial reporting as of January 28, 2007, based on the COSO criteria. Management's assessment of the effectiveness of our internal control over financial reporting as of January 28, 2007 has been audited by PricewaterhouseCoopers LLP, an independent registered public accounting firm, as stated in their report which appears in this Annual Report on Form 10-K.

EXHIBIT 5.2
**Trade-Off Between
Tests of Controls and
Substantive Testing**

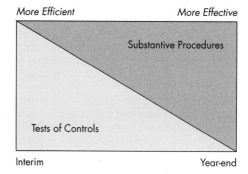

high-quality external evidence and lower-quality internal evidence (*nature*). Of course, auditors may assess control risk between "low" and "maximum" (e.g., "moderate," "high," or "slightly below maximum") and adjust the substantive procedures accordingly. Exhibit 5.2 illustrates the trade-off between tests of controls and substantive procedures. It also illustrates the trade-off between audit *effectiveness* (catching errors or fraud) and audit *efficiency* (completing the audit in a timely fashion).[2]

A secondary reason for evaluating internal control is to provide information useful to management and directors for carrying out the entity's control mission. Regulators, Congress, and the public have been concerned about auditors' communication of internal control and other matters to high levels in public corporations. In response, the SEC, the Public Company Accounting Oversight Board (PCAOB), and the American Institute of CPAs (AICPA) Auditing Standards Board have issued pronouncements that address auditors' responsibilities to communicate internal control matters noted in an audit to the those charged with governance such as the audit committee of the entity's board of directors and directly to shareholders through their report on management's assertion of effective internal control in the annual report.

Review Checkpoints

5.1 What are managements' and auditors' respective responsibilities regarding internal control?

5.2 Define *control risk* and explain the role of control risk assessment in audit planning.

5.3 What are the primary and secondary reasons for conducting an evaluation of an audit client's internal control?

5.4 How does the control risk affect the *nature, timing,* and *extent* of substantive procedures?

5.5 Why do you think some firms use numeric control risk evaluations and others use words?

INTERNAL CONTROL DEFINED

**LEARNING
OBJECTIVE**

2. Define and describe
internal control.

In response to a report by the National Commission on Fraudulent Financial Reporting (referred to as the *Treadway Commission* after its first chairman, former SEC Commissioner James Treadway) on problems in financial reporting, a group of professional organizations met to determine what organizations could do to improve financial reporting. Representatives from the Financial Executives Institute (FEI), the American Accounting Association (AAA), the Institute of Internal Auditors (IIA), the Institute of Management Accountants (IMA), and the AICPA (collectively referred to as the *Committee of*

[2] A recent white paper co-authored by representatives of the Big Four and five other major firms ("A Framework for Evaluating Control Exceptions and Deficiencies," December 20, 2004) states that a high level of assurance means at least a 90 percent level of confidence that the controls are working at least 90 percent of the time (pp. 3–4).

Sponsoring Organizations, or *COSO*) debated internal control theory and definitions. Given that these professional groups have quite divergent interests, the fact that their representatives reached a consensus on internal control was quite momentous. The resulting report (the COSO Report) defined **internal control** as follows:

> Internal control is a process, effected by an entity's board of directors, management and other personnel, designed to provide reasonable assurance regarding the achievement of objectives in the following three categories:
>
> - Reliability of financial reporting.
> - Effectiveness and efficiency of operations.
> - Compliance with applicable laws and regulations.

Internal control is designed to achieve *control objectives* (measurable targets) in three categories. In the *financial reporting category,* the control objectives are publishing reliable financial reports (e.g., annual financial statements, interim financial reports) and safeguarding assets from unauthorized use (e.g., embezzlement, theft, damage, unauthorized purchase, or unauthorized disposal). Financial reporting controls enable an entity to *safeguard its assets* from unauthorized disposal and *prepare financial statements in conformity with GAAP*. In the *operations category,* some examples of control objectives are good business reputation, return on investment, market share, new product introduction, and using assets effectively and efficiently. The operations control objectives cover business strategy and tactics. In the *compliance category,* the broad control objective is compliance with laws and regulations that affect the entity.

External auditors are primarily concerned with the financial reporting controls. However, some controls related to operations and compliance can be relevant to the external audit. For example, controls over developing nonfinancial data such as scrap reports can be relevant if the audit team uses such information in analytical procedures or to evaluate inventory valuation. Compliance controls related to laws and regulations directly affecting the financial statements (e.g., income taxes) are also relevant to the external audit.

People are the key component of an entity's internal control. An entity may have policy manuals, forms, computer-controlled information and accounting, and other features of control, but people make the system work. People establish the control objectives, put controls in place, and operate them.

Internal control provides *reasonable assurance*, not absolute assurance, that control objectives will be achieved. Because people operate the controls, breakdowns can occur. Human error, deliberate circumvention, management override, and improper collusion among people who are supposed to act independently can cause failure to achieve control objectives. Internal control can help prevent and detect these people-caused failures, but it cannot guarantee that they will never happen. In auditing standards, the concept of **reasonable assurance** recognizes that the costs of controls should not exceed the benefits that are expected from the controls. Hence, an entity can decide that certain controls are too costly in light of the risk of loss that can occur.

Internal control is a *process*, not an end in itself, but a means to ends (i.e., the control objectives). It is a dynamic process operating every day within an entity's operating structure.

Review Checkpoints

5.6 What are the three categories of control objectives according to the COSO Report? Which is most important to auditors?

5.7 Why are people the most important component of internal control?

5.8 What four types of control breakdowns can cause failure to achieve control objectives?

AUDITING INSIGHT Sarbanes-Oxley Definition of Internal Control

The Sarbanes-Oxley Act of 2002's definition of "internal control over financial reporting" is very similar to the COSO definition, although it focuses primarily on internal control over financial reporting:

> Internal control is a process designed by, or under the supervision of, the registrant's principal executive and principal financial officers, or persons performing similar functions, and effected by the registrant's board of directors, management and other personnel, to provide reasonable assurance regarding the reliability of financial reporting and the preparation of financial statements for external purposes in accordance with generally accepted accounting principles and includes those policies and procedures that
>
> 1. pertain to the maintenance of records that in reasonable detail accurately and fairly reflect the transactions and dispositions of the assets of the registrant;

> 2. provide reasonable assurance that transactions are recorded as necessary to permit preparation of financial statements in accordance with generally accepted accounting principles, and receipts and expenditures of the registrant are being made only in accordance with authorizations of management and directors of the registrant; and
>
> 3. provide reasonable assurance regarding prevention or timely detection of unauthorized acquisition, use or disposition of the registrant's assets that could have a material effect on the financial statements.

Source: U.S. Congress, *Sarbanes-Oxley Act of 2002*, Pub. L. No. 107–204, 116 Stat. 745 (2002).

COMPONENTS OF INTERNAL CONTROL

LEARNING OBJECTIVE

3. Define and describe the five basic components of internal control and specify some of their characteristics.

The COSO Report defined each of the three control objectives and stated that management should enact the five components related to each of them (Exhibit 5.3). The control components are relevant for each of the control objectives categories. The financial reporting control objectives (shaded area of Exhibit 5.3) are the focus of the rest of the material in this chapter.

Just as *management* is responsible for an organization's financial statements, Sarbanes-Oxley states that *management* is responsible for the components of its internal control. *Management* establishes a control environment, identifies risks facing the entity and assesses those risks it wishes to control, specifies information and communication channels and content (including the accounting system and its reports), designs and implements control procedures, and monitors, supervises, and maintains the controls. For these reasons, the COSO framework is intended to be a guide for *management* of organizations. Hence, *management* is used to describe the five interrelated components of internal control (Exhibit 5.4)—*management*'s control environment, *management*'s risk assessment, *management*'s control procedures, *management*'s monitoring, and the *management* information and communication systems that link all components. Even though the COSO framework is a tool for *management,* the components also provide a framework for auditors' evaluation of internal control.

Control Environment

The control environment sets the tone of the organization. It is the foundation for all other components of internal control. It provides discipline and structure. Control environment factors include the integrity, ethical values, and competence of the entity's people. The following are general elements of an internal control environment:

* Management's philosophy and operating style.
* Management and employee integrity and ethical values.
* Existence and implementation of an entity code of conduct.
* Management's financial reporting attitudes (e.g., conservative, aggressive).

EXHIBIT 5.3
Internal Control—
Integrated Framework
(COSO)

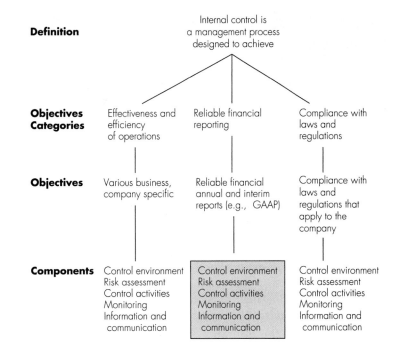

Definition — Internal control is a management process designed to achieve

Objectives Categories	Effectiveness and efficiency of operations	Reliable financial reporting	Compliance with laws and regulations
Objectives	Various business, company specific	Reliable financial annual and interim reports (e.g., GAAP)	Compliance with laws and regulations that apply to the company
Components	Control environment Risk assessment Control activities Monitoring Information and communication	Control environment Risk assessment Control activities Monitoring Information and communication	Control environment Risk assessment Control activities Monitoring Information and communication

- Degree of emphasis on meeting performance targets.
- The entity's organizational structure.
- Methods of assigning authority and responsibility.
- Human resource policies and practices.
- The entity's commitment to competence—job skills and knowledge.
- Formal and informal job descriptions.
- Nature of employee candidate background checks.
- Type of action taken when employee misconduct (e.g., theft, embezzlement, fraudulent reporting) is discovered.
- Membership and operation of the board's audit committee.
- Presence of an internal audit function.

As noted earlier, the most important feature of the control environment is the people who make the system work. An entity's personnel problems sometimes create internal control problems. High turnover in accounting jobs means that inexperienced people are performing the accounting and control tasks, and they generally make more mistakes than experienced people. New accounting officers and managers may not be familiar with entity accounting policies and could make technical and judgmental errors. Sometimes

EXHIBIT 5.4
Interrelated
Components of
Internal Control

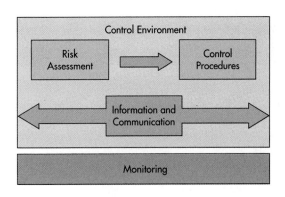

AUDITING INSIGHT "As Long as You Make Money, It's All Right"

At a worldwide meeting of **Enron**'s vice presidents, CFO Jeff Skilling singled out Louise Kitchen for praise. Ms. Kitchen had started the company's Internet-based trading operation, Enron Online, even though Mr. Skilling had repeatedly refused to allow her to do so. Instead, she pulled the new network together in secret, using funds allocated for other purposes. A former vice president who attended that meeting was aghast: "The moral of this story is, 'You can break the rules, you can cheat, you can lie, but as long as you make money, it's all right.'"

Source: "Darth Vader. Machiavelli. Skilling Set Intense Pace," *The New York Times,* February 7, 2002.

accounting officers and employees are fired because they refuse to comply with improper accounting procedures desired by a higher level of management. In general, high turnover among accounting personnel can be a warning signal to the audit team.

The entity's audit committee is a key factor in the control environment. An **audit committee** is a subcommittee of the board of directors that is generally composed of three to six "outside" members (those not involved in the entity's day-to-day management) of the organization's board of directors. Each member must be *financially literate,* and one member must be a "financial expert." The purpose of including outside members is to provide a buffer between the audit team and operating management. The buffer allows the audit team (and the corporate internal audit department) to report any controversial findings to members of the board of directors without fear of reprisal. For example, should the internal auditors find wrongdoing in the CEO's office, it would do no good to report the matter to the CEO. Similarly, if management does not have control over appointing auditors, management is prevented from threatening to fire the auditors if they do not go along with an inappropriate accounting practice. Some of the more important duties of the audit committee follow:

- Appointment, compensation, and oversight of the public accounting firm conducting the entity's audit.
- Resolution of disagreements between management and the audit team.
- Oversight of the entity's internal audit function.
- Approval of nonaudit services provided by the public accounting firm performing the audit engagement.

Small and midsize entities may implement the control environment factors differently than larger entities. For example, smaller entities might not have a written code of conduct but instead develop a culture that emphasizes the importance of integrity and ethical behavior through oral communication and by management example. Similarly, a smaller entity may not have an independent or outside member on its board of directors.

AUDITING INSIGHT The Audit Committee Strikes Back

Freddie Mac, one of the largest mortgage finance companies in the United States, fired David Glenn, its president and chief operating officer, and several other key executives for not fully cooperating with its audit committee. In its press release, the company said Glenn was fired "because of serious questions as to the timeliness and completeness of his cooperation and candor with the board's Audit Committee counsel."

Source: "Mortgage Concern in Broad Shake-Up," *The New York Times,* June 10, 2003.

Control Consciousness Self-Assessment

Is the organization's ethical tone at the top communicated in words and deeds?

Is an ethics program in place and does it include a meaningful code of conduct?

Is the board of directors active, independent, and well informed?

Are positions in the organization structured for optimum effectiveness in regard to productivity and communication?

Are all responsibilities and accountabilities clearly defined?

Is delegation of authority commensurate with responsibility?

Do formal or informal job descriptions include an analysis of the knowledge and skills needed to perform each position?

Does the organization hire qualified, ethical, and well-trained personnel?

Do frequent interactions occur between senior and operating management?

Are appropriate policies and procedures in place for hiring, training, promoting, and compensating employees?

Are background checks conducted for new hires, especially those in sensitive positions?

Source: Institute of Internal Auditors, *Tone at the Top*, November 2003, pp. 1–2.

Risk Assessment

To use the ill-fated White Star liner *Titanic* as an analogy, corporate management has often been accused of spending too much time making sure that the deck chairs are properly arranged rather than peering over the bow looking for icebergs. "Icebergs" represent **business risks:** factors, events, and conditions that can prevent the organization from achieving its business objectives. Of course, to know the risk of failure to meet objectives, management must set objectives in the first place. These range from overall strategy to specific entity and activity-level objectives.

Management should take steps to identify risks, estimate their significance and likelihood, and consider how to manage the risks. By setting control objectives, management can identify critical success factors and institute policies and procedures to ensure they are met. Using the enterprise risk management (ERM) framework discussed in Chapter 4 is an effective method for management to perform this function. (*Note:* The risk assessment element of the COSO framework is management's responsibility and does not include auditors' use of the audit risk model or assessment of control risk.) Basically, management should be able to address the following questions:

- How does management develop strategies and control objectives? Is the board of directors involved? Is the process formal and subject to review? Is the process updated periodically? Is the process realistic?

- How does management assess risks? Is sufficient information gathered? Are risks viewed in isolation, or are they linked? Are assumptions and forecasts realistic? Is the risk assessment updated periodically? Is risk assessment performed at all levels of the entity?

- How does management respond to prospects of risks that are significant and likely? What processes are in place? What key indicators are monitored? If other entities are involved in sharing the risk, are they evaluated for soundness?

AUDITING INSIGHT · The Paradox of Risk

The paradox of risk is that it results from the future being different from the past, while traditional risk management relies upon the future being similar to the past.

Frank Knight (as quoted in "Managing Risk from the Mailroom to the Boardroom," *Tone at the Top*, June 2003).

The basic concepts of the risk assessment process should be present in every entity, regardless of size, but the risk assessment process is likely to be less formal and less structured in small and midsize entities than in larger ones. All entities should have established financial reporting control objectives, but they may be recognized implicitly rather than explicitly in smaller entities. Management may be able to learn about risks related to these control objectives through direct personal involvement with employees and outside parties.

Review Checkpoints

5.9 What are the five components of management's internal control?

5.10 What is the *control environment*?

5.11 What is the purpose of risk assessment for an entity?

Control Procedures

Once risks to management's control objectives have been identified (risk assessment), internal control procedures need to be established to eliminate, mitigate, or compensate for the risks. **Control procedures** are specific actions taken by a client's management and employees to help ensure that management directives are carried out. Control procedures (both computerized and manual) are imposed on the accounting system for the purpose of *preventing*, *detecting*, and *correcting* errors and frauds that could enter and flow through to the financial statements. Clearly, procedures that prevent misstatements before they occur are preferable. Control procedures include the following:

- Performance reviews.
- Separation of duties.
- Physical controls.
- Information-processing controls.

We discuss each of these control procedures in the following sections.

Performance Reviews

Management has primary responsibility for ensuring that the organization's control objectives are being met. Performance reviews require management's active participation in the supervision of operations. Management's study of budget variances with follow-up action is an example of a performance review.

Managers also should provide for periodic comparison of the recorded amounts with independent evidence of existence and valuation. Periodic comparisons may include counts of cash on hand, reconciliation of bank statements, counts of securities, counts of inventories maintained on hand, confirmation of accounts receivable and accounts payable, and other such comparisons undertaken to determine whether accounting records represent real assets and liabilities.

Management that performs frequent performance reviews has more opportunities to detect errors in the records than management that does not. The frequency, of course, is governed by the costs and benefits. One should not try to count, compare, or confirm assets with great frequency unless they are especially susceptible to loss or error or are unusually valuable.

Subsequent action to investigate further or correct differences is also important. Periodic comparison and action to correct errors lowers the risk that material misstatements remain in the accounts. Such comparisons are frequently assigned to internal auditors and

other employees. Research has shown that companies with active internal auditors have fewer accounting errors.

Separation of Duties

A very important characteristic of effective internal control is an appropriate separation of functional responsibilities. Four types of functional responsibilities should be performed by different departments (see Exhibit 5.5), or at least by different persons on the entity's accounting staff:

1. *Authorization to execute transactions.* This duty belongs to people who have authority and responsibility for initiating or approving transactions. Authorization may be general, referring to a class of transactions (e.g., all purchases up to $100,000), or it may be specific (e.g., sale of a major asset).
2. *Recording transactions.* This duty refers to the accounting and record-keeping function, which in most organizations is delegated to a computerized information system. People who control computerized processing are the record keepers.
3. *Custody of assets involved in the transactions.* This duty refers to the actual physical possession or effective physical control of property.
4. *Periodic reconciliation of existing assets to recorded amounts.* This duty refers to making comparisons at regular intervals and taking appropriate action with respect to any differences.

EXHIBIT 5.5
Separation of Duties

Incompatible responsibilities are combinations of responsibilities that place a person alone in a position to *create* and *conceal* errors, frauds, and misstatements in her or his normal job. Duties should be divided so that no one person can control two or more of these responsibilities. If different departments or persons are forced to deal with these different facets of transactions, frauds are more difficult because they require collusion of two or more persons, and most people hesitate to seek the help of others to conduct wrongful acts.

AUDITING INSIGHT

Three can keep a secret if two of them are dead.

Benjamin Franklin

A second benefit of separating duties is that by acting in a coordinated manner (handling different aspects of the same transaction), innocent errors are more likely to be found and corrected. The old saying is "Two heads are better than one."

Many control procedures once performed by different individuals in manual systems can be concentrated in computerized systems. The number of people who handle a transaction is typically reduced, often to just the individual employee who enters the data into the computer. Therefore, individuals who have access to the computer can be in a position to perform incompatible functions. As a result, other control procedures

could be required in computerized systems to achieve the degree of control ordinarily accomplished by separating functions in manual systems. These can include such techniques as password control procedures to prevent incompatible functions from being performed by individuals who have access to assets and to records through an online terminal or by limiting the types of transactions that can be performed from certain computers.

In a simple environment, an individual manager may be responsible for managing and ensuring the quality of gathering, processing, and using information. In more complex environments, an individual manager may be responsible for only a portion of the processing and control. Unless carefully defined and monitored, this sharing of control responsibilities can result in loss of overall control.

AUDITING INSIGHT No Separation of Duties

A computer center employee instructed the company's computer to pay his wife rent for land she allegedly leased to the company by assigning her an alphanumeric code as a lessor and then ordering the payments. The control lesson: Never let a data entry clerk who processes payment claims also have access to the approved vendor master file for additions or deletions.

Source: G. J. Bologna and R. J. Lindquist, *Fraud Auditing and Forensic Accounting* (New York: John Wiley & Sons, 1995).

Physical Controls

Physical access to assets and important records, documents, and blank forms should be limited to authorized personnel. Such assets as inventory and securities should not be available to persons who have no need to handle them. Likewise, access to records should be denied to people who do not have a record-keeping responsibility for them. Some blank forms are very important for accounting and control, and their availability should be restricted. Someone not involved in accounting for payroll should not be able to pick up blank time cards. Only authorized persons should be able to obtain blank checks after signing for them. Sometimes access to blank forms is the equivalent of access to an important asset. For example, someone who has access to blank checks has a measure of actual custody and access to cash.

Physical security of computer equipment and limited access to computer program files and data files are as important as restricting access to blank checks or inventory. Access controls help prevent improper use or manipulation of data files, unauthorized or incorrect use of computer programs, and improper use of the computer equipment. Locked doors, security passes, passwords, and check-in logs can be used to limit access to the computer system hardware. Having definite schedules for running computerized applications is another way to detect unauthorized access because the computer system software can produce reports that can be compared to the planned schedule. Applications being run at unauthorized times then can be investigated for illicit use of computer resources.

Information-Processing Controls

The financial reporting objective of internal control is to ensure that the financial statements are presented in accordance with GAAP, and an important objective of financial reporting control procedures is to process transactions correctly. Correctly processed transactions produce correct account balances, which in turn help produce accurate and reliable assertions in the financial statements. Information-processing controls can be broken down into two categories: manual and computerized information processing control procedures.

Manual Information Processing Control Procedures Although it is rare today to find an entity that has not moved to some extent to computerized information processing, manual controls over information processing remain the backbone of any information processing

AUDITING INSIGHT When Good Controls Go Bad

Zondervan Corporation announced a $5 million pretax write-down for the year. The problem was in the accounting controls at its Family Bookstore division. Ten percent of the inventory was "missing." The company had unsalable finished products and $1 million in "overlooked liabilities."

Zondervan's workers were not putting purchasing records into their computers correctly. Only 20 percent of the bookstore managers were using the system correctly. The system was capable of handling 7,000 individual product identifiers for 30 store locations, but the company was processing 10,000 products for 87 stores. Employees improvised by bunching more than one product onto one identifier code. This activity made record-tracking virtually impossible.

Source: "Bible Bungle," *Forbes*, March 11, 1985, p. 135.

system. For example, important manual control procedures over the purchasing and cash disbursement cycle include using purchase orders to ensure proper authorization (the *occurrence* assertion), matching vendor invoices with receiving reports and purchase orders to ensure that the quantity billed agrees with the quantity ordered and received at previously agreed-upon prices (the *accuracy* assertion), and using prenumbered documents (checks, purchase orders, and receiving reports) to ensure that all transactions have been recorded (the *completeness* assertion). The specific manual control procedures for each cycle will be discussed in greater detail in Chapters 6 through 10.

Computerized Information Processing Controls Computerized information-processing controls are organized under two categories: *general* controls and *application* controls. **Information technology general controls (ITGC)** apply to all applications systems and help ensure their continued proper operations. They include controls over data center operations, system software acquisition and maintenance, access security, and application system development, including changes in software and databases. They include physical security, hardware controls, separation of duties within the computer center, documentation and backup procedures, and other controls discussed more thoroughly in Module H. They can be thought of in the same light as the control environment because if the general controls are weak, the application controls cannot be relied on.

Information technology application controls (ITAC) include computerized steps within the application software (and related manual procedures) to control the information processing. Application controls are specific to each cycle (e.g., revenue and collection, acquisition and expenditure). They are divided into the following categories: *input controls*, *processing controls*, and *output controls*.

The weakest point in computerized systems is input—the point at which transaction data are transformed from hard-copy source documents into machine-readable form, or when direct entry is made from the Internet or with a communication device such as a remote terminal. When undetected errors are entered originally, they may not be detected during processing, and, if detected, they are troublesome to correct. **Input controls** are designed to provide reasonable assurance that data received for processing by the information-processing department have been authorized properly and converted into machine-sensitive form and that information has not been lost, suppressed, added, duplicated, or improperly changed.

Processing controls refer to error-condition check routines written into the computer program. Processing controls are designed to provide reasonable assurance that information processing has been performed as intended without any omission or double counting of transactions. Many of the processing controls are the same as the input controls, but they are used in the actual processing phases rather than at the time input is verified.

Output control refers primarily to control over the distribution of reports, but feedback on errors and comparison of input totals to output totals also are part of this "last-chance" control point. **Output controls** are the final check on the accuracy of the results of

AUDITING INSIGHT | Walloping Water Bill

When Chuck Richison received a water bill in the mail last week, he had a hunch it wouldn't float. Richison's bill normally runs about $55, but the new one was for $7,714,510.21! "It was the 21 cents that got me," he said. "You're not too worried about it because you know even if it is real, you can't afford to pay it." Richison, whose meter had been replaced recently, called the Utility Business Office for help—only to be told the meter had not been misread. The city later adjusted the bill, acknowledging that he was overcharged. "It was just a timing issue," office manager Michelle Workman said. "It caused it to overbill." Richison, who kept the misprinted bill, had not yet received a new invoice by mail.

Source: CNN.com, Jan. 28, 2004.

computerized processing. These controls should be designed to ensure that only authorized persons receive reports or have access to files produced by the system. Some common application controls are described in Exhibit 5.6.

Spreadsheet controls are also included under the topic of application controls. Financial reporting controls extend over the entire process from initiation of transactions to the financial statements. Many of the final adjusting entries, consolidating entries, and footnote amounts are created by spreadsheet applications, which also must be controlled. A

EXHIBIT 5.6 Information Technology Application Controls

Input Controls

- *Input authorized and approved.* Only properly authorized and approved input should be accepted for processing by the information processing center.
- *Check digits.* A check digit is an extra number, precisely calculated from the other numbers, that is tagged onto the end of a basic identification number such as an employee number or credit card number. The program calculates the correct check digit and compares it to the one on the input data. When the digits do not match, an error message is indicated on the device or printed out on an input error report. Check digits are used only on identification numbers (not quantity or value fields) to detect coding errors or keying errors such as the transposition of digits (e.g., coding 387 as 837).
- *Record counts.* Counts of records are tallies of the number of transaction documents submitted for data conversion.
- *Financial totals.* These are the sum of some important quantity or amount (e.g., the total payroll dollars in a batch of invoices). Calculating financial totals is useful during the input, processing, and output stages.
- *Hash totals.* These totals are similar to financial totals except the hash total is not meaningful for accounting records (e.g., the sum of all invoice numbers on invoices submitted to the data input operator).
- *Limit or reasonableness tests.* These tests are computerized checks to see whether data values exceed or fall below some predetermined limit.
- *Error correction and resubmission.* It is a good idea to have a control group log the content of error reports to monitor the nature, disposition, and proper correction of rejected data. Unless properly supervised and monitored, the error-correction process itself can become a source of data input errors.

Processing Controls

- *Run-to-run totals.* "Run-to-run" refers to *sequential processing operations*—runs—on the same data. These totals can be record counts, financial totals, and/or hash totals obtained at the end of one processing run. The totals are passed to the next run and compared to corresponding totals produced at the end of the second run.
- *Control total reports.* Control totals—record counts, financial totals, hash totals, and run-to-run totals—should be produced during processing operations and printed out on a report.
- *File and operator controls.* External and internal labels are means of ensuring that the proper files are used in applications. The systems software should produce a log to identify instructions entered by the operator and to make a record of time and use statistics for application runs. Supervisory personnel should review these logs on a periodic basis.
- *Limit and reasonableness tests.* These tests should be programmed to ensure that illogical conditions do not occur.

Output Controls

- *Control totals.* An independent control group should be responsible for the review of output control totals and investigation of differences.
- *Output distribution.* A distribution list should be maintained and used to deliver report copies. The number of copies produced should be restricted to the number needed.

AUDITING INSIGHT Recent Spreadsheet Goofs

- **TransAlta Corp.** confessed that a "clerical error" was a costly one for the power producer—$24 million to be exact. The Calgary-based company said a spreadsheet goof by an employee last April caused the company to pay higher than intended rates to ship power in New York. CEO Steve Snyder explained via a conference call yesterday that a "cut-and-paste" foul-up within an Excel spreadsheet on a bid to New York's power grid operator led TransAlta to secure 15 times the capacity of power lines at 10 times the price. The costly human error couldn't be reversed by the grid operator and while TransAlta has since tried to recoup the mammoth losses, it was left with a $24 million lesson.

- In October 2003, about two weeks after releasing its third-quarter earnings figures, **Fannie Mae** had to restate its unrealized gains by $1.2 billion for errors in "mark to market" calculations required by *SFAS 149*. This was apparently the result of "honest mistakes made in a spreadsheet used in the implementation of the new accounting standard."

 Sources: "Cut-and-Paste Oops Costly for TransAlta," *Canadian Press*, June 4, 2003; "Fannie Mae Corrects Mistakes in Results," *The New York Times*, October 30, 2003, p. C1.

summary of seven studies of spreadsheet errors concluded that 94 percent of the spreadsheets audited contained errors.[3] Embarrassing and high-profile errors and fraud have been attributed to spreadsheet errors.[4]

Spreadsheets can be evaluated using the following steps.[5]

1. Inventory the spreadsheets including name, description, department, frequency, and extent of changes.
2. Evaluate the use and complexity of the spreadsheets.
3. Determine the necessary level of controls for the spreadsheets.
4. Evaluate existing controls for the spreadsheets.
5. Develop action plans for remediating control deficiencies.

Controls should be placed to ensure that changes to spreadsheets are appropriate, only current versions of spreadsheets are used, access to spreadsheets is restricted, data input is accurate, data are secure, and the spreadsheets' documentation is appropriate. Procedures include life cycle analysis, backups, archiving, logic inspection, separation of duties, and overall analytics. The concepts underlying control activities in small or midsize organizations are likely to be similar to those in larger entities, but the formality with which they operate varies. Further, smaller entities can find that certain types of control activities are not relevant because of controls applied by management. For example, management's retention of authority for approving credit sales, significant purchases, and draw downs on lines of credit can provide strong control over those activities, lessening or removing the need for more detailed control activities. An appropriate separation of duties often appears to present difficulties in smaller organizations. Even companies that have only a few employees, however, can assign their responsibilities to achieve appropriate separation or, if that is not possible, to use management oversight of the incompatible activities to achieve control objectives.

Information and Communication

The information and communication component of internal control is a necessary prerequisite for achieving management's control objectives. To make effective decisions, managers must have access to timely, reliable, and relevant information. Information systems should be devised to identify data from external sources such as suppliers,

[3] R. Panko, "What We Know about Spreadsheet Errors," www.panko.cba.hawaii.edu/ssr/whatknow.htm.

[4] For examples, go to www.eusprig.org/stories.htm.

[5] PricewaterhouseCoopers, "The Use of Spreadsheets: Considerations for Section 404 of the Sarbanes-Oxley Act," July 2004.

customers, economic databases, and so on, as well as internal sources. Having superior information systems can be a part of an entity's strategy (e.g., Amazon, eBay, and Wal-Mart). Management evaluates the quality of information by determining whether the content is appropriate and the information is timely, current, accurate, and accessible. Note that these sometimes are contradictory. For example, waiting to ensure that information is accurate can cause it not to be timely.

Communication includes report production and distribution. The account balances are summarized in internal management reports and external financial statements. The internal reports are management's feedback for monitoring operations. The external reports are the financial information for outside investors, creditors, and others. Communication also involves expectations, responsibilities of individuals and groups, and other important matters. Specific duties must be made clear and people need to know how their activities relate to the work of others. People need to know what behavior is expected. Personnel also need to have a means of communicating significant information upstream in an organization. Outsiders also should know that fraudulent and unethical behavior by entity personnel is unacceptable and should be reported to management.

The information system produces a trail of operations (often referred to as an *audit trail*) from data identification to reports. You can visualize that the audit trail begins with the *source documents* (e.g., purchase orders, sales orders, etc.) and proceeds through to the financial reports.

Auditors often follow this trail frontward and backward, identifying and testing relevant control procedures along the way. They will follow it backward from the financial reports to the source documents to determine whether everything in the financial reports is supported by appropriate source documents (the *existence* or *occurrence* assertions). They will follow it forward from source documents to reports to determine whether everything that happened (transactions) was recorded in the accounts and reported in the financial statements (the *completeness* assertion).

Information systems in small or midsize organizations are likely to be less formal than in larger organizations, but their role is just as significant. Smaller entities with active management involvement may not need extensive descriptions of accounting procedures, sophisticated accounting records, or written policies. Communication may be less formal and easier to achieve in a small or midsize company than in a larger enterprise because the smaller organization has fewer levels and management has more visibility and availability.

Monitoring

Internal control systems need to be monitored. Management should assess the quality of control performance on a timely basis. Monitoring does *not* include regular management and supervisory control activities and other actions personnel take in performing their duties. It involves ongoing evaluation of the *controls*. Some monitoring controls include these:

- Operating managers' comparison of internal reports and published financial statements with their knowledge of the business.
- Analysis of customer complaints of amounts billed.
- Analysis of vendor complaints of amounts paid.
- Regulators' reports on compliance with laws and regulations (e.g., bank examiners' reports, IRS audits).
- Accounting managers' supervision of the accuracy and completeness of transaction processing.
- Periodic comparison of recorded amounts to actual assets and liabilities (e.g., internal auditors' inventory counts, receivables and payables confirmations, bank reconciliations).
- Internal auditors' reports on control effectiveness and recommendations for improvement.
- Training sessions for management and employees to heighten awareness of the importance of controls.

These elements of the monitoring component have a great deal in common with the controls included in the control procedures component. Indeed, some of the control procedures explained earlier in this chapter are monitoring activities as well (e.g., periodic comparison). For example, analyzing customer complaints for follow-up is a control procedure, but analyzing them to determine whether the complaints result from a weakness in other controls (e.g., a failure to compare shipping documents to customer orders) is a monitoring activity.

While the preceding procedures provide management daily monitoring opportunities, the audit committee provides the highest level of monitoring. The Treadway Commission stated, "To be effective, audit committees should exercise vigilant and informed oversight of the financial reporting process, including the entity's internal controls."[6]

Ongoing monitoring activities of small and midsize entities are more likely to be informal and are typically performed as a part of the overall management of the entity's operations. Management's close involvement in operations often will identify significant variances from expectations and inaccuracies in financial data.

Review Checkpoints

5.12 What is a control procedure?

5.13 What four general kinds of functional responsibilities should be performed by different departments or persons in a control system with good separation of duties?

5.14 What is an audit trail? Of what use is it in the audit process?

5.15 What is the difference between ITGCs and ITACs?

5.16 Describe five input controls that could be used to ensure that a customer's payment has been posted to the correct account.

5.17 Why are spreadsheet controls important to an auditor? Can you think of examples of complex calculations you have made with spreadsheets that might have contained errors?

5.18 Give some examples of everyday work an entity's management can use to enact the monitoring component of internal control. When are such activities control procedures and when are they monitoring activities?

INTERNAL CONTROL EVALUATION

LEARNING OBJECTIVE

4. Explain the phases of an evaluation of control and risk assessment and the documentation and extent of audit work required.

The five components of internal control are considered to be criteria for evaluating an entity's financial reporting controls and the bases for auditors' assessment of the risk of material misstatement (combined control and inherent risk) as it relates to financial statements. Thus, auditors must consider the five components in terms of (1) understanding a client's financial reporting controls and documenting that understanding, (2) assessing preliminary levels of control risk, and (3) testing the controls, reassessing control risk, and using that assessment to plan the remainder of the audit work.

Exhibit 5.7 places the internal control evaluation phases in perspective. In Phase 1, auditors are required to document their understanding of the client's internal control. For nonpublic entities, the audit team can halt the control evaluation process for the efficiency or effectiveness reasons. However, if the auditors want to justify a low-risk assessment to reduce the substantive audit procedures, the evaluation must be continued in Phase 3, the testing phase.

[6] Report of the National Commission on Fraudulent Financial Reporting, October 1987, p. 41.

EXHIBIT 5.7
**Phases of Internal
Control Evaluation**

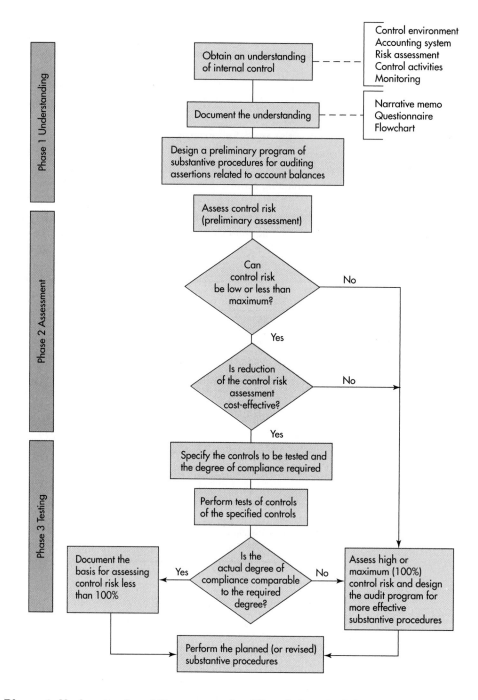

Phase 1: Understand and Document the Client's Internal Control

A major goal in audits is to be *efficient* without losing *effectiveness*. This means performing the work in minimum time and with minimum cost while still doing high-quality work to obtain sufficient appropriate evidence. The allocation of work times between control evaluation and substantive procedures is a cost–benefit trade-off. Generally, the more auditors know about good controls, the fewer substantive procedures they need to perform. Audit efficiency often can come at the cost of a loss of audit effectiveness (i.e., failure to find errors or frauds in the financial statements). This trade-off is one that keeps auditors awake at night.

Identifying Entity-Level Controls

The process of obtaining an understanding of internal control should occur early in the audit engagement. The procedures used to gain an understanding provide the audit team

EXHIBIT 5.8 Entity-Level Controls and Assessment

Entity-Level Controls	Assessment
Controls related to the control environment. Controls related to management override. Centralized processing and controls including shared service environments. Controls to monitor results of operations. Controls to monitor other controls.	The primary evidence is gathered through observation and inquiry and some examination of documents. The Phase 1 work should produce general knowledge of whether management's integrity, values, and operating style promote effective control consciousness throughout the entity.
Management's risk assessment.	The audit team next needs to gain an understanding of how the client assesses the control environment and responds to risk. If the client uses ERM, inquiring and obtaining documentation about other processes should suffice.
Period-end financial reporting process	After the audit team gains an understanding of the control environment and the client's risk assessment, its next task is to obtain an understanding of the accounting system's flow of transactions and other processes that mitigate financial reporting risk. This review should produce general knowledge about (1) the various classes of significant accounting transactions, (2) the types of material errors and frauds that could occur, and (3) the methods by which each significant class of transactions is authorized and initiated, documented and recorded, processed in the accounting system, and placed in financial reports and disclosures.
Policies that address significant business control and risk management practices	Accounting manuals should contain statements of control objectives and policies. Management should approve statements of specific accounting and control objectives and ensure that appropriate steps are taken to accomplish them. An entity's internal auditors and systems staff often review and evaluate this documentation. Independent auditors may review and study their work instead of doing the same tasks over again. Other sources of information include (1) previous experience with the entity as found in the prior year's audit, (2) responses to inquiries directed to client personnel, and (3) inspection of documents and records.

with an overall acquaintance with the control environment and management's risk assessment, the flow of transactions through the accounting system, and the design of some client control procedures. Gaining an understanding should be performed in a "top-down" risk-based manner that first examines entity-level controls (ELCs). Exhibit 5.8 presents the list of PCAOB's entity-level controls along with the auditors' methods of obtaining an understanding. Notice that they include parts or all of the COSO framework elements.

After identifying entity-level controls, the audit team next examines *significant accounts* and disclosures and their *relevant assertions*. An account's *significance* is based on the *inherent risk* of the account (i.e., the likelihood of containing a material misstatement before the consideration of internal control). While this determination is not based on quantitative measures alone, it is unlikely that a large account could be omitted from consideration. *Relevant assertions* are those that represent the possibility of a material misstatement. Thus, an assertion that does not represent meaningful risk of misstatement is not relevant (e.g., valuation of cash).

The most effective method used to gain an understanding of the flow of transactions, the points at which a misstatement could occur, and the controls management has implemented to address potential misstatements is through an observation of activities and operations made in a *walkthrough* of one or a few transactions. A **walkthrough** consists of a combination of inquiry and observation of entity operations while tracing one or more transactions through the audit trail from initiation of the transaction to its inclusion in the financial statements. Each client employee involved is asked to demonstrate the procedures that he

or she follows in processing the transaction. Additionally, reperformance of critical controls along the transaction trail can take place at this time to provide evidence of operating effectiveness. The walkthrough is an important step in gaining an understanding because often the information that is contained in manuals and understood by supervisors is not the same as the procedures actually being performed. People could change procedures to make them more efficient, they can forget procedures, or the procedures may not be passed along when new people are placed in the positions.

Document the Internal Control Understanding

Audit documentation of a decision to assess control risk as 100 percent (no reliance on internal control to reduce procedures) should explain reasons for the decision. However, for future reference in the following year's audit, the memorandum should contain an explanation of effectiveness-related or efficiency-related reasons for the assessment.

For decisions to assess control risk at lower than the maximum, audit documentation is required and should include records showing the audit team's understanding of the controls. The understanding can be summarized in the form of questionnaires, narratives, and flowcharts.

Internal Control Questionnaires The most efficient means to begin gathering evidence about an entity's internal control is to conduct a formal interview with knowledgeable managers, using the checklist form of **internal control questionnaire** illustrated in Exhibit 5.9. This questionnaire is organized under headings that identify questions related to relevant control objectives, as well as the overall control environment. All questionnaires are not organized like this, so auditors need to know the general transaction control objectives to know whether the questionnaire is complete. Likewise, if you are assigned to prepare an internal control questionnaire, you will need to be careful to include questions about each significant assertion.

Internal control questionnaires are designed to help the audit team obtain evidence about the control environment and about the accounting and control procedures that are considered good error-checking routines. Answers to the questions, however, should not be taken as final and definitive evidence about how well control actually functions. Evidence obtained through the interview process is hearsay evidence because its source is often the supervisor, not the person who actually performs the control work. This person could give answers that reflect what the system should be rather than what it really is. The person can be unaware of informal ways in which duties have been changed or can be innocently ignorant of the system details. Nevertheless, interviews and questionnaires are useful when a manager's responses suggest control weaknesses. An admission of weak control is fairly convincing.

An advantage of using internal control questionnaires is that auditors are less likely to forget to cover some important point. Questions generally are worded such that a "no" answer points out some weakness or control deficiency, thus making analysis easier. However, auditors should be aware that entity personnel know that "yes" answers are "good" and "no" answers are "bad," so they tend to tell auditors "yes" all the time. Also, internal control questionnaires tend to be inflexible. If a key question is not included on the list because the question is unique to a client, the auditor might not even know to ask the question. Thus, for new clients, other methods of gaining an understanding that are tailored to the client are preferable. (In practice, auditors typically use a combination of methods to document their understanding of the client's internal control.)

Narrative Descriptions One way to tailor inquiry procedures to a particular entity is to write a **narrative description** of each important control subsystem. Such a narrative would simply describe all environmental elements, the accounting system, and all control procedures. The narrative description can be efficient in audits of very small businesses. For larger companies, narratives can become too difficult to follow. They are also difficult to update.

EXHIBIT 5.9 Internal Control Questionnaire—Payroll Processing

	Yes/No	Comments
Control Environment		
1. Are all employees paid by check or direct deposit?		
2. Is a special payroll bank account used?		
3. Are payroll checks signed by persons who do not prepare checks or keep cash funds or accounting records?		
4. If a check-signing machine is used, are the signature plates controlled?		
5. Is the payroll bank account reconciled by someone who does not prepare, sign, or deliver paychecks?		
6. Are payroll department personnel rotated in their duties? Required to take vacations? Bonded?		
7. Is there a timekeeping department (function) independent of the payroll department?		
8. Are authorizations for deductions signed by the employees on file?		
Occurrence		
9. Are time cards or piecework reports prepared by the employee approved by her or his supervisor?		
10. Is a time clock or other electromechanical or computerized system used?		
11. Is the payroll register sheet signed by the employee preparing it and approved prior to payment?		
12. Are names of terminated employees reported in writing to the payroll department?		
13. Is the payroll periodically compared to personnel files?		
14. Are checks distributed by someone other than the employee's immediate supervisor?		
15. Are unclaimed wages deposited in a special bank account or otherwise controlled by a responsible officer?		
16. Do internal auditors conduct occasional surprise distributions of paychecks?		
Completeness		
17. Are names of newly hired employees reported in writing to the payroll department?		
18. Are blank payroll checks prenumbered and the numerical sequence checked for missing documents?		
Rights and Obligations		
19. Is a qualified person assigned to track retirement obligations?		
20. Is an actuary employed and are assumptions used reviewed by responsible officers?		
Valuation or Allocation		
21. Are all wage rates determined by contract or approved by a personnel officer?		
22. Are timekeeping and cost-accounting records (such as hours, dollars) reconciled with payroll department calculations of hours and wages?		
23. Are payrolls audited periodically by internal auditors?		
24. Are individual payroll records reconciled with quarterly tax reports?		
Classification		
25. Do payroll accounting personnel have instructions for classifying payroll debit entries?		
Cutoff		
26. Are monthly, quarterly, and annual wage accruals reviewed by an accounting officer?		

Accounting and Control System Flowcharts Another widely used method for documenting the auditors' understanding of accounting and control is to construct a flowchart. Many control-conscious companies have their own flowcharts and the auditors may use them instead of constructing their own. The advantages of flowcharts can be summarized by an old adage: "A picture is worth a thousand words." Flowcharts can enhance auditors' evaluations and annual updating of a chart is relatively easy with additions or deletions to the symbols and lines.

Construction of a flowchart takes time because an auditor must learn about the operating personnel involved in the system and gather samples of relevant documents. Thus, the information for the flowchart, like the narrative description, involves a lot of effort and

observation. When the flowchart is complete, however, the result is an easily evaluated, informative description of the system. Showing the various duties performed by one individual or group also provides graphic evidence of any conflicting responsibilities (i.e., lack of separation of duties).

For any flowcharting application, the chart must be understandable to an audit supervisor. Most flowcharts are now created with audit-specific flowcharting software, but also can be created with Excel or PowerPoint. The flowchart should communicate all relevant information and evidence about separation of responsibilities, authorization, and accounting and control procedures in an understandable, visual form. The starting point in the system, if possible, should be placed at the upper-left-hand corner. The flow of procedures and documents should be from left to right and from top to bottom as much as is possible. Narrative explanations should be written on the face of the chart as annotations or in a readily available reference key.

Exhibit 5.10 contains a flowchart representation of the beginning stages of a payroll processing system. This is a partial flowchart. The out connectors shown by the circled letters A and B indicate continuation on other flowcharts. Ultimately, the flowchart ends showing entries in accounting journals and ledgers. In Exhibit 5.10, you can see some characteristics of flowchart construction and some characteristics of this accounting system. By reading down the columns headed for each department, you can see that transaction initiation authority (both hiring and time card preparation) and custody of checks are separated.

Deciding Not to Test Controls Auditors of nonpublic entities can decide to stop the evaluation work in Phase 1 for either of two reasons. First, the audit team could conclude control is too poor to justify reductions of subsequent audit procedures. This conclusion is equivalent to assessing control risk at 100 percent and specifying extensive substantive procedures such as confirmation of all customer accounts as of year end. Essentially, this decision is a matter of audit *effectiveness*.

EXHIBIT 5.10 **Payroll System Flowchart**

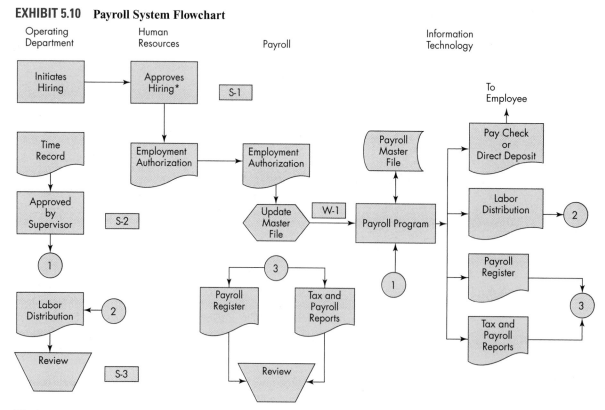

*Obtains W-4, determines wage rate based on contract or employment agreement, obtains deduction authorization.

AUDITING INSIGHT Bad Books Block County Audit

Travis County commissioners kept such poor financial records for four nonprofit entities they controlled that an audit could not be done. The four corporations were conduits for more than $630 million in low-interest financing for businesses. CPA D. Holliday of Holliday & Associates struggled to find words to describe the entities' records. "To say they are horrid is stretching it, because there weren't any records," Holliday told court commissioners.

Among the findings were (1) no records of purchase and redemption of certificates of deposit for hundreds of thousands of dollars, (2) the possibility that there may be certificates of deposit that the county officials do not know exist, (3) failure to keep bank statements, and (4) checking accounts that were not reconciled.

The former treasurer of the corporations said, "We had a very simple bookkeeping system. Money went in and went out. The system wasn't sophisticated because it wasn't needed."

Source: "Housing Programs Face Loss of U.S. Funds," *Austin American Statesman*, March 9, 1993, p. B-1.

Second, the audit team could decide that more time and effort would be spent testing controls to lower the control risk assessment than would be saved by being able to justify less-effective or fewer substantive procedures (providing the controls turn out to be working well). The cost of obtaining a low control risk assessment can be high. In this case, the conclusion is also equivalent to assessing control risk at 100 percent, but this time it is because the auditors lack knowledge about the effectiveness of controls, not because they have decided controls are poor. However, the result is the same: more extensive and effective substantive procedures are specified. For example, suppose the extensive testing of controls over the validity of payroll expenses is estimated to take 40 hours. If controls were excellent, suppose then the sample confirmation of payrolls as of November 1 (with subsequent review of the December 31 trial balance) would take 30 hours less to perform than confirmation of all accounts as of December 31. The additional work on controls is not economical. The decision to stop work on control risk assessment in this case is a matter of audit *efficiency*—it doesn't make sense to spend 40 hours testing controls to reduce substantive tests to 30 hours. Note again that this decision is appropriate for nonpublic companies; auditors must extensively test internal control over financial reporting for public companies.

Review Checkpoints

5.19 Must the overall understanding of internal control in Phase 1 always be followed by assessment and testing phases? Explain.

5.20 Where can an auditor find a client's documentation of the accounting system?

Phase 2: Assess the Control Risk (Preliminary)

After completing Phase 1—obtaining an understanding of control and designing a preliminary audit program—the audit team should be able to make a preliminary assessment of control risk. At this preliminary stage, the audit team also may use their internal control findings from the previous year's audit. One way to make the assessment is to analyze the control strengths and weaknesses. Strengths are specific features of good general and application controls. Weaknesses are the lack of controls in particular areas. The auditors' findings and preliminary conclusions should be written up for the audit files.

Strengths and weaknesses should be documented in a *bridge workpaper,* so called because it connects ("bridges") the control evaluation to subsequent audit procedures. The major strengths and weaknesses apparent in the flowchart (Exhibit 5.10) can be

EXHIBIT 5.11
Bridge Workpaper

Apollo Shoes, Inc
Payroll Processing Controls
December 31, 2008

Prepared by *RJR* *10/20/08*
Reviewed by *TJL* *10/21/08*

	Strength/Weakness	Audit Implication	Test of Controls Audit Program	Compensating Substantive Procedures
S-1	Supervisor approval is indicated on timecard.	This ensures that work was actually performed.	Select a sample of timecards and examine for supervisor signature.	
S-2	Hiring of employees is approved by personnel department.	This ensures that hiring is authorized and based on company policies.	Using the S-1 sample, examine personnel file for approval.	
S-3	Supervisor examines labor distribution.	Additional unauthorized payroll costs will not be charged to an operating department.	Using the S-1 sample, examine labor distribution for supervisor initials.	
W-1	Payroll master file update summaries are not returned to Personnel Department for review.	Errors in master file updates, which could result in incorrect payroll, will not be identified befor processing.		The information used in payroll calculations.

summarized as in Exhibit 5.11. On the flowchart, the strengths are indicated by the S-# and the weaknesses by W-#. In the bridge workpaper, the "Test of Controls Audit Program" column contains tests of controls for auditing the control strengths and "Compensating Substantive Procedures" are related to the weaknesses (the last column in Exhibit 5.11). Auditors do not need to perform tests of controls on weaknesses just to prove they are weaknesses. Doing so would be inefficient. Instead, the audit team identifies substantive procedures that compensate for the control weakness to obtain sufficient appropriate evidence regarding the fairness of the recorded amounts.

In terms of control risk assessment, at this stage the control risk related to the payroll cycle can be set very high (e.g., 95 or 100 percent). The three control strengths, however, relate to good control over payroll. The auditors probably will want to rely on these controls to reduce the substantive procedures related to payroll. Tests of controls must be performed to obtain evidence about whether controls that are apparent strengths actually operate as described. The "Test of Controls Audit Program" column of Exhibit 5.11 for each of the strengths is a statement of tests of controls, which consist of procedures designed to produce evidence of how effectively the controls operated in practice. If they operate with the required level of frequency (i.e., controls are followed by employees a high percentage of the time), control risk can be assessed below the maximum. If they do not operate with the required level of effectiveness, the final conclusion is to assess a high or maximum control risk, revise the account balance audit plan to take the control weakness into account, and then proceed with the audit work.

Apparent weaknesses in control procedures are matters of concern. However, absence of a control at one stage may be offset by *compensating controls* at another stage. For example, the supervisor's review of the labor distribution (S-3) can be sufficient to catch any master file errors (W-1). Of course, it usually is more efficient to catch errors early rather than late, but controls still can be considered effective for the accounting records and financial statements.

Weaknesses in manual and computerized controls become a part of independent auditors' assessment of control risk. Lack of input controls can permit data to be lost or double counted and poor processing controls can permit accounting calculation, allocation,

and classification errors to occur. Poor output controls over distribution of reports and other output (negotiable checks, for example) can be the source of misstatements that could make financial statements materially misleading.

The distinction between the understanding and documenting phase and the preliminary control risk assessment phase is useful for understanding the audit work. However, most auditors in practice do the two together, not as separate and distinct audit tasks.

Phase 3: Perform Tests of Controls and Reassess Risk of Material Misstatement

When auditors reach the third phase of an evaluation of internal control, they will have identified specific control procedures on which risk could be assessed below maximum (100 percent). To reduce the control risk assessment, auditors must determine (1) the required degree of control procedure effectiveness and (2) whether the control procedure is operating at that required level. The required level of effectiveness is the auditors' decision criterion for good control performance. Knowing that compliance cannot realistically be expected to be perfect, auditors could decide, for example, that evidence of using time cards to validate payroll recordings 96 percent of the time is sufficient to assess a low control risk for the audit of payroll (looking for overstatement in payroll expense).

A test of controls is a two-part statement. Part 1 is an identification of the data population from which a sample of items will be selected for audit. Tests of controls, when performed, should be applied to samples of transactions and control procedures executed *throughout the period* under audit. The reason for this requirement is that the conclusions about controls will be generalized to the whole period under audit. Part 2 is an expression of an action taken to produce relevant evidence. In general, the action is to determine whether (1) the selected items correspond to a standard (e.g., mathematical accuracy) and (2) the selected items agree with information in another data population.

Perform Tests of Controls

When the audit team determines that a specific control procedure could have a significant effect in reducing control risk to a low level for a specific assertion, they perform tests of controls to obtain sufficient audit evidence to support the conclusion about the effectiveness of the design or operation of that control procedure. There are four methods of testing controls: inquiry, observation, document examination, and reperformance.

Inquiry is a procedure that generally involves the collection of oral (but sometimes written) evidence from employees regarding the existence of control procedures. While very efficient, inquiry alone generally will not provide sufficient audit evidence to support a conclusion about the effectiveness of design or operation of a specific control. In other words, just because client employees say that they are performing a control procedure does not mean that they are actually doing so.

Generally, auditors will inquire about the existence of control procedures and then corroborate the oral evidence by observing that the client-described control procedures are actually being performed. *Observation* amounts to auditors' unobtrusive eyewitness observation of employees at their jobs performing control procedures. Observation is typically used when certain control procedures such as separation of employees' duties leave no documents behind. Observation also can produce evidence of access controls such as password-secured access to the computerized information system, locked doors, and security guards. The limitation of observation is that this test of control is performed as of one point in time (usually near year end) and what is observed at that point in time may not be representative of prior time periods.

Some tests of controls depend on documentary evidence such as a payroll entry supported by a time card. In these cases, *document examination* for evidence of signatures, initials, checklists, reconciliations, and the like provides better evidence than procedures that leave no documentary tracks. Inspection might be enough; the auditors may look to see whether the documents were marked with an initial, signature, or stamp to indicate

they had been checked. For example, auditors could examine canceled checks for authorized signatures, inspect voucher packets for the initials of the employee who matched vendor invoices with supporting purchase orders and receiving reports, or examine bank reconciliations to make sure that have been performed on a timely basis.

Generally, the most effective test of controls is reperformance. *Reperformance* can involve any client control procedure such as recalculating vendor invoice extensions. In this case, the auditors perform the arithmetic calculations and compare them to those that entity's employees were supposed to have performed. The key difference between document examination and reperformance is that, with the former, auditors inspect documents for evidence that employees have performed the control procedure; reperformance provides evidence that the control procedure was (or was not) done correctly.

The auditors' choice of which test of control to use depends on the nature and importance of the control. To obtain a lower risk of material misstatement, more persuasive forms of evidence need to be obtained. Exhibit 5.12 puts controls in the perspective of the payroll functions with examples of specific assertions.

Direction of the Tests of Controls The tests of controls in Exhibit 5.12 are designed to test the payroll accounting in two directions. One is the completeness direction, in which the control performance of audit interest is the matching of personnel file content to payroll department files and the payroll register. The objective of this test is to ensure that all

EXHIBIT 5.12 Assertions about Classes of Transactions and Events for the Period: Payroll Cycle

Assertion	Controls	Tests of Controls
Occurrence—Payroll and related events that have been recorded have occurred and pertain to the entity.	Payroll accounting is separated from personnel and supervision. Labor usage reports are compared to job time tickets or listings of time clocked. Labor usage approved by payroll supervisor.	Observe separation of duties. Vouch labor costs to labor reports. Vouch labor reports to time tickets or computerized listing. Examine documentary evidence of supervisor approval.
Completeness—All payroll events that occurred should have been recorded.	All documents are prenumbered and numerical sequence reviewed. Labor costs reviewed by supervisors and compared to budgets. The personnel department notifies the payroll department of new hires to include in payroll.	Account for numerical sequence of selected job cost tickets and paychecks. Examine documentary evidence of supervisor review of labor costs. Trace a sample of employees in the personnel file to payroll department files and the payroll register.
Accuracy—Payroll amounts and related data have been recorded accurately.	Payroll entries are reviewed by person independent of preparation. Payroll expenses are budgeted by department and compared to actual.	Examine evidence of review. Examine documentary evidence of budget comparison.
Classification—Payroll-related events are recorded in the proper accounts.	Job cost sheets are posted weekly and summary journal entries of work-in-process and of work completed prepared monthly. Payroll supervisor is required to approve distribution of payroll expense accounts and to compare payroll costs to budget.	Verify that payroll account distribution and job cost sheets agree. Examine supervisor signature on payroll reports. Note evidence of comparison to budget.
Cutoff—Payroll events have been recorded in the correct accounting period.	Payroll reports are prepared weekly and transmitted to cost accounting.	Check that the date of payroll reports agrees with dates in weekly journal entries.

EXHIBIT 5.13
Dual-Direction Test of Payroll Controls

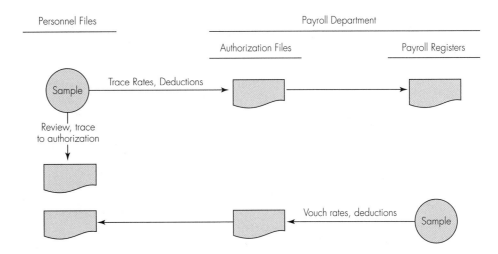

valid employees are included in the entity's payroll. Exhibit 5.13 shows that the sample for this direction is taken from the population of personnel files. The procedures trace the personnel department authorizations to the payroll department files.

The purpose of the occurrence test is to ensure that all employees included in the payroll are bona fide employees of the organization. Because payroll provides access to cash, this cycle is highly susceptible to fraudulent activity on the part of an organization's employees. If a fictitious employee were created and added to the payroll, his or her pay could be deposited into another person's account. This is relatively difficult to detect in the era of direct deposit of paychecks. As a result, this test is ordinarily considered far more important than the completeness direction.

Reassess the Control Risk

The audit team should evaluate the evidence obtained from an understanding of the client's internal control and from the related tests of control procedures. If control risk (and the related risk of material misstatement) is assessed very low, the substantive procedures on the account balances can be limited in cost-saving ways. As examples, a surprise payroll distribution might be considered unnecessary or the auditors might decide it is appropriate to place considerable reliance on management reports generated by the payroll system. On the other hand, if tests of control procedures reveal weaknesses (e.g., improper separation of duties, inaccurate cost reports, inaccurate tax returns, or lax personnel policies), substantive procedures need to be added to lower the risk of failing to detect material misstatements in the financial statements.

Final assessment of control risk (and consequently, the risk of material misstatement) is complicated. In the sampling modules (Modules E and F), you will find explanations of sampling methods for performing tests of controls of the type illustrated in Exhibit 5.12. Further discussion of assessing the risk of material misstatement (including control risk) will be saved for these modules. However, recognize that the final evaluation of an entity's internal control is the assessment of the control risk related to each assertion. These assessments are the auditors' expression of the effectiveness of control procedures for preventing, detecting, and correcting specific errors and frauds in management's financial statement assertions.

An assessment of control risk should be coordinated with the final audit plan. The final account balance audit plan includes the list of **substantive procedures** to detect material misstatements in account balances and financial statement disclosures. Note that the reassessment of control risk can go only one direction: upward. If the controls are not functioning as described, they cannot be relied on. On the other hand, even if weak controls are functioning, they are still weak and do not reduce risk of misstatement. One exception occurs: Should you find you were in error during the understanding of controls phase and there are additional controls you were not aware of. In that case, lowering control risk could be justified.

You have studied tests of controls and substantive procedures as if they were easily distinguishable. Be advised, however, that general audit procedures can be used as **dual-purpose tests** (i.e., both as tests of controls and as substantive procedures). A single procedure can produce both control and substantive evidence and, thus, serve both purposes. For example, a selection of recorded payroll entries could be used to (1) vouch payroll to time cards and (2) calculate the correct dollar amount of payroll. The first procedure provides relevant information about control compliance. The second provides dollar-value information that can help measure an amount of misstatement in the book balance of payroll. Another example is the confirmation of payroll procedure (sending letters to employees asking how much they were paid). This procedure has a primary substantive purpose, but when confirmation replies tell about significant or systematic errors, the evidence is relevant to control evaluation as well as to dollar-value measurement. Most audit procedures serve dual purposes and yield evidence about both controls and financial statement assertions.

Review Checkpoints

5.21 What are the advantages and disadvantages of documenting internal control by using (1) an internal control questionnaire, (2) a narrative memorandum, and (3) a flowchart?

5.22 What is a *bridge workpaper*? Describe its content and its connection to the tests of controls and account balance audit programs.

5.23 What are *tests of controls*?

5.24 What is the difference between inspection and reperformance in tests of controls?

5.25 What purposes are served by a dual-purpose test?

ADDITIONAL PROCEDURES REQUIRED BY *AUDITING STANDARD NO. 5*

LEARNING OBJECTIVE

5. Describe additional responsibilities for management and auditors of public companies required by Sarbanes-Oxley and *Auditing Standard No. 5.*

PCAOB *Auditing Standard No. 5 (AS 5)* details the work that external auditors of public entities must perform to comply with section 404 of Sarbanes-Oxley. The audit team must plan and perform the audit to obtain *reasonable assurance* about whether the entity maintained effective control over financial reporting. Reasonable assurance is understood by the SEC to be not absolute, but a "high level of assurance." For the auditors, this duty entails an increased amount of internal control testing concerning the client's financial reporting processes and procedures. The audit of internal controls must be integrated with the financial statement audit and cannot be performed as a separate engagement. The controls subject to the reports are those that exist at the end of the year being reported on.

The procedures listed in the previous section are those required by GAAS's second standard of field work. Auditors must obtain an understanding of internal controls to determine the *nature, timing,* and *extent* of audit procedures. If they plan to rely on controls to reduce substantive procedures, they must test the controls for effectiveness. However, GAAS are designed for an audit of *financial statements,* but Sarbanes-Oxley requires an audit of *financial reporting controls.* Thus, the procedures related to internal control in an integrated audit performed under *AS 5* are more extensive than those in a GAAS audit for a nonpublic entity.

Requirements

Much of the initial work, including documentation and testing of controls, is done by employees of the client including management, the internal audit staff, and outside parties hired by management. *AS 5* encourages the audit team to use the work of internal auditors,

but the audit team must evaluate the internal auditors' competence and objectivity and must perform some tests of their work. Additionally, the audit team's own work must provide the *principal evidence* for the audit opinion on internal controls.

Another important difference between *AS 5* and GAAS is that the audit of internal control is *as of the end of the fiscal year*. However, to meet the requirements of GAAS, the audit team must understand and evaluate internal control for the *entire period* to determine its effect on the nature, timing, and extent of substantive procedures.

	Internal Control Assessment	**Financial Statement Audit**
Scope	Test each relevant control procedure each year	Test relevant control procedures if relying on them
Reporting	Opinion on the operating effectiveness of internal control	Opinion on the conformity of the financial statements with GAAP
Timing	Evaluate operating effectiveness of internal control as of the fiscal year end	Evaluate operating effectiveness of internal control throughout the fiscal year

AS 5 emphasizes the use of a six-step audit procedure to evaluate the opertaing effectiveness of financial reporting controls:

1. *Planning the engagement.* The audit team must be aware of the additional requirements and incorporate into the planning of the engagement any additional knowledge required and tests that need to be performed. Evaluation must be done for all relevant assertions for all significant accounts or disclosures. Thus, significant accounts, locations, and assertions must be identified. A difficult decision in auditing controls of global organizations is deciding which locations are significant and must be visited. Each location is evaluated based on size, risks, and whether risks are mitigated by entitywide controls. The key to determining whether an account, location, or assertion is significant is whether there is a more-than-remote possibility that a material misstatement could be associated with it. Just as *control risk* is used to determine the nature, timing, and extent of substantive procedures, *inherent risk* is used to determine the nature, timing, and extent of tests of controls.

2. *Using a top-down approach to gain an understanding.* As mentioned earlier, the top-down approach focuses on the threats to the financial reporting process. The audit team's first step in gaining an understanding should focus on entity-level controls (ELCs) that have a pervasive impact on control procedures at the process, transaction, or application level. The team next moves down to the significant accounts and disclosures and their *relevant* assertions. By relevant, we mean that the assertion has a reasonable possibility of containing a material misstatement. The audit team is required to understand the working of the internal control process over financial reporting. This aspect of the standard emphasizes performance of a *walkthrough* of the internal control process by the audit team members. Typically, the use of a walkthrough in conducting internal control testing related to PCAOB is more comprehensive than the use of a walkthrough in the financial statement audit.

3. *Testing controls.* Based upon its identification of significant controls over financial reporting in the previous step, the audit team decides which controls to test. The audit team considers both *design effectiveness* as well as *operating effectiveness.*

- **Design effectiveness** determines whether the controls over financial reporting, *if operating effectively,* would be expected to prevent or detect errors or fraud that could result in a material misstatement in the financial statements. The evaluation and testing for each assertion must be performed annually. After an understanding of internal controls is gained through inquiry, inspection, and observation, the controls are evaluated for the possibility that the controls would not prevent or detect a misstatement. This includes examining general and application controls using techniques discussed in Module H.

- **Operating effectiveness** is whether the control is *operating as designed* and whether the person performing the control possesses the necessary authority and qualifications to perform the control effectively. The tests of operating effectiveness are similar to a test of controls discussed previously. A sample of transactions is examined using inquiry, observation, inspection, and reperformance. Tests of controls are not performed if design is not effective.

4. *Evaluating control deficiencies.* Whether the result of a design deficiency or an operating deficiency, an **internal control deficiency** exists when the design or operation of a control does not allow the entity's management or employees to detect or prevent misstatements in a timely fashion. A *design deficiency* is a problem relating to either a necessary control that is missing or an existing control that is so poorly designed that it fails to satisfy the control's objective. An *operating deficiency,* on the other hand, occurs when a properly designed control is either ignored or inappropriately applied (possibly because employees are poorly trained). More serious internal control deficiencies can be categorized into one of two groups, significant deficiencies or material weaknesses, depending on their severity.

- **Significant deficiencies** are defined as conditions, or combinations of conditions, that could adversely affect the organization's ability to initiate, record, process, and report financial data in the financial statements. While not material, they are important enough to bring to the attention of those charged with governance (usually the audit committee). Some examples follow:
 - Absence of appropriate separation of duties.
 - Absence of appropriate reviews and approvals of transactions.
 - Evidence of failure of control procedures.

- A **material weakness** in internal control is defined as a deficiency, or combination of deficiencies, that results in a *reasonable possibility* that a *material misstatement* would not be prevented or detected on a timely basis. The following circumstances should be regarded as strong indicators that a material weakness exists:
 - Restatement of previously issued financial statements to reflect the correction of a misstatement.
 - Evidence of material misstatements (caught by the audit team) that were not prevented or detected by the client's internal controls.
 - Ineffective oversight of the financial reporting process by the entity's audit committee.
 - Indication of fraud (either material or immaterial) by senior management.

The difference between a significant deficiency and a material weakness is the (1) *likelihood* and (2) *materiality* that a potential (or actual) misstatement would not be detected on a timely basis.

5. *Wrapping up: forming an opinion on the effectiveness of internal control over financial reporting.* Auditors are required to issue an opinion on the effectiveness of internal controls. They do so by evaluating evidence obtained from all sources, including the audit team's testing of controls, any misstatements detected during the financial statement audit, and any identified control deficiencies and material weaknesses. As with reports on financial statements, auditors can issue one of three types of opinions on internal controls:

- *Unqualified.* No material weaknesses exist.
- *A disclaimer of opinion.* The audit team cannot perform all of the procedures considered necessary.
- *Adverse opinion.* One or more material weaknesses exist.

Note that since the opinion on internal controls is as of the end of the fiscal year, the entity may be able to correct or remediate deficiencies or weaknesses after they are

AUDITING INSIGHT Where the Internal Control Problems Lie

Moody's Investor Service carefully examines the internal control reports of each company that it follows and recently published the results of the third year of reporting under Sarbanes-Oxley's Section 404. Notice that the number of problems appears to be declining as section 404's rigorous internal control guidelines are implemented.

	2004	2005	2006
Weaknesses related to entity-level controls	30	34	24
Weaknesses related to controls over account balances and transactions	50	20	15
Delinquent filers	17	21	16
	97	75	55

The most common entity-level control weaknesses involved ineffective accounting personnel in companywide functions, pervasive ineffective processes, and stock option backdating. The weaknesses in processing controls related to income taxes (36 percent), accounts payable and accrued liabilities, revenues and related receivables, derivative instruments, and leasing. In general, these areas are characterized by complex accounting involving estimates, judgments, and nonroutine transactions or events. Delinquent filers are those companies that missed filing deadlines because their evaluations were not complete; many of the current delinquent filers were also delinquent filers in either one or both of the previous reporting periods.

Source: Moody's Investor Service, "The Third Year of Section 404 Reporting on Internal Control," May 2007.

detected. However, the audit team must have sufficient time to test the design effectiveness and operating effectiveness of the remediated control before providing an unqualified opinion.[7]

In addition to expressing an opinion on the effectiveness of the entity's internal control over financial reporting, the audit team also should evaluate the completeness and presentation of **management's annual report on internal control over financial reporting.** The auditors also must obtain written representations from management (1) acknowledging its responsibility for establishing and maintaining effective internal control over financial reporting; (2) stating that it has performed an evaluation and made a conclusion about the effectiveness of the entity's internal control over financial reporting; (3) disclosing to the auditor any frauds resulting in a material misstatement to the entity's financial statements (as well as any other immaterial fraud that involves key managers), all significant deficiencies, and any material weaknesses identified during its evaluation; and (4) stating that management did not use the auditors' procedures performed during the audits of internal control over financial reporting or the financial statements as part of the basis for management's assessment of the effectiveness of internal control over financial reporting.

6. *Reporting on internal control.* The final step in the process is reporting on internal control over financial reporting. For the auditors' report on internal control, two options are available. One option is to have two separate reports: one on the fairness of the entity's financial statements (presented earlier in Chapter 2) and a separate report on internal control over financial reporting. Each report would be separately titled, dated (although using the same date), and signed. The auditors' separate report on internal control is discussed in detail in the following section. The second option is to prepare a *combined report* that expresses one opinion on the financial statements and a second on the effectiveness of internal control over financial reporting. An example of a combined auditors' report on internal control over financial reporting and financial statements is shown in Chapter 12.

[7] Clients may request auditors to report separately on elimination of material weaknesses. Guidance on preparing such a report is provided by PCAOB's *AS 4.*

Review Checkpoints

5.26 What is management's responsibility for reporting on internal control over financial reporting?

5.27 What are the six steps followed by auditors in examining internal control over financial reporting?

5.28 What is (a) a *significant deficiency* and (b) a *material weakness*?

5.29 What options are available to the auditor for presenting reports on the entity's financial statements and internal control over financial reporting?

AUDITOR REPORTS ON INTERNAL CONTROL OVER FINANCIAL REPORTING

LEARNING OBJECTIVE

6. List the major components of the auditors' report on internal control over financial reporting.

As noted earlier in this chapter, in addition to the auditors' report on the entity's financial statements, *AS 5* imposes the following reporting requirements for SEC registrants related to the entity's internal control over financial reporting at the balance sheet date:

- Management's report on its assessment of the internal control over financial reporting.
- The auditors' report on internal control over financial reporting.

The **auditors' report on internal control over financial reporting** provides an opinion on the effectiveness of the entity's internal control over financial reporting. This opinion will be based on tests of the operating effectiveness of the entity's internal control policies and procedures over financial reporting. An example of a standard, unqualified report is shown in Exhibit 5.14. Until recently, auditors were required to evaluate and express an opinion on *management's assessment* of its internal control over financial reporting, but this responsibility was eliminated by *AS 5*.

As the exhibit indicates, the auditors' report includes the following key components:

- A title that includes the word *independent*.
- Statements regarding the responsibility of the auditors and management with respect to the assessment and evaluation of internal control, as well as the title of management's report on internal control over financial reporting.
- A paragraph indicating that the engagement was conducted in accordance with standards established by the Public Company Accounting Oversight Board, with a brief description of the procedures performed in the engagement.
- The definition of internal control over financial reporting.
- An identification of the inherent limitations of internal control over financial reporting.
- The auditors' opinion on whether the entity maintained effective internal control over financial reporting. The opinion in the above report represents an **unqualified opinion on internal control over financial reporting.**
- A reference to the auditors' opinion on the financial statements, indicating the type of opinion expressed.
- The date of the report.

Review Checkpoints

5.30 Describe the major components of the auditors' standard, unqualified report on internal control over financial reporting.

EXHIBIT 5.14 **Standard Report on Internal Control over Financial Reporting**

Title	**Report of Independent Registered Public Accounting Firm**
Address	To the Board of Directors and Shareholders Vandalay Enterprises, Inc.
Introductory paragraph	We have audited Vandalay Enterprises, Inc.'s internal control over financial reporting as of December 31, 2008, based on control criteria established in Internal Control—Integrated Framework issued by the Committee of Sponsoring Organizations of the Treadway Commission (COSO). Vandalay Enterprises, Inc.'s management is responsible for maintaining effective internal control over financial reporting, and for its assessment of the effectiveness of internal control over financial reporting, included in the accompanying Management's Report on Internal Control over Financial Reporting. Our responsibility is to express an opinion on the company's internal control over financial reporting based on our audits.
Scope paragraph	We conducted our audits in accordance with the standards of the Public Company Accounting Oversight Board (United States). Those standards require that we plan and perform the audits to obtain reasonable assurance about whether effective internal control over financial reporting was maintained in all material respects. Our audit of internal control over financial reporting included obtaining an understanding of internal control over financial reporting, assessing the risk that a material weakness exists, and testing and evaluating the design and operating effectiveness of internal control based on the assessed risk. Our audits also included performing such other procedures as we considered necessary in the circumstances. We believe that our audit provides a reasonable basis for our opinion.
Definition paragraph	A company's internal control over financial reporting is a process designed to provide reasonable assurance regarding the reliability of financial reporting and the preparation of financial statements for external purposes in accordance with generally accepted accounting principles. A company's internal control over financial reporting includes those policies and procedures that (1) pertain to the maintenance of records that, in reasonable detail, accurately and fairly reflect the transactions and dispositions of the assets of the company; (2) provide reasonable assurance that transactions are recorded as necessary to permit preparation of financial statements in accordance with generally accepted accounting principles, and that receipts and expenditures of the company are being made only in accordance with authorizations of management and directors of the company; and (3) provide reasonable assurance regarding prevention or timely detection of unauthorized acquisition, use, or disposition of the company's assets that could have a material effect on the financial statements.
Inherent limitations paragraph	Because of its inherent limitations, internal control over financial reporting may not prevent or detect misstatements. Also, projections of any evaluation of effectiveness to future periods are subject to the risk that controls may become inadequate because of changes in conditions, or that the degree of compliance with the policies or procedures may deteriorate.
Opinion paragraph	In our opinion, Vandalay Enterprises, Inc., maintained, in all material respects, effective internal control over financial reporting as of December 31, 2008, based on control criteria established in Internal Control—Integrated Framework issued by the Committee of Sponsoring Organizations of the Treadway Commission (COSO).
Paragraph on financial statement report	We have also audited, in accordance with the standards of the Public Company Accounting Oversight Board (United States), the balance sheets of Vandalay Enterprises, Inc., as of December 31, 2008 and 2007 and related statements of income, comprehensive income, shareholders' equity, and cash flows for each of the three years in the period ended December 31, 2008 and our report dated March 7, 2009 expressed an unqualified opinion thereon.
Signature	*Costanza & Son, CPAs* New York, NY
Date	March 7, 2009

MODIFICATIONS TO THE AUDITORS' STANDARD REPORT ON INTERNAL CONTROL OVER FINANCIAL REPORTING

LEARNING OBJECTIVE

7. Describe situations in which the auditors' report on internal control over financial reporting would be modified.

The report in Exhibit 5.14 expresses an unqualified opinion on the effectiveness of the entity's internal control over financial reporting. The standard unqualified report on internal control may be modified for two reasons: (1) the existence of material weaknesses in internal control over financial reporting and/or (2) the existence of a limitation in the scope of the engagement. These modifications, along with modifications for other factors, are discussed in the following subsections.

Material Weaknesses in the Entity's Internal Control over Financial Reporting

Recall that a *material weakness* in internal control is defined as a deficiency, or combination of deficiencies, that results in a reasonable possibility that a material misstatement would not be prevented or detected on a timely basis. If the audit team identifies a material weakness in internal control, the firm expresses an *adverse opinion* on the effectiveness of the entity's internal control over financial reporting. As shown in Exhibit 5.15, the standard report on internal control over financial reporting would be modified (in the exhibit, modifications are shown in bold italic type) as follows:

- Include a paragraph immediately following the inherent limitations paragraph that defines a material weakness.
- Describe any material weakness(es) identified during the audit as well as an identification of the material weakness(es) described in management's assessment. (Note: If any identified material weakness has been omitted from or not presented fairly in management's assessment, the auditors' report should so state, as well as disclose any information necessary to fairly describe the material weakness.) The description should provide specific information about the nature of the material weakness and its effect on the presentation of the company's financial statements issued during the existence of the weakness.
- Modify the opinion paragraph to indicate that because of the effect of the material weakness(es) identified, the company has *not* maintained an effective internal control over financial reporting. This is referred to as an **adverse opinion on internal control over financial reporting.**

The firm also may express an adverse opinion if management's report on internal control is incomplete or improperly presents a disclosure about a material weakness. In addition to the adverse opinion, the auditors' report would include an explanatory paragraph describing the situation.

AUDITING INSIGHT Material Weaknesses

The first round of reports on internal control over financial reporting identified the following material weaknesses:

AIG	Ability of former executives to "circumvent internal controls over financial reporting"
General Electric	Accounting for hedge transactions
Kroger	Determination of deferred income tax balances
Princeton Review	Revenue recognition
Sharper Image	Net income overstated because of incorrect cost of goods sold
Toys "R" Us	Accounting for leases and leasehold improvements

Source: "Imagine All the Material Weaknesses," *Forbes*, August 15, 2005, p. 28.

EXHIBIT 5.15 Report on Internal Control over Financial Reporting If a Material Weakness Exists

Title	**Report of Independent Registered Public Accounting Firm**
Address	To the Board of Directors and Shareholders Apollo Shoes, Inc.
Introductory paragraph	[Standard introductory paragraph]
Scope paragraph	[Standard scope paragraph]
Definition paragraph	[Standard definition paragraph]
Inherent limitations paragraph	[Standard inherent limitations paragraph]
Explanatory paragraphs	*A material weakness in internal control is defined as a deficiency, or combination of deficiencies, that results in a reasonable possibility that a material misstatement would not be prevented or detected on a timely basis.* *During the fiscal year ended December 31, 2008, Apollo Shoes, Inc., senior managers were able to override internal controls over financial reporting. This material weakness resulted in accounting errors that were corrected prior to the issuance of the financial statements for the year ended December 31, 2008. Given the nature of the transactions and processes involved and the potential for a misstatement to occur as a result of the internal control deficiency existing on December 31, 2008, we have concluded that there is a reasonable possibility that a material misstatement in the annual or interim financial statements would not have been prevented or detected by internal controls over financial reporting.* *This material weakness was considered in determining the nature, timing, and extent of audit tests applied in our audit of the 2008 financial statements, and this report does not affect our report dated January 29, 2009 on those financial statements.*
Opinion paragraph	In our opinion, *because of the effect of the material weakness described above on the achievement of the objectives of the control criteria, Apollo Shoes, Inc., has not maintained* effective internal control over financial reporting as of December 31, 2008, in all material respects, based on the COSO criteria.
Paragraph on financial statement report	[Standard financial statement report paragraph]
Signature	Smith & Smith CPAs Shoetown, Maine
Date	January 29, 2007

Effect of an Adverse Opinion on Internal Control on Opinion on Financial Statements

One issue raised by the preceding discussion concerns how a material weakness that results in an adverse opinion on the effectiveness of the entity's internal control over financial reporting affects the opinion on the financial statements. For example, could the auditor still issue an unqualified opinion on the entity's financial statements? Assuming that no material misstatements were detected, the auditor could issue an unqualified opinion on the entity's financial statements. In addition, as shown earlier in Exhibit 5.15, the following language would be included in the report in the paragraph describing the material weakness(es): "This material weakness was considered in determining the nature, timing, and extent of audit tests applied in our audit of the 2008 financial statements, and this report does not affect our report dated January 29, 2009, on those financial statements."

Restriction on the Scope of the Engagement

During the engagement, auditors could encounter scope limitations on their ability to evaluate the effectiveness of the entity's internal control over financial reporting. In

AUDITING INSIGHT DOH! PricewaterhouseCoopers Issues
Disclaimer on Krispy Kreme

Recall the problems admitted by **Krispy Kreme's** management in its report on internal controls in Exhibit 5.1? **Pricewaterhouse-Coopers** found the following in its 2005 integrated audit of the company's internal control:

1. Krispy Kreme's management did not complete its assessment of internal control over financial reporting.
2. A total of 10 material weaknesses were identified, some of which represented very basic elements of the control environment.
3. The auditors acknowledged that these weaknesses resulted in financial statement restatements.
4. Krispy Kreme's management restricted PwC from completing its own assessment, resulting in a disclaimer of opinion on the effectiveness of internal control.

As a result, PwC was forced to issue the following disclaimer in its 2005 auditors' report on internal control over financial reporting at Krispy Kreme:

Since (a) the Company was unable to complete its assessment of the effectiveness of internal control over financial reporting as of January 30, 2005 and (b) management further restricted the scope of our work by directing that we not complete our (i) testing and evaluation of the effectiveness of the design of the Company's internal control over financial reporting, (ii) testing of operating effectiveness of the Company's internal control over financial reporting, and (iii) review and evaluation of the results of management's testing and of the control deficiencies noted in management's incomplete assessment, and because we were unable to complete our procedures to satisfy ourselves as to the effectiveness of the Company's internal control over financial reporting, the scope of our work was not sufficient to enable us to express, and we do not express, an opinion either on management's assessment or on the effectiveness of the Company's internal control over financial reporting, including identifying all material weaknesses that might exist as of January 30, 2005

addition to general scope limitations encountered as part of the audit engagement, an additional scope limitation related to internal control over financial reporting could arise when management has implemented new controls (or remediated existing controls) in response to one or more previously identified material weaknesses. In these cases, management may assess the new or remediated controls and conclude that the controls have been operating for a sufficient time to be judged as effective. If the auditor believes the time period is not sufficient to evaluate the operating effectiveness of the controls, a scope limitation exists. (*AS 4* provides guidance to the auditor for reporting on previously identified material weaknesses).

As with scope limitations related to the report on the entity's financial statements, a scope limitation may result in the issuance of a **disclaimer of opinion on internal control over financial reporting or a withdrawal from the engagement,** depending on the significance of the limitation. The standard report on internal control over financial reporting would be modified as shown in Exhibit 5.16.

Other Report Modifications

AS 5 identifies other situations that may result in modification to the auditors' report on internal control over financial reporting:

* If other auditors have audited the financial statements and internal control over financial reporting of one or more subsidiaries, the principal auditors need to determine whether to refer to the other auditors' report in their own report on internal control.
* If management's report on internal control contains additional information (such as corrective actions taken by the entity or the entity's plan to implement new controls), the auditors should disclaim an opinion on other information if they have not had an opportunity to evaluate the information.

EXHIBIT 5.16 Report on Internal Control over Financial Reporting If a Scope Limitation Exists

	Disclaimer of Opinion
Introductory paragraph	Change "we have audited" to "we *were engaged* to audit" since an audit could not be completed. Delete the sentence describing the auditors' responsibility for internal control over financial reporting. (It is inappropriate to indicate that the auditors' responsibility is to express an opinion, and then later say that an opinion could not be expressed.)
Scope paragraph	Delete the scope paragraph
Definition paragraph	No change.
Inherent limitations paragraph	No change.
Explanatory paragraphs	Provide an explanatory paragraph describing the scope limitation. If the scope limitation is related to the inability to gather sufficient evidence with respect to a potential material weakness, this paragraph also should include the definition of a material weakness.
Opinion paragraph	Modify the opinion paragraph to disclaim an opinion ("the scope of our work was not sufficient to enable us to express, and we do not express, an opinion . . .").

- If the auditors believe that management's annual certification (Section 302) is misstated, they should include an explanatory paragraph describing the reasons the auditors believe management's disclosures should be modified.
- If changes in internal control over financial reporting occur that materially and adversely affect the effectiveness of the entity's internal control subsequent to the date of the financial statements but prior to the issuance of the report, the auditors should issue an adverse opinion (if the subsequent event indicates a material weakness) or a disclaimer of opinion (if the auditor is unable to determine whether the subsequent event indicates a material weakness) on the effectiveness of the entity's internal control over financial reporting.

Exhibit 5.17 summarizes situations in which modifications are appropriate for the auditors' report on internal control over financial reporting.

EXHIBIT 5.17 Modifications to Auditors' Report on Internal Control over Financial Reporting

Situation	Effect on Opinion on Effectiveness of Internal Control
Material weaknesses in internal control over financial reporting	Issue an adverse opinion on internal control
Restriction on the scope of the engagement	Issue either a disclaimer of opinion or withdraw from the engagement, depending on the severity of the scope limitation
Reference to report of other auditors as the basis for the auditors' opinion	No effect, assuming other auditors' opinion is consistent with principal auditors' opinion (would refer to report of other auditors)
Other information contained in management's report on internal control	No effect, but should disclaim an opinion on other information
Management's annual certification (section 302) is misstated	Include an explanatory paragraph describing the reasons why management's disclosures should be modified
Significant subsequent event related to internal control	Issue either adverse opinion (if subsequent event adversely affects the effectiveness of internal control) or disclaimer of opinion (if auditor is unable to determine effects of subsequent event)

AUDITING INSIGHT Is Sarbanes-Oxley Working?

Since its inception in 2002, the Sarbanes-Oxley Act has been criticized for its rigourous internal control requirements (Section 404), which detractors have argued are too burdensome and costly. Ultimately, the question arises as to whether Sarbanes-Oxley is working as intended.

Listed below are some early effects of Section 404 on financial reporting:

- The provisions of Sarbanes-Oxley have resulted in a doubling of audit fees among the Big Four accounting firms. A survey of 43 companies (40 of which are Fortune 500 companies) indicated that these companies spent an average of $5 to $8 million in new audit fees related solely to Sarbanes-Oxley.

- More than 60 companies requested an additional 15 days to file their 2004 annual reports, citing issues relating to documenting internal controls as required under Sarbanes-Oxley. These companies included **American International Group, Fannie Mae, HealthSouth, EDS, Veritas Software,** and **Impax Laboratories.**

- Reviews of the first year of internal disclosures under Sarbanes-Oxley indicate that nearly 12 percent of companies (mostly smaller companies) reported material weaknesses. The most common general issues were deficiencies in documentation, weaknesses resulting in adjustments or restatements, and inadequate personnel competence. Specific areas related to tax accounting, revenue recognition, leases, and inventory.

- Compared to the general stock market, companies disclosing a material weakness in internal control over financial reporting experienced a decline in their stock prices of 0.67 percent on the day of disclosure; this decline increased to 4.06 percent during the next 60 days. The market performance was even worse when the company missed its filing deadline with the SEC.

Before you judge too harshly, let's take a look at some more recent evidence:

- Although a new record for financial statement restatements was set in 2006, with publicly traded companies correcting 1,876 financial results, the number of restatements by large companies that fell under Sarbanes-Oxley requirements plunged 20 percent to 196. On the other hand, smaller companies that do not yet follow Sarbanes-Oxley's internal control requirements jumped 42 percent. Restatements of financial results, a *bete noire* for both companies and their auditors, are akin to a product recall. Proponents of Sarbanes-Oxley view these results as supportive of the act's rigorous internal control measures, especially for smaller companies.

- A 2006 Financial Executives Institute survey of its members found that Sarbanes-Oxley average compliance costs fell 23 percent (to $2.9 million) from the previous year. This marked the third year in a row that compliance costs had fallen. Survey respondents indicated an average of 18,070 internal employee-hours; 3,382 external worker-hours (other than auditors); and $1.2 million in auditor attestation fees. All of these measures were lower than in past years. While this finding appears to refute critics' charges that the compliance is too expensive, 78 percent of those surveyed still believe that the benefits of compliance still do not outweigh the costs.

Sources: "Audit Fees Double Due to Sarbox," *CFO.com*, February 11, 2005; "Five Dozen Companies Seek Filing Delay," *CFO.com*, March 21, 2005; Deloitte & Touche, *Internal Control Disclosures: Key Trends to Watch*, May 11, 2005; "How Markets Punish Material Weaknesses," *CFO.com*, July 21, 2005; "Restatements Still Bedevil Firms," *The Wall Street Journal*, February 12, 2007, p. C7; "Study: Costs of 404 Drop 23 Percent," *CFO.com*, May 17, 2007; "Costs to Comply with Sarbanes Decline Again," *The Wall Street Journal*, May 16, 2007, p. C7.

Review Checkpoints

5.31 What are some major reasons for departing from the standard, unqualified report on internal control over financial reporting?

5.32 What type of opinion(s) would be issued by auditors on the effectiveness of internal control over financial reporting if a material weakness in internal control exists? How would the standard report be modified?

5.33 What type of opinion(s) would be issued by auditors as the result of a scope limitation on the examination of internal control over financial reporting?

INTERNAL CONTROL COMMUNICATIONS

LEARNING
OBJECTIVE

8. Explain the
communication of
internal control
deficiencies to the
those charged with
governance such as
the audit committee
and other key
management
personnel.

Whether auditing a nonpublic entity under GAAS or a publicly held entity in an examination conducted under Sarbanes-Oxley, auditors must communicate significant deficiencies and material weaknesses in internal control that come to their attention in the performance of the audit. Auditors' communications of significant deficiencies and material weaknesses are intended to help management carry out its responsibilities for internal control monitoring and change. However, external auditors' observations and recommendations are usually limited to external financial reporting matters.

For publicly held entities, the auditors' report must be in writing and presented to those in charge of governance (usually the audit committee) before its report on internal control over financial reporting is issued to the public. The report is to be addressed to the management, the board of directors, or its audit committee. An illustration of a report is in Exhibit 5.18.

If auditors do not identify any significant deficiencies, they should not issue a report stating that "no significant deficiencies were noted during the audit." Doing so might be

EXHIBIT 5.18
Internal Control Letter

Smith & Smith
Certified Public Accountants
Chicago, Illinois

January 31, 2009

Board of Directors
Apollo Shoes, Inc.
Shoetown, Maine

In planning and performing our audit of the financial statements of Apollo Shoes, Inc., for the year ended December 31, 2008, we considered its internal control in order to determine our audit procedures for the purpose of expressing our opinion on the financial statements as well as the effectiveness of the company's internal control over financial reporting. Our consideration of internal control would not necessarily disclose all deficiencies in internal control that might be significant deficiencies. However, we noted a certain matter involving the internal control and its operation that we consider to be a significant deficiency under standards established by the Public Company Accounting Oversight Board. A significant deficiency involves a matter coming to our attention relating to a weakness in the design or operation of the internal control that, in our judgment, could adversely affect the company's ability to initiate, record, process, and report financial data consistent with the assertions of management in the financial statements.

The matter noted is that shipping personnel have both transaction-initiation and alteration authority and custody of inventory assets. If invoice/shipping copy documents are altered to show shipment of smaller quantities than actually shipped, customers or accomplices can receive your products without charge. The sales revenue and accounts receivable could be understated, and the inventory could be overstated. This deficiency caused us to spend more time auditing your inventory quantities.

A material weakness in internal control is defined as a deficiency, or combination of deficiencies, that results in a reasonable possibility that a material misstatement would not be prevented or detected on a timely basis. We do not believe that the significant deficiency described above is a material weakness.

This report is intended solely for the information and use of the board of directors and its audit committee, and is not intended to be and should not be used by anyone other than these specified parties.

Respectfully yours,

Smith & Smith CPAs

misleading because an integrated audit is not designed to detect all significant deficiencies. A manager receiving such a report could conclude (incorrectly) that the auditors are stating positively that the entity has no internal control problems.

Auditors often issue another type of report to management called a *management letter.* This letter may contain commentary and suggestions on a variety of matters in addition to internal control matters. Examples include issues identified during the audit related to operational and administrative efficiency, business strategy, and profit-making possibilities. Auditing standards do not require management letters, but they represent a type of value-added management advice rendered as a part of an audit.

Review Checkpoints

5.34 What reports (other than auditors' report) on internal control do auditors give to an entity's management, board of directors, or audit committee?

INTERNAL CONTROL LIMITATIONS

LEARNING
OBJECTIVE

9. Explain the limitations of all internal control systems.

As noted at the beginning of the chapter, internal control provides *reasonable,* not *absolute,* assurance that category control objectives will be achieved. Internal control can help prevent and detect many errors, but it cannot guarantee that they will never happen. Several limitations to internal control systems prevent management (and auditors, for that matter) from obtaining complete assurance that entity controls are absolutely effective. For example, although controls are implemented to prevent and detect errors, human error due to mistakes in judgment, fatigue, and carelessness can still occur. Other limitations include deliberate circumvention, *management override,* and improper *collusion.*

Most internal controls are directed at lower-level employees, not management. Therefore, it is often possible for management to override controls by force of authority. Similarly, although separation of duties is an extremely effective control, collusion among people who are supposed to act independently can cause failure to achieve control objectives.

Additionally, internal control is subject to cost–benefit considerations. Internal control could be made perfect, or nearly so, at great expense. An inventory could be left unlocked and unguarded (no control against theft and no control expenses) or a fence could be used; locks could be installed; lighting could be used at night; television monitors could be put in place; armed guards could be hired. Each of these successive safeguards costs money, as does extensive supervision of clerical personnel in an office. At some point, the cost of protecting the inventory from theft (or of supervisors catching every clerical error) exceeds the benefit of control. Hence, an entity can decide that certain controls are too costly in light of the risk of loss that may occur. Reasonable assurance is thought to be enough.

The key person in internal control in a small business with few employees is the owner-manager. A diligent owner-manager may be able to oversee and supervise all the important authorization, record-keeping, and custodial functions, as well as be able to ensure satisfactory transaction-processing accuracy. Thus, an audit team evaluating control risk will study the extent of the owner-manager's involvement in the operation of the accounting and control system and evaluate the owner-manager's competence and integrity.

Review Checkpoints

5.35 What are some of the limitations of any entity's internal control?

5.36 What is the concept of reasonable assurance? Who is responsible for assessing it?

Summary

This chapter explains the theory and practice of auditors' involvement with a client's internal control. The purposes of audit team involvement are to assess the control risk (as part of the overall assessment of the risk of material misstatement) in order to plan the substantive audit program and to report control deficiencies to management and the board of directors. The PCAOB's *AS 5* defines additional responsibilities for management and public accounting firms' reports on internal control stipulated by the Sarbanes-Oxley Act.

Internal control consists of five components: management's control environment, management's risk assessment, management's information and communication system, management's control procedures, and management's monitoring of the control system. Each of these components is evaluated and documented in the audit files. The control environment and management's risk assessment are explained in terms of understanding the client's business. Elements of the accounting system are explained in conjunction with control procedures designed to prevent, detect, and correct misstatements that occur in transactions. The explanations of these controls integrate computerized information systems with control practice.

Documentation of an entity's internal control is accomplished through the use of questionnaires, flowcharts, and narratives. The understanding and the documentation are taken one step further to the test of controls phase and the cost reduction reasons for doing work to obtain a low control risk assessment. This assessed control risk is connected to the control risk component (CR) in the audit risk model discussed previously (in Chapter 3).

Control evidence is linked to substantive audit programs with a "bridge workpaper" presentation. The nature of tests of controls is explained in terms of a two-part statement that dictates identification of the data population, from which control evidence is drawn, and the action taken to produce the relevant evidence. It is important to distinguish the "client's control procedures" from the "auditors' tests of controls." Control procedures are part of the internal control designed and operated by the entity. The auditors' procedures are the auditors' own evidence-gathering work performed to obtain evidence about the client's control procedures.

AS 5 requires management to report on its assessment the effectiveness of its financial reporting controls. Auditors must provide an opinion on the controls over financial reporting. This may involve more extensive procedures than those required by GAAS.

The chapter closes with sections on the communication of internal control–related matters and the limitations of internal control systems, including cost–benefit and reasonable assurance considerations.

Key Terms

adverse opinion (internal control over financial reporting): Opinion issued when the company has *not* maintained an effective internal control over financial reporting, 188

audit committee: A subcommittee of the board of directors that is generally composed of three to six "outside" members of the organization's board of directors, 162

business risks: Those factors, events, and conditions that could prevent the organization from achieving its business objectives, 163

control procedures: Specific actions taken by a client's management and employees to help ensure that management directives are carried out, 164

control risk: The probability that an entity's controls will fail to prevent or detect errors and frauds that would otherwise have entered the system, 156

design effectiveness: A condition expressing whether controls would be expected to prevent or detect errors or fraud that could result in a material misstatement in the financial statements, 183

disclaimer of opinion (internal control over financial reporting): Situations in which auditors cannot provide assurance on the effectiveness of internal control over financial reporting; issued when a significant scope limitation exists, 190

dual-purpose tests: An audit procedure that can be used as both a test of controls and a substantive test, 182

information technology application controls (ITAC): Computerized steps with the application software and related manual procedures to control the processing of various types of transactions. Major categories of ITAC are input controls, processing controls, and output controls, 167

information technology general controls (ITGC): Controls that apply to all application systems and help ensure their continued proper operations. Major categories of ITGC are hardware controls, program development controls, program change controls, computer operations controls, and access to programs and data controls, 167

input controls: Controls designed to provide reasonable assurance that data received for processing by the information-processing department have been authorized properly and converted into machine-sensitive form and that information has not been lost, suppressed, added, duplicated, or improperly changed, 167

internal control: A process, effected by an entity's board of directors, management, and other personnel, designed to provide reasonable assurance regarding the achievement of objectives in the reliability of financial reporting, the effectiveness and efficiency of operations, and compliance with applicable laws and regulations, 159

internal control deficiency: A condition that exists when the design or operation of a control does not allow the entity's management or employees to detect or prevent misstatements in a timely fashion, 184

internal control questionnaire: A checklist of internal control–related questions used to gain and document an understanding of the client's internal control, 174

material weakness: A deficiency, or combination of deficiencies, that results in a *reasonable possibility* that a *material misstatement* would not be prevented or detected on a timely basis, 184

narrative description: Audit documentation that describes the environmental elements, the accounting system, and the control procedures in an entity's internal control, 174

operating effectiveness: A condition expressing whether a control is operating as designed and whether the person performing the control possesses the necessary authority and qualifications to perform the control effectively, 184

output controls: The final check on the accuracy of the results of computerized processing and controls designed to ensure that only proper persons receive reports or have access to files produced by the system, 167

processing controls: Error-condition check routines written into the computer program, 167

reasonable assurance: Concept that recognizes that the costs of control procedures should not exceed the benefits that are expected from the control procedures, 159

report on internal control over financial reporting (prepared by auditor): Report that expresses an opinion on the effectiveness of the entity's internal control over financial reporting, 186

report on internal control over financial reporting (prepared by management): Report that describes the process through which management assesses its internal control over financial reporting and that provides management's conclusion with respect to the effectiveness of its internal control over financial reporting, 185

significant deficiency: A condition, or combinations of conditions, that could adversely affect the organization's ability to initiate, record, process, and report financial data in the financial statements, 184

substantive procedures: Transaction detail audit and analytical procedures designed to detect material misstatements in account balances and footnote disclosures, 181

unqualified opinion (internal control over financial reporting): Issued when no material weaknesses in internal control over financial reporting are identified (effectiveness of internal control over financial reporting) and no scope limitations on the audit of internal control exist, 186

walkthrough: Tracing one or more transactions through the audit trail from initiation of the transaction to its inclusion in the financial statements, 173

Multiple Choice Questions for Practice and Review

5.37 The most important fundamental concept involved in an entity's internal control is
 a. Effectiveness and efficiency of operations.
 b. People who operate the control system.
 c. Reliability of financial reporting.
 d. Compliance with applicable laws and regulations.

5.38 The primary purpose for obtaining an understanding of an audit client's internal control is to
 a. Provide a basis for making constructive suggestions in a management letter.
 b. Determine the nature, timing, and extent of tests to be performed in the audit.
 c. Obtain sufficient appropriate audit evidence to afford a reasonable basis for an opinion on the financial statements under examination.
 d. Provide information for a communication of internal control–related matters to management.

5.39 Reductions of audit procedures can be characterized by

a. Selecting larger sample sizes for audit.

b. Performing audit procedures at the fiscal year-end date, as opposed to the interim period.

c. Deciding to obtain external evidence instead of internal evidence.

d. Selecting smaller sample sizes for audit.

5.40 Financial totals can be used for

a. Input controls.

b. Processing controls.

c. Output controls.

d. All of the above.

5.41 Which of the following is an application control?

a. Locked doors to the central server.

b. Change controls over new programs.

c. Backup controls.

d. An output control department that ensures that reports go to authorized recipients.

5.42 In the weekly payroll check run, a check was printed for an employee who had been terminated the previous week. Which of the following controls, if properly utilized, would have been most effective in preventing the error or ensuring its prompt detection?

a. A control total for hours worked prepared from time cards collected by the timekeeping department.

b. A requirement that the treasurer's office account for the numbers of the prenumbered checks issued to the information processing department for the processing of the payroll.

c. Use of the check digit for employee numbers.

d. Use of hash totals for the payroll input sheet.

5.43 In most audits of large entities, control risk assessment contributes to audit efficiency, which means that

a. The cost of substantive procedures will exceed the cost of control evaluation work.

b. Auditors will be able to reduce the cost of substantive procedures by an amount more than the control evaluation costs.

c. The cost of control evaluation work will exceed the cost of substantive procedures.

d. Auditors will be able to reduce the cost of substantive procedures by an amount less than the control evaluation costs.

5.44 Which of the following is a device designed to help the audit team obtain evidence about the accounting and control procedures of an audit client?

a. A narrative memorandum describing the control system.

b. An internal control questionnaire.

c. A flowchart of the documents and procedures used by the company.

d. All of the above.

5.45 A bridge workpaper shows the connection between

a. Control evaluation findings and subsequent audit procedures.

b. Control objectives and accounting system procedures.

c. Control objectives and entity control procedures.

d. Financial statement assertions and tests of controls.

5.46 Tests of controls in a GAAS audit are required for

a. Obtaining evidence about the financial statement assertions.

b. Accomplishing control over the occurrence of recorded transactions.

c. Applying analytical procedures to financial statement balances.

d. Obtaining evidence about the operating effectiveness of client control procedures.

5.47 A client's control procedure is

 a. An action taken by auditors to obtain evidence.

 b. An action taken by client personnel for the purpose of preventing, detecting, and correcting errors and frauds in transactions.

 c. A method for recording, summarizing, and reporting financial information.

 d. The functioning of the board of directors in support of its audit committee.

5.48 When planning an integrated audit under *AS 5,* the audit team should

 a. Identify significant accounts, locations, and assertions.

 b. Conduct a walkthrough of the internal control process.

 c. Make inquiries of employees regarding the existence of control procedures.

 d. Reperform control procedures performed by client employees to determine their effectiveness.

5.49 A material weakness is a situation in which

 a. It is probable that an immaterial financial statement misstatement would not be detected on a timely basis

 b. There is a remote likelihood that a material misstatement would be detected on a timely basis.

 c. It is reasonably possible that a material misstatement would not be detected on a timely basis.

 d. It is reasonably possible that an immaterial misstatement would not be detected on a timely basis.

5.50 Totals of amounts in computer-recorded data fields that are not usually added but are used only for data processing control purposes are called

 a. Record totals.

 b. Hash totals.

 c. Processing data totals.

 d. Field totals.

5.51 In updating a computerized accounts receivable file, which one of the following would be used as an input control to verify the accuracy of the posting of cash receipts remittances?

 a. The sum of the cash deposits plus the discounts less the sales returns.

 b. The sum of the cash deposits.

 c. The sum of the cash deposits less the discounts taken by customers.

 d. The sum of the cash deposits plus the discounts taken by customers.

5.52 *AS 5* requires auditors of public companies to audit internal controls over

 a. Operations.

 b. Compliance with regulations.

 c. Financial reporting.

 d. All of the above.

5.53 *AS 5* requires auditors of public companies to report on

	Management's Report on Internal Control	An Audit of Internal Control
a.	No	No
b.	Yes	No
c.	No	Yes
d.	Yes	Yes

5.54 *AS 5* requires auditors to test

 a. Operating effectiveness only.

 b. Design effectiveness only.

 c. Both operating and design effectiveness.

 d. Neither operating nor design effectiveness.

5.55 Which of the following would probably *not* be considered an indication of a material weakness?

 a. Evidence of a material misstatement.

 b. Ineffective oversight by the audit committee.

 c. An immaterial fraud committed by senior management.

 d. All of the above indicate material weaknesses.

5.56 Which report would not be appropriate for an audit firm to provide on financial reporting controls?

 a. Unqualified—no material weaknesses found.

 b. Disclaimer of opinion—unable to perform all necessary procedures.

 c. Qualified—significant deficiencies exist.

 d. Adverse—material weaknesses exist.

5.57 The purpose of separating the duties of hiring personnel and distributing payroll checks is to separate the

 (a.) Authorization of transactions from the custody of related assets.

 b. Operational responsibility from the record-keeping responsibility.

 c. Human resources function from the controllership function.

 d. Administrative controls from the internal accounting controls.

 (AICPA adapted)

5.58 Effective internal control procedures over the payroll function may include

 a. Reconciliation of totals on job time tickets with job reports by employees responsible for those specific jobs.

 b. Verification of agreement of job time tickets with employee clock card hours by a time-keeping department employee.

 c. Preparation of payroll transaction journal entries by an employee who reports to the supervisor of the personnel department.

 d. Custody of rate authorization records by the supervisor of the payroll department.

 (AICPA adapted)

5.59 Which of the following statements is *not* true with respect to the auditors' report on internal control over financial reporting?

 a. The report will be dated as of the balance sheet date.

 b. The report will express an opinion on the effectiveness of internal control over financial reporting.

 c. If one or more material weaknesses exist, the auditor will issue an adverse opinion.

 d. The report may be presented with the report on the entity's financial statements as a combined report.

5.60 If the auditors encounter a significant scope limitation in evaluating a publicly traded company's internal control over financial reporting, which of the following types of opinions on the effectiveness of the company's internal control over financial reporting would be appropriate?

 a. Unqualified opinion or adverse opinion.

 b. Qualified opinion or adverse opinion.

 c. Unqualified opinion or disclaimer of opinion.

 d. Disclaimer of opinion.

5.61 Which of the following information would be included in the introductory paragraph of the auditors' report on internal control over financial reporting if the report is presented separately from the auditors' report on the entity's financial statements?

 a. The fact that the auditors conducted an audit of the entity's financial statements.

 b. The definition of a material weakness in internal control over financial reporting.

 (c.) Statements identifying the responsibility of the auditors and management for internal control over financial reporting.

 d. A reference to the auditors' report and opinion on the entity's financial statements.

Exercises, Problems, and Simulations

5.62 **Internal Control Audit Standards.** Auditors are required to obtain a sufficient understanding of each of the components of a client's internal control. This understanding is used to assess control risk and plan the audit of the client's financial statements.

Required:

a. For what purposes should an auditors' understanding of the internal control components be used in planning an audit?

b. What is required for an audit team to assess control risk below the maximum level?

c. What should an audit team consider when seeking to reduce the planned assessed level of control risk below the maximum?

d. What are the documentation requirements concerning a client's internal control components and the assessed level of control risk?

(AICPA adapted)

5.63 **Costs and Benefits of Control.** Managers can mitigate risk three ways: avoid it, control it, and share it. Actually, another way is available: accept it and live with it! This "acceptance" comes in the form of deciding that the costs of unavoidable risks that remain after buying insurance (or some other form of sharing the risks) should not exceed the benefits of the control (e.g., profits, losses prevented). The following questions and cases deal with the subject of cost–benefit analysis of internal control. Some important concepts in cost–benefit analysis are

a. *Measurable benefit.* Benefits or cost savings may be measured directly or may be based on estimates of expected value. An expected loss is an estimate of the amount of a probable loss multiplied by the frequency or probability of the loss-causing event. A measurable benefit can arise from the reduction of an expected loss.

b. *Qualitative benefit.* Some gains or cost savings such as company public image, reputation for regulatory compliance, and customer satisfaction may not be measurable.

c. *Measurable costs.* Controls may have direct costs such as wages and equipment expenses.

d. *Qualitative cost factors.* Some costs such as lower employee morale created by overcontrolled work restrictions may be indirect.

e. *Marginal analysis.* Each successive control feature may have marginal cost and benefit effects on the control problem.

Required:

Use these concepts to answer the questions at the end of each case.

Case 1

Porterhouse Company has numerous bank accounts. Why might management hesitate to spend $10,000 (half of a clerical salary) to assign someone the responsibility of reconciling each account every month for the purpose of catching the banks' accounting errors? Do other good reasons exist to justify spending $10,000 each year to reconcile bank accounts monthly?

Case 2

Harper Hoe Company keeps a large inventory of hardware products in a warehouse. Last year, it lost $500,000 to thieves who broke in through windows and doors. Joyce Harper figures that installing steel doors with special locks and burglar bars on the windows at a cost of $25,000 would eliminate 90 percent of the loss. Hiring armed guards to patrol the building 16 hours a day at a current annual cost of $75,000 would eliminate all loss, according to officials of Holmes Security Agency. Should Joyce arrange for one, both, or neither of the control measures?

Case 3

The Merry Mound Cafeteria formerly collected from each customer at the end of the food line. A cashier, seated at a point-of-sale terminal, rang up the amount (displayed on a digital screen) and collected money. Management changed the system and now a clerk at the end of the line operates a calculator and gives each customer a paper tape. The calculator accumulates a running total internally. The customers present the tape at the cash register as they exit the cafeteria and pay.

The cafeteria manager justified the direct cost of $10,000 annually for the additional salary and $500 for the new calculator by pointing out that this would enable the cafeteria to serve four more people each weekday (Monday through Friday) and 10 more people on

both Saturday and Sunday. The food line now moves faster and customers are more satisfied. (The average meal tab is $6 and total costs of food and service are considered fixed.) "Besides," the manager said, "my internal control is better." Evaluate the manager's assertions.

5.64 **Audit Simulation: Separation of Duties.** Your small business client, Phillip's Computer Repair Shop, is experiencing hard times and has to lay off one of its four employees in the accounting area. Phillip has asked you to determine what duties should be assigned to the three remaining employees—Abigail, Bryan, and Chris—to maintain the best separation of duties.

Required:

Assign the following 10 duties to each of the three employees.

a. Reconcile bank statement.

b. Open mail and list checks.

c. Prepare checks for Phillip's signature.

d. Prepare payroll checks.

e. Maintain personnel records.

f. Prepare deposit and take to bank.

g. Maintain petty cash.

h. Maintain accounts receivable records.

i. Maintain general ledger.

j. Reconcile accounts receivable records to general ledger account.

5.65 **Effects of Sarbanes-Oxley Act.** Your long-time client, Central Office Supply, has been rapidly expanding and the board of directors is considering taking the company public. CEO Terry Puckett has heard that costs of operating a public company have increased significantly as a result of the Sarbanes-Oxley Act. Puckett is particularly concerned with reports that audit fees have doubled because of internal control provisions of the act and *AS 5*. Puckett has asked you to explain the possible effects on the audit of complying with the requirements of Sarbanes-Oxley.

Required:

Draft a letter to Puckett outlining the changes in the company's responsibilities for internal control and changes in the audit due to Sarbanes-Oxley and *AS 5*.

5.66 **Internal Control Questionnaire Items: Assertions, Tests of Controls, and Possible Errors or Frauds.** Following is a selection of items from the payroll processing internal control questionnaire in Exhibit 5.9.

1. Are names of terminated employees reported in writing to the payroll department?

2. Are authorizations for deductions signed by the employee on file?

3. Is there a timekeeping department (function) independent of the payroll department?

4. Are timekeeping and cost accounting records (such as hours, dollars) reconciled with payroll department calculations of hours and wages?

Required:

For each of the above questions

a. Identify the assertion to which the question applies.

b. Specify one test of controls an auditor could use to determine whether the control was operating effectively.

c. Provide an example of an error or fraud that could occur if the control were absent or ineffective.

d. Identify a substantive auditing procedure that could detect errors or frauds that could result from the absence or ineffectiveness of the control items.

5.67 **Obtaining a "Sufficient" Understanding of Internal Control.** The 12 partners of a regional CPA firm met in special session to discuss audit engagement efficiency. Jones spoke up, saying, "We all certainly appreciate the firmwide policies set up by Martin and Smith, especially in connection with the audits of the large clients that have come our way recently. Their experience with a large accounting firm has helped build our practice. But I think the

standard policy of conducting reviews and tests of internal control on all audits is raising our costs too much. We can't charge our smaller clients fees for all of the time the staff spends on this work. I would like to propose that we give engagement partners discretion to decide whether to do a lot of work on assessing control risk. I may be old-fashioned, but I think I can finish a competent audit without it." Discussion on the subject continued but ended when Martin said, with some emotion, "But we can't disregard generally accepted auditing standards like Jones proposes!"

Required:

What do you think of Jones' proposal and Martin's view of the issue? Discuss.

5.68 **Fraud Opportunities.** Simon Blfpstk Construction Company has two divisions. The president (Simon) manages the roofing division. Simon delegated authority and responsibility for management of the modular manufacturing division to John Gault. The company has a competent accounting staff and a full-time internal auditor. Unlike Simon's procedures, however, Gault and his secretary handle all bids for manufacturing jobs, purchase all materials without competitive bids, control the physical inventory of materials, contract for shipping by truck, supervise the construction activity, bill the customer when the job is finished, approve all bid changes, and collect the payment from the customer. With Simon's tacit approval, Gault has asked the internal auditor not to interfere with his busy schedule.

Required:

Discuss this situation in terms of internal control and identify frauds that could occur.

5.69 **Internal Control Questionnaire Items: Errors That Could Occur from Control Weaknesses.** Refer to the internal control questionnaire on a payroll system (Exhibit 5.9) and assume that the answer to each question is No. Prepare a table matching the questions to errors or frauds that could occur because of the absence of the control. Your column headings should be

Question	Possible Error or Faud Due to Weakness

5.70 **Reports on Internal Control over Financial Reporting (Report Modifications).** For each of the following situations, describe how the auditors' report on internal control over financial reporting would be modified from the standard, unqualified report. Do *not* write the actual reports.

 a. A material weakness in the processing of sales transactions has been identified by the auditors.

 b. Because of a relatively short period of time since a control weakness has been remediated, the auditors do not believe that sufficient evidence can be obtained with respect to the operating effectiveness of the entity's internal control over financial reporting.

 c. Other auditors have audited a significant component of the company, including internal controls over financial reporting relating to that component.

 d. The auditors believe that the entity's management has not adequately disclosed a material weakness in its internal control over financial reporting.

5.71 **Audit Simulation: Reports on Internal Control over Financial Reporting (Identify Report Deficiencies).** Sorrell, CPA, is auditing the financial statements of Van Dyke as of December 31, 2008. Sorrell's substantive procedures and other tests indicated that Van Dyke's financial statements were prepared in accordance with generally accepted accounting principles and, accordingly, Sorrell expressed an unqualified opinion on those financial statements. Because Van Dyke's securities are registered with the Securities and Exchange Commission, Van Dyke is subject to the reporting requirements of *AS 5*. During its assessment of internal control over financial reporting, Van Dyke's management identified material weaknesses related to (1) the method of accounting for sales commissions and (2) segregation of duties related to purchase transactions. Sorrell was able to gather sufficient evidence and did not encounter any limitations with respect to her evaluation of Van Dyke's internal control over financial reporting. Sorrell prepared the following draft report on Van Dyke's internal control over financial reporting:

Report of Independent Registered Public Accounting Firm

To the Board of Directors and Shareholders of Van Dyke:

We have audited management's assessment, included in the accompanying Management's Report on Internal Control over Financial Reporting, that Van Dyke has not maintained effective internal control over financial reporting as of December 31, 2008, based on criteria established in Internal Control—Integrated Framework issued by the Committee of Sponsoring Organizations of the Treadway Commission (COSO criteria). Van Dyke's management is responsible for assessing the effectiveness of internal control over financial reporting. Our responsibility is to express an opinion on management's assessment and an opinion on the effectiveness of the company's internal control over financial reporting based on our audit.

We conducted our audits in accordance with the standards of the Public Company Accounting Oversight Board (United States). Those standards require that we plan and perform the audit to obtain reasonable assurance about whether effective internal control over financial reporting was maintained in all material respects. Our audit included obtaining an understanding of internal control over financial reporting, evaluating management's assessment, testing and evaluating the design and operating effectiveness of internal control, and performing such other procedures as we considered necessary in the circumstances. We believe that our audit provides a reasonable basis for our opinion.

A company's internal control over financial reporting is a process designed to provide reasonable assurance regarding the reliability of financial reporting and the preparation of financial statements for external purposes in accordance with generally accepted accounting principles. A company's internal control over financial reporting includes those policies and procedures that (1) pertain to the maintenance of records that, in reasonable detail, accurately and fairly reflect the transactions and dispositions of the assets of the company; (2) provide reasonable assurance that transactions are recorded as necessary to permit preparation of financial statements in accordance with generally accepted accounting principles, and that receipts and expenditures of the company are being made only in accordance with authorizations of management and directors of the company; and (3) provide reasonable assurance regarding prevention or timely detection of unauthorized acquisition, use, or disposition of the company's assets that could have a material effect on the financial statements.

Two material weaknesses were identified in the design and operation of internal controls over the accounting for sales commissions and segregation of duties related to purchases of inventory. Given the nature of the transactions and processes involved and the potential for a misstatement to occur as a result of the internal control deficiencies existing on December 31, 2008, we have concluded that there is more than a remote likelihood that a material misstatement in the annual or interim financial statements would not have been prevented or detected by internal controls.

These material weaknesses were considered in determining the nature, timing, and extent of audit tests applied in our audit of the 2008 financial statements.

In addition to the material weaknesses noted above, we identified several deficiencies in internal control over financial reporting that we deemed to be less significant than a material weakness. These deficiencies have been separately communicated to Van Dyke's management.

In our opinion, because Van Dyke has not maintained an effective internal control over financial reporting, we are unable to evaluate management's assessment that Van Dyke did not maintain effective internal control over financial reporting as of December 31, 2008. Also in our opinion, because of the effect of the material weaknesses described above on the achievement of the objectives of the control criteria, Van Dyke has not maintained, in all material respects, effective internal control over financial reporting as of December 31, 2008, based on the COSO criteria.

We have also audited, in accordance with the standards of the Public Company Accounting Oversight Board (United States), the balance sheets of Van Dyke as of December 31, 2008 and 2007 and related statements of income, comprehensive income, shareholders' equity, and cash flows for each of the three years in the period ended December 31, 2008.

Sorrell, CPA

December 31, 2008

Required:

Identify the deficiencies in the audit report drafted by Sorrell. Group the deficiencies by paragraph and in the order in which they appear. Do not rewrite the report. Cite the relevant sections from the professional standards.

5.72 **Kaplan CPA Exam Simulation: Internal Control Components.**

Required:

Go to the Kaplan Web site at www.mhhe.com/louwers3e, click on AUD: Earhart & King case and the "Components of Internal Control" tab, and complete the assigned task.

5.73 **Kaplan CPA Exam Simulation: Internal Control Evaluation.**

Required:

Go to the Kaplan Web site at www.mhhe.com/louwers3e, click on AUD: Peters Michael case and the "Communication" tab, and complete the assigned task.

5.74 **Mini-Case: Control environment.** Refer to the mini-case "Unhealthy Accounting at HealthSouth" shown on page ••• and respond to Questions 3 and 4.

5.75 **Mini-Case: Effect of Internal Control Evaluation on Auditors' Fees.** Refer to the mini-case "How Much are Auditors Paid?" shown on page 843 and respond to Questions 5 and 6.

Employee Fraud and the Audit of Cash

Professional Standards References

Compendium Section	Document Reference	Topic
Various[1]	AS 5	"An Audit of Internal Control over Financial Reporting That Is Integrated with an Audit of Financial Statements"
AU 110	SAS 1	"Responsibilities and Functions of the Independent Auditor"
	ISA 200	"Objective and General Principles Governing Audits of Financial Statements"
AU 230	SAS 1	"Due Care in the Performance of Work"
	SAS 104	"Amendment to 'Due Care in the Performance of Work'"
AU 311	SAS 108	"Planning and Supervision"
	ISA 300	"Planning an Audit of Financial Statements"
AU 312	SAS 107	"Audit Risk and Materiality in Conducting an Audit"
	ISA 320	"Audit Materiality"
AU 316	SAS 99	"Consideration of Fraud in a Financial Statement Audit"
	ISA 240	"The Auditor's Responsibility to Consider Fraud in an Audit of Financial Statements"
AU 319	SAS 109	"Understanding the Entity and Its Environment and Assessing the Risks of Material Misstatements"
	ISA 315	"Understanding the Entity and Its Environment and Assessing the Risks of Material Misstatements"
AU 321	SAS 99	"Consideration of Fraud in a Financial Statement Audit"
	ISA 240	"The Auditor's Responsibility to Consider Fraud in an Audit of Financial Statements"
AU 323	SAS 54	"Illegal Acts by Clients"
	ISA 250	"Consideration of Laws and Regulations in an Audit of Financial Statements"
AU 326	SAS 106	"Evidential Matter"
	ISA 500	"Audit Evidence"
	ISA 501	"Audit Evidence—Additional Consideration for Specific Items"
AU 329	SAS 56	"Analytical Procedures"
	ISA 520	"Analytical Procedures"
AU 330	SAS 67	"The Confirmation Process"
	ISA 505	"External Confirmations"
AU 334	SAS 45	"Related Parties"
	ISA 550	"Related Parties"
AU 9334		"Interpretations: Related Parties"
AU 336	SAS 73	"Using the Work of a Specialist"
	ISA 620	"Using the Work of an Expert"
AU 339	SAS 103	"Audit Documentation"
	AS 3	"Audit Documentation"
	ISA 230	"Documentation"
AU 342	SAS 57	"Auditing Accounting Estimates"
	ISA 540	"Auditing Accounting Estimates"
AU 9342		"Interpretation: Auditing Accounting Estimates"
AU 380	SAS 114	"Audit Committee Communications"
	ISA 620	"Communications of Audit Matters with Those Charged with Governance"

[1]*AS 5* amends AU 230, AU 310, AU 312, AU 313, AU 315, AU 316, AU 319, AU 322, AU 325, AU 328, AU 332, AU 333, AU 341, AU 342, AU 380, AU 508, AU 530, AU 543, AU 560, AU 561, AU 711, AU 722, *AS 3,* and *AS 4.*

When a man tells you that he got rich through hard work, ask him: "Whose?"

Don Marquis, humorist (1878–1937)

Rather fail with honor than succeed by fraud.

Sophocles, philosopher (496–406 BCE)

Learning Objectives

Fraud auditing can be very exciting. It has the aura of detective work—finding things people want to keep hidden. However, fraud auditing and fraud examination are not easy and are not activities to be pursued without special training, experience, and care. Employee thieves and their primary target (cash) are the focus of this chapter, enabling you to not only get an introduction to employee fraud, but also heighten your awareness of employee theft during your audit of cash.

After reading this chapter, you should be able to achieve these learning objectives:

1. Define and explain the differences among several kinds of employee frauds that might occur in an entity.

2. List and explain some conditions that can lead to frauds.

3. Describe ways and means for preventing employee frauds.

4. Describe the controls over the receipt and disbursement of cash.

5. Design and perform substantive procedures for the audit of cash.

6. Discuss actual cash fraud cases and describe how the schemes were uncovered.

7. Describe some extended procedures for detecting employee fraud schemes involving cash.

EMPLOYEE FRAUD OVERVIEW

LEARNING OBJECTIVE

1. Define and explain the differences among several kinds of employee frauds that might occur in an entity.

The years-old "Nigerian Fraud" had snagged another victim. The fraud scheme involving Nigerian "government officials" (or their "widows") with access to millions in Nigerian government funds has been e-mailed throughout the world. One especially heinous version involves an auditor(!) who has discovered a secret government account. In order to gain access to the millions in the account, the funds must be transferred out of the country. For a small transfer fee (or authorized access to a bank account), the victim can have a big percentage. The fees (e.g., "currency fluctuation marginal differences," "Drug, Terrorists and Money Laundering Clearance Certificate," etc.) continue to grow as complications arise. That's what happened to Ann Marie Poet, a 59-year-old part-time law firm bookkeeper. FBI investigators say Poet sent $2.3 million, in payments ranging from $72,000 to $175,000, in an attempt to get 25 percent of a supposed $18 million treasure. Where did she get such money? She embezzled it from her employer, draining the entity's entire cash reserve.[1]

An entity's internal control cannot thwart or detect all fraud schemes. Inherent limitations in internal control (such as *collusion* and *management override*) prevent complete assurance that every fraud scheme will be detected before a loss is incurred. For this reason, the entity's auditors, accountants, and security personnel must be acquainted with the basics of fraud awareness. While the AICPA auditing standards concentrate on management fraud—the production of materially false and misleading financial statements (i.e., fraudulent financial reporting)—professional standards also require auditors to pay some attention to employee fraud perpetrated against a client. Attention to employee fraud is important in the context that the cover-up may create financial statement misstatements (e.g., overstating an inventory to disguise unauthorized removal of valuable products).

[1] "An Updated Scam: Black Money," *CBS Evening News,* October 14, 2002.

AUDITING INSIGHT The Case of the Extra Checkout

The district grocery store manager could not understand why receipts and profitability had fallen and inventory was hard to manage at one of the largest stores in her area. She hired an investigator who covertly observed the checkout clerks and reported that no one had shown suspicious behavior at any of the nine checkout counters. Nine? That store only has eight, she exclaimed! (The store manager had installed another checkout aisle, not connected to the cash receipts and inventory maintenance central computer, and was pocketing all the receipts from that register.)

Source: Association of Certified Fraud Examiners (ACFE), "Auditing for Fraud."

Fraud consists of knowingly making material misrepresentations of fact with the intent of inducing someone to believe the falsehood and act upon it and, thus, suffer a loss or damage. This definition encompasses all the varieties by which people can lie, cheat, steal, and deceive other people. **Employee fraud** (often referred to as **misappropriation of assets** or **defalcation**) is the use of fraudulent means to take money or other property from an employer. It usually involves falsifications of some kind—false documents, lying, exceeding authority, or violating an employer's policies. **Embezzlement** is a type of fraud involving employees or nonemployees wrongfully taking money or property entrusted to their care, custody, and control, often accompanied by false accounting entries and other forms of lying and cover-up. **Larceny** is simple theft—for example, an employee taking an employer's money or property that has not been entrusted to the custody of the employee.

Employee frauds generally consist of (1) the fraud act itself, (2) the conversion of assets to the fraudster's use (very easy if cash is involved), and (3) the cover-up. Catching people in the fraud act is difficult and unusual. The act of conversion is equally difficult to observe since it typically takes place in secret away from the entity's offices (e.g., fencing stolen inventory). By noticing signs and signals of fraud, and then following the trail of missing, mutilated, or false documents that are part of the accounting records cover-up, alert auditors uncover many frauds. Being able to notice "red flags," oddities, and unusual events takes some experience, but this chapter can provide you with some starting places.[2]

Employee Fraud Red Flags

Employee fraud can involve all employees from high-level executives to hourly employees in production and on the clerical staff. For most people, the commitment and continuation of fraudulent activity is a stressful situation. Observation of changes in persons' habits and lifestyles may reveal some red flags. Fraudsters often exhibit these characteristics:

- Lose sleep.
- Drink too much.
- Take drugs.
- Become irritable easily.
- Can't relax.
- Get defensive, argumentative.
- Can't look people in the eye.
- Sweat excessively.
- Go to confession (e.g., priest, psychiatrist).

[2] Long lists of red flags can be found in G. J. Bologna and R. J. Lindquist, *Fraud Auditing and Forensic Accounting* (New York: John Wiley & Sons, 1995), pp.49–56; W. S. Albrecht et al., in R. K. Elliott and J. J. Willingham, *Management Fraud: Detection and Deterrence* (New York: Petrocelli Books, Inc., 1980), pp. 223–26; *Statement on Auditing Standards No. 99* (New York: AICPA, 2002); "Auditing for Fraud" courses of the Association of Certified Fraud Examiners; and courses offered by other organizations such as the AICPA and The Institute of Internal Auditors.

Management fraud is deliberate fraud committed by management that injures investors and creditors through materially misleading information.

Errors are unintentional misstatements or omissions of amounts or disclosures in financial statements.

Direct-effect illegal acts are violations of laws or government regulations by the company or its management or employees that produce direct and material effects on dollar amounts in financial statements.

- Find excuses and scapegoats for mistakes.
- Work standing up.
- Work alone; work late.

Personality red flags are difficult because (1) honest people sometimes show them, (2) they often are hidden from view, and (3) auditors are not in a good position to notice these characteristics. Managers are in the best position to notice changes, especially when a person changes his or her lifestyle or spends more money than the salary justifies—for example, on homes, furniture, jewelry, clothes, boats, autos, vacations, and the like. Therefore, it is imperative that the auditor make specific inquiries of management regarding changes in the employee's demeanor and lifestyle.

Often, auditors can notice telltale hints of the cover-up. These generally appear in the accounting records. The key is to notice exceptions and oddities such as the following transactions:

- Transactions recorded at unusual times of the day, month, or year.
- An unusual (either large or small) number or dollar amount of transactions.
- Transactions associated with unusual branches or locations of a multilocation entity.
- Transactions for "round" dollar amounts (e.g., $5,000).

Exceptions and oddities like these can appear:

- Missing documents.
- Cash shortages and overages.
- Excessive voids and credit memos.
- Customer complaints.
- Common names or addresses for refunds.
- Unusual adjustments to receivables and Payables, especially with insufficient documentation.
- General ledgers that do not balance.
- Increased past due receivables.
- Inventory shortages.
- Increased scrap.
- Alterations on documents.
- Duplicate payments.
- Employees who cannot be located.
- Second endorsements on checks.
- Use of copies instead of originals.
- Dormant accounts that become active.

Characteristics of Fraudsters

White-collar criminals are not like typical bank robbers, who are often described as "young and dumb." Bank robbers and other strong-arm artists often make comical mistakes like writing their holdup note on the back of a probation identification card, leaving

AUDITING INSIGHT | High Style in the Mailroom

A female mailroom employee started wearing designer clothes (and making a big deal about it). She drove a new BMW to work. An observant manager who had known her as an employee for seven years and knew she had no outside income became suspicious. He asked the internal auditors to examine her responsibilities extra carefully. They discovered she had stolen $97,000 over a two-year period.

Source: Association of Certified Fraud Examiners (ACFE), "Auditing for Fraud."

the getaway car keys on the convenience store counter, using a zucchini as a holdup weapon, going through a fast-food restaurant's drive-through window backwards, and timing the holdup to get stuck in rush hour traffic. Then there's the classic about the robber who ran into his own mother at the bank (she turned him in!).

Burglars and robbers average about $400–$500 for each hit. Employee frauds often range from $20,000 on up to $500,000 if a computer is used. Yet, employee frauds are not usually the intricate, well-disguised ploys you find in espionage novels. Who are these thieves wearing ties? What do they "look like"? Unfortunately, they look like most everybody else, including you and me. They have these characteristics:

- Likely to be married.
- Not likely to be divorced.
- Probably not tattooed.
- Member of a church.
- Educated beyond high school.
- No arrest record.
- Range in age from teens to over 60.
- Socially conforming.
- Employment tenure from 1 to 20 years.
- Usually act alone (70 percent or more of incidents).

White-collar criminals do not make themselves obvious, although there may be telltale signs, which we call "red flags." Older individuals (usually over 50) who hold high executive positions, have long tenure, and are respected and trusted employees often have gained the trust and confidence of others and, therefore, are in the position to commit the largest frauds. After all, these are the people who have access to the largest amounts of money and have the power to give orders and override controls. When managers minimize the significance of a weak or missing control by rationalizing that the employee involved is a *"long-time trusted employee,"* most experienced auditors escalate their level of fraud risk awareness.

Review Checkpoints

6.1 What are the defining characteristics of employee fraud? embezzlement? larceny? defalcation?

6.2 What does a fraud perpetrator look like? How does one act?

6.3 Is there anything odd about these situations? (a) Auditors performed a surprise payroll distribution and J. Jones, S. Smith, and D. Douglas were absent from work. (b) A check to Larson Electric Supply was endorsed with "Larson Lectric" above the signature of "Eloise Garfunkle." (c) Numerous checks were issued dated September 7, November 26, December 25, January 1, May 25, and July 4.

AUDITING INSIGHT Who Does It?

Alex W was a 47-year-old treasurer of a credit union. Over a seven-year period, he stole $160,000. He was a good husband and the father of six children, and he was a highly regarded official of the credit union. His misappropriations came as a stunning surprise to his associates. He owed significant amounts on his home, cars, college for two children, two side investments, and five credit cards. His monthly payments significantly exceeded his take-home pay.

Source: Association of Certified Fraud Examiners (ACFE), "Auditing for Fraud."

CONDITIONS THAT MAKE EMPLOYEE FRAUD POSSIBLE, EVEN EASY (SAS 99)

LEARNING OBJECTIVE

2. List and explain some conditions that can lead to frauds.

When can fraud occur? Imagine the probability of fraud being a function of three factors—motive, opportunity, and rationalization (Exhibit 6.1). When one or two of these factors are present, the probability of fraud increases. When three of them are present, fraud almost certainly will occur.[3]

Motivation

A **motive** is some type of pressure experienced by a person and believed unshareable with friends and confidants. Psychotic motivation is relatively rare, but it is characterized by the "habitual criminal," who steals simply for the sake of stealing. Egocentric motivations drive people to steal to achieve more personal prestige. Ideological motivations are held by people who think their cause is morally superior and they are justified in making someone else a victim. However, economic motives are far more common in business frauds than the other three.

The economic motive is simply a need for money, and at times it can be intertwined with egocentric and ideological motivations. Ordinary honest people can fall into circumstances where they have a new or unexpected need for money and the normal options for

EXHIBIT 6.1
Fraud Elements

Source: W. Hillison, D. Sinason, and C. Pacini, "The Role of the Internal Auditor in Implementing *SAS 82*," *Corporate Controller*, July/August 1998, p. 20.

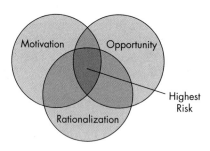

[3] For further reference, see D. R. Cressey, "Management Fraud, Accounting Controls, and Criminological Theory," pp. 117–47, and Albrecht et al., "Auditor Involvement in the Detection of Fraud," pp. 207–61, both in R. K. Elliott and J. J. Willingham, *Management Fraud: Detection and Deterrence* (New York: Petrocelli Books, Inc., 1980); J. K. Loebbecke, M. M. Eining, and J. J. Willingham, "Auditors' Experience with Material Irregularities: Frequency, Nature, and Detectability," *Auditing: A Journal of Practice and Theory*, Fall 1989, pp. 1–28.

AUDITING INSIGHT I Couldn't Tell Anyone

A young unmarried woman stole $300 from her employer to pay for an abortion. Coming from a strict religious family, she felt her only alternative was to have the secret abortion. Once she realized how easy it was to steal, however, she took another $86,000 before being caught.

Source: W. S. Albrecht, "How CPAs Can Help Clients Prevent Employee Fraud," *Journal of Accountancy*, 1988, pp. 110–14.

talking about it or going through legitimate channels seem to be closed. Consider these needs to

- Pay college tuition.
- Pay uninsured medical bills.
- Pay gambling debts.
- Pay for drugs and alcohol.
- Pay alimony and child support.
- Pay for high lifestyle (homes, cars, boats).
- Finance business or stock speculation losses.

Opportunity

An opportunity is an open door for solving the unshareable problem by violating a trust. The violation may be a circumvention of internal control policies and procedures or it may be simply taking advantage of an absence or lapse of control in an entity. The higher the position in an organization, the greater the degree of trust, the more likely that controls can be overridden, and, hence, the greater the opportunity for larger frauds. Here are some examples:

- Inventory is not counted on a regular basis, so inventory shortages and losses are not known.
- The petty cash box is often left unattended.
- Supervisors set a bad example by taking supplies home.
- The finance vice president has investment authority without any review.
- Frequent emergency jobs leave a lot of excess material just lying around.

AUDITING INSIGHT When Facing Adversity, Become a Model Employee

A supervisor for a state university health service was facing great financial difficulty. Her husband had permanently injured his back and no longer worked. One of her children was in a serious automobile accident requiring large payments to cover the uninsured portion of the medical bills.

Despite these personal problems the supervisor was considered a model employee. She would come to work early, stay late, never call in ill, and only took vacation time between semesters when the health service facility was closed. When she was ill with something contagious, she would come in to work after all other employees had left.

A newly hired director of health services noticed that although the number of students and number of services had increased, health services was having unexplained cash flow problems. An investigation revealed that the supervisor had embezzled $757,000 over a 13-year period. She was sentenced to five years in prison and ordered to repay the university $208,000 and perform 250 hours of community service.

Source: "Catching Fraudsters with Their Hands in the Till," *CPA Journal*, May 2005, pp.13–15.

AUDITING INSIGHT No Locks on the Door

Perini Corporation kept blank checks in an unlocked storeroom to which every clerk and secretary had access. Also in the storeroom was the automatic check signing machine. The prenumbered checks were not logged when used. The bookkeeper was very surprised to open the bank statement one month and find that $1.5 million in stolen checks had been paid on the account.

Source: Association of Certified Fraud Examiners (ACFE), "Auditing for Fraud."

Rationalization or Lack of Integrity

Practically everyone, even the most violent criminal, knows the difference between right and wrong. Unimpeachable integrity is the ability to act in accordance with the highest moral and ethical values all the time. Thus, it is the lapses and occasional lack of integrity that permit motive and opportunity to take form as fraud. But people normally do not make deliberate decisions to "lack integrity today while I steal some money." They find a way to describe (rationalize) the act in words that make it acceptable for their self-image. Here are some of these rationalizations:

- I need it more than the other person (Robin Hood theory).
- I'm borrowing the money and will pay it back.
- Nobody will get hurt.
- The company is big enough to afford it.
- A successful image is the name of the game.
- Everybody is doing it.
- I am underpaid, so this is due compensation.

Review Checkpoints

6.4 What are some of the pressures that can cause honest people to contemplate theft? List some egocentric and ideological ones as well as economic ones.

6.5 What kinds of conditions provide opportunities for employee fraud?

6.6 Give some examples of "rationalizations" that people have used to excuse fraud. Can you imagine using them?

6.7 Is capability required to commit a fraud? Is capability part of opportunity or should it be considered a separate element of fraud?

AUDITING INSIGHT What's Your Excuse?

A manager at **Andersen Consulting** (currently **Accenture**) stole $240,000 by abusing the expense reimbursement procedures in her company. She claims that she suffers from severe depression and her only remedy is exorbitant shopping sprees for jewelry and fine clothing.

Source: M.F. Zimbelman, "Student Shares Insights about Expense Fraud," *Fraud Magazine*, December 2004, pp. 15–19.

FRAUD PREVENTION

3. Describe ways and means for preventing employee frauds.

Building a good fraud prevention program is an extremely difficult task. Most day-to-day business activities require some trust and processes where controls will never be absolute. For example, if we entrust an individual with check authorization, at the instant they sign the check they have physical custody of the asset. Management cannot add controls that reduce the effectiveness of the business process.

Accountants and auditors have often been exhorted to be the leaders in fraud prevention by employing their skills in designing "tight" control systems. This strategy is, at best, a short-run solution to a large and pervasive problem. Business activity is built on the trust that people at all levels will do their jobs properly. Control systems limit trust and, in the extreme, can strangle business in bureaucracy. The challenge is to have useful controls and to avoid picky rules that are "fun to beat." The challenge of "beating the system," which can lead to bigger and better things, is an invitation to fraudulent types of behavior. (How many college students find ways to get into course registration before their scheduled times?)

Accountants and auditors must be sensitive to the needs of the business by instituting controls that will prevent or detect fraud without impeding business activity. Managers and employees must have freedom to do business, which may mean giving them some freedom to commit frauds. Effective long-run prevention measures are complex and difficult, involving the elimination of the causes of fraud by mitigating the effect of motive, opportunity, and lack of integrity.

Managing People Pressures in the Workplace

From time to time, people will experience financial and other pressures. The pressures cannot be eliminated, but the facilities for sharing them can be created. Some companies have "ethics officers" to serve this purpose. Their job is to be available to talk over the ethical dilemmas faced in the workplace and help people adopt legitimate responses. However, the ethics officers are normally not psychological counselors.

Many companies have "hot lines" for anonymous reporting of ethical problems. Indeed, companies that must comply with the PCAOB standards must implement an employee "hot line." Usually, the best kind of hot-line arrangement is to have the responding party be a third-party agency outside the organization. In the United States, some external providers are in the business of being the recipients of hot-line calls, coordinating their activities with the management of various organizations to whom they provide this service.

The most effective method of long-run fraud prevention, however, lies in the practice of management by caring for people. Managers and supervisors at all levels can exhibit a genuine concern for the personal and professional needs of their subordinates and fellow managers and subordinates can show the same concern for each other and their managers. Many companies facilitate this caring attitude with an organized employee assistance program (EAP). They offer a range of counseling referral services dealing with substance abuse, mental health, family problems, crisis help, legal matters, health education, retirement, career paths, job loss troubles, and family financial planning.

When external auditors are engaged in the audit of an entity's financial statements, they must obtain an understanding of the control environment, which relates to the overall scheme of management activity in the company. The audit team should consider how management addresses these employee issues. Using devices such as the above enhances the entity's control environment and represents the beginnings of an effective control system.

Internal Control Procedures and Employee Monitoring

Auditors would be aghast at an entity that had no controls. Controls in the form of job descriptions and performance specifications are needed to help people know the jobs they are supposed to accomplish. An entity whose only control is "trustworthy

AUDITING INSIGHT The Trusted Employee

A small business owner hired his best friend to work as his accountant. The friend was given full, unlimited access to all aspects of the business and was completely responsible for the accounting. Five years later, the owner finally terminated the friend because the business was not profitable. Upon taking over the accounting, the owner's wife found that cash receipts from customers were twice the amounts formerly recorded by the accountant "friend." An investigation revealed that the friend had stolen $450,000 in cash sales receipts from the business, while the owner had never made more than $16,000 a year. (The friend had even used the stolen money to make loans to the owner to keep the business going!)

employees" has no control.[4] Unfortunately, "getting caught" is an important consideration for many people when coping with their problems. Controls provide the opportunity to get caught.

As previously discussed, concealment of the crime is a distinguishing attribute of a fraud. Often the auditors' first indication of a fraud is the identification of a control violation or the attempt to conceal a control violation. Such red flags may include[5]

- Missing documents.
- Second endorsements on checks.
- Unusual endorsements on checks.
- Unexplained adjustments to inventory balances.
- Unexplained adjustments to accounts receivable.
- Old items in bank reconciliations.
- Old outstanding checks.
- Customer complaints.
- Unusual patterns in deposits in transit.

As noted previously in Chapter 5, an important feature of effective internal control is the separation of duties and responsibilities for (1) transaction authorization, (2) record-keeping, (3) custody of or access to assets, and (4) reconciliation of actual assets to the accounting records. Generally, a person who, acting alone or in a conspiracy, can perform two or more of these functions also can commit a fraud by taking assets, converting them, and covering up. (Other control features were explained in Chapter 5.)

AUDITING INSIGHT Too Perfect!

Because of allegations of fraud and abuse, Congress mandated that all clubs in the U.S. military system be audited. These audits included inspecting various reports generated by the clubs including cash count sheets, physical inventory counts, and reconciliations of accounts. When the auditors reviewed these reports, there were never any discrepancies: cashiers were never short; inventory always balanced; and there was never an unexplained variance in any reconciliation. Because of this "perfection," the auditors decided to do additional testing. The auditors found modified shot glasses (shorting each customer on every drink) and filler being placed in hamburgers to cover theft of ground beef inventory. It is believed that approximately 20 percent of the sales were skimmed by employees, with almost every employee at the club involved. This high degree of collusion among employees allowed for the *perfect* cover-up!

Source: "Right Controls, Wrong Culture," *Internal Auditor,* April 2004, p. 85.

[4] W. S. Albrecht, "How CPAs Can Help Clients Prevent Employee Fraud," *Journal of Accountancy,* December 1988, pp. 110–14.
[5] Ibid., pp. 113–14.

AUDITING INSIGHT She Can Do Everything

Mrs. Lemon was the only bookkeeper for an electrical supply company. She wrote the checks and reconciled the bank account. In the cash disbursements journal, she coded some checks as inventory, but she wrote the checks to herself, using her own true name. When the checks were returned with the bank statement, she simply destroyed them. She stole $416,000 over five years. After being caught and sentenced to prison, she testified to having continuous guilt over doing something she knew was wrong.

Source: Association of Certified Fraud Examiners (ACFE), "Auditing for Fraud."

Fraud awareness auditing involves perceptions of the client controls installed (or not installed), plus "thinking like a crook" to imagine ways and means of stealing. When controls are absent, the ways and means may be obvious. Otherwise, it might take some scheming to figure out how to steal from an employer.

Integrity by Example and Enforcement

The key to integrity in business is "accountability"—that is, each person must be willing to put his or her decisions and actions in the open, for all to see. Many organizations begin by publishing codes of conduct. Some of these codes are simple and some are very elaborate. Government agencies and defense contractors typically have the most elaborate rules for employee conduct. Sometimes these codes are effective; sometimes they are not effective. A code can be effective only if the "tone at the top" supports it. When the chairman of the board and the president make themselves visible examples of the code, other people will then believe it is real. Subordinates tend to follow the boss's lead.

Hiring and firing are important. Background checks on prospective employees are advisable. A new employee who has been a fox in some other organization's hen house will probably be a fox in a new place. Organizations have been known to hire private investigators to make these background checks. Fraudsters should be fired and, in most cases, prosecuted. They have a low rate of recidivism (repeat offenses) if they are prosecuted, but they have a high rate if not.[6] Prosecution has the added benefit of sending the message that management does not believe that "occasional dishonesty" is acceptable.

AUDITING INSIGHT You're Not Supposed to Audit Me!

One of the large professional services firms was conducting an "ethical compliance" audit of a Fortune 500 company. An ethical compliance audit is an attestation engagement to ensure, among other things, that client personnel are following the company's code of conduct. Believing that the "tone at the top" was the most important element of the client's ethical compliance control system, the assurance team started in the CEO's office. They found that the CEO was using the company plane to fly his fashion designer wife and her friends back and forth to Paris on a regular basis. When confronted in a board of directors meeting with the evidence, the CEO chastised the assurance team: "You weren't supposed to check on me; you were supposed to check on the employees." The board of directors disagreed, requesting the CEO's resignation.

[6] Ibid., p. 114.

┌───┐
│ **AUDITING INSIGHT** Where Did He Come From? │
└───┘

The controller defrauded the company for several million dollars. As it turned out, he was no controller at all. He didn't know a debit from a credit. The fraudster had been fired from five previous jobs where money had turned up missing. He was discovered one evening when the president showed up unexpectedly at the com-pany and found a stranger in the office with the controller. The stranger was doing all of the accounting for the bogus controller.

Source: Association of Certified Fraud Examiners (ACFE), "Auditing for Fraud."

Review Checkpoints

6.8 Make a two-column list with fraud-prevention management-style characteristics in one column and, opposite each of these, management-style characteristics that might lead to fraud.

CASH INTERNAL CONTROL CONSIDERATIONS

LEARNING OBJECTIVE

4. Describe the controls over the receipt and disbursement of cash.

After the discussion of employee fraud, we focus on the audit of cash. We make this transition for two reasons. First, cash is the primary target of employee fraud, and consequently inherent risk for cash is generally highest among all the account groups. Cash is highly liquid (easily converted into cash!), not easily identifiable as company property, and highly portable. For these reasons, cash is the favorite target of employee thieves, although theft of inventory is a close second. As a consequence, controls over cash must be unusually strong.

Second, because cash is endemic to each of a client's accounting cycles, the discussion of cash should naturally precede the audits of the different cycles in the following chapters. For example, the basic activities in the revenue and collection cycle (Chapter 7) are (1) receiving and processing customer orders, including credit granting; (2) delivering goods and services to customers; (3) billing customers and accounting for accounts receivable; (4) *collecting and depositing cash received from customers; and* (5) *reconciling bank statements.* The basic acquisition and expenditure activities (Chapter 8) are (1) purchasing goods and services and (2) *paying the bills.* Similarly, the production and conversion cycle (Chapter 9) and the investing and financing cycle (Chapter 10) also feature the collection or expenditure of cash. For our discussion, we will focus on (1) cash collections, (2) cash disbursements, and (3) reconciling cash balances.

Control Considerations for Cash Collections

Cash can be received in several ways—over the counter, through the mail, by electronic funds transfer, and by receipt in a "lockbox." In a **lockbox** arrangement, payments are remitted by customers to an external location (lockbox); a fiduciary (e.g., a bank) opens the box, lists the receipts, deposits the money, and sends the remittance advices (stubs showing the amount received from each customer) to the company. Exhibit 6.2 shows some cash receipts processing procedures in a manual accounting setting.

Some individual employee will always initially receive cash and checks and thus has custody of the physical cash for a time. Since this initial custody cannot be avoided, it is always good control to (1) have two people open the mail containing customer receipts (joint custody), (2) restrictively endorse the checks immediately after removing them from the envelope, (3) prepare a list of the cash receipts as early in the process as possible, and then (4) separate the actual cash from the recordkeeping documents. The cash

EXHIBIT 6.2 Cash Receipts Processing

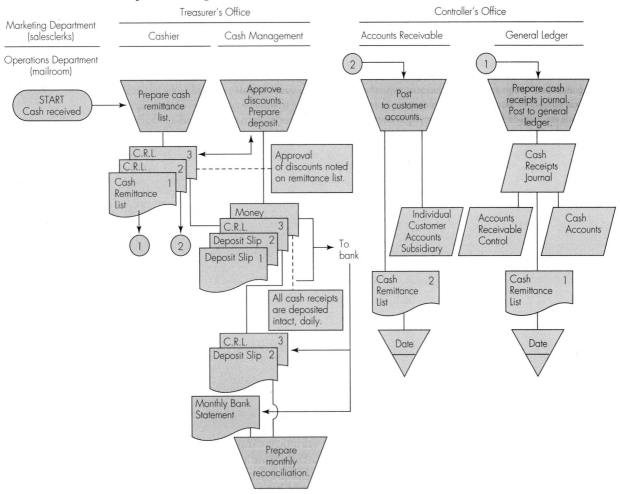

should be sent to the cashier or treasurer's office, where a bank deposit is prepared and the money is sent to the bank *daily* and *intact* (no money should be withheld from the deposit). The list or remittance advices go to the accountants, who record the cash receipts. (You have prepared a "remittance advice" each time you write the "amount enclosed" on part of your credit card bill, tear it off, and enclose it with your check.)

The accountants who record cash receipts and credits to customer accounts should never handle the cash. They should use the remittance list or remittance advice to make entries to the cash and accounts receivable control accounts and to the customers' accounts receivable subsidiary account records. A good error-checking activity is to have control account and subsidiary account entries made by different people, then later the accounts receivable entries and balances can be compared (reconciled) to determine whether they agree in total. Most computerized accounting programs post the customers' accounts automatically by keying on the customer identification number, and agreement is controlled by the computer program.

At the end of the day, an independent person can receive (1) a copy of the check listing, (2) a report of payments recorded in accounts payable, and (3) a copy of the deposit slip from the bank. (Commercial deposit slips have multiple copies. The bank runs these copies through the teller machine, which imprints the time, date, account, and amount on each copy. At least one copy is returned to the person making the deposit, who returns the copy to the company as evidence that the deposit was made.) If the cash received during the day is maintained intact, the information on all three items should match.

AUDITING INSIGHT Lapping up the Profits

Stephan Winkler was the controller and director of accounting for a beverage distributing company in Florida. Some customers paid the route drivers by cash or check when beverages were delivered; other customers mailed payments directly the company. Winkler performed the final accounting before the bank deposits were made and was able to skim cash collected by the route drivers by covering the customers' account with payments received in the mail from other customers. In this manner, Winkler stole approximate $350,000 from his employer.

Source: A. McNeal, "Lapping up the Profits," *Internal Auditor,* December 2006, pp. 85–87.

Take a close look at Exhibit 6.2. Suppose the cashier who prepares the remittance list had misappropriated and converted Customer A's checks to personal use. It might work for a short time until Customer A complained that the entity had not credited their account for payments. The cashier knows this. So, the cashier later puts Customer B's check in the bank deposit, but shows Customer A on the remittance list; thus, the accountants give Customer A credit. So far, so good for preventing Customer A's complaint. But now Customer B needs to be covered. To detect this **lapping** scheme, a detailed audit should include comparison of the checks listed on a sample of deposit slips (Customer B) to the detail of customer remittances recorded to customer accounts (Customer A). It is an attempt to find credits given to customers for whom no payments were received on the day in question.

Employees outside the normal cash operations (recording and custody) should prepare bank account reconciliations on a timely basis. Deposit slips should be compared to the details on cash remittance lists and the total should be traced to the general ledger accounts receivable entries. (This reconciliation would reveal if money was withheld from the deposit.) This care is required to establish that all the receipts recorded in the books were deposited and that credit was given to the right customer.

A common feature of cash management is to require that persons who handle cash be insured under a fidelity bond. A **fidelity bond** is an insurance policy that covers most kinds of cash embezzlement losses. Fidelity bonds do not prevent or detect embezzlement, but the failure to carry the insurance exposes the company to complete loss if embezzlement occurs. Moreover, bonding companies often perform their own background checks of employees before bonding them. Auditors may recommend fidelity bonding to companies that do not know about such coverage.

Information about a company's controls often is gathered by completing an internal control questionnaire. A selection of other questionnaires for both general (manual) controls and computer controls over cash receipts is in Appendix 6A at the end of this chapter. You can study these questionnaires for details of desirable control procedures. They are organized under headings that identify the important control objectives over cash transactions—occurrence, accuracy, completeness, classification, and cutoff.

Another way to obtain general information about controls is called a "walkthrough." In conducting walkthroughs, the auditors select examples of a transaction (in this case, customer remittance advices) and "walk them through" the information-processing system from its receipt to its recording in the accounting records. Sample documents are collected, and employees in each department are questioned about their specific duties. The walkthrough, combined with inquiries, can contribute evidence about appropriate separation of duties, which might be a sufficient basis for assessing control risk slightly below the maximum. However, a walkthrough is too limited in scope to provide evidence of whether the client's control activities were operating effectively during the period under audit. Usually, a larger sample of transactions for detail testing of control performance is necessary to justify a low control risk assessment based on actual control performance evidence.

AUDITING INSIGHT The Consequence of a Lack of Separation of Duties

PBS&J is a Miami, Florida–based engineering firm with 75 offices and 3,900 employees. In September 2006, the ex-CFO and two former subordinates waived indictment concerning a $36 million embezzlement. Their attorneys stated that the three employees will plead guilty.

Between 1993 and 2005, the three defendants issued company checks to themselves and funneled money from the company's health care benefit fund. One defendant purchased a home in the Florida Keys, another purchased an interest in a local restaurant, and the third bought property in Florida and Nicaragua as well as financing high-dollar gambling activities. Sentencing guidelines call for prison terms of 78 to 97 months for each of these individuals.

Source: P. Danner and D. Christensen, "Three Charged in Embezzlement Scheme," *Miami Herald*, September 19, 2006, p. A1.

Tests of Controls over Cash Receipts

An entity should establish input, processing, and output control activities to prevent, detect, and correct accounting errors. Auditors can perform tests of controls to determine whether client personnel are properly performing the prescribed activities essential to the correct handling of cash receipts. If personnel in the organization are not performing cash control activities very well, auditors will need to expand substantive audit procedures to detect possible frauds and to ensure control failures have not produced materially misleading cash balances.

Exhibit 6.3 contains a selection of tests of controls for cash receipts transactions. Many of these procedures can be characterized as steps taken to verify the content and character of sample documents from one file with the content and character of documents in another file. These steps are designed to enable the audit team to obtain objective evidence about the *effectiveness* of controls and about the *reliability* of accounting records. Exhibit 6.3 also shows the control objectives (management assertions) tested by the audit procedures. Thus, the test of controls procedures produces evidence that helps auditors determine whether the specific control objectives were achieved.

Control Considerations for Cash Disbursements

For cash disbursements, effective internal control begins with appropriate separation of duties. Proper separation involves different people and different departments handling the

EXHIBIT 6.3
Test of Controls for Cash Receipts

Internal Control	Control Objective (Management Assertion)	Test of Control
• Cash receipts are deposited intact and daily.		1. For a sample of recorded cash receipts in the cash receipts journal, . . .
	Occurrence	a. Vouch to deposits in the bank statement.
	Accuracy	b. Recalculate the cash summarized for a daily deposit or posting.
	Cutoff	c. Compare the date of receipt to the recording date.
	Completeness	d. Trace the receipts to postings in the correct customers' accounts.
• Deposits are reconciled with totals posted to the accounts receivable subsidiary ledger.	Completeness	2. For a sample of daily cash deposits from the client's bank statement, trace to the cash receipts journal.

cash disbursement *authorization; custody* of blank documents (checks); *record keeping* for payments; and bank *reconciliation:*

- *Custody.* Blank documents such as blank checks should be kept secure at all times. If unauthorized persons can obtain a blank check, they can be in another country before the embezzlement is detected.

- *Authorization.* Cash disbursements are authorized by an accounts payable department's assembly of purchase orders, vendor invoices, and internal receiving reports to show a valid obligation to pay. This assembly of supporting documents is called a *voucher* and will be discussed in greater detail in a Chapter 8. (Accounts payable obligations usually are recorded when the purchaser receives the goods or services ordered.) A person authorized by the management or the board of directors signs checks. A company may have a policy to require two signatures on checks over a certain amount (e.g., $50,000). Vouchers should be marked "PAID" or otherwise stamped to show that they have been processed completely so they cannot be paid a second time.

- *Recording.* When checks are prepared, entries are made to debit the accounts payable and credit cash. Someone without access to the check-writing function should perform the recording function.

- *Reconciliation.* Monitoring of the internal control over cash can be provided by timely bank reconciliations by individuals outside of the normal cash operations.

Combinations of two or more of these responsibilities in one person, one office, or one computerized system may open the door for errors and frauds. In addition, the control system should provide for detailed information processing control procedures.

Information about the control system often is gathered initially by completing an internal control questionnaire. A selection of questionnaires for both general (manual) controls and computer controls is in Appendix 6A.

Tests of Controls over Cash Disbursements

An entity should have detailed controls in place and operating to prevent, detect, and correct accounting errors. Exhibit 6.4 identifies common tests of controls over cash disbursements. Auditors can perform tests of controls to determine whether company personnel actually are performing controls that are said to be in place and operating properly.

EXHIBIT 6.4 **Tests of Controls over Cash Disbursements**

Internal Control	Control Objective (Transation Assertion)	Test of Control
• Checks are not printed until voucher packets are prepared. • An employee compares printed checks with voucher packets (documents used to authorize payments) prior to submission for signature.	Occurrence Cutoff Accuracy	1. For a sample of recorded cash disbursements from the cash disbursements journal, vouch to supporting documentation for evidence of mathematical accuracy, correct classification, properapproval, and proper date of entry.
• Only authorized signers are permitted to sign checks.	Occurrence	
• Checks are prenumbered and accounted for.	Completeness	2. Scan checks for sequence. Look for gaps in sequence and duplicate numbers.
• Bank reconciliations are prepared on a timely basis.	Completeness Accuracy	3. For a sample of cancelled checks received back from the bank, vouch to supporting documentation for evidence of mathematical accuracy, proper classification, proper approval, and proper date of entry.

AUDITING INSIGHT Too Much Trouble

A trucking company self-insured claims of damage to goods in transit, processed claims vouchers, and paid customers from its own bank accounts. Several persons were authorized to sign checks. One person thought it "too much trouble" to stamp the vouchers PAID and said: "That's textbook stuff anyway." Numerous claims were recycled to other check signers and $80,000 was paid for duplicate claims before the problem was discovered.

Summary: Cash Considerations in the Risk of Material Misstatement

The audit manager or senior accountant in charge of the audit should evaluate the evidence obtained from an understanding of the internal control system and from the tests of controls. If the control risk is assessed very low, the substantive procedures for the cash account balances can be limited in cost-saving ways. For example, internal auditors could be used to assist in the audit the bank reconciliations. On the other hand, if tests of controls reveal weaknesses, the substantive procedures will need to be more effective to lower the risk of failing to detect material misstatement in the cash balances. Descriptions of major deficiencies, control weaknesses, and inefficiencies should be incorporated in a letter to the client describing "significant internal control deficiencies."

Review Checkpoints

6.9 What is the basic sequence of activities in the cash collection process?

6.10 Why should a list of cash remittances be made and sent to the accounting department? Wouldn't it be easier to send the cash and checks to the accountants so they can enter the credits to customers' accounts accurately?

6.11 What is *lapping*? What procedures can auditors employ to detect lapping?

6.12 What feature of the acquisition and expenditure control would be expected to prevent an employee from embezzling cash through creation of fictitious vouchers?

AUDIT EVIDENCE IN MANAGEMENT REPORTS AND DATA FILES

Audit evidence can be found in a number of different management reports and documents, which are discussed in this section.

Cash Receipts Journal

The cash receipts journal contains all the detailed entries for all receipts of cash by the entity (debits to the cash account), including cash deposits. It contains the population of credit entries that should be reflected in the credits to accounts receivable for customer payments. It also contains the adjusting and correcting entries that can result from the bank account reconciliation. These entries are important because they may signal the types of accounting errors or manipulations that occur in the cash receipts accounting.

Cash Disbursements Journal

The cash disbursements journal is the company's checkbook. It contains all the detailed entries for checks written during the period being audited (cash disbursements). Since all cash disbursements (other than those from a petty cash account) should be made via

AUDITING INSIGHT Who Was That Check From Again?

Four people were under investigation for an easily discovered counterfeit check-cashing scheme. Despite using high-tech computer equipment to generate the counterfeit checks, the fraudsters mistakenly misspelled the payer (Broyhill Furniture) as "Boryhill Furniture."

Source: "News of the Weird," *Funny Times*, May 2003.

check, the cash disbursements journal contains the cash credit entries that provide a population for testing cash disbursements. It also contains the adjusting and correcting entries that can result from the bank account reconciliation. These entries are important because they may signal the types of accounting errors or manipulations that occur in the cash disbursements accounting. The cash disbursements journal is usually scanned for suspect items such as checks made out to "cash" or "bearer." In addition, company procedures should require that "voided" checks be retained and auditors should review these checks to ensure they were actually voided.

Bank Reconciliations

The company's bank reconciliation is the primary means of valuing cash in the financial statements. The amount of cash in the bank is almost always different from the amount in the general ledger (financial statements) and the reconciliation purports to explain the difference. A bank account reconciliation to compare book cash balances to bank cash balances provides management an opportunity to monitor the separation of duties for both cash receipts as well as cash disbursements.

Canceled Checks

Exhibit 6.5 describes the information found on a typical check. Whether the auditor examines the actual check or a scanned image obtained from the bank, knowledge of the codes for federal reserve districts, offices, states, and bank identification numbers could enable an auditor to spot a crude check forgery.

A forger's mistake with the optional identification printing or the magnetic check number might supply a tip-off. If the amount of a check is altered after it has cleared the bank, the alteration would be noted by comparing the magnetic imprint of the amount paid to the amount written on the check face. The reverse side of a check carries the endorsement(s) of the payees and holders in due course; the date and the name and routing number of the bank where the check was deposited; and the date, identification of the Federal Reserve office, and its routing number for the Federal Reserve check clearing. (Sometimes there is no Federal Reserve clearing identification when local checks are cleared locally without going through a Federal Reserve office.) Auditors can follow the path of a canceled check by following the banks where it was deposited and cleared. This route may or may not correspond with the characteristics of the payee. (For example, ask why a check to a local business in Texas was deposited in a small Missouri bank and cleared through the St. Louis Federal Reserve office.)

AUDITING INSIGHT Who Endorsed That Check?

The distribution manager called internal audit and asked why his predecessor's endorsement was on a $600 check payable to the company and why it appeared to be deposited in his personal account. Further investigation revealed that the former manager had been selling company inventory without recording the sale and keeping the payments when received. The result? Over 60 payments were identified totaling approximately $70,000. However, a count of physical inventory revealed an inventory variance of more than $200,000. Keep an eye on those endorsements!

Source: "Purchasing Below the Radar," *Internal Auditor*, August 2003, pp. 95–97.

EXHIBIT 6.5 How to Read a Canceled Check and Endorsement

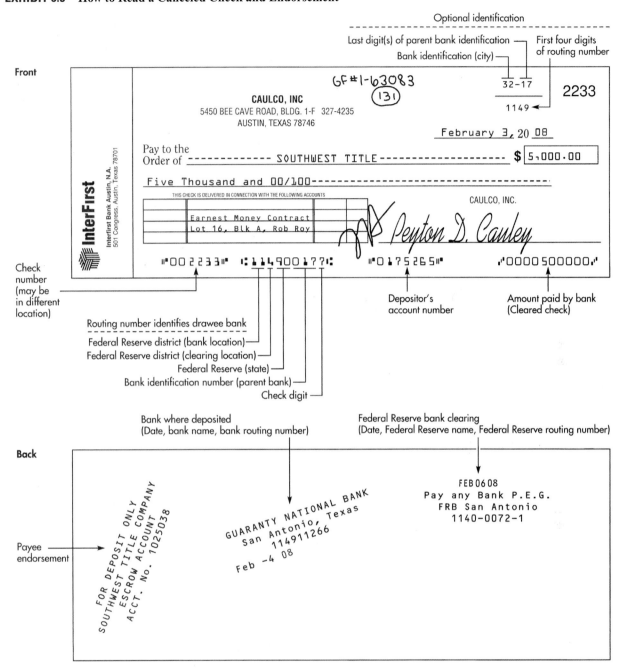

It should be noted that many banks no longer return the canceled checks to their customers. Instead, they send photocopies of the front of the checks. While this information is sufficient for reconciling an account, it does not provide the information that may assist a company or auditor in detecting or investigating possible irregularities. Many banks will return the canceled checks to the company for a small fee. Other banks retain images of checks (front and back) on the bank's Internet site. Auditors, controllers, and CFOs should strongly recommend that their client or company ensure that access to canceled checks is available, even if additional fees are required.

Individuals engaging in fraudulent schemes involving cash often try to conceal their defalcations by removing canceled checks they made payable to themselves or endorsed on the back with their own names. Missing canceled checks are a signal (red flag).

However, people who reconcile bank accounts may not notice missing checks if the bank reconciliation is performed using only the numerical listing printed in the bank statement. Now consider the case of truncated bank statements, when the bank does not even return the canceled checks to the payor. All the checks are "missing" and the bank reconciler has no opportunity to notice anything about canceled checks.

Bank Statements

Most of the information shown on the bank statement in Exhibit 6.6 is self-explanatory. However, auditors should not overlook the usefulness of some of the information: the number and dollar amount of deposits and checks can be compared to the detail data on the bank statement; the account holder's federal business identification number is on the statement, and this can be used in other databases (for individuals, this is a place to get a person's Social Security number); and the statement itself can be studied for alterations.

EXHIBIT 6.6
Small Business Bank Statement

```
                                                                    27
    ☒ First RepublicBank

    FIRST REPUBLICBANK AUSTIN, N.A.                          ACCOUNT
    P.O. BOX 908                          ---          604017-526-5
    AUSTIN, TEXAS  78781
                                          ---    ---
                                          ---                  PAGE
                                                ---               1

    CAULCO INC                                         SSN/TAX ID
    BLDG 1 OFFICE F                                    74-2076251
    5450 BEE CAVE RD
    AUSTIN,  TX                                       CYC MC FREQ
    78746                                             01 01 M0000

    **  YOUR CHECKING ACCOUNT        01-29-08 THRU 02-28-08  **

    TO YOUR PREVIOUS BALANCE OF - - - - - - - -        7,559.06
    YOU ADDED        1 DEPOSITS FOR  - - - - - -        5,654.16
    YOU SUBTRACTED  26 WITHDRAWALS FOR - - - - -       10,838.29
    GIVING YOU A CURRENT BALANCE OF - - - - - - -       7,374.93

    NUMBER OF DAYS USED FOR AVERAGES  - - - - - -             31
    YOUR AVERAGE LEDGER BALANCE - - - - - - - - -        4,014.67
    YOUR LOW BALANCE OCCURRED ON 02-22 AND WAS  -        2,374.93

                    THANK YOU

    ------------------------------------------------------------
    ------------------------------------------------------------
                    DEPOSITS AND OTHER ADDITIONS

        DATE     AMOUNT   ✔
        0204     5654.16
    ------------------------------------------------------------
                    CHECKS AND OTHER WITHDRAWALS

    CHECK DATE   AMOUNT CHECK DATE    AMOUNT CHECK DATE    AMOUNT
    2201 0211     57.83✔ 2214 0203    403.92✔ 2225 0217  ✔182.77
     **                  2215 0203    135.59✔    **
    2205 0222     16.72✔ 2216 0216      6.16✔ 2231 0205  ✔254.37
    2206 0203    533.28✔ 2217 0217    138.43✔ 2232 0210  ✔ 60.61
    2207 0203   1312.15✔ 2218 0217    131.92✔
     **                  2219 0217     82.97✔ 2234 0217  ✔ 64.69
    2209 0203    247.10✔ 2220 0217     87.49✔ 2235 0218  ✔279.97
    2210 0203    249.98✔ 2221 0217     85.68✔    **
    2211 0203    255.26✔ 2222 0217     84.69✔ 2238 0219  ✔ 90.00
    2212 0203    242.09✔    **
    2213 0203    384.91✔ 2224 0217    449.71✔
```

Review Checkpoints

6.13 How can you tell whether the amount on a check was altered after it was paid by a bank?

6.14 Take a closer look at Exhibit 6.6. Is there anything wrong with the bank statement? What are some ways to tell whether any of the amounts have been altered?

THE AUDIT OF CASH

LEARNING OBJECTIVE

5. Design and perform substantive procedures for the audit of cash.

The first procedure in an audit of cash is to obtain the entity-prepared bank reconciliations and audit them, focusing on some of the reconciling items discussed in the preceding section. Auditors should not perform the company's control function of preparing the reconciliation.

Bank Reconciliation

A client-prepared bank reconciliation is shown in Exhibit 6.7. Auditors verify the bank balance using a confirmation (Exhibit 6.8) received directly from the bank and cross-reference this balance to the bank reconciliation. Other procedures used in auditing the bank reconciliation are as follows:

- Verify the mathematical accuracy of the reconciliation, including the listing of outstanding checks and deposits in transit.
- Examine reconciling items to ensure they are appropriately classified (i.e., were outstanding checks written but not paid and deposits in transit mailed to the bank but not recorded).
- Agree the book balance to the trial balance, which has been traced to the general ledger.

The auditors' information source for validating the bank reconciliation items is a **cutoff bank statement,** which is a complete bank statement including all paid checks and deposit slips. The client requests the bank to send this bank statement directly to the auditor. It is usually for a 10- to 20-day period following the reconciliation date. (It also can be the next regular monthly statement, received directly by the auditors.)

The *tracing* of outstanding checks is a matter of comparing checks that cleared in the cutoff bank statement (and were either returned with that statement or identified in that statement) with the client's list of outstanding checks for evidence that all checks that were written prior to the reconciliation date were on the list of outstanding checks. The deposits shown in transit should be recorded by the bank in the first business days of the cutoff period. If recorded later, the inference is that the deposit may have been made up from receipts of the period after the reconciliation date. For large outstanding checks not clearing in the cutoff period, other documentation supporting the disbursement may be used. These procedures are keyed and described by tick marks in Exhibit 6.7. For cash disbursements, canceled checks should be traced to the cash disbursements listing (journal).

Confirmation of Cash Balances

The auditor should confirm account balances for all accounts, both deposit and loan, from each bank the client utilizes in the business. The standard bank confirmation form, approved by the AICPA, the American Bankers Association, and the Bank Administration Institute, is shown in Exhibit 6.8. This form is used to obtain bank confirmation of deposit and loan balances. (Other confirmation letters are used to obtain confirmation of contingent liabilities, endorsements, compensating balance agreements, lines of credit, and other financial instruments and transactions.) A word of caution is in order: While financial

EXHIBIT 6.7
Bank Reconciliation

C-2

| Prepared By | SSS, III | Date | 1/24/2009 |
| Reviewed By | SSS, Jr. | Date | 1/28/2009 |

Apollo Shoes, Inc.
Bank Reconciliation
12/31/2008

Prepared by Client

Balance per bank statement		343,055.04 ᵉ
Add:		
Deposits in transit		0.00
		343,055.04

Deduct O/S Checks

3086	12/27/06	8,533.12 ˣ
3087	12/27/06	4,741.30 ˣ
3088	12/27/06	14,122.85 ˣ
3089	12/28/06	6,707.05 ˣ
3090	12/28/06	10,587.77 ˣ
3091	12/28/06	7,566.07 ˣ
3092	12/28/06	5,684.08 ˣ
3093	12/28/06	18,421.90 ˣ
3094	12/28/06	12,741.49 ˣ
3095	12/28/06	988.55 ˣ
3096	12/28/06	10,014.94 ˣ
3097	12/28/06	15,746.44 ˣ
3098	12/28/06	16,472.00 ˣ
3099	12/28/06	12,610.96 ˣ

	−144,938.52 F
Adjust bank balance	198,116.52 T/B-1
	F

F Footed

ˣ Traced from bank statement on page C-2-2

ᵉ Confirmed by bank, confirmation on page C-2-1

institutions may note exceptions to the information typed in a confirmation and may confirm items omitted from it, the AICPA warns auditors that sole reliance on the form to satisfy the completeness assertion, insofar as cash and loan balances are concerned, is unwarranted. Officers and employees of financial institutions cannot be expected to search their information systems for balances and loans that may not be immediately evident as assets and liabilities of the client company. However, it is a good idea to send confirmations on accounts the company represents as closed during the year to get the bank to confirm zero balances. (If a bank confirms a nonzero balance, the auditors have evidence that some asset accounting is omitted in the company records.)

Schedule of Interbank Transfers

Auditors usually prepare a **schedule of interbank transfers** to determine whether transfers of cash from one bank to another were recorded properly (correct amount and correct date). Auditors also should be alert to the possibility of a company's practice of illegal

EXHIBIT 6.8 **Bank Confirmation**

STANDARD FORM TO CONFIRM ACCOUNT
BALANCE INFORMATION WITH FINANCIAL INSTITUTIONS

C-2-1

Apollo Shoes, Inc.
CUSTOMER NAME

FINANCIAL INSTITUTION'S NAME AND ADDRESS

Twenty-First National Bank

Post Office Box 1

Shoetown, ME 00002

We have provided to our accountants the following information as of the close of business on 12/31/2006, regarding our deposit and loan balances. Please confirm the accuracy of the information, noting any exceptions to the information provided. If the balances have been left blank, please complete this form by furnishing the balance in the appropriate space below.* Although we do not request nor expect you to conduct a comprehensive, detailed search of your records, if during the process of completing this confirmation additional information about other deposit and loan accounts we may have with you comes to your attention, please include such information below. Please use the enclosed envelope to return the form directly to our accountants.

1. At the close of business on the date listed above, our records indicated the following deposit balance(s):

ACCOUNT NAME	ACCOUNT NO.	INTEREST RATE	BALANCE*	
Checking Account	604-17-526-5	n/a	*343,055.04*	*REF C-2*
Payroll Account	604-29-016-3	n/a	*0*	
Savings Account	604-03-739-8	3.2%	*4,150,947.95*	

2. We were directly liable to the financial institution for loans at the close of business on the date listed above as follows:

ACCOUNT NO./ DESCRIPTION	BALANCE*	DATE DUE	INTEREST RATE	DATE THROUGH WHICH INTEREST IS PAID	DESCRIPTION OF COLLATERAL
Note#106316	10,000,000	1/1/2008	8.75%	11/30/2008	None
Line of Credit, Acct#7500438	44,053,000	2007 (revolving)	9.75%	11/30/2008	None

E.P. Unum 1/3/2009
(Customer's Authorized Signature) (Date)

The information presented above by the customer is in agreement with our records. Although we have not conducted a comprehensive, detailed search of our records, no other deposit or loan accounts have come to our attention except as noted below.

I.M Rich 1/10/2009
(Financial Institution Authorized Signature) (Date)

Account Confirmation Specialist
(Title)

EXCEPTIONS AND OR COMMENTS
No exceptions noted.

Please return this form directly to our accountants:

Smith & Smith, CPAs
31st Financial Avenue
Shoetown, ME 00002

*Ordinarily, balances are intentionally left blank if they are not available at the time this form is prepared.
Approved 1990 by American Bankers Association, American Institute of Certified Public Accountants, and Bank Administration Institute. Additional forms available from: AICPA–Order Department, P.O. Box 1003 NY, NY 10108-1003.

AUDITING INSIGHT "The Darn Stuff Is So Easy To Count"

Through the use of discretionary estimates, HealthSouth, one of the largest health care providers in the United States, inflated its assets by $1.5 billion. In an even more bizarre twist, prosecutors allege the company overstated its cash by more than $300 million. Because auditors use standardized forms to confirm cash balances with financial institutions, how the auditors missed the cash overstatement is a mystery. "I'm shocked that cash is manipulated and overstated, because the darn stuff is so easy to count," states one audit expert.

Source: "Did HealthSouth Auditor Ernst Miss Key Clues to Fraud Risks?" *The Wall Street Journal*, April 10, 2003.

[handwritten: using float system]

"kiting." **Check kiting** is the deliberate floating of funds between two or more bank accounts. When a check is deposited in one bank, the cash receipts journal immediately includes that deposit. At the same time, the check, drawn on a different bank account, does not appear in the cash disbursements journal for several days. By this method, an entity uses the time required for checks to clear to inflate the cash amount on the entity's books. The transactions shown in Exhibit 6.9 describe a simple check kiting scheme.

Start with no money in the First National Bank and none in the Last National Bank. Run the kite quickly from July 3 (Monday) through July 12 (next Wednesday)—taking advantage of the holiday and the weekend to float the hot checks.

A. Deposit a $15,000 check drawn on First National Bank to the Last National account. Simultaneously, deposit a $10,000 check drawn on Last National Bank to the First National account. Do not record the deposits and disbursements in the general ledger. Note that, if auditors were to confirm the bank balances with these two banks on July 3, the total cash would appear to be $25,000 ($10,000 at First National Bank and $15,000 at Last National Bank); however, the actual cash is $0.

B. Deposit an $11,000 check drawn on First National Bank to the Last National account. Simultaneously, deposit a $13,000 check drawn on Last National Bank to

EXHIBIT 6.9 Illustrative Check Kiting Transactions *[handwritten: bank #1] [handwritten: bank #2]*

Index	Date	Transaction	First National Bank At Bank (1)	First National Bank Actual (2)	Last National Bank At Bank (1)	Last National Bank Actual (2)	Total Actual Cash (Sum of 2's)
A	July 3	1st Transfers	0	$ (15,000)	$15,000	15,000	
A	July 3		$10,000	10,000		(10,000)	
		Balances	10,000	(5,000)	15,000	5,000	0
B	July 5	2nd Transfers		(11,000)	11,000	11,000	
B	July 5		13,000	13,000		(13,000)	
		Balances	23,000	(3,000)	26,000	3,000	0
C	July 6	Mercedes payment	(8,000)	(8,000)			
		Balances	15,000	(11,000)	26,000	3,000	(8,000)
D	July 7	1st Transfer (A) clears	(15,000)		(10,000)		
E	July 7	3rd Transfer		(16,000)	16,000	16,000	
E	July 7		14,000	14,000		(14,000)	
		Balances	14,000	(13,000)	32,000	5,000	(8,000)
F	July 8	Pay Travel		(14,000)		(32,000)	
		Balances	14,000	(27,000)	32,000	(27,000)	(54,000)
G	July 10	2nd Transfer clears	(11,000)		(13,000)		
G	July 12	3rd Transfer clears	(16,000)		(14,000)		
G	July 12		(14,000)		(32,000)		
			(27,000)		(27,000)		(54,000)

[handwritten annotations in table: "Per bank recs", "Per GL Opt comp", "net" (circled at (5,000), 5,000, (3,000), 3,000), "nothing recorded on books", "claimed amount"]

(1) "At Bank" means the bank's records of deposits received and checks paid (cleared).
(2) "Actual" means the amounts the general ledger would have had the transfers been recorded.

[handwritten: only mercedes payment 8,00 recorded]

the First National account. Do not record the deposits and disbursements in the general ledger.

C. Purchase an $8,000 certified check from First National Bank to make a down payment on a Mercedes automobile. Record the check in the general ledger.

D. The first transfer checks (part A) clear each bank.

E. Deposit a $16,000 check drawn on First National Bank to the Last National account. Simultaneously, deposit a $14,000 check drawn on Last National Bank to the First National account. Do not record the deposits and disbursements in the general ledger.

F. Write checks for $14,000 drawn on First National Bank and $32,000 drawn on Last National Bank payable to a travel agent and take a long trip (preferably to a country with no extradition treaty!).

G. When the checks are presented to the banks for payment, the accounts are empty. A total of $79,000 was kited, of which $25,000 cleared during the kite period (the first transfers in A), so the "take" was $54,000. The criminals got the Mercedes ($8,000) and the vacation funds ($46,000).

These are some characteristic signs of check kiting schemes:

- Frequent deposits and checks in same amounts.
- Frequent deposits and checks in round amounts.
- Frequent deposits with checks written on the same (other) banks.
- Short time lags between deposits and withdrawals.
- Frequent ATM account balance inquiries.
- Many large deposits made on Thursday or Friday to take advantage of the weekend.
- Large periodic balances in individual accounts with no apparent business explanation.
- Low average balance compared to high level of deposits.
- Many checks made payable to other banks.
- Bank willingness to pay against uncollected funds.
- "Cash" withdrawals with deposit checks drawn on another bank.
- Checks drawn on foreign banks with lax banking laws and regulations.

Auditors can detect the above signs of check kiting by reviewing bank account activity. The only trouble is that criminal check kiters often destroy the banking documents. A company should provide the auditor with access to all deposit slips and canceled checks. However, in today's computerized banking environment, many documents exist only in electronic form or as scanned images. The auditor may need to review the client's account activity directly on the bank's Internet site.

If these cash transfers are recorded in the books, a company will show the negative balances that result from checks drawn on insufficient funds. However, perpetrators may try to hide the kiting by not recording the deposits and checks. Such maneuvers may be detected by using a schedule of interbank transfers.

Assume the facts given in the preceding kiting illustration and the following: (1) the First National Bank account is the company's general bank account and the Last National Bank account is the payroll account, (2) the company pays its payroll on the 15th and 30th days of each month, and (3) the company transfers the net amount of each payroll from the general account to the payroll account. A "schedule of interbank transfers" prepared from the recorded entries in the general ledger would look like the one in Panel A of Exhibit 6.10.

However, we know that the managers performed a check kite and did not record several transfers between these accounts. Auditors should review the bank statements, find the other transfers, and put them on the schedule (shown in Panel B in Exhibit 6.10). Panel B shows how the auditors can document the unrecorded transfers.

Currently, banks are implementing the Check Clearing for the 21st Century Act, referred to as Check 21. In this system, checks will be converted to digital images allowing

EXHIBIT 6.10 Illustration of Interbank Transfer Schedule

Check Number	Bank (Disbursing Account)	Amount	Date per Books	Date per Bank	Bank (Receiving Account)	Date per Books	Date per Bank
Panel A							
7602	First National	$24,331	Jul 14	Jul 18	Last National	Jul 14	Jul 14
8411	First National	36,462	Jul 28	Aug 1	Last National	Jul 28	Jul 28
Panel B							
6722	First National	15,000	none	Jul 7	Last National	none	Jul 3
11062	Last National	10,000	none	Jul 7	First National	none	Jul 3
6793	First National	11,000	none	Jul 10	Last National	none	Jul 5
11097	Last National	13,000	none	Jul 10	First National	none	Jul 5
6853	First National	16,000	none	Jul 12	Last National	none	Jul 7
11106	Last National	14,000	none	Jul 12	First National	none	Jul 7

for a dramatic increase in speed in clearing checks. The benefit is that the "float" on the check is virtually eliminated and kiting becomes difficult to perform and conceal. However, in the Check 21 system, the paper check is usually destroyed and a hard copy of the check is never returned to the customer or their bank. In such a system, the nature of the audit trail is significantly different. In investigating possible irregularities, the auditor will only be able to obtain an electronic copy of the check and the controls over the safeguarding of the imaging files will be of great importance.[7]

Proof of Cash

Auditors can use another method to discover unrecorded cash transactions. It is called a "proof of cash." You may have studied this method in your intermediate accounting course under the name of "four-column bank reconciliation." The **proof of cash** is a reconciliation in which the bank balance, the bank report of cash deposited, and the bank report of cash paid are all reconciled to the corresponding records maintained in the entity's general ledger. Exhibit 6.11 illustrates a proof of cash. The illustration assumes some bank reconciliation

EXHIBIT 6.11 Illustration of Proof of Cash—First National Bank

	Balance June 30	Month of July Deposits	Month of July Payments	Balance July 31
Bank statement amounts	$264,322	$398,406	$390,442	$272,286
Deposits in transit				
June 30	76,501	(76,501)		
July 31		79,721		79,721
Outstanding checks				
June 30	(89,734)		(89,734)	
July 31			62,958	(62,958)
Unrecorded bank interest (recorded in the next month)				
June 30	(162)	162		
July 31		(155)		(155)
Unrecorded service charges (recorded in the next month)				
June 30	118		118	
July 31			(129)	129
Unrecorded transfers received from Last National Bank		(37,000)		(37,000)
Unrecorded transfers to Last National Bank			(42,000)	42,000
General ledger amounts	$251,045	$364,633	$321,655	$294,023

[7]A white paper entitled "Is Your Check 21 Implementation a Fraud Hazard" by Frank Abagnale (the main character played by Leonardo DiCaprio in the movie *Catch Me If You Can?*) is available on Frank Abagnale's Web site, www.abagnale.com.

AUDITING INSIGHT As Simple as Flying a Kite

Four employees of Detroit-based **Simplified Employment Services** were charged with defrauding banks of at least $32 million in a complex check-kiting scheme. Using seven corporate entities holding 21 separate checking accounts, the fraudsters were able to commingle legitimate company transactions with fraudulent ones to conceal overdrawn bank accounts.

Source: "4 Charged in $32 Million Check-Kiting Scheme," *Detroit News*, January 24, 2002.

information, some transaction activity, and the unrecorded transfers for the First National Bank account used in the previous illustrations of kiting and interbank transfers. (Changing the kiting illustration: the bank accounts did not start with zero balances.)

The proof of cash attempts to reconcile the deposits and payments reported by the bank to the deposits and payments recorded in the general ledger will reveal the unrecorded transfers. The amounts will not reconcile until the auditors inspect the bank statement and find the bank amounts that are not in the general ledger. (Likewise, the attempt to reconcile the July 31 bank balance will show a $5,000 difference, which is explained by the $37,000 unrecorded deposits and the $42,000 unrecorded payments.)

Review Checkpoints

6.15 What is a cutoff bank statement? How is it used by auditors?

6.16 What is *check kiting*? How might auditors detect kiting?

6.17 How does a schedule of interbank transfers show improper cash transfer transactions?

6.18 How can a *proof of cash* reveal unrecorded cash deposit and cash payment transactions?

AUDIT CASES: MORE SCHEMES AND WAYS TO DETECT THEM

LEARNING OBJECTIVE

6. Discuss actual cash fraud cases and describe how the schemes were uncovered.

As discussed previously, many cases of fraud occur in the cash collections and disbursements areas. In this section, we will try a new approach. Instead of discussing lists of schemes and detection procedures in the abstract, the following illustrative cases tell the actual stories of some of these cash embezzlement schemes. The cases follow a standard format in two major parts: (1) case situation and (2) audit approach. Some problems at the end of the chapter will give the case situation and you will be assigned to write the audit approach section.

Case 6.1

Case of the Missing Petty Cash

PROBLEM

Petty cash embezzlement.

METHOD

The petty cash custodian (1) brought postage receipts from home and paid them from the fund, (2) persuaded the supervisor to sign blank authorization slips the custodian could use when the supervisor was away and used these to pay for fictitious meals and minor supplies, and (3) took cash to get through the weekend, replacing it the next week.

AUDIT TRAIL

Postage receipts were from a distant post office station the company did not use. The blank authorization slips were dated on days the supervisor was absent. The fund was cash short during the weekend and for a few days the following week.

AMOUNT

The fund was small ($500), but the custodian replenished it about every two working days, stealing about $50 each time. With about 260 working days per year and 130 reimbursements, the custodian was stealing about $6,500 per year. The custodian was looking forward to getting promoted to general cashier and bigger and better things!

AUDIT APPROACH

OBJECTIVE

Obtain evidence of the existence of the petty cash fund and validity of petty cash transactions.

CONTROL

A supervisor is assigned to approve petty cash disbursements by examining them for validity and signing an authorization slip.

TEST OF CONTROLS

Inquire of the custodian and supervisor regarding petty cash procedures, especially those that relate to situations where the custodian or supervisor is not available to provide needed petty cash. Audit for transaction authorization and validity. Select a sample of petty cash reimbursement check copies with receipts and authorization slips attached; study them for evidence of authorization and validity (vouching procedure). Notice the nature and content of the receipts. Obtain supervisor's vacation schedule and compare dates to authorization slip dates.

AUDIT OF BALANCE

On Friday, count the petty cash and receipts to see that they total $500. Then, count the fund again later in the afternoon. (Be sure the second count is a surprise and that the custodian and supervisor sign off on the count documentation so the auditor will not be accused of theft.)

DISCOVERY SUMMARY

Knowing the location of the nearby post office branch used by the company, the auditor noticed the pattern of many receipts from a distant branch, which was near the custodian's apartment. Several authorizations were dated during the supervisor's vacation and he readily admitted signing the forms in blank so his own supervisor "wouldn't be bothered." The second count on the same day was a real surprise and the fund was found $65 short.

Case 6.2

The Laundry Money Skim

PROBLEM

Cash receipts skimmed from collections.

Albert owned and operated 40 coin laundries around town. As the business grew, he could no longer visit each one, empty the cash boxes, and deposit the receipts. Each location grossed about $140 to $160 per day, operating 365 days per year. (Gross receipts of about $2 million per year.)

METHOD

Four part-time employees each visited 10 locations, collecting the cash boxes and delivering them to Albert's office, where he would count the coins and currency (from the change machine) and prepare a bank deposit. One of the employees skimmed $5 to $10 from each location visited each day.

AUDIT TRAIL

None, unfortunately. The first paper that gets produced is Albert's bank deposit, and the money is gone by then.

AMOUNT

The daily theft does not seem like much, but at an average of $7.50 per day from each of 10 locations, it was about $27,000 per year. If all four of the employees had stolen the same amount, the loss could have been over $100,000 per year.

AUDIT APPROACH

OBJECTIVE

Obtain evidence of the completeness of cash receipts—that is, that all the cash received is delivered to Albert for deposit.

CONTROL

Controls over the part-time employees were nonexistent. There was no overt or covert surprise observation and no times when two people went to collect cash (thereby needing to agree, in collusion, to steal). There was no rotation of locations or other indications to the employees that Albert was concerned about control.

TEST OF CONTROLS

With no controls, there is no test of control procedures. Obviously, however, "thinking like a crook" leads to the conclusion that the employees could simply pocket money.

AUDIT OF BALANCE

Assuming some employees are honest, periodically rotating the stores assigned to each employee and performing revenue comparisons (analytical procedures) on a store-by-store basis may be helpful. If revenues consistently decline for stores assigned to a specific employee, further investigation may be warranted.

The "balance" in this case is the total revenue that should have been deposited, and auditing for completeness is always difficult. Albert marked a quantity of coins with an etching tool and marked some $1 and $5 bills with ink. Unknown to the employees, he put these in all the locations, carefully noting the coins and bills in each.

DISCOVERY SUMMARY

Sure enough, a pattern of missing money emerged. When confronted, the employee confessed.

Review Checkpoints

6.19 In Case 6.1, if the petty cash custodian were replaced and the frequency of fund reimbursement decreased from every two days to every four days, what might you suspect?

6.20 Give some examples of control omissions that would make it easy to "think like a crook" and see opportunities for fraud.

"EXTENDED PROCEDURES" TO DETECT FRAUD (*SAS 99*)

LEARNING
OBJECTIVE

7. Describe some extended procedures for detecting employee fraud schemes involving cash.

The auditing literature often refers to "extended procedures." *SAS 99* calls them "specific responses to fraud risk factors" and lists a few. An exhaustive list would be very lengthy. Moreover, authorities fear that a definitive list might limit the range of such procedures, so "extended procedures" are generally left as an open-ended identified as "whatever is necessary in the circumstances." This section describes some of the "extended procedures" and warns that (1) some auditors may consider them ordinary and (2) other auditors may consider them unnecessary in any circumstances. They are useful detective procedures in either event.[8]

[8] Further explanation of these and other procedures can be found in the books and articles cited in preceding footnotes and in these sources: AICPA Technical Practice Aids; D. Churbuck, "Desktop Forgery," *Forbes*, November 27, 1989, pp.246–54; O. Hilton, *Scientific Examination of Questioned Documents*, rev. ed. (New York: Elsevier North Holland, 1982); A. C. Levinston, "40 Years of Embezzlement Tracking," *Internal Auditor*, April 1991, pp.51–55.

AUDITING INSIGHT | Helping Those Less Fortunate?

Ocean World Seafood has been charged with food stamp fraud. According to investigators, a store of Ocean World's size would normally make approximately $3,000 a month of sales paid using food stamps. Over the last 13 months, over $1 million in food stamps were accepted by Ocean World. Apparently the store would provide cash for food stamps, paying approximately 50 cents for $1 of food stamps.

Source: "Store Owner Charged in $1 Million Food Stamp Fraud," *Associated Press Wire*, April 15, 2005.

Count the Petty Cash Twice in a Day

The second count is unexpected, and auditors might catch an embezzling custodian, who incorrectly believes that "the auditors are gone, so now it's safe!"

Examine Endorsements on Canceled Checks

Most business payments are deposited with one (usually stamped) endorsement. Look for handwritten endorsements and second endorsements, especially those of employees. The second endorsee indicates that the payee (possibly a "ghost employee") may not have received the benefit of the payment. Be sure to include checks payable to "cash" or to a bank for purchase of cashiers' checks.

Retrieve Customers' Checks

If an employee has diverted customer payments for his or her own use, the canceled checks showing endorsements and deposits to a bank where the company has no account are not available because they are returned to the issuing customer. Ask the customer to give originals or copies (front and back), or to provide access for examination.

Use Marked Coins and Currency

Plant marked money in locations where cash collections should be gathered and turned over for deposit.

Analyze the Mix of Cash and Checks in Deposits

Noting a significant change in the mix of cash and checks on bank deposit slips over time, a government auditor became suspicious enough to set up a hidden camera. The camera caught a county tax clerk "skimming" cash from daily property tax deposits. The clerk would pocket most of the cash, leaving the checks to be deposited. The fraud perpetrator was able to conceal the theft by replacing the missing cash with checks written to the county for other, miscellaneous purposes for which established procedures were not closely followed. This procedure is most effective for retail operations in which cashiers receive significant amounts of both cash and checks.

Measure Deposit Lag Time

Compare the dates of cash debit recording and deposit slip dates to dates credited by the bank. Someone who takes cash, then holds the deposit for the next cash receipts to make up the difference, causes a delay between the date of recording and the bank's date of deposit.

Document Examination

Look for erasures, alterations, copies where originals should be filed, telltale lines from a copier when a document has been pieced together, handwriting, and other oddities. Auditors should always insist on seeing original documents instead of photocopies. Professional document examination is a technical activity that requires special training (e.g., IRS, FBI), but crude alterations may be observed, at least enough to bring them to specialists' attention.

AUDITING INSIGHT A Little Training Goes a Long Way

Naomi, an employee at a check-cashing business in Brooklyn, New York, received only the basics of detecting check fraud from her supervisors: look for watermarks, compare encoded check numbers, and question customers to see if they can keep their stories straight if a check looks suspicious.

Earlier in the month, the main office of Naomi's business warned workers to look for a Roberta Kane who had been successfully passing false checks in other branches. When Roberta walked into Naomi's branch, Naomi closely examined her ID and the $200 check. The check's routing numbers were larger than they should be, the check felt softer than others, and there was no watermark. Naomi asked Roberta how she had received the

check and Roberta said it was a paycheck from her employer. Naomi called the number of the company that supposedly wrote the check. When the number appeared to be out of service, Naomi told Roberta that she had presented a false check and that the police would have to get involved. Roberta frantically ran for the door, leaving behind her fake check and ID.

Even with the most basic knowledge of detecting check fraud, this teller was able to deter a thief. It's even more important for auditors to review the fundamentals of check fraud detection.

Source: Suzanne Mahadeo, "Check Fraud: Separating Money from Worthless Paper," *Fraud Magazine*, September/October 2005, pp. 21–23, 50

Inquire

Be careful not to discuss fraud possibilities with the managers who might be involved. It gives them a chance to cover up or run. Wells described fraud audit questioning (FAQ) as a nonaccusatory method of asking key questions of personnel during a regular audit to give them an opportunity to furnish information about possible misdeeds. Fraud possibilities are addressed in a direct manner, so the FAQ approach must have the support of management. Example questions are: "Do you think fraud is a problem for business in general?" "Do you think this company has any particular problem with fraud?" "In your department, who is beyond suspicion?" "Is there any information you would like to furnish regarding possible fraud within this organization?"[9]

Covert Surveillance

Observe activities while not being seen. External auditors might watch employees clocking onto a work shift, observing whether they use only one time card. Auditors of casinos actually get paid to gamble so they can observe cash-handling procedures. Traveling hotel auditors may check in unannounced, use the restaurant and entertainment facilities, and watch the employees skimming receipts and tickets. (Trailing people on streets, undercover surveillance, and maintaining a "stake-out" should be left to trained investigators.)

Horizontal and Vertical Analyses

These ratio analysis procedures are very similar to preliminary analytical procedures explained in earlier chapters. Horizontal analysis refers to changes of financial statement numbers and ratios across several years. Vertical analysis refers to financial statement amounts expressed each year as proportions of a base such as sales for the income statement accounts and total assets for the balance sheet accounts. Auditors look for relationships that do not appear logical as indicators of potential large misstatement and fraud.

Net Worth Analysis

This is used when fraud has been discovered or strongly suspected and the information to calculate a suspect's net worth can be obtained (e.g., asset and liability records, bank accounts). The method is to calculate the suspect's net worth (known assets minus known liabilities) at the beginning and end of a period (months or years), then try to account for the difference as (1) known income less living expenses and (2) unidentified difference. The unidentified difference may be the best available approximation of the amount of a theft.

[9] Joseph T. Wells, "From the Chairman: Fraud Audit Questioning," *The White Paper*, National Association of Certified Fraud Examiners, May–June 1991, p. 2. This technique must be used with extreme care and practice.

AUDITING INSIGHT · Thank Goodness Its Payday!

Five individuals have been charged with tax and insurance fraud in the operation of a temporary employment agency in Southeastern Massachusetts. From January 1993 through June 2001, the agency paid a large portion of its payroll in cash in order to avoid employment taxes (e.g., social security and Medicare) and to reduce payments for workers' compensation insurance. Why would a company pay its employees in cash? Is there a legitimate reason to do this? Even if the employees wanted cash, would there be a better way to provide it?

Source: "Five Charged in $30 Million 'Under-the-Table' Payroll Fraud, Reports U.S. Attorney," *PR Newswire*, January 27, 2005.

Expenditure Analysis

This is similar to net worth analysis, except the data is the suspect's spending for all purposes compared to known income. If spending exceeds legitimate and explainable income, the difference may be the amount of a theft.

Reasonableness Test

Often auditors become so involved in ticking and tying numbers that they forget to ask themselves the simplest questions: Where is the cash going? For what purpose? Does this make sense? The answers to these often motivate the auditor to ask more penetrating questions of management and to dig for more evidence.

Review Checkpoints

6.21 What is the difference between a "normal procedure" and an "extended procedure?"

6.22 What might be indicated by two endorsements on a canceled check?

6.23 What can an auditor find using net worth analysis? Expenditure analysis?

Summary

While auditing standards concentrate on management fraud—the production of materially false and misleading financial statements (i.e., fraudulent financial reporting), professional standards also require auditors to consider employee fraud perpetrated against an entity. Attention to employee fraud is important in the context that the cover-up may create financial statement misstatements (e.g., overstating an inventory to disguise unauthorized removal of valuable products). Fraud may be contemplated when people have motives, usually financial needs, for stealing money or property. Motive, combined with opportunity and a lapse of integrity, generally makes the probability of fraud or theft very high. Opportunities arise when an entity's management has lax attitudes about setting examples for good behavior and about maintenance of a supportive control environment. The fear of getting caught by control procedures deters some fraudsters. Otherwise, attentive management of personnel can ease the pressures people feel and, thus, reduce the incidence of fraud.

Auditors need to know about the "red flags," those telltale signs and indications that have accompanied many frauds. When studying a business operation, auditors' ability to

"think like a crook" to devise ways to steal can help in planning procedures designed to determine whether fraud has happened. Often, imaginative "extended procedures" can be employed to unearth evidence of fraudulent activity. Auditors must always exercise technical and personal care, however, because accusations of fraud are taken very seriously. For this reason, after preliminary findings indicate fraud possibilities, auditors should enlist the cooperation of management and assist fraud examination professionals when bringing an investigation to a conclusion.

Cash is highly liquid, not easily identifiable, and very portable. For these reasons, cash is the primary target of fraudulent activities, and consequently has a high inherent risk. Controls over cash receipts and disbursements accordingly must be strong. With respect to auditing cash, the combination of all the procedures performed on the bank reconciliation provides evidence of existence, valuation, and proper cutoff of the bank cash balances. Auditors use a cutoff bank statement to obtain independent evidence of the proper listing of outstanding checks and deposits in transit on a bank reconciliation.

Additional procedures can be performed to try to detect attempts at lapping accounts receivable collections and kiting checks. For lapping, these procedures include auditing the details of customer payments listed in bank deposits in comparison to details of customer payment postings (remittance lists). For kiting, these procedures include being alert to the signs of kiting activity and preparing a schedule of interbank transfers and a proof of cash.

Key Terms

check kiting: The practice of building up balances in one or more bank accounts based on uncollected (float) checks drawn against similar accounts in other banks, 228

cutoff bank statement: A client bank statement (usually sent directly to the auditor) that includes all paid checks and deposits slips through a certain date, usually the middle of the month, 225

defalcation: Another term used to describe employee fraud and embezzlement, 207

direct-effect illegal acts: Violations of laws or government regulations by the company or its management or employees that produce direct and material effects on dollar amounts in financial statements, 208

embezzlement: A type of fraud involving employees or nonemployees wrongfully taking money or property entrusted to their care, custody, and control, often accompanied by false accounting entries and other forms of lying and cover-up, 207

employee fraud (also called misappropriation of assets): The use of fraudulent means to take money or other property from an employer. It consists of three phases: (1) the fraudulent act, (2) the conversion of the money or property to the fraudster's use, and (3) the cover-up, 207

errors: Unintentional misstatements or omissions of amounts or disclosures in financial statements, 208

fidelity bond: An insurance policy that covers most kinds of cash embezzlement losses, 218

fraud: Knowingly making material misrepresentations of fact with the intent of inducing someone to believe the falsehood and act upon it and, thus, suffer a loss or damage, 207

lapping: The theft of a payment and the application of subsequent payments to cover the theft, 218

larceny: Simple theft of an employer's property that is not entrusted to an employee's care, custody, or control, 207

lockbox: An arrangement in which a fiduciary (e.g., a bank) receives the payments, lists the receipts, deposits the money, and sends the remittance advices (stubs showing the amount received from each customer) to the company, 216

management fraud: Deliberate fraud committed by management that injures investors and creditors through materially misleading information, 208

motive: Pressure experienced by a person and believed unshareable with friends and confidants, 210

proof of cash: A reconciliation in which the bank balance, the bank report of cash deposited, and the bank report of cash paid are all reconciled to the company's general ledger, 230

schedule of interbank transfers: An analysis used to determine whether transfers of cash from one bank to another were recorded properly (correct amount and correct date), 226

Multiple Choice Questions for Practice and Review

6.24 When auditing with "fraud awareness," auditors should especially notice and follow up employee activities under which of these conditions?

 a. The company always estimates the inventory but never takes a complete physical count.

 b. The petty cash box is always locked in the desk of the custodian.

 c. Management has published a company code of ethics and sends frequent communication newsletters about it.

 d. The board of directors reviews and approves all investment transactions.

6.25 The best way to enact a broad fraud-prevention program is to

 a. Install airtight control systems of checks and supervision.

 b. Name an "ethics officer" who is responsible for receiving and acting upon fraud tips.

 c. Place dedicated "hot line" telephones on walls around the workplace with direct communication to the company ethics officer.

 d. Practice management "of the people and for the people" to help them share personal and professional problems.

6.26 A good fraud prevention program should address employees' motivation to steal from the company. The best method for doing this is to

 a. Establish employee assistance programs.

 b. Require a fidelity bond on all employees.

 c. Require reconciliations of all accounts to be reviewed by a supervisor.

 d. Ensure audits of all accounts with high inherent risk of fraud.

6.27 A code of ethics is an important element of a fraud prevention program. Which of the following would diminish the effectiveness of a company's code of conduct?

 a. The establishment of a chief ethics officer.

 b. The establishment of a "hot line" for reporting unethical behavior.

 c. The violation of the code of ethics by senior management.

 d. The posting of the code of ethics in the company workplace.

6.28 Which of the following is *least* indicative of fraudulent activity?

 a. Numerous cash refunds have been made to different people at the same post office box address.

 b. Internal auditors cannot locate several credit memos to support reductions of customers' balances.

 c. Bank reconciliation has no outstanding checks or deposits older than 15 days.

 d. Three people were absent the day the auditors handed out the paychecks and have not picked them up four weeks later.

6.29 Which of the following combinations is a good means of concealing employee fraud but a poor means of perpetrating management (financial reporting) fraud?

 a. Overstating sales revenue and overstating customer accounts receivable balances.

 b. Overstating sales revenue and overstating bad debt expense.

 c. Understating interest expense and understating accrued interest payable.

 d. Omitting the disclosure information about related-party sales to the president's relatives at below-market prices.

6.30 Allison, an employee in accounts payable, believes she can run a fictitious invoice through the accounts payable system and collect the money. She knows payments are subject to an audit. Which account would be the best place to hide the fraud?

 a. Inventory.

 b. Wage expense.

 c. Consulting service expense.

 d. Property tax expense.

6.31 Which of these arrangements of duties could most likely lead to an embezzlement or theft?

 a. Inventory warehouse manager has responsibility for making the physical inventory observation and reconciling discrepancies to the perpetual inventory records.

 b. Cashier prepared the bank deposit, endorsed the checks with a company stamp, and delivered the cash and checks to the bank for deposit (no other bookkeeping duties).

 c. Accounts receivable clerk received a list of payments received by the cashier so she could make entries in the customers' accounts receivable subsidiary accounts.

 d. Financial vice president received checks made out to suppliers and the supporting invoices, signed the checks, and mailed the checks.

6.32 Which of the following would the auditor consider to be an incompatible operation if the cashier receives remittances?

 a. The cashier prepares the daily deposit.

 b. The cashier makes the daily deposit at a local bank.

 c. The cashier posts the receipts to the accounts receivable subsidiary ledger cards.

 d. The cashier endorses the checks.

6.33 Which of the following is an effective audit procedure that might be used by an auditor to detect kiting between intercompany banks?

 a. Review composition of authenticated deposit slips.

 b. Review subsequent bank statements.

 c. Prepare a schedule of the bank transfers.

 d. Prepare a year-end bank reconciliation.

6.34 Immediately upon receipt of cash, a responsible employee should

 a. Record the amount in the cash receipts journal.

 b. Prepare a remittance listing.

 c. Update the subsidiary accounts receivable records.

 d. Prepare a deposit slip in triplicate.

<div align="right">(AICPA adapted)</div>

6.35 Each morning the assistant controller gets the prior day's listing of remittances, a copy of the payment report, and a copy of the deposit slip returned from the bank. When comparing these items, the individual would be able to determine that

 a. No checks were returned for insufficient funds.

 b. The cash received and remittance advice received were mantained in a single batch.

 c. The accounts receivable system has controls over unauthorized access.

 d. The assistant controller does not also reconcile the subsidiary accounts payable.

6.36 Upon receipt of customers' checks in the mail room, a responsible employee should prepare a remittance listing that is forwarded to the cashier. A copy of the listing should be sent to the

 a. Internal auditor to investigate the listing for unusual transactions.

 b. Treasurer to compare the listing with the monthly bank statement.

 c. Accounts receivable bookkeeper to update the subsidiary accounts receivable records.

 d. Entity's bank to compare the listing with the cashier's deposit slip.

<div align="right">(AICPA adapted)</div>

6.37 Cash receipts from sales on account have been misappropriated. Which of the following acts would conceal this defalcation and be least likely to be detected by an auditor?

 a. Understating the sales journal.

 b. Overstating the accounts receivable control account.

 c. Overstating the accounts receivable subsidiary ledger.

 d. Overstating the sales journal.

6.38 Embezzlement is a type of fraud that involves

 a. An employee's misappropriating an employer's money or property not entrusted to him or her.

 b. A manager's falsification of financial statements for the purpose of misleading investors and creditors.

 c. An employee's mistaken representation of opinion that causes incorrect accounting entries.

 d. An employee misappropriating an employer's money or property entrusted to the employee's control in the employee's normal job.

6.39 An effective control procedure that protects against the preparation of improper or inaccurate cash disbursements would be to require that all checks be

a. Signed by an officer after necessary supporting evidence has been examined.

b. Reviewed by the treasurer before mailing.

c. Sequentially numbered and accounted for by internal auditors.

d. Perforated or otherwise effectively canceled when they are returned with the bank statement.

6.40 During an audit of cash, the auditor is most concerned with the management assertion of

a. Existence.

b. Rights and obligations.

c. Valuation or allocation.

d. Occurrence.

6.41 In preparing for the audit of cash, the auditors perform analytical procedures concerning cash. Which of the following would be the best source of information for use in the estimate of cash?

a. Prior-years' balances.

b. Management inquiry.

c. Cash budgets.

d. Aged accounts receivable reports.

6.42 Which of the following is a control procedure that could prevent a paid disbursement voucher from being presented for payment a second time?

a. Vouchers should be prepared by individuals who are responsible for signing disbursement checks.

b. Disbursement vouchers should be approved by at least two responsible management officials.

c. The date on a disbursement voucher should be within a few days of the date the voucher is presented for payment.

d. The official signing the check should compare the check with the voucher and should stamp "paid" on the voucher documents.

Exercises, Problems, and Simulations

6.43 **Tests of Controls over Cash Disbursements.** The Runge Controls Corporation manufactures and markets electrical control systems: temperature controls, machine controls, burglar alarms, and the like. Electrical and semiconductor parts are acquired from outside vendors, and systems are assembled in Runge's plant. The company incurs other administrative and operating expenditures. Liabilities for goods and services purchased are entered in a vouchers payable journal, at which time the debits are classified to the asset and expense accounts to which they apply.

The company has specified control procedures for approving vendor invoices for payment, for signing checks, for keeping records, and for reconciling the checking accounts. The procedures appear to be well specified and placed in operation.

You are the senior auditor on the engagement and you need to specify a program (list) of test of controls procedures to evaluate the effectiveness of the controls over cash disbursements.

Required:

Using the management's assertions over transactions as a guide, specify two or more test of controls procedures to audit the effectiveness of typical control procedures. (*Hint*: From one sample of recorded cash disbursements, you can specify procedures related to several objectives. See Exhibit 6.4 for examples of test of controls procedures over cash disbursements.) Organize your list according to the example shown below for the "completeness" assertion.

Completeness Assertion	Test of Controls Program
All valid cash disbursements are recorded and none are omitted.	Determine the numerical sequence of checks issued during the period and scan the sequence for missing numbers.

(AICPA adapted)

6.44 **Internal Control Questionnaire for Book Buy-Back Cash Fund.** Taylor, a CPA, has been engaged to audit the financial statements of University Books, Incorporated. University Books maintains a large, revolving cash fund exclusively for the purpose of buying used books from students for cash. The cash fund is active all year because the nearby university offers a large variety of courses with varying starting and completion dates throughout the year.

Receipts are prepared for each purchase. Reimbursement vouchers periodically are submitted to replenish the fund.

Required:

Construct an internal control questionnaire to be used in evaluating the internal control over University Books' repurchasing process using the revolving cash fund. The internal control questionnaire should elicit a yes or no response to each question. *Do not discuss the internal controls over books that are purchased from publishers.*

(AICPA adapted)

6.45 **Audit Simulation: Test of Controls over Cash Receipts.** You are the in-charge auditor examining the financial statements of the Gutzler Company for the year ended December 31. During late October, with the help of Gutzler's controller, you completed an internal control questionnaire and prepared the appropriate memoranda describing Gutzler's accounting procedures. Your comments relative to cash receipts are as follows:

- All cash receipts are sent directly to the accounts receivable clerk with no processing by the mail department. The accounts receivable clerk keeps the cash receipts journal, prepares the bank deposit slip in duplicate, posts from the deposit slip to the subsidiary accounts receivable ledger, and mails the deposit to the bank.

- The controller receives the validated deposit slips directly (unopened) from the bank. She also receives the monthly bank statement directly (unopened) from the bank and promptly reconciles it.

- At the end of each month, the accounts receivable clerk notifies the general ledger clerk by journal voucher of the monthly totals of the cash receipts journal for posting to the general ledger.

- Each month, with regard to the general ledger cash account, the general ledger clerk makes an entry to record the total debits to cash from the cash receipts journal. In addition, the general ledger clerk, on occasion, makes debit entries in the general ledger cash account from sources other than the cash receipts journal; for example, funds borrowed from the bank.

Certain standard audit procedures listed below already have been performed by you in the audit of cash receipts:

- All columns in the cash receipts journal have been totaled and cross-totaled.

- Postings from the cash receipts journal have been traced to the general ledger.

- Remittance advices and related correspondence have been traced to entries in the cash receipts journal.

Required:

Considering Gutzler's internal control over cash receipts and the standard audit procedures already performed, list all other audit procedures that should be performed to obtain sufficient appropriate audit evidence regarding controls over cash and give the reasons for each procedure. Do not discuss the procedures for cash disbursements and cash balances. Also, do not discuss the extent to which any of the procedures are to be performed. Assume adequate controls exist to ensure that all sales transactions are recorded. Organize your answer sheet as follows:

Other Audit Procedure	Reason for Other Audit Procedures

(AICPA adapted)

6.46 **Establishing Internal Control over Sales Returns.** You are the auditor for Konerko's Office supply store, which is opening for business next week. The owner of the store has established all the controls you have recommended for ensuring sales are recorded properly and cash is accounted for. The owner has heard from other small business owners that returned goods are often used by employees as means of skimming money from the register.

Required:

 a. How might an employee use returned goods to skim money from the register?

 b. What controls would you recommend to prevent or detect fraudulent returns?

 c. What audit procedures might you perform to detect fraudulent returns?

6.46 **Procedures for Auditing a Client's Bank Reconciliation.** Auditors normally will find the items lettered A–F in a client-prepared bank reconciliation.

GENERAL COMPANY
BANK RECONCILIATION: 1ST NATIONAL BANK
SEPTEMBER 30

A.	Balance per bank		$ 28,375
B.	Deposits in transit		
	Sept 29	$ 4,500	
	Sept 30	1,525	6,025
			$ 34,400
C.	Outstanding checks		
	# 988 Aug 31	$ 2,200	
	# 1281 Sept 26	675	
	# 1285 Sept 27	850	
	# 1289 Sept 29	2,500	
	# 1292 Sept 30	7,255	(11,450)
			$ 20,950
D.	Customer note collected by the bank		(3,000)
E.	Error: Check # 1282, written on Sept. 26 for $270, was erroneously charged by bank as $720; bank was notified Oct. 2		450
F.	Balance per books		$ 20,400

Required:

Assume these facts: On October 11, the auditor received a cutoff bank statement dated October 7. The September 30 deposit in transit; the outstanding checks #1281, #1285, #1289, and #1292; and the correction of the bank error regarding check #1282 appeared on the cutoff bank statement.

 a. For each of the lettered items A–F above, select one or more of the procedures 1–10 below that you believe the auditor should perform to obtain evidence about the item. These procedures may be selected once, more than once, or not at all. Be prepared to explain the reasons for your choices.

 1. Trace to cash receipts journal.

 2. Trace to cash disbursements journal.

 3. Compare to the September 30 general ledger.

 4. Confirm directly with the bank.

 5. Inspect bank credit memo.

 6. Inspect bank debit memo.

 7. Ascertain reason for unusual delay, if any.

 8. Inspect supporting documents for reconciling items that do not appear on the cutoff bank statement.

 9. Trace items on the bank reconciliation to the cutoff bank statement.

 10. Trace items on the cutoff bank statement to the bank reconciliation.

 b. Auditors ordinarily foot a client-prepared bank reconciliation. If the auditors had performed this recalculation on the bank reconciliation shown above, what might they have found? Be prepared to discuss any findings.

 (AICPA adapted)

6.48 **Proof of Cash.** You can use the computer-based *Electronic Audit Documentation* on the textbook Web site to prepare the proof of cash required in this problem.

The auditors of Steffey, Ltd., decided to study the cash receipts and disbursements for the month of July of the current year under audit. They obtained the bank reconciliations and the cash journals prepared by the company accountants, which revealed the following:

June 30: Bank balance $355,001; deposits in transit $86,899; outstanding checks $42,690; general ledger cash balance $399,210.

July 1: Cash receipts journal $650,187; cash disbursements journal $565,397.

July 31: Bank balance $506,100; deposits in transit $51,240; outstanding checks $73,340; general ledger cash balance $484,000. Bank statement record of deposits: $835,846; of payments: $684,747.

Required:

Prepare a four-column proof of cash (see Exhibit 6.11 for an example) covering the month of July of the current year. Identify problems, if any.

6.49 **Audit Simulation: Interbank Transfers.** You can use the computer-based *Electronic Workpapers* on the textbook Web site to prepare the schedule of interbank transfers required in this problem.

EverReady Corporation is in the home building and repair business. Construction business has been in a slump and the company has experienced financial difficulty over the past two years. Part of the problem lies in the company's desire to avoid laying off its skilled crews of bricklayers and cabinetmakers. Meeting the payroll has been a problem.

The auditors are engaged to audit the 2008 financial statements. Knowing of EverReady's financial difficulty and its business policy, the auditors decided to prepare a schedule of interbank transfers covering the 10 days before and after December 31, which is the company's balance sheet date.

First, the auditors used the cash receipts and disbursements journals to prepare part of the schedule shown in Exhibit 6.49.1. They obtained the information for everything except the dates of deposit and payment in the bank statements (disbursing date per bank and receiving date per bank). They learned that EverReady always transferred money to the payroll account at 1st National Bank from the general account at 1st National Bank. This transfer enabled the bank to clear the payroll checks without delay. The only bank accounts in the EverReady financial statements are the two at 1st National Bank.

Next, the auditors obtained the December 2008 and January 2009 bank statements for the general and payroll accounts at 1st National Bank. They recorded the bank disbursement and receipt dates in the schedule of interbank transfers. For each transfer, these dates are identical because the accounts are in the same bank. An alert auditor noticed that the 1st National Bank general account bank statement also contains deposits received from Citizen National Bank and canceled check number 1799 dated January 5 payable to Citizen National Bank. This check cleared the 1st National Bank account on January 8 and was marked "transfer of funds." This led to the auditors' decision to inquire of EverReady's chief financial officer.

Asked about the Citizen National Bank transactions, EverReady's chief financial officer readily admitted the existence of an off-books bank account. He explained that it was used for financing transactions in keeping with normal practice in the construction industry. He gave the auditors the

EXHIBIT 6.49.1 **Schedule of Interbank Transfers**

C-5

EVERREADY CORPORATION

Schedule of Interbank Transfers

December 31, 2008

Prepared _____

Date _____

Reviewed _____

Date _____

	Disbursing Account				Receiving Account		
Check #	Bank	Amount	Date per Books	Date per Bank	Bank	Date per Books	Date per Bank
1417	1st National	9,463 ✓	24-Dec	24-Dec *m*	1st National Payroll	24-Dec *t*	24-Dec *n*
1601	1st National	11,593 ✓	31-Dec *b*	31-Dec *m*	1st National Payroll	31-Dec *t*	31-Dec *n*
1982	1st National	9,971 ✓	08-Jan	08-Jan *m*	1st National Payroll	08-Jan *t*	08-Jan *n*

✓ Traced from cash disbursements journal.

b Check properly listed as outstanding on bank reconciliation.

m Vouched to check cleared in bank statement.

t Traced from cash receipts journal.

n Vouched deposit cleared in bank statement.

Note: We scanned the cash disbursements and cash receipts journals for checks to and deposits from other bank accounts.

December and January bank statements for the account at Citizen National Bank. In it, the auditors found the following:

Citizen National Bank

Check #	Payable to	Amount	Dated	Cleared Bank
4050	1st National	$10,000	23-Dec	29-Dec
4051	Chase Bank	12,000	28-Dec	31-Dec
4052	1st National	12,000	30-Dec	05-Jan
4053	Chase Bank	14,000	4-Jan	07-Jan
4054	1st National	20,000	8-Jan	13-Jan

Deposits

Received from	Amount	Date
Chase Bank	$11,000	22-Dec
Chase Bank	15,000	30-Dec
1st National	10,000	05-Jan
Chase Bank	12,000	07-Jan

When asked about the Chase Bank transactions, EverReady's chief financial officer admitted the existence of another off-books bank account, which he said was the personal account of the principal stockholder. He explained that the stockholder often used it to finance EverReady's operations. He gave the auditors the December and January bank statements for this account at Chase Bank; in it, the auditors found the following:

Chase Bank

Payments

Check Number	Payable to	Amount	Dated	Cleared Bank
2220	Citizen National Bank	11,000	22-Dec	28-Dec
2221	Citizen National Bank	15,000	30-Dec	05-Jan
2222	Citizen National Bank	12,000	7-Jan	12-Jan

Deposits

Received froma	Amount	Dated
Citizen National Bank	12,000	28-Dec
Citizen National Bank	14,000	04-Jan

An abbreviated calendar for the Period is in Exhibit 6.49.2

EXHIBIT 6.49.2

	S	M	T	W	T	F	S
December 2008	20	21	22	23	24	25	26
	27	28	29	30	31		
January 2009						1	2
	3	4	5	6	7	8	9
	10	11	12	13	14	15	16

Required:

 a. Complete the Schedule of Interbank Transfers (document C-5, Exhibit 6.49.1) by entering the new information.

 b. What is the actual cash balance for the three bank accounts combined, considering only the amounts given in this case information, as of December 31, 2008 (before any of the December 31 payroll checks are cashed by employees)? As of January 8, 2009 (before any of the January 8 payroll checks are cashed by employees)? (Hint: Prepare a schedule of bank and actual balances.)

6.50 **Manipulated Bank Reconciliation.** You can use the computer-based *Electronic Workpapers* on the textbook Web site to prepare the bank reconciliation solution.

 Caulco, Inc., is the audit client. You have obtained the client-prepared bank reconciliation as of February 28 (below). The February bank statement in is shown in Exhibit 6.6 in the text.

Required:

Check #2231 was the first check written in February 2009. All earlier checks cleared the bank, some during January and some during February. Assume that the only February-dated canceled checks returned in the March bank statement are #2239 and #2240, showing the amounts listed in the February bank reconciliation. They cleared the bank on March 3 and March 2, respectively. The first deposit on the March bank statement was $1,097.69, credited on March 3. Assume further that all checks entered in Caulco's cash disbursements journal through February 28 have either cleared the bank or are listed as outstanding checks in the February bank reconciliation.

Determine whether any errors exist in the following bank reconciliation. If errors exist, prepare a corrected reconciliation and explain the problem.

CAULCO, INC.
Bank Reconciliation
February 28

Balance per bank				$7,374.93
Deposit in transit				1,097.69

Outstanding checks

#	Date	Payee	Amount	
2239	Feb 26	Alpha Supply	500.00	
2240	Feb 28	L. C. Stateman	254.37	
Total outstanding				(754.37)
General ledger balance Feb. 28				$7,718.25

6.51 **Investigating a Fraud.** Suppose you are auditing cash disbursements and discover several payments to a company you were unfamiliar with and cannot find information about this company on the Internet or in the local telephone directory. The invoices from this company have numbers very close to each other in the sequence, there is no phone number on the invoice, and each bill is for a dollar amount just under the amount that would require additional approvals before payment. Based on this information, you now suspect this may be a fraud.

Required:

Based on your suspicions, how would you change the audit procedures you would perform and how might you change the evidence you gather?

6.52 **Audit Simulation: Fraud in Purchasing.** Consider the following scenario:

Adam worked for the local hardware store as an outside sales representative. His job was to visit local companies and contractors in an attempt to identify their needs for tools and materials and provide a bid to supply those items. When a new job was accepted by a local contractor, Adam would get their material requirements, come back to the store, and prepare and submit a proposal for the items. After some initial success with Big Builder, a large contractor, the number of jobs awarded to Adam had decreased dramatically.

One day Adam was back at the store after losing a bid to Big Builder when he noticed someone in the store purchasing the exact items and quantities that were in the specification for that bid. The combination of items was unusual and it would be an unlikely coincidence for someone else to want such a combination in that exact quantity. The customer paid the retail price for the merchandise and left.

Adam decided to contact Big Builder, but he knew he could not do so and make any accusations. Adam set up a meeting with the president of Big Builder and inquired as to how Adam might "increase his business and better meet the needs of Big Builder." Eventually the recent bid entered the conversation. Adam showed his copy of the bid to the president. The president retrieved a copy of the purchase order and recognized that the purchase order was for more money than the bid Adam had submitted. The company that submitted the bid was K. A. Supplies, Inc. Adam had never heard of K. A. Supplies and noted the address of K. A. Supplies on the purchase order. The president of Big Builder promised to investigate the bidding process.

Adam drove to the address of K. A. Supplies and found a packaging and shipping store at that address. Further, Adam went to the county court house and inquired about K. A. Supplies. The company was listed in the county records and one of the purchasing agents for the contractor was listed as an officer.

Required:

 a. Given the information that Adam knows, what do you believe is occurring at the contractor?

 b. What other information would you want to obtain and how might you retrieve that information?

 c. What controls might be instituted at the contractor to prevent improprieties in the bidding and purchasing process?

6.53 **The Perfect Crime?** Consider the following story of an actual embezzlement.

This was the ingenious embezzler's scheme: (a) He hired a print shop to print a private stock of Ajax Company checks in the company's numerical sequence. (b) In his job as an accounts payable clerk, he intercepted legitimate checks written by the accounts payable department and signed by the Ajax treasurer, then destroyed them. (c) He substituted the same-numbered check from the private stock, payable to himself in the same amount as the legitimate check, and he "signed" it with a rubber stamp that looked enough like the Ajax Company treasurer's signature to fool the paying bank. (d) He deposited the money in his own bank account. The bank statement reconciler (a different person) was able to correspond the check numbers and amounts listed in the cleared items in the bank statement to the recorded cash disbursement (check number and amount), thus he did not notice the trick. The embezzler was able to process the vendor's "past due" notice and next month statement with complete documentation, enabling the Ajax treasurer to sign another check the next month paying both the past due balance and current charges. The embezzler was careful to scatter the double-expense payments among numerous accounts (telephone, office supplies, inventory, etc.) so the double-paid expenses did not distort any accounts very much. As time passed, the embezzler was able to recommend budget amounts that allowed a large enough budget so his double-paid expenses in various categories did not often pop up as large variances from the budget.

Required:

List and explain the ways and means you believe someone might detect the embezzlement. Think first about the ordinary everyday control activities. Then, think about extensive detection efforts assuming a tip or indication of a possible fraud has been received. Is this a "perfect crime?"

6.54 **Select Effective Extended Procedures.** Given below are some "suspicions"; you have been requested to select some effective extended procedures designed to confirm or deny the suspicions.

Required:

Write the suggested procedures for each case in definite terms so another person can know what to do.

 a. The custodian of the petty cash fund may be removing cash on Friday afternoon to pay for weekend activities.

b. A manager noticed that eight new vendors were added to the purchasing department's approved vendor list after the assistant purchasing agent was promoted to chief agent three weeks ago. She suspects all or some of them might be fictitious companies set up by the new chief purchasing agent.

c. The payroll supervisor may be stealing unclaimed paychecks of employees who resigned and did not collect the last check.

d. Although no customers have complained, cash collections on accounts receivable have decreased and the counter clerks may have stolen customers' payments.

e. The cashier may have "borrowed" money, covering it by holding each day's deposit until cash from the next day(s) collection is enough to make up the shortage from an earlier day, then sending the deposit to the bank.

6.55 **Forensic Accounting: Assurance Engagement 1: Expenditure Analysis.** Expenditure analysis is used when fraud has been discovered or strongly suspected and the information to calculate a suspect's income and expenditures can be obtained (e.g., asset and liability records, bank accounts). Expenditure analysis consists of establishing the suspect's known expenditures for all purposes for the relevant period, subtracting all known sources of funds (e.g., wages, gifts, inheritances, bank balances, and the like), and identifying the difference as "expenditures financed by unknown sources of income."

You have been hired by the law firm of Gleckel and Morris. The lawyers have been retained by Blade Manufacturing Company in a case involving a suspected kickback by a purchasing employee, E. J. Cunningham. Cunningham is suspected of taking kickbacks from Mason Varner, a salesman for Tanco Metals. He has denied the charges, but Lanier Gleckel, the lawyer in charge of the case, is convinced the kickbacks have occurred.

Gleckel filed a civil action and subpoenaed Cunningham's financial records, including his last year's bank statements. The beginning bank balance January 1 was $3,463 and the ending bank balance December 31 was $2,050. Over the intervening 12 months, Cunningham's gross salary was $3,600 per month, with a net of $2,950. His house payments were $1,377 per month. In addition, he paid $2,361 per month on a new Mercedes 500 SEL and paid a total of $9,444 last year toward a new Nissan Maxima (including $5,000 down payment). He also purchased new state-of-the-art audio and video equipment for $18,763, with no down payment, and total payments on the equipment last year of $5,532. A reasonable estimate of his household expenses during the period is $900 per month ($400 for food, $200 for utilities, and $300 for other items).

Required:

Using expenditure analysis, calculate the amount of income, if any, from "unknown sources."

6.56 **Forensic Accounting: Assurance Engagement 2: Net Worth Analysis.** Net worth analysis is used when fraud has been discovered or strongly suspected and the information to calculate a suspect's net worth can be obtained (e.g., asset and liability records, bank accounts). The procedure is to calculate the person's change in net worth (excluding changes in market values of assets) and to identify the known sources of funds to finance the changes. Any difference between the change in net worth and the known sources of funds is called "funds from unknown sources," which might include ill-gotten gains.

Nero has worked for Bonne Consulting Group (BCG) as the executive secretary for administration for nearly 10 years. His dedication has earned him a reputation as an outstanding employee and has resulted in increasing responsibilities. Nero is a suspect in fraud.

This is the hindsight story. During Nero's first five years of employment, BCG subcontracted all of its feasibility and marketing studies through Jackson & Company. This relationship was terminated because Jackson & Company merged with a larger, more expensive consulting group. At the time of termination, Nero and his supervisor were forced to select a new firm to conduct BCG's market research. However, Nero never informed the accounting department that the Jackson & Company account had been closed.

Since his supervisor allowed Nero to sign the payment voucher for services rendered, Nero was able to continue to process checks made payable to Jackson's account. Nero was trusted to be the only signature authorizing payments less than $10,000. The accounting department continued to write the checks and Nero took responsibility for delivering them. Nero opened a bank account in a nearby city under the name of Jackson & Company, where he made the deposits.

Nero's financial records have been obtained by subpoena. Exhibit 6.56.1 provides a summary of the data obtained from Nero's records.

EXHIBIT 6.56-1
Nero's Subpoenaed Records

	Year One	Year Two	Year Three
Assets:			
Residence	$100,000	$100,000	$100,000
Stocks and bonds	30,000	30,000	42,000
Automobiles	20,000	20,000	40,000
Certificate of deposit	50,000	50,000	50,000
Cash	6,000	12,000	14,000
Liabilities:			
Mortgage balance	90,000	50,000	—
Auto loan	10,000	—	—
Income:			
Salary		34,000	36,000
Other		6,000	6,000
Expenses:			
Scheduled mortgage payments		6,000	6,000
Auto loan payments		4,800	—
Other living expenses		20,000	22,000

Required:

You have been hired to estimate the amount of loss by estimating Nero's "funds from unknown sources" that financed his comfortable life style. Hint: Set up a working paper like this:

	End Year 1	End Year 2	End Year 3
Assets (list)			
Liabilities (list)			
Net worth (difference)			
Change in net worth			
Add total expenses			
= Change plus expenses			
Subtract known income			
= Funds from unknown sources			

6.57 **Mini-Case: Cash confirmations.** Refer to mini-case "Something Went Sour at Parmalat" shown on page 839 and respond to question 1.

6.58 **Employee Embezzlement via Cash Receipts and Payment of Personal Expenses.** This case is designed in a manner similar to the cases in the chapter. It identifies the problem, the method, the audit trail, and the amount. In this case, you can assume you have received the informant's message. Your assignment is to write the "audit approach" portion of the case, organized around these sections:

Objective: Express the objective in terms of the facts supposedly asserted in financial records, accounts, and statements. (Refer to the "assertions" explained in Chapter 1.)

Control: Write a brief explanation of desirable controls, missing controls, and especially the kinds of "deviations" that might arise from the situation described in the case. (Refer to controls explained in Chapter 5.)

Test of controls: Develop some procedures for obtaining evidence about existing controls, especially procedures that could discover deviations from controls. If there are no controls to test, then there are no procedures to perform; go then to the next section. (Refer to test of controls procedures explained in this chapter.) An audit "procedure" should instruct someone about the source(s) of evidence to obtain and the work to perform.

Audit of balance: Write some procedures for getting evidence about the existence, completeness, valuation, ownership, or disclosure assertions identified in your objective section above. Discovery summary: Write a short statement about the discovery you expect to accomplish with your procedures.

The Extra Bank Account

Problem: Cash receipts pocketed and personal expenses paid from business account.

Method: The Ourtown Independent School District, like all others, had formal, often bureaucratic, procedures regarding school board approval of cash disbursements. To get around the rules, and to make timely payment of selected bills possible, the superintendent of schools had a school bank account that was used in the manner of a petty cash fund. The board knew about it and had given blanket approval in advance for its use to make timely payment of minor school expenses. The board, however, never reviewed the activity in this account. The business manager had sole responsibility for the account, subject to the annual audit. The account received money from transfers from other school accounts and from deposit of cafeteria cash receipts. The superintendent did not like to be bothered with details and he often signed blank checks so the business manager would not need to obtain a signature all the time. The business manager sometimes paid her personal American Express credit card bills, charged personal items to the school's VISA account, and pocketed some cafeteria cash receipts before deposit.

Audit trail: An informant called the state education audit agency and told the story that this business manager had used school funds to buy hosiery. When told of this story, the superintendent told the auditor to place no credibility in the informant, who is "out to get us." The business manager had, in fact, used the account to write unauthorized checks to "cash," put her own American Express bills in the school files (the school district had a VISA card, not American Express), and signed on the school card for gasoline and auto repairs during periods of vacation and summer when school was not in session. (As for the hosiery, she purchased $700 worth with school funds one year.) The superintendent was genuinely unaware of the misuse of funds.

Amount: The business manager had been employed for six years, was trusted, and embezzled an estimated $25,000.

6.59 **Kaplan CPA Simulation: Audit Objectives for Cash.** You are an auditor working for Burton & Associates CPAs (Burton), a local CPA firm. Burton is examining the financial statements of Harrison Homes, Inc. (Harrison). Harrison is a custom home builder incorporated under the laws of Anystate, USA. You have been assigned as the auditor in charge of field work for the Harrison audit.

Required:

Go to the Kaplan Web site at www.mhhe.com/louwers3e and click on AUD: Harrison Homes case and the "audit objectives" tab and complete the assigned task.

6.60 **Kaplan CPA Simulation: Audit of Cash.** Peters & Michael CPA (P&M) is the incumbent auditor for the financial statements of Lakeland Supermarkets, Inc. (Lakeland) for the year ended December 31, Year 2. Lakeland is a relatively small and new company that is, nevertheless, publicly traded on a major U.S. stock exchange. P&M has previously obtained and documented its understanding of Lakeland's internal controls for cash receipts, cash disbursements, and cash balances. No significant weaknesses were found. It is now January 31, Year 3, and the audit field work for Year 2 is just beginning to commence. You are an auditor with P&M and have been assigned to specifically audit Lakeland's cash accounts as part of your duties. Materiality for the overall financial statements is set at $20,000.

The lead schedule for cash has been prepared and is shown below.

Account Number	Account	Description	Unaudited Year 2	Audited Year 1	Change from Prior Year
100	First National Bank	General checking	$573,250	$599,623	(26,373)
101	Second Federal Bank	Payroll	42,401	36,888	5,513
102	Cash at Store 1	Cash at store	4,250	6,698	(2,448)
103	Cash at Store 2	Cash at store	4,977	5,454	(477)
104	Cash at Store 3	Cash at store	4,338	8,239	(3,901)
105	Cash on Hand	Petty Cash	2,000	2,000	0
	Total Cash		631,216	658,902	(27,686)

Required:

Go to the Kaplan Web site at www.mhhe.com/louwers3e and click on AUD: Peter Michaels case.

a. Click on the "Bank Reconciliation" tab and complete the assigned task.

b. Click on the "Confirmation" tabs (note: there are two tabs for confirmations) and complete the assigned task.

c. Click on the "Obtaining Evidence" tab and complete the assigned task.

d. Click on the "Communication" tab and complete the assigned task.

CPA REVIEW

6.61 **Kaplan CPA Simulation: *SAS 99* Requirements.** Ridge & Associates (Ridge), a local CPA firm, is examining the financial statements of Western Water Company for the year ended December 31, 2008. This is Ridge's first audit of Western and you are the in-charge auditor. Western Water was previously audited for several years by another local CPA firm. Ridge has already reviewed the prior auditors' audit documentation. During late October, with the help of Western's controller, you completed an internal control questionnaire and prepared the appropriate memoranda describing Western Water's accounting procedures. Your comments relative to accounts receivable and cash receipts are as follows:

The utility billing clerk (who has been with the company for 12 years, ever since the water treatment plant was put in operation) prepares all new water tap orders and collects the associated tap-in fee. When the customer pays the tap-in fee, the water tap orders are written on preprinted forms that have not been prenumbered and one copy of the order is forwarded to the maintenance department for installation. The other copy of the order is used by the utility billing clerk to post to the cash receipts journal.

The utility billing clerk also prepares and mails the monthly water bills. All cash receipts for monthly water bills are collected in person by the utility billing clerk or are mailed directly to the utility billing clerk, who then posts them to the customer accounts. The utility billing clerk posts these receipts to the cash receipts journal as well.

Cash receipts are in the form of both cash and customer checks for both water tap-in fees and monthly water bills. The cash receipts journal is totaled daily by the utility billing clerk, who then prepares the bank deposit slip in duplicate and takes the deposit to the bank. The controller, who is a CPA and has been with Western Water for 10 years, receives the monthly bank statement directly from the bank and promptly reconciles it.

The utility billing clerk's compensation is based upon a salary schedule that is adjusted from time to time for the cost of living. It is common knowledge that the utility billing clerk makes frequent visits to a nearby casino and has incurred a large number of personal debts.

Western Water Company invested in a state-of-the-art accounting system three years ago. Both the utility billing clerk and the controller are satisfied with the system and think that it meets the company's needs. The system was tested by the prior auditors and found to be operating effectively.

Required:

Go to the Kaplan Web site at www.mhhe.com/louwers3e and click on AUD: Ridge Associates case and the "research" tab and complete the assigned task.

Appendix 6A

Internal Control Questionnaires

APPENDIX 6A.1 Internal Control Questionnaire—Cash Receipts Processing

	Yes	No	Comments
Control Environment:			
1. Are receipts deposited daily, intact, and without delay?			
2. Does someone other than the cashier or accounts receivable bookkeeper take the deposits to the bank?			
3. Are the duties of the cashier entirely separate from record keeping for notes and accounts receivable? From general ledger record keeping?			
4. Is the cashier denied access to receivables records or monthly statements?			
Existence or Occurrence Objective:			
5. Is a bank reconciliation performed monthly by someone who does not have cash custody or record-keeping responsibility?			
6. Are the cash receipts journal entries compared to the remittance lists and deposit slips regularly?			
Completeness Objective:			
7. Does the person who opens the mail make a list of cash received (a remittance list)?			
8. Are currency receipts controlled by mechanical devices? Are machine totals checked by the internal auditor?			
9. Are prenumbered cash receipts listings used? Is the numerical sequence checked for missing documents?			
10. Does the accounting manual contain instructions for dating cash receipts entries the same day as the date of receipt?			
Valuation or Allocation Objective:			
11. Is a duplicate deposit slip retained by the internal auditor or someone other than the employee making up the deposit?			
12. Is the remittance list compared to the deposit by someone other than the cashier?			
Presentation and Disclosure Objective:			
13. Does the accounting manual contain instructions for classifying cash receipts credits?			
14. Does someone reconcile the accounts receivable subsidiary to the control account regularly (to determine whether all entries were made to customers' accounts)?			

APPENDIX 6A.2 Cash Disbursements Processing

	Yes	No	Comments
Control Environment:			
1. Are persons with cash custody or check-signing authority denied access to accounting journals, ledgers, and bank reconciliations?			
2. Is access to blank checks denied to unauthorized persons?			
3. Are all disbursements except petty cash made by check?			
4. Are check signers prohibited from drawing checks to cash?			
5. Is signing blank checks prohibited?			
6. Are voided checks mutilated and retained for inspection?			
Existence or Occurrence Objective:			
7. Are invoices, receiving reports, and purchase orders reviewed by the check signer?			
8. Are the supporting documents stamped "paid" (to prevent duplicate payment) before being returned to accounts payable for filing?			
9. Are checks mailed directly by the signer and not returned to the accounts payable department for mailing?			
10. Do checks require two signatures? Is there dual control over machine signature plates?			
Completeness Objective:			
11. Are blank checks prenumbered and the numerical sequence checked for missing documents?			
12. Are checks dated in the cash disbursements journal with the date of the check?			
Valuation or Allocation Objective:			
13. Are bank accounts reconciled by personnel independent of cash custody or record keeping?			
Presentation and Disclosure Objective:			
14. Does the chart of accounts and accounting manual give instructions for determining debit classifications of disbursements not charged to accounts payable?			
15. Is the distribution of charges checked periodically by an official? Is the budget used to check on gross misclassification errors?			
16. Are special disbursements (e.g., payroll and dividends) made from separate bank accounts?			
17. Is the bank reconciliation reviewed by an accounting official with no conflicting cash receipts, cash disbursements, or record keeping responsibilities?			
18. Do internal auditors periodically conduct a surprise audit of bank reconciliations?			

Appendix 6B

Audit Program Questionnaires

APPENDIX 6B.1 Audit Program—Tests of Controls—Cash

	Workpaper Reference	Performed by
1. Inquire of management concerning employees that a) Receive remittances from customers. b) Record payments in accounts payable. c) Prepare and deliver payments to the bank.		
2. Observe the opening of the mail and ensure that a) Two employees are opening the mail. b) Checks are restrictively endorsed. c) A listing of all checks is being prepared.		
3. Observe the flow of checks and remittance advices and ensure that a) Checks are delivered directly to the cashier. b) Remittance advices are delivered to the accounting department.		
4. Review reconciliations of cash listings, accounts receivable payments, and bank deposits.		
5. Review reconciliations of bank statements for a) Initials of proper review. b) Investigation of all outstanding items reviewed for propriety.		

APPENDIX 6B.2 Audit Program—Selected Substantive Procedures—Cash

	Documentation Reference	Performed by
1. Obtain confirmations from banks (standard bank confirmation).		
2. Obtain reconciliations of all bank accounts. a. Trace the bank balance on the reconciliation to the bank confirmation. b. Trace the reconciled book balance to the general ledger. c. Verify the mathematical accuracy of client-prepared bank reconciliations.		
3. Review the bank confirmation for evidence of loans and collateral.		
4. Ask the client to request a cutoff bank statement for each account, to be mailed directly to the audit firm. a. Trace deposits in transit on the reconciliation to bank deposits returned with the cutoff statement. b. Trace outstanding checks on the reconciliation to checks returned with the cutoff statement.		
5. Prepare a schedule of interbank transfers for a period of 10 business days before and after the year-end date. Document dates of book entry transfer and correspondence with bank entries and reconciliation items, if any.		
6. Count cash funds in the presence of a client representative. Obtain a receipt for return of the funds.		
7. Obtain management representations concerning compensating balance agreements.		

Revenue and Collection Cycle

Professional Standards References

Compendium Section	Document Reference	Topic
Various*	AS 5	"An Audit of Internal Control over Financial Reporting That Is Integrated with an Audit of Financial Statements"
AU 311	SAS 108	"Planning and Supervision"
	ISA300	"Planning an Audit of Financial Statements"
AU 312	SAS 107	"Audit Risk and Materiality in Conducting an Audit"
AU 313	SAS 110	"Performing Audit Procedures in Response to Assessed Risks and Evaluating the Audit Evidence Obtained"
	ISA 330	"The Auditor's Procedures in Response to Assessed Risks"
AU 316	SAS 99	"Consideration of Fraud in a Financial Statement Audit"
	ISA 240	"The Auditor's Responsibility to Consider Fraud in an Audit of Financial Statements"
AU 319	SAS 109	"Understanding the Entity and Its Environment and Assessing the Risks of Material Misstatement"
	ISA 315	"Understanding the Entity and Its Environment and Assessing the Risks of Material Misstatement"
AU 326	SAS 106	"Audit Evidence"
	ISA 500	"Audit Evidence"
AU 329	SAS 56	"Analytical Procedures"
	ISA 520	"Analytical Procedures"
AU 330	SAS 67	"The Confirmation Process"
AU 9330		"Use of Electronic Confirmations"
	ISA 505	"External Confirmations"
AU 333A	SAS 85	"Management Representations"
	ISA 580	"Management Representations"
AU 334	SAS 45	"Related Parties"
	ISA 550	"Related Parties"
AU 339	SAS 103	"Audit Documentation"
	AS 3	"Audit Documentation"
	ISA 230	"Audit Documentation"
AU 342	SAS 57	"Auditing Accounting Estimates"
	ISA 540	"Audit of Accounting Estimates"

*AS 5 amends AU 310, AU 319, AU 325, AU 326, AU 329, AU 339, AU 380, AT 501, ET 101, and ET 191.

What at first was plunder assumed the softer name of revenue.

Thomas Paine

Learning Objectives

This is the first of four "cycle chapters" in which you will go through the steps of the audit risk model. First, we will discuss the inherent risks particular to the revenue cycle. Many recent frauds have consisted of improper revenue recognition, which generally also results in overstatement of receivables. Next, we will examine controls normally included in the cycle. Finally, we will discuss substantive procedures, including common analytical procedures. Accounts receivable confirmations are a central part of accounts receivable auditing and are required by GAAS. You will see examples of confirmations and a discussion of procedures auditors perform when sending those confirmations.

Your objectives are to be able to

1. Discuss inherent risks related to the revenue and collection cycle with a focus on improper revenue recognition.
2. Describe the revenue and collection cycle, including typical source documents and control procedures.
3. Give examples of tests of controls over customer credit approval, delivery, and accounts receivable accounting.
4. Give examples of substantive procedures in the revenue and collection cycle and relate them to assertions about account balances at the end of the period.
5. Describe some common errors and frauds in the revenue and collection cycle and design some audit and investigation procedures for detecting them.

INTRODUCTION

MiniScribe Corporation was a manufacturer of hard drives that owned several distribution warehouses around the country and in Canada and operated as a "just-in-time" supplier for distributors. Using fraudulent **bill and hold** transactions, MiniScribe booked sales when goods were shipped to the distribution warehouses rather than when they were shipped to customers. Consequently, MiniScribe increased sales by simply shipping goods to its own warehouses. These aggressive accounting practices helped MiniScribe report sales of $362 million in 1987, a 95 percent increase over the previous year. Growth was so rapid that *Electronic Business Magazine* named MiniScribe one of the top growth companies in the electronics industry. Eventually, the company became so bold that it started packaging bricks as finished products and shipping them to distributors at the end of the year. In 1989, things began to fall apart. The CEO resigned and the company's stock price fell from a high of $15 per share to $1 per share. Ultimately, the SEC charged the CEO, two corporate controllers, and 13 other corporate officers with falsifying financial records. In addition, Coopers & Lybrand, MiniScribe's auditor, paid a $140 million settlement to defrauded shareholders.

OVERALL AUDIT APPROACH FOR THE REVENUE AND COLLECTION CYCLE

Chapter 3 introduced the audit risk model. As noted there, this model allows auditors to control audit risk to desired levels. *Audit risk* is defined as the risk that auditors will issue an unqualified opinion on financial statements that contain a material misstatement. Audit risk is manifested when a material misstatement enters the financial reporting process (inherent risk) that the client's internal controls do not prevent or detect (control risk) and that the auditors' substantive procedures do not detect (detection risk). Recall the basic three-step approach for using the audit risk model to plan an engagement:

- Set audit risk at desired levels (normally, low).
- Assess risk of material misstatement, which incorporates inherent risk based on the nature of the account balance or class of transactions and control risk based on gaining an understanding of internal control.
- Determine detection risk based on the level of audit risk and risk of material misstatement.

The components of the audit risk model are assessed on an assertion-by-assertion basis. This assessment recognizes that certain assertions assume an increased level of importance and are of greater interest to auditors than others are. For example, because of the

tendency to overstate assets and revenues, the *existence* assertion is relatively important in the audit of assets such as accounts receivable and *occurrence* is important for revenues such as sales. Thus, auditors may assess inherent risk for the *existence* assertion to be higher than for the *completeness* assertion for these accounts, all other things being equal.

After considering the inherent risk associated with each assertion, the auditors identify important control procedures implemented by the client for the assertion. Once the control procedures have been determined to be in place through inquiry, observation, and walkthrough, auditors estimate the control risk. Based upon the combined inherent and control risk assessments (referred to as *the risk of material misstatement*), auditors calculate detection risk and determine the nature, timing, and extent of evidence to gather by substantive procedures. If the audit team estimates that control risk is below the maximum, they will perform tests of controls to confirm that the control procedures are operating effectively and that the auditors' initial strategy is sound.[1] If the tests of controls reveal that control risk is higher than originally estimated, the audit team would *decrease* detection risk and modify the *nature, timing, and extent* of substantive procedures. Using a matrix such as the following one (which assumes a low desired overall audit risk), the maximum allowable level of detection risk can be determined by finding the intersection of the row (representing inherent risk) and column (representing control risk).

		CONTROL RISK		
		Low	Moderate	High
INHERENT RISK	Low	High detection risk	Moderate to high detection risk	Moderate detection risk
	Moderate	Moderate to high detection risk	Moderate detection risk	Low to moderate detection risk
	High	Moderate detection risk	Low to moderate detection risk	Low detection risk

Later in the chapter, we present a specific example of how the audit team might go through this process.

INHERENT RISKS IN THE REVENUE AND COLLECTION CYCLE

LEARNING
OBJECTIVE

1. Discuss inherent risks related to the revenue and collection cycle with a focus on improper revenue recognition.

Revenue Recognition

MiniScribe Corporation is an extreme example of the violation of accounting standards related to **revenue recognition** (recording revenues in the general ledger). To be recognized, revenues must be (1) realized or realizable and (2) earned.[2]

> An entity's revenue-earning activities involve delivering or producing goods, rendering services, or other activities that constitute its ongoing major or central operations, and

[1] Note that PCAOB *AS 5* requires auditors of public companies to test *all relevant* controls over *significant accounts* for design and operating effectiveness.

[2] *SFAC No. 5,* "Recognition and Measurement in Finance Statements."

revenues are considered to have been earned when the entity has substantially accomplished what it must do to be entitled to the benefits represented by the revenues.[3]

Similarly, the SEC believes that revenue generally is realized or realizable and earned when *all* of the following criteria are met:

• Persuasive evidence of an arrangement exists.
• Delivery has occurred or services have been rendered.
• The seller's price to the buyer is fixed or determinable.
• Collectibility is reasonably assured.[4]

The SEC and the popular press have expressed concern about appropriate recognition of revenue in financial statements. A study by the Government Accountability Office (GAO) of 919 financial statement restatements from 1997 through June 2002 showed that 37.9 percent of the restatements were due to misstatements of revenue that eventually resulted in market losses of $56 billion.[5] Some recent restatements are listed in Exhibit 7.1. The fact that the financial statements were restated means that the auditors missed the original misstatement or went along with the company's accounting treatment. In some

EXHIBIT 7.1 Revenue Recognition Rogues

Company	Cause of Misstatement	Alleged Amount
Bristol-Myers	Company offered incentives to wholesalers to build their inventories so Bristol-Meyers could meet sales forecasts (*channel stuffing*).	$2.5 billion
Computer Associates	Company recognized revenue from several contracts in which either (1) the company had agreed to make offsetting purchases (*round trips*) or (2) the contracts contained undisclosed side letters that could have canceled the contracts.	$2.2 billion
Qwest Communication	Company used fiber-optic "swaps." It recorded sales of equipment when it agreed to pay hundreds of millions of dollars for Internet services. It recognized the revenue for the equipment, but deferred the cost of the Internet services.	$2.2 billion
Nortel	Company prematurely recorded revenue from equipment sales before the buyer had taken title to the equipment.	$1.5 billion
Sea View Video Technology	Company prematurely recorded revenues and accounts receivable for customer orders for security camera products prior to shipping.	$1.4 billion
Safety-Kleen Corporation	Company recorded contingent revenues and contract claims that were not probable and recorded revenue for property not yet sold.	$534 million
Household International	Company employed incorrect timing of recognizing costs and revenues related to its MasterCard and Visa co-branding and affinity credit card relationships, as well as a credit card marketing agreement with a third party.	$386 million
Xerox	Several senior managers colluded to circumvent company's accounting policies and administrative procedures. The restatement related to uncollectible long-term receivables, failure to record liabilities for amounts due to concessionaires, and, to a lesser extent, recording revenue for contracts that did not fully meet the requirements of sales-type leases.	$207 million
AOL (now Time Warner)	AOL recorded advertising revenue, some of which included one-time payments, stock sales, and "round-trip" deals in which money flowed both ways between AOL and the advertiser.	$190 million
Interpublic	Company improperly booked credits, creating double-counting; included insurance proceeds that had not been realized; and understated liabilities.	$181 million
Gemstar	Subsidiary TV Guide recorded $113 million in patent-licensing revenue from an expired Scientific-Atlanta Inc. contract.	$113 million

[3] Ibid., 83(b).

[4] *Staff Accounting Bulletin No. 104,* "Securities and Exchange Commission."

[5] Government Accountability Office (GAO), *Financial Statement Restatements,* October 2002, www.gao.gov.

Under its Name Your Own Price® services, **Priceline.com** takes bids from customers for airline tickets, rental cars, hotel rooms, and other services. If the supplier agrees to the price, the customer pays Priceline, who deducts their commission and pays the airline, hotel, or car rental company. If Priceline receives $175 for a ticket and pays the airline $150, what should the company record as revenue? Priceline contends they should record $175 because they take ownership of the ticket and do not receive a fee or commission. Moreover, Priceline argues that they assume the risk of uncollectible accounts, even though they receive the customer's credit card number before they award the ticket. The SEC staff generally believes companies should report this type of transaction on a net basis (i.e., $25), but they have gone along with Priceline so far. For the year ended December 31, 2006, Priceline reported $904 million of "merchant" revenues and $722 million as the cost of "merchant" revenues.

Source: Priceline.com Incorporated Form 10-K.

cases, predecessor auditors accepted the accounting treatment, but the successor auditors demanded the restatement.

The SEC issued *Staff Accounting Bulletin (SAB) 104* in December 2003 to provide examples of situations in which revenue should not be recorded. In 2005, the percentage of restatements related to revenue recognition dropped below restatements for lease and other expenses,[6] but it is still a significant cause of financial statement restatements.

Risks of improper revenue recognition are greater in developing companies, which are often valued by financial analysts at a multiple of total revenues. In addition, companies with complex transactions, related-party transactions, and reciprocal transactions have a higher likelihood of inflating revenues. An example of the latter occurred in the telecom industry where **Global Crossing** and other companies are alleged to have traded line rights in one geographic area to other companies for rights in another area. The rights given up were recorded in revenue while the rights received were capitalized and the expense was spread out over several years.

Collectibility of Accounts Receivable

Estimation of the allowance for doubtful accounts can be subjective and difficult for the client and the auditor. This is particularly true where the client has changed products or its customer base, so there is little experience on which to base estimates. Changing economic conditions also make it difficult to estimate collectibility.

Customer Returns and Allowances

Clients may enter into informal right of return agreements with customers unknown to the auditors. Even liabilities for known rights of return, warranties, and other potential obligations are very difficult to estimate. Companies with new products or technologies have a high inherent risk.

According to the SEC, **Take-Two Interactive Software, Inc.**, best-known for its blockbuster "Grand Theft Auto" series, systematically recognized sales revenue from about 180 "parking" transactions in which the company, at or near the end of fiscal quarters or fiscal years, shipped hundreds of thousands of video games to distributors who had no obligation to pay for the products. After they had "fraudulently recorded the shipments as if they were sales," the company accepted the sales returns in subsequent reporting periods. In many cases, Take-Two created fraudulent invoices to disguise the returns as "purchases of assorted product." Take-Two also improperly recognized sales revenue for games that were still being manufactured and could not be shipped.

Source: "Take-Two, Executives Settle with SEC," *CFO.com*, June 13, 2005.

[6] "Restatements Surged in 2005," *CFO.com*, March 6, 2006.

Review Checkpoints

7.1 What do we mean by "revenue recognition"? What do GAAP say about proper revenue recognition?

7.2 Why do you think companies use revenue recognition as a primary means for inflating profits?

7.3 What are "bill and hold" sales?

REVENUE AND COLLECTION CYCLE: TYPICAL ACTIVITIES

LEARNING
OBJECTIVE

2. Describe the revenue and collection cycle, including typical source documents and control procedures.

STAGES OF AN AUDIT

 Obtain (or Retain) Engagement

 Engagement Planning

 Risk Assessment

 Substantive Procedures

 Reporting

The basic activities in the revenue and collection cycle are (1) receiving and processing customer orders, including credit granting; (2) delivering goods and services to customers; (3) billing customers and accounting for accounts receivable; and (4) collecting and depositing cash received from customers. Exhibit 7.2 shows the activities and transactions involved in a revenue and collection cycle. As you follow the exhibit, you can track some of the highlighted elements of internal control.

Receiving and Processing Customer Orders, Including Credit Granting

Customers initiate sales orders in a variety of ways. They may send in purchase orders, call in orders by phone or over the Internet, or simply come to the company's place of business and buy their goods. In some cases, companies are directly linked to production schedules in their customers' computer files, so they can ship goods automatically as the customer needs them. Electronic or Web-based sales orders require special software controls that protect against unauthorized orders and that protect customer information.

It is important that someone authorize credit sales to ensure that the customer will be able to pay for the goods or service. Since various authorizations are imbedded in a computerized system, access to the master file for additions, deletions, and other changes must be limited to responsible people. If these controls fail, orders might be processed for fictitious customers, credit might be approved for bad credit risks, and shipping documents might be created for goods that do not exist in the inventory.

Customer orders, shipping documents, and invoices should be in numerical sequence so the system can check the sequence and determine whether any transactions have not been completed (*completeness* assertion) or have been duplicated (*occurrence* assertion).

Another authorization in the system is the price list master file. This file contains the product unit prices for billing customers. Persons who have power to alter this file have the power to authorize price changes and customer billings.

Delivering Goods and Services to Customers

Physical custody of inventory goods starts in the storeroom or warehouse where inventory is kept. Custody is transferred to the shipping department upon the authorization of the shipping order that permits storekeepers to release goods to the shipping area. Proper authorization is important—employees performing each of these steps should

EXHIBIT 7.2 Revenue and Collection Cycle

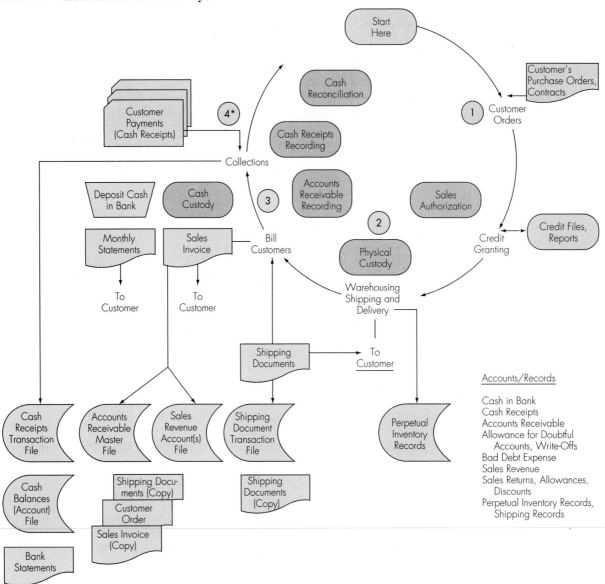

*Processing customer payments is discussed in the Cash Receipts section of Chapter 6.

sign transfer documents so they are held accountable. This control procedure will prevent them from misappropriating the goods or shipping them to friends without billing them. A **bill of lading** is a form that is signed by the carrier to verify the goods are shipped. A **packing slip,** which describes the goods being shipped, is often included with the shipment.

AUDITING INSIGHT Price Manipulation

A computer programmer was secretly paid by one of his employer's customers to bill the customer at prices lower than list prices. The programmer wrote a subroutine that was invoked when the billing system detected the customer's regular code number. This subroutine instructed the computerized billing system to reduce all unit prices 9.5 percent. The company relied on the computerized billing system and no one rechecked the actual prices billed.

AUDITING INSIGHT Shipping Employee Caught by Computer!

A customer paid off a shipping department employee to enter smaller quantities than actually shipped on the packing slip and bill of lading. This caused the customer's invoices to be understated. Unknown to the employee, a computerized log recorded all the entries that altered the original packing slip record. An alert internal auditor noticed the pattern of "corrections" made by the shipping employee. A trap was laid by initiating fictitious orders for this customer; the employee was observed making the alterations.

Billing Customers and Accounting for Accounts Receivable

When a delivery or shipment is complete, the system finishes the transaction by filing a shipment record and preparing a final invoice for the customer (which is recorded as sales revenue and accounts receivable). A **sales invoice** is the bill sent to the customer that indicates the amount due. Any person who has the power to enter or alter these transactions or to change the invoice before it is mailed to the customer has an undesirable combination of authorization, custody, and recording responsibilities.

Access to accounts receivable records implies the power to alter them directly or enter transactions to alter them (e.g., transfers, returns and allowance credits, write-offs). Personnel with this power have a combination of authorization and recording responsibility. Another important facet of control is physical protection of the files. If the files are lost or destroyed, it is unlikely the accounts will be collected, so the records are truly assets. Limited access, backup, and disaster recovery plans are important controls to ensure the files remain safe. Moreover, customer and employee information must be protected.

The most frequent reconciliation is the comparison of the sum of customers' unpaid balances with the accounts receivable control account total. This reconciliation is accomplished by preparing a trial balance of the accounts receivable (a list of customers and amounts), adding it, and comparing the total to the control account balance. Internal auditors can perform periodic comparisons of the customers' balances by sending confirmations to the customers.

AUDIT EVIDENCE IN MANAGEMENT REPORTS AND DATA FILES

Exhibit 7.3 represents a computerized system for processing customer orders. Computerized processing of revenue and cash receipts transactions enables management to generate several reports that can provide important audit evidence.

Pending Order Master File

This file contains sales transactions that were initiated but are not yet completed, and thus not yet recorded as sales. Long-standing orders may represent unfilled sales to a customer, which results in ill will and lack of revenue. They also may represent shipments that actually were made, but for some reason the shipping department did not enter the shipping information (or entered an incorrect code that did not match the pending order file). The pending orders can be reviewed for evidence of the *completeness* of recorded sales and accounts receivable.

AUDITING INSIGHT Maxxed Out?

TJX, operator of discount chains including **T.J. Maxx** and **Marshalls**, said its computers were hacked, putting shoppers at risk of identity fraud. Intruders accessed systems used to process and store customer transaction data, the Framingham, Massachusetts–based TJX said in a statement. "It is pretty obvious that it was a very well orchestrated, targeted attack," said Avivah Litan, an analyst with Gartner. Litan suspects the perpetrators are the same people who have broken into systems at other retailers. "These people are piecing together information on millions of Americans. It is quite scary."

Source: "T.J.Maxx Hack Exposes Consumer Data," *C-Net News.com*, January 18, 2007.

EXHIBIT 7.3 Computerized Sales and Accounts Receivable Processing

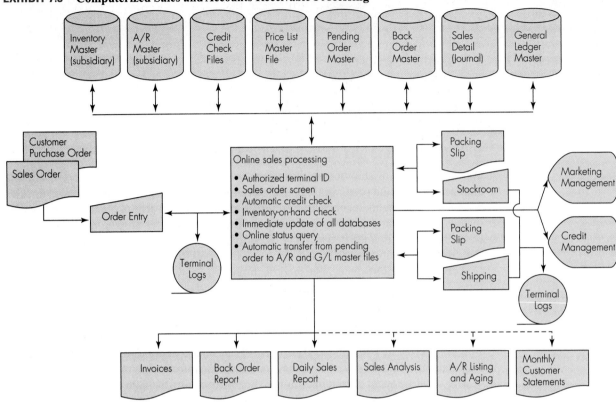

Credit Check Files

The computerized system may make automatic credit checks, but up-to-date maintenance of the credit information is very important. Credit checks based on dated or incomplete information are not good credit checks. A sample of the files can be tested for current status. Alternatively, the company's data change controls can be reviewed to ensure the files are accurately maintained.

Price List Master File

The computerized system may produce customer invoices automatically, but, if the master price list is incorrect, the billings will be incorrect. The computer file can be compared to an official price source for accuracy. The company should perform this comparison every time the prices are changed.

Sales Detail (Journal) File

This file should contain the detail sales entries, including the shipping references and dates. The file can be scanned using CAATs for entries without shipping references (fictitious sales?) and for match of recording dates with shipment dates (sales recorded before shipment?). Daily totals should be compared to a computer-generated list of debits to accounts receivable.

Sales Analysis Reports

A variety of sales analyses may be produced. Sales that are classified by product lines are information for the business segment disclosures. Sales classified by sales employee or region can show unusually high or low volume that might bear further investigation if an error is suspected.

Accounts Receivable Listing and Aging

This list of customers' balances is the actual accounts receivable. If the control account total is larger than the sum of the trial balance, it will have to be adjusted after the difference is thoroughly investigated. A receivable amount that cannot be identified with a customer

AUDITING INSIGHT Peaks and Valleys

During the year-end audit, the independent auditors reviewed the weekly sales volume reports classified by region. They noticed that sales volume was very high in Region 2 the last two weeks of March, June, September, and December. The volume was unusually low in the first two weeks of April, July, October, and January.

In fact, the peaks far exceeded the volume in all the other six regions. Further investigation revealed that the manager in Region 2 was holding open the sales recording at the end of each quarterly reporting period (i.e., including sales from the next period) in an attempt to make the quarterly reports look good.

cannot be collected! The trial balance is used as the starting point for selecting accounts for confirmation. The aging information is used in connection with assessing the allowance for doubtful accounts. Auditors must ensure that the calculation of the aging is accurate to verify that customers are not listed as current when they are in fact past due. An example of this listing, also called an **aged trial balance** is presented at Exhibit 7.7 (on page 269).

Cash Receipts Listing

The cash receipts journal contains all the detail entries for cash deposits and credits to various accounts. It contains the population of credit entries that should be reflected in the credits to accounts receivable for customer payments. It also contains adjusting and correcting entries that can result from the bank account reconciliation. These entries are important because they may signal the types of accounting errors or manipulations that occur in the cash receipts accounting.

Customer Statements

Probably the best control over whether cash is received and recorded is the customer. Therefore, sending customers monthly statements of what has been billed, what has been paid, and ending monthly balances enables them to spot discrepancies and notify the company. Statements should be sent even if the ending balances are zero.

Review Checkpoints

7.4 What is the basic sequence of activities and accounting in a revenue and collection cycle?

7.5 What purpose is served by prenumbering sales orders, shipping documents, and sales invoices?

7.6 What controls should be implemented to safeguard accounts receivable files?

7.7 What computer-based files might auditors examine to find evidence of unrecorded sales? Of inadequate credit checks? Of incorrect product unit prices?

7.8 Suppose you selected a sample of customers' accounts receivable and wanted to find supporting evidence for the entries in the accounts. Where would you go to vouch the debit entries? What would you expect to find? Where would you go to vouch the credit entries? What would you expect to find?

CONTROL RISK ASSESSMENT

LEARNING OBJECTIVE

3. Give examples of tests of controls over customer credit approval, delivery, and accounts receivable accounting.

Control risk assessment is important because it governs the nature, timing, and extent of substantive procedures that will be applied in the audit of account balances in the revenue and collection cycle. These account balances (listed in the corner of Exhibit 7.2) include

- Cash in bank.
- Accounts receivable.
- Allowance for doubtful accounts.
- Bad debts expense.

- Sales revenue.
- Sales returns, allowances, and discounts.

Control Considerations

Controls for proper separation of responsibilities should be in place and operating. By referring to Exhibit 7.2, you can see that proper separation involves different people and different departments performing the sales and credit authorization; custody of goods and cash; and record keeping for sales, receivables, inventory, and cash receipts. Combinations of two or more of these responsibilities in one person, one office, or one computerized system may open the door for errors and fraud.

It is not always possible to have complete separation of duties in a small business with few employees because the benefits of controls do not outweigh the costs involved. In order to obtain *reasonable assurance* that financial controls are intact, the owner must have active involvement in the accounting process—approving credit and discounts, reviewing the aged accounts receivable listing, and occasionally opening mail. The owner will usually be in direct contact with customers and can ensure that shipments are received. The owner also can follow up on past due accounts.

In addition, control procedures should be in place to prevent and detect the following errors:

- No sales order should be entered without a customer order.
- A credit-check code or manual signature should be recorded for authorization.
- Access to inventory and the shipping area should be restricted to authorized persons.
- Access to billing terminals and blank invoice forms should be restricted to authorized personnel.
- Accountants should be instructed to record sales and accounts receivable when all the supporting documentation of shipment is in order.
- Care should be taken to record sales and receivables as of the date the goods and services were shipped and the cash receipts on the date the payments were received.
- Customer invoices should be compared with bills of lading and customer orders to determine that the customer is sent the goods ordered at the proper location for the proper prices and that the quantity being billed is the same as the quantity shipped.
- Pending order files should be reviewed frequently to avoid failure to bill and record shipments.

Finally, procedures must be in place to ensure errors noted by these steps are properly corrected. An error control log monitored by the information systems supervisor ensures this is done.

Information about a company's controls often is gathered by completing an internal control questionnaire. Questionnaires for both manual controls and computerized controls over the revenue and collection cycle are in Appendix 7A. You can study these questionnaires for details of desirable control procedures. They are organized under headings that address the assertions regarding classes of transactions. Auditors should perform a *walkthrough* to verify their understanding of the procedures. The revenue and collection cycle walkthrough involves following a sale from the initial customer order through credit approval, billing, and delivery of goods, to the entry in the sales journal and subsidiary accounts receivable records, then its subsequent collection and cash deposit.

Tests of Controls

An organization should have control procedures in place and operating to prevent, detect, and correct accounting errors. Exhibit 7.4 puts these in the perspective of revenue cycle activity with examples of specific assertions.

Auditors can perform tests of controls to determine whether company personnel are properly performing controls that are said to be in place. In general, the actions in tests of

EXHIBIT 7.4 Assertions about Classes of Transactions and Events for the Period: Revenue and Collection Cycle

Assertion	Controls	Tests of Controls
Occurrence—Sales and related events that have been recorded have occurred and pertain to the entity.	Invoices supported by customer purchase orders. Bills of lading or other shipping documents exist for all invoices. Recorded sales in Sales Revenue account file supported by invoices.	Check agreement of sales in sales detail file to invoices, supporting shipping documents, and customer purchase orders for customer name, product description, terms, dates, and quantities. Vouch debits from Accounts Receivable accounts to supporting sales invoices.
Completeness—All sales and related events that should have been recorded have been recorded.	Invoices, shipping documents, and sales orders are prenumbered and the numerical sequence is checked. Overall comparisons of sales are made periodically by a statistical or product-line analysis.	Scan documents for numerical sequence. Observe client checking sequence. Trace shipping documents to recording in sales detail file. Examine evidence of client review and follow-up of analytical sales data.
Accuracy—Amounts and other data related to sales transactions and events have been recorded properly.	Credit sales are approved by the credit department. Prices used to prepare invoices are from the authorized price schedule. Invoice quantities are compared to shipment and customer order quantities. Prices and mathematical accuracy are independently checked after the invoice is prepared.	Examine invoices for credit approval. Compare prices to approved price listing. Observe client comparing shipping quantities. Examine evidence of client making the comparison. Recalculate price extensions and discounts. Examine evidence of client checking prices.
Cutoff—Sales and related events have been recorded in the correct period.	Date of shipping document is compared to invoice date.	Check agreement of date of shipment to sales invoice date. Check FOB terms.
Classification—Sales and related events have been recorded in the proper accounts.	Sales to subsidiaries and affiliates are classified as intercompany sales and receivables. Credit sales are posted to customers' individual accounts.	Trace posting of intercompany sales, sales returns, etc. to sales.

controls involve vouching, tracing, observing, scanning, and recalculating. If personnel in the organization are not performing their control procedures effectively, auditors will need to design substantive procedures to try to detect whether control failures have produced materially misstated account balances.

Tests of controls can be used to audit the accounting for transactions in two directions (see Exhibit 7.5). This dual-direction testing involves selecting samples to obtain evidence

EXHIBIT 7.5
Dual Direction of Test
Audit Samples

Did all recorded sales actually occur?

Sales Invoice File (Journal)

Completeness Assertions

Vouch sample of invoices to shipping documents (occurrence)

Trace sample of shipping documents to invoices (completeness)

Shipping documents

Were all shipments invoiced?

about control over *completeness* in one direction and control over *occurrence* in the other direction. The completeness direction determines whether all transactions that occurred were recorded (none omitted), and the occurrence direction determines whether recorded transactions actually occurred (were valid). An example of the *completeness* direction is the examination of a sample of shipping documents (from the file of all shipping documents) to determine whether invoices were prepared and recorded. An example of the *occurrence* direction is the examination of a sample of sales invoices (from the file representing all recorded sales) to determine whether supporting shipping documents exist to verify the fact of an actual shipment. The content of each document or file is compared with its related supporting document or file.

Appendix 7.B.1 contains a test of controls audit program. These steps are designed to enable the audit team to obtain objective evidence about the effectiveness of controls and about the reliability of accounting records. Thus, the tests of controls produce evidence that helps auditors determine whether the specific control assertions listed in Exhibit 7.4 were achieved.

When the business receives many payments from customers, a detailed audit should include comparison of the checks listed on a sample of deposit slips to the detail of customer credits listed on the day's posting to customer accounts receivable (daily remittance list or other record of detail postings). This procedure is a test for accounts receivable *lapping* (see Chapter 6). Auditors look for credits given to customers for whom no payments were received on the day in question.

Summary: Control Risk Assessment

Auditors must evaluate the evidence obtained from an understanding of internal control and from tests of controls. The initial process of obtaining an understanding of the company's controls and the later process of obtaining evidence from actual tests of controls are two of the phases of control risk assessment. If the control risk is assessed very low, the substantive procedures on the account balances can be reduced in cost-saving ways. For example, the accounts receivable confirmations can be sent on a date prior to the year end and the sample size can be small.

On the other hand, if tests of controls reveal weaknesses (such as posting sales without shipping documents, charging customers the wrong prices, or recording credits to customers without supporting credit memos), the substantive procedures will need to be designed to lower the risk of failing to detect material misstatement in the account balances. For example, the confirmation procedure could need to be scheduled on the year-end date with a large sample of customer accounts.

Review Checkpoints

7.9 What account balances are included in a revenue and collection cycle?

7.10 What specific control procedures (in addition to separation of duties and responsibilities) should be in place and operating in internal controls governing revenue recognition and cash accounting?

7.11 What is a "walkthrough" of a sales transaction? How can the walkthrough work complement the use of an internal control questionnaire?

7.12 What assertions are made about classes of transactions and events in the revenue and collection cycle?

7.13 What "actions" are typically contemplated by such a procedure?

7.14 What is "dual direction test of controls sampling"?

SUBSTANTIVE PROCEDURES IN THE REVENUE AND COLLECTION CYCLE

LEARNING OBJECTIVE

4. Give examples of substantive procedures in the revenue and collection cycle and relate them to assertions about account balances at the end of the period.

STAGES OF AN AUDIT

Obtain (or Retain) Engagement Engagement Planning Risk Assessment Substantive Procedures Reporting

Exhibit 7.6 illustrates the assertions about the account balances in the revenue and collection cycle and some illustrated substantive procedures the audit team might use to test those assertions. When considering assertions and obtaining evidence about accounts receivable and other assets, auditors must put emphasis on the *existence* assertion. This emphasis on existence is rightly placed because companies and auditors often have found themselves in malpractice trouble by giving unqualified reports on financial statements that overstated assets and revenues. For example, credit sales recorded too early or fictitious sales result in overstated accounts receivable and overstated sales revenue.

Discerning the population of assets to audit for existence is easy because the company has asserted their existence by putting them on the balance sheet. The audit procedures described in the following sections can be used to obtain evidence about the existence of accounts receivable.

EXHIBIT 7.6
Assertions and Substantive Procedures in the Revenue and Collection Cycle

Assertions about Account Balances	Substantive Procedures
Existence—Accounts receivable exist.	Confirm a sample of accounts receivable and perform follow-up procedures.
Accuracy—Receivables are recorded accurately.	Vouch sales invoices to customer orders and shipping documents.
Rights and obligations—The entity holds or controls the rights to accounts receivable.	Inquire whether any receivables have been sold or factored.
	Review bank confirmations, loan agreements, and minutes of the board for indications of pledged, discounted, or assigned receivables.
Completeness—All receivables that should have been recorded are recorded.	Perform sales cutoff tests.
	Include a sample of zero-balance accounts in the confirmation process.
Valuation or allocation—Receivables are included in the financial statements at appropriate amounts and any resulting valuation adjustments are properly recorded.	Obtain an aged trial balance of individual customer accounts and test the aging.
	Compare current year write-off experience to the prior-year allowance for bad debts.
	Examine cash receipts after the balance sheet date for collections on past-due accounts. For large past-due accounts, obtain financial statements or credit reports and discuss with the credit manager.
	Calculate an allowance estimate using prior relations of write-offs and sales, taking under consideration current economic events.

AUDITING INSIGHT Simple Analytical Comparison

The auditors prepared a schedule of the monthly credit sales totals for the current and prior years. They noticed several variations, but one in November of the current year stood out in particular. The current-year credit sales were almost twice as large as in any prior November. Further investigation showed that a computer error had caused the November credit sales to be recorded twice in the control accounts. The accounts receivable and sales revenue were materially overstated as a result.

Analytical Procedures

A variety of analytical comparisons might be employed, depending on the circumstances and the nature of the business. Comparisons of asset and revenue balances with recent history might help detect overstatements. Such relationships as receivables turnover and days of sales in receivables, aging, gross margin ratio, and sales/asset ratios can be compared to historical data and industry statistics for evidence of overall reasonableness. Account interrelationships also can be used in analytical procedures. For example, sales returns and allowances and sales commissions generally vary directly with dollar sales volume, bad debt expense usually varies directly with credit sales, and freight expense varies with the physical sales volume. Accounts receivable write-offs should be compared with earlier estimates of doubtful accounts.

Confirmation of Accounts and Notes Receivable

In general, the use of confirmations for trade accounts receivable is considered a required audit procedure by GAAS. If auditors decide not to use them, the burden of proof is on the auditors to justify their position. Auditors should document justifications for the decision not to use confirmations for trade accounts receivable in a particular audit. Justifications might include (1) receivables are not material; (2) confirmations would be ineffective, based on prior years' experience or knowledge that responses could be unreliable; and (3) analytical procedures and other substantive procedures provide sufficient, competent evidence.

Confirmations provide evidence of *existence* and, to a limited extent, *valuation* of accounts and notes receivable. The accounts and notes to be confirmed should be documented with an aged trial balance. (An aged trial balance annotated to show the auditors' work is shown in Exhibit 7.7.) Accounts for confirmation can be selected at random or in accordance with another sampling method consistent with the audit objectives. Statistical methods may be useful for determining the sample size. Audit software can be used to access computerized receivables files, select, and even print the confirmations.

Two widely used confirmation forms are positive confirmations and negative confirmations. A **positive confirmation** asks the customer to respond whether the balance is correct or incorrect. An example of a positive confirmation is shown in Exhibit 7.8. A variation of the positive confirmation is the *blank form*. A blank confirmation does not

AUDITING INSIGHT A Decision Not to Use Accounts Receivable Confirmations

Sureparts Manufacturing Company sold all its production to three auto manufacturers and six aftermarket distributors. All nine of these customers typically paid their accounts in full by the tenth of each following month. The auditors were able to vouch the cash receipts for the full amount of the accounts receivable in the bank statements and cash receipts records in the month following the Sureparts year end. Confirmation evidence was not considered necessary in these circumstances.

EXHIBIT 7.7 Accounts Receivable Aged Trial Balance

C-2

	Prepared by	RJR	3/15/09
	Reviewed by	TJL	3/16/09

APOLLO SHOES, INC.
Accounts Receivable Aged Trial Balance
For Year Ended 12/31/2008
(Prepared by Client)

	2008 Total Balance	Conf. No.	Date Mailed	Date Rec'd	Current < 30 Days	30–60 Days	Past Due 60-90 Days	> 90 Days
Pay More Shoes	$173,406.37					$173,406.37		
Nuke Me	$11,630.14				$11,630.14			
Run For Your Life Shoes	$718,986.45	1 C	1/15	1/22	$718,986.45			
Shoe Shack	$242,568.88				$242,568.88			
Tread	$461.09						$461.09	
Mall-Wart	$6,822,725.10	2 C	1/15	1/27	γ$5,765,081.85			$1,057,643.25
Wall of Shoes	$3,181.49						$3,181.49	
Shack's Shoe Shine	$1,644.41				$1,644.41			
Imelda's Closet	$32,023.89	3 E	1/15	1/21	$32,023.89			
Hip Hop Shoes	$230,932.95					$230,932.95		
International Soccer Federation	$405,846.10				$405,846.10			
Eight East	$15,026.57	4 E	1/15	1/25	γ($1,388.75)	γ$16,415.32		
Feet Lamour	$127,907.18β	5 NR	1/15α	n/a			$127,907.18	
Neutralizer	$1,013,239.57	6 E	1/15	2/2	$1,013,239.57			
Doug's Shoes	$879.43				$879.43			
Total	$16,410,902.71CF				$10,233,296.72	$536,874.60	$746,034.56	$4,894,696.83
	u TB				u	u	u	u

α Second request mailed 2/1.
γ Tested calculation of aging.
C Confirmation received without exception.
E Confirmation received with exception. See C-2.1 for follow up.

β Examined related invoices and shipping documents.
u Footed
CF Cross footed
TB Agreed to trial balance.

NR Confirmation not returned. See C-3 for application of subsequent cash receipts.

269

EXHIBIT 7.8
Positive Confirmation Letter

Apollo Shoes, Inc.
Shoetown, ME

Neutralizer
1359 Central Boulevard
Derma, MS 39530
Attn: Accounts Payable Dept.

Our auditors, Smith & Smith, are making their regular audit of our financial statements. Part of this audit includes direct verification of customer balances.

PLEASE EXAMINE THE DATA BELOW CAREFULLY AND EITHER CONFIRM ITS ACCURACY OR REPORT ANY DIFFERENCES DIRECTLY TO OUR AUDITORS USING THE ENCLOSED REPLY ENVELOPE.

This is not a request for payment. Please do not send your remittance to our auditors.

Your prompt attention to this request will be appreciated.

Samuel Carboy
Samuel Carboy, Controller

The balance due Apollo Shoes as of December 31, 2008, is
$1,013,239.57 C-2

This balance is correct except as noted below:

Our records indicate that we wrote a check to Apollo on 12/28 for this amount. ✓

Date: __1/21/09__ By: *Rudy Robinson*
 Title: *Accounts Payable*

✓ *Check Received 1/3/09 RJR*

contain the balance; customers are asked to fill it in themselves. The blank positive confirmation may produce better evidence because the recipients need to get the information directly from their own records instead of just signing the form and returning it with no exceptions noted. (However, the effort involved on the part of the recipient may cause a lower response rate.) In the examples below, the auditors must follow up on the exception. For example, they may choose to examine the bank deposit that includes the check mentioned by the customer. The reason for any discrepancy will have to be investigated by the client, and the audit team will examine corroborative evidence of the client's resolution.

The **negative confirmation** form for the same request shown in Exhibit 7.8 is in Exhibit 7.9. The positive form asks for a response. The negative form asks for a response *only if something is wrong with the balance;* thus, lack of response to negative confirmations is considered evidence that the account is fairly stated.

The positive form is by far the most common and is used when individual balances are relatively large or when accounts are in dispute. Positive confirmations may ask for information about either the account balance or specific invoices, depending on knowledge about how customers maintain their accounting records. The negative form is used mostly when the risk of material misstatement is considered low, when a large number of small balances is involved, and when the client's customers can be expected

EXHIBIT 7.9
Negative Confirmation Letter

Apollo Shoes, Inc.
Shoetown, ME

Neutralizer
1359 Central Boulevard
Derma, MS 39530
Attn: Accounts Payable Dept.

 Our auditors, Smith & Smith, are making their regular audit of our financial statements. Part of this audit includes direct verification of customer balances.

 PLEASE EXAMINE THE DATA BELOW CAREFULLY AND COMPARE THEM TO YOUR RECORDS OF YOUR ACCOUNT WITH US. IF THE INFORMATION IS NOT IN AGREEMENT WITH YOUR RECORDS, PLEASE STATE ANY DIFFERENCES BELOW AND RETURN DIRECTLY TO OUR AUDITORS IN THE RETURN ENVELOPE PROVIDED. **IF THE INFORMATION IS CORRECT, NO REPLY IS NECESSARY.**

 This is not a request for payment. Please do not send your remittance to our auditors.

 Your prompt attention to this request will be appreciated.

 Samuel Carboy

 Samuel Carboy, Controller

The balance due Apollo Shoes as of December 31, 2008, is
$1,013,239.57 C-2

This balance is correct except as noted below:

Our records indicate that we wrote a check to Apollo on 12/28 for this amount. ✓

Date: _1/21/09_____ By: _Rudy Robinson_____
 Title: _Accounts Payable_____

✓ *Check Received 1/3/09 RJR*

to consider the confirmations properly. Auditors must use these confirmations with great care. Occasionally, both forms are used by sending positive confirmations on some (large) customers' accounts and negative confirmations on others (usually smaller account balances).

Getting confirmations delivered to the intended recipient requires auditors' careful attention. Auditors need to control mailing the confirmations, including the addresses to which they are sent, and the confirmations should be returned directly to the auditors. The confirmations should normally be addressed to the customer's accounts payable department. There have been cases where confirmations were mailed to company accomplices, who provided false responses. The auditors should carefully consider features of the reply, such as postmarks, fax and telegraph responses, letterhead, electronic mail, telephone, or other characteristics that may give clues to indicate false responses. Auditors should follow up electronic and telephone responses to determine their origin (e.g., returning the telephone call to a known number, looking up telephone numbers to determine addresses, or using a directory to determine the location of a respondent). On the other hand, an electronic confirmation process that creates a secure confirmation environment may mitigate

EXHIBIT 7.10
Responses to Positive Confirmations (December 31)

Response	Follow-Up Action
"This amount was paid on December 28."	This account is probably valid as the check was probably received after year-end. However, it should be treated as an exception and the date of the receipt should be verified.
"We are unable to confirm this amount."	This is treated the same as a nonresponse and alternative procedures should be performed.
"We returned these items."	This is an exception that should be discussed with the client. The auditor should verify that there are no other returns included in receivables.
"We received these goods on January 3."	This is also probably valid as the shipment was probably made in late December. However, this should also be treated as an exception and the shipment should be verified. The auditor should also make sure the goods were removed from the year-end inventory.

the risks of human intervention and misdirection. For example, encryption, electronic digital signatures, and procedures to verify Web site authenticity may improve the security of the electronic confirmation process.[7] Second and third requests should be sent to prompt responses to positive confirmations and auditors should audit nonresponding customers by alternative procedures. Furthermore, the lack of response to a negative confirmation is no guarantee that the intended recipient received it or read it. Exhibit 7.10 illustrates some common confirmation responses and the appropriate follow-up action.

If an exception cannot be resolved or it appears to indicate a misstatement, auditors should (1) determine the cause of the misstatement, (2) extrapolate the misstatements over the population, and (3) consider whether fraud may have occurred. If similar misstatements could exist, additional procedures are generally necessary to determine the extent of misstatements. In the case of fraud, an extensive investigation may be necessary.[8]

Confirmation of receivables may be performed at a date other than the year end. When confirmation is done at an interim date, the audit firm is able to spread work throughout the year and avoid the pressures of overtime that typically occur during "busy season." In addition, the audit can be completed sooner after the year-end date if confirmation has been done earlier. The primary consideration when planning confirmation of accounts before the balance sheet date is the client's internal control over transactions affecting receivables. When confirmation is performed at an interim date, the following additional procedures should be considered:

1. Obtain a summary of receivables transactions from the interim date to the year-end date and review them for unusual items.
2. Vouch a selected sample of transactions for the period.
3. Obtain a year-end trial balance of receivables, compare it to the interim trial balance, and obtain evidence and explanations for large variations.
4. Consider the necessity for additional confirmations as of the balance sheet date if balances have significantly increased.

One final note about confirmations: Confirmations of accounts, loans, and notes receivable may not produce sufficient evidence of *ownership* by the client (rights assertion). Debtors may not be aware that the client sold the accounts, notes, or loans receivable to financial institutions or to the public (collateralized securities). Auditors need to perform additional inquiry and detail procedures to get evidence of the ownership of the receivables and the appropriateness of disclosures related to financing transactions secured by receivables.

[7] *AU 9330,* 06.
[8] "AICPA Practice Alert 03-1: Audit Confirmations," June 2007.

Alternative Procedures

Often the client's customer will not be willing or able to return the confirmation. They may not be able if, for example, they are on a voucher system that lists payables by invoice instead of by vendor account. The U.S. government is notorious for not returning confirmations because records may be kept at various agencies. In these cases, auditors have to perform alternative procedures to ensure existence. These include examining (1) subsequent cash receipts; (2) sales orders, invoices, and shipping documents; and (3) correspondence files for past due accounts. Examining subsequent cash receipts is a particularly effective test because if the customer paid the account, it is strong evidence the receivable existed. It is often done even when the customer has confirmed the account. The cash receipt should be traced to the remittance advice and the deposit into cash.

Review for Collectibility

Even if the customer confirms that the account exists, it does not necessarily follow that the customer can or will pay it! Thus, the audit team must review accounts for collectibility and determine the adequacy of the allowance for doubtful accounts (*valuation* assertion). To do this, auditors review subsequent cash receipts from the customer, discuss unpaid accounts with the credit manager, and examine the credit files. These should contain the customer's financial statements, credit reports, and correspondence between the client and the customer. Based on this evidence, the audit team estimates the likely amount of nonpayment for the customer, which is included in the estimate of the allowance for doubtful accounts. In addition, an allowance should be estimated for all other customers, perhaps as a percentage of the current accounts with a higher percentage of past-due accounts. The auditors compare their estimate to the recorded balance in the allowance account and propose an adjusting entry for the difference.

Cutoff and Sales Returns

Auditors must make sure that sales are recorded in the proper period. To do this, **sales cutoff tests** are employed. Procedures include obtaining used and unused shipping documents at year end, which are traced into current-year and subsequent-year sales, respectively. Credit memos for returns after year end are traced to receiving reports. Any goods returned after year end that were sold during the year being audited should be deducted from sales.

Adjusting entries for cut-off errors (i.e., sales recorded for next month's shipments) must be considered carefully because not only is Accounts Receivable and Sales overstated, but also Inventory is understated and Cost of Goods Sold is overstated.

Rights and Obligations

Companies may sell or **factor** their accounts receivable to a financial institution to obtain cash immediately. It is difficult to determine if receivables have been sold because the customers usually do not know that their account is actually owned by someone else. The cash goes to the original seller, who passes it on to the factor. Inquiring of management and examining support for large cash receipts is the best way to detect these transactions.

Presentation and Disclosure

Once auditors are satisfied that controls have been examined and transactions and balances have been appropriately tested, the job is not over. The accounts in the revenue cycle require certain disclosures. Revenue recognition policies and the amount of the allowance for doubtful accounts are some of the items requiring specific presentation and disclosures. These disclosures must ensure that the presentation and disclosure assertions of *occurrence, rights and obligations, completeness, classification, accuracy and valuation*, and *understandability* have been met.

AUDITING INSIGHT Oracle Doesn't Tell

Delphi Corp., the nation's largest auto supplier, said its audit committee had found undisclosed off-balance-sheet debt ranging from $187 million to $374 million per quarter. The debt stemmed from a factoring facility that allowed Delphi to borrow money against receivables. The accounting problems led to the resigna-

tions of the company's CEO, CFO, treasurer, and other members of the treasury staff.

Source: "Delphi Discloses New Accounting Irregularities," *The Wall Street Journal*, June 10, 2005, p. A1.

Review Checkpoints

7.15 Why is it important to place emphasis on the *existence* assertion when auditing accounts receivable?

7.16 Which audit procedures are usually the most useful for auditing the existence assertion?

7.17 What analytical procedures might be informative regarding the existence assertion?

7.18 Distinguish between "positive" and "negative" confirmations. Under what conditions would you expect each type of confirmation to be appropriate?

7.19 What are some of the justifications for not using confirmations of accounts receivable on a particular audit?

7.20 What special care should be taken with regard to examining the sources of accounts receivable confirmation responses?

7.21 What alternative procedures should be applied to accounts that do not return confirmations?

7.22 What procedures should be performed to determine the adequacy of the allowance for doubtful accounts?

AUDIT RISK MODEL SUMMARY

Now that the control and inherent risk elements for the revenue and collection cycle have been presented, along with some of the important substantive procedures, let's examine how an audit team might apply the audit risk model for the *existence* assertion.

AUDITING INSIGHT Time Doesn't Fly

The Securities and Exchange Commission filed an action alleging that **Sirena Apparel Group, Inc.,** a women's swimwear manufacturer, held open the March fiscal quarter until the company had reached its sales target for that period. The fraud was accomplished by resetting the date on the company's computer clock to the end of the month. Manipulation of the computer clock allowed April shipments to be recorded as March revenue because the computer clock controlled the date that was printed on the company's invoices. The computerized system also automatically

recorded revenue earned as of the date of the invoice. The bills of lading for the out-of-period shipments reflected April shipping dates. When management learned that the company's independent auditors would be testing shipping cutoff for the March 31 quarter, they instructed a subordinate to create false bills of lading to reflect March shipping dates in order to conceal the fraud from the auditors.

Source: *SEC Accounting and Auditing Enforcement Release No. 1325*, September 27, 2000.

HEALTHY DELIGHTS ICE CREAM, INC.

Healthy Delights is a publicly held company that sells health-based ice cream to grocery store chains in the United States. Annual sales have steadily remained at around $100 million. Marsha Fields had been assigned as the senior auditor. Marsha's firm's policy is always to set overall audit risk as low. She knows previous years' errors were few and the food industry is sound. The company is generally profitable; management's compensation is based on long-term performance, not short-term goals; and the overall economy is strong at the time of the audit, so she assesses inherent risk as low to moderate. Controls have been historically strong including hiring of competent people; maximum use of computer technology, which is reviewed by internal auditors; and careful reviews of detailed sales analyses by management. Testing of controls in accordance with *AS 5* found no design or operating deficiencies. Thus, Marsha assesses risk of material misstatement as low, which is confirmed by tests of controls. In this situation, Marsha can be comfortable setting detection risk at a moderate to high level. This will allow her to limit her sample of accounts for confirmation to the largest accounts, with a small random sample of smaller accounts. The confirmations will be sent at an interim date. She also can rely heavily on analytical procedures. This combination of low risk of material misstatement and moderate to high detection risk should lead Marsha to an acceptably low overall audit risk.

FRAUD CASES: EXTENDED AUDIT PROCEDURES (*SAS 99*)

LEARNING OBJECTIVE

5. Describe some common errors and frauds in the revenue and collection cycle and design some audit and investigation procedures for detecting them.

The audit procedures to gather evidence on the assertions in account balances are called *substantive procedures*. Some amount of substantive procedures must be performed in all audits. Auditors should not place total reliance on controls to the exclusion of other procedures. Substantive procedures differ from tests of controls in their basic purpose. Substantive procedures are designed to obtain direct evidence about the dollar amounts in account balances, while tests of controls are designed to obtain evidence about the company's performance of its own control procedures. Sometimes an audit procedure can be used for both purposes; then it is called a **dual-purpose procedure.**

Dual-Purpose Nature of Accounts Receivable Confirmations

Accounts receivable confirmation is a substantive procedure designed to obtain evidence of the existence and gross amount (valuation) of customers' balances directly from the customer. If such confirmations show numerous exceptions, auditors will be concerned with the controls over the details of sales and cash receipts transactions even if previous control evaluations seemed to show little control risk.

The goal in performing substantive procedures is to detect evidence of any material misstatement due to errors or fraud. If there is a risk of material misstatement involving revenue recognition, auditors should consider confirming contract terms and the absence of side agreements with customers. Items to be considered would be acceptance criteria, delivery and payment terms, and the absence of future or continuing vendor obligations, rights of return, guaranteed resale, and cancellation or refund provisions.

The remainder of this part of the chapter uses a set of cases that contain specific examples of tests of controls and substantive procedures (recalculation, observation, confirmation, inquiry, vouching, tracing, scanning, and analytical procedures). The case stories are better than listing schemes and detection procedures in the abstract. (A selection of substantive procedures for accounts receivable is in Appendix 7B.)

The cases follow a standard format that first tells about an error or fraud situation in terms of the problem, the audit approach, and the discovery. The first part of each case gives you the "inside story" that auditors seldom know before they perform the audit work. The next part is an "audit approach" section, which tells about the audit objective (assertion), controls, tests of controls, and substantive procedures that could be considered in approaching the situation. The audit approach section presumes that the auditors do not know everything about the situation.

At the end of the chapter, some similar discussion cases are presented and you can write the audit approach to test your ability to design audit procedures for detecting errors and frauds. Appendix 7B contains a substantive audit program for reference.

Case 7.1

The Canny Cashier

PROBLEM

D. Bakel was the assistant controller of Sports Equipment, Inc. (SEI), an equipment retailer. SEI maintained accounts receivable for school districts in the region; otherwise, customers received credit by using their own credit cards.

As company cashier, Bakel received all incoming mail payments on school accounts, the credit card account, and cash and checks taken over the counter. He prepared the bank deposit, listing all the checks and currency, and also prepared a remittance worksheet (daily cash report) that showed amounts received, discounts allowed on school accounts, and amounts to credit to the accounts receivable. The remittance worksheet was used by another accountant to post credits to the accounts receivable. Bakel delivered the deposit to the bank and reconciled the bank statement. No one else reviewed the deposits or the bank statements except the independent auditors.

Bakel opened a bank account in the name of Sport Equipment Company (SEC), after properly incorporating the company in the secretary of state's office. Over-the-counter cash, checks, and school district payments were taken from the SEI receipts and deposited in the SEC account. (None of the customers noticed the difference between the rubber stamp endorsements for the two similarly named corporations, and neither did the bank.) SEC kept the money awhile, earning interest, and then Bakel wrote SEC checks to SEI to replace the "borrowed" funds, in the meantime taking new SEI receipts for deposit to SEC.

Bakel also stole payments made by the school districts, depositing them to SEC. Later, Bakel deposited SEC checks in SEI, giving the schools credit, but approved an additional 2 percent discount in the process. Thus, the schools received proper credit later and SEC paid less by the amount of the extra discounts.

SEI's bank deposits systematically showed small currency deposits. Bakel was nervous about taking too many checks, so cash was preferred. The deposit slips had to include the SEC checks because bank tellers compare the deposit slip listing to the checks submitted. The remittance worksheet showed different details: Instead of showing SEC checks, it showed receipts from school districts and currency, but not many over-the-counter checks from customers.

The transactions became complicated enough that Bakel had to use the office computer to keep track of the school districts that needed to receive credit. There were no vacations for this hardworking cashier because the discrepancies might be noticed by a substitute and Bakel needed to give the districts credit later.

Over a six-year period, Bakel built up a $150,000 average balance in the Sport Equipment Company (SEC) account that earned a total of $67,500 interest that should have been earned by Sports Equipment, Inc. (SEI). By approving the "extra" discounts, Bakel skimmed 2 percent of $1 million in annual sales, for a total of $120,000. Since SEI would have had net income before taxes of about $1.6 million over these six years (about 9 percent of sales), Bakel's embezzlement took about 12.5 percent of the income.

AUDIT APPROACH

Authorization related to cash receipts, custody of cash, recording cash transactions, and bank statement reconciliation should be separate duties designed to prevent errors and frauds. Some supervision and detail review of one or more of these duties should be performed as a next-level control designed to detect errors and frauds, if they have occurred. For example, someone else should prepare the remittance worksheet, or at least the controller should approve the discounts; someone else should prepare the bank reconciliation.

Bakel performed incompatible duties. (While recording was not actually performed, Bakel provided the source document—the remittance worksheet—the other accountant used to make the cash and accounts receivable entries.) According to the company president, the "control" was the diligence of "our long-time, trusted, hardworking assistant controller." Note: A vigilant auditor who "thought like a crook" might have been able to imagine ways Bakel could have committed fraud and thus prevented or detected this cash embezzlement and accounts receivable lapping scheme.

Since the "control" purports to be Bakel's honest and diligent performance of the accounting and control procedures that might have been performed by two or more people, the test of controls is an audit of cash receipts transactions as they relate to accounts receivable credit. The dual-direction samples and procedures are these:

Occurrence direction: The auditors selected a sample of customer accounts receivable and vouched payment credits to remittance worksheets and bank deposits, including recalculation of discounts allowed in comparison to sales terms (2 percent), classification (customer name) identification, and correspondence of receipt date to recording date.

Completeness direction: The auditors selected a sample of remittance worksheets (or bank deposits), vouched details to bank deposit slips (trace details to remittance worksheets if the sample is bank deposits), and traced forward to complete accounting posting in customer accounts receivable.

Because there was a control risk of incorrect accounting, accounts receivable were confirmed as of year-end using positive confirmations. The "sample" included all school district accounts.

When prompted by notice of an oddity (noted in the discovery summary below), the audit team can use the telephone book, chamber of commerce directory, local criss-cross directory, and a visit to the secretary of state's office to determine the location and identity of Sport Equipment Company.

DISCOVERY SUMMARY

The test of controls samples showed four cases of discrepancy, one of which is shown below.

Bank Deposit Slip		Cash Remittance Report				
		Name	Amount	Discount	AR	Sales
Jones	25	Jones	25	0	0	25
Smith	35	Smith	35	0	0	35
Hill District	980	Hill District	980	20	1,000	0
Sport Equipment	1,563	Marlin District	480	20	500	0
Currency	540	Waco District	768	32	800	0
Deposit	3,143	Currency	855	0	0	855
		Totals	3,143	72	2,300	915

The auditors sent positive confirmations on all 72 school district accounts. Three of the responses stated the districts had paid the balances before the confirmation date. Follow-up procedures on their accounts receivable credit in the next period showed they had received credit in remittance reports and the bank deposits had shown no checks from the districts but had contained a check from Sports Equipment Company.

Investigation of SEC revealed the connection of Bakel, who was confronted and then confessed.

Case 7.2

The Taxman Always Rings Twice

PROBLEM

J. Shelstad was the tax assessor-collector in the Ridge School District, serving a large metropolitan area. The staff processed tax notices on a computerized system and generated 450,000 tax notices each October. An office copy was printed and used to check off "paid" when payments were received. Payments were processed by computer and a master file of "accounts receivable" records (tax assessments, payments) was kept on the computer hard disk.

Shelstad was a good personnel manager, who often took over the front desk at lunchtime so the teller staff could enjoy lunch together. During these times, Shelstad took payments over the counter, gave the taxpayers a counter receipt, and pocketed some of the money, which was never entered in the computerized system.

Shelstad resigned when he was elected to the Ridge school board. The district's assessor-collector office was eliminated upon the creation of a new countywide tax agency.

The computerized records showed balances due from many taxpayers who had actually paid their taxes. The book of printed notices was not marked "paid" for many taxpayers who had received counter receipts. These records and the daily cash receipts reports (cash receipts journal) were available at the time the independent auditors performed the most recent annual audit in April. When Shelstad resigned in August, a power surge permanently destroyed the hard disk receivables file and the cash receipts journals could not be found.

The new county agency managers noticed that the total of delinquent taxes disclosed in the audited financial statements was much larger than the total turned over to the county attorney for collection and foreclosure.

Shelstad had been the assessor-collector for 15 years. The "good personnel manager" pocketed 100–150 counter payments each year, in amounts of $500–$2,500, stealing about $200,000 a year for a total of approximately $2.5 million. The district had assessed about $800–$900 million per year, so the annual theft was less than 1 percent. Nevertheless, the taxpayers got mad.

AUDIT APPROACH

The school district had a respectable system for establishing the initial amounts of taxes receivable. The professional staff of appraisers and the independent appraisal review board established the tax base for each property. The school board set the price (tax rate). The computerized system authorization for billing was validated on these two inputs.

The cash receipts system was well designed, calling for preparation of a daily cash receipts report (cash receipts journal that served as a source input for computerized entry). The "boss," Shelstad, always reviewed this report.

Unfortunately, Shelstad had the opportunity and power to override the controls and become both cash handler and supervisor. Shelstad made the decisions about sending delinquent taxes to the county attorney for collection, and the ones known to have been paid but stolen were withheld.

The auditors performed dual-direction sampling to test the processing of cash receipts.

Occurrence direction: The auditors selected a sample of receivables from the computer hard disk and vouched (1) charges to the appraisal record, recalculating the amount using the authorized tax rate, and (2) payments, if any, to the cash receipts journal and bank deposits. (The auditors found no exceptions.)

Completeness direction: The auditors selected a sample of properties from the appraisal rolls and determined that tax notices had been sent and tax receivables (charges) recorded in the computer file. They next selected a sample of cash receipts reports, vouched them to bank deposits of the same amount and date, and traced the payments forward to credits to taxpayers' accounts. They also selected a sample of bank deposits and traced them to cash receipts reports of the same amount and date. Finally, they compared the details on bank deposits to the details on the cash receipts reports to determine whether the same taxpayers appear on both documents. (The auditors found no exceptions.)

The auditors confirmed a sample of unpaid tax balances with taxpayers. In such cases, response rates may not be high and follow-up procedures determining the ownership (county title files) may need to be performed, and new confirmations may need to be sent.

DISCOVERY SUMMARY

Shelstad persuaded the auditors that the true "receivables" were the delinquencies turned over to the county attorney. The confirmation sample and other work were based on this population. Thus, confirmations were not sent to fictitious balances that Shelstad knew had been paid, and the auditors never had the opportunity to receive "I paid" complaints from taxpayers.

Shelstad did not influence the new managers of the countywide tax district. They questioned the discrepancy between the delinquent taxes in the audit report and the lower amount turned over for collection. Since the computer file was not usable, the managers had to use the printed book of tax notices, where paid accounts had been marked "paid." (Shelstad had not marked the stolen ones "paid"

so the printed book would agree with the computer file.) Tax due notices were sent to the taxpayers with unpaid balances and they began to show up bringing their counter receipts and loud complaints.

In a fit of audit overkill, the independent auditors had earlier photocopied the entire set of cash receipts reports (cash journal) and they were then able to determine that the counter receipts (all signed by Shelstad) had not been deposited or entered. Shelstad was prosecuted and sentenced to a jail term.

Case 7.3

Bill Often, Bill Early

PROBLEM

McGossage Company experienced profit pressures for two years in a row. Actual profits were squeezed in a recessionary economy, but the company reported net income decreases that were not as severe as other companies in the industry were.

Sales were recorded in the grocery products division for orders that had been prepared for shipment but not actually shipped until later. Employees backdated the shipping documents. Gross profit on these "sales" was about 30 percent. Customers took discounts on payments, but the company did not record them, leaving the debit balances in the customers' accounts receivable instead of charging them to discounts and allowances expense. Company accountants were instructed to wait 60 days before recording discounts taken.

The division vice president and general manager knew about these accounting practices, as did a significant number of the 2,500 employees in the division. The division managers were under orders from headquarters to achieve profit objectives they considered unrealistic.

The customers' accounts receivable balances contained amounts due for discounts the customers already had taken. The cash receipts records showed payments received without credit for discounts. Discounts were entered monthly by a special journal entry.

The unshipped goods were on the shipping dock at year end with papers showing earlier shipping dates.

As misstatements go, some of these were on the materiality borderline. Sales were overstated 0.3 percent and 0.5 percent in the prior and current year, respectively. Accounts receivable were overstated 4 percent and 8 percent. The combined effect was to overstate the division's net income by 6 percent and 17 percent. Selected data were

	One Year Ago*		Current Year*	
	Reported	Actual	Reported	Actual
Sales	$330.0	$329.0	$350.0	$348.0
Discounts expense	1.7	1.8	1.8	2.0
Net income	6.7	6.3	5.4	4.6

*Dollars in millions.

AUDIT APPROACH

The accounting manual should provide instructions to record sales on the date of shipment (or when title passes, if later). Management subverted this control procedure by having shipping employees date the shipping papers incorrectly.

Cash receipts procedures should provide for authorizing and recording discounts when customers take them. Management overrode this control instruction by giving instructions to delay the recording.

Questionnaires and inquiries should be used to determine the company's accounting policies. It is possible that employees and managers would lie to the auditors to conceal the policies. It is also possible that pointed questions about revenue recognition and discount recording policies would elicit answers to reveal the practices.

For detail procedures, the auditors will select a sample of cash receipts, examine them for authorization, recalculate the customer discounts, and trace them to accounts receivable input for recording of the proper amount on the proper date. Select a sample of shipping documents and vouch them to customer orders, then trace them to invoices and to recording in the accounts receivable input with proper amounts on the proper date. These tests follow the tracing direction—starting with data that represent the beginning of transactions (cash receipts, shipping) and tracing them through the company's accounting process.

The audit team should confirm a sample of customer accounts and use analytical procedures to determine relationships of past years' discount expense to a relevant base (sales, sales volume) to calculate an overall test of the discounts expense.

DISCOVERY SUMMARY

The managers lied to the auditors about their revenue and expense timing policies. The sample of shipping documents showed no dating discrepancies because the employees had inserted incorrect dates. The analytical procedures on discounts did not show the misstatement because the historical relationships were too erratic to show a deficient number. However, the sample of cash receipts transactions showed that discounts were not calculated and recorded at time of receipt. Additional inquiry led to discovery of the special journal entries and knowledge of the recording delay. Two customers in the sample of 65 confirmations responded with exceptions that turned out to be unrecorded discounts.

Two other customers in the confirmation sample complained that they did not owe for late invoices on December 31. Follow-up showed the shipments were goods noticed on the shipping dock. Auditors taking the physical inventory noticed the goods on the shipping dock during the December 31 inventory taking. Inspection revealed the shipping documents dated December 26. When the auditors traced these shipments to the sales recording, they found them recorded "bill and hold" on December 29. (These procedures were performed and the results obtained by a successor audit firm in the third year!)

Case 7.4

Thank Goodness It's Friday

PROBLEM

Alpha Brewery Corporation generally has good controls related to authorization of transactions for accounting entry and the accounting manual has instructions for recording sales transactions in the proper accounting period. The company regularly closes the accounting process each Friday at 5 p.m. to prepare weekly management reports. The year-end date (cutoff date) is December 31 and, this year, December 31 was a Monday. However, the accounting was performed through Friday as usual and the accounts were closed for the year on January 4.

All the entries were properly dated after December 31, including the sales invoices, cash receipts, and shipping documents. However, the trial balance from which the financial statements were prepared was dated December 31, (this year). Nobody noticed the slip of a few days because the Friday closing was normal.

Alpha recorded sales of $672,000 and gross profit of $268,800 over the January 1–4 period. Cash collections on customers' accounts were recorded in the amount of $800,000.

AUDIT APPROACH

The company had in place the proper instructions for people to date transactions on the actual date on which they occurred, to enter sales and cost of goods sold on the day of shipment, and to enter cash receipts on the day received in the company offices. An accounting supervisor should have checked the entries through Friday to make sure the dates corresponded with the actual events and that the accounts for the year were closed with Monday's transactions.

In this case, the auditors need to be aware of the company's weekly routine closing and the possibility that the intervention of the December 31 date might cause a problem. Asking the question: "Did you cut off the accounting on Monday night this week?" might elicit the "Oh, we forgot!" response. Otherwise, it is normal to sample transactions around the year-end date to determine whether they were recorded in the proper accounting period.

The auditors would select transactions 7–10 days before and after the year-end date and inspect the dates on supporting documentation for evidence of accounting in the proper period.

The audit for sales overstatement is partly accomplished by auditing the cash and accounts receivable at December 31 for overstatement. Confirm a sample of accounts receivable. If the accounts are too large, the auditors expect the debtors to say so, thus leading to detection of sales overstatements.

Cash overstatement is audited by auditing the bank reconciliation to see whether deposits in transit (the deposits sent late in December) actually cleared the bank early in January. Obviously, the January 4 cash collections could not reach the bank until at least Monday, January 7. That is too long for a December 31 deposit to be in transit to a local bank.

The completeness of sales recordings is audited by selecting a sample of sales transactions (and supporting shipping documents) in the early part of the next accounting period (January next year). One way this year's sales could be incomplete would be to postpone recording December shipments until January, and this procedure will detect them if the shipping documents are dated properly.

The completeness of cash collections (and accounts receivable credits) is examined by auditing the cash deposits early in January to see whether there is any sign of holding cash without entry until January.

In this case, the existence objective is more significant for discovery of the problem than the completeness objective. After all, the January 1–4 sales, shipments, and cash collections did not "exist" in December this year.

DISCOVERY SUMMARY

The test of controls sample from the days before and after December 31 quickly revealed the problem. Company accounting personnel were embarrassed, but there was no effort to misstate the financial statements. This was a simple error. The company readily made the following adjustment:

	Debit	Credit
Sales	$672,000	
Inventory	403,200	
Accounts receivable	800,000	
Accounts receivable		$672,000
Cost of goods sold		403,200
Cash		800,000

Review Checkpoints

7.23 What are the goals of dual-direction testing regarding an audit of the accounts receivable and cash collection system?

7.24 In the case of The Canny Cashier, name one control that could have revealed signs of the embezzlement.

7.25 What feature(s) could SEI have installed in their cash receipts internal controls that would have been expected to prevent the cash receipts journal and recorded cash sales from reflecting more than the amount shown on the daily deposit slips?

7.26 In the case of The Taxman Always Rings Twice, what information could have been obtained from confirmations directed to the real population of delinquent accounts?

7.27 In the case of Bill Often, Bill Early, what information might have been obtained from inquiries? From tests of controls? From observations? From confirmations?

7.28 With reference to the case of Thank Goodness It's Friday, what contribution could an understanding of the business and the management reporting system have made to discovery of the open cash receipts journal cutoff error?

AUDITING INSIGHT PCAOB Inspections and the Revenue and Collections Cycle

- The Firm failed in the following respects to obtain sufficient competent evidential matter to support its audit opinion—The issuer entered into multiple-element software sales contracts that generally included a license fee and a maintenance element. Documentation of the issuer's revenue recognition policies was limited to an issuer-prepared memorandum dated in 2002. Since that time, the issuer has acquired three additional entities; however, the Firm failed to consider the appropriateness of the issuer's methods of recognizing revenues with respect to each acquired entity's unique software license and maintenance contracts. In addition, there was no evidence in the audit documentation, and no persuasive other evidence, that the Firm had assessed whether a change in a maintenance renewal rate on its standard price list affected the timing of the issuer's recognition of revenue.

- More than half of the issuer's revenue was realized through partnering relationships with indirect channel partners and independent software vendors that develop and market applications using the issuer's technology. The issuer has extensive information available about its partnering programs. The descriptions appear to indicate that the issuer is providing its partners with assistance in several areas, including marketing and developing enhanced application solutions. The Firm, however, failed to consider the specific terms of the issuer's various partnering relationships and whether they fell within the provisions of EITF No. 01–9, *Accounting for Consideration Given by a Vendor to a Customer (Including a Reseller of the Vendor's Products)* ("EITF No. 01–9"). The work papers simply included a check mark on a checklist indicating that EITF No. 01–9 did not apply.

- The Firm sent confirmations to test accounts receivable and identified errors based on the responses; however, the Firm failed to adequately evaluate the extent of the errors. The Firm noted errors both in invoices with debit balances and in invoices with credit balances. The Firm estimated the total amount of the errors in the debit balances and performed certain procedures to evaluate the errors noted in the credit balances; however, the Firm failed to estimate a total amount of the errors noted in the credit balances in order to adequately evaluate the issuer's assertion that the errors netted to an immaterial amount.

- The Firm failed in the following respects to obtain sufficient competent evidential matter to support its audit opinion—
 - The Firm's audit procedures to test revenue consisted primarily of analytical procedures. The Firm analyzed revenue

at the companywide level, even though the issuer operated in more than 250 locations and provided different products and services. The Firm's analytical procedures were therefore not disaggregated to a level that would provide the Firm with reasonable assurance of detecting misstatements that are material, individually or when aggregated with other misstatements. Further, the Firm failed to seek corroboration of management's explanation for a difference from the Firm's expectation that was greater than its threshold of significant differences.

- To test accounts receivable, the Firm performed substantive analytical procedures rather than sending confirmation requests. These analytical procedures consisted primarily of comparing reported subsequent cash receipts to the Firm's expectation of subsequent cash receipts. The reported subsequent cash receipts differed from the Firm's expectation by an amount greater than the Firm's established threshold of significant differences. The Firm revised its expectation based upon its discussions with the issuer. The reported cash receipts were within this revised expectation; however, the Firm failed to obtain corroboration of management's explanations that resulted in the revised expectation. The Firm also tested a sample of subsequent cash receipts. The Firm did not compare the sample items to the recorded accounts receivable, nor was the sample size sufficient to provide the Firm with the necessary level of assurance regarding the accuracy of the recorded accounts receivable.

- The Firm limited its tests of the existence and accuracy of accounts receivable to tests of controls and analytical procedures. The analytical procedures did not qualify as substantive analytical procedures because there was no evidence in the audit documentation, and no persuasive other evidence, that the Firm had established precise enough expectations or obtained corroboration of management's explanations of certain significant differences. Further, the Firm failed to perform other substantive tests of significant receivables.

Source: 2005 PCAOB Inspection of Deloitte & Touche (November 30, 2006); 2006 PCAOB Inspection of Ernst & Young (May 2, 2007); 2005 Inspection of KPMG (January 11, 2007); and 2005 Inspection of PricewaterhouseCoopers (December 14, 2006). All reports can be found on the PCAOB's Web site www.pcaob.org/Inspections/Public_Reports/index.aspx.

Summary

The revenue and collection cycle consists of customer order processing, credit checking, shipping goods, billing customers, accounting for accounts receivable, and collecting and accounting for cash receipts. Companies reduce control risk by having a suitable separation of authorization, custody, recording, and periodic reconciliation duties. Error-checking activities of comparing customer orders and shipping documents are important for billing customers the right prices for the delivered quantities. Otherwise, many things could go wrong—ranging from making sales to fictitious customers

or customers with bad credit to erroneous billings for the wrong quantities at the wrong prices at the wrong time.

Confirmation is the primary substantive audit procedure accompanied by analytical procedures, application of subsequent cash receipts and other alternative procedures. Confirmations of loans, accounts receivable, and notes receivable are required, unless auditors can justify substituting other procedures in the circumstances of a particular audit. Confirmations for accounts and notes receivable can be in positive or negative form, and the positive form may be a blank confirmation. Confirmations yield evidence about *existence* and gross *valuation*. Other procedures must be undertaken to audit the collectibility of the accounts. Nevertheless, confirmations can give some clues about collectibility when customers tell about balances in dispute. Confirmations of accounts, notes, and loans receivable should not be used as the only evidence of the ownership (*rights* assertions) of these financial assets.

Although these procedures may seem like common sense, auditing the revenue and collection cycle is not straightforward. Some deficiencies the PCAOB noted in its inspections of Big Four audit firms regarding audits of this cycle are described on the previous page.

Key Terms

aged trial balance: A schedule that lists each individual receivable and indicates whether it is current or past due, and how long it is past due. The total should equal the accounts receivable general ledger balance, 263

bill and hold: A fraudulent financial reporting activity whereby a company recognizes a sale even though it does not ship the merchandise to the customer, but instead holds it in its own warehouse, 255

bill of lading: A document signed by a common carrier to verify shipment of goods, 260

dual-purpose procedure: An audit procedure that simultaneously serves the substantive purpose (obtain direct evidence about the dollar amounts in account balances) and the test of controls purpose (obtain evidence about the company's performance of its own control activities), 275

factor: To sell accounts receivable to another party (a factor) at a discount from face value, 273

negative confirmation: A letter sent to a customer by auditors requesting that the customer respond only if the balance is incorrect, 270

packing slip: A document included with a shipment that shows the description and quantity of the goods being shipped, 260

positive confirmation: A letter sent to a customer by auditors requesting that the customer respond whether the balance is correct or not, 268

revenue recognition: Recording revenues in the general ledger. This is often done fraudulently by schemes such as bill and hold, 256

sales cutoff tests: Tests that ensure sales are recorded in the proper period—generally, when they are shipped—and that the cost of sales is recorded and removed from inventory, 273

sales invoice: A bill sent to customers for payment showing the amount due and payment terms, 261

Multiple Choice Questions for Practice and Review

7.29 Revenues are considered to have been earned when
 a. All possibility of return has expired.
 b. The company has substantially accomplished what it must to be entitled to the benefits.
 c. The cash is collected.
 d. Goods have been shipped.

7.30 Sales are normally recorded on the date of the
 a. Customer purchase order.
 b. Bill of lading.
 c. Sales invoice.
 d. Payment check.

7.31 When auditing the revenue and collection cycle, auditors normally select balances to confirm from the

 a. Sales journal.

 b. Accounts receivable listing.

 c. General ledger.

 d. Cash receipts listing.

7.32 Which of the follow accounts is not normally part of the revenue and collection cycle?

 a. Sales.

 b. Accounts Receivable.

 c. Cash.

 d. Purchases, Returns, and Allowances.

7.33 The control procedure "credit sales approved by credit department" is directed toward which assertion?

 a. Occurrence.

 b. Completeness.

 c. Accuracy.

 d. Cutoff.

7.34 Which of the following would be the best protection for a company that wishes to prevent the "lapping" of trade accounts receivable?

 a. Separate duties so that the bookkeeper in charge of the general ledger has no access to incoming mail.

 b. Separate duties so that no employee has access to both checks from customers and currency from daily cash receipts.

 c. Have customers send payments directly to the company's depository bank.

 d. Request that customer's payment checks be made payable to the company and addressed to the treasurer.

7.35 Which of the following internal control procedures will most likely prevent the concealment of a cash shortage from the improper write-off of a trade account receivable?

 a. Write-offs must be approved by a responsible officer after review of credit department recommendations and supporting evidence.

 b. Write-offs must be supported by an aging schedule showing that only receivables overdue several months have been written off.

 c. Write-offs must be approved by the cashier who is in a position to know if the receivables have, in fact, been collected.

 d. Write-offs must be authorized by company field sales employees who are in a position to determine the financial standing of the customers.

7.36 Auditors sometimes use comparisons of ratios as audit evidence. An unexplained decrease in the ratio of gross profit to sales may suggest which of the following possibilities?

 a. Unrecorded purchases.

 b. Unrecorded sales.

 c. Merchandise purchases being charged to selling and general expense.

 d. Fictitious sales.

7.37 An audit team is auditing sales transactions. One step is to vouch a sample of debit entries from the accounts receivable subsidiary ledger back to the supporting sales invoices. The purpose of this audit procedure is to establish that

 a. Sales invoices represent bona fide sales.

 b. All sales have been recorded.

 c. All sales invoices have been properly posted to customer accounts.

 d. Debit entries in the accounts receivable subsidiary ledger are properly supported by sales invoices.

7.38 To conceal defalcations involving receivables, a dishonest bookkeeper might charge which of the following accounts?

 a. Miscellaneous income.

 b. Petty cash.

 c. Miscellaneous expense.

 d. Sales returns.

7.39 Which of the following responses to an accounts receivable confirmation at December 31 would cause an audit team the most concern?

 a. "This amount was paid on December 30."

 b. "We received this shipment on January 2."

 c. "These goods were returned for credit on November 15."

 d. "The balance does not reflect our sales discount for paying by January 5th."

7.40 Audit documentation often includes a client-prepared, aged trial balance of accounts receivable as of the balance sheet date. The audit team uses this aging primarily to

 a. Evaluate internal control over credit sales.

 b. Test the accuracy of recorded charge sales.

 c. Estimate credit losses.

 d. Verify the existence of the recorded receivables.

7.41 Which of the following might be detected by auditors' cutoff review and examination of sales journal entries for several days prior to the balance sheet date?

 a. Lapping year-end accounts receivable.

 b. Inflating sales for the year.

 c. Kiting bank balances.

 d. Misappropriating merchandise.

7.42 Confirmation of individual accounts receivable balances directly with debtors will, of itself, normally provide the strongest evidence concerning the

 a. Collectibility of the balances confirmed.

 b. Ownership of the balances confirmed.

 c. Existence of the balances confirmed.

 d. Internal control over balances confirmed.

7.43 Which of the following is the best reason for prenumbering in numerical sequence such documents as sales orders, shipping documents, and sales invoices?

 a. Enables company personnel to determine the accuracy of each document.

 b. Enables personnel to determine the proper period recording of sales revenue and receivables.

 c. Enables personnel to check the numerical sequence for missing documents and unrecorded transactions.

 d. Enables personnel to determine the validity of recorded transactions.

7.44 When a sample of customer accounts receivable is selected for vouching debits, auditors will vouch them to

 a. Sales invoices with shipping documents and customer sales invoices.

 b. Records of accounts receivable write-offs.

 c. Cash remittance lists and bank deposit slips.

 d. Credit files and reports.

7.45 In the audit of accounts receivable, the most important emphasis should be on the

 a. Completeness assertion.

 b. Existence assertion.

 c. Rights and obligations assertion.

 d. Presentation and disclosure assertion.

7.46 When accounts receivable are confirmed at an interim date, auditors need not be concerned with

 a. Obtaining a summary of receivables transactions from the interim date to the year-end date.

 b. Obtaining a year-end trial balance of receivables, comparing it to the interim trial balance, and obtaining evidence and explanations for large variations.

 c. Sending negative confirmations to all the customers as of the year-end date.

 d. Considering the necessity for some additional confirmations as of the balance sheet date if balances have increased materially.

7.47 The negative request form of accounts receivable confirmation is useful particularly when the

Assessed level of risk of material misstatement relating to receivables is	Number of small balances is	Proper consideration by the recipient is
a. Low	Many	Likely
b. Low	Few	Unlikely
c. High	Few	Likely
d. High	Many	Likely

(AICPA adapted)

7.48 When an audit team traces a sample of shipping documents to the related sales invoice copies, they are trying to find relevant evidence that

 a. Shipments to customers were invoiced.

 b. Shipments to customers were recorded as sales.

 c. Recorded sales were shipped.

 d. Invoiced sales were shipped.

(AICPA adapted)

7.49 Write-offs of doubtful accounts should be approved by

 a. The salesperson.

 b. The credit manager.

 c. The treasurer.

 d. The cashier.

7.50 When an audit team does not receive a response on a positive accounts receivable confirmation, auditors should do all of the following except:

 a. Send a second request.

 b. Do nothing for immaterial balances.

 c. Examine shipping documents.

 d. Examine client correspondence files.

7.51 Cash receipts from sales on account have been misappropriated. Which of the following acts would conceal this defalcation and be least likely to be detected by an auditor?

 a. Understating the sales journal.

 b. Overstating the accounts receivable control account.

 c. Overstating the accounts receivable subsidiary ledger.

 d. Understating the cash receipts journal.

(AICPA adapted)

7.52 Which of the following internal control procedures most likely would deter lapping of collections from customers?

 a. Independent internal verification of dates of entry in the cash receipts journal with dates of daily cash summaries.

 b. Authorization of write-offs of uncollectible accounts by a supervisor independent of credit approval.

 c. Separation of duties between receiving cash and posting the accounts receivable ledger.

 d. Supervisory comparison of the daily cash summary with the sum of the cash receipts journal entries.

(AICPA adapted)

7.53 The financial records of the Movitz Company show that Mr. Dennis owes $4,100 on an account receivable. An independent audit is being carried out and the auditors send a positive confirmation to Mr. Jones. What is the most likely reason as to why a positive confirmation rather than a negative confirmation was used here?

 a. Control risk was particularly low for accounts receivable.

 b. Inherent risk was particularly high for accounts receivable.

 c. Mr. Dennis's account was not yet due.

 d. Mr. Dennis's account was not with a related party.

Exercises, Problems, and Simulations

7.54 **Control Objectives and Procedures Associations.** Exhibit 7.54.1 contains an arrangement of examples of transaction errors (lettered a–g) and a set of client control procedures and devices (numbered 1–15). You should photocopy the exhibit page or obtain a full-size copy from your instructor for the following requirements.

Required:

 a. Opposite the examples of transaction errors lettered a–g, write the name of the transaction assertion clients wish to achieve to prevent, detect, or correct the error.

 b. Opposite each numbered control procedure, place an "X" in the column that identifies the error(s) the procedure is likely to control by prevention, detection, or correction.

EXHIBIT 7.54.1

a.	Sales recorded, goods not shipped
b.	Goods shipped, sales not recorded
c.	Goods shipped to a bad credit risk customer
d.	Sales billed at the wrong price or wrong quantity
e.	Product line A sales recorded as Product line B
f.	Failure to post charges to customers for sales
g.	January sales recorded in December

	CONTROL PROCEDURES
1.	Sales order approved for credit
2.	Prenumbered shipping doc prepared. sequence checked
3.	Shipping document quantity compared to sales invoice
4.	Prenumbered sales invoices, sequence checked
5.	Sales invoice checked to sales order
6.	Invoiced prices compared to approved price list
7.	General ledger code checked for sales product lines
8.	Sales dollar batch totals compared to sales journal
9.	Periodic sales total compared to same period accounts receivable postings
10.	Accountants have instructions to date sales on the date of shipment
11.	Sales entry date compared to shipping doc date
12.	Accounts receivable subsidiary totaled and reconciled to accounts receivable control account
13.	Intercompany accounts reconciled with subsidiary company records
14.	Credit files updated for customer payment history
15.	Overdue customer accounts investigated for collection

7.55 **Control Assertion Associations.** Exhibit 7.54.1 contains an arrangement of examples of transaction errors (lettered a–g) and a set of client control procedures and devices (numbered 1–15).

Required:

For each error/control objective, identify the assertion about classes of transactions and events most benefited by the control.

7.56 **Client Control Procedures and Audit Tests of Controls.** Exhibit 7.54.1 contains an arrangement of examples of transaction errors (lettered a–g) and a set of client control procedures and devices (numbered 1–15).

Required:

For each client control procedure numbered 1–15, write a test of controls that could produce evidence on the question of whether the client's control procedure has been implemented and is in operation.

7.57 **Confirmation of Trade Accounts Receivable.** King, CPA, is auditing the financial statements of Cycle Company, a client that has receivables from customers arising from the sale of goods in the normal course of business. King is aware that the confirmation of accounts receivable is a generally accepted auditing procedure.

Required:

a. Under what circumstances could King justify omitting the confirmation of Cycle's accounts receivable?

b. In designing confirmation requests, what factors are likely to affect King's assessment of the reliability of confirmations that King sends?

c. What alternative procedures could King consider performing when replies to positive confirmation requests are not received?

7.58 **Audit Objectives and Procedures for Accounts Receivable.** In the audit of trade accounts receivable, auditors develop specific audit assertions related to the receivables. They then design specific substantive procedures to obtain evidence about each of these assertions. Here is a selection of accounts receivable assertions:

a. Accounts receivable represent all amounts owed to the client company at the balance sheet date.

b. The client company has a legal right to all accounts receivable at the balance sheet date.

c. Accounts receivable are stated at net realizable value.

d. Accounts receivable are properly described and presented in the financial statements.

Required:

For each of these assertions, select the audit procedure (below) that is best suited for the audit program. Select only one procedure for each audit objective. A procedure may be selected once or not at all.

1. Analyze the relationship of accounts receivable and sales and compare with relationships for preceding periods.

2. Perform sales cutoff tests to obtain assurance that sales transactions and corresponding entries for inventories and cost of goods sold are recorded in the same and proper period.

3. Review the aged trial balance for significant past-due accounts.

4. Obtain an understanding of the business purpose of transactions that resulted in accounts receivable balances.

5. Review loan agreements for indications of whether accounts receivable have been factored or pledged.

6. Review the accounts receivable trial balance for amounts due from officers and employees.

7. Analyze unusual relationships between monthly accounts receivable and monthly accounts payable balances.

(AICPA adapted)

7.59 **Overstated Sales and Accounts Receivable.** This case is designed like the ones in the chapter. Your assignment is to write the "audit approach" portion of the case, organized around these sections:

Objective: Express the objective in terms of the facts supposedly asserted in financial records, accounts, and statements.

Control: Write a brief explanation of desirable controls, missing controls, and especially the kinds of "deviations" that might arise from the situation described in the case.

Tests of controls: Write some procedures for getting evidence about existing controls, especially procedures that could discover deviations from controls. If there are no controls to test, then there are no procedures to perform; go then to the next section. A "procedure" should instruct someone about the source(s) of evidence to tap and the work to do.

Audit of balance: Write some procedures for getting evidence about the existence, completeness, valuation, ownership, or disclosure assertions identified in your objective section above.

Discovery summary: Write a short statement about the discovery you expect to accomplish with your procedures.

Ring around the Revenue

Mattel Toy Manufacturing Company had experienced several years of good business. Income had increased steadily and the common stock was a favorite among investors. Management had confidently predicted continued growth and prosperity. However, business turned worse instead of better. Competition became fierce.

In earlier years, Mattel had accommodated a few large retail customers with the practice of field warehousing coupled with a "bill and hold" accounting procedure. These large retail customers executed noncancelable written agreements, asserting their purchase of toys and their obligation to pay. The toys were not actually shipped because the customers did not have available warehouse space. They were set aside in segregated areas on the Mattel premises and identified as the customers' property. Mattel would later ship the toys to various retail locations upon instructions from the customers. The "field warehousing" was explained as Mattel's serving as a temporary warehouse and storage location for the customers' toys. In the related bill and hold accounting procedure, Mattel prepared invoices billing the customers, mailed the invoices to the customers, and recorded the sales and accounts receivable.

When business took a downturn, Mattel expanded its field warehousing and its bill and hold accounting practices. Invoices were recorded for customers who did not execute the written agreements used in previous arrangements. Some customers signed the noncancelable written agreements with clauses permitting subsequent inspection, acceptance, and determination of discounted prices. The toys were not always set aside in separate areas and this failure later gave shipping employees problems with identifying shipments of toys that had been "sold" earlier and those that had not.

Mattel also engaged in overbilling. Customers who ordered closeout toys at discounted prices were billed at regular prices, even though the customers' orders showed the discounted prices agreed by Mattel sales representatives.

In a few cases, the bill and hold invoices and the closeout sales were billed and recorded in duplicate. In most cases, the customers' invoices were addressed and mailed to specific individuals in the customers' management instead of the routine mailing to the customers' accounts payable departments.

Audit Trail: The field warehousing arrangements were well known and acknowledged in the Mattel accounting manual. Related invoices were stamped "bill and hold." Customer orders and agreements were attached in a document file. Sales of closeout toys also were stamped "closeout," indicating the regular prices (basis for salespersons' commissions) and the invoice prices. Otherwise, the accounting for sales and accounts receivable was unexceptional. Efforts to record these sales in January (last month of the fiscal year) caused the month's sales revenue to be 35 percent higher than the January of the previous year.

In the early years of the practice, inventory sold under the field warehousing arrangements (both regular and closeout toys) was segregated and identified. The shipping orders for these toys left the "carrier name" and "shipping date" blank, even though they were signed and dated by a company employee in the spaces for the company representative and the carrier representative signatures.

The lack of inventory segregation caused problems for the company. After the fiscal year end, Mattel solved the problem by reversing $6.9 million of the $14 million bill-and-hold sales. This caused another problem because the reversal was larger than the month's sales, causing the sales revenue for the first month of the next year to be a negative number!

Amount: Company officials gave persuasive reasons for the validity of recognizing sales revenue and receivables on the bill and hold procedure and field warehousing. After considering the facts and circumstances, the company's auditors agreed that the accounting practices appropriately accounted for revenue and receivables.

Mattel's abuse of the practices caused financial statements to be materially misstated. In January of the year in question, the company overstated sales by about $14 million, or 5 percent of the sales that should have been recorded. The gross profit of $7 million on these sales caused the income to be overstated by about 40 percent.

7.60 **CAATs Application—Receivables Confirmation.** You are using computer audit software to prepare accounts receivable confirmations during the annual audit of the Eastern Sunrise Services Club. The company has the following data files:

Master file—debtor credit record.

Master file—debtor name and address.

Master file—account detail:

Ledger number.

Sales code.

Customer account number.

Date of last billing.

Balance (gross).

Discount available to customer (memo account only).

Date of last purchase.

The discount field represents the amount of discount available to the customer if the customer pays within 30 days of the invoicing date. The discount field is cleared for expired amounts during the daily updating. You have determined that this is properly executed.

Required:

From the data files shown above, list the information that you would include on the confirmation requests. Identify the file from which the information can be obtained.

7.61 **Audit Simulation—Rock Island Quarry—Evidence Collection in an Online System.** Your firm has audited the Rock Island Quarry Company for several years. Rock Island's main revenue comes from selling crushed rock to construction companies from several quarries owned by the company in Illinois and Iowa. The rock is priced by weight, quality, and crushed size.

Past Procedure: Trucks owned by purchasing contractors or by Rock Island needed to display a current certified empty weight receipt or be weighed in. The quarry yard weigh master recorded the empty weight on a handwritten "scale ticket" along with the purchasing company name, the truck number, and the date. After the truck was loaded, it was required to leave via the scale where the loaded weight and rock grade were recorded on the scale tickets. The scale tickets were sorted weekly by grade and manually recorded on a summary sheet that was forwarded to the home office. Scale tickets were prenumbered and an accountant in the home office checked the sequence for missing numbers.

Revenue (and receivables) audit procedures involved evaluating the controls at selected quarries (rotated each year) and vouching a statistical sample of scale tickets to weekly summaries. Weekly summaries were traced through pricing and invoicing to the general ledger on a sample basis and general ledger entries were vouched back to weekly summaries on a sample basis. Few material discrepancies were found.

New Procedures: At the beginning of the current year, Rock Island converted to a local area network of personal computers to gather the information formerly entered manually on the scale ticket. This conversion was done with your knowledge but without your advice or input. Now, all entering trucks must weigh in. The yard weigh master enters NEW on the terminal keyboard and a form appears on the screen that is similar to the old scale ticket, except the quarry number, transaction number, date, and incoming empty weight are automatically entered. Customer and truck numbers are keyed in. After the weigh-in, the weigh master enters HOLD through the terminal. The weight ticket record is stored in the computer until weigh-out.

When a truck is loaded and stops on the scale, the weigh master enters OLD and a directory of all open transactions appears on the screen. The weigh master selects the proper one and enters OUT. The truck out-weighs and the rock weights are computed and entered automatically. The weigh master must enter the proper number for the rock grade. The weigh master cannot change any automatically entered field. When satisfied that the screen weight ticket is correct, the weigh master enters SOLD and the transaction is automatically transmitted to the home office computer and the appropriate accounting database elements are updated. One copy of a scale ticket is printed and given to the truck driver. No written evidence of the sale is kept by Rock Island.

Required:

It is now midyear for Rock Island and you are planning for this year's audit.

a. What control procedures (manual and computerized) should you expect to find in this system for recording quarry sales?

b. The computer programs that process the rock sales and perform the accounting reside at the home office and at the quarries. What implication does this have for your planned audit procedures?

c. What are you going to do to gather substantive audit evidence now that there are no written "scale tickets"?

7.62 **Organizing a Risk Analysis.** You are the director of internal auditing of a large municipal hospital. You receive monthly financial reports prepared by the accounting department and your review of them has shown that total accounts receivable from patients has steadily and rapidly increased over the past eight months.

Other information in the reports shows the following conditions:

a. The number of available hospital beds has not changed.

b. The bed occupancy rate has not changed.

c. Hospital billing rates have not changed significantly.

d. The hospitalization insurance contracts have not changed since the last modification 12 months ago.

Your internal audit department audited the accounts receivable 10 months ago. The audit file for that assignment contains financial information, a record of the risk analysis, documentation of the study and evaluation of management and internal risk mitigation controls, documentation of the evidence-gathering procedures used to produce evidence about the existence and collectibility of the accounts, and a copy of your report, which commented favorably on the controls and collectibility of the receivables.

However, the current increase in receivables has alerted you to a need for another audit, so things will not get out of hand. You remember news stories last year about the manager of the city water system who got into big trouble because his accounting department double-billed all the residential customers for three months.

Required:

You plan to perform a risk analysis to get a handle on the problem, if indeed a problem exists. Write a memo to your senior auditor listing at least eight questions he should use to guide and direct the risk analysis. (Hint: The questions used last year were organized under these headings: (1) Who does the accounts receivable accounting? (2) What information processing procedures and policies are in effect? and (3) How is the accounts receivable accounting done? This time, you will add a fourth category: What financial or economic events have occurred in the last 10 months?)

(CIA adapted)

7.63 **Study and Evaluation of Management Control.** The study and evaluation of management risk mitigation control is not easy. First, auditors must determine the risks and the controls subject to audit. Then, they must find a standard by which performance of the control can be evaluated. Next, they must specify procedures to obtain the evidence on which an evaluation can be based. Insofar as possible, the standards and related evidence must be quantified. The description below gives certain information (in italics) that internal auditors would know about or be able to figure out on their own. Fulfilling the requirement thus amounts to taking some information from the scenario below and figuring out other things by using accountants' and auditors' common sense.

The Scenario

Ace Corporation ships building materials to more than a thousand wholesale and retail customers in a five-state region. The company's normal credit terms are net/30 days and no cash discounts are offered. Fred Clark is the chief financial officer, and he is concerned about risks related to maintaining control over customer credit. In particular, he has stated two management control principles for this purpose.

1. Sales are to be billed to customers accurately and promptly. *Fred knows that errors will occur but thinks company personnel ought to be able to hold quantity, unit price, and arithmetic errors down to 3 percent of the sales invoices. He considers an invoice error of $1 or*

less not to matter. He believes prompt billing is important since customers are expected to pay within 30 days. *Fred is very strict in thinking that a bill should be sent to the customer one day after shipment*. He believes he has staffed the billing department well enough to be able to handle this workload. The relevant company records consist of an accounts receivable control account; a subsidiary ledger of customers' accounts in which charges are entered by billing (invoice) date and credits are entered by date of payment receipts; a sales journal that lists invoices in chronological order; and a file of shipping documents cross-referenced by the number on the related sales invoice copy kept on file in numerical order.

2. Accounts receivable are to be aged and followed up to ensure prompt collection. *Fred has told the accounts receivable department to classify all the customer accounts in categories of (a) current, (b) 31–59 days overdue, (c) 60–90 days overdue, and (d) more than 90 days overdue. He wants this trial balance to be complete and to be transmitted to the credit department within five days after each month-end. In the credit department, prompt follow-up means sending a different (stronger) collection letter to each category, cutting off credit to customers over 60 days past due (putting them on cash basis), and giving the over-90-days accounts to an outside collection agency. These actions are supposed to be taken within five days after receipt of the aged trial balance.* The relevant company records, in addition to the ones listed above, consist of the aged trial balance, copies of the letters sent to customers, copies of notices of credit cutoff, copies of correspondence with the outside collection agent, and reports of results—statistics of subsequent collections.

Required:

Take the role of a senior internal auditor. You are to write a memo to the internal audit staff to inform them about comparison standards for the study and evaluation of these two management control policies. You also need to specify two or three procedures for gathering evidence about performance of the controls. The body of your memo should be structured as follows:

1. Control: Sales are billed to customers accurately and promptly.
 a. Accuracy.
 (1) Policy standard . . .
 (2) Audit procedures . . .
 b. Promptness.
 (1) Policy standard . . .
 (2) Audit procedures . . .
2. Control: Accounts receivable are aged and followed up to ensure prompt collection.
 a. Accounts receivable aging.
 (1) Policy standard . . .
 (2) Audit procedures . . .
 b. Follow-up prompt collection.
 (1) Policy standard . . .
 (2) Audit procedures . . .

7.64 **Audit Simulation: Cash Receipts and Billing Control.** The narrative description (below) of a company's cash receipts and billing system is in the auditors' audit files.

Rural Building Supplies, Inc., is a single-store retailer that sells a variety of tools, garden supplies, lumber, small appliances, and electrical fixtures. About half of the sales are to walk-in customers and about half to construction contractors. Rural employs 12 salaried sales associates, a credit manager, three full-time clerical workers, and several part-time cash register clerks and assistant bookkeepers. The full-time clerical workers are the cashier who handles the cash and the bank deposits, the accounts receivable supervisor who prepares invoices and does the accounts receivable work, and the bookkeeper who keeps journals and ledgers and sends customer statements. Their work is described more fully in the narrative.

Control Narrative

Rural's retail customers pay for merchandise by cash or credit card at cash registers when they purchase merchandise. A building contractor can purchase merchandise on account if approved by the credit manager. The credit manager bases approvals on general knowledge of the contractor's reputation. After credit is approved, the sales associate files a prenumbered

charge form with the accounts receivable (A/R) supervisor to set up the contractor's account receivable.

The A/R supervisor independently verifies the pricing and other details on the charge form by reference to a management-authorized price list, corrects any errors, prepares the sales invoice, and supervises a part-time employee who mails the invoice to the contractor. The A/R supervisor electronically posts the details of the invoice in the A/R subsidiary ledger and the computerized system simultaneously transmits the transaction details to the bookkeeper. The A/R supervisor also prepares (1) a monthly computer-generated A/R subsidiary ledger without reconciliation to the A/R control account and (2) a monthly report of overdue accounts.

The cashier performs the cash receipts functions, including supervising the cash register clerks. The cashier opens the mail, compares each check with the enclosed remittance advice, stamps each check "for deposit only," and lists the checks for the deposit slip. The cashier then gives the remittance advices to the bookkeeper for recording. The cashier deposits the checks each day and prepares a separate deposit of the cash from the cash registers. The cashier retains the verified bank deposit slips (stamped and dated at the bank) to use in reconciling the monthly bank statements. The cashier sends to the bookkeeper a copy of the daily cash register summary. The cashier does not have access to the bookkeeper's journals or ledgers.

The bookkeeper receives information for journalizing and posting to the general ledger from the A/R supervisor (details of credit transactions) and from the cashier (cash reports). After recording the remittance advices received from the cashier, the bookkeeper electronically transmits the information to the A/R supervisor for subsidiary ledger updating. Upon receipt of the A/R supervisor's report of overdue balances, the bookkeeper sends monthly statements of account to contractors with unpaid balances. The bookkeeper authorizes the A/R supervisor to write off accounts as uncollectible six months after sending the first overdue notice. At this time, the bookkeeper notifies the credit manager not to approve additional credit to that contractor.

Required:

Take the role of the supervising auditor on the Rural engagement. Your assistants prepared the narrative description. Now, you must analyze it and identify the internal control weaknesses. Organize them under the heading of employee job functions: credit manager, accounts receivable supervisor, cashier, and bookkeeper. (Do not give advice about correcting the weaknesses.)

Optional Requirement:

Discuss the possibilities for fraud you notice in this control system.

7.65 **Tests of Controls and Errors/Frauds.** The four questions below are taken from an internal control questionnaire. For each question, state (a) one test of controls procedure you could use to find out whether the control technique was really functioning and (b) what error or fraud could occur if the question were answered "no," or if you found the control was not effective.

1. Are blank sales invoices available only to authorized personnel?

2. Are sales invoices checked for the accuracy of quantities billed? Prices used? Mathematical calculations?

3. Are the duties of the accounts receivable bookkeeper separate from any cash functions?

4. Are customer accounts regularly balanced with the control account?

7.66 **Kaplan CPA Simulations: Internal Control Questionnaire.**

Required:

Go to the Kaplan Web site at www.mhhe.com/louwers3e and click on AUD: Earhart & King case and the "Internal Control Sales and Accounts Receivable" tab and complete the assigned task.

7.67 **Kaplan CPA Simulations: Confirmation Form.**

Required:

a. Go to the Kaplan Web site at www.mhhe.com/louwers3e and click on AUD: Abernathy and Chapman case and the "confirmation" tab and complete the assigned task.

b. Go to the Kaplan Web site at www.mhhe.com/louwers3e and click on AUD: Abernathy and Chapman case and the "communication" tab and complete the assigned task.

7.68 **Kaplan CPA Simulations: Alternative Procedures.**

Required:

 a. Go to the Kaplan Web site at www.mhhe.com/louwers3e and click on AUD: Amberly case and the "Gathering Evidence—Accounts Receivable" tab and complete the assigned task.

 b. Go to the Kaplan Web site at www.mhhe.com/louwers3e and click on AUD: Amberly case and the "Gathering Evidence—Sales and Expenses" tab and complete the assigned task.

 c. Go to the Kaplan Web site at www.mhhe.com/louwers3e and click on AUD: Amberly case and the "Communication" tab and complete the assigned task.

7.69 **Kaplan CPA Simulations: Timing of Confirmations.**

Required:

 Go to the Kaplan Web site at www.mhhe.com/louwers3e and click on AUD: Ridge Associates case and the "Communication" tab and complete the assigned task.

7.70 **Kaplan CPA Simulations: Audit Evidence and the Confirmation Process.**

Required:

 a. Go to the Kaplan Web site at www.mhhe.com/louwers3e and click on AUD: Tomaszeski case and the "Audit Evidence and the Confirmation Process" tab and complete the assigned task.

 b. Go to the Kaplan Web site at www.mhhe.com/louwers3e and click on AUD: Tomaszeski case and the "Communication" tab and complete the assigned task.

7.71 **Mini-Case: Confirmations.** Refer to the mini-case "Something Went Sour at Parmalat" shown on page 839 and respond to Question 2.

Appendix 7A

Internal Control Questionnaires

APPENDIX 7A.1 **Internal Control Questionnaire—Revenue and Collection Cycle**

	Yes/No	Comments
Occurrence		
1. Are customer subsidiary records maintained by someone who has no access to cash?		
2. Is access to sales invoice blanks restricted?		
3. Are prenumbered bills of lading or other shipping documents prepared or completed in the shipping department?		
4. Are customers' statements mailed monthly by the accounts receivable department?		
5. Are direct confirmations of accounts and notes obtained periodically by the internal auditor?		
6. Are differences reported by customers routed to someone outside the accounts receivable department for investigations?		
7. Are returned goods checked against receiving reports?		
8. Are returned sales credits and other credits supported by documentation as to receipt, condition, and quantity and approved by a responsible officer?		
9. Are write-offs, returns, and discounts allowed after discount date subject to approval by a responsible officer?		
10. Are large loans or advances to related parties approved by the directors?		
Completeness		
11. Are sales invoice forms prenumbered?		
12. Is the sequence checked for missing invoices?		
13. Is the shipping document numerical sequence checked for missing bills of lading numbers?		
14. Are credit memo documents prenumbered and the sequence checked for missing documents?		
Accuracy		
15. Is customer credit approved before orders are shipped?		
16. Are delinquent accounts listed periodically for review by someone other than the credit manager?		
17. Is the credit department separated from the sales department?		
18. Are sales prices and terms based on approved standards?		
19. Are shipped quantities compared to invoice quantities?		
20. Are sales invoices checked for errors in quantities, prices, extensions and footings, and freight allowances, and checked with customers' orders?		
21. Do the internal auditors confirm customer accounts periodically to determine accuracy?		
22. Does someone reconcile the accounts receivable subsidiary to the control account regularly?		
Cutoff		
23. Does the accounting manual contain instructions to date sales invoices on the shipment date?		
Classification		
24. Does the accounting manual contain instructions for classifying sales?		
25. Are summary journal entries approved before posting?		
26. Are sales of the following types controlled by the same procedures described above: sales to employees, COD sales, disposals of property, cash sales, and scrap sales?		
27. Are receivables from officers, directors, and affiliates identified separately in the accounts receivable records?		

APPENDIX 7A.2 **Internal Control Questionnaire—Sales and Accounts Receivable Computerized Controls**

	Yes/No	Comments
1. Does each terminal perform only designated functions? For example, the terminal at the shipping dock cannot be used to enter initial sales information or to access the payroll database.		
2. Is an identification number and password (issued on an individual person basis) required to enter the sale and each command that a subsequent action has been completed? Unauthorized entry attempts are logged and immediately investigated. Further, certain passwords have "read-only" (cannot change any data) authorization. For example, the credit manager can determine the outstanding balance of any account or view online "reports" summarizing overdue accounts receivable but cannot enter credit memos to change the balances.		
3. Is all input information immediately logged to provide restart processing should any terminal become inoperative during the processing?		
4. Does a transaction code call up on the terminals a full-screen "form" that appears to the operator in the same format as the original paper documents? Each clerk must enter the information correctly or the computer will not accept the transaction. This is called *online input validation* and utilizes validation checks such as missing data, check digit, and limit tests.		
5. Are all documents prepared by the computer numbered with the number stored as part of the sales record in the accounts receivable database?		
6. Is a daily search of the pending order database made by the computer with sales orders outstanding more than seven days listed on the terminal in marketing management?		

Appendix 7B

Audit Program

APPENDIX 7B.1

APOLLO SHOES, INC.
Audit Program for Tests of Controls in the Revenues and Collection Cycle
12/31/08

	Performed by	Ref.
Sales		
1. Select a sample of recorded sales invoices from the sales journal.		
a. Vouch to supporting shipping documents.		
b. Inspect for credit approval.		
c. Vouch prices to the approved price list.		
d. Compare the quantity billed to the quantity shipped.		
e. Recalculate the invoice arithmetic.		
f. Compare the shipment date with the invoice record date.		
g. Trace the invoice to posting in the general ledger control account and in the correct customer's account.		
h. Note the type of product shipped and determine proper classification in the right product-line revenue account.		
2. Select a sample of shipping documents from the shipping department file and trace shipments to recorded sales invoices.		
3. Scan recorded sales invoices and shipping documents for missing numbers in sequence.		
Accounts Receivable		
1. Select a sample of customers' accounts.		
a. Vouch debits in them to supporting sales invoices.		
b. Vouch credits in them to supporting cash receipts documents and approved credit memos.		
2. Select a sample of credit memos.		
a. Review for proper approval.		
b. Trace to posting in customers' accounts.		
3. Scan the accounts receivable control for postings from sources other than the sales and cash receipts journals (e.g., general journal adjusting entries, credit memos). Vouch a sample of such entries to supporting documents.		

APPENDIX 7B.2

APOLLO SHOES, INC. Audit Program for Accounts and Notes Receivable and Revenue 12/31/08	Performed by	Ref.
A. Accounts and Notes Receivable		
1. Obtain an aged trial balance of individual customer accounts. Recalculate the total and trace to the general ledger control account.		
2. Review the aging for large and unusual items.		
3. Send confirmations to all accounts over $X. Select a random sample of all remaining accounts for confirmation.		
a. Investigate exceptions reported by customers.		
b. Perform alternative procedures on accounts that do not respond to positive confirmation requests.		
(1) Vouch cash receipts after the confirmation date for subsequent payment.		
(2) Vouch sales invoices and shipping documents.		
4. Evaluate the adequacy of the allowance for doubtful accounts.		
a. Vouch a sample of current amounts in the aged trial balance to sales invoices to determine whether amounts aged current should be aged past due.		
b. Compare the current-year write-off experience to the prior-year allowance.		
c. Vouch cash receipts after the balance sheet date for collections on past-due accounts.		
d. Obtain financial statements or credit reports and inquire of the credit manager about collections on large past-due accounts.		
e. Calculate an allowance estimate using prior relations of write-offs and sales, taking under consideration current economic events.		
5. Inspect the bank confirmations, loan agreements, and minutes of the board for indications of pledged, discounted, or assigned receivables.		
6. Inspect or obtain confirmation of notes receivable.		
7. Recalculate interest income and trace to the income account.		
8. Obtain management representations regarding pledge, discount, or assignment of receivables, and about receivables from officers, directors, affiliates, or other related parties.		
9. Review the adequacy of control over recording of all charges to customers (completeness) audited in the sales transaction test of controls audit program.		
B. Revenue		
1. Select a sample of recorded sales invoices and vouch to underlying shipping documents.		
2. Select a sample of shipping documents and trace to sales invoices.		
3. Obtain production records of physical quantities sold and calculate an estimate of sales dollars based on average sale prices.		
4. Compare revenue dollars and physical quantities with prior-year data and industry economic statistics.		
5. Select a sample of sales invoices prepared a few days before and after the balance sheet date and vouch to supporting documents for evidence of proper cutoff.		

Acquisition and Expenditure Cycle

Professional Standards References

Compendium Section	Document Reference	Topic
Various*	AS 5	"An Audit of Internal Control over Financial Reporting That Is Integrated with an Audit of Financial Statements"
AU 311	SAS 108	"Planning and Supervision"
	ISA 300	"Planning an Audit of Financial Statements"
AU 312	SAS 107	"Audit Risk and Materiality in Conducting an Audit"
AU 313	SAS 110	"Performing Audit Procedures in Response to Assessed Risks and Evaluating the Risks of Material Misstatement"
	ISA 330	"The Auditor's Procedures in Response to Assessed Risks"
AU 316	SAS 99	"Consideration of Fraud in a Financial Statement Audit"
	ISA 240	"The Auditor's Responsibility to Consider Fraud in an Audit of Financial Statements"
AU 319	SAS 109	"Understanding the Entity and Its Environment and Assessing the Risks of Material Misstatement"
	ISA 315	"Understanding the Entity and Its Environment and Assessing the Risks of Material Misstatement"
AU 326	SAS 106	"Audit Evidence"
	ISA 500	"Audit Evidence"
AU 329	SAS 59	"Analytical Procedures"
	ISA 520	"Analytical Procedures"
AU 330	SAS 67	"The Confirmation Process"
	ISA 505	"External Confirmations"
AU 333A	SAS 85	"Management Representations"
AU 339	SAS 103	"Audit Documentation"
	AS 3	"Audit Documentation"
	ISA 230	"Audit Documentation"
AU 342	SAS 57	"Auditing Accounting Estimates"
	ISA 540	"Audit of Accounting Estimates"

*AS 5 amends AU 310, AU 319, AU 325, AU 326, AU 329, AU 339, AU 380, AT 501, ET 101, and ET 191.

> Show those numbers to the damn auditors and I'll throw you out the $%*@@ window.
>
> *Buddy Yates, director of WorldCom, Inc., general accounting, to an employee asking for an explanation of a large accounting discrepancy*

Learning Objectives

This chapter contains a concise overview of a cycle for the acquisition of goods and services as well as the expenditure of cash in connection with paying for the purchases and acquisitions. This cycle affects more general ledger accounts than any other. Major accounts discussed include accounts payable and long-term assets. For accounts payable, the focus shifts from the *existence* assertion to the *completeness* assertion. A series of short cases is used to show the application of audit procedures in situations in which errors and frauds might be discovered. Payroll is a subcycle related to the acquisition and expenditure cycle and to the production cycle. A discussion of payroll controls and audit tests is included in Appendix 8C.

Your objectives are to be able to:

1. Identify significant inherent risks in the acquisition and expenditure cycle.

2. Describe the acquisition and expenditure cycle, including typical source documents and controls.

3. Give examples of tests of controls over purchases of inventory and services.

4. Explain the importance of the *completeness* assertion for the audit of accounts payable and list some procedures for a *search for unrecorded liabilities*.

5. Discuss audit procedures for other accounts affected by the acquisition and expenditure cycle.

6. Specify some ways fraud can be found in accounts payable and cash disbursements.

7. Describe some common errors and frauds in the acquisition and expenditure cycle and design some audit and investigation procedures for detecting them.

8. Describe the payroll cycle, including typical source documents and controls. [Appendix 8C]

INTRODUCTION

A headline in the March 14, 2003, issue of *The Wall Street Journal* announced that **WorldCom, Inc.,** was going to write down assets by more than $70 *billion* to correct the company's accounting records for a massive fraud that had been uncovered. To put this number in perspective, the amount of the writeoff almost equaled the entire gross domestic product for the country of Ireland.[1] How did the books of WorldCom become so inflated? A large part of the restatement was a result of the company's practice of capitalizing (rather than properly expensing) certain transactions to fixed asset accounts. The improper charges were not part of the regular system but were hidden in computerized files of adjusting entries to intercompany receivables. Only the dogged pursuit of the facts, led by the company's director of internal audit and 2002 *Time* Person of the Year Cynthia Cooper, uncovered the massive fraud. The internal auditors' search included midnight hacking into the computerized system to sort through hundreds of thousands of transactions—a process that discovered $2 billion of questionable items in the first week! When **Arthur Andersen,** the company's public accounting firm, was first apprised of the problems, the firm allegedly told Ms. Cooper that it had approved some of the very accounting practices she questioned.[2]

The WorldCom fraud represented the largest fraud ever perpetrated in the United States. However, as you will see, understating or capitalizing expenses is a means often used to mislead financial statement users. GAAP prescribes that expenses be charged to income to reflect the consumption of economic benefits. The FASB *Statement of Concepts* discusses three ways to recognize expenses:

1. They are recognized when they can be **matched** with related revenues (e.g., cost of goods sold with sales) and those revenues are recognized, or

2. They are recognized in the period in which they are incurred, or

3. They are allocated to the future periods benefited by a "systematic and rational" process (e.g., depreciation).[3]

[1] www.infoplease.com/IPA/A0874911.html.
[2] S. Pulliam and D. Soloman, "Uncooking the Books," *The Wall Street Journal*, October 10, 2002, p. A1.
[3] *SFAC No. 5*, "Recognition and Measurement in Finance Statements."

INHERENT RISKS IN THE ACQUISITION AND EXPENDITURE CYCLE

LEARNING
OBJECTIVE

1. Identify significant inherent risks in the acquisition and expenditure cycle.

The Government Accountability Office's (GAO) report on financial statement restatements between 1997 and 2002 found that the second most common reason for restatements (after improper revenue recognition) was misstated costs and expenses. This category included improperly recognizing costs or expenses, improperly **capitalizing** expenditures, and improperly accounting for taxes.[4] WorldCom, Inc., is an example of a company that simply placed expenses in capital accounts (accounts that will be expensed over a number of years as depreciation or amortization). Although the expenses do not go away, capitalizing them increases net income in the year when they should have been completely expensed. These restatements led to nearly $5 billion in immediate market losses when they were announced. (This disturbing trend has continued according to a 2006 survey by Audit Analytics.[5]) Some recent restatements are summarized in Exhibit 8.1. Note that in at least one case (**Cablevision**), expenses were *accelerated* to an earlier period.

In addition to improperly recognizing expenses, other concerns (inherent risks) in the acquisition and expenditure cycle include *unrecorded liabilities* and *noncancelable purchase agreements*. In many accounting systems, liabilities are not recorded until receiving reports have been matched to purchase orders and invoices. Often when there is a problem in matching the documents, the liability is not recorded, thus understating costs and overstating profits. Under noncancelable purchase agreements, companies order goods for future delivery to obtain volume discounts or favorable pricing. However, if market forces or technology causes a permanent decline in the value of those goods, the company must recognize any related losses immediately.

Review Checkpoint

8.1 What are the short-term effect and the long-term effect on the financial statements for improperly capitalizing expenditures?

EXHIBIT 8.1 **Cost and Expense Capers**

Company	Alleged Fraud Strategy	Restatement Amount
MCI (WorldCom)	The telecommunications company improperly capitalized expense items.	$74.4 billion
Waste Management, Inc.	The waste disposal giant used "top-level adjustments" to improperly eliminate and defer current period expenses and avoided depreciation on garbage trucks by assigning unsupported, inflated, and arbitrary salvage values and extending the useful lives.	$1.1 billion
Adelphia Communications Corporation	The cable company did not report off-balance-sheet liabilities.	$210.0 million
Orbital Sciences Corporation	The satellite manufacturer improperly capitalized costs.	$124.0 million
Aurora Foods, Inc.	The food company did not record trade marketing expenses (e.g., case discounts to induce grocery stores to stock its goods)	$81.5 million
Collins and Aikman	The automotive supply company booked rebates as lump sums that should have been spread out over time.	$16.0 million
Cablevision	The cable company improperly *accelerated* marketing expenses in the programming division.	$15.0 million

[4] GAO, *Financial Statement Restatements* (GAO, October 2002).
[5] M. Cheffers, D. Whalen, and D Tanona, *2006 Financial Restatements: A Six Year Comparison,* AuditAnalytics.com.

ACQUISITION AND EXPENDITURE CYCLE: TYPICAL ACTIVITIES

LEARNING
OBJECTIVE

2. Describe the
acquisition and
expenditure cycle,
including typical
source documents
and controls.

STAGES OF AN AUDIT

| Obtain (or Retain) Engagement | Engagement Planning | Risk Assessment | Substantive Procedures | Reporting |

The basic acquisition and expenditure activities include (1) purchasing goods and services, (2) receiving the good or service, (3) recording the asset or expense and related liability, and (4) paying the vendor. Exhibit 8.2 shows the activities and transactions involved in an acquisition and expenditure cycle. The exhibit also lists the accounts and records typically found in this cycle. As you follow the exhibit, you can track the elements of internal control described in the following sections.

EXHIBIT 8.2 ACQUISITION AND EXPENDITURE CYCLE

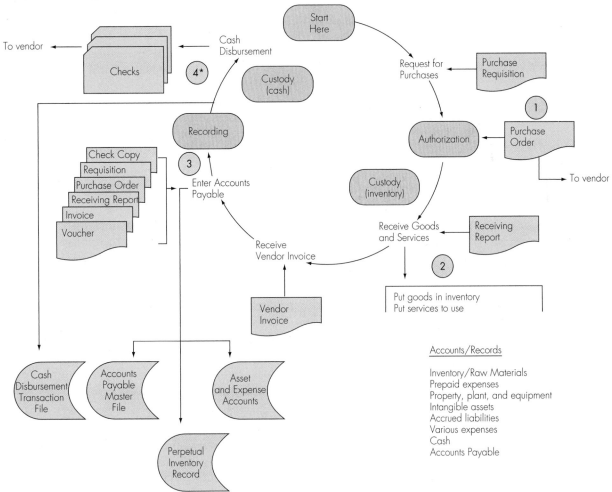

Accounts/Records

Inventory/Raw Materials
Prepaid expenses
Property, plant, and equipment
Intangible assets
Accrued liabilities
Various expenses
Cash
Accounts Payable

*Paying the vendor is discussed in the Cash Disbursements section of Chapter 6.

AUDITING INSIGHT My Place or Mine?

Facts: The construction manager of a national restaurant chain was responsible for entering into contracts with local building suppliers for materials for new restaurants. After the manager left the company, it was discovered that he had several thousand dollars of materials delivered to his home for home improvements. The materials were billed with the legitimate materials used in the new stores.

Question: How can a company prevent such activities?

Answer: Companies must have clear policies that prevent employees from taking personal gifts and communicate them to its vendors. These policies have to be strictly enforced and violators severely punished. Purchases must be based on budgets approved by senior management. Internal auditors should review significant purchase contracts. Finally, human resources should provide background checks on employees and see that they receive training in company ethics policies.

Purchasing Goods and Services ①

Purchases are requested (requisitioned) by people who know the needs of the organization. A purchasing department seeks the best prices and quality and issues a purchase order to a selected vendor from an approved vendor list. Obtaining competitive bids is a good practice because it tends to produce the best prices and involves several legitimate suppliers in the process. Inventory is often ordered automatically from approved vendors through **electronic data interchange (EDI).** When production plans indicate a need for the inventory, automatic links to the vendor's computerized system generate a purchase order.

The purchasing department is an area of high fraud risk because employees who have authority to purchase assets and services for the company are in a unique position to take advantage of their authority to enrich themselves or their friends. The abuse can simply be to give business to vendors who do not supply the best quality or price to the company in return for favors, perquisites, or even friendship. The abuse can extend to misdirecting purchases to the employee's personal benefit. These abuses are difficult to detect because vendors are often reluctant to lose favor with purchasing decision makers.

Receiving the Goods or Services ②

A receiving department inspects the goods received for quantity and quality (producing a receiving report) and then puts them in the hands of other responsible persons (e.g., inventory warehousing, fixed asset installation). A receiving report is completed indicating the quantity and description of the item. Receiving departments should obtain a "blind" purchase order that has all purchase information except the quantity, which is left blank for the receiving department to fill in after an independent inspection and count. Services are not "received" in this manner, but responsible persons indicate the service was satisfactorily performed by signing the invoice or some other form.

Recording the Asset or Expense and Related Liability ③

Accounts payable usually are recorded when the purchaser receives the goods or services ordered. The accounts payable department attaches a **voucher** to the purchase order, vendor's invoice, and receiving report. The voucher shows the accounts that are debited and indicates who checked the invoice for proper date, price, math, and supporting documentation. After the voucher package has been completed, accountants enter the accounts (or vouchers) payable with debits to proper inventory, fixed asset, and expense accounts and with a credit to accounts payable.

AUDIT EVIDENCE IN MANAGEMENT REPORTS AND DATA FILES

Computerized processing of acquisition and payment transactions enables management to generate several reports that can provide important audit evidence.

Open Purchase Orders

Purchase orders are "open" from the time they are issued until the goods and services are received. They are held in an *open purchase order file*. Generally, no liability exists until the transactions are complete (i.e., the merchandise or services are received). However, auditors can find evidence of losses on purchase commitments in this file if market prices have fallen below the purchase price shown in purchase orders.

Unmatched Receiving Reports

Liabilities should be recorded on the date the goods and services are received and accepted by the receiving department or by another responsible person. Sometimes, however, vendor invoices arrive later. In the meantime, the accounts payable department holds the receiving reports *unmatched* with invoices, awaiting enough information to record an accounting entry. Auditors can inspect the unmatched receiving report file to determine whether the company has material unrecorded liabilities on the financial statement date for goods that were received but not matched to invoices.

Unmatched Vendor Invoices

Sometimes vendor invoices arrive in the accounts payable department before the receiving activity is complete. Such invoices are held *unmatched* with receiving reports, awaiting information that the goods and services were actually received and accepted. Auditors can inspect the *unmatched invoice file* and compare it to the *unmatched receiving report file* to determine whether liabilities are unrecorded. Systems failures and human coding errors can cause unmatched invoices and related unmatched receiving reports to sit around unnoticed when all of the information for recording a liability is actually in hand.

Accounts (Vouchers) Payable Trial Balance

This trial balance is a list of payable amounts by vendor and the sum should agree with the accounts payable control account. (Some organizations keep records by individual vouchers instead of vendor names, so the trial balance is a list of unpaid vouchers. The sum still should agree with the control account balance.) The best type of trial balance for audit purposes is one that contains the names of *all* vendors with whom the organization has done business, even those whose balances are zero. The *search for unrecorded liabilities* should emphasize accounts with the small and zero balances, especially for regular vendors, because these accounts can be the places where liabilities are unrecorded.

AUDITING INSIGHT Thinking Ahead

Lone Moon Brewing purchased bulk aluminum sheets and manufactured its own cans. To ensure a source of raw materials supply, the company entered into a long-term purchase agreement for 6 million pounds of aluminum sheeting at 40 cents per pound. At the end of the year, 1.5 million pounds had been purchased and used, but the market price had fallen to 32 cents per pound. Lone Moon was on the hook for a $360,000 (4.5 million pounds @ 8 cents) purchase commitment in excess of current market prices that should be recognized as a loss in the period.

Purchases Journal

A list of all purchases may or may not be printed out. It may exist only in a computer transaction file. In either event, it provides information for (1) CAATs analysis of purchasing patterns that can exhibit characteristics of errors and frauds and (2) sample selection of transactions for tests of controls. (A company could have already performed analyses of purchases and auditors can use these for analytical procedures, provided the analyses are produced under reliable control conditions.)

Fixed Asset Reports

These reports show the details of fixed assets in control accounts. They can be used for scanning and sample selection. The information for depreciation calculation (cost, useful life, method, salvage) can be used for the audit of depreciation on a sample basis or by computerized applications to recalculate all the depreciation.

Review Checkpoints

8.2 What is a voucher?

8.3 How can purchasing managers use their position to defraud the company? What can be done to prevent it?

8.4 Why is a "blind" purchase order used as a receiving report document?

8.5 Where could an auditor look to find evidence of (a) losses on purchase commitments or (b) unrecorded liabilities to vendors?

8.6 List the management reports and data files that can be used for audit evidence. What information in them can be useful to auditors?

CONTROL RISK ASSESSMENT

LEARNING
OBJECTIVE

3. Give examples of tests of controls over purchase of inventory and services.

Control risk assessment is important because it governs the nature, timing, and extent of substantive procedures that will be applied in the audit of account balances in the acquisition and expenditure cycle. These account balances include

- Inventory.
- Prepaid and other assets.
- Fixed assets.
- Accounts payable.
- Accrued liabilities.
- Cash.
- Various expenses:
 - Administrative: supplies, legal fees, audit fees, and taxes.
 - Selling: commissions, travel, delivery, repairs, and advertising.
 - Manufacturing: maintenance, freight-in, utilities, etc.

Control Considerations

Control procedures for proper separation of responsibilities should be in place and operating. By referring to Exhibit 8.2, you can see that proper separation involves different people and different departments performing the purchasing, receiving, and cash disbursement authorization; custody of inventory, fixed assets, and cash; record keeping for purchases

and payments; and reconciliation of assets, cash, and accounts payable. Combinations of two or more of these responsibilities in one person, one office, or one computerized system can open the door for errors and frauds. Specifically, the persons authorizing purchases should not be responsible for recording them. Persons who actually handle the receipt and storage of goods should neither authorize nor account for them. The persons who sign checks should not prepare the vouchers, nor should they mail the checks.

In addition, the internal controls should provide for detailed control-checking activities. For example, purchase requisitions and purchase orders should be signed or initialed by authorized personnel. (Computer-generated purchase orders should come from a system whose master file specifications for reordering and vendor identification are restricted to changes only by authorized persons.)

Accountants should be instructed to record accounts payable only when all supporting documentation is in order and care should be taken to record purchases and payables as of the date goods and services are received. Vendor invoices should be compared to purchase orders and receiving reports to determine that the vendor is charging the approved price and that the quantity being billed is the same as the quantity received.

Custody

Access to inventory and other physical assets must be restricted by placing them in locked areas when possible. Responsibility must be established by having someone sign for receiving the assets when they are moved. Cash "custody" rests largely in the hands of the person or persons authorized to sign checks.

Another aspect of "custody" involves access to blank documents such as purchase orders, receiving reports, and blank checks. If unauthorized persons can obtain blank copies of these internal business documents, they can forge a false purchase order to a fictitious vendor, forge a false receiving report, send a false invoice from a fictitious supplier, and prepare a company check to the fictitious supplier, thereby accomplishing embezzlement.

Periodic Reconciliation

A periodic comparison or reconciliation of existing assets to recorded amounts is not shown in Exhibit 8.2, but it occurs in several ways, including the following:

- Physical inventory taking to compare inventory on hand to perpetual inventory records.
- Inspection of fixed assets to compare to detail fixed asset records.
- Preparation of an accounts payable trial balance to compare the detail of accounts payable to the control account.
- Internal audit confirmation of accounts payable to compare vendors' reports and monthly statements to recorded liabilities.
- Follow-up of old unmatched purchase orders, receiving reports, and invoices.

Information about the control system is often initially gathered by completing an *internal control questionnaire*. A selection of questionnaires for both manual controls and computer controls is in Appendix 8A. These questionnaires can be studied for details of desirable control procedures. They are organized under headings that identify the management assertions.

Tests of Controls

An organization should have controls in place and operating to prevent, detect, and correct accounting errors. Exhibit 8.3 puts controls in the perspective of purchasing activity with examples of specific assertions. You should study this exhibit carefully. It expresses the general control assertions in specific examples related to purchasing.

Auditors can perform tests of controls to determine whether company controls actually are in place and operating effectively. Tests of controls consist of (1) identification of the

EXHIBIT 8.3 **Assertions about Classes of Transactions and Events for the Period: Acquisition and Expenditure Cycle**

Assertion	Controls	Tests of Controls
Occurrence—Purchases and related events that have been recorded have occurred and pertain to the entity.	Separation of duties between purchasing, receiving, and accounting.	Observe separation of duties.
	Purchase orders support invoices. Receiving documents exist for all invoices. Recorded purchases and expenditures supported by invoices.	Check agreement of purchases in purchases detail file to invoices, supporting receiving documents, and customer purchase orders for customer name, product description, terms, dates, and quantities.
	Managers compare actual expenses to budgeted amounts.	Examine evidence of managers' reviews of actual versus budget and of follow-up on unusual items.
	Invoices are canceled with a PAID stamp when paid.	Examine paid vouchers for PAID stamp.
Completeness—All purchases and related events that should have been recorded have been recorded.	Vouchers, receiving reports, purchase orders, and checks are prenumbered and the numerical sequence is checked.	Trace receiving reports to recording in purchases detail file. Scan documents for numerical sequence. Observe client checking sequence.
	Overall comparisons of purchases are made periodically by a statistical or product line analysis.	Examine evidence that managers review statistical analyses and follow up on exceptions.
Accuracy—Amounts and other data related to purchase transactions and events have been recorded properly.	Purchase contracts are authorized at the appropriate level and accounting is made aware of all significant terms.	Examine contracts for authorization. Inquire how accounting is notified.
	Invoice quantities and prices are compared to purchase orders and receiving reports.	Observe client comparing receiving quantities.
	Prices and mathematical accuracy are independently checked before voucher prepared.	Compare prices to approved price listing. Examine evidence of client checking. Recalculate price extensions and discounts.
	Journal entries are reviewed by appropriate level.	Examine evidence of approval.
	Individual accounts payable are reconciled to general ledger.	Examine reconciliation and support for reconciling items.
	Statements are reviewed and approved at senior level.	Examine evidence of financial statement review by senior officials.
Cutoff—Purchases and related events have been recorded in the correct period.	Date of receiving report is compared to invoice date.	Check date of receipt to date recorded in voucher journal. Examine evidence of client comparison of dates.
Classification—Purchases and related events have been recorded in the proper accounts.	Chart of accounts is used for classifying purchase entries.	Observe use of chart of accounts.
	Purchases from subsidiaries and affiliates are classified as intercompany purchases and payables. Purchases returns and allowance are properly classified.	Observe correct account classification.
	Journal entries are reviewed by appropriate level.	Examine evidence of journal entry review.

EXHIBIT 8.4
Direction of Tests

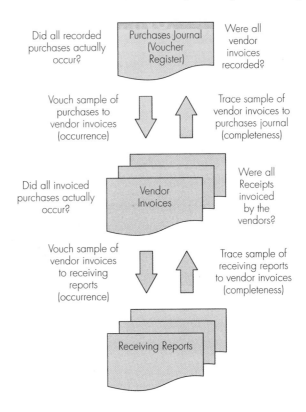

control that will be relied on to reduce assessed control risk and (2) identification of the data population from which a sample of items will be selected for audit. In general, the actions in tests of controls involve vouching, tracing, observing, scanning, and recalculating.

Procedures such as matching, recalculating, and scanning for unusual items often can be performed electronically using CAATs. If personnel in the organization are not performing control procedures effectively, auditors will need to design substantive procedures to try to detect whether control failures have produced materially misleading account balances.

Tests of controls over *occurrence* involve tests of the additions to the expense accounts. Exhibit 8.4 pictures the *direction of the test* for tests of controls in the acquisition and expenditure cycle. The samples from the source documents (receiving reports, invoices) meet the *completeness* direction requirement to determine whether everything received was recorded as an addition to the balance. The sample from the purchase records meets the *occurrence* direction requirement to determine whether everything recorded as an addition is supported by receiving reports and invoices.

Summary: Control Risk Assessment

The auditor should evaluate the evidence obtained from understanding internal controls and from the tests of controls. If the control risk is assessed below the maximum, the substantive procedures can be reduced in cost-saving ways. For example, if *completeness* controls are strong, only larger items will be examined in the search for unrecorded liabilities, and if *occurrence* controls are strong, vouching of expenses can be limited to significant items. On the other hand, if the tests of controls reveal weaknesses, the substantive procedures will need to be designed to lower the detection risk for the account balances. For example, if *completeness* controls are weak, the auditor might send confirmation letters to vendors with small or zero balances. If *occurrence* controls are weak, the auditor may have to perform substantive tests of transactions by recalculating and testing a sample of payments for the period for monetary errors rather than just evidence of control effectiveness. Other substantive procedures that can be affected include vouching of debits to assets and expenses.

Review Checkpoints

8.7 What are the primary functions that should be separated in the acquisition and expenditure cycle?

8.8 What feature of the acquisition and expenditure control would be expected to prevent an employee's embezzling cash through creation of fictitious vouchers?

8.9 How would substantive procedures for accounts payable be affected by (a) a low risk of material misstatement or (b) a high risk of material misstatement?

SUBSTANTIVE PROCEDURES IN THE ACQUISITION AND EXPENDITURE CYCLE

LEARNING OBJECTIVE

4. Explain the importance of the *completeness* assertion for the audit of accounts payable liabilities and list some procedures for a search for unrecorded *liabilities*.

STAGES OF AN AUDIT

| Obtain (or Retain) Engagement | Engagement Planning | Risk Assessment | Substantive Procedures | Reporting |

The Completeness Assertion

Exhibit 8.5 lists assertions related to account balances in the acquisition and expenditure cycle and some illustrative substantive procedures. When considering assertions and obtaining evidence about accounts payable and other liabilities, auditors must emphasize the *completeness* assertion. (For asset accounts, the emphasis is on the *existence* assertion.) This emphasis on completeness is rightly placed because financial statement users are typically more concerned if a company understates expenses and liabilities than if management overstates those accounts. Additional procedures are included in a sample audit program in Appendix 8B.

Evidence is much more difficult to obtain to verify the *completeness* assertion than the *existence* assertion. Auditors cannot rely entirely on a management assertion of *completeness*, even in combination with a favorable assessment of control risk. The **search for unrecorded liabilities** is the set of procedures designed to yield audit evidence of liabilities that were not recorded in the reporting period. Such a search normally should be performed from the audit client's balance sheet date up to the date of the auditors' report.

EXHIBIT 8.5 Assertions about Account Balances at the Period End and Substantive Procedures in the Acquisition and Expenditure Cycle

Assertions about Account Balances	Substantive Procedures
Existence—Accounts receivable exist	Vouch payables to vendor invoices, receiving reports, and purchase orders.
Rights and obligations—The company has all rights to items purchased. Liabilities are obligations of the entity	Review bank confirmations, loan agreements, and minutes of the board for indications that property has been pledged as collateral.
Completeness—All payables that should have been recorded are recorded	Perform search for unrecorded liabilities. Include a sample of zero-balance accounts in confirmation process.
Valuation or allocation—Purchases and related events have been recorded at the proper amount	Test math on payable listing. Select accounts due and test math and terms on invoices.

The following is a list of procedures useful in the *search for unrecorded liabilities*. The audit objective is to search all places where evidence of liabilities could exist.

- Inquire of client personnel about their procedures for ensuring that all liabilities are recorded.
- Scan the open purchase order file at year end for indications of material purchase commitments at fixed prices. Obtain current prices and determine whether any adjustments for loss and liability for purchase commitments are needed.
- Examine the unmatched vendor invoices listing and determine when the goods were received, looking to the unmatched receiving report file and receiving reports prepared around year end. Determine which invoices, if any, should be recorded by tracing them to the payables listing.
- Trace the unmatched receiving reports to accounts payable entries and determine whether entries recorded in the next accounting period need to be recorded in the current accounting period under audit.
- Select a sample of cash disbursements from the accounting period following the balance sheet date. Vouch them to supporting documents (invoice, receiving report) to determine whether the related liabilities were recorded in the proper accounting period.
- Confirm accounts payable with vendors, especially those most likely to be understated (regular suppliers showing small or zero balances in the year-end accounts payable ledger). Unlike accounts receivable confirmations, accounts payable confirmations are not required by GAAS. Such confirmations are not commonly used because they are primarily directed at the *existence* assertion, and the main concern regarding liabilities is *completeness*. However, accounts payable confirmations might be used under the following circumstances:
 - Internal controls are weak.
 - The company is in a tight cash position and bill paying is slow.
 - Physical inventories exceed general ledger inventory balances by significant amounts.
 - Certain vendors do not send statements.
 - Vendor accounts are pledged by assets.
 - Vendor accounts include unusual transactions.
- Apply analytical procedures appropriate in the circumstances. In general, accounts payable volume and period-end balances should increase when the company experiences increases in physical production volume or engages in inventory stockpiling. Some liabilities can be functionally related to other activities; for example, sales taxes are functionally related to sales dollar totals, payroll taxes to payroll totals, excise taxes to sales dollars or volume, and income taxes to income.
- Purchase cut-off must be tested both at year end and in conjunction with the observation of the physical inventory count. Receiving reports issued and unissued at the end of the period are examined and listed. Later, auditors check to ensure the goods received on the issued reports are included in inventory and payables and to ensure no goods are recorded for the unissued receiving reports.

Review Checkpoints

8.10 Describe the purpose and give examples of audit procedures in the *search for unrecorded liabilities.*

8.11 In substantive procedures, why is the emphasis on the *completeness* assertion for liabilities instead of on the *existence* assertion as in the audit of assets?

LEARNING
OBJECTIVE

5. Discuss audit
 procedures for other
 accounts affected by
 the acquisition and
 expenditure cycle.

Auditing Other Accounts in the Acquisition and Expenditure Cycle

Prepaid Expenses and Accrued Liabilities

Some of the other accounts affected by the acquisition and expenditure cycle are listed in Exhibit 8.2. Performing substantive procedures for cash and inventory accounts are discussed in other chapters. Many accounts, particularly expense accounts, can be tested using analytical procedures, such as horizontal and vertical analyses. Other accounts such as prepaid expenses can be analyzed by a schedule similar to Exhibit 8.6. In addition to vouching payments, related expense accounts are cross-referenced to expense workpapers (X-10, 11, 12 in Exhibit 8.6). A sample audit program for prepaid, deferred, and accrued expenses is shown at Appendix 8B.2.

Accrued Income Taxes

Income taxes are a special audit area because the accounting and underlying federal tax laws are so complex. State and local tax differences add to the complexity. Approximately one-third of the first round of adverse opinions on internal controls under Sarbanes-Oxley requirements cited tax accounting control weaknesses.[6] In addition, income tax expense is one of the largest items on the income statement. *Statement of Financial Accounting Standard No. 109 (SFAS 109)* requires companies to estimate deferred income tax assets and liabilities, both of which are very subjective. The adoption of *FASB Interpretation No. 48 (FIN 48)*, "Accounting for Uncertainty in Income Taxes," dramatically changed how companies account for uncertain income tax positions. *FIN 48* mandates a higher standard that tax benefits must meet before they can be recognized in a company's financial statements. Public accounting firms normally include tax specialists on the audit team to assess tax liabilities and estimates. The procedures for auditing estimates (discussed in detail later in Chapter 10) are generally followed, including evaluating controls over management's procedures for determining assumptions and calculating the amounts. Basic audit procedures are similar to those discussed for accrued liabilities above: auditors vouch payments, test

EXHIBIT 8.6 **Account Analysis for Prepaid Expenses**

APOLLO SHOES, INC. **Prepaid Expenses** **For Year Ended 12/31/2008** **Prepared by Client**					**E-1**
				Prepared by	RJR 1/16/09
				Reviewed by	TJL 1/18/09

Acct #	Account Title	(Audited) Balance 12/31/2007	Additions	Amortization/ Disposals	Unaudited Balance 12/31/2008
14100	Prepaid insurance	$706,148.66 PY	$941,531.55 v	$904,365.83 C X-10	$743,314.38
14200	Prepaid rent	$190,000.00 PY	$760,000.00 v	$750,000.00 C X-11	$200,000.00
14300	Office supplies	$7,036.48 PY	$26,025.00 v	$25,654.66 C X-12	$7,406.82
		$903,185.14	$1,727,556.55	$1,680,020.59	$950,721.20 CF
		F	F	F	F TB

PY = Agreed to prior year documentation.
PY = Agreed to prior-year documentation.
 v = Vouched to policies or agreements and vendor invoice.
 F = Footed

CF = Cross-footed.
 C = Calculated.
TB = Agreed to Trial Balance.

[6] K. Frieswick, *CFO Magazine*, November 7, 2005, www.cfo.com/article.cfm/5077959/c_2984354/?f=archives.

AUDITING INSIGHT H&R Block Accounting Is Taxing

As part of its ongoing work to remediate control weaknesses in its corporate tax function, **H&R Block** said that it will restate its results for fiscal years 2005 and 2004, as well as previously reported quarterly results for fiscal 2006. The restatement pertains principally to errors in determining the company's state effective income tax rate, resulting in a cumulative understatement of its state income tax liability of approximately $32 million as of April 30, 2005.

Source: H&R Block press release, February 23, 2006.

the expense, and recalculate the liability. All tax returns and government communications are carefully reviewed.

Property, Plant, and Equipment and Intangible Assets

Assertions Management makes assertions about *existence, completeness, rights and obligations,* and *valuation and allocation.* Typical specific assertions relating to property, plant, and equipment (PP&E) and intangible assets include these:

- Recorded PP&E exist.
- All PP&E are recorded (completeness).
- PP&E are owned (rights).
- Repairs and maintenance expense does not include items that should have been capitalized (completeness).
- Freight-in is included as part of purchases and added to equipment costs (valuation).
- Purchased goodwill is properly valued (valuation).
- Goodwill is not impaired (valuation).
- Capitalized intangible costs relate to intangibles acquired in exchange transactions (existence).
- Amortization and depreciation expenses are properly calculated (valuation).

Audit Procedures The two primary means of gathering evidence supporting management's assertions with respect to PP&E are physical inspection and vouching. The principal goal of the physical inspection of PP&E is to determine actual *existence* and condition of the property (*valuation*). The inspection of equipment should be compared to detailed PP&E records. Unlike current assets, most of the items in PP&E were also in the account in the previous year. Therefore, if the company was audited last year, the audit team can trace existing items to the previous year's audit documentation. The cost of newly acquired real and personal property can be vouched to invoices or other purchase documents (*existence, valuation*) and title documents (such as on land, buildings) may be inspected (*rights and obligations*). Disposals of items that were on last year's list also should be traced to cash receipts records if they were sold or to other documentation if they were traded in or abandoned. Auditors also should prepare or obtain a schedule of casualty insurance on buildings and equipment and determine the adequacy of insurance in relation to asset market values.

The depreciation schedule is audited by recalculating the depreciation expense (*valuation or allocation*), using the company's methods, estimates of useful life, and estimates of residual value. Auditors also must evaluate the useful lives and residual values assigned by the client for reasonableness. Industry groups often publish tables of useful lives of assets commonly found in the industry.

The asset acquisition and disposition information in the schedule gives auditors some points of departure for auditing the asset additions and disposals. When the schedule covers hundreds of assets and numerous additions and disposals, auditors can (1) use CAATs to recalculate the depreciation expense and (2) use sampling to choose additions and disposals for tests of controls and substantive procedures. An abbreviated illustration

EXHIBIT 8.7 Sample PP&E and Depreciation Documentation

	APOLLO SHOES, INC.							F-1
	Building and Land Improvements for Year Ended 12/31/2008 Prepared By Client					Prepared by		RJR 2/18/09
						Reviewed by		TJL 2/20/09

	Asset Cost ($s)				Accumulated Depreciation ($s)			
Description	**Beginning Balance**	**Added**	**Sold**	**Ending Balance**	**Beginning Balance**	**Depreciation Expense**	**Sold**	**Ending Balance**
Building 1	$218,367 PY	$0	$0	$218,367	$54,591 PY	$10,918 C	$0	$65,509
Building 2	0	155,976 v	0	155,976	0	1,050 C	0	1,050
Building 1 improvements	149,737 PY	109,825 v	10,000 E	249,562	37,434 PY	10,232 C	2,500 C	45,166
Total buildings and improvements	$368,104	$265,801	$10,000	$623,905 TB	$92,025	$22,200 TB	$2,500	$111,725 TB
	F	F	F	F/CF	F	F	F	F/CF

PY = Agreed to prior-year documentation.
v = Vouched to purchase contract.
E = Examined sales agreement and related cash receipts.
F = Footed.

CF = Cross-footed.
C = Recalculated.
TB = Carried forward to the Trial Balance.

of audit documentation for property, plant, and equipment and depreciation is shown in Exhibit 8.7. Note that the ending balances of PP&E, accumulated depreciation, and depreciation expense are carried forward to the trial balance.

With respect to intangible assets, official documents of patents, copyrights, and trademark rights can be inspected to see that they are recorded in the name of the client. Goodwill must be reviewed for impairment; in other words, does the goodwill still have value. Amortization of other intangibles should be recalculated. Similar to depreciation expense, this expense owes its existence to a calculation, and recalculation based on audited costs and rates is sufficient appropriate audit evidence.

Auditors inquire of company counsel about knowledge of any lawsuits or defects relating to patents, copyrights, trademarks, or trade names. Questions about lawsuits challenging patents, copyrights, or trade names can produce early knowledge of problem areas for further investigation. Likewise, discussions and questions about research and development successes and failures can alert the audit team to problems of valuation of intangible assets and related amortization expenses. Responses to questions about licensing of patents can be used in the audit of related royalty revenue accounts. Auditors can confirm royalty income from patent licenses received from a single licensee and review licensing and royalty contracts. However, such income amounts usually are audited by vouching the licensee's reports and the related cash receipt.

Vouching may be extensive in the areas of research and development (R&D) and deferred software development costs. The principal evidence problem is to determine whether costs are properly classified as assets or as R&D expenses. Recorded amounts generally are selected on a sample basis and the purchase orders, receiving reports, payroll records, authorization notices, and management reports are compared to them. Some R&D costs can resemble non-R&D cost (such as supplies, payroll costs), so auditors must be very careful in the vouching to be alert for costs that appear to relate to other operations.

Merger and acquisition transactions should be reviewed in terms of the appraisals, judgments, and allocations used to assign portions of the purchase price to tangible assets, intangible assets, liabilities, and goodwill. In the final analysis, nothing really substitutes for the inspection of transaction documentation, but verbal inquiries can help auditors to understand the circumstances of a merger. An illustrative program of substantive procedures for PP&E and related accounts can be found in Appendix 8B.3.

AUDITING INSIGHT — The Sign of the Credit Balance

Auto Parts & Repair, Inc., kept perpetual inventory records and equipment records on a computerized system. Because of the size of the files (8,000 parts in various locations and 1,500 asset records), the company never printed reports for visual inspection. Auditors ran a computer-audit "sign test" on inventory balances and equipment net book balances that called for a printed report for all balances less than zero. The auditors discovered 320 negative inventory balances that were caused by employees' failure to record purchases and 125 negative net asset balances caused by depreciating assets more than their cost.

Other Expenses

As mentioned earlier, most expense accounts can be tested in conjunction with tests of related assets and liabilities (e.g., depreciation) or through analytical procedures. However, if risk of material misstatement is high, expenses can be tested by **substantive tests of transactions** whereby a sample of transactions is tested much like a test of controls, except auditors look for evidence that the accounts contain monetary errors, rather than if controls are operating. Payroll expense is usually audited by testing controls or using substantive tests of transactions and performing analytical procedures (see Appendix 8C). Some expenses should be examined separately because of their unique nature. For example, legal and professional expenses should be listed by the client and significant amounts should be vouched so the auditors can determine what legal and professional services the client is using. Miscellaneous expenses likewise should be listed and examined for significant unusual items. Finally, maintenance and repairs should be examined to determine whether any items should be capitalized.

Presentation and Disclosure

Once auditors are satisfied that controls have been examined and transactions and balances have been appropriately tested, the job is not over. The accounts in the acquisition and expenditure cycle require many disclosures. Depreciation methods, asset impairments, leases, and details about income taxes are only a few of the essential items with specific presentation and disclosures requirements. These disclosures must ensure that the presentation and disclosure assertions of *occurrence* and *rights and obligations, completeness, classification and understandability,* and *accuracy and valuation* are all met.

Review Checkpoints

8.12 How do audit procedures for prepaid expenses and accrued liabilities also provide audit evidence about related expense accounts?

8.13 What are some of the typical assertions found in PP&E, investments, and intangibles accounts?

8.14 What items in a client's PP&E and depreciation schedule give auditors points of departure (assertions) for audit procedures?

8.15 What four methods are used to audit other expense accounts?

AUDIT RISK MODEL SUMMARY

Now that the elements of risk of material misstatement for the acquisition and expenditure cycle have been presented, along with some of the important substantive procedures, let's examine how auditors might apply the audit risk model for the completeness and classification assertions.

CHI-CHI'S CLOTHING STORES, INC.

Chi-Chi's Clothing Stores, Inc., is a chain of women's clothing stores that sells upscale fashions, mostly in the northeastern United States. The company is publicly held and annual sales have been increasing at a rate of almost 30 percent per year. David Escobar has been assigned as the senior auditor. The policy of David's firm is to always set overall audit risk as low. Chi-Chi's accounting department and systems have not kept up with the rapid growth. As a result, numerous audit adjustments have been required every year and the company received an adverse report on internal controls in the previous year. One problem has been that invoices do not come in from the stores on a timely basis. The company has been very profitable, causing enormous increases in management stock options, which are a significant part of management compensation. Although the economy has taken a downturn, management and analyst forecasts still project a 30 percent growth rate. David is concerned that management could be biased toward understating costs and liabilities and therefore sets inherent risk at high.

As mentioned, controls have not kept pace with company growth. Chi-Chi's has been working to improve the systems in the current year, but the accounting department and internal audit department are overworked. Their staff members have not had time to sufficiently test new systems or train new personnel. Thus, David assesses control risk as high and plans to test only year-end controls sufficiently to comply with *AS 5*. In this situation, David believes he must set risk of material misstatement as high and set detection risk at low. He will perform an extensive search for unrecorded liabilities, examining a large sample of disbursements after the balance sheet date, and he will send confirmations to vendors that historically have had activity but have small or zero year-end balances. David also will vouch a sample of additions to PP&E accounts to ensure they are not items that should be properly expensed. The combination of high risk of material misstatement, and low detection risk should lead David to an acceptably low overall audit risk.

FINDING FRAUD SIGNS IN ACCOUNTS PAYABLE

LEARNING OBJECTIVE

6. Specify some ways fraud can be found in accounts payable and cash disbursements.

Fraudsters can have a field day generating false payments through a company's acquisition and expenditure systems. A common scheme is to send false invoices on the letterhead of a fictitious vendor to the company and have an insider manipulate supporting documents or controls to make payments. Sometimes a company's own employees engage in unauthorized "business" as suppliers to their employers.

These frauds can proceed undetected for a long time as long as auditors and managers do not identify the signs and signals they leave behind. If the *SAS 99* review for fraud risk indicates that a potential significant risk of fraud could exist in the acquisition and expenditure cycle, auditors can try several kinds of searches and matches in the company's records. These searches and matches are often performed using CAATs.

- Look for photocopies of invoices in the files. Fraudsters alter real invoices for false or duplicate payments and make photocopies to hide whiteout and cut-and-paste changes.

- Look for a vendor's invoices submitted in numerical order. False vendors sometimes use the same pad of prenumbered invoices (standard office supply store printing) to send bills to the company. Either the company is the vendor's only customer or the company is a victim of a false billing scheme.

- Look for a vendor's invoice amounts always in round numbers. Prices, shipping charges, and taxes too often come in penny amounts to expect a vendor's invoices always to round to even dollars.

- Look for a vendor's invoices that are always slightly lower than a review threshold. Insiders know that a company gives special attention and approval to invoices over a specified dollar amount (e.g., $10,000). Therefore, the fraudster always avoids invoices that are too large.

- Look for vendors with only post office box addresses. While many businesses use post office box addresses for receiving payments, invoices also should show a street address location.

- Look for vendors with no listed telephone number. Legitimate businesses normally do not hide behind unlisted telephone numbers. Also, cheap fraudsters sometimes do not buy a phone line for their false companies.

- Match vendor and employee addresses and telephone numbers. Many companies have policies that their employees cannot also be vendors. Insiders (employees) often know how to circumvent controls and their business with the employer could be suspicious.
- Look for multiple vendors at the same address and telephone number. Many invoices from the same location, especially invoices for different kinds of products and services, could simply come from a front organization conducting a false invoice scheme. However, legitimate suppliers often operate under several company names and conduct business from the same location.
- Look for vendors not on the approved vendor list.

Review Checkpoints

8.16 What items could indicate a significant risk of fraud in the acquisition and expenditure cycle (i.e., be "red flags")?

8.17 Describe the purpose and give examples of specific fraud detection procedures in the acquisition and expenditure cycle.

8.18 Are these specific fraud detection procedures designed to detect fraudulent financial reporting or misappropriation of assets? Explain.

FRAUD CASES: EXTENDED AUDIT PROCEDURES (*SAS 99*)

LEARNING OBJECTIVE

7. Describe some common errors and frauds in the acquisition and expenditure cycle and design some audit and investigation procedures for detecting them.

The audit of account balances consists of procedural efforts to detect errors and frauds that could exist in the balances, thus making them misleading in financial statements.

Case 8.1

Printing (Copying) Money

PROBLEM

Argus Productions, Inc., a motion picture and commercial production company, assigned M. Welby the authority and responsibility for obtaining copies of scripts used in production. Established procedures permitted Welby to arrange for outside script-copying services, receive the copies, and approve the bills for payment. In effect, Welby was the "purchasing department" and the "receiving department" for this particular service. To a certain extent, Welby was also the "accounting department" by virtue of approving bills for payment and coding them for assignment to projects. Welby did not make the actual accounting entries or sign the checks.

Welby set up a fictitious company under the registered name of Quickprint Company with himself as the incorporator and stockholder, complete with a post office box number, letterhead stationery, and nicely printed invoices but no printing equipment. Legitimate copy services were "subcontracted" by Quickprint to real printing businesses, which billed Quickprint. Welby then prepared Quickprint invoices billing Argus, usually at the legitimate shop's rate, but for a few extra copies each time. Welby also submitted Quickprint bills to Argus for fictitious copying jobs on scripts for movies and commercials that never went into production. As the owner of Quickprint, Welby endorsed Argus's checks with a rubber stamp and deposited the money in the business bank account, paid the legitimate printing bills, and took the rest for personal use.

Argus's production cost files contained all of the Quickprint bills sorted under the names of the movie and commercial production projects. Welby even created files for proposed films that never

went into full production and thus should not have had script-copying costs. There were no copying service bills from any shop other than Quickprint Company.

Welby conducted this fraud for five years, embezzling $475,000 in false and inflated billings. (Argus's net income was overstated a modest amount because copying costs were capitalized as part of production cost and then amortized over a two- to three-year period.)

AUDIT APPROACH

Management should assign the authority to request copies and the purchasing authority to different responsible employees. Other persons also should perform the accounting, including coding cost assignments to projects. Managerial review of production results could result in notice of excess costs.

The request for the quantity (number) of copies of a script should come from a person involved in production who knows the number needed. This person also should sign off for the receipt (or approve the bill) for this requested number of copies, thus acting as the "receiving department." This procedure could prevent waste (excess cost), especially if the requesting person also were held responsible for the profitability of the project. A company agent always performs actual purchasing, and, in this case, the agent was M. Welby. Purchasing agents generally have latitude to seek the best service at the best price, with or without bids from competitors. A requirement to obtain bids is usually a good idea, but much legitimate purchasing is done with sole-source suppliers without bid. However, an approval process should be employed before vendors are placed on the approved vendor list.

Someone in the accounting department should be responsible for coding invoices for charges to authorized projects, thus making it possible to detect costs charged to projects not actually in production. Someone with managerial responsibility should review project costs and the purchasing practices. However, this is an expensive use of executive time. It was not spent in the Argus case. Too bad.

In gaining an understanding of the internal controls, auditors could learn of the trust and responsibility vested in M. Welby. Because the embezzlement was about $95,000 per year, the total copying cost under Welby's control must have been around $1 million or more. (It might attract unwanted attention to inflate a cost more than 10 percent.)

Controls were very weak, especially in the combination of duties performed by Welby and in the lack of managerial review. For all practical purposes, there were no controls to test other than to see whether Welby had approved the copying cost bills and coded them to active projects. This provides an opportunity because proper classification is a control objective.

The auditors should select a sample of project files and vouch costs charged to them to support in source documents (*occurrence* direction of the test). Select a sample of expenditures and trace them to the project cost records shown coded on the expenditures (*completeness* direction of the test).

Substantive procedures are directed to obtaining evidence about the *existence* of film projects, *completeness* of the costs charged to them, *valuation* of the capitalized project costs, *rights* in copyright and ownership, and proper *disclosure* of amortization methods. The most important procedures are the same as the tests of control procedures; thus, when performed at the year-end date on the capitalized cost balances, they are dual-purpose audit procedures. Either of the procedures described earlier as tests of controls should show evidence of projects that had never gone into production. (Auditors should be careful to obtain a list of actual projects before they begin the procedures.) Chances are good that the discovery of bad project codes with copying cost will reveal a pattern of Quickprint bills.

Knowing that controls over copying cost are weak, auditors could be tipped off to the possibility of a Welby-Quickprint connection. Efforts to locate Quickprint should be taken (telephone book, chamber of commerce, other directories). Inquiry with the secretary of state for names of the Quickprint incorporators should reveal Welby's connection. The audit findings can then be turned over to a trained investigator to arrange an interview and confrontation with M. Welby.

DISCOVERY SUMMARY

In this case, internal auditors performed a review of project costs at the request of the manager of production, who was worried about profitability. They performed the procedures described earlier, noticed the dummy projects and the Quickprint bills, investigated the ownership of Quickprint, and discovered Welby's association. They had first tried to locate Quickprint's shop but could not find

it in the telephone, chamber of commerce, or other city directories. They were careful not to direct any mail to the post office box for fear of alerting the then-unknown parties involved. A sly internal auditor already had used a ruse at the post office and learned that Welby rented the box, but they did not know whether anyone else was involved. Alerted, the internal auditors gathered all Quickprint bills and determined the total charged for nonexistent projects. Carefully, under the covert observation of a representative of the local district attorney's office, Welby was interviewed and readily confessed.

Case 8.2

Real Cash Paid to Phony Doctors

PROBLEM

As manager of the claims processing department, Martha Lee was considered one of Beta Magnetic's best employees. She had never missed a day of work in 10 years and her department had one of the company's best efficiency ratings. Controls were considered good, including the verification by a claims processor that (1) the patient was a Beta employee, (2) medical treatments were covered in the plan, (3) the charges were within approved guidelines, (4) the cumulative claims for the employee did not exceed $50,000 (if over $50,000, a claim was submitted to an insurance company), and (5) the calculation for payment was correct. After verification processing, claims were sent to the claims payment department to pay the doctor directly. No payments ever went directly to employees. Martha Lee prepared false claims on real employees, forging the signatures of various claims processors, adding her own review approval, and naming bogus doctors who would be paid by the payment department. The payments were mailed to various post office box addresses and to her husband's business address.

Nobody ever verified claims information with the employees. The employees received no reports of medical benefits paid on their behalf. Although the department had performance reports by claims processors, these reports did not show claim-by-claim details. No one verified the credentials of the doctors.

As noted, Martha never missed a day of work for vacation or sickness. She was considered an ideal employee.

The falsified claim forms were in Beta's files, containing all fictitious data on employee names, processor signatures, doctors' bills, and phony doctors and addresses. The canceled checks were returned by the bank and were kept in Beta's files, containing "endorsements" by the doctors. Martha Lee and her husband were clever: They deposited the checks in various banks in accounts opened in the names of the "doctors."

Martha Lee did not stumble on the audit trail. She drew the attention of an auditor who saw her take her 24 claims processing employees out to an annual staff appreciation luncheon in a fleet of stretch limousines.

Over the seven years, Martha Lee and her husband stole $3.5 million and, until the last, no one noticed anything unusual about the total amount of claims paid.

AUDIT APPROACH

The controls were good as far as they went. The claims processors used internal data in their work: employee files for identification, treatment descriptions submitted by doctors with comparisons to plan provisions, and mathematical calculations. This work amounted to all approval necessary for the claims payment department to prepare a check. No controls connected the claims data with outside sources such as employee acknowledgment or doctor investigation. Employees certainly should be notified of any payments made on their behalf.

By never taking a day off, Martha was able to make sure she saw all documents related to her scheme. The company needed an enforced vacation and employee rotation policy.

The processing and control work in the claims payment department can be audited for deviations from controls.

The auditors should select a sample of paid claims and reperform the claims processing procedures to verify the employee status, coverage of treatment, proper guideline charges, cumulative

amount of less than $50,000, and accurate calculation. However, this procedure would not help answer the question "Does Martha Lee steal the money to pay for the limousines?"

"Thinking like a crook" points out the holes in the controls. Nobody seeks to verify data with external sources. However, the audit team must be careful in an investigation not to cast aspersions on a manager by letting rumors start by interviewing employees to find out whether they actually had the medical claim paid on their behalf. If money is being taken, the company check must be intercepted in some manner.

The balance under audit is the sum of the charges in the employee medical benefits expense account and the objective relates to the valid existence of the payments.

The first procedure can be as follows: Obtain a list of doctors paid by the company and look them up in the state medical society directory. Look up their addresses and determine whether they are valid business addresses. You could try comparing claims processors' signatures on various forms, but this is difficult and requires training. An extended procedure would be as follows: Compare the doctors' addresses to addresses known to be associated with Martha Lee and other claims processing employees.

DISCOVERY SUMMARY

The comparison of doctors to the medical society directory showed eight "doctors" who were not licensed in the current period. Five of these eight had post office box addresses and discrete inquiries and surveillance showed them rented to Martha Lee. The other three had the same mailing address as her husband's business. Further investigation involving the district attorney and police was necessary to obtain personal financial records and reconstruct the thefts from prior years.

Review Checkpoints

8.19 What key control concept was missing at Argus Productions?

8.20 What evidence could the *verbal inquiry* audit procedure provide in Printing (Copying) Money?

8.21 If Martha Lee had not been seen taking employees out in a limousine, how else could she have been caught?

8.22 How would a policy of mandatory vacations helped discover the Beta fraud?

Summary

The acquisition and expenditure cycle consists of purchase requisitioning, purchase ordering, receiving goods and services, recording vendors' invoices, accounting for accounts payable, and making cash disbursements. Companies reduce control risk by having a suitable separation of authorization, custody, recording, and periodic reconciliation duties. Error-checking procedures of comparing purchase orders and receiving reports to vendor invoices are important for recording proper amounts of accounts payable liabilities. Having a separation of duties between preparing cash disbursement checks and actually signing them provides supervisory control. Otherwise, many things could go wrong, ranging from processing false or fictitious purchase orders to failing to record liabilities for goods and services received.

The *completeness* assertion is very important in the audit of liabilities because misleading financial statements often have involved unrecorded liabilities and expenses. The search for unrecorded liabilities is an important set of audit procedures. The section Finding Fraud Signs in Accounts Payable suggests some methods for finding signs that could indicate false payments to fictitious vendors.

Auditing the acquisition and expenditure cycle is not straightforward. Here are some deficiencies the PCAOB noted in its inspections of Big Four audit firms regarding the audits of this cycle.

AUDITING INSIGHT | PCAOB Inspections and the Acquisition and Expenditure Cycle

- The audit documentation did not evidence sufficient testing of . . . fair values allocated to certain assets and liabilities, useful lives assigned to the acquired assets, and the amount of the asset retirement obligation. In addition, there was no evidence that the Firm (1) evaluated the qualifications and relationships to the issuer of the specialists used to determine the fair values of certain of the acquired assets and liabilities, (2) obtained an understanding of the methods and assumptions used by the specialists, or (3) tested the data used by the specialists.

- The Firm's analytical procedures to test operating expenses did not meet the requirements for substantive analytical

procedures because, in one procedure, the Firm did not set a threshold for investigation and evaluation that allowed it to achieve the desired level of assurance and, in another procedure, there was no evidence in the audit documentation, and no persuasive other evidence, that the Firm had obtained corroboration of management's explanations for significant differences from the Firm's expectations.

Sources: 2005 PCAOB Inspection of Deloitte & Touche (November 30, 2006); 2006 PCAOB Inspection of Ernst & Young (May 2, 2007); 2005 Inspection of KPMG (January 11, 2007); and 2005 Inspection of PricewaterhouseCoopers (December 14, 2006). All reports can be found on the PCAOB's Web site, www.pcaob.org/Inspections/Public_Reports/index.aspx.

Key Terms

capitalizing: Recording expenditures as assets and charging them to expense by a systematic allocation over a number of years, 300

electronic data interchange (EDI): The transfer of data between different companies using networks such as the Internet, 302

matching: Recognizing expenses in the same period as associated revenues, 299

search for unrecorded liabilities: A substantive procedure to test the completeness assertion for accounts payable, 308

substantive test of transactions: A test of a sample of transactions during the period for monetary errors, 313

voucher: A document used as a source for recording payables. It shows approvals, accounts, and amounts to be recorded, usually attached to the supporting purchase order, receiving report, and vendor invoice, 302

Multiple Choice Questions for Practice and Review

8.23 Which of the following accounts does not appear in the acquisition and expenditure cycle?
 a. Cash.
 b. Purchases Returns.
 c. Sales Returns.
 d. Prepaid Insurance.

8.24 For which of the following accounts would the matching concept be the most appropriate?
 a. Cost of Goods Sold.
 b. Research and Development.
 c. Depreciation Expense.
 d. Sales.

8.25 Which of the following would *not* overstate current period net income?
 a. Capitalizing an expenditure that should be expensed.
 b. Failing to record a liability for an expenditure.
 c. Failing to record a check paying an item in Vouchers Payable.
 d. All of the above would overstate net income.

8.26 A client's purchasing system ends with the recording of a liability and its eventual payment. Which of the following best describes auditors' primary concern with respect to liabilities resulting from the purchasing system?

 a. Accounts payable are not materially understated.

 b. Authority to incur liabilities is restricted to one designated person.

 c. Acquisition of materials is not made from one vendor or one group of vendors.

 d Commitments for all purchases are made only after established competitive bidding procedures are followed.

8.27 Which of the following is an internal control activity that could prevent a paid disbursement voucher from being presented for payment a second time?

 a. Vouchers should be prepared by individuals who are responsible for signing disbursement checks.

 b. Disbursement vouchers should be approved by at least two responsible management officials.

 c. The date on a disbursement voucher should be within a few days of the date the voucher is presented for payment.

 d. The official who signs the check should compare the check with the voucher and should stamp "PAID" on the voucher documents.

8.28 Budd, the purchasing agent of Lake Hardware Wholesalers, has a relative who owns a retail hardware store. Budd arranged for hardware to be delivered by manufacturers to the retail store on a COD basis, thereby enabling his relative to buy at Lake's wholesale prices. Budd was probably able to accomplish this because of Lake's poor internal control over

 a. Purchase requisitions.

 b. Cash receipts.

 c. Perpetual inventory records.

 d. Purchase orders.

8.29 Which of the following is the best audit procedure for determining the existence of unrecorded liabilities?

 a. Examine confirmation requests returned by creditors whose accounts are on a subsidiary trial balance of accounts payable.

 b. Examine a sample of cash disbursements in the period subsequent to year end.

 c. Examine a sample of invoices a few days prior to and subsequent to the year end to ascertain whether they have been properly recorded.

 d. Examine unusual relationships between monthly accounts payable and recorded purchases.

8.30 Which of the following procedures is least likely to be performed before the balance sheet date?

 a. Observation of inventory.

 b. Review of internal control over cash disbursements.

 c. Search for unrecorded liabilities.

 d. Confirmation of receivables.

8.31 To determine whether accounts payable are complete, auditors perform a test to verify that all merchandise received has been recorded. The population for this test consists of all

 a. Vendors' invoices.

 b. Purchase orders.

 c. Receiving reports.

 d. Canceled checks.

(AICPA adapted)

8.32 When verifying debits to the perpetual inventory records of a nonmanufacturing company, auditors would be most interested in examining a sample of purchase

 a. Approvals.

 b. Requisitions.

 c. Invoices.

 d. Orders.

8.33 A furniture company ordered 84 tables from a supplier. The supplier accidentally sent only 48 tables. The tables were accepted by the receiving department at the furniture company. The invoice was eventually received but was for the original 84 tables. The furniture company paid the entire amount. Which of the following controls would have been *least* likely to have prevented this erroneous payment?

a. The copy of the purchase order sent to the furniture company's receiving department should not have shown an expected quantity.

b. Personnel in the furniture company's accounts payable department should compare the receiving report to the purchase invoice before creation of the voucher.

c. Personnel in the furniture company's cash disbursements department should compare the check that is prepared to all of the backup documentation.

d. Personnel in the furniture company's purchasing department should compare the purchase requisition to the purchase order.

8.34 Curtis, a maintenance supervisor, submitted maintenance invoices from a phony repair company and received the checks at a post office box. This should have been prevented by

a. Comparison of the company name to the approved vendor list by the check signer.

b. Recognition of the excess maintenance costs by Curtis's supervisor.

c. Refusal by the purchasing department to approve the vendor.

d. All of the above.

8.35 An audit team would most likely examine the detail support for which of the following charges?

a. Payroll Expense.

b. Cost of Goods Sold.

c. Supplies Expense.

d. Legal Expense.

8.36 Which of the following accounts would most likely be audited in connection with a related balance sheet account?

a. Property Tax Expense.

b. Payroll Expense.

c. Research and Development.

d. Legal Expense.

8.37 When auditing liabilities account balances, auditors are most concerned with management's assertion about

a. Existence.

b. Rights and Obligations.

c. Completeness.

d. Valuation and allocation.

8.38 In a test of controls, auditors may trace receiving reports to vouchers recorded in the voucher register. This is a test for

a. Occurrence.

b. Completeness.

c. Classification.

d. Cutoff.

Exercises, Problems, and Simulations

8.39 **Payable ICQ Items: Assertions, Tests of Controls, and Possible Errors or Frauds.** Following is a selection of items from internal control questionnaires.

1. Are purchase orders above a certain level approved by an officer?

2. Are quantity and quality of goods received determined at time of receipt by receiving personnel independent of the purchasing department?

3. Are vendors' invoices matched against purchase orders and receiving reports before a liability is recorded?

4. Are journal entries authorized at appropriate levels?

Required:

For each preceding item:

a. Identify the management assertion to which it applies.

b. Specify one test of controls auditors could use to determine whether the control was operating effectively.

c. Give an example of an error or fraud that could occur if the control were absent or ineffective.

d. Write a substantive procedure that could find errors or frauds that could result from the absence or ineffectiveness of the control items.

8.40 **Unrecorded Liabilities Procedures.** You are in the final stages of your audit of the financial statements of Ozine Corporation for the year ended December 31, 2008, when you are consulted by the corporation's president. The president believes there is no point to your examining the 2009 voucher register and testing data in support of 2009 entries. He stated that any bills pertaining to 2008 that were received too late to be included in the December voucher register were recorded by a year-end journal entry and the internal auditor tested for unrecorded liabilities after the year end. The president will provide you a letter certifying that there are no unrecorded liabilities.

Required:

a. Should your procedures for unrecorded liabilities be affected by the fact that the client made a journal entry to record 2008 bills that were received later? Explain.

b. Should your test for unrecorded liabilities be affected by the fact that a letter is obtained in which a responsible management official certifies that, to the best of that person's knowledge, all liabilities have been recorded? Explain.

c. Should your test for unrecorded liabilities be eliminated or reduced because of the internal audit work? Explain.

d. What sources, in addition to the 2009 voucher register, should you consider for locating possible unrecorded liabilities?

(AICPA adapted)

8.41 **Accounts Payable Confirmations.** Partners Clark and Kent, both CPAs, are planning their audit program for the audit of accounts payable on Marlboro Corporation's annual audit. Saturday afternoon they reviewed the thick file of last year's documentation and they both remembered too well the six days they spent last year on accounts payable.

Last year, Clark had suggested that they mail confirmations to 100 of Marlboro's suppliers. The company regularly purchases from about 1,000 suppliers and these account payable balances fluctuate widely, depending on the volume of purchase and the terms Marlboro's purchasing agent is able to negotiate. Clark's sample of 100 was designed to include accounts with large balances. In fact, the 100 accounts confirmed last year covered 80 percent of the total accounts payable. Both Clark and Kent had spent many hours tracking down minor differences reported in confirmation responses. Nonresponding accounts were investigated by comparing Marlboro's balance with monthly statements received from suppliers.

Required:

a. Identify the accounts payable audit objectives that auditors must consider in determining the audit procedures to be performed.

b. Identify situations when auditors should use accounts payable confirmations and discuss whether they are required to use them.

c. Discuss why the use of large dollar balances as the basis for selecting accounts payable for confirmation is not the most effective approach and indicate a more effective sample selection procedure that could be followed when choosing accounts payable for confirmation.

8.42 **Search for Unrecorded Liabilities.** Marsh, CPA, is the independent auditor for Compufast Corporation (Compufast). Compufast sells personal computers, peripheral equipment (printers, data storage), and a wide variety of programs for business and games. From experience on Compufast's previous audits, Marsh knew that the company's accountants were very much concerned with timely recording of revenues and receivables and somewhat less concerned with keeping up-to-date records of accounts payable and other liabilities. Marsh knew that the control environment was strong in the asset area and weak in the liability area.

Required:

List substantive procedures that Marsh and the audit staff can perform to obtain reasonable assurance that Compufast's unrecorded liabilities are discovered and adjusted in the financial statements currently under audit.

The following cases in Problems 8.43 and 8.44 are designed like the ones in the chapter.

8.43 **Fictitious Vendors, Theft, and Embezzlement.** Your assignment is to write the audit approach portion of the cases organized around these sections:

Objective: Express the objective in terms of the facts supposedly asserted in financial records, accounts, and statements.

Control: Write a brief explanation of desirable controls, missing controls, and especially the kinds of "deviations" that could arise from the situation described in the case.

Tests of controls: Write some procedures for getting evidence about existing controls, especially procedures that could discover deviations from controls. If there are no controls to test, then there are no procedures to perform; go to the next section. A "procedure" should instruct someone about the source(s) of evidence to tap and the work to do.

Audit of balance: Write some procedures for getting evidence about the existence, completeness, valuation, ownership, or disclosure assertions identified in your objective section above.

Discovery summary: Write a short statement about the discovery you expect to accomplish with your procedures.

Purchasing Stars Bailey Books, Inc., is a retail distributor of upscale books, periodicals, and magazines. Bailey has 431 retail stores throughout the southeastern states. Three full-time purchasing agents work at corporate headquarters. They are responsible for purchasing all inventory at the best prices available from wholesale suppliers. They can purchase with or without obtaining competitive bids. The three purchasing agents are R. McGuire in charge of purchasing books, M. Garza in charge of purchasing magazines and periodicals, and L. Collins (manager of purchasing) in charge of ordering miscellaneous items such as paper products and store supplies.

One of the purchasing agents is suspected of taking kickbacks from vendors. In return, Bailey is thought to be paying inflated prices, which first go to inventory and then to cost of goods sold and other expense accounts as the assets are sold or used.

The duties of L. Collins, the manager in charge, do not include audit or inspection of the performance of the other two purchasing agents. No one audits or reviews Collins's performance.

The purchasing system is computerized and detail records are retained. An extract from these records is in Exhibit 8.43.1.

This kickback scheme has been going on for two or three years. Several hundred thousand dollars could have been overpaid by Bailey Books.

EXHIBIT 8.43.1

BAILEY BOOKS, INCORPORATED
Selected Purchases 2006–2008

Vendor	Items Purchased	2006	2007	2008	Date of Last Bid	Percent of Purchases Bid (3-yr. period)
Armour	Books	$ 683,409	$ 702,929	$ 810,103	12/01/08	87%
Burdick	Sundries	62,443	70,949	76,722	—	—
Canon	Magazines	1,404,360	1,947,601	2,361,149	11/03/08	94
DeBois, Inc.	Paper	321,644	218,404	121,986	06/08/08	57
Elton Books	Books	874,893	781,602	649,188	07/21/08	91
Fergeson	Books	921,666	1,021,440	1,567,811	09/08/08	88
Guyford	Magazines	2,377,821	2,868,988	3,262,490	10/08/08	81
Hyman, Inc.	Supplies	31,640	40,022	46,911	10/22/08	—
Intertec	Books	821,904	898,683	949,604	11/18/08	86
Jerrico	Paper	186,401	111,923	93,499	10/04/08	72
Julian-Borg	Magazines	431,470	589,182	371,920	02/07/08	44
King Features	Magazines	436,820	492,687	504,360	11/18/08	89
Lycorp	Sundries	16,280	17,404	21,410	—	—
Medallian	Books	—	61,227	410,163	12/15/08	99
Northwood	Books	861,382	992,121	—	12/07/07	—
Orion Corp.	Paper	86,904	416,777	803,493	11/02/07	15
Peterson	Supplies	114,623	—	—	N/A	N/A
Quick	Supplies	—	96,732	110,441	11/03/08	86
Robertson	Books	2,361,912	3,040,319	3,516,811	12/01/08	96
Steele	Magazines	621,490	823,707	482,082	11/03/08	90
Telecom	Sundries	81,406	101,193	146,316	—	—
Union Bay	Books	4,322,639	4,971,682	5,368,114	12/03/08	97
Victory	Magazines	123,844	141,909	143,286	06/09/08	89
Williams	Sundries	31,629	35,111	42,686	—	—

(ACFE adapted)

8.44 **Grounds for Dismissal.** Ary Doe, IT Application Manager for The Coffee Company, signed a consulting services agreement with Fictitious Consulting Company (FCC). Doe was required to obtain written approval of the contract from a supervisor but forged the supervisor's signature. More than 100 invoices came in, which were approved with Doe's initials. Even though Doe's approval authority was only $5,000, many of the invoices were for more than $40,000.

FCC was not registered in the state or listed in telephone directories. The phone number was for a cell phone registered to Doe and the mailing address was a post office box. When Doe's supervisor asked to meet the FCC consultants, Doe was evasive, saying they "had just left" or "they were working away from the office." Ultimately Doe told her supervisor she had dismissed FCC, but she simply moved the charges to capital accounts the supervisor did not monitor. The Coffee Co. paid more than $3.7 million to FCC between December 1999 and August 2000. (M. Atkinson and M. Biliske, "Grounds for Dismissal," *Internal Auditor*, Feb. 2005.)

8.45 **Audit Simulation: Audit the PP&E and Depreciation Schedule.** Bart's Company has prepared the PP&E and depreciation schedule shown in Exhibit 8.45.1.

The following information is available (assume the beginning balance has been audited.):

* The land was purchased eight years ago when Building 1 was erected. The location was then remote but now is bordered by a major freeway. The appraised value of the land is $35 million.
* Building 1 has an estimated useful life of 35 years and no residual value.
* Building 2 was built by a local contractor this year. It also has an estimated useful life of 35 years and no residual value. The company occupied it on May 1 this year.
* Computer A system was purchased January 1 six years ago when the estimated useful life was eight years with no residual value. It was sold on May 1 for $500,000.
* Computer B system was placed in operation as soon as Computer A system was sold. It is estimated to be in use for six years with no residual value at the end.
* The company estimated the useful life of the press at 20 years with no residual value.
* Auto 1 was sold during the year for $1,000.
* Auto 2 was purchased on July 1. The company expects to use it five years and then sell it for $2,000.
* All depreciation is calculated on the straight-line method using months of service.

EXHIBIT 8.45.1 PP&E and Depreciation

| Description | Asset Cost ($000s) | | | | Accumulated Depreciation ($000s) | | | |
	Beginning Balance	Added	Sold	Ending Balance	Beginning Balance	Added	Sold	Ending Balance
Land	10,000			10,000				
Bldg 1	30,000			30,000	6,857	857		7,714
Bldg 2		42,000		42,000		800		800
Computer A	5,000		5,000	0	3,750	208	3,958	0
Computer B		3,500		3,500		583		583
Press	1,500			1,500	300	150		450
Auto 1	15		15	0	15		15	0
Auto 2		22		22		2		2
Total	46,515	45,522	5,015	87,022	10,922	2,600	3,973	9,549

Required:

a. Audit the depreciation calculations. Are there any errors? Put the errors in the form of an adjusting journal entry, assuming that 90 percent of the depreciation on the buildings and the press has been charged to Cost of Goods Sold and 10 percent is still capitalized in the inventory, and the other depreciation expense is classified as General and Administrative Expense (i.e., building and press depreciation is considered a product cost; inventory on hand includes 10 percent of the depreciation expense for buildings and the press: $180,700; COGS contains the other 90 percent: $1,626,300).

b. List two audit procedures for auditing the additions to PP&E.

c. What will auditors expect to find in the Gain and Loss on Sale of Assets account? What amount of cash flow from investing activities will be in the statement of cash flows?

8.46 **PP&E Assertions and Substantive Procedures.** This question contains three items that are management assertions about property and equipment. Following them are several substantive procedures for obtaining evidence about management's assertions.

Assertions

D ~ 1. The entity has legal right to property and equipment acquired during the year. *rights*

G ~ 2. Recorded property and equipment represent assets that actually exist at the balance sheet *- oc* date.

B ~ 3. Net property and equipment are properly valued at the balance sheet date. *- valuation*

Substantive Procedures

 A. Trace opening balances in the summary schedules to the prior-year audit documentation.

 B. Review the provision for depreciation expense and determine whether depreciable lives and methods used in the current year are consistent with those used in the prior year.

 C. Determine whether the responsibility for maintaining the property and equipment records is separated from the responsibility for custody of property and equipment.

 D. Examine deeds and title insurance certificates.

 E. Perform cutoff tests to verify that property and equipment additions are recorded in the proper period.

 F. Determine whether property and equipment are adequately insured.

 G. Physically examine all major property and equipment additions.

Required:

For each of the three assertions (1, 2, and 3), select the one best substantive audit procedure (A–G) for obtaining competent evidence. A procedure may be selected only once or not at all.

(AICPA adapted)

8.47 **Assertions and Substantive Procedures for Property, Plant, and Equipment (PP&E).** Following are the four assertions about account balances that can be applied to the audit of a company's PP&E, including assets the company has constructed itself: existence, rights and obligations, completeness, and valuation and allocation.

Required:

For each of the following substantive procedures, (a) cite one assertion most closely related to the evidence the procedure will produce (the primary assertion) and (b) when appropriate, cite one or more other assertions that also are related to the evidence the procedure will produce—the secondary assertion(s).

1. For major amounts charged to PP&E and a sample of smaller charges, examine supporting documentation for expenditure amounts, budgetary approvals, and capital work orders.

2. For a sample of capitalized PP&E, examine construction work orders in detail.

3. For a sample of construction work orders, vouch time and material charges to supporting payroll and material usage records. Review the reasonableness of the hours worked, the work description, and the material used.

4. Evaluate the policy and procedures for allocating overhead to the work orders and recalculate their application.

5. Determine whether corresponding retirements of replaced PP&E have occurred and have been properly entered in the detail records.

6. Select major additions for the year and a random sample of other additions and inspect the physical assets.

7. Vouch a sample of charges in the Repairs account and determine whether they are proper repairs and not capital items.

8. Review the useful lives, depreciation methods, and salvage values for reasonableness. Recalculate depreciation.

9. Study loan documents for terms and security of loans obtained for purchase of PP&E.

10. Inspect title documents for automotive and real estate assets.

11. Analyze the productive economic use of PP&E to determine whether any other-than-temporary impairment is evident.

(AICPA adapted)

8.48　**CAATs Application—PP&E.**　You are supervising the audit field work of Sparta Springs Company and need certain information from Sparta's equipment records, which are maintained on computer disk. The particular information is (1) net book value of assets so that your assistant can reconcile the subsidiary ledger to the general ledger control accounts (the general ledger contains an account for each asset type at each plant location) and (2) sufficient data to enable your assistant to find and inspect selected assets. Record layout of the master file:

　Asset number.

　Description.

　Asset type.

　Location code.

　Year acquired.

　Cost.

Accumulated depreciation, end of year (includes accumulated depreciation at the beginning of the year plus depreciation for year to date).

　Depreciation for the year to date.

　Useful life.

Required:

From the data file described earlier,

a. List the information needed to verify correspondence of the subsidiary detail records with the general ledger accounts. Does this work complete the audit of PP&E?

b. What additional data are needed to enable your assistant to inspect the assets?

8.49　**Audit Simulation: Search for Unrecorded Liabilities.**　The list of vouchers payable for Potter's Magic Shoppe at December is as follows:

Vendor	Invoice Date	Amount
Hagrid Cleaning Services	11/15	$ 4,322.43
Hermione's Hats	12/02	2,167.76
Lockhart Magic Books	12/31	6,489.11
Malfoy Financial Consultants	12/28	23,752.63
McGonagall Veterinary Supplies	12/23	4,590.60
Moaning Myrtle's Mystical Capes	10/14	11,529.88
Nicholas Fancy Headwear	12/29	51,268.62
Snape's Snakes	12/28	36,152.45
Weasley's Wands	12/28	6,400.55
Hogwart's Rentals	12/15	53,000.00
Total vouchers payable		$146,674.03

(handwritten annotations):

ⓑ Adjustments.

1. CK 1844 Jan rent exp. ~~Back~~ Sub out of total, should be in Jan, Not dec.

2. CK 1846

3. CK 1851 & 1847

4. CK 1853

5. CK 1854

Checks written in the following January are as follows

Check Number	Payee	Description	Invoice Date	Amount
1842	Malfoy Financial Consultants	Professional services	12/28	$23,752.63
1843	Hagrid Cleaning Services	October monthly cleaning	11/15	4,322.43
1844	Hogwart's Rentals	January rent	12/15	53,000.00
1845	Lockhart Magic Books	Inventory	12/31	6,489.11
1846	Dudley Pastries	Catering for office Christmas party	1/15	6,300.00
1847	Weasley's Wands	Inventory	12/28	6,400.55
1848	Rowlin's Enterprises	Trademark	1/1	10,000.00
1849	McGonagall Veterinary Supplies	Inventory	12/23	4,590.60
1850	Nicholas Fancy Headwear	Inventory	12/29	51,268.62
1851	Weasley's Wands	Inventory	12/31	6,400.55
1852	Hermione's Hats	Inventory	12/02	2,167.76
1853	Lockhart Magic Books	Inventory	12/31	6,489.11
1854	Hagrid Cleaning Service	November monthly cleaning	12/15	4,322.43
1855	Malfoy Financial Consultants	Professional services	1/28	13,888.56

[handwritten margin note: Just list out the problems, not the adj entry]

[handwritten margin note: Sales?]

Required:

a. Prepare an audit program for the audit of unrecorded liabilities for Potter's Magic Shoppe.

b. Prepare an adjusting journal entry to correct accounts payable. Potter's maintains perpetual inventory records and the inventory was counted and adjusted on December 31.

8.50 **Kaplan CPA Exam Simulation: Obtaining Evidence—Sales and Expense.**

Required:

Go to the Kaplan Web site at www.mhhe.com/louwers3e, click on AUD: Amberly Tool & Die case and the "Obtaining Evidence—Sales and Expense" tab, and complete the assigned task.

CPA REVIEW

8.51 **Kaplan CPA Exam Simulation: Accounts Payable Confirmations.**

Required:

a. Go to the Kaplan Web site at www.mhhe.com/louwers3e, click on AUD: Earhart&King case and the "Accounts Payable—Confirmations" tab, and complete the assigned task.

b. Go to the Kaplan Web site at www.mhhe.com/louwers3e, click on AUD: Earhart&King case and the "Obtaining Evidence—Accounts Payable" tab, and complete the assigned task.

CPA REVIEW

8.52 **ACL Assignment.**

Required:

Go to the ACL link at www.mhhe.com/louwers3e, click on "ACL Assignments," and complete the assignment for Chapter 8.

Appendix 8A

Internal Control Questionnaires

APPENDIX 8A.1 Internal Control Questionnaire—Acquisitions and Expenditures

	Yes/No	Comments

Occurrence

1. Are the purchasing department, accounting department, receiving department, and shipping department independent of each other?
2. Are receiving reports prepared for each item received and copies transmitted to inventory custodians? To purchasing? To the accounting department?
3. Are purchases made for employees authorized through the regular purchases procedures?
4. Are quantity and quality of goods received determined at the time of receipt by receiving personnel independent of the purchasing department?
5. Are vendors' invoices matched against purchase orders and receiving reports before a liability is recorded?
6. Do managers compare actual expenses to budget?
7. Are vouchers cancelled with a PAID stamp when paid?
8. Are shipping documents authorized and prepared for goods returned to vendors?
9. Are invoices approved for payment by a responsible officer?

Completeness

10. Are the purchase order forms prenumbered and the numerical sequence checked for missing documents?
11. Are receiving report forms prenumbered and the numerical sequence checked for missing documents?
12. Is the accounts payable department notified of goods returned to vendors?
13. Are vendors' invoices listed immediately on receipt?
14. Are unmatched receiving reports reviewed frequently and investigated for proper recording?
15. Is statistical analysis used to examine overall purchasing levels?
16. Are vendors' monthly statements reconciled with individual accounts payable accounts?

Accuracy

17. Are competitive bids received and reviewed for certain items?
18. Are all purchases made only on the basis of approved purchase requisitions?
19. Are all purchases, whether for inventory or expense, routed through the purchasing department for approval?
20. In the accounts payable department, are invoices checked against purchase orders and receiving reports for dates, quantities, prices, and terms?
21. Does the accounting department check invoices for mathematical accuracy?
22. Is the accounts payable listing balanced periodically with the general ledger control account?
23. Are purchase prices approved by a responsible purchasing officer?
24. Is accounts payable reconciled to the general ledger every period?
25. Are monthly statements reviewed by senior officials?

Classification

26. Do the chart of accounts and the accounting manual give instructions for classifying debit entries when purchases are recorded?
27. Are journal entries authorized at appropriate levels?

Cutoff

28. Does the accounting manual give instructions to date purchase/payable entries on the date of receipt of goods?

APPENDIX 8A.2 **Acquisitions and Expenditures—Computerized Controls**

	Yes/No	Comments
1. Does each terminal perform only designated functions? For example, the receiving clerk's terminal cannot accept a purchase order entry.		
2. Are an identification number and password (used on an individual basis) required to enter the nonautomatic purchase orders, vendors' invoices, and the receiving report information? Certain passwords have "read only" authorization. These are issued to personnel authorized to determine the status of various records, such as an open voucher, but not authorized to enter data.		
3. Are all input immediately logged to provide restart processing should any terminal become inoperative during the processing?		
4. Do transaction codes call up a full screen "form" on the terminals that appears to the operators in the same format as the original paper documents? Each clerk must enter the information correctly (online input validation) or the computer will not accept the data.		
5. Are all printed documents computer numbered and are the numbers stored as part of the record? All records in the open databases have the vendor's number as the primary search and matching field key. Of course, status searches could be made by another field. For example, the inventory number can be the search key to determine the status of a purchase of an item in short supply.		
6. Is a daily search of the open databases made? Purchases outstanding for more than 10 days and the missing "document" records are printed out on a report for investigation of the delay.		
7. Is the check signature printed, using a signature plate that is installed on the computer printer only when checks are printed? A designated person in the treasurer's office maintains custody of this signature plate and must take it to the computer room to be installed when checks are printed. This person also has the combination to the separate document storage room where the blank check stock is kept and is present at all check printing runs. The printed checks are taken immediately from the computer room for mailing.		

APPENDIX 8A.3 **Internal Control Questionnaire—PP&E and Related Transactions Processing**

	Yes/No	Comments
Occurrence:		
1. Is the accounting department notified of actions of disposal, dismantling, or idling a productive asset? For terminating a lease or rental?		
2. Are assets inspected periodically and physically counted?		
Completeness		
3. Are detailed property records maintained for the various assets included in PP&E?		
4. Are property tax assessments periodically analyzed? When was the last analysis?		
5. Are purchase contracts for major assets provided to the accounting department?		
Accuracy		
6. Are capital expenditure and leasing proposals prepared for review and approval by the board of directors or by responsible officers?		
7. When actual expenditures exceed authorized amounts, is the excess approved?		
8. Is there a uniform policy for assigning depreciation rates, useful lives, and salvage values?		
9. Are depreciation calculations checked by internal auditors or other officials?		
10. Are subsidiary records periodically reconciled to the general ledger accounts?		
Classification		
11. Does the accounting manual contain policies for capitalization of assets and expensing repair and maintenance?		
12. Are memorandum records of leased assets maintained?		
Cutoff		
13. Does the accounting manual give instructions for recording PP&E additions on a proper date of acquisition?		

APPENDIX 8A.4 Selected Computerized Questionnaire Items—General and Application Controls (PP&E)

	Yes/No	Comments
General Controls		
1. Are computer operators and programmers excluded from participating in the input and output control functions?		
2. Are programmers excluded from operating the computer?		
3. Is there a database administrator who is independent of computer operations, systems, programming, and users?		
4. Are computer personnel restricted from initiating, authorizing, or entering transactions or adjustments to the general ledger master database or the subsidiary ledger master database?		
5. Is access to the computer room restricted to authorized personnel?		
6. Is online access to data and programs controlled through the use of department account codes, personal ID numbers, and passwords?		
7. Are systems, programs, and documentation stored in a fireproof area?		
8. Can current files, particularly master files, be reconstructed from files stored in an off-site location?		
PP&E Application Controls		
1. Is terminal entry of asset data done on the basis of up-to-date written instructions?		
2. Are important asset data fields subject to input validation tests—missing data tests, limit and range tests, check digits, valid codes, and so forth?		
3. Does the computer print an input error report? Is this returned to the accounting department for correction of errors?		
4. Is an accounting department person assigned the responsibility for promptly correcting errors in asset input data and reentering the data for inclusion with the next batch?		
5. Are batch control totals used to reconcile computerized asset output to input control data?		
6 Is asset computerized output reviewed for reasonableness, accuracy, and legibility by the computer department personnel and the asset accounting personnel?		

Appendix 8B

Audit Programs

APPENDIX 8B.1

APOLLO SHOES, INC
Audit Program for Accounts Payable
12/31/08

	Performed by	Ref.
1. Obtain a trial balance of recorded accounts payable as of year end. a. Foot and trace the total to the general ledger account. b. Vouch a sample of balances to vendors' statements. Review the trial balance for related-party payables.		
2. Send confirmations to creditors, especially those with small or zero balances and those with whom the company has done significant business.		
3. Inquire of client personnel about their procedures for ensuring that all liabilities are recorded.		
4. Scan the open purchase order file at year end for indications of material purchase commitments at fixed prices. Obtain current prices and determine whether any adjustments for loss are needed.		
5. Obtain a list of unmatched vendor invoices and determine when the goods were received.		
6. If the goods were received before year end, trace the unmatched receiving reports to accounts payable and determine whether items recorded in the next accounting period need to be adjusted.		
7. Select a sample of cash disbursements from the accounting period following the balance sheet date. Vouch them to supporting documents (invoice, receiving report) to determine whether the related liabilities were recorded in the proper accounting period.		

APPENDIX 8B.2

APOLLO SHOES, INC Audit Program for Prepaid, Deferred, and Accrued Expenses 12/31/08	Performed by	Ref.
1. Obtain a schedule of all prepaid expenses, deferred costs, and accrued expenses. 2. Review documentation to determine whether each item is properly allocated to the current or future accounting periods. 3. Select significant additions to deferred and accrued amounts and vouch them to supporting invoices, contracts, or calculations. 4. Determine the basis for deferral and accrual and recalculate the recorded amounts. 5. Review the nature of each item, inquire of management, and determine whether the remaining balance will be recovered from future operations. 6. Scan income and expense items for items that should be considered prepaid, deferred, or accrued and allocated to current or future accounting periods. 7. Scan the expense accounts in the trial balance and compare to prior year. Investigate unusual difference that could indicate failure to account for a prepaid or accrual item. 8. Review each item to determine the proper current or noncurrent balance sheet classification.		

APPENDIX 8B.3

APOLLO SHOES, INC Audit Program for PPE and Related Accounts 12/31/08	Performed by	Ref.
Property, Plant, and Equipment 1. Summarize and foot detailed asset subsidiary records and reconcile to general ledger control account(s). 2. Select a sample of detail asset subsidiary records: a. Perform a physical observation (inspection) of the assets recorded. b. Inspect title documents, if any. 3. Prepare, or have client prepare, a schedule of asset additions and disposals for the period: a. Vouch to documents indicating proper approval. b. Vouch costs to invoices, contracts, or other supporting documents. c. Review all costs of shipment, installation, testing, and the like for proper capitalization. d. Vouch proceeds (on dispositions) to cash receipts or other asset records. e. Recalculate gain or loss on dispositions. f. Trace amounts to detail asset records and general ledger control account(s). 4. Observe a physical inventory taking of the assets and compare with detailed assets records. 5. Obtain written representations from management regarding pledge of assets as security for loans and leased assets. **Depreciation** 1. Analyze depreciation expense for overall reasonableness with reference to costs of assets and average depreciation rates. 2. Prepare, or have client prepare, a schedule of accumulated depreciation showing beginning balance, current depreciation, disposals, and ending balance. a. Trace to depreciation expense and asset disposition analyses. b. Recalculate depreciation expense and trace to general ledger account(s). c. Trace amounts to general ledger account(s). **Other Accounts** 1. Analyze insurance for adequacy of coverage. 2. Analyze property taxes to determine whether taxes due on assets have been paid or accrued. 3. Recalculate prepaid and/or accrued insurance and tax expenses. 4. Select a sample of rental expense entries. Vouch to rent/lease contracts to determine whether any leases qualify for capitalization. 5. Select a sample of repair and maintenance expense entries and vouch them to supporting invoices for evidence of property that should be capitalized.		

(continued)

APPENDIX 8B.3 *(continued)*

	Performed by	Ref.
Intangibles and Related Expenses		
1. Review merger documents for proper calculation of purchased goodwill.		
2. Inquire of management about legal status of patents, leases, copyrights, and other intangibles.		
3. Review documentation of new patents, copyrights, leaseholds, and franchise agreements.		
4. Select a sample of recorded R&D expenses. Vouch to supporting documents for evidence of proper classification.		
5. Recalculate amortization of goodwill, patents, and other intangibles.		
6. Perform tests for goodwill impairment.		

Appendix 8C

The Payroll Cycle

LEARNING OBJECTIVE

8. Describe the payroll cycle, including typical source documents and controls.

Every company has payroll. It can include manufacturing labor, research scientists, administrative personnel, or all of these. Payroll may take different forms. Personnel management and the payroll accounting cycle not only include transactions that affect the wage and salary accounts but also the transactions that affect pension benefits, deferred compensation contracts, compensatory stock option plans, employee benefits (such as health insurance), payroll taxes, and related liabilities for these costs. An important aspect of the payroll cycle is that it is self-policing. If employees are not paid, they will complain. If someone commits fraud by overpaying an employee and then diverts the difference, the employee will complain because his or her W-2 will be overstated and the employee will owe too much tax.

Typically, balance sheet accounts such as accrued payroll and accrued taxes are not material to companies' financial position. Also, because of the self-policing nature of the accounts and the regulatory restrictions of the internal revenue service and the department of labor, controls over payroll are normally stronger than in other areas. Therefore, most audit procedures related to payroll consist of evaluation of internal control and analytical procedures.

INHERENT RISKS

The major risks in the payroll cycle include
- Paying **ghost employees,** employees who do not exist (invalid transactions).
- Paying terminated employees (who have not been removed from payroll), whose paychecks are then endorsed with forged signatures by their supervisors.
- Overpaying for time or production (inaccurate transactions, improper valuation).
- Accounting incorrectly for costs and expenses (incorrect classification, improper or inconsistent presentation and disclosure).

AUDITING INSIGHT A Dedicated Employee

Prosecutors told the Winchester Crown Court in southern England that Jaswinder Bains, 45, was "blatantly dishonest" on the time cards for his job as a social worker on at least 24 occasions. In one instance, Bains allegedly claimed he worked 23 hours in one day on 29 case files, even though his credit card records show he was on a shopping spree in Paris that day. Bains testified that he did not falsify his work hour records. "I was working very long hours without sleep," he said. "I do not need a lot of sleep." He didn't explain what was behind his records on another day, when he claimed he worked 28 hours.

Source: SocietyGuardian.co.UK, May 9, 2005.

TYPICAL ACTIVITIES

Exhibit 8C.1 shows a payroll cycle. It starts with hiring (and firing) people and determining their wage rates and deductions, then proceeds to attendance and work (timekeeping), and ends with payment followed by preparation of governmental (tax) and internal reports.

The elements that follow are part of the payroll internal control system.

Personnel ①

A human relations department that is independent of the other functions should have authority to add new employees to the payroll, delete terminated employees, obtain authorizations for deductions, and transmit authority for pay rate changes to the payroll department. Terminated employees should have exit interviews so that this department's personnel can remove them from payroll. Final checks and W-2s should be mailed to the employee's home.

Supervision ②

Supervisors assign the employees to their jobs. Supervisors also approve any overtime. The immediate supervisor should approve all pay base data (number of hours worked, job number, absences, time off allowed for emergencies, and the like). Finally, supervisors compare production plans and budget reports to actual employee costs for discrepancies.

Timekeeping ③

Employees paid by the hour or on various incentive systems require records of time, production, piecework, or other measures of the basis for their pay. (Salaried employees do not require such detailed records.) Timekeeping or similar records are collected in a variety of ways. The traditional time clock is still used. More sophisticated computerized systems perform the same function without the paper time card. Production employees may clock in for various jobs or production processes in the system for assigning labor cost to various stages of production.

EXHIBIT 8C.1 **Typical Activities in the Payroll Cycle**

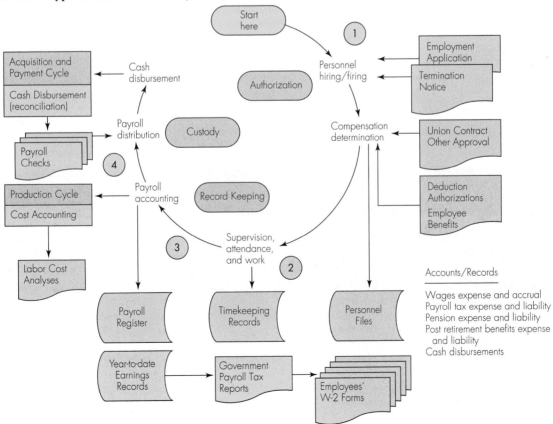

Supervisors should approve timekeeping records. In computerized systems, this approval may be automatic by virtue of the supervisory passwords used to input data into a computerized payroll system.

Record Keeping ④

The payroll accounting function should prepare individual paychecks, pay envelopes, or electronic transfers using rate and deduction information supplied by the personnel function and data supplied by the timekeeping–supervision functions. Persons in charge of the hiring, supervision, and timekeeping functions should not also prepare the payroll. They could be tempted to get checks for fictitious or terminated employees.

Payroll accounting maintains individual year-to-date earnings records and prepares the state and federal tax reports. The payroll tax returns and the annual W-2 report to employees are useful records for audit recalculation and analytical procedures.

The main feature of custody in the payroll cycle is the possession of the paychecks, cash, or electronic transfer codes for direct payments. A payroll distribution function should control the delivery of pay to employees so that unclaimed checks, cash, or incomplete electronic transfers are not returned to persons involved in any of the other functions.

Employees on Fixed Salary

The functional duties and responsibilities just described relate primarily to nonsalaried (hourly) employees. For salaried employees, the system is simplified by not having to collect timekeeping data. In nonmanufacturing businesses, the cost accounting operations can be very simple or even nonexistent.

The relative importance of each of these four areas should be determined for each engagement in light of the nature and organization of the company's operations.

Review Checkpoints

8C.1 What functional responsibilities are associated with the payroll cycle?

8C.2 Which duties should be separated in the payroll cycle?

8C.3 How does a company ensure that terminated employees are removed from the payroll?

8C.4 Describe a walk-through of the payroll transaction flow from hiring authorization to payroll check disbursement. (a) What document copies would be collected? (b) What controls should be noted?

AUDITING INSIGHT Not Enough Control, No Feedback, Bye-Bye Money

Homer had been in payroll accounting for a long time. He knew it was not uncommon to pay a terminated employee severance benefits and partial pay after termination. Homer received the termination notices and the data for the final paychecks. However, he also knew how to keep the terminated employee on the payroll for another week, pay a full week's compensation, change the electronic transfer code, and take the money for himself. The only things he could not change were the personnel department's copy of the termination notices, the payroll register, and the individual employee pay records used for withholding tax and W-2 forms.

Fortunately, nobody reconciled the cost accounting labor charges to the payroll. The supervisors did not get a copy of the payroll register for post payment approval, so they did not have any opportunity to notice the extra week. Nobody ever reviewed the payroll with reference to the termination notices. Former employees never complained about more pay and withholding reported on their W-2s than they actually received.

Homer and his wife retired comfortably to a villa in Spain on a nest egg that had grown to $450,000. After his retirement, the company experienced an unexpected decrease in labor costs and higher profits.

AUDIT EVIDENCE IN MANAGEMENT REPORTS AND FILES

Payroll systems produce numerous reports. Some are internal reports and bookkeeping records. Others are government tax reports.

Personnel Files

The personnel, human relations, or labor relations department keeps individual employee files. The files usually include an employment application, a background investigation report, a notice of hiring, a job classification with pay rate authorization, and employee authorizations for deductions. When employees retire, resign, or are otherwise terminated, appropriate notices of termination are filed.

A personnel file should establish a person's existence and employment. The background investigation report is important for employees in such sensitive areas as accounting, finance, and asset custody positions. News accounts are rich with reports of errors and frauds perpetrated by people who falsified their credentials.

Payroll Register

The *payroll register* is a special journal. It typically contains a row for each employee with columns for the gross regular pay, gross overtime pay, income tax withheld, Social Security and Medicare tax withheld, other deductions, and net pay. The net pay amount usually is transferred from the general bank account to a special **imprest bank account** that maintains a zero or fixed balance.

Payroll department records contain the canceled checks (or a similar computerized deposit record). The checks will contain the employees' endorsements on the back.

Labor Cost Analysis

One of the internal reports in the payroll cycle is a report of labor cost to the cost accounting department, thus linking the payroll cycle with cost accounting in the production cycle. The cost accounting department can receive its information in more than one way. Some companies have systems that independently report time and production work data from the production floor directly to the cost accounting department. Other companies let their cost accounting department receive labor cost data from the payroll department. When the data are received independently, they can be reconciled with a report from the payroll department.

The cost accounting department (or a similar accounting function) is responsible for the labor distribution. This is the most important part of the presentation and disclosure assertion with respect to payroll. The labor distribution is an assignment of payroll to the accounts where it belongs for internal and external reporting.

Payroll data flow from the hiring process, through the timekeeping function, into the payroll department, then to the cost accounting department, and finally to the accounting entries that record the payroll for inventory cost determination and financial statement presentation. The same data are used for various governmental and tax reports.

AUDITING INSIGHT Look at the Endorsements

Marsha, an assistant accountant was instructed to look at the endorsements on the back of a sample of canceled payroll checks. Marsha noticed three occurrences of the payee's signature followed by a second signature. Although scrawled almost illegibly, the second signatures were identical and were later identified as Fred's (the payroll accountant) handwriting. Fred had taken unclaimed checks and converted (stolen) them. When cashing these "third-party checks," banks and stores had required Fred to produce identification and endorse the checks that already had been "endorsed" by the employee payee. The lesson is that second endorsements are a red flag.

Beware the "Clearing Account"

Clearing accounts are temporary storage places for transactions awaiting final accounting. All clearing accounts should have zero balances after the accounting is completed. A balance in a clearing account means that some amounts have not been classified properly in the accounting records.

Governmental and Tax Reports

Payroll systems have complications introduced by the federal income and Social Security tax laws. Several reports are produced. Auditors can use them in tests of controls and substantive procedures produced by accumulating numerous payroll transactions.

Companies in financial difficulty have been known to try to postpone payment of employee taxes withheld. However, the consequences can be serious. The IRS can and will padlock the business and seize its assets for nonpayment.

Year-to-Date Earnings Records

The year-to-date (YTD) earnings records are the cumulative subsidiary records of each employee's gross pay, deductions, and net pay. Each time a periodic payroll is produced, the YTD earnings records are updated for the new information. The YTD earnings records are a subsidiary ledger of the wages and salaries cost and expense in the financial statements. Like any subsidiary and control account relationship, their sum (i.e., the gross pay amounts) should be equal to the costs and expenses in the financial statements. These YTD records provide the data for periodic governmental tax forms. They can be reconciled to the tax reports. Details can be compared to the company's YTD earnings records.

Employee W-2 Reports

The **W-2** is the annual report of gross salaries and wages and the income, Social Security, and Medicare taxes withheld. Copies are filed with the Social Security Administration and the IRS, and copies are sent to employees for use in preparing their income tax returns. The W-2s contain the annual YTD accumulations for each employee. Auditors can use the name, address, Social Security number, and dollar amounts in certain procedures to obtain evidence about the existence of the employees. The W-2s can be reconciled to the payroll tax reports.

W-2s should be mailed directly to employees' homes so if someone has been collecting additional pay in an employee's name (for example, if an employee leaves and the supervisor continues to send in a time card), the employee can spot the added income.

The assessment of payroll cycle control risk normally takes on added importance because most companies have fairly elaborate and well-controlled personnel and payroll functions. The transactions in this cycle are numerous during the year yet result in small amounts in balance sheet accounts at year end. Therefore, in most audit engagements, the review of controls, tests of controls, and substantive tests of transactions constitute the major portion of the evidence gathered for these accounts. On most audits, the substantive procedures devoted to auditing the payroll-related account balances are limited.

Control Considerations

Control procedures for proper separation of responsibilities should be in place and operating. By referring to Exhibit 8C.1, you can see that proper separation involves authorization (personnel department hiring and firing, pay rate, and deduction authorizations) by persons who do not have payroll preparation, paycheck distribution, or reconciliation duties. Payroll distribution (custody) is in the hands of persons who do not authorize employees' pay rates or time or prepare the payroll checks. Record keeping is performed by payroll and cost accounting personnel who do not make authorizations or distribute pay. Combinations of two or more of the duties of authorization, payroll preparation and record keeping, and payroll distribution in one person, one office, or one computerized system can open the door for errors and frauds.

In addition, the internal controls should provide for detailed control checking procedures. Examples of these controls follow:

- Periodic comparison of the payroll register to the personnel department files to check hiring authorizations and any terminated employees who have not been deleted.
- Periodic rechecking of wage rate and deduction authorizations.
- Reconciliation of time and production paid to cost accounting calculations.
- Quarterly reconciliation of YTD earnings records with tax returns.
- Payroll bank account reconciliation.

Some companies send each supervisor a copy of the payroll register, showing the employees paid under the supervisor's authority and responsibility. The supervisor has a chance to reapprove the payroll after it is completed. Managers also should receive a comparison of actual labor costs to standards to review any unusual differences.

The payroll report sent to cost accounting can be reconciled to the labor records used to charge labor cost to production. The cost accounting function should determine whether the labor paid is the same as the labor cost used in the cost accounting calculations. Finally, the payroll bank account can be reconciled like any other bank account.

Information about the payroll cycle control often is gathered initially by completing an internal control questionnaire (ICQ). An example of an ICQ for payroll controls is in Exhibit 5.9. You can study this questionnaire for details of desirable controls. It is organized with headings that identify the important assertions.

Computerized Payroll

Complex computerized systems that gather payroll data, calculate payroll amounts, print checks, and transfer computerized deposits are found in many companies. Even though the technology is complex, the basic management and control functions of ensuring a flow of data to the payroll department should be in place. Various paper records and approval signatures may not exist. They may be imbedded in computerized payroll systems. Companies often use computer service organizations to process their payroll because it is a specialized function that can be performed effectively and efficiently by an organization whose specialty is to keep up with and apply changes in tax laws and rates. Thus, auditors should refer to the requirements of *SAS 70* (Service Organizations) in addressing this function.

Review Checkpoints

8C.5 What documents should be included in an employee's personnel file?

8C.6 What features of a payroll system could be expected to prevent or detect (a) payment of a fictitious employee and (b) omission of payment to an employee?

8C.7 What are the most common errors and frauds in the personnel and payroll cycle? Which control characteristics are auditors looking for to prevent or detect these errors and frauds?

FRAUD CASE: EXTENDED AUDIT PROCEDURES (SAS 99)

Case 8C.1

Time Card Forgeries

PROBLEM

A personnel agency assigned Nurse Jane to work at County Hospital. She claimed payroll hours on agency time cards that showed approval signatures of a hospital nursing shift supervisor. The shift supervisor had been terminated by the hospital several months prior to the periods covered by the

time cards in question. Nurse Jane worked one or two days per week but submitted time cards for a full 40-hour workweek. The leasing agency paid Nurse Jane and then billed County Hospital for the wages and benefits. Supporting documents were submitted with the leasing agency's bills.

Each hospital workstation keeps ward shift logs, which are sign-in sheets showing nurses on duty at all times. Nurses sign in and sign out when going on and going off duty. County Hospital maintains personnel records showing, among other things, the period of employment of its own nurses, supervisors, and other employees.

Nurse Jane's wages and benefits were billed to the hospital at $22 per hour. False time cards overcharging about 24 extra hours per week cost the hospital $528 per week. Nurse Jane was assigned to County Hospital for 15 weeks during the year, so she caused overcharges of about $7,900. However, she told three of her friends about the procedure and they overcharged the hospital another $24,000.

AUDIT APPROACH

Control procedures should include a hiring authorization to put employees on the payroll. When temporary employees are used, this authorization includes contracts for nursing time, conditions of employment, and terms including the contract reimbursement rate. Control records of attendance and work should be kept (ward shift log). Supervisors should approve time cards or other records used by the payroll department to prepare paychecks. In this case, the contract with the leasing agency provided that approved time cards had to be submitted as supporting documentation for the agency billings.

Although the procedures and documents for control were in place, the controls did not operate because no one at the hospital ever compared the ward shift logs to time cards and no one examined the supervisory approval signatures for their validity. The fraud was easy in the personnel agency situation because the nurses submitted their own time cards to the agency for payment. The same fraud could be operated by the hospital's own employees if they, too, could write their time cards and submit them to the payroll department.

Auditors should make inquiries (e.g., internal control questionnaire) about the error-checking activities performed by hospital accounting personnel. Tests of controls are designed to determine whether control procedures are followed properly by the organization. Because the comparison and checking activities were not performed, there is nothing to test.

Select a sample of leasing agency billings and their supporting documentation (time cards). Vouch rates billed by the agency to the contract for agreement to proper rate. Vouch time claimed to hospital work attendance records (ward shift logs). Obtain handwriting examples of supervisors' signatures and compare them to the approval signatures on time cards. Use personnel records to determine whether supervisors were actually employed by the hospital at the time they approved the time cards. Use available work attendance records to determine whether supervisors were actually on duty at the time they approved the time cards.

DISCOVERY SUMMARY

The auditors quickly found that Nurse Jane (and others) had not signed in on ward shift logs for days they claimed to have worked. Further investigation showed that the supervisors who supposedly signed the time cards were not even employed by the hospital at the time their signatures were used for approvals. Handwriting comparison showed that the signatures were not written by the supervisors.

The leasing agency was informed and refunded the $31,900 overpayment that the auditors had proved. The auditors continued to comb the records for more!

(Adapted from vignette published in *Internal Auditor*.)

Key Terms	
	clearing accounts: Temporary storage places for transactions awaiting final accounting. They should eventually have zero balances, 336
	ghost employees: Fictitious or separated employees fraudulently maintained on the payroll to obtain checks, 332
	imprest bank account: An account that is maintained at a zero or fixed balance in the general ledger. Checks written on the account are offset by deposits of the same amount. Used for special purposes such as payroll or branch banking, 335
	W-2: The annual report of gross salaries and wages and the income, Social Security, and Medicare taxes withheld, 336

Multiple Choice Questions for Practice and Review

8C.8 An audit team most likely would assess control risk at the maximum if the payroll department supervisor is responsible for
 a. Examining authorization forms for new employees.
 b. Comparing payroll registers with original batch transmittal data.
 c. Authorizing payroll rate changes for all employees.
 d. Hiring all subordinate payroll department employees.

 (AICPA adapted)

8C9 Which of the following departments most likely would approve changes in pay rates and deductions from employee salaries?
 a. Personnel.
 b. Treasurer.
 c. Controller.
 d. Payroll.

 (AICPA adapted)

8C.10 Matthew Corp. has changed from a system of recording time worked on clock cards to a computerized payroll system in which employees record time in and out with magnetic cards. The computerized system automatically updates all payroll records. Because of this change
 a. A generalized computer audit program must be used.
 b. Part of the audit trail is altered.
 c. The potential for payroll-related fraud is diminished.
 d. Transactions must be processed in batches.

 (AICPA adapted)

8C.11 Effective control over the cash payroll function would mandate which of the following?
 a. The payroll clerk should fill the envelopes with cash and a computation of the net wages.
 b. Unclaimed payroll envelopes should be retained by the paymaster.
 c. Each employee should be asked to sign a receipt.
 d. A separate checking account for payroll should be maintained.

 (AICPA adapted)

8C.12 A large retail enterprise has established a policy that requires the paymaster to deliver all unclaimed payroll checks to the internal audit department at the end of each payroll distribution day. This policy was most likely adopted to
 a. Assure that employees who were absent on a payroll distribution day are not paid for that day.
 b. Prevent the paymaster from cashing checks that are unclaimed for several weeks.
 c. Prevent a bona fide employee's check from being claimed by another employee.
 d. Detect any fictitious employee who may have been placed on the payroll.

 (AICPA adapted)

8C.13 Auditors will ordinarily ascertain whether payroll checks are properly endorsed during the audit of
 a. Clock cards.
 b. The voucher system.
 c. Cash in bank.
 d. Accrued payroll.

 (AICPA adapted)

8C.14 In determining the effectiveness of an entity's policies and procedures relating to the occurrence assertion for payroll transactions, auditors most likely would inquire about and
 a. Observe the separation of duties concerning personnel responsibilities and payroll disbursement.
 b. Inspect evidence of accounting for prenumbered payroll checks.
 c. Recompute the payroll deductions for employee fringe benefits.
 d. Verify the preparation of the monthly payroll account bank reconciliation.

 (AICPA adapted)

8C.15 Which of the following activities most likely would be considered a weakness in an entity's internal control over payroll?

 a. A voucher for the amount of the payroll is prepared in the general accounting department based on the payroll department's payroll summary.

 b. Payroll checks are prepared by the accounts payable department and signed by the treasurer.

 c. The employee who distributes payroll checks returns unclaimed payroll checks to the payroll department.

 d. The personnel department sends employees' termination notices to the payroll department.

(AICPA adapted)

Exercises, Problems, and Simulations

8C.16 **Major Risks in Payroll Cycle.** Prepare a schedule of the major risks in the payroll cycle. Identify the financial statement assertions related to each. Lay out a two-column schedule like this:

Payroll Cycle Risk	Assertion

8C.17 **Payroll Authorization in a Computerized System.** Two accountants were discussing control procedures and tests of controls for payroll systems. The senior accountant in charge of the engagement said: "It is impossible to determine who authorizes transactions when the payroll account is computerized."

Required:

Evaluate the senior accountant's statement about control in a computerized payroll system. List the points in the flow of payroll information where authorization takes place.

8C.18 **Audit Simulation: Payroll Processed by a Service Organization.** Assume that you are the audit senior conducting a review of the payroll system of a new client. In the process of interviewing the payroll department manager, she makes the following statement: "We don't need many controls since our payroll is done outside the company by Automated Information Processing, a service bureau."

Required:

Evaluate the payroll department manager's statement and describe how a service organization affects an auditors' review of controls.

8C.19 **Audit Simulation: Payroll Audit Procedures, Computers, and Sampling.** You are the senior auditor in charge of the annual audit of Onward Manufacturing Corporation for the year ending December 31. The company is of medium size, having only 300 employees. All 300 employees are union members paid by the hour at rates set forth in a union contract, a copy of which is furnished to you. Job and pay rate classifications are determined by a joint union–management conference and a formal memorandum is placed in each employee's personnel file.

Every week, clock cards prepared and approved in the shop are collected and transmitted to the payroll department. The total of labor hours is summed on a calculator and entered on each clock card. Batch and hash totals are obtained for the following: (1) labor hours and (2) last four digits of Social Security numbers. These data are input into a disk file, batch balanced, and batch processed. The clock cards (with cost classification data) are sent to the cost accounting department.

The payroll system is computerized. As each person's payroll record is processed, the Social Security number is matched to a table (in a separate master file) to obtain job classification and pay rate data, then the pay rate is multiplied by the number of hours and the check is printed. (Ignore payroll deductions for the following requirements.)

Required:

 a. What audit procedures would you recommend to obtain evidence that payroll data are accurately totaled and transformed into machine-readable records? What deviation rate might you expect? What tolerable deviation rate would you set? What "items" would you sample? What factors should be considered in setting the size of your sample?

 b. What audit procedures would you recommend to obtain evidence that the pay rates are appropriately assigned and used in figuring gross pay? In what way, if any, would these procedures be different if the gross pay were calculated by hand instead of on a computer?

8C.20 **Payroll Tests of Controls.** The diagram in Exhibit 8C.20.1 describes several payroll tests of controls. It shows the direction of the tests, leading from samples of clock cards, payrolls, and cumulative year-to-date earnings records to blank squares.

Required:

For each blank square in Exhibit 8C.20.1, write a payroll test of controls procedure and describe the evidence it can produce. (Hint: Refer to Exhibit 5.12.)

EXHIBIT 8C.20.1
Diagram of Payroll Tests of Controls

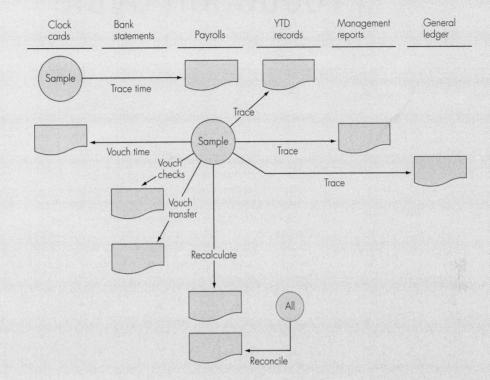

Production Cycle

Professional Standards References

Compendium Section	Document Reference	Topic
Various*	AS 5	"An Audit of Internal Control over Financial Reporting That Is Integrated with an Audit of Financial Statements"
AU 311	SAS 108	"Planning and Supervision"
	ISA 300	"Planning an Audit of Financial Statements"
AU 312	SAS 107	"Audit Risk and Materiality in Conducting an Audit"
AU 313	SAS 110	"Performing Audit Procedures in Response to Assessed Risks and Evaluating the Audit Evidence Obtained"
	ISA 330	"The Auditor's Procedures in Response to Assessed Risks"
AU 316	SAS 99	"Consideration of Fraud"
	ISA 240	"The Auditor's Responsibility to Consider Fraud in an Audit of Financial Statements"
AU 319	SAS 109	"Understanding the Entity and Its Environment and Assessing the Risks of Material Misstatement"
	ISA 330	"The Auditor's Procedures in Response to Assessed Risks"
AU 324	SAS 70	"Service Organizations"
AU 326	SAS 106	"Audit Evidence"
	ISA 500	"Audit Evidence"
AU 329	SAS 56	"Analytical Procedures"
	ISA 520	"Analytical Procedures"
AU 333A	SAS 85	"Management Representations"
	ISA 580	"Management Representations"
AU 339	SAS 103	"Audit Documentation"
	AS 3	"Audit Documentation"
	ISA 230	"Audit Documentation"
AU 342	SAS 57	"Auditing Accounting Estimates"
	ISA 540	"Audit of Accounting Estimates"
AU 901	SAS 1	"Public Warehouses—Controls and Auditing Procedures for Goods Held"

*AS 5 amends AU 230, AU 310, AU 312, AU 313, AU 315 AU 316, AU 319, AU 322, AU 325, AU 328, AU 332, AU 333, AU 341, AU 342, AU 380, AU 508, AU 530, AU 543, AU 560, AU 561, AU 711, AU 722, AS 3, and AS 4.

> There is one rule for industrialists and that is: Make the best quality of goods possible at the lowest cost possible, paying the highest wages possible.
>
> *Henry Ford*

Learning Objectives

In the production cycle, materials, labor, and overhead are converted into finished goods (inventory) and services. Even companies that do not sell products sell services that are generated solely from the labor of employees. These services still represent costs that have to be accounted for and recovered by revenues. This chapter covers the production cycle, focusing on determining inventory valuation and cost of goods sold. Observation of the client's physical inventory count is such an important audit procedure that it is required by GAAS. This chapter discusses procedures to be followed in observing the physical

inventory count. It also discusses procedures for auditing the accumulation and pricing of the inventory and recording it in the general ledger.

This chapter includes several short cases to illustrate the application of audit procedures in situations in which errors and frauds can be discovered.

Your objectives are to be able to:

1. Describe the production cycle, including typical source documents and controls.

2. Give examples of tests of controls over conversion of materials and labor in a production process.

3. Identify and describe considerations involved in the observation of physical inventory and tests of inventory pricing and compilation.

4. Describe some common errors and frauds in the accounting for production costs and related cost of goods sold and design some audit and investigation procedures for detecting these errors and frauds.

PHAR-MOR, INC.

From his childhood, Mickey Monus loved all sports, especially basketball. However, with limited talents and height (5 foot 9 on a good day), he would never play on a professional team. Monus did have one trait, however, shared by top athletes: an unquenchable thirst for winning.

Monus transferred his boundless energy from the basketball court to the boardroom. He acquired a single drugstore in Youngstown, Ohio, and, within 10 years, he had built 299 more stores and formed the national chain **Phar-Mor.** Unfortunately, it was all built on ghost goods—undetected inventory overstatements—and phony profits that eventually would be the downfall of Monus and his company and would cost the company's auditors millions of dollars. Here is how it happened.

After acquiring the first drugstore, Monus dreamed of building his modest holdings into a large pharmaceutical empire using power buying, that is, offering products at deep discounts. First, he took his one unprofitable, unaudited store and increased the profits with the stroke of a pen by adding phony inventory figures. Armed only with his gift of gab and a set of inflated financials, Monus bilked money from investors, bought eight stores within a year, and began the mini-empire that grew to 300 stores. Monus became a financial icon and his organization gained near-cult status in Youngstown. He decided to fulfill a sports fantasy by starting the World Basketball League (WBL) in which no players would be over six feet five inches tall. He pumped $10 million of Phar-Mor's money into the league.

However, the public did not like short basketball players and were not buying tickets, so Monus poured more Phar-Mor money into the WBL. One day a travel agent who booked flights for league players received a $75,000 check for WBL expenses, but it was disbursed from a Phar-Mor bank account. The employee thought it odd that Phar-Mor would be paying the team's expenses. Because she was an acquaintance of one of Phar-Mor's major investors, she showed him the check. Alarmed, the investor began conducting his own investigation into Monus's illicit activities and helped expose an intricate financial fraud that caused losses of over $1 billion.

The Game Is Over

Generating phony profits over an entire decade was no easy feat. Phar-Mor's CFO said the company was losing serious money because it was selling goods for less than it had paid for them. A significant mantra of Phar-Mor was "we will not be undersold by Wal-Mart." (Remember that a highly competitive industry can be an important red flag for management fraud.) Nevertheless, Monus argued that through Phar-Mor's *power buying,* it would become so large that it could sell its way out of trouble. Eventually, the CFO caved in—under extreme pressure from Monus—and for the next several years, he and some of his staff kept two sets of books: the ones they showed the auditors and the ones that reflected the awful truth.

Phar-Mor's management dumped the losses into the "bucket account" and then used "blow-out" entries to reallocate the sums to the company's hundreds of stores in the form of increases in inventory costs. They issued fake invoices for merchandise purchases, made phony journal entries to increase inventory and decrease cost of sales, recognized inventory purchases but failed to accrue a liability, and overcounted and double-counted merchandise. The finance department was able to conceal the inventory shortages because the auditors observed inventory in only four stores out of 300 and they informed Phar-Mor, months in advance, which stores they would visit. Phar-Mor executives fully stocked the four selected stores but allocated the phony inventory increases to the other 296 stores. Regardless of the accounting tricks, Phar-Mor was heading for collapse. During its last audit, cash was so tight suppliers threatened to cut the company off for nonpayment of bills.

The auditors never uncovered the fraud, for which they paid dearly. This failure cost the audit firm over $300 million in civil judgments. The CFO, who did not profit personally, was sentenced to 33 months in prison. Monus himself went to jail for five years.[1]

INHERENT RISKS IN THE PRODUCTION CYCLE

The Phar-Mor case illustrates how even a relatively simple inventory can be manipulated and misstated. Many other corporate frauds like Crazy Eddie's, Leslie Fay, and Health Management were concealed by creating nonexistent or overvalued inventory. Inventory is often the largest current asset on a company's balance sheet, and it is also likely to be the most complex account. Imagine trying to value the cars at General Motors, the computers at IBM, or the oil reserves at ExxonMobil. How about the $500 million of livestock at Tyson Foods? Even inventories of simple commodities present issues of measurement and valuation. Inventories of more complex items such as electronics or biochemicals can require specialists.

A number of problems can arise in accounting for inventory. Some inventories are very susceptible to theft. Others require complex cost build-ups (especially if they are valued at LIFO). GAAP require inventory to be stated at the lower of cost or market. Cost is the total price paid, including freight-in, or estimates of actual costs using LIFO, FIFO, or an average. Market is replacement cost limited by a ceiling—**net realizable value (NRV)**—or floor—NRV less a normal profit. Items should be added to inventory when the company has title to them and removed to cost of goods sold when the related revenue is recognized.[2] These multiple and often subjective evaluations make inventory a high-risk area that is often used by management to overstate assets.

Unethical managers might prefer to manipulate cost of goods sold (and the related inventory account) instead of other expenses because of the double effect on the financial statements. When ending inventory is overstated, assets are overstated and cost of goods sold is understated, thereby increasing both total assets and income. Analysts often look at a company's profit margins to determine how well it is managing costs and to determine whether the company can maintain sufficient markup to cover other operating and nonoperating costs and be competitive. Another reason that inventory is an inviting target for manipulation is the complexity and subjectivity involved in accounting for it.

TYPICAL ACTIVITIES IN THE PRODUCTION CYCLE

LEARNING
OBJECTIVE

1. Describe the production cycle, including typical source documents and controls.

When auditing a manufacturer, whether that manufacturer is a small entity producing specialty goods or a Fortune 100 Corporation making millions of units each year, it is paramount that an auditor understand all the stages involved with converting raw materials into finished goods. If this process is not properly controlled, not only are financial misstatements likely, but mismanagement can quickly put a company out of business.

[1] J. T. Wells, "Ghost Goods: How to Spot Phantom Inventory," *Journal of Accountancy*, June 2001.
[2] AICPA, *Restatement and Revision of Accounting Research Bulletin No. 43* (New York: AICPA, June 1953).

EXHIBIT 9.1
Relationship of Business Cycles

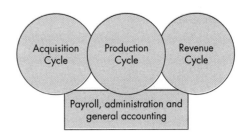

The production cycle links the acquisition cycle, in which goods and services are purchased, to the revenue cycle, in which the inventory is sold (see Exhibit 9.1) These cycles, along with the payroll cycle, account for all additions and reductions of inventory items. Thus, the production cycle is mostly concerned with accounting for inventory as it moves through the production stages from raw materials to work-in-process to finished goods and for accumulating accurate costs of the inventory items.

Sales Forecasts

Production activities start with a sales forecast. A production planner compares a marketing projection of product sales, based on past performance and marketing initiatives, with current finished goods inventory. Based on this forecast and other pertinent factors (e.g., production setup costs, scheduled equipment maintenance, and raw material inventories) the production planner can determine both the type and quantity of products that need to be produced to meet anticipated demand and can schedule the products in a production plan.

Production Planning

The goal of production planning is to provide a schedule, called the **production plan,** for manufacturing such that quality products will be available at the appropriate time for the least cost. For example, production planners must balance the finished-goods warehousing costs associated with making large (high-quantity) production runs with the changeover costs of making several smaller (low-quantity) production runs. In addition, production planners must integrate corporate strategies such as long-range plans and just-in-time (JIT) inventory management. Exhibit 9.2 shows the activities and accounting involved in a production cycle. As you follow the exhibit, you can track the elements of a control system that are described in the following sections.

The physical output of a production cycle is inventory (starting with raw materials, proceeding to work-in-process and then to finished goods). Exhibit 9.2 shows in greater detail the connection of inventory to the revenue and collection cycle in terms of orders and deliveries.

Most of the transactions in a production cycle are cost accounting allocations, unit cost determinations, and standard cost calculations. These are internal transactions produced entirely within the company's accounting system. Exhibit 9.2 shows the elements of depreciation cost calculation, cost of goods sold determination, and production cost analysis as examples of these transactions.

Production

The job of the production planner is one of the most critical in any manufacturing operation. Not only does the production planner create a production plan, but based on the production plan and the **bill of materials** (a specification of the type and quantity of component materials authorized for the production), the production planner must identify the total quantity of raw materials necessary for production. Once the planner knows what raw materials are required (from the bill of materials), he or she will use the **raw material inventory status report** to determine if enough raw materials are in stock to complete production. If insufficient raw materials exist, additional materials must be purchased and,

EXHIBIT 9.2 **Production Cycle**

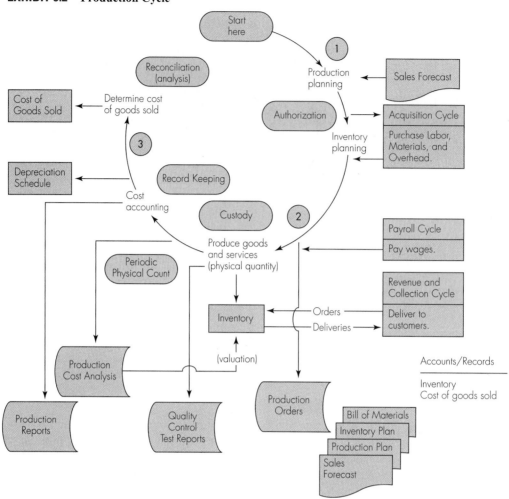

if required, the planner must send a purchase requisition to purchasing (which begins the expenditure cycle as discussed in Chapter 8). Because of purchase lead times, a change to the production plan may be necessary.

Once the production schedule has been finalized, it is generally shared with managers in the sales/marketing department, production department, and possibly human resources who may be required to "sign off" as evidence of their approval of the plan. Managers may request adjustments to the schedule or may need to adjust personnel, maintenance schedules, even overtime to ensure that production operates efficiently. As you can see, an error in the production plan may mean insufficient raw materials and personnel, excessive warehousing of finished goods, an oversupply of raw materials, unnecessary personnel, or insufficient finished goods to meet demand. All of these conditions represent real costs to the entity.

Inventory Control

As the time for production nears, the production planner issues a **production order** to the appropriate production personnel including inventory control and production managers. Inventory control will receive a **materials requisition** or **materials transfer ticket** that authorizes inventory to release raw materials and supplies to production. These documents are the inventory record keepers' authorizations to update the raw materials inventory files by recording the reductions in the raw materials inventory.

Cost Accounting

When production is completed, production orders and the related records of materials and labor used are sent to the cost accounting department. Labor is reported by various means from time sheets to computerized clocks. Employees designate what job or product they worked on, or the labor is automatically assigned based on the department or machinery to which the employee is assigned. Because these accounting documents can come from the production workers, the effective separation of the record-keeping function depends on accounting also receiving independent notices from other sources (e.g., notifications of materials from the inventory custodian or labor costs assigned from the payroll department).

Cost accounting records generally record goods at **standard costs.** Developing standard costs is a difficult, time-consuming process, even for relatively simple products. All materials, supplies, labor, and overhead that go into the product must be measured based on the bill of materials and associated with a cost. Differences between standard costs and actual costs are recorded in variance accounts and reviewed by supervisors. (*Note:* GAAP do not recognize standard costs per se. GAAP recognize specific-item, FIFO, LIFO, and weighted-average costing. The auditor must ensure that standard costs are not materially different from the GAAP method that the client has adopted.)

The cost accounting department produces analyses of actual cost per unit, standard cost, and variances. Cost accounting also may determine the **overhead allocation** to production in general, to production orders, and to finished units. Depending on the design of the company's cost accounting system, these costs are used to value inventory and ultimately to determine the cost of goods sold. In addition, production reports are authorization for the finished goods inventory custodian to place the units in the finished goods inventory. They also authorize the inventory record keepers to update

AUDITING INSIGHT Overhead Allocation

The cost accounting department at **Pointed Publications, Inc.,** routinely allocated overhead to book printing runs at the rate of 40 percent of materials and labor cost. The debit was initially to the finished books inventory while the credit went to an "overhead allocated" account that was offset against other entries in the cost of goods sold calculation, which included all actual overhead incurred. During the year, 10 million books were produced and $40 million of overhead was allocated to them. The auditors noticed that actual overhead expenditures were $32 million and 3 million books remained in the ending inventory. This finding resulted in the conclusion that the inventory was overstated by $2.4 million, the cost of goods sold was understated by $2.4 million, and the income before taxes was overstated by 8.2 percent. 8.2 percent.

Overhead Allocation		
	Company Accounting	**Proper Accounting**
Books produced	10 million	10 million
Books sold	7 million	7 million
Labor and materials cost	$100 million	$100 million
Overhead allocated	$40 million	$32 million (actual cost)
Cost per book	$14.00	$13.20
Cost of goods sold:		
Labor and materials cost	$100 million	$100 million
Overhead allocated to books	40 million	
Overhead incurred	32 million	32 million
Overhead credited to cost	(40 million)	
Ending inventory	(42 million)	(39.6 million)
Total cost of goods sold	$ 90 million	$ 92.4 million

the finished goods inventory. In many cases, the cost accounting department also is responsible for calculating the depreciation of fixed assets and the amortization of intangibles.

Review Checkpoints

9.1 What functions are normally associated with the production cycle?

9.2 What inventory costing methods are recognized by GAAP?

AUDIT EVIDENCE IN MANAGEMENT REPORTS AND FILES

Most production systems produce timely reports that managers need to monitor and control production. Auditors can use these reports as supporting evidence for assertions about raw materials inventories, work-in-process inventories, finished goods inventories, and cost of goods sold.

Sales Forecast

Management's sales forecast provides the basis for several aspects of business planning, notably the planning of production and inventory levels. Forecasts can be used in gaining an understanding of management's plans for the year under audit, most of which will have already been completed when the audit work begins. Forecasts help auditors understand the nature and volume of production orders and the reasons for inventory levels. Forecasts of the following year can be used in valuing the inventory at lower of cost or market (e.g., identifying slow-moving and potentially obsolete inventory). Special care must be taken when using the forecast for the next year in valuing inventory because an overly optimistic forecast can lead to a failure to write down inventory, accelerate the depreciation of fixed assets, and account for more cost of goods sold.

If the auditors want to use the forecast for audit decisions, some work should be performed to obtain assurance about its reasonableness. For example, the auditor can inquire about how the forecast was prepared, what assumptions were made, and how the client ensures its accuracy. The auditor also can compare previous forecasts with actual results. In addition, some work on the mechanical accuracy of the forecast should be performed to avoid a reliance on faulty calculations. This work can usually be limited to overall tests for reasonableness.

AUDITING INSIGHT The SALY Forecast

The auditors were reviewing the inventory items that had not been issued for 30 days or more, considering the need to write some items down to market lower than cost. The production manager showed them the SALY forecast that indicated continuing need for the materials in products that are expected to have reasonable demand. The auditors agreed that the forecasts supported the prediction of future sales of products at prices that would cover the cost of the slow-moving material items.

Unfortunately, the auditors neglected to ask the meaning of *SALY* in the designation of the forecast and therefore did not learn that it meant "same as last year." It was not a forecast at all. The products did not sell at the prices expected, and the company experienced losses the following year that should have been charged to cost of goods sold earlier.

Inventory Reports

Companies can produce a wide variety of inventory reports useful by auditors in conducting analytical procedures. These reports should include a list of the items in inventory and their costs and should agree with the inventory control account. Auditors can use this list (1) to scan for unusual conditions (e.g., negative item balances, overstocking, and valuation problems) and (2) as a population for sample selection for a physical inventory observation. The scanning and sample selection may be performed by computer assisted audit techniques (CAATs) on computerized inventory report file.

Production Plans and Reports

Based on the sales forecast, management should develop a plan for the amount and timing of production.

The production plan provides general information to the auditors, but the production orders and inventory plan associated with the production plan are even more important. The production orders carry the information about requirements for raw materials, labor, and overhead, including the requisitions for purchase and use of materials and labor. These documents are the initial authorizations for control of the inventory and production.

Production reports record the completion of production quantities. When coupled with the related cost accounting reports, they are the company's record of the cost of goods placed into the finished goods inventory. In most cases, auditors will examine the cost reports in connection with determining the cost valuation of inventory and cost of goods sold.

Review Checkpoints

9.3 Describe a walkthrough of a production transaction from receiving production orders to making an entry in the finished goods perpetual inventory records. What document copies would be collected? What controls noted? What duties separated?

9.4 When auditors want to use a client's sales forecast for general familiarity with the production cycle or for evaluation of slow-moving inventory, what kind of procedures should be performed with respect to the forecast?

9.5 If the actual sales for the year are substantially lower than the sales forecasted at the beginning of the year, what potential valuation problems could arise in the production cycle accounts?

CONTROL RISK ASSESSMENT

LEARNING OBJECTIVE

2. Give examples of tests of controls over conversion of materials and labor in a production process.

Control risk assessment is important because it governs the *nature, timing,* and *extent* of substantive procedures that will be performed in the audit of account balances in the production cycle. These account balances include

- Raw materials inventory.
- Work-in-process inventory.
- Finished goods inventory.
- Cost of goods sold.

With respect to inventory valuation, this chapter discusses the cost accounting function and its role in determining the cost valuation of manufactured finished goods.

Control Considerations

Control procedures for proper segregation of responsibilities should be in place and operating. By referring to Exhibit 9.2, you can see that proper segregation involves authorization (production planning, inventory planning, and purchase requisitions) by persons who do not have custody, record-keeping, or cost accounting and reconciliation duties. Custody of inventories (raw materials, work-in-process, and finished goods) is in the hands of persons who do not authorize the amount or timing of production or the purchase of materials and labor, perform the cost accounting record keeping, or prepare cost analyses (reconciliations). Cost accounting (a recording function) is performed by persons who do not authorize production or have custody of assets in the process of production. Combinations of two or more of the duties of authorization, custody, and cost accounting in one person, one office, or one computerized system could open the door for errors and frauds.

In addition, the controls should provide for detailed control-checking activities, for example:

- Production orders should contain a list of materials and their quantities and they should be approved by a production planner/scheduler.
- Materials requisitions should be compared in the cost accounting department with the list of materials on the production order and the materials requisitions should be signed by the production operator and the materials inventory storekeeper.
- Labor time records on jobs should be signed by production supervisors (or reviewed if the time is kept electronically) and the cost accounting department should reconcile these cost amounts with the labor report from the payroll department.
- Production reports of finished units should be reviewed by the production supervisor and finished goods inventory custodian and then forwarded to cost accounting.
- Inventory should be periodically counted, with the counts agreed to perpetual inventory records.

These control operations track the raw materials and labor from the beginning of production to completion in the production process. With each internal transaction, the responsibility and accountability for assets are passed from one person or location to another.

Complex computer systems to manage production and materials flow are found in many entities. Even though the technology is complex, the basic management and control functions of ensuring the flow of labor and materials to production and the control of waste should be in place. Manual signatures, paper production orders, and requisitions might not exist but could be imbedded in computer-controlled manufacturing systems.

AUDITING INSIGHT Overcharging the Government

Government contracting periodically is in the news in exposés of companies charging unrelated costs to government contracts of various kinds (e.g., defense production, research contracts). Although the production plans and orders do not specifically allow costs for building the company baseball field or paying for the president's kennel fees while on business trips, such costs have found their way into government contract reimbursement claims. Government contract auditors have found them and companies have incurred penalties and requirements to reimburse the costs wrongly charged. Some companies summarily fire cost accountants who engage in cost manipulation on government contracts (e.g., **McDonnell Douglas Company,** now **Boeing**). Other organizations suffer in the glare of adverse publicity (e.g., **Northrop Corporation,** Massachusetts Institute of Technology, and Stanford University).

Custody

Supervisors and production workers have physical custody of materials and labor documents (time cards, job tickets, etc.) while the production work is performed. Authorized employees can requisition materials from the raw materials inventory, assign people to jobs, and control the pace of work. In a sense, they have custody of a "moving inventory." The work-in-process (WIP) is literally "moving" and changing form in the process of being transformed from raw materials into finished goods.

Inventory warehouses and fixed asset locations should be under adequate physical security (storerooms, fences, locks, and the like). However, control over goods in process is more difficult than control over a warehouse of raw materials or finished goods where unauthorized individuals cannot gain access. Control over WIP can be exercised by holding supervisors and workers accountable for the use of materials specified in the production orders, for the timely completion of production, and for the quality of the finished goods. This accountability can be achieved with effective cost accounting, cost analysis, and quality control testing. Accountability may be evident by ensuring that supervisors and management are analyzing the costs of production orders, comparing the costs to prior experience or to standard costs, and determining lower-of-cost-or-market (LCM) valuations. When costs of material or labor, scrap rates for materials, or production numbers do not meet expectations, management should require a documented assessment by cost accounting or internal audit to determine the cause and corrective action required.

AUDITING INSIGHT Is Your Inventory on eBay?

Kevin Lee Ruff, a warehouse supervisor for Sacred Heart Medical Center, was given access to the computerized inventory system. Mr. Ruff took boxes of inventory including medical and office supplies and sold them on eBay. In court Mr. Ruff said, "I took several inventory items and sold them . . . Made adjustments to the inventory . . . so they would not be shown as missing." The FBI solved the case by investigating Mr. Ruff's PayPal account, which identified each eBay transaction he made. His take? More than $664,000.

Source: Thomas Clouse, "Man Pleads Guilty to Fraud: Stolen Items Were Sold on eBay," *Spokesman-Review* (Spokane, Washington), December 21, 2006.

Internal Control Questionnaire

Information about the production cycle control often is gathered initially by completing an *internal control questionnaire (ICQ)*. An ICQ for control procedures commonly found in the production cycle is included in Appendix 9A.1. You can study this questionnaire for details of desirable control procedures. It is organized with headings that identify the important transaction assertions: *occurrence, completeness, accuracy, cutoff,* and *classification*.

Tests of Controls

An entity should have detailed control procedures in place and operating to prevent, detect, and correct accounting errors. Exhibit 9.3 puts controls in the perspective of production activity with examples of specific assertions. This exhibit expresses the transaction assertions in specific examples related to production.

Auditors can perform tests of controls to determine whether company personnel are effectively performing controls that are said to be in place and operating properly. Exhibit 9.3 includes a selection of tests of controls for the accumulation of costs for WIP

EXHIBIT 9.3 **Assertions about Classes of Transactions and Events: Production Cycle**

Transaction Assertion	Controls	Tests of Controls
Occurrence—Production and related events that have been recorded have occurred and pertain to the entity.	Cost accounting is separated from production, payroll, and inventory control.	Observe segregation of cost accounting function from production, payroll, and inventory control.
	Material usage reports are compared to raw material stores issue slips.	Examine evidence of comparisons between documents.
Completeness—All production events that should have been recorded have been recorded.	All documents are prenumbered and numerical sequence reviewed.	Examine evidence of review of numerical sequence. Select a sample of documents and examine numerical sequence.
	Periodic count of inventory is compared to perpetual records.	Examine evidence that inventory counts are compared to perpetual records.
	Open production cost reports are reconciled to the WIP inventory cost report.	Examine reconciliation of production cost reports to WIP inventory control report.
	Receiving reports and material usage are posted to perpetual inventory records.	Trace receiving reports to perpetual inventory. Trace materials used reports to production cost reports.
	Job cost sheets are posted weekly and summary journal entries of work in process and work completed are prepared monthly.	Check that journal entries agree with approved cost sheets. Compare costs to standard cost listing.
Accuracy—Production information including costs has been properly calculated and recorded.	Labor usage reports are compared to job time tickets.	Examine evidence of comparison by client.
	Material usage and labor usage are prepared by floor supervisor and approved by production supervisor.	Examine evidence of approval of material and labor usage reports.
	Periodic count of inventory is compared to perpetual records.	Examine evidence of comparison of counts to perpetual records.
	Receiving reports are posted to perpetual inventory on a timely basis.	Compare dates on receiving reports to posting in perpetual inventory records.
Cutoff—Production events have been recorded in the correct accounting period.	Receiving reports are posted to perpetual inventory in the proper period.	Check that the dates of inventory records agree with receiving reports.
	Finished goods are recorded in the proper period.	Check that production data agree with finished goods inventory status reports.
	Production reports of material and labor are prepared weekly and transmitted to cost accounting.	Check that date of production reports agrees with dates in weekly journal entries.
Classification—Classification-related events are recorded in the proper accounts.	Production supervisor is required to account for all material and labor as direct or indirect and to identify appropriate job classifications.	Observe supervisor allocation. Test allocation. Examine supervisor signature.

inventory. This is the stage of inventory that is in the production process. Upon completion, the accumulated costs become the value of the finished goods inventory. The illustrative procedures presume the existence of production cost reports that are updated as production takes place, labor reports that assign labor cost to the job, materials used and materials requisitions charging raw materials to the production order, and overhead allocation calculations. Some or all of these documents may be in the form of computerized records.

It is important for the auditor performing tests of controls in the production cycle to recognize that most of the company's documentation is internal. Production reports,

EXHIBIT 9.4
Test of Production
Cost Controls:
Completeness
Direction

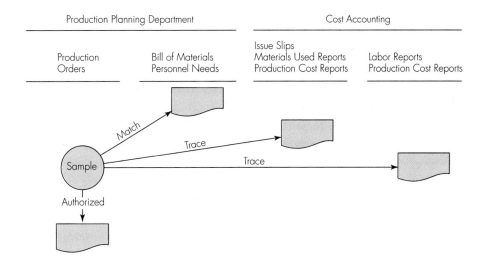

inventory reports, material and labor distribution reports, and other documents relied on by auditors are generated by the entity's reporting system. The auditor must pay close attention to general and application controls over the production reporting system in order to have some assurance that reports can be relied on for testing.

Direction of Tests of Controls

The tests of controls are designed to test the production accounting in two directions. One is the *completeness* direction, in which the auditors are interested in determining that all production that was started was recorded. Exhibit 9.4 shows that the sample for this direction is taken from the population of production orders found in the production-planning department. The procedures trace the cost accumulation forward to the production cost reports in the cost accounting department.

Testing the other direction relates to the *occurrence* of production. The auditors are interested in determining that WIP and finished goods inventories recorded in the general ledger were produced. Exhibit 9.5 shows that the sample for this test is from the general ledger. This sample is vouched to the production reports (quantity and cost) recorded in the inventory accounts. Further testing may include vouching from the production reports

EXHIBIT 9.5
Test of Production
Cost Controls:
Occurrence Direction

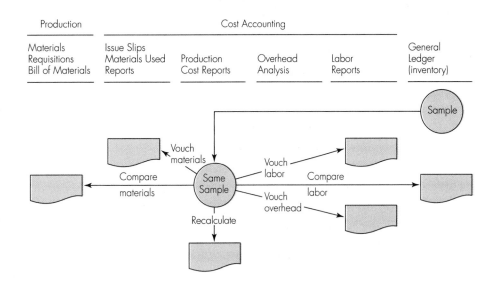

to the recorded material, labor, and payroll reports. Potential findings include errors in the *accuracy* of the recorded inventory cost. Of course, CAATs could be used to perform a 100 percent match that would accomplish both goals.

Summary: Control Risk Assessment

The audit manager or senior accountant in charge of the audit should evaluate the evidence obtained from an understanding of the internal controls and from the tests of controls. The evaluation of control risk along with the assessment of inherent risk will provide the auditors with an assessment of the risk of material misstatement. Given the assessed inherent risk, if the control risk is assessed very low, the substantive procedures on the account balances can be reduced. For example, if inventory observation test counts are performed on a date prior to the year end, fewer counts would be made and the inventory valuation procedures can be reduced in scope (i.e., smaller sample size). Further, substantive analytical procedures can be used with more confidence in detecting material misstatements not otherwise evident in the accounting details.

On the other hand, if tests of controls reveal weaknesses, the substantive procedures will need to be designed to lower detection risk in the inventory and cost of goods sold account balances. For example, a large number of inventory production reports may be selected for valuation calculations and the inventory observation may be scheduled nearer the year-end date with the audit team making a large number of test counts. Descriptions of significant deficiencies, control weaknesses, and inefficiencies may be incorporated in a letter to the client and must be communicated to the audit committee.

Review Checkpoints

9.6 What features of the cost accounting system would be expected to prevent the omission of recording materials used in production?

9.7 Describe how the functions of (a) authorization of production transactions, (b) recording of these transactions, and (c) physical custody of inventories can be separated among the production, inventory, and cost accounting departments.

9.8 How does the production order record provide a control over the quantity of materials used in production?

9.9 From what population of documents would an auditor sample to determine whether (a) all authorized production was completed and placed in inventory or recorded as scrap and (b) finished goods inventory was actually produced and properly costed?

SUBSTANTIVE PROCEDURES IN THE PRODUCTION CYCLE

LEARNING OBJECTIVE

3. Identify and describe considerations involved in the observation of physical inventory and tests of inventory pricing and compilation.

Exhibit 9.6 illustrates the assertions and primary substantive procedures used for accounts in the production cycle. Inventory is the primary account balance to apply substantive procedures in this cycle. When inventory is significant, GAAS require auditors to be present to observe the client's physical inventory count. After the inventory has been counted, the client summarizes the count by item number and then applies standard costs to determine the total amount of inventory owned on that date, which is compared to the amount in the general ledger. This step is normally referred to as the *compilation and pricing procedure,* which the auditors also test. Differences between the inventory count and the perpetual records are adjusted by increasing or decreasing cost of goods sold.

EXHIBIT 9.6 Account Balance Assertions and Substantive Procedures in the Production Cycle

Balance Assertions	Substantive Procedures
Existence—Inventory exists.	Observe client's physical inventory count. Confirm inventory held by others. Trace items from inventory count tags to inventory listing. Analytical procedures: Compare inventory turnover and gross margin to budget and previous periods and discuss differences with client personnel.
Rights and obligations—The entity holds or controls the rights to inventory.	Inquire whether any inventory is on consignment. Inquire whether inventory has been pledged as collateral or security.
Completeness—All inventory that should have been recorded has been recorded.	Review inventory subsidiary accounts and trace to inventory control account. Review physical inventory to ensure all items were counted. Trace test inventory counts to inventory subsidiary accounts and control account.
Valuation and Accuracy—Inventory is included in the financial statements at appropriate amounts and any resulting valuation adjustments are properly recorded.	Perform lower-of-cost-or-market tests. Examine calculation of cost of goods sold. Check that inventory cost agrees with standard costs or purchase invoices. Inquire whether any inventory is obsolete or unsalable. Examine loans and other agreements for the use of inventory as collateral.

Analytical Procedures

The production cycle is an excellent area for auditors to employ analytical procedures. Inventory turnover, days' sales in inventory, and simple trend analysis can indicate whether the client is able to sell the inventory or if inventory is slow-moving and becoming obsolete. In addition, an unexpected increase in inventory may be a red flag indicating bribes and kickbacks in purchasing or production. The gross margin percentage reveals whether the client is able to price the inventory to earn an acceptable profit. Moreover, comparing current-year gross margin to prior years can uncover fraudulent inventory accounting. These ratios should be disaggregated to specific product lines or geographic regions to make them more meaningful. They can be compared to those budgeted, in previous years, of competitors, and industry averages.

AUDITING INSIGHT Really Gross Margins

A popular move among online retailers has been to include shipping costs and discounts into selling expenses to inflate their gross margins. **FogDog,** a popular online sporting goods retailer, monthly gives hundred of thousands in goodies like free pizza and golf lessons for buying its goods. Placing these costs in selling expense instead of cost of goods sold has a big effect on gross margin. Say a company sells a $1,200 bicycle that cost $600 but takes a $500 coupon for it. Gross margin is 14 percent—right? Not if you bury the coupon in selling costs; then the margin becomes 50 percent, a number sure to catch Wall Street's eye. According to Lehman Brothers, Amazon.com inflated its gross margin in the first quarter of 2000 from 10 to 22.9 percent, Etoys reported 20.5 percent when it should have reported a negative 6.5 percent, and Drugstore.com reported 5 percent instead of a negative 15 percent. Because analysts value new companies more on their potential than their results, inflating gross margins can make a big difference in stock prices. Accounting rules have been adopted to prevent the abuse, but these actions illustrate the importance companies place on gross margins.

Source: "Fess-Up Time," *Forbes,* September 18, 2000.

Physical Inventory Observation

The auditing procedures for inventory and related cost of sales accounts frequently are extensive in an audit engagement. A material error or fraud in inventory has a pervasive effect on financial statements. Misstatements in inventory cause misstatements in many important financial statement subtotals (such as current assets, working capital, total assets, cost of sales, gross margin, and net income). While analytical procedures can help indicate inventory misstatements, the auditor's best opportunity to detect inventory errors and frauds is during a **physical inventory observation,** an observation of the client's **physical inventory count** taken by company personnel. (Auditors observe the inventory taking and make test counts, but they seldom actually count the entire inventory.)

This section gives details about auditors' observation of physical inventory taking. The first task is to review the client's inventory-taking instructions, which should include the following:

1. Names of client personnel responsible for the count.
2. Dates and times of inventory taking.
3. Names of client personnel who will participate in the inventory taking.
4. Instructions for recording accurate descriptions of inventory items, for count and double count, and for measuring or translating physical quantities (such as counting by measures of gallons, barrels, feet, dozens).
5. Instructions for making notes of obsolete or worn items.
6. Instructions for the use of tags, punched cards, count sheets, computers, or other media devices and for their collection and control (a typical inventory count sheet is illustrated at Exhibit 9.7).
7. Plans for shutting down plant operations or for taking inventory after store closing hours and plans for having goods in proper places (such as on store shelves instead of on the floor, or of raw materials in a warehouse rather than in transit to a job).

EXHIBIT 9.7
Inventory Count Sheet

8. Plans for counting or controlling movement of goods in receiving and shipping areas if those operations are not shut down during the count.

9. Instructions for computer compilation of the count media (such as tags, count sheets) into final inventory lists or summaries.

10. Instructions for review and approval of the inventory count; notations of obsolescence or other matters by supervisory personnel.

11. Instructions for making changes and corrections to count tickets.

These instructions characterize a well-planned counting operation. As the plan is carried out, the independent auditors should be present to hear the count instructions being given to the client's count teams and to observe the instructions being followed. In addition, the auditor should make selected test counts and record these in the audit documentation.

Manual Physical Inventory

An example of an audit program for observing a physical inventory count is presented in Appendix 9.B.1. Note the requirement for obtaining tag numbers. It is critically important to know which tag numbers or count sheets were and were not used to prevent the client from simply adding inventory items by creating more tags at a later date. Also, note the cutoff procedures of examining shipping and receiving documents issued immediately before and after the count. The items that are included in the count must be the same as those recorded in the inventory records, and any items that have been sold or are not yet received must be excluded from the count and the records.

The auditors can perform dual-direction testing by (1) selecting inventory items from a perpetual inventory master file, going to the location, and obtaining a test count, which produces evidence for the *existence* balance assertion, and (2) selecting inventory from locations on the warehouse floor, obtaining a test count, and tracing the count to the final inventory compilation, which produces evidence for the *completeness* balance assertion. If the company does not have perpetual records and a file to test for *existence*, the auditors must be careful to obtain a record of all counts and use it for the existence-direction tests. In addition to the test counts, the auditor should document whether client personnel were following the inventory instructions, the tag or count sheet numbers used and unused, the last shipping and receiving reports issued before the inventory count, the condition of the inventory, any inventory on hand that is not owned by the client, and any unusual items noticed during the count.

Inventory Count and Measurement Challenges		
Examples	**Challenges**	**Special Procedures**
Lumber	Problem identifying quality or grade	Employ a specialist.
Piles of sugar, coal, scrap steel	Geometric computations, aerial photos	Employ a specialist.
Items weighed on scales	Accuracy of scales	Examine certification.
Bulk materials (oil, grain, liquids in storage tanks)	Measuring volume, ensuring composition of content	Climb the tanks. Dip measuring rods. Sample for assay or chemical analysis.
Diamonds, jewelry	Identification and quality determination problems	Employ a specialist.
Pulp wood	Quantity measurement estimation	Examine aerial photos.
Livestock	Movement not controllable	Use chutes to control animals.

EXHIBIT 9.8
Example of Inventory
Bar Code Scanners
Phaser memory scanners
P360 and P460 by
Barcoding Incorporated

Using Bar-Codes and Computers in Physical Inventory

Many organizations are now using the bar codes located on almost every product to improve the efficiency and effectiveness of monitoring the movement of physical inventory. Maybe on a trip to the grocery store or department store you have seen an individual with a handheld device scanning the store shelves. This device (see Exhibit 9.8) is designed to scan the bar code located on the front of the shelf. That bar code records the product type, manufacturer, and size in the hand unit. Once the individual counts the number of units in inventory, the count can be entered and stored in the scanner by using the number pad located on the top of the scanner. When the counts are completed, the unit can be brought back to the physical inventory supervisor, who can download the data to the computer program being used to manage the physical inventory.

While the use of scanners and computers greatly improves the accuracy (all product descriptions are identical) and efficiency (product descriptions and counts do not need to be written), there is still a need to follow the basic elements of a physical inventory count. For example, all items still should be counted twice. However, the computer program can match first and second counts and, if they are identical, accept and record the count. If the counts are not identical, the item can be flagged for review by the physical inventory supervisor.

RFID Physical Inventory

Many people driving in cities with toll roads and bridges now bypass the toll booths because of Radio Frequency Identification (RFID). These devices send a signal to an RFID reader that identifies the automobile or truck as it travels and charges the driver's account for the toll. This same technology is beginning to be used in warehouses and stores around the world. As more and more products are tagged with RFID chips, most about the size of a nickel, companies will be able to scan each product as it enters or leaves the warehouse or store and count the inventory by moving an RFID reader down the aisles.

Will this eliminate the need for a physical inventory? Probably not. But it will change the focus of the audit of the physical inventory. If the RFID reader is connected to a computer, a completely accurate count of the RFID signals can be made without the need for a second count. The major focus may be a sampling of items to ensure the actual goods are contained in the carton and not just an RFID chip.

AUDITING INSIGHT Using RFID to Combat Counterfeit Fraud

Intelligenz Corporation, a subsidiary of **Unisone Corporation,** is utilizing RFID technology to help eliminate counterfeit drugs. It is estimated that there are approximate $10 billion in counterfeit drugs in the marketplace. RFID chips located in bottles will send out a unique code that cannot be duplicated. The codes will correspond to a specific bottle, case, and pallet and the system will be continuously updated as the medicine moves through the system. Each customer will be able to determine the origin of the medical product, ensuring its authenticity.

Source: "RFID Regulates Pharmaceutical Frauds," *Business Wire, Inc.,* October 6, 2006.

Difficult Circumstances

The following are some unusual circumstances that present difficulties for the auditors:

Physical Inventory Not on Year-End Date Often clients count the inventory before or after the balance-sheet date. When the auditors are present to make their physical observation, they follow the procedures outlined for observation of the physical count. However, with a period intervening between the count date and the year end, additional **inventory roll-forward** auditing procedures must be performed on transactions during that period. The inventory on the count date is reconciled to the year-end inventory by appropriate addition or subtraction of the intervening receiving and issue transactions.

Cycle Inventory Counting **Cycle counts** are physical counts of selected inventory throughout the year (i.e., different parts of the inventory throughout the year). They are most appropriate when internal control over inventory is effective (that is, a low level of control risk is present). Other companies use a statistical counting plan. In these circumstances, the auditors must understand the cycle or sampling plan and evaluate its appropriateness. In this situation, the auditors are present for some counting operations. Only under unusual circumstances and as an "extended procedure" are auditors present every month (or more frequently) to observe all counts. Businesses that count inventory in this manner purport to have accurate perpetual records and carry out the counting as a means of testing the records and maintaining their accuracy.

The auditors must be present during some counting operations to evaluate the counting plans and their execution. The procedures for an annual count enumerated as described are used, test counts are made, and the audit team is responsible for making a determination concerning the accuracy of perpetual records.

Auditors Not Present for Client's Inventory Count This situation can arise on a first audit when the accounting firm is appointed after the beginning inventory already has been counted. Because the beginning inventory amount affects cost of goods sold, the auditors will have to disclaim an opinion on the income statement unless they can be satisfied of the beginning number through alternative measures. For example, the auditors must review the client's plan for the already completed count as described earlier. Some test counts of current inventory should be made and traced to current records to determine the reliability of perpetual records. If the actual count was recent, intervening transaction activity might be reconciled back to the beginning inventory. The reconciliation of more than a few months' transactions to unobserved beginning inventories could be very difficult. The auditors can employ analytical procedures using such interrelationships as sales activity, physical volume, price variation, standard costs, and gross profit margins for the decision about beginning inventory reasonableness. Nevertheless, much care must be exercised in "backing into" the audit of inventory previously taken.

Inventories Located off the Client's Premises The auditors must determine where and in what dollar amounts inventories are located off the client's premises, in the custody of consignees, or in public warehouses. If amounts are material and if control procedures are not exceptionally strong, the audit team may wish to visit these locations and conduct on-site test counts. However, if amounts are not material, alternative evidence is adequate (such as periodic reports, cash receipts, receivables records, shipping records), or control risk is low, then direct confirmation with the custodian may be considered sufficient appropriate evidence of the existence of quantities.

Pricing and Compilation

The physical observation procedures are designed to audit for *existence* and *completeness* (physical quantities). The **pricing and compilation** tests examine *valuation* (recalculation of appropriate FIFO, LIFO, or other pricing at cost, and lower-of-cost-or-market, and write-down of obsolete or worn inventory). After the observation is complete,

auditors should have sufficient appropriate evidence of the following physical quantities and valuations:

- Goods in the perpetual records but not owned were excluded from the inventory compilation.
- Goods on hand were counted and included in the inventory compilation.
- **Consignment** (consigned-out) **goods** or goods stored in outside warehouses (goods owned but not on hand) were included in the inventory compilation.
- Goods in transit (goods actually purchased and recorded but not received) were added to the inventory count and included in the inventory compilation.
- Goods on hand that have been recorded as sold but have not been delivered were not counted and were excluded from the inventory compilation.
- Consignment goods (consigned-in) were excluded from the inventory compilation.

The compilation and pricing stage starts by listing all inventory items counted. The auditor foots the list and tests the mathematical accuracy by multiplying the quantities and the price to get the total value for each item. Test counts taken by the auditor at the physical count are traced into the list and other items from the list are traced back to inventory count tags. The unit price is compared to the purchase price for raw materials and to standard cost for in-process and finished goods. Many of these tests can be performed automatically using CAATs.

Lower-of-cost-or-market testing is an important step toward the *valuation* assertion. Market price can be obtained by examining the client's catalogue and actual sales in the subsequent period. Items that are slow-moving or obsolete can be spotted during the inventory observation if they demonstrate evidence of unsalability (e.g., old inventory tags, dust, rust). Appendix 9.B.2 illustrates a program for inventory pricing and compilation tests.

AUDITING INSIGHT Chips Ahoy!

In May 2001, Cisco took a $2.25 billion inventory write-down of excess inventory it had purchased during the technology boom of the 1990s. The company was simply caught unaware by the economic downturn of 2001. It was ordering materials based on sales forecasts instead of actual orders. Most of the write-down was to raw materials, including microprocessors, memory chips, and lasers. The company said it would scrap most of the inventory because it was custom-built for Cisco and could not be sold. Parts not destroyed would be sold to recycling companies that salvage metal components and resell them to brokers or other distributors.

Source: "Cisco's $2.25 Billion Mea Culpa," *News.Com*, May 9, 2001.

Inventory—A Ripe Field for Fraud

These problems have arisen in entities' inventory frauds:

- Auditors were fooled as a result of taking a small sample for test counting, thus missing important information.
- Entities included inventory they pretended to have ordered.
- Entities stacked inventory on pallets in such a manner that "empty spaces" were not visible to auditors, resulting in overstatements of inventory.
- Auditors permitted company officials to follow them and notice their counts. Then the managers falsified counts for inventory the auditors did not count.
- Shipments between plants (transfers) were reported as inventory at both plant locations.
- Auditors spotted a barrel whose contents management had valued at thousands of dollars, but it was filled with sawdust. The auditors required management to exclude the value from the inventory, but it never occurred to them that they had found just one instance in an intentional and pervasive overstatement fraud.

- Auditors observed inventory at five store locations and told the management in advance of the specific stores. Management took care not to make fraudulent entries in these five stores, instead making fraudulent adjustments in many of the other 236 stores.
- After counting an inventory of computer chips, the auditors received a call from the client's controller: "Just hours after you left the plant, 2,500 chips arrived in a shipment in transit." The auditors included them in inventory but never checked to see whether the chips were actually received.[3]

Accounting Firm Tips

To help detect inventory fraud, Grant Thornton, an accounting firm, advised its audit personnel:

- Focus test counts on high-value items and sample lower-value items. Test count a sufficient dollar amount of the inventory.
- If all locations will not be observed, do not follow an easily predictable pattern. Advise client personnel as late as possible of the locations to be visited.

- Be skeptical of large and unusual test count differences or of client personnel making notes or displaying particular interest in our procedures and test counts.
- Be alert for inventory not used for some time, stored in unusual locations, or showing signs of damage, obsolescence, or excess quantities.

Presentation and Disclosure Assertions

Once the auditor is satisfied that controls have been examined and transactions and balances are fairly presented according to GAAP, the job is not over. The aspects of production, especially inventory, require many disclosures. The components of inventory (raw materials, work-in-process, finished goods), inventory valuation method, lower of cost or market, and allocation of fixed costs are only a few of the essential items with specific presentation and disclosure requirements. These disclosures must ensure that the presentation and disclosure assertions of *occurrence, rights and obligations, completeness, classification and understandability,* and *accuracy and valuation* are all met. Exhibit 9.9 contains excerpts from the footnote contained in Boeing Corporation's 2006 financial statements.

EXHIBIT 9.9 **Excerpts from Inventory Footnote in Boeing Aircraft 2006 Annual Report**

Disclosure Assertion	Excerpt from Boeing Footnote
Classification of items included in inventory costs	To the extent a material amount of such costs are related to an abnormal event or are fixed costs not appropriately attributed to our programs or contracts, they will be expensed in the current period rather than inventoried.
Occurrence	In accordance with industry practice, inventoried cost includes amounts relating to programs and contracts with long production cycles, a portion of which is not expected to be realized within one year.
Accuracy and valuation of inventoried parts	We review our commercial spare parts and general stock materials each quarter to identify impaired inventory, including excess or obsolete inventory, based on historical sales trends, expected production usage, and the size and age of the aircraft fleet using the part.

Review Checkpoints

9.10 What characteristics do auditors consider in reviewing a client's inventory-taking instructions?

9.11 Explain dual-direction sampling in the context of inventory test counts.

9.12 Why is it important for auditors to obtain control information over inventory count sheets or tickets?

[3] Examples cited in this list have been taken from *The Wall Street Journal.*

9.13 What information should be documented by auditors?

9.14 Why is it important to obtain shipping and receiving cutoff information during the inventory observation?

9.15 What procedures are employed to audit inventory when the physical inventory is taken on a cycle basis or on a statistical plan but never a complete count on a single date?

9.16 What could be happening when a client's managers take notes of auditors' test counts while an inventory is being counted?

9.17 What analytical procedures might reveal obsolete or slow-moving inventory?

AUDIT RISK MODEL SUMMARY

Now that the control and inherent risk elements for the production cycle and some of the important substantive procedures have been presented, let's examine how an auditor might apply the audit risk model for the account balance assertion of existence. First we show a table relating levels of detection risk to extent of substantive procedures; then we provide an example of how they might be employed in practice. It is important to note that similar examples could be provided for the remaining material financial statement assertions related to inventory.

Extent of Substantive Inventory Procedures for Balance Assertion of Existence	
Low detection risk	Observe physical inventory count at end of year. Take substantial number of test counts and use large sample for vouching inventory purchases. Perform analytical procedures during planning and at audit completion.
Moderate detection risk	Observe inventory count at interim date. Test roll-forward to year end. Use moderate vouching of purchases. Perform analytical procedures during planning and at audit completion.
High detection risk	Rely heavily on analytical procedures. Observe cycle counts of inventory. Rely on roll-forward procedures with minimal testing.

Insight Electronics, Inc.

Martin Phelps has been assigned as audit manager for **Insight Semiconductor, Inc.,** a medium-size publicly held manufacturer of semiconductors used in the computer industry. It has four manufacturing facilities, located in Lexington, Kentucky; Dublin, Ireland; Barcelona, Spain; and Bangkok, Thailand. Insight uses just-in-time inventory management at all plants so that when a plant receives a customer order, it electronically forwards a purchase order for the materials to vendors. The company takes cycle counts of its inventory so it will not disrupt production. When goods are received, the receiving clerk enters the receipt into the system, which automatically updates the perpetual inventory. Likewise, as semiconductors are completed, they are scanned and automatically moved from in-process to finished goods. The computerized controls were reviewed and tested by the audit firm's computer audit specialist, who noted no exceptions. Therefore, Martin has set control risk as low. Control risk also has been set as low in the acquisition cycle and the revenue cycle.

The company is a leader in the industry, and management has a very good reputation. The semiconductor industry is experiencing strong growth and the company is consistently profitable. There have been only minor audit adjustments in previous years and the company has moved quickly to correct the cause of the adjustments. Consequently, Martin also has set inherent risk as low. Therefore, risk of material misstatement is assessed as low and detection risk has been set as high. As a result, Martin can select a sample of the cycle counts to observe on a surprise basis. He can record limited test counts and rely on limited testing of the computer records that roll forward the perpetual inventory until year end. Because risk of material misstatement is low in the acquisition cycle, Martin can limit vouching of invoices to test the prices of raw materials. Finally, Martin will rely heavily on analytical procedures, particularly gross margin percentages, to ensure that no serious errors or frauds have occurred. The combination of a low risk of material misstatement and a high detection risk combine to give Martin an acceptably low audit risk.

FRAUD CASE: EXTENDED AUDIT PROCEDURES (*SAS 99*)

LEARNING OBJECTIVE

4. Describe some common errors and frauds in the accounting for production costs and related cost of goods sold and design some audit and investigation procedures for detecting these errors and frauds.

The case refers to the Phar-Mor case discussed at the beginning of this chapter and Chapter 2. The first part reiterates the "inside story," which auditors seldom know before they perform the audit procedures. The second part of the case, under the heading Audit Approach, tells a structured story about the audit objective, controls, tests of controls, substantive procedures, and discovery summary. At the end of the chapter, some similar discussion cases are presented and you can prepare the audit approach to test your ability to design audit procedures for the detection of errors and frauds.

Case 9.1

The Players Weren't All That Was Short![4]

PROBLEM

Phar-Mor dumped losses in the "bucket account" and spread them over the individual stores by increasing inventory amounts. When company personnel found out which stores the auditors would be visiting for inventory observation, they simply moved goods from the stores that were not visited to make up for shortages. Phar-Mor used an outside service for inventory counting, but after receiving the results, Phar-Mor personnel would inflate the amounts during the pricing and compilation process. In some cases, the compilations were altered after the auditors tested them. When Phar-Mor rolled forward the inventory from the count date, the inventory showed large increases right at year end. These increases were due to the "blow-out" entries allocating the losses in the bucket account to stores' inventory. One entry was as high as $139 million. Finally, Phar-Mor did not have perpetual records but used the retail inventory method instead. Employees used distorted margin percentages to increase the estimated cost of the inventory on hand.

Phar-Mor issued fictitious invoices for purchases, made fictitious journal entries to increase inventory and decrease cost of sales, recognized purchases but failed to record the liabilities, and overcounted the merchandise.

The fraud lasted over a 10-year period, resulting in losses of over $1 billion.

AUDIT APPROACH

The primary control should have been an environment that discouraged false accounting. However, this clearly was not the case. Other controls that should have prevented or detected these misstatements include a review of nonstandard journal entries, comparison of inventory records to actual periodic counts, and management analysis of gross margins and cash flows. Most controls involving senior management can be easily overridden. Doing so requires only employees who can be bribed, threatened, or intimidated into going along.

How does one test the control environment? In the client acceptance/continuation stage of planning, the auditors should obtain evidence about management's reputation for integrity. In this case, many vendors were complaining because they were "squeezed" by Phar-Mor to provide rebates and promotion allowances, and some were threatening to cut the company off for nonpayment of bills. Many employees, including the controller, were very concerned about the company's practices and might have been persuaded to come clean had the auditors approached the audit with skepticism. However, because the client's chief financial officer was a former partner of the auditor, the auditors appeared to lack skepticism.

[4] Additional data taken from D. Cottrell and S. Glover, "Finding Auditors Liable for Fraud: What the Jury Heard in the Phar-Mor Case," *CPA Journal*, July 1997, pp. 14–21.

It is not practical to observe inventory at all stores. However, because the auditors had identified inventory valuation as a high-risk area, they probably should have visited more than four! Moreover, the actual stores that the auditors visited for inventory observation should have been kept secret until the day of the count to prevent movement of goods and randomized from one year to the next.

The auditors performed only a reasonableness test of the margins used in the retail method. They selected a sample of items in a "haphazard" method that turned out not to be representative. When the sample margins differed from the company's margins, the auditors explained the difference away without expanding their sample. In vouching the costs of inventory, the auditors should have been alert to phony documentation. Finally, large nonstandard journal entries at the end of the year should have been thoroughly scrutinized.

DISCOVERY SUMMARY

When a travel agent noticed that a bill for the World Basketball League (WBL) was paid with a Phar-Mor check, she asked a neighbor, who was a major shareholder, why Phar-Mor would pay the WBL's expenses. The neighbor phoned a board member, who initiated the investigation that uncovered the fraud.

Review Checkpoints

9.18 What steps should auditors take if the client has multiple locations being counted?

9.19 What is an inventory roll-forward? What roll-forward tests should be performed?

Summary

Production involves production planning; inventory planning; acquiring labor, materials, and overhead (acquisition and payment cycle); custody of assets; and cost accounting. Production information systems produce many internal documents, reports, and files that are sources of audit information as described in the chapter. This cycle is characterized by having mostly internal documentation as evidence and having relatively little external documentary evidence; therefore, the systems that produce these documents must be evaluated to ensure the validity of the information.

Companies reduce control risk by having a suitable separation of authorization, custody, recording, and periodic reconciliation duties. Error-checking procedures, including analyzing production orders and finished production cost reports, are important for the proper determination of inventory values and proper valuation of cost of goods sold. Otherwise, many things could go wrong, ranging from overvaluing the inventory to understating costs of production by deferring costs that should be expensed.

Cost accounting is a central feature of the production cycle. The illustrative case in the chapter tells the stories of financial reporting manipulations and the audit procedures that will detect them. The physical inventory observation audit work was discussed because actual contact with inventories provides auditors direct eyewitness evidence of important tangible assets.

While it may appear that production and related activities offer little risk, especially if the nature of inventory does not lend itself to high inherent risk (e.g., steel I-beams), even when production material is not highly susceptible to theft, many frauds have been hidden in the inventory accounts. Therefore, the auditors should pay attention to the inventory balance assertions of *existence* and *accuracy and valuation*. Here are some deficiencies the PCAOB noted in its inspections of the Big Four audit firms regarding audits of this cycle.

AUDITING INSIGHT PCAOB Inspections and the Production Cycle

- In connection with auditing inventory valuation, the Firm tested controls and performed substantive tests. The controls that the Firm identified and tested, however, did not address whether the inventory was properly valued or whether the variances were accounted for appropriately, and the substantive tests did not address whether inventory was properly valued at year end.

- When testing inventory, the Firm applied a controls reliance strategy, which included reliance on IT controls. The Firm's work papers indicated that the results of its tests of the issuer's information technology general controls did not support a conclusion that the issuer's information processing was reliable. The Firm, however, did not perform any additional procedures to address its finding, nor did it modify its audit strategy.

- Other than reviewing certain untested reports for reasonableness, there was no evidence that the Firm performed audit procedures, such as examination, observation, or reperformance, to obtain corroboration of management's explanations regarding a significant portion of the inventory controls identified for testing.

- There was no evidence in the audit documentation, and no persuasive other evidence, that the Firm, in evaluating the issuer's allocation of the costs of assets acquired in a series of business combinations, had tested management's assertion that the acquired inventory was recorded at an estimate of the selling price, less the cost of disposal and a reasonable profit allowance for the selling effort.

- The issuer maintained inventory at numerous locations and did not have a perpetual inventory system. The issuer performed one complete inventory count at each location per year. The Firm observed certain of these inventory counts at various times during the year. The Firm did not test inventory transactions between the dates of the interim physical inventory observations and year end, nor did it compare the interim balances with the year-end inventory balances; rather, its procedures were limited to comparing the inventory balances at year end with those at the prior year end.

- The Firm failed to perform sufficient procedures to test the valuation and existence assertions related to certain portions of the inventory. The deficiencies included

 a. The failure to test certain key factors used in calculating the LIFO cost of the inventory;

 b. The failure to perform inventory price testing;

 c. The failure to perform substantive procedures on the activity in inventory, at a location that the Firm had selected for testing, between the date as of which interim audit procedures were performed and the issuer's fiscal year end;

 d. The failure to establish a precise expectation, and to appropriately investigate or evaluate significant differences, when performing substantive analytical procedures; and

 e. The failure to test certain assumptions and underlying data used to calculate the inventory obsolescence reserve.

Key Terms

bill of materials: List of raw materials and supplies used to build a product that is used to develop standard costs, 345

consignment goods: Goods that are given by one party, the consignor, to another party, the consignee, to sell; however, title is retained by the consignee until the goods are sold, 360

cycle counts: A method of physically counting different areas of inventory throughout the year, 359

inventory roll-forward: Accounting process from date of physical inventory count to the end of the period; includes additions for purchases and production and reductions for sales, scrap, etc., 359

materials requisition (materials transfer ticket): Form used to obtain raw materials and supplies from inventory custodian, 346

net realizable value (NRV): Selling price less costs to sell (e.g., sales commissions), 344

overhead allocation: Accounting procedure used to assign indirect costs to various products, 347

physical inventory count: Client's procedure for determining actual amount of inventory on hand, 356

physical inventory observation: Auditor's procedures during client's physical inventory count. Includes observing inventory procedures and performing test counts on selected inventory items, 356

pricing and compilation: The procedure for translating units counted in the physical inventory count to amounts recorded in the accounting records, including gains or losses for shortages or overages; involves mathematically accumulating counts and applying standard costs, 359

production order: Document that communicates to production personnel the specific product, product quantity, and date a product is to be produced, 346

production plan: Schedule of goods to be produced for a period based on sales forecasts, 345

raw material inventory status report: Periodic report (usually daily or weekly) that includes a list of all raw materials and the inventoried quantity of each material, 345

standard costs: Estimates of cost to produce a product; used for transferring products between departments and to finished goods and to record cost of goods sold; compared to actual costs to obtain variances, 347

Multiple Choice Questions for Practice and Review

9. 20 Which of the following methods for determining inventory cost is not allowed by GAAP?
 a. Average cost.
 b. FIFO.
 c. LIFO.
 d. Standard cost.

9.21 Which cycle is *not* linked to the production cycle?
 a. Acquisition and expenditure cycle.
 b. Payroll cycle
 c. Revenue and collection cycle.
 d. Finance and investment cycle.

9.22 To determine the client's planned amount and timing of production of a product, the auditor will review the
 a. Sales forecast.
 b. Inventory reports.
 c. Production plan.
 d. Purchases journal.

9.23 An auditor reviews job cost sheets to test which *transaction assertion*?
 a. Occurrence.
 b. Completeness.
 c. Accuracy.
 d. Classification.

9.24 Which of the following is an internal control weakness for a company whose inventory of supplies consists of a large number of individual items?
 a. Supplies of relatively little value are expensed when purchased.
 b. The cycle basis is used for physical counts.
 c. The warehouse manager is responsible for maintenance of perpetual inventory records.
 d. Perpetual inventory records are maintained only for items of significant value.

9.25 To make a year-to-year comparison of inventory turnover *most* meaningful, the auditor will perform the analysis
 a. For the company as a whole.
 b. By division.
 c. By product.
 d. All of the above.

9.26 Which of the following procedures would best prevent or detect the theft of valuable items from an inventory that consists of hundreds of different items selling for $1 to $10 and a few items selling for hundreds of dollars?
 a. Maintain a perpetual inventory of only the more valuable items with frequent periodic verification of the accuracy of the perpetual inventory record.
 b. Have an independent accounting firm prepare an internal control report on the effectiveness of the controls over inventory.
 c. Have separate warehouse space for the more valuable items with frequent periodic physical counts and comparison to perpetual inventory records.
 d. Require a manager's signature for the removal of any inventory item with a value above $50

9.27 An auditor will usually trace the details of the test counts made during the observation of physical inventory counts to a final inventory compilation. This audit procedure is undertaken to provide evidence that items physically present and observed by the auditor at the time of the physical inventory count are
 a. Owned by the client.
 b. Not obsolete.
 c. Physically present at the time of the preparation of the final inventory schedule.
 d. Included in the final inventory schedule.

9.28 A retailer's physical count of inventory was higher than that shown by the perpetual records. Which of the following could explain the difference?

a. Inventory items had been counted but the tags placed on the items had not been taken off and added to the inventory accumulation sheets.

b. Credit memos for several items returned by customers had not been recorded.

c. No journal entry had been made on the retailer's books for several items returned to its suppliers.

d. An item purchased FOB shipping point had not arrived at the date of the inventory count and had not been reflected in the perpetual records.

9.29 From the auditors' point of view, inventory counts are more acceptable prior to the year end when

a. Internal control is weak.

b. Accurate perpetual inventory records are maintained.

c. Inventory is slow moving.

d. Significant amounts of inventory are held on a consignment basis.

9.30 Which of the following internal control procedures most likely addresses the completeness assertion for inventory?

a. The work-in-process account is periodically reconciled with subsidiary inventory records.

b. Employees responsible for custody of finished goods do not perform the receiving function.

c. Receiving reports are prenumbered and the numbering sequence is checked periodically.

d. There is a separation of duties between the payroll department and inventory accounting personnel.

(AICPA adapted)

9.31 When auditing inventories, an auditor would least likely verify that

a. All inventory owned by the client is on hand at the time of the count.

b. The client has used proper inventory pricing.

c. The financial statement presentation of inventories is appropriate.

d. Damaged goods and obsolete items have been properly accounted for.

(AICPA adapted)

9.32 A client maintains perpetual inventory records in quantities and in dollars. If the assessed risk of material misstatement is high, an auditor would probably

a. Apply gross profit tests to ascertain the reasonableness of the physical counts.

b. Increase the extent of tests of controls relevant to the inventory cycle.

c. Request the client to schedule the physical inventory count at the end of the year.

d. Insist that the client perform physical counts of inventory items several times during the year.

(AICPA adapted)

9.33 An auditor selected items for test counts while observing a client's physical inventory. The auditor then traced the test counts to the client's inventory listing. This procedure most likely obtained evidence concerning management's balance assertion of

a. Rights and obligations.

b. Completeness.

c. Existence.

d. Valuation or allocation.

(AICPA adapted)

9.34 Which of the following auditing procedures probably would provide the most reliable evidence concerning the entity's assertion of rights and obligations related to inventories?

a. Trace test counts noted during the entity's physical count to the entity's summarization of quantities.

b. Inspect agreements to determine whether any inventory is pledged as collateral or subject to any liens.

c. Select the last few shipping documents used before the physical count and determine whether the shipments were recorded as sales.

d. Inspect the open purchase order file for significant commitments that should be considered for disclosure.

(AICPA adapted)

9.35 An auditor most likely would analyze inventory turnover rates to obtain evidence concerning management's balance assertions about

a. Existence.

b. Rights and obligations.

c. Completeness.

d. Valuation or allocation.

9.36 When evaluating inventory controls, an auditor would be *least* likely to

a. Inspect documents.

b. Make inquiries.

c. Observe procedures.

d. Consider policy and procedure manuals.

9.37 When testing a company's cost accounting system, the auditor uses procedures that are primarily designed to determine that

a. Quantities on hand have been computed based on acceptable cost accounting techniques that reasonably approximate actual quantities on hand.

b. Physical inventories agree substantially with book inventories.

c. The system is in accordance with generally accepted accounting principles and is functioning as planned.

d. Costs have been properly assigned to finished goods, work-in-process, and cost of goods sold.

9.38 The auditor tests the quantity of materials charged to work-in-process by vouching these quantities to

a. Cost ledgers.

b. Perpetual inventory records.

c. Receiving reports.

d. Material requisitions.

9.39 Your client counts inventory three months before the end of the fiscal year because controls over inventory are excellent. Which procedure is not necessary for the roll-forward?

a. Check that shipping documents for the last three months agree with perpetual records.

b. Examine receiving reports for the last three months to perpetual records.

c. Compare gross margin percentages for the last three months.

d. Request the client to recount inventory at the end of the year.

9.40 An auditor is examining a nonpublic company's inventory procurement system and has decided to perform tests of controls. Under which of the following conditions do GAAS require tests of controls be performed by an auditor?

a. Significant weaknesses were found in the company's internal control.

b. The auditor hopes to reduce the amount of work to be done in assessing inherent risk.

c. The auditor believes that testing the controls could lead to a reduction in overall audit time and cost.

d. Tests of controls are always performed when the auditor begins to assess control risk.

Exercises, Problems, and Simulations

9.41 **Internal Control Questionnaire Items: Possible Error or Fraud Due to Weakness.** Refer to the internal control questionnaire for the production cycle (Appendix 9A.1) and assume that the answer to each question is "no." Prepare a table matching questions to errors or frauds that could occur because of the absence of the control. Your column headings should be as follows:

Question	Possible Error or Fraud Due to Weakness

9.42 **Tests of Controls Related to Controls and Assertions.** Each of the following tests of controls could be performed during the audit of the controls in the production cycle.

Required:

For each procedure, identify (a) the internal control procedure (strength) being tested and (b) the assertion(s) being addressed.

1. Balance and reconcile detailed production cost sheets to the work-in-process inventory control account.

2. Scan closed production cost sheets for missing numbers in the sequence.

3. Vouch a sample of open and closed production cost sheet entries to (i) labor reports and (ii) issue forms and materials used reports.

4. Locate the material issue forms and determine whether they are (i) prenumbered, (ii) kept in a secure location, and (iii) available to unauthorized persons.

5. Select several summary journal entries in the work-in-process inventory and (i) vouch them to weekly labor and material reports and to production cost sheets and (ii) trace them to the control account.

6. Select a sample of the material issue forms in the production department file. Examine them for

 (i) Issue date and materials used report date.

 (ii) Production order number.

 (iii) Floor supervisor's signature or initials.

 (iv) Name and number of material.

 (v) Raw material stores clerk's signature or initials.

 (vi) Material requisition in raw material stores file, noting the date of requisition.

7. Determine by inquiry and inspection whether cost clerks review dates on reports of units completed for accounting in the proper period.

9.43 **Cost Accounting Tests of Controls.** The diagram in Exhibit 9.43.1 describes several cost accounting tests of controls. It shows the direction of the tests, leading from samples of cost accounting analyses, management reports, and the general ledger to blank squares.

Required:

For each blank square in Exhibit 9.43.1, write a cost accounting test of controls procedure and describe the evidence it can produce. (*Hint:* Refer to Exhibits 9.4 and 9.5.)

EXHIBIT 9.43.1
Diagram of Cost Accounting Tests of Controls

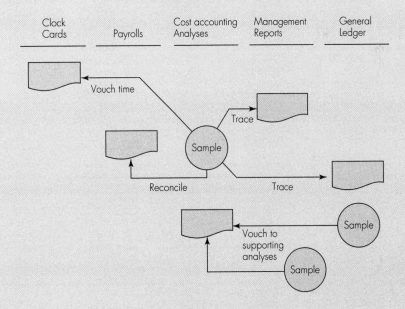

9.44 **Inventory Count Observation: Planning and Substantive Procedures.** Sammy Smith is the partner in charge of the audit of Blue Distributing Corporation, a wholesaler that owns one warehouse containing 80 percent of its inventory. Sammy is reviewing the audit documentation that was prepared to support the firm's opinion on Blue's financial statements and wants to be certain that essential audit procedures are well documented.

Required:

a. What evidence should Sammy expect to find indicating that the observation of the client's physical count of inventory was well planned and that assistants were properly supervised?

b. What substantive procedures should Sammy find in the audit documentation of management's balance assertions about existence and completeness of inventory quantities at the end of the year? (Refer to Appendix 9B.1 for the audit program's procedures.)

(AICPA adapted)

9.45 **Sales/Inventory Cutoff.** Your client took a complete physical inventory count under your observation as of December 15 and adjusted the inventory control account (perpetual inventory method) to agree with the physical inventory. After considering the count adjustments as of December 15 and after reviewing the transactions recorded from December 16 to December 31, you are almost ready to accept the inventory balance as fairly stated. However, your review of the sales cutoff as of December 15 and December 31 disclosed the following items not previously considered:

Sales		Date		
Cost	Price	Shipped	Billed	Credited to Inventory Control
$28,400	$36,900	12/14	12/16	12/16
39,100	50,200	12/10	12/19	12/10
18,900	21,300	1/2	12/31	12/31

Required:

What adjusting journal entries, if any, would you make for each of these items? Explain why each adjustment is necessary.

(AICPA adapted)

9.46 **Audit Simulation: Purchasing Cutoff.** When tracing in the cutoff information from the December 31 inventory count of Thermo-Tempur Mattresses, you note the following information:

Receiving Report Number	Date Received	Total Cost
1179	12/28	$12,433.61
1180	12/28	8,923.34
1181	12/29	15,448.22
1182	12/31	14,109.33
1183	12/31	11,482.57
1184	1/2	17,852.56
1185	1/3	8,753.95

The purchases list shows that the following items were recorded in December.

Receiving Report Number	Date Received	Total Cost
1179	12/28	$12,433.61
1180	12/28	8,923.34
1181	12/29	15,448.22
1182	12/31	14,109.33
1184	1/2	17,852.56

The documentation indicates that the last receiving report included in the inventory count was Receiving Report 1182. Receiving Reports 1183 and 1184 were for goods received on the company's truck but not unloaded.

Required:

Prepare a correcting journal entry assuming that Thermo-Tempur uses (a) a periodic inventory system and (b) a perpetual inventory system that was updated for the inventory count.

9.47 **Statistical Sampling Used to Estimate Inventory.** ACE Corporation does not conduct a complete annual physical count of purchased parts and supplies in its principal warehouse but uses statistical sampling to estimate the year-end inventory. ACE maintains a perpetual inventory record of parts and supplies. Management believes that statistical sampling is highly effective in determining inventory values and is sufficiently reliable, making a physical count of each item of inventory unnecessary.

Required:

a. List at least 10 normal audit procedures that should be performed to verify physical quantities whenever a client conducts a periodic physical count of all or part of its inventory (see Appendix 9B.1 for procedures).

b. Identify the audit procedures you should use that change or are in addition to normal required audit procedures (in addition to those listed in your solution to part a) when a client utilizes statistical sampling to determine inventory value and does not conduct a 100 percent annual physical count of inventory items.

(AICPA adapted)

9.48 **Inventory Procedures Using Computer-Assisted Audit Techniques (CAATs).** You are conducting an audit of the financial statements of a wholesale cosmetics distributor with an inventory consisting of thousands of individual items. The distributor keeps its inventory in its own distribution center and in two public warehouses. A perpetual inventory computer database is maintained on a computer disk. The database is updated at the end of each business day. Each individual record of the perpetual inventory database contains the following data:

Item number.

Location of item.

Description of item.

Quantity on hand.

Cost per item.

Date of last purchase.

Date of last sale.

Quantity sold during year.

You are planning to observe the distributor's physical count of inventories as of a given date. The client will provide a computer disk file of the preceding items taken from its database as of the date of the physical count. Your firm has a computer audit program that will be ideal for analyzing the inventory records.

Required:

List the basic inventory auditing procedures and, for each, describe how the use of CAATs and the computerized perpetual inventory database might be helpful to the auditor in performing such auditing procedures. (See Appendix 9B for substantive procedures for inventory.)

Organize your answer as follows:

Basic Inventory Auditing Procedures	How Audit Software and Copy of the Inventory Data File Might Be Helpful
Conduct an observation of the company's physical count.	Determine which items are to be test counted by selecting a random sample of a representative number of items from the inventory file as of the date of the physical count.

(AICPA adapted)

9.49 **CAATs Application: Inventory.** Your client, Boos & Becker, Inc., is a medium-size manufacturer of products for the leisure-time activities market (camping equipment, scuba gear, bows and arrows, and the like). During the past year, a computer system was installed, and inventory records of finished goods and parts were converted to computerized processing. Each record of the inventory master file contains the following information:

Item or part number.

Description.

Size.

Quantity on hand.

Cost per unit.

Total value of inventory on hand at cost.

Date of last sale or usage.

Quantity used or sold this year.

Reorder point (quantity).

Economic order quantity.

Code number of major vendor or code number of secondary vendor.

In preparation for year-end inventory, the client has two identical sets of preprinted inventory cards prepared from the master file. One set is for the client's inventory counts and the other is for your use to make audit test counts. The following information has been included on the preprinted cards:

Item or part number.

Description.

Size.

Unit of measure code.

In taking the year-end count, the client's personnel will write the actual counted quantity on the face of each card. When all counts are complete, the counted quantity will be processed against the master file, and quantity-on-hand figures will be adjusted to reflect the actual count. A computer list will be prepared to show any missing inventory count cards and all quantity adjustments of more than $100 in value. Client personnel will investigate these items and will make all required adjustments. When adjustments have been completed, the final year-end balances will be computed and posted to the general ledger.

Your firm has available an audit software package that will run on the client's computer and can process both cards and disk master files.

Required:

a. In general and without regard to the preceding facts, discuss the nature of CAATs and list the various audit uses of such packages.

b. List and describe at least five ways CAATs can be used to assist in all aspects of the audit of the inventory of Boos & Becker, Inc. (For example, CAATs can be used to read the inventory master file and list items and parts with a high unit cost or total value. Such items can be included in the test counts to increase the dollar coverage of the audit verification.) (*Hint:* Think of the normal audit procedures in gathering evidence on inventory when the client makes a periodic count; then think of how these could help in this particular client situation.)

(AICPA adapted)

9.50 **Audit Simulation: Inventory Evidence and Long-Term Purchase Contracts.** During the audit of Mason Company, Inc., for the calendar year 2008, you noted that the company produces aluminum cans at the rate of about 40 million units annually. On the plant tour, you noticed a large stockpile of raw aluminum in storage. Your inventory observation and pricing procedures showed this stockpile to be the raw materials inventory of 400 tons valued at $240,000 (LIFO cost). Inquiry with the production chief yielded the information that 400 tons was about a four-month supply of raw materials.

Suppose you learn that Mason had executed a firm long-term purchase contract with All Purpose Aluminum Company to purchase raw materials on the following schedule:

Delivery Date	Quantity (Tons)	Total Price
January 30, 2009	500	$300,000
June 30, 2009	700	420,000
December 30, 2009	1,000	500,000

Because of recent economic conditions, principally a decline in the demand for raw aluminum and a consequent oversupply, the price stood at 40 cents per pound as of January 15, 2009. Commodities experts predict that this low price will prevail for 12 to 15 months or until there is a general economic recovery.

Required:

a. Describe the procedures you would employ to gather evidence about this contract (including its initial discovery).

b. What facts recited in the problem would you have to discover for yourself in an audit?

c. Discuss the effect this contract has on the financial statements.

9.51 **Audit Simulation: Tracing the Inventory Count.** You have been assigned to trace the results of the observation of Brightware China's physical inventory count to its pricing and compilation. You note the following conditions.

1. The last inventory tag documented by Mark Hulse, the auditor who observed the inventory, was 1732, but you notice a number of items with count ticket numbers higher than 1732. You contact the client's controller, Marcia Vines, who tells you the client found a storage room full of a new product that Brightware had just produced and added it to the inventory.

2. The count tickets recorded by Hulse agree to the inventory list, but some of the other count tickets you select are substantially different from it. Vines tells you these are input errors and she will have them corrected.

3. Hulse described several boxes of goods as being dusty and even broken. They are included in the inventory at cost. Vines's explanation is that china never "goes bad" and the goods themselves were not broken.

Required:

a. Prepare an audit program for tracing the information from the inventory count to the compilation.

b. What might have caused the conditions you found? What effect might they have on the financial statements?

c. What steps will you take to follow up on Vines's explanations?

9.52 **Audit Simulation: FIFO Inventory Pricing.** You are auditing Martha's Prison Clothes, Inc., as of December 31, 2008. The inventory for orange jumpsuits shows 1,263 suits at $782 for a total of $987,666. When you look at the invoices for the jumpsuits, you see the following:

Inventory Number	Date	Quantity	Unit Price	Total
12732	11/22/08	1,000	$765	$765,000
12844	12/03/08	800	777	621,600
12905	12/28/08	600	782	469,200

Required:

a. Determine the adjusting entry, if any, for the cost of inventory at December 31, 2008.

b. Would your answer to part a be different if you saw an invoice dated January 9, 2009, for 500 suits at $750?

Instructions for Problems 9.53 and 9.54

The cases in Problems 9.53 and 9.54 are designed like the ones in the chapter. They give the problem and the amount. Your assignment is to write the audit approach portion of the case organized around these sections:

Objective: Express the objective in terms of the facts supposedly asserted in the financial records, accounts, and statements.

Control: Write a brief explanation of desirable controls, missing controls, and especially the types of deviations that might arise from the situation described in the case.

Tests of controls: Write some procedures for obtaining evidence about controls, especially procedures that could discover control deviations. If there are no controls to test, there are no procedures to perform; go to the next section. A *procedure* should instruct someone about the source(s) of evidence to tap and the work to do.

Audit of balance: Write some procedures for obtaining evidence about the balance assertions of existence, rights and obligations, completeness, valuation, and accuracy identified in your objective section.

Discovery summary: Write a short statement about the discovery you expect to accomplish with your procedures.

Inventory and deferred cost overstatement: Follow the preceding instructions. Write the audit approach section following the cases in the chapter.

9.53 **Toying around with the Numbers.** Mattel, Inc., a manufacturer of toys, failed to write off obsolete inventory, thereby overstating inventory and improperly deferred tooling costs, both of which understated cost of goods sold and overstated income.

"Excess" inventory was identified by comparing types of toys (wheels, general toys, dolls, games), parts, and raw materials with the forecasted sales or usage; lower-of-cost-or-market (LCM) determinations then were made to calculate the obsolescence write-off. Obsolescence was expected and the target for the year was $700,000. The first comparison computer run showed $21 million "excess" inventory! The company "adjusted" the forecast by increasing the quantities of expected sales for many toy lines. (Forty percent of items had forecasted sales more than their actual recent sales.) Another "adjustment" was to forecast toy closeout sales not at reduced prices but at regular prices. In addition, certain parts were labeled "interchangeable" without the normal reference to a new toy product. These adjustments to the forecast reduced the excess inventory exposed to LCM valuation and write-off.

The cost of setting up machines, preparing dies, and other preparations for manufacture are tooling costs. They benefit the lifetime run of the toy manufactured. The company capitalized them as prepaid expenses and amortized them in the ratio of current-year sales to expected product lifetime sales (much like a natural resource depletion calculation). To lower the amortization cost, the company transferred unamortized tooling costs from toys with low forecasted sales to ones with high forecasted sales. This caused the year's amortization ratio to be smaller, the calculated cost write-off lower, and the cost of goods sold lower than it should have been.

The computerized forecast runs of expected usage of interchangeable parts provided a space for a reference to the code number of the new toy where the part would be used. Some of these references contained the code number of the part itself, not a new toy. In other cases, the forecast of toy sales and parts usage contained the quantity on hand, not a forecast number.

In the tooling cost detailed records, unamortized cost was classified by lines of toys (similar to classifying asset cost by asset name or description). Unamortized balances were carried forward to the next year. The company changed the classifications shown at the prior year-end to other toy lines that had no balances or different balances. In other words, the balances of unamortized cost at the end of the prior year did not match the beginning balances of the current year except for the total prepaid expense amount.

For lack of obsolescence write-offs, inventory was overstated at $4 million. The company recorded a $700,000 obsolescence write-off. It should have been about $4.7 million, as later determined. The tooling cost manipulations overstated the prepaid expense by $3.6 million.

The company reported net income (after taxes) of $12.1 million in the year before the manipulations took place. If pretax income were in the $20 to $28 million range in the year of the misstatements, the obsolescence and tooling misstatements alone amounted to about 32 percent income overstatement.

9.54 **No Defense for These Charges.** Follow the instructions preceding Problem 9.53. Write the audit approach section following the cases in the chapter.

SueCan Corporation deferred costs under the heading of defense contract claims for reimbursement and deferred tooling labor costs, thus overstating assets, understating cost of goods sold, and overstating income.

SueCan manufactured electronic and other equipment for private customers and government defense contracts. Near the end of the year, the company used a journal entry to remove $110,000 from cost of goods sold and defer it as deferred tooling cost. This $110,000 was purported to be labor cost associated with preparing tools and dies for large production runs.

The company opened a receivables account for "cost overrun reimbursement receivable" as a claim for reimbursement on defense contracts ($378,000).

The company altered the labor time records for the tooling costs in an effort to provide substantiating documentation. Company employees prepared new work orders numbered in

the series used late in the fiscal year and attached labor time records dated much earlier in the year. The production orders originally charged with the labor cost were left completed but with no labor charges!

The claim for reimbursement on defense contracts did not have documentation specifically identifying the labor costs as being related to the contract. There were no work orders. (Auditors know that Defense Department auditors insist on documentation and justification before approving such a claim.)

SueCan reported net income of about $442,000 for the year, an overstatement of approximately 60 percent.

9.55 **Detection of Errors and Fraud.** For each of the following independent events, indicate the (1) effect of the error or fraud on the financial statements and (2) what auditing procedures could have detected the misstatement resulting from error or fraud.

 a. The physical inventory count of J. Payne Enterprises, which has a December 31 year end, was conducted on August 31 without incident. In September, the perpetual inventory was not reduced for the cost of sales.

 b. Holmes Drug Stores counted its inventory on December 31, which is its fiscal year end. The auditors observed the count at 20 of Holmes's 86 locations. The company falsified the inventory at 20 of the locations not visited by the auditors by including fictitious goods in the counts.

 c. Pope Automotive inadvertently included in its inventory automobiles that it was holding on consignment for other dealers.

 d. Peffer Electronics, Inc. overstated its inventory by pricing wiring at $200 per hundred feet instead of $200 per thousand feet.

 e. Goldman Sporting Goods counted boxes of baseballs as having one dozen baseballs per box when they only had six per box.

CPA REVIEW

9.56 **Kaplan CPA Exam Simulation: Inventory Assertions.** Rapport & Associates, LLC (Rapport) is auditing the financial statements of Amberly Tool & Die, Inc. (Amberly), which is publicly traded on the New York Stock Exchange, for Year 2. The year end is December 31 and Year 1 was audited by Rapport. Some interim work has already been performed starting in late October of Year 2.

It is now January 9, Year, and the field work for the end of Year 2 is about to commence. You are an audit senior with Rapport and have been assigned to the Amberly engagement.

Required:

Go to the Kaplan Web site at www.mhhe.com/louwers3e, click on AUD: Amberly Tool & Die case and the "Inventory" tab, and complete your answer.

CPA REVIEW

9.57 **Kaplan CPA Exam Simulation: Inventory Method.** Officials of Ferreira Company approach Riley & Associates, a local CPA firm, about the possibility of looking over the company's financial statements. All of the stock of Ferreira Company is privately owned by four unrelated shareholders. A partner with Riley & Associates has explained to the company officials that the financial statements could be subjected to an audit, a review, or a compilation.

Required:

Go to the Kaplan Web site at www.mhhe.com/louwers3e, click on AUD: Amberly Tool & Die case and the "Research" tab, and complete your answer.

Appendix 9A

Internal Control Questionnaires

APPENDIX 9A.1 Production Cycle

	Yes/No	Comments
Occurrence		
1. Is cost accounting separate from production, payroll, and inventory control?		
2. Is access to blank production order forms denied to unauthorized persons?		
3. Is access to blank bills of materials and labor needs forms denied to unauthorized persons?		
4. Is access to blank material requisition forms denied to unauthorized persons?		
5. Are production orders prepared by authorized persons?		
6. Are bills of materials and labor needs prepared by authorized persons?		
7. Are material usage reports compared to raw material stores issue forms?		
8. Are labor usage reports compared to job time tickets?		
9. Are material requisitions and job time tickets reviewed by the production supervisor after the floor supervisor prepares them?		
10. Are the weekly direct labor and materials used reports reviewed by the production supervisor after preparation by the floor supervisor?		
Completeness		
11. Are production orders prenumbered and the numerical sequence checked for missing documents?		
12. Are bills of materials and labor needs forms prenumbered and the numerical sequence checked for missing documents?		
13. Are material requisitions and job time tickets prenumbered and the numerical sequence checked for missing documents?		
14. Are inventory issue forms prenumbered and the numerical sequence checked for missing documents?		
15. Is accounting notified of terms of major agreements?		
16. Is accounting notified of orders received on consignment?		
Accuracy		
17. Are differences between inventory issue forms and materials used reports recorded and reported to the cost accounting supervisor?		
18. Are differences between job time tickets and the labor report recorded and reported to the cost accounting supervisor?		
19. Are standard costs used? If so, are they reviewed and revised periodically?		
20. Are differences between reports of units completed and products received reports recorded and reported to the cost accounting supervisor?		
Cutoff		
21. Does the accounting manual give instructions to date cost entries on the date of use?		
22. Does an accounting supervisor review monthly, quarterly, and year-end cost accruals?		
Classification		
23. Are summary entries reviewed and approved by the cost accounting supervisor?		
24. Does the accounting manual give instructions for proper classification of cost accounting transactions?		

APPENDIX 9A.2 Inventory Transaction Processing

	Yes/No	Comments
Occurrence		
1. Are perpetual inventory records kept for raw materials? Supplies? Work-in-process? Finished goods?		
2. Is merchandise or materials on consignment-in (not the property of the company) physically segregated from goods owned by the company?		
3. Are additions to inventory quantity records made only on receipt of a receiving report copy?		
4. Do inventory custodians notify inventory records of reductions of inventory?		
Completeness		
5. Are reductions of inventory record quantities made only on receipt of inventory issuance documents?		
6. Do inventory custodians notify the records department of additions to inventory?		
7. Are separate records maintained for consignment inventory?		
Accuracy		
8. Are perpetual records reconciled to general ledger control accounts?		
9. Do the perpetual records show both quantities and prices?		
10. Are inventory records maintained by someone other than the inventory stores custodian?		
11. Are the inventory records compared to physical counts?		
12. Are production reports of material and labor prepared weekly and transmitted to cost accounting?		
13. Are job cost sheets posted weekly and summary journal entries of work-in-process and work completed prepared monthly?		
14. Are job cost sheet entries reviewed by a person independent of the preparer?		
15. If standard costs have been used for inventory pricing, have they been reviewed for reasonableness and current applicability?		
16. Is there a periodic review for overstocked, slow-moving, or obsolete inventory? Have any adjustments been made during the year?		
17. Are periodic counts of physical inventory made to correct errors in the individual perpetual records?		
Cutoff		
18. Does the accounting manual give instructions to record inventory additions on the date of the receiving report?		
19. Does the accounting manual give instructions to record inventory issues on the issuance date?		
Classification		
20. Are perpetual inventory records kept in dollars periodically reconciled to general ledger control accounts?		

Appendix 9B

Audit Programs

APPENDIX 9B.1

Apollo Shoes, Inc. Audit Program for Physical Inventory Observation December 31, 2008		
	Performed by	**Ref.**
1. Obtain client's inventory-counting instructions and review for completeness.		
2. Tour facility before the inventory count looking for out-of-the-way items, obsolete items, and patterns of inventory flow.		
3. Observe client personnel taking inventory counts for compliance with instructions.		
(continued)		

APPENDIX 9B.1 *(continued)*

	Performed by	Ref.
4. Test count a selection of items throughout the facility and record a sample of your test counts. Note description, stage of completion, counting unit, and condition. 5. Inspect tags used and unused and obtain and record tag numbers used. 6. Select sample of used tags and trace them to the items on the floor. 7. Obtain number of last five receiving reports and last five shipping documents. Record numbers of next unused items in sequence. 8. Tour facilities to ensure all items have been counted.		

APPENDIX 9B.2

Apollo Shoes, Inc.
Audit Program for Inventory Pricing and Compilation
December 31, 2008

	Performed by	Ref
Inventory 1. Obtain client's inventory list, mathematically verify it, and check it against the general ledger. 2. Trace test counts from inventory observation to the final inventory compilation. 3. Select a sample of inventory items. Vouch unit prices to vendors' invoices or other cost records. Recalculate the multiplication of unit and price. 4. Scan the inventory compilation for items added from sources other than the physical count and items that appear to be large round numbers or systematic fictitious additions. 5. Recalculate the extensions and footings of the final inventory compilation for mathematical accuracy. Reconcile the total to the adjusted trial balance. 6. For selected inventory items and categories, determine the replacement cost and the applicability of lower-of-cost-or-market valuation. 7. Determine whether obsolete or damaged goods should be written down. 8. Inquire about obsolete, damaged, slow-moving, and overstocked inventory. 9. Scan the perpetual records for slow-moving items. 10. During the physical observation, be alert to notice damaged or scrap inventory. 11. Compare the list of obsolete, slow-moving, damaged, or unsalable inventory from last-year's audit to the current inventory compilation. 12. At year end, identify the numbers of the last shipping and receiving documents for the year. Compare these to the sales, inventory/cost of sales, and accounts payable entries for proper cutoff. 13. Read bank confirmations, debt agreements, and minutes of the board and make inquiries about pledge or assignment of inventory to secure debt. 14. Inquire about consigned-out inventory and about inventory on hand that is consigned-in from vendors. 15. Confirm or inspect inventories held in public warehouses. 16. Recalculate the amount of intercompany profit to be eliminated in consolidation. 17. Obtain management representations concerning pledging of inventory as collateral, intercompany sales, and other related-party transactions. **Cost of Sales** 1. Select a sample of recorded cost of sales entries and vouch to supporting documentation. 2. Select a sample of basic transaction documents (such as sales invoices, production reports) and determine whether the related cost of goods sold was figured and recorded properly. 3. Determine whether the accounting costing method used by the client (such as FIFO, LIFO, standard cost) was applied properly. 4. Compute the gross margin rate and compare to prior years. 5. Compute the ratio of cost elements (such as labor, material) to total cost of goods sold and compare this ratio to that for prior years.		

Finance and Investment Cycle

Professional Standards References

Compendium Section	Document Reference	Topic
Various*	AS 5	"An Audit of Internal Control over Financial Reporting That Is Integrated with an Audit of Financial Statements"
AU 311	SAS 108	"Planning and Supervision"
	ISA 300	"Planning an Audit of Financial Statements"
AU 312	SAS 107	"Audit Risk and Materiality in Conducting an Audit"
AU 313	SAS 110	"Performing Audit Procedures in Response to Assessed Risks and Evaluating the Audit Evidence Obtained"
	ISA 330	"The Auditor's Procedures in Response to Assessed Risks"
AU 316	SAS 99	"Consideration of Fraud in the Audit of Financial Statements"
	ISA 240	"The Auditor's Responsibility to Consider Fraud in an Audit of Financial Statements"
AU 319	SAS 109	"Understanding the Entity and Its Environment and Assessing the Risks of Material Misstatement"
	ISA 330	"The Auditor's Procedures in Response to Assessed Risks"
AU 326	SAS 106	"Audit Evidence"
	ISA 500	"Audit Evidence"
AU 328	SAS 101	"Auditing Fair Value Measurements and Disclosures"
AU 9101		"Interpretation: Auditing Investments in Securities Where a Readily Determinable Fair Value Does Not Exist"
AU 9328		"Interpretation: Auditing Interests in Trusts Held by a Third-Party Trustee and Reported at Fair Value"
AU 329	SAS 56	"Analytical Procedures"
	ISA 520	"Analytical Procedures"
AU 330	SAS 67	"The Confirmation Process"
AU 332	SAS 92	"Auditing Derivative Investments, Hedging Activities, and Investments in Securities"
AU 9332		"Interpretation: Auditing Derivative Investments, Hedging Activities, and Investments in Securities"
		"Interpretation: Auditing Interests in Trusts Held by a Third-Party Trustee and Reported at Fair Value"
AU 333A	SAS 85	"Management Representations"
	ISA 580	"Management Representations"
AU 334	SAS 110	"Performing Audit Procedures in Response to Assessed Risks and Evaluating the Audit Evidence Obtained"
AU 9334		"Interpretation: Related-party Transactions with a Component"
AU 336	SAS 73	"Using the Work of a Specialist"
AU 339	SAS 103	"Audit Documentation"
	AS 3	"Audit Documentation"
	ISA 230	"Audit Documentation"
AU 342	SAS 57	"Auditing Accounting Estimates"
	ISA 540	"Audit of Accounting Estimates"
AU 9342		"Interpretation: Fair Value Disclosures"
AU 431	SAS 32	"Adequacy of Disclosure of Financial Statements"

*AS 5 amends AU 230, AU 310, AU 312, AU 313, AU 315 AU 316, AU 319, AU 322, AU 325, AU 328, AU 332, AU 333, AU 341, AU 342, AU 380, AU 508, AU 530, AU 543, AU 560, AU 561, AU 711, AU 722, AS 3, and AS 4.

Credit has done a thousand times more to enrich mankind than all the goldmines in the world. It has exalted labor, stimulated manufacture and pushed commerce over every sea.

Daniel Webster, statesman, lawyer, and orator

Learning Objectives

The finance and investment cycle consists of planning for capital requirements and raising the required money by borrowing, selling stock, and entering into acquisitions and joint ventures. The finance part of the cycle involves obtaining money through stock or debt issues. The investment portion of the cycle encompasses using the funds for investments in property, plant, and equipment (covered in the acquisition and expenditure cycle chapter), marketable securities, joint ventures and partnerships, and subsidiaries. The transactions discussed in this chapter are generally large and infrequent. They can involve complex accounting issues and

receive much attention by management and the auditors.

Your objectives are to:

1. Describe the finance and investment cycle, including typical source documents and controls.

2. Give examples of tests of controls over debt and owners' equity transactions and investment transactions.

3. Describe substantive procedures for finance and investment accounts.

4. Describe common errors and frauds in the accounting for capital transactions and investments and design audit and investigation procedures for detecting them.

INTRODUCTION

Enron used hundreds of off-the-book arrangements known as **special purpose entities (SPEs)** ostensibly to create joint ventures for new businesses such as energy trading and on-demand movies. (The company created so many SPEs that officers named them after Star Wars characters (Chewco and Jedi), animals (raptors and bobcats), and even officers' children.) In point of fact, however, they were used to enrich company officers and hide more than a billion dollars of debt from the company's creditors, investors, and auditors. Rather than vehicles to fund expansion into new innovative markets, the SPEs brought down the company. Many of the SPEs were financed by pledges of Enron stock as collateral and their viability was dependent upon the company's stock price. When the company's stock started to fall, the structures collapsed. When the firm's stock price dropped from $80 to less than $1 in less than a year, millions of investors suffered losses and thousands of current and former company employees had their retirement plans wiped out. The restatement of the company's financial statements totaled $586 million. Although Arthur Andersen's obstruction of justice conviction for shredding Enron audit documentation was later overturned by the U.S. Supreme Court, the 86,000-employee accounting firm was ruined.

Enron was a spectacular business and audit failure that captured the attention of the country. However, hidden behind all of the headlines was the enormous difficulty the auditors faced in unraveling Enron's complex financing arrangements. Enron management had paid millions of dollars to Wall Street firms to design the SPEs so that they could be kept off the balance sheet. Early knowledge of the extent of Enron's deception might have caused its auditors to insist on consolidating the SPEs on Enron's books and thereby might have saved both Enron and Arthur Andersen.

This example illustrates the potential size and complexity of transactions in the finance and investment cycle. Transactions in this cycle are much less frequent than in the other cycles; however, they tend to be large and complex, although rarely as complex as Enron's. Thus, the focus of control procedures is on the authorization of transactions and competent accounting personnel who can understand the transactions and related accounting standards. The focus of substantive procedures is gaining an understanding of

the transactions, verifying the amounts and calculations, and ensuring proper presentation and disclosure. Finance and investment cycle transactions have become a leading cause of recent financial statement restatements. Some of the largest recent restatements are described in Exhibit 10.1.

EXHIBIT 10.1 **Finance and Investment Shenanigans**

Company	Cause of Misstatement	Amount
Fannie Mae	The mortgage lending giant used questionable methodology, assumptions, and documentation for applying cash flow hedge accounting.	$9.18 billion
Freddie Mac	The other mortgage lending giant similarly used improper accounting techniques and financial transactions structured to push unwanted earnings into the future and hide gains senior management thought would make the entity appear too volatile.	$4.5 billion
AIG	The insurance giant hid deferred compensation that some executives received through an investment entity, Starr International Co., with long ties to AIG. AIG disclosed the amounts in prior filings but did not run the cost through its financial statements, as it now admits it should have. In addition, the company had problems with accounting for investments by AIG's subsidiaries in synthetic-fuel production facilities, wrongly booked tax credits from the investments as net investment income or other revenue when it should have used them to reduce tax expenses, and accounted for syndication transactions from low-cost housing as sales, boosting net income by $209 million over five years.	$2.7 billion
El Paso	The energy company used improper hedges of anticipated natural gas production.	$2.4 billion
Tyco	Most of the substantive accounting changes centered on $50.6 million in pretax credits that it took to reverse merger reserves set up in prior periods but never used. The SEC said the reserves should either never have been set up or should have been reversed earlier. Additionally, a subsidiary, ADT, improperly carried canceled alarm accounts on its books.	$1.15 billion
Goodyear Tire Company	The company changed the way it accounted for income taxes and the costs of retirees' health and life insurance benefits.	$1.03 billion
General Electric	The company misapplied a rule on how to account for certain derivative deals.	$460 million
Millennium Chemicals	The company changed the accounting treatment on a five-year agreement for its requirements for gold used for production of acetyls that should have been accounted for as a secured financing rather than as an operating lease, underestimated the obligation due to its largest domestic pension plan, and understated deferred taxes.	$400 million
Xerox	Over a period of years, several senior managers in Mexico collaborated to circumvent Xerox's accounting policies and administrative procedures. The restatement related to uncollectible long-term receivables, to failure to record liabilities for amounts due to concessionaires, and, to a lesser extent, for contracts that did not fully meet the requirements to be recorded as sales-type leases.	$207 million
Gap, Inc.	The popular clothier used improper lease accounting related to accounting for rent holidays and tenant allowances.	$200 million
Nikko Cordial	The company falsified information on the timing of a derivative deal.	$119 million
Provident Financial Group	Auto leases were reported off the company's balance sheet as sale and lease-backs of operating leases, but, after a review, the company determined that none of the transactions should have been recorded that way. Instead, they should have been recorded as financing leases, with all assets and liabilities appearing on the company's balance sheet.	$114.7 million
Kroger	The grocery giant used improper lease accounting.	$25 million
Starbucks Corp.	The chain of popular coffee houses used lease accounting practices that were not consistent with generally accepted accounting principles.	$12.6 million
Wild Oats	The grocery chain specializing in healthy foods used improper lease accounting.	$3.2 million

INHERENT RISKS IN THE FINANCE AND INVESTMENT CYCLE

Lease Accounting

Although *SFAS 13* on lease accounting has been in effect since 1976, its implementation has recently come into question. The classification of leases as either operating or capitalized is based on assumptions that management can easily manipulate. For example, if the present value of lease payments is 90 percent or more of the property's value, the lease is capitalized; however, if it is only 89.9 percent of the value, the lease is classified as operating and is not reported as a liability on the balance sheet. The SEC has estimated that Fortune 500 companies have $482 billion of off-balance-sheet leases.[1] With the SEC providing additional scrutiny to lease accounting, over 200 companies recently announced restatements due to their lease accounting.

AUDITING INSIGHT Watch Out for Leases!!!

In a 2005 review of internal control disclosures, conducted by *Financial Executive* magazine, 58 companies disclosed material weaknesses in their internal controls over financial reporting. The largest type of disclosed weaknesses? Leases, accounting for 22.6 percent of the disclosed weaknesses.

Source: "Internal Control Weaknesses in April Highlight Leases," *Financial Executive* 21, no. 5 (June 2005), p. 14.

Loan Covenants

To protect themselves, banks usually insert clauses in loan agreements intended to keep the borrower's financial position at the same level as it was when the bank initiated the loan. These **loan covenants** may restrict payment of dividends, additional borrowings, or use of assets for collateral on other debt. They often require the borrower to maintain certain ratio levels (e.g., a current ratio of no less than 2:1). If borrowers violate these restrictions, the debt can be called (payment demanded) immediately. If the borrower cannot pay the debt when called, it could be forced into bankruptcy. Auditors must check to see that their clients are not in violation of their loan covenants. An additional risk is that companies' managements will misstate their other accounts to meet the covenant requirements.

Related-Party Transactions

Many of the examples of fraud in this chapter occurred through related-party transactions. *SFAS 57* provides the definition for related parties and the appropriate disclosure and accounting. Essentially, a **related party** is one that can exert significant influence over another party. Related parties are frequently used in fraudulent activity because they can

AUDITING INSIGHT The Importance of Disclosure

Bobby L. Jolly was the director of the War Fighting Center at I Corps at Fort Lewis, Washington. John P. Doran, Jolly's friend, was the owner of Walking D Ranch Adventures in Twisp, Washington. On May 16, 2006, the procurement fraud branch of the army's Legal Services Agency suspended Jolly and banned Doran from doing business with the government. The army alleged that Jolly shared sensitive bidding information with Doran leading

to a contract for the Walking D Ranch valued at $65,190. A major part of the allegations is that Jolly served as president of the U.S. Cavalry School, which is part of the Walking D Ranch Adventures, and this relationship was not disclosed.

Source: "Trading in Gray Areas," *Governmental Executive* 38, December 2006, pp. 28, 30.

[1] D. Gullapali, "Lease Restatements Are Surging," *The Wall Street Journal*, April 20, 2005.

conceal activities that the auditors would normally be aware of if the activity occurred between unrelated parties. *SAS 99,* "Consideration of Fraud in a Financial Statement Audit," specifically lists significant transactions with related parties not in the ordinary course of business as a risk factor relating to fraudulent financial reporting.

Complex Transactions

Clients often work with investment bankers to create investing and financing transactions that are structured to get around GAAP rules. Management may want to keep risky ventures off the financial statements to make the company look better. These transactions are usually complex, are difficult to audit, and can be used as vehicles to hide fraud.

Impairments

Large investments involve the risk of asset impairment (loss of value). GAAP require that these impairments normally be taken as losses when they occur. Valuing investments and determining possible impairment of related goodwill is very complex. Moreover, companies have been accused of taking a "big bath," which means writing off assets and building up reserves to reduce expenses in future years. This is more likely to happen when a company is experiencing a bad year or when it hires a new CEO (like a football coach going 1-11 his first year and blaming it on his predecessor's players). Thus, there is always a risk that the client will either overstate or understate the assets.

Presentation and Disclosure

As previously mentioned, it is important for auditors to determine if a lease is a capital or operating lease. In part, the importance stems from different disclosures for these types of leases. Capital leases are presented in a manner identical to purchased assets. Operating leases are disclosed solely in the footnotes to the financial statements. In addition, fixed assets not used in the operations or projected for future use in the operations should not be classified as property, plant, and equipment. For example, if a company owns a warehouse that is no longer in use and has no projected future use (possibly awaiting a buyer), it should be presented in "other assets." Impairments of tangible and intangible assets also must be disclosed in the proper places. These subtle, but important distinctions make the review of proper disclosure a greater risk for long-lived assets.

AUDITING INSIGHT Not Disclosing Information Can Hurt

The Securities and Exchange Commission has ruled that the city of San Diego committed securities fraud by failing to disclose that the unfunded liability in its pension plan was projected to dramatically increase from $284 million in the beginning of 2002 to an estimated $2 billion by 2009, and the liability for retiree health care was an estimated $1.1 billion. The city is now projected to have a shortfall in its retirement system of $1.4 billion. The ongoing investigations have led to a reduction in the city's credit rating and have essentially blocked San Diego from accessing the public bond market. The city had planned to issue more public bonds to pay for needed upgrades to its water and sewer infrastructure.

Source: "SEC Slams City on Pension Debt," *San Diego Union-Tribune,* November 15, 2006.

FINANCE AND INVESTMENT CYCLE: TYPICAL ACTIVITIES

LEARNING OBJECTIVE

1. Describe the finance and investment cycle, including typical source documents and controls.

The finance and investment cycle contains a large number of accounts and records, ranging across tangible (e.g., property, plant, and equipment—PP&E) and intangible assets (e.g., goodwill, patents), long-term liabilities, deferred credits, stockholders' equity, gains and losses, expenses, and income taxes. The major accounts and records are listed in Exhibit 10.2. These include some of the more complicated topics in accounting: equity method accounting for investments, consolidation accounting, goodwill, income taxes, and derivatives, to name a few. It is not the purpose of this chapter to explain the

EXHIBIT 10.2
Finance and Investment Cycle

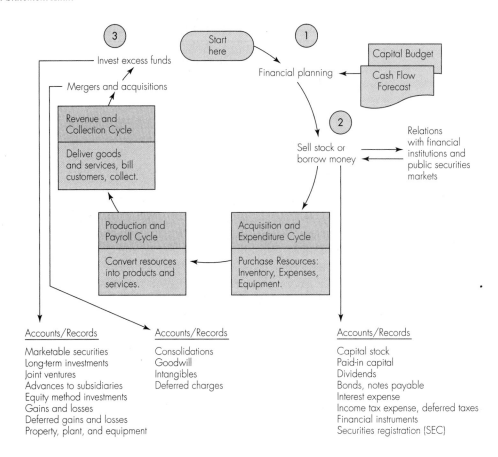

accounting for these balances and transactions. The chapter concentrates on a few important aspects of auditing them. Because the cycle generally involves large, one-of-a-kind transactions, auditors usually focus on substantive procedures.

Exhibit 10.2 is an outline of the finance and investment cycle, which interacts with all of the other cycles. Its major functions are financial planning, raising capital, and entering into mergers, acquisitions, and other investments.

Financing Transactions: Debt and Stockholder Equity Capital

Transactions in debt and stockholder equity capital are normally few in number but large in monetary amount. The highest levels of management handle them. The control-related duties and responsibilities reflect this high-level attention.

Financial Planning

Financial planning starts with the cash flow forecast by the chief financial officer (CFO). This forecast informs the board of directors and management of the business plans, the prospects for cash inflows, and the needs for cash outflows. The cash flow forecast usually is integrated with the capital budget, which contains the plans for asset purchases and business acquisitions. A capital budget approved by the board of directors constitutes the authorization for major capital asset acquisitions (acquisition cycle) and investments. Cash flow planning and capital budgeting are important controls over major management decisions.

Raising Capital

The board of directors usually authorizes sales of capital stock and debt financing transactions. All directors must sign registration documents for public securities offerings. However, authority normally is delegated to the CFO or treasurer to complete such transactions as periodic renewals of notes payable and other ordinary types of financing

transactions without specific board approval of each transaction. Auditors should expect to find the authorizing signatures of the chief executive officer (CEO), CFO, treasurer, chair of the board of directors, and perhaps other high-ranking officers on financing documents.

Company bonds and stocks are normally handled by an intermediary called a **transfer agent,** generally a bank or trust company. The transfer agent tracks securities owners for payment of interest or dividends. The certificate records are kept by a **registrar** who updates the records based on information from the transfer agent. Often the registrar and transfer agent are the same company.

Many financing transactions are off the balance sheet. Companies can enter into obligations and commitments that are not required to be recorded in the accounts. Examples of such authorizations include operating leases, endorsements on discounted notes or on other companies' obligations, letters of credit, guarantees, repurchase or remarketing agreements, commitments to purchase at fixed prices, commitments to sell at fixed prices, and certain kinds of stock options. The Enron debacle was a case of using SPEs to keep certain transactions off the company's balance sheet. Off-balance-sheet transactions often cause problems in financial reporting and disclosure.

AUDITING INSIGHT Synthetic Leases

A popular form of keeping liabilities off the balance sheet is a synthetic lease, which is simply a lease whose terms are structured to be treated as an operating lease for accounting purposes but as a capital lease for tax purposes. These lease arrangements allow companies to borrow money without recording liabilities on the balance sheet. Some large players include Cisco Systems ($1.9 billion), Continental Airlines ($324 million), H.J. Heinz ($220 million), HealthSouth ($207 million), and Human Genome Sciences ($200 million).

Source: "False Front," *Forbes*, October 14, 2002, p. 96.

Record Keeping for Long-Term Liabilities

The accounting department and the CFO or controller maintain records of notes and bonds payable. The record-keeping procedures should be similar to those used to account for vendor accounts payable: comparing payment notices from lenders to the accounting records, monitoring due dates, setting up interest in vouchers for payment, and making accruals for unpaid interest on financial reporting dates. If the company has only a few bonds and notes outstanding, it usually does not keep subsidiary records of them. All information is in the general ledger accounts. (Companies with a large number of bonds and notes may keep control and subsidiary accounts, as is done for accounts payable.) When all or parts of the notes become due within the next year, the CFO and controller have the necessary information for properly classifying current and long-term amounts.

Another class of credit balances is treated here under the heading of record keeping, for which the functions of authorization, custody, and reconciliation are not easy to describe. They are the "calculated liabilities and credits": lease obligations, deferred income taxes, pension and postretirement benefit liabilities, and foreign currency translation gains and losses, to name a few. These are accounting creations, calculated according to accounting rules using basic data from company plans and operations. Management usually has considerable discretion in structuring leases, tax strategies, pension plan and employee benefit terms, foreign holdings, and the like. These accounting calculations often involve significant accounting estimates made by management. Company accountants try to capture the economic reality of these calculated liabilities by following generally accepted accounting principles, which are often complex and difficult to understand.

Periodic Reconciliation

Most publicly traded corporations use registrars and transfer agents to issue certificates and track stock ownership. Reports can be obtained from registrars and transfer agents to verify that the company's record of the number of shares outstanding agrees with the registrar's number. (Without this reconciliation, counterfeit shares handled by the transfer agent and recorded by the registrar might go unnoticed.) A **trustee** having duties and responsibilities similar to those of registrars and transfer agents can handle ownership of bonds. Confirmations and reports from bond trustees can be used to reconcile the trustee's records to the company's records.

Some small, especially closely held corporations may issue stock certificates themselves. These companies utilize a stock certificate book to issue certificates as authorized by the board of directors. A responsible person should periodically inspect the stock certificate book to determine whether the only missing certificates are the ones known to be outstanding in the possession of bona fide owners. If necessary, officials in very small companies can confirm the ownership of shares with the holders of record.

Investing Transactions: Investments and Intangibles ③

Company investments can take many shapes. Investments in PP&E are discussed in the acquisition and expenditure cycle chapter. Investments in intangible assets may be in the form of purchased assets (e.g., patents, trademarks) or accounting allocations (e.g., goodwill, deferred charges). Finally, a company can have a variety of types of investments in marketable securities. The following sections are phrased in the context of a manufacturing or service company; however, financial institutions (banks, thrifts), investment companies (mutual funds, small business investment companies), and insurance companies have more elaborate systems for managing their investments and intangibles.

Authorization

The board of directors or its investment committee should approve all investment policies. It is not unusual to find board or executive committee approval required for major investment transactions. However, auditors should expect to find a great deal of variation across companies about the nature and amount of transactions that must have specific high-level approval. It is imperative that auditors understand the approval process and vouch major acquisitions to the appropriate documented approval.

A U D I T I N G I N S I G H T Authorization: Here Today, Gone Tomorrow

The treasurer of Travum County had many responsibilities as a chief financial officer. She invested several million dollars of county funds with a California-based investment money manager. Soon thereafter, news stories of the money manager's expensive personal lifestyle and questionable handling of clients' funds began to circulate, indicating that clients could lose much of their investments. At the same time, news stories about the county treasurer's own credit card spending habits were published locally, indicating that she had obtained a personal credit card by using the county's name. Although no county funds were lost and no improper credit card bills were paid, the county commissioners temporarily suspended the treasurer's authority to choose investment vehicles for county funds.

Custody

Negotiable certificates such as stocks and bonds may be kept in a brokerage account. Other negotiable certificates (such as titles to real estate) may be in the actual possession of the client. If the company keeps them, they should be in a safe or a bank safe deposit box. Only high-ranking officers (e.g., CFO, CEO, president, and chairman of the board) should have access and access should require two signatures (dual custody).

Patents, trademarks, copyrights, and similar legal intangible rights can be evidenced in legal documents and contracts. These seldom are negotiable and they usually are kept in ordinary company files.

AUDITING INSIGHT Don't Use Our Logo

The University of Texas at Austin has trademark rights over the "longhorn" symbol and a particular school color (burnt orange). The university actively prohibits businesses from using these symbols without permission. For example, a local cleaning business and a trash-hauling business were informed that they must cease and desist using the longhorn head logo on their buildings, signs, and trucks. The businesses complied by repainting and finding other ways to promote their business.

The Coalition to Advance the Protection of Sports Logos (CAPS), whose members are colleges and the professional leagues (NFL, NBA, MLB, and NHL), uses a national network of investigators to scour flea markets, customs ports, and parking lots on game days to ferret out unlicensed T-shirts, caps, and other gear. CAPS has seized $70 million of counterfeit and unlicensed products. NBA investigators alone have seized $87 million worth of counterfeits.

Record Keeping for Investments

The procedures for purchase of most investments involve the voucher system previously described in the acquisition and expenditure cycle chapter. Authorization by the board of directors or other responsible officials provides the approval for the purchasing department to acquire the assets and for the accounting department to prepare the voucher and the check. The treasurer or CFO signs the check for the investment.

The record keeping for many types of investments and intangibles can be complicated. The complications arise not so much from the original recording of transactions but from the maintenance of the accounts over time. This is where complex accounting standards for marketable securities, equity method accounting, consolidations, goodwill, intangibles amortization and valuation, depreciation, deferred charges, deferred taxes, pension and postretirement benefit liabilities, and various financial instruments enter the picture. High-level accountants who prepare financial statements are involved with the accounting rules and the management estimates required to account for such investments and intangibles. Management plans and estimates of future events and interpretations of the accounting standards often become elements of the accounting maintenance of these balances. These decisions are ripe areas for overstatement of assets, understatement of liabilities, and understatement of expenses.

Periodic Reconciliation

The most significant reconciliation opportunity for the investments in marketable securities is the inspection and count of negotiable securities certificates. This reconciliation is similar to a physical inventory count in consisting of an inspection of certificates on hand and comparison to the information recorded in the accounts. (When a brokerage firm holds the securities, the "inspection" is accomplished with a written confirmation.)

A securities count is not a mere handling of bits of paper. A securities count should include a record of the name of the company represented by the certificate, the interest rate for bonds, the dividend rate for preferred stocks, the due date for bonds, the serial numbers on the certificates (known as the CUSIP number), the face value of bonds, the number or face amount of bonds and stock shares, and notes on the name of the owner shown on the face of the certificate or on the endorsements on the back (should be the client company). Companies should perform this reconciliation reasonably often and not wait for an annual visit by the independent auditors. A securities count in a financial institution that holds thousands of shares in multimillion-dollar asset accounts is a major undertaking. A surprise count by the auditors may be done during the interim testing. As with other assets, the auditor should insist that client personnel are present during the entire count.

AUDITING INSIGHT A New Meaning for "Recycling"

Something strange must have happened on the way to the dump. Hundreds of issues of long-term bonds were redeemed early and presented to Citibank in New York, acting as agent for the issues. Many of the bonds still had not reached the maturity date marked on them. Citibank sent about $1 billion of the canceled U.S. corporate bonds to a landfill dump in New Jersey, but some of them turned up at banks in Europe and the United States. The banks have had a disturbing surprise: Although the bonds are worth-

less, they still might look genuine to a layman or even to some bankers. The FBI traced the canceled bonds to a defunct company in New Jersey that had a contract to destroy the bonds. *Note:* Companies obtain a destruction certificate when bonds and stock certificates are canceled. The certificate obtained by Citibank apparently was fraudulent.

Source: Securities Exchange Act Release No. 31612, December 17, 1992.

Review Checkpoints

10.1 What is a destruction certificate?

10.2 What constitutes the authorization for notes payable? What documentary evidence could auditors examine as evidence of this authorization?

10.3 What procedures can auditors employ in the audit of investment securities to obtain the names of the issuers and the number of shares held, certificate numbers, maturity value, and interest and dividend rates?

10.4 Describe the procedures and documentation of a controlled count of client's investment securities.

CONTROL RISK ASSESSMENT

LEARNING OBJECTIVE

2. Give examples of tests of controls over debt and owners' equity transactions and investment transactions.

In the finance and investment cycle, auditors look for control procedures such as authorization, custody, record keeping, and periodic reconciliation. They especially look for information about the level of management involved in these functions. Tests of controls generally amount to inquiries and observations related to these features. Because finance and investment transactions are usually individually material, each transaction usually is audited using substantive procedures. Auditors do not normally examine samples of transactions for tests of controls as they do in the other cycles because reliance on controls does not normally reduce the extent of substantive procedures on finance and investment cycle accounts. However, lack of control can lead to performance of significant extended procedures. Of course, for SEC clients where the auditors must issue a report on the effectiveness of controls over the financial reporting process, evaluation of controls over these transactions is essential.

Control Considerations

Control procedures for suitable handling of responsibilities should be in place and operating. By referring to the discussion accompanying Exhibit 10.2, you can tell that these responsibilities are primarily in the hands of senior management officials. You also can tell that different companies may have widely different policies and procedures.

It is difficult to have a strict separation of functional responsibilities when the principal officers of a company authorize, execute, and control finance and investment activities. It is not realistic to maintain that a CEO can authorize investments but cannot have access to stockholder records, securities certificates, and the like. Real separation of duties can be found in middle management and lower ranks, but it is difficult to create and enforce in upper-level management.

Because of this control problem, a company should have *compensating control procedures*. A **compensating control** is a control feature used when the company does not specify a standard control procedure (such as strict separation of functional responsibilities). In the area of finance and investment, the compensating control feature is the involvement of two or more persons in each area of important functional responsibility.

If involvement by multiple persons is not specified, an oversight or review can be substituted. For example, the board of directors can authorize the purchase of securities or the creation of a partnership. The CFO or CEO can carry out the transactions, have custody of certificates and agreements, manage the partnership or the portfolio of securities, oversee the record keeping, and make the decisions about valuations and accounting (authorizing the journal entries). These are normal management activities and they combine several responsibilities. The compensating control can exist in the form of periodic reports to the board of directors, oversight by the investment committee of the board, and internal audit involvement in making a periodic reconciliation of securities certificates in a portfolio with the amounts and descriptions recorded in the accounts.

Control over Accounting Estimates

An **accounting estimate** is an approximation of a financial statement element, item, or account. Estimates often are included in basic financial statements because (1) the measurement of some amount of valuation is uncertain, perhaps depending on the outcome of future events, or (2) relevant data cannot be accumulated on a timely, cost-effective basis (*SAS 57*). Some examples of accounting estimates in the finance and investment cycle include the following:

- Plant and equipment: Useful lives, salvage values.
- Financial instruments: Valuation of securities, including fair values assigned to debt and equity securities; classification into held-to-maturity, available-for-sale, and trading securities investment portfolios; probability of a correlated hedge; sales of securities with puts and calls; investment model assumptions, impairments.
- Accruals: Compensation in stock option plans, actuarial assumptions in pension costs.
- Leases: Initial direct costs, useful lives, executory costs, and residual values; capitalization interest rate.
- Rates: Imputed interest rates on receivables and payables.
- Other: Losses and net realizable value on segment disposal and business restructuring, fair values in nonmonetary exchanges, impairment of goodwill.

A client's management is responsible for making estimates and should have a process and controls designed to reduce the likelihood of material misstatements in them. According to auditing standards (*SAS 57*), specific relevant aspects of such controls include the following:

- Management communication of the need for proper accounting estimates.
- Accumulation of relevant, sufficient, and reliable data for estimates.
- Preparation of estimates by qualified personnel.
- Adequate review and approval by appropriate levels of authority.
- Comparison of prior estimates with subsequent results to assess the reliability of the estimation outcomes.
- Consideration by management as to whether particular accounting estimates are consistent with the company's operational plans.

Auditors' tests of controls over the estimation process include inquiries and observations. Inquiries would include such questions as: Who prepares estimates? When are they prepared? What data are used? Who reviews and approves the estimates? Have prior estimates been compared with subsequent actual events? Observations include study of data documentation, study of comparisons of prior estimates with subsequent

actual experience, and study of intercompany correspondence concerning estimates and operational plans. The audit of a valuation estimate starts with the tests of controls, much of which have a bearing on the quality of the estimation process and of the estimate itself.

AUDITING INSIGHT OOPS!

A large television manufacturer decided to extend its 90-day warranty on labor to one year. Because the company had no experience with such an extended warranty, it devised a complex formula to take into account the increased likelihood of repair and the associated cost. While going through the pages and pages of calculations with the warranty accountant to obtain an understanding, the auditor noticed one fraction used in the calculation was inverted. The error resulted in a $20,000,000 understatement of the warranty reserve.

Custody

In large companies, custody of stock certificate books is not a significant management problem because of the use of registrars and transfer agents. Small companies often keep their own stockholder records. A stock certificate book looks like a checkbook. It has perforated stubs for recording the number of shares, the owner's name and other identification, and the date of issue. Actual unissued share certificates are attached to the stubs, like blank checks in a checkbook. The missing certificates are the ones that are outstanding in the possession of owners. Custody of the stock certificate book is important because the unissued certificates are like money or collateral. If improperly removed, they can be sold to buyers who think they are genuinely issued or can be used as collateral with unsuspecting lenders.

Lenders have custody of debt instruments (e.g., leases, bonds, and notes payable). However, when a company repurchases its debt instruments, they come into the custody of trustees or company officials. Until they are canceled and destroyed, it is possible to misuse them by improperly reselling them to unsuspecting investors.

Summary: Control Risk Assessment

From the preceding discussion, you can tell that tests of controls take a variety of forms: inquiries, observations, studies of documentation, comparisons with related data, and detail audits of some transactions. Detail audits of transactions, however, represent a small part of the tests of controls because of the nature of the finance and investment transactions, their number (few), and their dollar amount (large). However, some companies have numerous debt-financing transactions and a more detailed approach to control risk assessment can be used, including the selection of a sample of transactions for control risk assessment evidence.

Internal control questionnaires for the finance and investment cycle are in Appendix 10A. They illustrate typical questions about the assertions. These inquiries give auditors insights into the client's specifications for review and approval of major investing and financing transactions, the system of accounting for them, and the provision for error-checking review activities.

The audit manager or senior accountant in charge of the audit should evaluate the evidence obtained from an understanding of the internal control system and from tests of controls. These tests can take many forms because management systems for finance and investment accounts can vary a great deal among clients. The involvement of senior officials in a relatively small number of high-dollar transactions makes control risk assessment a process tailored specifically to the company's situation. Some companies enter into complicated financing and investment transactions, while others keep to the simple transactions.

AUDITING INSIGHT Goodwill Impairment

Following the merger of **Time Warner** and **America Online** (to form **AOL Time Warner**) in 2001, a total of $103.5 billion of goodwill was recognized (to reflect the difference between the value of the AOL shares issued and the book value of the net assets of Time Warner). During the first quarter of 2002, the company took an impairment charge of $54 billion and later in the fourth quarter an additional $46 billion charge. The end result? AOL Time Warner wrote off almost the entire amount of goodwill that was recorded upon the merger. In addition, the market value of AOL Time Warner shares has decreased by $100 billion since the merger.

Source: "AOL Reports $98.7 Billion Loss and Says Ted Turner Will Resign," *The Wall Street Journal*, January 30, 2003, p. A2.

Review Checkpoints

10.5 What is a compensating control? Give some examples for finance and investment cycle accounts.

10.6 What are some of the specific relevant aspects of management's control over the estimation process? What are some inquiries auditors can make?

10.7 When a company has produced an estimate of an investment valuation based on a nonmonetary exchange, what source of comparative information can auditors use to audit the estimate's reasonableness?

10.8 Generally, how much emphasis is placed on adequate internal control in the audit of (a) long-term debt, (b) capital stock, (c) paid-in capital, (d) retained earnings?

FINANCING ACTIVITIES: ASSERTIONS AND SUBSTANTIVE PROCEDURES

LEARNING OBJECTIVE

3. Describe substantive procedures for finance and investment accounts.

This part of the chapter covers the audit of various account balances and transactions. It is presented in two sections: (1) financing activities (such as owners' equity, long-term liabilities, and related accounts) and (2) investing activities (PP&E, investments, and intangibles). This chapter provides some assertions and procedures related to accounts in each portion of the financing and investing cycle. As in previous chapters, some cases illustrating errors and frauds are used to describe useful audit approaches.

Long-Term Liabilities and Related Accounts

Exhibit 10.3 lists assertions for debt and equity accounts and some illustrative procedures for each assertion. The primary audit concern with the verification of long-term liabilities is that all liabilities are recorded and that the interest expense is properly paid or accrued. Therefore, the balance assertion of *completeness* is paramount. Alertness to the possibility of unrecorded liabilities during the performance of procedures in other areas frequently will uncover liabilities that have not been recorded. For example, when PP&E are acquired during the year under audit, auditors should inquire about the source of funds to finance the new assets. Auditors also should be alert for large cash disbursements and maintenance expenses for electrical, plumbing, and air-conditioning systems upgrades. These are all often indicators of the purchase and installation of equipment.

When auditing long-term liabilities, auditors usually obtain independent written confirmations for notes and bonds payable. In the case of notes payable to banks, the standard bank confirmation may be used. The amount and terms of bonds payable, mortgages payable, and other formal debt instruments can be verified by reading the bond **indenture,** the written agreement with the bondholders, and confirmed by requests to bond holders or the bond trustee. The confirmation request should include questions not only of

EXHIBIT 10.3 Account Balance and Presentation and Disclosure Assertions and Substantive Procedures for Debt and Equity Accounts

Account Balance Assertions	Substantive Procedures
Existence—Items in the debt and equity accounts exist.	Confirm debt balances with debtors, including terms, collateral, interest, etc. Confirm certificates issued and outstanding with registrar.
Completeness—All debt and equity that should have been recorded have been recorded.	Confirm debt and equity. Examine large cash receipts for related debt equity.
Rights and obligations—Obligations related to debt or equity are recorded.	Examine debt agreements and include information about restrictions, terms, and collateral on debt confirmations.
Valuation and Accuracy—Debt and equity are included in the financial statements at appropriate amounts and any resulting valuation adjustments are properly recorded.	Recalculate amortization or discount of premiums.
Presentation and Disclosure Assertions	**Substantive Procedures**
Classification—Debt is properly classified as current or noncurrent. Leasing arrangements are properly classified in financial.	Inquire and obtain representation from management. Read footnote disclosures and agree to debt instruments.
Completeness—Debt terms, collateral, leasing arrangements, and debt covenants are disclosed in footnotes.	Calculate ratios and balances required by debt covenants.

amount, interest rate, and due date but also of collateral, restrictive covenants, and other items of agreement between lender and borrower. Confirmation requests should be sent to lenders with whom the company has done business in the recent past, even if no liability balance is shown at the confirmation date. Such extra coverage is a part of the search for unrecorded liabilities. Exhibit 10.4 illustrates typical audit documentation for auditing

EXHIBIT 10.4 Audit Documentation—Long-Term Debt and Interest Expense

APOLLO SHOES, INC. M-1
Long-Term Debt, Accrued Interest Payable, and Interest Expense
For Year Ended 12/31/2008
Prepared by Client

Prepared by	RJR 3/10/09
Reviewed by	TJL 3/12/09

	Date Due	Long-Term Debt				Accrued Interest Payable			
		Balance 12/31/2007	Additions	Amortization/ Payments	Balance 12/31/2008	Balance 12/31/2007	Interest Expense	Payments	Balance 12/31/2006
5.25% senior subordinated debt	6/30/17	$2,500,000 PY	0	$250,000 v	$2,250,000 CF TB	$66,750	$131,437 C	$143,750 v	$54,437 CF
4% note payable— Bank One	9/30/10	0	$500,000 u	0	$500,000 CF TB	$5,000	$20,000 C $151,437	$20,000 v	$5,000 CF
Premium on long-term debt		$354,128 PY	0	$18,266 C	$335,862 CF TB		$18,266 C		
						$71,750 F PY	$169,703 F/TB	$163,750 F	$59,437 CF F/TB

PY = Agreed to prior year workpapers.
u = Agreed to copy of note and cash receipts journal.
v = Vouched to cash disbursement.
F = Footed.

CF = Cross-Footed.
C = Recalculated.
TB = Carried forward to the Trial Balance.

EXHIBIT 10.5 Off-Balance-Sheet Commitments

Type of Commitment	Typical Audit Procedures
Repurchase or remarketing agreements	Vouching of contracts, confirmation by customer, and inquiry of client management
Commitments to purchase at fixed prices	Vouching of open purchase orders, inquiry of purchasing personnel, and confirmation by supplier
Commitments to sell at fixed prices	Vouching of sales contracts, inquiry of sales personnel, and confirmation by customer
Loan commitments (as in a savings and loan association)	Vouching of open commitment file, inquiry of loan officers
Lease commitments	Vouching of lease agreement, confirmation with lessor or lessee

long-term debt and interest expense. Note that the interest expense consists of additions to the accrual account as well as amortization of premium on long-term debt. An illustrative program of substantive procedures for notes payable and long-term debt is in Appendix 10B.1.

Confirmation and inquiry procedures may be used to obtain responses on a class of items loosely termed off-balance-sheet information. Within this category are terms of loan agreements, leases, endorsements, guarantees, and insurance policies (whether issued by a client insurance company or owned by the client). Among these items is the difficult-to-define set of commitments and contingencies that often pose evidence-gathering problems. Some common types of commitments are shown in Exhibit 10.5.

Footnote disclosure should be considered for the types of commitments shown in Exhibit 10.5. Some of them can be estimated and valued and, thus, can be recorded in the accounts and shown in the financial statements themselves (such as losses on fixed-price purchase commitments and losses on fixed-price sales commitments). Interest expense generally is related item by item to interest-bearing liabilities. Based on the evidence of long-term liability transactions (including those that have been retired during the year), the related interest expense amounts can be recalculated. The amount of debt, the interest rate, and the time period are used to determine whether the interest expense and accrued interest are properly recorded. Interest expense also may be estimated by the analytical procedure of multiplying average debt outstanding by the average interest rate.

AUDITING INSIGHT Less Reasonable Assurance?

In a recent study conducted by researchers from Cornell University and Bentley College, auditors took a very different stance on whether to correct an error in lease costs and stock option accounting depending on whether the client's lease costs were directly included in the financial statements as capital leases or in the footnotes as operating leases even though the amount of the errors was the same in both cases. The researchers found similar results with stock option costs. The researchers said the auditors knowingly view misstatements of financial statement numbers as more important than footnote items. As one of them said, "Numbers may be less reliable if you put them in the footnotes."

Source: "Auditors May Let Footnote Errors Slide," *The Wall Street Journal*, March 30, 2005.

Owners' Equity: Audit Procedures

Owners' equity transactions usually are well documented in the minutes of the meetings of the board of directors, proxy statements, and securities offering registration statements. Transaction authorization can be vouched to these documents and the cash proceeds

can be traced to the bank accounts. Capital stock may be subject to confirmation when independent registrars and transfer agents are employed. Such agents are responsible for knowing the number of shares authorized and issued and for keeping lists of stockholders' names. The basic information about capital stock—such as number of shares, classes of stock, preferred dividend rates, conversion terms, dividend payments, shares held in the company name, expiration dates, and terms of warrants and stock dividends and splits—can be confirmed with the independent agents. The audit team's own inspection and reading of stock certificates, charter authorizations, directors' minutes, and registration statements can corroborate many of these items. However, when the client company does not use independent agents, most audit evidence is gathered by inspecting and vouching stock record documents (such as certificate book stubs). When circumstances call for extended procedures, information on outstanding stock in very small corporations having only a few stockholders may be confirmed directly with the holders. An illustrative program of substantive procedures for owners' equity is in Appendix 10B.2.

Review Checkpoints

10.9 What are some of the typical assertions found in owners' equity descriptions and account balances?

10.10 What are some of the typical assertions found in the long-term liability accounts?

10.11 How can confirmations be used in auditing (a) stockholder capital accounts and (b) notes and bonds payable?

10.12 What information about capital stock could be confirmed with outside parties? How could this information be corroborated by the auditors?

10.13 Define and give five examples of off-balance-sheet information. Why should auditors be concerned with such items?

10.14 If a company does not monitor notes payable for due dates and interest payment dates in relation to financial statement dates, what misstatements can appear in the financial statements?

INVESTING ACTIVITIES: ASSERTIONS AND SUBSTANTIVE PROCEDURES

Exhibit 10.6 lists assertions for investment accounts and related substantive procedures. In general, substantive procedures on finance and investment accounts are extensive. The number of transactions is usually not large and the audit cost is not high for complete coverage. Auditors often perform substantive procedures on 100 percent of these transactions and balances. Nevertheless, control deficiencies and unusual or complicated transactions can cause auditors to adjust the nature and timing of audit procedures. Complicated financial instruments, pension plans, exotic equity securities, related-party transactions, and nonmonetary exchanges of investment assets call for procedures designed to find evidence of errors and frauds in the finance and investment accounts. The next section deals with some of the finance and investment cycle assertions and presents some cases for your review.

Substantive procedures for estimates include determining whether (1) the valuation principles are acceptable under GAAP, (2) the valuation principles are consistently applied, (3) the valuation principles are supported by the underlying documentation, and (4) the method of estimation and the significant assumptions are properly disclosed according to GAAP. When auditors perform the securities inspection and count, all of this information should be recorded in the audit documentation. *Existence* is established by

EXHIBIT 10.6 Assertions and Substantive Procedures in Investment Accounts

Assertions about Account Balances	Substantive Procedures
Existence—Items in investment accounts exist.	Confirm stock investments with brokerage.
Completeness—All investments that should have been recorded have been recorded.	Examine documentation for large expenditures. Confirm stock investments with brokerage.
Rights and obligations—The entity holds or controls the rights to investments.	Examine documents for acquisitions.
Valuation and accuracy—Investments are included in the financial statements at appropriate amounts and any resulting valuation adjustments are properly recorded.	Obtain client documentation of review for impairment of goodwill and test. Inquire if management is aware of asset impairments. Obtain audited financial statements of investments accounted for by equity method and recalculate investment amount.
Presentation and disclosure—Investments are properly classified as current or noncurrent and as trading, available for sale, or hold to maturity. Hedging terms are properly disclosed in footnotes	Inquire of management as intent for holding investments. Read footnote disclosures and agree to investment documents. Calculate footnote disclosures required for derivatives. Ensure hedges meet requirements for hedging treatment.

inspecting the securities, ownership (*rights*) is established by viewing the client name as owner, and *valuation* evidence is added by finding the cost and market value. If a security certificate is pledged as collateral for a loan, it may not be available for inspection. It can be confirmed or inspected (if the extended procedure of visiting the creditor is necessary). The pledge as collateral may be important for a footnote disclosure. A securities count and reconciliation is important for management and auditors because companies have tried to substitute others' securities for missing ones. If securities have been sold and then replaced without any accounting entries, the serial numbers will show that the certificates recorded in the accounts are not the same as the ones on hand.

Derivative Instruments, Hedging Activities, and Investments in Securities (*SAS 92*)

Derivative instruments are those that take their value from another asset or index. For example, an option to buy Disney stock is a derivative instrument. Interest rate swaps, options, convertible bonds, futures contracts, and convertible preferred stock are also derivatives. Derivatives can be used as **hedging instruments** to protect companies from uncertainties in the marketplace. For example, a clothing manufacturer could buy futures contracts on cotton to lock the price of its main raw ingredient so that it can predict the future cost of goods sold. Likewise, companies selling overseas use currency futures to lock in the exchange rate for their sales. Accounting for derivatives is extremely complex and new derivatives are constantly being developed. There are even derivatives to protect against bad weather!

Companies can have a wide variety of investments and relationships with affiliates. Investments accounting may be on the market value method, cost method, equity method, or full consolidation, depending on the nature, size, and influence represented by the investment. Consolidations usually create problems of accounting for the fair value of acquired assets and the related goodwill.

An illustrative program of substantive procedures for investments and related accounts is presented in Appendix 10B.3. Part B of this program covers portfolio classification, fair value determination, and evidence about impairment.

Substantive Procedures

Unlike the current asset accounts, which are characterized by numerous small transactions, the noncurrent investment accounts usually consist of a few large entries. Consequently, the

auditors focus on the authorization of transactions because each individual transaction is likely to be material in itself and the authorization will give significant information about the proper classification and accounting method. The controls usually are not reviewed, tested, and evaluated at an interim date but are considered along with the year-end procedures when the transactions and their authorizations are audited.

Trouble Spots in Audits of Investments and Intangibles

- Valuation of investments at cost or market, or impairment that is other than temporary.
- Determination of significant influence relationship for equity method investments.
- Impairment of goodwill.
- Capitalization and continuing valuation of intangibles and deferred charges.
- Propriety, effectiveness, and risk disclosure of derivative securities used as hedges of exposure to changes in fair value (fair value hedge), variability in cash flows (cash flow hedge), or fluctuations in foreign currency.
- Determination of the fair value of derivatives and securities, including valuation models and the reasonableness of key assumptions.
- Realistic distinctions of research, feasibility, and production milestones for capitalization of software development costs.
- Adequate disclosure of restrictions, pledges, or liens related to investment assets.

The practice of obtaining independent written confirmation from outside parties is fairly limited in the area of investments, intangibles, and related income and expense accounts. Securities held by trustees or brokers should be confirmed and the confirmation request should seek the same descriptive information as that obtained in a physical inspection by the auditors.

Investment costs should be vouched to brokers' reports, monthly statements, or other documentary evidence of cost. At the same time, the amounts of sales are traced to gain or loss accounts and the amounts of sales prices and proceeds are vouched to the brokers' statements. Auditors should determine what method of cost-out assignment was used (i.e., FIFO, specific identification, or average cost) and whether it is consistent with prior years' transactions.

Market valuation of securities is required for securities classified in trading portfolios and available-for-sale portfolios. While management may assert that an investment valuation is not impaired, subsequent sale at a loss before the end of audit field work will indicate otherwise. Auditors should review investment transactions subsequent to the balance sheet date for this kind of evidence about value impairment.

Classification of marketable securities is another management judgment that auditors must evaluate. If management classifies securities as trading securities, net income includes unrealized gains. When the market is doing well, these gains can provide significant additions to the bottom line. When the market is down, management can classify the securities as available for sale, which removes the losses from net income. Similar judgments can move securities from noncurrent to current, thus affecting current ratios. Auditors must ensure management is basing its classifications on sound business judgments, not their financial statement effect.

By consulting quoted market values of securities, auditors can calculate market values and determine whether investments should be written down. If quoted market values are not available, financial statements related to investments must be obtained and analyzed for evidence of basic value. If such financial statements are unaudited, they provide extremely weak evidence.

Income amounts can be verified by consulting published or online dividend records for quotations of dividends actually declared and paid during a period (e.g., Moody's and Standard & Poor's dividend records). Because auditors know the holding period of securities, dividend income can be calculated and compared to the amount in the account. Any difference could indicate a cutoff error, misclassification, defalcation, or failure to record a dividend receivable. In a similar manner, application of interest rates to bond or

note investments produces a calculated interest income figure (considering amortization of premium or discount if applicable).

Inquiries should deal with the nature of investments and the reasons for holding them, especially derivative securities used for hedging activities. The classification affects the accounting treatment of market values and the unrealized gains and losses on investments. Due to the complexity of *SFAS 133,* "Accounting for Derivative Securities and Hedging Activities," auditors may need special skills or knowledge to understand clients' hedging transactions, to ensure that effective controls are in place to monitor them, and to audit the transactions.

When equity method accounting is used for investments, auditors need to obtain financial statements of the investee company. These should be audited statements. The inability to obtain financial statements from a closely held investee could indicate that the client investor does not have the significant controlling influence required by APB Opinion No. 18. When available, these statements are used as the basis for recalculating the amount of the client's share of income to recognize in the accounts. In addition, these statements can be used to audit the disclosure of investees' assets, liabilities, and income presented in footnotes (a disclosure recommended when investments accounted for by the equity method are material).

Auditing Fair Value Measurements (*SAS 101*)

GAAP pronouncements increasingly require the use of fair value for measurement of transactions and disclosure amounts. Auditing these measurements is similar to auditing accounting estimates. As with other estimates, management has primary responsibility for determining fair value in accordance with GAAP. Observable market-based values are generally preferred. However, if market prices are not readily available, clients should incorporate assumptions that would have been used by the marketplace. If information about the assumptions is not readily available, management can use their own assumptions "as long as there are no contrary data . . ." (*SAS 101*). Thus, auditors first must determine whether a market-based value is available; if not, they must evaluate whether clients' assumptions would have been used by the marketplace or there are data contrary to what the client used—very murky waters, indeed.

Review Checkpoints

10.15 What are some of the typical assertions found in investment accounts?

10.16 What are some of the typical areas of concern to auditors involving investment accounts?

10.17 How can confirmations be used in auditing investments in stocks?

FRAUD CASES: EXTENDED AUDIT PROCEDURES (*SAS 99*)

LEARNING OBJECTIVE

4. Describe common errors and frauds in the accounting for capital transactions and investments and design audit and investigation procedures for detecting them.

The cases first set the stage with a story about an accounting estimate, error, or fraud. The first part of each case gives you the "inside story," which auditors seldom know before they perform the audit work. The second part of each case, under the heading "Audit Approach," tells a structured story about the audit objective, desirable controls, test of control procedures, and audit of balance procedures and the third part wraps up the case with a discovery summary. At the end of the chapter, some similar discussion cases are presented and you can write the audit approach to test your ability to design audit procedures for the detection of mistaken accounting estimates, errors, and frauds. Some substantive audit programs are in Appendix 10B.

Case 10.1

Unregistered Sale of Securities

PROBLEM

A.T. Bliss & Company (Bliss) salespeople contacted potential investors and sold limited partnership interests. The setup deal called for these limited partnerships to purchase solar hot water heating systems for residential and commercial use from Bliss. All partnerships entered into arrangements to lease the equipment to Nationwide Corporation, which then rented the equipment to end users. The limited partnerships were, in effect, financing conduits for obtaining investors' money to pay for Bliss's equipment. The investors depended on Nationwide's business success and ability to pay under the lease terms for their return of capital and profit.

Bliss published false and misleading financial statements, which used a non-GAAP revenue recognition method and failed to disclose cost of goods sold. Bliss overstated Nationwide's record of equipment installation and failed to disclose that Nationwide had little cash flow from end users (resulting from rent-free periods and other inducements). Bliss knew—and failed to disclose to prospective investors—the fact that numerous previous investors had filed petitions with the U.S. tax court to contest the disallowance by the IRS of all their tax credits and benefits claimed in connection with their investments in Bliss's tax-sheltered equipment lease partnerships.

All of the money put up by the limited partnership investors was at risk but was not disclosed to investors.

AUDIT APPROACH

Management should employ experts—attorneys, underwriters, and accountants—who can determine whether securities and investment contract sales require registration. Auditors should learn the business backgrounds and securities industry expertise of the client's senior managers. They should study the minutes of board of directors meetings for authorization of the fund-raising method, obtain and study opinions rendered by attorneys and underwriters about the legality of the fund-raising methods, and inquire about management's interaction with the SEC in any presale clearance. (The SEC will give advice about the necessity for registration.)

Auditors should study the offering documents and literature used in the sale of securities to determine whether financial information is being used properly. In this case, the close relationship with Nationwide and the experience of earlier partnerships give reasons for extended procedures to obtain evidence about the representations concerning Nationwide's business success (in this case, lack of success).

DISCOVERY SUMMARY

The auditors gave unqualified reports on Bliss's materially misstated financial statements. They apparently did not question the legality of the sales of the limited partnership interests as a means of raising capital. They apparently did not perform procedures to verify representations made in offering literature reflecting Bliss or Nationwide finances. Two partners in the audit firm were enjoined because of violations of the securities laws. The partners resigned from practice before the SEC and were ordered not to perform any attest services for companies making filings with the SEC. According to SEC Litigation Release 10274, AAER 20, and AAER 21, they later were expelled from the AICPA as reported in *The CPA Letter* for failure to cooperate with the Professional Ethics Division in its investigation of alleged professional ethics violations.

Case 10.2

Off-Balance-Sheet Inventory Financing

PROBLEM

Verity Distillery Company's president incorporated the Veritas Corporation, making him and two other Verity officers the sole stockholders. The president arranged to sell $40 million of Verity's inventory of whiskey in the aging process to Veritas, showing no gain or loss on the transaction. The

officers negotiated a 36-month loan with a major bank to get the money Veritas used for the purchase, pledging the inventory as collateral. Verity pledged to repurchase the inventory for $54.4 million, which amounted to the original $40 million plus 12 percent interest for three years.

The contract of sale was in the files, specifying the name of the purchasing company, the $40 million amount, and the cash consideration. Nothing mentioned the relationship of Veritas to the officers. Nothing mentioned the repurchase obligation. However, the sale amount was unusually large.

The $40 million amount was 40 percent of the normal inventory. Verity's cash balance increased 50 percent. The current asset total was not changed, but the inventory ratios (e.g., inventory turnover, days' sales in inventory) and quick ratio were materially altered. Long-term liabilities were understated by not recording the liability. The ploy was actually a secured loan with inventory pledged as collateral, but this reality was neither recorded nor disclosed. The total effect would be to keep debt off the books, to avoid recording interest expense, and later to record inventory at a higher cost. Subsequent sale of the whiskey at market prices would not affect the ultimate income results, but the unrecorded interest expense would be buried in the cost of goods sold. The net income in the first year when the "sale" was made was not changed, but the normal relationship of gross margin to sales was distorted by the zero-profit transaction.

	Before Transaction	Recorded Transaction	Should Have Recorded
Assets	$530	$530	$570
Liabilities	390	390	430
Stockholder equity	140	140	140
Debt/equity ratio	2.79	2.79	3.07

AUDIT APPROACH

The relevant control in this case would rest with the integrity and accounting knowledge of the senior officials who arranged the transaction. Authorization in the board minutes might detail the arrangements, but, if the officials wanted to hide it from the auditors, they also would suppress the telltale information in the board minutes.

Inquiries should be made about large and unusual financing transactions. This might not elicit a response because the event is a sales transaction, according to Verity. Other audit work on controls in the revenue and collection cycle might turn up the large sale. Fortunately, this one sticks out as a large one.

Analytical procedures to compare monthly or seasonal sales probably will identify the sale as large and unusual. This identification should lead to an examination of the sales contract. Auditors should discuss the business purpose of the transaction with knowledgeable officials. If being this close to discovery does not result in an admission of the loan and repurchase arrangement, the auditors nevertheless should investigate further. Even if the "customer" name were not a giveaway, a quick inquiry of the corporation records office at the secretary of state office will show the names of the officers and the auditors will know the related-party nature of the deal. A request for the financial statements of Veritas should be made.

DISCOVERY SUMMARY

The auditors found the related-party relationship between the officers and Veritas. Confronted, the president admitted the attempt to make the cash position and the debt/equity ratio look better than they were. The financial statements were adjusted to reflect that the "should-have-recorded" set of figures shown earlier.

Case 10.3

Go for the Gold

PROBLEM

In 1989, Alta Gold Company was a public "shell" corporation that was purchased for $1,000 by the Blues brothers. Operating under the corporate names of Silver King and Pacific Gold, the brothers purchased numerous mining claims in auctions conducted by the U.S. Department of

the Interior. They invested a total of $40,000 in 300 claims. Silver King sold limited partnership interests in its 175 Nevada silver claims to local investors, raising $20 million to begin mining production. Pacific Gold then traded its 125 Montana gold mining claims for all of the Silver King assets and partnership interests, valuing the silver claims at $20 million. (Silver King valued the gold claims received at $20 million as the fair value in the exchange.) The brothers then put $3 million obtained from dividends into Alta Gold and, with the aid of a bank loan, purchased half of the Silver King gold claims for $18 million. The Blues brothers then obtained another bank loan of $38 million to merge the remainder of Silver King's assets and all of Pacific Gold's mining claims by purchase. They paid off the limited partners. At the end of 1989, Alta Gold had cash of $16 million and mining assets valued at $58 million and liabilities on bank loans of $53 million.

Alta Gold had in its files the partnership-offering documents, receipts, and other papers showing partners' investment of $20 million in the Silver King limited partnerships. The company also had Pacific Gold and Silver King contracts for the exchange of mining claims. The $20 million value of the exchange was justified in light of the limited partners' investments.

Appraisals in the files showed one appraiser's report that there was no basis for valuing the exchange of Silver King claims, other than the price limited partner investors had been willing to pay. The second appraiser reported a probable value of $20 million for the exchange based on proved production elsewhere, but no geological data on the actual claims had been obtained. The $18 million paid by Alta to Silver King also had similar appraisal reports.

The transactions occurred over a period of 10 months. The Blues brothers had $37 million cash in Silver King and Pacific Gold, as well as the $16 million in Alta (all of which was the gullible bank's money, which the bank had loaned to Alta with the mining claims and production as security). The mining claims that had cost $40,000 were now in Alta's balance sheet at $58 million, the $37 million was about to flee, and the bank was about to be left holding the bag containing 300 mining claim papers.

AUDIT APPROACH

Alta Gold, Pacific Gold, and Silver King had no internal controls. The Blues brothers engineered all transactions and hired friendly appraisers. The only control that might have been effective was at the bank in the loan-granting process, but the bank failed.

The only vestige of control could have been the engagement of competent, independent appraisers. Because the auditors need to use (or try to use) the appraisers' reports, the procedures involve investigating the reputation, engagement terms, experience, and independence of the appraisers. The auditors can use local business references, local financial institutions that keep lists of approved appraisers, membership directories of the professional appraisal associations, and interviews with the appraisers themselves (*SAS 73*, "Using the Work of a Specialist").

The procedures for auditing the asset values include analyses of each of the transactions through all of their complications, including obtaining knowledge of the owners and managers of the several companies and the identities of the limited partner investors. If the Blues brothers have not disclosed their connection with the other companies (and perhaps with the limited partners), the auditors will need to inquire at the secretary of state's offices where Pacific Gold and Silver King are incorporated and try to discover the identities of the players in this flip game. Numerous complicated premerger transactions in small corporations and shells often signal manipulated valuations.

Loan applications and supporting papers should be examined to determine the representations made by Alta in connection with obtaining the bank loans. These papers may reveal some contradictory or exaggerated information.

Ownership of the mining claims might be confirmed with the Department of Interior auctioneers or be found in the local county deed records (spread all over Nevada and Montana).

DISCOVERY SUMMARY

The inexperienced audit staff were unable to unravel the Byzantine exchanges and they never questioned the relation of Alta Gold to Silver King and Pacific Gold. They never discovered the Blues brothers' involvement in the other side of the exchange, purchase, and merger transactions. They accepted the appraisers' reports because they had never worked with appraisers before and thought all appraisers were competent and independent. The bank lost $37 million. The Blues brothers changed their names.

Case 10.4

No Treasure in This Treasure Planet[2]

PROBLEM

In 2002 Disney had to take a last-minute write-down of motion picture production costs for the movie *Treasure Planet*. The set-in-space version of Robert Louis Stevenson's *Treasure Island* cost $140 million to make, but opening five-day revenues were only $16.7 million, compared to relatively successful *Lilo & Stitch*, which grossed $35.3 million in its first weekend.

Revenue forecasts are based on many factors, including facts and assumptions about number of theaters, ticket prices, receipt-sharing agreements, domestic and foreign reviews, and moviegoer tastes. Several publications track the box office records of movies. You can find them in newspaper entertainment sections and in industry trade publications. Of course, the production companies themselves are the major source of the information. However, company records also show the revenue realized from each movie. Revenue forecasts can be checked against actual experience and the company's history of forecasting accuracy can be determined by comparing actual to forecast over many films and many years.

The write-down in 2002 was $74 million.

AUDIT APPROACH

Revenue forecasts should be prepared in a controlled process that documents the facts and underlying assumptions built into the forecast. Forecasts should break down the revenue estimate by years and the accounting system should produce comparable actual revenue data so forecast accuracy can be assessed after the fact. Forecast revisions should be prepared in as much detail and documentation as original forecasts.

The general procedures and methods used by personnel responsible for revenue forecasts should be studied (inquiries and review of documentation), including their sources of information, both internal and external. Procedures for review of mechanical aspects (arithmetic) should be tested: Select a sample of finished forecasts and recalculate the final estimate.

Specific procedures for forecast revision also should be studied in the same manner. A review of the accuracy of forecasts for other movies with hindsight on actual revenues helps in a circumstantial way, but past accuracy on different film experiences do not directly influence the forecasts on a new, unique product.

The audit of motion picture development costs concentrates on the content of the forecast itself. The preparation of forecasts used in the impairment calculation should be studied to distinguish underlying reasonable expectations from hypothetical assumptions. A hypothetical assumption is a statement of a condition that is not necessarily expected to occur, but nonetheless is used to prepare an estimate. For example, a hypothetical assumption is like an "if-then" statement: "If *Treasure Planet* sells 15 million tickets in the first 12 months of release, then domestic revenue and product sales will be $40 million, and foreign revenue can eventually reach $10 million." Auditors need to assess the reasonableness of the basic 15-million-ticket assumption. It helps to have some early actual data from the film's release in hand before the financial statements need to be finished and distributed. For actual data, industry publications should be reviewed, with special attention to competing films and critics' reviews (yes, movie reviews!).

DISCOVERY SUMMARY

The company was too optimistic in its revenue forecasts and management did not weigh unfavorable actual/forecast history comparisons heavily enough. Apparently, management let itself be convinced that the movie was comparable to recent animated hits from other studios like *Shrek* and *A Bug's Life*. One of the possible problems was the long development time—17 years from conception. The audit of forecasts and estimates used in accounting determinations is very difficult, especially when company personnel have incentives to hype the numbers, seemingly with conviction about the artistic and commercial merit of their productions. The high production costs finally came home to roost in big write-offs when the film was released.

[2] F. Ahrens, "Is Disney Losing Its Boy Appeal?" *Washington Post*, December 19, 2002.

Review Checkpoints

10.18 What unfortunate lesson did the auditors learn from the situation in Case 10.1 (Unregistered Sale of Securities)? What should auditors do when a violation of U.S. securities laws is suspected?

10.19 How could auditors have discovered the off-balance-sheet financing described in Case 10.2 (Off-Balance-Sheet Inventory Financing)?

10.20 What effect can related-party transactions have in some cases of asset valuation? (Refer to Case 10.3, Go for the Gold.)

10.21 How should an audit team assess the reasonableness of a film studio's estimate of film revenues?

Summary

The finance and investment cycle contains a wide variety of accounts: capital stock, dividends, long-term debt, interest expense, income tax expense and deferred taxes, financial instruments, marketable securities, equity method investments, related gains and losses, consolidated subsidiaries, goodwill, and other intangibles. These accounts involve some of the most technically complex accounting standards. They create most of the difficult judgments for financial reporting.

Senior officials generally authorize these transactions and maintain control of them in these accounts. Therefore, internal control is centered on the integrity and accounting knowledge of these officials. The procedural controls over details of transactions are not very effective because senior managers can override them and order their own desired accounting presentations. As a consequence, auditors' work on the assessment of control risk is directed toward the senior managers and the board of directors, as well as their authorizations and design of finance and investment details. Because of the threat of management override and the high dollar value of many of these transactions, auditors ensure the occurance and valuation of transactions as well as the existence and valuation of year-end balances. Here are some deficiencies the PCAOB noted in its inspections of the Big Four audit firms regarding audits of this cycle.

AUDITING INSIGHT · PCAOB Inspections and the Finance and Investment Cycle

- For fixed assets, the Firm failed to test a sufficient number of items to obtain the desired level of assurance (and failed to test items representing one-third of the sample size that the Firm had determined was necessary).

- The issuer exchanged certain of its debt for debt at a lower interest rate and extended maturity and for cash. There was no evidence in the audit documentation, and no persuasive other evidence, that the firm had performed procedures to test the issuer's accounting for the debt exchange, including testing the issuer's assumptions and calculations and analyzing the terms of the new debt.

- In connection with a merger, the issuer assumed convertible debt securities and, as a result of the merger, certain terms and features of the convertible debt securities were changed. The Firm failed to evaluate the effect of the changes on the accounting for securities. These changes include changes to the conversion and settlement options and certain contingent features.

- The Firm's work papers did not address whether the issuer's investments in marketable securities or U.S. government securities were appropriately classified, and the Firm did not test the issuer's evaluation of a financial derivative, even though the issuer used different inputs for that evaluation than the forward price curve would indicate.

- The Firm failed to test the fair market values of marketable securities, beyond obtaining a confirmation from the investment broker.

- The Firm failed to evaluate the appropriateness of an issuer's classification of certain investments as cash equivalents. The issuer subsequently determined that approximately 89 percent of its reported cash and cash equivalents were invested in securities that were not appropriate for classification as cash or cash equivalents under *SFAS No. 95,* "Statement of Cash Flows."

Key Terms

accounting estimate: An approximation of a financial statement element, item, or account, 389

compensating control: A control instituted by a company to offset the risk imposed by a weakness in another procedure, 389

derivative instrument: A financial instrument whose value is based on an index or value of another financial instrument, 395

hedging instrument: An investment made in order to reduce the risk of adverse price movements in a security or future transaction by taking an offsetting position in a related security such as an option or a short sale, 395

indenture: A written agreement between the issuers of bonds and the bondholders, usually specifying interest rate, maturity date, convertibility, and other terms, 391

loan covenant: Provision in a loan agreement that requires the borrower to undertake or refrain from specified actions and to maintain specified financial levels and ratios, 382

registrar: Financial institution appointed to record issue and ownership of company securities, 385

related party: Party with which an enterprise may deal if one party controls or can significantly influence the management or operating policies of the other to an extent that one of the transacting parties might be prevented from fully pursuing its own separate interests, 382

special purpose entity (SPE): A partnership formed by a company to pursue particular lines of business, often used to keep risky enterprises off the company's books, 380

transfer agent: A bank or other company employed by a corporation to maintain shareholder records, including purchases, sales, and account balances, 385

trustee: Agent of a bond issuer who handles the administrative aspects of a loan and ensures that the borrower complies with the terms of the bond indenture, 386

Multiple Choice Questions for Practice and Review

10.22 Which of the following approaches is most suitable for auditing the finance and investment cycle?

 a. Perform extensive tests of controls and limit substantive procedures to analytical procedures.

 b. Ignore internal controls and perform extensive substantive procedures.

 c. Review internal controls and perform extensive substantive procedures.

 d. Ignore internal controls and limit substantive procedures to analytical procedures.

10.23 Loan covenants are used for which of the following reasons?

 a. To protect the lender from the borrower substantially weakening the borrower's financial position.

 b. To protect the borrower from the lender calling the loan early.

 c. To protect the auditors from false information by the borrower.

 d. To protect shareholders from management taking on too much debt.

10.24 A related party is a person or entity that

 a. Has a family tie to a management member.

 b. Does business with the company.

 c. Can exert significant influence over or be influenced by the company.

 d. Is a member of the company's management.

10.25 Jones was engaged to examine the financial statements of Gamma Corporation for the year ended June 30. Having completed an examination of the investment securities, which of the following is the best method of verifying the accuracy of recorded dividend income?

 a. Tracing recorded dividend income to cash receipts records and validated deposit slips.

 b. Performing analytical procedures and statistical sampling.

 c. Comparing recorded dividends with amounts appearing on federal information Form 1099.

 d. Comparing recorded dividends with a standard financial reporting service's record of dividends.

10.26 When the client holds a large amount of negotiable securities, auditors need to plan to guard against

 a. Unauthorized negotiation of the securities before they are counted.

 b. Unrecorded sales of securities after they are counted.

 c. Substitution of securities already counted for other securities that should be on hand but are not.

 d. Substitution of authentic securities with counterfeit securities.

10.27 In connection with the audit of an issue of long-term bonds payable, the audit team should
 a. Determine whether bondholders are persons other than owners, directors, or officers of the company issuing the bond.
 b. Calculate the effective interest rate to see if it is substantially the same as the rates for similar issues.
 c. Decide whether the bond issue was made without violating state or local law.
 d. Ascertain that the client has obtained the opinion of counsel on the legality of the issue.

10.28 Which of the following is the most important audit consideration when examining the stockholders' equity section of a client's balance sheet?
 a. Changes in the capital stock account are verified by an independent stock transfer agent.
 b. Stock dividends and stock splits during the year under audit were approved by the stockholders.
 c. Stock dividends are capitalized at par or stated value on the dividend declaration date.
 d. Entries in the capital stock account can be traced to resolutions in the minutes of meetings of the board of directors.

10.29 If the auditors discover that the carrying amount of a client's investments is overstated because of a loss in value that is other than a temporary decline in market value, they should insist that
 a. The approximate market value of the investments be shown in parentheses on the face of the balance sheet.
 b. The investments be classified as long term for balance sheet purposes with full disclosure in the footnotes.
 c. The loss in value be recognized in the financial statements.
 d. The equity section of the balance sheet separately show a charge equal to the amount of the loss.

10.30 The primary reason for preparing a reconciliation between interest-bearing obligations outstanding during the year and interest expense in the financial statements is to
 a. Evaluate internal control over securities.
 b. Determine the validity of prepaid interest expense.
 c. Ascertain the reasonableness of imputed interest.
 d. Detect unrecorded liabilities.

10.31 The auditors should insist that a representative of the client be present during the inspection and count of securities to
 a. Lend authority to the auditors' directives.
 b. Detect forged securities.
 c. Coordinate the return of all securities to proper locations.
 d. Acknowledge the receipt of securities returned.

10.32 When independent stock transfer agents are not employed and the corporation issues its own stock and maintains stock records, canceled stock certificates should
 a. Be defaced to prevent reissuance and attached to their corresponding stubs.
 b. Not be defaced but be segregated from other stock certificates and retained in a canceled certificates file.
 c. Be destroyed to prevent fraudulent reissuance.
 d. Be defaced and sent to the secretary of state.

10.33 When a client company does not maintain its own capital stock records, the auditors should obtain written confirmation from the transfer agent and registrar concerning
 a. Restrictions on the payment of dividends.
 b. The number of shares issued and outstanding.
 c. Guarantees of preferred stock liquidation value.
 d. The number of shares subject to agreements to repurchase.

(AICPA adapted)

10.34 All corporate capital stock transactions should ultimately be traced to the

 a. Minutes of the meetings of the board of directors.

 b. Cash receipts journal.

 c. Cash disbursements journal.

 d. Numbered stock certificates.

10.35 An audit program for the examination of the retained earnings account should include a step that requires verification of the (choose two steps)

 a. Market value used to charge retained earnings to account for a 2-for-1 stock split.

 b. Approval of the adjustment to the beginning balance as a result of a write-down of account receivables.

 c. Authorization for both cash and stock dividends.

 d. Gain or loss resulting from disposition of treasury shares.

10.36 When an entity uses a trust company as custodian of its marketable securities, the possibility of concealing fraud most likely would be reduced if the

 a. Trust company has no direct contact with the entity employees responsible for maintaining investment accounting records.

 b. Securities are registered in the name of the trust company rather than the entity itself.

 c. Interest and dividend checks are mailed directly to an entity employee who is authorized to sell securities.

 d. The trust company places the securities in a bank safe deposit vault under the custodian's exclusive control.

 (AICPA adapted)

10.37 An audit team would most likely verify the interest earned on bond investments by

 a. Vouching the receipt and deposit of interest checks.

 b. Confirming the bond interest rate with the issuer of the bonds.

 c. Recomputing the interest earned on the basis of face amount, interest rate, and period held.

 d. Testing internal controls relevant to cash receipts.

 (AICPA adapted)

10.38 A client has a large and active investment portfolio that is kept in a bank safe deposit box. If the auditors are unable to count securities at the balance sheet date, they most likely will

 a. Request the bank to confirm to the auditors the contents of the safe deposit box at the balance sheet date.

 b. Examine supporting evidence for transactions occurring during the year.

 c. Count the securities at a subsequent date and confirm with the bank whether securities were added or removed since the balance sheet date.

 d. Request the client to have the bank seal the safe deposit box until the auditors can count the securities at a subsequent date.

 (AICPA adapted)

10.39 An audit team testing long-term investments would ordinarily use analytical procedures to ascertain the reasonableness of the

 a. Existence of unrealized gains or losses.

 b. Completeness of recorded investment income.

 c. Classification as available-for-sale or trading securities.

 d. Valuation of trading securities.

 (AICPA adapted)

10.40 In auditing for unrecorded long-term bonds payable, an audit team most likely will

 a. Perform analytical procedures on the bond premium and discount accounts.

 b. Examine documentation of assets purchased with bond proceeds for liens.

 c. Compare interest expense with the bond payable amount for reasonableness.

 d. Confirm the existence of individual bondholders at year-end.

 (AICPA adapted)

10.41 An audit program to examine long-term debt most likely would include steps that require

a. Comparing the carrying amount of held-to-maturity securities with their year-end market values.

b. Correlating interest expense recorded for the period with outstanding debt.

c. Verifying the existence of the holders of the debt by direct confirmation.

d. Inspecting the accounts payable subsidiary ledger for unrecorded long-term debt.

(AICPA adapted)

10.42 Which of the following questions would auditors most likely include on an internal control questionnaire for notes payable?

a. Are assets that collateralize notes payable critically needed for the entity's continued existence?

b. Are two or more authorized signatures required on checks that repay notes payable?

c. Are the proceeds from notes payable used for the purchase of noncurrent assets?

d. Are direct borrowings on notes payable authorized by the board of directors?

(AICPA adapted)

10.43 An audit team's purpose in reviewing the documentation concerning the renewal of a note payable shortly after the balance sheet date most likely is to obtain evidence concerning management's assertions about

a. Existence.

b. Valuation.

c. Completeness.

d. Classification.

(AICPA adapted)

10.44 Which of the following audit procedures would *not* likely be performed for audits of investments?

a. Read board of directors' minutes for authorization of investment strategies.

b. Confirm investments with registrar.

c. Confirm investments with broker or trustee.

d. Compare valuation to published market prices.

10.45 Which of the following audit procedures would *not* likely be performed for audits of shareholders' equity?

a. Read board of directors' minutes for authorization of equity transactions.

b. Confirm outstanding common and preferred stock with stock registrar.

c. Compare valuation of stock to published market prices.

d. Obtain management representation about number of shares issued and outstanding.

Exercises, Problems, and Simulations

10.46 **ICQ for Equity Investments.** Cassandra Corporation, a manufacturing company, periodically invests large sums in marketable equity securities. The investment policy is established by the investment committee of the board of directors. The treasurer is responsible for carrying out the investment committee's directives. All securities are stored in a bank safe deposit vault. Your internal control questionnaire with respect to Cassandra's investments in equity securities contains the following three questions:

1. Is investment policy established by the investment committee of the board of directors?

2. Is the treasurer solely responsible for carrying out the investment committee's directive?

3. Are all securities stored in a bank safe deposit vault?

Required:

In addition to these three questions, what questions should your internal control questionnaire include with respect to the company's investment in marketable equity securities? (*Hint:* Prepare questions to cover management's transaction assertions *occurrence, completeness, cutoff, accuracy, classification.*)

(AICPA adapted)

10.47 **Audit Simulation: Held-to-Maturity Investment Securities.** You are engaged in the audit of the financial statements of Bass Corporation for the year ended December 31 and you are about to begin an audit of the held-to-maturity investment securities. Bass's records indicate

that the company owns various bearer bonds, as well as 25 percent of the outstanding common stock of Commercial Industrial, Inc. All securities in Bass's portfolio are actively traded in a broad market. You are satisfied with evidence that supports the presumption of significant influence over Commercial Industrial, Inc. The various securities are at two locations as follows:

1. Recently acquired securities are in the company's safe in the custody of the treasurer.

2. All other securities are in the company's bank safe deposit box.

Required:

a. Assuming that the internal controls over securities are satisfactory, what are the objectives (specific assertions) for the audit of the held-to-maturity securities?

b. What audit procedures should you undertake with respect to obtaining audit evidence for the existence and cost valuation of Bass's securities in the held-to-maturity classification?

c. What audit procedures should you undertake with respect to obtaining audit evidence against Bass's investment in Commercial Industrial, Inc.?

d. What audit procedures should you undertake with respect to obtaining audit evidence about the classification of held-to-maturity securities in the Bass portfolio? (*Hint:* Review the audit program in Appendix 10B.3.)

e. Suppose that the held-to-maturity portfolio (excluding the investment in Commercial Industrial, Inc.) is carried at cost in the amount of $3,450,000. What audit procedures should you undertake with respect to obtaining audit evidence about the fair market value of this portfolio?

f. Suppose that the auditors determine that the held-to-maturity portfolio (excluding the investment in Commercial Industrial, Inc.) has an aggregate fair market value of $2,970,000. What audit procedures should they undertake with respect to obtaining audit evidence regarding a value impairment that might be "other than temporary?" (*Hint:* Review the audit program in Appendix 10B.3.)

(AICPA adapted)

10.48 **Audit Simulation: Lease Accounting.** Union Pacific Corp. opened its new 19-story, $260 million headquarters in Omaha, Nebraska. The railroad operator is the owner of the city's largest building, the Union Pacific Center. Under an initial operating lease, Union Pacific guaranteed 89.9 percent of all construction costs through the building's completion date. After completing the building, the company signed a new operating lease, which guarantees 85 percent of the building's costs. Both were "synthetic" leases, which allow the company to take income tax deductions for interest and depreciation while maintaining complete operational control (Jonathan Weil, "Open Secrets: How Leases Play a Shadowy Role in Accounting," *The Wall Street Journal,* September 22, 2004).

Required:

a. Explain why Union Pacific would want to structure the lease to be an operating lease.

b. What audit evidence would you require for testing the appropriate accounting for this lease?

10.49 **Audit Simulation: Securities Examination and Count.** You are in charge of the audit of the financial statements of Demot Corporation for the year ended December 31. The corporation has a policy of investing its surplus funds in marketable securities. Its stock and bond certificates are kept in a safe deposit box in a local bank. Only the president and the treasurer of the corporation have access to the box.

You were unable to obtain access to the safe deposit box on December 31 because neither the president nor the treasurer was available. Arrangements were made for your assistant to accompany the treasurer to the bank on January 11 to examine the securities. Your assistant should be able to inspect all securities on hand in an hour. Your assistant has never examined securities in the safe deposit box and requires instructions.

Required:

a. List the instructions that you should give to your assistant regarding the examination of the stock and bond certificates kept in the safe deposit box. Include in your instructions the details of the securities to be examined and the reasons for examining these details.

b. After returning from the bank, your assistant reports that the treasurer had entered the box on January 4 to remove an old photograph of the corporation's original building. The photograph was loaned to the local chamber of commerce for display purposes. List the additional audit procedures that are required because of the treasurer's action.

(AICPA adapted)

10.50 **Audit Objectives and Procedures for Investments.** In the audit of investment securities, auditors develop specific audit assertions related to the investments. They then design specific substantive procedures to obtain evidence about each of these assertions. Following is a selection of investment securities assertions:

1. Investments are properly described and classified in the financial statements.
2. Recorded investments represent investments actually owned at the balance sheet date.
3. Investments are properly valued at the balance sheet date.

Required:

For each of these assertions, select the following audit procedure that is best suited for the audit program. Select only one procedure for each assertion. A procedure may be selected once or not at all.

a. Trace opening balances in the general ledger to prior-year audit documentation.

b. Determine whether employees who are authorized to sell investments have access to cash.

c. Examine supporting documents for a sample of investment transactions to verify that prenumbered documents are used.

d. Determine whether any other-than-temporary impairments in the carrying value of investments have been properly recorded.

e. Verify that transfers from the trading portfolio to the held-to-maturity investment portfolio have been properly recorded.

f. Obtain positive confirmations as of the balance sheet date of investments held by independent custodians.

g. Trace investment transactions to minutes of the board of directors meetings to determine that transactions were properly authorized.

(AICPA adapted)

10.51 **Audit Simulation: Intangibles.** Sorenson Manufacturing Corporation was incorporated on January 3, 2007. The corporation's financial statements for its first year's operations were not examined by a CPA. You have been engaged to audit the financial statements for the year ended December 31, 2008, and your work is substantially completed. A partial trial balance of the company's accounts follows:

SORENSON MANUFACTURING CORPORATION
Trial Balance
at December 31, 2008

	Debit	Credit
Cash	$11,000	
Accounts receivable	42,500	
Allowance for doubtful accounts		$ 500
Inventories	38,500	
Machinery	75,000	
Equipment	29,000	
Accumulated depreciation		10,000
Patents	85,000	
Leasehold improvements	26,000	
Prepaid expenses	10,500	
Organization expenses	29,000	
Goodwill	24,000	
Licensing Agreement No. 1*	50,000	
Licensing Agreement No. 2*	49,000	

*An intangible asset representing the right to use a patent.

The following information relates to accounts that may yet require adjustment:

1. Patents for Sorenson's manufacturing process were purchased January 2, 2008, at a cost of $68,000. An additional $17,000 was spent in December 2008 to improve machinery

covered by the patents and charged to the Patents account. The patents had a remaining legal term of 17 years.

2. On January 3, 2007, Sorenson purchased two licensing agreements; at that time they were believed to have unlimited useful lives. The balance in the Licensing Agreement No. 1 account included its purchase price of $48,000 and $2,000 in acquisition expenses. Licensing Agreement No. 2 also was purchased on January 3, 2007, for $50,000, but it has been reduced by a credit of $1,000 for the advance collection of revenue from the agreement.

3. In December 2007, an explosion caused a permanent 60 percent reduction in the expected revenue-producing value of Licensing Agreement No. 1 and, in January 2009, a flood caused additional damage, which rendered the agreement worthless.

4. A study of Licensing Agreement No. 2 made by Sorenson in January 2008 revealed that its estimated remaining life expectancy was only 10 years as of January 1, 2008.

5. The balance in the Goodwill account includes $24,000 paid December 30, 2007, for an advertising program, which it is estimated will assist in increasing Sorenson's sales over a period of four years following the disbursement.

6. The Leasehold Improvement account includes (a) the $15,000 cost of improvements with a total estimated useful life of 12 years, which Sorenson, as tenant, made to leased premises in January 2007; (b) movable assembly-line equipment costing $8,500, which was installed in the leased premises in December 2008; and (c) real estate taxes of $2,500 paid by Sorenson, which, under the terms of the lease, should have been paid by the landlord. Sorenson paid its rent in full during 2008. A 10-year nonrenewable lease was signed January 3, 2007, for the leased building that Sorenson used in manufacturing operations.

7. The balance in the Organization Expenses account includes preoperating costs incurred during the organizational period.

Required:

Prepare adjusting entries as necessary.

(AICPA adapted)

10.52 **Loan Covenants.** A loan covenant is a condition requiring the borrower to comply with the terms of a loan agreement. If the borrower does not act in accordance with the covenants, the loan can be considered in default and the lender has the right to demand payment (usually in full).

Required:

a. Why do banks add covenants to loan agreements?

b. The following is a list of common loan covenants. For each covenant, indicate what the bank is trying to accomplish by requiring it.

(1) Maintain hazard insurance/content insurance.

(2) Maintain key-person life insurance.

(3) Make all payments of taxes/fees /licenses.

(4) Provide financial information on borrower and guarantor.

(5) Maintain a certain level in key financial ratios such as

(a) Minimum quick and current ratios (liquidity).

(b) Minimum return on assets and return on equity (profitability).

(c) Minimum equity and minimum working capital.

(d) Maximum debt to worth (leverage).

(6) Make no change of management or merger without prior approval.

(7) Obtain no more loans without prior approval.

(8) Make no dividends/withdrawals or limited dividend withdrawals.

10.53 **Long-Term Financing Agreement.** You have been engaged to audit the financial statements of Broadwall Corporation for the year ended December 31, 2008. During the year, Broadwall obtained a long-term loan from a local bank pursuant to a financing agreement, which provided the following:

1. The loan is to be secured by the company's inventory and accounts receivable.

2. The company is to maintain a debt-equity ratio not to exceed 2:1.

3. The company is not to pay dividends without permission from the bank.

4. Monthly installment payments to commence July 1, 2008.

In addition, during the year, the company also borrowed, on a short-term basis, substantial amounts just prior to the year end from the president of the company.

Required:

a. For the purposes of your audit of the Broadwall Corporation's financial statements, what procedures should you employ in examining the described loans? Do not discuss internal control.

b. What are the financial statement disclosures that you should expect to find with respect to the loan from the president?

10.54 **Bond Indenture Covenants.** The following covenants are extracted from the indenture of a bond issue. The indenture provides that failure to comply with its terms in any respect automatically advances the due date of the loan to the date of noncompliance (the stated date is 20 years hence).

Give any audit steps or reporting requirements you believe should be taken or recognized in connection with each of the following:

1. "The debtor company shall endeavor to maintain a working capital ratio of 2:1 at all times and, in any fiscal year following a failure to maintain said ratio, the company shall restrict compensation of officers to a total of $500,000. Officers for this purpose shall include the board chair, president, all vice presidents, secretary, and treasurer."

2. "The debtor company shall keep all property that is security for this debt insured against loss by fire to the extent of 100 percent of its actual value. Policies of insurance comprising this protection shall be filed with the trustee."

3. "The debtor company shall pay all taxes legally assessed against property that is security for this debt within the time provided by law for payment without penalty and shall deposit receipted tax bills or equally acceptable evidence of payment of same with the trustee."

(AICPA adapted)

10.55 **Common Stock and Treasury Stock Audit Procedures.** You are the continuing auditor of Sussex, Inc., and are beginning the audit of the common stock and treasury stock accounts. You have decided to design substantive procedures with reliance on internal controls.

Sussex has no-par, no-stated-value common stock and acts as its own registrar and transfer agent. During the past year, Sussex both issued and reacquired shares of its own common stock, some of which the company still owned at year end. Additional common stock transactions occurred among the shareholders during the year.

Common stock transactions can be traced to individual shareholders' accounts in a subsidiary ledger and to a stock certificate book. The company has not paid any cash or stock dividends. There are no other classes of stock, stock rights, warrants, or option plans.

Required:

What substantive procedures should you apply in examining the common stock and treasury stock accounts? Organize your answer as a list of audit procedures organized by the financial statement assertions. (See Appendix 10B.1 for examples of substantive procedures for owners' equity.)

(AICPA adapted)

10.56 **Stockholders' Equity.** You are a CPA engaged in an audit of the financial statements of Pate Corporation for the year ended December 31. The financial statements and records of Pate Corporation have not been audited by a CPA in prior years.

The stockholders' equity section of Pate Corporation's balance sheet at December 31 follows:

Stockholders' equity:	
Capital stock—10,000 shares of $10 par value authorized; 5,000 shares issued and outstanding	$ 50,000
Capital contributed in excess of par value of capital stock	32,580
Retained earnings	47,320
Total stockholders' equity	129,900

Pate Corporation was founded in 1985. The corporation has 10 stockholders and serves as its own registrar and transfer agent. There are no capital stock subscription contracts in effect.

Required:

a. Prepare the detailed audit program for the examination of the three accounts composing the stockholders' equity section of Pate Corporation's balance sheet. Organize the audit program under broad financial statement assertions. (Do not include in the audit program the audit of the results of the current-year operations.)

b. After every other figure on the balance sheet has been audited, it might appear that the retained earnings figure is a balancing figure and requires no further audit work. Why do auditors audit retained earnings as they do the other figures on the balance sheet? Discuss.

(AICPA adapted)

10.57 **Audit Simulation: Intercompany and Interpersonal Investment Relations.** You have been engaged to audit the financial statements of Hardy Hardware Distributors, Inc., as of December 31. In your review of the corporate nonfinancial records, you have found that Hardy Hardware owns 15 percent of the outstanding voting common stock of Hardy Products Corporation. Upon further investigation, you learn that Hardy Products Corporation manufactures a line of hardware goods, 90 percent of which is sold to Hardy Hardware.

Mr. James L. Hardy, president of Hardy Hardware, has supplied you objective evidence that he personally owns 30 percent of the Hardy Products voting stock and the remaining 70 percent is owned by Ms. Juana Hardy Lewis, his sister and president of Hardy Products. James Hardy also owns 20 percent of the voting common stock of Hardy Hardware Distributors, another 20 percent is held by an estate of which James and Juana are beneficiaries, and the remaining 60 percent is publicly held. The stock is listed on the American Stock Exchange.

Hardy Hardware consistently has reported operating profits higher than the industry average. Hardy Products Corporation, however, has a net return on sales of only 1 percent. The Hardy Products investment always has been reported at cost and no dividends have been paid by the company. During the course of your conversations with the Hardy siblings, you learn that you were appointed as auditor because they had a heated disagreement with the former auditors over the issues of accounting for the Hardy Products investment and the prices at which goods have been sold to Hardy Hardware.

Required:

Discuss the following.

a. Identify the issues in this situation as they relate to (1) conflicts of interest and (2) controlling influences among individuals and corporations.

b. Should the investment in Hardy Products Corporation be accounted for using the equity method?

c. What evidence should the auditor seek with regard to the prices paid by Hardy Hardware for products purchased from Hardy Products Corporation?

d. What information would you consider necessary for adequate disclosure in the financial statements of Hardy Hardware Distributors?

Instructions for Discussion Cases 10.58–60

These cases are designed like the ones in the chapter. They give the problem, and your assignment is to write the audit approach portion of the case, organized around these sections:

Objectives: Express the objective in terms of the facts supposedly asserted in financial records, accounts, and statements.

Control: Write a brief explanation of control considerations, especially the kinds of manipulations that could arise from the situation described in the case.

Tests of controls: Write some procedures for getting evidence about existing controls, especially procedures that could discover management manipulations. If there are no controls to test, there are no procedures to perform; go on then to the next section. A "procedure" should instruct someone about the source(s) of evidence to tap and the work to do.

Audit of balance: Write some procedures for getting evidence about the *existence*, *completeness*, *valuation*, *rights*, and *disclosure* assertions identified in your objective section above.

Discovery summary: Write a short statement about the discovery you expect to accomplish with your procedures.

10.58 **Related-Party Transaction "Goodwill."** Write the audit approach section like the cases in the chapter.

Hide the Loss under the Goodwill

Gulwest Industries, a public company, decided to discontinue its unprofitable line of business of manufacturing sporting ammunition. Gulwest had capitalized the startup cost of the business and, with its discontinuance, the $7 million deferred cost should have been written off. Instead, Gulwest formed a new corporation, Amron, and transferred the sporting ammunition assets (including the $7 million deferred cost) to it in exchange for all of the Amron stock. In the Gulwest accounts, the Amron investment was carried at $12.4 million, which was the book value of the assets transferred (including the $7 million deferred cost).

Gulwest and a different public company (Big Industrial) created another company (BigShot Ammunition). Gulwest transferred all Amron assets to BigShot in exchange for (1) common and preferred stock of Big Industrial, valued at $2 million, and (2) a note from BigShot in the amount of $3.4 million. Big Industrial thus acquired 100 percent of the stock of BigShot. Gulwest management reasoned that it had "given" Amron stock valued at $12.4 million to receive stock and notes valued at $5.4 million, so the difference must be goodwill. Thus, the Gulwest accounts carried amounts for Big Industrial Stock ($2 million), BigShot Note Receivable ($3.4 million), and Goodwill ($7 million).

Gulwest directors included in the minutes of board meetings an analysis of the sporting ammunition business's lack of profitability. The minutes showed approval of a plan to dispose of the business, but they did not use the words "discontinue the business." The minutes also showed approval of the creation of Amron, the deal with Big Industrial along with the formation of BigShot, and the acceptance of Big's stock and BigShot's note in connection with the final exchange and merger.

10.59 **Related-Party Transaction Valuation.** Follow the instructions preceding Case 10.58. Write the audit approach section like the cases in the chapter.

In Plane View

Whiz Corporation owned 160,000 shares of Wing Company stock, carried on the books as an investment in the amount of $6,250,000. Whiz bought a used airplane from Wing, giving in exchange (1) $480,000 cash and (2) the 160,000 Wing shares. Even though the quoted market value of the Wing stock was $2,520,000, Whiz valued the airplane received at $3,750,000, indicating a stock valuation of $3,270,000. Thus, Whiz recognized a loss on disposition of the Wing stock in the amount of $2,980,000.

Whiz justified the airplane valuation with another transaction. On the same day it was purchased, Whiz sold the airplane to the Mexican subsidiary of one of its subsidiary companies (two layers down, but Whiz owned 100 percent of the first subsidiary, which in turn owned 100 percent of the Mexican subsidiary). The Mexican subsidiary paid Whiz with US$25,000 cash and a promissory note for US$3,725,000 (market rate of interest).

The transaction was within the authority of the chief executive officer and company policy did not require a separate approval by the board of directors. A contract of sale and correspondence with Wing detailing the terms of the transaction were in the files. Likewise, a contract of sale to the Mexican subsidiary, along with a copy of the deposit slip, and a memorandum of the promissory note were on file. The note itself was kept in the company vault. None of the Wing papers cited a specific price for the airplane.

Whiz overvalued the Wing stock and justified it with a related-party transaction with its own subsidiary company. The loss on the disposition of the Wing stock was understated by $750,000.

10.60 **Lack of Controls Over Investments.** Follow the instructions preceding Case 10.58. Write the audit approach section like the cases in the chapter.

Rogue Trader

In February 1989, 22-year old Nicholas Leeson joined Baring Investment Bank. In 1993, he began trading on behalf of the Baring group as a "proprietary trader" on the Singapore

International Monetary Exchange (SIMEX). By 1995 he had wiped out the 233-year-old bank, which had counted Queen Elizabeth as a client. He left behind liabilities totaling $1.3 billion. As a proprietary trader, Leeson was to arbitrage or take advantage of differences between the prices quoted for identical contracts on SIMEX and on other exchanges. This was supposed to be achieved by entering into matching purchase and sale contracts simultaneously to capture favorable price differences. Unfortunately, Leeson entered into very large contracts that were not matched, exposing the bank to enormous potential losses from even small market movements. These trades were hidden in a separate account 88888. Transactions were transferred from other Baring accounts into account 88888 to artificially generate a profit for the other accounts.

During the period, Baring was reorganizing and Leeson reported to local managers in Singapore and product managers in London. Neither set of managers checked Leeson's activities. An internal audit report had criticized the reporting structure, but its recommendations were never implemented. Funds to finance Leeson's trades were requested from him to ostensibly fund client positions and were recorded as receivables from clients. The credit control group never reviewed the creditworthiness of the clients because they said they were never informed of the remittances.

Leeson's managers accepted reports of his profitability with admiration. They did not question the unusually large profits from his trading that would have been unlikely from an arbitrage operation.

KAPLAN

CPA REVIEW

10.61 **Kaplan CPA Exam Simulations: Related Parties.** Peters & Michael CPA (P&M) are the incumbent auditors for the audit of Lakeland Supermarkets, Inc. (Lakeland) for the year ended December 31, Year 2. P&M has previously obtained and documented its understanding of Lakeland's internal controls for cash receipts, cash disbursements, and cash balances. No significant weaknesses were found.

It is now January 31 and the field work is just beginning. You are an auditor with P&M and have been assigned specifically to audit Lakeland's cash accounts as part of your duties. Materiality for the overall financial statements is set at $20,000.

Required:

Go to the Kaplan Web site at www.mhhe.com/louwers3e, click on AUD: Peters Michael case and the "Research" tab, and complete the assigned task.

APPENDIX 10A

Internal Control Questionnaires

APPENDIX 10A.1 Internal Control Questionnaire: Notes Payable

	Yes/No	Comments
Environment		
1. Are notes payable records kept by someone who cannot sign notes or checks?		
2. Are direct borrowings on notes payable authorized by the directors? By the treasurer or by the chief financial officer?		
3. Are two or more authorized signatures required on notes?		
Occurrence		
4. Are paid notes canceled, stamped "paid," and filed?		
Completeness		
5. Is all borrowing authorization by the directors checked to determine whether all notes payable are recorded?		
Accuracy		
6. Are loan documents forwarded to accounting for review?		
7. Are bank due notices compared with records of unpaid liabilities?		
8. Is the subsidiary ledger of notes payable periodically reconciled with the general ledger control account(s)? Are interest payments and accruals monitored for due dates and financial statement dates?		
Cutoff		
9. Are new notes recorded in the appropriate period?		
Classification		
10. Is sufficient information available in the accounts to enable financial statement preparers to classify current and long-term debt properly?		

APPENDIX 10A.2 Internal Control Questionnaire: Investments

	Yes/No	Comments
Environment		
1. Are investment strategies authorized by the board of directors?		
2. Are investment structures based on legitimate business goals?		
3. Are trading guidelines and limits established by company policy?		
4. Are derivatives used for legitimate company objectives?		
5. Are brokerage relationships reviewed for potential conflicts of interests?		
Occurrence		
6. Are brokerage statements reconciled to the general ledger monthly?		
Completeness		
7. Are company traders monitored in their discussions with brokers?		
Accuracy		
8. Does accounting review all significant transactions?		
9. Are purchases and sales of investments listed on brokerage statements compared to changes in the investment account?		
10. Are purchases and sales of investments listed on brokerage statements compared to receipts and disbursements?		
(continued)		

APPENDIX 10A.2 *(continued)*

	Yes/No	Comments
11. Are changes in investments accounted for on the equity method monitored and recorded in the financial statements?		
12. Are accounting personnel trained in standards for hedge accounting?		
Cutoff		
13. Are purchases and sales of investments listed on brokerage statements compared to changes in the investment account to ensure they were recorded in the proper period?		
Classification		
14. Are investment classifications based on legitimate management intentions?		
15. Are disclosures reviewed by senior management?		

APPENDIX 10B

Substantive Audit Programs

APPENDIX 10B.1

APOLLO SHOES, INC. Audit Program for Notes Payable and Long-Term Debt December 31, 2008		
	Performed by	**Ref.**
1. Obtain a schedule of notes payable and other long-term debt (including capitalized lease obligations) showing beginning balances, new notes, repayment, and ending balances. Trace to general ledger accounts.		
2. Confirm liabilities with creditor: amount, interest rate, due date, collateral, and other terms. Some of these confirmations may be standard bank confirmations.		
3. Review the standard bank confirmation for evidence of assets pledged as collateral and for unrecorded obligations.		
4. Read loan agreements for terms and conditions that need to be disclosed and for pledge of assets as collateral.		
5. Recalculate the current portion of long-term debt classified as a current liability and trace to the trial balance.		
6. Inspect lease agreements for indications of need to capitalize leases. Recalculate the capital and operating lease amounts for required disclosures.		
7. Recalculate interest expense on debts and trace to the interest expense and accrued interest accounts.		
8. Obtain written representations from management concerning notes payable, collateral agreements, and restrictive covenants.		

APPENDIX 10B.2

APOLLO SHOES, INC. Audit Program for Owners' Equity December 31, 2008		
	Performed by	**Ref.**
1. Obtain an analysis of owners' equity transactions. Trace additions and reductions to the general ledger. a. Vouch additions to directors' minutes and cash receipts. b. Vouch reductions to directors' minutes and other supporting documents. 2. Read the directors' minutes for owners' equity authorization. Trace to entries in the accounts. Determine whether related disclosures are adequate. 3. Confirm outstanding common and preferred stock with stock registrar. 4. Vouch stock option and profit-sharing plan disclosures to contracts and plan documents. 5. Vouch treasury stock transactions to cash receipts and cash disbursement records and to directors' authorization. Inspect treasury stock certificates. 6. When the company keeps its own stock records: a. Inspect the stock record stubs for certificate numbers and number of shares. b. Inspect the unissued certificates. 7. Obtain management representations about the number of shares issued and outstanding.		

APPENDIX 10B.3

APOLLO SHOES, INC. Audit Program for Investments and Related Accounts December 31, 2008		
	Performed by	**Ref.**
A. Investments and Related Accounts 1. Obtain a schedule of all investments, including purchase and disposition information for the period. Reconcile with investment accounts in the general ledger. 2. Inspect or confirm with a trustee or broker the name, number, identification, interest rate, and face amount (if applicable) of securities held as investments. 3. Vouch the cost of recorded investments to brokers' reports, contracts, canceled checks, and other supporting documentation. 4. Vouch recorded sales to brokers' reports and bank deposit slips and recalculate gain or loss on disposition. 5. Recalculate interest income and verify dividend income from a dividend-reporting service (such as Moody's or Standard & Poor's annual dividend record). 6. Obtain market values of investments and determine whether any write-down or write-off is necessary. Scan transactions soon after the client's year end to see if any investments were sold at a loss. Recalculate the unrealized gains and losses required for fair value securities accounting. 7. Read loan agreements and minutes of the board of directors and inquire of management about pledges of investments as security for loans. 8. Obtain audited financial statements of joint ventures, investee companies (equity method of accounting), subsidiary companies, and other entities in which an investment interest is held. Evaluate indications of significant controlling influence. Determine proper balance sheet classification. Determine appropriate consolidation policy in conformity with accounting principles. 9. Obtain management representations concerning pledge of investment assets as collateral. *(continued)*		

APPENDIX 10A.2 *(continued)*

	Performed by	Ref.
B. Investments in Debt and Equity Securities		
1. Determine the proper classification of securities in the categories of held-to-maturity, available-for-sale, and trading securities.		
a. Inquire about management's intent regarding classifications.		
b. Inspect written records of investment strategies.		
c. Review records of past investment activities and transactions.		
d. Review instructions to portfolio managers.		
e. Inspect minutes of the investment committee of the board of directors.		
2. Determine whether facts support management's intent to hold securities to maturity.		
a. Consider the company's financial position, working capital requirements, results of operations, debt agreements, guarantees, and applicable laws and regulations.		
b. Inspect the company's cash flow forecasts.		
c. Obtain management representations confirming proper classification with regard to intent and ability.		
3. Audit value when appropriate by performing the following:		
a. Obtain published market quotations.		
b. Obtain market prices from broker-dealers who are market makers in particular securities.		
c. Obtain valuations from expert specialists.		
d. Determine whether proprietary market valuation models are reasonable and the data and assumptions in them are appropriate.		
4. Determine whether value impairments are "other than temporary," considering evidence of the following:		
a. Fair market is materially below cost.		
b. The value decline is due to specific adverse conditions.		
c. The value decline is industry or geographically specific.		
d. Management does not have both the intent and ability to hold the security long enough for a reasonable hope of value recovery.		
e. The fair value decline has existed for a long time.		
f. A debt security has been downgraded by a rating agency.		
g. The financial condition of the issuer has deteriorated.		
h. Dividends of interest payments have been reduced or eliminated.		

Completing the Audit

Professional Standards References

Compendium Section	Document Reference	Topic
Various*	AS 5	"An Audit of Internal Control over Financial Reporting That Is Integrated with an Audit of Financial Statements"
AU 161	SAS 25	"The Relationship of Generally Accepted Auditing Standards to Quality Control Standards"
	ISA 220	"Quality Control for Audits of Historical Financial Information"
AU 312	SAS 107	"Audit Risk and Materiality in Conducting an Audit"
AU 313	SAS 45	"Substantive Tests Prior to the Balance Sheet Date"
AU 325	SAS 112	"Communicating Internal Control Related Matters Identified in an Audit"
AU 329	SAS 56	"Analytical Procedures"
	ISA 520	"Analytical Procedures"
AU 333	SAS 85	"Management Representations"
	ISA 580	"Management Representations"
AU 9333		"Interpretation: Violations of Laws and Regulations; When Current Management Not Present"
AU 337	SAS 12	"Inquiry of a Client's Lawyer Concerning Litigation"
AU 337C	SAS 12	"American Bar Association Statement of Policy Regarding Lawyers' Responses to Auditors' Requests for Information"
AU 9337		"Interpretations: Inquiry of a Client's Lawyer"
AU 339	SAS 103	"Audit Documentation"
	AS 3	"Audit Documentation"
	ISA 230	"Audit Documentation"
AU 341	SAS 59	"The Auditor's Consideration of an Entity's Ability to Continue as a Going Concern"
	ISA 570	"Going Concern"
AU 380	SAS 114	"The Auditor's Communication with Those Charged with Governance"
	ISA 260	"Communication of Audit Matters with Those Charged with Governance"
AU 390	SAS 46	"Consideration of Omitted Procedures after the Report Date"
AU 530	SAS 1	"Dating the Independent Auditor's Report"
AU 560	SAS 1	"Subsequent Events" (amended by SAS 98 and SAS 113)
	ISA 560	"Subsequent Events"
AU 561	SAS 1	"Subsequent Discovery of Facts Existing at the Date of the Auditor's Report"
AU 9561		"Interpretation: Subsequent Discovery When the Auditor Has Resigned or Been Discharged"

*AS 5 amends AU 230, AU 310, AU 312, AU 313, AU 315, AU 316, AU 319, AU 322, AU 325, AU 328, AU 332, AU 333, AU 341, AU 342, AU 380, AU 508, AU 530, AU 543, AU 560, AU 561, AU 711, AU 722, AS 3, and AS 4.

It ain't over till it's over.

Yogi Berra, former catcher for the New York Yankees

Learning Objectives

This chapter discusses the completion of the audit examination and identifies major events and auditors' responsibilities in three time periods: (1) prior to the audit completion date, (2) between the audit completion date and audit report release date, and (3) following the audit report release date.

Your objectives are to be able to:

1. Describe the approach used to examine major revenue and expense accounts.

2. Identify procedures performed by auditors to evaluate contingencies, including the use of an attorney letter, during the completion of the audit.

3. Explain why auditors obtain management representations and identify the key components of management representations.

4. Identify the two major categories of subsequent events and describe the proper handling of these events by auditors.

5. Identify the final steps in the completion of an audit.

6. Following the audit report release date, identify auditors' responsibilities for (1) facts that may have existed at the date of the auditors' reports and (2) omitted audit procedures.

7. Summarize important communications made by auditors following completion of the audit and audit report release date.

OVERVIEW

So the completion of the audit is a *fait accompli?* Try telling that to **Adecco,** a Swiss staffing firm. On January 12, 2004, Adecco announced that its auditors (**Ernst & Young**) refused to sign off on the company's 2003 financial statements, citing "material weaknesses in internal control." On that day alone, the value of shares of Adecco's stock declined by 35 percent; Adecco's chief financial officer was fired shortly thereafter. However, that was only the beginning of Adecco's problems. Four months later, after an investigation of more than 22 million pages of documents, more than 150 interviews with company managers, and €100m ($121 million) paid to Ernst & Young and other advisers and consultants, Adecco released its financial results with an unqualified opinion from Ernst & Young and no restatements. While Adecco's stock price slightly recovered, it was still down 20 percent from its January level and remained at that level for the next 18 months.[1]

Thus far in this text, we have discussed auditors' use of the audit risk model to limit exposure to audit risk, auditors' tests of controls to determine the operating effectiveness of internal control and to assess control risk (and the risk of material misstatement), and auditors' substantive procedures to determine the fairness of the account balances and classes of transactions. At this point, it seems as though little work remains to be done! Although the audit is concluding, the potential for audit failure is at its highest. Consider just a few of these questions that auditors may be asking as the audit is concluding:

- Are there year-end adjustments that significantly affect the financial statements?
- What events that occur after year end could affect the current-year's financial statements?
- What potential exposure does the client have for pending litigation?
- Has the client provided all relevant information to auditors during the engagement?
- What matters need to be discussed with the individuals charged with governance of the client (normally, the audit committee)?

As shown in the Auditing Insight, the completion of the audit is far from a straightforward, "checking the boxes" matter and involves significant auditor judgment and attention. These matters were identified by the Public Company Accounting Oversight Board (PCAOB) during its annual inspections in 2006 for audits conducted by the Big Four firms (**Deloitte & Touche, Ernst & Young, KPMG,** and **PricewaterhouseCoopers**). In this excerpt, "the firm" refers to one of these firms.

[1] "Crisis? What Crisis?" *CFO.com*, July 24, 2004.

AUDITING INSIGHT PCAOB Inspections and Completing the Audit

- The firm identified known errors that it concluded did not warrant further investigation, discussion, or adjustment to the financial statements. Some of these errors were left in the audit documentation without final disposition, despite the fact that they exceeded the firm's posting threshold.
- The firm's analytical procedures for testing operating expenses did not appropriately set a threshold for investigation of significant differences between the recorded balance and the firm's expectations; further, the firm did not document its corroboration of management's explanations for significant differences between the recorded balance and the firm's expectations.
- The firm did not perform sufficient audit procedures with respect to income tax contingencies (assessing the likelihood of occurrence, testing the amount of the estimate accrued by the client, evaluating whether the client's policy on establishing reserves was consistent with GAAP, and evaluating the

client's conclusion that no reserve was required for items that were disallowed in a report received in connection with an Internal Revenue Service audit).
- In its response to the PCAOB's inspection report, one firm noted that it performed additional auditing procedures in cases where the PCAOB felt that sufficient evidence was not obtained to support the firm's opinion. In five cases, these procedures did not affect the financial statements or the firm's opinion on the financial statements; in one case, the client restated its financial statements to correct for an error identified by the firm's additional procedures.

Sources: 2005 PCAOB Inspection of Deloitte & Touche, November 30, 2006; 2005 PCAOB Inspection of Ernst & Young, January 11, 2007; 2005 Inspection of KPMG, January 11, 2007; and 2005 Inspection of PricewaterhouseCoopers, December 14, 2006. All reports can be found on the PCAOB's Web site, www.pcaob.org/Inspections/Public_Reports/index.aspx.

This chapter discusses the completion (or wrap-up) of the audit. During this time, many important issues arise and many other issues that have served as the focus of auditors' work need to be documented. To provide an overview of the general timeframe of the audit and the potential emergence of issues and matters for the auditors' consideration, consider the following broad timeline.

Beginning of Year	End of Year	Audit Completion Date	Audit Report Release Date
Time period A:	Time period B:	Time period C:	Time period D:
Interim testing • Tests of controls • Substantive procedures	"Roll-forward" work Revenue and expense accounts Attorney's letters Management representations Going-concern assessment Adjusting journal entries Subsequent events Audit documentation review	Subsequent events (dual dating)	Subsequent discovery of facts Omitted audit procedures Management letter Communications with those charged with governance

For the current audit (say, December 31, 2008), auditors often do a significant amount of tests of controls and substantive procedures prior to year end to "spread" the audit work over a more extended period. This *interim testing* occurs during time period A (between the beginning of the year and the end of the year under audit).

Obviously, auditors cannot issue an opinion on financial statements without examining the entire period covered by these statements. Thus, auditors extend the work from the interim period through year end. For example, assume that that work was carefully planned in such a manner that auditors' interim work satisfied them that the financial statements were fairly presented as of October 15, 2008. In this case, auditors would perform additional tests of controls and substantive procedures on transactions occurring from October 16, 2008, through December 31, 2008 (assuming the client has a December 31, 2008,

fiscal year end). These procedures are often referred to as *roll-forward* work because they allow auditors to *roll* the conclusion *forward* to the end of the year under audit.

In addition to roll-forward work, auditors perform other procedures and gather other audit evidence during time period B. The significant characteristic of time period B is that auditors are still conducting the audit examination and obtaining sufficient appropriate evidence. At some point, auditors will have gathered sufficient appropriate evidence on which to base their opinions on the financial statements and internal control over financial reporting; *SAS 103* notes that this includes the review of audit documentation, preparation of the financial statements and related disclosures, and management's assertion that they take responsibility for the financial statements and disclosures. We will refer to this as the **audit completion date** and this is the date auditors will use for their opinions on the client's financial statements and internal control over financial reporting. Recall that auditors' report on the entity's financial statements covers all events that occur up to this date and, as a result, auditors need to continue to be alert for developments affecting the client.

In some instances, auditors become aware of a development affecting the client *after* the audit completion date but *prior* to the **audit report release date** (date on which auditors allow the client to use the auditors' reports in conjunction with the financial statements)[2] (time period C). The audit report release date is also the date on which the client's financial statements are issued. These events present significant challenges to auditors, who are no longer actively obtaining audit evidence; however, auditors' reports have yet to be issued. The auditors' dilemma is simple: how to report on the new development without increasing the responsibility for other (unknown) developments. As discussed later in this chapter, auditors may consider dual dating the report on the entity's financial statements to limit responsibility for other developments.

Finally, some issues can come to auditors' attention after the audit report release date and the client's financial statements are issued (time period D).[3] Although the entity's Form 10-K and auditors' reports have been released, it is important that auditors take important steps to ensure that the reports are not inappropriately relied on by third parties. In addition, following the audit report release date, auditors make other communications to the client and individuals charged with governance based on observations during the audit examination.

This chapter focuses on a number of the topics addressed in the preceding timeline. In considering auditors' responsibility for various matters, it is important to consider the timing of these topics in the above timeline.

PROCEDURES PERFORMED DURING FIELD WORK

LEARNING OBJECTIVE

1. Describe the approach used to examine major revenue and expense accounts.

Revenue and Expense Accounts

As noted, following the fiscal year end, auditors perform various types of roll-forward work to allow their conclusions to be extended to the date of the financial statements. Typically, these procedures will include confirmations of accounts receivable with customers, confirmations of cash balances with banks, searches for unrecorded liabilities, price tests and test counts for inventory, and so on. These procedures are performed after year end out of necessity; for example, significant customer accounts may not be known with certainty until after year end and, thus, cannot be confirmed with the customer until that time.

[2] These reports include opinions on (1) the entity's financial statements and (2) the effectiveness of the entity's internal control over financial reporting. As noted in Chapter 12, both auditors' reports are dated on the audit completion date and included with the entity's 10-K filed with the Securities and Exchange Commission.
[3] Beginning in 2007, the largest public companies must file annual reports with the U.S. Securities and Exchange Commission (SEC) within 60 days after the balance sheet date. Thus, audit field work must be completed and auditors' reports for these companies must be dated earlier than 60 days after an entity's fiscal year end.

EXHIBIT 11.1
Audit of Revenue and Expense Accounts

Revenue and Expense Account	Balance Sheet Account	Transaction Cycle
Sales Revenue and Sales Returns	Receivables	Revenue/Collection
Dividend and Interest Revenue	Receivables, Investments	Finance/Investment
Gain or Loss on Asset Disposals	PPE	Acquisition/Expenditure
	Receivables, Investments	Finance/Investment Production
Cost of Goods Sold	Inventories	Acquisition/Expenditure
Interest Expense	Liabilities	Finance/Investment

As a result of this roll-forward work and interim tests, the major revenue and expense accounts typically will have been audited in connection with related balance sheet accounts. Exhibit 11.1 summarizes a sample of revenue and expense accounts as well as the related balance sheet accounts and transaction cycles. For example, during the audit of receivables and the revenue/collection cycle, auditors also have gathered some degree of audit evidence as to the fair presentation and disclosure of sales revenue and sales returns. To the extent that these items have been audited in conjunction with the related balance sheet accounts, the audit documentation should cross-reference the revenue accounts in the client's working trial balance.

Although Exhibit 11.1 suggests that many revenue and expense accounts have been examined during the audit of balance sheet accounts and examination of transaction cycles, not all revenue and expense accounts have been examined in this manner. Normally, the remaining accounts are not individually material and the relative risk that they could result in material financial statement misstatement is small. However, if material, auditors can vouch details included in the account balance to the appropriate documentation supporting those entries.

In addition to procedures related to revenue and expense accounts on which evidence has not been obtained, auditors extensively use *analytical procedures* to verify the overall reasonableness of all revenue and expense accounts. These analytical procedures complement the substantive procedures performed in the examination of these accounts and may compare the recorded revenues and expenses with the following benchmarks:

- Prior-year balances.
- Expected balances determined using a statistical analysis or relationship among accounts.
- Internal budgets and reports.

When using analytical procedures in this fashion, auditors are attempting to identify accounts that do not look appropriate based on prior relationships. To illustrate, if an account typically does not change much from one year to another, a significant fluctuation can suggest the existence of a misstatement. In contrast, if the client's operations have changed in such a way that the account balances should be significantly different from those observed in prior years, the failure to observe a major change might suggest the existence of a misstatement. As with all analytical procedures, auditors should corroborate the findings with inquiry of the client's management. *SAS 56* (AU 329) requires auditors to use analytical procedures in the final review stages of the audit to assess the conclusions reached and evaluate the overall financial statement presentation.

In addition to the preceding, auditors should be alert for "miscellaneous," "other," and "clearing" accounts classified as revenues or expenses, particularly when they result from adjustments made at the end of the year or quarter. In many cases, these items reflect adjustments made to meet analysts' earnings expectations (known as *earnings management*) and should be more appropriately classified as *deferred items, assets, liabilities, contra-assets, or contra-liabilities*. **HealthSouth, Sunbeam,** and **WorldCom** used adjustments

AUDITING INSIGHT — DNY?

A governmental auditor was examining year-end adjusting entries made at a state university. In doing so, he was perplexed that there were no explanations for the entries but only the initials "DNY." When trying to track down the mysterious DNY who made these entries, the auditor was shocked when told "DNY isn't a person but means 'Don't know why.'" The auditors disclaimed an opinion on the university's financial statements.

(which did not comply with generally accepted accounting principles) near the end of a reporting period to improve their reported earnings.

"Miscellaneous," "other," and "clearing" items are typically identified by scanning accounts for large and unusual debit (expense) or credit (revenue) entries. To verify whether current classification as a revenue or expense is appropriate, auditors should examine related documentation and inquire of the client. In addition to classification issues, these accounts may reveal the existence of unrecorded asset disposals, expiration of prepaid assets, and other types of transactions. To the extent that auditors identify evidence of these types of transactions (for example, a gain on sale of property, plant, and equipment—PPE), they should verify that the related asset or liability also has been accounted for properly (PPE has been properly reduced for the historical cost and accumulated depreciation).

Review Checkpoints

11.1 Identify four primary time periods in an audit examination and the tasks and activities that occur in each time period.

11.2 Identify the balance sheet accounts and transaction cycles that are most closely associated with the following revenue and expense accounts: Sales Revenue and Sales Returns, Dividend and Interest Revenue, Gain or Loss on Asset Disposals, Cost of Goods Sold, Interest Expense.

11.3 Other than any work with the related balance sheet accounts and transaction cycles, what is the general approach used to examine revenue and expense accounts?

11.4 What additional issues are involved with miscellaneous, other, and clearing accounts?

Contingencies

LEARNING OBJECTIVE

2. Identify procedures performed by auditors to evaluate contingencies, including the use of an attorney letter, during the completion of the audit.

For financial statements to be presented according to GAAP, all material contingencies (contingent gains or losses) must be properly accounted for and disclosed in the financial statements. According to *FASB Statement No. 5 (SFAS 5)*, a **contingency** is

> an existing condition, situation, or set of circumstances involving uncertainty as to possible gain ("gain contingency") or loss ("loss contingency") to an enterprise that will ultimately be resolved when one or more future events occur or fail to occur.

Because of their negative impact on an entity's financial condition, auditors are generally more concerned with loss contingencies (which would require recognizing a contingent liability). Examples of contingent liabilities include warranties, tax disputes involving the Internal Revenue Service, and guarantees of debt. *SFAS 5* sets forth standards for the accrual and disclosure of contingent liabilities based on the classification of the likelihood of occurrence as either "probable," "reasonably possible," or "remote." Contingent liabilities may be identified during the *search for unrecorded*

liabilities discussed in Chapter 8. As noted therein, some of the procedures performed by auditors include:

- Inquiring of client personnel.
- Reviewing the open purchase order files, unmatched vendor invoices, and unmatched receiving reports.
- Vouching cash disbursements made after year end to supporting documentation.
- Confirming accounts payable with vendors, particularly those having small or zero balances at year end.

A common contingent liability is the uncertain outcome of litigation, claims, and assessments pending against the entity. From the auditors' standpoint, two important issues relating to pending litigation, claims, and assessments are ensuring that all pending litigation, claims, and assessments (1) have been disclosed to auditors and (2) are properly presented and disclosed in the client's financial statements. Because the client's attorney(s) is (are) most familiar with the existence and classification of pending litigation, claims, and assessments, this party plays a very important role in auditors' evaluation of these matters.

Auditors should inquire of management and discuss potential litigation, claims, and assessments. Once this inquiry has resulted in identifying litigation, claims, and assessments, auditors perform the following procedures:

- Obtain from management a description and evaluation of litigation, claims, and assessments.
- Examine documents in the client's possession concerning litigation, claims, and assessments, including correspondence and invoices from attorneys.
- Obtain assurance from management that it has disclosed all material unasserted claims the attorney has advised them are likely to be litigated.
- Read minutes of meetings of stockholders, directors, and appropriate committees.
- Read contracts, loan agreements, leases, and correspondence from taxing or other governmental agencies.
- Obtain information concerning guarantees from bank confirmations.
- Review the legal expense account, cash disbursements records, and invoices related to legal services.

The client's responsibility is to respond to auditors' inquiries and provide auditors with a description and evaluation of litigation, claims, and assessments. Based on the auditors' request, the client then would send an **attorney letter** (or letter of inquiry) to all attorneys who worked for the client during the period under audit. It is important to note that the client should make this request because it informs the attorney that the client is waiving the attorney-client privilege and is authorizing the attorney to provide information to auditors. The attorney letter should contain the following information (prepared from the client's perspective):

- A list of pending or threatened litigation, claims, or assessments.
- A description of each item, including the nature of the case and management responses or intended responses to the case.
- An evaluation of the likelihood of an unfavorable outcome.
- An estimate of the range of potential loss.

See the following diagram for the flow of correspondence related to the attorney letter. The process begins when auditors request the client to send a letter to its attorney(s) (step 1). In step 2, the attorney receives the letter from the client asking to respond to the letter (step 3). The *attorney's response* should be provided *directly* to auditors for purposes of control and should explain any matters noted in the attorney letter in which the attorney's view differs from the information in the letter. For example, the client may indicate

that the likelihood of an unfavorable outcome is "remote," but the attorney may believe that it is higher than "remote." In addition, the attorney may inform auditors of pending litigation, claims, or assessments not included in the attorney letter.

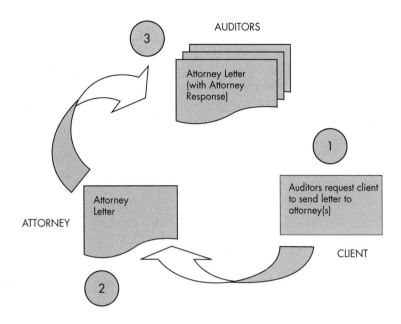

The general roles of the client, auditors, and attorney(s) in this process are summarized in Exhibit 11.2.

EXHIBIT 11.2
Role of Various Parties in Audit of Litigation, Claims, and Assessments

Party	Responsibilities
Auditors	• Inquire of client regarding the existence of litigation, claims, and assessments. • Perform various procedures regarding litigation, claims, and assessments. • Initiate request to the client for attorney letter.
Client	• Respond to auditors' inquiries regarding litigation, claims, and assessments. • Provide auditors with a list, description, and evaluation of litigation, claims, and assessments. • Send letter to attorney (attorney letter) that includes information related to litigation, claims, and assessments.
Attorney	• Respond to auditors regarding client's description of litigation, claims, and assessments contained in the attorney letter.

A sample attorney letter is shown in Exhibit 11.3.

Unasserted claims raise additional issues for attorney letters. An **unasserted claim** represents that no formal lawsuit or claim has been filed or threatened on behalf of others but that circumstances such as a catastrophe, accident, or other physical occurrence could result in a suit or claim being filed in the future. In these cases, attorneys must consider the likelihood that a lawsuit or claim will be filed as well as the possibility of an unfavorable outcome when responding to the attorney letter.

Because unasserted claims have not been filed, the issue of client disclosure of these matters to auditors is less clear. *SAS 12* (AU 337C) notes that attorneys should encourage their clients to disclose this information to auditors when the assertion of a claim is at least *probable*. However, the American Bar Association's guidelines to attorneys do not require them to disclose unasserted claims to auditors unless they are specifically listed by the client in the attorney letter. Thus, auditors must rely on the attorney to inform the

EXHIBIT 11.3 **Sample Attorney Letter**

Source: Adapted from *SAS 12* (AU 337A).

VANDALAY INDUSTRIES
P.O. BOX 2121
NEW YORK, NY 21001

March 2, 2009

To: Jackie Childs
Childs and Dunn
280 East 23rd Street
New York, NY 21005

In connection with an audit of our financial statements at December 31, 2008, and for the year then ended, management of Vandalay Industries has prepared, and furnished to George Costanza, CPA, P.O. Box 10024, New York, NY 21001, a description and evaluation of certain contingencies, including those set forth below involving matters with respect to which you have been engaged and to which you have devoted substantive attention on behalf of Vandalay Industries in the form of legal consultation or representation. These are regarded by the management of Vandalay Industries as material for this purpose. Your response should include matters that existed at December 31, 2008, and during the period from that date to the date of your response.

[Add description of pending or threatened litigation]

Please furnish to our auditors such explanation, if any, that you consider necessary to supplement the foregoing information, including an explanation of those matters as to which your views may differ from those stated and an identification of the omission of any pending or threatened litigation, claims, and assessments or a statement that the list of such matters is complete.

[Add description of unasserted claims and assessments]

Please furnish to our auditors such explanation, if any, that you consider necessary to supplement the foregoing information, including an explanation of those matters as to which your views may differ from those stated.

We understand that whenever, in the course of performing legal services for us with respect to a matter recognized to involve an unasserted possible claim or assessment that may call for financial statement disclosure, if you have formed a professional conclusion that we should disclose or consider disclosure concerning such possible claim or assessment, as a matter of professional responsibility to us, you will so advise us and will consult with us concerning the question of such disclosure and the applicable requirements of Statement of Financial Accounting Standards No. 5. Please specifically confirm to our auditors that our understanding is correct.

Please specifically identify the nature of and reasons for any limitation on your response.

Signed:

Cosmo Kramer
Cosmo Kramer, Chief Executive Officer

client (not the auditors) if an unasserted claim must be disclosed. As shown in Exhibit 11.3, the attorney letter explicitly asks that this understanding be communicated to the client's auditors through the attorney's response. If the attorney tells the client that a

matter must be disclosed and the client does not disclose it, auditors should assume that the attorney will resign, which is a signal that something is amiss.

Interpreting Attorney Letters

Because open disclosure of information about litigation could result in negative reactions by shareholders and other third parties (courts may view this as an admission of guilt), responses to attorney letters often contain vague wording. According to AU 9337, the following responses can be interpreted to mean that the likelihood of an unfavorable outcome is "remote":

- We are of the opinion that this action will not result in any liability to the entity.
- It is our opinion that the possible liability to the entity is nominal in amount.
- We believe the entity will be able to defend this action successfully.
- We believe that the plaintiff's case against the entity is without merit.

In contrast, the following wording in attorney responses should be viewed as providing no information about the likelihood of an unfavorable outcome:

- We believe the plaintiff will have serious problems establishing the entity's liability; nevertheless, if the plaintiff is successful, the damage award could be substantial.
- It is our opinion the entity will be able to assert meritorious defenses.
- We believe the lawsuit can be settled for less than the damages claimed.
- We are unable to express an opinion on the merits of the litigation, but the entity believes there is absolutely no merit.

In addition, some differences in terminology exist between *SFAS 5* and the American Bar Association. For example, *SFAS 5* defines *remote* as "[t]he chance of the future event or events occurring as slight"; the American Bar Association defines it as "prospects for the client not succeeding in its defense are judged to be extremely doubtful and the prospects of success by the claimant are judged to be slight."

Research on 126 lawsuits successfully brought against public companies revealed that 72 companies (57.2 percent) provided satisfactory disclosure of the litigation while 54 companies (42.8 percent) did not. Amazingly, in almost 36 percent of the lawsuits that public companies lost, the companies' prior-years' financial statements did not even mention the pending litigation![4]

AUDITING INSIGHT Merck Litigation

Merck, a developer, manufacturer, and marketer of pharmaceutical products, disclosed that as of December 31, 2006, it had been served or was aware that it had been named in over 27,400 lawsuits related to the use of Vioxx, an arthritis and acute pain medication. Merck voluntarily withdrew Vioxx from the market on September 30, 2004, because of concerns about side effects related to cardiovascular diseases (such as heart attacks and strokes). Thus far, a total of 14 cases have come to trial, with the following results:

- Four verdicts in favor of the plaintiff, with damages ranging from $7.75 million to $26.1 million (which was reduced from the original damages of $253.4 million awarded by the jury); Merck is appealing all four of these verdicts.

- Seven verdicts in favor of Merck; plaintiffs have moved for new trials in five of these cases.
- One case where the judge overthrew a verdict in favor of Merck, with a new trial ordered.
- One mistrial because of a deadlocked jury.

To the extent that external attorneys are involved in this litigation, issues related to Merck's Vioxx litigation would be included in attorney letters.

Source: Merck & Co. 2006 10-K.

[4] "Disclosure of Litigation Contingencies Faulted," *Journal of Accountancy,* July 1990, pp. 15–16.

Review Checkpoints

11.5 What are the responsibilities of (a) client management, (b) auditors, and (c) the client's attorneys with respect to obtaining evidence regarding litigation, claims, and assessments?

11.6 What is the typical content of attorney letters?

11.7 In addition to obtaining responses to attorney letters, what other procedures can be used to gather audit evidence regarding litigation, claims, and assessments?

Management Representations

LEARNING
OBJECTIVE

3. Explain why auditors obtain management representations and identify the key components of management representations.

Under Section 302 of the Sarbanes-Oxley Act of 2002 (Sarbanes-Oxley), all 10-Q and 10-K filings with the Securities and Exchange Commission are required to include certifications from the chief executive officer and chief financial officer related to the fairness of the entity's financial statements and effectiveness of the entity's internal control over financial reporting. However, these are only some representations that are made by the client. As noted in previous chapters, an important source of audit evidence is inquiries of client personnel. Many of the responses to these inquiries are very important. To the extent that additional evidence is obtainable through other procedures, auditors should corroborate these representations.

SAS 85 (AU 333) requires that auditors obtain **management representations** (also known as *written representations* or *client representations*) on matters of audit importance. The representations take the form of a letter on the client's letterhead addressed to auditors and signed by responsible officers of the client (normally the chief executive officer [CEO], chief financial officer [CFO], and other appropriate officers). These representations are dated as of the date of the auditors' reports, which is the audit completion date (in fact, the audit completion date is dependent upon auditors receiving assertions from management regarding its responsibility for the fairness of the financial statements and related disclosures). Thus, the letter covers events and representations running beyond the balance sheet date up to this date.

It is important to note that management representations are not substitutes for corroborating evidence obtained by applying other substantive procedures. That is, auditors cannot substitute client inquiry (and representations regarding that inquiry) for substantive procedures. For example, the representation that "management told us that the inventory costing method was FIFO and adequate allowance for obsolescence was provided" is not a good excuse for failing to obtain the evidence from the records and other sources.

However, in some cases, management representations are the only available evidence about important matters of management intent. For example, the following representations (written by the client's management) provide auditors important audit evidence regarding presentation and disclosure matters:

- "We will discontinue the parachute manufacturing business, wind down the operations, and sell the remaining assets" (classification of the parachute manufacturing business as a discontinued operation).
- "We will exercise our option to refinance the maturing debt on a long-term basis" (classification of the maturing debt as long-term debt).

One of the major purposes of management representations is to impress on management its primary responsibility for establishing and maintaining effective internal control over financial reporting and for the fairness of the financial statements. These representations also may establish the auditors' defense if a question of management integrity arises later. If management does not respond truthfully and completely to auditors' inquiries, management representations may serve as important evidence in support of auditors.

Exhibit 11.4 provides sample management representations in the form of a letter from the client to auditors. As noted earlier, it is written by the client (specifically, key officers) to auditors and is dated March 2, 2009 (the audit completion date). Management representations

EXHIBIT 11.4 Sample Management Representations

Source: Modified from Appendix to AU 333 to include internal control representations from *AS 5*.

VANDALAY INDUSTRIES
P.O. BOX 2121
NEW YORK, NY 21001

March 2, 2009

To: George Costanza, CPA

We are providing this letter in connection with your audit of the balance sheet, income statement, statement of comprehensive income, statement of stockholders' equity, and statement of cash flows of Vandalay Industries as of December 31, 2008, and for the year ended December 31, 2008, for the purpose of expressing an opinion as to whether the consolidated financial statements present fairly, in all material respects, the financial position, results of operations, and cash flows in conformity with accounting principles generally accepted in the United States of America.

Certain representations in this letter are described as being limited to matters that are material. Items are considered material, regardless of size, if they involve an omission or misstatement of accounting information that, in the light of surrounding circumstances, makes it probable that the judgment of a reasonable person relying on the information would be changed or influenced by the omission or misstatement.

We confirm, to the best of our knowledge and belief, as of March 2, 2009, the following representations made to you during your audit.

1. We are responsible for the fair presentation in the financial statements of financial position, results of operations, and cash flows and believe that the financial statements referred to above are fairly presented in conformity with accounting principles generally accepted in the United States of America.
2. We have made available to you all the financial records and related data.
3. We have made available to you all minutes of the meetings of stockholders, directors, and committees of directors.
4. There are no material transactions that have not been properly recorded in the accounting records.
5. We believe that the effects of any uncorrected financial statement misstatements summarized in the accompanying schedule are immaterial, both individually and in the aggregate, to the financial statements taken as a whole.
6. There are no:
 a. Communications from regulatory agencies concerning noncompliance with or deficiencies in financial reporting practices.
 b. Violations or possible violations of laws or regulations whose effects should be considered for disclosure in the financial statements.
 c. Unasserted claims or assessments that our lawyer has advised us are probable of assertion and must be disclosed in accordance with Statement of Financial Accounting Standards No. 5.
7. With respect to our internal control over financial reporting:
 a. We are responsible for establishing and maintaining effective internal control over financial reporting.
 b. We have performed an assessment of the effectiveness of our internal control over financial reporting based on criteria established in Internal Control — Integrated Framework issued by the Committee on Sponsoring Organizations of the Treadway Commission (COSO criteria). *
 c. Based on this assessment, we conclude that we have maintained effective internal control over financial reporting as of December 31, 2008. *
 d. We have disclosed to you all deficiencies in the design or operation of internal control over financial reporting, including separate disclosure of any deficiencies that we believe to be significant deficiencies or material weaknesses.
 e. There are no instances of material fraud or fraud involving senior management or management or other employees who have a significant role in our internal control over financial reporting.
 f. There are no control deficiencies communicated to the audit committee from prior engagements that have not been appropriately resolved. *
 g. There are no subsequent changes in internal control over financial reporting or other factors that may significantly affect internal control over financial reporting. *
8. We acknowledge our responsibility for the design and implementation of programs and controls to prevent and detect fraud.

Signed:

Cosmo Kramer
Cosmo Kramer, Chief Executive Officer

Newman Post
Newman Post, Chief Financial Officer

*Included if the client is a publicly traded entity, subject to assessment and reporting requirements for internal control over financial reporting under *AS 5*.

should discuss only material matters facing the client. Auditing standards provide that the following representations must appear in the letter without limitation based on materiality:

1. Management's acknowledgment of its responsibility for fair presentation of financial statements in conformity with U.S. generally accepted accounting principles.

2. Availability of all financial records and related data and completeness of the minutes of meetings of stockholders, directors, and important committees. (In some cases, management also may provide a "minute representation letter" that lists the dates of all directors' and shareholders' meetings during the period under audit).

3. Management's acknowledgement of its responsibility for the design and implementation of programs and controls to prevent and detect fraud.

4. Disclosure of all significant deficiencies in internal control.

5. Information concerning fraud involving management, employees who have significant roles in internal control, or cases in which the fraud could have a material effect on the financial statements.

AS 5 requires an extensive number of representations related to the audit of internal control over financial reporting (see items marked * in item 7 in Exhibit 11.4). Similar to the representations related to the financial statement audit, these items provide auditors important evidence regarding management's responsibility for internal control over financial reporting and ensure that all important facts have been properly disclosed to auditors.

Clearly, management representations are a critical part of auditors' overall ability to support the opinion on the financial statements. As a result, management's refusal to furnish representations constitutes a scope limitation, which requires a qualification in the auditors' report on the entity's financial statements (*SAS 85*, AU 333) or a disclaimer of opinion (AU 9333). Auditors should be very skeptical of any situation in which the client's management refuses to furnish representations.

AUDITING INSIGHT Can You Trust Management Representations?

Gemstar-TV Guide International, Inc., a media, entertainment, and technology company headquartered in Los Angeles, California, engaged in a massive scheme to inflate its revenue; the most significant fraudulent transaction was $100 million in revenue from an expired contract with **Scientific-Atlanta, Inc.** Gemstar's auditor (**KPMG**) raised specific questions about the Scientific-Atlanta transaction and received written assurance from Henry Yuen (then-CEO of Gemstar) and Elsie Leung (then-

CFO) that the revenue from Scientific-Atlanta was legitimate and would be received. Brian Palbaum, the KPMG partner involved with this audit, indicates that Mr. Yuen and Ms. Leung "may have misled [him] about the status of the settlement negotiations with Scientific-Atlanta."

Source: "As Fraud Case Unravels, Executive Is at Large," *The Wall Street Journal,* April 25, 2007, pp. A1, A9.

Review Checkpoints

11.8 What is the purpose of management representations? What representations must always be provided regardless of materiality?

11.9 If the entity is subject to the requirements of *AS 5*, what management representations should auditors obtain from the client with respect to internal control over financial reporting?

11.10 Why are management representation and attorney letters obtained near the end of the evidence-gathering process and dated on or near the audit report release date?

11.11 How should auditors respond if the client refuses to furnish management representations?

Subsequent Period and Events

LEARNING
OBJECTIVE

4. Identify the two major
categories of
subsequent events and
describe the proper
handling of these
events by auditors.

The **subsequent period** is the period of time between the balance sheet date and the audit report release date. During this period, auditors should perform certain procedures to evaluate the existence of events that occur after the balance sheet date that could affect the presentation and disclosure in the client's financial statements. Some important procedures performed by auditors in this regard include these:

- Read the latest interim financial statements and compare them with the financial statements being reported on.
- Inquire of officers and other executives having responsibility for financial and accounting matters about contingent liabilities or commitments; significant changes in capital stock, long-term debt, or working capital since the balance sheet date; and unusual adjustments since the balance sheet date.
- Read minutes of meetings of shareholders, directors, and appropriate committees.
- Obtain responses to attorney letters from any legal counsel engaged by the client (see earlier discussion).
- Obtain management representations (see earlier discussion).

Events occurring between the balance sheet date and the audit report release date are referred to as **subsequent events.** The auditors' primary objective is to ensure that any major events that affect the fairness of the client's financial statements and disclosures are properly identified. These procedures should alert auditors to these types of changes.

Types of Subsequent Events

The two types of subsequent events are distinguished by whether the underlying conditions existed at the date of the financial statements. **Type I subsequent events** provide new information regarding a condition that *existed at the balance sheet date*. Because the condition existed at that time, some information related to these events may have been disclosed; as a result, a Type I subsequent event requires adjustment of amounts or disclosures in the financial statements for new information identified during the period under audit.

The following examples of Type I subsequent events are provided by *SAS 1* (AU 560):

- A loss on uncollectible trade accounts receivable as a result of the bankruptcy of a major customer. (The customer's deteriorating financial condition existed prior to the balance sheet date.)
- The settlement of litigation for an amount different than estimated (assuming the litigation had taken place prior to the balance sheet date).

Type II subsequent events involve occurrences whose cause and manifestation both arose *after the balance sheet date*. Recall that the responsibility for adequate disclosure runs to the date corresponding to the audit report release date. Consequently, even for events that occurred after the balance sheet date, auditors must consider their importance and may insist that disclosure be made.

Type II events that occur after the balance sheet date could be of such magnitude that disclosure is necessary to keep the financial statements from being misleading. Disclosure normally is in a narrative note. Occasionally, however, an event can be so significant that the best disclosure would be **pro forma financial data,** which refers to the presentation of the financial statements "as if" the event had occurred as of the beginning of the period.

Examples of Type II subsequent events in *SAS 1* (AU 560) include these:

- Loss on an uncollectible trade receivable resulting from a customer's loss from fire or flood subsequent to the balance sheet date (as contrasted with a customer's slow decline into bankruptcy cited as a Type I event above).
- Sale of a bond or capital stock issue.

AUDITING INSIGHT Subsequent Events

The following are examples of Type II subsequent events disclosed by companies in their footnotes to the financial statements:

• **Wal-Mart** increased its annual dividend from $0.60 to $0.67 per share on March 2, 2006, and entered into a £150 million revolving credit facility in the United Kingdom during February 2006 (Wal-Mart's fiscal year end was January 31, 2006).

• **Cisco Systems** made an acquisition of **Meetinghouse Data Communications, Inc.,** and a significant investment in Nuova **Systems, Inc.** during the first quarter of 2007 (Cisco's fiscal year end was July 31, 2006).

Sources: Wal-Mart 2006 10-K; Cisco Systems 2006 10-K.

• Settlement of litigation when the event giving rise to the claim took place after the balance sheet date.
• Loss of plant or inventories as a result of fire or flood.

Effect of Subsequent Events on Auditors' Reports

Depending on the timing, subsequent events can affect the date of the auditors' report on the entity's financial statements. Recall that the date of the auditors' report (the audit completion date) indicates the degree of responsibility assumed—that is, auditors are responsible for matters affecting the client's financial statements until that date. If auditors learn of subsequent events and can perform the appropriate procedures prior to the audit completion date, these events will not influence the date of the auditors' report or the responsibility assumed by the auditors.

In some circumstances, auditors could learn of subsequent events *after the audit completion date* but *prior to the audit report release date*. Because it would be misleading for the client to issue financial statements that did not reflect the subsequent events, auditors must perform additional procedures and evaluate the appropriateness of the disclosure of these events. One option would be to do so and change the date on the auditors' report to reflect the new (later) audit completion date. However, a disadvantage of this approach is that the responsibility for *all events* is now extended to this later date.

In cases such as this, auditors normally choose to **dual date** the report (that is, to give it two dates). For example, **Ernst & Young** completed the field work of its 2001 audit of **Hewlett-Packard** on November 13, 2001 (Hewlett-Packard had an October 31 year end). On December 6, 2001, Hewlett-Packard made an offering of $1 billion of debt, which it disclosed in Note 19 to its financial statements. The date used by Ernst & Young in its 2001 auditors' report of Hewlett-Packard was as follows:

November 13, 2001, except for Note 19, as to which the date is December 6, 2001.

In this instance, Ernst & Young has full responsibility for all subsequent events through November 13, 2001, except for the issuance of debt. Ernst & Young has responsibility for this event through December 6, 2001.

AUDITING INSIGHT No Responsibility

BMC Software's financial statements for the year ended March 31, 2001, included a subsequent event related to a 6 percent worldwide reduction in the company's workforce and a corresponding restructuring charge of $14 million to be taken in the first quarter of 2002. This subsequent event was included in the footnotes to the financial statements and marked as "unaudited" by BMC Software's auditors (at that time, **Arthur Andersen**). A single date was used for the report on the company's financial statements.

Source: BMC Software 2006 10-K.

Dual dating serves two important functions. First, it provides a means of modifying the financial statements and disclosures for information discovered by auditors after the audit completion date. This provides financial statement users the most complete set of information about the entity. Second, it limits auditors' liability for events after the audit completion date to the subsequent event specifically identified in the report date.

Review Checkpoints

11.12 What is a *subsequent event?*

11.13 What procedures are performed during the subsequent period?

11.14 Identify the two types of subsequent events. How is information about these events reflected in the financial statements?

11.15 What is the purpose of dual dating the auditors' report?

Ability to Continue as a Going Concern

LEARNING OBJECTIVE

5. Identify the final steps in the completion of an audit.

As auditors gather evidence throughout the engagement, information may be encountered that raises questions as to the client's ability to continue as a going concern. *SAS 59* (AU 341) limits auditors' responsibility for evaluating the client's ability to continue operations as a going concern to a period of time not to exceed one year beyond the date of the financial statements being audited. Factors that may raise questions about the client's ability to continue as a going concern include

- Negative trends such as recurring operating losses, working capital deficiencies, and negative cash flow from operations.
- Indications of financial difficulties such as default on loans, restructuring of debts, or arrearages in dividends.
- Other internal or external matters such as work stoppages, legal proceedings, or other needs to significantly revise operations.

If the above factors are identified, auditors should obtain information about management's plans to mitigate the effect of these factors and assess the likelihood that these plans can be effectively implemented. If, after this evaluation, auditors still believe substantial doubt exists about the client's ability to continue as a going concern, they should ensure that appropriate disclosures related to going concern are provided in the financial statements and modify their opinion on the client's financial statements. The specific report modifications for going concern uncertainties are discussed in Chapter 12.

Adjusting Entries and Financial Statement Disclosure

The financial statements, including the accompanying footnotes, are the responsibility of management, although auditors frequently draft them. Thus, although auditors could detect some misstatements in the financial statements during the examination, it is the responsibility of the client to adjust the financial statements. Even in instances when the failure to adjust the financial statements would result in materially misstated financial statements, it is the client's decision as to whether to accept auditors' proposed adjustments.

Exhibit 11.5 is a summary worksheet ("score sheet") showing the effect of proposed adjusting journal entries. In this example, three potential adjustments were noted during the audit: (1) recording payments to vendors on account made prior to year end, (2) reversing sales entries that were incorrectly recorded in the current year, and (3) recording items discovered during the auditors' search for unrecorded liabilities. In addition, a

EXHIBIT 11.5
Proposed Adjusting Journal Entries (Score Sheet)

	Income Statement	Balance Sheet		
	Increase (Decrease) Net Income	Increase (Decrease) Assets	Increase (Decrease) Liabilities	Increase (Decrease) Equity
(1) Unrecorded cash disbursements				
Accounts payable			($42,000)	
Cash		($42,000)		
(2) Improper sales cutoff:				
Sales	($13,000)			($13,000)
Inventory		7,800		
Cost of goods sold	7,800			7,800
Accounts receivable		(13,000)		
(3) Unrecorded liabilities:				
Utilities expense	(700)			(700)
Commissions expense	(3,000)			(3,000)
Wage expense	(2,500)			(2,500)
Accounts payable			700	
Accrued expenses payable			5,500	
Net effect before taxes	($11,400)	($47,200)	($35,800)	($11,400)
(4) Reduction in income taxes ($11,400 × 0.35)				
Income tax expense	3,990			3,990
Income taxes payable			(3,990)	
Current-year effects	($7,410)	($47,200)	($39,790)	($7,410)
Uncorrected waived adjustments from prior audits	($18,000)			($18,000)
Cumulative effect of waived adjustments	($25,410)			($25,410)

Conclusion: Waived and uncorrected adjustments from previous audits had a net debit effect of $18,000 on the income statement (decrease in net income) and balance sheet (decrease in net assets, or equity). When considered with the $7,410 effect noted in the current year, the cumulative waived adjustments are less than materiality. As a result, no adjustment to the financial statements is considered necessary.

fourth adjustment reflects the income tax effects of these adjustments (if recorded by the client). These entries are labeled as *proposed* to indicate the responsibility of management for the financial statements. This summary indicates how the proposed adjustments would affect the financial statements and helps auditors decide which adjustments must be made to support an unqualified opinion on the financial statements and which adjustments may be waived. A **waived adjustment** is a proposed adjustment auditors decide not to insist that the client make because it does not have a material effect on the financial statements. Prior to the issuance of Sarbanes-Oxley, evidence suggests that a large number of adjustments were waived in practice.[5]

As shown in Exhibit 11.5, the misstatements have a $7,410 debit (decrease) effect on net income and a $7,410 credit (decrease) effect on net assets. If materiality were established at $100,000, adjustment of these misstatements could be waived by auditors because the failure to make them will not result in materially misstated financial statements. However, *Staff Accounting Bulletin No. 99* notes that auditors and clients should not simply waive "apparently" immaterial adjustments without giving consideration to a number of other factors (such as the effect of the adjustment on debt covenants).

An important issue with respect to waived adjustments is whether a number of waived adjustments in previous years will accumulate over time to have a material effect on an

[5] For example, an academic study of audits performed by Deloitte & Touche (then Deloitte, Haskins & Sells) reported that 75 percent of all detected errors were waived (C. Houghton and J. Fogarty, "Inherent Risk," *Auditing: A Journal of Practice & Theory* 10, no. 1 [1991], pp. 1–21). A similar study of audits conducted by an unnamed international accounting firm found a corresponding 65 percent (A. Wright and S. Wright, "An Examination of Factors Affecting the Decision to Waive Audit Adjustments," *Journal of Accounting, Auditing, & Finance* 12, no. 1 [1997], pp. 15–36).

entity's financial statements in a future year. For example, if materiality is $100,000 and an entity fails to accrue a $25,000 liability for unused sick pay (which will not be paid until employees retire) each year for four years, this matter will not have a material effect on the income statement in any individual year. However, assuming this obligation has not been paid, at least in part, by the end of year 4, the cumulative effect on the entity's balance sheet would become material ($100,000).

SAS 107 allows auditors to use either of two methods to evaluate the materiality of waived adjustments. The **rollover method** considers only the current period income effect(s); in the example shown in Exhibit 11.5, when using the rollover method, auditors would consider the misstatement to be $7,410. In contrast, the **iron curtain method** considers the aggregate effect of the adjustments on the entity's balance sheet; when using the iron curtain method, auditors would consider the misstatement to be $25,410. In September 2006, the Securities and Exchange Commission issued *Staff Accounting Bulletin No. 108,* which requires auditors to evaluate misstatements using both methods and propose an adjustment if either method indicates that the misstatement is material. Since neither the amount of the current-year's waived adjustment in Exhibit 11.5 ($7,410) nor the cumulative effect of waived adjustments ($25,410) exceeds materiality of $100,000, no adjustment is required.

SAS 114 (AU 380) requires auditors to communicate all adjustments and misstatements detected during the audit to the client's audit committee (or other individuals charged with governance). These should be communicated regardless of whether they have a material effect on the financial statements. *AS 5* and *SAS 112* note that auditors' identification of

AUDITING INSIGHT Auditors and Restatements

The following excerpts (both pre- and post-Sarbanes-Oxley) illustrate the changing degree of attention paid to adjustments proposed by auditors.

PRE-SARBANES-OXLEY
At the Securities and Exchange Commission's Hearings on Auditor Independence (September 20, 2000), the following testimony from Mr. Roderick M. Hills, founder and partner of the accounting firm Hills & Sterns, illustrates the role and responsibility of auditors and management for adjusting the financial statements:

> Each time [an audit committee has replaced the audit firm or audit team], we checked and found out that auditors had raised significant accounting issues with the management that they had not raised with the audit committee . . . it happens for the simple fact that the auditors are much more afraid of being fired by management than by an audit committee. And there are too many managers that are willing to use perhaps a subtle threat just to lose the audit assignment if the audit partner is reluctant to accept some kind of accounting irregularity.

POST-SARBANES-OXLEY
Xerox
In 2003, the Securities and Exchange Commission filed suit against **KPMG** for civil fraud and accused the firm of "knowingly and recklessly" misleading investors on its audits of **Xerox**. However, when it came to adjustments, KPMG's main partner on the Xerox audit (Ronald Safan) was extremely stringent. Mr. Safan insisted that virtually every audit adjustment be recorded, including immaterial amounts that were not required for the financial statements to be prepared in conformity with generally accepted accounting principles. In fact, during 2001, Xerox had to delay filing its annual report due to a disagreement with KPMG over accounting issues.

Epilogue: On April 11, 2002, Xerox agreed to a $10 million fine with the Securities and Exchange Commission and restated its financial statements from 1997 to 2001; on April 21, 2005, KPMG agreed to pay $22.5 million to the SEC to settle charges related to its audits of Xerox.

Bristol-Myers Squibb
A recent restatement made by **Bristol-Myers Squibb** (a New York producer and distributor of pharmaceutical products) illustrates the role that auditors play in the financial statement adjustment process. In 2002, Bristol-Myers Squibb officials decided to restate sales and earnings for at least the last two years. Peter Dolan, chairman and chief executive officer, noted that "[w]e're doing it based on further review and consideration of the company's accounting and on the recent advice of our auditors, **PricewaterhouseCoopers.**"

Epilogue: These restatements were part of a scheme to artificially inflate sales; to date, Bristol-Myers Squibb has paid $839 million in restitution to shareholders and penalties to the Securities and Exchange Commission.

Sources: "KPMG's Auditing with Xerox Tests Toughness of SEC," *The Wall Street Journal,* May 6, 2002, p. A10; "Xerox: New Lease on Life," *CFO.com,* October 24, 2003; "KPMG Settles Xerox Charges with SEC," *CFO.com,* April 21, 2005; "Bristol-Myers to Restate Results," *The Wall Street Journal,* October 25, 2002, p. A3; and "Bristol's Former CFO Indicted," *CFO.com,* June 17, 2005.

material misstatements is a "strong indicator" of a material weakness in internal control over financial reporting, even if these misstatements are ultimately adjusted by the client. In addition, *SAS 107* (AU 312) requires auditors to communicate and distinguish between known and likely misstatements.

Audit Documentation Review

During the field work, the audit supervisor, and sometimes the audit manager, review the audit documentation soon after the audit staff complete it. The general purpose of this review is to ensure that all appropriate steps in the audit program were performed, the referencing among audit documentation is clear, and the explanations contained in the audit documentation are understandable. In general, the supervisor is attempting to determine that the work was performed with due professional care and that, if necessary, the work can be reperformed or verified by another party. A common outcome of this review is a set of "review notes" prepared by the audit supervisor that are to be completed or addressed by the audit staff; these notes address the procedures performed, the referencing among audit documentation, and the appropriateness of the audit staff member's conclusions based upon the procedures performed. This review process provides evidence of compliance with the first standard of field work, which requires proper planning and supervision.

When this initial review has been completed, the audit manager and audit partner review the audit documentation. This review focuses more on the overall scope of the audit and whether the overall conclusions in the audit documentation are sufficient to provide support for the opinion on the financial statements. Current GAAS require the audit documentation to be reviewed by a partner who has not been involved with the audit (known as a *reviewing partner*). This **second-partner review** (or *concurring-partner review*) is undertaken to ensure that the quality of audit work and reporting is in keeping with the accounting firm's quality standards. In addition, the second-partner review provides a very-high-level review of whether the evidence obtained during the audit is sufficient to support the opinion on the client's financial statements.

Audit documentation review provides a number of benefits to the firm, including these:

- Because audit documentation is the primary evidence of the audit procedures performed and conclusions reached by auditors, the review ensures that the audit is conducted in accordance with generally accepted auditing standards.

- Audit documentation review provides the firm an opportunity to evaluate the overall quality of the firm's audit practices as a method of quality control.

- Audit documentation review often serves as an important component of the training and evaluation of audit staff members.

- Audit documentation review allows the firm to adhere to the first standard of field work that auditors adequately plan the work and properly supervise any assistants.

Review Checkpoints

11.16 Why are adjusting entries and note disclosures labeled "proposed"?

11.17 What is a waived adjustment? What is the auditors' responsibility for communicating adjustments and misstatements detected during the audit?

11.18 Identify the two methods of evaluating the materiality of waived adjustments. What are the requirements of *Staff Accounting Bulletin No. 108* for evaluating the materiality of these adjustments?

11.19 Describe the audit documentation review process in an accounting firm.

11.20 What is a second-partner review?

11.21 What are some of the benefits of audit documentation review to an accounting firm?

RESPONSIBILITIES AFTER THE AUDIT REPORT RELEASE DATE

LEARNING OBJECTIVE

6. Following the audit report release date, identify auditors' responsibilities for (1) facts that may have existed at the date of the auditors' reports and (2) omitted audit procedures.

Subsequent Discovery of Facts

Earlier, we discussed auditors' responsibility for subsequent events when they were discovered prior to the audit report release date. In such cases, auditors should undertake procedures related to the subsequent event and determine that the financial statements properly present and disclose the subsequent event. In addition, if the subsequent event is identified after the audit completion date but prior to the audit report release date, the reports may be dual dated. These actions are shown on the following timeline.

End of Year	Audit Completion Date	Audit Report Release Date
• Perform procedures related to subsequent event • Adjust financial statements or disclose subsequent event	• Perform procedures related to subsequent event • Adjust financial statements or disclose subsequent event • Extend audit completion date or dual date auditors' report on financial statements	• Ensure that facts are reliable • Ensure that facts affect financial statements and auditors' reports • Ensure that persons are relying on the financial statements and auditors' reports • Request client disclosure of facts to users or provide disclosure to regulatory agencies

In some cases, auditors can become aware of facts that *existed* at the date of the reports *following* the audit report release date. This is referred to as a **subsequent discovery of facts**. In such cases, auditors should require the client to disclose the facts and their impact on the financial statements to persons relying on the financial statements (shareholders and other third-party users) if the following conditions exist:

1. The facts are reliable and existed at the report date.
2. The facts affect the financial statements and auditors' reports.
3. Persons are continuing to rely on the financial statements and auditors' reports.

If the client refuses to make appropriate disclosures, auditors should notify each member of the board of directors that they will notify regulatory agencies having jurisdiction over the client (such as the Securities and Exchange Commission) as well as other persons who currently rely on the reports.

Omitted Procedures

Although auditors have no responsibility to continue to review their work after the audit report release date, auditors' reports and audit documentation may be subjected to review by an outside peer review or the firm's internal inspection program.[6] A **peer review** is a quality assurance review by another firm or professional body of an accounting firm's

[6] See *Statement on Auditing Standards No. 25,* "The Relationship of Generally Accepted Auditing Standards to Quality Control Standards" (AU 161), and *Statements on Quality Control Standards* (QC 20–40).

AUDITING INSIGHT | Discovering Facts . . . 10 Years Later

A Russian unit of **PricewaterhouseCoopers** (PwC) recently withdrew its audits and reports from 1995–2004 for oil company **OAO Yukos.** PwC officials indicated that Yukos's management may have provided inaccurate information to auditors and that the PwC only recently became aware of new evidence that suggested Yukos's management had misled PwC auditors. PwC indicated that its decision to formally withdraw the reports "was influenced by the fact that some former shareholders and management of Yukos are continuing to encourage others to rely on PwC's audit reports."

Source: "PwC Withdraws a Decade of Yukos Audits," *The Wall Street Journal,* June 25, 2007, p. A3.

quality control policies and procedures and the compliance with those policies and procedures. Section 104 of Sarbanes-Oxley requires peer reviews to be conducted annually by the PCAOB (if the firm provides services for more than 100 public audit clients) or every three years (if the firm provides services for less than 100 public audit clients). These reviews could reveal that a situation exists in which an audit was not performed in accordance with generally accepted auditing standards. In particular, situations exist in which necessary audit procedures were not performed prior to the audit report release date (referred to as **omitted procedures**).

Statement on Auditing Standards No. 46 (AU 390) provides guidance for such situations. If (1) the omitted procedures are important in supporting the auditors' opinion and (2) individuals are currently relying on the client's financial statements (and auditors' reports), auditors should perform the omitted procedure or alternative procedure(s). Assuming that the procedures allow auditors to support the previously expressed opinion, no further action is necessary. However, if they do not, auditors should formally withdraw the original report, issue revised reports, and inform persons currently relying on the financial statements.

Review Checkpoints

11.22 What is the difference between a "subsequent event" and a "subsequent discovery of facts existing at the report date"? Describe auditors' responsibility for each.

11.23 If, subsequent to the audit report release date, the audit partner discovers information that existed at the report date and materially affects the financial statements, what action(s) should the partner take if the client consents to disclose the information? What actions should be taken if the client (including the board of directors) refuses to make the disclosure?

11.24 What are the steps auditors should take if, after the audit report release date, someone discovers that an important audit procedure was omitted?

COMMUNICATIONS AFTER THE AUDIT IS COMPLETED

LEARNING OBJECTIVE

7. Summarize important communications made by auditors following completion of the audit and audit report release date.

Following the conclusion of the audit, a number of communications are made about matters observed during the audit (in addition to auditors' opinions on the financial statements and the effectiveness of the entity's internal control over financial reporting). Although in some cases these matters may be communicated as they are encountered during the engagement (particularly if they are significant in nature), auditors typically accumulate them and communicate them after the audit report release date.

Communications with Individuals Charged with Governance (SAS 112, SAS 114, AS 5)

During the engagement, matters can arise that are of such importance that they be communicated with "individuals charged with governance." **Individuals charged with governance** are person(s) responsible for overseeing the client's financial reporting process, including the internal control over financial reporting. While this phrase can include the client's management and full board of directors, for public entities it would typically be the audit committee of the board of directors. Audit committees are required for registrants under Sarbanes-Oxley and must be comprised of only independent directors. Audit committees are an important element in the governance process, as they are directly responsible for the appointment, compensation, and oversight of auditors and the audit examination.

Sections 204 and 404 of Sarbanes-Oxley both address required communications between auditors and the client's audit committee; these communications have been formally incorporated into professional standards relating to the communication of internal control–related issues (*SAS 112* and *AS 5*) and communication of other matters (*SAS 114*). *SAS 112* (AU 325) and *AS 5* require auditors to communicate all significant internal control deficiencies and material weaknesses to the client and individuals charged with governance in writing. For public entities, *AS 5* requires the communication to be made prior to the audit report release date. For nonpublic entities, *SAS 112* notes that it is preferable to provide this communication prior to the audit report release date, but it should be made no later than 60 days following the audit report release date. While auditors may decide to communicate significant deficiencies and material weaknesses to the client as they are discovered during the audit, if these deficiencies or weaknesses have not been corrected (or remediated) by the client, they must be communicated again in writing at the conclusion of the audit.

For nonpublic entities, auditors' communication would acknowledge that the purpose of the audit is to express an opinion on the financial statements and not internal control over financial reporting; further, the communication would explicitly state that auditors are not expressing an opinion on internal control over financial reporting. For public entities subject to the reporting requirements of Sarbanes-Oxley, this communication would parallel the form and content of the auditors' report on internal control over financial reporting, which expresses an opinion on internal control over financial reporting. These communications are governed by *AS 5*.

In addition to internal control deficiencies, *SAS 114* (AU 380) requires auditors to communicate various other matters to the client. As with internal control communications, auditors ordinarily make these communications with individuals charged with governance after the conclusion of the audit; however, if the matters are particularly significant, they should be communicated during the audit. These communications may be made either orally or in writing (however, because of the important nature of these matters, one would anticipate that they be made in writing).

Auditors should communicate the following information to individuals charged with governance:

- Auditors' responsibility under generally accepted auditing standards.
- An overview of the planned scope and timing of the audit.
- Auditors' judgment about the quality of the client's accounting policies, accounting estimates, and financial statement disclosures.
- Any significant difficulties encountered during the audit.
- Any uncorrected misstatements identified during the audit, other than those auditors believe to be trivial.
- Any disagreements with management.
- Material, corrected misstatements that were brought to the attention of management.
- Representations requested from the client's management.
- Any management consultations with other auditors.

AUDITING INSIGHT Communications with Individuals Charged with Governance

DVI, a company that finances diagnostic imaging equipment for outpatient clinics, recently underwent Chapter 11 bankruptcy proceedings because of "recent discovery of apparent improprieties." These improprieties occurred despite the fact that DVI's auditors **(Deloitte & Touche)** made numerous communications to DVI's board of directors regarding DVI's failure to provide for loan loss reserves and loan write-offs, DVI's policy of recording income on contracts more than 180 days in arrears, and DVI's failure to properly approve certain loans.

Source: Phyllis Berman, "Master of Disguises," *Forbes*, July 26, 2004, p. 88.

- Any significant issues arising from the audit that were discussed with management.
- Other findings or issues that are significant and relevant to individuals charged with governance.

Auditors also should determine that individuals charged with governance have received copies of written communications regarding material issues between auditors and management such as engagement letters, management representations, and reports on deficiencies in internal control over financial reporting.

Management Letter

During the engagement (particularly the study and evaluation of the client's internal control, assessment of the risk of material misstatement, and evaluation of the effectiveness of internal control over financial reporting), matters are noted that can be made as recommendations to the client. These recommendations may allow the client to improve the efficiency and effectiveness of their operations. After the conclusion of the audit, these matters are summarized in a letter (commonly referred to as the **management letter**) that is delivered to and discussed with the client. Management letters are not required by generally accepted auditing standards but are considered an important method of adding value to clients beyond that provided by the audit examination. In this spirit, some firms encourage consulting and tax professionals to participate in preparing the management letter.

Management letters are a service provided as a by-product of the audit. The management letter is an excellent opportunity to develop rapport with the client and to make the client aware of other business services offered by the accounting firm.

Summary of Audit Communications

Many types of formal communications have been mentioned in this text. Because you are learning the final procedures to complete the audit, this is a good place to summarize these various communications. Exhibit 11.6 is a summary of audit correspondence other than auditors' reports on the entity's financial statements and internal control over financial reporting (which are discussed in Chapter 12).

Review Checkpoints

11.25 Identify information that auditors are required to communicate to individuals charged with governance of the client.

11.26 What is a *management letter* and is one required by generally accepted auditing standards?

EXHIBIT 11.6 Audit Communications

Type	From	To	Timing	Reference	Method
Engagement letter	Auditors	Client	Before engagement	*SAS 83* (AU 310)	Written
Acceptance letter (signed copy of engagement letter)	Client	Auditors	Before engagement	*SAS 83* (AU 310)	Written
Attorney letter response	Attorney	Auditors	Near audit completion date	*SAS 12* (AU 337)	Written
Management representations	Client	Auditors	Audit completion date	*SAS 85* (AU 333)	Written
Internal control deficiencies	Auditors	Individuals charged with governance (audit committee)	Prior to audit report release date (for public entities) or within 60 days of audit report release date (for nonpublic entities)*	*SAS 112* (AU 325) and *AS 5*	Written
Communications with individuals charged with governance	Auditors	Individuals charged with governance (audit committee)	After audit*	*SAS 114* (AU 380); *AS 5*	Oral or written
Management letter	Auditor	Client	After audit	None	Oral or written

*If matters are significant, they may be communicated as they are identified.

Summary

This chapter begins by identifying four major time periods during an audit: (1) prior to year end, (2) between year end and the audit completion date, (3) between the audit completion date and the audit report release date, and (4) following the audit report release date. As various matters are discussed, it is important to determine the time period in which auditors identify issues because this will affect their responsibility.

Within the context of the four time periods, the chapter discusses several aspects of completing an audit. These events include (1) examining revenue and expense accounts, (2) obtaining responses to attorney letters, (3) obtaining management representations, (4) identifying and examining subsequent events, (5) evaluating the entity's ability to continue as a going-concern, (6) summarizing proposed adjustments to the financial statements, (7) reviewing audit documentation, (8) considering subsequent discovery of facts and the effect of audit procedures omitted during the audit examination, and (9) providing communications at the conclusion of the audit. The purpose of these procedures is to enable auditors to issue and support opinions on financial statements and internal control over financial reporting.

Key Terms

attorney letter: A communication sent from the client to its attorney(s) that details a list of pending litigation, claims, and assessments involving the client. The attorney(s) is (are) requested to comment on these matters directly to the client's auditors, 424

audit completion date: The date on which auditors have gathered sufficient appropriate evidence on which to base their opinions on the financial statements and internal control over financial reporting; this evidence includes the review of audit documentation, preparation of the financial statements and related disclosures, and management's assertion that they assume responsibility for the financial statements and disclosures, 421

audit report release date: The date on which auditors allow the client to use auditors' reports in conjunction with the financial statements; this is also the date on which the client's financial statements are issued, 421

contingency: An existing condition, situation, or set of circumstances involving uncertainty as to possible gain ("gain contingency") or loss ("loss contingency") to an enterprise that will ultimately be resolved when one or more future events occur or fail to occur, 423

dual date: To provide two dates by which auditors limit the responsibility beyond the audit completion date to a specific subsequent event identified in the report, 432

individuals charged with governance: Person(s) responsible for overseeing the client's financial reporting process, including the internal control over financial reporting. While this phrase can include the client's management and full board of directors, for public entities it would typically be the audit committee of the board of directors, 439

iron curtain method: When evaluating the effect of waived adjustments, this method considers the aggregate effect of current and prior misstatements in the entity's balance sheet, 435

management letter: A summary of recommendations made by auditors resulting from the audit engagement that allow the client to improve the effectiveness and efficiency of its operations, 440

management representations: Written assertions provided by management to auditors on matters such as the fairness of the organization's financial statements, availability of all financial records and related data, internal control over financial reporting, and other important matters, 428

omitted procedures: Situations in which a necessary audit procedure is inadvertently not performed by auditors prior to the audit report release date, 438

peer review: A quality assurance review by another firm or professional body of an accounting firm's quality control policies and procedures and the compliance with those policies and procedures, 437

pro forma financial data: The presentation of financial statements "as if" some important subsequent event had occurred at the balance sheet date, 431

rollover method: When evaluating the effect of waived adjustments, this method only considers the current period income effect(s) of the potential adjustment, 435

second-partner review: A review of audit documentation by a partner who has not been involved with the audit; its purpose is to ensure that the quality of the audit work and reporting is consistent with the quality standards of the accounting firm, 436

subsequent discovery of facts: A situation in which auditors become aware of facts (unknown prior to the report release date) after the audit report release date, 437

subsequent events: Events occurring between the balance sheet date and audit report release date, 431

subsequent period: Time period between the balance sheet date and the audit report release date, 431

Type I subsequent events: Subsequent events that provide new information about a condition that existed (and could have been disclosed in the financial statements) at the balance sheet date, 431

Type II subsequent events: Events that did not exist (and were not disclosed in the financial statements) at the balance sheet date but occurred prior to the audit report release date, 431

unasserted claim: A representation that no formal lawsuit or claim has been filed or threatened on behalf of others but that circumstances such as a catastrophe, accident, or other physical occurrence could result in a suit or claim being filed in the future, 425

waived adjustment: A proposed adjustment auditors decide not to insist that the client make because it does not have a material effect on the financial statements, 434

Multiple Choice Questions for Practice and Review

11.27 Which of the following would most likely be audited in conjunction with the examination of the client's interest-bearing notes payable?

 a. Interest income.

 b. Interest expense.

 c. Amortization of goodwill.

 d. Royalty revenue.

11.28 The main purpose of management representations is to

 a. Shift responsibility for financial statements from the management to auditors.

 b. Provide a substitute source of audit evidence for substantive procedures that auditors would otherwise perform.

 c. Provide management an opportunity to make assertions about the quantity and valuation of the physical inventory.

 d. Impress on management its ultimate responsibility for the financial statements and disclosures.

11.29 Which of these substantive procedures or sources is *not* used to obtain evidence about contingencies?

 a. Scan expense accounts for credit entries.

 b. Obtain a letter from the client's attorney.

 c. Read the minutes of the board of directors' meetings.

 d. Examine terms of sale in sales contracts.

11.30 A Type I subsequent event involves subsequent information about a condition that existed at the balance sheet date. Subsequent knowledge of which of the following would cause the entity to adjust its December 31 financial statements?

 a. Sale of an issue of new stock for $500,000 on January 30.

 b. Settlement of a damage lawsuit for a customer's injury sustained February 15 for $10,000.

 c. Settlement of litigation in February for $100,000 that had been estimated at $12,000 in the December 31 financial statements.

 d. Storm damage of $1 million to the entity's buildings on March 1.

11.31 A. Griffin audited the financial statements of Dodger Magnificat Corporation for the year ended December 31, 2008. She completed gathering sufficient appropriate evidence on January 30 and later learned of a stock split voted by the board of directors on February 5. The financial statements were changed to reflect the split, and she now needs to dual date the report on the company's financial statements before sending it to the company. Which of the following is the proper form?

 a. December 31, 2008, except as to Note X, which is dated January 30, 2009.

 b. January 30, 2009, except as to Note X, which is dated February 5, 2009.

 c. December 31, 2008, except as to Note X, which is dated February 5, 2009.

 d. February 5, 2009, except for the audit completion date, for which the date is January 30, 2009.

11.32 Prior to the audit report release date, auditors have a responsibility related to management's disclosure of subsequent events until

 a. The year-end balance sheet date.

 b. The auditors' report date.

 c. The audit report release date.

 d. The following year's balance sheet date.

11.33 The auditing standards regarding "subsequent discovery of facts that existed at the balance sheet date" refers to knowledge obtained after

 a. The audit report release date.

 b. The auditors' report date.

 c. The entity's year-end balance sheet date.

 d. The date interim audit work was complete.

11.34 Which of the following is *not* required by generally accepted auditing standards?

 a. Management representations.

 b. Attorney letter.

 c. Management letter.

 d. Engagement letter.

11.35 Which of these persons generally does *not* participate in writing the management letter (client advisory comments)?

 a. Client's outside attorneys.

 b. Client's accounting and production managers.

 c. Accounting firm's audit team on the engagement.

 d. Accounting firm's consulting and tax experts.

11.36 Which of the following is ordinarily performed *last* in the audit examination?

 a. Securing a signed engagement letter from the client.

 b. Performing tests of controls.

 c. Performing a review for subsequent events.

 d. Obtaining signed management representations.

11.37 Which of the following normally occurs *earliest* in the audit examination?

 a. Discovery of an omitted audit procedure.

 b. Dual dating the auditors' report on the entity's financial statements for subsequent events that exist at the balance sheet date.

 c. Preparation of the management letter.

 d. Review of audit documentation.

11.38 Which of the following procedures is *least likely* to be performed in conjunction with the audit of revenue and expense accounts?

 a. Analytical procedures to evaluate the overall reasonableness of revenue and expense accounts.

 b. Sampling and investigation of individual transactions affecting revenue and expense accounts.

 c. Consideration of evidence obtained in the examination of related balance sheet accounts.

 d. Scanning revenue and expense accounts for large and unusual entries.

11.39 Which of the following statements is *most likely* to be included in an attorney letter?

 a. "Certain representations in this letter are described as being limited to matters that are material."

 b. "If any unasserted claims or assessments are omitted from this disclosure, please provide this information directly to our auditors."

 c. "Our work enabled us to notice some actions that could enhance the profitability of the Company."

 d. "Please furnish to our auditors such explanation, if any, that you consider necessary to supplement the foregoing information."

11.40 If, after the audit report release date, auditors determine that an important auditing procedure was omitted, which of the following initial courses of action is most appropriate?

 a. Perform the omitted procedure or an alternative procedure.

 b. Notify the board of directors and regulatory agencies that are currently relying on auditors' reports.

 c. Determine whether the omitted procedure is important in supporting the auditors' opinion on the entity's financial statements.

 d. Engage another accounting firm to conduct a quality assurance review.

11.41 Which of the following statements is *not* true with respect to management representations?

 a. The failure of management to furnish representations is a significant scope limitation, resulting in either an adverse opinion or disclaimer of opinion.

 b. Management representations must address the disclosure of all significant deficiencies in internal control, regardless of materiality.

 c. Management representations are used by auditors to corroborate information received during the audit from the client and its employees.

 d. Management representations are dated the same date as the auditors' reports.

11.42 Hall accepted an engagement to audit the Year 1 financial statements of XYZ Company. XYZ completed the preparation of the Year 1 financial statements on February 13, Year 2, and Hall began the field work on February 17, Year 2. Hall completed gathering sufficient appropriate evidence on March 24, Year 2, and completed the report on March 28, Year 2. The management representations normally would be dated

 a. February 13, Year 2.

 b. February 17, Year 2.

 c. March 24, Year 2.

 d. March 28, Year 2.

(AICPA adapted)

11.43 A charge in the subsequent period to a notes receivable account from the cash disbursements journal should alert auditors to the possibility that a

 a. Contingent asset has come into existence in the subsequent period.

 b. Contingent liability has come into existence in the subsequent period.

 c. Provision for contingencies is required.

 d. Contingent liability has become a real liability and has been settled.

(AICPA adapted)

11.44 Which of the following substantive procedures should auditors ordinarily perform regarding subsequent events?

 a. Compare the latest available interim financial statements with the financial statements being audited.

 b. Send second requests to the client's customers who failed to respond to initial accounts receivable confirmation requests.

 c. Communicate material weaknesses in internal control to the client's audit committee.

 d. Review the cutoff bank statements for several months after the year end.

<div align="right">(AICPA adapted)</div>

11.45 Which of the following substantive procedures would auditors most likely perform to obtain evidence about the occurrence of subsequent events?

 a. Recompute a sample of large-dollar transactions occurring after year end for arithmetic accuracy.

 b. Investigate changes in shareholders' equity occurring after year end.

 c. Send confirmations to vendors with whom the client normally does business but for whom no balance in accounts payable is noted.

 d. Confirm bank accounts established after year end.

<div align="right">(AICPA adapted)</div>

11.46 The primary reason auditors request responses to attorney letters is to provide auditors

 a. The probable outcome of asserted claims and pending or threatened litigation.

 b. Corroboration of the information furnished by management about litigation, claims, and assessments.

 c. The attorney's opinions of the client's historical experiences in recent similar litigation.

 d. A description and evaluation of litigation, claims, and assessments that existed at the balance sheet date.

<div align="right">(AICPA adapted)</div>

11.47 The scope of an audit is *not* restricted when an attorney letter limits the response to

 a. Matters to which the attorney has given substantive attention in the form of legal representation.

 b. An evaluation of the likelihood of an unfavorable outcome of the matters disclosed by the entity.

 c. The attorney's opinion of the entity's historical experience in recent similar litigation.

 d. The probable outcome of asserted claims and pending or threatened litigation.

<div align="right">(AICPA adapted)</div>

Exercises, Problems, and Simulations

11.48 **Management Representations.** Hart, an assistant accountant with the firm of Better & Best, CPAs, is auditing the financial statements of Tech Consolidated Industries, Inc. The firm's audit program calls for the preparation of management representations.

Required:

 a. In an audit of financial statements, in what circumstances are auditors required to obtain management representations?

 b. What are the purposes of obtaining representations?

 c. To whom should the representations be addressed and as of what date should they be dated?

 d. Who should sign the representations and what would be the effect of the refusal to sign them?

 e. In what respects may auditors' other responsibilities be relieved by obtaining management representations?

<div align="right">(AICPA adapted)</div>

11.49 **Management Representations Omissions.** During the audit of the annual financial statements of Amis Manufacturing, Inc., the company's president, Vance Molar, and Wanda Dweebins, the engagement partner, reviewed matters that were supposed to be included in management representations. Amis Manufacturing is not subject to the reporting requirements of *AS 5*. Upon receipt of the following representations, Dweebins contacted Molar to state that they were incomplete.

To John & Wayne, CPAs:

In connection with your examination of the balance sheet of Amis Manufacturing, Inc., as of December 31, 2008, and the related statements of income, comprehensive income, retained earnings, and cash flows for the year then ended, for the purpose of expressing an opinion on whether the financial statements present fairly the financial position, results of operations, and cash flows of Amis Manufacturing, Inc., in conformity with generally accepted accounting principles, we confirm, to the best of our knowledge and belief, the following representations made to you during your audit. There were no

- Plans or intentions that could materially affect the carrying value or classification of assets or liabilities.
- Communications from regulatory agencies concerning noncompliance with, or deficiencies in, financial reporting practices.
- Agreements to repurchase assets previously sold.
- Violations or possible violations of laws or regulations whose effects should be considered for disclosure in the financial statements or as a basis for recording a contingent liability.
- Unasserted claims or assessments that our lawyer has advised are probable of assertion that must be disclosed in accordance with *Statement of Financial Accounting Standards No. 5.*
- Capital stock purchase options or agreements or capital stock reserved for options, warrants, conversions, or other requirements.
- Compensating balance or other arrangements involving restrictions on cash balances.

<div style="text-align:right">

Vance Molar, President
Amis Manufacturing, Inc.
March 14, 2009

</div>

Required:

Identify the other matters that Molar's representations should specifically confirm.

<div style="text-align:right">(AICPA adapted)</div>

11.50 **Management Representations.** Each of the following statements is a communication from management. Indicate whether the inclusion of each statement in management representations is appropriate. Provide your rationale for any statements whose inclusion in management representations is not appropriate.

a. "Certain representations in this letter are described as being limited to matters that are material."

b. "No frauds involving management, employees who have significant roles in internal control, or other frauds that could have a material effect on the financial statements have occurred during the year under audit."

c. "Based on our assessment, we conclude that the Company has maintained an effective internal control over financial reporting as of December 31, 2008."

d. "We have prepared a description and evaluation of certain contingencies for which our attorneys have devoted substantive attention on our behalf in the form of legal representation."

e. "There are no significant deficiencies, including material weaknesses, in the design or operation of internal controls that could adversely affect our ability to record, process, summarize, and report financial data."

f. "Summarized below are important actions taken in response to comments provided by you in the management letter dated March 22, 2008, based on your prior audit."

g. "Our assessment of internal control over financial reporting provides us with absolute assurance that no material misstatements will occur and be undetected by our internal control."

h. "We have made available to you all financial records and related data."

11.51 **Management Representations.** For each of the following issues, classify them according to whether they will be (1) included in management representations if material, (2) included in management representations regardless of materiality, or (3) not included in management representations.

2 a. Management acknowledgement of its responsibility for the fairness of the financial statements in conformity with accounting principles generally accepted in the United States of America.

3 b. A list of pending or threatened litigation, claims, or assessments currently outstanding against the client.

3 c. A description of recommendations that allow the client to improve the efficiency and effectiveness of its operations.

2 d. Availability of all financial records and related data.

1 e. Information related to the presentation and disclosure of items within the financial statements.

2 f. Disclosure of all significant deficiencies in internal control.

2 g. Information concerning fraud involving management and employees who have significant roles in internal control.

3 h. Auditors' judgment about the quality of the client's accounting principles. *Communicated through audit committee*

1 i. Information about violations or possible violations of laws or regulations that should be considered for disclosure in the financial statements.

3 j. A statement that the financial statements are prepared according to U.S. generally accepted accounting principles.

11.52 **Client Request for Attorney Letter.** Cole & Cole, CPAs, are auditing the financial statements of Consolidated Industries Co. for the year ended December 31, 2008. On May 6, 2009, C. R. Brown, Consolidated's chief financial officer, gave Cole a draft of an attorney letter for Cole's review before mailing it to J. J. Young, Consolidated's outside counsel. This letter is intended to elicit the attorneys' responses to corroborate information furnished to Cole by management concerning pending and threatened litigation, claims, and assessments, and unasserted claims and assessments.

Client's Attorney Letter Request

May 6, 2009

J. J. Young, Attorney at Law
123 Main Street, Anytown, USA

Dear J. J. Young:

 In connection with an audit of our financial statements at December 31, 2008, and for the year then ended, management of the Company has prepared, and furnished to our auditors, Cole & Cole, CPAs, a description and evaluation of certain contingencies, including those set forth below, involving matters with respect to which you have been engaged and to which you have devoted substantive attention on behalf of the Company in the form of legal consultation or representation. Your response should include matters that existed at December 31, 2008. Because of the confidentiality of all these matters, your response may be limited.

 In November 2008, an action was brought against the Company by an outside salesman alleging breach of contract for sales commissions and asking an accounting with respect to claims for fees and commissions. The causes of action claim damages of $3,000,000, but the Company believes it has meritorious defenses to the claims. The possible exposure of the Company to a successful judgment on behalf of the plaintiff is slight.

 In July 2008, an action was brought against the Company by Industrial Manufacturing Company (Industrial) alleging patent infringement and seeking damages of $20,000,000. The action in U.S. District Court resulted in a decision on October 16, 2008, holding that the Company infringed seven Industrial patents and awarded damages of $14,000,000. The Company vigorously denies these allegations and has filed an appeal with the U.S. Court of Appeals. The appeal process is expected to take approximately two years, but there is some chance that Consolidated may ultimately prevail.

 Please furnish to our auditors such explanation, if any, that you consider necessary to supplement this information, including an explanation of those matters as to which your

views may differ from those stated, and an identification of the omission of any pending or threatened litigation, claims, and assessments or a statement that the list of such matters is complete. Your response may be quoted or referred to in the financial statements without further correspondence with you.

You also consulted on various other matters considered to be pending or threatened litigation. However, you may not comment on these matters because publicizing them may alert potential plaintiffs to the strengths of their cases. In addition, various other matters probable of assertion that have some chance of an unfavorable outcome, as of December 31, 2008, are presently considered unasserted claims and assessments.

Respectfully,

C. R. Brown

Chief Financial Officer

Required:

Describe the omissions, ambiguities, and inappropriate statements and terminology in Brown's letter. Remember, this is Brown's letter requesting a response to auditors, but it must request responses in the manner most useful to auditors.

(AICPA adapted)

11.53 **Attorney Letters.** Jaworski, CPA, is auditing the financial statements of Fulbright Company. As she is nearing the audit completion date, Jaworski realizes that she needs to evaluate whether all material contingencies are properly accounted for and disclosed in Fulbright's financial statements. Because of its size, Fulbright has retained external counsel (Vinson, LLP) to handle its various legal matters.

Required:

a. List some common procedures that Jaworski will perform with respect to Fulbright's litigation, claims, and assessments.

b. What are the responsibilities of Jaworski, Fulbright, and Vinson with respect to litigation, claims, and assessments?

c. Attorney letters are used to provide corroboration of litigation, claims, and assessments against the client. Briefly describe the process through which attorney letters are prepared, sent, and used in the audit examination.

d. What information is normally included in an attorney letter?

11.54 **Subsequent Events.** Michael Ewing is auditing the financial statements of Dallas Company for the year ended December 31, 2008. In concluding the process of gathering sufficient appropriate evidence, Michael has asked to meet with his supervisor on the audit (John Ross) to discuss responsibility for events occurring after the balance sheet date.

Required:

a. What is a subsequent event? During what time period is Michael Ewing responsible for subsequent events?

b. List some procedures that Michael may perform to assist him in identifying subsequent events.

c. What are the two types of subsequent events? How should information related to these types of subsequent events be reflected in Dallas's financial statements?

d. Assume that on January 8, 2009, Dallas Company agreed to acquire Houston, Inc., in a significant transaction. Michael's audit completion date was February 7, 2009, and Dallas issued their financial statements (and Michael's reports on its financial statements and internal control over financial reporting) on February 14, 2009. How would Michael proceed if he became aware of this subsequent event on the following dates?

1. January 10, 2009.

2. February 10, 2009.

3. February 20, 2009.

e. On March 2, 2009, Dallas announced that it also will acquire San Antonio Company in a significant transaction. What is Michael Ewing's responsibility with respect to this acquisition in the audit of Dallas's financial statements for the year ended December 31, 2008?

11.55 **Audit Simulation: Subsequent Events and Contingent Liabilities.** Crankwell, Inc., is preparing its annual financial statements and annual report to stockholders. Management wants to be sure that all of the necessary and proper disclosures are incorporated into the financial statements and the annual report. Two classes of items that have an important bearing on the financial statements are subsequent events and contingent liabilities. The financial statements could be materially inaccurate or misleading if proper disclosure of these items is not made. In providing your responses, please reference the appropriate professional literature when appropriate.

Required:

 a. With respect to subsequent events

 1. Define what is meant by a *subsequent event*.

 2. Identify the two types of subsequent events and explain the appropriate financial statement presentation of each type.

 3. What are the procedures that should be performed to ascertain the occurrence of subsequent events?

 b. With respect to contingent liabilities

 1. Identify the essential elements of a contingent liability.

 2. Explain how a contingent liability should be disclosed in the financial statements.

 c. Explain how a subsequent event may relate to a contingent liability. Give an example to support your answer.

<div align="right">(CMA adapted)</div>

11.56 **Subsequent Events Procedures.** You are in the process of completing the gathering of sufficient appropriate evidence for Top Stove Corporation, a company engaged in the manufacture and sale of kerosene space-heating stoves. To date there has been every indication that the financial statements of the client present fairly the position of the company at December 31 and the results of its operations and cash flows for the year then ended. Top Stove had total assets at December 31 of $4 million and a net profit for the year (after deducting federal and state income taxes) of $285,000. The principal records of the company are a general ledger, cash receipts record, voucher register, sales register, check register, and general journal. Financial statements are prepared monthly. Your audit completion date is February 20 and you plan to deliver the reports to the client by March 12.

Required:

 a. Write a brief statement about the purpose and period to be covered in a review of subsequent events.

 b. Outline the program you would follow to determine what transactions involving material amounts, if any, have occurred since the balance sheet date.

<div align="right">(AICPA adapted)</div>

11.57 **Subsequent Events—Cases.** In connection with your examination of the financial statements of Olars Manufacturing Corporation for the year ended December 31, your postbalance sheet substantive procedures disclosed the following items:

 1. *January 3:* The state government approved a plan for the construction of an express highway. The plan will result in the appropriation of a portion of the land area owned by Olars. Construction will begin late next year. No estimate of the condemnation award is available.

 2. *January 4:* Mr. Olars (president of Olars Manufacturing Corporation) loaned the company $25,000. He obtained these funds on July 15 by borrowing against a personal life insurance policy. The loan from Olars to Olars Manufacturing Corporation was recorded in the account Loan Payable to Officers. Mr. Olars's source of the funds was not disclosed in the company records. The corporation pays the premiums on the life insurance policy and Mrs. Olars, the president's wife, is the owner and beneficiary of the policy.

 3. *January 7:* The mineral content of a shipment of ore in transit on December 31 was determined to be 72 percent. The shipment was recorded at year end at an estimated content of 50 percent by a debit to Raw Material Inventory and a credit to Accounts Payable in the amount of $20,600. The final liability to the vendor is based on the actual mineral content of the shipment.

 4. *January 15:* A series of personal disagreements have arisen between Mr. Olars, the president, and Mr. Tweedy, his brother-in-law, the treasurer. Mr. Tweedy resigned, effective

immediately, under an agreement whereby the corporation would purchase his 10 percent stock ownership at book value as of December 31. Payment is to be made in two equal amounts in cash on April 1 and October 1. In December, the treasurer had obtained a divorce from Mr. Olars's sister.

5. *January 31:* As a result of reduced sales, production was curtailed in mid-January and some workers were laid off. On February 5, all remaining workers went on strike. To date the strike is unsettled.

Required:

Assume that the preceding items came to your attention prior to completion of your audit work on February 15. For each item,

a. Give the substantive procedures, if any, that would have brought the item to your attention. Indicate other sources of information that may have revealed the item.

b. Discuss the disclosure that you would recommend for the item, listing all details that should be disclosed. Indicate those items or details, if any, that should not be disclosed. Give your reasons for recommending or not recommending disclosure of the items or details.

(AICPA adapted)

11.58 **Subsequent Discovery of Facts.** On June 1, Albert Faultless of A. J. Faultless & Co., CPAs, noticed some disturbing information about his client, Hopkirk Company. A story in the local paper mentioned the indictment of Tony Baker, whom A. J. knew as the assistant controller at Hopkirk. The charge was mail fraud. A. J. made discreet inquiries with the controller at Hopkirk's headquarters and learned that Baker had been speculating in foreign currency futures. In fact, part of Baker's work at Hopkirk involved managing the company's foreign currency. Unfortunately, Baker had violated company policy, lost a small amount of money, and then decided to speculate some more, lost some more, and eventually lost $7 million in company funds.

The mail fraud was involved in Baker's attempt to cover his activity until he recovered the original losses. Most of the events were in process on March 1, when A. J. had signed and dated the unqualified opinion on Hopkirk's financial statements for the year ended on the previous December 31.

A. J. determined that the information probably would affect the decisions of external users and advised Hopkirk's chief executive to make the disclosure. She flatly refused to make any disclosure, arguing that the information was immaterial. On June 17, A. J. provided the subsequent information in question to a news reporter, and it was printed in *The Wall Street Journal* with a statement that the financial statements and accompanying auditors' report on the company's financial statements could not be relied on.

Required:

Evaluate the actions of Faultless & Co., CPAs, with respect to the subsequent information discovered. What other action could Faultless & Co. have taken? What are the possible legal effects of the firm's actions, if any?

11.59 **Omitted Audit Procedures.** The following are independent situations that have occurred in your accounting firm, Arthur Hurdman:[7]

Case 1

During the internal inspection review by the regional office of Arthur Hurdman, one of your clients, Wildcat Oil Suppliers, was selected for review. The reviewers questioned the thoroughness of inventory obsolescence procedures, especially in light of the depressed state of the oil exploration industry at the time. They believed that specific substantive procedures, which they considered appropriate, were not performed by your audit team.

Case 2

Top Stove, one of your clients, installed an automated system in July 2008 to process part of the accounting transactions. You completed the audit of Top Stove's December 31, 2008,

[7] Situation derived from examples given in Thomas R. Weirich and Elizabeth J. Ringelberg, "Omitted Audit Procedures," *CPA Journal,* March 1984, pp. 34–39.

statements on February 15, 2009. During the April 2009 review work on Top Stove's first-quarter financial information, you discovered that during the audit of the 2008 statements, only the manual records were investigated in the search for unrecorded liabilities.

Required:

a. Without regard to the specific situation given, answer the following questions:

1. What are the proper steps auditors should take if it is discovered, after the report date, that an important substantive procedure was omitted?

2. How are auditors' decisions affected if, after review of the audit documentation, they determine that other substantive procedures produced the sufficient appropriate audit evidence?

3. If, in subsequently applying the omitted procedure, auditors become aware of material new information that should have been disclosed in the financial statements, how should they proceed?

b. Describe the proper action to take in each of the preceding situations, given the following additional information:

Case 1: You thoroughly consider the scope of the audit of Wildcat Oil Suppliers and made a detailed review of the audit documentation. You have concluded that compensating procedures were conducted sufficient to support the valuation of inventory.

Case 2: Your subsequent investigation of the automated system's records of Top Stove revealed that material liabilities were not recorded as of December 31.

11.60 **Subsequent Events, Subsequent Discovery of Facts, and Omitted Procedures.** Ralph completed the December 31, 2008, audit of Raider Company on February 3, 2009; his reports on Raider's financial statements and internal control over financial reporting were issued on February 12, 2009. During April 2009, Ralph's firm conducted a quality review over selected audits that were completed during the most recent year and the audit of Raider Company was randomly selected for review. The reviewer identified the following matters that were not addressed by Ralph during the audit of Raider:

a. On February 9, 2009, Ralph learned of the following events during his post-audit meeting with Raider's chief operating officer.

1. A class action lawsuit was brought against Raider Company by some of its former employees for workplace discrimination. The lawsuits were filed by an attorney on behalf of a class of employees on January 10, 2009. This lawsuit was not identified in the letter from Raider's attorneys.

2. One of Raider's major customers is experiencing significant financial difficulties; this customer's account receivable balance on December 31, 2008, was $1.2 million, which represented 2 percent of Raider's total accounts receivable on that date.

Because of an important deadline for submitting the financial statements to lenders for evaluation, Raider did not modify its financial statements for the above events, despite the fact that they were material. Their justification was that since the events occurred after the balance sheet date, they were not required to be disclosed in the financial statements. Ralph acquiesced to Raider's wishes and did not modify his report on Raider's financial statements.

b. On March 16, 2009, Ralph initially learned of the following events affecting Raider Company, neither of which was disclosed in Raider's financial statements:

1. Raider Company declared a significant dividend payable to its shareholders. This dividend was declared on March 14, 2009, to be paid to Raider's shareholders of record on May 16, 2009.

2. Raider Company activated a portion of its line of credit on February 8, 2009, by borrowing $2.5 million. This additional obligation increased Raider Company's long-term liabilities by 10 percent.

c. Reviewing Ralph's audit documentation, it does not appear that he conducted any tests to evaluate the need for impairment of the carrying value of Raider Company's property, plant, and equipment.

Required:

For each of the above items, describe what actions Ralph should take after these issues were identified by the firm's quality review.

11.61 **Audit Simulation: Various Completion Matters.** For each of the following independent situations, describe the most appropriate course of action that should be taken by auditors. Where possible, please cite the relevant professional standards that apply to the situation.

a. Allison is conducting the audit of Anderson, Inc. as of December 31, 2008. As she is beginning to complete her evidence gathering, she becomes aware that one of Anderson's major customers (Jones) is experiencing significant financial difficulties. Jones normally accounts for 5 percent of Anderson's net sales. After performing the necessary procedures, Allison believes that $2.8 million of Jones's receivable balance will ultimately become uncollectible. Allison further believes this amount is material to Anderson's financial condition and results of operations.

b. Carmelo is completing the December 31, 2008, audit of Nugget Company. As part of his final procedures, he has requested representations from Nugget's management regarding their assertion as to the fairness of the financial statements and other important matters addressed by professional standards. Because Nugget's management is attending an analyst briefing in the upcoming week, Carmelo receives these signed representations dated February 6, 2009. Carmelo has a few remaining items to complete, does so, and dates his auditors' report February 9, 2009.

c. Colt completed the December 31, 2008, audit of Manning and issued an unqualified opinion on Manning's financial statements dated March 15, 2009. Colt's opinion was released, along with Manning's financial statements, on March 21, 2009. During his review of Manning's first quarter 10-Q in late April, Colt became aware of Manning's settlement with a customer over a product warranty lawsuit; this case was settled on March 13, 2009. While Colt received the necessary letter from Manning's attorneys, these letters were received prior to the settlement of the case and did not mention this development. After reviewing the information related to the settlement, Colt does not believe that the settlement is material to Manning's financial condition or results of operations and believes he is still able to support his opinion on Manning's financial statements.

d. Alta completed the December 31, 2008, audit of Saxe Company on February 10, 2009. Saxe is planning on releasing its financial statements, along with Alta's opinion on these financial statements and internal control over financial reporting, on February 17, 2009. On February 12, 2009, a flood in one of Saxe's warehouses located in the Gulf Coast region destroyed over $10 million of inventory. While the extent to which this loss is recoverable through Saxe's insurance is uncertain at this time, Alta believes that this loss could have a material impact on Saxe's financial condition and results of operations.

e. During the audit of Glomco, Myron has identified a number of misstatements. These misstatements are not material in dollar amount, do not appear to represent any discernable pattern, and do not represent fraudulent activity. As a result, Myron has decided that Glomco's financial statements do not need to be adjusted to reflect the known or likely effect of these misstatements.

f. Following the completion of the 2008 audit of Blankenship Corporation and release of the financial statements and auditors' reports, Jill met with the manager on the engagement to conduct a post-mortem on the engagement and identify how changes in Blankenship's operations noted during the most recent audit may affect future audits. During this review, Jill became aware that she did not consider Blankenship's process for evaluating goodwill related to an acquisition made by Blankenship during the most recent year for potential impairment. Jill believes that the omitted procedure is important in supporting her opinion on Blankenship's financial statements and that persons are continuing to rely on the financial statements and her report.

11.62 **Attorney Letter Responses.** Omega Corporation is involved in a lawsuit brought by a competitor for patent infringement. The competitor is asking $14 million actual damages for lost profits and unspecified punitive damages. The lawsuit has been in progress for 15 months and Omega has worked closely with its outside counsel preparing its defense. Omega recently requested its outside attorneys with the firm of Wolfe & Goodwin to provide information to its auditors.

The managing partner of Wolfe & Goodwin asked four different lawyers who have worked on the case to prepare a concise response to auditors. The partners received these responses from the lawyers:

1. The action involves unique characteristics wherein authoritative legal precedents bearing directly on the plaintiff's claims do not seem to exist. We believe the plaintiff will have serious problems establishing Omega's liability; nevertheless, if the plaintiff is successful, the damage award may be substantial.

2. In our opinion, Omega will be able to defend this action successfully, and, if not, the possible liability to Omega in this proceeding is nominal in amount.

3. We believe the plaintiff's case against Omega is without merit.

4. In our opinion, Omega will be able to assert meritorious defenses and has a reasonable chance of sustaining an adequate defense, with a possible outcome of settling the case for less than the damages claimed.

Required:

a. Interpret each of the four responses separately. Decide whether each is (i) adequate to conclude that the likelihood of an adverse outcome is "remote," requiring no disclosure in financial statements, or (ii) too vague to serve as adequate information for a decision, requiring more information from the lawyers or from management.

b. What response do you think auditors would get if they asked the plaintiff's counsel about the likely outcome of the lawsuit? Discuss.

11.63 **Accounting for a Contingency: Attorney Letter Information.** Central City was involved in litigation brought by Mexican-American Legal Defense Fund (MALDEF) over the creation of single-member voting districts for city council positions. Auditors were working on the financial statements for the year ended December 31, 2008, and had almost completed gathering sufficient appropriate evidence by February 12, 2009.

The court heard final arguments on February 1 and rendered its judgment on February 10. The ruling was in favor of MALDEF and required the creation of certain single-member voting districts. This ruling did not impose a monetary loss on Central City, but the court also ruled that MALDEF would be awarded a judgment of court costs and attorney fees to be paid by Central City.

Local newspaper reports stated that MALDEF would seek a $250,000 recovery from the city. Auditors obtained an attorney letter dated February 15 that stated the following:

In my opinion, the court will award some amount for MALDEF's attorney fees. In regard to your inquiry about an amount or range of possible loss, I estimate that such an award could be anywhere from $30,000 to $175,000.

Required:

a. What weight should be given to the newspaper report of the $250,000 amount MALDEF might ask? What weight should be given to the attorney's estimate?

b. How should this subsequent event be reflected in the 2008 financial statements of Central City?

CPA REVIEW

11.64 **Kaplan CPA Exam Simulation: Audit Committee Communications.**

Required:

Go to the text Web site at www.mhhe.com/louwers3e, click on the AUD: Harrison Homes and the "Communicating with the Audit Committee" tab, and complete the assigned task.

Reports on Audited Financial Statements

Professional Standards References

Compendium Section	Document Reference	Topic
	AS 1	"Reference in Auditors' Reports to the Standards of the Public Company Accounting Oversight Board"
Various*	AS 5	"An Audit of Internal Control over Financial Reporting That Is Integrated with an Audit of Financial Statements"
AU 339	SAS 103	"Audit Documentation"
	AS 3	"Audit Documentation"
	ISA 230	"Audit Documentation"
AU 341	SAS 59	"Auditor's Consideration of an Entity's Ability to Continue as a Going Concern" (amended by SAS 64, SAS 77, and SAS 96)
	ISA 570	"Going Concern"
AU 410	SAS 1	"Adherence to Generally Accepted Accounting Principles"
AU 9410		"Interpretation: Impact of FASB Statement Prior to Effective Date"
AU 411	SAS 69	"The Meaning of 'Present Fairly in Conformity with GAAP'"
AU 420	SAS 1	"Consistency of Application of Generally Accepted Accounting Principles" (amended by SAS 88)
AU 431	SAS 32	"Adequacy of Disclosure in Financial Statements"
AU 504	SAS 26	"Association with Financial Statements"
AU 9504		"Interpretation: Interim and Condensed Information, Lack of Independence"
AU 508	SAS 58	"Reports on Audited Financial Statements" (amended by SAS 79 and SAS 93)
	ISA 700	"The Independent Auditor's Report on a Complete Set of General Purpose Financial Statements"
	ISA 701	"Modifications to the Independent Auditor's Report"
AU 9508		"Interpretations: Reports on Audited Financial Statements"
AU 530	SAS 1	"Dating of the Independent Auditor's Report"
AU 543	SAS 1	"Part of Audit Performed by Other Independent Auditors"
AU 9543		"Interpretations: Other Auditors"
	ISA 600	"Using the Work of Another Auditor"
AU 544	SAS 1	"Lack of Conformity with Generally Accepted Accounting Principles" (Regulated Companies)
AU 550	SAS 8	"Other Information in Documents Containing Audited Financial Statements"
	ISA 720	"Other Information in Documents Containing Audited Financial Statements"
AU 9550		"Interpretation: Other Information in Electronic Sites"
AU 552	SAS 42	"Reporting on Condensed Financial Statements and Selected Financial Data"
AU 558	SAS 52	"Required Supplementary Information"
AU 9558		"Interpretation: Supplementary Oil and Gas Reserve Information"

*AS 5 amends AU 230, AU 310, AU 312, AU 313, AU 315, AU 316, AU 319, AU 322, AU 325, AU 328, AU 332, AU 333, AU 341, AU 342, AU 380, AU 508, AU 530, AU 543, AU 560, AU 561, AU 711, AU 722, AS 3, and AS 4.

The television industry doesn't like to see the complexity of the world. It prefers simple reporting, with simple ideas: this is white, that's black; this is good, that's bad.

Filmmaker Krisztof Kieslowski

In our opinion . . .

Beginning of the opinion paragraph of most auditors' reports on financial statements

Learning Objectives

Management has the primary responsibility for the effectiveness of the entity's internal control over financial reporting and fair presentation of financial statements in conformity with generally accepted accounting principles. Auditors have primary responsibility for expressing an opinion, based on their audits, on internal control over financial reporting and the fairness of the financial statements in auditors' reports. The accounting firm partner's signature on these reports concludes the last stage of the audit engagement, as shown here:

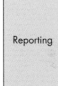

| Obtain (or Retain) Engagement | Engagement Planning | Risk Assessment | Substantive Procedures | Reporting |

While the majority of audits involve "clean" reports (unqualified opinions), this chapter covers the most frequent variations in auditors' reports. The standard report is a starting place and you must understand the reasons for changing the standard language when auditors cannot issue a "clean" opinion.

Your objectives are to be able to:

1. Provide an overview of the types of reports that accompany an entity's financial statements.

2. List three general functions of the auditors' report on an entity's financial statements.

3. Explain the significance of each of the paragraphs in the auditors' standard report on an entity's financial statements.

4. Describe the types of auditors' reports that may be issued if an entity's financial statements contain a departure from generally accepted accounting principles.

5. Describe the types of auditors' reports that may be issued if auditors are unable to comply with generally accepted auditing standards.

6. Describe how the standard report is modified when auditors issue unqualified opinions but reference other matters affecting the audit or the client.

7. Identify other circumstances affecting auditors' reporting responsibilities and explain how they affect auditors' reports on an entity's financial statements.

OVERVIEW

Founded in 1952 by John Rigas and his brother Gus, **Adelphia Communications Corporation** (Adelphia is the Greek word for "brothers") was one of the largest operators of cable systems in the United States. It experienced financial success in the late 1990s and, to promote its brand and increase its exposure, paid $30 million to secure the naming rights to the National Football League's Tennessee Titans' stadium for 15 years. The "Music City Miracle" (a kickoff return featuring two laterals in the final seconds of a playoff game against the Buffalo Bills) and the subsequent appearance of the Titans in the 2000 Super Bowl had the name "Adelphia" splashed over the media across the United States. At that time, Adelphia's stock traded for over $60 per share.

In the early 2000s, the name "Adelphia" became featured for another reason. The company was rocked by a scandal involving members of the Rigas family, who were members of Adelphia's management team (including chairman, president, and CEO John J. Rigas) and were found to have misappropriated billions of dollars from the company for such purposes as using the company plane to transport a Christmas tree and the purchase of 22 automobiles for Rigas's sons, who were all officers of the company. Many referred to these abuses as the Rigas family using the company as its private "piggy bank."[1] As a result of this scandal, as well as other operating problems, in June 2002 Adelphia was forced to file a voluntary petition for bankruptcy reorganization under Chapter 11 of the U.S. Bankruptcy Code.

For its 2005 fiscal year, Adelphia's financial statements showed operating income of $34 million (from revenues of $4.3 billion) and a shareholders' deficit of over $8 billion. (Adelphia lost $1.9 billion and $839 million in 2005 and 2004, respectively). Its stock was trading at less than $1 per share in the over-the-counter markets. What should Adelphia's auditors (**PricewaterhouseCoopers**) have done in this situation? Clearly, some significant questions existed about Adelphia's ability to continue to exist as a going concern. However, if Adelphia's management disclosed these going-concern uncertainties, did this affect the conformity of Adelphia's financial statements with generally accepted accounting principles (GAAP)? And how should PricewaterhouseCoopers' report have reflected these uncertainties?

In its March 28, 2006, report on Adelphia's financial statements, PricewaterhouseCoopers concluded that Adelphia's financial statements were fairly presented in conformity with GAAP. However, they expanded their report to include the recognition of Adelphia's going-concern uncertainties to the users of Adelphia's financial statements:

> The consolidated financial statements listed in the accompanying index have been prepared assuming that the Company will continue as a going concern. As discussed in Note 2 to the consolidated financial statements, on June 25, 2002, Adelphia and substantially all of its domestic subsidiaries filed a voluntary petition for reorganization under Chapter 11 of the United States Bankruptcy Code. In addition, the Company is involved in material litigation, the ultimate outcome of which is not presently determinable. The uncertainties inherent in the bankruptcy and litigation process, the Company's net capital deficiency and the expiration of the Company's extended debtor-in-possession credit facility on August 7, 2006 raise substantial doubt about its ability to continue as a going concern. The financial statements do not include any adjustments to reflect the possible future effects on the recoverability and classification of assets or the amount and classification of liabilities that may result from the outcome of these uncertainties.

As shown above, the auditors' report on an entity's financial statements does more than simply report on whether the entity's financial statements are fairly presented in conformity with GAAP. In this case, professional standards required PricewaterhouseCoopers to inform users about Adelphia's potential going-concern problems, despite the fact that this information was disclosed by Adelphia and that its financial statements were in conformity with GAAP.

This chapter discusses auditors' reports on an entity's financial statements. As with the Adelphia example shown above, auditors' reports serve as an important tool to communicate to third-party users both the conformity of the entity's financial statements with GAAP as well as other important matters affecting the entity.

REPORTS ACCOMPANYING THE ENTITY'S FINANCIAL STATEMENTS

LEARNING OBJECTIVE

1. Provide an overview of the types of reports that accompany an entity's financial statements.

Within 60 days of their fiscal year end, large public entities subject to the reporting requirements of the Securities and Exchange Commission (SEC) are required to file certain financial information with the SEC. This information, which includes the entity's audited financial statements and footnotes and other required disclosures related to the financial statements, is filed using Form 10-K.

Until recently, this financial information was accompanied by a single report: the **auditors' report on the financial statements and related disclosures.** It either provides (or

[1] "Adelphia: A Cable Dynasty Unravels," *The Wall Street Journal*, July 25, 2002, p. A3.

disclaims) an opinion on whether the entity's financial statements and related disclosures are presented in conformity with generally accepted accounting principles (GAAP). This opinion is based on the tests of controls and substantive procedures that have been performed during the audit engagement and discussed throughout this text.

Recently, the Sarbanes-Oxley Act of 2002 and *Accounting Standard 5 (AS 5)* have mandated two additional types of reports for SEC registrants:

1. A report, prepared by the entity's management, on the effectiveness of the entity's internal control over financial reporting.
2. A report, prepared by the auditors, on the effectiveness of the entity's internal control over financial reporting.

Management's report on internal control over financial reporting was discussed in Chapter 5. As noted there, management's report includes the following major components:

- A statement indicating that management is responsible for establishing and maintaining adequate internal control over financial reporting.
- A statement identifying the framework used by management to assess the effectiveness of the entity's internal control over financial reporting.
- Management's opinion on the effectiveness of the entity's internal control over financial reporting, including an explicit statement as to whether the internal control over financial reporting is effective.
- A statement that the registered accounting firm auditing the financial statements (auditor) has issued an attestation report on the entity's internal control over financial reporting (see following paragraph).

The **auditors' report on internal control over financial reporting** provides an opinion on the effectiveness of the entity's internal control over financial reporting. This opinion will be based on tests of the operating effectiveness of the entity's internal control policies and procedures over financial reporting. Until recently, auditors were required to evaluate and express an opinion on management's assessment of its internal control over financial reporting, but this responsibility was eliminated by *AS 5*.

Exhibit 12.1 summarizes the reports that accompany an entity's financial statements. Note that auditors can issue either two separate reports (one related to the financial statements and one related to internal control over financial reporting) or a single combined report addressing both the financial statements and internal control over financial reporting. You also should note that management's report on internal control over financial reporting will accompany the entity's financial statements. It is important to reiterate that *AS 5* reports on internal control over financial reporting are required only for SEC registrants.

EXHIBIT 12.1
Reports Accompanying the Entity's Financial Statements

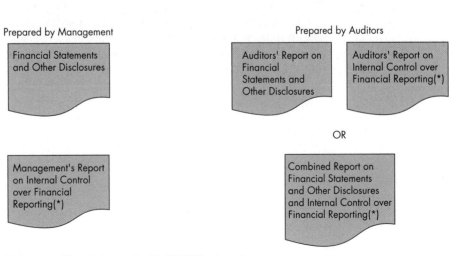

*Only presented if required to comply with *AS 5* (SEC registrants).

In the remainder of this chapter, we discuss the reports prepared by auditors on the entity's financial statements and internal control over financial reporting.

Review Checkpoints

12.1 List the reports that accompany the entity's financial statements along with the party or parties that prepare each report.

12.2 What are the major elements included in management's report on internal control over financial reporting?

REPORTING ON THE ENTITY'S FINANCIAL STATEMENTS

Purpose of the Report

LEARNING
OBJECTIVE

2. List three general
functions of the
auditors' report on an
entity's financial
statements.

The American Accounting Association's definition of auditing concludes with the phrase ". . . communicating those results [of the audit] to interested users." The auditors' report serves to communicate to users three specific comments with respect to the financial statements, the conduct of the audit, and the entity in general:

1. The report indicates *whether the financial statements are presented in conformity with GAAP.* If the entity's financial statements do not conform with GAAP, the auditors must indicate how the financial statements would appear if they did. Additionally, the auditors must disclose any material omissions from the financial statements. For example, if the entity omits a footnote, the auditors must disclose the GAAP departure in the report as well as the information that was omitted.

2. Auditors use their reports to *highlight any unusual aspects of the audit examination.* The audit team may not have been able to examine all facets of the entity due either to the timing of the audit, the nature of the entity, or entity-imposed restrictions. For example, if the entity has never been audited before, the auditors have the nearly impossible task of recreating financial statements from the previous year. In a more ominous scenario, the entity may not allow the auditors access to all relevant information, thereby prohibiting the auditors from gathering sufficient evidence to express an opinion on the financial statements. Auditors also may use their reports to indicate a division of responsibility if auditors from another firm conducted a significant portion of the audit.

3. Even if the financial statements are fairly presented in conformity with GAAP and the audit was conducted in accordance with GAAS, *auditors may wish to reference other matters affecting the audit or the client.* Auditors, for example, can highlight a change in an entity's accounting principles that could result in a comparability problem when comparing prior-years' results with those of the current year. When an entity is experiencing significant financial difficulties, auditors can express their concerns ("substantial doubt") about the entity's ability to continue as a going concern. Auditors also can use their reports to emphasize matters such as subsequent events, significant related-party transactions, or other events and transactions that they believe are material to financial statement users.

In the following sections of this chapter, we discuss how the various conditions, events, and transactions just mentioned affect the auditors' report.

Review Checkpoints

12.3 What are three general functions of the auditors' report?

The Standard Report

LEARNING
OBJECTIVE

3. Explain the
significance of each of
the paragraphs in the
auditors' standard
report on an entity's
financial statements.

Auditors issue a standard report when (1) the financial statements present fairly the financial condition, results of operations, and cash flows of the entity in conformity with GAAP; (2) there are no unusual issues related to the conduct of the audit; and (3) the auditors do not need to highlight any entity transactions or events to financial users. The auditors' standard report contains four basic components: (1) the **introductory paragraph,** (2) the **scope paragraph,** (3) the **opinion paragraph,** and (4) the **internal control paragraph.** An example is given in Exhibit 12.2.

The report shown in Exhibit 12.2 would be issued for public entities subject to the requirements of *AS 5*. Differences between this report and a *SAS 58* report for a nonpublic entity (or a public entity not yet subject to the requirements of *AS 5*) are highlighted using callouts in Exhibit 12.2. As shown therein, most of the differences are relatively minor, with the exception of the absence of an internal control paragraph in the *SAS 58* report. This

EXHIBIT 12.2 Auditors' Standard Report

Title	**Report of Independent Registered Public Accounting Firm** *(SAS 58 report is titled "report of Independent Auditors")*
Address	To the Board of Directors and Shareholders Apollo Shoes, Inc.
Introductory Paragraph	We have audited the accompanying balance sheets of Apollo Shoes, Inc. as of December 31, 2008 and 2007, and the related statements of income, comprehensive income, shareholders' equity, and cash flows for each of the years in the three-year period ended December 31, 2008. These financial statements are the responsibility of Apollo Shoes, Inc.'s management. Our responsibility is to express an opinion on these financial statements based on our audits.
Scope Paragraph	We conducted our audits in accordance with the standards of the Public Company Accounting Oversight Board (United States). Those standards require that we plan and perform the audit to obtain reasonable assurance about whether the financial statements are free of material misstatement. An audit includes examining, on a test basis, evidence supporting the amounts and disclosures in the financial statements. An audit also includes assessing the accounting principles used and significant estimates made by management, as well as evaluating the overall financial statement presentation. We believe that our audits provide a reasonable basis for our opinion. *(SAS 58 report uses "auditing standards generally accepted in the United States of America")*
Opinion Paragraph	In our opinion, the financial statements referred to above present fairly, in all material respects, the financial position of Apollo Shoes, Inc., at December 31, 2008, and 2007, and the results of their operations and their cash flows for each of the years in the three-year period ended December 31, 2008, in conformity with accounting principles generally accepted in the United States of America.
Internal Control Paragraph	We have also audited, in accordance with the standards of the Public Company Accounting Oversight Board (United States), Apollo Shoes, Inc.'s internal control over financial reporting as of December 31, 2008, based on criteria established in *Internal Control — Integrated Framework* issued by the Committee of Sponsoring Organizations of the Treadway Commission and our report dated January 29, 2009, expressed an unqualified opinion thereon. *(SAS 58 report does not include this paragraph)*
Signature	*Smith & Smith, CPAs* Shoetown, Maine
Date	January 29, 2009

omission is consistent with the lack of requirements for auditors to evaluate and opine on the operating effectiveness of internal control over financial reporting for nonpublic entities.

All standard reports contain these features:

1. *Title.* The title should contain the word *independent,* as in "independent registered public accounting firm" (for public entities) or "independent auditors" (for nonpublic entities).

2. *Address.* The report should be addressed to the client, which occasionally may be different from the auditee. A **client** is the person (entity, board of directors, agency, or some other person or group) who retains the auditors and pays the fee. In financial audits, the client and the auditee usually are the same economic entity. An **auditee** is the actual designation of the entity or other entity whose financial statements are being audited. Occasionally, the client and the auditee are different. For example, if Conglomerate Corporation hires and pays the auditors to audit Newtek Company in connection with a proposed acquisition, Conglomerate is the client and Newtek is the auditee.

3. *Notice of audit.* A sentence should identify the financial statements and declare that they were audited. This appears in the *introductory paragraph.*

4. *Responsibilities.* The report should state management's responsibility for the financial statements and the auditors' responsibility for the report. These statements are also in the *introductory paragraph.*

5. *Description of the audit.* The second paragraph *(scope paragraph)* should declare that the audit was conducted in accordance with the standards of the Public Company Accounting Oversight Board (PCAOB) (which represent generally accepted auditing standards (GAAS) for the audits of public entities). The scope paragraph also should describe the principal characteristics of an audit, including a statement of belief that the audit provides a reasonable basis for the opinion.

6. *Opinion.* The report should express an opinion *(opinion paragraph)* regarding conformity of the financial statements with generally accepted accounting principles. In this example, the conclusion that Apollo Shoes' financial statements are presented in conformity with GAAP is referred to as an *unqualified opinion.*

7. *Internal control.* The report should reference the auditors' report and opinion on the client's internal control over financial reporting *(internal control paragraph).* These reports and engagements were initially discussed in Chapter 5. As noted later in this chapter, auditors may prepare a combined report that expresses opinions on both the financial statements and internal control over financial reporting.

8. *Signature.* The auditors (partner of the audit team) should sign the report, manually or otherwise.

9. *Date.* The report should be dated with the date when the auditors have obtained sufficient appropriate evidence to support the opinion (the **audit completion date**).

Introductory Paragraph

The introductory paragraph indicates that an audit has been conducted and identifies the financial statements the auditors examined. Identifying the financial statements is important because the opinion paragraph expresses an opinion on these financial statements. In some instances, entities engage auditors to audit and report on only one of the financial statements but not on the others (although GAAP requires that an income statement always be accompanied by a statement of cash flows). Most often, such an engagement is for the audit of the balance sheet only. Audit standards make a special exception for this type of engagement referred to as a *limited reporting engagement.* A report on only one financial statement is permitted. In the introductory paragraph, the auditors state that only one statement (e.g., the balance sheet) has been audited. In the opinion paragraph, the opinion on presentation in conformity with GAAP is limited to one characteristic (e.g., financial position). If one or more of the basic financial statement(s) is not identified in the introductory paragraph, the opinion paragraph likewise should not express an opinion on these statement(s).

The introductory paragraph also explicitly states that the financial statements are the responsibility of management. This statement was added to ensure that users did not mistakenly attribute responsibility for the preparation and presentation of the financial statements to the auditors. Instead, auditors are responsible for expressing an opinion on the financial statements based on the audit work performed.

Scope Paragraph

The scope paragraph is the description of the character of the work in the audit. The sentence "We conducted our audits in accordance with the standards of the Public Company Accounting Oversight Board (United States)" refers primarily to the general standards and standards of field work. Its message is that the auditors (1) were trained and proficient, (2) were independent, (3) exercised due professional care, (4) planned and supervised the work, (5) obtained a sufficient understanding of the entity and its environment, including internal control, and (6) gathered sufficient appropriate evidence. For public and nonpublic entities subject to *SAS 58* (and not *AS 5*), the scope paragraph will reference "auditing standards generally accepted in the United States of America."

To the extent that one or more of the general standards and standards of field work is not actually satisfied during an audit, the scope paragraph must be modified to identify which standard was not satisfied. Such modifications can be caused by a lack of independence, lack of sufficient appropriate evidence, or restrictions on procedures that could be performed by the auditors. In practice, auditors also will modify the standard opinion paragraph language when the scope paragraph is modified.

Opinion Paragraph

Users of audited financial statements are generally most interested in the opinion paragraph. This long sentence contains the conclusions about the financial statements. This conclusion is in the form of an *opinion* on whether the entity's financial statements present its financial condition, results of operations, and cash flows in conformity with generally accepted accounting principles. It is the public manifestation of the private audit decision process.

With regard to the fourth standard of reporting, auditors may issue four types of opinions:

- An **unqualified opinion,** in which the conclusion is that the financial statements present the financial condition, results of operations, and cash flows in conformity with GAAP. The *auditors' standard report* shown in Exhibit 12.2 is an example of an unqualified opinion; however, unqualified opinions can be issued in forms other than the standard report. Interestingly, while the term "unqualified" normally has a negative connotation, an unqualified opinion is the most favorable opinion auditors can issue.

- A **qualified opinion,** in which the conclusion is that, with the exception of one or more issues, the financial statements present the financial condition, results of operations, and cash flows in conformity with GAAP. Qualified opinions use the phrase "except for" in describing the issues that give rise to the qualification. Interestingly, while the term "qualified" normally has a positive connotation, qualified opinions are issued when one or more issues are encountered during the audit.

- An **adverse opinion,** in which the conclusion is that the financial statements *do not* present the financial condition, results of operations, and cash flows in conformity with GAAP.

- A **disclaimer of opinion,** in which the auditors do not express an opinion on the fairness of the entity's financial statements.

Internal Control Paragraph

As noted in Chapter 5, *AS 5* requires auditors to evaluate and report on the operating effectiveness of the entity's internal control over financial reporting. Auditors can fulfill their reporting responsibility in two ways. First, they can issue two separate reports (one

on the financial statements and one on internal control over financial reporting); if this option is selected, each of these reports will carry a reference to the other report. As a result, the auditors' report on the entity's financial statements will reference the evaluation of the internal control over financial reporting as well as the auditors' opinion on the effectiveness of internal control over financial reporting. Reviewing Exhibit 12.2, the last paragraph of the auditors' report on the financial statements states that Apollo Shoes' internal control over financial reporting was effective based on criteria established by the Committee of Sponsoring Organizations of the Treadway Commission (COSO) and refers to the auditors' report expressing an unqualified opinion on internal control. This report (not shown) would, in turn, refer to Smith & Smith, CPAs' audit of Apollo Shoes' financial statements and refer to the unqualified opinion issued on those financial statements.

The second option for Smith & Smith would be to issue a single report that expresses opinions on both Apollo Shoes' financial statements and internal control over financial reporting. This report (sometimes referred to as an **integrated report**) is shown in Exhibit 12.3. This report essentially combines the report on Apollo Shoes' financial statements (shown in Exhibit 12.2) with a report on its internal control (for examples, see Chapter 5). A review of this report in Exhibit 12.3 reveals the introductory, scope, and opinion paragraphs are modified to describe the additional responsibilities assumed (introductory paragraph), engagement scope (scope paragraph), and conclusions (opinion paragraph) resulting from the examination of Apollo Shoes' internal control over financial reporting. In addition, two explanatory paragraphs (the definition and inherent limitations paragraphs) are included to provide readers with additional information about Apollo Shoes' internal control over financial reporting.

For the 2006 fiscal year, auditors of the Fortune 100 companies (largest 100 U.S. companies based on revenues) are relatively evenly split in terms of the presentation of reports on the financial statements and internal control over financial reporting. Of those subject to Sarbanes-Oxley's reporting requirements, 58 percent used a single report and 42 percent used two separate reports. Because the focus of this chapter is on reports on the fairness of the entity's financial statements, we will illustrate report modifications assuming that separate reports are prepared.

Reports Other Than the Standard Report

Subsequent sections of this chapter explain the major variations on the standard report on the financial statements. There are three basic reasons for issuing a report other than the standard report.

- If the financial statements contain a *departure from GAAP*, including inadequate disclosure, the auditors must choose between an *unqualified opinion* (including the standard report), a *qualified opinion,* or an *adverse opinion*. The choice depends on the nature and materiality of the effects of the GAAP departure.

- If matters affect the ability of auditors to comply with GAAS, the auditors may deviate from the standard report. For example, when the audit has a *scope limitation* (*a departure from GAAS,* in which the extent of audit work was limited) and the auditors have not been able to obtain sufficient appropriate evidence on a particular account balance or disclosure, the auditors must choose between an *unqualified opinion* (including the standard report), a *qualified opinion,* or a *disclaimer of opinion*. The choice again depends on the materiality of the matter for which evidence is not sufficient.

- If the auditors believe it important to *bring certain information to financial statement users' attention,* the auditors may highlight the information by adding an additional explanatory paragraph to or otherwise modifying the language in the standard report. These situations include changes in an entity's accounting methods, financial difficulties facing the entity, justified departures from accounting principles, a division of

EXHIBIT 12.3 **Combined Report on Financial Statements and Internal Control over Financial Reporting**

Title	**Report of Independent Registered Public Accounting Firm**
Address	To the Board of Directors and Shareholders Apollo Shoes, Inc.
Introductory Paragraph	We have audited the accompanying balance sheets of Apollo Shoes, Inc. as of December 31, 2008 and 2007, and the related statements of income, comprehensive income, shareholders' equity, and cash flows for each of the years in the three-year period ended December 31, 2008. We have also audited Apollo Shoes, Inc.'s internal control over financial reporting as of December 31, 2008, based on criteria established in *Internal Control — Integrated Framework* issued by the Committee of Sponsoring Organizations of the Treadway Commission (COSO criteria). Apollo Shoes, Inc.'s management is responsible for these financial statements, for maintaining effective internal control over financial reporting, and for its assessment of internal control over financial reporting, included in the accompanying "Management's Report to Shareholders" under the caption "Report on Internal Control Over Financial Reporting." Our responsibility is to express an opinion on these financial statements and an opinion on the company's internal control over financial reporting based on our audits.
Scope Paragraph	We conducted our audits in accordance with the standards of the Public Company Accounting Oversight Board (United States). Those standards require that we plan and perform the audits to obtain reasonable assurance about whether the financial statements are free of material misstatement and whether effective internal control over financial reporting was maintained in all material respects. Our audits of the financial statements included examining, on a test basis, evidence supporting the amounts and disclosures in the financial statements, assessing the accounting principles used and significant estimates made by management, and evaluating the overall financial statement presentation. Our audit of internal control over financial reporting included obtaining an understanding of internal control over financial reporting, assessing the risk that a material weakness exists, and testing and evaluating the design and operating effectiveness of internal control based on the assessed risk. Our audits also included performing such other procedures as we considered necessary in the circumstances. We believe that our audits provide a reasonable basis for our opinions.
Definition Paragraph	A company's internal control over financial reporting is a process designed to provide reasonable assurance regarding the reliability of financial reporting and the preparation of financial statements for external purposes in accordance with generally accepted accounting principles. A company's internal control over financial reporting includes those policies and procedures that (1) pertain to the maintenance of records that, in reasonable detail, accurately and fairly reflect the transactions and dispositions of the assets of the company; (2) provide reasonable assurance that transactions are recorded as necessary to permit preparation of financial statements in accordance with generally accepted accounting principles, and that receipts and expenditures of the company are being made only in accordance with authorizations of management and directors of the company; and (3) provide reasonable assurance regarding prevention or timely detection of unauthorized acquisition, use, or disposition of the company's assets that could have a material effect on the financial statements.
Inherent Limitations Paragraph	Because of its inherent limitations, internal control over financial reporting may not prevent or detect misstatements. Also, projections of any evaluation of effectiveness to future periods are subject to the risk that controls may become inadequate because of changes in conditions, or that the degree of compliance with the policies or procedures may deteriorate.
Opinion Paragraph	In our opinion, the financial statements referred to above present fairly, in all material respects, the financial position of Apollo Shoes, Inc. as of December 31, 2008 and 2007, and the results of its operations and cash flows for each of the years in the three-year period ended December 31, 2008, in conformity with accounting principles generally accepted in the United States of America. Also, in our opinion, Apollo Shoes, Inc. maintained, in all material respects, effective internal control over financial reporting as of December 31, 2008, based on the COSO criteria.
Signature	*Smith & Smith, CPAs* Shoetown, Maine
Date	January 29, 2009

responsibility involving other auditors, and the desire to emphasize some matter with respect to the entity. In many of these cases, the fairness of the entity's financial statements is not affected, so an *unqualified opinion* is still appropriate. However, the modifications made to the report to address these issues would result in this report differing from the standard report.

Review Checkpoints

12.4 What are the important elements of the auditors' standard report?

12.5 Regarding the standard introductory and scope paragraphs, (a) what do they identify as the objects of the audit and (b) what does the sentence "We conducted our audit in accordance with the standards of the Public Company Accounting Oversight Board" mean?

12.6 Identify the major differences between the auditors' standard report issued for public entities (under the requirements of *AS 5*) and nonpublic entities (under the requirements of *SAS 58*).

12.7 What are the major reasons for deviating from the wording in the auditors' standard report?

AUDITORS' REPORTS ON DEPARTURES FROM GAAP

LEARNING OBJECTIVE

4. Describe the types of auditors' reports that may be issued if an entity's financial statements contain a departure from generally accepted accounting principles.

An entity's management may decide to present financial statements containing an accounting treatment or disclosure that is not in conformity with GAAP. This situation is unusual, but the reasons for it vary. Perhaps management does not wish to capitalize leases and show the related debt, wants to calculate earnings per share using a more favorable (non-GAAP) methodology, does not accrue unbilled revenue at the end of a period, makes unreasonable accounting estimates, or is reluctant to disclose all known details of a contingency. Whatever the reason, the fact is that a departure from GAAP exists in the financial statements. Now the auditors must decide the type of opinion to render (see Exhibit 12.4).

EXHIBIT 12.4
GAAP Departures

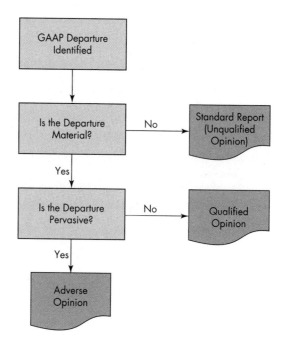

As with any issue, a departure from GAAP may not be material to the entity's financial statements. Recall the wording of the opinion paragraph in the auditors' standard report: "In our opinion, the financial statements referred to above present fairly, *in all material respects . . .*" [italics added]. As a result, if a departure from GAAP is immaterial, the auditors would treat the departure as if it did not exist. In this case, the auditors can express an unqualified opinion and issue the standard report.

If the departure is sufficiently material to affect users' decisions based on the financial statements but can be "compartmentalized," the auditors must *qualify* the opinion. By "compartmentalized," we mean that the departure can be isolated to a particular account group (e.g., accounts receivable not valued at net realizable value) or transactions (e.g., failure to capitalize leases) without affecting other accounts to any material extent. In these cases, the qualification takes the "except for" language form. This "except for" qualification isolates a particular departure but indicates that the financial statements are otherwise in conformity with GAAP. The nature of the GAAP departure must be explained in a separate paragraph in the report, as shown in Exhibit 12.5.

On the other hand, if the GAAP departure is pervasive, affecting numerous accounts and financial statement relationships, or "super material" to the point that the financial statements as a whole are misleading, the auditors must issue an adverse opinion. As noted earlier, in an adverse opinion, auditors conclude that the financial statements *do not present fairly* the financial position, results of operations, and cash flows in conformity with GAAP. The introductory and scope paragraphs should not be modified because, in order to decide to issue an adverse opinion, the audit team must possess all evidence necessary to reach the decision. When this opinion is issued, all substantive reasons must be disclosed in the report in explanatory paragraphs.

EXHIBIT 12.5
Qualified Opinion

Report of Independent Registered Public Accounting Firm[2]

To the Board of Directors and Shareholders, Apollo Shoes, Inc.

[Standard Introductory Paragraph]

[Standard Scope Paragraph]

As discussed in Note 16, an additional provision in the amount of $30,000,000 for possible uncollectible receivables at December 31, 2007, was charged to operations during the year ended December 31, 2008, which, in our opinion, should have been reflected in the financial statements for 2007. Had this provision been properly recorded in the 2007 financial statements, the net loss in that year would have been increased by $30,000,000 and shareholders' equity would have been decreased by that amount, and Apollo Shoes, Inc., would have reported net earnings of $700,000 for the year ended December 31, 2008, rather than the net loss of $29,300,000 as reflected in the statements of income, comprehensive income, shareholders' equity, and cash flows for that period.

In our opinion, *except for the effects of the provision for possible uncollectible receivables reported in the preceding paragraph,* the financial statements referred to above present fairly, in all material respects, the financial position of Apollo Shoes, Inc., at December 31, 2008 and 2007, and the results of operations and cash flows for each of the years in the three-year period ended December 31, 2008, in conformity with accounting principles generally accepted in the United States of America.

[Standard Internal Control Paragraph]

Smith & Smith, CPAs
Shoetown, Maine
January 29, 2009

[2] For easier reference, all revisions to the auditors' standard report in Exhibit 12.2 in reports presented throughout this chapter are shown in color.

EXHIBIT 12.6
Adverse Opinion

Report of Independent Registered Public Accounting Firm

To the Board of Directors and Shareholders, Apollo Shoes, Inc.:

[Standard Introductory Paragraph]

[Standard Scope Paragraph]

As discussed in Note 16, an additional provision in the amount of $30,000,000 for possible uncollectible receivables at December 31, 2007, was charged to operations during the year ended December 31, 2008, which, in our opinion, should have been reflected in the financial statements for 2007. Had this provision been properly recorded in the 2007 financial statements, the net loss in that year would have been increased by $30,000,000 and shareholders' equity would have been decreased by that amount, and Apollo Shoes, Inc., would have reported net earnings of $700,000 for the year ended December 31, 2008, rather than the net loss of $29,300,000 as reflected in the statements of income, comprehensive income, shareholders' equity, and cash flows for that period.

In our opinion, *because of the effects of the matters discussed above,* the aforementioned balance sheet as of December 31, 2007, and the statements of income, comprehensive income, shareholders' equity, and cash flows for the years ended December 31, 2007 and 2008, *do not* present fairly the financial position of Apollo Shoes, Inc., as of December 31, 2007, or the results of its operations or its cash flows for the years ended December 31, 2007 and 2008, in conformity with accounting principles generally accepted in the United States of America.

However, in our opinion, the balance sheet as of December 31, 2008, presents fairly, in all material respects, the financial position of Apollo Shoes, Inc., as of December 31, 2008, and the statements of income, comprehensive income, shareholders' equity, and cash flows present fairly the results of operations and cash flows for the year ended December 31, 2006, in conformity with accounting principles generally accepted in the United States of America.

[Standard Internal Control Paragraph]

Smith & Smith, CPAs
Shoetown, Maine
January 29, 2009

Because of an SEC prohibition against accepting financial statements containing a material GAAP departure, "real world" examples of adverse opinions are difficult to find. The example in Exhibit 12.6 assumes that the same departure in GAAP that served as the focus of the qualified opinion in Exhibit 12.5 reached a level of materiality to warrant an adverse opinion. The adverse opinions relate to the results of operations and cash flows for 2007 and 2008 and to the financial position as of December 31, 2007. However, as noted in the last paragraph, the balance sheet for 2008 and statements of income, comprehensive income, shareholders' equity, and cash flows for 2006 were presented in conformity with GAAP. This report illustrates the fact that auditors can issue different opinions on different financial statements in the same report.

The report in Exhibit 12.6 illustrates how different opinions on financial statements in comparative years can be issued (i.e., an unqualified opinion on the statements of income, comprehensive income, shareholders' equity, and cash flows in 2006 and adverse opinions on these statements in 2007 and 2008). This report also illustrates how different opinions on different financial statements within the same year may be appropriate. For example, because the timing of the provision for uncollectible accounts did not affect the ending account receivable balance in 2008, an unqualified opinion on the 2008 balance sheet is appropriate. However, since the timing of recognizing this provision did materially impact the results of operations for both 2007 and 2008, Smith & Smith's report appropriately expressed an adverse opinion on the 2008 statements of income, comprehensive income, shareholders' equity, and cash flows.

Review Checkpoints

12.8 Explain the effect of pervasiveness on the auditors' report when the entity uses an accounting method that departs from generally accepted accounting principles.

12.9 What are the major differences in wording for qualified opinions and adverse opinions issued as a result of departures from generally accepted accounting principles?

AUDITORS' REPORTS FOR DEPARTURES FROM GAAS

LEARNING OBJECTIVE

5. Describe the types of auditors' reports that may be issued if auditors are unable to comply with generally accepted auditing standards.

Auditors use reports not only to document unusual issues related to the entity's financial statements (i.e., GAAP departures) but also to document unusual aspects related to the conduct of the audit. In this section, we discuss the two unusual aspects of the audit (scope limitations and lack of independence) that may be highlighted in the report.

Scope Limitation Reports

Auditors are most comfortable when they have all of the evidence they need to reach their conclusion as to whether the financial statements present the financial condition, results of operations, and cash flows in conformity with GAAP. However, two situations may create **scope limitations,** in which auditors are unable to obtain sufficient appropriate evidence. The two arise from (1) management's deliberate refusal to let auditors perform auditing procedures (known as a **client-imposed scope limitation**) and (2) circumstances beyond the auditors' and client's control such as the late appointment of the auditors that lead to auditors' inability to perform certain auditing procedures (known as a **circumstance-imposed scope limitation**). The nature of auditors' reports depends on the nature and materiality of the scope limitation (see Exhibit 12.7).

EXHIBIT 12.7
GAAS Departures

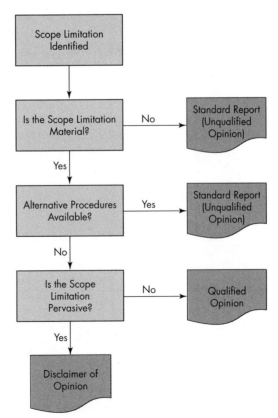

If management's refusal or the circumstances affect the scope of the audit in an immaterial manner, the audit can be considered unaffected and the auditors can issue the standard report (and express an *unqualified opinion*) as if the limitation had never occurred. This response is consistent with auditors' actions when an immaterial departure from GAAP was identified. Similarly, if *alternative procedures* are available to the auditors and they can obtain sufficient evidence despite the scope limitation, the auditors may still issue the standard report. For example, assume a large chain of funeral homes did not want its auditors to send confirmations to its (deceased) customers' families. This request would normally be considered a scope limitation, but assume that the audit team was able to gather sufficient evidence by examining supporting documentation (signed contracts, newspaper obituaries, and subsequent cash receipts) to support the entity's accounts receivable balance. In this situation, since sufficient appropriate evidence has been gathered, the standard report (and an *unqualified opinion*) can be issued.

While the funeral home chain's request in the above scenario was reasonable under the circumstances, management's deliberate refusal to give auditors access to documents or otherwise limit the application of auditing procedures is a most serious condition. It casts doubt on management's integrity. (Why would management refuse access or limit the work?) In these *client-imposed scope limitations,* the opinion is either qualified or disclaimed, depending on the materiality of the financial items affected. *SAS 58* (AU 508.24) notes that auditors would ordinarily disclaim an opinion on the financial statements when they encounter client-imposed scope limitations. This disclaimer reflects auditors' inability to gather sufficient appropriate evidence in cases where clients feel it necessary to limit the nature of the auditors' examination.

Exhibit 12.8 provides examples of two reports that illustrate reporting alternatives when scope limitations are encountered. The failure to take physical counts of inventory could have been based on a request from the client's management *(client-imposed)* or it could have resulted from other circumstances such as the entity's not anticipating the need for an audit and appointing the auditors after the latest year end *(circumstance-imposed).*

EXHIBIT 12.8
Scope Limitation Reports

Panel A: Qualified Opinion

Report of Independent Registered Public Accounting Firm

To the Board of Directors and Shareholders, Apollo Shoes, Inc.:

[Standard Introductory Paragraph]

Except as discussed in the following paragraph, we conducted our audits in accordance with the standards of the Public Company Accounting Oversight Board (United States). [Remainder of paragraph the same as the standard unqualified scope paragraph] . . .

Apollo Shoes, Inc., did not make a count of its physical inventory in 2008 or 2007, stated in the accompanying financial statements at $10 million as of December 31, 2008, and at $15 million as of December 31, 2007, and we were unable to observe the physical quantities on hand. Apollo Shoes, Inc.'s records do not permit the application of other auditing procedures to the audit of the inventories.

In our opinion, *except for the effects of such adjustments, if any, as might have been determined to be necessary had we been able to examine evidence regarding the inventories described above,* the financial statements referred to above present fairly, in all material respects, the financial position of Apollo Shoes, Inc., at December 31, 2008 and 2007, and the results of operations and cash flows for each of the years in the three-year period ended December 31,2008, in conformity with accounting principles generally accepted in the United States of America.

[Standard Internal Control Paragraph]

Smith & Smith, CPAs
Shoetown, Maine
January 29, 2009

Panel B: Disclaimer of Opinion

Report of Independent Registered Public Accounting Firm

To The Board of Directors and Shareholders. Apollo Shoes, Inc.:

*We **were engaged to audit*** the accompanying balance sheets of Apollo Shoes, Inc. as of December 31, 2008 and 2007, and the related statements of income, comprehensive income, shareholders' equity, and cash flows for the years then ended. These financial statements are the responsibility of Apollo Shoes, Inc.,'s management. *[Sentence on auditors' responsibility is omitted.]*

[Standard Scope Paragraph Omitted]

Apollo Shoes, Inc., did not make a count of its physical inventory in 2008 or 2007, stated in the accompanying financial statements at $10 million as of December 31, 2008, and at $15 million as of December 31, 2007, and we were unable to observe the physical quantities on hand. Apollo Shoes, Inc.,'s records do not permit the application of other auditing procedures to the audit of the inventories.

Since Apollo Shoes, Inc., did not take physical inventories and we were not able to apply other auditing procedures to satisfy ourselves as to inventory quantities and cost, the scope of our work was not sufficient to enable us to express, and we do not express, an opinion on these financial statements.

[Standard Internal Control Paragraph]

Smith & Smith, CPAs
Shoetown, Maine
January 29, 2009

In Panel A, the opinion is qualified, using "except for" language. In this case, the lack of evidence is considered material but not pervasive (or "supermaterial") to overwhelm the meaning of a qualified opinion and the usefulness of the unaffected parts of the financial statements. Note that the qualification is based on the fact that the auditors are not able to determine whether the inventory is fairly stated, not the inability to perform the procedure *per se*. The report in Panel A of Exhibit 12.8 "compartmentalizes" the inventory from the audit reporting responsibility, indicating no audit responsibility for this part of the financial statements.

Notice that the introductory paragraph in Panel A is the same as for an unqualified opinion. However, the scope paragraph is qualified because the audit was not conducted entirely in accordance with standards of the PCAOB. Specifically, the audit team was unable to obtain sufficient appropriate evidence about the inventories. When the scope paragraph is qualified for an important omission of audit work, the opinion paragraph also should be qualified.

In Panel B, the situation is fatal to the auditors' opinion. The auditors believe that the inventories are too large and too important in this case to say "except for adjustments, if any." The report then must express a disclaimer of opinion. Notice that the introductory paragraph in Panel B is different from the introductory paragraph in the standard report. This paragraph indicates "[w]e *were engaged to audit* . . .," instead of "[w]e have audited . . ." The introductory paragraph omits the last sentence in which the auditors normally take responsibility for an opinion; in this case, there is no opinion. Notice also that the scope paragraph is entirely omitted. The standard scope paragraph says the audit was conducted in accordance with the standards of the PCAOB and that the audit provided a reasonable basis for the opinion. These statements are not true when a pervasive scope limitation exists. It is important to note that this scope limitation does not necessarily preclude auditors from reporting on the client's internal control over financial reporting (see the reference to the internal control paragraph in Panel B of Exhibit 12.8).

Lack of Independence

When auditors lack independence, an audit in accordance with PCAOB standards is impossible. An audit is not just the application of tools, techniques, and procedures of auditing; it also requires the independence in mental attitude of the auditors. This idea is set forth clearly in the following excerpt from *SAS 26*, "Association with Financial Statements":

> When an accountant is not independent, any procedures he might perform would not be in accordance with generally accepted auditing standards, and he would be precluded from expressing an opinion on such statements. Accordingly, he should disclaim an opinion with respect to the financial statements and should state specifically that he is not independent. (AU 504.09)

This standard applies to the financial statements of public entities. In keeping with this standard, evidence obtained by auditors who are not independent is not considered sufficient appropriate evidence. In such cases, a disclaimer like the one shown in Exhibit 12.9 is appropriate.

Notice that the report below is not titled or addressed to specific users because the auditors did not complete the engagement. Whenever financial statements are unaudited, the following additional guidelines should be observed:

1. If a disclaimer is issued because of a lack of independence, the report should not mention any reasons for not being independent because the readers might erroneously interpret them as unimportant.
2. The report should not mention any auditing procedures applied because readers might erroneously conclude that they were sufficient to enable an opinion to be expressed on the financial statements.
3. If the auditors should learn that the financial statements are not in conformity with generally accepted accounting principles (including adequate disclosures), the departures should be explained in the disclaimer.
4. If prior-years' unaudited financial statements are presented, the disclaimer should cover them as well as the current-year statements.
5. Each page of the financial statements should be labeled clearly as being "unaudited."

The report shown in Exhibit 12.9 for situations in which auditors are not independent provides guidance for unusual circumstances. Clearly, a public entity would not hire auditors who are not independent. However, issues can arise during the audit that impair independence. Several years ago, a bank's management became irate with its auditors over the auditors' insistence on increasing the allowance for loan losses. The bank's management filed a lawsuit against the auditors. Under ethics interpretations, such circumstances impair the auditors' independence and the disclaimer described in Exhibit 12.9 would be the appropriate report. Because the bank needed the report to meet a reporting deadline, the bank had to forgo its lawsuit and the auditors were able to issue a standard report (after the bank recorded additional charges for loan losses that the auditors believed necessary.)

EXHIBIT 12.9
Disclaimer of Opinion When Auditors Are Not Independent

> We are not independent with respect to the Apollo Shoes, Inc., and the accompanying balance sheet as of December 31, 2008, and the related statements of income, comprehensive income, shareholders' equity, and cash flows for the year then ended were not audited by us and, accordingly, we do not express an opinion on them.
>
> Smith & Smith, CPAs
> Shoetown, Maine
> January 29, 2009

Review Checkpoints

12.10 Distinguish between client-imposed scope limitations and circumstance-imposed scope limitations. Which of these scope limitations is generally of greater concern to auditors?

12.11 When a scope limitation exists, how would the standard report be modified to express (1) a qualified opinion and (2) a disclaimer of opinion?

12.12 If auditors are not independent with respect to a public entity, what type of opinion must be issued? Why?

AUDITORS' REPORTS REFERENCING OTHER MATTERS ENCOUNTERED DURING THE AUDIT

LEARNING OBJECTIVE

6. Describe how the standard report is modified when auditors issue unqualified opinions but reference other matters affecting the audit or the client.

Several circumstances may permit an unqualified opinion paragraph but require additional information to be added to the standard report. Five such situations are covered in this section.

1. *Consistency.* An explanatory paragraph identifies a change in accounting principles.
2. *Going concern.* An explanatory paragraph draws attention to problems of the entity's ability to continue as a going concern.
3. *Justified departures from GAAP.* An explanatory paragraph describes a departure from GAAP, which the auditors believe to be appropriate because GAAP would be misleading.
4. *Division of responsibility.* The introductory paragraph, scope paragraph, and opinion paragraph are modified to note a division of responsibility when other auditors are involved in conducting a portion of the examination.
5. *Emphasis paragraph(s).* Additional explanatory paragraph(s) emphasize a matter of importance.

Because the only change is the addition of a fourth paragraph appended to an otherwise standard report (or, in the case of division of responsibility, modifications to three paragraphs of the standard report), these reports are commonly referred to as *modified unqualified opinions* (or "*standard plus reports*"). It is not unusual to see the report express an unqualified opinion with an additional explanatory paragraph (most commonly for a consistency exception). Exhibit 12.10 presents an unqualified opinion on the financial statements of **Time Warner** (formerly, AOL Time Warner) with *two* additional explanatory paragraphs (a standard plus, plus, report?) and a reference to other financial information. The following sections describe the circumstances in which auditors consider such reports (and disclosures) necessary.

Consistency

The second standard of reporting (the consistency standard) requires that the auditors' report refer to the consistent application of accounting principles only when the entity has changed accounting principles during the year. The objective of this standard is to ensure that the auditors give users appropriate notice if the comparability of an entity's financial statements from year to year has been materially affected by a change in accounting principles (such as depreciation methods and inventory cost flow assumptions).

Statement of Financial Accounting Standards 154 (SFAS 154), "Accounting Changes and Error Corrections," specifies the accounting principles regarding changes in principles, estimates, the accounting entity, and correction of errors. Auditing standards parallel the requirements of *SFAS 154* and require a notification be added to the report for changes in accounting principles and discretionary changes in the accounting entity.

EXHIBIT 12.10 **Auditors' Report for Time Warner**

REPORT OF INDEPENDENT REGISTERED PUBLIC ACCOUNTING FIRM

**The Board of Directors and Shareholders of
Time Warner Inc.**

We have audited the accompanying consolidated balance sheets of Time Warner, Inc. ("Time Warner"), as of December 31, 2004 and 2003, and the related consolidated statements of operations, shareholders' equity and cash flows for each of the three years in the period ended December 31, 2004. Our audits also included Financial Statement Schedule II and Supplementary Information listed in the index at Item 15 (a). These financial statements, schedule and supplementary information are the responsibility of Time Warner's management. Our responsibility is to express an opinion on these financial statements, schedule and supplementary information based on our audits.

We conducted our audits in accordance with the standards of the Public Company Accounting Oversight Board (United States). Those standards require that we plan and perform the audit to obtain reasonable assurance about whether the financial statements are free of material misstatement. An audit includes examining, on a test basis, evidence supporting the amounts and disclosures in the financial statements. An audit also includes assessing the accounting principles used and significant estimates made by management, as well as evaluating the overall financial statement presentation. We believe that our audits provide a reasonable basis for our opinion.

In our opinion, the financial statements referred to above present fairly, in all material respects, the consolidated financial position of Time Warner at December 31, 2004 and 2003, and the consolidated results of its operations and its cash flows for each of the three years in the period ended December 31, 2004, in conformity with U.S. generally accepted accounting principles. Also, in our opinion, the related financial statement schedule and supplementary information, when considered in relation to the basic financial statements taken as a whole, present fairly in all material respects the information set forth therein.

As discussed in Note 1 to the accompanying consolidated financial statements, in 2004 and 2003 Time Warner changed its method of accounting for certain variable interest entities. Additionally in 2003, Time Warner changed its accounting for financial instruments with characteristics of both liabilities and equity and in 2002 Time Warner changed its method of accounting for goodwill and indefinite lived intangible assets.

As discussed in Note 1 to the accompanying consolidated financial statements, Time Warner has restated its financial statements for the years ended December 31, 2003 and 2002.

We also have audited, in accordance with the standards of the Public Company Accounting Oversight Board (United States), the effectiveness of Time Warner's internal control over financial reporting as of December 31, 2004, based on criteria established in Internal Control—Integrated Framework issued by the Committee of Sponsoring Organizations of the Treadway Commission and our report dated March 9, 2005 expressed an unqualified opinion thereon.

ERNST & YOUNG LLP

New York, New York
March 9, 2005

Accounting changes that affect consistency and may require modification of the report include (1) changes in accounting principles (from one GAAP method to another GAAP method); (2) changes in the form of the reporting entity; (3) changes from an accounting principle that is not GAAP to one that is GAAP; (4) changes in accounting principles inseparable from changes in estimates; and (5) changes in the presentation and definition of cash equivalents in the statement of cash flows. Changes in accounting estimates, corrections in errors not involving accounting principles, and changes in classification and reclassifications do not involve the consistency standard and these matters are not recognized in the report.

In Exhibit 12.10, Time Warner's auditors (Ernst & Young) identified accounting changes affecting consistency with respect to Time Warner's accounting for (1) variable interest entities, (2) financial instruments with characteristics of both liabilities and equity, and (3) goodwill and indefinite lived intangible assets. These changes are identified in the report through the addition of an explanatory paragraph following the opinion paragraph. Note that the opinion paragraph still expresses an *unqualified opinion* on Time Warner's financial statements.

When evaluating a change in accounting principle, auditors must be satisfied that management's justification for the change is reasonable and that it has accounted for the

change properly (i.e., restating prior-years' financial statements versus accounting for the change prospectively). For example, an entity's decision to change from accelerated depreciation to the straight-line method "to increase profits" could be preferable from management's viewpoint, but such a reason is not a reasonable justification for most auditors. If the auditors do not agree that a change is to a preferable accounting principle, an opinion qualification based on a departure from GAAP is appropriate. (The SEC requires auditors to submit a letter stating whether a change is to a preferable principle that provides a better measure of business operations.) In addition, if the change has not been accounted for properly, auditors should treat this as a departure from GAAP. In auditors' reports on financial statements in years following the change in accounting principle, an appropriate consistency reference must be included as long as the financial statements for the year of the change are included in the years presented.

Reporting on "Going-Concern" Uncertainties *(SAS 59)*

Generally accepted accounting principles are based on the *going-concern* principle, which means the entity is expected to continue in operation and meet its obligations as they become due without substantially disposing of its assets outside the ordinary course of business, restructuring its debt, significantly revising its operations based on external forces (e.g., a bank reorganization forced by the Federal Deposit Insurance Corporation), or similar actions. Hence, an opinion that financial statements are in conformity with GAAP means that continued existence may be presumed for a "reasonable time" not to exceed one year beyond the date of the financial statements. As noted in Chapter 11, one of the activities performed by auditors during the completion of the audit is assessing the entity's ability to continue as a going concern.

Situations in which questions are raised about the entity's ability to continue in operation and meet its obligations as they become due are known as **going-concern uncertainties.** Managers and auditors view news of financial troubles in the auditors' report (an attention-directing paragraph or a disclaimer based on going-concern uncertainty) as a *self-fulfilling prophecy* that causes bankruptcy because of the disclosure's effect on the actions of investors, suppliers, and creditors. However fallacious this view might be, it still prevails and sometimes inhibits auditors' appropriate consideration of going-concern questions. Auditors are responsible for determining any substantial doubt about an entity's ability to continue as a going concern. Careful auditors should not ignore signs of financial difficulty and operate entirely on the assumption that the entity will continue indefinitely. Financial difficulties, labor problems, loss of key personnel, litigation, and other such matters may

AUDITING INSIGHT The Watchdog That Didn't Bark

In a report filed with the U.S. Bankruptcy Court, a court-appointed examiner criticized **KPMG** for its failure to modify its auditors' report for going-concern uncertainties for **Polaroid** prior to the company's 2001 bankruptcy filing. An observer of the proceedings noted that while each decision KPMG made with respect to Polaroid's financial condition appeared to be justifiable in isolation, "when you step back, the impression of a company that was manipulating its accounting to satisfy its debt covenants was inescapable. What surprised me is how aware KPMG was of the issues and how it looked for flimsy fig leafs to justify Polaroid's decisions." For example, Polaroid reversed a $5.8 million restructuring charge to avoid violating its debt covenants.

In KPMG's defense, the decision to issue a report modified for going-concern uncertainties is a difficult one. In this case, KPMG relied heavily on an investment banker's oral assertion that there was a 90 percent plus chance that his bank would refinance Polaroid's troubled debt. Additionally, KPMG did ensure that Polaroid's financial difficulties were disclosed (albeit in the financial statement footnotes rather than in KPMG's report).

Source: "KPMG Defends Audit Work for Polaroid," *The Wall Street Journal,* August 25, 2003, p. B4.

be important signals of financial distress. Likewise, elements of financial flexibility (salability of assets, availability of lines of credit, debt extension, and dividend elimination) may be available as survival strategies. (In the auditing standards, these elements of financial flexibility and management strategy are known as **mitigating factors** that may reduce the financial difficulty problems.)

The most common report issued when going-concern uncertainties exist is an unqualified opinion with an explanatory paragraph following the opinion paragraph that directs users' attention to management's disclosures about going-concern uncertainties and specifically includes the words "substantial doubt" and "going concern." Auditing standards recommend this paragraph when the audit team concludes that the entity may not be able to continue in existence as a going concern (for example, see the paragraph included by PricewaterhouseCoopers in its report on Adelphia Communications Company in the introduction to this chapter). However, in practice, an entity in financial distress may present explanatory notes describing its financial problems and its auditors may decide that they are not serious enough to warrant modification of the report. For very severe going-concern uncertainties, auditors may issue a disclaimer of opinion, reflecting auditors' inability to value business assets at their liquidation (instead of historic cost) values if necessary.

AUDITING INSIGHT Research on Going-Concern Reports

An academic study reported in the *Journal of Accounting Research* found that negative media coverage (from *The Wall Street Journal* as well as other media outlets) of a company's potential bankruptcy increased the likelihood that auditors would issue reports modified for going-concern uncertainties. The author concluded that the greater scrutiny and awareness of these cases influenced auditors' reporting decisions, despite the fact that auditors' perceptions of the probability of bankruptcy were not influenced.

An analysis by Geiger et al. of 226 companies entering into bankruptcy between 2000 and 2003 revealed that auditors were more likely to issue reports modified for going-concern uncertainties after December 2001 (70 percent) than prior to December 2001 (40 percent). This tendency is attributed to legislative and media scrutiny resulting from the scandals at **Enron** and **WorldCom** as well as the regulation brought by the Sarbanes-Oxley Act of 2002.

Geiger and Rama found that the going-concern reporting decisions of Big Four firms were more accurate regarding the company's ability to continue in existence compared to the decisions of non–Big Four firms. In other words, for companies that ultimately experienced bankruptcy, Big Four firms were more likely to issue going-concern modifications prior to that bankruptcy than non–Big Four firms. Geiger and Rama attribute these differences to higher-quality reporting decisions made by the largest international accounting firms.

Sources: J. Joe, "Why Press Coverage of a Client Influences the Audit Opinion," *Journal of Accounting Research*, March 2003, pp. 109–33; M. A. Geiger, K. Raghunandan, and D. V. Rama, "Recent Changes in the Association between Bankruptcies and Prior Audit Opinions," *Auditing: A Journal of Practice & Theory*, May 2005, pp. 21–35; and M. A. Geiger and D. V. Rama, "Audit Firm Size and Going-Concern Reporting Accuracy," *Accounting Horizons*, March 2006, pp. 1–17.

Justified Departures from GAAP

Although an *unqualified opinion* is normally issued only when the entity's financial statements are presented in conformity with GAAP, Rule 203 of the AICPA Code of Professional Conduct provides for the possibility (although remote) that adherence to GAAP might create misleading financial statements:

> *Rule 203.* A member [auditor] shall not (1) express an opinion or state affirmatively that financial statements or other financial data of an entity are presented in conformity with generally accepted accounting principles or (2) state that he or she is not aware of any material modifications that should be made to such statements or data in order for them to be in conformity with generally accepted accounting principles, if such statements or data contain any departure from an accounting principle promulgated by bodies designated by Council to establish such principles that has a material effect on the statements taken as a whole. *If, however, the statements or data contain such a departure and the member can*

demonstrate that due to unusual circumstances the financial statements or data would otherwise have been misleading, the member can comply with the rule by describing the departure, its approximate effects, if practicable, and the reasons why compliance with the principle would result in a misleading statement. [emphasis added]

Earlier, we discussed auditors' reports when departures from GAAP exist. However, in some highly unusual circumstances, the use of GAAP may result in misleading financial statements. These situations are sometimes referred to as **justified departures from GAAP.** Rule 203 has the effect of allowing financial statements to contain a departure from a Financial Accounting Standards Board (FASB) or Governmental Accounting Standards Board (GASB) (or their predecessors') accounting standard, permitting the auditors to explain why the departure was necessary and then allowing the departure to be "in conformity with generally accepted accounting principles" as indicated by the unqualified opinion. An example of such a report that refers to a FASB statement is presented in Exhibit 12.11; current auditing standards permit the explanatory paragraph to be placed either prior to or following the opinion paragraph. Notice that the standard opinion paragraph would be used in this report, indicating an unqualified opinion.

EXHIBIT 12.11
Report Conforming to Rule 203

Report of Independent Registered Public Accounting Firm

To the Board of Directors and Shareholders of Apollo Shoes, Inc.

[Standard Introductory Paragraph]

[Standard Scope Paragraph]

As described in Note 3, in May 2008, Apollo Shoes, Inc., exchanged shares of its common stock for $5,060,000 of its outstanding public debt. The fair value of the common stock issued exceeded the carrying amount of the debt by $466,000, which has been shown as an extraordinary loss in the 2008 income statement. Because a portion of the debt exchanged was convertible debt, a literal application of Statement of Financial Accounting Standards No. 84, "Induced Conversions of Convertible Debt," would have resulted in a further reduction in net income of $3,611,000, which would have been offset by a corresponding $3,611,000 increase in additional paid-in capital; accordingly, there would have been no net effect on shareholders' equity. In the opinion of Apollo Shoes, Inc.'s management, with which we agree, a literal application of accounting standards would have resulted in misleading financial statements that do not properly portray the economic consequences of the exchange.

[Standard Opinion Paragraph]

[Standard Internal Control Paragraph]

Smith & Smith, CPAs
Shoetown, Maine
January 29, 2009

Division of Responsibility

In some cases, **principal auditors** perform the audit of a material portion of an entity's assets, liabilities, revenues, and expenses while other independent auditors may be engaged to audit subsidiaries, divisions, branches, components, or investments that are included in the entity's financial statements. Situations such as this are not common for the largest public accounting firms (which have offices located throughout the world) but may occur if clients have significant remote subsidiaries or if clients have an investment in another entity that is accounted for using the equity method. Because the principal auditors' signature appears in the report on the financial statements of a consolidated or parent entity, the principal auditors must make decisions regarding the use of the work and reports of

the other independent auditor(s). It is important to note that these situations involve one or more other auditors concurrently examining elements of the financial statements for the current year and not situations in which other auditors examined one or more prior-years' financial statements *(predecessor auditors)* and newly engaged auditors examine the current-year financial statements *(successor auditors)*.

The principal auditors must first obtain information about the independence and professional reputation of the other auditors. If the principal auditors are satisfied with these qualities, they must next communicate with the other auditors and decide whether to refer to the other auditors in the principal auditors' report. The principal auditors may decide to make no reference and the principal auditors' report will follow the form and wording of the standard report. In this case, the principal auditors take full responsibility for the other auditors' work.

On the other hand, the principal auditors may decide to refer to the work and reports of the other auditors; this is referred to as a **division of responsibility.** Such a reference is not in itself a scope limitation and the report should not be considered to be inferior to a standard report that does not contain such a reference. The explanation should show very clearly the extent of the *division of responsibility* by disclosing the percent or amount of assets, revenues, and expenses covered by other auditors' work. However, the opinion paragraph must be consistent with the sufficiency and appropriateness of evidence gathered by all auditors. If other auditors have rendered opinions that are qualified in some way, the principal auditors must consider the circumstances when deciding whether to qualify, modify, or expand the report on the consolidated financial statements.

When the principal auditors refer to the other auditors' work, the other auditors are ordinarily not identified by name. In fact, the other auditors may be named in the principal auditors' report only by express permission and with publication of their report along with the principal auditors' report. The options available to principal auditors for reporting a division of responsibility are summarized in Exhibit 12.12.

EXHIBIT 12.12
Reporting Options for Division of Responsibility

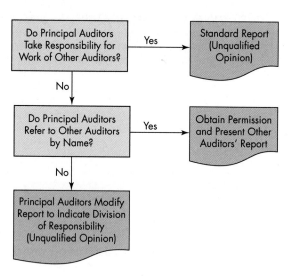

Exhibit 12.13 provides an example of a principal auditors' report that has been modified to express an unqualified opinion on financial statements while indicating a division of responsibility. Note from this report that the principal auditors do not identify the "other auditors" by name.

EXHIBIT 12.13
Report Modified for Division of Responsibility

Report of Independent Registered Public Accounting Firm

To the Board of Directors and Shareholders, Apollo Shoes, Inc.

We have audited the accompanying consolidated balance sheets of Apollo Shoes, Inc., and subsidiaries as of December 31, 2008 and 2007, and the related consolidated statements of income, comprehensive income, shareholders' equity, and cash flows for each of the years in the three-year period ended December 31, 2008. These financial statements are the responsibility of Apollo Shoes, Inc.'s management. Our responsibility is to express an opinion on these financial statements based on our audits. *We did not audit the financial statements of American Reserve Company, a consolidated subsidiary, which statements reflect total assets constituting 35 percent in 2008 and 36 percent in 2007, and total revenues constituting 13 percent in 2008, 14 percent in 2007, and 17 percent in 2006 of the related consolidated totals. Those statements were audited by other auditors whose reports have been furnished to us, and our opinion, insofar as it relates to the amounts included for American Reserve Company, is based solely on the reports of the other auditors.*

We conducted our audits in accordance with the standards of the Public Company Accounting Oversight Board (United States). Those standards require that we plan and perform the audit to obtain reasonable assurance about whether the financial statements are free of material misstatement. An audit includes examining, on a test basis, evidence supporting the amounts and disclosures in the financial statements. An audit also includes assessing the accounting principles used and significant estimates made by management, as well as evaluating the overall financial statement presentation. We believe that our audits *and the reports of other auditors* provide a reasonable basis for our opinion.

In our opinion, *based on our audits and the reports of other auditors,* the financial statements referred to above present fairly, in all material respects, the consolidated financial position of Apollo Shoes, Inc., and subsidiaries at December 31, 2008 and 2007, and the consolidated results of operations and their cash flows for each of the years in the three-year period ended December 31, 2008, in conformity with accounting principles generally accepted in the United States of America.

[Standard Internal Control Paragraph]

Smith & Smith, CPAs
Shoetown, Maine
January 29, 2009

AUDITING INSIGHT How Many Auditors?

In its March 31, 1999, 10-K, **BMC Software** (a systems software developer headquartered in Houston, Texas) had the reports of three different CPA firms presented along with its financial statements: (1) **Arthur Andersen,** the principal auditor, which reported on BMC Software's consolidated financial statements for the three-year period ended March 31, 1999; (2) **Ernst & Young,** which reported on **Boole & Babbage's** financial statements for the three-year period ended September 30, 1998; and (3) **PricewaterhouseCoopers,** which reported on **MAXM Systems'** financial statements for the year ended September 30, 1996. Why so many reports? Boole & Babbage acquired MAXM Systems in 1997; Boole & Babbage was, in turn, acquired by BMC Software during 1999. Because BMC Software's consolidated financial statements included the financial position, results of operations, and cash flows for each of these entities, the division of responsibility was necessary. In 2001, Arthur Andersen's report no longer referred to this division of responsibility since all three years (and the related components) had been examined by Andersen.

Emphasis Paragraph

Beyond the wording contained in the standard report, auditors have one avenue for enriching the information content in auditors' reports. They can add one or more paragraphs to emphasize something they believe readers should consider important or useful. In the auditing standards, this type of addition to the report is known as the **emphasis of a matter**

paragraph. An emphasis paragraph can be added when the auditors intend to express an unqualified opinion. Indeed, the matter emphasized is not supposed to be mentioned in the opinion paragraph because the financial statements as presented may be in conformity with GAAP and there were not any issues in the conduct of the audit engagement.

Although auditing standards place no official limits on the content of an emphasis paragraph, auditors often use these paragraphs to describe circumstances that present some business or information risk. Matters that may be emphasized include a warning that a bankruptcy filing may be imminent, a description of the auditee as a subsidiary of a larger entity, the effects of business events on the comparability of financial statements, the interaction of the auditee with related parties, and the effect of events that occur after the balance sheet date (commonly referred to as *subsequent events*). In Exhibit 12.10, **Time Warner's** auditors (**Ernst & Young**) added an explanatory paragraph following the opinion paragraph to emphasize the fact that Time Warner's comparative financial statements have been restated.

Review Checkpoints

12.13 What circumstances cause auditors to recognize inconsistent applications of GAAP in their report?

12.14 What circumstances lead auditors to have substantial doubt about an entity's ability to continue as a going concern?

12.15 What are auditors' reporting options when going-concern uncertainties are noted?

12.16 What is the purpose of the Code of Professional Conduct Rule 203 and how does the rule affect audit reporting?

12.17 What options are available to principal auditors when other auditors are involved in the examination of a subsidiary or division?

12.18 Is the reference in the auditors' report to work performed by other auditors a scope limitation? Explain.

12.19 List some circumstances, events, or transactions that auditors may want to emphasize to financial statement users in an emphasis of a matter paragraph.

OTHER REPORTING TOPICS

LEARNING OBJECTIVE

7. Identify other circumstances affecting auditors' reporting responsibilities and explain how they affect auditors' reports on an entity's financial statements.

A great deal of financial information is distributed publicly in annual reports, SEC filings, and other documents containing audited financial statements. The entity president's letter to shareholders, management's discussion and analysis of results of operations, interim financial statements, and supplemental schedules all contain financial information that is not mentioned explicitly in the auditors' report. Auditors have professional responsibilities, however, with regard to much of this information. When this other information is inaccurate, inconsistent, or unusual, auditors should expand their reports. In this section, we discuss this topic and several other reporting topics that are somewhat outside the mainstream of the basic auditors' report modification topics covered to this point in this chapter.

Association with Financial Statements

In some cases, auditors may consent to the use of their name in some form of communication containing the entity's financial statements. In other situations, the auditors may submit to their clients or others (such as third-party users) financial statements they have

EXHIBIT 12.14
Disclaimer of Opinion on Unaudited Financial Statements

> The accompanying balance sheet of Apollo Shoes, Inc., as of December 31, 2008, and the related statements of income, comprehensive income, shareholders' equity, and cash flows for the year then ended were not audited by us and, accordingly, we do not express an opinion on them.
>
> *Smith & Smith, CPAs*
> Shoetown, Maine
> January 29, 2009

prepared or assisted in preparing. These situations are referred to as being **associated with financial statements.** In these cases, we refer to the financial statements of public entities subject to audit requirements and not the financial statements of nonpublic entities, whose financial statements may either be compiled or reviewed by independent accounts. These engagements for nonpublic entities are discussed further in Module A.

In cases where auditors are associated with the financial statements of a public entity, they must specifically disclaim an opinion, as shown in Exhibit 12.14 above.

As with disclaimers when the auditors were not independent (see Exhibit 12.9), this report is not titled or addressed to specific users because the auditors were not engaged to conduct an audit. In addition, similar to disclaimers for a lack of independence, the following additional guidelines should be observed:

1. The report should not mention any auditing procedures applied because readers might erroneously conclude that they were sufficient to enable an opinion to be expressed on the financial statements.
2. If the auditors should learn that the financial statements are not in conformity with generally accepted accounting principles (including adequate disclosures), the departures should be explained in the disclaimer.
3. If prior-years' unaudited financial statements are presented, the disclaimer should cover them as well as the current-year statements.
4. Each page of the financial statements should be labeled clearly as being "unaudited."

Reporting on Comparative Statements

The SEC requires public entities to present comparative balance sheets for two years and comparative statements of income, comprehensive income, shareholders' equity, and cash flows for three years. Financial statement footnotes contain disclosures in comparative form for two or three years. Together, these comparative financial statements and footnotes are the "financial statements as a whole" mentioned in the fourth standard of reporting of GAAS.

When auditors issue a report on the current-year financial statements, they are required to update the report previously issued on the prior-years' financial statements. For example, for Exhibit 12.2, Apollo Shoes' auditors previously issued reports (not shown in the exhibit) on the 2007 and 2006 financial statements. As shown in Exhibit 12.2, after the most recent audit, their report dated January 29, 2009, covers the 2008 and 2007 financial statements (for all financial statements) and 2006 financial statements (for the statements of income, comprehensive income, shareholders' equity, and cash flows). The **updated report** on the 2007 and 2006 financial statements is based not only on the prior-year audits but also on information that has come to light since then (particularly in the course of the most recent audit). An updated report may express the same opinion as that originally expressed, or it may express a different opinion if current information causes a change in the auditors' reporting decision. An updated report carries the most recent audit completion date and the auditors' responsibility for the comparative financial statements now extends to the most recent date.

An updated report differs from a **reissued report.** When auditors reissue a report, they simply provide additional copies of a previously issued report or grant permission to use a previously issued report in another document sometime after its original delivery date. However, auditors do not attempt to update the report or otherwise consider events that have occurred since the date of the original report. The report date of a reissued report is the audit completion date for that year's audit, indicating a cutoff date for the auditors' responsibility.

AUDITING INSIGHT Audit Them? No, You Audit Them

In the wake of the Enron debacle, **PricewaterhouseCoopers** (PwC) required one of its clients, **Amerco** (the holding company for **U-Haul International**), to restate its prior-year financial statements to consolidate a number of special purpose entities (SPEs). Unfortunately for PwC, prior to the consolidation, **Ernst & Young** had audited the unconsolidated SPEs. Because the SPEs were to be consolidated into Amerco's financial statements, PwC simply needed to obtain permission from Ernst & Young to allow its report to be included in Amerco's 10-K report to the Securities and Exchange Commission. However, because of a misunderstanding between Ernst & Young and PwC, Ernst & Young declined. Consequently, PwC was forced to reperform auditing procedures related to the (already-audited) SPEs prior to issuing an opinion on Amerco's consolidated financial statements, thereby delaying the submission of Amerco's 10-K to the SEC.

Source: "PricewaterhouseCooper's Goof Is Now U-Haul's Big Problem," *Fortune*, June 23, 2003, pp. 110–11.

The situation in Exhibit 12.2 is a common one in which the same auditors audited the comparative-years' financial statements. If the entity has changed auditors, the introductory paragraph would have identified only the current financial statements examined by the new (successor) auditors. If Smith & Smith were engaged by Apollo Shoes for the 2008 audit, a sentence would be added to the introductory paragraph providing facts about the former (predecessor) auditors' report: "The financial statements of Apollo Shoes, Inc. as of December 31, 2007 and 2006, were audited by other auditors whose report dated February 4, 2008, expressed an unqualified opinion on those statements." The opinion paragraph would cite only the current-year financial statements audited by Smith & Smith (the successor auditors). For example, in 2005, **Best Buy** (an electronics retailer headquartered in Richfield, Minnesota), switched auditors from **Ernst & Young** to **Deloitte & Touche** because of a compensated personal services agreement between one of Best Buy's directors and Ernst & Young. Deloitte & Touche's report expresses an opinion on Best Buy's 2006 financial statements and the introductory paragraph identifies that "other auditors" (Ernst & Young) examined the 2005 and 2004 financial statements and expressed an unqualified opinion on those financial statements.

Auditors can express different opinions on comparative-years' financial statements in the same report. Exhibit 12.6 shows the situation in which the prior-year financial statements were considered materially misstated, but the most recent balance sheet was presented in conformity with GAAP. You can see that the opinion on the misstated financial statements is an adverse opinion and the opinion on the most recent balance sheet is an unqualified opinion.

Auditors also can change the opinion expressed on prior-years' financial statements if circumstances have changed in the intervening period. The auditors must have good reasons for such a change, which must be explained in the report. For example, consider the adverse opinion issued in Exhibit 12.6. Suppose that Apollo Shoes had originally failed to record the additional $30 million provision for uncollectible receivables in the 2007 financial statements and Smith & Smith issued an adverse opinion in that year. Assume that, in 2008, Apollo Shoes restated its 2007 financial statements, recording the additional provision in the proper period. The report on the 2008 and 2007 comparative financial statements should contain the explanation shown in Exhibit 12.15.

EXHIBIT 12.15
Comparative Financial Statement Opinion Changed from Adverse to Unqualified

Report of Independent Registered Public Accounting Firm

To the Board of Directors and Shareholders, Apollo Shoes, Inc.:

[Standard Introductory Paragraph]

[Standard Scope Paragraph]

In our report dated January 30, 2008, we expressed an opinion that the balance sheet as of December 31, 2007, and the statements of income, comprehensive income, shareholders' equity, and cash flows for the year then ended did not fairly present financial position, results of operations, and cash flows in conformity with accounting principles generally accepted in the United States of America because Apollo Shoes, Inc., did not record an additional $30,000,000 provision for uncollectible receivables as of December 31, 2007. As described in Note 2 in these financial statements, Apollo Shoes, Inc., has restated its 2007 financial statements to record the provision in conformity with accounting principles generally accepted in the United States of America. Accordingly, our present opinion on the 2007 financial statements, as presented herein, is different from the opinion we expressed in our previous report.

In our opinion, the financial statements referred to above present fairly, in all material respects, the financial position of Apollo Shoes, Inc., as of December 31, 2008 and 2007, and the results of its operations and its cash flows for each of the years in the two-year period ended December 31, 2008 in conformity with accounting principles generally accepted in the United States of America.

[Standard Internal Control Paragraph]

Smith & Smith, CPAs
Shoetown, Maine
January 29, 2009

Reporting on Condensed Financial Statements

Published financial statements are lengthy and often complex. Entities sometimes have occasion to present the financial statements in considerably less detail (for example, summary totals of current assets, current liabilities, long-term liabilities, operating income, etc.). Generally, such condensed financial statements are derived directly from the full audited financial statements. However, condensed financial statements are not a fair presentation of financial position, results of operations, and cash flows in conformity with GAAP. Auditors who report on such statements cannot issue the standard report (and an unqualified opinion) even if an unqualified opinion was issued on the full financial statements.

Auditors may issue a report on condensed financial statements derived from full financial statements that have been audited. The report must refer to the auditors' report on the full financial statements, giving the date and the type of opinion, and state whether the information in the condensed financial statements is fairly stated in all material respects in relation to the complete financial statements. An example is shown in Exhibit 12.16.

In addition to a separate report, reporting on condensed information may be done within the auditors' report on the entity's financial statements. For example, referring to Exhibit 12.10, Ernst & Young identifies Financial Statement Schedule II and Supplementary Information in the introductory paragraph and the opinion paragraph. Note that the conclusion with respect to this other information is that it is fairly stated in relation to the financial statements "taken as a whole."

Other Information Accompanying Audited Financial Statements *(SAS 8)*

All annual reports to shareholders and SEC filings contain such sections as a president's letter and management's discussion and analysis (MD&A) of operations. These sections are separate from the audited financial statements and are not covered by the auditors'

EXHIBIT 12.16
Report on Condensed Financial Statements Derived from Audited Financial Statements

Report of Independent Registered Public Accounting Firm

To the Board of Directors and Shareholders, Apollo Shoes, Inc.:

We have audited, in accordance with the standards of the Public Company Accounting Oversight Board (United States), the balance sheet of Apollo Shoes as of December 31, 2008 and 2007, and the related statements of income, comprehensive income, shareholders' equity, and cash flows for each of the years in the three-year period ended December 31, 2008; and in our report dated January 29, 2009, we expressed an unqualified opinion on those financial statements.

In our opinion, the information set forth in the accompanying condensed financial statements is fairly stated, in all material respects, in relation to the financial statements from which it has been derived.

Smith & Smith, CPAs
August 21, 2009

opinion. Nevertheless, auditors have an obligation to read (study) the other information and determine whether it is consistent with the audited financial statements. However, auditors are not obligated to review press releases, analysts' interviews, or other forms of irregular financial news releases unless specifically engaged by the entity. In addition, an entity's financial statements and other information placed on a Web site are not considered "documents," and, consequently, auditors are not required to review them for inconsistencies or material misstatements. This interpretation is likely to change as publication of financial statements on corporate Web sites becomes more commonplace.

Other information is subject to "exception-based" reporting (that is, auditors' reports will only mention the other information if inconsistencies or misstatements exist). For example, consider the following remark from a president's letter: "Earnings increased from $1 million to $2 million, an increase of 50 cents per share." This statement can be corroborated by comparison to the audited financial statements. The president's comment would be considered inconsistent if the $1 million was income before an extraordinary loss and the $2 million was income after an extraordinary gain, or if the 50 cent change in earnings per share (EPS) was the difference between last year's fully diluted EPS and this year's primary EPS. The president could have selected numbers without due regard to their meaningful comparison.

If misstatements or inconsistencies exist with respect to other information accompanying audited financial statements and the client chooses not to revise the other information, the auditors should (1) notify the client in writing of the auditors' views, (2) consult with legal counsel about appropriate action to take, and (3) consider whether this inconsistency affects the opinion on the financial statements. If so, the auditors should revise their opinion on the financial statements; if not, the auditors should expand their report to add an explanatory paragraph (similar to an *emphasis of a matter* paragraph). It is important to note that, in this latter case, auditors may still conclude that the financial statements are presented in conformity with GAAP but are emphasizing that the other information accompanying the audited financial statements is not consistent with the financial statements.

Quarterly and Supplemental Information

As part of an audit engagement, auditors typically review an entity's quarterly financial statements. Accounting principles, however, do not require that such interim (quarterly) financial information be disclosed as a basic and necessary element of financial statements conforming to GAAP. The SEC, on the other hand, does require the presentation of interim information as supplemental information outside the basic financial statements. Thus, interim information is voluntary insofar as the FASB is concerned but is required insofar as the SEC is concerned. However, the FASB may require supplemental information to be presented outside the basic financial statements. Oil, gas, and other mineral reserve information are currently required to be presented as supplemental information.

Problems with supplemental information arise when (1) required information is omitted, (2) the information departs materially from GAAP, (3) the auditors cannot perform necessary procedures to evaluate the information, (4) management's presentation of the information indicates the auditors performed review procedures without also indicating the auditors do not express an opinion on it, or (5) management places the information close to, or within, the basic financial statements (e.g., in a financial statement footnote) and does not label it unaudited. When these problems arise, auditors should expand their report on the entity's financial statements or disclaim an opinion on the supplemental information.

Review Checkpoints

12.20 What is meant when auditors are "associated with" a public entity's financial statements? In connection with unaudited statements, which general reporting guides should the auditors follow for public entities?

12.21 What is an updated report? What is a reissued report?

12.22 What two types of disclosure problems must auditors be alert to detect when reading "other information" in an annual report?

12.23 Why do you think auditors are prohibited from issuing a standard report on condensed financial statements?

12.24 What issues may arise with respect to supplemental information required by the SEC? How does the auditors' report address these issues?

Summary

This chapter has discussed a wide range of reporting issues. While the array and variety of reports may seem confusing, a couple of simple rules will enable you to remember the basics of auditors' reports on financial statements. First, begin with the standard report shown in Exhibit 12.2. Keeping the four paragraphs in mind, the following basic rules apply (modifications to the *internal control paragraph* were previously discussed in Chapter 5):

- The *introductory paragraph* is modified when the financial statements examined or responsibility assumed by auditors changes (for example, in a limited reporting engagement to audit the balance sheet, for a division of responsibility, or for a pervasive scope limitation).

- The *scope paragraph* is modified when the scope of the audit is not in accordance with PCAOB standards (most notably, when a scope limitation exists).

- The *opinion paragraph* is modified when an opinion other than an unqualified opinion is issued.

- An *explanatory paragraph* is added to the report when an opinion other than an unqualified opinion is issued or when some other matter arises. A general rule for the placement of the explanatory paragraph is that, if an unqualified opinion is issued, the explanatory paragraph follows the opinion paragraph; if an opinion other than unqualified is issued, the explanatory paragraph precedes the opinion paragraph.

Like all general guidelines, exceptions to the above rules can be found. For example, when a division of responsibility is encountered, an explanatory paragraph *would not* be added, which contradicts the general rule related to explanatory paragraphs (however, the introductory, scope, and opinion paragraphs are modified in this situation!). Exhibit 12.17 provides a comprehensive summary of auditors' reports discussed in this chapter. In reviewing Exhibit 12.17, it is important to note that if any of the issues does not have a material effect on the financial statements, auditors can issue the standard report without any reference to the issue (except for a lack of independence, which can never be immaterial).

EXHIBIT 12.17 Summary of Reporting Issues

	Significance of the Matter		Paragraphs Modified				Other Comments
	Material	Pervasive	Introductory	Scope	Opinion	Explanatory	
Departure from GAAP	Qualified opinion	Adverse opinion			X	X	
Scope limitation	Qualified opinion	Disclaimer of opinion		X	X	X	• Can issue standard report if alternative procedures are available and performed • Should consider disclaimer if client-imposed limitation
Lack of independence	Disclaimer of opinion	Disclaimer of opinion					Would issue single-paragraph disclaimer of opinion
Consistency	Unqualified opinion	Unqualified opinion				X	
Going-concern	Unqualified opinion	Disclaimer of opinion			X	X	Opinion paragraph only modified if disclaimer is issued
Justified departure from GAAP	Unqualified opinion	Unqualified opinion				X	Explanatory paragraph can be placed before or following opinion paragraph
Division of responsibility	Unqualified opinion	Unqualified opinion	X	X	X		Can issue standard report if assume responsibility for other auditors' work
Emphasis of a matter	Unqualified opinion	Unqualified opinion				X	
Association with unaudited financial statements	Disclaimer of opinion	Disclaimer of opinion					Would issue single-paragraph disclaimer of opinion

Key Terms

adverse opinion: Issued when the auditors conclude that the financial statements do not present the financial condition, results of operations, or cash flows in conformity with GAAP, 461

association with financial statements: Cases when auditors consent to the use of their name in some form of communication containing the entity's financial statements or submit to their clients or others (such as third-party users) financial statements they have prepared or assisted in preparing. Auditors should issue a one-paragraph disclaimer when they are associated with (but did not audit or review) financial statements, 479

audit completion date: The date on which auditors have obtained sufficient appropriate evidence to support the opinion; this is the date that should be used in the auditors' report, 460

auditee: The company or other entity whose financial statements are being audited, 460

circumstance-imposed scope limitation: Situation in which auditors cannot gather sufficient appropriate evidence because of circumstances beyond the auditors' and client's control such as late appointment of the auditors, 467

client: The person (entity, board of directors, agency, or some other person or group) who retains the auditors and pays the fee, 460

client-imposed scope limitation: Situation in which auditors cannot gather sufficient appropriate evidence because of the client's deliberate refusal to provide access to documents or otherwise limit the auditors' application of auditing procedures, 467

departure from GAAP: Situation in which an entity does not follow GAAP in preparing its financial statements. Auditors can issue qualified or adverse opinions if departures from GAAP have a material effect on the entity's financial statements, 475

disclaimer of opinion: Issued when auditors do not express an opinion on the fairness of the entity's financial statements. Disclaimers of opinion are issued for pervasive going-concern uncertainties, pervasive scope limitations, and situations in which the auditors are not independent, 461

division of responsibility: Situation in which the other auditors are involved with the examination of a subsidiary, branch, component, or investment that is included in the financial statements audited by principal auditors, 476

emphasis of a matter: One or more paragraphs auditors can add to a report to emphasize something they believe readers should consider important and useful, 477

going-concern uncertainties: Situations in which questions are raised about the entity's ability to continue in operation and meet its obligations as they become due without substantially disposing of its assets outside the ordinary course of business, restructuring its debt, significantly revising its operations based on external forces, or similar actions, 473

integrated report: A single report issued by auditors that expresses the auditors' opinion on the fairness of the financial statements and effectiveness of internal control over financial reporting, 462

internal control paragraph: Paragraph in the auditors' report that refers to the auditors' report on the effectiveness of the entity's internal control over financial reporting, 459

introductory paragraph: Paragraph in the auditors' report that identifies the financial statements examined by the auditors and the responsibility of auditors and management with respect to the financial statements, 459

justified departures from GAAP: Situations in which an entity does not follow GAAP in preparing its financial statements because the use of GAAP would result in materially misleading financial statements. If auditors agree with the departure, an unqualified opinion is issued, 475

mitigating factors: Elements of financial flexibility (salability of assets, lines of credit, debt extensions, dividend elimination) available as survival strategies in circumstances of going-concern uncertainty that may reduce financial difficulty problems, 474

opinion paragraph: Paragraph in the auditors' report that expresses an opinion on whether the financial statements are presented in conformity with GAAP, 459

principal auditors: Auditors who examine the majority of the assets, liabilities, revenues, and expenses included in an entity's financial statements and whose signature appears in the auditors' opinion on that entity's financial statements, 475

qualified opinion: Issued when the auditors conclude that, with the exception of one or more issue(s), the financial statements present the financial condition, results of operations, and cash flows in conformity with GAAP. Qualified opinions can be issued for material departures from GAAP and material scope limitations, 461

reissued report: A copy of a previously-issued report that auditors provide or grant permission to use in another document after its delivery date; the report is not modified to consider events occurring subsequent to the date of the original report, 480

report on financial statements and related disclosures: A report prepared by the auditors that expresses an opinion on whether the entity's financial statements and disclosures are prepared and presented in conformity with GAAP, 457

report on internal control over financial reporting (prepared by auditors): Report that expresses an opinion on the effectiveness of the entity's internal control over financial reporting, 457

report on internal control over financial reporting (prepared by management): Report that describes the process through which management assesses its internal control over financial reporting and that provides management's conclusion with respect to the effectiveness of its internal control over financial reporting, 457

scope limitation: A condition in which the auditors are unable to obtain sufficient appropriate evidence. If material, a scope limitation results in the issuance of either a qualified opinion or disclaimer of opinion, 467

scope paragraph: Paragraph in the auditors' report that indicates the engagement was performed in accordance with the standards of the PCAOB and provides a general description of an audit, 459

unqualified opinion: Issued when the auditors conclude that the financial statements present the financial condition, results of operations, and cash flows in conformity with GAAP, 461

updated report: Auditors' report on prior-year financial statements that is based on both the prior-year audit and information that has come to light in the most recent audit, 479

Multiple Choice Questions for Practice and Review

12.25　Some of the GAAS standards of reporting require certain statements in all auditors' reports ("explicit") and others require statements only under certain conditions ("implicit"). Which combination that follows correctly describes these features of the standards of reporting?

Standards	(a)	(b)	(c)	(d)
1. GAAP	Explicit	Explicit	Implicit	Implicit
2. Consistency	Implicit	Explicit	Explicit	Implicit
3. Disclosure	Implicit	Implicit	Explicit	Explicit
4. Opinion	Explicit	Explicit	Implicit	Implicit

12.26　Auditors found that the entity has not capitalized a material amount of leases in the financial statements. When considering the materiality of this departure from GAAP, the auditors would choose between which reporting options?

　　a.　Unqualified opinion or disclaimer of opinion.

　　b.　Unqualified opinion or qualified opinion.

　　c.　Unqualified opinion with emphasis paragraph or an adverse opinion.

　　d.　Qualified opinion or adverse opinion.

12.27　The auditors determined that the entity is suffering financial difficulty and the going-concern status is seriously in doubt. Assuming the entity adequately disclosed this matter in the financial statements, the auditors must choose between which of the following auditors' report alternatives?

　　a.　Unqualified opinion with a going-concern explanatory paragraph or disclaimer of opinion.

　　b.　Standard report or a disclaimer of opinion.

　　c.　Qualified opinion or adverse opinion.

　　d.　Standard report or adverse opinion.

12.28　An entity accomplished an early extinguishment of debt and the auditors believe that literal application of *SFAS No. 98* would cause recognition of a loss that would materially distort the financial statements and cause them to be misleading. Given these facts, the auditors would probably choose which reporting option?

　　a.　Explain the situation and issue an adverse opinion.

　　b.　Explain the situation and issue a disclaimer of opinion.

　　c.　Explain the situation and issue an unqualified opinion, relying on Rule 203 of the AICPA Code of Professional Conduct.

　　d.　Issue the standard report.

12.29 Which of these situations would require auditors to append an explanatory paragraph about consistency to an otherwise unqualified opinion?

 a. Entity changed its estimated allowance for uncollectible accounts receivable.

 b. Entity corrected a prior mistake in accounting for interest capitalization.

 c. Entity sold one of its subsidiaries and consolidated six subsidiaries this year compared to seven last year.

 d. Entity changed its inventory costing method from FIFO to LIFO.

12.30 Wolfe became the new auditor for Royal Corporation, succeeding Mason, who audited the financial statements last year. Wolfe needs to report on Royal's comparative financial statements and should disclose in his report an explanation about other auditors having audited the prior year

 a. Only if Mason's opinion last year was qualified.

 b. Describing the prior audit and the opinion but not naming Mason as the predecessor auditor.

 c. Describing the audit but not revealing the type of opinion Mason gave.

 d. Describing the audit and the opinion and naming Mason as the predecessor auditor.

12.31 When other independent auditors are involved in the current audit of parts of the entity's business, the principal auditors may issue a report that (two answers)

 a. Mentions the other auditors, describes the extent of the other auditors' work, and expresses an unqualified opinion.

 b. Does not mention the other auditors and expresses an unqualified opinion in a standard report.

 c. Places primary responsibility for the reporting on the other auditors.

 d. Names the other auditors, describes their work, and presents only the principal auditors' report.

12.32 An "emphasis-of-a-matter" paragraph inserted in a standard report causes the report to be characterized as a(n)

 a. Unqualified opinion.

 b. Division of responsibility.

 c. Adverse opinion.

 d. Disclaimer of opinion.

12.33 Under which of the following conditions can a disclaimer of opinion *never* be issued?

 a. Going-concern problems are highly material and significant.

 b. The entity does not allow the auditors to have access to evidence about important accounts.

 c. The auditors own stock in the entity.

 d. The auditors have determined that the entity uses the NIFO (next-in, first-out) inventory costing method.

12.34 How is the auditors' own responsibility for expressing the opinion on financial statements disclosed in the report?

 a. Stated explicitly in the introductory paragraph of the standard report.

 b. Unstated but understood in the introductory paragraph of the standard report.

 c. Stated explicitly in the opinion paragraph of the standard report.

 d. Stated explicitly in the scope paragraph of the standard report.

12.35 Company A hired Samson & Delilah, CPAs, to audit the financial statements of Company B and deliver the report to Megabank. Who is the client?

 a. Megabank.

 b. Samson & Delilah.

 c. Company A.

 d. Company B.

12.36 Which of the following is *not* included in the standard report on the financial statements?

a. An identification of the financial statements that were audited.

b. A general description of an audit.

c. An opinion that the financial statements present financial position in conformity with GAAP.

d. An emphasis paragraph commenting on the effect of economic conditions on the entity.

12.37 If the auditors decide to present separate reports on the entity's financial statements and internal control over financial reporting, which of the following reports should be modified to reference the other report?

	Report on Financial Statements	Report on Internal Control over Financial Reporting
a.	Yes	Yes
b.	Yes	No
c.	No	Yes
d.	No	No

Exercises, Problems, and Simulations

12.38 **Audit Simulation: Reports on Financial Statements (Deficiencies and Omissions in the Auditors' Report).** On September 23, 2009, at the audit completion date, Betsy Ross drafted the following report on Continental Corporation's financial statements to the directors of Continental Corporation. Continental Corporation's stock is publicly traded and, accordingly, Continental is subject to the reporting requirements of *AS 5*. Ross has decided to present separate reports on Continental's financial statements and internal control over financial reporting.

To Whom It May Concern:

The accompanying balance sheet of Continental Corporation and the related statements of income, comprehensive income, and shareholders' equity as of July 31, 2009, are the responsibility of management.

In accordance with your instructions, we have conducted a complete audit. We planned and performed the audit to obtain reasonable assurance about whether the financial statements are free of material misstatement. An audit includes examining, on a test basis, evidence supporting the amounts and disclosures in the financial statements. An audit also includes assessing the accounting principles used and significant estimates made by management, as well as evaluating the overall financial statement presentation. We believe that our audit provides a reasonable basis for our opinion.

In many respects this was an unusual year for the Continental Corporation. The weakening of the economy in the early part of the year and the strike of plant employees in the summer led to a decline in sales and net income. After making several tests of the sales records, nothing came to our attention that would indicate sales have not been properly recorded.

In our opinion, with the explanation given above, and with the exception of some minor errors we consider immaterial, the aforementioned financial statements present the financial position of Continental Corporation at July 31, 2009, and the results of its operations, and its cash flows for the year then ended in conformity with pronouncements of the Financial Accounting Standards Board.

We have also audited, in accordance with the standards of the Public Company Accounting Oversight Board (United States), Continental Corporation's internal control over financial reporting as of July 31, 2009, based on criteria established in *Internal Control – Integrated Framework* issued by the Committee of Sponsoring Organizations of the Treadway Commission and our report dated July 31, 2009, expressed an unqualified opinion thereon.

Betsy Ross & Co., CPA
July 31, 2009

Required:

List and explain the deficiencies and omissions in Ross's report on Continental Company's financial statements.

12.39 **Reports on Financial Statements (Consistency).** Various types of "accounting changes" can affect the second standard of reporting under generally accepted auditing standards. This standard indicates that the auditors' report should be modified to identify situations in which accounting principles have not been consistently observed in relation to prior years.

Assume that the following list describes changes that have a material effect on an entity's financial statements for the current year:

1. A change from the completed-contract method to the percentage-of-completion method of accounting for long-term construction-type contracts.
2. A change in the estimated useful life of previously recorded fixed assets based on newly acquired information.
3. Correction of a mathematical error in inventory pricing made in a prior period.
4. A change from prime costing to full absorption costing for inventory valuation.
5. A change from presentation of statements of individual entities to presentation of consolidated statements.
6. A change from deferring and amortizing preproduction costs to recording such costs as an expense when incurred because future benefits of the costs have become doubtful. The new accounting method was adopted in recognition of the change in estimated future benefits.
7. A change to including the employer's share of FICA taxes in "retirement benefits" on the income statement from including it in "other taxes."
8. A change from the FIFO method of inventory pricing to the LIFO method of inventory pricing.

Required:

Identify the type of change described in each preceding item as a change in accounting principle, change in the reporting entity, error correction, combined error correction and change in principle, or change in an accounting estimate. State whether any explanatory paragraph is required in the auditors' report as it relates to the second standard of reporting. Organize your answer sheet as in the following table. For example, a change from the LIFO method of inventory pricing to the FIFO method of inventory pricing would appear as follows:

Item No.	Type of Change	Should the Auditors' Report Be Modified?
Example	An accounting change from one generally accepted accounting principle to another generally accepted accounting principle	Yes
1.		
2.		
3.		
4.		
5.		
6.		
7.		
8.		

12.40 **Reports on Financial Statements (Errors in an Adverse Opinion).** The board of directors of Cook Industries, Inc. engaged Brown & Brown, CPAs, to audit the financial statements

for the year ended December 31, 2008. Because Cook Industries is publicly traded, Brown & Brown will issue reports on the financial statements and internal control over financial reporting; they will present separate reports on each of these areas. Maria Brown has decided an adverse opinion is appropriate on Cook Industries' financial statements, despite the fact that she agrees with Cook's management's assessment that Cook Industries maintained an effective internal control over financial reporting.

Maria Brown also became aware of a March 14, 2009, subsequent event, which Cook Industries' financial vice president properly disclosed in the notes to the financial statements. Brown wants responsibility for subsequent events to be limited to this specific event after the audit completion date of March 7.

Required:

Identify the deficiencies in the following draft of the report. Do not rewrite the report.

Report of Independent Registered Public Accounting Firm

To the President of Cook Industries, Inc.:

We have audited the accompanying financial statements of Cook Industries, Inc., for the year ended December 31, 2008. We conducted our audits in accordance with the standards of the Public Company Accounting Oversight Board (United States). Those standards require that we plan and perform the audit to obtain reasonable assurance about whether the financial statements are free of material misstatement. An audit includes examining, on a test basis, evidence supporting the amounts and disclosures in the financial statements. An audit also includes assessing the accounting principles used and significant estimates made by management, as well as evaluating the overall financial statement presentation. We believe that our audit provides a reasonable basis for our opinion.

As discussed in Note K to the financial statements, the Company has properly disclosed a subsequent event dated March 14, 2009.

As discussed in Note G to the financial statements, the Company carries its property and equipment at appraisal values, and provides depreciation on the basis of such values. Further, the Company does not provide for income taxes with respect to differences between financial income and taxable income arising from the use, for income tax purposes, of the installment method of reporting gross profit from certain types of sales.

In our opinion, the financial statements referred to above do not present fairly the financial position of Cook Industries, Inc., as of December 31, 2008, and the results of its operations and its cash flows for the year then ended in conformity with accounting principles generally accepted in the United States of America.

We have also audited, in accordance with the standards of the Public Company Accounting Oversight Board (United States), Cook Industries' internal control over financial reporting as of December 31, 2008, based on criteria established in *Internal Control – Integrated Framework* issued by the Committee of Sponsoring Organizations of the Treadway Commission; because of our adverse opinion on Cook Industries' financial statements, our report dated March 14, 2009 does not express an opinion thereon.

Brown & Brown
Certified Public Accountants
March 14, 2009

(AICPA adapted)

12.41 **Reports on Financial Statements (Errors in a Comparative Report with Change from Prior Year).** The following auditors' report was drafted by an assistant at the completion of the audit of Cramdon, Inc., on March 1, 2009. The partner in charge of the engagement has decided the opinion on the 2008 financial statements should be modified only with reference to the change in the method of computing the cost of inventory. In 2007, Cramdon used the NIFO method, which is not permissible under generally accepted accounting principles, but in 2008 changed to FIFO and restated the 2007 financial statements. (The auditors' report on the 2007 financial statements expressed an adverse opinion.) The 2007 auditors' report (prepared by the same firm) was dated March 5, 2008.

Report of Independent Registered Public Accounting Firm

To the Board of Directors of Cramdon, Inc.:

We have audited the accompanying financial statements of Cramdon, Inc., as of December 31, 2008 and 2007. These financial statements are the responsibility of Cramdon, Inc.'s management. Our responsibility is to express an opinion on these financial statements based on our audits.

We conducted our audits in accordance with the standards established by the Public Company Accounting Oversight Board (United States). Those standards require that we plan and perform the audit to obtain reasonable assurance about whether the financial statements are free of material misstatement. An audit includes examining, on a test basis, evidence supporting the amounts and disclosures in the financial statements. An audit also includes assessing the accounting principles used and significant estimates made by management, as well as evaluating the overall financial statement presentation. We believe that our audit provides a reasonable basis for our opinion.

As discussed in Note 7 to the financial statements, the company changed its method of accounting for inventory cost from NIFO to FIFO. The 2007 financial statements have been restated to reflect this change. Accordingly, our present opinion on the 2007 financial statements, as presented herein, is different from the opinion we expressed in our previous report dated December 31, 2007.

In our opinion, based on the preceding, the financial statements referred to above present fairly, in all material respects, the financial position of Cramdon, Inc., as of December 31, 2008, and the results of its operations and its cash flows for the period then ended in conformity with accounting principles generally accepted in the United States of America, consistently applied, except for the changes in the method of computing inventory cost as described in Note 7 to the financial statements.

We have also audited, in accordance with the standards of the Public Company Accounting Oversight Board (United States), Cramdon, Inc.'s internal control over financial reporting as of December 31, 2008, based on criteria established in *Internal Control – Integrated Framework* issued by the Committee of Sponsoring Organizations of the Treadway Commission and our report dated March 5, 2009 expressed an unqualified opinion thereon.

George Costanza, CPA
March 5, 2009

Required:

Identify the deficiencies and errors in the draft report and write an explanation of the reasons they are errors and deficiencies. Do not rewrite the report.

12.42 **Reports on Financial Statements (Division of Responsibility).** Lando Corporation is a domestic company with two wholly-owned subsidiaries. Michaels, CPA, has been engaged to audit the financial statements of the parent company and one of the subsidiaries and to act as the principal auditor. Thomas, CPA, has audited the financial statements of the other subsidiary, whose operations are material in relation to the consolidated financial statements.

The work performed by Michaels is sufficient for him to serve as the principal auditor and to report as such on the financial statements. Michaels has not yet decided whether to refer to the part of the audit performed by Thomas.

Required:

a. What responsibilities does Michaels have with respect to Thomas when deciding on whether a division of responsibility is appropriate?

b. What are the reporting requirements with which Michaels must comply if he decides to name Thomas and refer to the work done by Thomas?

c. What report should be issued if Michaels can neither assume responsibility for Thomas's work nor indicate a division of responsibility by referring to his work?

12.43 **Reports on Financial Statements (Division of Responsibility and Other Operating Matters).** Following is Rex Wolf's report on Bonair Corporation's financial statements. Bonair Corporation is profit-oriented and publishes general-purpose financial statements for distribution to owners, creditors, potential investors, and the general public.

Report of Independent Registered Public Accounting Firm

To the Board of Directors and Shareholders, Bonair Corporation

We have audited the accompanying consolidated balance sheet of Bonair Corporation and subsidiaries as of December 31, 2008, and the related statements of income, comprehensive income, and shareholders' equity for the year then ended. Our responsibility is to express an opinion on these financial statements based on our audit. We did not examine the financial statements of Caet Company, a major consolidated subsidiary. These statements were examined by Nero Stout, CPA, whose report thereon has been furnished to us, and our opinion expressed herein, insofar as it relates to Caet Company, is based solely upon the other auditors' report on Caet Company.

Except as stated in the paragraph above, we conducted our audit in accordance with the standards established by the Public Company Accounting Oversight Board (United States). Those standards require that we plan and perform the audit to obtain reasonable assurance about whether the financial statements are free of material misstatement. An audit includes assessing control risk and examining on a test basis evidence supporting the amounts and disclosures in the financial statements. An audit also includes assessing the accounting principles used and significant estimates made by management, as well as evaluating the overall financial statement presentation. We believe that our audit provides a reasonable basis for our opinion.

In our opinion, except for the matter of the report of the other auditors, the financial statements referred to above present fairly, in all material respects, the financial position of Bonair Corporation and subsidiaries as of December 31, 2008, and the results of their operations and their cash flows for the year then ended.

We have also audited, in accordance with the standards of the Public Company Accounting Oversight Board (United States), Bonair Corporation's internal control over financial reporting as of December 31, 2008, based on criteria established in *Internal Control – Integrated Framework* issued by the Committee of Sponsoring Organizations of the Treadway Commission and our report dated March 5, 2009 expressed an unqualified opinion thereon.

Rex Wolf, CPA
March 5, 2009

Required:

Describe the reporting deficiencies and explain why they are considered deficiencies. Organize your response according to each of the paragraphs in the standard report.

12.44 **Reports on Financial Statements: Various Reporting Situations.** Assume that the auditors encountered the following separate situations when deciding on the report to issue for the current-year financial statements.

1. The auditors decided that sufficient appropriate evidence could not be obtained to complete the audit of significant investments the entity held in a foreign entity.

2. The entity failed to capitalize lease assets and obligations but explained them fully in the notes to the financial statements.

3. The entity is defending a lawsuit on product liability claims. (Customers allege that power saw safety guards were improperly installed.) All facts about the lawsuit are disclosed in the notes to the financial statement, but the auditors believe the entity should record a loss based on a probable settlement mentioned by the entity's attorneys.

4. The entity hired the auditors after taking inventory on December 31. The accounting records and other evidence are not reliable enough to enable the auditors to have sufficient evidence about the proper inventory amount.

5. The oil company is required by the FASB to present supplemental oil and gas reserve information outside the basic financial statements. The auditors find that this information, which is not required as a part of the basic financial statements, is omitted.

6. The auditors are principal auditors of the parent company, but they decide not to take responsibility for the work of the other auditors on three subsidiary companies included in the consolidated financial statements. The principal auditors reviewed the other auditors' work and reputation, but they still do not wish to take responsibility for the other auditors' work, which amounts to 32 percent of the consolidated assets and 39 percent of the consolidated revenues.

7. The entity changed its depreciation method from units of production to straight line and the auditors believe the straight-line method is the more appropriate method in the circumstances. The change, fully explained in the notes to the financial statements, has a material effect on the year-to-year comparability of the comparative financial statements.

8. Because the entity has experienced significant operating losses and has had to obtain waivers of debt payment requirements from its lenders, the auditors decide that there is substantial doubt that the entity can continue in existence as a going concern. The entity has fully described all the problems in a note in the financial statements and the auditors feel that, while material, the uncertainty is not serious enough to warrant a disclaimer of opinion.

Required:

a. What kind of opinion should the auditors express in each separate case?

b. What other modification(s) or addition(s) to the standard report is (are) required for each separate case?

12.45 **Reports on Financial Statements (Explain Deficiencies in a Disclaimer of Opinion).** Your partner drafted the following auditors' report yesterday. You need to describe the reporting deficiencies, explain the reasons for them, and discuss with him how the report should be corrected. You have decided to prepare a three-column worksheet showing the deficiencies, reasons, and corrections needed. Your partner's report is shown below.

> I made my examination in accordance with standards of the Public Company Accounting Oversight Board (United States). However, I am not independent with respect to Mavis Corporation because my wife owns 5 percent of the outstanding common stock of the company. The accompanying balance sheet as of December 31, 2008, and the related statements of income, comprehensive income, shareholders' equity, and cash flows for the year then ended were not audited by me. Accordingly, I do not express an opinion on them.

Required:

Prepare the three-column worksheet described.

12.46 **Reports on Financial Statements (Evidence Required for Various Auditors' Reports).** Auditors' alternatives for reporting on financial statements offer many choices among unqualified, qualified, adverse, disclaimers, and modified opinions with expanded report language.

Required:

a. List the report(s) that require fully sufficient appropriate evidence.

b. List the report(s) that would be issued because of pervasive evidence deficiencies.

c. List the report(s) that would be issued because of "compartmentalized" (or material, but not pervasive) evidence deficiencies.

12.47 **Reports on Financial Statements (Unqualified Opinion, Accounting Change, and Uncertainty).** The following auditors' report was drafted by Moore, a staff auditor with Tyler & Tyler, CPAs, at the completion of the audit of the financial statements of Park Publishing Company for the year ended September 30, 2008. The engagement partner reviewed the audit documentation and properly decided to issue an unqualified opinion. In drafting the report, Moore considered the following:

- During fiscal year 2008, Park changed its depreciation method. The engagement partner concurred with this change in accounting principles and its justification, and Moore included an explanatory paragraph in the report.

- The 2008 financial statements are affected by an uncertainty concerning a lawsuit, the outcome of which cannot presently be estimated. Moore included an explanatory paragraph in the report to emphasize this uncertainty.

- The financial statements for the year ended September 30, 2007, are to be presented for comparative purposes. Tyler & Tyler previously audited these statements and expressed an unqualified opinion.

- Because Park Publishing Company is publicly traded, Tyler & Tyler also prepared a separate report on Park Publishing's internal control over financial reporting. This report expressed an unqualified opinion on the effectiveness of Park's internal control over financial reporting.

Report of Independent Registered Public Accounting Firm

To the Board of Directors of Park Publishing Company:

We have audited the accompanying balance sheets of Park Publishing Company as of September 30, 2008 and 2007, and the related statements of income, comprehensive income, shareholders' equity, and cash flows for each of the years in the three-year period ended September 30, 2008. These financial statements are the responsibility of Park Publishing Company's management.

We conducted our audits in accordance with the standards of the Public Company Accounting Oversight Board (United States). Those standards require that we plan and perform the audit to obtain reasonable assurance about whether the financial statements are fairly presented. An audit includes examining, on a test basis, evidence supporting the amounts and disclosures in the financial statements. An audit also includes assessing significant estimates made by management, as well as evaluating the overall financial statement presentation. We believe that our audits provide a basis for determining whether any material modifications should be made to the accompanying financial statements.

As discussed in Note X to the financial statements, the company changed its method of computing depreciation in fiscal 2008.

In our opinion, except for the accounting change, with which we concur, the financial statements referred to above present fairly, in all material respects, the financial position of Park Publishing Company as of September 30, 2008, and the results of its operations and its cash flows for each of the years in the three-year period ended September 30, 2008, in conformity with accounting principles generally accepted in the United States of America.

As discussed in Note Y to the financial statements, the company is a defendant in a lawsuit alleging infringement of certain copyrights. The company has filed a counteraction, and preliminary hearings on both actions are in progress. Accordingly, any provision for liability is subject to adjudication of this matter.

We have also audited, in accordance with the standards of the Public Company Accounting Oversight Board (United States), Park Publishing Company's internal control over financial reporting as of September 30, 2008, based on criteria established in *Internal Control – Integrated Framework* issued by the Committee of Sponsoring Organizations of the Treadway Commission and our report dated November 5, 2008, expressed an unqualified opinion thereon.

Tyler & Tyler, CPAs
November 5, 2008

Required:

Identify the deficiencies in the auditors' report as drafted by Moore. Group the deficiencies by paragraph and in the order in which they appear. Do not rewrite the report.

(AICPA adapted)

12.48 **Reports on Financial Statements (Reports and the Effect of Materiality).** The concept of materiality is important to auditors in examinations of financial statements and expressions of opinion on these statements.

Required:

How will materiality influence auditors' reporting decisions in the following circumstances?

a. The entity prohibits confirmation of accounts receivable, and sufficient and appropriate evidence cannot be obtained using alternative procedures.

b. The entity is a gas and electric utility company that follows the practice of recognizing revenue when it is billed to customers. At the end of the year, amounts earned but not yet billed are not recorded in the accounts or reported in the financial statements.

c. The entity leases buildings for its chain of transmission repair shops under terms that qualify as capital leases under *SFAS 13*. These leases are not capitalized as leased property assets and lease obligations.

d. The entity has lost a lawsuit in federal district court. The case is on appeal in an attempt to reduce the amount of damages awarded to the plaintiffs. No loss amount is recorded.

12.49 **Reports on Financial Statements (Internet Exercise).** One of the great resources on the World Wide Web for auditors is the SEC's EDGAR (Electronic Data Gathering, Analysis and Retrieval system) database at www.sec.gov. Most publicly traded companies

file SEC-required documents electronically. The SEC makes this information available on its Web page.

Required:

Choose five publicly traded companies with which you are familiar. After accessing the EDGAR database, download copies of auditors' reports from the Form 10-K filings and check the boxes in the following table that apply. The first has been done for you. (*Hint:* Search the 10-K filings. Once you have accessed the 10-K filing, use the "Find in page" function in your Internet browser to locate the auditors' report using the key word "independent," as in "Report of Independent Registered Public Accounting Firm.") Do not evaluate the auditors' report on internal control over financial reporting.

(*Note:* U = unqualified opinion; Q = qualified opinion; D = disclaimer of opinion; A = adverse opinion; C = consistency; GC = going concern; E = emphasis paragraph; IC = reference to report on internal control over financial reporting.)

Company Name	Type of Opinion				Additional Explanatory Paragraph?			
	U	Q	D	A	C	GC	E	IC
Time Warner (2005)	X				X		X	X

12.50 **Reports on Internal Control over Financial Reporting (Internet Exercise).** One of the great resources on the World Wide Web for auditors is the SEC's EDGAR (Electronic Data Gathering, Analysis and Retrieval) system database at www.sec.gov. Most publicly traded companies file SEC-required documents electronically. The SEC makes this information available on its Web page.

Required:

Choose five publicly traded companies with which you are familiar. After accessing the EDGAR database, download copies of auditors' reports on the internal control over financial reporting from the Form 10-K filings and check the boxes in the following table that apply. The first has been done for you. (*Hint:* Search the 10-K filings. Once you have accessed the 10-K filing, use the "Find in page" function in your Internet browser to locate the auditors' report using the key word "independent," as in "Report of Independent Registered Public Accounting Firm.")

Company Name	Auditors' Opinion on Internal Control over Financial Reporting				
	Unqualified Opinion	Qualified Opinion	Disclaimer of Opinion	Adverse Opinion	Separate or Combined Report
BMC Software (2005)				X	Separate

Report-Writing Cases

Cases 12.51 through 12.57 require you to draft auditors' reports. The *Electronic Workpapers* (available on the textbook Web site listed on the back cover of the text) has a Word file (file name AUDIT) containing the standard report, which can be used as the starting place for a nonstandard report requirement. You can read this file into many word processing programs to make your report-writing task easier and more professional.

Unless instructed otherwise, assume the following in drafting your reports: (1) your firm Anderson, Olds, & Watershed (AOW) conducted the audit examination of the identified client; (2) the fiscal year end is December 31, 2008; (3) the audit completion date is February 10, 2009; and (4) the client is publicly traded and, therefore, subject to the auditing and reporting requirements of *AS 5*.

12.51 **Financial Difficulty: The "Going-Concern" Problem.** Pitts Company has experienced significant financial difficulty. Current liabilities exceed current assets by $1 million, cash has decreased to $10,000, the interest on the long-term debt has not been paid, and a customer has brought a lawsuit against Pitts for $500,000 on a product liability claim. Significant questions concerning the going-concern status of the company exist. The lawsuit and information about the going-concern status have been appropriately described in footnote 3 to the financial statements.

Required:

a. Draft Anderson, Olds, & Watershed's report, assuming that they decide that an unqualified opinion instead of a disclaimer of opinion is appropriate in the circumstances.

b. Draft Anderson, Olds, & Watershed's report, assuming that they decide the uncertainties are so overwhelming that they do not wish to express an opinion on Pitts' financial statements (assume they are still able to express an opinion on Pitts' internal control over financial reporting).

12.52 **Disagreement with Auditors.** Officers of Richnow Company do not wish to disclose information about a product liability lawsuit filed by a customer seeking $500,000 in damages. They believe the suit is frivolous and without merit. Outside counsel is more cautious. The auditors insist on disclosure. Angered, the chair of the board of Richnow Company threatens to sue Anderson, Olds, & Watershed if a standard report is not issued within three days.

Required:

Draft Anderson, Olds, & Watershed's report appropriate in the circumstances.

12.53 **Late Appointment of Auditors.** Anderson, Olds, & Watershed (AOW) have completed the audit of the financial statements of Musgrave Company for the year ended December 31, 2008, and is now preparing the report.

AOW has audited the financial statements for several years, but this year Musgrave delayed the start of the audit work, so AOW was not present to observe the taking of the physical inventory on December 31, 2008. The inventory balance is $194,000, which represents 39 percent of Musgrave's total assets and 69 percent of its current assets. However, AOW performed alternative procedures, including (1) examination of shipping and receiving documents with regard to transactions since the year end, (2) extensive review of the inventory count sheets, and (3) discussion of the physical inventory procedures with responsible company personnel. AOW also satisfied themselves about the propriety of the inventory valuation calculations and the consistency of the valuation method. Musgrave determines year-end inventory quantities solely by means of physical count.

Required:

Draft AOW's report on the balance sheet at the end of the current year and on the statements of operations, comprehensive income, shareholders' equity, and cash flows for the year then ended. (*Hint*: Did the alternative procedures produce sufficient appropriate evidence?)

12.54 **Division of Responsibility.** The firm of Anderson, Olds, & Watershed (AOW) is the principal auditor for the December 31, 2008, consolidated financial statements of Ferguson Company and subsidiaries. However, other auditors perform the work on certain subsidiaries for the year under audit amounting to

	2008	2007
Total assets	29%	31%
Total revenues	36	41

AOW investigated the other auditors, as required by auditing standards, and they furnished AOW with their auditors' reports. AOW has decided to rely on their work and to refer to the other auditors in their report. None of the audit work revealed any issues with respect to Ferguson Company or its subsidiaries.

Required:

Draft AOW's report indicating the division of responsibility.

12.55 **Other Information in a Financial Review Section of an Annual Report.** Mr. Humphreys (chair of the board) and Ms. VanEns (vice president, finance) prepared the draft of the financial review section of the annual report. You are reviewing it for consistency with the audited financial statements. The draft contains the following explanation about income coverage of interest expense:

Last year, operating income before interest and income taxes covered interest expense by a ratio of 6:1. This year, on an incremental basis, the coverage of interest expense increased to a ratio of 6.59:1.

The relevant portion of the audited financial statements showed the following:

	Current Year	Prior Year
Operating income	$400,000	$360,000
Extraordinary gain from realization of tax benefits	100,000	
Interest expense	(81,250)	(60,000)
Income taxes	(127,500)	(120,000)
Net income	$291,250	$180,000

Required:

a. Determine whether the financial review section statement about coverage of interest is or is not consistent with the audited financial statements. Be able to show your conclusion with calculations.

b. Assume that you find an inconsistency and the officers disagree with your conclusions. Draft the explanatory paragraph you should put in your auditors' report.

12.56 **Departures from GAAP.** On January 1, Graham Company purchased land (the site of a new building) for $100,000. Soon thereafter, the state highway department announced that a new feeder roadway route would run next to the site. The effect was a dramatic increase in local property values. Comparable land located nearby sold for $700,000 in December of the current year. Graham presents the land at $700,000 in its accounts and, after reduction for implicit taxes at 33 percent, the fixed asset total is $400,000 higher than historical cost, with the same amount shown separately in the shareholder equity account "Current Value Increment." The valuation is fully disclosed in a footnote to the financial statements, along with a letter from a certified property appraiser attesting to the $700,000 value.

Required:

a. Draft the appropriate auditors' report, assuming that you believe the departure from GAAP is material but not pervasive enough to cause you to issue an adverse opinion.

b. Draft the appropriate auditors' report, assuming that you believe an adverse opinion is necessary.

c. Discuss whether you should (could) issue a report conforming to Rule 203 of the AICPA Code of Professional Conduct.

12.57 **Reporting on an Accounting Change.** In December of the current year, Williams Company changed its method of accounting for inventory and cost of goods sold from LIFO to FIFO. The account balances shown in the trial balance have already been recalculated and adjusted retroactively, as required by *SFAS 154*. The accounting change and the financial effects are described in Note 2 in the financial statements.

Required:

a. Assume that you believe the accounting change is justified as required by *SFAS 154*. Draft the report appropriate in the circumstances.

b. Assume that you believe the accounting change is not justified and causes the financial statements to be materially distorted. Inventories that would have been reported at

$1.5 million (LIFO) are reported at $1.9 million (FIFO); operating income before tax that would have been $130,000 is reported at $530,000. As a result of this change, current assets, total assets, and shareholders' equity have increased by 17 percent, 9 percent, and 14 percent, respectively. Draft the report appropriate in the circumstances.

12.58 **Mini-Case: Other Auditors.**

Refer to the mini-case "Something Went Sour at Parmalat" and respond to Question 4.

12.59 **Kaplan CPA Exam Simulation: Reports on Financial Statements (General Auditors' Reports).**

Required:

Go to the text Web site at www.mhhe.com/louwers3e, click on AUD: Kerklaan Enterprises and the "Audit Opinions" tab, and complete the assigned task.

12.60 **Kaplan CPA Exam Simulation: Reports on Financial Statements (Opinions and Report Modifications).**

Required:

Go to the text Web site at www.mhhe.com/louwers3e, click on AUD: Riley & Associates and the "Audit Opinions" tab, and complete the assigned task.

12.61 **Kaplan CPA Exam Simulation: Reports on Financial Statements (Comparative Financial Statements).**

Required:

Go to the text Web site at www.mhhe.com/louwers3e, click on AUD: Ridge and Associates and the "Fin. Reptg." tab, and complete the assigned task.

12.62 **Kaplan CPA Exam Simulation: Reports on Financial Statements (Comparative Financial Statements).**

Required:

Go to the text Web site at www.mhhe.com/louwers3e, click on AUD: Kerklaan Enterprises and the "Comparative Financial Statements" tab, and complete the assigned task.

Other Public Accounting Services

Professional Standards References

Compendium Section	Document Reference	Topic
Attestation Engagements		
Various	AS 5	"An Audit of Internal Control over Financial Reporting That Is Integrated with an Audit of Financial Statements"
AT 20	SSAE 13	"Defining Professional Requirements in Statements on Standards for Attestation Engagements"
AT 50	SSAE 14	"SSAE Hierarchy"
AT 101	SSAE 10	"Attest Engagements"
AT 201	SSAE 10	"Agreed Upon Procedures Engagements"
	ISA 4400	"Engagement to Perform Agreed-Upon Procedures Regarding Financial Information"
AT 301	SSAE 10	"Financial Forecasts and Projections"
	ISA 3400	"The Examination of Prospective Information"
AT 401	SSAE 10	"Reporting on Pro Forma Financial Information"
AT 501	SSAE 10	"Reporting on an Entity's Internal Control over Financial Reporting"
AT 601	SSAE 10	"Compliance Attestation"
AT 701	SSAE 10	"Management's Discussion and Analysis"
	ISA 3000	"Assurance Engagements Other Than Audits or Reviews of Historical Information"
Review and Compilation of Unaudited Financial Statements		
AR 50	SSARS 11	"Standards for Accounting and Review Services"
AR 100	SSARS 1	"Compilation and Review of Financial Statements"
	SSARS 8	"Amendment to Statement on Standards for Accounting and Review Services No. 1, Compilation and Review of Financial Statements"
	SSARS 10	"Performance of Review Engagements"
	ISA 2400	"Engagements to Review Financial Statements"
	ISA 4410	"Engagements to Compile Financial Statements"
AR 110	SSARS 13	"Compilation of Specified Elements, Accounts, or Items of a Financial Statement"
AR 120	SSARS 14	"Compilation of Pro Forma Financial Information"
AR 200	SSARS 2	"Reporting on Comparative Financial Statements"
AR 300	SSARS 3	"Compilation Reports on Financial Statements Included in Certain Prescribed Forms"
AR 400	SSARS 4	"Communications between Predecessor and Successor Accountants"
AR 600	SSARS 6	"Reporting on Personal Financial Statements Included in Written Personal Financial Plans"
Various	SSARS 9	"Omnibus 2002"
Various	SSARS 12	"Omnibus Statement on Standards for Accounting and Review Services—2005"
Various	SSARS 15	"Elimination of Certain References to Statements on Auditing Standards and Incorporation of Appropriate Guidance Into Statements on Standards for Accounting and Review Services"
Various		"Omnibus Statement on Standards for Accounting and Review Services—2007"

Special Reports		
AU 324	SAS 70	"Reports on the Processing of Transactions by Service Organizations"
	SAS 88	"Service Organizations and Reporting on Consistency"
AU 544	SAS 1	"Lack of Conformity with GAAP—Regulated Companies"
AU 623	SAS 62	"Special Reports"
	ISA 800	"The Independent Auditor's Report on Special Purpose Audit Engagements"
AU 9623		"Interpretation: Reporting on Supplementary Current-Value Information"
AU 625	SAS 50	"Reports on the Application of Accounting Principles"
	SAS 97	"Amendment to Statement on Audit Standard No. 50, Reports on the Application of Accounting Principles"
AU 722	SAS 100	"Interim Financial Information"
	ISA 2410	"Review of Interim Financial Information Performed by the Independent Auditor of the Entity"

There's no business like show business, but there are several businesses like accounting.

David Letterman, late-night talk-show host

Learning Objectives

Certified Public Accountants (CPAs) are trusted professionals with a reputation for objectivity and integrity. The reputation has its foundation in a long history of service to the business community and the general public. Despite recent problems, individuals and businesses still view their CPAs as trusted business professionals who add value to their businesses and provide valuable guidance concerning difficult business decisions. In this tradition, CPAs and other accountants[1] offer numerous assurance and attestation services on information other than audited financial statements. These services result from consumer demand for assurance by objective experts. This module covers several areas of public accounting practice related to accountants' association with information other than complete, audited historical financial statements.

This module is broken into five parts. The first part defines and further explores assurance services. The second part is devoted to (nonaudit) attestation engagements. The third part deals with reviews and compilations of unaudited financial statements. The fourth part discusses the auditors' responsibility related to interim financial information. The module concludes with other topics, including special and restricted-use reports.

Your objectives are to be able to:

1. Explain and provide examples of assurance services engagements.
2. Explain and provide examples of attestation engagements.
3. Write appropriate reports for review and compilation of unaudited financial statements, given specific factual circumstances.
4. Explain auditors' responsibilities related to reporting on interim financial information.
5. Define, explain, and give examples of other comprehensive bases of accounting (OCBOA), distinguishing them from generally accepted accounting principles (GAAP).

ASSURANCE SERVICES

LEARNING OBJECTIVE

1. Explain and provide examples of assurance services engagements.

Why Develop New Assurance Services?

While auditing courses focus on policy, procedure, service to the client, and ethical and professional conduct, you should not lose sight of the fact that public accounting firms are businesses and require sufficient revenue to cover expenses, provide profit for the firm's partners, and provide funds for the continued growth of the firm. One of the objectives of the American Institute of Certified Public Accountants (AICPA) has been to identify

[1] While only CPAs can express opinions on audited financial statements, the terms *accountants* and *accounting practitioners* generally refer to those engaged to perform the wider set of public accounting services discussed in this module.

additional niche services that accountants might offer to enhance their value to the client, attract new clients, and improve the potential for growth as a business. The AICPA's Special Committee on Assurance Services (SCAS) identified eight megatrends that can affect public accounting firms' business. Each presents opportunities to provide assurance service products, and each presents business risks. Consider the bright side—the opportunities:

- *Information technology* promises vast databases and easy user access. Accountants can offer services related to database content and design.

- *Competition* among CPA and non-CPA service providers sometimes may favor CPAs because of their reputations for expertise in internal control and measurement methods.

- *Corporate structure changes* that encourage outsourcing and temporary ventures create (1) needs for corporate partners' assurance of other partners' accountability and (2) services for which the public accounting firms can be the outsource providers (e.g., internal audit, pension plan administration).

- *Accountability*—the interdependence among businesses, not-for-profit organizations, management, government (Congress, legislatures, regulators), and public interest groups (environmentalists, educators, capital market participants)—creates various arrangements for grants, ventures, alliances, and similar contracts in which the participants will seek assurance about other participants' performance and accomplishments.

- *Investment capital* is already becoming institutionalized in large mutual funds, and many more individuals are managing their assets in defined contribution retirement plans. Services related to evaluating mutual fund managers' performance, giving investment advice to corporations and individuals, evaluating the riskiness of hedge funds, and managing pension plans fall within many CPAs' financial expertise.

- *Aging* of the U.S. population has created the need for advisory expertise in connection with retirement benefit plans, Social Security financing, school financing, medical services, and the efficiency, effectiveness, and accomplishment of other issues that affect an older population.

- *Globalization* of trade can involve CPAs in creating common standards for accounting reports and other forms of information flow (e.g., databases) as well as services in foreign regulations and taxation.

- In regard to *education*, some school districts currently allow students to attend public schools in districts other than the ones in which they reside. In addition, some districts provide vouchers to assist students in paying for private schools. University education now includes complete degree programs via the Internet. In the future, students and their families may have even more education choices. Families may look for independent counseling concerning the quality of the education as well as the costs and funding available to complete school—all of which accountants may learn to provide.

Definition: Assurance Services

The SCAS provides a concise definition for assurance services: "**Assurance services** are independent professional services that improve the quality of information, or its context, for decision makers." A large group of activities can fit within this definition. In addition, although attestation and audit services are highly structured and intended to be useful for large groups of decision makers (e.g., investors, lenders), assurance services are more customized and intended to be useful to smaller, targeted groups of decision makers. In this sense, assurance services resemble consulting services. The major elements, and boundaries, of the definition follow:

- *Independence.* CPAs want to preserve their attestation and audit reputations and competitive advantages by preserving integrity and objectivity when performing assurance services.

- *Professional services.* Virtually all work performed by CPAs (accounting, auditing, information management, taxation, management, marketing, finance) is defined as a

"professional service" as long as it involves some element of judgment based on education and experience in accounting or auditing.

- *Improving the quality of information.* The emphasis on "information" is CPAs' traditional stock in trade. CPAs can enhance quality by assuring users about the reliability and relevance of information, and these two features are closely related to the familiar credibility-lending products of attestation and audit services.

- *Improving the context of information.* "Context" is relevance in a particular situation. For assurance services, "improving the context of information" refers to improving its usefulness when targeted to particular decision makers in the surroundings of particular decision problems. Accountants will need time and experience in various assurance services to more fully develop this concept of context.

- *For decision makers.* They are the "consumers" of assurance services and they personify the consumer focus of new and different professional work. They may or may not be the "client" that pays the fee and they may or may not be one of the parties to an assertion or other information. The decision makers are the beneficiaries of the assurance services. Depending on the assignment, decision makers may be a very small, targeted group (e.g., managers of a database) or a large targeted group (e.g., potential investors interested in a mutual fund manager's performance).

While there are seemingly unlimited assurance opportunities, assurance service engagements proposed to date include CPA WebTrust, CPA SysTrust, CPA ElderCare/PrimePlus, and CPA Performance View services. These four assurance services are described in the following sections.

CPA WebTrust and CPA SysTrust

Electronic commerce (or e-commerce), the sale of goods and services via the Internet, is exploding. According to a leading marketing research group, U.S. retail e-commerce sales will exceed $131 billion in 2007.[2] Although the growth of e-commerce continues unabated, security issues, both real and perceived, have prevented many potential customers from purchasing goods and services via the Internet. Many customers and business owners distrust the Internet as a medium of conducting business. Indeed, a general lack of security is the top reason given by nonbuyers for not purchasing products online, as well as the top concern among current online buyers. Specifically, prospective buyers have expressed concerns about ascertaining whether an e-commerce company is authentic (*authentication*), is trustworthy (*transaction integrity,* the e-tailer will do what it says it will do), and will safeguard buyers' personal information (*information security*). Customers also want to be reassured that they can get their products, services, and repairs on a timely basis. Despite growing familiarity with doing business on the Internet, these security issues have not diminished for potential customers.

According to the U.S. Census Bureau, 92 percent of e-commerce in 2005 was business to business (B-to-B).[3] For significant customer–supplier business relationships, company computers are often directly linked through Internet-based virtual private networks (VPNs). Purchase orders for goods are made via computer and payment is made automatically through electronic funds transfer (EFT) directly to the vendor's bank. The primary benefit of such a relationship is an increase in the timeliness of the process; transactions that once took several weeks to complete manually (from customer purchase order generation to final payment being deposited to the supplier's bank account) now take only as long as it takes to ship and receive the goods. However, just as Internet customers are wary of purchasing online, business customers are often cautious about entering into such relationships with other businesses.

The AICPA and the Canadian Institute of Chartered Accountants (CICA) developed the WebTrust Service to provide assurance to the consumer on the reliability of Internet

[2] "US Retail E-Commerce: Entering the Multi-Channel Era," *eMarketer,* May 1, 2007, available at www.marketresearch.com.
[3] "E-Stats Reports," U.S. Census Bureau, May 25, 2007, available at www.census.gov/estats.

Web sites and the SysTrust Service to focus on a company's systems as a means of increasing the reliability of B-to-B computer transactions. Because these two services have a common framework to address risks and technological opportunities, the AICPA has adopted the term **trust services** to define these assurance examinations.

Generally speaking, accountants performing a trust service must address the following principles:

- *Security.* Because parties to business transactions will transmit and store important and often confidential information regarding its business partners, the security principle requires that the entity's system be protected from unauthorized access. This includes protection concerning both unauthorized physical and logical access to computer systems.

- *Availability.* The availability principle requires the system, products, or services to be obtainable as indicated by the seller or service provider. The principle does not set any standard for availability but states that the product or service provider performs in accordance with the terms indicated on its Web site or in agreements with customers.

- *Processing integrity.* This principle refers to the completeness, accuracy, timeliness, and authorization of information system processing. There should be adequate system protection to ensure that the user will receive the product or service correctly in accordance with specifications of the order.

- *Privacy.* Personal information collected by an entity must be safeguarded against unauthorized use. While this principle is associated with the security principle, it includes situations in which the access to computers and information is appropriate but the subsequent distribution and use of the information is not. Privacy covers all personal information concerning customers and business partners. New laws greatly restrict the dissemination of any information concerning customers to outside organizations.

- *Confidentiality.* Related to the privacy principle, the principle of confidentiality includes the assurance that other information is safeguarded from unauthorized users. For example, a company may learn that a business partner is going to introduce a new product. This information is not personal in nature and is not covered under privacy rules. However, within the confines of ethical business practices, this information should not be disseminated to other organizations.

Accountants offering **WebTrust Services** and **SysTrust Services** can issue opinions and corresponding "seals of assurance" on individual principles or a combination of the principles. An actual WebTrust report is reproduced in Exhibit A.1.

PrimePlus/ElderCare Services

Given improved health care and the aging of the "baby boomer" generation, the U.S. population's average age is increasing at a significant rate. In 1998, the SCAS introduced *ElderCare Services* as a new assurance growth area. These services were designed to provide assurance to family members that appropriate care was provided to elderly family members no longer able to be totally independent. In conducting ElderCare Services, accountants acted as an assuror of the quality of the services provided based on criteria and goals set by the client.

ElderCare Services were successful, but accountants believed that the term *ElderCare* limited the target market to issues concerning health care. In addition, *elder* had negative connotations to potential customers. In 2002, the CICA and the AICPA changed the name to **PrimePlus/ElderCare Services** to encompass traditional financial and tax-planning services provided by accountants. Under PrimePlus/ElderCareServices, accountants can assist individuals with estate planning, financial planning, tax preparation, and cash flow management. In addition, accountants may continue to provide guidance and assurance to families concerning health care services and residence choices.

CPA Performance View

Performance measurement has been defined as "the identification of critical success factors that lead to measures that can be tracked over time to assess progress made in achieving

EXHIBIT A.1 **Example of WebTrust Report**

Report of Independent Accountants

To the Management of Nexity Bank:

We have examined Nexity Bank's management assertion that during the period March 15, 2005 through March 14, 2006, it:

- Maintained effective controls over its Banking System to provide reasonable assurance that the System was protected against unauthorized access (both physical and logical) and complied with the commitments regarding the security of its Banking System, as described in Nexity Bank's description of security commitments;

- Maintained effective controls over the privacy of personal information collected by its Banking System to provide reasonable assurance that the personal information was collected, used, retained, and disclosed based on its commitments in the privacy notice related to the System, and complied with its commitments in the privacy notice, as described in Nexity Bank's description of commitments;

based on the AICPA/CICA Trust Services Security and Privacy Criteria. This assertion is the responsibility of Nexity Bank management. Our responsibility is to express an opinion based on our examination.

Our examination was conducted in accordance with attestation standards established by the American Institute of Certified Public Accountants and, accordingly, included (1) obtaining an understanding of Nexity Bank's relevant security controls and the controls over the privacy of personal information, (2) testing and evaluating the operating effectiveness of the controls, (3) testing compliance with its commitments regarding the security of its System and the commitments in the privacy notice, and (4) performing such other procedures as we considered necessary in the circumstances. We believe that our examination provides a reasonable basis for our opinion.

Because of inherent limitations in controls, error or fraud may occur and not be detected. Furthermore, the projection of any conclusions, based on our findings, to future periods is subject to the risk that the validity of such conclusions may be altered because of changes made to the system or controls, the failure to make needed changes to the system or controls, or deterioration in the degree of effectiveness of the controls.

In our opinion, Nexity Bank's management's assertion referred to above is fairly stated, in all material respects, based on the AICPA/CICA Trust Services Security Criteria and the AICPA/CICA Trust Services Privacy Criteria.

Nexity Bank's use of the WebTrust Seal constitutes a symbolic representation of the contents of this report and it is not intended, nor should it be construed, to update this report or provide any additional assurance.

/s/ Ernst & Young, LLP
www.ey.com
Atlanta, Georgia
March 15, 2006

specific targets linked to an entity's vision." Developed jointly by the AICPA and the CICA, **CPA Performance View** identifies and measures key activities that are critical to the entity. Rather than relying strictly on historical financial information, CPA Performance View uses nonfinancial information such as customer satisfaction, employee training and satisfaction, and product quality to identify critical success factors that can lead to organizational change, better performance, and increased revenue for an organization.

Review Checkpoints

A.1 In what ways are assurance services similar to attestation services (including audits of financial statements)?

A.2 What are the five major elements of the broad definition of assurance services?

A.3 Why do you think the AICPA is so interested in developing CPAs' expertise in assurance services?

A.4 Briefly describe the four assurance engagements proposed by the SCAS in terms of services provided and intended customers.

ATTESTATION ENGAGEMENTS

LEARNING
OBJECTIVE

2. Explain and provide
 examples of attestation
 engagements.

Introduction to Attestation Engagements

While the majority of this textbook is devoted to auditing financial statements, audit services are really a subset of a larger group of services referred to as *attestation services.* An **attestation** is defined as an engagement

> in which a practitioner is engaged to issue or does an examination, a review, or an agreed-upon procedures report on subject matter, or an assertion about the subject matter . . ., that is the responsibility of another party. (AT 101.01)

The definition incorporates three types of attestation engagements: examination, review, and agreed-upon procedures. An **examination** is similar in substance to an audit. Accountants review internal controls and assess the risk of material misstatement, gather evidence in support of the assertions, and render opinions that represent a high level of assurance. A **review** provides only a moderate level of assurance. The procedures performed in a review engagement are generally limited to inquiries and analytical procedures, although the accountants may decide that other procedures are necessary. The third type of attestation engagement, discussed in more detail later in this module, is an **agreed-upon procedure** engagement in which the client delineates exactly what functions they want accountants to perform. Therefore, the level of assurance provided by such an engagement varies, depending on the procedures requested.

The purpose of differentiating attestation engagements from audits is to provide accountants with a framework that allows them to perform other services often requested by their clients. For example, clients may want a public accounting firm to lend its name to a report on compliance with a contract or an environmental regulation. Public accounting firms have even attested to success rates at fertility clinics!

Professional standards for performing attest engagements are provided by *Statements on Standards for Attestation Engagements (SSAEs)* in the AT section of the AICPA's Professional Standards. *SSAE 10* lists standards similar to the 10 generally accepted auditing standards on which *SASs* are based (see Exhibit A.2).

As you can see, attestation standards are similar to auditing standards; however, they have some important differences. The general standards are concerned with the *practitioner's* knowledge about the *subject matter* of the engagement and having suitable *criteria to measure* it by. To be suitable, the criteria must be objective, measurable, complete, and relevant. The standards of field work do not require an evaluation of internal controls, although such an evaluation may be necessary, particularly in an examination engagement. In financial statement audits, the measurement criteria are generally accepted accounting principles (GAAP) or other comprehensive bases of accounting (OCBOA); therefore, the determination of suitable measurement criteria has already been established. In engagements in which GAAP or OCBOA are not suitable measurement criteria, the identification of the appropriate criteria may be difficult and time consuming. The reporting standards restrict the distribution of the reports to persons who will understand the subject matter.

Attestation engagements include engagements related to

- Agreed-Upon Procedures (AT 201).
- Financial Forecasts and Projections (AT 301).
- *Pro Forma* Financial Information (AT 401).
- An Entity's Internal Control over Financial Reporting (AT 501).
- Compliance Attestation (AT 601).
- Management's Discussion and Analysis (AT 701).

We briefly discuss these types of attestation engagements in the following sections.

EXHIBIT A.2 **Generally Accepted Attestation Standards**

Attestation Standards	Generally Accepted Auditing Standards
1. The *practitioner* must have adequate technical training and proficiency to perform the *attest engagement.*	1. The auditor must have adequate technical training and proficiency to perform the audit.
2. The *practitioner* must have adequate knowledge of the subject matter.	
3. The *practitioner* must have reason to believe that the subject matter is capable of evaluation against criteria that are suitable and available to users.	
4. The *practitioner* must maintain independence in mental attitude in all matters relating to the *engagement.*	2. The auditor must maintain independence in mental attitude in all matters relating to the audit.
5. The *practitioner* must exercise due professional care in the planning and performance of the *engagement* and the preparation of the report.	3. The auditor must exercise due professional care in the performance of the audit and the preparation of the report.
6. The *practitioner* must adequately plan the work and must properly supervise any assistants.	4. The auditor must adequately plan the work and must properly supervise any assistants.
[Depending upon the subject matter, internal control evaluation may not be required for an attestation engagement.]	5. The auditor must obtain a sufficient understanding of the entity and its environment, including its internal control, to assess the risk of material misstatement of the financial statements whether due to error or fraud, and to design the nature, timing, and extent of further audit procedures.
7. The *practitioner* must obtain sufficient evidence to provide a reasonable basis for *the conclusion that is expressed in the report.*	6. The auditor must obtain sufficient appropriate audit evidence by performing audit procedures to afford a reasonable basis for an opinion regarding the financial statements under audit.
8. The *practitioner* must state the *practitioner's* conclusion about the *subject matter or the assertion* in relation to *criteria against which the subject matter was evaluated* in the report.	7. The auditor must state in the auditor's report whether the financial statements are presented in accordance with generally accepted accounting principles (GAAP).
	8. The auditor must identify in the auditor's report those circumstances in which such principles have not been consistently observed in the current period in relation to the preceding period.
9. The *practitioner* must state all of the *practitioner's significant reservations about the engagement,* the *subject matter,* and, if applicable, the *assertion* related thereto in the report.	9. When the auditor determines that informative disclosures are not reasonably adequate, the auditor must so state in the auditor's report.
10. The *practitioner* must identify the *subject matter* or the assertion being reported on and state the character of the *engagement* in the report.	10. The auditor must either express an opinion regarding the financial statements, taken as a whole, or state that an opinion cannot be expressed, in the auditor's report. When the auditor cannot express an overall opinion, the auditor should state the reasons therefor in the auditor's report. In all cases where an auditor's name is associated with financial statements, the auditor should clearly indicate the character of the auditor's work, if any, and the degree of responsibility the auditor is taking, in the auditor's report.
11. The *practitioner* must state in the report that the report is intended solely for the information and use of the *specified parties* under the following circumstances [detail omitted].	

Applying Agreed-Upon Procedures (AT 201)

Clients sometimes engage auditors to perform specified procedures, known as agreed-upon procedures, to examine a particular element, account, or item in financial statements or to perform a special engagement. For example, a restaurant may ask their accountants

to classify and summarize customer comment cards and a composer might ask an accountant to verify the mathematics on a royalty report. Such work should not be considered an audit because the specified set of agreed-upon procedures is usually not sufficient to be considered an audit in accordance with GAAS. Agreed-upon procedures engagements have a limited scope, so the second and third standards of field work (assessing the risk of material misstatement and obtaining sufficient appropriate evidence for an opinion) and the standards of reporting do not apply.

According to attestation standards for agreed-upon procedures engagements, auditors must reach a clear understanding with the client and the report users about the users' needs and the procedures to be performed. Reports are to be restricted to the specified users who participate in and take responsibility for defining the work on the engagement.

A report on an agreed-upon procedures engagement is quite different from the standard audit report. In particular, the report should identify the specified users and describe in detail the procedures the users decided were necessary; state that the work is not an audit or review that results in an overall opinion or assurance; and describe each of the agreed-upon procedures and the specific audit findings related to each procedure. No overall "opinion" or "negative assurance" is given as a conclusion to the report.

Financial Forecasts and Projections (AT 301) and *Pro Forma* Financial Information (AT 401)

Prospective financial information (PFI) is financial information representing the financial position, results of operations, and cash flows for some period of time in the future. For example, a **financial projection** is PFI based on the occurrence of one or more hypothetical events that change the entity's existing business structure (e.g., possible addition of a new distribution center: Should the entity continue to distribute goods from only one distribution center?) A **financial forecast** is PFI based on expected conditions and courses of action (e.g., no new distribution center). In contrast, **pro forma** financial information shows the effect of a proposed or consummated transaction on the *historical* financial statements "as if" that transaction had occurred by a specific date.

In many cases, the entity is negotiating directly with a single user (limited use) who has requested prospective financial information for use in economic decisions. Any PFI can be used for limited purposes. In other instances, the entity may be preparing financial statements that it intends to present to a large number of users (general use), none of whom it is negotiating with at the current time.

The PFI may contain amounts similar to historical financial statements (single-point estimates) or ranges of amounts. If ranges are used, care should be taken to indicate that the endpoints of this range do not represent best- and worst-case scenarios. In addition, the PFI should disclose the significant accounting policies and procedures used to generate the statements. If the basis in the PFI is different from that used in the historical financial statements, a reconciliation of the two bases must be shown. In addition, the entity must disclose all significant assumptions used to prepare prospective financial statements, indicate that actual events or conditions may not be consistent with these assumptions, and, for financial projections, indicate the limited usefulness of the projection.

To perform an attestation engagement on either PFI or *pro forma* information, accountants must evaluate the preparation of the financial information, the support underlying the assumptions, and the presentation of the information. To accomplish these objectives, accountants must (1) obtain knowledge about the entity's business, accounting principles, and factors affecting the events and transactions in question; (2) obtain an understanding of the process through which the information was developed (e.g., determine whether all relevant information was considered in developing assumptions); (3) evaluate the assumptions (and their underlying support) used to prepare the information; (4) identify key factors affecting the information; and (5) evaluate the preparation and presentation of the financial information (e.g., consistency with AICPA guidelines).

AUDITING INSIGHT Attestation Expectation Gap?

The results of a recent academic study indicate significant differences in beliefs between accountants, users, and preparers of prospective financial information concerning forecast reliability and the role and responsibilities of auditors and management. Contrary to the usual published studies on expectation gap between auditors and the public, researchers found that auditors believe that forecasts are more reliable than users or preparers do. Auditors also believe that they have a higher level of responsibility and accountability than is attributed to them by users or preparers.

Source: P. Schelluch and G. Gay, "Assurance Provided by Auditors' Reports on Prospective Financial Information: Implications for the Expectation Gap," *Accounting and Finance* 46 (Dec 2006), p. 653.

Reporting on an Entity's Internal Control over Financial Reporting (AT 501)

Auditing Standard 5 requires the management of SEC-regulated companies to assess and report on their internal control over financial reporting and also requires auditors to express an opinion on the effectiveness of internal control based on established criteria (generally, based on criteria established by the Committee of Sponsoring Organizations, or COSO). These reports are covered in Chapter 5.

Non-SEC companies may engage accountants to evaluate and report on their assertions concerning the effectiveness of internal controls in their organization. The attestation standards that govern accountants' reports on an entity's internal control (*SSAE 10*, AT 501) specify that accountants' public reports can be issued only when management issues a separate written report containing assertions about its internal control. In such a case, the accountants' report is an opinion on the fair presentation of management's assertions.

An internal control examination is an attestation engagement because, like an audit, it produces an opinion. These conditions must be met before accountants can conduct an examination on an entity's internal control:

- Management accepts responsibility for the effectiveness of its internal control.
- Management's evaluation of control is based on reasonable criteria (e.g., the Committee of Sponsoring Organizations (COSO) Report; see Chapter 5).
- Management's evaluation of control can be supported by sufficient evidence.
- Management presents a written assertion about the effectiveness of its internal control.

An internal control examination is similar to an audit. The work must be in accordance with the attestation standards, which bear many points of similarity to generally accepted auditing standards (refer to Exhibit A.2 for a direct comparison). An examination of management's assertion about the effectiveness of internal control involves (*SSAE 10*, AT 501)

- Planning the engagement.
- Obtaining an understanding of the internal control.
- Evaluating the design effectiveness of internal control activities.
- Testing and evaluating the operating effectiveness of internal control activities.
- Forming an opinion about the fair presentation of management's assertion regarding internal control effectiveness.

Audit procedures for testing and evaluating design and operating effectiveness are very similar to the procedures described in other chapters in this textbook. They include inquiries, document examination, observation, and reperformance (test of detail controls) performed on samples of transactions. The standard "unqualified" report on an entity's internal control is shown in Exhibit A.3.

EXHIBIT A.3 Standard Report on an Entity's Internal Control (*SSAE 10*, AT 501)

Report Title	Independent Accountants' Report
Introductory paragraph	We have examined management's assertion concerning maintenance of effective internal control over financial reporting as of December 31, 2008, included in the accompanying management report.
Scope paragraph	Our examination was made in accordance with standards established by the American Institute of Certified Public Accountants, and, accordingly, included obtaining an understanding of the internal control over financial reporting, testing and evaluating the design and operating effectiveness of the internal control, and such other procedures as we considered necessary in the circumstances. We believe that our examination provides a reasonable basis for our opinion.
Inherent limitations paragraph	Because of inherent limitations in any internal control, errors or irregularities may occur and not be detected. Also, projections of any evaluation of the internal control over financial reporting to future periods are subject to the risk that the internal control may become inadequate because of changes in conditions, or that the degree of compliance with the policies or procedures may deteriorate.
Opinion paragraph	In our opinion, management's assertion that the company maintained effective internal control over financial reporting as of December 31, 2008, is fairly stated, in all material respects, based upon suitable control criteria [may cite the COSO report on Internal Control—Integrated Framework].
Signature	*Mickey and Roger, CPAs*
Date	January 15, 2009

AUDITING INSIGHT Why Would a Company Voluntarily Audit Its Internal Control If It Didn't Have to?

A recent study of 397 mid-sized companies indicated that voluntary management reports on internal control (prior to the requirements of section 404 of Sarbanes-Oxley) were more likely for larger companies, companies with more active audit committees, companies with a greater level of institutional ownership, and companies with more rapid sales growth. In addition, none of these reports discussed a material weakness or included an auditor's attestation.

Source: S. Bronson, J. Carcello, and K. Raghunandan, "Firm Characteristics and Voluntary Management Reports on Internal Control," *Auditing: A Journal of Practice & Theory*, November 2006, pp. 25–39.

Compliance Attestation (AT 601)

Management often must report its compliance with contractual obligations to third parties. For example, entities may have restrictive covenants in loan agreements and lenders may require a periodic report on whether they have complied with such contractual agreements. Contractual agreements could include dividend limitations, loan limitations, prescribed debt/equity ratios, and limitations on geographic operations. Governmental agencies must comply with applicable laws and regulations. Accountants may accept engagements to attest to (1) an entity's compliance with the requirement of the laws, regulations, rules, and so forth, to (2) the effectiveness of an entity's internal controls that ensure compliance with the requirements. Accountants also can perform *agreed-upon procedures* regarding compliance. A *review* of compliance is not appropriate.

For a compliance attestation engagement, three conditions must be met: (1) management accepts responsibility for compliance, (2) management's evaluation of compliance or the controls over compliance is capable of evaluation and measurement against reasonable criteria, and (3) sufficient evidence must be available to support management's evaluation. Management may either make an assertion in a written report or as a written

representation to the accountants. The accountants then *examine* or perform *agreed-upon procedures* that evaluate management's written assertion about the entity's compliance with the reasonable criteria.

Attestation standards direct accountants to consider inherent risk, control risk, and detection risk in connection with *examination* engagements for compliance. These considerations are very similar to the risk elements in financial statement audits. However, consideration of materiality in compliance engagements may be difficult; sometimes monetary measures can be applied and sometimes they cannot. Nevertheless, risk and materiality are as important in compliance attestation as they are in financial statement audits.

Exercise of due care and professional skepticism about noncompliance are prerequisites for a compliance attestation examination. Otherwise, the major steps in a compliance attestation engagement are these:

- Understand the specific compliance requirements; assess planning materiality.
- Plan the engagement; assess inherent risk.
- Understand relevant controls over compliance; assess control risk with or without tests of controls; design tests of compliance with detection risk in mind.
- Obtain sufficient evidence of compliance with specific requirements, including a written letter of management representations. (This work represents the *substantive procedures* in a compliance attestation.)
- Consider subsequent events: subsequent information that bears on the management assertion and subsequent events of noncompliance after the assertion date.
- Form an opinion and write the report.

These standards call for work that is directly parallel to that in financial statement audits. The standard unqualified report (Exhibit A.4) is likewise very similar to the standard audit report. Accountants can write an unqualified report or, if findings dictate, prepare (1) a report modified to disclose a noncompliance event, (2) a qualified report stating material noncompliance, or (3) an adverse report stating that the entity is not in compliance.

Similar assurance may be given with regard to federal and state regulatory requirements. Examples include limitations on investments for mutual funds or state insurance department regulations about the nature of insurance company investments. Regulatory agencies may seek assertions in prescribed report language that goes beyond acceptable professional reporting responsibilities and involve accountants in areas outside their function and responsibility. In such cases, accountants should insert additional wording in the

EXHIBIT A.4
Standard Unqualified Compliance Attestation Report

Independent Accountant's Report

To the Agency:

We have examined the Agency's compliance with Department of Employment Regulation JR-52 during the year ended December 31, 2008. Management is responsible for the Agency's compliance with Regulation JR-52. Our responsibility is to express an opinion on the Agency's compliance based on our examination.

Our examination was made in accordance with standards established by the American Institute of Certified Public Accountants and, accordingly, included examining, on a test basis, evidence about the Agency's compliance with Regulation JR-52 and performing such other procedures as we considered necessary in the circumstances. We believe that our examination provides a reasonable basis for our opinion. Our examination does not provide a legal determination on the Agency's compliance with specified requirements.

In our opinion, the Agency complied, in all material respects, with Regulation JR-52 for the year ended December 31, 2008.

Mickey and Roger, CPAs
February 15, 2009

prescribed report language or write a completely revised report that reflects adequately their position and responsibility.

Management's Discussion and Analysis (AT 701)

Accountants also can examine or review **management's discussion and analysis** (MD&A) that usually accompanies the audited financial statements in corporate annual reports. Under existing audit standards (*SAS No. 8*, "Other Information in Documents Containing Audited Financial Statements"), auditors are required to read the MD&A section to ensure that this information accompanying the audited financial statements is consistent with them. The attestation engagement allows accountants to undertake engagements to additionally *examine* or *review* the MD&A section. The performance of the attestation engagement and subsequent reporting responsibilities are similar to other attestation engagements and would result in the accountants issuing an opinion on the MD&A based on the engagement performed.

Review Checkpoints

A.5 Regarding attestation, (a) what is it and (b) provide some examples of attestation engagements.

A.6 Identify several points of similarity between a compliance attestation engagement and an audit of financial statements.

UNAUDITED FINANCIAL STATEMENTS: REVIEWS AND COMPILATIONS

LEARNING OBJECTIVE

3. Write appropriate reports for review and compilation of unaudited financial statements, given specific factual circumstances.

Many public accounting firms perform bookkeeping, financial statement preparation, and financial statement review to help small businesses prepare financial communications. A subset of attestation engagements, these services are collectively referred to as *accounting and review services*. The Accounting and Review Services Committee has continuing responsibility for developing and issuing pronouncements of standards concerning the services and reports accountants may render in connection with unaudited financial statements. This committee issues *Statements on Standards for Accounting and Review Services (SSARS). SSARS* apply to work on unaudited financial statements of *nonpublic companies*.[4]

Review Services

The review services explained in this section apply specifically to accountants' work on the *unaudited* financial statements of *nonpublic* companies. In a review services engagement, accountants perform some procedures to achieve a level of assurance. This level is not the same that could be attained by performing an audit in accordance with GAAS. According to *SSARS 1* (AR 100), "Compilation and Review of Financial Statements," the objective of a review of financial statements is

> to provide a reasonable basis for expressing limited assurance that there are no material modifications that should be made to the financial statements in order for them to be in conformity with generally accepted accounting principles or, if applicable, with another comprehensive basis of accounting (OCBOA).[5]

Review work on unaudited financial statements consists primarily of (1) inquiry, (2) analytical procedures, and (3) the obtaining of written representations from management

[4] According to *SSARS,* a public company is one (1) whose securities trade in a public market such as a stock exchange, over the counter, and on locally quoted markets; (2) that files with a regulatory agency in preparation for the sale of securities in a public market; or (3) that is a subsidiary, joint venture, or other entity controlled by a company meeting either criterion (1) or (2). All other organizations are considered nonpublic.

[5] *Omnibus Statement on Standards for Accounting and Review Services—2007.*

EXHIBIT A.5 Representative Review Procedures

- *Obtain* an understanding with management about the nature and limitations of a review engagement (engagement letter).
- *Obtain* knowledge of the entity's business, the accounting principles of the entity's industry, and the entity's organization and operations.
- *Inquire* about the accounting system and bookkeeping procedures.
- *Perform and document* analytical procedures to identify relationships and individual items that appear to be unusual.
- *Inquire* about actions taken at meetings of stockholders, directors, and other important executive committees.
- *Read* (study) the financial statements for indications that they conform with generally accepted accounting principles or OCBOA.
- *Obtain* reports from other accountants who audit or review significant components, subsidiaries, or other investees.
- *Inquire* of management and directors about:
 - The preparation of financial statements in accordance with GAAP or OCBOA.
 - Accounting principles, practices, and methods used in applying those principles and procedures.
 - Unusual or complex situations that may affect the financial statements.
 - Significant transactions that occurred or were recognized near the end of the reporting period.
 - The status of uncorrected misstatements identified during the previous engagement.
 - Questions that have arisen in the course of applying review procedures.
 - Subsequent events that could have a material effect on the financial statements.
 - Significant journal entries and other adjustments.
 - Communications with regulatory agencies.
- *Perform* any other procedures considered necessary if the financial statements appear to be incorrect, incomplete, or otherwise unsatisfactory.
- *Prepare* documentation showing the matters covered by the inquiry and analytical procedures, especially the resolution of unusual problems and questions.
- *Obtain* from management written representations concerning its responsibility for the fair presentation of financial statements in accordance with GAAP or OCBOA, its belief that the financial statements are fairly presented, its belief that it has responded fully and truthfully to all inquiries and the information provided is complete, its disclosure of information concerning subsequent events, its acknowledgement of its responsibility to prevent and detect fraud, as well as its knowledge of any known or suspected fraud affecting the entity, involving management or others.

for all financial statements and periods covered by the accountants' review report. While the information gained through these procedures is similar to audit evidence, the recommended review procedures shown in Exhibit A.5 are much more limited in scope than the typical auditing procedures for assessing the risk of material misstatement, conducting physical observation of tangible assets, sending confirmations, or examining documentary details of transactions.

Professional standards (e.g., *SSARS 10*, "Performance of Review Engagements") require accountants to provide adequate documentation for the review engagement. Accountants are required to describe

- Matters covered in the accountants' inquiries.
- Analytical procedures performed.
- Significant expectations used in analytical procedures and factors used in determining the expectations.
- Results of the comparison of the expectations to the recorded amounts or ratios.
- Additional procedures performed in response to significant unexpected differences arising from the analytical procedures and the results of such procedures.
- Unusual matters that the accountants considered during the performance of the review procedures and their disposition.
- The written management representations.

Given the limited procedures performed (basically, inquiry of management, analytical procedures, and the obtaining of management's written representations), a review engagement does *not* provide a basis for expressing an opinion on financial statements. In a standard unqualified report for an audit engagement, auditors provide *positive assurance* (a forthright and factual statement of the auditors' opinion based on an audit) that the financial statements are fairly presented. For engagements less than an audit, accountants do not provide positive assurance. For example, a negative assurance conclusion typical in the review report on unaudited financial statements reads like this:

> Based on our review, *we are not aware* of any material modifications that should be made to the accompanying financial statements in order for them to be in conformity with generally accepted accounting principles.

(*SSARS 1*, AR 100). This conclusion is called *negative assurance* because it uses the phrase "we are *not aware*" to give assurance about conformity with GAAP. While auditing standards (e.g., *SAS 26*) prohibit the use of negative assurance in reports on audited financial statements (because it is considered too weak a conclusion for the audit effort), negative assurance is permitted in reviews of unaudited financial statements, in letters to underwriters, and in reviews of interim financial information.

Each page of the financial statements should be marked "See accountants' review report." The report on a complete review services engagement should include the following statements:

- A review service was performed in accordance with Statements on Standards for Accounting and Review Services issued by the AICPA.
- All information included in the financial statements is the representation of the management or owners of the business.
- A review consists primarily of inquiries of entity personnel, analytical procedures applied to financial data, and written representations from the entity's management.
- A review service is substantially less in scope than an audit, and an opinion on financial statements is not expressed. (This is a disclaimer of any audit opinion.)
- The accountants are not aware of any material modifications that should be made or, if aware of any, the report includes a disclosure of departure(s) from generally accepted accounting principles. (This is a *negative assurance*.)

When other independent accountants are involved in an audit or review of parts of the business, a principal reviewer can divide responsibility by referring to the other accountants in the review report. You can follow the spirit of the auditing standards (*SAS 1*, AU 543) to write the form and content of the reference to the work and reports of other auditors. Accountants who are not independent may not issue a review services report. An example of a review report is in Exhibit A.6.

Compilation Services

In your first principles of accounting course, you were probably given a list of account balances and accounting information and asked to prepare basic financial statements. In essence, you were being asked to do a compilation service. Compilation is a synonym for an older term, *write up*. Both terms refer to accountants helping clients "write up" the financial information in the form of financial statements. A **compilation service** is accounting work in which accountants perform few, if any, procedures, and it is substantially less than a review service. The objective of a compilation of financial statements, according to *SSARS 1* (AR 100) is

> to present in the form of financial statements information that is the representation of the management or owners. A compilation does not contemplate performing inquiry, analytical or any other procedures ordinarily performed in a review. Therefore, a compilation engagement is not designed to provide and does not provide assurance on the financial statements.[6]

[6] *Omnibus Statement on Standards for Accounting and Review Services—2007.*

EXHIBIT A.6
Example Review Report

Board of Directors, Children's Shoe House, Inc.:

We have reviewed the accompanying balance sheet of Children's Shoe House, Inc., as of January 31, 2008 and 2007, and the related statements of income, comprehensive income, and cash flows for the years then ended in accordance with Statements on Standards for Accounting and Review Services issued by the American Institute of Certified Public Accountants. All information included in these financial statements is the representation of the management of Children's Shoe House, Inc.

A review consists principally of inquiries of company personnel and analytical procedures applied to financial data. It is substantially less in scope than an audit in accordance with generally accepted auditing standards, the objective of which is the expression of an opinion regarding the financial statements taken as a whole. Accordingly, we do not express such an opinion.

Based on our review, we are not aware of any material modifications that should be made to the accompanying financial statements in order for them to be in conformity with generally accepted accounting principles.

Tosh & Company
February 25, 2009

In providing a compilation service, accountants should obtain an engagement letter, understand the entity's business and applicable accounting standards, read (study) the financial statements looking for obvious clerical or accounting principle errors, and follow up on information that is incorrect, incomplete, or otherwise unsatisfactory. Accountants are *not* required to assess control risk or to perform any other evidence-gathering procedures (e.g., observation, confirmation, document examination, inquiry, analytical procedures).

In a compilation engagement, given the very limited procedures performed, accountants explicitly state that no opinion and no assurance are expressed (basically issuing a disclaimer of opinion), thus taking no responsibility for a report on the fair presentation of financial statements in conformity with GAAP. The conclusion sentence in the compilation report on unaudited financial statements specifically states: "We have not audited or reviewed the accompanying financial statements and, accordingly, do not express an opinion or any other form of assurance on them" (*SSARS 1*, AR 100.14). Accountants who are not independent can issue a compilation report, provided the lack of independence is disclosed in the report.

Each page of the financial statements should be marked "See accountants' compilation report." The report should contain the following statements (see Exhibit A.7):

- That a compilation service has been performed in accordance with *Statements on Standards for Accounting and Review Services* issued by the AICPA.

- That the financial statement information is the representation of the management or owner(s) of the business.

- That the financial statements have not been audited or reviewed and the accountants do not express an opinion or any other form of assurance on them.

Three types of reports on compiled financial statements can be given:

1. The management or owners may not wish to present all footnote disclosures required by GAAP (believing such disclosures are not needed for their purposes). Accountants can issue a compilation report that notifies users of the omission and states that if they were included, they might influence users' conclusions about the business (provided the accountant has no reason to believe the footnotes were omitted to mislead the financial statement user).

EXHIBIT A.7
Example Compilation Report Modified for Omission of GAAP Disclosures and Accountants' Lack of Independence

President and Sole Stockholder, Petro-Chem Producing Corporation:

We have compiled the accompanying balance sheets of Petro-Chem Producing Corporation as of August 31, 2008 and 2007, and the related statements of income, comprehensive income, and cash flows for the years then ended, in accordance with Statements on Standards for Accounting and Review Services issued by the American Institute of Certified Public Accountants.

A compilation is limited to presenting in the form of financial statements information that is the representation of management. We have not audited or reviewed the accompanying financial statements and, accordingly, we do not express an opinion or any other form of assurance on them.

Management has elected to omit all the disclosures required by generally accepted accounting principles. If the omitted disclosures were included in the financial statements, they might influence users' conclusions about the company's financial position, results of operations, and cash flows. Accordingly, these financial statements are not designed for persons who are not informed about such matters.

We are not independent with respect to Petro-Chem Producing Corporation.

Tosh & Company
October 20, 2009

2. The management or owners may engage accountants who are not independent. In this case, the accountants can issue a compilation report stating their lack of independence.

3. The management or owners can also choose to present GAAP financial statements complete with all disclosures required by GAAP.

Exhibit A.7 shows a compilation report modified for these first two matters.

With the passage of *SSARS 8*, accountants can perform compilation engagements in which no compilation report is necessary (referred to as "plain-paper" engagements). Instead of issuing a compilation report, accountants have the option to document an understanding with the entity (through an engagement letter) regarding the services to be performed and the limitations on the use of those financial statements.

AUDITING INSIGHT Do Plain-Paper Financial Statements Have Any Value?

A survey of practicing CPAs and bankers found that both groups reported confidence and were likely to place some reliance on plain-paper statements. This confidence was even greater when a CPA was involved with the financial statements.

Source: Alan Reinstein, Brian Patrick Green, and Cathleen L. Miller, "Evidence of Perceived Quality of 'Plain-Paper Statements,'" *Auditing: A Journal of Practice & Theory* 25, no. 2 (November 2006), pp. 85–94.

Other Review and Compilation Topics

Additional *SSARS* statements explain standards for review and compilation engagements and reports that differ from audit standards. These topics point out some of the different problems in dealing with unaudited financial statements.

Reviews, Compilations, and Fraud

SSARS No. 12 requires accountants to establish an understanding with the entity, preferably in writing, that the accountants will inform the appropriate level of management if any evidence of fraud or illegal acts comes to the accountants' attention during the performance of compilation or review procedures. However, the accountants need not report matters regarding illegal acts that are clearly inconsequential.

Comparative Financial Statements

SSARS 2 (AR 200), "Reporting on Comparative Financial Statements," deals with reporting variations that turn out to be rather complex. The complexity arises from the several possible combinations of prior and current services. The following sections contribute some organization to the technical details found in *SSARS 2*.

Same or Higher Level of Service

These combinations are (in prior-year/current-year order) (1) compilation followed by compilation, (2) compilation followed by review, and (3) review followed by review. The essence of comparative reporting is to report on the current service and update the report on the statements of the prior period. Examples of report language are given in *SSARS 2* (AR 200). When the current-year work is an audit, the report is governed by auditing standards, not by SSARS (See *SAS 26.*).

When the current-year service is being performed by successor accountants, they cannot update the predecessors' report. In this case, the successors can request that the predecessors reissue the prior report and distribute it and the current report (in which case the predecessors must decide whether to reissue). Alternatively, the successors can simply indicate in the current report a paragraph describing the predecessors' report on the prior period. The paragraph (1) states that prior-period financials were compiled or reviewed by other accountants, (2) gives the date of the previous report, (3) describes the compilation disclaimer or review report with negative assurance rendered last year, and (4) describes any modifications written in the prior-year report (See AR 200 for examples.).

Lower Level of Service

These combinations are (in prior-year/current-year order) (1) review followed by compilation, (2) audit followed by compilation, and (3) audit followed by review. The essence of comparative reporting is to report on the current service and reissue (and not update) the report on the statements of the prior period. The underlying theory calling for reissuance in such cases is that accountants cannot update a previous report when currently performing a lower level of work compared to that performed in the prior year.

The alternative to reissuing a prior report is to include in the current report a paragraph describing the report on the prior-year financial statements. When the current-year service is being performed by successor accountants, the predecessors can be asked to reissue the prior report (subject to decisions to do so, AR 200). When the predecessors' report is not presented, the descriptive paragraph about the report can be added to the current-year report.

Prescribed Forms

Industry trade associations, banks, government agencies, and regulatory agencies often use prescribed forms (standard preprinted documents) to specify the content and measurement of accounting information required for special purposes. Such forms may not request disclosures required by GAAP or may specify measurements and disclosures that do not conform to GAAP. When such forms are compiled (not when reviewed) by accountants, the compilation report does not need to call attention to GAAP departures or GAAP disclosure deficiencies. The presumption is that the organization that prescribed the form knew what it was doing and does not need to be informed of the ways the form calls for GAAP departures. The reporting obligation is satisfied by adding the following paragraph (*SSARS 3*, AR 300.03) to the standard compilation report:

> The financial statements are presented in accordance with the requirements of (name of trade association, bank, agency, or other body), which differ from generally accepted accounting principles. Accordingly, these financial statements are not designed for those who are not informed about such differences.

However, departures from the information specified by a prescribed form should be treated in the report as the accountants otherwise would treat GAAP departures: by

disclosing them in the body of the accountants' report. Likewise, GAAP departures that are not specified in the prescribed form should still be treated as GAAP departures.

Communications between Predecessors and Successors

In the case of audits, successor auditors are required to make certain inquiries of predecessor auditors when a new client is obtained (*SAS 84*, AU 315). However, in compilation and review work, successor accountants are not required to communicate with predecessor accountants.

Nevertheless, *SSARS 4* (AR 400) advises accountants who decide to communicate with the predecessors. The standard suggests that inquiries may be a good idea if the successors do not know much about the new client, if the change in accountants occurred long after the end of the client's fiscal year (hinting at problems between the client and the predecessors), and if the client changes accountants frequently. When inquiries are made, the successors must obtain the client's permission for the predecessors to disclose confidential information. Otherwise, *SSARS 4* gives advice about inquiries that will give the successor a chance to learn about problem areas. When the successors make inquiries and the client gives the predecessors permission to respond to these inquiries, the predecessors are required to respond.

Personal Financial Plans

Personal financial planning provides a significant source of business for public accounting firms. Most personal financial plan documentation includes personal financial statements. Ordinarily, accountants associated with such statements would need to issue the standard compilation report (disclaimer), which seems rather awkward in a personal financial planning engagement when the client is the only one using the statements. *SSARS 6*, "Reporting on Personal Financial Statements Included in Written Personal Financial Plans" (AR 600.05), exempts such personal financial statements from the *SSARS 1* reporting requirement. However, the following report must be given, with each page of the financial report marked "See accountants' report":

> The accompanying Statement of Financial Condition of Rooster Cogburn, as of December 31, 2008, was prepared solely to help you develop your personal financial plan. Accordingly, it may be incomplete or contain other departures from generally accepted accounting principles and should not be used to obtain credit or for any purposes other than developing your financial plan. We have not audited, reviewed, or compiled the statement.

Note on GAAP Departures and Rule of Conduct 203

An accountants' report of known GAAP departures must be treated carefully in review and compilation reports. *SSARS* interpretations (AR 9100) carefully point out that the conclusion that "the financial statements are not in conformity with GAAP" is not appropriate in review and compilation reports because it is an adverse opinion that should be based only on audit evidence. Review and compilation engagements are not audits and the adverse opinion sentence cannot be included in either report. After all, both the review and compilation reports contain disclaimers of any audit-based opinion.

As in auditors' reports, however, accountants can and should add an explanatory paragraph pointing out known departures from GAAP, including omitted disclosures. This paragraph is placed after the normal standard report that gives the disclaimer on compiled financial statements, but the standard disclaimer is still given. In the case of a review report, the knowledge of GAAP departures means that the accountants must take exception to the departure in the negative assurance sentence, using the following language: "Based on our review, with the exception of the matter described in the following paragraph, we are not aware of any material modifications that should be made . . ." (AR 100.47).

Rule 203 of the AICPA Code of Conduct is explicitly worded to cover the negative assurance given in the standard review report. (The application of this rule in audits is explained in Chapter 12.) In review engagements, justifiable departures from official

pronouncements are treated in the same manner that they are in audits. The accountants add a paragraph explaining why adherence to an official pronouncement would cause financial statements to be misleading and the departure necessary in the circumstances; then the negative assurance paragraph is written in its standard, unmodified wording (AR 9100.73–.75).

The situation is different in a compilation engagement, however, because the accountants are giving neither an opinion nor a negative assurance. When compiled financial statements contain a known departure from an official pronouncement, the compilation report with its unmodified disclaimer is presented as usual. Then an explanatory paragraph is added, pointing out the departure and the financial effects, if known. If the accountants believe that the GAAP departure causes the financial statements to be misleading, they can refuse to give the compilation report and resign from the engagement.

Review Checkpoints

A.7 In what area(s) of practice are the Accounting and Review Service Committee pronouncements applicable?

A.8 What is the difference between a review service engagement and a compilation service engagement regarding historical financial statements? Compare both of these to an audit engagement.

RESPONSIBILITIES RELATED TO REPORTING ON INTERIM FINANCIAL INFORMATION

LEARNING OBJECTIVE

4. Explain auditors' responsibilities related to reporting on interim financial information.

Interim financial information refers to financial information or statements covering a period that ends on a date other than the entity's fiscal year end. Entities often provide interim financial information to owners and other financial statement users or attach such information to the audited annual financial statements. Companies that are under the jurisdiction of the Securities and Exchange Commission (SEC) are required to engage independent accountants to review interim financial information filed with the SEC. In addition, when a non-SEC entity is required to file with a regulatory agency in preparation for a public offering or listing, the interim information included in the filing must be reviewed. In each case, the accountants performing the review must have audited or be in the process of auditing the entity's latest annual financial statements.

A review of interim financial information differs considerably from an audit. According to *SAS 100*, the objective of a review of interim financial information is to provide the accountants a basis for communicating whether material modifications should be made to interim financial information to ensure conformity with GAAP. In this respect, the interim information review is very similar to a review of unaudited financial statements of a nonpublic company. The interim information review does not require a complete assessment of control risk each quarter or the gathering of sufficient appropriate evidential matter on which to base an opinion on interim financial information.

In reviewing interim financial information, the accountants need to acquire a sufficient knowledge of the entity's business and its internal control, just as if the engagement were an audit. This information will help the accountants identify the types of potential misstatements and select the inquiries and analytical procedures that will allow the accountants to communicate to management any modifications that must be made for the information to conform with GAAP. Basically, the extent of review procedures depends on the accountants' professional judgment about deficiencies in the internal control, the severity of unique accounting principles problems, and the errors that have occurred in the past. With knowledge of these areas, the accountants can direct and fine-tune the review procedures in the interest of improving the quality of the interim information. Many of the procedures outlined by *SAS 100* are provided in Exhibit A.8.

EXHIBIT A.8 *SAS 100* **Procedures for Reviewing Interim Financial Information**

- *Compare*
 - ✓ Interim financial information with comparable information for the immediately preceding interim periods.
 - ✓ Recorded amounts and ratios to expectations developed by the accountant.
 - ✓ Disaggregated revenue data (e.g., by month, product, business segment, etc.).
- *Consider plausible relationships* among both financial and nonfinancial information.
- *Read the minutes* of stockholder, board of director, and appropriate committee meetings to identify actions or events that may affect interim financial information.
- *Obtain reports* from other accountants who have been engaged to perform a review of interim financial information of significant components of the reporting entities.
- *Inquire of members* of management concerning
 - ✓ Conformity with generally accepted accounting principles.
 - ✓ Consistent application of accounting principles.
 - ✓ Unusual or complex situations that may have an effect on interim financial information.
 - ✓ Significant transactions occurring or recognized at the end of the period.
 - ✓ The status of uncorrected misstatements identified during previous audits and reviews.
 - ✓ Changes in the client's business or accounting practices.
 - ✓ Matters about which questions have arisen as a result of applying other procedures.
 - ✓ Events subsequent to the date of the interim information.
 - ✓ Knowledge of any fraud or suspected fraud affecting the entity.
 - ✓ Significant journal entries and other adjustments.
 - ✓ Communications from regulatory agencies.
 - ✓ Significant deficiencies in the design and operations of internal controls that could adversely affect the recording, processing, summarizing, and reporting of financial data.
 - ✓ The entity's ability to continue as a going concern.
- *Obtain evidence* that the interim financial information agrees or reconciles with accounting records.
- *Obtain written representations* from management about interim information matters including
 - ✓ Acknowledgment that management is responsible for
 The fair presentation of the company's financial statements.
 The financial statements' presentation in accordance with GAAP.
 The design and implementation of internal controls.
 - ✓ Disclosure of any internal control deficiencies.
 - ✓ Knowledge of fraud or suspected fraud.
 - ✓ Availability of financial information.
 - ✓ Absence of unrecorded transactions.
 - ✓ Completeness of
 All minutes of meetings.
 Communications with regulatory agencies.
 - ✓ The aggregate of unrecorded misstatements are immaterial.
 - ✓ Plans or intentions that may affect the interim financial information.
 - ✓ Significant estimates.
 - ✓ Violations or possible violations of laws or regulations.
 - ✓ Disclosure of all contingent liabilities and contingent losses.

Accountants may report on interim information presented separately from audited financial statements provided that a review has been satisfactorily completed. The basic content of the report is (*SAS 100*)

- A title that includes the word *independent.*
- Identification that the interim financial information was reviewed.
- A statement that the information is the responsibility of management.
- A statement that a review was made in accordance with standards established by the AICPA.
- A description of the review procedures.
- A statement that a review is substantially less in scope than an audit in accordance with GAAS.

EXHIBIT A.9
Report on Interim
Information in a
Company's Quarterly
Report

Independent Accountant's Report

The Board of Directors and Stockholders,
Fine Devices, Inc.:

We have reviewed the accompanying unaudited condensed balance sheets of Fine Devices, Inc., at April 28, 2008, and April 29, 2007, the related unaudited consolidated statements of income and comprehensive income for the three- and six-month periods ended April 28, 2008, and April 29, 2007, and the unaudited consolidated statements of cash flows for the six-month periods ending April 28, 2008, and April 29, 2007. This interim financial information is the responsibility of the company's management.

We conducted our review in accordance with standards established by the American Institute of Certified Public Accountants. A review of interim financial information consists principally of applying analytical procedures and making inquiries of persons responsible for financial and accounting matters. It is substantially less in scope than an audit conducted in accordance with generally accepted auditing standards, the objective of which is the expression of an opinion regarding the financial statements taken as a whole. Accordingly, we do not express such an opinion.

Based on our review, we are not aware of any material modifications that should be made to the accompanying financial information for it to be in conformity with generally accepted accounting principles in the United States.

Ernest & Somebody
Certified Public Accountants
May 16, 2009

- A statement about whether the accountants are aware of any material modifications that should be made so that the information conforms with GAAP.
- A disclaimer of opinion on the interim information.
- Public accounting firm's signature and date of the report.
- Each page should be marked "unaudited."

A report on reviewed interim information presented in a quarterly report (not within an annual report) is shown in Exhibit A.9.

Interim financial information may be presented as supplementary information accompanying audited financial statements or in a note to audited annual financial statements. This information should be clearly labeled "Unaudited." The audit report for the audited financial statements need not refer to the reviewed information. The audit report must refer to the interim financial information if the information

- Has not been marked "Unaudited."
- Is not in conformity with GAAP.
- Is required and omitted.
- Has not been reviewed.

Review Checkpoints

A.9 In what respects is a review of interim financial information similar to a review of the unaudited annual financial statements of a nonpublic company?

A.10 Is interim financial information required to be presented in order for annual financial statements to be in conformity with (a) GAAP and (b) SEC filing requirements?

A.11 When interim information is presented in a note to annual financial statements, under what circumstances would an audit report on the annual financial statements be modified with respect to the interim financial information?

OTHER TOPICS: SPECIAL AND RESTRICTED-USE REPORTS

LEARNING OBJECTIVE

5. Define, explain, and give examples of other comprehensive bases of accounting (OCBOA), distinguishing them from generally accepted accounting principles (GAAP).

Auditors may issue special reports in connection with the following:

- Conducting engagements to report on specified elements, accounts, or items of a financial statement *(SAS 62)*.
- Reporting on other comprehensive bases of accounting *(SAS 62)*.
- Reporting on the application of accounting principles *(SAS 50, SAS 97)*.
- Reporting on service organizations *(SAS 70, SAS 88)*.

Specified Elements, Accounts, or Items *(SAS 62)*

Special engagements with limited objectives enable auditors to provide needed services to entities. Auditors may be requested to render special reports on such things as rentals, royalties, profit participations, or a provision for income taxes. The first reporting standard does not apply because the specified element, account, or item does not purport to be a financial statement of financial position or results of operations. The second AICPA reporting standard (consistency) applies only if the element, account, or item is measured according to some provision of generally accepted accounting principles.

The auditors' report on elements, accounts, or items is very similar to the standard auditors' report. A GAAS audit is performed on specified elements, accounts, or items instead of financial statements. The auditors express an opinion on whether the element, account, or item is fairly stated in accordance with GAAP. Exhibit A.10 contains an illustrative report on a company's accounts receivable. If an adverse opinion or disclaimer of opinion is issued for the financial statements taken as a whole, the public accounting firm may not accept the engagement; this would prevent an entity from "negotiating" with the auditors for a positive opinion on a component of the financial statements if the opinion on the overall financial statements is not favorable.

Other Comprehensive Bases of Accounting

For a long time, controversy has existed concerning "Big GAAP–Little GAAP." Many accountants have been dismayed by the complexity of generally accepted accounting principles and have openly questioned their relevance to small businesses with uncomplicated operations. They believe that business managers and users of the financial statements care little about accounting for such things as pension obligations, capitalized leases, deferred taxes, and similar complicated topics. They characterize such topics as "standards overload" that may be necessary for "big business" but are largely superfluous for "small business."

EXHIBIT A.10
Report on a Financial Element

> **Independent Auditor's Report**
>
> To ABC Company Board of Directors:
>
> We have audited the accompanying schedule of accounts receivable of ABC Company as of December 31, 2008. This schedule is the responsibility of the Company's management. Our responsibility is to express an opinion on this schedule based on our audit.
>
> (Standard scope paragraph here, referring to the accounts receivable schedule)
>
> In our opinion, the schedule of accounts receivable referred to above presents fairly, in all material respects, the accounts receivable of ABC Company as of December 31, 2008, in conformity with generally accepted accounting principles.
>
> *David and Manny, CPAs*
> January 21, 2009

For a while, the "little GAAP" advocates lobbied for formal GAAP exemptions for small businesses. They actually won some battles. For example, earnings per share is an FASB requirement only for public companies. However, resistance arose in the counterargument that there was a danger of creating "second-class GAAP" for small business while reserving "real GAAP" for big companies. Bankers and other users of financial statements were not nearly so eager to have little GAAP financial statements as some accountants were. Anyway, many small businesses aspire to be large businesses and their managers may not want to be stigmatized by little GAAP beginnings.

The little GAAP fallback position has been the accounting known as **other comprehensive bases of accounting (OCBOA).** Companies that are not subject to SEC regulations and filing requirements can choose to present financial information in accordance with OCBOA. A *comprehensive basis* in this context refers to a coherent accounting treatment in which substantially all important financial measurements are governed by criteria other than GAAP. Some examples include (1) insurance company statements conforming to state regulatory agency accounting rules, (2) tax basis accounting, (3) **cash basis** accounting (i.e., no accruals) or **modified cash basis** (i.e., limited accruals such as long-term assets and liabilities or inventory), and (4) some other methods such as constant-dollar, price-level-adjusted, and current-value financial statements.

The Private Companies Practice Section (PCPS) of the AICPA Division for Firms has promoted OCBOA to its members as a way to accomplish little GAAP. The position is that OCBOA financial statements can be less expensive to produce and easier to interpret than full GAAP statements. Surveys report that 50 percent of OCBOA financial statements are on the tax basis of accounting and 49 percent are on the cash basis. However, PCPS also notes that OCBOA are appropriate only when they meet user needs.

SAS 62 warns that OCBOA financial statements should not use the titles normally associated with GAAP statements such as balance sheet, statement of financial position, statement of operations, income statement, statement of comprehensive income, and statement of cash flows. Even the titles are said to suggest GAAP financial statements. Instead, OCBOA statements should use titles like these:

* Statement of Assets and Liabilities—Regulatory Basis.
* Statement of Assets and Liabilities—Cash Basis.
* Statement of Admitted Assets, Liabilities, and Surplus—Statutory Basis Required by the Insurance Department of the State of (name).
* Statement of Assets, Liabilities, and Capital—Income Tax Basis.
* Statement of Income—Regulatory Basis.
* Statement of Revenue and Expenses—Income Tax Basis.
* Statement of Revenue Collected and Expenses Paid—Cash Basis.
* Statement of Changes in Partners' Capital Accounts—Income Tax Basis.

OCBOA statements can be audited, reviewed, or compiled like any other financial statements. All general and field work auditing standards and the standards for review and compilation apply, just as they apply for GAAP financial statements. The reporting standards regarding consistency, adequate disclosure, and report responsibility (fourth reporting standard) also apply to OCBOA statements. OCBOA do not reduce disclosure requirements. However, the first reporting standard, which requires the audit report statement on whether the financial statements are presented in conformity with GAAP, is handled differently.

When OCBOA are used, the first reporting standard is satisfied by a sentence in the report that presents the OCBOA basis of accounting; the opinion sentence refers to the OCBOA instead of to GAAP. Disclosures in the financial statements should (1) contain an explanation of the OCBOA and (2) describe in general how the OCBOA differ from GAAP. However, the differences between GAAP and the OCBOA do not have to be quantified; that is, the OCBOA do not need to be reconciled to GAAP with dollar amounts. For all practical purposes, the GAAP criteria are replaced by criteria applicable to the OCBOA. An example of a special report on cash basis statements is in Exhibit A.11.

EXHIBIT A.11
Special Report on OCBOA (Cash Basis Statements)

Independent Auditor's Report

To Natalia National Bank Association (Trustee)
and the Unit Holders of the Mega Offshore Trust:

We have audited the accompanying statements of assets, liabilities, and trust corpus—cash basis, of the Mega Offshore Trust as of December 31, 2008 and 2007, and the related statements of changes in trust corpus—cash basis, for each of the three years in the period ended December 31, 2008. These financial statements are the responsibility of the Company's management. Our responsibility is to express an opinion on these financial statements based on our audits.

(Standard scope paragraph here)

As described in Note 2, these financial statements were prepared on the cash receipts and disbursements basis of accounting, which is a comprehensive basis of accounting other than generally accepted accounting principles.

In our opinion, the financial statements referred to above present fairly, in all material respects, the assets, liabilities, and trust corpus arising from cash transactions of the Mega Offshore Trust as of December 31, 2008 and 2007, and the related changes in trust corpus arising from cash transactions for each of the three years in the period ended December 31, 2008, on the basis of accounting described in Note 2.

George Costanza, CPA
March 18, 2009

Reporting on the Application of Accounting Principles *(SAS 50, SAS 97)*

The subject of "reporting on the application of accounting principles" touches a sensitive nerve in the public accounting profession. It arose from entities' searching for a public accounting firm that would agree to give an unqualified audit report on a questionable accounting treatment. *Opinion shopping* often involved auditor–client disagreements, after which the client said, "If you won't agree with my accounting treatment, then I'll find an auditor who will." These disagreements often involved early revenue recognition and unwarranted expense or loss deferral. A few cases of misleading financial statements occurred after shopping resulted in clients switching to more agreeable auditors. However, the practice is not entirely undesirable because "second opinions" on complex accounting matters often benefit from consultation with other auditors.

The auditing standard "Reporting on the Application of Accounting Principles" *(SAS 50)* established procedures for dealing with requests for consultation from parties other than auditors' own clients. These parties can include other companies (nonclients who are shopping), attorneys, investment bankers, and perhaps other people. *SAS 50* is applicable in these situations:

- When preparing a written report or giving oral advice on specific transactions, either completed or proposed.
- When preparing a written report or giving oral advice on the type of audit opinion that might be rendered on specific financial statements.

Providing a written report on a hypothetical transaction is prohibited. Also, the standard does not apply to conclusions about accounting principles offered in connection with litigation support engagements or expert witness work, nor does it apply to advice given to another CPA in public practice. It also does not apply to an accounting firm's expressions of positions in newsletters, articles, speeches, lectures, and the like, provided that the positions do not give advice on a specific transaction or apply to a specific company.

When auditors evaluate the application of accounting principles, they are not required to issue written reports. However, a written report or oral advice that is provided to an entity regarding this application of accounting principles should

- Describe the engagement and state that it was performed in accordance with appropriate standards *(SAS 50)*.
- Identify the entity and describe the transactions, circumstances, and sources of information.
- Provide the conclusion about appropriate accounting principles or the type of audit report, including reasons for the conclusions, if appropriate.
- State that the entity's management is responsible for proper accounting treatments in consultation with its own auditors.
- State that any differences in facts, circumstances, or assumptions might change the conclusions.
- Include a separate paragraph that indicates (1) the report is for the sole use of specified parties, (2) the specified parties for whom the report is intended, and (3) the information should not be used by anyone else.

The purpose of *SAS 50* is to impose some discipline on the process of shopping/consultation and to erect a barrier to some companies' quest for willing accountants.

Special Reports: Service Organizations *(SAS 70, SAS 88)*

Occasionally, some clients' transactions are handled by a **service organization,** another business that executes or records transactions on behalf of the client. Examples of service organizations include payroll processing companies, computerized information processing service centers, trust departments of banks, insurers that maintain the accounting records for ceded insurance (reinsurance transactions), mortgage bankers and savings and loan associations that service loans for owners, and transfer agents that handle the shareholder accounting for mutual and money market investment funds. The fact that management is *outsourcing* some of its noncore functions does not absolve management of its responsibility for internal control over those functions. Management (as well as the audit team) must somehow gain comfort that controls are in place and effective. The solution to this dilemma is a special-purpose report on internal control (referred to as a *SAS 70* report) in which the service organization's auditors report on the effectiveness of the service organization's internal control to the service organization's customers (and their auditors). This situation is described in Exhibit A.12.

EXHIBIT A.12
Special Reports:
Service Organization
Controls

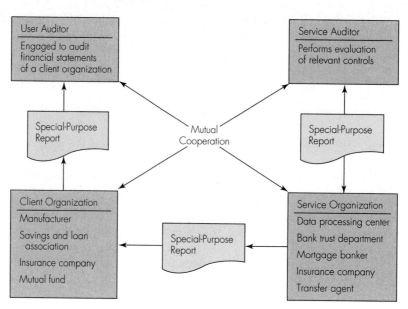

AUDITING INSIGHT Increase in *SAS 70* Reports Tied to Sarbanes-Oxley

With increased outsourcing of activities that are not company core competencies, the emphasis on *SAS 70* reports takes on increased importance. Take, for example, **Service Corporation International (SCI)**, the largest provider of funeral, cemetery, and cremation services in North America. SCI's funeral homes are spread across 48 states, Canada, and Puerto Rico. The company outsources both generic activities (e.g., payroll) as well as some activities specific to its industry (e.g., the management of trust accounts held for future funeral and cremation services). While it would not be cost-effective for the company's management to examine the controls over all of these activities (as required by Sarbanes-Oxley), they rely on service auditors to do the work for them—the company will collect over 40 *SAS 70* reports this year.

Source: "SAS 70 Reports Continue to Grow in Demand and Utility for Sarbanes-Oxley Compliance," available at www.Protiviti.ca.

There are two types of *SAS 70* reports. A Type I report describes the service organization's internal controls placed in operation at a specific point in time but does not report on the effectiveness of the controls. A Type II report not only includes a description of the controls, but also reports on the service organization's auditors' testing of the controls over a minimum six-month period. Only the Type II reports are useful with respect to meeting Sarbanes-Oxley's rigorous internal control requirements. Ordinarily, service auditors' reports are not public reports on internal controls but are used only by service organization customers' auditors to assess internal controls at the service organization. Another note of caution: The auditors for the service organization customer must be read the *SAS 70* report carefully and consider the effect of any necessary controls that are missing or otherwise ineffective.

AUDITING INSIGHT *SAS 70* and Sarbanes-Oxley

Evidence exists that both auditors and clients attribute a greater level of assurance in the areas of privacy and security than is intended or actually provided by *SAS 70* reports. Some common misperceptions about the level of assurance that *SAS 70* reports provide with respect to privacy and security include the following. First, the outsourcing services auditors only review controls deemed relevant by *its* client, the services provider (not the customer or the customer's auditors). Second, the service organization auditors make one overall evaluation rather than addressing each control by control. Additionally, the user auditors may not agree with the service auditors' findings; worse, "they might just look for a clean opinion, locate it, and stow the document away without reading further." Finally, "*SAS 70* is intended to be a service-auditor-to-client auditor communication tool. But some [information technology] people think it affirms privacy and security. It doesn't," says Everett Johnson, president of the Information Systems Audit and Control Association.

Source: "*SAS 70* Weak on Data Security: Experts," *CFO.com*, November 28, 2006.

Review Checkpoints

A.12 Regarding OCBOA, (a) why do they exist and (b) can their financial statements be audited?

A.13 What are some examples of (a) OCBOA and (b) entities for which current value is GAAP?

A.14 How could "opinion shopping" be (a) suspect or (b) beneficial?

A.15 What must a CPA do when reporting on the application of accounting principles?

Summary

Public accounting firms are highly regarded for their attestation services. Many forms of services, in addition to audits of historical financial statements, have arisen or have been proposed. Managers of companies often develop innovative financial presentations and want to give the public some assurance about them, so they engage auditors. Regulators also often become interested in auditors' communication of information and press for attestation involvement. Guided by the general attestation standards, auditing standards, and accounting and review services standards, auditors offer services and render reports in several areas.

Unaudited financial statements have been around for a long time. Work on them is known in public practice as review *and compilation.* The differences lie in the amount of work performed and the level of assurance given in an accountants' report. Review engagements involve less work than an audit and the report gives a low level of negative assurance instead of an audit opinion. Compilation engagements merely involve writing up the financial statements, which is less work than a review, and the report gives no assurance in the form of an outright disclaimer. See Exhibit A.13 for a summary of the differences among services commonly provided by public accounting firms.

Another type of review is a review of interim financial information (e.g., quarterly financial reports). This review is technically similar to a review of unaudited financial statements and the report on free-standing interim financial statements gives the negative assurance.

Some entities have the option to prepare their statements for public use on other comprehensive bases of accounting (OCBOA). Auditors can audit and report on such financial statements. This option gives managers an opportunity to avoid the complications of many of the GAAP rules. OCBOA audits and reporting are discussed in the auditing standards under the heading of "special reports." Other types of special audit reports can be given on particular elements, accounts, or items in a financial statement.

EXHIBIT A.13
Summary of Differences among Audits, Reviews, and Compilations

	Audit	**Review**	**Compilation**
Objective	To provide a reasonable basis for expressing an opinion regarding the financial statements taken as a whole	To provide a reasonable basis for expressing limited assurance that there are no material modifications that should be made to the financial statements in order for the statements to be in conformity with GAAP or, if applicable, OCBOA	To present in the form of financial statements information that is the representation of the management or owners
Procedures	Audit procedures required by generally accepted auditing standards (GAAS)	Inquire Perform analytical procedures Obtain management representation letter	Read the financial statements and look for obvious errors
Assurance	Positive	Negative	No assurance
Independence required?	Yes	Yes	No (although independence for compilations is currently being discussed)
Professional standards	PCAOB *Auditing Standards (ASs)* ASB *Statements on Auditing Standards (SASs)*	AICPA *Statements on Standards for Accounting and Review Services (SSARS)*	

Key Terms

agreed-upon procedures: An engagement in which users participate in determining the scope of procedures performed by the accountants, 505

assurance services: Professional services aimed at improving the quality of information for decision makers; include a variety of information including nonfinancial information, 501

attestation: Professional services resulting in a report on subject matter or an assertion about subject matter that is the responsibility of another party, 505

cash basis: A comprehensive basis of accounting that includes no accruals, 522

compilation service: An accounting service in which the practitioner assists in assembling information that is the representation of management but provides no assurance, 513

CPA Performance View: An assurance service that takes a prospective look at company performance, 504

examination: An attestation engagement similar in nature to an audit, 505

financial forecast: Prospective financial information reflecting an entity's estimates of what is likely to occur in a future period, 507

financial projection: Prospective financial information reflecting a transaction or event that may occur in the future, 507

interim financial information: Financial information or statements covering a period that ends on a date other than the entity's fiscal year end, 518

management's discussion and analysis: A required section of financial reports of public companies that analyzes the results of operations and cash flows for the periods presented, 511

modified cash basis: A comprehensive basis of accounting that provides limited accruals for items such as fixed assets and/or inventories and long-term debt, 522

other comprehensive bases of accounting (OCBOA): A coherent accounting treatment in which substantially all important financial measurements are governed by criteria other than GAAP, 522

PrimePlus/ElderCare Services: An assurance service that focuses on a variety of financial, health care, and living decisions for senior citizens as well as financial planning, tax assistance, and cash management, 503

pro forma: Financial information reflecting historical data as if a certain transaction had occurred, 507

review: An engagement whereby a practitioner provides limited assurance about financial information, 505

service organization: An entity that processes transactions for another entity, 524

SysTrust Services: An assurance service that reviews an entity's computer system to provide assurance to business partners and customers concerning the security, privacy, and confidentiality of information in addition to system availability and processing integrity, 503

trust services: Category of assurance on the reliability of Web sites to consumers (WebTrust) and of business-to-business computer transaction (SysTrust), 503

WebTrust Services: An assurance service designed to reduce the concerns of Internet users regarding the existence of a company and the reliability of key business information placed on its Web site, 502

Multiple Choice Questions for Practice and Review

A.16 In providing assurance services to clients, public accounting firms are building on their reputations for

a. Knowledge and integrity.

b. Objectivity and integrity.

c. Independence and due professional care.

d. Professionalism and trust.

A.17 The AICPA Special Committee on Assurance Services identified eight mega trends that can affect a CPA's business. Which of the following is *not* one of these mega trends?

a. The decreasing supply of natural resources.

b. Information technology.

c. Changes in corporate structure.

d. Changes in investment capital.

A.18 An *assurance service* is defined as a service that

a. Provides auditing services to nonfinancial information.

b. Reviews unaudited financial information.

c. Improves the quality of information for decision makers.

d. Reduces the risk in management decision making.

A.19 Bill is surfing the Internet and finds a great pair of rollerblades at a really low price. He has never heard of the company and is concerned that he may not receive the product he orders. Bill may be more willing to place an order with this company if

a. The Web site displays the WebTrust seal.

b. The company provides its annual report and the report of the independent auditors on its Web site.

c. The company provides a money-back guarantee.

d. Only a partial payment is required prior to receiving the product.

A.20 Which of the following is *not* a principle of Trust Services?

a. Security.

b. Authentication.

c. Privacy.

d. Confidentiality.

A.21 Which of the following is *not* an assurance service provided by public accounting firms?

a. SysTrust.

b. PrimePlus.

c. Performance View.

d. ValueCare.

A.22 Practice in connection with unaudited historical cost financial statements is conducted by

a. International accounting firms only.

b. Regional and local public accounting firms.

c. Local public accounting firms only.

d. All public accounting firms.

A.23 The official *Statements on Standards for Accounting and Review Services* are applicable to practice with

a. Audited financial statements of public companies.

b. Unaudited financial statements of public companies.

c. Unaudited financial statements of nonpublic companies.

d. Audited financial statements of nonpublic companies.

A.24 Which of the following is a general standard of generally accepted attestation standards but *not* a general standard of generally accepted auditing standards?

a. Adequate training and proficiency.

b. Adequate knowledge in the subject matter.

c. Independence.

d. Due professional care.

A.25 In performing an attestation on prospective financial information (PFI), which of the following is *not* required?

a. If the basis of the PFI is different than the financial statements, a reconciliation of the two must be provided.

b. Management must disclose all significant assumptions used.

c. Management must disclose significant accounting policies and procedures used in generating the PFI.

d. Management must disclose the probability of obtaining the results included in the PFI.

A.26 To perform an attestation on prospective information or *pro forma* information, accountants must do all of the following except

a. Obtain knowledge about the entity's business and accounting principles.

b. Understand the internal controls used in the processes that generated the information.

c. Obtain an understanding of the process through which the information was developed.

d. Evaluate the assumptions used to prepare the information.

A.27 A review service engagement involving unaudited financial statements involves
 a. More work than a compilation and an audit.
 b. Less work than an audit but more work than a compilation.
 c. Less work than a compilation but more work than an audit.
 d. More work than an audit but less work than a compilation.

A.28 When accountants are not independent, which of the following reports can nevertheless be issued?
 a. Compilation report.
 b. Standard unqualified audit report.
 c. Examination report on a forecast.
 d. Review report on unaudited financial statements.

A. 29 For a compliance engagement, three conditions must be met. Which of the following is *not* one of the three conditions?
 a. Management accepts responsibility for compliance.
 b. Management's evaluation of compliance is capable of evaluation and is measured against reasonable criteria.
 c. Sufficient evidence is available to support management's evaluation.
 d. Management provides a report attesting to the satisfactory compliance.

A.30 Accountants are permitted to express "negative assurance" in which of the following reports?
 a. Standard unqualified audit report on audited financial statements.
 b. Compilation report on unaudited financial statements.
 c. Review report on unaudited financial statements.
 d. Adverse opinion report on audited financial statements.

A.31 When a company's financial statements in a review or compilation engagement contain a known material departure from an FASB statement on financial accounting standards that is acceptable to the accountants, the accountants' report can
 a. Make no mention of the departure in a compilation report because it contains an explicit disclaimer of opinion.
 b. Express an adverse opinion.
 c. Explain the departure as necessary to make the statements not misleading and then express a disclaimer.
 d. Explain the departure as necessary to make the statements not misleading and then provide negative assurance.

A.32 When interim financial information is presented in a footnote to annual financial statements, the standard audit report on the annual financial statements should
 a. Not mention the interim information unless there is an exception the auditors need to include in the report.
 b. Contain an audit opinion paragraph that specifically mentions the interim financial information if it is not in conformity with GAAP.
 c. Contain an extra paragraph that gives negative assurance on the interim information if it has been reviewed.
 d. Contain an extra explanatory paragraph if the interim information note is labeled "unaudited."

A.33 During a review of a nonpublic entity's financial statements, accountants are required to make certain inquiries of management. Which of the following inquiries is *not* required by the *SSARS*?
 a. The basis for the preparation of financial statements.
 b. Internal control deficiencies.
 c. Significant transactions occurring near the end of the reporting period.
 d. Material subsequent events.

A.34 According to auditing standards, financial statements presented on another comprehensive basis of accounting should not

 a. Contain a note describing the other basis of accounting.

 b. Describe in general how the other basis of accounting differs from generally accepted accounting principles.

 c. Be accompanied by an audit report that gives an unqualified opinion with reference to the other basis of accounting.

 d. Contain a note with a quantified dollar reconciliation of the assets based on the other comprehensive basis of accounting with the assets based on generally accepted accounting principles.

A.35 For which two of the following reports is an expression of negative assurance *not* permitted?

 a. A review report on unaudited financial statements.

 b. An audit report on financial statements prepared on a comprehensive basis of accounting other than GAAP.

 c. An examination report on a financial forecast.

 d. A review report on interim financial information.

A.36 In a current-value presentation of the balance sheet of a manufacturing company,

 a. The basis of valuation must always be explained in notes to the financial statements.

 b. The basis of valuation is well known as a comprehensive basis of accounting other than GAAP.

 c. Auditors can attest to the fair presentation of financial position in conformity with GAAP.

 d. The company must follow the AICPA guides for presentation of a financial forecast.

Exercises, Problems, and Simulations

A.37 **Assurance Services.** In 1995, the AICPA Special Committee on Assurance Services identified eight megatrends that can affect a CPA's business.

Required:

 a. Review the megatrends that were identified. Are these trends still viable in today's society and economy? Which trends, if any, need to be reconsidered due to current conditions in society and the economy?

 b. Are there additional trends in the marketplace that could affect a public accounting firm's business?

A.38 **Internet Exercise: Assurance Services.** Go to the Internet and identify a company that uses the WebTrust seal. (*Hint:* The AICPA provides a list on its Web site.)

Required:

Click on the WebTrust seal and identify the information available for Internet customers. Continue to search other information that may be linked to that Web site. Is the information sufficient to provide an Internet user with assurance about the company and its Web site?

A.39 **Assurance Services.** Dave has a store that sells old baseball cards. To expand the business, he has decided to open an Internet site where potential customers can view the cards and place orders. Dave hires Karen, who is an expert in constructing Web sites for small businesses. Karen explains that even with a quality Web site and pictures of the merchandise for sale, customers may be reluctant to purchase baseball cards from his Web site.

Required:

 a. Explain the reasons for Karen's concerns.

 b. What steps can Dave and Karen take to reduce customer's reluctance to make purchases on the Internet?

A.40 **Assurance Services.** Henry's Health Food Store maintains a perpetual inventory on its computer. The sales representative from A-Plus Vitamins has recommended the following to Henry:

- All the files should have password protection.

- A-Plus Vitamins should be given the telephone number and the password for the inventory file on the computer, which is connected to a dedicated phone line and can be accessed from outside.

- A-Plus Vitamins will search the inventory for items that fall below an established re-order point and will automatically ship a set amount of product to its store.

Required:

 a. What are the advantages of this arrangement for Henry? For A-Plus Vitamins?

 b. What concerns might Henry have in this arrangement?

 c. How might his concerns be addressed?

A.41 **PrimePlus/ElderCare Services.** Mary has contacted you as a CPA who performs Prime-Plus/ElderCare Services. Her mother, Pat, is a widow who has lived alone for the last five years. Pat is now 80 years old and, although she is in good health, she and Mary have agreed that she needs more assistance in her daily life. They have agreed that Pat should move to an assisted-living facility. Further, they agree that the facility will provide Pat with her own apartment, cleaning services, emergency services, and a dining room for meal service. Several facilities in the area appear to meet these requirements.

Required:

 As a CPA performing PrimePlus Services, how can you assist Mary and Pat in this decision?

A.42 **Attestation Evaluation Criteria.** The local high school experienced trouble two years ago. Its graduation rates had declined to the bottom 10 percent in the state, college admission rates were low, and graduates had a high unemployment rate. The school board and administration have notified the state Department of Education and the taxpayers in the school district that these problems have been fixed. Graduation rates have increased, a higher percentage of students are continuing with their education, and a higher percentage of students have jobs. The Department of Education wants an independent attestation to these assertions. It is concerned not only about the numbers claimed by the school board and administration, but also about the underlying process and means used to obtain these numbers.

Required:

 Establish a list of criteria you would use to validate the claim of the school board and administration and to determine the processes and means used to obtain these numbers.

A.43 **Errors in an Accountants' Review Report.** Jordan & Stone, CPAs, audited the financial statements of Tech Company, a nonpublic entity, for the year ended December 31, 2007, and expressed an unqualified opinion. For the next year, ended December 31, 2008, Tech issued comparative financial statements. Jordan & Stone reviewed Tech's 2008 financial statements and Kent, an assistant on the engagement, drafted the accountants' review report that follows. Stone, the engagement supervisor, decided not to reissue the prior-year audit report but instructed Kent to include a separate paragraph in the current-year review report describing the responsibility assumed for the prior-year audited financial statements. This is an appropriate reporting procedure.

 Stone reviewed Kent's draft and indicated in the following supervisor's review notes that the draft contained several deficiencies.

Accountants' Review Report—Kent's Draft

 We have reviewed and audited the accompanying balance sheets of Tech Co. as of December 31, 2008 and 2007, and the related statements of income and comprehensive income, retained earnings, and cash flows for the years then ended, in accordance with Statements on Standards for Accounting and Review Services issued by the American Institute of Certified Public Accountants and generally accepted auditing standards. All information included in these financial statements is the representation of the management of Tech Company.

 A review consists principally of inquiries of company personnel and analytical procedures applied to financial data. It is substantially less in scope than an audit in accordance with generally accepted auditing standards, the objective of which is the expression of an opinion regarding the financial statements taken as a whole.

 Based on our review, we are not aware of any material modifications that should be made to the accompanying financial statements. Because of the inherent limitations of a review engagement, this report is intended for the information of management and should not be used for any other purpose.

 The financial statements for the year ended December 31, 2007, were audited by us and our report was dated March 2, 2008. We have no responsibility for updating that report for events and circumstances occurring after that date.

Jordan and Stone, CPAs

March 1, 2009

 (AICPA adapted)

Required:

These supervisor's review notes may or may not be correct. For each item 1–14, indicate whether Stone is correct (C) or incorrect (I) in the criticism of Kent's draft.

1. The report should contain no reference to the prior-year audited financial statements in the first (introductory) paragraph.

2. All current-year basic financial statements are not properly identified in the first (introductory) paragraph.

3. The report should contain no reference to the American Institute of Certified Public Accountants in the first (introductory) paragraph.

4. Accountants' review and audit responsibilities should follow management's responsibilities in the first (introductory) paragraph.

5. The report should contain no comparison of the scope of a review to an audit in the second (scope) paragraph.

6. Negative assurance should be expressed on the current-year reviewed financial statements in the second (scope) paragraph.

7. The report should contain a statement that no opinion is expressed on the current-year financial statements in the second (scope) paragraph.

8. The report should contain a reference to "conformity with generally accepted accounting principles" in the third paragraph.

9. The report should not express a restriction on the distribution of the accountants' review report in the third paragraph.

10. The report should not contain a reference to "material modifications" in the third paragraph.

11. The report should contain an indication of the type of opinion expressed on the prior-year audited financial statements in the fourth (separate) paragraph.

12. The report should indicate that no auditing procedures were performed after the date of the report on the prior-year financial statements in the fourth (separate) paragraph.

13. The report should not contain a reference to "updating the prior-year auditors' report for events and circumstances occurring after that date" in the fourth (separate) paragraph.

14. The description of procedures performed in a review engagement in the second (scope) paragraph is incomplete.

A.44 **Review of Forecast Assumptions.** Dodd Manufacturing Corporation has engaged you to attest to the reasonableness of the assumptions underlying its forecast of revenues, costs, and net income for the next calendar year, 2009. Four of the assumptions follow.

a. The company intends to sell certain real estate and other facilities held by Division B at an after-tax profit of $600,000; the proceeds of this sale will be used to retire outstanding debt.

b. The company will call and retire all outstanding 9 percent subordinated debentures (callable at 108). The debentures are expected to require the full call premium given present market interest rates of 8 percent on similar debt. A rise in market interest rates to 9 percent would reduce the loss on bond retirement from the projected $200,000 to $190,000.

c. Current labor contracts expire on September 1, 2009, and the new contract is expected to result in a wage increase of 5.5 percent. Given the forecasted levels of production and sales, after-tax operating earnings would be reduced approximately $50,000 for each percentage point of wage increase in excess of the expected contract settlement.

d. The sales forecast for Division A assumes that the new Portsmouth facility will be complete and operating at 40 percent of capacity on February 1, 2009. It is highly improbable that the facility will be operational before January 2009. Each month's delay would reduce Division A sales by approximately $80,000 and operating earnings by $30,000.

Required:

For each assumption, state the evidence sources and procedures you would use to determine the reasonableness.

A.45 **Compilation and Review Procedures.** The following numbered items 1–10 state procedures accountants should consider in review engagements and compilation engagements on the annual financial statements of nonpublic entities (performed in accordance with AICPA *Statements on Standards for Accounting and Review Services*).

Required:

For each item (taken separately), tell whether the item is (a) required in all review engagements, (b) not required in review engagements, (c) required in all compilation engagements, (d) not required in compilation engagements. For each item, give two responses, one regarding review engagements and the other regarding compilation engagements.

1. The accountants should establish an understanding with the entity's management regarding the nature and limitations of the services to be performed.

2. The accountants should make inquiries concerning actions taken at the board of directors' meetings.

3. The accountants, as the entity's successor accountants, should communicate with the predecessor accountants to obtain access to the predecessors' audit documentation.

4. The accountants should obtain a level of knowledge of the accounting principles and practices of the entity's industry.

5. The accountants should obtain an understanding of the entity's internal control.

6. The accountants should perform analytical procedures designed to identify relationships that appear to be unusual.

7. The accountants should assess the risk of material misstatement.

8. The accountants should obtain a letter from the entity's attorney to corroborate the information furnished by management concerning litigation.

9. The accountants should obtain management representations from the entity.

9. The accountants should study the relationship of the financial statement elements that would be expected to conform to a predictable pattern.

(AICPA adapted)

A.46 **Compilation Presentation Alternatives.** Jimmy C operates a large service station, garage, and truck stop on Interstate 95 near Plainview. His brother, Bill, has recently joined as a partner, even though he will continue his small CPA practice. One slow afternoon, they were discussing financial statements with Bert, the local CPA who operates the largest public practice in Plainview.

Jimmy: The business is growing, and sometimes I need to show financial statements to parts suppliers and the loan officers at the bank.

Bert: That so?

Jimmy: Yea-boy, and they don't like the way I put 'em together.

Bert: That so?

Bill: Heck, Jimmy, I know all about that. I can compile a jim-dandy set of financial statements for us.

Jimmy: What does Jim Dan over at the cafe have to do with it?

Bert: Never mind, Jimmy. Bill can't do compiled financial statements for you. He's not independent.

Jimmy: I know. Momma didn't let him outa the house 'til he was 24. The neighbors complained.

Bert: That so?

Bill: Shucks.

Jimmy: But, Bert, those fellas are always asking me about accounting policies, contingencies, and stuff like that. Said something about "footnotes." I don't want to fool with all that small print.

Required:

Think about the financial disclosure problems of Jimmy and Bill's small business. What types of compiled financial statements can be prepared for them and by whom?

A.47 **Negative Assurance in Review Reports.** One portion of the report on a review services engagement is the following: "Based on my review, I am not aware of any material modifications that should be made to the accompanying financial statements in order for them to be in conformity with generally accepted accounting principles."

Required:

a. Is this paragraph a "negative assurance" given by the accountants?

b. Why is "negative assurance" generally prohibited in audit reports?

c. What justification is there for permitting "negative assurance" in a review services report on unaudited financial statements and on interim financial information?

A.48 **Audit Simulation: Deficiencies in an Internal Control Communication.** Land & Hale, CPAs, are auditing the financial statements of Marlowe Company, a nonpublic entity, for the year ended December 31, 2008. Land, the engagement supervisor, anticipates expressing an unqualified opinion on May 20, 2009, at the end of the field work. Wood, an assistant on the engagement, drafted the auditors' communication of internal control matters that Land plans to send to Marlowe's board of directors with the May 20 audit report.

Land reviewed Wood's draft, which follows, and indicated in the supervisor's review notes certain deficiencies.

Independent Auditor's Report
To the Board of Directors of Marlowe Company:

In planning and performing our audit of the financial statements of Marlowe Company for the year ended December 31, 2008, we considered its internal control to determine our auditing procedures for the purpose of expressing our opinion on the financial statements and to provide assurance on the internal control system. However, we noted certain matters involving internal control and its operations that we consider to be significant deficiencies under standards established by the American Institute of Certified Public Accountants. Significant deficiencies involve matters coming to our attention relating to significant deficiencies in the design or operation of the internal controls that, in our judgment, could adversely affect the organization's ability to record, process, summarize, and report financial data consistent with our assessment of control risk.

We noted that deficiencies in the internal control design included inadequate provisions for the safeguarding of assets, especially concerning cash receipts and inventory stored at remote locations. Additionally, we noted failures in the operation of the internal controls. Reconciliations of subsidiary ledgers to control accounts were not timely prepared and senior employees in authority intentionally overrode the internal control procedures concerning cash payments to the detriment of the overall objectives of control.

A material weakness is not necessarily a significant deficiency, but is a design defect in which the internal control elements do not reduce to a relatively low level the risk that errors or frauds in amounts that would be material in relation to the financial statements being audited may occur and not be detected by the auditors during the audit.

Our consideration of the internal control system will not necessarily disclose all matters of internal control that might be significant deficiencies and, accordingly, will not necessarily disclose all significant deficiencies that are also considered to be material weaknesses as defined above. However, none of the significant deficiencies described above is believed to be a material weakness.

This report is intended solely for the information and use of the Board of Directors of Marlowe Co. Accordingly, it is not intended to be distributed to stockholders, management, or those who are not responsible for these matters.

Land & Hale, CPAs
May 4, 2009

Required:

These supervisor's review notes may or may not be correct. For each item 1–15, indicate whether Land is correct (C) or incorrect (I) in the criticism of Wood's draft. (*Hint*: Refer to *SAS 112* and *SSAE 10* for details not in the textbook chapter.)

In the 1st paragraph

1. There should be no reference to "our audit of the financial statements."

2. The report should indicate that providing assurance is not the purpose of our consideration of internal control.

3. The reference to "our assessment of control risk" at the end of the paragraph should have been a reference to "the assertions of management in the financial statements."

4. There should be a reference to "conformity with generally accepted accounting principles."

In the 2nd paragraph

5. There should be no reference to deficiencies because such reference is inconsistent with the expression of an unqualified opinion on the financial statements.

6. When deficiencies (reportable conditions) are noted, the report should include a description of the assessed level of control risk.

In the 3rd paragraph

7. The definition of material weakness is incorrect. A material weakness is a significant deficiency.

8. The report should indicate that the auditors assume no responsibility for errors or frauds resulting from the deficiencies identified in the report.

9. The report should refer at the end of the paragraph to detection by the entity's employees, not by the auditors.

In the 4th paragraph

10. The report should indicate that our consideration of the internal control system is expected to disclose all reportable conditions.

11. It is inappropriate to state that "none of the reportable conditions... is believed to be a material weakness."

In the final paragraph

12. The restriction on the report's distribution is inadequate because management ordinarily would receive the report.

13. The report should indicate that the financial statement audit resulted in an unqualified opinion.

14. The report should indicate that the auditors are not responsible for updating the report for events or circumstances occurring after the date of the report.

Dating the report

15. The report may not be dated before the auditors' report on the financial statements.

(AICPA adapted)

A.49 **Reporting on an Other Comprehensive Basis of Accounting.** The following abstracted report is an actual report on a pension fund that refers to a statutory basis of accounting (OCBOA) as well as to generally accepted accounting principles (GAAP).

Report of Independent Auditors

Board of Trustees
The Church Pension Fund

[#1: Standard introductory paragraph here]
[#2: Standard scope paragraph here]

(#3) As described in the Financial Review under the heading "Accounting Principles and Practices," the accompanying financial statements have been prepared on the basis of accounting practices prescribed by the New York Insurance Department, whose statutory accounting practices vary from generally accepted accounting principles for defined benefit pension plans, principally with respect to the valuation of bonds and the computation of pension obligations.

(#4) In our opinion, for the reasons set forth in the preceding paragraph, the financial statements referred to above are not intended to and do not present fairly, in conformity with certain generally accepted accounting principles for defined benefit pension plans, the assets and liabilities of The Fund at March 31, 2008 and 2007, or the changes in funded reserve for the years then ended.

(#5) Also, in our opinion, the financial statements referred to above present fairly, in all material respects, the assets and liabilities of The Fund at March 31, 2008 and 2007, and the changes in its funded reserve for the year then ended, in conformity with accounting practices prescribed or permitted by the New York Insurance Department.

/s/ Auditor signature
New York, New York
June 8, 2008

Required:

a. What is the purpose of paragraph #3 in relation to paragraph #4? (*Hint:* Consider the fourth reporting standard of GAAS.)

b. What is the message in paragraph #4? What is the name for the message under GAAS?

c. What is the message in paragraph #5? What is the name for the message under GAAS?

Instructions for Cases A.50–A.55

These cases require a written report. The Electronic Workpapers on the textbook Web site have four ASCII files (filenames AUDIT, REVIEW, COMPILE, and INTERIM) containing the standard reports for these services. These can be used as the starting place for the report-writing requirements in these cases. You can read this file into many word processing programs to make your report-writing task easier and more professional.

A.50 **Prepare a Compilation Report.** The Coffin brothers have engaged you to compile their financial schedules from books and records maintained by James Coffin. The brothers own and operate three auto parts stores in Central City. Even though their business is growing, they have not wanted to employ a full-time bookkeeper. James specifies that all he wants is a balance sheet, a statement of operations, and a statement of cash flows. He does not have time to write up footnotes to accompany the statement.

James directed the physical count of inventory on June 30 and adjusted and closed the books on that date. You find that he actually is a good accountant, having taken some night courses at the community college. The accounts appear to have been maintained in conformity with generally accepted accounting principles. At least you have noticed no obvious errors.

Required:

You are independent with respect to the Coffin brothers and their Coffin Auto Speed Shop business. Prepare a report on your compilation engagement.

A.51 **Reporting on Comparative Unaudited Financial Statements.** Anson Jones, CPA, performed a review service for the Independence Company in 2008. He wants to present comparative financial statements. However, the 2007 statements were compiled by Able and Associates, CPAs, and Able does not want to cooperate with Jones by reissuing the prior-year compilation report. Jones has no indication that any adjustments should be made to either the 2008 or 2007 statements, which are to be presented with all necessary disclosures. However, he does not have time to perform a review of the 2007 statements. Jones completed his work on January 15, 2009, for the statement dated December 31, 2008.

Required:

Write Jones's review report and include the paragraph describing the report on the 2007 statements.

A.52 **Audit Simulation: Interim Financial Information.** June's Java provides coffee services (coffee, cups, cream, sugar, and coffee makers) to local companies for use in their offices. Each of five drivers has a truck with inventory and has a different route each day to replenish coffee supplies to the companies on the route. In past audits, the accountant found that June's Java was having difficulty properly recognizing revenue, usually due to timing issues. In addition, the internal control over inventory on each driver's truck was weak.

June's Java has prepared its third-quarter financial statements and the owners want a review of the information. The accountants have audited the financial statements for the past three years but have never been asked to review any interim financial information until now.

Required:

Prepare a review plan that lists the procedures that accountants should perform to do a professional review in accordance with *SAS 100* (AU 722). Be as specific as possible in planning your procedures.

A.53 **Erroneous Reporting on Interim Financial Information.** The following report was prepared by Baker & Baker, CPAs, on the interim financial information of Micro Mini Company. The interim financial information was presented in the first quarterly report for the three-month period ended March 31, 2009. No comparative quarterly information of the first quarter of the prior year was presented. Baker & Baker completed a review in accordance with standards established by the AICPA and found that, to the best of their knowledge, the information was presented in conformity with FASB requirements. In an audit report dated January 21, 2009, Baker & Baker had given a standard unqualified audit report on Micro Mini's 2008 and 2007 annual financial statements.

Required:

a. Review the report and list, with explanation, the erroneous portions in it.

b. Rewrite the report.

Report of Independent Auditors

Board of Directors and Stockholders,
Micro Mini Company:

We have made a review of the balance sheet of Micro Mini Company at March 31, 2009, the related statement of income and comprehensive income for the three-month period ended March 31, 2009, and the statement of cash flows for the three-month period ended March 31, 2009, in accordance with standards established by the American Institute of Certified Public Accountants.

A review of interim financial information consists principally of obtaining an understanding of the system for the preparation of the interim financial information, applying analytical review procedures to financial data, and making inquiries to persons responsible for financial and accounting matters.

In our opinion, the accompanying interim financial information presents fairly, in all material respects, the financial position of Micro Mini Company at March 31, 2009, and the results of its operations and its cash flows for the three-month period then ended in conformity with generally accepted accounting principles.

Baker & Baker, CPAs
June 15, 2009

A.54 **Report on Comprehensive Basis Other Than GAAP.** Brooklyn Life Insurance Company prepares its financial statements on a statutory basis in conformity with the accounting practices prescribed and permitted by the Insurance Department of the State of New York. This statutory basis produces financial statements that differ materially from statements prepared in conformity with generally accepted accounting principles. On the statutory basis, for example, agents' first-year commissions are expensed instead of being partially deferred.

The company engaged its auditors, Major and Major Associates, to audit the statutory basis financial statements and report on them. Footnote 10 in the statements contains a narrative description and a numerical table explaining the differences between the statutory basis and GAAP accounting. Footnote 10 also reconciles the statutory basis assets, liabilities, income, expense, and net income (statutory basis) to the measurements that would be obtained using GAAP.

Required:

Write the audit report appropriate in the circumstances. The year-end date is December 31, 2008, and the audit field work was completed on February 20, 2009. (The company plans to distribute this report to persons other than the department of insurance regulators, so the auditors will need to follow *SAS 1*.)

A.55 **Internet Exercise: CPA WebTrust.** Visit the AICPA WebTrust site (www.webtrust.org).

Required:

a. What is WebTrust?

b. Why is WebTrust needed?

c. How does an Internet user know that a Web site has received the WebTrust service?

d. Does the WebTrust seal cover security and privacy of the Internet service provider (ISP) that hosts a Web site?

e. Where can a person obtain copies of the WebTrust standards?

A.56 **Kaplan CPA Exam Simulation: Compilation Presentation Alternatives.**

Required:

Go to the Kaplan Web site at www.mhhe.com/lowers3e, click on AUD: Riley & Associates and the "performing a review" tab, and complete the assigned task.

CPA REVIEW

A.57 **Kaplan CPA Exam Simulation: Special Reports.**

Required:

Go to the Kaplan Web site at www.mhhe.com/louwers3e, click on AUD: Kerklaan Enterprises case and the "special reports" tab, and complete the assigned task.

CPA REVIEW

A.58 **Kaplan CPA Exam Simulation: Special Reports: Service Organizations.**

Required:

Go to the Kaplan Web site at www.mhhe.com/louwers3e, click on AUD: Harrison Homes case and the "research" tab, and complete the assigned task.

Professional Ethics

Professional Standards References

Compendium Section	Document Reference	Topic
AU 220	SAS 1	"Independence"
AU 9326	SAS 106	"Interpretation: Inability to Obtain Audit Evidence Relating to Income Tax Accruals"
QC 20	SQCS 2	"System of Quality Control for a CPA Firm's Accounting and Auditing Practice"
ET 51–57		"Principles of Professional Conduct"
ET 91–92		"Definitions and Applicability of Rules"
ET 101–191		"Rules of Conduct, Interpretations, and Rulings on Independence, Integrity, and Objectivity"
ET 201–291		"Rules of Conduct, Interpretations, and Rulings on General and Technical Standards"
ET 301–391		"Rules of Conduct, Interpretations, and Rulings on Responsibilities to Clients"
ET 501–591		"Rules of Conduct, Interpretations, and Rulings on Other Responsibilities and Practices"
ET Appendix A		"Resolution Designating Bodies to Promulgate Technical Standards" (Rules 201, 202, and 203)
ET Appendix B		"Resolution Concerning Form of Organization and Name" (Rule 505)
BL 100–900		"Bylaws of the AICPA"
	ISB 1	"Independence Discussion with Audit Committees"
	ISB 2	"Certain Independence Implications of Audits of Mutual Funds and Related Entities"
	ISB 3	"Employment with Audit Clients"

To educate a person in mind and not in morals is to educate a menace to society.

Theodore Roosevelt

Always do right—this will gratify some and astonish the rest.

Mark Twain

Learning Objectives

Previous chapters have focused on the theory and practice of auditing. This module tells you about the regulation of accountants and accounting practice. Regulation and discipline depend on published codes of ethics and on effective enforcement practices.

Your objectives are to be able to:

1. Understand general ethics and a series of steps for making ethical decisions.

2. Reason through an ethical decision problem using the imperative, utilitarian, and generalization principles of moral philosophy.

3. Identify the different entities that make ethics rules for CPAs and public accounting firms.

4. With reference to American Institute of Certified Public Accounting (AICPA), Public Company Accounting Oversight Board (PCAOB), Securities and Exchange Commission (SEC), and Independence Standards Board (ISB) rules, analyze factual situations and decide whether an accountant's conduct does or does not impair independence.

5. With reference to AICPA rules on topics other than independence, analyze factual situations and decide whether an accountant's conduct does or does not conform to the AICPA Rules of Conduct.

6. Explain the types of penalties that can be imposed on accountants.

INTRODUCTION

Florencio López-de-Silanes was a tenured professor of finance and economics at Yale University. Among his many published works was an article "What Works in Securities Laws?" in which he concluded that the best way to keep dishonest corporate executives under control is to sue them.

Professor López-de-Silanes resigned from Yale University in June 2005. According to a Yale spokesperson:

> He has resigned from Yale as a result of financial misconduct and irregularities as the director of the International Institute for Corporate Governance. Appropriate actions have been taken.[1]

Professor López-de-Silanes' departure from Yale was the consequence of the discovery that he had double billed his travel expenses for the International Institute for Corporate Governance for the past several years. In addition to his termination, he was forced to re-pay $150,000 to Yale. Professor López-de-Silanes' consulting contracts with the World Bank also have come under scrutiny.

Why would a professor actively involved in working toward better corporate governance, a man who has written about dishonesty in corporate management, ruin his career through unethical behavior? There may not be an answer to this question. However, the lesson to be learned is that unethical behavior often comes from those individuals whom we would least expect.[2]

Clearly, users of audited financial statements lose confidence in the public accounting profession when accountants fail to act in the public's best interest. Third-party users begin to question the motives of the public accounting firms and the goals and objectives of audits themselves. Ethical questions related to the auditors' concern for the shareholders and the public trust arise when it appears the auditors have personal financial interests. Beyond the philosophical ethical issues, most organizations have established minimal professional standards for ethical behavior. For auditors to both be ethical and appear ethical to the community, an understanding of ethical philosophy and ethical standards discussed in this module is imperative.

GENERAL ETHICS

LEARNING OBJECTIVE

1. Understand general ethics and a series of steps for making ethical decisions.

What is ethics? Wheelwright defined *ethics* as "that branch of philosophy which is the systematic study of reflective choice, of the standards of right and wrong by which it is to be guided, and of the goods toward which it may ultimately be directed."[3] In this definition, you can detect three key elements: (1) ethics involves questions requiring reflective choice *(decision problems)*, (2) ethics involves guides of right and wrong *(moral principles)*, and (3) ethics is concerned with the consequences *(good or bad)* of decisions.

What is an ethical problem? A *problem situation* exists when you must make a choice among alternative actions and the right choice is not absolutely clear. An *ethical problem situation* may be described as one in which the choice of alternative actions affects the well-being of other persons.

What is *ethical behavior*? You can find two standard philosophical answers to this question: (1) ethical behavior is that which produces the greatest good and (2) ethical behavior is that which conforms to moral rules and principles. The most difficult problem situations arise when two or more rules conflict or when a rule and the criterion of "greatest good" conflict.

Why does an individual or group need a code of ethical conduct? A *code* makes explicit some of the criteria for conduct unique to the profession. *Codes of professional ethics* provide

[1] J. Gravois "Yale Forces Out Tenured Professor for Financial Misconduct," *Chronicle of Higher Education*, January 21, 2005.
[2] Marianne M. Jennings, "Conspicuous Governance Failures: Why Sarbanes-Oxley Is Not an Ethics Warranty," *Internal Auditing*, July/August 2005.
[3] Philip Wheelwright, *A Critical Introduction to Ethics*, 3rd ed. (Indianapolis, IN: Odyssey Press, 1959).

In a famous experiment, subjects were told to ask questions of an individual in another room. If the individual answered incorrectly, the subjects were told to inflict an electric shock as punishment. In reality, no shock was actually administered; however, the subjects believed they were administering a shock and could hear shouts, cries, and appeals to stop emanating from the next room. The experimenter ordered the subject to continue to apply the shocks, often at ever increasing amounts. Many subjects increased the voltage to areas labeled as dangerous and continued even after the individual in the next room asked for a doctor.

guidance in addressing situations that may not be specifically available in general ethics theories. An individual is better able to know what the profession expects. From the viewpoint of the organized profession, a *code* is a public declaration of principled conduct and a means of facilitating *enforcement* of standards of conduct. Practical enforcement and professionwide internal discipline are impossible if members are not first notified of the standards.

While one of the main purposes of ethics is to guide the actions of decision makers, the role of decision maker does not fully describe a professional person's entire obligation. Each person acts not only as an individual but also as a member of a profession and as a member of society. Hence, accountants and auditors are also *spectators* (observing the decisions of colleagues), *advisers* (counseling with co-workers), *instructors* (teaching accounting students or new employees on the job), *judges* (serving on disciplinary committees of a state society, a state board of accountancy, or the AICPA), and *critics* (commenting on the ethical decisions of others). All of these roles are important in the practice of professional ethics.

AN ETHICAL DECISION PROCESS

LEARNING OBJECTIVE

2. Reason through an ethical decision problem using the imperative, utilitarian, and generalization principles of moral philosophy.

In considering general ethics, your primary goal is to arrive at a framework for making ethical decisions. Perhaps if the subjects described in the preceding experiment had a framework for making ethical decisions, they might not have blindly followed the orders of the experimenter. Consequently, an understanding of some of the general principles of ethics can contribute background for a detailed consideration of the behavior directed by the bodies responsible for setting standards for professional conduct.

In the earlier definition of ethics, one of the key elements was *reflective choice*. It involves an important sequence of events beginning with the recognition of a decision problem. Collection of evidence, in the ethics context, refers to thinking about rules of behavior and outcomes of alternative actions. The process ends with analyzing the situation and taking an action. Ethical decision problems almost always involve projecting yourself into the future to live with your decisions. Professional ethics decisions usually turn on these questions: "What written and unwritten rules govern my behavior?" and "What are the possible consequences of my choices?" *Principles of ethics* can help you think about these two questions in real situations.

A good way to approach ethical decision problems is to think through several steps:

1. Define all facts and circumstances known at the time you need to make the decision. They are the "who, what, where, when, and how" dimensions of the situation. Identify the actor who needs to decide what to do.

2. a. Because ethical decision problems are defined in terms of their effects on people, identify the people involved in the situation or affected by the situation. These are the "stakeholders"; be careful not to expand the number of stakeholders beyond the bounds of reasonable analysis.

 b. Identify and describe the stakeholders' rights and obligations in general and to each other.

3. Specify the actor's major alternative decision actions and their consequences (good, bad, short run, long run).

4. The actor must choose among the alternative actions.

Let's apply the preceding ethical framework to Ethical Example 2.

Ethical Example 2

Step 1: Kathy (the chief financial officer) ordered Jorge (a staff accountant) to "enhance" the financial statements in a loan application to Spring National Bank by understating the allowance for uncollectible accounts receivable, saying, "It's an estimate anyway and we need the loan for a short time to keep from laying off loyal employees." What should Jorge do?

Step 2a: The stakeholders include the direct participants—Kathy, Jorge, Luis (Spring National Bank's loan officer)—and some indirect participants—bank stockholders and loyal employees. Other people may be affected—Jorge's mother, citizens who depend on the solvency of the banking system as a whole, taxpayers who eventually need to bail out the insolvent banking system, and others—but identifying them probably will not improve the analysis.

Step 2b: *Obligations:* Kathy and Jorge should act with integrity and Kathy should not pressure Jorge to cut corners with financial statements. Luis should make careful loan approval decisions. *Rights:* Jorge should not be subject to pressures to cut corners with "enhanced financial statements," Luis should receive information that is not materially misstated or manipulated. (Some rights of employees and bank stockholders also could be identified.)

Step 3: (1) Jorge can follow orders: Kathy is happy, he keeps his job, Luis gets fooled and approves the loan, the employees keep their jobs, the company fails, the bank loses, the employees are laid off anyway, Kathy and Jorge are prosecuted and convicted of making false statements to a federal institution and go to federal prison. (2) Jorge can refuse to "enhance" the financial statements: Kathy is not happy, Jorge is fired, Kathy prepares the financial statements herself, etc. (3) Jorge persuades Kathy of the potential problems and Luis refuses the loan, and the company must find another way to survive, or Luis approves the loan anyway and the bank takes the risk; or Kathy does not agree, and Jorge must again face alternatives (1) and (2) anyway.

In addition to weighing the consequences, Jorge also should consider general and professional rules. If Jorge is a CPA, some of the relevant professional rules relate to maintaining integrity (AICPA rule 102), application of accounting standards (AICPA rule 203), and the prohibition of discreditable acts (AICPA rule 501). Jorge needs to decide whether to follow rules or balance the expected consequences in the particular situation.

Step 4: As the actor, Jorge must choose one of the alternative actions and justify it by presenting a convincing argument for its superiority. Jorge can base the argument on rules, consequences, or a combination of both.

PHILOSOPHICAL PRINCIPLES IN ETHICS

We could skip a discussion of ethical theories if we were willing to accept a simple rule: "Let your *conscience* be your guide." Such a rule is appealing because it calls on an individual's own judgment, which may be based on wisdom, insight, adherence to custom, or an authoritative code. However, it also might be based on caprice, immaturity, ignorance, stubbornness, or misunderstanding. The problem with using conscience as a guide is that it tells you about a wrong decision after you act!

In a similar manner, reliance on the opinions of others or on the weight of opinions of a particular social group is not always enough. Another person or a group of persons may perpetuate a custom or habit that is wrong. To adhere blindly to custom or to group habits is to abdicate individual responsibility. Titus and Keeton summarized this point succinctly: "Each person capable of making moral decisions is responsible for making his own decisions. The ultimate locus of moral responsibility is in the individual."[4] Thus, the function of *ethical principles* is not to provide a simple and sure rule but to provide some guides for your individual decisions and actions.

The Imperative Principle

The *imperative principle* directs a decision maker to act according to the requirements of an ethical rule. Strict versions of imperative ethics maintain that a decision should be made without trying to predict whether an action will probably create the greatest balance

[4] Harold H. Titus and Morris Keeton, *Ethics for Today,* 4th ed. (New York: American Book–Stratford Press, 1966), p. 131.

of good over evil. Ethics in the *imperative* sense is a function of moral rules and principles and does not involve a situation-specific calculation of the consequences.[5]

The philosopher Immanuel Kant (1724–1804) was perhaps the foremost advocate of the imperative school. Kant maintained that *reason* and the strict *duty to be consistent* should govern our actions. He believed that individuals should act only as they think everyone should act all of the time. This law of conduct is known as Kant's **categorical imperative,** meaning that it specifies an *unconditional obligation*. One such maxim (rule), for example, is "Lying is wrong."

Suppose you believe that Jorge (from Ethical Example 2) should agree with Kathy and do everything she asked for "enhancing the financial statements," thus participating in a lie (knowingly misrepresenting the facts about the allowance for uncollectible accounts receivable). The Kantian test of the morality of such a lie is this: Can this maxim be a moral rule that should be followed without exception by all persons who have the opportunity to fool a bank loan officer for a good cause? If Jorge refuses to manipulate the financial statement and the loan is refused, the result may be economic hardship and employee layoffs. Kant maintained that motive and duty alone define a moral act, not the consequences of the act. This reasoning places the highest value on the duty to be consistent and a lower value on the consequences, in this case the fate of the employees.

The general objection to the imperative principle is the belief that so-called universal rules always turn out to have exceptions. The general response to this objection is that if the rule is stated properly to include the exceptional cases, the principle is still valid. The problem with this response, however, is that human experience is complicated and extremely complex universal rules would have to be constructed to try to cover all possible cases.[6]

Most professional codes of ethics have characteristics of the imperative type of theory. As a general matter, professionals are expected to act in a manner in conformity with the rules. However, society frequently questions not only conduct itself but also the rules on which conduct is based. Thus, a dogmatic imperative approach to ethical decisions may not be completely sufficient for the maintenance of professional standards. Society may question the rules and conflicts among them are always possible. A means of estimating the consequences of alternative actions may be useful; see Ethical Example 3.

Ethical Example 3

Consolidata, Inc., was a tax client of **Alexander Grant & Company, CPAs (AG).** Consolidata prepared payrolls for 38 customers, received the customers' money, and then paid the payrolls. AG learned that Consolidata was in serious financial difficulty and advised the company to inform its customers, but company officials did not do so. When AG learned that the company's officers and directors had resigned, AG telephoned 12 Consolidata customers who were also AG clients, told them of the situation, and advised them not to entrust further payroll funds to Consolidata. The 12 were spared the risk of losing their money and Consolidata went out of business one month later.

Consolidata accused AG of breach of contract for breaking an obligation of confidentiality required by the AICPA Code of Professional Conduct. One SEC attorney said she thought AG should have alerted all 38 customers, not just the 12 AG clients. Accountants and SEC officials viewed the situation as a balancing of confidentiality (AICPA rule) against the public interest (Consolidata customers who needed a warning).

The Principle of Utilitarianism

The *principle of utilitarianism* emphasizes examining the *consequences* of action rather than following some rules. The criterion of producing the greater good is made an explicit

[5] I. Kant, *Foundations of the Metaphysics of Morals,* trans. Lewis W. Beck (Indianapolis, IN: Bobbs-Merrill, 1959; originally published in 1785).

[6] Several rules in the AICPA Rules of Conduct are explicitly phrased to provide for exceptions to the general rules, notably Rules 203 and 301. Imperative rules also seem to generate borderline cases, so the AICPA Ethics Division issues interpretations and rulings to explain the applicability of the rules.

part of the decision process. The *principle* is very useful, but be sure to notice that it does not specify the *values* that enable you to determine the good or evil of an action. In **act-utilitarianism,** the center of attention is the *individual act* as it is affected by the specific circumstances of a situation. The general difficulty with act-utilitarianism is that it seems to permit too many exceptions to well-established rules. By focusing attention on individual acts, the long-run effect of setting examples for other people appears to be ignored. If an act-utilitarian decision is to break a moral rule, the decision's success usually depends on everyone else's adherence to the rule. For example, to benefit from tax evasion for a good reason depends on everyone else not having an equally good reason for not paying their taxes.

Rule-utilitarianism, on the other hand, emphasizes the centrality *of rules for ethical behavior* while still maintaining the criterion of the greatest universal good. This kind of utilitarianism means that decision makers must first determine the rules that will promote the greatest general good for the largest number of people. The initial question is not which *action* has the greatest utility but which *rule*. The statement of the rule-utilitarian's problem may be given a very commonsense expression: "What would happen if everybody acted this way?" In this form, the question is known as *generalization*.

The Generalization Argument

The generalization argument may be considered a judicious combination of the imperative and utilitarian principles. Basically, the **generalization argument** considers the consequences of a decision made by similar persons acting under similar circumstances.[7] A more everyday expression of the argument is this question: "What would happen if everyone acted in that certain way?" If the answer to the question is that the consequences would be undesirable, the conclusion, according to the generalization test, is that the way of acting is unethical and should not to be done.

The key ideas in the generalization test are *similar persons* and *similar circumstances*. These features provide the needed flexibility to consider the many variations that arise in real problem situations. They also demand considerable judgment in determining whether persons and circumstances are genuinely different or are just arbitrarily rationalized as different so that a preconceived preference can be "explained" as right.

In Ethical Example 2, Jorge's problem as a professional accountant and as an employee arose when Kathy asked him to "enhance the financial statements" and he saw the enhancement as a lie. His generalization question may be something like this: "What if all accountants fudged financial statements and fooled loan officers when their companies needed to obtain loans?" Most people will see an easy answer: The result would be undesirable (because it might succeed often and cause considerable losses to banks along with other undesirable personal consequences for the actors, in addition to the problem of having broken a rule that requires truth-telling). Another kind of conflict subject to the generalization test is illustrated by a public accounting firm's desire for service and need for independence (see the Auditing Insight "Service versus Independence.").

AUDITING INSIGHT Service versus Independence

For many years, a national public accounting firm encouraged its professionals to become active members of the boards of directors of corporations. The purpose was to provide expertise to businesses in the metropolitan area and to enable the accounting firm to become well known and well respected. The firm changed its policy to prohibit such service after it had the opportunity to obtain some of these corporations as audit clients, but it was forced to refuse or delay the CPA–client relationship.

The firm's audit independence was considered impaired when a member of the firm had served in a director or management capacity during the period covered by the financial statements the corporations wanted the firm to audit. The generalization test was this: If members of the firm serve on the boards of directors of all corporations that may become audit clients, none of these corporations can be accepted as audit clients—a result that is undesirable.

[7] Marcus G. Singer, *Generalization in Ethics* (New York: Atheneum Publishers, 1961, 1971), esp. pp. 5, 10–11, 61, 63, 73, 81, 105–22.

This brief review of principles in ethics provides some guide to the ways many people approach difficult decision problems. The greatest task is to take general notions of ethics—the imperative, utilitarian, and generalization—and apply them to a real decision. Their application through codes of professional conduct is a challenge.

Review Checkpoints

B.1 What roles must a professional accountant be prepared to perform in regard to ethical decision problems?

B.2 When might the rule "Let your conscience be your guide" not be a sufficient basis for (a) your personal ethical decisions and (b) your professional ethical decisions?

B.3 Assume that you accept the following ethical rule: "Failure to tell the whole truth is wrong." In the textbook illustration about Jorge's problem with Kathy's instructions, (a) what would this rule require Jorge to do and (b) why is an unalterable rule like this classified as an element of imperative ethical theory?

B.4 How do utilitarian ethics differ from imperative ethics?

AN "ALPHABET SOUP" OF ETHICS RULE MAKERS

LEARNING OBJECTIVE

3. Identify the different entities that make ethics rules for CPAs and public accounting firms.

Independence, professionalism, and integrity have long been concerns of the accounting profession, but the scandals of Enron, WorldCom, and others have brought renewed cries and placed additional emphasis on these issues. The Public Company Accounting Oversight Board (PCAOB) was created to bring a new level of independence and integrity to the profession. Many services formally provided to public accounting firm clients can no longer be offered. Further, public accounting firms and CPAs also must follow rules set forth by the U.S. Securities and Exchange Commission (SEC) and the AICPA Professional Ethics Executive Committee (PEEC), respectively. The rules established by the Independence Standards Board (ISB), disbanded in 2001, still prevail (some have been superseded). If you are an internal auditor, you will be expected to observe the rules of conduct of the Institute of Internal Auditors (IIA). As a management accountant, the Institute of Management Accountants' (IMA) standards of ethical conduct for management accountants will apply to you. Certified Fraud Examiners are expected to observe the Association of Certified Fraud Examiners' (ACFE) Code of Ethics. If you find this "alphabet soup" of ethics rule makers confusing, imagine those CPAs who have to deal with complex and often conflicting rules on a daily basis. As a CPA, you will be expected to observe rules of conduct published in several codes of ethics. If you join the AICPA and a state society of CPAs and practice before the U.S. Securities and Exchange Commission (SEC), you will be subject to the following:

Source of Rules of Conduct	Applicable to
State board of accountancy	Persons licensed by the state to practice accounting
American Institute of CPAs	Members of AICPA
State society of CPAs	Members of state society of CPAs
U.S. Securities and Exchange Commission	Persons who practice before the SEC as accountants and auditors for SEC-registered companies
Public Company Oversight Accounting Board	Registered firms and individuals who perform audits of companies under the jurisdiction of the PCAOB

AUDITING INSIGHT | Fraud Auditor Expelled for Committing Fraud

Curtis C. was expelled by the board of regents of the ACFE at its regular meeting. Mr. C. was formerly a municipal internal auditor, but the trial board found that Mr. C. had wrongfully represented himself as a certified internal auditor when in fact he did not hold the CIA designation. Such conduct is in violation of Article 1.A.4 of the Certified Fraud Examiners Code of Professional Ethics.

L. Jackson Shockey, CFE, CPA, CISA, chairperson of the board of regents, said: "We are saddened that a member has been expelled for such conduct. However, in order to maintain the integrity of the CFE program, the trial board vigorously investigates violations of the Code of Professional Ethics. When appropriate, the board of regents will not hesitate to take necessary action."

Source: *CFE News.*

U.S. Securities and Exchange Commission (SEC)

The SEC has federal statutory authority to regulate the public accounting profession for the purposes of (1) protecting the reliability and integrity of the financial statements of public companies and (2) promoting investor confidence in financial statements and the securities markets. The SEC's jurisdiction covers only public companies that are required by federal securities laws to file financial statements audited by independent accountants. SEC rules have ultimate authority in defining independence standards for over 16,000 publicly traded companies in the United States. In addition to the duties outlined earlier, the passage of the Sarbanes-Oxley Act in 2002 requires the SEC to oversee the PCAOB.

The Public Company Accounting Oversight Board (PCAOB)

The PCAOB has been given the responsibility to set public accounting firm standards and oversee quality control, ethics, and independence issues for accounting professionals who audit financial statements of public companies. Students are urged to review the PCAOB Web site (www.pcaobus.org) to review the latest standards issued by the PCAOB.

While the PCAOB has almost the same authority as the SEC, the SEC must approve all PCAOB proposed rules before they are final. Also, while the PCAOB has authority over only publicly traded companies, it would be a mistake to view the PCAOB as having influence over *only* publicly traded audit clients. Several states (e.g., California) have passed legislation that incorporates PCAOB rules into state law applicable to all companies, both public and private. In addition, the AICPA may enact some provisions that would create similar restrictions for nonpublicly traded clients.

The Professional Ethics Executive Committee (PEEC) of the American Institute of CPAs (AICPA)

The PEEC is the AICPA committee that makes and enforces all rules of conduct for CPAs (the AICPA Code of Professional Conduct) who are AICPA members. You might think that if you were not in public accounting and not a member of the AICPA, the rules would not apply. However, state and federal court proceedings and disciplinary bodies have consistently upheld that CPAs must adhere to professional ethical standards even if they are not members of the AICPA or not in public accounting. The AICPA Code of Professional Conduct contains two basic sections. The first section is the Principles of Professional Conduct, a set of six positive essays expressing the profession's high ideals:

I. *Responsibilities.* In carrying out their responsibilities as professionals, members should exercise sensitive professional and moral judgments in all of their activities.

II. *The public interest.* Members should accept the obligation to act in a way that will serve the public interest, honor the public trust, and demonstrate commitment to professionalism.

III. *Integrity*. To maintain and broaden public confidence, members should perform all professional responsibilities with the highest sense of integrity.

IV. *Objectivity and independence*. A member should maintain objectivity and be free of conflicts of interest in discharging professional responsibilities. A member in public practice should be independent in fact and appearance when providing auditing and other attestation services.

V. *Due care*. A member should observe the profession's technical and ethical standards, strive continually to improve competence and quality of services, and discharge professional responsibility to the best of the member's ability.

VI. *Scope and nature of services*. A member in public practice should observe the Principles of the Code of Professional Conduct in determining the scope and nature of services to be provided.

"A distinguishing mark of a profession is acceptance of its responsibility to the public."[8] This *responsibility to the public interest* requires that CPAs' work must reflect high ideals about moral judgment, commitment to the public interest, and skillful performance. The scope and nature of services refers to the issue of balancing public accounting firms' commitment to clients (giving business advice and consulting) and commitment to the public (giving opinions on financial statements).

While the first section embodies principles that CPAs should adhere to, they are very general in nature, and thus not enforceable. The second section, however, contains the enforceable Rules of Conduct that were derived from the six principles:

AICPA Rules of Conduct[9]

Section 100: Independence, Integrity, and Objectivity
 Rule 101: Independence
 Rule 102: Integrity and Objectivity
Section 200: General and Technical Standards
 Rule 201: General Standards
 Rule 202: Compliance with Standards
 Rule 203: Accounting Principles
Section 300: Responsibilities to Clients
 Rule 301: Confidential Client Information
 Rule 302: Contingent Fees

Section 400: (No title or rules are in the 400 series.)
Section 500: Other Responsibilities and Practices
 Rule 501: Acts Discreditable
 Rule 502: Advertising and Other Forms of Solicitation
 Rule 503: Commissions and Referral Fees
 Rule 504: (No Rule 504.)
 Rule 505: Form of Practice and Name

The PEEC also publishes Interpretations of Rules of Conduct, which are detailed explanations of specific rules necessary to help members understand particular applications. Finally, the PEEC also publishes "rulings" on the applicability of rules in specific situations.[10]

Principles		**Rules**		**Interpretations**
Aspirational goals of behavior.	→	Enforceable ethical regulations that CPAs must follow.	→	Applications of rules to specific business situations.

[8] Robert H. Colson, "On CPAs and the Public Interest," *The CPA Journal*, February 2004.

[9] In light of the numbering system for the Rules of Conduct, you might wonder why no rule is numbered in the 400 series (formerly "Responsibilities to Colleagues"). Rules in this section were repealed by vote of the AICPA membership in 1979 after the rules were challenged by the U.S. Department of Justice as an unwarranted restraint on competition. The AICPA simply has not changed the numbering system.

[10] The full text of the interpretations and rulings are available on the AICPA Web site (www.aicpa.org).

The Independence Standards Board (ISB)

The Independence Standards Board (ISB) was created in 1997 and was located and funded in the SEC Practice Section of the AICPA Division for Firms. The ISB goals were to (1) serve the public interest and (2) promote investors' confidence in the securities markets. The ISB and the SEC cooperated to make private-sector independence rules applicable to auditors of public companies (the same jurisdiction as the SEC). On July 17, 2001, the AICPA and the SEC announced that the ISB had "largely fulfilled its mission" and disbanded it. The ISB's rules will continue to be enforced until they are superseded by new standards.

The Relationships among the Ethics Rule Makers

There is an intricate association for standard setting among the various groups. Although the SEC has ultimate authority for audits of public companies, it was mandated to create the PCAOB. The PCAOB creates independence rules that *public accounting firms* must follow in their audits of publicly traded companies. The AICPA provides ethics rules for *individual CPAs,* who are the only ones with the legislative mandate to express opinions on financial statements. However, states license the individual CPAs and have their own ethics rules. Sometimes there are different ethics rules; sometimes the rules conflict. The relationships among the different rule-making bodies continue to evolve.

Review Checkpoints

B.5 In regard to ethics rules, what are the jurisdictions of the (a) AICPA PEEC, (b) SEC, (c) PCAOB, and (d) ISB?

B.6 What organizations and agencies have rules of conduct that you must observe when you practice (a) public accounting, (b) internal auditing, (c) management accounting, and (d) fraud examination?

AN EMPHASIS ON INDEPENDENCE

LEARNING OBJECTIVE

4. With reference to AICPA, PCAOB, SEC, and ISB rules, analyze factual situations and decide whether an accountant's conduct does or does not impair independence.

A lack of public accounting firm independence has been blamed for several of the recent financial accounting frauds. For example, many have argued that Arthur Andersen's independence was impaired on the Enron engagement because of the large consulting fees ($27 million per year) that the firm was receiving, which exceeded the audit fees ($25 million per year) for the engagement. The argument goes that Andersen partners were so concerned about losing the lucrative consulting engagement fees that they compromised their professional skepticism when dealing with Enron's questionable accounting practices. The recent attention has resulted in several new rules aimed at bolstering public accounting firm independence. Not surprisingly, ethics rule-making bodies discussed in the previous section have developed their own solutions, each of which is discussed below.

American Institute of Certified Public Accountants

The PEEC makes independence rules for *CPAs* that are applicable not only for audits of public companies, but also for all other audits (audits of nonpublic companies, not-for-profit organizations, and government units) and attestation engagements. Independence is required for audit as well as attestation engagements (governed by *Statements on Standards for Attestation Engagements (SSAEs)* dealing with assertions other than financial statements) in which some form of assurance is provided *(Interpretation 101-11).* Its

✱ Know.

EXHIBIT B.1
Summary of Rule 101
Interpretations

A covered member cannot
- Have a direct financial interest in a client.
- Have a material indirect financial interest in a client.
- Be a trustee or administrator of an estate that has a direct or material indirect financial interest in a client.
- Have a joint investment with a client that is material to the covered member.
- Have a loan to or from a client, any officer of the client, or any individual owning more than 10 percent of the client (except as specifically described in interpretation 101-5).
- Participate on an attest engagement if they were formally employed by the client in a position to influence the audit or acted as an officer, director, promoter, underwriter, or trustee of a pension or profit-sharing trust of the client.

A covered member's immediate family cannot
- Have a direct financial interest in a client.
- Have a material indirect financial interest in a client.

A covered member's close relatives cannot
- Have a key position with a client.
- Have a material financial interest in a client that is known to the covered member.
- Have a financial interest in a client that allows the relative to have significant influence in a client.
- Be in a position to influence the audit.

A partner or a professional employee cannot
- Be associated with a client as a director, officer, employee, promoter, underwriter, voting trustee, or trustee of a pension or profit-sharing trust of the client.

independence rule (Rule 101) is derived from the AICPA Code of Professional Conduct's objectivity and independence principle:

Rule 101: Independence

Rule 101. A member in public practice shall be independent in the performance of professional services as required by standards promulgated by bodies designated by Council.[11]

Rule 101 itself has no substantive content. Instead, it incorporates PEEC interpretations that are explained in the following paragraphs. Exhibit B.1 summarizes the PEEC interpretations and other independence matters. The fundamental thrust of these interpretations is that auditors preserve **independence,** the mental attitude and appearance that auditors are not influenced by others in making judgments and decisions, by (a) avoiding financial connections that make it appear that the auditor's wealth depends on the outcome of the audit and (b) avoiding managerial connections that make it appear that the auditors are involved in management decisions for the audit client (thus auditing their own work).

Essentially, a *covered member* is prohibited from having any financial interest in a client that could affect its audit judgment *(independence in fact)* or would appear to others to have an influence on the auditor's judgment *(independence in appearance)*. In addition, immediate family members are under the same restrictions as the auditor. Again, the appearance of independence would be jeopardized if the auditor's child owned stock in a client. Similarly, if a close relative or immediate family member worked for a client in a position that could influence the audit (e.g., a controller) or is in a key position, independence in appearance, if not in fact, is impaired. Exhibit B.2 provides important definitions (both AICPA and SEC) used in delineating these issues.

So what do all of the definitions presented in Exhibit B.2 mean for applying the independence rules? For most practical purposes, the people who are prohibited from having

[11]The "bodies designated by Council" to produce them refers to the PEEC.

applies attestation engagements to Audits and reviews

EXHIBIT B.2 Comparison of SEC and AICPA Selected Definitions

AICPA Definition	SEC Definition
Engagement team	
Individuals participating in the attest engagement, including those who perform reviews. The attest engagement team includes all employees and contractors who participate in the attest engagement, irrespective of their functional classification (for example, audit, tax, or management consulting services). The attest engagement team excludes specialists and individuals who perform only routine clerical functions.	All partners, principals, shareholders, and professional employees participating in an audit, review, or attestation engagement of an audit client, including those conducting reviews and all persons who consult with others on the audit engagement team during the audit, review, or attestation engagement regarding technical or industry-specific issues, transactions, or events.
Chain of command	
Partner: A proprietor, shareholder, equity or nonequity partner, or any individual who assumes the risks and benefits of firm ownership or who is held out by the firm to be the equivalent of an owner or partner. **Manager:** A professional employee of the firm who has either of the following responsibilities: 1. Continuing responsibility for the overall planning and supervision of engagements for specified clients. 2. Authority to determine that an engagement is complete subject to final partner approval.	All persons who (1) supervise or have direct management responsibility for the audit, including at all successively senior levels through the accounting firm's chief executive, (2) evaluate the performance or recommend the compensation of the audit engagement partner, or (3) provide quality control or other oversight of the audit.
Covered person	
The following are considered covered members: (1) An individual on the attest engagement team; (2) An individual in a position to influence the attest engagement; (3) A partner or manager who provides nonattest services to the attest client beginning once he or she provides 10 hours of nonattest services to the attest client within any fiscal year and ending on the later of the date (i) the firm signs the report on the financial statements for the fiscal year during which those services were provided or (ii) he or she no longer expects to provide 10 or more hours of nonattest services to the attest client on a recurring basis; (4) A partner in the office in which the lead attest engagement partner primarily practices in connection with the attest engagement; (5) The firm, including the firm's employee benefit plans; or (6) An entity whose operating, financial, or accounting policies can be controlled (as defined by generally accepted accounting principles [GAAP] for consolidation purposes) by any of the individuals or entities described in (1) through (5) or by two or more such individuals or entities if they act together.	The following partners, principals, shareholders, and employees of an accounting firm: (1) An individual on the audit engagement team, (2) An individual in the chain of command, (3) Any other partner, principal, shareholder, or managerial employee of the firm who has provided 10 or more hours of nonaudit services to the audit client for the period beginning on the date such services are provided and ending on the date the accounting firm signs the report on the financial statements for the fiscal year during which those services are provided, or who expects to provide 10 or more hours of nonaudit services to the audit client on a recurring basis, and (4) Any other partner, principal, or shareholder from an office of the accounting firm in which the lead audit engagement partner primarily practices in connection with the audit. *Authors' Note:* In essence the "covered members" are the firm's professionals closely connected to the audit engagement and the firm's owners who are located in the office where the lead engagement partner practices. However, the SEC added the category of manager-level professionals and owners who provide nonaudit (tax, consulting) services for the audit client. Therefore, almost everyone who provides services of any type for an audit client must observe the independence rules.
Close family members	
Parent, sibling, or nondependent child.	Person's spouse, spousal equivalent, parent, dependent child, nondependent child, and sibling.
Immediate family members	
Spouse, spousal equivalent, or dependents (whether or not related).	Person's spouse, spousal equivalent, and dependents.

financial and managerial relationships with the client are the audit engagement team, the people in the chain of command, the covered persons in the firm, close family members, and immediate family members.

When a questionable practice or relationship arises, the PEEC evaluates whether the practice or relationship poses an unacceptable risk to CPAs' independence.[12] The PEEC uses a three-step risk-based approach that involves (1) identifying and evaluating threats to independence, (2) determining whether safeguards eliminate or sufficiently mitigate the identified threats, and (3) determining whether independence is impaired. Identified threats to independence include the following:

1. *Familiarity threat.* CPAs having a close or longstanding relationship with a client (e.g., a spouse is in a key client position or a partner has served a prolonged tenure with the client).

2. *Adverse interest threat.* CPAs acting in opposition to clients (e.g., through litigation).

3. *Undue influence threat.* Attempts to coerce or otherwise influence the CPA member (e.g., significant gifts or threats to replace the auditor over an accounting principles disagreement).

4. *Self-review threat.* CPAs reviewing their own work.

5. *Financial self-interest threat.* CPAs having a financial relationship with a client.

6. *Management participation threat.* CPAs taking on the role of client management or otherwise performing management functions.

7. *Advocacy threat.* CPAs promoting a client's interests or position.

Next, we take a closer look at threats to independence and their related interpretations that address those threats.

Familiarity Threat (Interpretations 101-1, 101-2, and 101-6)

An immediate family member may not hold a position of influence (key position) in an audit client.[13] The close family members' definition comes into play in connection with (1) ownership or control of an audit client or (2) employment with an audit client. An example of (1) is the impairment of the public accounting firm's independence when a close family member of a covered person in the firm owns a material investment in an audit client or is in a position to exert significant influence over an audit client. An example of (2) is the impairment of the public accounting firm's independence when a close family member works in an accounting or financial reporting role at an audit client or was in such a role during any period covered by an audit for which the person in the firm is a covered person. (Neither an immediate family member nor a close family member can work in a capacity such as a member of the board of directors, chief executive officer, president, chief financial officer, chief operating officer, general counsel, chief accounting officer, controller, director of internal audit, director of financial reporting, treasurer, or vice president of marketing).

Independence problems do not end when owners (partners, shareholders) and professional employees retire, resign, or otherwise leave an accounting firm. A former owner or professional can cause independence to be impaired if a relationship continues with a client of the former firm. However, the problems are solved and independence is not impaired if (1) the person's retirement benefits are fixed, (2) the person is no longer active in the accounting firm (sometimes retired owners remain "active"), and (3) the former owner is not held out to be associated with the accounting firm.

In addition to the preceding consideration, the public accounting firm must ensure that appropriate consideration is given to any increase in risks that may exist due to the former

[12] In April 2006, the PEEC adopted the *Conceptual Framework for AICPA Independence Standards,* which describes the PEEC's risk-based approach to analyzing independence issues that arise.

[13] However, employment relationships at an existing attest client that existed as of November 2001 are not deemed to impair independence provided such relationships were allowed under the ethics rules in effect at that time.

partner's or professional's knowledge of the firm's audit plan and procedures. The firm must consider the following:

- The interaction with the former partner or professional.
- The ability of attest team members to manage the interaction with the former partner or professional employee.
- Modification of the engagement procedures.
- The appropriateness of the review to determine that an appropriate level of skepticism was maintained.

Adverse Interest and Undue Influence Threats (Interpretation 101-6)

Conditions can arise when a CPA and a client move into an adversary relationship instead of the cooperative relationship needed in an attest engagement. CPAs are considered not independent when company management threatens or actually initiates a lawsuit against the CPA alleging deficiencies in audit or other attestation work or a covered member threatens or initiates litigation against the company management alleging fraud or deceit *(Interpretation 101-6)*. Such cases may be rare, but the AICPA has provided auditors a way out of the difficult audit situation by this rule requiring them to declare "nonindependence" and the ability to give only a disclaimer on financial statements or other information. Essentially, the CPA–client relationship ends and the litigation begins a new relationship.

Occasionally, the public accounting firm may find that it is a defendant in a lawsuit initiated by a third party or parties. Normally, this type of litigation is not considered to adversely impact the independence of the firm. However, sometimes these lawsuits result in claims from management that existing problems are the result of audit deficiencies or claims from the auditor that deficiencies are the result of fraud or deceit on the part of management. When such cross-claims are threatened or filed, independence may be impaired.

Self-Review Threat (Interpretation 101-3)

Independence is impaired if the public accounting firm performs the bookkeeping or makes accounting or management decisions for a company whose management does not know enough about the financial statements to take primary responsibility for them. The problem in this situation is the appearance of the public accounting firm having both prepared the financial statements or other information and provided the auditors' report or other attestation on its own work. In the final analysis, the management must be able to say, "These are our financial statements (or other information); we made the choices of accounting principles; we take primary responsibility for them." The auditors cannot authorize transactions, have control of assets, sign checks or reports, prepare source documents, supervise the client's personnel, or serve as the client's registrar, transfer agent, or general counsel.

Financial Self-Interest Threat (Interpretations 101-1, 101-5, 101-8, 101-12, and 101-15)

Interpretation 101-1 deals with the financial interests in a client. Any direct financial interest (e.g., common stock, preferred stock, bonds) is prohibited. This requirement is the strictest one in the code. The words of the rule offer no exceptions. Indirect financial interests, on the other hand, are allowed up to the point of materiality (with reference to the member's wealth). This provision permits members to have some limited business transactions with clients so long as they do not reach material proportions. Other provisions define certain specific types of prohibited and allowed indirect financial interests. *Immediate family members* are subject to the same provisions that prescribe the acceptable actions of the covered person. Like the covered person, an immediate family member may not have a direct financial or material indirect financial interest in a client.

We already understand that a covered member cannot have a financial relationship with a client. However, suppose the client is an investor in another company and the covered member has also invested in that company? Has independence been impaired? Under Interpretation 101-8, if the covered member's investment is a direct or material indirect financial interest in a nonclient investee, independence is considered to be

impaired. The reasoning for the basic rule is that the client investor, through its ability to influence a nonclient investee, can increase or decrease the CPA's financial stake in the investee by an amount material to the CPA and, therefore, the CPA may not appear to be independent. If the investment by the client is not material to the nonclient (i.e., there does not appear to be any influence over the investee), then independence is not impaired unless the covered member's investment allows the member to exercise significant influence over the nonclient.

Material cooperative arrangements with clients (i.e., joint participation in a business activity) also impair independence (Interpretation 101-12). Examples include joint ventures to develop or market products or to market a package of client and CPA services or one party working to market the products or services of the other.

Interpretation 101-5 prohibits most loans to or from audit clients: "Independence is considered impaired if a covered member has a loan from a client, officer, director, or any individual owning 10 percent or more of a client." Similarly, independence is impaired if there are unpaid fees or a note receivable arising from unpaid fees from the client outstanding for over a year (ET 191.52). The only loans permitted are "grandfathered loans" and "other permitted loans."

Grandfathered loans are those loans that were obtained either (1) before the independence rules changed (but met the requirements of Rule 101 in effect at that time or (2) from a financial institution before it became a client for services requiring independence. These grandfathered loans must at all times be current under all of their terms and the terms shall not be renegotiated. The specific types of loans that are grandfathered are home mortgages, loans not material to the CPA's net worth, and secured loans for which the collateral value must exceed the balance of the loan at all times.

Other permitted loans include

- Auto loans and leases collateralized by the automobile.
- Insurance policy loans based on policy surrender value.
- Loans collateralized by cash deposits at the same financial institution.
- Credit card balances and cash advances of $10,000 or less.

Thus, an individual involved in the audit of a bank can have an auto loan at the bank, borrow money secured by cash in a certificate of deposit, and have the bank's credit card with a balance of less than $10,000 as long as the loans are at normal lending terms. However, notice that these loans are limited to personal loans, with the unwritten understanding that they are for personal convenience, not large loans for business purposes.

An important part of Interpretation 101-1 is the recognition that ethics rules do not cover all circumstances in which the appearance of independence might be questioned. It is the member's responsibility to determine if the personal and business relationships would lead a reasonable person aware of all the relevant facts to conclude that there is an unacceptable threat to the member's and the firm's independence.

Management Participation and Advocacy Threats (Interpretations 101-1, 101-3, and 101-4)

In addition to prohibitions against financial relationships with clients, Interpretation 101-1 also prohibits a covered member from acting in the capacity of a manager, employee, promoter, or trustee of a client. Generally, independence is impaired if the public accounting firm even *appears* to outside observers to be working in the capacity of management or employees of the client. The client management (including its board of directors and audit committee) must understand that they are responsible for establishing and maintaining internal control and directing the internal audit function, if any. The board of directors and/or audit committee must understand their roles and responsibilities with regard to extended audit services including the establishment of guidelines for both management and the public accounting firm to follow in carrying out these responsibilities and monitoring how well the respective responsibilities have been met.

In addition to the guidance discussed in the previous paragraphs, Interpretation 101-3 lists additional activities that would impair independence:[14]

- Performing ongoing monitoring activities or control activities.
- Determining which, if any, recommendations for improving internal control should be implemented.
- Reporting to the board of directors or audit committee on behalf of management or the individual responsible for the internal audit function.
- Authorizing, executing, or consummating transactions or otherwise exercising authority on behalf of the client.
- Preparing source documents on transactions.
- Having custody of assets.
- Approving or being responsible for the overall internal audit work plan including the determination of the internal audit risk and scope project priorities and frequency of performance of audit procedures.
- Performing forensic accounting services, litigation support work, or any other service in which it appears that the CPA is taking an advocacy position on the client's behalf. While performing tax compliance work would not normally impair independence, certain tax work in which an advocacy position is required does (e.g., representing a client in a court to resolve a tax dispute).
- Being connected with the client as an employee or in any capacity equivalent to a member of client management (for example, being listed as an employee in client directories or other client publications, permitting himself or herself to be referred to by title or description as supervising or being in charge of the client's internal audit function, or using the client's letterhead or internal correspondence forms in communications).

While this list is not all-inclusive, prohibited activities are those that force CPAs to act in the capacity of either management or an advocate for management.

As noted above, independence is ordinarily impaired if a CPA serves on an organization's board of directors. However, members can be *honorary* directors of organizations such as charity hospitals, fund drives, symphony orchestra societies, and similar not-for-profit organizations so long as (1) the position is purely honorary, (2) the CPA is identified as an honorary director on letterheads and other literature, (3) the only form of participation is the use of the CPA's name, and (4) the CPA does not vote with the board or participate in management functions (Interpretation 101-4). When all of these criteria are satisfied, the CPA/board member can perform audit and attest services because the appearances of independence will have been preserved.

Other Rule 101 interpretations include relationships with governmental entities (Interpretation 101-10) and alternative practice structures (Interpretation 101-14). The full list of interpretations, with accompanying detail, can be found on the AICPA's Web site (www.aicpa.org). You will need to study these interpretations to understand the full details of the AICPA independence requirements.

SEC and PCAOB Independence Rules

Until fairly recently, the SEC accepted most of the independence rules established by the PEEC. However, the SEC became concerned even before Enron about the public

[14] Although the following information does not prohibit auditors from providing internal audit and a variety of other services, it should be emphasized that the interpretation covers client companies that are public and private. Audits of public companies must comply with the rules of the SEC, the appropriate stock exchange, and the PCAOB. These agencies have rules that prohibit auditors from providing internal audit services to audit clients in most cases and have more stringent requirements regarding extended services.

accounting profession's emphasis on consulting fees and the resulting effect on public accounting firm independence. The SEC issued its comprehensive independence rule in November 2000. The rule is based upon two premises: (1) *independence in fact* is a mental state of objectivity and lack of bias and (2) *independence in appearance* depends on whether a reasonable investor, with knowledge of all relevant facts and circumstances, can conclude that the auditor is not capable of exercising objective and impartial judgment. Hence, an auditor's independence depends on auditors both having the proper mental state and passing the appearance test.

In a preface to the rule, the SEC stated four principles for determining whether a public accounting firm is independent of an audit client, factors the SEC will first consider when making independence determinations in controversial cases. Auditors are *not* independent if they have a relationship that

- Creates a mutual or conflicting interest between the auditors and the audit client.
- Places the public accounting firm in the position of auditing its own work.
- Results in the public accounting firm personnel acting as management or employees of the audit client.
- Places the public accounting firm in a position of being an advocate for the audit client.

The SEC independence rules relating to financial relationships are very similar to the AICPA Code of Professional Conduct Rule 101 Interpretations explained earlier. The most significant categories addressed by the SEC rules are in the areas of financial and employment relationships, nonaudit services (e.g., taxation, consulting), and disclosure of fees.

AUDITING INSIGHT Sometimes a Few Problems Occur

In January 1999, the Securities and Exchange Commission censured **PricewaterhouseCoopers** for violation of auditor independence rules and improper professional conduct. The firm's partners reported a total of 8,064 independence violations with an average of 5 violations per offender. Most of the violations were by partners (81.3 percent) and half of the violations involved direct financial interests in clients. Peter Franks, the firm's global managing partner of risk management, stated, "We have to do a much better job of teaching our people the intricacies of the rules and the importance of compliance."

Source: "PricewaterhouseCoopers Addresses SEC Report on Independence Violations," *CPA Journal*, March 2000.

Nonaudit Services

The SEC is very concerned about the fact and appearance of independence when public accounting firms perform consulting services for audit clients. A major issue in the Enron case was that over half of the fee it paid to Arthur Andersen was for consulting services. This fact exacerbated the concern that auditors would allow a client's improper financial reporting for the sake of preserving lucrative fees from other services. The SEC's concern in this regard is controversial, but the PCAOB has reinforced it. The SEC and PCAOB independence rules prohibit or place restrictions on the following 14 types of nonaudit services provided to audit clients. (No such restrictions apply to these services when they are performed for clients who are not audit clients.)

- Bookkeeping or other services related to the audit client's accounting records or financial statements (including maintaining or preparing the accounting records, preparing the financial statements, or preparing or originating source data underlying the financial statements *except* in emergency situations).

- Financial information systems design and implementation (including operating or supervising the client's information system, designing or implementing a hardware or software system that generates information that is significant to the client's financial statements *unless* the audit client's management takes full and complete responsibility for all design, implementation, internal control, and management decisions about the hardware and software).

- Appraisal or valuation services or fairness opinions (including any such services material to the financial statements when the auditor might audit the results of the public accounting firm's own work, *but* the public accounting firm's valuation experts may audit actuarial calculations, perform tax-oriented valuations, and perform nonfinancial valuations for audit clients).

- Actuarial services (including determination of actuarial liabilities *unless* the audit client management first uses its own actuaries and accepts responsibility for significant actuarial methods and assumptions).

- Internal audit services (including those related to the client's internal accounting controls, financial systems, or financial statements).

- Management functions (including acting temporarily or permanently as a director, officer, or employee of an audit client, or performing any decision-making, supervisory, or ongoing monitoring function for the audit client).

- Human resources (including all aspects of executive search activities, reference checking, status and compensation determination, and hiring advice).

- Broker-dealer services (including acting as a broker-dealer, promoter, or underwriter on behalf of an audit client; making investment decisions or otherwise having discretionary authority over investments; executing a transaction to buy or sell investments; or having custody of assets).

- Legal services (including any service under circumstances in which the person providing the service must be admitted to practice before the courts of a U.S. jurisdiction).

- Expert services (including providing expert opinions or other services to an audit client or legal representative of an audit client for the purpose of advocating that audit client's interests in litigation, regulatory, or administrative investigations or proceedings; the auditor may perform internal investigations at the direction of the audit committee or its legal council).

The PCAOB has restricted the following services:

- Performing any service for a contingent fee or commission for an audit client.
- Providing tax services that are based on judicial proceedings or aggressive interpretations of tax law.
- Planning or opining on the tax consequence of a transaction.
- Providing tax services for key company executives.

AUDITING INSIGHT E&Y, PeopleSoft, and a Loss of Independence

An administrative law judge recommended that **Ernst & Young** pay the government $1.7 million and be barred from taking new auditing clients for six months for violating SEC conflict-of-interest regulations involving a joint marketing agreement with **People-Soft,** a former audit client. The judge found that E&Y had "engaged in improper professional conduct because it violated applicable professional standards for auditors by conduct that was both reckless and negligent." Further, the Big Four firm had displayed "an utter disdain for the commission's rules and regulations of auditor independence." Although no wrongdoing was alleged in its auditing of the software company, the joint marketing agreement violated SEC rules against having anything more that a "consumer" relationship with audit clients. The firm sold its consulting arm that created the conflict of interest.

Source: "Ernst & Young Hit Hard in PeopleSoft Case," April 16, 2004, available at www.TheStreet.com.

Disclosures about Fees

The SEC believes that people who use financial statements and auditors' reports can be enlightened with information about auditors' fee arrangements with clients. Hence, SEC rules require that companies (not auditors) disclose the following in proxy statements delivered to their shareholders:

- Total audit fees to the public accounting firm for the annual audit and the reviews of quarterly financial information.
- Total fees to the public accounting firm for tax and other advisory work (over and above the audit fees).
- Whether the audit committee or the board of directors considered the public accounting firm's advisory work to be compatible with maintaining the auditor's independence.
- If more than 50 percent, the percentage of the audit hours performed by persons other than the principal auditor's full-time, permanent employees. (This disclosure refers to "leased employees" in an "alternative practice structure" arrangement.)

Other Effects of Sarbanes-Oxley on Auditor Independence

The Sarbanes-Oxley Act of 2002 required the SEC to modify its position on auditor independence in several ways. Perhaps the most important change in independence arises from the changing role of the audit committee. Since the inception of the principle of the independence for auditors, it has been the auditor who was responsible for evaluating and determining the independence of the individual and firm. While auditors still must be vigilant in establishing and monitoring independence policy to ensure that they are in fact independent, Sarbanes-Oxley has placed the responsibility for the determination of independence in appearance at the door of the audit committee. This is particularly evident by the fact that the audit committee bears the responsibility for determining the scope of services provided by the auditor and reviewing independence issues prior to the appointment of the auditor. The audit committee may do this on a case-by-case basis or may establish a set of policies and procedures that establish acceptable and nonacceptable services.

In addition, Sarbanes-Oxley limits the engagement and concurring audit partners on an engagement to five-year terms. Other partners associated with the engagement are limited to seven-year terms with that client. Partners also are deemed as nonindependent if they receive compensation that is based on selling to an audit client services other than audit, review, and attestation services.

In the past, it was not unusual for a member of an audit team, usually a manager or higher, to leave the public accounting firm to take a financial management position with a client. Under the rules established by Sarbanes-Oxley, a public accounting firm cannot perform an audit of a company in which an individual with financial reporting oversight responsibilities was a member of the audit engagement team during the fiscal year under audit.

Independence Standards Board

Between the time of its creation in 1997 and its disbanding in July 2001, the ISB issued three standards and several interpretations.

ISB Standard No. 1 (ISB 1): Independence Discussions with Audit Committees[15]

ISB 1 requires that the public accounting firm each year

- Disclose in writing to the audit client's board of directors and its audit committee all relationships between the auditor and the company the auditor thinks may be reasonably related to consideration of the auditor's independence.

[15] On July 24, 2007, the PCAOB proposed Rule 3526, Communication with Audit Committees Concerning Independence, which requires that registered public accounting firms communicate with public company client audit committees about any relationships between the firm and the client that might affect the firm's independence. This rule, if approved by the SEC, would supersede ISB No. 1

- Confirm to the board of directors that, in the auditor's professional judgment, the public accounting firm is independent in accordance with SEC rules.
- Discuss its independence with the audit committee or the board of directors.

The intent of this standard is to ensure that public company audit committees and boards of directors consider their auditors' independence at least once each year. If the discussion is not held, auditors are supposed to withhold the auditors' report.

ISB Interpretation 00-1 added the additional requirement that when more than one auditor is involved in the audit of a consolidated group of companies, the primary auditor is the firm that must produce the required disclosures and conduct the discussion, but any other auditors ("secondary auditors") also must comply with respect to their audit clients. ISB Interpretation 00-2 amended Interpretation 00-1 with the requirement that the primary public accounting firm must disclose all relationships with domestic and foreign public accounting firms involved in the audit and describe the other auditors' relationships, if possible.

ISB Standard No. 2 (ISB 2): Certain Independence Implications of Audits of Mutual Funds and Related Entities

An investment company "complex" can consist of several related entities involved in mutual fund management: the fund sponsor, banks, broker-dealers, investment advisers, insurance companies, trustees, transfer agents, and "sister funds" (other mutual funds in the same family). Imagine a complex consisting of TruFund (sponsor); the sister funds TruFundDiversified, TruFundIndex, and TruFundInternational; Faithful & Co. (broker-dealer); BigBank (transfer agent); and Big Deal Investment Management (investment advisers).

When auditing one mutual fund in the complex (e.g., TruFundDiversified) or a nonfund entity (e.g., Faithful & Co.), the public accounting firm, the audit engagement team, and the persons in the chain of command (refer to the earlier SEC definitions) must be independent of all entities in the complex. This independence refers to all the financial, employment, and nonaudit services explained in the SEC rules.

ISB 2 rules that independence is not impaired (1) when anyone in the public accounting firm who is not on the audit engagement team and not in the chain of command holds investments in nonclient sister funds and (2) when anyone who is not on the audit engagement team or in the chain of command, including firm owners and their immediate family members, hold investments in audit client mutual funds through their employment benefit plans. The first exception means that owners and employees in the public accounting firm who are not connected with the audit of TruFundDiversified can own shares in TruFundInternational (sister fund that is not an audit client). The second exception means, for example, that the husband of the partner in charge of the TruFundDiversified audit can own shares in TruFundIndex (also an audit client but not led by the partner-wife) so long as the shares are acquired in connection with his employment benefit plan at AnyCompany (the husband's employer).

ISB Standard No. 3: Employment with Audit Clients

This standard deals with the threat to audit independence when public accounting firm professionals consider or take jobs with audit clients. The threat is that the auditor considering a job offer from a client might not perform audit work properly while on the audit team. Likewise, after the professional takes a job with the audit client, he or she might improperly influence the audit performed by former colleagues in the public accounting firm. It is important to note that the Sarbanes-Oxley Act has similar provisions. Students should be familiar with both sets of requirements.

The public accounting firm's independence is considered impaired unless it undertakes certain safeguards, which follow:

- Audit professionals must report to the firm any conversations with an audit client about possible employment. Then the public accounting firm must
 (1) Remove the person from the audit engagement team.
 (2) Review the person's audit work to date to determine whether he or she exercised proper skepticism while on the audit.

- When a former owner or professional employee of the firm joins an audit client within one year after leaving the firm and this person has significant interaction with the continuing audit engagement team, the public accounting firm must perform additional review of the next annual audit. The purpose of the review is to determine whether
 (1) The former firm professional circumvented the audit because of familiarity with design, approach, and strategy.
 (2) The remaining members of the audit engagement team maintained objectivity when auditing the work and representations of the former firm professional.

In addition, for persons who leave the public accounting firm to take client employment, the public accounting firm must (1) liquidate former owners' capital balances, (2) settle all material retirement account balances unless the payments are fixed as to timing and amount (but the former professional does not have to liquidate balances held under a defined contribution retirement plan), and (3) settle all immaterial retirement account balances when in the five years following separation from the public accounting firm the former professional becomes a client officer named in a proxy statement or annual report filed with the SEC. This last requirement dictates complete separation of financial connections with the public accounting firm when the person becomes a highly ranked officer in a public company.

The potential problems involved when public accounting firm owners or professional employees take jobs with audit clients is one of the topics that should be discussed with the client's audit committee or board in accordance with ISB 1.

ISB Interpretation 99-1: Assisting Clients with Implementation of FAS 133 (Derivatives)

The ISB's first pronouncement drew attention to a situation in which an auditor might have to audit her or his own work. For example, accounting for derivatives is a very complicated issue and many audit clients seek assistance from their auditors, yet the auditor will have to audit derivatives during the audit. Interpretation 99-1 rules that such assistance is permitted and independence is not impaired so long as the auditors (1) do not prepare accounting entries, (2) do not compute derivative values (even with a firm-developed valuation model), and (3) do not take responsibility for valuation assumptions and inputs. These three features are the essence of accounting for derivatives and the client must perform them. The auditors can give advice and then audit the client's results.

Governmental Accountability Office (GAO) Independence Requirements

Many state agencies and local municipalities use public accounting firms to perform audits required by government charters, laws, or contractual obligations (usually as part of a grant). During these audits, the public accounting firm is required to follow all GAO standards included in the Government Auditing Standards manual (also called the *Yellow Book*). These standards require the auditor to be independent with respect to the government entity. These standards differ from the SEC, AICPA, and Sarbanes-Oxley requirements in the following ways:

- Nonaudit services are allowed providing that the audit organization does not perform management functions, make management decisions, or audit their own work. However, the audit organization must employ the following safeguards:
 (1) Personnel who provide nonaudit services are prohibited from planning, conducting, or reviewing audit work related to the nonaudit services.
 (2) The audit organization may not reduce the scope or extent of work performed on the audit because the nonaudit work was performed by a member of the firm. The extent of the audit work may be reduced by an amount consistent with a reduction had the nonaudit been performed by another public accounting firm.
 (3) The audit organization must document its reasons that the nonaudit services do not affect the firm's independence.

(4) The audit organization must document an understanding with the client regarding the objectives, scope, and work product for the nonaudit service.

(5) The audit organization must have established policies and procedures to ensure that effects of nonaudit services on the present and future audits are considered.

(6) The audit organization must communicate to the government entity any situation in which the nonaudit service would prohibit it from performing the audit.

(7) When subjected to a peer review, the audit organization must identify all nonaudit services provided to the audited entity.

Review Checkpoints

B.7 Yolanda is the executive in charge of the Santa Fe office of Best & Co, an international public accounting firm. She is responsible for the practice in all areas of audit, tax, and consulting, but she does not serve as a field audit partner or a reviewer. Javier is the partner in charge of the Besame, Inc. audit (an SEC filing). Is Best & Co independent if (a) Yolanda owns common stock of Besame or (b) Yolanda's brother owns 10 shares of the common stock of Besame?

B.8 Can audit managers on the audit engagement team who are also attorneys admitted to the state bar assist in the defense of a lawsuit against an audit client for product liability defects?

B.9 Why do you think the SEC requires companies to disclose fees paid to independent accounting firms for audit and consulting services? What must be disclosed?

B.10 What do the SEC disclosure rules and ISB Standard No. 1 have in common in connection with auditors' relations with an audit client's board of directors and its audit committee?

B.11 What is the perceived independence problem concerning members of an audit engagement team entertaining employment offers from audit clients?

AICPA RULES OF CONDUCT: INTEGRITY AND OBJECTIVITY, RESPONSIBILITIES TO CLIENTS, AND OTHER RESPONSIBILITIES

LEARNING OBJECTIVE

5. With reference to AICPA rules on topics other than independence, analyze factual situations and decide whether an accountant's conduct does or does not conform to the AICPA Rules of Conduct.

Now that we have discussed independence (Rule 101), we can turn to the other AICPA rules of conduct. Ten such rules are in sections 100, 200, 300, and 500.

Rule 102: Integrity and Objectivity

> **Rule 102.** In the performance of any professional service, a member shall maintain objectivity and integrity, shall be free of conflicts of interest, and shall not knowingly misrepresent facts or subordinate his or her judgment to others.

Rule 102 applies not only to CPAs in public practice but also to CPAs working in government and industry. (Jorge, the staff accountant in the decision process illustration in Ethics Example 2, is a government and industry CPA.) The rule requires integrity and objectivity in all types of professional work—tax practice and consulting practice as well as audit practice for public accountants—and all types of accounting work performed by CPAs employed in corporations, not-for-profit organizations, governments, and individual practices. In addition to integrity and objectivity, Rule 102 emphasizes (1) being free from conflicts of interest between CPAs and others, (2) representing facts truthfully in reports and discussions, and (3) not letting other people dictate or influence the CPA's judgment and professional decisions.

Conflicts of interest cited in Rule 102 refer to the need to avoid having business interests in which the accountant's personal financial relationships or the accountant's

relationships with other clients might tempt the accountant to fail to serve the best interests of a client or the public that uses the results of the engagement. Some examples of conflicts of interest are these in which the CPA

- Is engaged to perform litigation support services for a plaintiff in a lawsuit filed against a client.
- In a personal financial planning engagement, recommends client investment in a business in which the CPA has a financial interest.
- Provides tax services for several members of a family who have opposing interests.
- Performs management consulting for a client and has a financial or managerial interest in a major competitor.
- Serves on a city board of tax appeals, which hears matters involving clients.
- Refers a tax client to an insurance broker, who refers clients to the CPA under an exclusive agreement.
- Charges a contingent fee to a client for expert witness litigation support services when the fee can be affected by the opinion the CPA expresses.

The phrases "shall not knowingly misrepresent facts" (Interpretation 102-1) and "shall not subordinate his or her judgment to others" (Interpretation 102-4) emphasize conditions people ordinarily identify with the concepts of integrity and objectivity. Accountants who know about a client's lies in a tax return, about false journal entries, about material misrepresentations in financial statements, and the like have violated both the spirit and the letter of rule 102.[16] Furthermore, the defense that "my boss made me do it" is unacceptable.

AUDITING INSIGHT An Auditor's Downfall

MIAMI: Jose Gomez, former partner of a large public accounting firm, surrendered to begin a 12-year prison term. As auditor of **ESM,** Jose Gomez knowingly approved the company's false financial statements for five years, allowing the massive fraud to continue, ultimately costing investors $320 million. Just days after being promoted to partner, two ESM officers told him about an accounting ruse that was hiding millions of dollars in losses. He had missed it in two previous audits. They said: "It's going to look terrible for you, a new partner." Jose Gomez didn't want to face his superiors at the firm with the admission of the failed audits. He decided to go along with ESM because he thought the company could make up the losses and get everybody out of it.

Jose Gomez: "I never evaluated a criminal side to what I was doing. It was a professional decision, a judgment decision that it would eventually work itself out. It's the only thing I never discussed with my wife." ESM loaned Jose Gomez $200,000 to help out with his financial problems. "I never related my actions to the money. I just didn't want to face up that I had missed it originally."

On being prepared for prison: "I don't know. What can I bring, a typewriter, computer? I'd like to read and work on things."

Source: *The Wall Street Journal.*

The prohibition of misrepresentations in financial statements (Interpretation 102-1) applies to the management accountants who prepare companies' statements. Government and industry CPAs should not subordinate their professional judgment to superiors who try to produce materially misleading financial statements and fool their external auditors. Government and industry CPAs must be candid and not knowingly misrepresent facts or fail to disclose material facts when dealing with their employer's external auditor. Government and industry CPAs cannot have conflicts of interest in their jobs and

[16] However, in tax practice, an accountant can act as an advocate to resolve doubt in favor of a taxpayer–client as long as the tax treatment has a reasonable or justifiable basis.

their outside business interests that are not disclosed to their employers and approved. The importance of integrity and objectivity for government and industry CPAs cannot be overemphasized. Too often, CPAs relate the Code of Professional Conduct only to CPAs in public practice.

Rule 102 has two other applications. One concerns serving as a client advocate (Interpretation 102-6), which occurs frequently in taxation and rate regulation practice and in supporting clients' positions in FASB and SEC proceedings. Client advocacy in support or advancement of client positions is acceptable only so long as the member acts with integrity, maintains objectivity, and does not subordinate judgment to others. (Accountants-as-advocates do not adopt the same attitude as defense attorneys in a courtroom.) The other application is directed specifically to your college professors: They are supposed to maintain integrity and objectivity, be free of conflicts of interest, and not knowingly misrepresent facts to students (Interpretation 102-5).

Rule 201: General Standards

Rule 201. A member shall comply with the following standards and with any interpretations thereof by bodies designated by Council:

A. *Professional competence.* Undertake only those professional services that the member or the member's firm can reasonably expect to be completed with professional competence.
B. *Due professional care.* Exercise due professional care in the performance of professional services.
C. *Planning and supervision.* Adequately plan and supervise the performance of professional services.
D. *Sufficient relevant data.* Obtain sufficient relevant data to afford a reasonable basis for conclusions or recommendations in relation to any professional services performed.

Rule 201 is a comprehensive statement of general standards that accountants are expected to observe in all areas of practice. This is the rule that enforces the various series of professional standards. The AICPA Council has authorized the following agencies, boards, and committees to issue standards enforceable under Rule 201:

- Public Company Accounting Oversight Board.
- Auditing Standards Board.
- Accounting and Review Services Committee.
- Tax Executive Committee.
- Management Consulting Services Executive Committee.

Rule 201 effectively prohibits the acceptance of any engagement that the CPA cannot competently complete. Such engagements may involve audits that require specialized industry knowledge or technical expertise not possessed by the practitioner. Practitioners are allowed to accept an engagement if, through education, hiring of additional staff, or contracting with specialists, the practitioner can obtain the required knowledge *prior to the conclusion* of the engagement. This rule covers all areas of public accounting practice except personal financial planning and business valuation. Of course, a CPA may have to do some research to learn more about a unique problem or technique and may need to engage a colleague as a consultant.

Rule 202: Compliance with Standards

Rule 202. A member who performs auditing, review, compilation, management consulting, tax, or other professional services shall comply with standards promulgated by bodies designated by Council.

Rule 202 requires adherence to duly promulgated technical standards in all areas of professional service. These areas include the ones cited in the rule: auditing, review and

compilation (unaudited financial statements), consulting, tax, or "other" professional services. The "bodies designated by Council" are the Auditing Standards Board, the Accounting and Review Services Committee, the Tax Executive Committee, and the Consulting Services Executive Committee. The practical effect of Rule 202 is to make noncompliance with all technical standards (in addition to the Rule 201 general standards) subject to disciplinary proceedings. Therefore, failure to follow auditing standards, accounting and review standards, tax standards, and consulting standards is a violation of Rule 202.

Rule 203: Accounting Principles

Rule 203. A member shall not (1) express an opinion or state affirmatively that the financial statements or other financial data of any entity are presented in conformity with generally accepted principles or (2) state that he or she is not aware of any material modifications that should be made to such statements or data in order for them to be in conformity with generally accepted accounting principles, if such statements or data contain any departure from an accounting principle promulgated by bodies designated by Council to establish such principles that has a material effect on the statements or data taken as a whole. If, however, the statements or data contain such a departure and the member can demonstrate that due to unusual circumstances the financial statements or data would otherwise have been misleading, the member can comply with the rule by describing the departure, its approximate effects, if practicable, and the reasons why compliance with the principle would result in a misleading statement.

The AICPA Council has designated three rule-making bodies to pronounce accounting principles under Rule 203. The Financial Accounting Standards Board (FASB) and its predecessors are designated to pronounce standards in general. Therefore, Rule 203 requires adherence to Accounting Research Bulletins of the Committee on Accounting Procedure (issued before 1959), Opinions of the Accounting Principles Board (1959–1973), and statements and interpretations of financial accounting standards adopted by the Financial Accounting Standards Board (1973 to present). The Council also has designated the Governmental Accounting Standards Board (GASB) to pronounce accounting standards for state and local government entities and the Federal Accounting Standards Advisory Board (FASAB) with respect to statements of federal accounting standards.

You may wonder about the two parts at the beginning of Rule 203: "(1) express an opinion or state affirmatively . . . or (2) state that he or she is not aware of any material modifications . . ." These two parts are intended to cover two types of attestation reports regarding the conformity of financial statements or other information with generally accepted accounting principles. The first part refers to *opinions* on financial statement and other information, for example, the standard unqualified auditors' report on audited financial statements. The second part refers to reports in which *negative assurance* is permitted, for example, the review report on unaudited financial statements.

Rule 203 requires adherence to official pronouncements unless such adherence would be misleading. The consequences of misleading statements to outside decision makers would be financial harm, so presumably the greater good would be realized by explaining a departure and thereby "breaking the rule of officially promulgated accounting principles." Such an instance occurs in very rare situations and the burden of proving that following pronouncements would be misleading is the responsibility of the auditor.

Members in government and industry also can be subject to Rule 203. These accountants produce and certify financial statements and sign written management representation letters for their external auditors. They also present financial statements to regulatory authorities and creditors. Government and industry accountants generally "report" that the company's financial statements conform to GAAP and this report is taken as an expression of opinion (or negative assurance) of the type governed by Rule 203.

The result is that accountants who present financial statements containing any undisclosed departures from official pronouncements face disciplinary action for violating the rule.

Rule 301: Confidential Client Information

 Rule 301. A member in public practice shall not disclose any confidential information without the specific consent of the client.

Confidential information is information that should not be disclosed to outside parties unless demanded by a court or an administrative body having subpoena or summons power. *Privileged information* is information that cannot even be demanded by a court. Common-law privilege exists for husband–wife and attorney–client relationships. Physician–patient and priest–penitent relationships have obtained the privilege through state statutes. No accountant–client privilege exists under federal law and no state-created privilege has been recognized in federal courts. In all recognized privilege relationships, the professional person is obligated to observe the privilege, which can be waived only by the client, patient, or penitent. (These persons are said to be the *holders of the privilege*.)

The rules of privileged and confidential communication are based on the belief that they facilitate a free flow of information between parties to the relationship. The nature of accounting services makes it necessary for the accountant to have access to information about salaries, products, contracts, merger or divestment plans, tax matters, and other information required for the best possible professional work. Managers would be less likely to reveal such information if they could not trust the accountant to keep it confidential. If accountants were to reveal such information, the resulting reduction of the information flow might be undesirable, so no accountant should break the confidentiality rule without a good reason.

AUDITING INSIGHT Spies, Lies, and Client Confidentiality

What would you do if a government intelligence agent approached you to assist him in a "top secret" assignment involving national security? Guy Enright, an accountant with KPMG's Financial Advisory Services Ltd. in Bermuda, said "yes" to Nick Hamilton, a British intelligence officer, and agreed to deposit confidential audit documents in plastic containers at "dead drop" sites located throughout Bermuda. Unfortunately for Enright, KPMG, and their client, IPOC International Growth Fund Ltd. (IPOC), "Nick Hamilton" was in fact Nick Day, a co-founder of Diligence Inc., a Washington-based private intelligence firm that was gathering information for one of IPOC's business competitors.

The setup was quite elaborate. "Hamilton" required Enright to undergo a detailed background check, even producing an official-looking questionnaire with a British government seal at the top, before he could participate on "Project Yucca." The undercover mission came to an abrupt end when someone (still unknown) dropped off a package of Diligence business records and e-mails involving "Project Yucca" at KPMG's Montvale office. After KPMG sued, Diligence ended up paying $1.7 million.

Source: "Spies, Lies, and KPMG," *BusinessWeek*, February 26, 2007.

Difficult problems arise over auditors' obligations to "blow the whistle" about clients' shady or illegal practices. Auditing standards deal with this problem: If a client refuses to accept an auditors' report that has been modified because of the inability to obtain sufficient competent evidence about a suspected illegal act, failure to account for or disclose properly a material amount connected with an illegal act, or inability to estimate amounts involved in an illegal act, the public accounting firm should withdraw from the engagement and give the reasons in writing to the board of directors. In such an extreme case, the withdrawal amounts to whistle-blowing, but the action results from the client's decision not to disclose the information. For all practical purposes, information is not considered confidential if its disclosure is necessary to make financial statements not misleading.

Auditors are not, in general, legally *obligated* to blow the whistle on clients. However, circumstances in which auditors are legally *justified* in making disclosures to a regulatory agency or a third party may exist. Such circumstances include (1) when a client has intentionally and without authorization associated or involved a CPA in its misleading conduct, (2) when a client has distributed misleading draft financial statements prepared by a CPA for internal use only, or (3) when a client prepares and distributes in an annual report or prospectus misleading information for which the CPA has not assumed any responsibility.[17] In addition, the Private Securities Litigation Reform Act of 1995 imposed another reporting requirement in connection with clients' illegal acts (see Module C).

Rule 301 possibly provides accountants the most difficulties and may be the most violated procedure. First, in its strictest interpretation, the principle of confidentiality applies to the communication of information to anyone that is not involved in the audit except as noted by the rule. Over lunch or after hours, however, you might find auditors discussing the day's work with other members of the firm or company. Second, CPAs should not view Rule 301 on confidential information as an excuse for inaction when action may be appropriate to right a wrongful act committed or about to be committed by a client. In some cases, auditors' inaction may be viewed as part of a conspiracy or willingness to be an accessory to a wrong. Such situations are dangerous and potentially damaging. A useful initial course of action is to consult with an attorney about possible legal pitfalls of both whistle-blowing and silence. In both situations, the auditor's personal standard of ethics will determine the individual's course of action.

Accountants can permit other accountants to review confidential working papers and other information about clients in connection with arrangements to sell or merge an accounting practice. The AICPA advises accountants to have an agreement among themselves that extends the confidentiality safeguard to the prospective purchasing accountant as it existed with the original accountant.

CPAs also may disclose confidential information without the client's permission to remain in compliance with applicable laws (e.g., responding to a subpoena), as part of an ethics investigation *(of a CPA)*, or as part of a peer review or PCAOB investigation of *public accounting firm* practices. The exception related to ethic violations applies only to investigative or disciplinary bodies under the AICPA's jurisdiction, namely the AICPA Professional Ethics Division, the ethics enforcement committees in the various state societies of CPAs, and state Boards of Accountancy. Thus, the ethics and law enforcement agencies in the United States (SEC, Internal Revenue Service [IRS], and such other agencies as the U.S. Department of Justice, Federal Trade Commission [FTC], Equal Employment Opportunity Commission, and local police and district attorneys) are not within the exception. Voluntary disclosure to these agencies is not explicitly permitted under Rule 301 (i.e., subpoenas are required).

Rule 302: Contingent Fees — *non attest*

Rule 302. A member in public practice shall not

(1) Perform for a contingent fee any professional services for, or receive such a fee from, a client for whom the member or the member's firm performs

 (a) an audit or review of a financial statement; or

 (b) a compilation of a financial statement when the member expects, or reasonably might expect, that a third party will use the financial statement and the member's compilation report does not disclose a lack of independence; or

 (c) an examination of prospective financial information; or

(2) Prepare an original or amended tax return or claim for a tax refund for a contingent fee for any client.

[17] C. Chazen, R. L. Miller, and K. I. Solomon, "When the Rules Say: 'See Your Lawyer,'" *Journal of Accountancy,* January 1981.

Suppose you are a shareholder in New Medical Corporation. You have some concerns about the company's revenue practices, but the fact that New Medical Corporation received an unqualified audit opinion reassures you. Now let's assume that you discover that New Medical Corporation's contract with its auditor paid the auditor more for an unqualified opinion than a qualified opinion. How might that affect the value you placed on the auditor's report?

A **contingent fee** is a fee established for the performance of any service in an arrangement in which no fee will be charged unless a specific finding or result is attained or the fee otherwise depends on the result of the service. (Fees are not contingent if they are fixed by a court or other public authority or, in tax matters, determined as a result of the findings of judicial proceedings or the findings of government agencies; nor are fees contingent when they are based on the complexity or time required for the work.) Under Rule 302, CPAs can charge contingent fees for work such as representing a client in an IRS tax audit and certain other tax matters, achieving goals in a consulting service engagement, or helping a person obtain a bank loan in a financial planning engagement. However, the PCAOB has proposed (but not issued at the date of publication) an independence rule that would prohibit all contingent fees for audit clients of registered public accounting firms. CPAs can charge contingent fees as investment bankers do in merger deals and lawyers do in injury lawsuits.

Rule 302 permits CPAs to receive contingent fees *except* from clients for whom the CPAs perform attest services when users of financial information may be relying on the CPAs' work. The prohibitions in item 1(a), 1(b), and 1(c) all refer to attest engagements in which independence is required. Acceptance of contingent fee arrangements during the period in which the member or the member's firm is engaged to perform any of these attestations or during the period covered by any historical financial statements involved in any of these engagements is considered an impairment of independence.

Rule 302 also prohibits contingent fees in connection with the everyday tax practice of preparing original or amended tax returns. This prohibition arose from an interesting conflict of government agencies. The Federal Trade Commission (FTC) wanted to see contingent fees permitted, but the IRS objected on the grounds that such fees might induce accountants and clients to "play the audit lottery": understate tax improperly in the hope of escaping audit. The IRS asserted that if the AICPA permitted such contingent fees, the IRS would make its own rules prohibiting them. The FTC agreed that the AICPA rule could contain this prohibition.

Rule 501: Acts Discreditable

Rule 501. A member shall not commit an act discreditable to the profession.

Rule 501 may be called the moral clause of the code, but it is only occasionally the basis for disciplinary action. Penalties normally are invoked automatically under the AICPA Bylaws, which provide for expulsion of members found by a court to have committed any fraud, filed false tax returns, been convicted of any criminal offense, or found by the AICPA Trial Board to have been guilty of an act discreditable to the profession.

AUDITING INSIGHT Discreditable Act

The Enforcement Committee found that Respondent drew a gun from his desk drawer during a dispute with a client in his office in contravention of Section 501.41 [discreditable acts prohibition] of the [Texas] Rules of Professional Conduct. Respondent agreed to accept a private reprimand to be printed . . . in the Texas State Board Report.

Source: Texas State Board of Accountancy Report.

AICPA interpretations consider discreditable acts to include these:

- Withholding a client's books and records and important documentation when the client has requested their return.

AUDITING INSIGHT What Are Accountants Doing?

According to the Pennsylvania CPA Journal, documentation reten-
tion complaints by clients are "by far the most common issue
brought before the Ethics Committee" in the state of Pennsylvania.

Source: Cherie L. Craft, "Keeping Ethics Quandaries at Bay," *Pennsylvania
CPA Journal,* Summer 2005.

- Being found guilty by a court or administrative agency to have violated employment an-
 tidiscrimination laws, including ones related to sexual and other forms of harassment.
- Failing to follow government audit standards and guides in governmental audits when
 the client or the government agency expects such standards to be followed.
- Failure to follow the requirements of governmental bodies, commissions, or other reg-
 ulatory bodies including the PCAOB.
- Soliciting or disclosing CPA Examination questions and answers from the closed CPA
 Examination.
- Failing to file tax returns or remit payroll and other taxes collected for others (e.g., em-
 ployee taxes withheld).
- Making, or permitting others to make, false and misleading entries in records and
 financial statements.

This last item is specifically applicable to members in government and industry as well as
members in public practice. Any management accountant who participates in the produc-
tion of false and misleading financial statements commits a discreditable act.

Rule 502: Advertising and Other Forms of Solicitation

Rule 502. A member in public practice shall not seek to obtain clients by advertising or
other forms of solicitation in a manner that is false, misleading, or deceptive. Solicitation
by the use of coercion, overreaching, or harassing conduct is prohibited.

Advertising consists of messages designed to attract business that are broadcast widely to
an undifferentiated audience (e.g., print, radio, television, billboards). Rule 502 permits
advertising with only a few limitations. The current rule applies only to CPAs practicing
public accounting and relates to their efforts to obtain clients. The guidelines basically
prohibit false, misleading, and deceptive messages:

- Advertising may not create false or unjustified expectations of favorable results.
- Advertising may not imply the ability to influence any court, tribunal, regulatory
 agency, or similar body or official.
- Advertising may not contain a fee estimate when the CPA knows it is likely to be sub-
 stantially increased unless the client is notified.
- Advertising may not contain any other representation likely to cause a reasonable per-
 son to misunderstand or be deceived.

Most CPAs carry out only modest advertising efforts, and many do no advertising at
all. Public practice is generally marked by decorum and a sense of good taste. However,
there are exceptions, and they tend to get much attention—most of it disapproving—from
other CPAs and the public in general. The danger in bad advertising lies in creating the
image of a professional huckster, which may backfire on efforts to build a practice.

Solicitation generally refers to direct contact (e.g., in person, mail, telephone) with a
specific potential client. In regard to solicitation, Rule 502 basically prohibits extreme bad
behavior (coercion, overreaching, or harassing conduct). Many CPAs abhor solicitation
and many state boards of accountancy try to prohibit direct, uninvited approaches to
prospective clients, especially when the client already has a CPA. Nevertheless, the U.S.
Supreme Court has struck down state solicitation prohibitions, declaring them to be an in-
fringement of personal and business rights to free speech and due process.

AUDITING INSIGHT Felicity and Solicitations

CPA Fane moved to Florida and conducted face-to-face meetings to obtain clients. The Florida Board of Accountancy brought suit to enforce its anti-solicitation rule but lost in a Supreme Court decision. At present, some state boards try to discourage solicitation with restrictive rules they hope will not run afoul of the Supreme Court decision. Other state boards are trying to put anti-solicitation rules into their state laws when they think they will be shielded from the U.S. Supreme Court. At the present, solicitation is legal, but be aware that your local state board may have rules or laws prohibiting it.

Source: *Edenfield v. Fane,* 507 U.S. 761 (1993).

CPAs sometimes hire marketing firms to obtain clients. In years past, this arrangement was designed to avoid direct involvement in advertising and solicitation efforts that might violate Rule 502. The AICPA permits such arrangements but warns that all such "practice development" activity is subject to Rule 502 because members cannot do through others things they are prohibited from doing themselves.

Rule 503: Commissions and Referral Fees

Rule 503. A. Prohibited Commissions

A member in public practice shall not for a commission recommend or refer to a client any product or service, or for a commission recommend or refer any product or service to be supplied by a client, or receive a commission, when the member or the member's firm also performs for that client:

Software package put together by an accounting firm.

(a) an audit or review of a financial statement; or
(b) a compilation of a financial statement when the member expects, or reasonably might expect, that a third party will use the financial statement and the member's compilation report does not disclose a lack of independence; or
(c) an examination of prospective financial information.

This prohibition applies during the period in which the member is engaged to perform any of the services listed above and the period covered by any historical financial statements involved in such listed services.

B. Disclosure of Permitted Commission

A member in public practice who is not prohibited by this rule from performing services for or receiving a commission and who is paid or expects to be paid a commission shall disclose that fact to any person or entity to whom the member recommends or refers a product or service to which the commission relates.

C. Referral Fees

Any member who accepts a referral fee for recommending or referring any service of a CPA to any person or entity or who pays a referral fee to obtain a client shall disclose such acceptance or payment to the client.

A **commission** is generally defined as a percentage-based fee charged for professional services in connection with executing a transaction or performing some other business activity. Examples are insurance sales commissions, real estate sales commissions, and securities sales commissions. A CPA can earn commissions except in connection with any client for whom the CPA performs attestation services.

Part A of Rule 503 treats commissions as an impairment of independence just as Rule 302 treats contingent fees. Recall that *contingent fees* are based upon attaining a specific finding or result and are prohibited for attestation clients. When involved in an attest engagement with a client, the CPA cannot receive a commission from anyone for (1) referring a product or service to the client or (2) referring to someone else a product or service supplied by the client. It does not matter which party actually pays the commission.

Part B of Rule 503 *permits commissions* provided that the engagement *does not involve attestation* of the types cited in Part A of the rule. This permission is tempered by the requirement that the CPA must disclose to clients an arrangement to receive a commission.

Most of the commission fee activity takes place in connection with personal financial planning services. CPAs often recommend insurance and investments to individuals and families. Some critics point out that clients cannot always trust commission agents (e.g., insurance salespersons, securities brokers) to have clients' best interests in mind when the agents' own compensation depends on clients' buying the product that produces commissions.

Part C of Rule 503 deals with **referral fees,** which are (1) fees a CPA receives for recommending another CPA's services and (2) fees a CPA pays to obtain a client. Such fees may or may not be based on a percentage of the amount of any transaction. Referral involves the practice of sending business to another CPA and paying other CPAs or outside agencies for drumming up business. Some CPAs have hired services that solicit clients on their behalf, paying a fixed or percentage fee. Many CPAs frown on these arrangements, but they are permitted. However, CPAs must disclose such fees to clients.

Rule 505: Form of Organization and Name

Rule 505. A member may practice public accounting only in a form of organization permitted by law or regulation whose characteristics conform to resolutions of Council. A member shall not practice public accounting under a firm name that is misleading. Names of one or more past owners may be included in the firm name of a successor organization. A firm may not designate itself as "Member of the American Institute of Certified Public Accountants" unless all of its CPA owners are members of the Institute.

Rule 505 allows CPAs to practice public accounting in any form of organization permitted by a state board of accountancy and authorized by law. Organization forms include sole proprietorship, partnership, limited partnership, limited liability partnership (LLP), professional corporation (PC), limited liability corporation (LLC), and ordinary corporation (Inc.). You may have noticed that the large international accounting firms now place LLP after their firm names. Many small accounting firms include PC in their names.

However, the AICPA Council limits this privilege of organizational form by expressing certain requirements for ownership and control, especially regarding non-CPAs who have ownership interests in an organization that practices public accounting. (See the Council Resolution provisions in the boxed feature. The purpose of the Council Resolution is to conform the operations of an accounting organization as closely as possible to the traditional accounting firm and to ensure control of professional services in the hands of CPAs).

CPAs in public practice cannot use misleading firm names. For example, suppose CPAs Dave and Tim, who are not in partnership, agree to share expenses for office

Council Resolution Concerning Form of Organization and Name

(EXCERPTS)
The characteristics of an accounting organization under Rule 505 are as follows:

- A majority (50 percent +) ownership and voting rights must belong to CPAs.
- Non-CPA owners must be active in the firm, not passive investors.
- A CPA must have ultimate responsibility for the firm's services.
- Non-CPA owners can use titles such as "principal, owner, officer, member, and shareholder" but cannot hold out to be a CPA.

- Non-CPA owners must abide by the AICPA Code of Professional Conduct.
- Non-CPA owners must hold a bachelor's degree, and after the year 2010 must have 150 semester hours of college education.
- Non-CPA owners must complete the same continuing education requirements as CPAs who are members of the AICPA.
- Non-CPA owners are not eligible to be members of the AICPA.

support, advertising, and continuing education. They cannot put up a sign that states "Dave & Tim CPAs" because this name suggests a partnership where there is none.

The last paragraph of Rule 505 permits a mixed accounting organization consisting of CPA and non-CPA owners to designate itself "Members of the AICPA" if all of the CPA owners are actually AICPA members. (People who are not CPAs, including owners of public accounting firms, are not eligible to be members of the AICPA.)

A member who practices public accounting also can participate in the operation of another business organization (e.g., a consulting or tax preparation firm) that offers professional services of the types offered by public accounting firms. If this business is permitted to practice public accounting under state law, the member also is considered to be in the practice of public accounting in it and must observe all rules of conduct.

CPAs who work in alternative practice structures occupy an odd position. They can prepare compiled (unaudited) financial statements, which is considered a form of public accounting practice. In such a case, CPA employees of the alternative practice structure (e.g., "PublicCo") must take final responsibility for the accountants' compilation report and must sign it with their own personal names (not the name of "PublicCo").

Review Checkpoints

B.12 What ethical responsibilities do members of the AICPA have for acts of nonmembers who are under their supervision (e.g., recent college graduates who are not yet CPAs)?

B.13 What rules of conduct apply specifically to members in government and industry?

B.14 What provisions of the AICPA Council Resolution on form of organization place control of accounting services in the hands of CPAs?

B.15 Can you envision a situation that is not addressed by these ethics rules? If such a situation existed, how should the auditor address that situation?

REGULATION, QUALITY CONTROL, AND SELF-REGULATORY DISCIPLINE

LEARNING OBJECTIVE

6. Explain the types of penalties that can be imposed on accountants.

Public accounting firms and responsible professional accountants understand the importance of ethics to the profession and seek to ensure that the organization and all employees are acting in an ethical manner. Unethical behavior can have not only financial implications (e.g., fines, lawsuits) but also reputation implications that may be difficult to change. Quality control practices and disciplinary proceedings provide the mechanisms of *self-regulation*. **Self-regulation** refers to the quality control reviews and disciplinary actions conducted by fellow CPAs—professional peers.

AUDITING INSIGHT How Do You Ensure That You Are Ethical?

Moss Adams LLP (Seattle) and **BKD LLP** (Springfield, Missouri) have instituted programs to help ensure ethical behavior throughout their organizations. Moss Adams has established an independent ethics officer within its firm and BKD has formed an advisory council of independent experts. The mission statement of the council is as follows:

Mission Statement

The council's mission is to help ensure BKD, acting of its own accord, meets its obligations and high duty to the public and its clients.

The council will fulfill that charge by autonomously monitoring and evaluating the firm's independence standards and other internal policies and procedures designed to establish and maintain the quality, objectivity, and competency of BKD's people and services, and by examining any other matters deemed appropriate. The goal of these efforts is to assist BKD in achieving its ongoing commitment to the highest ethical, professional, and business standards.

Source: Rick Telberg, "Two Firms Launch New Ethics Programs," *Journal of Accountancy*, July 2004.

Self-Regulatory Discipline

Individual persons (not accounting firms) are subject to the rules of conduct of state CPA societies and the AICPA only if they choose to join these organizations. The AICPA and most of the state societies have entered into a Joint Ethics Enforcement Program through which the AICPA can refer complaints against CPAs to state societies or state societies can refer them to the AICPA. Both organizations have ethics committees to hear complaints. They can (1) acquit an accused CPA, (2) find the CPA in violation of rules and issue a Letter of Required Corrective Action, or (3) refer serious cases to an AICPA trial board. The Letter of Required Corrective Action ordinarily admonishes the CPA and requires specific continuing education courses to bring the CPA up to date in technical areas.

The trial board panel has the power to (1) acquit the CPA, (2) admonish the CPA, (3) suspend the CPA's membership in the state society and the AICPA for up to two years, or (4) expel the CPA from the state society and the AICPA. The AICPA Bylaws (not the Code of Professional Conduct) provide for automatic expulsion of CPAs judged to have committed a felony, failed to file their tax returns, or aided in the preparation of a false and fraudulent income tax return. The trial board panels are required to publish the names of the CPAs disciplined in their proceedings. Published details about these disciplinary actions are on the AICPA Web site at www.aicpa.org/pubs/cpaltr/index.htm.

The AICPA also has a *settlement offer* procedure designed to impose penalties for rule violations. When the preliminary investigation of a complaint against a CPA shows clear evidence of a violation, the AICPA can (1) proceed with the full investigation and documentation leading to a trial board hearing or (2) offer the CPA the opportunity to plead and accept the penalties proposed by the Professional Ethics Executive Committee. The penalties are typically the same ones that would result from a trial board panel hearing—resignation, continuing professional education (CPE) requirement, and suspension or termination of membership with publication—but the lengthy process of investigation, documentation, and formal hearing is not carried out. When a CPA agrees, the penalty is presented to the Joint Trial Board for endorsement. The settlement offer procedure is a means of closing cases without the time-consuming investigation and trial board hearing that burdens both the CPA and the AICPA Professional Ethics Division.

The expulsion penalty, while severe, does not prevent a CPA from continuing to practice accounting. Membership in the AICPA and state societies, while beneficial, is not required. However, a CPA must have a valid state license in order to practice. State boards of accountancy are the agencies that can suspend or revoke the license to practice.

Public Regulation Discipline

State boards of accountancy are government agencies consisting of CPA and non-CPA officeholders. They issue licenses to practice accounting in their jurisdictions. Most state laws require a license to use the designation CPA or Certified Public Accountant and limit the attest (audit) function to license holders.

State boards have rules of conduct and trial board panels. They can admonish a license holder; more importantly, they can suspend or revoke the license to practice. Suspension and revocation are severe penalties because a person no longer can use the CPA title and cannot sign auditors' reports. When candidates have successfully passed the CPA examination and are ready to become CPAs, some state boards administer an ethics examination or an ethics course intended to familiarize new CPAs with the state rules.

AUDITING INSIGHT The AICPA Joint Trial Board in Action

At a meeting of a hearing panel of the joint trial board in Delta, Michigan, Willie of Delta was suspended from membership in the AICPA and the Michigan Association of CPAs for one year for violating the Rules of Conduct. The violations involved his undertaking an engagement that he or his firm could not reasonably expect to complete with professional competence, permitting his name to be associated with financial statements so as to imply that he was acting as an independent accountant without complying with generally accepted auditing standards and statements on auditing standards, and expressing an opinion that

financial statements conformed with GAAP when they contained material departures therefrom. In addition to the suspension, he was required to complete 64 hours of CPE and to submit a list of engagements which his firm will be performing within the next year, from which two engagements will be selected by the AICPA and the Michigan Association of CPAs for their review.

Willie, who was present at the hearing, did not request a review of the decision which, therefore, became effective.

Note: The names of the auditor and city have been changed.

Source: *The CPA Letter,* www.aicpa.org/pubs/capltr/index.htm.

The SEC and the PCAOB also conduct public disciplinary actions. Their authority comes from their rules of practice, of which Rule 102(e) provides that the SEC can deny, temporarily or permanently, the privilege of practice before the SEC to any person found to have engaged in unethical or improper professional conduct. When conducting a "Rule 102(e) proceeding," the SEC acts in a quasi-judicial role as an administrative agency.

AUDITING INSIGHT Be Audit You Can Be

Reuben E. Price & Co., a firm with a single office in San Francisco, California, was censured when one of its clients issued an annual report that gave the appearance that an audit was conducted. The client (Universal Communication Systems, Inc.) filed its annual report and included a document that it alleged to be an auditors' report issued by Price. While Price provided Universal

with a draft auditors' report, it had not completed the audit. Price was found negligent for not taking action to inform users that an audit had not been conducted when it had knowledge that the document was included along with the financial statements.

Source: "PCAOB Censures California Auditor," *CFO.com,* April 24, 2006.

The SEC penalty bars an accountant from signing any documents filed by an SEC-registered company. The penalty effectively stops the accountant's SEC practice. In a few severe cases, Rule 102(e) proceedings have resulted in settlements barring not only the individual accountant but also her or his accounting firm or certain of its practice offices from accepting new SEC clients for a period of time.

The IRS also can discipline accountants as a matter of public regulation. The IRS can suspend or disbar from practice before the IRS any CPA shown to be incompetent or disreputable or who refuses to comply with tax rules and regulations. The IRS also can levy monetary fines for improper practices.

AUDITING INSIGHT What Do Other Countries Do?

Different countries have different penalties for accountants caught not honoring the public trust. In China, the *death sentences* for Zhou Limin, the former head of the China Construction Bank, and Liu Yibing, an accountant, were upheld by China's

State Supreme Court. The pair was found guilty of stealing over $60 million by offering fake accounts with high interest rates.

Source: "Accountant Gets Death Penalty," *CFO.com,* December 14, 2006.

Review Checkpoints

B.16 What penalties can be imposed by the AICPA and the state societies on CPAs in their "self-regulation" of ethics code violators?

B.17 What penalties can public regulatory agencies impose on CPAs who violate rules of conduct?

Summary

This module begins with philosophers' considerations of moral philosophy, explains the AICPA Rules of Conduct as well as the SEC, PCAOB, and ISB rules related to auditors' independence, and ends with a review of enforcement actions against those CPAs who choose not to follow the rules. Professional ethics for accountants is not simply a matter covered by a few rules in a formal Code of Professional Conduct. Concepts of proper professional conduct permeate all areas of practice. Ethics and accompanying sanctions for ethical failures provide the foundation for public accountants' self-regulatory efforts.

The spirit of the AICPA Code of Professional Conduct is that, while independence is required for audit and attest services, integrity and objectivity are required in connection with all professional services. In this context, integrity and objectivity are the larger concepts and "independence" is a special condition largely defined by the matters of appearance specified in the interpretations of Rule 101. The ethics rules may appear to be restrictive, but they are intended for the benefit of the public as well as for the discipline of CPAs.

Specific rules in the AICPA Rules of Conduct may not necessarily be classified under one of the ethics principles. Decisions based on a rule may involve imperative, utilitarian, or generalization considerations, or elements of all three. The rules have the form of imperatives because that is the nature of a code. However, elements of utilitarianism and generalization seem to be apparent in the underlying rationale for most of the rules. If this perception is accurate, auditors may use these two principles in difficult decision problems for which adherence to a rule could produce an undesirable result. Your knowledge of philosophical principles in ethics—the imperative, utilitarian, and generalization—will help you make decisions about the AICPA, SEC, and ISB rules. This structured approach to thoughtful decisions is important not only when you are employed in public accounting but also when you work in government, industry, and education.

Public accountants must be careful in all areas of practice. As an accountant, you must not lose sight of the nonaccountants' perspective. No matter how complex or technical a decision may be, a simplified view of it always tends to cut away the details of special technical issues to get directly to the heart of the matter. A sense of professionalism coupled with a sensitivity to the effect of decisions on other people is invaluable in the practice of accounting and auditing.

Key Terms

act-utilitarianism (in moral philosophy): Emphasis on an individual act as it is affected by the specific circumstances of a situation, 544

categorical imperative (in moral philosophy): Kant's specification of an unconditional obligation, to act as one thinks others should act regardless of circumstances, 543

commission: A percentage fee charged for professional services in connection with executing a transaction or performing some other business activity, 568

contingent fee: A fee established for the performance of any service in an arrangement in which no fee will be charged unless a specific finding or result is attained or the fee otherwise depends on the result, 566

generalization argument (in moral philosophy): A judicious combination of the imperative and utilitarian principles, to act as one thinks others should act in a similar circumstance, 544

independence: A mental attitude and appearance that the auditor is not influenced by others in judgments and decisions, 549

referral fees: (1) Fees a CPA receives for recommending another CPA's services and (2) fees a CPA pays to obtain a client. Such fees may or may not be based on a percentage of the amount of any transaction, 569

rule-utilitarianism (in moral philosophy): Emphasis on the centrality of rules for ethical behavior while still maintaining the criterion of the greatest universal good, 544

self-regulation: Quality control reviews and disciplinary actions conducted by fellow CPAs—professional peers, 570

Multiple Choice Questions for Practice and Review

B.18 Auditors are interested in having independence in appearance because
 a. They want to impress the public with their independence in fact.
 b. They want the public at large to have confidence in the profession.
 c. They need to comply with the standards of field work of GAAS.
 d. Audits should be planned and properly supervised.

B.19 Assuring that the auditor is independent in appearance is the responsibility of
 a. The public accounting firm.
 b. Senior management.
 c. The audit committee.
 d. The PCAOB.

B.20 If a public accounting firm says it always follows the rule that requires adherence to FASB pronouncements in order to give a standard unqualified auditors' report, it is following a philosophy characterized by
 a. The imperative principle in ethics.
 b. The utilitarian principle in ethics.
 c. The generalization principle in ethics.
 d. Reliance on members' collective conscience.

B.21 Which of the following agencies issues independence rules for the auditors of public companies?
 a. Financial Accounting Standards Board (FASB).
 b. Government Accountability Office (GAO).
 c. Public Company Accounting Oversight Board (PCAOB)
 d. AICPA Accounting and Review Services Committee (ARSC).

B.22 Audit independence in fact is most clearly lost when
 a. A public accounting firm audits competitor companies in the same industry (e.g., Coke and Pepsi).
 b. An auditor agrees to the argument of the client's financial vice president that deferring losses on debt refinancing is in accordance with generally accepted accounting principles.
 c. An audit team fails to discover the client's misleading omission of disclosure about permanent impairment of asset values.
 d. A public accounting firm issues a standard unqualified report, but the reviewing partner fails to notice that the assistant's observation of inventory was woefully incomplete.

B.23 The audit committee's responsibility for auditor independence concerns
 a. Ensuring that partners of the public accounting firm are not stockholders in the company.
 b. Ensuring that nonaudit services provided by the auditor do not impair independence.
 c. Reporting on auditor independence to the PCAOB.
 d. Ensuring that all nonaudit services are provided by auditors who do not provide the financial statement audit.

B.24 AICPA members who work in industry and government must always uphold which two of the following AICPA rules of conduct?

 a. Rule 101—Independence.

 b. Rule 102—Integrity and Objectivity.

 c. Rule 301—Confidential Client Information.

 d. Rule 501—Acts Discreditable.

B.25 A public accounting firm's independence is not impaired when members of the audit engagement team perform for an audit client

 a. Preparation of special purchase orders for active plutonium in secure national defense installations.

 b. Operational internal audit assignments under the directions of the client's director of internal auditing.

 c. Outsourced internal audit work on the client's financial accounting control monitoring.

 d. Preparation of actuarial assumptions used by the client's actuaries for life insurance actuarial liability determination.

B.26 When the public accounting firm audits FUND-A in a mutual fund complex that has sister funds FUND-B and FUND-C, independence for the audit of FUND-A is not impaired when

 a. Manager-level professionals located in the office where the engagement audit partner is located but who are not on the engagement team own shares in FUND-B, which is not an audit client.

 b. The wife of the FUND-A audit engagement partner owns shares in FUND-C (an audit client of another of the firm's offices) and these shares are held through the wife's employee benefit plan funded by her employer, the AllSteelFence Company.

 c. Both (a) and (b).

 d. Neither (a) nor (b).

B.27 Which of the following is considered a close relative (but not an immediate family member) as defined by the AICPA?

 a. Spouse.

 b. Spousal equivalent.

 c. Parent.

 d. Uncle.

B.28 Which of the following is true if an auditor performs nonaudit services for a government entity?

 a. The scope of the audit must be reduced so that the auditor does not audit the area for which the nonaudit work was performed.

 b. Nonaudit work in areas directly related to the production of accounting information is prohibited.

 c. The senior members of the government entity must document their review of the nonaudit service and indicate why it is appropriate for the auditors to perform this service.

 d. The scope of the audit cannot be reduced because the nonaudit work was performed by the public accounting firm.

B.29 Which of the following is true?

 a. Members of an audit engagement team cannot speak with audit client officers about employment possibilities with the client while the audit work is in progress.

 b. Audit team members who leave the public accounting firm for employment with audit clients can provide audit efficiencies (next year) because they are very familiar with the firm's audit programs.

 c. Audit team partners who leave the public accounting firm for employment with audit clients can retain variable annuity retirement accounts established in the person's former firm retirement plan.

 d. The public accounting firm must discuss with the audit client's board or its audit committee the independence implications of the client's having hired the audit engagement team manager as its financial vice president.

B.30 Which of the following "bodies designated by Council" have been authorized to promulgate general standards enforceable under Rule 201 of the AICPA Code of Professional Conduct?

a. AICPA Division of Professional Ethics.

b. Financial Accounting Standards Board.

c. Government Accounting Standards Board.

d. Accounting and Review Services Committee.

B.31 Which of the following "bodies designated by Council" have been authorized to promulgate accounting principles enforceable under Rule 203 of the AICPA Code of Professional Conduct?

a. Auditing Standards Board.

b. Federal Accounting Standards Advisory Board.

c. Consulting Services Executive Committee.

d. Accounting and Review Services Committee.

B.32 Phil Greb has a thriving practice in which he assists attorneys in preparing litigation dealing with accounting and auditing matters. Phil is "practicing public accounting" if he

a. Uses his CPA designation on his letterhead and business card.

b. Is in partnership with another CPA.

c. Practices in a professional corporation with other CPAs.

d. Never lets his clients know that he is a CPA.

B.33 The AICPA removed its general prohibition of CPAs taking commissions and contingent fees because

a. CPAs prefer more price competition to less.

b. Commissions and contingent fees enhance audit independence.

c. Nothing is inherently wrong about the form of fees charged to nonaudit clients.

d. Objectivity is not always necessary in accounting and auditing services.

B.34 CPA Rambo is the auditor of Ajax Corporation. Her audit independence will not be considered impaired if she

a. Owns $1,000 worth of Ajax stock.

b. Has a husband who owns $1,000 worth of Ajax stock.

c. Has a sister who is the financial vice president of Ajax.

d. Owns $1,000 worth of the stock of Pericles Corporation, which is controlled by Ajax as a result of Ajax's ownership of 40 percent of Pericles' stock, and Pericles contributes 3 percent of the total assets and income in Ajax's financial statements.

B.35 When a client's financial statements contain a material departure from an FASB *Statement on Accounting Standards* and the public accounting firm believes the departure is necessary to ensure that the statements are not misleading,

a. The public accounting firm must qualify the auditors' report for a departure from GAAP.

b. The public accounting firm can explain why the departure is necessary and then give an unqualified opinion paragraph in the auditors' report.

c. The public accounting firm must give an adverse auditors' report.

d. The public accounting firm can give the standard unqualified auditors' report with an unqualified opinion paragraph.

B.36 Which of the following would not be considered confidential information obtained in the course of an engagement for which the client's consent would be needed for disclosure?

a. Information about whether a consulting client has paid the CPA's fees on time.

b. The actuarial assumptions used by a tax client in calculating pension expense.

c. Management's strategic plan for next year's labor negotiations.

d. Information about material contingent liabilities relevant for audited financial statements.

B.37 Which of the following would probably not be considered an "act discreditable to the profession"?

a. Numerous moving traffic violations.

b. Failing to file the CPA's own tax return.

c. Filing a fraudulent tax return for a client in a severe financial difficulty.

d. Refusing to hire Asian Americans in an accounting practice.

B.38 According to the AICPA Code of Conduct, which of the following acts is generally forbidden to CPAs in public practice?

 a. Purchasing bookkeeping software from a hi-tech development company and reselling it to tax clients.

 b. Being the author of a "TaxAid" newsletter promoted and sold by a publishing company.

 c. Having a commission arrangement with an accounting software developer to receive 4 percent of the price of programs recommended and sold to audit clients.

 d. Engaging a marketing firm to obtain new financial planning clients for a fixed fee of $1,000 for each successful contact.

B.39 A CPA's legal license to practice public accounting can be revoked by the

 a. American Institute of Certified Public Accountants.

 b. State Society of CPAs.

 c. Auditing Standard Board.

 d. State board of accountancy.

B.40 According to Rule 501, which of the following is not a "discreditable act"?

 a. Withholding a client's sales records.

 b. Failing to file or remit tax payments.

 c. Failing to follow requirements of the PCAOB during the audit of an SEC client.

 d. Advertising that indicated the firm can reduce IRS penalties.

B.41 An auditor's independence would not be considered impaired if he had

 a. Owned common stock of the audit client but sold it before the company became a client.

 b. Sold short the common stock of an audit client while working on the audit engagement.

 c. Served as the company's treasurer for six months during the year covered by the audit but resigned before the company became a client.

 d. Performed the bookkeeping and financial statement preparation for the company, which had no accounting personnel and for which the president had no understanding of accounting principles.

B.42 When a CPA knows that a tax client has skimmed cash receipts and not reported the income in the federal income tax return but signs the return as a CPA who prepared the return, the CPA has violated which of the following AICPA Rules of Conduct?

 a. Rule 301—Confidential Client Information.

 b. Rule 102—Integrity and Objectivity.

 c. Rule 101—Independence.

 d. Rule 203—Accounting Principles.

B.43 An auditor recommends a local computer company to a client that is trying to upgrade its computerized sales records. The client purchases $25,000 worth of equipment and sends a check to the auditor for 5 percent of the total sales. This is an example of a

 a. Commission.

 b. Contingent fee.

 c. Referral fee.

 d. Nonaudit fee.

B.44 Which of the following ownership situations is permissible for a public accounting firm?

 a. A partner of the firm is responsible for fraud issues related to audits and audit clients. He owns 20 percent of the firm and is not a CPA.

 b. Because the firm now specializes in fraud auditing and fraud investigation, the managing partner of the firm has a background in law enforcement and fraud investigation. He is not a CPA.

 c. A partner of the firm is responsible for fraud issues related to audits and audit clients. He owns 50 shares of stock in an audit client of the firm.

 d. A partner of the firm is responsible for fraud issues related to audits and audit clients. He has 20 years of experience in law enforcement and fraud investigation. He began his career as a police officer after receiving a law enforcement degree from a local community college.

Exercises, Problems, and Simulations

B.45 **SEC Independence Rules.** Is independence impaired for the individual or the public accounting firm on these SEC filing audits according to SEC independence rules?

a. CPA Yolanda is the Best & Co engagement partner on the Casa Construction Company (CCC) audit supervised from the Santa Fe office of the firm. Yolanda owns 100 shares of CCC.

b. CPA Yolanda sold the 100 CCC shares to CPA Javier, who is another partner in the Santa Fe office but who is not involved in the CCC audit.

c. CPA Javier transferred ownership of the 100 CCC shares to his wife.

d. CPA Javier's wife gave the shares to their 12-year-old son.

e. CPA Javier's son sold the shares to Javier's father.

f. CPA Javier's father was happy to combine the 100 CCC shares with shares he already owned because now he owns 25 percent of CCC and can control many decisions of the board of directors.

g. CPA Javier's father declared personal bankruptcy and sold his CCC stock. CCC then hired him to fill the newly created position of director of financial reporting.

B.46 **SEC Independence and Nonaudit Services.** Is independence impaired on these SEC filing audits according to SEC independence rules regarding nonaudit services?

a. CPA Tidrick is a staff assistant II auditor on the Section Co. audit. Upon the audit completion date in January, Tidrick drafted the balance sheet, income statement, comprehensive income statement, statement of cash flows, and notes for review by the engagement partner before the auditors' report was finalized.

b. CPA Carnes is a manager in the firm's consulting division. He spent 100 hours with the Section Co. audit client on an accounts payable information system study, which involved selecting the preferred software and supervising Section Co.'s employees in startup operations.

c. CPA Webber, working in the public accounting firm's asset valuation consulting division located in Chicago, prepared for Section Co. an appraisal of the fair value of assets purchased in Section's merger with the Group Co. These valuations were then audited by the engagement team located in Dallas in connection with the purchase accounting for the merger.

d. CPA Young is the engagement partner on the Section Co. audit; he is also an actuarial consultant in the firm's consulting division. He personally audited the client's post-employment benefits calculations, which had been prepared by Section's actuaries.

e. Section Co. appointed its own employee, certified internal auditor (CIA) Mumta, to be director of internal auditing with complete responsibility for planning, management, and review of all internal audit work. Mumta engaged Section Co.'s independent public accounting firm to supply staff to perform all operational audit studies of efficiency and effectiveness in Section's domestic subsidiary companies. The public accounting firm used half of these same staff professionals to work on the audit of Section's financial statement audit.

f. CPA Churyk is the partner in charge of the Dallas office where the Section Co. audit is managed (by engagement partner Jack). She has no direct role on the audit engagement team. However, Section relies on Churyk to prepare the confidential papers for the board of directors' stock options and she signs the release forms for option grants.

g. CPA Mantzke works in the executive search department of the public accounting firm's consulting division, located in New York City. In connection with Section Co.'s hiring of its new vice president for marketing, Mantzke checked the references on the lead candidate Smith and performed a thorough background investigation that led to the firm's advice that Smith was the best person for the appointment. Section Co. board members investigated other candidates and hired Smith in Dallas without further interaction with Mantzke.

h. Section Co. completed a private placement of long-term bonds during the year under audit. The bonds were distributed to 40 qualified-exempt investors through the brokerage firm of Amalgamated Exchange, Inc., which is 50 percent owned by the public accounting firm and 50 percent owned by Merrill Lynch Investment Corporation.

i. The public accounting firm's tax consulting division prepared Section Co.'s export-import tax reports, which involved numerous interpretations of complicated export-import tax law provisions.

B.47 **Audit Simulation: Independence, Integrity, and Objectivity Cases.** Read the following cases.

Required:

For each case, state whether the action or situation shows a violation of the AICPA Code of Professional Conduct, explain why, and cite the relevant rule or interpretation.

a. CPA R. Stout performs the audit of the local symphony society. Because of her good work, she was elected an honorary member of the board of directors.

b. CPA N. Wolfe practices management consulting in the area of computerized information systems under the firm name of Wolfe & Associates. The "associates" are not CPAs and the firm is not an accounting firm. However, Wolfe shows "CPA" on business cards and uses these credentials when dealing with clients.

c. CPA Archie Goodwin performs significant day-to-day bookkeeping services for Harper Corporation and supervises the work of the one part-time bookkeeper employed by Marvin Harper. This year, Marvin wants to engage CPA Goodwin to perform an audit.

d. CPA H. Poirot bought a home in 1989 and financed it with a mortgage loan from Farraway Savings and Loan. Farraway was merged into Nearby S&L and Poirot became the manager in charge of the Nearby audit.

e. Poirot inherited a large sum of money from old Mr. Giraud in 2000. Poirot sold his house, paid off the loan to Nearby S&L, and purchased a much larger estate, a mansion in fact. Nearby S&L provided the financing.

f. Poirot and Ms. Lemon (a local real estate broker) formed a partnership to develop apartment buildings. Ms. Lemon is a 20 percent owner and managing partner. Poirot and three partners in the accounting firm are limited partners. They own the remaining 80 percent of the partnership but have no voice in everyday management. Ms. Lemon obtained permanent real estate financing from Nearby S&L.

g. Ms. Lemon won the lottery and purchased part of the limited partners' interests. She now owns 90 percent of the partnership and remains general partner while the CPAs remain limited partners with 10 percent interest.

h. CPA Shultz purchased a variable annuity insurance contract that offered her the option to choose the companies in which this contract will invest. At Schultz's direction, the insurance company purchased common stock in one of her audit clients.

B.48 **Audit Simulation: Independence, Integrity, and Objectivity Cases.** Read the following cases.

Required:

For each separate case, state whether the action or situation shows a violation of the AICPA Code of Professional Conduct, explain why, and cite the relevant rule or interpretation.

a. Your client, Contrary Corporation, is very upset over the fact that your audit last year failed to detect an $800,000 inventory overstatement caused by employee theft and falsification of the records. The board discussed the matter and authorized its attorneys to explore the possibility of a lawsuit for damages.

b. Contrary Corporation filed a lawsuit alleging negligent audit work, seeking $1 million in damages.

c. In response to the lawsuit by Contrary, you decided to bring litigation against certain officers of the company alleging management fraud and deceit. You are asking for a damage judgment of $500,000.

d. The Allright Insurance Company paid Contrary Corporation $700,000 under a fidelity bond covering an inventory theft by employees. Allright is suing your public accounting firm for damages on the grounds of negligent performance of the audit, claiming a proper audit would have uncovered the theft sooner and the amount would have been considerably less.

e. Your audit client, Science Tech, Inc., installed a cost accounting system devised by the consulting services department of your firm. The system failed to account properly for certain product costs (according to management) and the system had to be discontinued. Science Tech management was very dissatisfied and filed a lawsuit demanding return of the $10,000 consulting fee. The audit fee is normally about $50,000 and $10,000 is not an especially large amount for your firm. However, you believe that Science Tech

management operated the system improperly. While you are willing to do further consulting work at a reduced rate to make the system operate, you are unwilling to return the entire $10,000 fee.

f. A group of dissident shareholders filed a class action lawsuit against both you and your client, Amalgamated, Inc., for $30 million. They allege there was a conspiracy to present misleading financial statements in connection with a recent merger.

g. CPA Lisa, a shareholder in the firm of Eden, Benjamin, and Block, P.C. (a professional accounting corporation), owns 25 percent of the common stock of Dove Corporation (not a client of Eden, Benjamin, and Block). This year, Dove purchased a 32 percent interest in Tale Company and is accounting for the investment using the equity method of accounting. The investment amounts to 11 percent of Dove's consolidated net assets. Tale Company has been an audit client of Eden, Benjamin, and Block for 12 years.

h. CPAs Mark and Ben are the father-and-son partners of Queens, LLP. They have a 12 percent joint private investment in ownership of the voting common stock of Hydra Corporation, which is not an audit client of Queens, LLP. However, their audit client, Howard Company, owns 46 percent of Hydra and this investment accounts for 20 percent of Howard's assets (using the equity method of accounting).

i. Francie & Brian, CPAs, regularly perform the audit of the First National Bank and the firm is preparing for the audit of the financial statements for the year ended December 31, 2008.

 (1) Two directors of the First National Bank became partners in Francie and Brian, CPAs, on July 1, 2008, resigning their directorship on that date. They will not participate in the audit.

 (2) During 2008, the former controller of the First National Bank, now a partner of Francie and Brian, was frequently called on for assistance regarding loan approvals and the bank's minimum checking account policy. In addition, he conducted a computer feasibility study for First National.

j. The Cather Corporation is indebted to a CPA for unpaid fees and has offered to give the CPA unsecured interest-bearing notes. Alternatively, Cather Corporation offered to give two shares of its common stock, after which 10,002 shares would be outstanding.

k. Debra is not yet a CPA but is doing quite well in her first employment with a large public accounting firm. She has been on the job two years and has become an "experienced assistant". If she passes the CPA exam this year, she will be promoted to senior accountant. This month, during the audit of Row Lumber Company, Debra told the controller that she is remodeling an old house. The controller likes Debra and had a load of needed materials delivered to the house, billing Debra at a 70 percent discount—a savings over the normal cash discount of about $300. Debra paid the bill and was happy to have the materials that she otherwise could not afford on her meager salary.

l. Groaner Corporation is in financial difficulty. You are about to sign the report on the current audit when your firm's office manager informs you the audit fee for last year has not yet been paid.

m. CPA Lily Rowan prepared Goodwin's tax return this year. Last year, Goodwin prepared the return and paid too much income tax because the tax return erroneously contained "income" in the amount of $300,000 from an inheritance received when dear Aunt Martha died. This year, Goodwin sold the inherited property for $500,000. Goodwin argued with Rowan, who agreed to omit the sale of the property and the $200,000 gain this year on the grounds that Goodwin had already overpaid tax last year and this omission would make things even.

n. CPA D. Watson is employed by Baker Street Company as its chief accountant. M. Lestrade, also a CPA and the financial vice president of Baker, owns a trucking company that provides shipping services to Baker in a four-state area. The trucking company needs to buy 14 new trailers and Lestrade authorized a payment to finance the purchase in the amount of $750,000. The related document cited repayment in terms of reduced trucking charges for the next seven years. M. Lestrade created the journal entry for this arrangement, charging the $750,000 to prepaid expenses. Watson and Lestrade signed the representation letter to Baker's external auditors and stated that Baker had no related-party transactions that were not disclosed to the auditors.

B.49 **Integrity and Objectivity.** In 1997, a disagreement arose between Livent Inc. and its auditor Deloitte and Touche. Livent, which operated several theaters for live stage production, had sold the naming rights to one of its theaters to AT&T for $12.5 million. The agreement was oral and one of the theaters was under construction. The auditors for Deloitte believed that only a portion of the deal should be included in revenue, but Livent wanted to book the entire $12.5 million. Livent retained Ernst & Young (E&Y) to provide an opinion on the transaction. E&Y's report indicated that all $12.5 million could be recorded as revenue. Deloitte hired Price Waterhouse (currently PricewaterhouseCoopers) to review the transaction. Price Waterhouse agreed with E&Y and Livent and Deloitte allowed Livent to book the $12.5 million. In 1998, Livent issued a series of press releases indicating the discovery of significant account irregularities and, later in 1998, declared bankruptcy.

Required:

Comment on the inclusion of Ernst & Young and Price Waterhouse concerning the $12.5 million transaction. What would your position be on the need for other opinions? What would your position be for the disposition of the transaction?

B.50 **Audit Simulation: General and Technical Rule Cases.** Read the following cases. For each case, state whether the action or situation shows a violation of the AICPA Code of Professional Conduct, explain why, and cite the relevant rule or interpretation.

 a. CPA J. Cheese became the new auditor for Python Insurance Company. Cheese knew a great deal about insurance accounting, but he had never conducted an audit of an insurance company. Consequently, he hired CPA T. Gilliam, who had six years of experience with the State Department of Insurance Audit. Gilliam managed the audit and Cheese was the partner in charge.

 b. CPA M. Palin practices public accounting and is a director of Comedy Company. Palin's firm performs consulting and tax services for Comedy. Palin prepared unaudited financial statements on Comedy's letterhead and submitted them to First National Bank in support of a loan application. Palin's accounting firm received a fee for this service.

 c. CPA E. Idle audited the financial statements of Monty Corporation and gave an unqualified report. Monty is not a public company, so the financial statements did not contain the SEC-required reconciliation of deferred income taxes.

 d. CPA G. Chapman audited the financial statement of BTV. Ltd. These financial statements contain capitalized leases that do not meet FASB criteria for capitalization. They resemble more closely the criteria for operating leases. The effect is material, adding $4 million to assets and $3.5 million to liabilities. However, BTV has a long experience with acquiring such property as its own assets after the "lease" terms end. Chapman and BTV management believe the financial statements should reflect the operating policy of the management instead of the technical requirements of the FASB. Consequently, the auditors' report explains the accounting and gives an unqualified opinion.

B.51 **Audit Simulation: Responsibilities to Clients' Cases.** Read the following cases. For each case, state whether the action or situation shows a violation or potential for violation of the AICPA Code of Professional Conduct, explain why, and cite the relevant rule or interpretation.

 a. CPA Sally Colt has discovered a way to eliminate most of the boring work of processing routine accounts receivable confirmations by contracting with the Cohen Mail Service. After the auditor has prepared the confirmations, Cohen will stuff them in envelopes, mail them, receive the return replies, open the replies, and return them to Sally.

 b. Cadentoe Corporation, without consulting Jora Cramer, its CPA, has changed its accounting so that it is not in conformity with generally accepted accounting principles. During the regular audit engagement, Cramer discovers that the statements based on the accounts are so grossly misleading that they might be considered fraudulent. CPA Cramer resigns the engagement after a heated argument. Cramer knows that the statements will be given to Saul Panzer, her friend at the Last National Bank, and that Panzer is not a very astute reader of complicated financial statements. Two days later, Panzer calls Cramer and asks some general questions about Cadentoe's statements and remarks favorably on the very thing that is misrepresented. Cramer corrects the erroneous analysis and Panzer is very much surprised.

c. A CPA who had reached retirement age arranged for the sale of his practice to another certified public accountant. Their agreement called for the review of all working papers and business correspondence by the accountant purchasing the practice.

d. Martha Jacoby, CPA, withdrew from the audit of Harvard Company after discovering irregularities in Harvard's income tax returns. One week later, Jacoby received a phone call from Jake Henry, CPA, who explained that he had just been retained by Harvard Company to replace her. Henry asked Jacoby why she withdrew from the Harvard engagement and she told him.

e. CPA Wallace has two audit clients: Willingham Corporation owned by J. Willingham and Ward Corporation owned by B. Ward. Willingham Corp. sells a large proportion of its products to Ward Corp., which amounts to 60 percent of Ward Corp.'s purchases in most years. J. Willingham and B. Ward are also Wallace's tax clients as individuals. This year, while preparing B. Ward's tax return, Wallace discovered information that suggested Ward Corporation is in a failing financial position. In consideration of the fact that the companies and individuals are mutual clients, Wallace discussed Ward Corporation's financial difficulties with J. Willingham.

f. Amos Fiddle, CPA, prepared an uncontested claim for a tax refund on Faddle Corporation's amended tax return. The fee for the service was 30 percent of the amount the IRS rules to be a proper refund. The claim was for $300,000.

g. After Faddle had won a $200,000 refund and Fiddle collected the $60,000 fee, Jeremy Faddle, the president, invited Amos Fiddle to be the auditor for Faddle Corporation.

h. Burgess Company engaged CPA Kim Philby to audit Maclean Corporation in connection with a possible initial public offering (IPO) of stock registered with the SEC. Burgess Company established a holding company named Cairncross Inc. and asked Philby to issue an engagement letter addressed to Cairncross stating that Cairncross would receive the auditors' report. Cairncross has no assets and Philby agreed to charge a fee for the audit of Maclean only if the IPO is successful.

B.52 **Audit Simulation: Other Responsibilities and Practices Cases.** Read the following cases. For each case, state whether the action or situation shows a violation or potential for violation of the AICPA Code of Professional Conduct, explain why, and cite the relevant rule or interpretation.

a. CPA R. Stout completed a review of the unaudited financial statements of Wolfe Gifts. Arvida Wolfe was very displeased with the report. An argument ensued and she told Stout never to darken her door again. Two days later, she telephoned Stout and demanded that he return (1) Wolfe's cash disbursement journal, (2) Stout's documentation schedule of adjusting journal entries, (3) Stout's inventory analysis documentation, and (4) all other documentation prepared by Stout. Wolfe had not yet paid her bill, so Stout replied that state law gave him a lien on all of the records and he would return them as soon as she paid his fee.

b. CPA May teaches a CPA review course at the university. He needs problem and question material for students' practice, but the CPA examination questions and answers are no longer published. He pays $5 to students who take the exam for each question they can "remember" after taking the examination.

c. CPA Blitz has been invited to conduct a course in effective tax planning for the City Chamber of Commerce. The Chamber's president said a brochure would be mailed to members giving the name of Blitz's firm, his educational background and degrees held, professional society affiliations, and testimonials from participants in the course held last year comparing his excellent performance with other CPAs who have offered competing courses in the city.

d. CPA Philby is a member of the state bar. Her practice is a combination of law and accounting and she is heavily involved in estate planning engagements. Her letterhead has the following: Member, State Bar of Illinois, and Member, AICPA.

e. The public accounting firm of Burgess & Maclean has made a deal with Brit & Company, a firm of management consulting specialists, for mutual business advantage. B&M agreed to recommend Brit to clients who need management consulting services. Brit agreed to recommend B&M to clients who need improvements in their accounting systems. During the year, both firms would keep records of fees obtained by these mutual referrals. At the end of the year, Brit and B&M would settle the net differences based on a referral rate of 5 percent of fees.

f. Jack Robinson and Archie Robertson (both CPAs) are not partners, but they have the same office, the same employees, and a joint bank account and work together on audits. A letterhead they use shows both their names and the description "Members, AICPA."

g. CPA Dewey retired from the two-person firm of Dewey & Cheatham. One year later, D&C merged practices with Howe & Company to form a regional firm under the name of Dewey, Cheatham, & Howe Company.

B.53 **AICPA Independence and Other Services.** AICPA Interpretation 101-3 (Performance of Other Services: www.aicpa.org) cites several "other services" that do and do not impair audit independence.

Required:

Go to the AICPA Web site and find whether the following items impair independence (Yes) or do not impair independence (No) when performed for audit clients.

a. Post the client-approved entries to a client's trial balance.

b. Authorize the client's customer credit applications.

c. Use CPA's information-processing facilities to prepare the client's payroll and generate checks for the client treasurer's signature.

d. Sign the client's quarterly federal payroll tax return.

e. Advise client management about the application or financial effect of provisions in a employee benefit plan contract.

f. Have emergency signature authority to cosign cash disbursement checks in connection with a client's hospital benefit plan.

g. As an investment advisory service, provide analyses of a client's investments in comparison to benchmarks produced by unrelated third parties.

h. Take temporary custody of a client's investment assets each time a purchase is made as a device to reduce cash float expense.

B.54 **General Ethics.** Is there any moral difference between a disapproved action in which you are caught and the same action that never becomes known to anyone else? Do many persons in business and professional society make a distinction between these two circumstances? If you respond that you do (or do not) perceive a difference while persons in business and professional society do not (or do), how do you explain the differences in attitudes?

B.55 **Competition and Audit Proposals.** Accounting firms are often asked to present "proposals" to companies' boards of directors. These proposals are comprehensive booklets, accompanied by oral presentations, telling about the firm's personnel, technology, special qualifications, and expertise in the hope of convincing the board to award the work to the firm.

Dena has a new job as staff assistant to Michael, chairman of the board of Granof Grain Company. The company has a policy of engaging new auditors every seven years. The board will hear oral proposals from 12 accounting firms. This is the second day of the three-day meeting. Dena's job is to help evaluate the proposals. Yesterday, the proposal by Eden, Benjamin, and Block was clearly the best.

Then Dena sees Michael's staff chief slip a copy of Eden, Benjamin, and Block's written proposal into an envelope. He tells Dena to take it to a friend who works for Hunt and Hunt, a public accounting firm scheduled to make its presentation tomorrow. He says: "I told him we'd let him glance at the best proposal." Michael is absent from the meeting and will not return for two hours.

Required:

What should Dena do? What should CPA Hunt do if he receives the Eden, Benjamin, and Block proposal, assuming he has time to modify the Hunt and Hunt proposal before tomorrow's presentation?

B.56 **Engagement Timekeeping Records.** A time budget is always prepared for audit engagements. Numbers of hours are estimated for various segments of the work, for example, internal control evaluation, cash, inventory, and report review. Audit supervisors expect the work segments to be completed "within budget" and staff accountants' performance is evaluated in part on the ability to perform audit work efficiently within budget.

Sara is an audit manager who has worked hard to get promoted. She hopes to become a partner in two or three years. Finishing audits on time is heavily weighted on her performance

evaluation. She assigned the cash audit work to Ed, who has worked for the firm for 10 months. Ed hopes to get a promotion and salary raise this year. Twenty hours were budgeted for the cash work. Ed is efficient, but it took 30 hours to finish because the company had added seven new bank accounts. Ed was worried about his performance evaluation, so he recorded 20 hours for the cash work and put the other 10 hours under the internal control evaluation budget.

Required:

What do you think about Ed's resolution of his problem? Was his action a form of lying? What would you think of his action if the internal control evaluation work was presently under budget because it was not yet complete and another assistant was assigned to finish that work segment later?

B.57 **Audit Overtime.** The performance evaluation of all accountants is based in part on their ability to do audit work efficiently and within the time budget planned for the engagement. New staff accountants, in particular, usually have some early difficulty learning speedy work habits, which demand that no time be wasted.

Elizabeth started work for Julie and Jacob CPAs in September. After attending the staff training school, she was assigned to the Rising Sun Company audit. Her first work assignment was to complete the extensive recalculation of the inventory compilation, using the audit test counts and audited unit prices for several hundred inventory items. Her time budget for the work was six hours. She started at 4 p.m. and was not finished when everyone left the office at 6 p.m. Not wanting to stay downtown alone, she took all necessary documentation working papers home. She resumed work at 8 p.m. and finished at 3 a.m. The next day, she returned to the CPA offices, put the completed documentation in the file, and recorded six hours in the time budget/actual schedule. Her supervisor was pleased, especially about her diligence in taking the work home.

Required:

a. What do you think about Elizabeth's diligence and her understatement of the time she took to finish the work?

b. What would you think of the case if she had received help at home from her husband Paul?

c. What would you think of the case if she had been unable to finish and had left the work at home for her husband to finish while he took off a day from his job interviews?

B.58 **Conflict of Client's Interests.** Jon Williams, CPA, is in the middle of the real-life soap opera, "Taxing Days of Our Lives."

The Cast of Characters:

Oneway Corporation is Jon's audit and tax client. The three directors are the officers and the only three stockholders, each owning exactly one-third of the shares.

President Jack founded the company and is now nearing retirement. As an individual, he is also Jon's tax client.

Vice President Jill manages the day-to-day operations. She has been instrumental in increasing the business and its profits. Jill's individual tax work is done by CPA Phil.

Treasurer Bill has been a long-term, loyal employee and has been responsible for many innovative financial transactions and reports of great benefit to the business. He is Jon's close personal friend and an individual tax client.

The Conflict:

President Jack discussed with CPA Jon the tax consequences to him as an individual of selling his one-third interest in Oneway Corporation to Vice President Jill. Later, meeting with Bill to discuss his individual tax problems, Jon learns that Bill fears that Jack and Jill will make a deal, put him in a minority position, and force him out of the company. Bill says, "Jon, we have been friends a long time. Please keep me informed about Jack's plans, even rumors. My interest in Oneway Corporation represents my life savings and my resources for the kid's college. Remember, you're little Otto's godfather."

Thinking back, Jon realized that Vice President Jill has always been rather hostile. Chances are that Phil would get the Oneway engagement if Jill acquires Jack's shares and controls the corporation. Nevertheless, Bill will probably suffer a great deal if he cannot learn about Jack's plans, and Jon's unwillingness to keep him informed will probably ruin their close friendship.

Later, on a Dark and Stormy Night:

Jon ponders the problem. "Oneway Corporation is my client, but a corporation is a fiction. Only a form. The stockholders personify the real entity, so they are collectively my clients, and I can transmit information among them as though they were one person. Right? On the other hand, Jack and Bill engage me for individual tax work, and information about one's personal affairs is really no business of the other. What to do? What to do?"

Required:

Give Jon advice about alternative actions, considering the constraints of the AICPA Code of Conduct.

B.59 **Managerial Involvement and Audit Independence.** CPA P. Marlowe is the partner in charge of the audit practice in the midsize public accounting firm of Marlowe & Chandler, PC. CPA R. Chandler is the overall managing partner of the firm. They founded the firm 20 years ago. CPA Marlowe is also a member of the board of directors of Hobart Arms Hotel Corporation, one of the firm's tax clients. Hobart wanted to acquire the Bristol Apartment Company, and the Los Angeles National Bank insisted on an independent audit of Hobart's financial statements in connection with its loan application for $3 million. Marlowe & Chandler knew they were not independent for this audit because of Marlowe's position on the board.

To solve this problem, Hobart engaged Wilde & Associates, LLP to perform the audit. The Wilde firm was not very large, so the following arrangement was made: CPA Wilde was the partner in charge of the audit, CPA Linda (a Wilde professional) was the manager of the audit, and CPAs Lacosta and Martinez were the staff assistants. Lacosta and Martinez were employed by Marlowe & Chandler and they were loaned to Wilde & Associates for the purpose of staffing the Hobart audit. They performed almost all of the detailed field work.

Wilde & Associates, LLP completed the audit and delivered an unqualified auditors' report. Fees were paid to Wilde & Associates for the work of its professionals. Fees were billed separately by Marlowe & Chandler, PC for the work performed by Lacosta and Martinez, and Hobart paid these directly to Marlowe & Chandler.

Required:

Analyze this situation. Do you see any lack of independence in connection with the audit? Discuss.

B.60 **Disciplinary Action.** Go to the Web site for the CPA Society and for the Department of Professional Regulation in the state where you live. Search the Web sites for disciplinary action taken against CPAs for violation of the code of ethics. If you cannot find a list of disciplinary action taken in your state, go to the Web site for the Illinois CPA Society (www.icpas.org). Move your mouse to "Advocacy." A drop-down menu should appear. Click on "Regulation of the Profession" and then "Resolution of Ethics Cases."

Required:

Review the ethics cases and list the violations and penalties indicated in each case.

B.61 **Audit Simulation: Ethics Case.**[18] Sally is a sole proprietor CPA who runs a successful practice with five employees. Several years ago, Sally purchased an office building; she relocated her practice in about 20 percent of the space and rented out the remaining portion. Things went well for the first few months, but then two of Sally's tenants ran into financial difficulties and had to vacate the building. Sally was unable to quickly find new tenants for the space.

Sally struggled to keep current with the mortgage payments for a few months, but the loss of tenant income combined with the expense of operating a building became a large burden. Cash flow became very tight, and Sally stopped remitting the employee payroll taxes withheld.

The IRS filed a lien for nonpayment of employee payroll taxes, which was published in a local newspaper. A concerned citizen filed an ethics complaint.

[18] The following information was obtained from the *Pennsylvania CPA Journal* and is adopted from a case brought before the Pennsylvania Ethics Committee (Robert J. DePasquale and Colleen Williams, "The CPA's Taxes and the Code of Ethics," *Pennsylvania CPA Journal,* Winter 2004).

Investigation found that although Sally had been delinquent in remitting employee payroll taxes and a federal tax lien had been filed, she had brought her tax liabilities into current status and produced evidence that the IRS lien had been released.

Required:

a. What code violation(s) have occurred in this case?

b. What is the range of penalties that could be levied against Sally?

c. What do you think is the appropriate penalty?

B.62 **Kaplan CPA Exam Simulation: Independence.**

Required:

Go to the text Web site at www.mhhe.com/louwers3e, click on AUD: Abernathy and Chapman and the "Independence" tab, and complete the assigned task.

B.63 **Kaplan CPA Exam Simulation: Independence.**

Required:

Go to the text Web site at www.mhhe.com/louwers3e, click on AUD: Hardi Risk and Independence and the "Independence" tab, and complete the assigned task.

B.64 **Mini-Case: Ethics.** Refer to the mini-case "Andersen: An Obstruction of Justice?" shown on page 829 and respond to question 6.

B.65 **Mini-Case: Non-Audit Services and Independence.** Refer to the mini-case "KPMG: How Many Firms?" shown on page 836 and respond to Questions 1, 2, and 3.

B.66 **Mini-Case: Non-Audit Services and Independence.** Refer to the mini-case "How Much are Auditors Paid?" shown on page 843 and respond to Questions 1 and 2.

B.67 **Mini-Case: Effect of Sarbanes-Oxley on Fees.** Refer to the mini-case "How Much are Auditors Paid?" shown on page 843 and respond to Questions 3 and 4.

B.68 **Mini-Case: Indemnity Clauses and Independence.** Refer to the mini-case "To Indemnify or Not to Indemnify: That is the Question" shown on page 842 and respond to Questions 1 through 5.

Legal Liability

Privity: A relationship between persons who successively have a legal interest in the same right or property (2) an interest in a transaction contract or legal action (3) a joint knowledge of a private matter.

Professional Standards References

Compendium Section	Document Reference	Topic
AU 311	*SAS 108*	"Planning and Supervision"
AU 316	*SAS 99*	"Consideration of Fraud in a Financial Statement Audit"
	ISA 240	"The Auditor's Responsibility to Consider Fraud in an Audit of Financial Statements"
AU 317	*SAS 54*	"Illegal Acts by Clients"
AU 9317		"Interpretations: Illegal Acts by Clients (FCPA)"
	ISA 250	"Consideration of Laws and Regulations in an Audit of Financial Statements"
AU 634	*SAS 72*	"Letters for Underwriters and Certain Other Requesting Parties" (amended by *SAS 76* and *SAS 86*)
AU 711	*SAS 37*	"Filings under Federal Securities Statutes"
AU 9711		"Interpretations: Filings under Federal Securities Statutes"

When men are pure, laws are useless; when men are corrupt, laws are broken.

Benjamin Disraeli, Former British Prime Minister

Learning Objectives

Module B on professional ethics dealt mainly with auditors' self-regulation. This module focuses on public regulation enforced by the Securities and Exchange Commission (SEC) and state and federal court systems. The discussion will help you understand auditors' legal liability for professional work.

Your objectives are to be able to:

1. Identify and describe auditors' exposure to lawsuits and loss judgments.

2. Specify the characteristics of auditors' liability under common law and cite some specific case precedents.

3. Describe auditors' liability to third parties under statutory law.

4. Specify the civil and criminal liability provisions of the Securities Act of 1933.

5. Specify the civil and criminal liability provisions of the Securities Exchange Act of 1934.

6. Understand recent developments that affect auditors' liability to clients and third parties.

Other than the "Big Four," **BDO Seidman LLP** (BDO) is one of the nation's largest accounting firms (ranking eighth in the United States) with revenues of $440 million. Investors of **E.S. Bankest** (a Miami, Florida, factoring firm) are bringing a $170 million lawsuit against BDO for losses they incurred because of the alleged failure of BDO to detect a fraud that led to E.S. Bankest's collapse. BDO is not willing to settle the case out of court, but is risking a trial . . . a trial that could lead to the demise of the entire firm. Scott

Univer, BDO's general counsel, noted that "we do settle cases. But there are situations where, if we're accused of fraud or collaboration or misconduct, we have to draw a line. We'll see you in court."[1] Prior to the Bankest case, BDO has taken six cases to trial over the last 12 years and prevailed in each one.

However, on June 16, 2007, a Florida jury concluded that BDO exhibited gross negligence in its audits of Bankest, exposing the accounting firm to potential liability of $510 million (treble damages of the $170 million of investor losses). BDO is appealing the jury's decision and countersuing **Banco Espirito Santo** (the original claimant), alleging that the directors Banco appointed to Bankest's board were negligent in fulfilling their duties. Clearly, future developments in this case will have a significant impact on BDO's survival (these potential damages are nearly equal to BDO's firmwide revenue of $550 million in 2006).[2]

BDO's track record in court is unusual, simply because most legal actions against auditors and accounting firms do not actually make it to trial. Accounting firms have generally found it preferable to settle cases out of court instead of risking a trial and significant monetary judgments. As Michael Young, an attorney who has represented the Big Four firms as well as BDO, noted, "the practical reality is that our system of justice breaks down when you're talking about the Big Four. The damages sought are often so big that a rational approach is to settle."[3] In addition to the potential monetary damages, firms consider the opportunity costs of their professionals' time as well as negative publicity surrounding an extensive legal proceeding when making decisions whether to risk a trial.

Legal liability continues to be an important consideration for auditors and accounting firms as they conduct business. Recent settlements involving the largest accounting firms reveal that our litigious society has spilled into the auditing domain. In addition to the settlements summarized in the accompanying Auditing Insight, **Fannie Mae** and **Fortress Re Inc.** have recently filed $2 billion lawsuits against their auditors (**KPMG and Deloitte & Touche,** respectively).[4] While the intentions of these accounting firms are not known at this time, it is possible that these lawsuits might lead to further settlements. This chapter summarizes the legal liability of auditors and the burden of care they owe to various parties who rely upon their work.

AUDITING INSIGHT Recent Settlements Involving Accounting Firms

Firm	Settlements	Firm	Settlements
Arthur Andersen	**WorldCom** ($65 million) **Dynegy** ($1 million)	PricewaterhouseCoopers	**Tyco** ($225 million) **Safety-Kleen** ($48 million) **Raytheon** ($50 million) **Amerco** ($50 million)
Deloitte & Touche	**Adelphia Communications** ($167.5 million) **Parmalat, SpA** ($149 million)		
Ernst & Young	**Bank of New England** ($84 million) **Cendant** ($335 million)		
KPMG	**Xerox** ($22 million) Tax shelter purchasers ($456 million)		

Sources: "Deloitte to Be Latest to Settle in Accounting Scandals," *The Wall Street Journal*, April 26, 2005, p. B1; "Big Accounting Firms Still Pay for Scandals," *The Wall Street Journal*, January 13, 2007, p. B5; "PwC Sets Accord in Tyco Case," *The Wall Street Journal*, July 7–8, 2007, p. A3; "Deloitte to Pay $167.5M in Adelphia Case," *CFO.com*, August 6, 2007, p. C4.

[1] "BDO Prepares to Fight Lawsuit, with Survival Possibly at Stake," *The Wall Street Journal*, January 24, 2007, p. C2.
[2] "BDO Is Found Guilty of Negligence in Fraud," *The Wall Street Journal*, July 16, 2007, p. B2; "BDO is Ordered to Pay Negligence Damages," *The Wall Street Journal*, August 14, 2007, p. C4.
[3] "BDO Prepares to Fight Lawsuit," p. C2.
[4] "Deloitte Sued for $2 Billion," *CFO.com*, November 12, 2004; "Fannie Mae Sues KPMG," *CFO.com*, December 12, 2006.

THE LEGAL ENVIRONMENT

LEARNING
OBJECTIVE

1. Identify and describe auditors' exposure to lawsuits and loss judgments.

How does legal liability arise? Consider the following schematic that summarizes the relationship between auditors and two key parties: the client and third-party users.

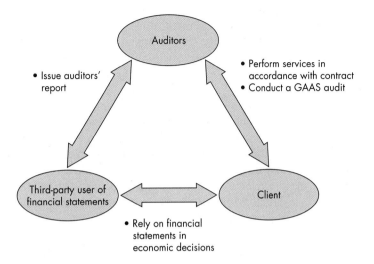

As shown above, auditors owe clients a responsibility to conduct an audit in accordance with generally accepted auditing standards (GAAS) consistent with the terms in the *engagement letter,* that serves as a contract between auditors and their clients. Clients may suffer losses related to these responsibilities for two reasons. First, breach of contract between auditors and the client (for example, auditors' failure to complete the engagement by a specified deadline) may cause economic losses to the client resulting from delays such as failing to receive funding through loans or investments or issuing its shares through a public offering at a less favorable price. Second, clients may suffer economic losses from acts of fraud or other misappropriation of assets by employees that *should have been identified* during a GAAS audit. In either case, if the client's loss is caused by the breach of contract or failure to exercise the appropriate level of professional care (substandard performance) by auditors, the client may seek legal action.

With respect to third-party users, auditors are responsible for issuing a report based on a GAAS audit that provides reasonable assurance that the financial statements on which these users base their economic decisions (lending decisions and investment decisions) are presented according to generally accepted accounting principles (GAAP). For third-party users, economic losses are either related to the inability of the client to repay loans or other obligations or to a decline in the value of the user's investment in the client (in the form of a partnership interest or publicly traded shares of stock). If the user's loss is caused by reliance on financial statements and those financial statements were not presented according to GAAP, users may seek legal action against auditors.

The main defense for auditors is that they followed GAAS and performed their audits with due professional care. Plaintiff attorneys usually exclude from juries individuals who have an understanding or sense of the nature and difficulty of an audit. Therefore, many of these cases are decided on other issues. Small individual investors often testify concerning the loss of their retirement fund, loss of children's college funds, or changes in their life necessitated by the loss. Auditors are often portrayed as wealthy professionals who should have known better. In many cases, lawsuits are brought against auditors not because they are necessarily at fault, but in the case of client failure, they are the only party with resources against which recovery can be made (the **"deep pockets" theory**).

Many users of auditors' reports expect auditors to detect and report fraud, theft, and illegal acts, despite the fact that a GAAS audit cannot be expected to identify all items of this nature. Some financial statement users' expectations are very high and, for this

reason, an **expectation gap** often exists between the diligence that users expect and the diligence that auditors are able to provide. For example, in performing an audit on a multibillion-dollar corporation, auditors may choose to exclude testing transactions of $50,000, $100,000, $500,000, or more as immaterial. Certainly, a $1 million error in the financial statements of **General Motors** (2006 revenues of $207 billion) would be immaterial to auditors. However, it would be difficult to convince an individual investor with $25,000 of retirement money invested that $1 million is not a significant amount of money. Clearly, many financial statement users believe auditors are looking at most, if not every, transaction; are evaluating each transaction, event, person, and department for fraud; and are certifying that financial statements are accurate. No auditors would, however, accept an engagement for which any of these objectives was required.

When auditors do not meet the expectations of clients or financial statement users, they may be held liable under common law or statutory law, depending on the nature of the action and relationship of the party to the auditors. **Common law** uses legal precedent to identify the fault and responsibility of parties where there is no violation of a written law or statute. In a common law action, the judge evaluates prior decisions looking for legal precedent. When no legal precedent can be found, the judge follows a sense of justice or morality, considering the prevailing customs and moral standards. Common law liability against auditors is available to clients and nonshareholder third parties; the jurisdiction for common law actions is typically a court in the state in which the alleged action occurred.

Statutory law is based on laws passed by legislative bodies and compiled in federal, state, and municipal codes. In a statutory case, the primary basis for a decision is whether the party's actions have violated the law as written in the code. A lawsuit claiming that auditors did not perform the audit in an appropriate manner is a common law action. A charge by the district attorney or U.S. attorney that auditors participated in a financial statement fraud in violation of a written law or statute is an action under statutory law. The primary statutory laws relevant to the audit of financial statements are laws governing the purchase and sale of securities; as a result, auditors' liability under statutory law is primarily to third-party shareholders. The Securities Act of 1933 and Securities and Exchange Act of 1934 (discussed later in this module) provide U.S. district courts with jurisdiction for violations of these acts.

Review Checkpoints

C.1 Identify the general responsibilities auditors owe to clients and third parties.

C.2 Distinguish between *common law* liability and *statutory law* liability. Which parties generally bring suit against auditors under common law and statutory *law* liability?

LIABILITY UNDER COMMON LAW

LEARNING OBJECTIVE

2. Specify the characteristics of auditors' liability under common law and cite some specific case precedents.

Under common law liability, lawsuits may be brought against auditors based on the law of contracts or as tort actions for failure to exercise the appropriate level of professional care. **Breach of contract** is a claim that accounting or auditing services were not performed in the manner proscribed in the contract. This basis is most characteristic of lawsuits involving auditors and their clients. **Tort** actions cover other civil complaints (e.g., fraud, deceit, injury) arising from auditors' failure to exercise the appropriate level of professional care (substandard performance). Tort actions can be initiated by clients or users of financial statements.

Suits for damages under common law usually result when someone suffers a financial loss after relying on financial statements later found to be materially misstated. The popular

press calls such unfortunate events *audit failures*. **Plaintiffs** generally assert all possible causes of action, including breach of contract, tort, deceit, fraud, and whatever else may be relevant to the claim. Various legal terms that will be used throughout this module are summarized in the accompanying textbox for reference.

AUDITING INSIGHT Summary of Legal Terminology

Breach of contract: Failing to abide by or fulfill the terms of a contract.

Constructive fraud: A failure to provide any care in fulfilling a duty owed to another including a reckless disregard for the truth. Constructive fraud is similar in nature to gross negligence (see below).

Foreseeable party: A wide range of individuals or organizations that might rely on auditors' work.

Foreseen party: A limited class of individuals or organizations that could be reasonably expected to rely on auditors' work.

Fraud: Misrepresentations of fact that the individual knows to be false.

Gross negligence: Breach of duty owed to another party due to the lack of minimal care.

Ordinary negligence: Unintentional breaches of duty owed to another party due to a lack of reasonable care.

Plaintiff: The person or organization that initiates a lawsuit (client or third-party user of financial statements).

Primary beneficiary: A person named in a contract for whom the services provided are intended who is known by name to auditors.

Privity of contract: Situation in which parties have a contractual relationship

Liability to Clients

Clients may bring a lawsuit for breach of contract and other tort actions. The relationship of direct involvement between parties to a contract is known as **privity of contract.** When privity exists, plaintiffs must demonstrate all of the following:

1. They suffered an economic loss.
2. Auditors did not perform in accordance with the terms of the contract (for breach of contract).
3. Auditors failed to exercise the appropriate level of professional care (for tort actions).
4. The loss was the result of the breach of contract or failure to exercise the appropriate level of professional care.

The first case in the United States involving an auditor and client dispute *(Smith v. London Assurance Corp.)* established auditors' obligation for breach of contract.

Legal Precedent

SMITH V. LONDON ASSURANCE CORP. (1905)

This was the first U.S. case involving auditors. Smith, the auditor, sued for an unpaid fee and London Assurance Corp. counterclaimed for a large sum that had been embezzled by one of its employees, which it claimed would not have occurred except for the auditors' breach of contract. The evidence indicated that auditors had indeed failed to audit the cash accounts at one branch office as stipulated in an engagement contract. The court recognized auditors as skilled professionals and held Smith liable for the embezzlement losses that could have been prevented by non-negligent performance under the terms of the contract.

In addition to breach of contract, auditors also may be liable to clients for tort liability. Because of the very close relationship between auditors and their clients, auditors have a high level of responsibility to their clients. This responsibility is to conduct an audit in accordance with GAAS; if auditors exhibit *ordinary negligence* (the lack of reasonable care in performing an audit), clients will typically prevail in their legal actions against auditors. (Auditors are also liable to their clients for *gross negligence* and *fraud*).

Auditors may attempt to mitigate clients' claims through one of the following three defenses:

1. Auditors exercised the appropriate level of professional care (tort) or performed the engagement in accordance with terms of the contract (breach of contract).
2. The client's economic loss was caused by a factor other than auditors' failure to exercise appropriate levels of professional care or breach of contract (the **causation defense**).
3. Actions on the part of the client were, in part, responsible for the loss (for example, failure of the client to establish effective internal control to prevent embezzlement losses). This is referred to as **contributory negligence** and is available to auditors in certain jurisdictions.

AUDITING INSIGHT — Who's Suing Whom?

In an interesting twist, **KPMG** is suing one of its audit clients (**Federal National Mortgage Association**, or **Fannie Mae**) for withholding and distorting its accounting and engaging in fraudulent misrepresentations and other wrongdoings. This suit is in response to a suit Fannie Mae filed against KPMG for negligence and breach of contract, which the mortgage giant claims resulted in KPMG's failure to detect $6.3 billion in accounting misstatements.

Source: "In Rare Move, Auditor Sues Client," *CFO.com*, April 24, 2007.

Liability to Third Parties

In the early part of the 20th century, parties other than clients had difficulty succeeding in lawsuits against auditors. Parties not in privity of contract have no cause of action for breach of contract. However, these parties can bring lawsuits against auditors for failure to exercise appropriate levels of professional care (tort action). In these cases, third parties suffer an economic loss because of reliance on the audited financial statements and auditors' reports on those statements. The three levels of failure to exercise the appropriate level of professional care that have emerged through various cases are **ordinary negligence** (lack of reasonable care), **gross negligence** (lack of minimal care), and **fraud** (intention to deceive).

It has been well established that auditors are liable to all third parties for levels of performance representing gross negligence and fraud. However, auditors' liability to various third parties for ordinary negligence has been debated and has changed significantly over time. Further, the extent of liability for ordinary negligence to third parties varies by jurisdiction (state in which the action is brought). As a result, the evolution of auditors' liability to third parties for ordinary negligence through common law precedents has been carefully monitored by both auditors and third-party users. This is particularly important, because it is relatively easier for third parties to demonstrate ordinary negligence compared to either gross negligence or fraud.

To bring a suit against auditors under common law, third parties must demonstrate all of the following:

1. They suffered an economic loss (normally, a decline in the value of an investment or failure to be repaid for a loan or other obligation).
2. Auditors failed to exercise the appropriate level of professional care (ordinary negligence, gross negligence, or fraud).
3. The financial statements were materially misstated.
4. The loss was caused by reliance on the materially misstated financial statements.

One early and important case involving auditors' liability to third parties was in the case known as *Ultramares*. The *Ultramares* opinion expressed the view that, if auditors' failure to exercise the appropriate level of professional care were so great as to constitute gross negligence, grounds might exist for concluding that auditors had engaged in *constructive fraud*. While **constructive fraud** may not have the same element of intent associated with fraud, it results in depriving or injuring the rights of an unsuspecting party in the same manner as fraud. The significance of the *Ultramares* case is that it established an obligation to third parties and others not in privity with auditors for gross negligence and fraud. *Ultramares* has been cited in numerous third-party common law cases against auditors.

Legal Precedent

ULTRAMARES CORP. V. TOUCHE (1931)

In 1924, **Touche, Niven & Co.** was engaged to audit the 1923 balance sheet of **Fred Stern & Co.**, a rubber importer. Based on the audited balance sheet, **Ultramares**, a factoring business, made numerous loans to Stern & Co. In January 1925, Stern & Co. went bankrupt and was unable to repay Ultramares (this represented the economic loss). While the New York court of appeals denied Ultramares' negligence claim, the court *did not assert that privity of contract was a requirement for third parties to sue auditors*. As a result, auditors' potential liability to third parties and the right for these parties to bring suit against auditors was permitted.

In part, the court's decision established criteria for auditors' liability to third parties for constructive fraud. To do so, third parties must prove all of the following:

1. There was a misrepresentation of a material fact (usually in the financial statements).
2. The misrepresentation was made knowingly or without adequate knowledge to know if it was true.
3. There was knowledge *(scienter)* and intent to induce action in reliance on the information.

4. The damaged party justifiably relied on the misrepresentation.
5. There was resulting damage.

The court held that auditors could be liable when they did not have sufficient information (audit evidence) to lead to an opinion. Therefore, the auditors' opinion is deceitful when auditors claim to have knowledge that they do not possess. The court also wrote that when the degree of negligence is gross, it may amount to a constructive fraud and auditors could be liable to a third-party user. *Case conclusion: Ultramares* contributed to the development of common law liability to third parties by establishing that

1. Third parties not in privity with auditors can bring suit against auditors.
2. Auditors may be liable to parties who are not in privity in cases representing constructive fraud (gross negligence) or fraud.
3. Auditors are generally not liable for ordinary negligence to parties who are not in privity.

The *Ultramares* decision was upheld in *State Street Trust Co. v. Ernst*, in which the courts identified auditors' liability to third parties for gross negligence in the following opinion:

> [Auditors], however, may be liable to third parties, even where there is lacking deliberate or active fraud . . . A representation certified as true to the knowledge of the accountants when knowledge there is none, a reckless misstatement, or an opinion based upon grounds so flimsy... In other words, heedlessness and reckless disregard of consequence may take the place of deliberate intention.[5]

While the *Ultramares* case opened the door for lawsuits by third parties in which fraud or constructive fraud was present, for many years only parties that had privity of contract (typically, the client) could bring legal action against auditors for ordinary negligence. **Primary beneficiaries** are third parties for whose primary benefit the audit or other accounting service is performed (also referred to as *near privity*). In some legal jurisdictions, a beneficiary must be named in the contract; in other jurisdictions, the beneficiary need only be identified to auditors prior to or during the engagement. For example, an accounting firm may be informed that the report is needed for a bank loan

[5] *State Street Trust Co. v. Ernst*, 278 N.Y. 105, 15 N.E.2d 415 (1938).

application at the First National Bank; in this case, First National Bank is a primary beneficiary because they are known *by name* to auditors. Many cases (for example, *CIT v. Glover*) indicate that proving ordinary negligence may be sufficient to hold auditors liable for damages to primary beneficiaries. *Credit Alliance v. Arthur Andersen* identified specific criteria that must be met for primary beneficiaries to prevail against auditors for ordinary negligence.

Legal Precedent

CREDIT ALLIANCE V. ARTHUR ANDERSEN (1985)

In this landmark case, **Credit Alliance** (a financial services firm) provided financing for equipment to L.B. Smith, Inc. In 1978, Credit Alliance advised Smith that any future extensions of credit would require audited financial statements, which Smith subsequently provided for fiscal years 1976 through 1979. In 1980, L.B. Smith filed for bankruptcy. The New York court of appeals provided a three-pronged test for Credit Alliance's right to sue:

1. Auditors were aware that a particular party intended to rely on the auditors' opinion and financial statements.
2. The third party was specifically identified.

3. Some action by auditors showed that they had acknowledged the third-party's identification and intent to rely on the opinion and financial statements.

This test has been used as precedent in many cases in determining whether the third party was an intended beneficiary of the auditors' work.

Case conclusion: In many jurisdictions, third parties may bring suit against auditors for ordinary negligence, even if they are not in privity of the contract. However, they must meet the three-pronged test established by the New York court of appeals.

In some jurisdictions, auditors also may be liable for ordinary negligence to **foreseen parties.** In these jurisdictions, the *restatement of torts* doctrine specifies that auditors are liable if they are aware that the auditors' opinion and financial statements are to be used by some third party. Auditors need not know the exact identity of the third party but are presumed to owe a duty to persons who they are actually aware will rely on the information. For example, if a client informs auditors that it will be using audited financial statements to obtain financing but does not identify any specific banks, under the doctrine of *restatement of torts,* any bank that uses the audited financial statements in making lending decisions may have legal standing to sue auditors for ordinary negligence. For example, *Rusch Factors v. Levin* concluded that auditors were liable to a lender (**Rusch Factors**) because the auditors were aware that the financial statements were to be shown to potential lenders, despite the fact that the auditors were not aware of their actual identity. *Fleet National Bank v. Gloucester Co.* affirmed auditors' obligation to third parties who are foreseen parties, but are not known by name to auditors (and, therefore, do not qualify as primary beneficiaries).

Legal Precedent

FLEET NATIONAL BANK V. GLOUCESTER CO. (1994)

Fleet Bank relied on financial statements audited by **Tonneson** when making loans to **Gloucester.** Tonneson was named in the suit brought by Fleet National Bank. The court applied the *restatement of torts* doctrine to identify Fleet Bank as a beneficiary of the audit contract. These points were made: (1) Tonneson knew about Fleet Bank's loans to Gloucester, (2) Tonneson reviewed the loan agreements between Gloucester and Fleet Bank, (3) Tonneson knew the loan agreements

required submission of audited financial statements, and (4) Tonneson believed and expected Gloucester would provide the audited financial statements to Fleet Bank.

Case conclusion: Auditors may be liable to third parties for ordinary negligence, even if the third party is not named in the engagement contract. If auditors have knowledge that financial statements will be provided to third parties for the purpose of making a decision, in some jurisdiction auditors may be liable to such a third party.

Lastly, in other jurisdictions auditors may be liable to reasonably **foreseeable parties.** These parties include creditors, investors, or potential investors whose decisions normally rely on audited financial statements and opinions on those financial statements. If auditors are reasonably able to *foresee* a limited class of potential users (e.g., local banks, regular suppliers) of their reports, liability may be imposed for ordinary negligence. This, however, is an uncertain area and liability in a particular case depends entirely on the unique facts and circumstances of the case and the jurisdiction of the legal action. This is the most liberal interpretation of the third-party liability and is used in only two states, Mississippi and Wisconsin. *Rosenblum, Inc. v. Adler* establishes auditors' liability for ordinary negligence to individuals who are "reasonably foreseeable."[6]

Legal Precedent

ROSENBLUM, INC. V. ADLER (1983)

Giant Stores Corporation acquired the retail catalog showroom business owned by **Rosenblum,** giving stock in exchange for the business. Fifteen months after the acquisition, Giant Stores declared bankruptcy. **Adler** had audited Giant Stores' financial statements and issued unqualified opinions on those financial statements for several prior years. These financial statements turned out to be misstated because Giant Stores had engaged in a fraudulent scheme to misstate its financial statements.

In finding for Rosenblum on certain motions, the New Jersey Supreme Court held, "Independent auditors have a duty of care to all persons whom the auditor should *reasonably foresee* as recipients of the statements from the company for proper business purposes, provided that the recipients rely on those financial statements. . . . It is well recognized that audited financial statements are made for the use of third parties who have no direct relationship with the auditor. . . . Auditors have responsibility not only to the client who pays the fee but also to investors, creditors, and others who rely on the audited financial statements."

Case conclusion: In some jurisdictions, auditors may be liable for ordinary negligence to a large class of users that are reasonably foreseeable but may not be known to the auditor at the time of the audit.

Additional note: While the opinion in the *Rosenblum* case is an excellent example of a court opinion that extends liability to foreseeable parties, it should be noted that subsequent legislation (1995) in New Jersey has moved that state to a *near privity* standard. However, the *Rosenblum* opinion has been used as precedent in other states. This is an example of how state law can change and how court decisions can provide an impetus to legislatures to enact new law.

It should be noted that these classes of third parties are based on legislation and legal precedents. For example, for primary beneficiaries, auditors know both the name of the party and the intended use of the financial statements; for foreseen parties, auditors know the financial statements will be used by third parties; for foreseeable parties, auditors *should be* aware that the financial statements *could be used* by third parties. In all jurisdictions, auditors will generally be liable for acts of gross negligence and fraud; auditors' liability to third parties for ordinary negligence depends upon the doctrine in effect in the jurisdiction in which auditors practice. Clearly, limiting auditors' liability for acts of ordinary negligence to only primary beneficiaries is most advantageous to auditors, while exposing auditors to liability for ordinary negligence to foreseeable parties is most disadvantageous to auditors. One study[7] classified various jurisdictions (as of 2000) as follows:

* Privity or near-privity: Arkansas, Idaho, Illinois, Kansas, Louisiana, Michigan, Montana, Nebraska, New Jersey, New York, Pennsylvania, Utah, Virginia, Wyoming.
* *Restatement of torts* (foreseen): Alabama, Alaska, Arizona, California, Colorado, Florida, Georgia, Hawaii, Iowa, Massachusetts, Missouri, New Hampshire, North Carolina, Ohio, South Carolina, Tennessee, Texas, Washington, West Virginia.
* Reasonable foreseeability: Mississippi, Wisconsin.

[6] F. D. Greene, A. R. Petrocine, and R. C. FitzPatrick, "Holding Accountants Accountable: The Liability of Accountants to Third Parties," *Employee Responsibilities and Rights Journal,* March 2003, p. 27.

[7] C. Pacini, M. J. Martin, and L. Hamilton, "At the Interface of Law and Accounting: An Examination of a Trend toward a Reduction in the Scope of Auditor Liability to Third Parties in the Common Law Countries," *American Business Law Journal,* Winter 2000, pp. 171–225.

EXHIBIT C.1
**Summary of Auditors'
Liability to Third
Parties under
Common Law**

Auditors' legal liability to third parties as established by these and other cases under common law is summarized in Exhibit C.1.

As with their liability to clients, auditors can defend a common law action by presenting arguments and evidence to mitigate third-party plaintiffs' claims and evidence. Assuming that the plaintiff has demonstrated an economic loss and materially misstated financial statements, defenses available to auditors against third parties include

1. The third party did not have appropriate standing to sue in that jurisdiction (for example, bringing suit for ordinary negligence if the appropriate relationship between auditors and third party does not exist).
2. The third party did not rely on the financial statements but on some other source of information.
3. The third-party's loss was caused by some other events beyond the auditors' scope of responsibility (causation defense).
4. Auditors' work was performed in accordance with professional standards (e.g., GAAS for audits of financial statements).

Liability for Compilation and Review Services

People find it easy to think about common law liability in connection with audited financial statements. Do not forget, however, that accountants also render compilation and review services and are associated with the resultant *unaudited* financial information. Users expect public accountants to perform these services in accordance with professional standards and courts can impose liability for accounting work found to be substandard. Accountants have been assessed damages for work on such statements, as shown in the *1136 Tenants' Corporation v. Max Rothenberg & Co.* case. In this case, the court concluded that accountants engaged to perform "write-up" (compilation) work had a duty to inform clients of indicators of fraud that were identified during the engagement. Liability for these types of engagements is important, since approximately 11 percent of losses to the AICPA professional liability insurance plan involve compilation and review engagements and unaudited financial statements.

One significant risk involved with compilation and review engagements is that the client may fail to understand the nature of the service being given. Accountants should use a conference and an engagement letter to explain clearly that a compilation engagement ("write-up") does not involve gathering sufficient appropriate evidence and is lesser in scope than a review engagement. Similarly, a review service should be explained in terms of being less extensive than an audit engagement conducted in accordance with GAAS. Clear understandings at the outset (along with clearly worded engagement letters) can enable accountants and clients to avoid later disagreements. In *Iselin v. Landau* (1992), the court decided that the lack of an opinion on reviewed financial statements precluded the

third party (**William Iselin & Company**) from bringing a lawsuit against the auditors (**Mann Judd Landau**) because of losses suffered from the bankruptcy of one of Iselin's customers. (Mann Judd Landau had performed a review engagement on the financial statements of Iselin's customer.)

Review Checkpoints

C.3 For what type of actions can clients bring suit against auditors under common law? What must clients prove prior to bringing suit in each case?

C.4 In terms of tort liability, what level of responsibility do auditors owe clients under common law?

C.5 What must third parties prove in a common law action seeking recovery of damages from auditors?

C.6 What legal theory is derived from the *Ultramares* decision? Can auditors rely on the *Ultramares* decision today?

C.7 Define and explain *privity, primary beneficiary, foreseen,* and *foreseeable party* in terms of the degree of failure to exercise the appropriate level of professional care on the part of auditors that would trigger the liability.

C.8 What defenses are available to auditors against suits brought by clients under common law? Against suits brought by third parties under common law?

C.9 What additional defenses can accountants use in lawsuits related to compilation and review engagements?

LIABILITY UNDER STATUTORY LAW

LEARNING OBJECTIVE

3. Describe auditors' liability to third parties under statutory law.

Auditors can be liable to individuals when they violate a specific law or statute when performing professional services; this liability is referred to as *statutory liability*. Several federal statutes provide sources of potential liability for auditors, including the Federal False Statements Statute, the Federal Mail Fraud Statute, the Federal Conspiracy Statute, the Securities Act of 1933 (Securities Act), the Securities Exchange Act of 1934 (Securities Exchange Act), and the Sarbanes-Oxley Act. The Securities Act and Securities Exchange Act contain provisions defining certain civil and criminal liabilities of auditors. Because a significant segment of accounting practice is under the jurisdiction of these acts, the following discussion concentrates on duties and liabilities under these laws.

Federal securities regulation in the United States was enacted in the 1930s not only as a reaction to the events of the early years of the Great Depression but also in the spirit of the New Deal era and as a culmination of attempts at "blue-sky" regulation by the states.[8] The Securities Act of 1933 and the Securities Exchange Act of 1934 require registrants to disclose important financial and nonfinancial information required for informed investment decisions. This information is provided in the form of financial statements and related disclosures on both an annual basis (**Form 10-K,** which must be audited by independent auditors) and quarterly basis (**Form 10-Q,** which must be reviewed by independent auditors) (see Module A for a discussion of review engagements). The securities acts and the SEC operate for the protection of investors and for the facilitation of orderly capital markets. Even so, no federal government agency, including the SEC, rules on the *quality* of investments. The securities acts have been characterized as "truth-in-securities" law. Their spirit favors the otherwise uninformed investing public and caveat vendor—let the seller beware of violations—is applied to the issuer.

[8] The term *blue sky* comes from a state judge's remark during a securities fraud case. He said: "These securities have no more substance than a piece of blue sky."

The form and content of 10-K and 10-Q filings are governed by the SEC through **Regulation S-X** (which covers the annual and interim financial statements) and **Regulation S-K** (which covers other supplementary disclosures). In addition to these two regulations, auditors must be familiar with **Financial Reporting Releases (FRRs),** which express new rules and policies about disclosure, and **Staff Accounting Bulletins (SABs),** which provide unofficial, but important, interpretations of Regulations S-X and S-K. Taken together, these four pronouncements provide the authoritative literature for information that must be filed with the SEC.

Registrant entities are required to provide annual reports to shareholders, file annual reports with the SEC on Form 10-K, and file registration statements (discussed later) with the SEC when securities are initially offered to the public. Under the SEC's integrated disclosure system, entities can prepare the annual report to shareholders in conformity with Regulations S-X and S-K and use the annual report as the filing in a registration statement.

Auditors' liability under the Securities Act and the Securities Exchange Act arises from the requirement for registrants to file audited financial statements with the SEC. If purchasers and sellers of securities suffer an economic loss through a change in the price of securities following a purchase or sale and the financial statements contain a material misstatement, auditors may be held liable for failure to detect the material misstatement. The following sections discuss auditors' liability under the two securities acts in greater detail.

Review Checkpoints

C.10 What are (a) Regulation S-X, (b) Regulation S-K, (c) Financial Reporting Releases, and (d) Staff Accounting Bulletins?

C.11 How does the SEC's integrated disclosure system simplify and coordinate various SEC report filings?

C.12 How does auditors' liability under statutory law arise?

THE SECURITIES ACT OF 1933 (SECURITIES ACT)

LEARNING OBJECTIVE

4. Specify the civil and criminal liability provisions of the Securities Act of 1933.

The Securities Act of 1933 regulates the initial issuance of securities by registrants to the investing public through a market (primarily through an **initial public offering,** or **IPO**). The Securities Act provides that no person may lawfully buy, sell, offer to buy, or offer to sell any security by means of interstate commerce unless a registration statement is "effective" (a legal term essentially meaning "filed and accepted" by the SEC). This prohibition should be interpreted literally: *No person can buy or sell any security* by means of *interstate commerce* (e.g., telephone, mail, highway, national bank) unless a registration statement is *effective.* This registration statement includes a **prospectus,** which is a legal document offering securities for sale and includes the terms of the issue, name of the issuer, planned use of the proceeds, and historical financial statements. Certain exemptions exist for limited offerings, offerings by small investors, and offerings involving financially sophisticated investors; these exemptions can be found in section 3, section 4, and Regulation D of the Securities Act.

The general point concerning the Securities Act is that, with some minor exceptions, *all* issuances of securities to the public must be registered with the SEC. One fine point of the law is that *offerings* are registered but specific securities are not. This means that a corporation holding treasury stock or a large shareholder (holding 10 percent or more of a stock) must consult the law before selling large holdings. Even if the shares held were acquired through an earlier registration, subsequent sales could have to be registered anew.

From the auditors' point of view, the key issue under the Securities Act is that the *registration statement* filed with the SEC includes financial statements and required disclosures under Regulations S-X and S-K. The Securities Act notes that this information "shall be certified by an independent public or certified accountant"; this language requires an audit examination. This audit requirement provides the basis for auditors' liability to investors under the Securities Act.

Section 11: Civil Liability

Section 11 of the Securities Act is of great interest to auditors because of the duties and responsibilities it establishes. This section discusses the principal criteria defining civil liabilities under the statute. Portions of section 11 pertinent to auditors' liability are discussed next.

Section 11, Securities Act of 1933

Section 11(a): ... any person acquiring such security [in a registered offering] ... may sue:

- Every person who signed the registration statement.
- Every person who was a director of ... or partner in, the issuer.
- Every accountant, engineer, or appraiser.
- Every underwriter with respect to such security.

If such person acquired the security after the issuer has made generally available to its security holders an earnings statement covering a period of at least 12 months beginning after the effective date of the registration statement, then the right of recovery ... shall be conditioned on proof that such person acquired the security relying upon ... the registration statement. ...

Section 11(b): Notwithstanding the provisions of subsection (a), no person, other than the issuer, shall be liable as provided therein who shall sustain the burden of proof that (A) as regards any part of the registration statement not purporting to be made on the authority of an expert, ... he had, after reasonable investigation, reasonable grounds to believe ... that the statements therein were true and that

there was no omission to state a material fact ... and (B) as regards any part of the registration statement purporting to be made upon his authority as an expert ... he had, after reasonable investigation, reasonable grounds to believe ... that the statements therein were true and that there was no omission to state a material fact ... and (C) as regards any part of the registration statement purporting to be made on the authority of an expert (other than himself) ... he had no reasonable grounds to believe ... that the statements were untrue or that there was an omission to state a material fact. ...

Section 11(c): In determining, for the purpose of ... subsection (b) of this section, what constitutes reasonable investigation and reasonable ground for belief, the standards of reasonableness shall be that required of a prudent man in the management of his own property. ...

Section 11(e): ... if the defendant proves that any portion or all of such damages [claimed in a lawsuit] represents other than the depreciation in value of such security resulting from such part of the registration statement, with respect to which his liability is asserted, not being true or omitting to state a material fact required to be stated therein ... such portion of or all such damages shall not be recoverable.

In section 11(*b*)(B), auditors are considered the *experts* on the financial statements covered by the auditors' opinion and, therefore, must perform a reasonable investigation: an audit in accordance with GAAS using due professional care. This requirement imposes an obligation for *ordinary negligence* on the part of auditors. Read carefully again section 11(*b*)(C); all other people who might be included in a registration legal action do not need to prove that they made a "reasonable investigation" of the financial statements because they relied on the authority of the expert (auditors providing the opinion). Thus, the other parties would like auditors to expand the opinion to cover as much as possible and auditors must be careful to specify exactly which statements, including footnotes, are covered by their opinion.

Auditors commonly provide assurance to underwriters, who act as intermediaries between the offering entity and investing public by purchasing securities for investment or resale. Auditors provide **"comfort letters"** to underwriters that address, among other information, the independence of auditors and the fairness of the registrant's financial statements. (See *SAS 72, SAS 76,* and *SAS 86* for more information about the content of comfort letters.)

Section 11 includes two other very important implications for auditors. First, reviewing the first two words in section 11(*a*), "*any person*" (emphasis added) may bring suit against auditors. Essentially, the Securities Act treats *all* persons as being *reasonably foreseeable* and holds auditors liable to these persons. In addition, section 11 shifts the major burden of proof from the plaintiff (investor) to the expert auditors; essentially, plaintiffs must prove each of the following:

1. They suffered an economic loss.
2. The financial statements contained a material misstatement.

Recall that under common law liability, plaintiffs had to also allege and prove some level of failure to exercise the appropriate level of professional care and that the loss was caused by reliance on the misstated financial statements. Thus, under the Securities Act, the plaintiff is *not* required to demonstrate that the loss was caused by the misstated financial statements; the burden of proof regarding professional care rests with auditors. Taken together, these three major implications associated with section 11 (liability for ordinary negligence, liability to a large number of persons, and auditors' burden of proof) provides greater exposure to auditors to a wide range of potential plaintiffs.

Section 11 was written with the protection of the investing public in mind, not the protection of the expert auditors. The first significant court case under section 11 was *Escott v. BarChris Construction Corporation*. The ruling in this case was that auditors did not conduct a reasonable investigation of subsequent events and, thus, did not satisfy section 11(*b*)(B).

Legal Precedent

ESCOTT V. BARCHRIS CONSTRUCTION CORP. (1968)

BarChris Construction Corporation built bowling alleys. In 1961, BarChris issued convertible bonds to the public that were subject to the provisions of the Securities Act. BarChris issued a registration statement that included financial statements audited by **Peat, Marwick, Mitchell & Co.** (now KPMG). Investors sued Peat, Marwick, Mitchell & Co. under the provisions of the Securities Act, citing lack of appropriate level of professional care during the conduct of the audit.

The judge ruled that the auditors had failed to perform a diligent and reasonable investigation (section 11(*b*)(B)). The judge found that the auditor had spent "only" 20.5 hours on the subsequent events review, had read no important documents, and "He asked questions, he got answers that he considered satisfactory, and he did nothing to verify them. . . . He was too easily satisfied with glib answers to his inquiries." The judge also said, "Accountants should not be held to a standard higher than that recognized in their profession. I do not do so here. The senior accountant's review [of subsequent events] did not come up to that standard. He did not take some of the steps which [the] written program prescribed. He did not spend an adequate amount of time on a task of this magnitude."

Section 11(*a*) Exemption

Financial reporting has changed since 1933. The SEC now requires some larger entities to present interim financial statements and encourages the presentation of forecasts. To remove the legal liability barrier to auditors' association with such information, the SEC has exempted auditors from section 11 liability related to interim information and has enacted a safe harbor with respect to forecasts. A **safe harbor** means that plaintiffs in a lawsuit must show that auditors did not act in good faith when reporting on a forecast, effectively placing the burden of proof on the plaintiff and requiring a more significant lack of care (gross negligence) to be demonstrated.

Auditors' Defenses under the 1933 Act

Section 11 provides two possible defenses to auditors, assuming that purchasers of securities are able to demonstrate they suffered a loss and the financial statements are materially misstated. First, the "due diligence" defense is established under section 11(*b*)(B); auditors who can prove they conducted a "reasonable investigation" will not be held liable under the Securities Act. Further, section 11(*c*) states the standard of reasonable degree of

care to be "that of a prudent person in the management of her or his own property." In a context more specific to auditors, a reasonable investigation can be shown by the conduct of an audit in accordance with GAAS.

Section 11(*b*)(C) also gives a *diligence* defense standard for portions of a registration statement made on the authority of an expert. Auditors who rely on the work and opinions of specialists (such as actuaries or engineers) need not make a personal independent investigation of that expert's areas. Similarly, any officer, director, attorney, or underwriter connected with a registration has less obligation for information covered by the expert auditors' opinion. In the *BarChris* judgment, officers, attorneys, and underwriters were found lacking in diligence except with respect to audited financial statements.

In addition to the due diligence defense, section 11(*e*) establishes the *causation defense*. Essentially, if auditors can prove that all or part of the plaintiffs' damages were caused by something other than the materially misstated financial statements included in the registration statement, they are not required to pay all or part of the damages. This defense may create some imaginative "other reasons." In the *BarChris* case, at least one plaintiff had purchased securities *after* the company had gone bankrupt. This claim was settled out of court.

Section 13: Statute of Limitations

Section 13 of the Securities Act requires any suits to be brought within one year after discovery of the materially misstated statement or omission or within three years after the public offering. These limitations restrict auditors' liability exposure to a determinable time span. In many cases, the statute of limitations is a viable defense available to auditors.

Section 17: Antifraud

Section 17 of the Securities Act is the antifraud section. This section makes it unlawful to "use the mails or instruments of transportation in interstate commerce" in an effort to defraud others. As with section 11, plaintiffs are not required to demonstrate reliance on the fraudulent information or that the fraudulent information resulted in their loss. Therefore, the burden of proof still rests with auditors.

Section 24: Criminal Liability

Section 24 sets forth the criminal penalties imposed by the Securities Act. Criminal penalties are characterized by monetary fines, prison terms, or both. The key words in section 24 are "willful" violation and "willfully" causing materially misstated statements to be filed. Thus, while auditors have civil liability to third parties under section 11 in cases where ordinary negligence can be demonstrated (failure to conduct a GAAS audit), criminal penalties are possible under the 1933 Securities Act only for instances in which auditors act with knowledge of the materially misstated financial statements (fraud and, perhaps, gross negligence). Section 24 establishes these penalties for fines at $10,000 and imprisonment for up to five years. The *United States v. Benjamin* case is an example of how auditors may be found criminally liable under the Securities Act.

Legal Precedent

UNITED STATES V. BENJAMIN (1964)

The judgment in this case resulted in the conviction of auditors for willingly conspiring by use of interstate commerce to sell unregistered securities and to defraud investors in the sale of securities, in violation of section 24 of the Securities Act. The auditors had prepared *pro forma* balance sheets and claimed that use of the words *pro forma* absolved them of responsibility. The auditors also claimed they did not know their reports would be used in connection with securities sales. The court found otherwise, showing that the auditors did in fact know about the use of their reports and that certain statements about asset values and acquisitions were materially misstated. The court made two significant findings: (1) the willfulness requirements of section 24 may be proved by showing that due diligence would have revealed the materially misstated statements and (2) use of limiting words such as *pro forma* do not justify showing false ownership of assets in any kind of financial statements.

Review Checkpoints

C.13 How is section 11 of the Securities Act different from the legal environment that exists under common law?

C.14 What must (a) the plaintiff prove in a suit under section 11 of the Securities Act seeking recovery of damages from independent auditors of financial statements and (b) the defendant auditors do in such a court action?

C.15 Why should officers, directors, and underwriters want auditors to include under the auditors' opinion such information as the plan for use of the proceeds of an offering, the description of the organization and business, the description of physical properties, and other quasi-financial information such as plant floor space and sales order backlog?

C.16 What liability exposure for auditors is found in the Securities Act in (a) section 17 and (b) section 24?

C.17 How did auditors violate generally accepted auditing standards in the *BarChris* decision?

THE SECURITIES EXCHANGE ACT OF 1934 (SECURITIES EXCHANGE ACT)

LEARNING OBJECTIVE

5. Specify the civil and criminal liability provisions of the Securities Exchange Act of 1934.

The Securities Exchange Act regulates daily trading of securities and requires most entities whose securities are traded in interstate commerce to register and file pertinent information with the SEC. Entities having total assets of $10 million or more and 500 or more stockholders are required to register under the Securities Exchange Act. The purpose of these size and share criteria is to define securities in which there is a significant public interest. (These criteria are subject to change by the SEC.)

For auditors and accountants, the most significant aspect of the Securities Exchange Act is the requirement for registrant entities to file annual reports (Form 10-K), quarterly reports (Form 10-Q), and periodic special reports (Form 8-K) with the SEC. The Securities Exchange Act requires the information on Form 10-K to be audited by independent or certified auditors and the information on Form 10-Q to be reviewed by an independent or certified accountant. This requirement forms the basis for auditors' liability to either purchasers or sellers of securities (under the Securities Act of 1933, liability is limited to purchasers of securities since the entity itself is issuing securities to the public).

Section 10 and Rule 10*b*-5: Antifraud

Section 10 of the Securities Exchange Act is used against auditors quite frequently. Like section 17 of the Securities Act, section 10 is a general antifraud section that makes it unlawful for persons to use "manipulative" or "deceptive" devices in connection with the purchase or sale of securities. Rule 10*b*-5, made by the SEC staff under their authority to create administrative rules related to the statute, is more explicit than section 10 in identifying auditors' specific responsibilities.

Rule 10*b*-5. Securities Exchange Act of 1934

Rule 10*b*-5. Employment of Manipulative and Deceptive Devices. It shall be unlawful for any person, directly or indirectly, by the use of any means or instrumentality of interstate commerce, or of the mails, or of any facility of any national securities exchange,

1. To employ any device, scheme, or artifice to defraud.

2. To make any untrue statement of material fact or to omit to state a material fact necessary in order to make the statements made,

in the light of the circumstances under which they were made, not misleading.

3. To engage in any act, practice, or course of business which operates or would operate as a fraud or deceit upon any person in connection with the purchase or sale of any security.

An important point about Rule 10*b*-5 liability is that plaintiffs must prove **scienter** (auditors had knowledge of the misstatement and intentionally failed to disclose the misstatement in their reports) to impose liability under the rule. Mere failure to exercise the appropriate level of professional care is not enough cause for liability. Two cases (*Ernst & Ernst v. Hochfelder* and *Denise L. Nappier et al. v. Pricewaterhouse-Coopers*) illustrate the need for purchasers and sellers of securities to prove scienter on the part of auditors and confirm the inability for these parties to bring suit against auditors for ordinary negligence. The *Hochfelder* case was also significant in that it provided exposure for auditors in cases of gross negligence, even in the absence of scienter.

Legal Precedent

ERNST & ERNST V. HOCHFELDER (U.S. SUPREME COURT, 1976)

The decision in this case established precedent for the plaintiff's need to allege and prove scienter to impose section 10(*b*) liability under the Securities Exchange Act. The issue was whether failure to exercise the appropriate level of professional care alone is sufficient. In this case, **Hochfelder** represented investors in an escrow account with **First Securities of Chicago;** this account was maintained by Lester Nay (president of First Securities), who diverted funds for his own personal use through a fraudulent scheme that was revealed in a suicide note prepared by Nay. The plaintiff (Hochfelder) specifically disclaimed any allegations of fraud or intentional misconduct on the part of **Ernst & Ernst,** but they wanted to see liability under section 10(*b*) imposed for ordinary negligence in the auditors' failure to uncover the fraudulent scheme.

The Court reasoned that section 10(*b*) in its reference to "employment of any manipulative and deceptive device" meant that intention to deceive, manipulate, or defraud is necessary to support a private cause of action under section 10(*b*) and failure to exercise the appropriate level of professional care is not sufficient. This decision is considered a landmark for auditors because it relieved them of liability for ordinary negligence under section 10(*b*) of the Securities Exchange Act and its companion SEC Rule 10(*b*)-5.

However, a footnote in this opinion (footnote 12) noted that "[in] certain areas of the law recklessness is considered to be a form of intentional conduct for purposes of imposing liability for some act. We need not address here the question whether, in some circumstances, reckless behavior is sufficient for civil liability under 10(b) and Rule 10b-5." This footnote provides potential exposure to auditors for gross negligence under the Securities Exchange Act, even in the absence of scienter.

DENISE L. NAPPIER ET AL. V. PRICEWATERHOUSECOOPERS (2002)

A class action suit brought on behalf of the shareholders was successful in asserting a claim against **Campbell Soup Company** and its directors for violations of the Securities Exchange Act. The shareholders then attempted to assert an additional claim against **PricewaterhouseCoopers.** The claim was that PricewaterhouseCoopers violated the provisions of the Securities Exchange Act by being a party to the preparation and certification of fraudulent financial statements. The case was dismissed when the shareholders could not prove the allegation that the firm operated with scienter in certifying Campbell's statements.

Section 18: Civil Liability

Section 18 sets forth the pertinent civil liability under the Securities Exchange Act. Under Rule 10*b*-5 and section 18, plaintiffs have the same burden of proof as under common law (that is, they must demonstrate that the loss was caused by reliance on the materially misstated financial statements and that auditors failed to exercise the appropriate level of professional care). However, under the Securities Exchange Act, plaintiffs must demonstrate scienter on the part of auditors. Thus, plaintiffs must demonstrate all of the following:

1. They suffered an economic loss
2. The financial statements were materially misstated.
3. The loss was caused by reliance on the materially misstated financial statements.
4. Auditors were aware that the financial statements were materially misstated (recall that, under *Hochfelder,* auditors may be held liable for gross negligence).

AUDITING INSIGHT Prove It!

The importance of placing the burden of proof on plaintiffs is demonstrated by two recent decisions by U.S. Courts of Appeals (*Tricontinental Industries v. PricewaterhouseCoopers, LLP* and *Lattanzio v. Deloitte & Touche, LLP*). In both cases, the courts dismissed charges against the accounting firms because plaintiffs failed to demonstrate that their losses were caused by materially misstated financial statements. The following excerpt from the Seventh Circuit Court in the former case is of particular note:

> Although we agree with the district court that **Tricontinental's** scienter allegations are problematic, we believe that Tricontinental's claim for pre-closing fraud suffers from a more fundamental

infirmity . . . Tricontinental's claim falls short with respect to the last requirement: Tricontinental does not allege how PwC's fraud caused its losses.

Clearly, the shift of burden of proof from auditors (in the Securities Act) to plaintiffs (in the Securities Exchange Act) is an important distinction and determinant in plaintiffs' ability to successfully prevail in securities actions.

Source: *Tricontinental Industries v. PricewaterhouseCoopers LLP,* 2007 U.S. App. LEXIS 7247 (7th Cir. January 17, 2007); *Lattanzio v. Deloitte & Touche LLP,* 476 F.3d 147 (2d Cir. 2007).

As a defense, auditors can attempt to demonstrate that they acted in good faith and had no knowledge of the material misstatement. This requirement parallels the *Ultramares* rule written into statute to the extent that proving good faith is equivalent to demonstrating that auditors' failure to exercise the appropriate level of professional care was no greater than ordinary negligence. (The *Ultramares* decision information was presented earlier in this module.)

Section 32: Criminal Liability

Section 32 states the criminal penalties for violation of the Securities Exchange Act. Like section 24 of the Securities Act, the critical test is whether the violator acted "willfully and knowingly." Therefore, in order to be subject to criminal liability, auditors must be shown to be guilty of fraud. The criminal penalties for violating the Securities Exchange Act were markedly increased by the Sarbanes-Oxley Act of 2002; currently, violators may be fined up to $5 million and imprisoned for up to 20 years. In addition, Sarbanes-Oxley provides that if the "person" was not a natural person (for example, an accounting firm), fines of up to $25 million can be assessed. The *United States v. Natelli* (better known as the "National Student Marketing" case) illustrates potential criminal liability for auditors charged with violations of section 32.

Legal Precedent

UNITED STATES V. NATELLI ("NATIONAL STUDENT MARKETING" CASE) (1975)

In this case, two auditors were convicted because of their involvement with materially misstated financial statements in the proxy statement of **National Student Marketing Corporation.** These materially misstated financial statements were related to the failure to reveal a $1 million write-off of "sales" (about 20 percent of the amount previously reported) and a corresponding large adjustment to National Student Marketing's operating income.

The court stated: "It is hard to probe the intent of a defendant. . . . When we deal with a defendant who is a professional accountant, it

is even harder at times to distinguish between simple errors of judgment and errors made with sufficient criminal intent to support a conviction, especially when there is no financial gain to the accountant other than his legitimate fee."

Both the audit partner and the supervisor were fined and received jail sentences of one year each. While a federal appeals court reversed the supervisor's conviction, it upheld the partner's conviction because of this apparent motive and action to conceal the effect of some accounting adjustments.

Foreign Corrupt Practices Act

In 1977, Congress passed the Foreign Corrupt Practices Act, which

- Made it illegal for corporations or their officers to knowingly bribe foreign officials or participate in bribery schemes involving foreign officials to obtain or retain business.
- Required entities to develop and maintain effective internal controls.

In 1988, the Foreign Corrupt Practices Act eventually became codified as an amendment to the Securities Exchange Act. As a result, auditors may be liable for violations of this act if they should have identified these violations during their examination.

SUMMARY OF AUDITORS' LIABILITY TO CLIENTS AND THIRD PARTIES

Thus far, we have discussed auditors' potential liability to clients and third parties under both common law and statutory law. Exhibit C.2 summarizes various elements of this liability, including (1) the level of professional care (performance) owed to various parties

EXHIBIT C.2 Summary of Auditors' Liability

Source of Liability	Party(ies) Involved	Plaintiff Proof	Type of Offense	Auditors' Defenses
Common law	Client	• Economic loss • Auditors' breach of contract or failure to exercise the appropriate level of professional care • Loss caused by breach of contract or failure to exercise appropriate level of professional care	• Breach of contract • Ordinary negligence • Gross negligence • Fraud	• No breach of contract or no failure to exercise the appropriate level of professional care • Economic loss caused by other factors (causation) • Clients partially responsible for loss (contributory negligence)
	Third parties	• Economic loss • Auditors' failure to exercise the appropriate level of professional care • Material misstatements in financial statements • Loss caused by reliance on materially misstated financial statements	• Ordinary negligence (depends upon jurisdiction and standing of party) • Gross negligence • Fraud	• Lack of appropriate standing (relationship) between third party and auditors • Third party did not rely on financial statements in decision • Loss caused by other factors • Work performed in accordance with GAAS or other professional standards
Securities Act of 1933	Purchasers of securities in an initial registration	• Economic loss • Material misstatements in financial statements	• Ordinary negligence • Gross negligence • Fraud	• "Due diligence" (auditors conducted a GAAS audit) • Loss caused by other factors
Securities Exchange Act of 1934	Purchasers and sellers of securities through ongoing exchanges	• Economic loss • Material misstatements in financial statements • Loss caused by reliance on materially misstated financial statements • Auditors were aware of material misstatements and acted with intent (scienter)	• Gross negligence • Fraud	• Auditors acted in good faith • Auditors had no knowledge of material misstatements

by auditors, (2) the burden of proof, and (3) various defenses available to auditors. Most noteworthy in Exhibit C.2 is that plaintiffs have the burden of proving that auditors' failure to exercise the appropriate level of professional care caused the loss ("burden of proof") under common law and the Securities Exchange Act of 1934; however, the burden of proof is with auditors under the Securities Act of 1933.

Review Checkpoints

C.18 Who may bring suit against auditors under the Securities Exchange Act? What must these parties demonstrate in order to bring suit?

C.19 What defenses are available to auditors under the Securities Exchange Act?

C.20 What are the criminal penalties associated with violations of the Securities Exchange Act?

C.21 What is *scienter*? How do the findings in *Ernst & Ernst v. Hochfelder* and *Denise L. Nappier et al. v. PricewaterhouseCoopers* relate to scienter?

C.22 What are the major differences in auditors' liability under the Securities Act of 1933 and the Securities Exchange Act of 1934?

THE CHANGING LANDSCAPE OF AUDITORS' LIABILITY

LEARNING OBJECTIVE

6. Understand recent developments that affect auditors' liability to clients and third parties

Legal defense expenses and liabilities for large damage awards consume approximately 10 percent of audit service revenues of the large accounting firms. The profession considers the U.S. tort liability system a crisis of expanding liability exposure in need of reform. Some important reforms that have been implemented or are currently being discussed in response to these damages are summarized in the remainder of this section. Some of these reforms influence auditors' liability under common law and statutory law described in the preceding sections.

Sarbanes-Oxley

The corporate scandals of Enron and WorldCom were the impetus for the creation and passage of the *U.S. Public Company Reform and Investor Protection Act of 2002,* better known as the Sarbanes-Oxley Act. Sarbanes-Oxley is aimed at strengthening corporate accountability and governance of public entities. While the more publicized aspects of Sarbanes-Oxley affect corporate officers and directors, some of its provisions affect auditors' statutory liability under the securities acts by increasing the penalties for auditors' involvement in financial statement fraud. Many of the aspects of Sarbanes-Oxley that affect auditors' planning, implementation, and reporting processes are discussed in other chapters in this book. Sarbanes-Oxley has impacted auditors' liability as follows:

- Sarbanes-Oxley extended the statute of limitations for bringing suit under the Securities Exchange Act to the earlier of (1) two years after the discovery of facts relating to violations of the act or (2) five years following the violation of the act. In addition, as noted earlier, the penalties for securities fraud have been increased to provide for fines of up to $5 million and imprisonment of up to 20 years for violations of the Securities Exchange Act.

- Sarbanes-Oxley increased penalties for mail fraud and wire fraud from five years of imprisonment to 20 years of imprisonment.

- Sarbanes-Oxley addressed the destruction, alteration, or falsification of records in federal investigations and bankruptcies. While these issues are addressed in laws regarding obstruction of justice and were the means by which the Department of Justice successfully prosecuted Arthur Andersen, Sarbanes-Oxley adds another avenue to

pursue accounting firms that fail to cooperate with federal investigations. Firms and individuals that are found to have altered or destroyed documents with the intent to impede an investigation may be subject to fines and imprisonment for up to 20 years. In addition, accountants performing an audit or review must maintain all engagement documentation for a period of five years. Firms that do not comply with the record-retention provision are subject to fines and imprisonment of up to 10 years. This provision of Sarbanes-Oxley has forced many firms to review and revise their record-retention policies.

In addition to the above, Sarbanes-Oxley amended federal sentencing guidelines that increase financial and criminal penalties when securities fraud, obstruction of justice, and criminal fraud exist. This means not only that auditors face a higher liability risk but also that Sarbanes-Oxley may influence the courts in decisions regarding awards in civil cases. These provisions are considered a setback for the accounting profession's initiative to reduce auditors' liability.

AUDITING INSIGHT When Does the Auditors' Responsibility End?

A recent case may expand liability under the Securities Exchange Act by requiring auditors to evaluate the appropriateness of previously-issued opinions. In *Overton v. Todman & Co, CPAs PC*, plaintiffs alleged that **Todman & Co.** (auditors) became aware of misstatements in the financial statements of **Direct Brokerage** following the issuance of their unqualified opinion on Direct Brokerage's financial statements in 2002 (these misstatements existed at the date of Todman & Co.'s opinion, but Todman & Co. was unaware of these misstatements at that time). These financial statements were subsequently used by David Overton to invest and loan over $2 million to

Direct Brokerage, which was lost when Direct Brokerage ceased operations in 2004.

The U.S. Court of Appeals for the Second District ruled that Todman & Co.'s failure to correct or withdraw its previously issued opinion resulted in liability under section 10(*b*) and Rule 10*b*-5. The court did note that its findings only required auditors to correct previous opinions for facts existing at the date of these opinions, not update these opinions based on subsequent developments.

Source: *David Overton and Jerome Kransdorf v. Todman & Co., CPAs, PC, and Trien, Rosenberg, Rosenberg, Weinberg, Ciulo & Fazzari,* 478 F.3d 479 (2d Cir. 2007).

Racketeer Influenced and Corrupt Organizations Act

The U.S. Supreme Court ruled that auditors are not subject to civil Racketeer Influenced and Corrupt Organizations Act (RICO) complaints unless they actually participated in the management or operation of a corrupt business. The important requirement is "active participation"; failure to exercise the appropriate level of professional care in an audit or advisory capacity is not enough to subject auditors to RICO. RICO was originally intended to combat organized crime in businesses and other organizations. Before this Supreme Court ruling, lawyers used RICO to subject auditors to threats of characterization as "racketeers" and imposition of treble damages under the law.

Aiding and Abetting

The U.S. Supreme Court limited the extent to which the doctrine of "aiding and abetting" could be used against auditors. Aiding and abetting means that plaintiffs could argue that auditors' failure to exercise the appropriate level of professional care or failure to find fraud and illegal acts amounted to complicity in a management's strategy to mislead investors and creditors; hence, auditors could be found liable for losses.

Organization of Accounting Firms as Limited Liability Partnerships

Almost all of the major accounting firms have names that end with the designation "LLP" (standing for limited liability partnership). Prior to 1990, accounting firms were organized as partnerships. One of the major disadvantages of the partnership form of organization is

that the personal assets of all partners within the firm were "at risk" (i.e., were subject to loss via litigation) for the actions of all others within the firm. In the early 1990s, decisions in New York and Hawaii to permit and recognize limited liability partnerships to practice within their jurisdictions led to accounting firms reorganizing themselves as limited liability partnerships.

A **limited liability partnership** combines the advantages of the traditional partnership form of organization (taxation of partnership income to the partners, limited ownership of partnership interests) with the liability protection afforded to corporations. Specifically, in a limited liability partnership, any claims against the partnership are limited to partnership assets, unless an individual partner directly participated in the action giving rise to the claim. After the Department of Justice indicted Arthur Andersen over the audits of Enron, some partners of the firm expressed concern about whether their limited liability partnership agreement would shield nonparticipating partners from claims (this was never strictly tested in the courts).[9] It is important to note that organization of the firm as a limited liability partnership does not affect the firm's legal liability, only the extent to which the individual partners' assets were subject to loss via litigation.

Proportionate Liability

One significant concern for auditors is the doctrine of **joint and several liability,** which allows a successful plaintiff to recover the full amount of a damage award from any defendant found to have failed to exercise the appropriate level of professional care, regardless of the relative guilt of this defendant compared to other defendant(s). Stated another way, if both the auditors and the client are found to have been responsible for misstatements in the client's financial statements, plaintiffs can seek recovery from either or both parties. Often in cases of business failures, auditors are the only parties with "deep pockets" of financial resources to pay damages. Thus, when a group of defendants (auditors, management, and client) is found liable for damages, auditors may be required to pay the entire amount even though they may be only partially at fault. In contrast, under **proportionate liability,** a defendant is required to pay a proportionate share of the court's damage award depending on the degree of fault determined by a judge and jury (e.g., 20 percent, 30 percent, but not 100 percent).

Proportionate liability was largely accomplished at the federal level in 1995 with the passage of the *Private Securities Litigation Reform Act*. Civil lawsuits for damages now are governed by these proportionate liability terms:

- The total responsibility for loss is divided among all parties responsible for the loss.
- If other defendant(s) are insolvent, a solvent defendant's liability is extended to 50 percent more than the proportion found at trial. (For example, if an accounting firm is found 20 percent responsible for a loss and the client and its managers are insolvent, the accounting firm will have to pay 30 percent of the loss but not 100 percent as before.)
- Only the defendants who knowingly committed a violation of securities laws remain jointly and severally liable for all of the plaintiffs' damages. (This is the imposition of penalty for actively participating in an actual fraud.)

The Private Securities Litigation Reform Act has included an exception to these provisions to compensate smaller investors. If plaintiffs have a net worth of less than $200,000 and lost 10 percent or more of the net worth because of auditors' failure to exercise appropriate levels of professional care, auditors will remain jointly and severally liable.

[9] "Partners Forever? Within Andersen, Personal Liability May Bring Ruin," *The Wall Street Journal*, April 2, 2002, pp. C1, C16.

AUDITING INSIGHT Joint and Several Liability

In July 2005, a federal jury found **Coopers & Lybrand** (which has since merged with Price Waterhouse to form Pricewaterhouse-Coopers) and the president of the client (**Ambassador Insurance Company**) to be jointly liable for losses incurred by policyholders of Ambassador, which became insolvent in 1983. While the jury assigned the liability as 60 percent against Arnold Chait (president of Ambassador) and 40 percent against Coopers & Lybrand,

Chait died during the 1990s with insufficient assets in his estate. As a result, PricewaterhouseCoopers is required to pay the entire $182.9 million settlement for an audit conducted over 20 years ago!

Sources: "PwC to Pay $182.9M for Coopers Audit," *CFO.com*, October 3, 2005; "Pricewaterhouse Is Ordered to Pay $182.9 million," *The Wall Street Journal*, October 5, 2005, p. B6.

Class Action Suits

It is not unusual for shareholders or investors who have suffered losses to band together and bring legal action against entities and/or auditors. In a **class action** suit, a relatively small number of aggrieved plaintiffs with small individual claims can bring suit for large damages in the name of an extended class. After a bankruptcy, for example, 50 bondholders who lost $40,000 might decide to sue, and can do so on behalf of the entire class of bondholders for *all* of their alleged losses (say $40 million). Attorneys take these cases on a contingency fee basis (a percentage of the judgment, if any). The size of the claim and the zeal of the attorneys can make the class action suit a serious matter. For example, the recent decision of an appeals court to "certify" a class action suit against **Wal-Mart** for sexual discrimination exposes the retailer to liability and potential damages to 1.5 million past and present female employees.

In the past, most class action lawsuits were adjudicated in state courts, and a great deal of "jurisdiction shopping" was performed to find a court that might be more sympathetic to the plaintiffs. Some of the large corporate failures (e.g., **Lincoln Savings and Loan, Enron, WorldCom**) have resulted in class action lawsuits that have proven costly for defendants to defend and difficult for them to win. In February 2005, the *Class Action Fairness Act* was signed into law. This act is designed to expand federal jurisdiction over class action lawsuits and is estimated to result in the movement of 40 percent of class action lawsuits from various state courts to federal court. Federal courts are preferable venues for defendants in class action lawsuits because

- Class action lawsuits come under more scrutiny in federal court compared to state courts.
- Federal courts have more resources at their disposal in managing class action cases than state courts.
- State courts have been alleged to unfairly discriminate against defendants from other jurisdictions.
- State court verdicts often affect plaintiffs in other jurisdictions (states). A verdict in federal court is regarded as more appropriate when it is applied to multiple jurisdictions.

It is important to note that not all class action lawsuits will come under federal jurisdiction and the rules for determining whether a state or federal court has jurisdiction over a case are complex. It is too early to determine the exact effects of the Class Action Fairness Act on lawsuits against auditors, but initial perceptions are that it may reduce class action lawsuits and provide a more impartial venue for auditors in defending themselves against class action lawsuits.

In addition to the Class Action Fairness Act, Congress enacted the *Securities Litigation Uniform Standards Act* in 1998. The most significant provision of this legislation requires that class action lawsuits with 50 or more parties must be filed in the federal courts. As noted earlier, federal courts are generally more favorable venues for class action lawsuits for the defendants (auditors).

AUDITING INSIGHT How Big Is the Class?

While the number of recent class action lawsuits brought by shareholders has declined, the average dollar amount of settlements has risen. From 2005 to 2006, the number of lawsuits filed by shareholders decreased from 178 to 110 (a decline of 38 percent). This is the smallest number of filings in a year since the passage of the Private Securities Litigation Reform Act. Of these cases, accounting-related issues comprise a larger proportion, increasing from 44 percent of the cases in 2005 to 68 percent in 2006.

However, all of the news is not favorable. The average dollar amount of corporate settlements rose from $73.6 million in 2005 to $86.7 million in 2006. This average was skewed by five large settlements during 2006 (these settlements were against the companies and/or their officers): $2.7 billion by **AOL Time Warner** (now **Time Warner**); $1.1 billion by **Royal Ahold NV**; two separate $1.1 billion settlements by **Nortel Networks**; and an unspecified portion of the total $7.1 billion settlement by **Enron**. These settlements are particularly noteworthy since prior to 2006, only three settlements of greater than $1 billion had been reached.

Sources: "Securities Class-Action Suits Sharply Decline," *CFO.com*, January 3, 2007; "Class-Action Settlement Size Is Surging," *CFO.com*, January 4, 2007.

Legal Precedent

DURA PHARMACEUTICALS V. BROUDO (2005)

Michael Broudo and others (class action lawsuit) purchased stock in **Dura Pharmaceuticals** and suffered a loss when the stock price declined. The plaintiff's case included allegations of securities fraud and misrepresentation regarding a new product, leading to an artificially high stock price at the time of purchase. In a unanimous opinion, the U.S. Supreme Court held that an allegation of inflated purchase price is insufficient by itself to demonstrate loss and causation for purposes of a private damages action for securities fraud under section 10(b) of the Securities Exchange Act and Securities and Exchange Commission Rule 10b-5.

Case conclusions: Two important aspects of this case follow:

1. It affirms the need to prove cause between the actions and damages.

2. Because many class action lawsuits are based on the decline in stock price following the actions of the defendant, this decision is likely to reduce the frequency of class action lawsuits.

Sources: *Dura Pharmaceuticals, Inc. et al. v. Michael Broudo et al.*, 544 U.S. 336 (2005); "Supreme Court Reverses Ninth Circuit's Loss Causation Standard," *Insights: The Corporate & Securities Law Advisor*, May 2005.

Auditors' Liability Caps

A final development in the legal liability arena is related to various measures of limiting (or "capping") auditors' liability to both clients and third parties. In their engagement letters, auditors are attempting to limit their potential liability to clients through wording such as the following (excerpted from **United Rental's** 2006 proxy statement):

> In connection with the audit of the 2005 financial statements, the company entered into an engagement agreement with **Ernst & Young LLP** . . . That agreement is subject to alternative dispute resolution procedures and an exclusion of punitive damages.

A strict reading of this language suggests that United Rental is barred from bringing suit against Ernst & Young and would need to seek redress through mediation and arbitration; further, it suggests that Ernst & Young would only be liable for compensatory (and not the often more costly punitive) damages. While the effectiveness of this language in limiting auditors' liability has not been legally tested, some negative publicity over these agreements has resulted in Ernst & Young recently deciding to no longer include language related to exclusion of punitive damages in its engagement letters (it continues to include the language related to alternative dispute resolution).[10]

[10] "More Companies are Disclosing Pacts with Auditors on Liability Caps," *The Wall Street Journal*, June 22, 2006, p. C4.

In addition to liability to clients, some recent actions have been taken to potentially limit auditors' liability to third parties. In late 2006, the Committee on Capital Markets Regulation (a group of business, financial, investor, legal, and accounting leaders) was formed in response to evidence that the U.S. public markets are losing registrants to foreign and private equity markets. Among other areas, their report addressed liability issues facing public entities and other parties (including auditors). While this group did not provide a specific recommendation, their report suggested dollar liability caps and safe harbors against certain types of auditing activities as a possible mechanism for protecting accounting firms against large monetary losses.[11] In addition, Conrad Hewitt (the SEC's chief accountant) recently called for limiting the exposure of accounting firms to lawsuits citing concerns if one of the remaining Big Four were to be forced out of business because of litigation.[12]

Review Checkpoints

C.23 List some of the major changes in auditors' liability provided by Sarbanes-Oxley.

C.24 What is the difference between *joint and several liability* and *proportionate liability?*

C.25 What changes did the Private Securities Litigation Reform Act make? What changes did the Class Action Fairness Act make?

C.26 What new requirement was enacted in the Securities Litigation Uniform Standards Act that affected class action lawsuits?

Summary

This module summarizes the potential liability auditors have to clients and third parties who rely upon their work. Auditors can be liable under either common law (based on prior legal decisions and precedents) or statutory law (violating a written law). Auditors' liability to clients arises through an economic loss suffered because of failure to perform in accordance with the contract (breach of contract) or because of auditors' failure to exercise the appropriate level of professional care (tort liability). Because of the close relationship between auditors and clients, auditors owe their clients a very high degree of performance and are liable when they commit ordinary negligence (lack of reasonable care), gross negligence (lack of minimal care), or fraud (knowledge and intent to deceive).

Auditors' liability to third-party investors or creditors under common law arises because of economic decisions made by these parties using audited financial statements. Under common law, auditors are liable to all third-party users for levels of failure to exercise the appropriate level of professional care representing gross negligence or fraud. With respect to ordinary negligence, three separate approaches to liability are for third parties who are primary beneficiaries *(Credit Alliance v. Arthur Andersen)*, foreseen third parties *(restatement of torts, Fleet National Bank v. Gloucester Co.)*, or foreseeable third parties *(Rosenblum, Inc. v. Adler)*. Auditors' liability to third parties for ordinary negligence is determined by the legal precedent in the jurisdiction in which the action is brought.

Liability to investors in securities is dictated by statutory law, the Securities Act of 1933 and the Securities Exchange Act of 1934. These acts differ based on both the burden of proof as well as the level of failure to exercise the appropriate level of professional care required to bring suit. Under the Securities Act, the burden of proof is on auditors; purchasers

[11] "Panel Seeks Cap on Liability of Accounting Firms," *The Wall Street Journal,* November 30, 2006, p. C3. The report of the committee can be found at www.capmktsreg.org/pdfs/11.30Committee_Interim_ReportREV2.pdf.
[12] "SEC's Hewitt: Indemnify the Big Four," *CFO.com,* January 29, 2007.

of securities may bring suit for ordinary negligence, gross negligence, or fraud. Under the Securities Exchange Act, the burden of proof is on purchasers or sellers of securities and suit can only be brought for gross negligence or fraud. Clearly, the Securities Act imposes the highest degree of care on auditors and the lowest barriers for plaintiffs to bring suits against auditors.

While the Sarbanes-Oxley Act has expanded both the statute of limitations as well as the penalties to auditors under the Securities Exchange Act, other recent developments have reduced (or advocate a reduction in) auditors' exposure to legal liability. These developments include the Private Securities Litigation Reform Act, the Class Action Fairness Act, and various calls for liability limitations (or caps).

Key Terms

breach of contract: A claim that a party to the contract did not perform in the manner prescribed in the contract, 590

causation defense: A defense available to auditors who can show that a plaintiff's economic loss was caused by a factor other than failure to exercise the appropriate level of professional care or breach of contract, 592

class action: A group of plaintiffs that come together in a legal action, 609

comfort letter: Letter issued by auditors to underwriters of securities that provides an opinion on the fairness of the issuers' financial statements, 599

common law: Liability for injuries that is based on reasons other than violation of a written law or statute. Under common law, legal precedent is used in assessing the degree of responsibility or fault of the parties, 590

constructive fraud: A failure to provide any care in fulfilling a duty owed to another including a reckless disregard for the truth, 593

contributory negligence: A legal defense theory in which the plaintiff's own failure to perform with the appropriate level of professional care bars recovery from auditors, 592

"deep pockets" theory: Situations in which lawsuits may be brought against auditors not because they are necessarily at fault, but because they are the only part with resources against which recovery can be made, 589

expectation gap: The difference between the actual work and assurance required by GAAS and the expectation of that work by the general public, 590

Financial Reporting Releases (FRRs): SEC staff reports that express new rules and policies about disclosure, 598

foreseeable parties: A wide range of individuals or organizations that might rely on auditors' work, 595

foreseen parties: A limited class of individuals or organizations that could be reasonably expected to rely on auditors' work, 594

Form 10-K: Financial statements and related disclosures provided by public companies on an annual basis under the securities acts, 597

Form 10-Q: Financial statements and related disclosures provided by public companies on a quarterly basis under the securities acts, 597

fraud: Misrepresentations of fact that an individual knows to be false, 592

gross negligence: Breach of duty owed to another party due to lack of minimal care, 592

initial public offering (IPO): The initial issuance of securities by a registrant entity to the investing public through a market. IPOs are subject to the provisions of the Securities Act of 1933, 598

joint and several liability: The legal doctrine that when multiple defendants are named, the full amount of a damage award may be collected from any of the defendants named in the lawsuit, even though they may be only partially at fault, 608

limited liability partnership: A form of organization adopted by most large accounting firms that combines the advantages of a traditional partnership with the liability protection afforded to corporations, 608

ordinary negligence: Unintentional breaches of duty owed to another due to a lack of reasonable care, 592

plaintiff: The person or organization that initiates a lawsuit, 591

privity of contract: Situations in which parties have a contractual relationship, 591

primary beneficiary: A person named in a contract for whom the services provided are intended who is known to auditors by name, 593

proportionate liability: Payment by a convicted defendant based on a share of the court's damage award that is proportional to the degree of fault determined by a judge and jury, 608

prospectus: A legal document offering securities for sale that includes the terms of the issue, name of the issuer, planned use of the proceeds, and historical financial statements, 598

Regulation S-K (SEC): Contains requirements relating to all business, analytical, and supplementary financial disclosures other than financial statements themselves, 598

Regulation S-X (SEC): Contains accounting requirements for annual and interim financial statements filed under both the Securities Act and the Securities Exchange Act, 598

safe harbor: Doctrine that holds blameless a person who acts in good faith. The burden of proof that the defendant did not act in good faith lies with the plaintiff, 600

scienter: Intent or knowledge of inappropriate actions prior to committing those actions (for example, auditors' knowledge of a misstatement in the financial statements and the intentional failure to disclose this misstatement in their report), 603

Staff Accounting Bulletins (SABs): Unofficial but important interpretations of Regulation S-X and Regulation S-K by SEC staff, 598

statutory law: Liability that is based on violations of written laws or statutes, 590

tort: Civil complaint that the action of one person caused injury (personal or financial) to another; such action against auditors is normally initiated by users of financial statements, 590

Multiple Choice Questions for Practice and Review

C.27 A lack of reasonable care that may be characterized by the failure of auditors to follow GAAS in the conduct of the audit is known as
 a. Constructive fraud.
 b. Fraud.
 c. Gross negligence.
 d. Ordinary negligence.

C.28 From the auditors' point of view, which of the following is a preferable provision for imposition of civil liability in a lawsuit for financial damages?
 a. Joint and several liability.
 b. Reasonably foreseeable users' approach to privity.
 c. Foreseen third parties' approach to privity.
 d. Proportionate liability.

C.29 Users of financial statements have a different perception concerning the nature of auditors' services than the actual objectives of an audit. This difference is known as
 a. Diverse liability perception.
 b. Reasonable foreseeable third parties.
 c. Insurance hypothesis.
 d. Expectations gap.

C.30 Individuals that believe they relied on misstated financial statements to make a decision and have lost money as a result will issue an action known as a
 a. Breach of contract.
 b. Tort.
 c. Securities litigation.
 d. Constructive fraud.

C.31 If auditors lost a civil lawsuit for damages, the court found total losses of $5 million, the auditors were found 30 percent at fault, the auditors were the only solvent defendant, and the court followed Private Securities Litigation Reform Act rules of proportionate liability, the court would order the auditors to pay
 a. $ 5,000,000.
 b. Zero.
 c. $2,250,000.
 d. $1,500,000.

C.32 Suppose the auditors in Question C.31 participated knowingly in commission of violations of securities laws (with managers and directors of the audit client); the court would order the auditors to pay

 a. $5,000,000.

 b. Zero.

 c. $2,250,000.

 d. $1,500,000.

C.33 When a client sues an accountant for failure to perform consulting work properly, the accountants' best defense is probably based on the idea of

 a. Lack of privity of contract.

 b. Contributory negligence on the part of the client.

 c. Lack of any measurable dollar amount of damages.

 d. No negligence on the part of the consultant.

C.34 When creditors who relied on an entity's audited financial statements lose money after a customer (the auditors' client) goes bankrupt, what must the plaintiff creditors in a lawsuit for damages show in a court that follows the limited exposure *(Credit Alliance)* privity doctrine?

 a. The auditors knew and specifically acknowledged identification of the creditors.

 b. The auditors could reasonably foresee them as beneficiaries of the audit because entities such as this client use financial statements to get credit from vendors.

 c. They were foreseen users of the audited financial statements because they were vendors of long standing.

 d. All of the above.

C.35 When accountants agree to perform a compilation or review of unaudited financial statements, the best way to avoid clients misunderstanding the nature of the work is to describe it completely in

 a. An engagement letter.

 b. The auditors' opinion.

 c. A report to the clients' board of directors at the close of the engagement.

 d. A management letter to the board of director's audit committee.

C.36 Entities desiring to sell stocks and bonds must provide a set of financial statements to any prospective purchaser. This set of financial statements and other information for prospective purchasers is known as a

 a. Prospectus.

 b. Review.

 c. Patron's acquisition statement.

 d. Projected audited financial information.

C.37 The Securities Act of 1933 and Securities Exchange Act of 1934 contain

 a. Civil liability provisions applicable to auditors.

 b. Criminal liability provisions applicable to auditors.

 c. Neither *a* nor *b*.

 d. Both *a* and *b*.

C.38 Which of the following third parties is known by name to auditors as the audit is conducted?

 a. Foreseeable third party.

 b. Foreseen third party.

 c. General third party.

 d. Primary beneficiary.

C.39 Which of the following would be auditors' most likely defense in an action brought under the Securities Exchange Act of 1934?

 a. The investor did not have privity with auditors.

 b. The investor did not suffer a loss based on the materially misstated financial statements.

 c. The auditors acted in good faith and were not aware of the materially misstated financial statements.

 d. The financial statements were not filed with the Securities and Exchange Commission.

C.40 Which of the following statements regarding auditors' liability under the Securities Act of 1933 is *not* true?

 a. This act relates to the initial issuance of securities to the public, normally through an initial public offering.

 b. Auditors' liability arises because of audited financial information filed with the SEC under this act.

 c. Third parties must demonstrate that they relied upon misstated financial statements that were examined by auditors.

 d. Auditors may be liable if they are found to have engaged in ordinary negligence.

C.41 Under the Securities Exchange Act of 1934, entities are required to report to the public about changing auditors on

 a. Form 10-K.

 b. Form S-1.

 c. Form 10-Q.

 d. Form 8-K.

C.42 Section 11(*b*) of the Securities Act of 1933 provides that people can be sued and may be liable for investors' losses in connection with a public securities offering under which of these circumstances?

 a. The chair of the board of directors performed a reasonable investigation of facts in connection with writing the section in the registration statement concerning the specification of the use of the proceeds of the offering.

 b. A consulting engineer performed a reasonable investigation and reported in the registration statement on the feasibility of construction of a roadway to be financed with the offering proceeds.

 c. The president of the issuing entity had no reason to doubt the report of the consulting engineer, although the president did not perform a separate reasonable investigation of her own.

 d. The officers of the issuing entity were relieved that the independent auditors did not make an issue about the excessive valuation of inventory held to support construction in progress.

C.43 In comparison to the burden of affirmative proof required of plaintiffs in civil lawsuits against independent auditors under the common law, section 10(*b*) of the Securities Exchange Act of 1934

 a. Is the same regarding plaintiffs' need to prove damages or losses.

 b. Is the same regarding plaintiffs' need to establish privity or a beneficiary relationship with auditors.

 c. Does not require that plaintiffs prove their reliance on materially misstated financial statements.

 d. Does not require that plaintiffs prove that relying on the materially misstated financial statements caused their losses.

C.44 Which of the following cases provides auditors with the broadest exposure for liability to third parties for ordinary negligence under common law?

 a. *Credit Alliance v. Arthur Andersen.*

 b. *Fleet National Bank v. Gloucester Co.*

 c. *Rosenblum, Inc. v. Adler.*

 d. *Ultramares.*

C.45 Which of the following is a major difference in auditors' liability under the Securities Act of 1933 and the Securities Exchange Act of 1934?

 a. The burden of proving reliance on misstated financial statements and the relationship between these financial statements and the economic loss.

 b. The auditors' required degree of professional care (level of substandard performance).

 c. Both of the above.

 d. None of the above.

C.46 When an entity registers a security offering under the Securities Act of 1933, the law provides an investor with

 a. An SEC guarantee that the information in the registration statement is true.

 b. Insurance against loss from the investment.

 c. Financial information examined by independent auditors.

 d. Inside information about the entity's trade secrets.

C.47 A group of investors sued Anderson, Olds, and Watershed, CPAs (AOW) for alleged damages suffered when the entity in which they held common stock went bankrupt. To avoid liability under the common law, AOW must prove which of the following?

 a. The investors actually suffered a loss.

 b. The investors relied on the financial statements audited by AOW.

 c. The investors' loss was a direct result of their reliance on the audited financial statements.

 d. The audit was conducted in accordance with generally accepted auditing standards and with due professional care.

C.48 The Securities and Exchange Commission document that governs accounting in financial statements filed with the SEC is

 a. Regulation D.

 b. Form 8-K.

 c. Form SB-1.

 d. Regulation S-X.

C.49 Which of the following cases upheld the requirement that plaintiffs demonstrate scienter when bringing action under the Securities Exchange Act of 1934?

 a. *Ernst & Ernst v. Hochfelder.*

 b. *Escott v. BarChris Construction Corp.*

 c. *Smith v. London Assurance Corp.*

 d. *Ultramares.*

C.50 A "public company" subject to the periodic reporting requirements of the Securities Exchange Act of 1934 must file an annual report with the SEC known as the

 a. Form 10-K.

 b. Form 10-Q.

 c. Form 8-K.

 d. Regulation S-X.

C.51 When investors sue auditors for damages under section 11 of the Securities Act of 1933, they must allege and prove

 a. Scienter on the part of auditors.

 b. The audited financial statements were materially misstated.

 c. They relied on the materially misstated financial statements.

 d. Their reliance on the materially misstated financial statements was the direct cause of their loss.

C.52 The official name of the Sarbanes-Oxley Act is

 a. The U.S. Corporate Governance Act of 2002.

 b. The U.S. Fair Reporting Act of 2002.

 c. The U.S. Public Company Reform and Investor Protection Act of 2002.

 d. The U.S. Executive and Director Liability Act of 2002.

C.53 Which of the following is not part of the Sarbanes-Oxley Act?

 a. An increased duty on the part of auditors to identify financial statement fraud.

 b. A requirement that the CEO and CFO certify the financial statements.

 c. Increased penalties for destruction of records in federal investigations.

 d. Increased penalties for mail fraud and criminal violations of the Securities Exchange Act of 1934.

Exercises, Problems, and Simulations

C.54 Breach of Contract. While large-dollar lawsuits brought by shareholders grab the headlines, auditors are most often sued by the client for breach of contract.

Required:

a. How can auditors be in breach of contract with a client?

b. How can a client be in breach of contract with auditors?

c. What are the best defenses for auditors against breach of contract lawsuits brought by their clients?

C.55 Common Law Responsibility for Errors and Fraud. Huffman & Whitman (H&W), a large regional accounting firm, was engaged by Ritter Tire Wholesale Company to audit its financial statements for the year ended January 31. H&W had a busy audit engagement schedule from December 31 through April 1 and decided to audit Ritter's purchase vouchers and related cash disbursements on a sample basis. The firm instructed staff members to select a random sample of 130 purchase transactions and gave directions about the important deviations, including missing receiving reports. Boyd, the assistant in charge, completed the audit documentation, properly documenting the fact that 13 of the purchases in the sample had been recorded and paid without including the receiving report (required by stated internal control procedures) in the file of supporting documents. Whitman, the partner in direct charge of the audit, showed the findings to Lock, Ritter's chief accountant. Lock appeared surprised but promised that the missing receiving reports would be inserted into the files before the audit was over. Whitman was satisfied, noted in the audit documentation that the problem was solved, and did not say anything to Huffman about it.

Unfortunately, H&W did not discover the fact that Lock was involved in a fraudulent scheme in which he diverted shipments of tires to a warehouse leased in his name and sent the invoices to Ritter for payment. He then sold the tires for his own profit. Internal auditors discovered the scheme during a study of slow-moving inventory items. Ritter's inventory was overstated by about $500,000 (20 percent), the amount Lock had diverted.

Required:

a. With regard to the 13 missing receiving reports, does a material weakness in internal control exist? If so, does Huffman & Whitman have any further audit responsibility? Explain.

b. Did Huffman & Whitman fail to exercise the appropriate level of professional care? Why or why not?

C.56 Common Law Responsibility for Errors and Fraud. Herbert McCoy is the president of McCoy Forging Corporation. For the past several years, Donovan & Company, CPAs, has performed the company's compilation and some other accounting and tax work. McCoy decided to have an audit. He had recently received a disturbing anonymous letter that stated, "Beware; you have a viper in your nest. The money is literally disappearing before your very eyes! Signed: A friend." He told no one about the letter.

McCoy Forging engaged Donovan & Company, CPAs, to render an opinion on the financial statements for the year ended June 30. McCoy told Donovan he wanted to verify that the financial statements were "accurate and proper." He did not mention the anonymous letter. The usual engagement letter providing for an audit in accordance with generally accepted auditing standards (GAAS) was drafted by Donovan & Company and signed by both parties.

The audit was performed in accordance with GAAS. The audit did not reveal a clever defalcation plan. Harper, the assistant treasurer, was siphoning off substantial amounts of McCoy Forging's money. The defalcations occurred both before and after the audit. Harper's embezzlement was discovered by McCoy's new internal auditor in October after Donovan had delivered the auditors' opinion. Although the scheme was fairly sophisticated, it could have been detected if Donovan & Company had performed additional procedures. McCoy Forging demands reimbursement from Donovan for the entire amount of the embezzlement, some $40,000 of which occurred before the audit and $65,000 after. Donovan has denied any liability and refuses to pay.

Required:

Discuss Donovan's responsibility in this situation. Do you think McCoy Forging could prevail in whole or in part in a lawsuit against Donovan under common law? Explain your conclusions.

(AICPA adapted)

C.57 **Auditors' Liability for Fraud.** Auditors may be liable to third parties for fraud in several ways.

Required:

a. Identify auditors' liability for fraud to third parties.

b. Distinguish between fraud and constructive fraud.

c. What is auditors' liability for constructive fraud to third parties?

d. In your opinion, is auditors' liability to third parties for fraud and constructive fraud appropriate (or "fair")?

C.58 **Audit Simulation: Accusation of Fraud.** (This exercise is based on the actual case of **Health Management, Inc.**) During the audit of the 1995 financial statements of Health Management Inc., $1.8 million of inventory in transit was placed on the entity's balance sheet. The auditors never obtained evidence of the existence of this inventory even though several questions were raised concerning the excessively large amount of inventory in transit at year end. In 1996, Health Management announced that it had discovered a series of accounting irregularities.

Required:

a. Do legal grounds exist to claim that the auditors committed fraud?

b. What would be the auditors' defense if such grounds exist? Why or why not?

C.59 **Common Law Liability Exposure.** An accounting firm was engaged to examine the financial statements of Martin Manufacturing Corporation for the year ending December 31. Martin needed cash to continue its operations and agreed to sell its common stock investment in a subsidiary through a private placement. The buyers insisted that the proceeds be placed in escrow because of the possibility of a major contingent tax liability that could result from a pending government claim against Martin's subsidiary. The payment in escrow was completed in late November. Martin's president told the audit partner that the proceeds from the sale of the subsidiary's common stock, held in escrow, should be shown on the balance sheet as an unrestricted current account receivable. The president held the opinion that the government's claim was groundless and that Martin needed an "uncluttered" balance sheet and a "clean" auditors' opinion to obtain additional working capital from lenders. The audit partner agreed with the president and issued an unqualified opinion on the Martin financial statements, which did not refer to the contingent liability and did not properly describe the escrow arrangement.

The government's claim proved to be valid and, pursuant to the agreement with the buyers, the purchase price of the subsidiary was reduced by $450,000. This adverse development forced Martin into bankruptcy. The accounting firm is being sued for deceit (fraud) by several of Martin's unpaid creditors who extended credit in reliance on the accounting firm's unqualified opinion on Martin's financial statements.

Required:

a. What deceit (fraud) do you believe the creditors are claiming?

b. Is the lack of privity between the accounting firm and the creditors important in this case?

c. Do you believe the accounting firm is liable to the creditors? Explain.

(AICPA adapted)

C.60 **Common Law Liability Exposure.** Risk Capital Limited, a Delaware corporation, was considering the purchase of a substantial amount of treasury stock held by Florida Sunshine Corporation, a closely held corporation. Initial discussions with the Florida Sunshine Corporation began late in 2008.

Wilson and Wyatt, Florida Sunshine's auditors, regularly prepared quarterly and annual unaudited financial statements. The most recently prepared financial statements were for the year ended September 30, 2008.

On November 15, 2008, after extensive negotiations, Risk Capital agreed to purchase 100,000 shares of no par, class A capital stock of Florida Sunshine at $12.50 per share. However, Risk Capital insisted on audited statements for calendar year 2008. The contract that was made available to Wilson and Wyatt specifically provided:

> Risk Capital shall have the right to rescind the purchase of said stock if the audited financial statements of Florida Sunshine for the calendar year 2008 show a material adverse change in the financial condition of the corporation.

The audited financial statements furnished to Florida Sunshine by Wilson and Wyatt showed no such material adverse change. Risk Capital relied on the audited statements and purchased the treasury stock of Florida Sunshine. It was subsequently discovered that, as of the balance sheet date, the audited statements were incorrect and that in fact there had been a material adverse change in the financial condition of the corporation. Florida Sunshine is insolvent and Risk Capital will lose virtually its entire investment.

Risk Capital seeks recovery against Wilson and Wyatt.

Required:

Assuming that only ordinary negligence is proved, will Risk Capital prevail

a. Under a privity of contract standard?

b. Under a primary beneficiary standard?

c. Under a foreseen parties standard?

C.61 **Common Law Liability Exposure.** Smith, CPA, is the auditor for Juniper Manufacturing Corporation, a privately owned entity that has a June 30 fiscal year. Juniper arranged for a substantial bank loan, which depended on the bank receiving audited financial statements showing a current ratio of at least 2 to 1. The bank's deadline for receiving these financial statements was September 30. On September 25, just before the auditors' opinion was to be issued, Smith received an anonymous letter on Juniper's letterhead indicating that a five-year lease by Juniper, as lessee, of a factory building that was in the financial statements as an operating lease was in fact a capital lease. The letter stated that Juniper had a secret written agreement with the lessor modifying the lease and creating a capital lease.

Smith confronted the president of Juniper, who admitted that a secret agreement existed but said it was necessary to treat the lease as an operating lease to meet the current ratio requirement of the pending loan and that nobody would ever discover the secret agreement with the lessor. The president said that if Smith did not issue a report by September 30, Juniper would sue Smith for substantial damages that would result from not getting the loan. Under this pressure and because the audit documentation contained a copy of the five-year lease agreement supporting the operating lease treatment, Smith issued the report with an unqualified opinion on September 29. In spite of the fact that the loan was received, Juniper went bankrupt. The bank is suing Smith to recover its losses on the loan and the lessor is suing Smith to recover uncollected rents.

Required:

Answer the following, setting forth reasons or any conclusions stated.

a. Is Smith liable to the bank?

b. Is Smith liable to the lessor?

c. Was Smith independent?

(AICPA adapted)

C.62 **Liability in a Review Engagement.** Mason & Dilworth (M&D), CPAs, were auditors for Hotshot Company, a closely held corporation owned by 30 residents of the area. Hotshot had previously engaged M&D to perform some compilation and tax work. Bubba Crass, Hotshot's president and holder of 15 percent of the stock, said he needed something more than these services. He told Mason, the partner in charge, that he wanted financial statements for internal use, primarily for management purposes but also to obtain short-term loans from financial institutions. Mason recommended a "review" of the financial statements. Mason did not prepare an engagement letter.

During the review work, Mason had some reservations about the financial statements. Mason told Dilworth at various times he was "uneasy about certain figures and conclusions," but he would "take Crass's word about the validity of certain entries since the review was primarily for internal use in any event and was not an audit."

M&D did not discover a material act of fraud committed by Crass. The fraud would have been detected had Mason not relied so much on the unsupported statements Crass made concerning the validity of the entries about which he had felt so uneasy.

Required:

a. What potential liability might M&D have to Hotshot Company and other stockholders?

b. What potential liability might M&D have to financial institutions that used the financial statements in connection with making loans to Hotshot Company?

(AICPA adapted)

C.63 **Class Action Lawsuits.** In the United States, it has become common to seek recovery of financial losses from other parties, often even if that other party is not at fault. Frequently this occurs by means of a class action lawsuit.

Required:
a. Define class action lawsuit.
b. What advantages does a class action lawsuit have for the plaintiffs?
c. What disadvantages does a class action lawsuit have for the defendant?
d. How has recent legislation affected class action lawsuits?
e. Review *The Wall Street Journal*, *Barron's*, or other major newspapers and business periodicals for class action lawsuits against auditors. What are the (1) particulars of the lawsuit and (2) auditors' defenses?

C.64 **Liability under Common Law and the Securities Act of 1933.** Butler Manufacturing Corporation raised capital for a plant expansion by borrowing from a bank and making a stock offering. Butler engaged Weaver, CPA, to audit its December 2008 financial statements. Butler told Weaver that the financial statements would be given to Union Bank and certain other named banks and included in a registration statement for the stock offering.

In performing the audit, Weaver did not confirm accounts receivable and therefore failed to discover a material overstatement. Weaver also was aware of a pending class action product liability lawsuit that was not disclosed in Butler's financial statements. Despite being advised by Butler's legal counsel that the entity's potential liability under the lawsuit would result in material losses, Weaver issued an unqualified opinion on Butler's financial statements.

In May 2009, Union Bank relied on the financial statements and Weaver's opinion to grant Butler a $500,000 loan.

Butler raised additional funds in November 2009 with a $14,000,000 unregistered offering of preferred stock. This offering was sold directly by the entity to 40 nonaccredited private investors during a one-year period.

Shortly after obtaining the Union Bank loan, Butler experienced financial problems but was able to stay in business because of the money raised by the stock offering. Butler lost the product liability suit, resulting in a judgment the entity could not pay. Butler also defaulted on the Union Bank loan and was involuntarily petitioned into bankruptcy. This caused Union Bank to sustain a loss and Butler's stockholders' investments became worthless.

Union Bank sued Weaver for failure to provide the appropriate level of professional care and common law fraud. The stockholders who purchased Butler's stock through the offering sued Weaver, alleging fraud under section 17 of the Securities Act of 1933.

These transactions took place in a jurisdiction providing for auditors' liability for ordinary negligence to known and intended users of financial statements.

Required:
Answer the following questions and give the reasons for your conclusions.
a. Will Union Bank be successful in its suit against Weaver under common law for (1) ordinary negligence and (2) fraud?
b. Will the stockholders who purchased Butler's stock through the offering succeed against Weaver under the antifraud provisions of section 17 of the Securities Act of 1933?

(AICPA adapted)

C.65 **Audit Simulation: Liability under the Securities Acts.** One of your firm's clients, Fancy Fashions, Inc., is a highly successful, rapidly expanding entity. It is owned predominantly by the Munster family and key corporate officials. Although additional funds would be available on a short-term basis from its bankers, they would represent only a temporary solution of the entity's need for capital to finance its expansion plans. In addition, the interest rates being charged are not appealing. Therefore, Chris Munster, Fancy's chairman of the board, in consultation with the other shareholders, has decided to explore the possibility of raising additional equity capital of approximately $15 million to $16 million. This will be Fancy's first public offering.

At a meeting of Fancy's major shareholders, its attorneys and a member of your firm spoke about the advantages and disadvantages of "going public" and registering a stock offering. One of the shareholders suggested that Regulation D under the Securities Act of 1933 might be a preferable alternative.

Required:

a. Assume that Fancy makes a public offering for $16 million and, as a result, more than 1,000 persons own shares of the entity. Following the public offering, what are the implications with respect to the Securities Exchange Act of 1934? (*Hint:* You can identify the thresholds for being subject to the reporting requirements of the Securities Exchange Act of 1934 through reference to the SEC's Web site, www.sec.gov).

b. What federal civil and criminal liabilities under the Securities Act of 1933 could apply in the event that Fancy sells the securities without registration and a registration exemption is not available?

c. Using the SEC's Web site (www.sec.gov) as a reference, define "accredited investor" and discuss the exemption applicable to offerings made under Regulation D for accredited investors.

(AICPA adapted)

C.66 **Audit Simulation: Section 11 of Securities Act of 1933: Liability Exposure.** Chriswell Corporation decided to raise additional long-term capital by issuing $20 million of 12 percent subordinated debentures to the public. May, Clark & Company, CPAs, the company's auditors, were engaged to examine the June 30, 2009, financial statements, which were included in the bond registration statement.

May, Clark & Company completed its examination and submitted an unqualified auditors' report dated July 15, 2009. The registration statement was filed and became effective on September 1, 2009. On August 15, one of the partners of May, Clark & Company called on Chriswell Corporation and had lunch with the financial vice president and the controller. He questioned both officials on the company's operations since June 30 and inquired whether there had been any material changes in the company's financial position since that date. Both officers assured him that everything had proceeded normally and that the financial condition of the company had not changed materially.

Unfortunately, the officers' representation was not true. On July 30, a substantial debtor of the company failed to pay the $400,000 due on its account receivable and indicated to Chriswell that it would probably be forced into bankruptcy. This receivable was shown as a collateralized loan on the June 30 financial statements. It was secured by stock of the debtor corporation, which had a value in excess of the loan at the time the financial statements were prepared but was virtually worthless at the effective date of the registration statement. This $400,000 account receivable was material to the financial condition of Chriswell Corporation and the market price of the subordinated debentures decreased by nearly 50 percent after the foregoing facts were disclosed.

The debenture holders of Chriswell are seeking recovery of their loss against all parties connected with the debenture registration.

Required:

Are May, Clark & Company liable to the Chriswell debenture holders under section 11 of the Securities Act of 1933? Explain. (*Hint:* Review the *BarChris* case in this chapter.)

(AICPA adapted)

C.67 **Rule 10b-5 Liability under the Securities Exchange Act of 1934.** Gordon & Groton (G&G), CPAs, were auditors of Bank & Company, a brokerage firm and member of a national stock exchange. G&G examined and reported on the financial statements of Bank, which were filed with the Securities and Exchange Commission.

Several of Bank's customers were swindled by a fraudulent scheme perpetrated by Bank's president, who owned 90 percent of the voting stock of the company. The facts establish that G&G failed to perform the audit with the appropriate level of professional care but neither participated in the fraudulent scheme nor knew of its existence.

The customers are suing G&G under the antifraud provisions of section 10(b) and Rule 10b-5 of the Securities Exchange Act of 1934 for aiding and abetting the fraudulent scheme

of the president. The customers' suit for fraud is predicated exclusively on G&G's failure to conduct a proper audit, thereby failing to discover the fraudulent scheme.

Required:

Answer the following, setting forth reasons for any conclusions stated:

a. What is the probable outcome of the lawsuit?

b. What might be the result if plaintiffs had sued under common law for ordinary negligence? Explain.

(AICPA adapted)

C.68 **Audit Simulation: Independence and Securities Exchange Act of 1934.** Anderson, Olds, and Watershed (AOW) has been the independent auditors for Accord Corporation since 1990. Accord is a public entity obligated to file periodic reports under the Securities Exchange Act of 1934.

Beginning in January 2008, the AOW litigation support consulting division performed a special engagement for Accord. The work involved a lawsuit that Accord had filed against Civic Company for patent infringement on microchip manufacturing processes. AOW personnel compiled production statistics—costs and lost profits—under various volume assumptions and then testified in court about the losses to Accord that resulted from Civic's improper use of patented processes. The amounts at issue were very large, with claims of $50 million for lost profits and a plea for $150 million punitive damages. Accord won a court judgment for a total of $120 million and Civic has appealed the damage award. The case remained pending throughout 2008 and into 2009. By March 1, 2009, AOW had billed Accord $265,000 for the litigation support work.

In November 2008, AOW started the audit work on Accord's financial statements for the fiscal year ending December 31, 2008. During this work, AOW auditors found that Accord's management and board of directors did not fully disclose the stage of the appeal of the Civic case, had improperly deferred a material loss on new product start-up costs as an element of its inventory, and had accrued sales revenue for promotional chip sales that carried an unconditional right of return. As partner in charge of the engagement, D. Ward agreed with the president that the accounting and disclosure were suitable to protect Accord's shareholders from adverse business developments and he issued a standard unqualified opinion that was included in the entity's 10-K annual report filed with the SEC and dated April 1, 2009.

AOW then billed Accord for the $200,000 audit fee and sent a reminder for payment of the $265,000 consulting fee; both billings were dated April 2, 2009.

Required:

a. Was AOW independent for the audit of Accord for the fiscal year ended December 31, 2008? Explain.

b. Did Ward and AOW follow generally accepted auditing standards in the audit? Cite any specific standards that might have been violated and explain your reasoning.

c. Did Ward and AOW violate any section(s) of the Securities Exchange Act of 1934? Explain.

C.69 **Audit Simulation: Auditors' Liability under Securities Exchange Act of 1934.** Adam, an Illinois resident, was interested in purchasing stock in Joshua Foods, Inc. Joshua Foods has corporate headquarters in Fond du Lac, Wisconsin, and is incorporated in Delaware. Adam e-mailed Joshua Foods' Investor Relations Department and requested its 2008 annual report including the financial statements. Adam also reviewed several analysts' opinions on the Internet, including the opinions provided from his Internet broker, Matthew & Co. Express-Trade. Adam received the annual report in the mail. Based on the increasing revenues, the $8 million net income indicated on the financial statements, and the other information received from the analysts, Adam purchased $350,000 worth of stock.

Three months later, Joshua Foods announced that over the last three years, the company had included $25 million of fictitious revenue and had capitalized more than $30 million of charges that should have been expensed. These irregularities will result in a restatement of the fiscal 2006 financial statements resulting in a $1,250,000 loss for fiscal 2008. The press release from the company says that it will likely declare bankruptcy in the next few weeks. In the following two weeks, the value of Adam's holdings in the stock declined to $50,000.

Required:

a. You are Adam's attorney. List the various legal issues and precedents that you will use in trying to recover the losses Adam sustained.

b. You are the attorney for Joshua Foods' auditors. It is apparent that Adam will try to recover losses from your firm. List the defenses you would prepare to protect auditors from liability.

c. How does Sarbanes-Oxley affect the position of either Adam's attorney or the auditors' attorney? You may find www.sarbanes-oxley.com helpful.

C.70 **Mini-Case: Limiting Legal Liability.**
Refer to the mini-case "To Indemnify or Not to Indemnify: That is the Question" and respond to Questions 1 through 3.

C.71 **Mini-Case: Litigation.**
Refer to the mini-case "Unhealthy Accounting at HealthSouth" and respond to Question 6.

C.72 **Mini-Case: Ethics.**
Refer to the mini-case "Andersen: An Obstruction of Justice?" and respond to Questions 1, 2, 3, 4, 5, and 7.

C.73 **Kaplan CPA Exam Simulation: Securities Act of 1933.**

Required:

Go to the Kaplan Web site at www.mhhe.com/louwers3e, click on AUD: Hardi Risk and Independence and the "Research" tab, and complete the assigned task.

Internal, Governmental, and Fraud Audits

Professional Standards References

Compendium Section	Document Reference	Topic
AU 322	SAS 65	"The Auditor's Consideration of the Internal Audit Function in an Audit of Financial Statements"
	ISA 610	"Considering the Work of Internal Auditing"
AU 316	SAS 99	"Consideration of Fraud in a Financial Statement Audit"
	ISA 240	"The Auditor's Responsibility to Consider Fraud in an Audit of Financial Statements"
AU 317	SAS 54	"Illegal Acts by Clients"
AU 319	SAS 78	"Consideration of Internal Control in a Financial Statement Audit: An Amendment to Statement on Auditing Standards No. 55"
AU 801	SAS 74	"Compliance Auditing Considerations in Audits of Governmental Entities and Recipients of Governmental Financial Assistance"
AT 601	SSAE 10	"Compliance Attestation"
	IIA 1100	"Independence and Objectivity"
	IIA 1110	"Organizational Objectivity"
	IIA 1120	"Individual Objectivity"
	IIA 1210	"Proficiency"
	IIA 2000	"Managing the Internal Audit Activity"
	IIA 2100	"Nature of Work"
	IIA 2110	"Risk Management"
	IIA 2120	"Control"
	IIA 2130	"Governance"
	IIA 2200	"Engagement Planning"
	IIA 2201	"Planning Considerations"
	IIA 2210	"Engagement Objectives"
	IIA 2220	"Engagement Scope"
	IIA 2300	"Performing the Engagement"
	IIA 2400	"Communicating Results"
	IIA 2410	"Criteria for Communicating"
	IIA 2420	"Quality of Communications"
	IIA 2600	"Management's Acceptance of Risks"
ET 101.12		"Ethics Interpretation 101-10. The Effect on Independence of Relationships with Entities Included in the Governmental Financial Statements"
ET 501.04		"Ethics Interpretation 501-3. Failure to Follow Standards and/or Procedures in Governmental Audits"
ET 501.06		"Ethics Interpretation 501-5. Failure to Follow Requirements of Governmental Bodies in Attest or Similar Services"

I predict that audit committees will look increasingly to internal audit departments to be their eyes and ears across the corporation

Jacqueline K. Wagner, General Auditor, General Motors Corporation, and past chair of the Institute of Internal Auditors

Learning Objectives

This module introduces governmental, internal, and fraud auditing. These fields differ in important respects from financial statement auditing practiced by independent CPAs in public accounting. However, you will find that all the fields of auditing share many similarities. Fraud auditing can be very exciting. It has the aura of detective work—finding things people want to keep hidden. The explanations and examples in this module will help you understand the working environment, objectives, and procedures that characterize governmental, internal, and fraud auditing.

Your learning objectives are to be able to:

1. Define *internal auditing;* describe internal audit institutions (e.g., IIA); describe how internal auditors interact with independent auditors; explain internal auditors' independence problems; and list features of internal reports.

2. Define *governmental auditing;* describe governmental audit institutions (e.g., GAO); describe how governmental auditors interact with independent auditors; explain governmental auditors' independence problems; and list features of governmental audit reports.

3. Explain the function of standards and measurements in economy, efficiency, and program results audits.

4. Describe the Single Audit Act of 1984 in relation to audits of governmental fund recipients.

5. Define *fraud auditing* and describe various engagements performed by fraud auditors.

6. Describe the elements necessary for a successful fraud examination and explain the differences between how fraud examiners and external auditors handle evidence.

7. Describe the ways CPAs can assist in prosecuting fraud perpetrators.

INTRODUCTION

In the summer of 2002, **WorldCom** announced that its financial statements were misstated by more than $7 billion. The misstatement was the result of capitalizing ordinary expenses. The accounting fraud was discovered by WorldCom's Vice President of Internal Audit, Cynthia Cooper. Despite opposition from WorldCom's chief financial officer, Ms. Cooper took her findings to the chairman of the audit committee of WorldCom's board of directors. The actions of WorldCom's internal auditors led to the disclosure of one of the largest financial statement frauds in history. Ms. Cooper was subsequently named one of *Time* magazine's three "2003 Persons of the Year."

"EXTERNAL," GOVERNMENTAL, AND INTERNAL AUDITS

In today's environment of Sarbanes-Oxley, the Public Company Accounting Oversight Board (PCAOB), and increased public scrutiny, public accounting firms are being asked to do more. While public accounting firms are no longer able to provide internal audit services to their publicly traded audit clients, nonclients in need of assistance have turned to other public accounting firms for internal audit, fraud assistance, and other related services. Currently, one of the fastest-growing segments in most large public accounting firms is outsourced internal audit services and this opportunity has led to several new business ventures focused primarily on providing internal audit and other (nonaudit) services to clients (e.g., **Protiviti Inc.**).

Many of the tasks and processes performed by internal auditors and government auditors are similar to those tasks performed by external auditors when expressing an opinion

on financial statements. However, services performed by government and internal auditors vary considerably. When internal and governmental auditors perform audits of financial information, the scope of the engagement typically is greater than the scope of an audit performed by an external auditor. Internal auditors and governmental auditors often have objectives that go beyond the fair presentation of the financial numbers such as the efficiency of the financial reporting process. Further, these auditors often audit monthly statements or financial reports to ensure reliable information for management decisions. In this module, we will explore the services provided by internal auditors and government auditors and gain an understanding of the elements that delineate a quality audit.

There is often confusion when discussing internal auditing, government auditing, and financial statement auditing performed by public accounting firms. Many governmental and internal auditors are CPAs and perform services similar to those performed by public accounting firms. Indeed, several state audit organizations are considered independent auditors and issue opinions on the financial statements of government agencies. At the same time, many public accounting firms are employed to audit the financial statements of government entities such as counties, cities, and school districts. To further complicate the discussion, many public accounting firms offer internal audit services to non-SEC clients and non–financial statement audit clients alike. It is important to note that while the Public Company Accounting Oversight Board (PCAOB) prohibits auditors of public companies from providing internal audit services to their public audit clients, auditors of privately held companies may still provide both internal and external audit services to their clients. For purposes of this module, therefore, external auditing will be used to refer to financial statement auditing performed by CPAs in public accounting firms and thereby distinguish public practice from governmental and internal practice.

INTERNAL AUDITS

LEARNING OBJECTIVE

1. Define *internal auditing;* describe internal audit institutions (e.g., IIA); describe how internal auditors interact with independent auditors; explain internal auditors' independence problems; and list features of internal reports.

In the past, *internal auditors* have been defined as auditors working for the organization that they were auditing. Internal auditors were employed by an organization such as a bank, hospital, city government, or industrial company. However, in recent years, many external auditors are providing internal audit services to the business community. Therefore, internal auditors may now be employed by either the organization they are auditing or an independent professional services firm.[1] Many corporations believe that they gain expertise and improve control over audit costs when the internal audit function is "outsourced" to an external audit firm. Conversely, many companies believe that an "in-house" internal audit function is better aligned with the company's goals and objectives and auditors gain more experience and expertise with the company's organization and business. Currently we are seeing more firms implementing a "co-sourcing strategy," where the company retains an "in-house" internal audit department augmented with auditors from an outside firm. This strategy allows the company to have a core audit group dedicated to the company with specialized "institutional knowledge" in company policy, procedure, and strategy, yet the company can employ the expert industry and audit knowledge of a professional services firm directly to specific engagements or projects.

The Institute of Internal Auditors (IIA), the organization that sets standards and governs the internal audit profession, defines **internal auditing** and states its objective as follows:

> Internal auditing is an independent, objective, assurance and consulting activity designed to add value and improve an organization's operations. It helps an organization accomplish its objectives by bringing a systematic, disciplined approach to evaluate and improve effectiveness of risk management, control, and governance processes.

There are several key elements in this definition that warrant further evaluation.

[1] Professional services firms include public accounting firms that offer a variety of auditing, accounting, and consulting services and some consulting firms that do not perform financial statement audit services but do provide other services including internal audit services (e.g., Protiviti).

Independence

You may be wondering how internal auditors employed by the company being audited can classify themselves as independent and objective. Although internal auditors employed by the entity under audit cannot be disassociated from their employers in the eyes of the public, they seek organizational and individual independence. Internal auditors achieve independence during the audit process when they are free from direction or constraint by the managers of the business unit under audit. To establish this organizational independence, many internal audit organizations report directly to the audit committees of the boards of directors. Such a reporting relationship reduces management's influence over the audit scope and reporting (IIA *Standards 1100* and *1110*).

An element that greatly assists the internal audit department in establishing an independent and objective organization is the audit charter. While many departments and organizations have charters, it is particularly important for the internal audit department. An internal audit charter approved by senior management and the board of directors provides

- A commitment from management to the establishment of an independent and objective audit organization.
- A definition of the authority and responsibility of the audit department.
- A definition of the scope of the audit department's activities.
- The department's authorization to perform audits, request materials, and gather evidence.
- The performance and reporting requirements for the audit department.

These elements provide a tremendous foundation for building an independent department. The audit charter for the Chicago Mercantile Exchange is provided in Exhibit D.1.

The other key aspect of independence and objectivity concerns the attitude of the individuals engaged in the audit. An internal auditor must have an impartial, unbiased attitude in performing the audit. In addition, individual auditors must not have any conflicts of interests. Such conflicts may result when the same company employs family members or outside business interests appear to affect audit judgments (See IIA *Standard 1120* and the IIA Code of Ethics).

As previously mentioned, many public accounting firms are performing internal audit work for clients. While this is strictly prohibited for public companies by Sarbanes-Oxley, the Public Company Accounting Oversight Board, and the Securities and Exchange Commission, public accounting firms can provide internal audit services to clients that are not publicly traded and to publicly traded companies who are not audit clients. However, great care should be given concerning independence issues, both independence in fact and independence in appearance. Auditors should take great care to avoid even the appearance that they are auditing their own work or are biased in their audit judgments due to revenue and relations emanating from internal audit work.

AUDITING INSIGHT Does Everyone Know What They're Doing?

An auditor was reviewing the mortgage procedures at a large bank including a discussion with a clerk in charge of escrow accounts. The clerk knew about receiving funds and placing them in the escrow account. The clerk knew to pay for surveys, inspections, title investigations, and other fees from the escrow account. However, the clerk was not aware that once the property sale was completed, any remaining funds were to be taken by the bank as revenue. The auditor found $77,000 in unrecorded revenue.

Value-Added Audit

The objectives of an internal audit and an external audit are vastly different. Generally speaking, internal auditors perform little of their work on the financial statements. In-house internal auditors audit their companies all year, often months removed from both

CHICAGO MERCANTILE EXCHANGE INC.

Internal Audit Charter

MISSION and SCOPE of WORK

Chicago Mercantile Exchange Inc.'s (CME) Internal Audit Department serves the Audit Committee of the Board of Directors and management as an independent, objective assurance, and consulting activity designed to add value and to improve CME's operations. The Internal Audit Department will:

- Assist CME in accomplishing its objectives by partnering with management to provide solution-oriented quality audit services.
- Bring a systematic, disciplined approach to evaluating and improving the effectiveness of risk management and control processes.

The scope of work of the Internal Audit Department is to determine whether the organization's network of risk management and control processes, as designed and represented by management, is adequate and functioning in a manner to ensure:

- Risks are appropriately identified and managed.
- Significant financial, managerial, and operating information is accurate, reliable, and timely.
- Employees' actions are in compliance with policies, standards, procedures, and applicable laws and regulations.
- Resources are acquired economically, used efficiently, and adequately protected.
- Significant legislative or regulatory issues impacting the organization are recognized and addressed appropriately.

Opportunities for improving management control, profitability, and the organization's image may be identified during audits. These opportunities will be communicated to the appropriate level of management.

RESPONSIBILITY

The Internal Audit Department is responsible for:

- Providing an annual assessment on the adequacy and effectiveness of the organization's internal control processes and management of risks in the areas set forth above.
- Developing, implementing, and communicating to the Audit Committee and management an annual audit plan using an appropriate risk-based methodology. The plan will give consideration to risks, control concerns, and special projects identified by management and the Audit Committee. To address changing risk situations, modifications to the plan may be required on an ongoing basis.
- Issuing periodic reports to the Audit Committee and management summarizing the results of internal audit activities.
- Reporting significant issues and potential improvements via a written report at the conclusion of each audit, as appropriate.
- Maintaining an audit staff with sufficient knowledge, skills, experience, and professional certifications to meet the requirements of this Charter. The adequacy of department staffing resources will be periodically communicated to the Audit Committee.
- Conducting follow-up audits with the auditee at appropriate intervals until all significant open corrective plans have been closed.
- Assisting in the investigation of significant suspected fraudulent activities within the organization and notifying management and the Audit Committee of the results.
- Considering the scope of work of the independent accountants, regulators, and other control and monitoring functions for the purpose of providing optimal audit coverage to the organization at a reasonable overall cost.

INDEPENDENCE and AUTHORITY

The Internal Audit Department reports functionally and administratively to the Managing Director and Chief Financial Officer and periodically to the Audit Committee of the Board of Directors in the manner outlined in the Responsibility section above.

The Internal Audit Department is authorized to:

- Have unrestricted access to all functions, records, property, and personnel.
- Have full and free access to the Audit Committee.
- Allocate resources, set frequencies, select subjects, determine scopes of work, and apply the techniques required to accomplish audit objectives.
- Obtain the necessary assistance of personnel in units of the organization where they perform audits, as well as other specialized services from within or outside the organization.

The Internal Audit Department is not authorized to:

- Perform any operational duties for the organization or its affiliates.
- Initiate or approve accounting transactions external to the Internal Audit Department.
- Direct the activities of any organization employee not employed by the Internal Audit Department, except to the extent such employees have been appropriately assigned to auditing teams or to otherwise assist the Internal Audit Department.

STANDARDS of AUDIT PRACTICE

The Internal Audit Department will meet or exceed the *Standards for the Professional Practice of Internal Auditing* of The Institute of Internal Auditors.

the previous or next issue of annual financial statements. Internal auditors are primarily concerned with affecting the company's bottom line; hence, the definition includes the phrase *to add value and improve an organization's operations*. Internal auditors add value to a company primarily by following four audit objectives:

1. Recognizing and analyzing industry, business, and operational risks.
2. Improving the economy and efficiency of the operations.
3. Ensuring compliance with management directives.
4. Serving as management's representative.

Recognizing and Analyzing Industry, Business, and Operational Risks

A major goal of an internal audit organization is to gain as much expertise as possible concerning the industry, business, and operational areas of the company. This expertise allows the internal auditors to recognize and evaluate changes in the economy, business environment, technology, regulatory environment, and management. These types of changes often result in additional risks faced by the organization. The internal audit department must take a proactive approach to reduce or eliminate these risks. By reducing or eliminating risks that might create potential losses, the internal audit organization adds value to the company.

Improving Economy and Efficiency of the Operations

Over a period of a few years, an internal auditor will have evaluated almost every department and almost every aspect of a company's business. This experience makes the auditor a valuable asset to the organization. Indeed, many organizations use internal audit as a training ground for management and they highly value the experience gained by an employee as a member of the internal audit organization. This experience also enables the internal auditor to evaluate many aspects regarding the performance of a particular department or process. For example, an internal auditor for Sears may visit five or six distribution centers in a given year. A particular distribution center may have developed a procedure that enables orders to be processed faster. The internal auditor may be able to recommend this "best practice" to other facilities.

An important ingredient in successfully recommending changes in a company's operations is for the auditor to have a complete business and technical perspective of the operation under evaluation. For example, auditors will not be successful in implementing meaningful change in a marketing department without completely considering the marketing perspective on the processes and procedures used in that specialty. Many internal audit organizations enhance this critical element of internal audit by adding personnel with backgrounds in production, engineering, computer science, and other relevant disciplines to the internal audit staff (IIA *Standard 1210*).

Ensuring Compliance with Management Directives

Management provides all departments and operations with directives regarding the desired performance of the company's business. These directives are designed to ensure that the company complies with laws and regulations; that departments are operating efficiently and effectively; and that risks are minimized. Many of these directives are found in the policy and procedure manuals maintained by each functional area. Internal audit is charged with reporting on departments' compliance with these directives. Often these directives delineate the internal controls established by management to reduce or eliminate risk within a functional area.

It is important to recognize the distinction between the compliance issues of internal auditors and those of external auditors. External auditors review compliance with internal controls that are relevant to the financial reporting process. The internal auditors are concerned with any noncompliance that (1) increases the risk faced by the company or (2) diminishes the efficiency or effectiveness of the company's operations. Basically, internal auditors are concerned with any noncompliance that might adversely affect the company's likelihood of meeting its goals and objectives.

Serving as Management's Representative

The complexities of managing a large organization often prohibit senior management from visiting locations and departments critical to the success of the organization. For example, it would not be feasible for the vice president of materials management for Sears to visit each distribution center. Therefore, the reports from the internal audit department may be the only critical objective evaluations received by that manager regarding certain distribution centers and other key operations.

It should be evident that the four audit objectives discussed above are not mutually exclusive. For example, the evaluation of compliance with company policies and procedures includes elements of risk reductions, economy and efficiency, and management's representative.

Scope of Service

Internal auditors make recommendations that result in additional profits or cost savings for their companies. In this capacity, they function as management consultants. Within the IIA definition of *to evaluate and improve effectiveness of risk management, control, and governance processes,* almost any type of assessment of any aspect of the organization is feasible. In fact, it is difficult to define the variety of audits that the modern internal audit department performs.

The stated objective of internal auditing is phrased in terms of *helping the organization accomplish its objectives.* To achieve this goal internal auditors provide services including (1) financial audits of financial reports and accounting control systems; (2) compliance audits that ensure conformity with company policies, plans, and procedures and with laws and regulations; (3) operational audits that evaluate the economy and efficiency of business process; and (4) audits of effectiveness in achieving program results in comparison to established objectives and goals (IIA *Standards 2100* and *2210*).

Financial Audits

Internal auditors usually do not audit quarterly or year-end financial statements in the same manner as external auditors. However, internal auditors may evaluate areas that management believes may be of concern to the external auditors such as areas that were found to have problems in the prior audit. Such a preliminary evaluation may allow for correction of errors prior to the arrival of the external auditors.

Internal auditors more likely will perform audits of financial reports for internal use. This type of audit provides managers with assurance that the information they are using in the decision-making process is relevant and reliable. Such an assurance function reduces management's risk in making daily operating decisions or in determining appropriate action to address a unique problem. This type of auditing is similar to the auditing described elsewhere in this textbook.

AUDITING INSIGHT Who's Minding the Cash?

Lisa Bisel was the only person in charge of cash at the *Topeka-Capital Journal.* The internal audit department examined 142 deposits made during 2004 and found 104 (73.2 percent) to have cash shortages. Bisel is charged with stealing $25,000 although over $445,000 is unaccounted for.

Source: "Auditor Says System Lacked Checks and Balances," *Topeka Capital Journal*, January 30, 2007.

Compliance Audits

In many functional areas, management's primary concern is compliance with policies, procedures, laws, and regulations—thus, **compliance audits.** The degree of management's concern may vary by industry or by functional area. For example, compliance with laws will

be of greater concern in the banking, insurance, and health care industries as compared with a company in the retail industry. Also, in an audit of the human resource department, the main audit objective may be compliance with policies and procedures designed to ensure conformity with laws regarding fair hiring and proper dismissals of employees.

AUDITING INSIGHT How Hard Did You Study for Your Last Exam?

An internal audit at Auburn University found a grade for a scholarship athlete was changed without the knowledge of the professor, raising the athlete's grade for the semester just over the 2.0 minimum for graduation.

Source: "An Audit Reveals More Academic Questions at Auburn," *The New York Times,* December 10, 2006.

Operational Audits

In the past, the terms *internal auditing* and *operational auditing* were used almost interchangeably because the vast majority of audits performed by internal auditors were operational audits. The internal auditing activity known as **operational auditing** refers to auditors' study of business operations for the purpose of making recommendations about economic and efficient use of resources, effective achievement of business objectives, and compliance with company policies. The goal of operational auditing is to help managers discharge their management responsibilities and improve profitability. Therefore, operational auditing is included in the definition of internal auditing given previously. In a similar context, an AICPA committee defined operational auditing performed by independent public accounting firms as a distinct type of consulting service having the goal of helping a client improve the use of its capabilities and resources to achieve its objectives. So, internal auditors consider operational auditing an integral part of internal auditing and external auditors define it as a type of consulting service offered by public accounting firms.

Governance Audits

The definition of internal auditing includes evaluating the *governance process.* General Motors' general auditor and IIA Chairman Jacqueline Wagner predicted that

> [t]he changes that began with the top members of our governing bodies are now enabling internal auditors to take on a greater role in corporate governance. I predict that audit committees and boards of directors will look increasingly to internal audit departments to be their eyes and ears across the operations.[2]

In this role as management's representative, the auditor reports on a wide variety of critical information. It is essential that management understand the risks that the business and industry are facing. It is also imperative that management receive objective, timely feedback concerning corporate strategies and initiatives in order to effectively guide the corporation and fulfill their fiduciary responsibilities. **Governance audits** ensure that senior management receives accurate and timely information concerning management and leadership throughout the organization as well as the proper implementation and execution of company strategy and plans. This function of internal audit is continuing to grow in both scope and importance.

Other Audits

Internal auditors may perform audits that are specific to the nature of the business they service. For example, auditors that work with manufacturing companies may provide **quality audits,** audits designed specifically to determine if the product meets the standards established by management. Customer service departments also may be subject to a quality audit to ensure that customers are being served in the manner prescribed by the company. The auditors are not a substitute for the quality control department but can review the

[2] Jacqueline K. Wagner, "Leading the Way," *Internal Auditor,* August 2000, p. 37.

AUDITING INSIGHT — Internal Auditors Produce Interest Income

During an audit of the cash management operations at branch offices, internal auditors found that bank deposits were not made until several days after cash and checks were received. Company policy was to complete the bookkeeping before making the deposit.

The auditors showed branch managers a cost-efficient way to capture the needed bookkeeping information that would permit release of the cash and checks. Management agreed to implement the timely deposit of checks and transfer to headquarters through an electronic funds transfer system from local banks to the headquarters bank, performing the bookkeeping afterward.

The change resulted in additional interest income in the first year in the amount of $150,000.

work of quality control, quality control reports, and the responses of manufacturing management to issues raised by quality control.

Another type of audit performed in some organizations is an **environmental audit.** Many organizations deal with materials that must be handled in manners prescribed by law (e.g., what does Sears do with those old batteries, tires, and oil?). Auditors can review procedures, record keeping, liability issues, and compliance as they relate to environmental issues of the organization. In addition, auditors can make recommendations to reduce waste (e.g., reusable shipping containers) and make products that are more environmentally friendly (e.g., recyclable packaging materials).

Internal Audit Standards

The IIA is the international organization that governs the standards, continuing education, and general rules of conduct for internal auditors as a profession. The IIA also sponsors research and development of practices and procedures designed to enhance the work of internal auditors wherever they are employed.

The *International Standards for the Professional Practice of Internal Auditing* (IIA *Standards*) are issued by the IIA (see the IIA Web site at www.theiia.org). The IIA standards are classified in three major categories:

1. Attribute standards
2. Performance standards
3. Implementation standards

Aptly named, the attribute standards address the *characteristics of internal auditors* (e.g., independence, objectivity) *and organizations* performing internal audit activities. Performance standards relate to the *conduct of internal audit activities* and provide a *measure of quality* against which the performance of internal audit activities can be measured. The attribute and the performance standards are similar to the general standards in GAAS: they apply to internal audit services in general. Implementation standards, on the other hand, are specific applications of the attribute and performance standards to specific types of engagements (e.g., attestations and consulting engagements).

Internal auditors are expected to comply with the IIA's standards of professional conduct. IIA audit standards are recommended and encouraged, but compliance with them depends on their acceptance, adoption, and implementation by practicing internal auditors. Many internal audit organizations include compliance with IIA standards in their department charters and in their audit reports (note the reference to the IIA standards in the audit charter of the Chicago Mercantile Exchange in Exhibit D.1)The IIA standards require internal auditors to be skilled in dealing with people and in communicating effectively. Such a requirement may be considered implicit in GAAS related to training and proficiency, but little is said in GAAS about effective communication, perhaps because the audit report language is so standardized. External auditors tend to believe the public has the responsibility to learn how to understand their audit reports, while internal auditors believe it is their responsibility to see that audit findings and recommendations are understood by management and the audit committee.

The IIA also issues practice advisories. Because of the diversity of entities serviced by internal auditors, guidance from practice advisories is not mandatory. Practice advisories suggest "best practices" in internal audit and internal audit organizations are encouraged to implement those practices that are applicable to the business and industry they serve.

Many of the IIA standards deal with the organization and management of the internal audit department. CPAs in public practice have similar standards, but their standards are included in the AICPA quality control standards, rather than in GAAS. However, observance of quality control standards is considered essential for proper auditing practice in accordance with GAAS. The AICPA quality control standards are incorporated by reference in GAAS and enforced through the peer reviews and monitoring activities of accounting firms.

While the four AICPA reporting standards for financial statements are comprehensive, the related IIA standards are very brief. It would be extremely difficult to provide detailed specifications on internal audit reports since the reports vary by entity and audit objective. The best the IIA can provide is an outline of desirable audit report characteristics.

The IIA also controls the Certified Internal Auditor (CIA) program. This certification is a mark of professional achievement that has gained international acceptance. To become a CIA, a candidate must hold a college degree and pass an examination on internal auditing and related subjects. The exam has four parts:

- Part 1—The internal audit activity's role in governance, risk, and control.
- Part 2—Conducting the internal audit engagement.
- Part 3—Business analysis and information technology.
- Part 4—Business management skills.

Candidates also must have two years of audit experience (internal audit or public accounting audit) obtained before or after passing the examination. Holders of masters' degrees need only one year of experience. You can sit for the CIA exam prior to completion of your bachelor's degree. For more details, consult the IIA's Web site (www.theiia.org).

Internal Audit Reports

Internal audit reports are not standardized like external auditors' reports on financial statements. Each report is different because internal auditors need to communicate findings on a variety of assignments and audit objectives. The key criterion for an internal audit report is clear and concise communication of findings and recommendations.

The reporting stage is the internal auditors' opportunity to capture management's undivided attention. To be effective, a report cannot be unduly long, tedious, technical, or laden with minutiae. It must be accurate, concise, clear, and timely. It must speak directly to the risks the auditors evaluated. Most quality audit reports ensure that significant issues are described by five elements:

- The *condition* the auditor identified.
- The *criteria* that renders the condition inappropriate.
- The *cause* of the condition.
- The *effect* the condition may have on the company.
- The *recommendation* that may eliminate or mitigate the condition.

For example, let's say that, during a compliance audit of the human resource area, you notice that a recent candidate for an accounting position was asked several inappropriate questions on the employment application. An inappropriate question might be "have you ever been arrested?" (you may only ask if someone has ever been convicted since a person is considered innocent until proven guilty). After further investigation, you discover that the human resource department ran out of current job applications and decided to use some old applications kept in storage.

- Condition—inappropriate questions asked of job candidates.
- Criteria—fair hiring laws and company policies.

- Cause—use of old job applications due to stock out of current applications.
- Effect—possible lawsuits and adverse publicity.
- Recommendation—destroy obsolete job applications to prevent further use and institute better monitoring of forms inventory.

Generally, internal auditors meet with the auditee and the auditee's management to review the audit report before it is distributed to senior management. This meeting is called the **exit conference.** The purpose of the exit conference is to inform the auditee's management of the audit results, reach an agreement on the correctness of the findings, and learn of the corrective action management plans to initiate. Sometimes disagreements concerning audit findings occur. In the interest of fair and complete disclosure, many auditors will include management's reasons for disagreement in the audit report.

Internal audit reports are sent to the highest level of management in the organization, often including the CEO and the audit committee. Usually the senior manager overseeing an auditee (e.g., the vice president of materials management for distribution centers and purchasing) would receive audit reports and respond to senior management and the audit committee regarding which recommendations will be implemented. The manager also must explain why certain recommendations will not be implemented. Top management and the audit committee may compel management to reconsider selected actions.

Once senior management agrees with acceptance or rejection of audit recommendations, the auditee is obligated to implement the accepted recommendations. The IIA standards include a requirement for a **follow-up** to ascertain that appropriate action is being taken on accepted recommendations. AICPA standards have no comparable follow-up requirement. Only after the follow-up is completed is the audit considered "closed."

Review Checkpoints

D.1 How can internal auditors achieve practical independence?

D.2 What auditing services do internal auditors provide?

D.3 What special professional certification is available for internal auditors?

D.4 Who is responsible for enforcing compliance with laws and regulations in business administration?

GOVERNMENTAL AUDITS

LEARNING OBJECTIVE

2. Define *governmental auditing;* describe governmental audit institutions (e.g., GAO); describe how governmental auditors interact with independent auditors; explain governmental auditors' ndependence problems; and list features of govern-mental audit reports.

Government officials and recipients of federal monies are responsible for carrying out public functions efficiently, economically, effectively, ethically, and equitably, while achieving desired public objectives. High-quality auditing is essential for government accountability to the public and transparency regarding linking resources to related program results.[3]

Many federal agencies (e.g., Army, Navy, Department of Transportation, etc.) have governmental auditors who are charged with ensuring compliance with agency and department policies and procedures. The accounting, auditing, and investigative agency of the federal government is the Government Accountability Office (GAO). The GAO audits the departments, agencies, and programs of the federal government (even if they are subject to audits by their own internal audit staffs) to determine whether the laws passed by the U.S. Congress are followed and to determine whether programs are being implemented with economy and efficiency and are achieving desired results. The U.S. Congress always receives copies of GAO reports.

[3] *Government Auditing Standards,* January 2007, p. 1.

When approving the Katrina Housing Tax Relief Act of 2007, the U.S. House Ways and Means Committee included an amendment requiring the GAO to report on any waste, fraud, or abuse.[1]

- "Congress did not write a blank check for spending in Iraq. We need to know funds are being used appropriately, which is what the GAO will do."—Senator Tom Harkins[2]

- "Every time we open these GAO reports we find more outrageous spending."—Senator Chuck Grassley[3]

- Senator Diane Feinstein asked the GAO to conduct an investigation of e-voting machines—especially those that fail to produce paper receipts for the ballots cast.[4]

- "The 2007 GAO High Risk Update correctly highlights the need for policy makers to conduct a critical review of existing transportation funding mechanisms."—Senator James Inhofe[5]

- "We will continue our work to transform [Department of Homeland Security] into a first class department, with a special emphasis on information sharing and the other areas on the GAO's high-risk list."—Senator Joe Lieberman[6]

- "It concerns me that some agencies are persistent perennials on GAO's high-risk list, such as DOD's contract management and financial management, protecting the nation's critical infrastructures and information systems, and managing federal real property."—Senator Susan Collins6

[1]"Katrina Relief Bill Contains Hulshof Provision," *States News Service*, March 29, 2007.

[2]"Harkin Calls on State Department to Allow GAO Auditors in Baghdad," *States News Service*, March 12, 2007.[3]

[3]"Grassley Time for Waste, Fraud and Abuse of Government," Capitol Hill Press Releases, March 7, 2007.

[4]"Feinstein Calls for Probe into E-voting Machines: Senator Asks GAO to Look at Potential for DRE Malfunctions, Election Fraud," *ComputerWorld*, February 23, 2007.

[5]"Inhofe Welcomes New GAO High-Risk Series Update," *States News Service*, February 1, 2007.

[6]"Sens. Lieberman, Collins Vow to Remove Department of Homeland Security from 'High-Risk' List," *US Fed News*, January 31, 2007.

The U.S. Comptroller General heads the GAO. In one sense, GAO auditors are the highest level of internal auditors for the federal government. State and federal agencies and other local governmental units use the GAO *Generally Accepted Government Auditing Standards* (GAGAS) to guide their audits. These standards are published in a book with a yellow cover, referred to as the **Yellow Book.**

Many states also have audit agencies similar to the GAO. They answer to state legislatures and perform the same types of work described herein as GAO auditing. In another sense, the GAO and many state agencies are really external auditors with respect to government agencies they audit because they are organizationally independent.

Many government agencies have their own internal auditors and inspectors general. Well-managed local governments also have internal audit departments. For example, most federal agencies (Department of Defense, Department of Human Resources, Department of the Interior), state agencies (education, welfare, controller), and local governments (cities, counties, tax districts) have internal audit staffs.

AUDITING INSIGHT · Million Dollar Pen

During the heat of the space race in the 1960s, the United States' National Aeronautics and Space Administration decided it needed a ballpoint pen to write in the zero gravity confines of its space capsules. After considerable research and development, the Astronaut Pen was developed at a cost of approximately $1 million. The pen worked and also enjoyed some modest success as a novelty item back here on Earth.

The Soviet Union, faced with the same problem, used a pencil.

Government auditors are charged with looking for projects that do not spend the taxpayers' money wisely. If you were a government auditor looking at this project, would you raise any issues?

Types of Audits

The GAO shares with internal auditors many of the same elements of expanded-scope services. The GAO, however, emphasizes the accountability of public officials for the efficient, economical, and effective use of public funds and other resources. The GAO

defines and describes *expanded-scope governmental auditing* in terms of three types of government audits:

1. Financial statement audits.
2. Attestation engagements.
3. Performance audits.

Financial Statement Audits

Financial statement audits determine whether the financial statements of an audited entity present fairly the financial position, results of operations, and cash flows in conformity with generally accepted accounting principles. In addition, financial audits can have other objectives, including

- Issuing special reports for specified elements, accounts, or items of a financial statement.
- Reviewing interim financial statements.
- Issuing letters for underwriters.
- Reporting on the processing of transactions by service organizations.
- Auditing compliance with regulations relating to federal award expenditures and other governmental financial assistance.

Attestation Engagements

Attestation engagements concern examining, reviewing, or performing agreed-upon procedures on a subject matter or assertion about a subject matter and reporting on the results. The subject matter of an attestation engagement may take many forms, including historical or prospective performance or condition, physical characteristics, historical events, analyses, systems and processes, or behavior. Examples of such engagements include reporting on

- Internal control over financial reporting or compliance with specified requirements.
- Compliance with requirements of specified laws, regulations, rules, contracts, or grants.
- Management's discussion and analysis presentation.
- Prospective or *pro forma* financial information.
- The reliability of performance measures.
- Whether proposed contract amounts are reasonable and allowable.
- Specified procedures performed on a subject matter.

Performance Audits

The GAO issued new standards in January 2007. One of the fundamental changes in these standards is the enhancement of performance auditing standards. According to the new standards,

> Performance audits provide objective analysis so that management and those charged with governance and oversight can use the information to improve program performance and operations, reduce costs, facilitate decision making by corrective action, and contribute to public accountability.[4]

Performance audits may be requested by management or legislative body or may be mandated by the law, grant, or contract under which an agency or company is operating or receiving money. Performance audits provide an objective and systematic examination of evidence of the performance and management of a program against objective criteria. Performance audits provide information to improve program operations and facilitate

[4] *Government Auditing Standard 1.25,* January 2007.

decision making by those with oversight responsibility. Examples of performance audits include assessing

- The extent to which legislative, regulatory, or organizational goals and objectives are being achieved.
- The relative ability of alternative approaches to provide better program performance or eliminate factors that inhibit program effectiveness.
- The relative cost and benefits or cost effectiveness of program performance.
- Whether a program produced the intended results.
- Whether a program produced unintended effects.
- The extent to which programs duplicate, overlap, or conflict with other related programs.
- Whether the audited entity is using sound procurement practices.
- The validity and reliability of performance measures and/or financial information related to the program.

The audit of a governmental organization, program, activity, or function may involve one or more of these audit types. The scope of the work is determined by the needs of the users of the audit results.

Audit Procedures—Economy, Efficiency, and Program Results Audits

LEARNING OBJECTIVE

3. Explain the function of standards and measurements in economy, efficiency, and program results audits.

The general evidence-gathering procedures used during the audit of financial statements in governmental audits are basically the same as the ones used by external auditors. These procedures are explained in other chapters in this textbook. However, the audit problems are usually different in audits of *economy, efficiency,* and *program results.* Also, while internal auditors occasionally perform audits of this nature, the vast majority of these audits are performed in the government sector.

Governmental and internal auditors must be as objective as possible when developing conclusions about efficiency, economy, and program results. This objectivity is achieved by (1) finding standards for evaluation, (2) determining the actual results of the program, and (3) comparing the actual results to the standards. Finding standards and deciding on relevant measurements is often difficult.

Students are often surprised by the difficulty in establishing standards and measurement criteria because these issues are not prominent during a financial statement audit. In a financial statement audit, the standards (which are the objective criteria) have already been set in the establishment of GAAP.

AUDITING INSIGHT Establishing Standards

In the mid 1990s, the Florida state legislature gave millions of dollars to school districts to improve education for the next millennium. The program was called "Blueprint 2000." The legislature asked the Office of the Auditor General to monitor the use and performance of these funds. It took a team of auditors almost a year to establish standards and measurement criteria so that successful audits could begin.

When dealing with standards, measurements, and comparisons, auditors must keep inputs and outputs in perspective. Evidence about inputs—personnel hours and cost, material quantities and costs, asset investment—are most important in connection with reaching financial audit conclusions. For economy, efficiency, and program results conclusions, however, output measurements are equally important. Management has the responsibility for devising information systems to measure output. Such measurements should correspond to program objectives set forth in laws, regulations, administrative

policies, legislative reports, or other such sources. Auditors must realize that output measurements are usually not expressed in financial terms (for example, water quality improvement, educational progress, weapons effectiveness, materials-inspection time delays, and test program reporting accuracy).

Many economy and efficiency audits and most program results audits are output-oriented. Auditors need to be careful not to equate program activity with program success without measuring program results. These features are significantly different from auditors' roles with respect to financial statement audits where the primary concern is with reporting on the accounting for inputs.

An Example of Setting Performance Audit Criteria

Kinerville has instituted a new program in its school system. The program provides a healthy balanced breakfast for underprivileged students in grades K–12. You have been asked to audit the effectiveness of the program. In planning this audit, the following issues must be resolved.

First, what is the goal of the program? If you said, "to feed hungry children," you would only be partially correct. The actual goal of school breakfast programs is based on the assumption that children do better in school when they have a good breakfast. Therefore, the main purpose of the program is to improve the educational experience for underprivileged children.

Second, by what standard would you measure success? A comparison to other students in the school who are not in the program? If these students are not "underprivileged," is this a fair measure? Should Kinerville's school district withhold breakfasts from some underprivileged children so there is a comparison group? Is there a moral issue with this type of evaluation? (This is an ethical question that the medical profession wrestles with on a regular basis since

placebos are given to ill patients when studying a new medicine.) Would a comparison with other schools in other districts be appropriate? Maybe. But the comparison group would have to be carefully selected and matched on many demographic factors.

Third, what is the measure that will be used for comparison? Increased grades? Higher standardized test scores? What are the problems with these measures? Will teachers change their teaching methods and focus exclusively on test preparation? Can there be other reasons for an increase in test scores?

Lastly, how large an improvement is required for the program to be successful?

You may want answers to all these questions, but real concrete answers do not exist. Most of these issues can be resolved with tests and measures that have some positive aspects and some negative aspects and the audit team may need several measures and have to make many judgments.

Review Checkpoints

D.5 What auditing services do government auditors provide?

D.6 What difficulties do auditors find when conducting a performance audit?

D.7 How can governmental and internal auditors try to achieve objectivity when developing conclusions about economy, efficiency, or program results?

GAO Government Auditing Standards

The GAO establishes *Generally Accepted Government Auditing Standards* (GAGAS) that guide all audits for federal government agencies and facilities and all audits of entities receiving federal funds. Note, these standards must be adhered to even if a CPA firm is engaged to perform one of these audits (rule 501 of the AICPA Code of Conduct makes the *failure to follow government standards during a government audit* an Act Discreditable (see Module B)).In addition, many state and local governments have adopted GAGAS as the audit standards for agencies, municipalities, and government districts (e.g., school districts).

In many areas, GAGAS are similar to the AICPA *Statements on Auditing Standards*. However, GAGAS go beyond the AICPA standards in several respects. Government auditing standards impose additional rules and regulations about handling government funds and accounts.[5] A sample of this literature includes the following:

- Single Audit Act of 1984. This is the federal law that established uniform requirements for audits of federal financial assistance provided to state and local governments.
- *OMB Circular A-133,* "Audits of States, Local Governments, and Non-profit Organizations." This Office of Management and Budget guidance helps auditors implement the Single Audit Act of 1984 for governmental units and a wide range of nonprofit organizations (e.g., colleges, universities, voluntary health and welfare organizations, hospitals). (The Single Audit Act is discussed later in this module.)
- *OMB Circular A-122,* "Cost Principles for Nonprofit Organizations."
- *OMB Circular A-110,* "Uniform Requirements for Grants to Universities, Hospitals, and Other Nonprofit Organizations."
- *OMB Circular A-102,* "Uniform Requirements for Grants to State and Local Governments."
- *OMB Circular A-87,* "Cost Principles for State and Local Governments."
- *OMB Circular A-21,* "Cost Principles for Educational Institutions."
- *AICPA Audit and Accounting Guide*, "Audits of State and Local Governments."

Since most governmental programs are created by grants and operate under laws and regulations, GAGAS explicitly require review and testing for compliance with applicable laws and regulations. Government auditors must be especially diligent when noncompliance with laws and regulations could result in errors or frauds that could be material to the financial statements. The Auditing Standards Board issued *SAS 74* (AU 801) to guide CPAs on governmental audits

GAGAS have more elaborate specifications for audit documentation and reporting than GAAS requires. The GAO standards require the following written reports in financial statement audits:

1. An audit report on financial statements.
2. A report on the auditee's compliance with applicable laws and regulations, including a report of irregularities, frauds, illegal acts, material noncompliance, and internal control deficiencies.
3. A report on the auditee's internal control and the control risk assessment.

GAGAS also contain an elaborate set of guidelines for reports on performance audits. These audits cover such a wide range of subjects (from food programs to military contracts) that no "standard" report is possible. The details of these standards can be found on the GAO Web site (www.gao.gov). These GAO standards are good guides for internal audit reports and for operational audit reports (consulting services engagements) prepared by CPAs in public practice.

In January 2007, the GAO updated the Government Auditing Standard. A review of these changes indicate six specific issues designed to increase the transparency and accountability of audits. A review of these changes indicates that the GAO is moving to increase audit consistency and quality in a manner similar to the Public Company Accounting Oversight Board (PCAOB) (see Exhibit D.2).

[5] Extensive government audit literature can be found at three important Web sites: (1) the OMB Web site (www.white-house.gov) (search "OMB" in the GO box), (2) the AICPA Web site (www.AICPA.org/belt/a133.htm), and (3) the GAO Web site (www.GAO.gov).

EXHIBIT D.2
Significant Revisions to Government Auditing Standards

Area	Emphasis or Nature of Revision
Ethics	Heightened emphasis on ethics principles
Nonaudit services	Additional guidance on the acceptance of professional services other than audit services and the impact on audit work
Recent developments in auditing and internal control	Revised standards that increase transparency concerning restatements, uncertainties, and unusual events
Performance auditing	Additional guidance on the overall framework for high-quality performance auditing including reasonable assurance and its relationship to risk and level of evidence used to support findings and conclusions
Audit language	Standardized audit language throughout the standards
Auditor responsibilities	Reinforcement of the auditors' role in accountability and improvements for government operations

Review Checkpoints

D.8 What scope of practice is suggested or required by GAGAS?

D.9 Why do GAGAS require a review for compliance with laws and regulations in conjunction with financial audits?

Single Audit Act of 1984 and Amendments of 1986

LEARNING OBJECTIVES

4. Describe the Single Audit Act of 1984 in relation to audits of governmental fund recipients.

The federal government requires audits of state and local governments that receive federal financial assistance through appropriations, grants, contracts, cooperative agreements, loans, loan guarantees, property, interest subsidies, and insurance. Prior to 1985, state and local governments often were visited by audit teams from several federal agencies. The Single Audit Act of 1984 (the Act) replaced the system of expensive and duplicative grant-by-grant audits with an organizationwide **single audit** encompassing all federal funds that a government unit receives. When a state or local government, university, or community organization receives federal financial assistance from several federal agencies, all of these agencies are supposed to rely on the single audit report instead of requiring other auditors to enter the same unit to audit various grants.

The act established an annual audit requirement for all governments, agencies, and nonprofit organizations that receive $500,000 or more of federal funds. A single audit, conducted in accordance with GAGAS, covering financial statements, compliance with laws and regulations, and internal control is required. The act does not require expanded scope audits of economy, efficiency, or program results. However, federal agencies may require, and pay for, additional audits of economy, efficiency, and program results to monitor the benefits of federal fund expenditures.

The auditors can be from public accounting firms or from state and local agencies, provided they meet the GAO independence and proficiency requirements. In a single audit, the auditors are supposed to determine and report whether

1. The financial statements present fairly the financial position and results of operations in accordance with generally accepted accounting principles.
2. The organization has internal controls to provide reasonable assurance that it is managing federal financial assistance programs in compliance with applicable laws and regulations.
3. The organization has complied with laws and regulations that may have a material effect on its financial statements and on each major federal assistance program.

OMB *Circular A-133* imposes additional audit and reporting requirements. These reports are directed toward information about the accountability of agencies that receive federal funds:

- A supplementary schedule of federal financial assistance programs showing expenditures for each program.
- A report of the compliance audit procedures showing the extent of testing and the amount and explanation of questioned expenditures.
- A report on internal control, identifying significant controls designed to provide reasonable assurance that federal programs are being managed in compliance with laws and regulations and identifying material weaknesses.
- A report of fraud, abuse, or illegal acts that become known to the auditors.

Government audits under the Yellow Book and the Single Audit Act Amendments of 1996 (including OMB *Circular A-133*) are difficult and time consuming. The GAO requires auditors to have 24 hours of continuing education in governmental auditing to qualify for planning an audit, conducting field work, and preparing reports. The GAO also imposes requirements for continuing education and participation in a peer review program.[6]

Government audits require more work on compliance and reporting on internal control than external auditors normally do in an audit of financial statements of a private business. The reason is the federal government's concern for laws, regulations, and control of expenditures. Over $100 billion of federal funds are used by state and local governments for various programs, so the stakes are high. Exhibit D.3 shows the State of Oregon Statewide Single Audit Report for the fiscal year ended June 30, 2006.

Review Checkpoint

D.10 What additional requirements for audit field work are imposed by GAGAS and the Single Audit Act of 1984 in comparison to the AICPA generally accepted auditing standards?

GAO Audit Reports

GAGAS has three sets of reporting standards: one for financial audits, one for attestation engagements, and another for performance audits.

Financial audit reports start with an audit report like the external auditors' standard report, except that the description of the audit in the scope paragraph must include a reference to generally accepted government auditing standards (GAGAS). The report on financial statements contains an opinion regarding conformity with generally accepted accounting principles, just like the reports independent auditors in public practice give on nongovernmental organizations. In addition, GAGAS include reports on internal control, fraud, illegal acts, violations of provisions of contracts, grant agreements, abuse of government assets, and tests of compliance with laws and regulations as part of the financial reporting requirements. The detailed financial reporting standards can be found on the GAO Web site (www.gao.gov).

Governmental auditors, like their public accounting firm counterparts, may be asked to perform attestation engagements. Attestation engagements provide an opinion or conclusion

[6] Most CPAs in public practice have similar continuing education and peer review requirements, though not specific to governmental auditing, in connection with their state licenses and voluntary membership in the AICPA. However, the GAO makes the requirements even for CPAs who do not have similar demands from their state boards or who choose not to belong to the AICPA. In this manner, the GAO exercises its own control over government audit quality.

EXHIBIT D.3
State of Oregon
Statewide Single Audit
Report for Fiscal Year
Ended June 30, 2006

The Honorable Theodore R. Kulongoski Governor of Oregon

We have conducted a statewide audit in accordance with the Single Audit Act Amendments of 1996, Government Auditing Standards, and U. S. Office of Management and Budget (OMB) Circular A-133, Audits of States, Local Governments, and Non-Profit Organizations. This report encompasses the year ended June 30, 2006, and is required for the State to continue receiving federal financial assistance, which, as shown in this report, totals approximately $5.9 billion.

As required by the Single Audit Act, we issued a report dated December 15, 2006, on the State of Oregon's financial statements. That report was included in the State of Oregon's *Comprehensive Annual Financial Report* for the year ended June 30, 2006.

This report contains the remaining components required by the Single Audit Act:

- *Report on Internal Control over Financial Reporting and on Compliance and Other Matters.* This component contains our report on the State of Oregon's internal control over financial reporting and compliance with laws, regulations, contracts and grant agreements that affect the financial statements. Part of the schedule of findings and questioned costs relates to this report.
- *Report on Compliance with Requirements Applicable to each Major Program and on Internal Control Over Compliance in Accordance with OMB Circular A-133.* This component contains our report on the State of Oregon's compliance with the requirements applicable to each of its major federal programs described in OMB Circular A-133 and internal controls over compliance. Part of the schedule of findings and questioned costs relates to this report. This component also contains our report on the State of Oregon's schedule of expenditures of federal awards for the year ended June 30, 2006.
- *Schedule of Expenditures of Federal Awards.* This schedule is not a required part of the State of Oregon's financial statements, but is required by OMB Circular A-133. The schedule shows State expenditures of federal awards, for the fiscal year ended June 30, 2006, excluding Oregon Health and Science University. The notes, which accompany the schedule, are considered an integral part of the schedule. They provide disclosures regarding the reporting entity, the significant accounting policies used in preparing the schedule, the value of federal awards expended in the form of non-cash assistance, the value of loans outstanding at year end, and the value of pass-through awards received by the State from non-federal entities.
- *Schedule of Findings and Questioned Costs.* This schedule lists 7 current audit findings regarding compliance and internal control related to financial reporting. It also lists 16 current audit findings regarding compliance with the requirements of major federal programs and related internal controls. Further, it lists the status of findings regarding compliance and internal control related to financial reporting and compliance with the requirements of major federal programs and related internal controls, which were included in our report for the fiscal year ended June 30, 2005. In addition, it lists the status of prior year audit findings for the fiscal year ended June 30, 2004, which were not previously corrected.
- OMB Circular A-133 requires management to provide a plan of corrective action on the findings and recommendations for the fiscal year ended June 30, 2006. Management's responses and planned corrective actions are included in this schedule.

OREGON AUDITS DIVISION

Charles A. Hibner, CPA Director

concerning a specific subject or an assertion about a subject. It is important when reporting on attestation engagements to clearly specify the subject matter or assertion, the conclusions, and any significant reservations concerning the subject matter or assertion addressed in the report.

Both attestation engagement reports and performance audit reports are altogether different from financial audit reports. Like internal auditors, the GAO objective is clear communication for the purpose of making recommendations and improving operations. Hence, GAGAS performance audit reporting standards require timely, well-written communications of findings and recommendations for action. The managers of an audited entity are expected to respond to the report and this response is usually included in the final version of the report. Unlike internal audit reports, most GAO reports are available to the public and can be requested from the Government Printing Office.

However, performance audits have another side. GAGAS requires the reports to tell about illegal acts, abuse of public money and property, noncompliance with laws and regulations, and internal control weaknesses. These matters reflect negatively on an organization's management. The details of performance audit reporting can be found on the Government Accountability Office Web site at www.gao.gov.

Review Checkpoints

D.11 What are the major differences between independent auditors' reports on financial statements and internal and governmental reports on efficiency, economy, and program results audits?

D.12 Why do you think the GAGAS reporting standards permit performance audit reports to include "views of responsible officials of the audited program concerning the auditors' findings, conclusions, and recommendations"?

FRAUD AUDITS

LEARNING OBJECTIVES

5. Define fraud auditing and describe various engagements performed by fraud auditors.

The responsibilities of external auditors, internal auditors, and government auditors often require the investigation of suspected fraud. *SAS 99* and *SAS 110* require auditors to use information obtained during the planning and performance of the audit to identify risks that may result in a material misstatement due to fraud. In addition, auditors need to be aware of the various types of frauds, their signs (red flags), and the need to follow up to determine whether a suspicion is justified. If justified, auditors need to alert their management to call in the experts.

> A focused effort by internal auditors on the prevention, deterrence, and detection of financial statement misstatements arising from asset misappropriation is consistent with their broad mission maximizing owners' wealth (which requires safeguarding the entity's assets). In carrying out their mission, internal auditors should be aware of the risks and warning signs of fraud.[7]

Most frauds are found through anonymous tips (34.2 percent) or by accident. Internal auditors uncover about 20.2 percent of discovered fraud while external auditors get credit for finding about 12.0 percent of the frauds.[8] Once a fraud is suspected a fraud examiner may be called in for further investigation.

For government auditors, the basic requirements are to know the applicable laws and regulations, to design the audit to detect abuse and illegal acts, and to report to the proper level of authority. Auditors are required to prepare a written report on their tests of compliance with applicable laws and regulations, including all material instances of noncompliance and all instances or indications of illegal acts that could result in criminal prosecution. Reports are directed to the top official of an organization and, in some cases, to an appropriate oversight body, including other government agencies and audit committees. Persons receiving the audit reports are responsible for reporting to law enforcement agencies.

Compliance auditing in governmental audits is a matter of considerable concern and the AICPA has issued *SAS 74* (AU 801) entitled "Compliance Auditing Applicable to Governmental Entities and Recipients of Governmental Financial Assistance." *SAS 74* tailors the discussion of responsibilities regarding errors, frauds, and illegal acts; GAO standards; and certain government bulletins to the special requirements of governmental entities and other recipients of government financial assistance.

[7] W. Hillison, D. Sinason, and C. Pacini, "The Role of the Internal Auditor in Implementing SAS 82," *Corporate Controller,* July/August 1998, p. 21. Although *SAS 82* has been superseded by *SAS 99,* the content of the quote is still valid.

[8] Association of Certified Fraud Examiners, *2006 Report to the Nation: Occupational Fraud and Abuse.*

The Art of Fraud Examinations

LEARNING
OBJECTIVE

6. Describe the elements
 necessary for a
 successful fraud
 examination and
 explain the differences
 between how fraud
 examiners and
 external auditors
 handle evidence.

Auditors are required to provide reasonable assurance that financial statements are free of material misstatements due to fraud. During the audit, auditors may uncover facts or circumstances that indicate that fraud may exist. At this point, a fraud examination may commence and may require the assistance of a Certified Fraud Examiner (CFE).[9]

Fraud examinations combine the expertise of auditors and criminal investigators. Fraud examiners are fond of saying that their successes are the result of accident, hunches, or luck. Nothing can be further from reality. Successes come from experience, logic, and the ability to see things that are not obvious (as Sherlock Holmes noticed the dog that did not bark). Fraud examinations, broadly speaking, involve familiarity with many elements: the human element, organizational behavior, common fraud schemes, evidence and its sources, standards of proof, and red flags.

Independent auditors of financial statements and fraud examiners approach their work differently. Some of the most important differences are

- Financial auditors follow a program/procedural approach designed to accomplish a fairly standard job, while fraud examiners work in unique and unusual situations where little is standard.

- Financial auditors make note of errors and omissions; while fraud examiners also focus on exceptions, they must be aware of peculiarities and patterns of conduct as well.

- Financial auditors assess control risk in general and specific terms to design audit procedures, while fraud examiners habitually "think like a crook" to imagine ways controls could be subverted for fraudulent purposes.

- Financial auditors use a concept of materiality (dollar size big enough to matter). Most fraud examiners believe that "immaterial fraud" is an oxymoron. Fraud is often larger than it appears, fraud left unchecked tends to grow, and fraud indicates a lack of integrity on the part of the person or persons involved. For these reasons, fraud examiners will often pursue even small frauds.

- Financial audits are based on theories of financial accounting and auditing logic, while fraud examination has a theory of behavioral motive, opportunity, and rationalization.

Financial auditors often use inductive reasoning—that is, they sample accounting data, derive audit findings, and project ("induct") the finding to a conclusion about the population of data sampled. Fraud examiners often enjoy the expensive luxury of using deductive reasoning—that is, after being tipped off that a certain type of loss occurred or probably occurred, they can identify the suspects, make clinical observations (e.g., stakeouts), conduct interviews and interrogations, eliminate dead-end results, and establish a legal case against the fraudster. They can conduct covert activities that usually are not used in the financial audit. The "expensive luxury" of the deductive approach involves surveying a wide array of information and information sources, eliminating the extraneous, and retaining the selection that proves the fraud.

Successfully identifying and catching fraud perpetrators often depends on awareness of auditors. The identification of evidence that may indicate a fraud, the handling of that evidence, and the timely involvement of the fraud examiner may mean the difference between stopping a fraud and recovering stolen assets, or the continued expansion of fraud in the client's business.

[9] The CFE designation is offered by the Association of Certified Fraud Examiners. Information concerning the designation and requirements can be found on its Web site (www.cfenet.com).

AUDITING INSIGHT What Car Are You Driving?

A government fraud auditor uncovered a fraud driving into the parking lot of the city hall of a small town. The auditor always parks in the employee lot (saving the customer parking for residents conducting business with city hall). In the parking lot, along with the Fords and Chevrolets, was a candy-apple red Porsche. After parking his car, the auditor went over to the Porsche and began to look the car over. When someone from city hall came out, the auditor began a conversation.

Auditor: This is certainly a beautiful car!

City hall employee: Yes, it is.

Auditor: Do you know how many horsepower it has?

City hall employee: Not a clue. The car belongs to Bob. I'm certain he'd tell you.

Auditor: Great. I would love to find out more about this car. Where would I find Bob?

City hall employee: Oh. Bob's a city inspector. You'll find him in the inspector's office.

Auditor: Thanks!

Further investigation revealed that Bob had been taking kickbacks.

Source: Story told by a government fraud auditor at an Association of Certified Fraud Examiner seminar.

Review Checkpoints

D.13 Compare and contrast the type of work performed by external auditors (auditing financial statements to render an opinion) and fraud examiners.

Fraud Examiner Responsibilities

When a fraud examiner is called, fraud is already known or strongly suspected. The Association of Certified Fraud Examiners (ACFE) indicates that assignments are initiated only with **predication,** which means a reason to believe fraud may have occurred.[10]

Fraud examiners' attitudes and responsibilities differ from those of other auditors in two additional respects: internal control and materiality. Fraud examiners' interest in internal control policies and procedures involves less evaluation of strengths and more evaluation of weaknesses. Fraud examiners "think like crooks" to imagine fraud schemes that get around an organization's internal controls.

Fraud examiners have four main objectives in performing an investigation. First, the fraud examiner must determine if a fraud does exist. Second, once the fraud examiner determines that a fraud does exist, the examiner must determine the scope of the fraud. For organizations that received an external audit, the average fraud, when discovered, had been in operation for over 23 months.[11] Therefore, a fraud examiner must attempt to determine when the fraud started and what assets have been misappropriated. Third, the fraud examiner must identify the perpetrators. Great care must be taken not to falsely accuse employees and not to solicit help from management personnel that might be involved in the fraud. Finally, the examiner must determine how the fraud occurred and if changes in controls or policy can eliminate this type of fraud in the future.

Fraud examiners have a different attitude about *materiality*. While other auditors may have a large-dollar amount as a criterion for an error that is big enough to matter, fraud

[10] The Professional Standards and Practices for Certified Fraud Examiners can be found on the association's Web site at www.acfenet.org.
[11] Association of Certified Fraud Examiners, *2006 Report to the Nation: Occupational Fraud and Abuse.*

examiners have a much lower threshold and many operate under the theory that there is no such thing as an immaterial fraud. In fact, fraud is sometimes compared to an iceberg in the sense that most of it is hidden and only a small part may be visible. A fraud loss of $20,000 this year may not be material to an external auditor, but $20,000 each year for a 15-year fraud career amounts to $300,000 in the fraud examiner's eyes—and it is big enough to matter!

Review Checkpoints

D.14 Internal auditors have one of the highest incidents of fraud detection (higher then external auditors). Why might this be true? To what extent would you think internal auditors include fraud detection responsibility in their normal audit assignments?

D.15 In fraud examiners' terminology, what is *predication*?

D.16 Why might fraud examiners have attitudes about control systems and materiality different from other auditors?

A Fraud Audit Example

Alice, a fraud examiner, has been called into Bulldog Corporation because an accounts payable fraud is suspected. Several vendor invoices were paid to Longhorn Enterprises, a vendor not on the approved vendor list. While this may indicate a fictitious vendor set up by someone in the company as a fraud, it also may be an indication of someone not following procedure. It is possible that the purchases from this vendor were valid, but the vendor did not get on the approved vendor list. The fraud examiner must make the determination if this is a fraud or just a case of not following procedure. The fraud examiner may take several steps to identify whether Longhorn Enterprises exists.

DOES FRAUD EXIST?
Alice has called the secretary of state's office, checked the telephone book, asked directory assistance, and searched the Internet and has not found any indication of a company called Longhorn Enterprises. In addition, the invoices from Longhorn Enterprises have no telephone number and only a P.O. Box as an address. Finally, there are no creases on the invoices in the file, indicating they were probably not mailed to the company.

HOW LARGE IS THE FRAUD?
Convinced that Longhorn Enterprises does not exist, Alice sets out to determine the extent of the fraud. She searches the cash disbursements journal and accounts payable records looking for checks paid to Longhorn Enterprises. She finds 32 invoices paid over the last two years. Alice retrieves the canceled checks from the file, copies them front and back, and places the originals in a plastic bag (they are evidence and may have fingerprints or other forensic information). She makes copies of all the invoices and places the originals in a plastic bag. All the originals are locked up for safekeeping. The total of the checks is $47,245.

WHO COMMITTED THE FRAUD?
Alice notices that the checks are endorsed by hand (most companies endorse checks with a stamp). She also notes the checks are deposited in Smalltime Regional Bank. Because Bulldog pays its employees through direct deposit, Alice can compare the banks used by employees with the bank used to deposit Longhorn Enterprises' checks. Alice compares that list with the list of employees that are involved in the purchasing and payables process. She finds three purchasing and payable employees that use the Smalltime Regional Bank. Alice takes the information she has to an attorney, who assists Alice in getting a subpoena for the bank records and postal information concerning the P.O. Box. She finds that both the P.O. Box and bank account are registered to Myrtle, an accounts payable clerk who uses Smalltime Regional Bank for her payroll deposits. The bank records also show transfers of money from the bank account, listed as LE Inc., to Myrtle's personal bank account.

Next, Alice talks with other employees in the accounts payable area. Alice discovers that Myrtle has purchased a new car and has taken an expensive vacation over the last year. Alice is now ready to confront Myrtle with the evidence and obtain a confession.

HOW COULD THIS FRAUD HAPPEN?
Finally, from Myrtle's confession, Alice determines that the assistant treasurer routinely approves small payments without any scrutiny of supporting documentation. Myrtle inserted fictitious invoices in stacks of other invoices for the assistant treasurer to sign. Alice's final report included that it was a failure of the assistant treasurer to follow procedure that allowed the fraud to occur.

After Discovering a Fraud

LEARNING
OBJECTIVE

7. Describe the ways
CPAs can assist in
prosecuting fraud
perpetrators.

Building a case against a fraudster is a task for trained investigators who know how to conduct interviews and interrogations, perform surveillance, use informants, and obtain usable confessions. In almost all cases, the post-discovery activity proceeds with a special prosecutorial attitude and with the cooperation or leadership of management. A district attorney and police officials also may be involved. Prosecution of fraudsters is advisable because, if left unpunished, they often go on to steal again. In addition, failure to prosecute sends a bad message to other potential fraudsters in the organization.

Consulting and Assisting

While engaged in the audit work, auditors should know how to preserve the *chain of custody* of evidence. The chain of custody is the crucial link of the evidence to the suspect, called the "relevance" of evidence by attorneys and judges. If documents are lost, mutilated, coffee-soaked, or compromised (so a defense attorney can argue that they were altered to frame the suspect), they can lose their effectiveness for the prosecution. Auditors should learn to mark the evidence, writing an identification of the location, condition, date, time, and circumstances as soon as it appears to be a signal of fraud. This marking may be on a separate tag or page or the original may be marked in a manner that preserves the integrity of the document. The original document should be put in a protective envelope (plastic) for preservation and audit work should proceed with copies of the documents instead of originals. A record should be made of the safekeeping and of all persons who use the original. Any eyewitness observations should be promptly recorded in a memorandum or on tape (audio or video), with corroboration of colleagues, if possible. Other features of the chain of custody relate to interviews, interrogations, confessions, documents obtained by subpoena, and other matters, but auditors usually do not conduct these activities.

Litigation Support

Independent CPAs often accept engagements for litigation support and expert witnessing. This work is often referred to as **forensic accounting,** which means the application of accounting and auditing evidence to legal problems, both civil and criminal. Litigation support can take several forms, but it usually amounts to consulting in the capacity of helping attorneys document cases and determine damages. Expert witness work involves testifying to findings determined during litigation support and testifying about accounting principles and auditing standards applications. The AICPA, ACFE, and IIA conduct continuing education courses for auditors who want to become experts in these fields.

Review Checkpoints

D.17 Why is prosecution of fraud perpetrators generally a good idea?

D.18 Why do fraud examiners handle information in a different manner than auditors? Why is this important?

Summary

Governmental and internal auditing standards include the essence of the AICPA generally accepted auditing standards (GAAS) and go much further by expressing standards for audits of economy, efficiency, and program results. In addition, the internal auditing standards contain many guides for the management of an internal audit department within a company.

All auditors hold independence as a primary goal, but internal auditors must establish an internal organizational independence from the managers and executives whose areas they audit. Governmental auditors must be concerned about factual independence with regard to social, political, and level-of-government influences.

Governmental auditing is complicated by the special context of audit assignments intended to accomplish accountability by agencies that handle federal funds—grants, subsidies, entitlement programs, and the like. The requirements of the GAO standards and the Single Audit Act of 1984 impose on the audit function the responsibility for compliance audit work designed to determine agencies' observance of laws and regulations, of which there are many. Auditors must report not only on financial statements but also on internal control, violations of laws and regulations, fraud, abuse, and illegal acts. These elements are all part of the federal oversight of federal spending, facilitated by auditors.

Governmental and internal audit reports are not standardized like the GAAS reports on audited financial statements. Auditors must be very careful that their reports communicate their conclusions and recommendations in a clear and concise manner. The variety of assignments and the challenge of reporting in such a free-form setting contribute to making governmental auditing, internal auditing, and consulting services exciting fields for career opportunities.

Fraud awareness auditing starts with knowledge of the types of errors, frauds, and illegal acts that can be perpetrated. External, internal, and governmental auditors all have standards for care, attention, planning, detection, and reporting of some kinds of errors, frauds, and illegal acts. Fraud examiners, on the other hand, have little in the way of standard programs or materiality guidelines to limit their attention to fraud possibilities. However, auditors must always exercise technical and personal care because accusations of fraud are always taken very seriously. For this reason, after preliminary findings indicate fraud possibilities, auditors should enlist the cooperation of management and assist fraud examination professionals when bringing an investigation to a conclusion.

Key Terms

compliance audits: Audits designed to ensure that an organization is following applicable laws, regulations, and management directives. Usually performed by internal auditors but may be performed by governmental or external auditors as well, 630

environmental audit: Audit designed to ensure that an organization is following environmental standards established by laws, regulations, and management directives. In addition, environmental audits may recommend methods of reducing environmental problems by reducing or reusing waste or by-products of an organization's processes, 632

exit conference: Meeting that occurs at the end of an internal audit between the auditors and management of the organization being audited. While many external audits include such a meeting, an exit conference is a required part of an internal audit, 634

follow-up: Internal auditors are required to ensure that significant audit findings have been addressed by the auditee in accordance with the agreement between the auditor and management, 634

forensic accounting: Application of accounting and auditing evidence to resolve legal issues in civil and criminal law, 645

governance audits: Audits designed to provide management with information required to make governance decisions or to ensure that high-quality information is provided for these decisions, 631

internal auditing: An audit service provided to a company to assist a company to meet the corporate goals and objectives through evaluation and recommendation concerning risk management, control, and governance processes, 626

operational audits: Audits designed to evaluate the processes and procedures of an organization or an area within an organization to ensure the process or area is operating efficiently and effectively, 631

performance audits: Audits designed to ensure that the resources of an organization are being used appropriately and the objectives of an organization are being met, 636

predication: A suspicion that a fraud may have occurred, 645

quality audit: Audit designed to ensure that an organization is meeting its quality control standards. Usually involves determining that personnel responsible for performing quality control are meeting the goals and objectives established and that quality information is being reported to appropriate members of management, 631

single audit: Government auditing standard that allows an entity to receive one audit of its financial statements, compliance with laws and regulations, and internal control that will be utilized by multiple agencies granting money to the entity, 640

Yellow Book: Common name used to refer to the Generally Accepted Government Auditing Standards (GAGAS), 635

Multiple Choice Questions for Practice and Review

D.19. Which of the following would be considered in determining if an internal audit department is independent?

a. The organizational level of the chief audit officer and the objectivity of the audit staff.

b. That the auditors report to the audit committee and the composition of the audit committee.

c. The organizational status of the audit committee and the individual independence of internal auditors in the department.

d. The nature of the audit charter and the objectivity of the audit staff.

D.20. Which of the following would be considered the greatest problem for internal audit if the chief audit officer reported to the controller?

a. The controller would amend the audit schedule so more audit time was spent on accounting issues.

b. The controller may have no training as an internal auditor.

c. During times when the budget needs to be cut, internal audit would likely be the first to lose funding.

d. The controller can control the scope of audits and censor audit reports before being sent to management and the audit committee.

D.21. Governmental auditors' independence and objectivity are enhanced when they report the results of an audit assignment directly to

a. Managers of the government agency under audit and in which the auditors are employed.

b. The audit committee of directors of the agency under audit.

c. Political action committees of which they are members.

d. The congressional committee that ordered the audit.

D.22 In all audits of governmental units performed according to GAGAS, the most important work is

a. Compliance auditing.

b. Obtaining a sufficient understanding of internal control.

c. Documentation of the audit.

d. Exit interviews with managers in the governmental unit.

D.23 Which of the following is considered different and more limited in objectives than the others?

a. Operational auditing.

b. Performance auditing.

c. Management auditing.

d. Financial statement auditing.

D.24 A typical objective of an operational audit is for the auditor to

a. Determine whether the financial statements fairly present the company's operations.

b. Evaluate the feasibility of attaining the company's operational objectives.

c. Make recommendations for achieving company objectives.

d. Report on the company's relative success in attaining profit maximization.

D.25 A government auditor assigned to audit the financial statements of the state highway department would not be considered independent if the auditor

 a. Also held a position as a project manager in the highway department.

 b. Was the state audit official elected in a general statewide election with responsibility to report to the legislature.

 c. Normally works as a state auditor employed in the department of human services.

 d. Was appointed by the state governor with responsibility to report to the legislature.

D.26 Government auditing can extend beyond audits of financial statements to include audits of an agency's efficient and economical use of resources and

 a. Constitutionality of laws and regulations governing the agency.

 b. Evaluation of the personal managerial skills shown by the agency's leaders.

 c. Correspondence of the agency's performance with public opinion regarding the social worth of its mission.

 d. Evaluations concerning the agency's achievements of the goals set by the legislature for the agency's activities.

D.27 Which of the following best describes how the detailed audit program of the external auditor who is engaged to audit the financial statements of a large publicly held company compares with the audit client's comprehensive internal audit program?

 a. The comprehensive internal audit program covers areas that would normally not be reviewed by an external auditor.

 b. The comprehensive internal audit program is more detailed although it covers fewer areas than would normally be covered by an external auditor.

 c. The comprehensive internal audit program is substantially identical to the audit program used by an external auditor because both review substantially identical areas.

 d. The comprehensive internal audit program is less detailed and covers fewer areas than would normally be reviewed by an external auditor.

D.28. Which of the following is usually *not* part of an internal audit department's audit charter?

 a. A commitment from management to ensure the independence of the internal audit department.

 b. A definition of the scope of the audit department's activities

 c. The organizational structure of the internal audit department.

 d. The reporting requirements of the internal audit department.

D.29 Which of the following would you not expect to see in an auditor's report(s) on the financial statements of an independent government agency?

 a. A statement that the audit was conducted in accordance with generally accepted government audit standards.

 b. A report on the agency's compliance with applicable laws and regulations.

 c. Commentary by the agency's managers on the audit findings and recommendations.

 d. A report on the agency's internal controls.

D.30 The federal Single Audit Act of 1984 requires auditors to determine and report several things about state and local governments that receive federal funds. Which of the following is not normally required to be reported?

 a. An opinion on the fair presentation of the financial statements in accordance with generally accepted accounting principles.

 b. A report on the government's internal control related to federal funds.

 c. The government's performance in meeting goals set in enabling legislation.

 d. A report on the government's compliance with applicable laws and regulations.

D.31. The Governmental Accountability Office (GAO) describes expanded-scope governmental auditing to include all of the following *except*

 a. Financial statement audits.

 b. Attestation engagements.

 c. Compliance audits.

 d. Performance audits.

D.32 In government and internal performance auditing, which of the following is the least important consideration when performing the field work?

a. Determining the applicable generally accepted government accounting principles pronounced by the GASB.

b. Defining problem areas or opportunities for improvement and defining program goals.

c. Selecting and performing procedures designed to obtain evidence about operational problems and production output.

d. Evaluating evidence in terms of economy, efficiency, and achievement of program goals.

D.33 Which of the following is the least important consideration for a government auditor who needs to be objective when auditing and reporting on an agency's achievement of program goals?

a. Measure the actual output results of agency activities.

b. Compare the agency's actual output results to quantitative goal standards.

c. Perform a comprehensive review of management controls.

d. Determine quantitative standards that describe goals the agency was supposed to achieve.

D.34 Compliance auditing in audits performed under the Single Audit Act of 1984 in accordance with GAGAS is necessary for an auditor's

a. Report on the auditee's internal control, including reportable conditions and material weaknesses.

b. Opinion on the auditee's observance, or lack thereof, of applicable laws and regulations.

c. Opinion on the auditee's financial statements.

d. Report of a supplementary schedule of federal assistance programs and amounts.

D.35 Which two of the following characterize the work of fraud examiners?

a. Analysis of control weaknesses for determination of acceptable fraud risk.

b. Analysis of control strengths as a basis for planning other audit procedures.

c. Determination of a materiality amount that represents a significant misstatement of the financial statements.

d. Thinking of a materiality amount in cumulative terms—that is, becoming large over a number of years.

D.36 When auditing with "fraud awareness," auditors should especially notice and follow up employee activities under which of these conditions?

a. The company always estimates the inventory but never takes a complete physical count.

b. The petty cash box is always locked in the desk of the custodian.

c. Management has published a company code of ethics and sends frequent communication newsletters about it.

d. The board of directors reviews and approves all investment transactions.

D.37 The best way to enact a broad fraud-prevention program is to

a. Install airtight control systems of checks and supervision.

b. Name an "ethics officer" who is responsible for receiving and acting upon fraud tips.

c. Place dedicated "hotline" telephones on walls around the workplace with direct communication to the company ethics officer.

d. Practice management "of the people and for the people" to help them share personal and professional problems.

D.38 A reason to believe that a fraud has occurred is called

a. Deliberation.

b. Forensics.

c. Predication.

d. Restitution.

D.39 An environmental audit might include all of following *except*

a. Determining that proper tracking of waste material is being maintained by the organization.

b. Reviewing the liability account established for pending environmental claims against the company.

c. Reviewing the environmental history of another company that the internal auditor's organization is interested in purchasing.

d. All of the above are appropriate issues for an environmental audit.

Exercises, Problems, and Simulations

D.40 **Identification of Audits and Auditors.** Audits may be characterized as (a) financial statement audits, (b) compliance audits, (c) economy and efficiency audits, and (d) program results audits. The work can be done by independent (external) auditors, internal auditors, or governmental auditors (including IRS auditors and federal bank examiners). Below is a list of the purpose or products of various audit engagements. [Students may need to refer to Chapter 1.]

1. Analyze proprietary schools' spending to train students for oversupplied occupations.
2. Determine the fair presentation in conformity with GAAP of an advertising agency's financial statements.
3. Study the Department of Defense's expendable launch vehicle program.
4. Determine costs of municipal garbage pickup services compared to comparable service subcontracted to a private business.
5. Audit tax shelter partnership financing terms.
6. Study a private aircraft manufacturer's test pilot performance in reporting on the results of test flights.
7. Periodically have U.S. comptroller of currency examine a national bank for solvency.
8. Evaluate the promptness of materials inspection in a manufacturer's receiving department.
9. Report on the need for the states to consider reporting requirements for chemical use data.
10. Render a public report on the assumptions and compilation of a revenue forecast by a sports stadium/racetrack complex.

Required:

Prepare a three-column schedule showing (1) each of the engagements listed above; (2) the type of audit (financial statement, compliance, economy and efficiency, or program results); and (3) the kind of auditors you would expect to be involved.

D.41 **Organizing a Risk Analysis.** You are the director of internal auditing of a large municipal hospital. You receive monthly financial reports prepared by the accounting department and your review of them has shown that total accounts receivable from patients has steadily and rapidly increased over the past eight months.

Other information in the reports shows the following conditions:

a. The number of available hospital beds has not changed.
b. The bed occupancy rate has not changed.
c. Hospital billing rates have not changed significantly.
d. The hospitalization insurance contracts have not changed since the last modification 12 months ago.

Your internal audit department audited the accounts receivable 10 months ago. The audit documentation file for that assignment contains financial information, a record of the risk analysis, documentation of the study and evaluation of management and internal risk mitigation controls, documentation of the evidence-gathering procedures used to produce evidence about the validity and collectibility of the accounts, and a copy of your report, which commented favorably on the controls and collectibility of the receivables.

However, the current increase in receivables has alerted you to a need for another audit so things will not get out of hand. You remember news stories last year about the manager of the city water system who got into big trouble because his accounting department double-billed all the residential customers for three months.

Required:

You plan to perform a risk analysis to get a handle on the problem, if indeed a problem exists. Write a memo to your senior auditor listing at least eight questions he should use to guide and direct the risk analysis. (*Hint:* The questions used last year were organized under these headings: (1) Who does the accounts receivable accounting? (2) What data processing procedures and policies are in effect? and (3) How is the accounts receivable accounting done? This time, you will add a fourth category: (4) What financial or economic events have occurred in the last 10 months?)

(CIA adapted)

D.42 **Audit Simulation: Study and Evaluation of Management Control.** The study and evaluation of management risk mitigation control in a governmental or internal audit is not easy. First, auditors must determine the risks and the controls subject to audit. Then, they must find a standard by which performance of the control can be evaluated. Next, they must specify procedures to obtain the evidence on which an evaluation can be based. Insofar as possible, the standards and related evidence must be quantified.

Students working on this case usually do not have the experience or theoretical background to determine control standards and audit procedures, so the description below gives certain information (in italics) that internal auditors would know about or be able to figure out on their own. Fulfilling the requirement thus amounts to taking some information from the scenario below and figuring out other things by using accountants' and auditors' common sense.

The Scenario

Ace Corporation ships building materials to more than a thousand wholesale and retail customers in a five-state region. The company's normal credit terms are net/30 days and no cash discounts are offered. Fred Clark is the chief financial officer and he is concerned about risks related to maintaining control over customer credit. In particular, he has stated two management control principles for this purpose.

1. Sales are to be billed to customers accurately and promptly. Fred knows that errors will occur but thinks company personnel ought to be able to hold quantity, unit price, and arithmetic errors down to 3 percent of the sales invoices. He considers an invoice error of $1 or less not to matter. He believes prompt billing is important since customers are expected to pay within 30 days. Fred is very strict in thinking that a bill should be sent to the customer one day after shipment. He believes he has staffed the billing department well enough to be able to handle this workload. The relevant company records consist of an accounts receivable control account; a subsidiary ledger of customers' accounts in which charges are entered by billing (invoice) date and credits are entered by date of payment receipts; a sales journal that lists invoices in chronological order; and a file of shipping documents cross-referenced by the number on the related sales invoice copy kept on file in numerical order.

2. Accounts receivable are to be aged and followed up to ensure prompt collection. Fred has told the accounts receivable department to classify all the customer accounts in categories of (a) current, (b) 31–59 days overdue, (c) 60–90 days overdue, and (d) more than 90 days overdue. He wants this trial balance to be complete and to be transmitted to the credit department within five days after each month end. In the credit department, prompt follow-up means sending a different (stronger) collection letter to each category, cutting off credit to customers over 60 days past due (putting them on cash basis), and giving the over-90-days accounts to an outside collection agency. These actions are supposed to be taken within five days after receipt of the aged trial balance. The relevant company records, in addition to the ones listed above, consist of the aged trial balance, copies of the letters sent to customers, copies of notices of credit cutoff, copies of correspondence with the outside collection agent, and reports of results—statistics of subsequent collections.

Required:

Take the role of a senior internal auditor. You are to write a memo to the internal audit staff to inform them about comparison standards for the study and evaluation of these two management control policies. You also need to specify two or three procedures for gathering evidence about performance of the controls. The body of your memo should be structured as follows:

1. Control: Sales are billed to customers accurately and promptly.
 a. Accuracy.
 (1) Policy standard . . .
 (2) Audit procedures . . .
 b. Promptness.
 (1) Policy standard . . .
 (2) Audit procedures . . .

2. Control: Accounts receivable are aged and followed up to ensure prompt collection.
 a. Accounts receivable aging.
 (1) Policy standard . . .
 (2) Audit procedures . . .
 b. Follow-up prompt collection.
 (1) Policy standard . . .
 (2) Audit procedures . . .

D.43 **Quality Audit of a University.** You have been engaged to perform a quality audit of your university.

Required:

 a. How do you measure quality in a university environment? What departments are responsible for measuring quality?
 b. What audit evidence would you look for in performing the quality audit?

D.44 **Analytical Audit of Inventory.** External auditors usually calculate inventory turnover (cost of goods sold for the year divided by average inventory) and use the ratio as a broad indication of inventory age, obsolescence, or overstocking. External auditors are interested in evidence relating to the material accuracy of the financial statements taken as a whole. Internal auditors, on the other hand, calculate turnover by categories and classes of inventory to detect problem areas that might otherwise get overlooked. This kind of detailed analytical audit might point to conditions of buying errors, obsolescence, overstocking, and other matters that could be changed to save money.

The data shown in Exhibit D.44.1 are turnover, cost of sales, and inventory investment data for a series of four history years and the current year. In each of the history years, the external auditors did not recommend any adjustments to the inventory valuations.

Required:

Calculate the current year inventory turnover ratios. Interpret the ratio trends and point out what conditions might exist; write a memo to the vice president for production explaining your findings and the further investigation that can be conducted.

EXHIBIT D.44.1 Inventory Data

	Inventory Turnover				Current-Year Inventory ($000)	
	2005	**2006**	**2007**	**2008**	**Beginning**	**Ending**
Total inventory	2.1	2.0	2.1	2.1	$3,000	$2,917
Materials and parts	4.0	4.1	4.3	4.5	1,365	620
Work-in-process	12.0	12.5	11.5	11.7	623	697
Finished products:						
Computer games	6.0	7.0	10.0	24.0	380	500
Floppy disk drives	8.0	7.2	7.7	8.5	64	300
Semiconductor parts	4.0	3.5	4.5	7.0	80	400
Electric typewriters	3.0	2.5	2.0	1.9	488	400

Additional Information

Current Year ($000)

	Transfers	Sales	Cost of Goods Sold	Gross Profit	Compared to prior year
Materials and parts	$3,970*	NA	NA	NA	
Work-in-process	7,988[†]	NA	NA	NA	
Computer games	2,320[‡]	$2,000	$2,200	$<200>	Sales volume declined 60%[§]
Floppy disk drives	2,236[‡]	3,000	2,000	1,000	Sales volume increased 35%
Semiconductor parts	2,720[‡]	4,000	2,400	1,600	Sales volume increased 40%
Electric typewriters	712[‡]	1,000	800	200	Sales volume declined 3%

NA means not applicable.
*Cost of materials transferred to Work-in-Process.
[†]Cost of materials, labor, and overhead transferred to Finished Goods.
[‡]Cost of goods transferred from Work-in-Process to Finished Product Inventories.
[§]Selling prices also were reduced and the gross margin declined.

D.45 **Audit Simulation: Internal Auditors in the Fast-Food Industry.** Internal auditors perform risk-based audits that go beyond the risks of the financial statements. Assume you are on the internal audit staff of McDonald's.

Required:

 a. Identify the risks in the fast food industry associated with

 1. Competition

 2. Customer preference

 3. The economy

 4. Technology

 5. Regulation

 6. Other risks

 b. Explain how each of the risks you identified could affect McDonald's

 c. Explain how these risks might affect the internal audits performed by the internal audit staff for McDonald's.

D.46 **CPA Involvement in an Expanded-Scope Audit.** A public accounting firm received an invitation to bid for the audit of a local food commodity distribution program funded by the U.S. Department of Agriculture. The audit is to be conducted in accordance with the audit standards published by the Government Accountability Office (GAO). The accountants have become familiar with the GAGAS and recognize that they incorporate the AICPA generally accepted auditing standards (GAAS).

 The public accounting firm has been engaged to perform the audit of the program and the audit is to encompass both financial and performance audits that constitute the expanded scope of a GAGAS audit.

Required:

 a. The accountants should perform sufficient audit work to satisfy the financial and compliance element of GAGAS. What is the objective of such audit work? (*Hint:* Go to the Generally Accepted Government Auditing Standards at www.gao.gov).

 b. The accountants should be aware of general and specific kinds of uneconomical or inefficient practices in such a program. What are some examples?

 c. What might be some standards and sources of standards for judging program results?

D.47 **Select Effective Extended Procedures.** Given below are some "suspicions"; you have been requested to select some effective extended procedures designed to confirm or deny the suspicions.

Required:

Write the suggested procedures for each case in definite terms so another person can know what to do.

 a. The custodian of the petty cash fund may be removing cash on Friday afternoon to pay for weekend activities.

 b. A manager noticed that eight new vendors were added to the purchasing department approved list after the assistant purchasing agent was promoted to chief agent three weeks ago. She suspects all or some of them might be phony companies set up by the new chief purchasing agent.

 c. The payroll supervisor may be stealing unclaimed paychecks of people who quit work and don't pick up the last check.

 d. Although no customers have complained, cash collections on accounts receivable are down and the counter clerks may have stolen customers' payments.

 e. The cashier may have "borrowed" money, covering it by holding each day's deposit until cash from the next day(s)'s collection is enough to make up the shortage from an earlier day, then sending the deposit to the bank.

D.48 **Internet Exercise: Government audit reports.** Go to the Web site of the town where you reside and find the Comprehensive Annual Financial Report (CAFR). Find and print the auditor's report. Warning: Be careful! CAFRs can be over 100 pages, so make certain you're just printing the auditor's report.

Required:

 a. Who audited the financial statements in the CAFR?

 b. How does the auditor's report compare to the three-paragraph standard report used when auditing for-profit companies' financial statements?

 c. What additional paragraphs were added to the report?

D.49 **Collecting Evidence in a Fraud Examination.** A fraud examiner was called into a business because of a suspicion of fraud. An assistant manager in a bookstore is taking books off the shelf, bringing them to the return book area, completing a customer return form, and pocketing the money. He does this late in the day when there are few other employees in the store and those employees are involved in closing activities that occupy them in other areas.

Required:

 a. What are the objectives of the fraud examiner in performing a fraud audit?

 b. What evidence could the fraud examiner obtain that would help reach the objectives of the audit?

 c. How should the fraud examiner handle the evidence he or she obtains?

D.50 **Simulation: Auditing the Effectiveness of a Loan Program.** The Office of Economic Opportunity (OEO) designed special impact programs to have a major impact on unemployment, dependency, and community tensions in urban areas with large concentrations of low-income residents or in rural areas having substantial migration to such urban areas. The purpose of these experimental programs—combining business, community, and manpower development—is to offer poor people an opportunity to become self-supporting through the free enterprise system. The programs are intended to create training and job opportunities, improve the living environment, and encourage development of local entrepreneurial skills.

One area chosen to participate in the special impact program was Bedford-Stuyvesant. The Bedford-Stuyvesant program was the first and largest such program to be sponsored by the federal government. It has received more than $30 million in federal funds from its inception through the current year. Another $7.7 million was obtained from private sources such as the Ford Foundation and the Astor Foundation.

Problems

Bedford-Stuyvesant is a five-square-mile area with a population of 350,000 to 400,000 in New York City's borough of Brooklyn. This area has serious problems of unemployment and underemployment and inadequate housing.

Bedford-Stuyvesant's problems are deep-seated and have resisted rapid solution. They stem primarily from the fact that local residents, to a considerable degree, lack the education and training required for the jobs available elsewhere in the city and from the lack of jobs in the area. Unemployment and underemployment, in turn, reduce buying power, which has a depressing effect on the area's economy.

The magnitude of the Bedford-Stuyvesant problems is indicated by the following data disclosed by the U.S. census:

1. Of the total civilian labor force, 8.9 percent were unemployed, compared with unemployment rates of 7.1 percent for New York City and 6.8 percent for the New York Standard Metropolitan Statistical Area (SMSA).

2. Per capita income was $7,106, compared with $10,720 for New York City and $13,909 for the SMSA.

3. Families below the poverty level made up 24.8 percent of the population, compared with 11.4 percent in New York City and 9.2 percent in the SMSA.

4. Families receiving public assistance made up 25.4 percent of the population, compared with 9.6 percent in New York City and 7.5 percent in the SMSA.

A number of factors serve to aggravate the area's economic problems and make them more difficult to solve. Some of these are

1. A reluctance of industry to move into New York City.

2. A net outflow of industry from New York City.

3. High city taxes and a high crime rate.

4. A dearth of local residents possessing business managerial experience.

The area's housing problems resulted from the widespread deterioration of existing housing and are, in part, a by-product of below-average income levels resulting from

unemployment and underemployment. They were aggravated by a shortage of mortgage capital for residential housing associated with a lack of confidence in the area on the part of financial institutions, which, as discussed later, seems to have been somewhat overcome.

Bedford-Stuyvesant was the target of several special impact programs. Included were programs designed to stimulate private business, to improve housing, to establish community facilities, and to train residents in marketable skills. There were two programs to stimulate private business: a program to loan funds to local businesses and a program to attract outside businesses to the area.

Under the business loan program begun five years ago, the sponsors proposed to create jobs and stimulate business ownership by local residents. At first, investments in local businesses were made only in the form of loans. Later, the sponsors adopted a policy of making equity investments in selected companies to obtain for the sponsors a voice in management. Equity investments totaling about $159,000 were made in four companies.

Loans were to be repaid in installments over periods of up to 10 years, usually with a moratorium on repayment for six months or longer. Repayment was to be made in cash or by applying subsidies allowed by the sponsors for providing on-the-job training to unskilled workers. Loans made during the first two years of the program were interest free. Later, the sponsors revised the policy to one of charging below-market interest rates. Rates charged were from 3 to 6.5 percent. This policy change was made to (1) emphasize to borrowers their obligations to repay the loan and (2) help the sponsors monitor borrowers' progress toward profitability.

Prospective borrowers learned of the loan program through (1) information disseminated at neighborhood centers, (2) advertisements on radio and television and in a local newspaper, and (3) word of mouth. Those who wished to apply for loans were required to complete application forms providing information relating to their education, their business and work experience, and their personal financial statements and references. The sponsors set up a management assistance division, which employed consultants to supplement its internal marketing assistance efforts and to provide management, accounting, marketing, legal, and other assistance to borrowers.

The sponsors proposed to create at least 1,700 jobs during the first four years of the loan program by making loans to some 73 new and existing businesses.

Required:

Put yourself in the position of the GAO manager in charge of all audits pertaining to the Office of Economic Opportunity. The New York City field office has been assigned the job of conducting a detailed review of the special impact program described above. Prepare a memo to the New York City field office in which you indicate, in as great detail as is possible from the information provided, the specific steps they should perform in conducting an evaluation of the program effectiveness of the special impact loan program.

D.51 **Audit Simulation: Operational Audit: Customer Complaints.** Danny Deck, the director of internal auditing for the Rice Department Stores, was working in his office one Thursday when Larry McMurray, president of the company, burst in to tell about a problem. According to Larry: "Customer complaints about delays in getting credit for merchandise returns are driving Sally Godwin up the wall! She doesn't know what to do because she has no control over the processing of credit memos."

Sally is the manager in charge of customer relations and she tries to keep everybody happy. Upon her recommendation, the company adopted an advertising motto: "Satisfaction Guaranteed and Prompt Credit When You Change Your Mind." The motto is featured in newspaper ads and on large banners in each store.

Danny performed a preliminary review and found the following:

1. Sally believes customers will be satisfied if they receive a refund check or notice of credit on account within five working days.

2. The chief accountant described the credit memo processing procedure as follows: When a customer returns merchandise, the sales clerks give a smile, a "returned merchandise receipt," and a promise to send a check or a notice within five days. The store copy of the receipt and the merchandise are sent to the purchasing department, where buyers examine the merchandise for quality or damage to decide whether to put it back on the shelves, return it to the vendor, or hold it for the annual rummage sale. The buyers then

prepare a brief report and send it with the returned merchandise receipt to the customer relations department for approval. The buyer's report is filed for reference and the receipt, marked for approval in Sally's department, is sent to the accounting department. The accounting department sorts the receipts in numerical order, checking the numerical sequence, and files them in readiness for the weekly batch processing of transactions other than sales and cash receipts, both of which are processed daily. When the customer has requested a cash refund, the checks and canceled returned merchandise receipts are approved by the treasurer, who signs and mails the check. When the credit is on a customer's charge account, it is shown on the next monthly statement sent to the customer.

3. The processing in each department takes two or three days.

Required:

 a. Analyze the problem. How much time does it take the company to process the merchandise returns?

 b. Formulate a recommendation to solve the problem. Write a brief report explaining your recommendation.

D.52 **GAO Auditor Independence.** The GAO reporting standards for performance audits state that each report should include "recommendations for action to correct the problem areas and to improve operations." For example, an audit of the Washington Metropolitan Area Transit Authority found management decision deficiencies affecting some $230 million in federal funds. The GAO auditors recommended that the transit authority could improve its management control over railcar procurement through better enforcement of contract requirements and development of a master plan to test cars.

Suppose the transit authority accepted and implemented specific recommendations made by the GAO auditors.

Required:

Do you believe these events would be enough to impair the independence of the GAO auditors in a subsequent audit of the transit authority? Explain and tell if it makes any difference to you whether the same or different person performs both the first and subsequent audits.

D.53 **Efficiency Standards.** The U.S. Postal Service (USPS) advertises prompt delivery schedules for express mail (overnight delivery) and priority mail (2–3-day delivery). The USPS knows various risks that may arise to thwart their work of timely (as advertised) delivery but believes that systems and controls are in place and operating to mitigate the risks. The USPS advertised that 94 percent of express mail and 87 percent of priority mail was delivered on time from the time the mail was postmarked to the time it reached the destination post office. However, a consulting firm studied the USPS operations and determined that the express mail arrived at the recipients' addresses 81 percent of the time (not 94 percent) and the priority mail arrived timely 75 percent of the time (not 87 percent).

Required:

What can account for the difference in these performance statistics between the USPS delivery rates and the consultant's rates? (*Hint:* Think in terms of orientation to customers and standards for measuring performance.)

D.54 **Audit Simulation: The Perfect Crime.** Embezzlers often try to cover up by removing canceled checks they made payable to themselves or endorsed on the back with their own names. Missing canceled checks are a signal (red flag). However, people who reconcile bank accounts may not notice missing checks if the bank reconciliation is performed using only the numerical listing printed in the bank statement. Now consider the case of truncated bank statements, when the bank does not even return the canceled checks to the payer. All the checks are "missing" and the bank reconciler has no opportunity to notice anything about canceled checks. Consider the following story of a real embezzlement.

The embezzler hired a print shop to print a private stock of Ajax Company checks in the company's numerical sequence. In his job as an accounts payable clerk, he intercepted legitimate checks written by the accounts payable department and signed by the Ajax treasurer, then destroyed them. He substituted the same-numbered check from the private stock, payable to himself in the same amount as the legitimate check, and he "signed" it with a rubber stamp that looked enough like the Ajax Company treasurer's signature to fool the paying bank. He deposited the money in his own bank account.

The bank statement reconciler (a different person) was able to agree the check numbers and amounts listed in the cleared items in the bank statement to the recorded cash disbursement (check number and amount), thus did not notice the trick. The embezzler was able to process the vendor's "past due" notice and next month statement with complete documentation, enabling the Ajax treasurer to sign another check the next month paying both the past due balance and current charges. The embezzler was careful to scatter the double-expense payments among numerous accounts (telephone, office supplies, inventory, etc.), so the double-paid expenses did not distort any accounts very much. As time passed, the embezzler was able to recommend budget figures that allowed a large enough budget so his double-paid expenses in various categories did not often pop up as large variances from the budget.

Required:

List and explain the ways and means you believe someone might detect this fraud scheme. Think first about the ordinary everyday control procedures. Then, think about extensive detection efforts assuming a tip or indication of a possible fraud has been received. Is this a "perfect crime"?

D.55 **Impact of Changing Rules.** Many companies outsourced their internal audit function to CPA firms.

Required:

a. What benefits might be gained from having a CPA firm provide its internal audit services?

b. What benefits might be gained from having an in-house internal audit department?

c. What concerns might arise from having a CPA firm provide its internal audit services?

D.56 **Audit Simulation: Looking for Evidence of Fraud.** Wen-Li is an internal auditor for Main Electrical Supply in Springfield, Illinois. During her audit, she came across the invoice shown in Exhibit D.56.1. The invoice is in almost pristine condition with few marks and no creases. The invoice was properly filed in a vendor folder marked Best Office Supply. Best Office Supply is on the approved vendor list, but the vendor review sheet, which is required to place a vendor on the approved vendor list, is missing from the file.

Three other invoices were in the file:

June 14, 2008	Invoice #0076	$238.99
July 17, 2008	Invoice #0082	$324.55
August 16, 2008	Invoice #0085	$386.82

Required:

a. Is this a legitimate invoice? What information might lead you to suspect that this invoice may indicate a fraud?

b. What type(s) of fraud might this indicate?

EXHIBIT D.56.1 **Vendor Invoice**

September 15, 2008

Best Office Supply Company
P.O. Box 1934
Springfield, Illinois 62705

Invoice #0089

Bill to:
Main Electrical Supply
506 Commerce Avenue
Springfield, IL 62707
217-555-2230

Product	Quantity	Price per Unit	Total Cost
Pens	10 Boxes	$3.65	$36.50
Copy paper	15 cases	$15.76	$236.40
Toner cartridges	8 units	$22.56	$180.48
Total			$453.38

Payment is due immediately upon receipt

CPA REVIEW

D.57 **Kaplan CPA Exam Simulation: Government Auditing Standards.** Ridge & Associates (Ridge), a public accounting firm, is examining the financial statements of Western Water Company (Western). This is Ridge's first audit and you are the in-charge auditor. Ridge has already reviewed the prior auditor's working papers. During late October, with the help of Western's controller, Ridge completed an internal control questionnaire and prepared the appropriate memoranda describing Western's accounting procedures.

Required:

Go to the Kaplan Web site at www.mhhe.com/louwers3e, click on AUD: Ridge Associates and the "Gov. Audit Standards" tab, and complete the assigned task.

Overview of Sampling

Professional Standards References

Compendium Section	Document Reference	Topic
Various*	AS 5	"An Audit of Internal Control over Financial Reporting That Is Integrated with an Audit of Financial Statements"
AU 312	SAS 107	"Audit Risk and Materiality in Conducting an Audit"
AU 313	SAS 110	"Performing Audit Procedures in Response to Assessed Risks and Evaluating the Audit Evidence Obtained"
	ISA 330	"The Auditor's Procedures in Response to Assessed Risks"
	ISA 320	"Audit Materiality"
AU 319	SAS 109	"Understanding the Entity and Its Environment and Assessing the Risk of Material Misstatement"
	ISA 330	"The Auditor's Procedures in Response to Assessed Risks"
	ISA 315	"Understanding the Entity and Its Environment and Assessing the Risks of Material Misstatement"
AU 326	SAS 106	"Audit Evidence"
	ISA 500	"Audit Evidence"
	ISA 501	"Audit Evidence—Additional Considerations for Specific Items"
AU 350	SAS 39	"Audit Sampling"
	SAS 111	"Amendment to Statement on Auditing Standards No. 39, *Audit Sampling*"
	ISA 530	"Audit Sampling and Other Means of Testing"
AU 9350		"Interpretation: Applicability of Audit Sampling"

**AS 5 amends AU 230, AU 310, AU 312, AU 313, AU 315, AU 316, AU 319, AU 322, AU 325, AU 328, AU 332, AU 333, AU 341, AU 342, AU 380, AU 508, AU 530, AU 543, AU 560, AU 561, AU 711, AU 722, AS 3, and AS 4.*

There are three kinds of lies: lies, damned lies, and statistics.

Benjamin Disraeli, former British Prime Minister

Learning Objectives

Module E introduces the sampling process and illustrates how sampling can be used during an assurance engagement.

Your objectives are to be able to:

1. Understand the basic principles of sampling, including the differences between statistical and nonstatistical sampling and sampling and nonsampling risk.

2. Understand the basic steps and procedures used in implementing a sampling plan.

3. Identify the two situations in which sampling is used in an audit examination.

4. Understand how the basic steps and procedures used in a sampling plan apply to an audit engagement.

INTRODUCTION

LEARNING
OBJECTIVE

1. Understand the basic
principles of sampling,
including the
differences between
statistical and
nonstatistical sampling
and sampling and
nonsampling risk.

Phar-Mor, a national chain of drugstores, inflated its profits by creating fictitious increases in inventory. How did the auditors fail to detect these misstatements? The auditors visited and observed inventory counts in only four of Phar-Mor's 300 stores. Even worse . . . they informed Phar-Mor months in advance which stores they would visit. Phar-Mor made sure that these stores would be fully stocked and the fictitious inventory was "allocated" to the remaining 296 stores. The auditors' failure to *sample* a representative number of stores (and do so on a surprise basis) eventually led to more than $300 million in judgments against the CPA firm.[1]

WHAT IS SAMPLING?

Consider the following information that we frequently hear and read in the media during an election year:

> Based on a sample of 1,000 eligible voters, Candidate A has 45 percent of the vote, with a margin for error of plus or minus 4 percent.

This statement means the pollsters have a certain level of confidence that Candidate A's true (but unknown) share of the vote is between 41 percent (45 percent minus 4 percent) and 49 percent (45 percent plus 4 percent). This range is based on the sample of 1,000 eligible voters.

Why do we not know the actual percentage of the vote? Because it would not be cost effective for any pollster to survey each and every possible voter. (In fact, it would probably be impossible to do so!) Pollsters cannot with any certainty provide a single estimate of the candidate's share of the vote unless all voters in the *population* are surveyed.[2] Instead, they provide a range of estimates that has a high (but unspecified) chance of including the true percentage of the vote.

This scenario is one example of the use of **sampling,** the objective of which is to make a statement about a **population** of interest (in this case, all eligible voters) by examining only a subset (or **sample**) of that population (in this case, the voters responding to the pollster's inquiries).

Just as surveying every eligible voter is not cost effective, it is not cost effective for an auditor to examine every item during an audit examination. Two major stages in the audit examination during which sampling is used are

- In the study and evaluation of a client's internal control to determine whether important control policies and procedures are functioning as intended to prevent and detect material financial statement misstatements.[3]

- In conducting substantive procedures to determine whether the client's account balances or classes of transactions are recorded and presented in conformity with generally accepted accounting principles.

The remainder of this module discusses sampling in a generic (nonaudit) context. In addition, we provide a broad overview of the use of sampling in these two audit contexts. The overview of sampling is followed by a brief introduction to audit sampling. Audit

[1] J. T. Wells, "Ghost Goods: How to Spot Phantom Inventory," *Journal of Accountancy,* June 2001, pp. 33–36.

[2] In addition, all voters surveyed would need to actually vote as they say they would vote.

[3] In this module, the focus on sampling with respect to internal control is the assessment of control risk to determine the nature, timing, and extent of substantive procedures. However, it is important to note that this discussion also applies to engagements subject to the provisions of PCAOB *Auditing Standard 5* with respect to the auditor's responsibility to evaluate a client's internal control under section 404 of the Sarbanes-Oxley Act.

sampling is somewhat different than sampling you learned in basic statistics. First, auditors are more concerned about incorrectly accepting a hypothesis (i.e., that the account is correctly stated). These were called *type II* or *beta errors* in your statistics classes. Normal hypothesis testing is concerned more with incorrectly rejecting hypotheses (*type I* or *alpha errors*). These types of errors are discussed in more detail later. Second, accounting distributions are generally more *skewed* than distributions of other data. In other words, there are generally many more low-dollar items or items without errors than high-dollar items or items with errors. Because accounting statisticians have developed helpful, time-saving tables to analyze these distributions, your study of audit sampling will focus more on the appropriate understanding and application of the tables than performing complex calculations. The two following modules provide detailed illustration of the use of sampling tables in the auditor's study of internal control (Module F) and the auditor's substantive procedures (Module G).

When Should Sampling Be Used?

To illustrate the basic concepts associated with sampling, assume that **Wilson Sporting Goods** (Wilson) was interested in determining whether amateur golfers could hit its golf balls farther than competitors' golf balls.[4] Wilson has determined that if its golf balls increase the distance of an amateur's shots by five or more yards, it can reliably claim that its ball can improve distances (or is "longer") relative to the competition. (It is not important for you to know how the distance five yards was determined, but it incorporates a margin for error or randomness.)

One possible way to test Wilson's claim is to have every amateur golfer in the world (a number totaling in the millions) hit both a competitor's golf ball and Wilson's golf ball. The distance each ball is hit would be determined and the difference in distances would be calculated. Assuming that no computational errors were made in the calculations, Wilson would know the average increase in distances (if any) with certainty.

Would an engagement team consider using sampling to answer this question? Sampling is typically used when the question of interest has the following two characteristics:

1. *The need for exact information is not important.* Considering the preceding example, the engagement team would be more interested in testing all golfers if it wanted to know an exact increase in distance (for example, does Wilson's golf ball increase distances by *7.5 yards* as opposed to *5 yards or more*?).
2. *The number of items comprising the population is large.* If the number of amateur golfers was 100, the engagement team would be more likely to test all 100 golfers than if the number of amateur golfers was over a million.

Essentially, sampling trades *effectiveness* for *efficiency*. That is, sampling allows an individual to obtain information about a population of interest in a fraction of the time it would take to examine the entire population. In other words, *sampling is more efficient*. However, because the individual is not examining all items in the population, there is a chance that sampling will not provide the correct answer to the question being examined *(sampling is less effective)*. Sampling is used when the gains associated with efficiency exceed the losses associated with effectiveness. As discussed later, certain types of sampling plans allow the losses associated with reduced effectiveness to be quantified and limited to relatively low levels.

Sampling Risk versus Nonsampling Risk

As noted, sampling can result in the loss of effectiveness; that is, basing conclusions about a population on a sample drawn from that population could fail to provide the correct conclusion. For example, assume that the engagement team tested 50 golfers, calculated the distances for the two golf balls, and concluded that Wilson's golf ball provided an average

[4] "After This, CPAs May Take Over Instant-Replay Duties for Football," *The Wall Street Journal*, July 9, 1991, p. B1.

EXHIBIT E.1
The Effect of Various Sample Averages on Conclusions

Cutoff = 5 yards
True average = 7 yards
Sample 1 average = 6 yards
Sample 2 average = 4 yards

increase in distance of six yards. Recall that the engagement team is interested in determining whether the increase in distance is more than five yards. If the true average increase in distance (which the engagement team would not know unless it tested all amateur golfers) is seven yards, the use of sampling has provided the engagement team the correct conclusion.

Now assume that the distances of the sample of 50 golfers provided an average increase in distance of four yards. In this case, the engagement team's conclusion that Wilson's golf ball did not increase the distances of shots of amateur golfers would be incorrect because the true average increase in distance (unknown to the engagement team) is seven yards.[5] This situation is an example of **sampling risk,** which is the possibility that the decision made based on the sample (in this case, that the increase in distance was four yards and Wilson's ball does not provide an increase in distance) differs from the conclusion that would have been made if the entire population had been examined (in this case, that the increase was seven yards and Wilson's ball does provide an increase in distance).

Obviously, other samples of 50 different golfers drawn from the population would provide the engagement team different averages. Some of these samples provide results consistent with the population and others do not. The ones that do not provide results consistent with the population (all samples providing an average increase in distance of less than five yards) represent examples of sampling risk. This relationship is shown in Exhibit E.1.

When decisions made based on the sample differ from decisions that would be made if the entire population were examined, sampling error has occurred. *Sampling error* is caused when the sample drawn from the population does not appropriately represent that population. *Sampling risk* is the likelihood of sampling error. In this instance, Wilson's golf ball did not provide the sample of golfers drawn from the population with as large of an increase in distance as it did for the average amateur golfer. This case is referred to as selecting a **nonrepresentative sample,** which differs substantially from the population from which the sample is drawn on one or more key characteristics of interest.

Sampling risk can never be eliminated (unless, of course, the engagement team were to test all amateur golfers in the population), but it can be controlled to relatively low levels. Three major steps can control sampling risk in the sampling process:

1. *Determining an appropriate sample size.* As a higher percentage of items in the population is examined, sampling risk decreases.
2. *Ensuring that all items have an equal opportunity to be selected.* If all items have an equal opportunity to be selected, the likelihood of sampling risk decreases.
3. *Evaluating sample results.* The results from a sample are "adjusted" to consider the possibility that the sample being evaluated does not appropriately represent the population. We discuss this "adjustment" later.

[5] Recall that the engagement team stipulated that the distance increase must equal or exceed five yards for it to reliably conclude that Wilson's ball will provide a distance increase. Therefore, even though Wilson's ball provided a distance increase of four yards in this sample, this difference is not large enough to provide the engagement team a reliable conclusion.

In both the Wilson assurance example and in an audit, sampling risk arises for the same reason: a nonrepresentative sample. Auditors using statistical sampling take appropriate measures to increase the likelihood that they select a representative sample for examination.

Nonsampling risk represents the probability that an incorrect conclusion will be reached due to reasons unrelated to the nature of the sample. Even if the auditors examine all items, they are still subject to nonsampling risk. Nonsampling risk typically arises because of errors in judgment or execution. For example, if the engagement team incorrectly measures the yardage, the sample average will be incorrect and can result in an inappropriate conclusion. Note that this error is not caused by a nonrepresentative sample but by an *evaluator error*. In an auditing context, *nonsampling error* arises when auditors use an inappropriate procedure or misinterpret evidence they have obtained.

AUDITING INSIGHT Polling Problems

Polling (or sampling) votes during the 2004 presidential election illustrated some of the problems that can result from sampling risk.

- Voter response rates are declining; according to the Pew Research Center, response rates in a poll conducted over five days were 36 percent in 1997 and 27 percent in 2003.

- Warren Mitofsky, one of the designers of the 2004 presidential election exit polls, noted that "Kerry voters were more anxious to participate in our exit polls than the Bush voters." Such a differential response bias can result in misleading results.

- Because laws prohibit pollsters from contacting voters on their mobile phones, pollsters are unable to survey 7 percent of the population who exclusively use mobile phones. This is a particular problem for voters under the age of 30, 20 percent of whom exclusively use mobile phones.

Because of these and other issues, pollster John Zogby notes that "[s]ome pundits are ready to declare polls are dead."

Source: "He Said, She Said, Nobody Knew," *The Economist*, November 20, 2004, p. 33.

Statistical Sampling versus Nonstatistical Sampling

The preceding section on the possible exposure to sampling risk notes a significant limitation with the use of sampling. This risk cannot be eliminated, but certain sampling plans allow the risk to be measured and controlled to acceptable levels. These plans are referred to as *statistical sampling plans*.

Statistical sampling plans apply the laws of probability to selecting sample items for examination and evaluating sample results. Specifically, statistical sampling methods provide the auditor the ability to make quantitative statements about the results and to measure the sufficiency of evidence gathered (i.e., determine a sufficient sample size) and evaluate the results in such a way to control sampling risk. **Nonstatistical sampling** plans do not meet either of these criteria. Thus, these two types of plans differ in terms of how sample size is determined and how the results are evaluated.

Although the phrase "nonstatistical sampling" sounds less professional and less favorable, nonstatistical sampling methods can be appropriate in some circumstances. In certain cases, it is not necessary (or desirable) to use the laws of probability to select sample items. For example, if a client's accounts receivable balance includes 1,000 individual customer accounts but a large percentage of the dollar amount is contained in only a few accounts, the auditor could reasonably decide to select only those few accounts for examination. In doing so, one of the provisions of statistical sampling (random selection of items) has been violated. However, it is both efficient and effective for the auditor to select the sample in this fashion!

Generally accepted auditing standards do *not* require the use of statistical sampling procedures. In fact, a survey of practicing auditors in public accounting, industry, and government revealed that 85 percent of all samples were *selected* using nonstatistical procedures and 64 percent of all samples were *evaluated* using nonstatistical evaluation

methods.[6] The use of nonstatistical sampling methods is often justifiable when the costs of using statistical sampling methods exceed the benefits of doing so. However, nonstatistical sampling should not be used as a means to reduce sample sizes. *SAS 111* suggests that sample sizes developed for a nonstatistical sampling plan should be comparable to those "resulting from an efficient and effectively designed statistical sample, considering the same sampling parameters" (AU 350).

The terms *statistical and nonstatistical sampling* and *sampling and nonsampling risk* are sometimes used interchangeably. However, it is important to note that they are indeed quite different. To see this, sampling risk exists in either a statistical or nonstatistical sample because either type of sampling plan can result in the selection of a sample that does not appropriately represent the population. However, statistical sampling plans allow sampling risk to be measured and controlled to acceptable levels. Similarly, nonsampling risk can exist in either type of sampling approach because an individual could make a mistake in evaluating sample results in either a statistical or nonstatistical sampling application.

Review Checkpoints

E.1 During what stages of the audit examination can sampling be used?

E.2 What is *sampling risk?* How does it arise?

E.3 What is *nonsampling risk?* How does it arise?

E.4 How is sampling risk controlled?

E.5 What is *statistical sampling?* How does it differ from nonstatistical sampling?

E.6 Is nonstatistical sampling permitted under generally accepted auditing standards?

THE BASIC STEPS INVOLVED WITH SAMPLING

LEARNING OBJECTIVE

2. Understand the basic steps and procedures used in implementing a sampling plan.

In general, sampling can be viewed as including the following major steps:

Planning
1. Determine the objective of sampling.
2. Define the characteristic of interest.
3. Define the population.

Performing
4. Determine the sample size.
5. Select the sample items.
6. Measure the sample items.

Evaluating
7. Evaluate the sample results.

Documentation

[6] T. W. Hall, J. E. Hunton, and B. J. Pierce, "Sampling Practices of Auditors in Public Accounting, Industry, and Government," *Accounting Horizons*, June 2002, p. 129.

As an example of the process illustrated, consider our example of determining whether Wilson's golf ball provides an increase in distance for amateur golfers. In this module, we provide a very nontechnical example of this process that does not involve calculations to illustrate how the sampling process works. Modules F and G provide a more comprehensive example of this process and how it is employed in various stages of the auditor's examination.

Planning

Determine the Objective, Define the Characteristic of Interest, and Define the Population

The *objective of the sampling application* is directly related to the question of interest. In this example, the objective is to determine whether Wilson's golf ball increases distance; because the engagement team's conclusion with respect to this question is evidenced by whether the increase exceeds five yards, the increase in distance is the *characteristic of interest*. Clearly defining the characteristic of interest in a sampling application is critical because it is the measure that will be obtained from the sample items and eventually evaluated against some criterion (related to the objective of the sampling application).

Defining the population can sound straightforward, but it must be defined carefully to be able to meet the objective of the sampling application. In our example, the population should be defined as all amateur golfers in the world. If the population is defined as amateur golfers who belong to country clubs, subscribe to *Golf Magazine,* or attend a Professional Golf Association (PGA) tournament each year, the results will not appropriately represent the entire population.

Performing

Determine Sample Size

While many factors are considered in determining the appropriate sample size, the acceptable level of sampling risk is one important factor. Recall that an advantage of *statistical* sampling plans is that they allow determining a sample size that measures sampling risk. An individual who wishes to reduce sampling risk to lower levels needs to select more items for examination as shown.

Assume that, based on an acceptable level of sampling risk of 10 percent (i.e., a 10 percent chance Wilson will claim its balls increase distance when, in fact, they *do not* or, conversely, that they do not increase distance when, in fact, *they do*), the engagement team determines that a sample size of 50 items is needed. Other factors also influence sample size; these factors will be discussed later in this module.

Review Checkpoints

E.7 What are the seven major steps involved with sampling?

E.8 What is the importance of carefully defining the population of interest?

E.9 How does sampling risk affect sample size?

Select the Sample Items

Once the sample size has been determined, the sample needs to be selected from the population. Recall that *population* is defined in this example as all amateur golfers throughout the world. Also recall that the acceptable level of sampling risk is 10 percent and that the sample size necessary to control sampling risk at this level is 50 amateur golfers (we illustrate the determination of these two factors as well as how they relate to one another in subsequent modules). Four methods that can be used to select a sample are discussed next.

Unrestricted Random Selection When using **unrestricted random selection** (often referred to as **random selection**), items are selected from a population so that each item has an equal chance of being selected. This type of selection process can be used only when items in the population are numbered or can easily be assigned a number. The use of random selection consists of a two-step procedure:

1. A series of random numbers is identified by either a random number table or a computer program.
2. The random numbers from step 1 are matched to numbered items in the corresponding population.

To illustrate the use of random selection, the engagement team selected the following numbers from a random number table: 120, 268, and 341. Using an alphabetical listing of amateur golfers throughout the world, the engagement team would test the 120th, 268th, and 341st golfers.[7] One key feature of random selection is that another individual is able to replicate the procedure and select exactly the same items. In addition, every item has an equal probability of being selected.

Systematic Random Selection When using **systematic random selection** (commonly referred to as **systematic selection**), the individual selects a starting point from within the population and examines every *n*th item thereafter, where *n* is determined based on the number of items in the population and the necessary sample size. Systematic selection has the advantage of ensuring that all items have an equal probability of selection while providing a more efficient method of selecting items than unrestricted random selection.

The following basic steps are used in systematic selection.

1. Determine the necessary **sampling interval.** The sampling interval identifies the frequency with which items are selected within the population. It is determined by dividing the number of items in the population by the necessary sample size.
2. Select a random starting point from within the population (a number equal to or less than the sampling interval).
3. Add the sampling interval to the random starting point. The item in the population corresponding to this number is the next item selected.
4. Add the sampling interval to the total from step 3. The item in the population corresponding to this number will be the next item selected.
5. Repeat step 4 until the number of items equal to the necessary sample size is selected.

To illustrate the use of systematic selection, recall that the population is all amateur golfers throughout the world and the necessary sample size is 50. For purposes of illustration, assume that the population of amateur golfers totaled 1,000 (it is surely much higher than this!). A sampling interval of 20 is calculated (1,000 golfers (50 items = 20); thus, every 20th item would be selected for examination. If the random starting point is 15, the first three items selected would be as follows:

Item 1: 15 (random starting point)
Item 2: 35 (15 + 20)
Item 3: 55 (35 + 20)

[7] Obviously, the definition of the population as including golfers from throughout the world introduces significant cost considerations. To offset these considerations, the engagement team may select a random number of cities throughout the world and sample amateur golfers living in those cities.

In some cases, several random starting points are used to ensure a more random sample. For example, in the preceding situation, the engagement team could use one random start and select the additional 49 items as noted. Alternatively, they could use five random starts and select an additional nine items for each of these starting points. In either case, a total of 50 items (the necessary sample size) would ultimately be selected.

Like random selection, systematic selection is advantageous because another individual can replicate the selection of the sample if both the random starting point and sampling interval are known. In addition, like random selection, every item in the population has an equal chance of being selected, which provides a reasonable likelihood of selecting a representative sample.

One limitation of systematic selection is that the population must be randomly ordered. Because systematic selection essentially bypasses a number of items, a nonrandomly ordered population can result in bypassing a number of items having similar characteristics. For example, if the population of amateur golfers were arranged alphabetically, bypassing a number of golfers whose last name begins with B (or any other letter) would not appear to influence the representativeness of the sample. However, if the population were arranged by ability (or golf handicap index), the use of systematic selection would essentially result in bypassing a large number of golfers of a certain level of ability. This could be problematic if the number of golfers with relatively high ability (low golf handicap indexes) is a relatively small percentage of the population.

Haphazard Selection When using **haphazard selection,** items are selected in a nonsystematic manner. Although this can be done in any number of ways, one way is to identify items (golfers) as they arrived at the clubhouse or flipping through membership rosters from country clubs selecting items until a total of 50 were selected.[8] Under haphazard selection, little thought is taken or effort made to identify items for selection.

One significant limitation of haphazard selection is that, unlike either random selection or systematic selection, the sampling method cannot be described in sufficient detail to permit another individual to replicate it. Some describe haphazard selection as a method of choosing items without any special reason for including or excluding items, thus obtaining a representative sample. However, haphazard selection methods do not permit individuals to measure the probability of selecting sample items. In addition, although items are selected in a nonsystematic manner, studies have found bias in selecting items (either conscious or unconscious) often exists.[9]

Block Selection The use of **block selection** involves selecting a series of contiguous (or adjacent) items from the population. One example of block selection is the selection of the first 10 golfers from the membership roster at each of five different country clubs for a total of 50 sample items. In this case, the population unit is really a list of golfers. Block selection is less desirable because it is difficult to efficiently obtain a representative sample; ordinarily, a relatively large number of blocks need to be selected to be representative.

Which Selection Method Should Be Used? The use of statistical or nonstatistical sampling procedures has a significant impact on the method of sample selection. Typically, random or systematic selection is used with statistical sampling because these methods (1) provide a reasonable likelihood of obtaining a representative sample, (2) allow the probability of obtaining sample items to be determined, and (3) allow the sample selection process to be replicated. As a result, these methods allow sampling risk to be measured and controlled to acceptable levels. In contrast, haphazard and block selection do not meet these criteria; they could result in a random sample, but quantitatively evaluating the randomness of the sample selected using them is difficult.

[8] Of course, the fact that the sample could be limited to golfers arriving at the clubhouse has some implications for the extent to which it is truly representative of the population. Presumably, golfers who are actively playing could have more ability than those who are not!

[9] T. W. Hall, T. L. Herron, and B. J. Pierce, "How Reliable Is Haphazard Sampling?" *The CPA Journal*, January 2006, p. 26.

In practice, computer software has greatly increased the efficiency and effectiveness of selecting sample items, particularly when using systematic random selection or unrestricted random selection. Software applications use client data files and parameters designated by the individual to select the appropriate sample items.

AUDITING INSIGHT Survey of Selection Methods

A survey of practicing auditors in public accounting, industry, and government accounting revealed that they used the following methods to select sample items (based on audits conducted by respondents during the most recent six months):

Statistical selection		Nonstatistical selection	
Random selection	3%	Haphazard selection	74%
Systematic selection (or variation)	12%	Block selection	3%
Total	15%	Other	8%
		Total	85%

In addition to illustrating the methods of sample selection used in practice, these results indicate the extent to which nonstatistical sampling methods are used in practice to select samples (85 percent of all audits).

Source: T. W. Hall, J. E. Hunton, and B. J. Pierce, "Sampling Practices of Auditors in Public Accounting, Industry, and Government," *Accounting Horizons*, June 2002, p. 129.

Measure the Sample Items

Once the sample size has been determined and the sample has been selected, the next step is to *measure the sample items*. In our example, measuring the sample items consists of having each golfer hit a series of shots with Wilson's golf ball and the competitors' golf balls and recording the distances.[10] It is at this point that nonsampling risk can occur. Examples of nonsampling risk include incorrectly transcribing a distance or making some other mathematical error during the measurement process. After selecting the 50 golfers and averaging the distances, assume that an average increase in distance of 6.7 yards for Wilson's golf ball is calculated.

Summary: Wilson Golf Ball Example

At this point, we have performed the following sampling procedures:

1. *Define the objective of sampling.* In this case, the objective of sampling is to determine whether using Wilson's golf ball provides amateur golfers an increase in distance.

2. *Define the characteristic of interest.* The characteristic of interest is the increase in distance gained by using Wilson's golf ball (specifically, whether this increase is at least five yards).

3. *Define the population.* The population is defined as all amateur golfers in the world.

4. *Determine the sample size.* Based on the acceptable exposure to sampling risk of 10 percent, a sample size of 50 has been determined.

5. *Select the sample items.* Items are selected using one of four selection methods (unrestricted random selection, systematic random selection, haphazard selection, or block selection).

6. *Measure the sample items.* Based on the distance using the golfers' existing golf ball and the Wilson golf ball, the average increase in distance is 6.7 yards.

Evaluating the Sample Results

Based on the sample average increase in distance of 6.7 yards, can the engagement team conclude that amateur golfers could hit the Wilson golf ball longer than its competitors'

[10] Of course, physical conditions such as type of club used, wind, and course altitude would have to be controlled.

golf balls? This average exceeds the five-yard criterion, but it is possible that the engagement team did not select a representative sample. (In addition, the engagement team could have made a computational error and introduced nonsampling risk, but we assume that no such errors of this sort were made.)

To evaluate the sample results, the sample average must be "adjusted" to control for the acceptable level of exposure to sampling risk. This is done by forming a range of estimates that have a certain probability of including the true (but unknown) population value. Although we illustrate the calculation of this range in a subsequent module, assume that we can conclude with 90 percent probability that the true population average increase in distance is between 5.2 yards and 8.2 yards (the sample estimate of 6.7 yards plus and minus a 1.5-yard point adjustment factor). The following concepts are introduced in the preceding example:

- The **precision** (or **allowance for sampling risk**) is the numeric distance from the estimated population value in which the true (but unknown) population value may lie with a given probability. In this case, the precision is 1.5 yards.

- The **reliability** (or **confidence**) is the likelihood of achieving a given level of precision. In the example, the reliability is 90 percent, which is equal to 100 percent minus the acceptable sampling risk of 10 percent.

- The **precision interval** is a range around the sample estimate that has a certain likelihood (equal to reliability) of including the true population value. In this example, the precision interval is 5.2 to 8.2 yards.

Note that, for any given level of reliability, a unique level of precision will exist (in this case, 1.5 yards). If the engagement team desires a higher level of confidence regarding the closeness of a sample estimate to the true population value (say 95 percent), the precision interval will be wider (say the sample estimate (3 yards). That is, one can be more confident a number falls within a range, the wider the range. Stated another way, each level of precision is associated with a given level of confidence.

What is the overall conclusion? Because the likelihood is 90 percent that the true population's average increase in distance is between 5.2 and 8.2 yards, the engagement team can reliably conclude that the average increase in distance is more than five yards. Therefore, it appears that Wilson's golf ball can be hit a longer distance than its competitors'. What is the chance that this conclusion is incorrect? The chance is less than 10 percent. Because this is less than the acceptable level of sampling risk, it is safe to conclude that Wilson does have a longer distance golf ball as evidenced by an increase of five yards. The relationship between this precision interval and the five-yard criterion is shown in Exhibit E.2.

On the other hand, would the engagement team's conclusion change if, for the same confidence level, the precision was determined to be three yards? In this case, the precision interval would be 3.7 yards to 9.7 yards (sample average of 6.7 yards ± 3 yards). As shown in Exhibit E.2, the results are a bit less certain because the lower level of the precision

EXHIBIT E.2
Precision Intervals for Two Hypothetical Sample Results

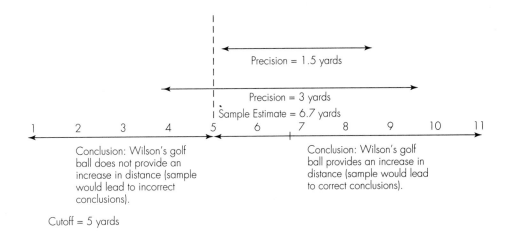

interval is below the criterion distance of five yards. In this case, statistical theory could be used to determine the precise probability that the true population's average was below five yards and compare that to the acceptable level of sampling risk of 10 percent. However, the evidence in this latter case is clearly less convincing than that for a precision of 1.5 yards.

In discussing the concept of precision, it is important to note that the terminology can be a bit misleading. Although the precision of 3.0 yards is larger than that of 1.5 yards, the latter is often referred to as being a *more precise* estimate because the precision interval is more closely centered around the sample estimate. In some instances, a more precise estimate is referred to as being characterized by higher precision.

Documenting the Sampling Procedure

For each of the seven major steps in the sampling process, important judgments and conclusions must be properly documented. Proper documentation for audit samples could be an element of supervisory or quality reviews. Some important information that would be documented in the Wilson example follows:

- *The objective of the sampling application, characteristic of interest, and definition of the population* (steps 1–3).
- *The factors affecting sample size (along with the method or rationale for those factors) and determination of sample size*; in this case, the engagement team would document the acceptable level of sampling risk of 10 percent, the rationale for this level of sampling risk, and the determination of the sample size of 50 items (step 4).
- *The method of selecting the sample and description of items selected for examination.* If systematic selection is used, the engagement team would document the random starting point and the sampling interval of 20 items, and the list the items selected (step 5).
- *The method of measuring sample items and summary of measurements.* In this case, the engagement team would document that golfers hit a series of shots with Wilson's golf ball and competitors' golf balls and the distances of each. In addition, the engagement team would document that the overall increase in distance using Wilson's golf ball is 6.7 yards (step 6).
- *The evaluation of sample results and overall conclusion with respect to the sample.* In this case, the engagement team would document the precision, reliability, and overall conclusions with respect to the sample (step 7).

Review Checkpoints

E.10 Briefly identify and explain the four methods used to select sample items.

E.11 What methods of sample selection are appropriate to use with a statistical sampling plan? Why?

E.12 Define the terms *precision* (allowance for sampling risk), *reliability* (confidence), and *precision interval.*

E.13 Describe the basic procedure used to evaluate sample results.

USE OF SAMPLING IN THE AUDIT

LEARNING OBJECTIVE

3. Identify the two situations in which sampling is used in an audit examination.

We have discussed some key concepts related to sampling and provided an example of how sampling can be used in a nonaudit setting. Our discussion has focused on the following questions:

- What is sampling?
- Why is sampling used?
- What are the different risks associated with the use of sampling?

- How does statistical sampling differ from nonstatistical sampling?
- What are the major steps involved with sampling?

Now we consider the use of sampling in the audit examination. *SAS 39* defines **audit sampling** as "the application of an audit procedure to less than 100 percent of the items within an account balance or class of transactions for the purpose of evaluating some characteristic of the account balance or class of transactions." Sampling is recognized in the scope paragraph of a standard auditors' opinion that says, "An audit includes examining, on a test basis, evidence supporting amounts and disclosures in the financial statements." As we have previously mentioned, auditors use sampling in one of two situations during their examination: (1) studying and evaluating the client's internal control and (2) performing substantive procedures on account balances and classes of transactions. *SAS 39* identifies certain types of controls whose evaluation would not involve sampling. These include (1) controls that are tested once or only infrequently when effective information technology general controls are present, (2) segregation of duties or other controls that do not provide documentary evidence of performance, and (3) certain controls related to the control environment when the auditor is not interested in estimating a rate of deviation (such as management integrity or audit committee effectiveness). Similarly, not all audit procedures are suitable for sampling. Inquiry and observation and analytical procedures would be difficult to perform by sampling.

The following three conditions must be met for an application to be classified as audit sampling:

1. Less than 100 percent of the items composing the population must be examined.
2. The results of the sample must be projected to the population being examined.
3. The projected results must be compared to some existing criterion.

With respect to the study and evaluation of the client's internal control, the auditor's objective is to determine whether important control policies and procedures are functioning effectively to prevent or detect financial statement misstatements. In making this evaluation, the auditor is interested in determining whether the rate at which internal control procedures are not functioning (referred to as the **deviation rate**) exceeds some rate permissible by the auditor (referred to as the *tolerable deviation rate*). The use of sampling in this context is referred to as *attribute sampling.*[11]

When used in substantive procedures, the auditor's objective is to determine whether an account balance or class of transactions is recorded and presented according to generally accepted accounting principles. In making this evaluation, the auditor is interested in determining whether the amount of dollar misstatement in the account balance or class of transactions exceeds some permissible amount (referred to as **tolerable error**). The end result of the auditor's substantive procedures is the determination as to whether the client's account balances are fairly stated according to generally accepted accounting principles. The use of sampling in this context is referred to as *variables sampling.*

The objectives, sampling units, and evaluations made by the auditor in these two situations are summarized in Exhibit E.3.

EXHIBIT E.3 **Use of Sampling during the Audit Examination**

Audit Application	Objective	Sampling Unit	Evaluation
Study and evaluation of internal control (attribute sampling)	Determine whether internal control policies and procedures are functioning in preventing or detecting misstatements	Instances in which control policies or procedures should have been applied	Compare deviation rate to tolerable rate
Substantive procedures (variables sampling)	Determine whether account balance or class of transactions is fairly recorded and presented	Transactions or components of account balances or classes of transactions	Compare misstatement to tolerable error

[11] Attribute sampling may be used in rare occasions for tests not related to internal controls. For example, auditors of insurance companies might use attribute sampling to test whether contracts are prepared in a prescribed format.

Attribute Sampling

Attribute sampling is used when the auditor examines a subset of items within a population to determine the extent to which a particular attribute exists within that population. To understand why the auditor uses attribute sampling, recall how the *audit risk model* is used in the audit examination. **Audit risk** is the risk that auditors will *unknowingly* fail to modify their opinion on financial statements that are materially misstated. That is, audit risk represents the likelihood that the auditor will issue an unqualified opinion on financial statements that are materially misstated.

The audit risk model that was introduced earlier in the text follows:[12]

$$AR = RMM \times DR$$

where

AR	=	Audit risk (the risk that a material misstatement occurs, is not detected by the client's internal control, and is not detected by the auditor's substantive procedures)
RMM	=	Risk of material misstatement (IR $\times$ CR)
IR	=	Inherent risk (the risk that an account balance or class of transactions contains a material misstatement in the absence of internal control)
CR	=	Control risk (the risk that the client's internal control policies and procedures fail to prevent or detect a material misstatement)
DR	=	Detection risk (the risk that the auditor's substantive procedures fail to detect a material misstatement)

The auditor uses *attribute sampling* in assessing control risk. Recall that auditors study and evaluate the client's internal control to determine the extent to which they can rely on specific internal control policies and procedures to prevent and detect misstatements. Based on the operating effectiveness of these policies and procedures, auditors will decide on the extent to which they can rely on the client's internal control. This degree of reliance, in turn, will influence the nature, timing, and extent of the auditors' substantive procedures.

How do auditors decide whether they can rely on internal control policies and procedures? In the planning stages of the audit, auditors assess control risk at a planned level; they then perform tests of controls to determine whether the controls are functioning (that is, the controls have been implemented and are performed by client employees) consistent with the planned level of control risk. The general procedure used by the auditor to assess control risk is summarized here:

Attribute sampling is used in the third (perform tests of controls on key controls) and fourth (assess effectiveness of key controls) steps illustrated. Based on the results of these

[12] *SAS 107* expresses the product of inherent risk and control risk as the *risk of material misstatement.* This standard notes that auditors may choose to make a combined assessment of the risk of material misstatement or separate assessments of inherent risk and control risk.

tests of controls, auditors evaluate their preliminary assessment of control risk and, ultimately, determine the *nature, timing,* and *extent* of substantive procedures. The following summarizes the auditor's study and evaluation of internal control (and possible decisions based on this study and evaluation):

- If the controls are operating at the planned level of effectiveness, auditors can support the reliance on internal control and maintain their assessment of control risk and detection risk at planned levels.

- If controls are not operating at the planned level of effectiveness, auditors could reduce the planned reliance on internal control and increase their assessment of control risk, which would result in performing substantive procedures for lower levels of detection risk (more effective substantive procedures).

Thus, attribute sampling provides the auditor an indication of the operating effectiveness of the client's internal control. This indication allows the auditor to determine the appropriate level of control risk that, with previous assessments of audit risk and inherent risk, allows the auditor to determine the necessary level of detection risk. The necessary level of detection risk determines the nature, timing, and extent of the auditor's substantive procedures.

Sampling Risks Associated with Attribute Sampling

Recall that *sampling risk* is the risk that the decision made based on the sample will differ from the decision that would have been made if the entire population had been examined. Also recall that sampling risk is the result of the possibility of selecting a nonrepresentative sample (one that does not appropriately represent the population of interest).

In attribute sampling, the auditor's ultimate objective is to provide a final assessment of control risk. In so doing, the auditor attempts to determine the extent to which the client's controls are functioning effectively in preventing or detecting misstatements. For a variety of reasons, it is neither practical nor realistic for the auditor to require controls to be functioning 100 percent of the time in order to be able to rely on them. When evaluating the effectiveness of the client's controls, auditors typically think in terms of the *maximum deviation rate* that could exist before they would reduce reliance on that control (**tolerable deviation rate** or **TDR**).

To illustrate, assume that the auditor decides that a control should function at least 96 percent of the time to be considered effective (we illustrate how this percentage is determined in a subsequent module). Stated another way, the auditor is willing to allow that the control does not function 4 percent of the time (100 percent – 96 percent). This 4 percent represents the TDR.

Once a TDR has been established, auditors compare this rate to the results of their sample. The decision made by the auditor will be as follows:

Although auditors will never know the true population deviation rate with any certainty, they can use sampling tables to "adjust" the sample deviation rate to one that has a certain probability of equaling or exceeding the true deviation rate. Simply stated, this adjusted rate (the **upper limit deviation rate,** or **ULDR**) provides a conservative measure of the sample deviation rate that allows the auditor to control exposure to sampling risk. If the ULDR is less than or equal to the tolerable deviation rate, auditors rely on controls as planned and maintain their assessment of control risk at planned (ordinarily lower) levels.

Why? They judge the control to be functioning effectively in preventing or detecting misstatements because the highest rate of deviations is less than the tolerable deviation rate. In contrast, if the ULDR is higher than the tolerable deviation rate, auditors reduce their planned reliance on controls and increase their assessment of control risk to higher levels. This decision is made because the control may not be functioning effectively (the highest rate of deviations exceeds the tolerable deviation rate).

Because sampling is being used to evaluate the operating effectiveness of controls, the auditor is exposed to sampling risk. Consider the following matrix. The two columns represent the two possible outcomes if the entire population were examined; the two rows represent the two possible decisions auditors could make based on their sample of controls (ADR = actual deviation rate, TDR = tolerable deviation rate, ULDR = upper limit deviation rate). Auditors calculate ULDR by adjusting the deviation rate in their sample for sampling error to determine the highest possible deviation rate for a given confidence level.

	Decision Based on True State of the Population	
	ADR ≤ TDR (rely on internal control as planned)	ADR > TDR (reduce planned reliance on internal control)
Decision Based on Examining Sample — ULDR ≤ TDR (rely on internal control as planned)	A: Correct decision	B: Risk of assessing control risk too low (risk of overreliance)
ULDR > TDR (reduce planned reliance on internal control)	C: Risk of assessing control risk too high (risk of underreliance)	D: Correct decision

Cells A and D do not expose the auditor to sampling risk because the decision to rely on the client's controls as planned (cell A) or to reduce the planned reliance on the client's controls (cell D) is consistent with the decision the auditor would have made had the entire population been examined.

Examine the outcome of cell C. In this instance, the auditors' sample of controls indicates that the deviation rate exceeds the tolerable deviation rate; as a result, they would choose to reduce the reliance on internal control and assess control risk at higher levels. However, unknown to the auditors, the deviation rate in the population is actually lower than the tolerable deviation rate. This situation is referred to as the **risk of assessing control risk too high** (or the **risk of underreliance**). In this instance, the auditors' sample results in the decision to reduce their reliance on internal control (i.e., *underrely on internal control*), which results in higher assessments of control risk.

In contrast, cell B represents a situation in which the auditors choose to reduce their reliance on internal control because the upper limit deviation rate is less than or equal to the tolerable deviation rate. However, in the population, the actual deviation rate exceeds the tolerable deviation rate. As a result, the auditors will inappropriately rely on internal control and maintain the assessment of control risk at lower levels. This is referred to as the **risk of assessing control risk too low** (or the **risk of overreliance**). In this instance, the sample will result in the auditors' decision to rely on internal control as planned (i.e., *overrely on internal control*), which results in lower assessments of control risk.

Which of these risks is of more concern to the auditor? If control risk is assessed at unnecessarily high levels (the risk of assessing control risk too high), the resulting detection risk will be lower than is necessary to reduce audit risk to acceptable levels. As a result, the nature, timing, and extent of the auditor's substantive procedures will be more effective than necessary. Ultimately, the overall level of audit risk that the auditors achieve will be lower than necessary. Thus, assessing control risk too high causes an

efficiency loss for the auditor because more extensive substantive procedures are performed than necessary.

If control risk is assessed too low, the resulting detection risk will be higher than appropriate in the circumstances. When this occurs, the auditors' substantive procedures will not reduce the overall audit risk to an acceptable level. This happens because the auditors believe that internal control is more effective in preventing or detecting misstatements than is the case. The ultimate result of failing to reduce audit risk to an acceptable level is issuing an unqualified opinion on financial statements that are materially misstated, resulting in a reputation loss or litigation by shareholders and other third parties relying on the auditors' work. Therefore, assessing control risk too low exposes the auditors to an *effectiveness loss.*

Given a choice of the two sampling risks, the risk of assessing control risk too low clearly is of more concern to auditors than the risk of assessing control risk too high. As a result, auditors explicitly control their exposure to this risk to acceptable levels when (1) determining the necessary sample size and (2) evaluating sample results.

Review Checkpoints

E.14 Define *attribute sampling.* When is it used in the audit examination?

E.15 What is the *tolerable deviation rate*? How does the auditor use it when deciding whether to rely on internal control?

E.16 What are the two sampling risks associated with attribute sampling? What types of losses are associated with each of these risks?

E.17 Why is the auditor more concerned with the risk of assessing control risk too low than with the risk of assessing control risk too high?

Variables Sampling

Variables sampling is used to examine a population when auditors want to estimate the amount (or value) of some characteristic of that population. Auditors use variables sampling when performing substantive procedures to evaluate the fairness of an account balance or class of transactions. Following the assessment of control risk, auditors use the audit risk model to determine the necessary level of detection risk for assertions related to account balances or classes of transactions. **Detection risk** is the risk that the auditors' substantive procedures (both tests of details and analytical procedures) will fail to detect a material misstatement that exists within an account balance or class of transactions.

The auditors' detection risk is embodied in the *nature, timing,* and *extent of substantive procedures.* Of these characteristics, the extent of substantive procedures is most closely associated with the use of variables sampling. Auditors increase the sample size in response to lower necessary levels of detection risk and decrease sample size in response to higher levels of detection risk.

When performing variables sampling, auditors select items for examination and evaluate the true ("correct") amount at which the item should be recorded, which is referred to as the **audited value** or **audited balance.** Depending on the method of variables sampling used, auditors use the evidence from the sample items to estimate either the (1) audited value of the account or (2) the amount of misstatement in the account.

Auditors can use one of two statistical sampling approaches with variables sampling. **Classical variables sampling** uses the laws of probability and the central limit theorem to estimate either the amount of misstatement in the account balance or class of transactions or the audited value. These procedures provide the auditors a range of estimates that has a specific probability of including the true amount of misstatement or the true account balance.

The second statistical sampling approach that auditors can use is **dollar unit sampling (DUS).** PPS sampling provides auditors an estimate of the amount of misstatement in the account balance or class of transactions. The distinguishing feature of DUS sampling is that it tends to select larger transactions (or components) within an account balance for examination.

In addition to these statistical sampling approaches to variables sampling, auditors can and in practice frequently do use nonstatistical sampling methods. As noted earlier in this module, the advantage of nonstatistical sampling methods is that they are normally less complex and costly to use. A disadvantage of them is that they do not permit the auditor to control the exposure to sampling risk.

Because the purpose of this module is to introduce the basic concepts of sampling, a more detailed discussion of both classical variables sampling and dollar unit sampling are beyond the scope of this module. These sampling methods are discussed in more detail in Module G.

Sampling Risks Associated with Variables Sampling

When performing substantive procedures, auditors evaluate the fairness of the account balance or class of transactions by estimating the difference between the recorded account balance and the audited account balance, which is referred to as the **sample estimate of misstatement.** This sample estimate of misstatement is then adjusted to control for sampling risk and (much like the sample deviation rate discussed in the preceding section) compared to an amount of misstatement that auditors are willing to allow in the account without concluding that it is materially misstated. This amount is one that presumably would not influence the judgments and perceptions of third-party investors and creditors and is known as *tolerable error* (see the earlier definition). Auditors set the level of tolerable error based on the magnitude of the account balance or class of transactions in relation to important financial statement subtotals such as total assets, total revenues, or net income.

As they do in attribute sampling, auditors compare the adjusted sample estimate of the misstatement to the tolerable error. The decision made by auditors will be as follows:

If the **upper error limit (UEL)** is less than or equal to the tolerable error, auditors will conclude that the account balance is fairly stated. Although auditors will not project discovered misstatements to the population and propose an adjustment to the account balance for these projected misstatements, the client should correct all misstatements discovered (unless clearly inconsequential). In contrast, if the upper error limit exceeds the tolerable error, auditors will conclude that the account balance is materially misstated and will propose an adjustment to the account balance.

Auditors may be exposed to sampling risk if the sample of components or transactions of the account balance is not representative of the population in terms of the extent to which they are misstated. Consider the following matrix. The two columns represent the two possible outcomes if the entire population were examined; the two rows represent the two possible decisions auditors could make based on the sample of transactions or

[13] Similar to attribute sampling, auditors cannot simply compare the sample estimate of misstatement to the tolerable error. Instead, the sample estimate of misstatement must be adjusted in a conservative direction (upward) to reflect potential sampling risks. This upward adjustment is discussed and illustrated in more detail in Module G.

components of the account balance (AM = actual misstatement, TE = tolerable error, UEL = upper error limit).

		Decision Based on True State of the Population	
		AM ≤ TE (conclude account is fairly stated)	AM > TE (conclude account is misstated)
Decision Based on Examining Sample	UEL ≤ TE (conclude account is fairly stated)	A: Correct decision	B: Risk of incorrect acceptance
	UEL > TE (conclude account is misstated)	C: Risk of incorrect rejection	D: Correct decision

Cells A and D do not represent sampling risk because the decision to conclude either that the account balance is fairly stated (cell A) or that the account balance is misstated (cell D) is consistent with the decision auditors would have made had the entire population been examined.

Examine the outcome of cell C. In this instance, the sample of transactions and components indicates that the misstatement might exceed the tolerable error; as a result, auditors would conclude that the account is misstated. However, the amount of misstatement in the population is actually less than the tolerable error, suggesting that the account balance is fairly stated. This risk is referred to as the **risk of incorrect rejection** because auditors' initial judgment is to *incorrectly reject* the account balance as fairly stated.

In contrast, cell B represents a situation in which auditors conclude that the account balance is fairly stated (because the upper error limit is less than or equal to the tolerable error); however, in the population, the actual misstatement exceeds the tolerable error. As a result, auditors will inappropriately conclude that the account balance is fairly stated. This is referred to as the **risk of incorrect acceptance** because the auditors' judgment is to *incorrectly accept* the account balance.

Which of these risks is of more concern to auditors? If the auditors commit the risk of incorrect rejection and initially conclude that the account balance is misstated, the client will typically request that the auditors expand the sample size or gather additional evidence before making an adjustment to the financial statements. As this occurs and as the sample becomes more representative of the population, the auditors will ultimately reach the correct conclusion. What is the cost to them? They were required to perform additional substantive procedures beyond those performed to control detection risk to acceptable levels. Thus, the risk of incorrect rejection causes an *efficiency loss* for the auditors.

If the auditors commit the risk of incorrect acceptance and conclude that the account is not misstated, they will most likely not perform additional procedures or examine additional items related to that account balance or class of transactions. As a result, the auditors will conclude that the account balance is fairly stated when, in fact, it is materially misstated. This is the basic definition of detection risk. The ultimate result of failing to propose an adjustment to materially misstated financial statements is issuing an unqualified opinion on financial statements that are materially misstated, resulting in a reputation loss or litigation by shareholders and other third parties relying on the auditors' work. This results in an *effectiveness loss* for the auditors because they made an incorrect conclusion with respect to the client's account balance.

This discussion should make clear that the risk of incorrect acceptance is of more concern to auditors than the risk of incorrect rejection. As with the risk of assessing control risk too low in attribute sampling, auditors explicitly control their exposure to the risk of incorrect acceptance when determining the necessary sample size and when evaluating sample results.

EXHIBIT E.4
Sampling Risks When Using Sampling in the Audit Examination

Type of Sampling	Risk	Type of Loss
Attribute	Risk of assessing control risk too low (overreliance)	Effectiveness
	Risk of assessing control risk too high (underreliance)	Efficiency
Variables	Risk of incorrect acceptance	Effectiveness
	Risk of incorrect rejection	Efficiency

Summary: Sampling Risks for Audit Sampling

Exhibit E.4 summarizes the sampling risks associated with attribute and variables sampling. Note that both types of sampling have risks that expose auditors to effectiveness and efficiency losses. Although any form of sampling risk is not desirable, auditors are particularly concerned with sampling risks that expose them to effectiveness losses.

Review Checkpoints

E.18 Define *variables sampling*. When is it used in the audit examination?

E.19 What is *tolerable error*? How do auditors use it when deciding whether account balances are fairly recorded?

E.20 What are the two sampling risks associated with variables sampling? What types of losses are associated with these risks?

E.21 Why are auditors more concerned with the risk of incorrect acceptance than the risk of incorrect rejection?

AN OVERVIEW OF AUDIT SAMPLING

LEARNING OBJECTIVE

4. Understand how the basic steps and procedures used in a sampling plan apply to an audit examination.

Earlier, we identified the following seven-step procedure used in any sampling application:

Planning
1. Determine the objective of sampling.
2. Define the characteristic of interest.
3. Define the population.

Performing
4. Determine the sample size.
5. Select the sample items.
6. Measure the sample items.

Evaluating
7. Evaluate the sample results.

Documentation

This subsection provides a brief overview of how this seven-step procedure is applied to sampling in an audit setting. Modules F and G apply this procedure using a comprehensive example for attribute and variables sampling, respectively.

Planning

In the planning stages, auditors determine the objective of the sampling application and define the characteristic of interest and the population. For attribute sampling, the objective is usually to assess the operating effectiveness of a key control, the characteristic of interest is the extent to which the control is functioning effectively (performed by client

EXHIBIT E.5
Factors Affecting Sample Size

Factor	Effect on Sample Size
Population size	*Direct* (as population size increases, sample size increases)
Expected deviation rate (expected error)	*Direct* (as expected deviation rate or expected error increases, sample size increases)
Tolerable deviation rate (tolerable error)	*Inverse* (as tolerable deviation rate or tolerable error increases, sample size decreases)
Sampling risk	*Inverse* (as acceptable sampling risk increases, sample size decreases)
Population variability	*Direct* (as variability increases, sample size increases)

personnel), and the population includes all possible applications of the control by client personnel. In a variables sampling application, the objective is to determine an estimate of the extent of misstatement in an account balance or class of transactions, the characteristic of interest is the extent of misstatement in the account balance or class of transactions, and the population includes all components or transactions composing the account balance or class of transactions. Auditors often perform **dual-purpose tests** whereby they examine documents for both attributes and monetary errors. For example an invoice might be examined for the attribute of a credit authorization signature (control test) and the monetary error of an incorrect price (substantive test).

Performing

Determine the Sample Size

In either type of sampling application, four key factors affect the auditors' determination of sample size: (1) the population size, (2) the expected deviation rate (or expected error), (3) the tolerable deviation rate (or tolerable error), and (4) the auditors' acceptable exposure to sampling risk. In addition, for certain types of variables-sampling applications, the population variability also affects the sample size. The effect of these factors on sample size is summarized in Exhibit E.5. At this point, students should attempt to *conceptually* understand how these factors affect sample size and not become overly concerned with how the auditors assess them. The method of assessing these factors is discussed in more detail in Modules F and G.

As the size of the population increases, a larger sample is typically necessary to support conclusions based on that population. This relationship is fairly logical; a sample of 50 items drawn from a population of 100 items is more likely to be representative than the same sample of 50 drawn from a population of 100,000 items. Therefore, we can state that population size has a *direct relationship* with sample size. That is, as the population size increases, the sample size will increase (and vice versa).[14]

As the expected deviation rate or expected error increases, the sample needs to be larger. Again, this relationship seems logical because higher rates of deviation (or higher levels of dollar misstatement) represent potential problems to the auditors, signaling the need for a larger sample size. As a result, like population size, expected deviation rates or expected errors have a *direct relationship* with sample size.

As the tolerable deviation rate (or tolerable error) decreases, the sample needs to be larger. This larger sample size results from the fact that auditors are requiring the client's (1) controls to operate extremely effectively (small tolerable deviation rate) or (2) account balance to be very accurately stated (small tolerable error). In this case, the tolerable deviation rate or tolerable error has an *inverse relationship* with sample size. That is, as the tolerable deviation rate (or tolerable error) decreases, sample size increases (and vice versa).

Sampling risk represents the risk that the auditors' decision based on the sample differs from the decision that would be made based on the population. Recall that sampling risk results from a nonrepresentative sample. To increase the representativeness of the sample

[14] However, once a population size reaches a certain level, additional increases in population size do not have significant effects on sample size. This relationship will be illustrated more completely in Module F.

and reduce sampling risk, the auditor should increase the size of the sample. Therefore, like the tolerable deviation rate (or tolerable error), sampling risk has an *inverse relationship* with sample size.

The variability of a population reflects differences between the value of individual items within the population and the mean of those items. Population variability is often measured as the **standard deviation** (or **standard error of the mean**). Clearly, as the components of a population differ more (i.e., have a greater level of variability), the auditor needs to examine a larger number of items to obtain a representative sample. As a result, population variability has a *direct relationship* with sample size. Because values in an attribute sampling application possess only one of two values (an attribute exists or does not exist), population variability is considered only by estimating the *expected deviation rate* (EDR) in the population.

Exhibit E.5 summarizes how the factors just discussed are related to sample size. The method of determining these factors, as well as calculations of sample size using these factors, will be presented in subsequent modules.

Select Sample Items

Once the sample size has been determined, the auditors select the sample. The items selected are either potential applications of important controls (attribute sampling) or components or transactions of an account balance or class of transactions (variables sampling). If *unrestricted random selection* is used, auditors use a list of random numbers either drawn from a random number table or generated from a computer program and then select items in the population corresponding to those random numbers. With *systematic random selection*, auditors select one or more random starting points from within the population and select every *n*th item thereafter until the appropriate number of items has been selected. Both unrestricted random selection and systematic random selection are appropriate for use with statistical sampling because all items in the population have an equal probability of selection and these methods allow another individual to replicate the sample selection process.

In contrast, *block selection* and *haphazard selection* do not provide auditors a method of identifying the likelihood that a specific item will be selected for examination. In addition, these methods do not permit another individual to replicate the sample based on stated criteria. As a result, they are not used with statistical sampling.

Measure Sample Items

After the sample items have been selected, auditors perform the appropriate audit procedures and measure each item. For attribute sampling, auditors perform tests of controls to evaluate whether client personnel have performed the control policy of interest. For variables sampling, auditors perform substantive procedures to determine the correct amount (audited balance) of each component or transaction selected for examination.

Evaluating

The final step in either attribute or variables sampling is evaluating the sample results. The evaluation of sample results involves the following four-step procedure:

1. Identify either the deviation rate (attribute sampling) or difference between audited values and recorded values (variables sampling) from the sample items.
2. Adjust the information in step 1 to control the auditors' exposure to sampling risk. This adjustment is referred to as the **allowance for sampling risk.**
3. Compare the adjusted estimate in step 2 to either the tolerable deviation rate (attribute sampling) or the tolerable error (variables sampling).
4. Based on the comparison in step 3, make the decision with regard to the effectiveness of the client's internal control (attribute sampling) or fairness of the account balance (variables sampling).

Documenting the Sampling Procedure

As the procedures in each of these steps are being performed, auditors should document important judgments, assumptions, and conclusions because this documentation will provide evidence of conclusions with respect to the operating effectiveness of the client's internal control and the fairness of the client's account balances. Documentation should be sufficient to enable another auditor to replicate the tests and for a reviewer to evaluate the results.

Review Checkpoints

E.22 What are the objectives of attribute and variables sampling?

E.23 What factors affect the sample size used in an attribute sampling application? How do these factors affect sample size?

E.24 What factors affect the sample size used in a variables sampling application? How do these factors affect sample size?

Summary

This module introduces the sampling process and illustrates how sampling is used in an assurance engagement. One of the major disadvantages of sampling is that the decision made based on the sample could differ from the decision that would have been made after examining the entire population. This disadvantage (referred to as *sampling risk*) can be overcome to some extent through the use of statistical sampling methods. Statistical sampling methods control the individual's exposure to sampling risk by selecting a sufficient sample size and evaluating sample results in such a way to control sampling risk.

Using sampling in practice often presents auditors problems. The following Auditing Insight presents some deficiencies noted by the PCAOB in their inspections of Big Four auditing firms.

AUDITING INSIGHT PCAOB Inspections and Sampling

- The Firm failed to perform sufficient procedures to test revenue and accounts receivable. Specifically, the Firm did not test a sufficient sample of sales and cash receipt transactions during the three-month period between the date as of which interim audit procedures were performed and the issuer's fiscal year end to achieve an appropriate level of assurance. The Firm's sample was approximately one-tenth of the sample size that the Firm later determined was necessary.

- The Firm also tested a sample of subsequent cash receipts. The Firm did not compare the sample items to the recorded accounts receivable, nor was the sample size sufficient to provide the Firm with the necessary level of assurance regarding the accuracy of the recorded accounts receivable.

- When testing certain significant components of supplier rebates receivable (including deferred rebate balances) and cost of sales adjustments related to supplier rebates, the Firm stratified the population subject to testing by selecting a sample of the largest supplier contracts in the population. The Firm's sample was not representative because it was selected from only one segment of the population and therefore the test results could not be extended to the entire population. Accordingly, the Firm failed to test a sufficient portion of supplier rebates receivable, deferred rebate balances, and cost of sales adjustments.

- During its testing of inventory valuation in this audit, the Firm identified certain errors. The Firm, however, did not ascertain whether the population it tested was complete, and the sample size for the test was too small to enable the Firm to make a meaningful estimate of the total error in the population.

Sources: 2005 PCAOB Inspection of Deloitte & Touche (November 30, 2006); 2006 PCAOB Inspection of Ernst & Young (May 2, 2007); 2005 Inspection of KPMG (January 11, 2007); and 2005 Inspection of Pricewaterhouse-Coopers (December 14, 2006). All reports can be found on the PCAOB Web site http://www.pcaob.org/Inspections/Public_Reports/index.aspx.

Two major approaches to sampling used in an audit examination are *attribute sampling* (in the study and evaluation of internal control) and *variables sampling* (in the auditors' substantive procedures). This chapter discussed the risks associated with these sampling approaches and the various factors that influence the sample size. Attribute sampling and variables sampling are discussed in more detail in Modules F and G, respectively.

Key Terms

allowance for sampling risk (precision): The numeric distance from the estimated population value in which the true (but unknown) population value may lie with a given probability. The allowance for sampling risk is used to adjust the sample estimate to measure exposure to sampling risk, 671, 682

attribute sampling: A form of sampling used to determine the extent to which some characteristic (attribute) exists within a population of interest; used by auditors during tests of controls, 674

audit risk: The risk that auditors will unknowingly fail to modify the opinion on financial statements that are materially misstated, 674

audit sampling: Applying an audit procedure to less than 100 percent of the items within an account balance or class of transactions to evaluate some characteristic of the account balance or class of transactions, 673

audited balance: See *audited value*, 677

audited value (audited balance): The amount at which an account balance or component should be recorded, assuming no departures from generally accepted accounting principles, 677

block selection: Method of selecting sample items in which a series of contiguous (or adjacent) items is selected from the population, 669

classical variables sampling: A variables sampling approach that uses the laws of probability and the central limit theorem to provide an estimate of either the amount of misstatement or the true balance of an account balance or class of transactions, 677

confidence: See *reliability*, 671

detection risk: The risk that the auditors' substantive procedures will fail to detect a material misstatement that exists within an account balance or class of transactions, 677

deviation rate: The rate at which internal control procedures are not functioning as intended, 673

dollar unit sampling (DUS): A variables sampling approach that provides auditors an estimate of the amount of misstatement in the account balance or class of transactions; tends to select larger transactions (or components) within an account balance for examination, 678

dual-purpose test: An audit procedure that can be used as both a test of controls and a substantive test, 681

haphazard selection: Method of selecting sample items in a nonsystematic manner, 669

nonrepresentative sample: A sample that differs substantially from the population from which it is drawn on one or more key characteristics of interest, 664

nonsampling risk: The risk that an incorrect conclusion will be reached because of reasons unrelated to the nature of the sample, 665

nonstatistical sampling: A sampling plan that does not apply the laws of probability to select sample items for examination and evaluate sample results; does not allow an individual to control exposure to sampling risk, 665

population: The entire group of items about which a conclusion is desired in a sampling application, 662

precision: See *allowance for sampling risk*, 671

precision interval: A range around the sample estimate that has a certain likelihood (equal to reliability) of including the true population value, 671

random selection: See *unrestricted random selection*, 668

reliability (confidence): The likelihood of achieving a given level of precision, 671

risk of assessing control risk too high (risk of underreliance): Risk that represents the likelihood that auditors' sample will provide evidence that the client's controls are not functioning effectively when the population would indicate that they are functioning effectively, 676

risk of assessing control risk too low (risk of overreliance): Risk that represents the likelihood that auditors' sample will provide evidence that the client's controls are functioning effectively when the population would indicate they are not functioning effectively, 676

risk of incorrect acceptance: The likelihood that auditors will conclude that the client's account balance is fairly stated when, in fact, it is materially misstated, 679

risk of incorrect rejection: The likelihood that auditors will conclude that the client's account balance is materially misstated when, in fact, it is fairly stated, 679

risk of overreliance: See *risk of assessing control risk too low*, 676

risk of underreliance: See *risk of assessing control risk too high*, 676

sample: A subset of items drawn from a population of interest, 662

sample estimate of misstatement: The difference between the recorded account balance and the audited account balance, 678

sampling: The process of making a statement about a population of interest based on examining only a subset (or sample) of that population, 662

sampling interval: The frequency with which items are selected within the population; determined by dividing the number of items in the population by the necessary sample size, 668

sampling risk: The risk that the decision made based on the sample will differ from the decision that would have been made if the entire population had been examined, 664

standard deviation (standard error of the mean): A measure of the variability of the population calculated by summing the squared differences between each item in the population and the population mean, 682

standard error of the mean: See *standard deviation*, 682

statistical sampling: A sampling plan that applies the laws of probability to select sample items for examination and evaluate sample results; allows an individual to control the exposure to sampling risk, 665

systematic random selection (systematic selection): Method of selecting sample items in which a starting point is selected and a fixed number of items are bypassed between selections, 668

systematic selection: See *systematic random selection*, 668

tolerable deviation rate (TDR): The maximum rate of deviations permissible by the auditor without modifying the planned reliance on an internal control policy or procedure, 675

tolerable error: The maximum amount by which an account balance or class of transactions can be misstated and be accepted by the auditor as fairly presented, 673

unrestricted random selection (random selection): Method of selecting sample items in which items in the population are assigned a number and selected based on random numbers picked from a random number table or generated from a computer program, 668

upper error limit: The amount that has a (1 – *risk of incorrect acceptance*) probability of equaling or exceeding the true amount of misstatement in the population, 678

upper limit deviation rate (ULDR): A measure that adjusts the sample deviation rate for the auditor's acceptable level of sampling risk; the deviation rate that has a (1 – *risk of assessing control risk too low*) probability of equaling or exceeding the true population deviation rate, 675

variables sampling: A form of sampling used to examine a population to estimate the amount or value of some characteristic of that population; used by auditors during their substantive procedures, 677

Multiple Choice Questions for Practice and Review

E.25 In an audit sampling application, an auditor

a. Performs procedures on all items in a balance and makes a conclusion about the entire balance.

b. Performs procedures on less than 100 percent of the items in a balance and formulates a conclusion about the entire balance.

c. Performs procedures on less than 100 percent of the items in a class of transactions to become familiar with the client's accounting system.

d. Performs analytical procedures on the client's unaudited financial statements when planning the audit.

E.26 Auditors consider statistical sampling to be characterized by the following:

a. Representative sample selection and nonmathematical consideration of the results.

b. Carefully biased sample selection and mathematical calculation of the results.

c. Representative sample selection and mathematical calculation of the results.

d. Carefully biased sample selection and nonmathematical consideration of the results.

E.27 In which of the following scenarios would the use of sampling be most appropriate?

　　a. The population consists of a relatively small number of items.

　　b. The need for precise information about the population is not important.

　　c. The decision to be made is relatively critical.

　　d. The costs associated with an incorrect decision are extremely high.

E.28 The risk that the decision made based on the sample will differ from the decision made based on the entire population is referred to as

　　a. Audit risk.

　　b. Examination risk.

　　c. Sampling risk.

　　d. Nonsampling risk.

E.29 Which of the following is not a method used by auditors to control their exposure to sampling risk during the examination?

　　a. Determining an appropriate sample size.

　　b. Performing the appropriate audit procedure.

　　c. Ensuring that all items have an equal opportunity to be selected.

　　d. Evaluating sample results using a mathematical basis.

E.30 Which of the following is an advantage of nonstatistical sampling?

　　a. It measures the auditor's exposure to sampling risk.

　　b. It is required by generally accepted auditing standards.

　　c. It ensures that samples are randomly selected.

　　d. It is typically less complex than statistical sampling.

E.31 Selecting a sample using a series of random numbers to identify sample items is referred to as

　　a. Block selection.

　　b. Haphazard selection.

　　c. Systematic random selection.

　　d. Unrestricted random selection.

E.32 If systematic selection is used with a starting point of 10, a population size of 100, and a necessary sample size of 20, the first three items selected for examination would be

　　a. 10, 110, 210.

　　b. 110, 210, 310.

　　c. 10, 15, 20.

　　d. 15, 20, 25.

E.33 A limitation of systematic random selection is that this method

　　a. Has a relatively low likelihood of yielding a representative sample.

　　b. Results in a larger sample size than other selection methods.

　　c. Can result in bypassing a number of items having similar characteristics.

　　d. Cannot be used with statistical sampling plans.

E.34 Which of the following is appropriately used for statistical sampling applications?

	Unrestricted Random Selection	Block Selection
a.	Yes	Yes
b.	Yes	No
c.	No	Yes
d.	No	No

E.35 Which of the following pairs of selection methods could appropriately be used in statistical sampling applications?

　　a. Unrestricted random selection, block selection.

　　b. Block selection, haphazard selection.

　　c. Systematic random selection, haphazard selection.

　　d. Unrestricted random selection, systematic random selection.

E.36 A range around the sample estimate that has a certain likelihood (equal to reliability) of including the true population value is known as the

a. Confidence.

b. Mean.

~~c.~~ Precision.

(d.) Precision interval.

E.37 The likelihood that an identified precision interval contains the true (but unknown) population value is the

(a) Confidence.

b. Mean.

c. Precision.

d. Sampling risk.

E.38 Which of the following statements is not true if the precision interval for a sampling risk of 10 percent ranges from 60 to 70?

a. A 10 percent probability exists that the true population value is less than 60 or more than 70.

b. A 90 percent probability exists that the true population value is less than 60 or more than 70.

c. The reliability is 90 percent.

d. The precision is 5.

E.39 In audit sampling applications, sampling risk is

a. A characteristic of statistical sampling applications but not of nonstatistical applications.

b. The probability that the auditor will fail to recognize erroneous accounting in the client's documentation.

c. The probability that accounting errors will arise in transactions and enter the accounting system.

(d.) The probability that an auditor's conclusion based on a sample might be different from the conclusion based on an audit of the entire population.

E.40 The risks of incorrect acceptance in variables sampling and of assessing control risk too low in attribute sampling both relate to

a. Effectiveness of an audit.

b. Efficiency of an audit.

c. Control risk assessment decisions.

d. Evidence about assertions in financial statements.

E.41 The type of sampling most frequently used by auditors during their study of internal control is referred to as

(a.) Attribute sampling.

b. Control sampling.

c. Probability proportional to size sampling.

d. Variables sampling.

E.42 Which of the following components of the audit risk model is most closely associated with attribute sampling?

a. Audit risk.

b. Control risk.

c. Detection risk.

d. Inherent risk.

E.43 The auditor will choose to reduce the reliance on controls if the _____ is greater than the _____.

a. Tolerable deviation rate; upper limit deviation rate.

b. Upper limit deviation rate; tolerable deviation rate.

c. Expected deviation rate; tolerable deviation rate.

d. Tolerable deviation rate; expected deviation rate.

E.44 An advantage of statistical sampling over nonstatistical sampling methods is that statistical methods

 a. Afford greater assurance than a nonstatistical sample of equal size.

 b. Provide an objective basis for quantitatively evaluating sampling risk.

 c. Can more easily convert the sample into a dual-purpose test useful for substantive procedures.

 d. Eliminate the need to use judgment in determining appropriate sample sizes.

<div align="right">(AICPA adapted)</div>

E.45 When using sampling in the study of internal control, the auditor would compare a conservative estimate of the deviation rate to the

 a. Expected deviation rate.

 b. Sample deviation rate.

 c. Statistical deviation rate.

 d. Tolerable deviation rate.

E.46 Which of the following would not result in exposure to nonsampling risk?

 a. Measuring the characteristic of interest in an inappropriate manner.

 b. Selecting items that are not representative of the population of interest.

 c. Making an unintentional mistake in measuring the characteristic of interest.

 d. All of the above would result in exposure to nonsampling risk.

E.47 Which of the following statements is not true with respect to nonstatistical sampling?

 a. Nonstatistical sampling cannot be used in an audit conducted in accordance with generally accepted auditing standards.

 b. Nonstatistical sampling considers a number of factors in determining the appropriate sample size.

 c. When using nonstatistical sampling, an individual makes some estimate of the characteristic of interest.

 d. Nonstatistical sampling requires the use of judgment on the part of the individual performing the sampling application.

E.48 In a sampling application to determine the average weight of students enrolled in a fitness class, if the sample estimate is 120 pounds, the precision is 10 pounds, and the reliability is 90 percent, which of the following statements is true?

 a. There is a 10 percent likelihood that the average weight of a student in the class is greater than 130 pounds.

 b. There is a 10 percent likelihood that the average weight of a student in the class is less than 110 pounds.

 c. There is a 90 percent likelihood that the average weight of a student in the class is less than 110 pounds or greater than 130 pounds.

 d. There is a 90 percent likelihood that the average weight of a student in the class is between 110 and 130 pounds.

E.49 Which of the following steps would normally be performed last in a sampling application?

 (a.) Examine sample items and determine the sample estimate.

 b. Determine the level of reliability for the sampling application.

 c. Identify the objective of the sampling application.

 d. Determine the appropriate sample size.

E.50 The risk of incorrect rejection and the likelihood of assessing control risk too high relate to the

 a. Effectiveness of the audit.

 b. Efficiency of the audit.

 c. Preliminary estimates of materiality.

 d. Tolerable error.

<div align="right">(AICPA adapted)</div>

Exercises, Problems, and Simulations

E.51 **Sampling Risk.** You and a friend are deciding whether to pack heavy clothing for a trip to the northeastern United States. You have decided that you would need heavy clothing only if the temperature is expected to fall below 50 degrees during your trip. You have studied the past 50 years' seasonal temperatures in the northeast. You are considering the use of sampling to calculate an expected average temperature; you will base your decision to pack heavy clothing on the results of your sample.

Required:

a. What is *sampling risk?* What two types of sampling risks are present in this context?

b. Describe the "costs" associated with the sampling risks in (*a*).

c. How would your sampling plan differ if you used statistical sampling versus nonstatistical sampling?

d. What are the advantages and disadvantages of using statistical sampling methods in an attempt to answer your question?

E.52 **Sampling and Nonsampling Risk.** This module provided a detailed example of the use of sampling to determine whether individuals could increase their driving distance by using a Wilson golf ball.

Required:

Indicate whether each of the following situations reflects sampling risk (S), nonsampling risk (NS), both sampling risk and nonsampling risk (B), or neither sampling risk nor nonsampling risk (N).

a. Distance markers on the practice range are incorrectly placed.

b. At one course, you arrive on the day of the club championship.

c. Some of the golfers are using 3-woods, not drivers, for their shots.

d. At one course, you arrive on ladies' day, on which females have exclusive access to the course.

e. The Wilson golf balls are all new, but some of the comparison golf balls are old.

f. Your assistant makes an error in recording several driving distances.

E.53 **Sampling and Nonsampling Risk.** Read the five independent sampling applications.

Required:

Indicate whether each situation is characteristic of sampling risk (S) or nonsampling risk (N). Provide a brief explanation for your answer.

1. You are estimating the average net income of passengers on a particular airline flight. You randomly select three rows of seats (a total of 18 passengers) and calculate the average income of those passengers.

2. When estimating the average time for swimmers in a 25-meter freestyle race, you inadvertently include the times of swimmers from other events (butterfly, breaststroke, and backstroke) in your sample.

3. When estimating the average time necessary to finish an examination, the class of students you randomly selected was an honors section of the course.

4. When estimating the percentage of sixth-grade students who plan to attend college, your sample includes a disproportionate number of students attending intermediate schools located in small college towns (many of the parents are affiliated with the local university).

5. When estimating the total amount of money held in savings accounts by people of various nationalities, you make some inadvertent mistakes in converting various currencies into U.S. dollars.

E.54 **Basic Sampling.** You are attempting to determine whether you are taller or shorter than the average of students currently enrolled in your university. You have just learned about sampling and have decided to sample students to determine the average height at your university.

Required:

a. Define *sampling.*

b. What are the advantages and disadvantages of using sampling to answer this question as opposed to examining the entire population?

c. In which situations would you be more likely to use sampling (applied to this particular example) as opposed to examining the entire population?

E.55 **Basic Sampling.** You are evaluating the feasibility of opening a new 10-screen movie theater in a town that has only one existing theater. To be viable, the proposed theater would need an average attendance of at least 15,000 patrons per month. The theater would show movies every day; each of the 10 screens would have a capacity of 120 patrons. An average month has the following characteristics with respect to potential patrons:

> Weekdays: 21 days with a total of 20 shows per day (2 show times × 10 screens)
> Weekends: 9 days with a total of 40 shows per day (4 show times × 10 screens)

Because the current theater maintains no records, you must physically visit the theater and count patrons.

Required:

a. What are some possible methods you can use to estimate the number of patrons on the evenings you visit?

b. What are some precautions that you should consider to ensure a representative sample?

c. What are two possible types of sampling risk that are present in this context? Which of these risks is of more concern to you?

d. Assume that your sampling procedure was employed to provide you 95 percent confidence. How would you react to the following independent outcomes?

1. Sample estimate of 600 patrons, precision of 30 patrons.
2. Sample estimate of 680 patrons, precision of 150 patrons.
3. Sample estimate of 490 patrons, precision of 35 patrons.

E.56 **Basic Sampling.** You are employed by Northeast Airlines and have been asked to determine the rate of on-time arrivals for competing airlines at a proposed hub location. Northeast is known for its outstanding customer service and constantly ranks in the top three among all airlines in on-time arrivals with an average rate of 82 percent of all flights. Because it would be a new entrant in this particular airport, Northeast does not believe it can compete unless its on-time arrival rate can surpass that of the airlines currently serving this hub.

Because each of the four major competitors has hundreds of flights arriving at the hub on a daily basis, you are considering the use of sampling to estimate an on-time arrival rate.

Required:

a. Define *sampling*. What are the primary advantages and primary disadvantages of using sampling in this application?

b. Briefly describe how you would identify the population of flights from which you intend to sample.

c. Define *sampling risk* and *nonsampling risk*. Provide an example of how each could be present in this situation.

d. List some characteristics of various flights that could give you increased exposure to sampling risk in this application.

e. Once you have estimated an on-time arrival rate for its competitors, what information can you provide to Northeast Airlines to assist it in its decision process?

E.57 **Sample Evaluation.** In the most recent local election between two candidates, you heard your local news anchor indicate that your preferred candidate had 48 percent of the vote with a margin for error (precision) of ±6 percent. The news anchor also indicated a reliability of 99 percent for these results.

Required:

a. Define the terms *sample estimate*, *precision*, and *reliability*.

b. Based on the information given, what is the possible range of support that your preferred candidate could have when all votes are counted?

c. Provide a brief summary (one sentence) describing what you can determine from the anchor's report.

d. How do you feel about your candidate's chances of winning the election?

e. How would you feel about your candidate's chances of winning if the anchor's report was identical except that the margin for error was only ±1 percent?

E.58 **Sample Evaluation.** For each of the following independent cases, identify the missing value(s).

	1	2	3
Precision	20	(C)	10
Sample estimate	56	80	(E)
Reliability	95%	(D)	98%
Precision interval	(A)	75 to 85	111 to 131
Sampling risk	(B)	10%	(F)

E.59 **Sample Evaluation.** The National Football League (NFL) is interested in determining whether the average age of its fan base is less than 35 years of age to identify this demographic for potential advertisers. Following are the results for three different stadiums for fans attending an NFL game on a given weekend. In all cases, assume a sampling risk of 5 percent.

	Sample 1	Sample 2	Sample 3
Precision	5	3	8
Sample estimate	26	34	40

Required:

a. Construct a precision interval for each of these samples.

b. Given the sampling risk of 5 percent, provide a single-sentence summary of the results to the NFL for each sample.

c. What is your basic conclusion regarding each sample?

d. If the NFL increased its acceptable level of sampling risk, how would that affect the precision interval and your conclusions? If they decreased the acceptable level of sampling risk, how would that affect the precision interval and your conclusions? Why?

E.60 **Sample Evaluation.** Gloria Bush has performed a sampling plan to estimate the number of children per household in her neighborhood. In doing so, she established a 10 percent acceptable level of sampling risk and found a sample estimate of 2.5 children per household. Based on the acceptable level of sampling risk, she calculated a precision of 0.7 child per household.

Required:

a. Define the terms *precision* and *reliability*. How are these terms related?

b. What is the precision interval in this example? What statement can Gloria make based on her sample evidence?

c. Assume that Gloria desires a lower sampling risk (5 percent). How will this affect the precision interval?

d. If Gloria is interested in knowing whether the number of children per household exceeds 1.5 children, how would you advise her based on the following outcomes? In all cases, assume that the sample estimate is 2.5 children per household.

 1. Reliability = 90 percent; precision = 0.7 child per household.

 2. Reliability = 95 percent; precision = 1.4 children per household.

 3. Reliability = 99 percent; precision = 1.8 children per household.

e. What causes the differences in the relationships noted in (*d*)?

E.61 **Sample Evaluation.** Your political consulting group (Electem, Inc.) is assisting a local political candidate (Alice Evans) to determine the likelihood of her election to office during the upcoming campaign. Alice would like to have an extremely high level of confidence (95 percent) that she would receive more than a majority of the ballots cast.

 After conducting an extensive survey, you have determined that 53 percent of voters would prefer Alice, with a precision of 5 percent and a corresponding reliability of 95 percent.

In determining this information, your notes of the sampling process revealed the following information:

1. The district that Alice would represent is composed of eight neighborhoods. You randomly chose four of these neighborhoods and, within each, had workers poll voters (using a door-to-door technique) from the first 25 households that responded.

2. Your workers canvassed the neighborhoods during the day from 12 p.m. to 3 p.m.

3. Your workers asked voters to respond to the following question: "Do you support Alice Evans during the upcoming election?"

4. In one neighborhood (a community with restricted access to nonresidents), your workers could not obtain a sample of 25 voters using a door-to-door polling technique. As a result, they used a telephone survey to obtain the 25 responses for this neighborhood.

5. Some of your workers observed that, at homes indicating they would support Alice for office, campaign signs for her chief rival were present. The workers were surprised that these same households indicated they would support Alice.

6. George Clinton, one of your workers, indicated that he misunderstood the survey instructions, which indicated that a voter could indicate "yes," "no," or "undecided." George thought that he was required to obtain a "yes" or "no" answer; when voters indicated they were undecided, he pressed them to make a decision (which they ultimately did).

7. Billy Bush, another worker, did not verify the names of the individuals to whom he was speaking.

Required:

a. Based on the sample results, without considering any of the information included in (1)–(7), what would you advise Alice about her electibility?

b. How would your advice to Alice change if she established the following levels of reliability (assume that the sample estimate of 53 percent is unchanged)?

 1. Reliability = 99 percent, precision = 8 percent.
 2. Reliability = 90 percent, precision = 2 percent.

c. Summarize why your advice to Alice would change based on the reliability and precision noted in (*b*).

d. For each of the seven issues included in your sampling notes, indicate how that issue could affect the advice you provide to Alice and her ability to rely on the sample evidence.

E.62 **Sample Evaluation.** Marts, Inc., a local fund-raising organization, is considering the feasibility of a fund-raising campaign to assist a youth organization build a new recreation center in College Bryan, Texas. Marts has been asked to determine whether this campaign would be successful in raising $1.5 million, the amount needed to construct and equip the center.

Because unsuccessful fundraising efforts have a negative impact on Marts' ability to obtain future clients and engagements, it has established a reliability of 99 percent; that is, Marts wants to have a very high level of confidence that the $1.5 million can be successfully raised in the local community. Because a total of 50,000 citizens live in the College Bryan area, the average gift necessary to ensure a successful campaign is $30 per person ($1,500,000 ÷ 50,000). Based on the sampling risk associated with a 99 percent reliability, Marts determined a sample size of 200 and surveyed each of these individuals with respect to their willingness to donate to the fund-raising campaign. The average level of support indicated by these 200 persons was $35 per person.

Required:

a. Based on Marts's sample, calculate the sample estimate for the total amount that could be raised under this fund-raising effort.

b. Based only on the sample estimate, how would you advise Marts as to the potential success of its fund-raising campaign?

c. What is the primary limitation to Marts in making its decision based only on the sample estimate?

d. What is sampling risk? What types of factors could influence Marts's exposure to sampling risk in this particular situation?

e. Using the sample estimate calculated in (*a*), determine the precision interval if the calculated precision were

 1. $100,000.

 2. $200,000.

 3. $300,000.

f. How would you advise Marts regarding the potential success of the fund-raising campaign based on the precision intervals calculated in (*e*)?

g. Assume that Marts believes that a 99 percent reliability is too stringent and is considering lowering the reliability to 95 percent. How will this change affect the precision interval and the likelihood that Marts will conclude that the fund-raising campaign will ultimately be successful?

E.63 **Basic Sampling: Comprehensive.** Reagan Russell is considering opening a multipurpose hardware and lawn store in Anytown, USA. Based on his knowledge of the industry, he believes that if the average household income is more than $35,000, the store will ultimately be successful. He was planning to attempt a census of the income levels in Anytown but has heard about sampling and is now considering using sampling to obtain the necessary information to make his decision.

Required:

a. What would you tell Reagan about the advantages and disadvantages of sampling?

b. Reagan is interested in knowing the advantages and disadvantages of statistical sampling. What would you tell him?

c. Reagan has heard about sampling and nonsampling risk and is concerned about them.

 1. Define *sampling risk* and *nonsampling risk*.

 2. How can Reagan control his exposure to sampling and nonsampling risk?

 3. What are some possible examples of sampling and nonsampling risk in this situation?

d. Assume that Reagan decided to use an unrestricted random selection to obtain a sample of households for examination. If he determined a sample size of 100 households, describe how he could select the sample from the city's property tax rolls.

e. Instead of unrestricted random selection, Reagan asked you whether he could just pick four or five streets and examine all of the households on those streets. What would you tell him?

f. Assume that Reagan has set a sampling risk of 10 percent and found a sample estimate of $39,000 with a precision of $3,000. How would you explain the results to Reagan? What advice would you give him?

g. Repeat (*f*) assuming that Reagan found a sample estimate of $42,000 and a precision of $10,000.

E.64 **Sample Selection.** Arianna Casey is trying to select a sample of registered voters in Hoops County to see how they intend to vote on funding a stadium for the local professional basketball team. She has determined that a sample of 1,000 voters will be necessary to provide an acceptable minimum level of sampling risk (15 percent). The state has more than 3 million registered voters who are listed (sorted by ZIP code) in an electronic data file maintained in the state commissioner's office. The commissioner has agreed to allow Arianna to have access to this data file for her project.

Required:

a. What is sampling risk? What steps can Arianna take to control her exposure to sampling risk?

b. How would Arianna define the population in this case?

c. What are some potential methods of selecting the sample (as specifically applied to this application)?

d. What precautions should Arianna take to ensure that she selects a representative sample?

E.65 **Sample Selection Methods.** You are employed by FishWrap, Ltd., a local newspaper distribution company, and are attempting to determine the average level of customer satisfaction with the newspaper's delivery service. All customers are included in a comprehensive

database that includes the following information: customer name, delivery address, telephone number, type of service (weekly only, weekend only, weekly/weekend), length of service (how long they have subscribed to the newspaper), and name of carrier.

Because the local area has 10,500 subscribers, FishWrap has decided to sample its customers instead of surveying the entire population of subscribers. Based on a number of factors (including precision and reliability), FishWrap has determined that a sample of 150 customers is necessary.

Required:

a. In this application, what are some of the major characteristics of subscribers that should be considered to ensure that a representative sample is selected?

b. Identify and briefly define four major methods used to select a sample.

c. How could you select a sample from the population using each of these methods?

d. The information in each list is arranged in descending order based on length of service. Indicate how each of the following factors could impact your ability to use the four methods of selecting a sample from a population:

1. The database is a typed list of information.

2. The database is an electronic list of information and cannot be sorted on any other characteristic.

3. The database is an electronic list of information and can be sorted on any characteristic.

e. How does each of the following factors impact your ability to evaluate whether you have selected a representative sample from the population?

1. Delivery address does not include ZIP code or other reasonable way of identifying physical location within the subscription area.

2. The length of service is classified as follows: less than six months, six months to one year, more than one year.

3. If customers have relocated within the subscription area, their length of service has been reset to zero even when they continued their subscriptions.

E.66 **Sampling and Nonsampling Risk.** Arthur Castle is interested in identifying the average number of family members living in each household in his neighborhood. He has heard about sampling and thinks that it could help him identify the number. In considering the application of sampling to this particular situation, he considers the following characteristics of his neighborhood:

a. Many of his neighbors are dual-income career couples and are away from home in the mornings and afternoons.

b. His neighborhood has two distinct types of homes. The value of the homes in the more established section is in the $300,000 price range and above; most of the individuals have resided in this section for quite some time. The value of homes in the newer section is in the $150,000–$200,000 range, most of which have been built and occupied within the last two years.

c. A small park has been built in the neighborhood. Because of safety considerations, many families with small children have chosen to live near the park.

d. A wooded area backs up to one section of his neighborhood. Because of the privacy offered by the wooded area, as well as the relative lack of traffic, older residents have chosen to live in this part of the neighborhood.

e. Several families have frequent visitors to their homes, particularly on the weekends.

Required:

For each of these characteristics, indicate whether it has the potential to affect sampling risk, nonsampling risk, both sampling risk and nonsampling risk, or neither sampling risk nor nonsampling risk.

E.67 **Sampling and Nonsampling Risk.** You are conducting a research study to determine the effect of a two-week workout and diet regimen on the weight loss experienced by individuals between the ages of 30 and 35 years. Health Busters, a local fitness club, has allowed

you access to some of its members for their voluntary participation. Your research study will use the following methodology:

1. Solicit participation from health club members.
2. Ask members who agree to participate to weigh themselves and self-report their weight to you at that time.
3. Provide members a scheduled set of workouts and dietary restrictions for the upcoming two weeks.
4. Via telephone survey, obtain the members' weights following the two-week period.
5. Based on the initial weight measurement and final weight measurement, calculate the net weight gain or loss.

Required:

a. How would each of the following characteristics of the methodology affect sampling risk and nonsampling risk?

1. You solicited member participation during the early morning hours when most of the members working out were doing so before going to work that day.
2. Males comprised 85 percent of your sample.
3. The health club is located near downtown, where most residents are either single or married without children.
4. Because of traffic, expensive parking, and reasonable proximity of their homes to their offices, most of the patrons walk to their offices (or, in inclement weather, take taxicabs or public transportation).
5. Because of privacy concerns, you agreed to allow participants to self-report their initial and final weight measurements.
6. Because of time constraints, you were unable to monitor participants' workouts or diets during the two-week period.

b. Suggest some improvements to the methodology described to reduce potential exposure to sampling risk and nonsampling risk.

E.68 **Sample Selection Methods.** You are interested in selecting a sample of 100 students on your campus to participate in a survey of the effects of coffee on students' ability to comprehend material from a faculty member's lecture. You have decided to limit your selection to business majors and have obtained a comprehensive list (ranked in descending order based on grade point average) of all business majors. This list is 22 pages long and contains the names of 2,200 business majors.

Required:

a. When selecting your sample, what precautions should you take to ensure a representative sample?

b. Briefly describe how you might select the sample using each of the following methods: (1) unrestricted random selection, (2) systematic random selection, (3) haphazard selection, and (4) block selection.

c. What are some of the advantages and disadvantages of using the selection methods described in (*b*)?

E.69 **Factors Affecting Sample Size.** Indicate how each of the following factors influences the sample size in an attribute and variables sampling application by using I (inverse relationship), D (direct relationship), or U (unrelated).

	Attribute Sampling	Variables Sampling
Population size		
Expected deviation rate (expected error)		
Tolerable deviation rate (tolerable error)		
Sampling risk		
Population variability		

E.70 **General Sampling.** Alex Fishkin is trying to decide on a new location for an ice cream and candy shop. He has decided that if the average number of children per household within a one-mile radius of a proposed shop exceeds 1.3, it would be financially successful and would provide him an annual net income of $50,000 (the minimum acceptable amount). If not, he would stand to lose his initial investment of $150,000.

Required:

a. What factors would influence Alex's decision to use sampling to answer this question?

b. What are some of the advantages and disadvantages of using sampling to answer this question?

c. Define *sampling risk*. Describe two different outcomes that may reflect Alex's exposure to sampling risk. Which of these outcomes would be of more concern to him?

d. If the initial investment was $10,000 instead of $150,000, how do you think Alex would evaluate the potential outcomes of the two sampling risks noted in (c)?

e. Define *nonsampling risk*. Describe some potential nonsampling risks that Alex could encounter in this application.

E.71 **Audit Sampling: Types of Audit Samples.** You have been assigned to the audit of Phillip's, Inc., a chain of convenience stores. As part of the audit planning, you decide to perform the following tests:

1. Perform a walkthrough of purchase transactions by selecting one purchase and following it through all procedures from the order to recording in the general ledger.

2. Select a sample of purchase vouchers and ensure they are supported by receiving documents.

3. Select a sample of payroll checks and agree the time to the time cards and ensure they have supervisor approval. Using the sample, project the total payroll expense for the year.

4. Select a sample from the inventory on hand and estimate the total inventory on hand at the balance sheet date.

5. Vouch all long-term debt added during the year to the loan agreement and the cash received.

6. Select a sample of long-term debt agreements and ensure they have been approved in the board of director minutes.

7. Evaluate the control environment by inquiring of personnel as to the existence of a code of conduct.

Required:

a. Define the terms *attribute sampling*, *variables sampling*, and *dual-purpose sampling*.

b. For each of the items listed above, indicate whether it indicates an attribute sample, a variables sample, or a dual-purpose sample or if it is not an example of sampling.

E.72 **Audit Simulation: Various Sampling Concepts.** You overheard the following comments during a conversation between Roger Roddick and Andrew Federer about a specific sampling application.

Required:

Refer to appropriate professional standards and comment on the validity of each of these statements.

a. "Using nonstatistical sampling is so much easier than using statistical sampling. Statistical sampling requires far too many judgments. Under nonstatistical sampling, I can just pick items, evaluate them, and make my decision."

b. "I wish nonstatistical sampling were allowable in generally accepted auditing standards audits. In some cases, the additional time required by statistical sampling just isn't worth the benefits."

c. "Once we control the sampling risk, we're home free. Assuming we select a representative sample, there's nothing else that we need to worry about."

d. "Be careful if you try to control sampling risk at too low a level. You will need to select more items, which will increase the amount of audit time."

 e. "Those transactions with Wimbledon are always so difficult to audit. Let's exclude them from our sampling frame. We can pick other items and have a sufficiently large sample to meet generally accepted auditing standards."

 f. "I'm about to perform a walkthrough on Flushing's processing of sales transactions to understand their nature. What level of sampling risk should I consider in planning my sample of transactions?"

E.73 **Audit Simulation: General Sampling.** The accounting firm of Mason & Jarr performed the work described in each of the following separate cases. The two partners are worried about properly applying auditing standards regarding sampling. They have asked your advice.

Required:

Write a report addressed to Mason & Jarr stating whether they did or did not observe the essential elements of auditing standards in each case. When applicable, refer to the appropriate professional standards regarding audit sampling.

 a. Mason selected three purchase orders for the purchase of raw materials from LIZ Corporation's files. He started at the beginning in the accounting process and traced each one through the accounting system. He saw the receiving reports, purchasing agent's approvals, receiving clerks' approvals, vendors' invoices (now stamped PAID), entry in the cash disbursement records, and canceled checks. This work gave him a first-hand familiarity with the cash disbursement system and he felt confident about understanding related questions in the internal control questionnaire completed later.

 b. Jarr observed the physical inventory at SER Corporation. She had a list of the different inventory descriptions with the quantities taken from the perpetual inventory records. She selected the 200 items with the largest quantities and counted them after the client's shop foreperson had completed his count. She decided not to verify the count accuracy of the other 800 items. The shop foreperson miscounted in 16 cases. Jarr concluded the rate of miscount was 8 percent and that as many as 80 of the 1,000 items might be counted incorrectly. As a result, she asked him to recount everything.

 c. CSR Corporation issued seven separate series of short-term commercial paper notes near the fiscal year-end to finance seasonal operations. Jarr confirmed the obligations under each series with the independent trustee for the holders, studied all seven indenture agreements, and traced the proceeds of each issue to the cash receipts records.

 d. At the completion of the EH&R Corporation audit, Mason obtained management representations as required by generally accepted auditing standards from the president, the chief financial officer, and the controller. He did not ask the chief accountant at headquarters or the plant controllers in the three divisions for management representations.

 e. Jarr audited the Repairs and Maintenance account of Kerr Corporation by vouching all entries over $5,000 (totaling $278,000) to supporting documents. She compared the sum of all remaining entries ($75,000, a materal amount) in relation to the prior-year total of $56,000 and decided the amounts were reasonable and did not perform any additional procedures with respect to these entries.

CPA REVIEW

E.74 **Kaplan CPA Exam Simulation: Sampling Terminology.**

Required:

Go to the text Web site at www.mhhe.com/louwers3e, click on the AUD: Ridge Associates case and the "Stat. Sampling" tab, and complete the assigned task.

Attribute Sampling

Professional Standards References

Compendium Section	Document Reference	Topic
Various*	AS 5	"An Audit of Internal Control over Financial Reporting That Is Integrated with an Audit of Financial Statements"
AU 312	SAS 107	"Audit Risk and Materiality in Conducting an Audit"
AU 319	SAS 109	"Understanding the Entity and Its Environment and Assessing the Risk of Material Misstatement"
	ISA 330	"The Auditor's Procedures in Response to Assessed Risks"
AU 319	SAS 94	"The Effect of Information Technology on the Auditor's Consideration of Internal Control in a Financial Statement Audit"
AU 326	SAS 106	"Audit Evidence"
	ISA 500	"Audit Evidence"
AU 339	SAS 103	"Audit Documentation"
	AS 3	"Audit Documentation"
	ISA 230	"Audit Documentation"
AU 350	SAS 39	"Audit Sampling"
AU 350	SAS 111	"Amendment to Statement on Auditing Standards No. 39, *Audit Sampling*"
	ISA 530	"Audit Sampling and Other Means of Testing"
AU 9350		"Interpretation: Applicability of Audit Sampling"

*AS 5 amends AU 230, AU 310, AU 312, AU 313, AU 315 AU 316, AU 319, AU 322, AU 325, AU 328, AU 332, AU 333, AU 341, AU 342, AU 380, AU 508, AU 530, AU 543, AU 560, AU 561, AU 711, AU 722, *AS 3*, and *AS 4*.

> There are five kinds of lies: lies, damned lies, statistics, politicians quoting statistics, and novelists quoting politicians on statistics.
>
> *Stephen K. Tagg, Marketing faculty member, University of Strathclyde*

Learning Objectives

Module F builds on the sampling overview presented in Module E and provides a comprehensive example of the use of attribute sampling in the auditor's study of internal control.

Your objectives are to be able to:

1. Identify the objectives of attribute sampling, define *deviation conditions*, and define the population for an attribute sampling application.

2. Understand how various factors influence the size of an attribute sample.

3. Determine the sample size for an attribute sampling application.

4. Identify various methods of selecting an attribute sample.

5. Evaluate the results of an attribute sampling application by determining the *upper limit deviation rate*.

6. Define *sequential sampling* and *discovery sampling* and identify when these types of sampling applications could be used.

7. Understand how to apply nonstatistical sampling to attribute testing.

INTRODUCTION

This module focuses on the use of attribute sampling in conducting tests of controls. Recall that **attribute sampling** is used to determine the extent to which some attribute (or characteristic) exists within a population of interest. In tests of controls, that attribute is whether a specific control was applied by client personnel and is functioning to prevent or detect financial statement misstatements.

The following seven-step procedure detailed in Module E serves as the basis for our illustration of attribute sampling. The procedure introduced there has been slightly revised to more closely fit an attribute sampling application.

To illustrate the application of the process, we focus on the auditor's study and evaluation of important controls for the revenue cycle of **AirCon Company,** a manufacturer of high-technology products.[1] In the revenue cycle, two important assertions about events or transactions are *occurrence* (that is, do recorded sales and accounts receivable represent bona fide sales?) and *accuracy* (are sales and accounts receivable recorded accurately?). The auditor uses the audit risk model to determine the necessary level of detection risk (nature, timing, and extent of substantive procedures) for these two assertions.

Attribute sampling is employed to confirm the auditor's assessment of control risk. That is, the auditor obtains evidence as to the operating effectiveness of key controls. This is the focus of the AirCon Company example.

ATTRIBUTE SAMPLING: PLANNING

LEARNING OBJECTIVE

1. Identify the objectives of attribute sampling, define *deviation conditions*, and define the population for an attribute sampling application.

Determining the Objective of Sampling

The objective of attribute sampling is related to the particular control policy or procedure being examined. The auditor begins by identifying relevant assertions related to account balances and classes of transactions. Then the key control objectives related to these assertions are matched to these assertions. The major categories of control objectives for the revenue cycle (which is the focus of the AirCon Company example we use in this module) are shown in Exhibit F.1.

[1] This module focuses on sampling with respect to internal control in assessing control risk to determine the nature, timing, and extent of substantive procedures. However, it is important to note that this discussion also applies to engagements subject to the provisions of PCAOB *Auditing Standard 5* with respect to the auditor's responsibility to audit internal control under section 404 of the Sarbanes-Oxley Act.

EXHIBIT F.1
Some Control Objectives for the Revenue Cycle

Occurrence	Does the recorded sale represent an actual sale made to a customer?
Completeness	Have all valid sales been recorded?
Accuracy	Has the sale been recorded at the proper dollar amount?
Classification	Have sales to subsidiaries and affiliates been classified as intercompany sales and receivables?

The first step in the attribute sampling process is to identify the objective of attribute sampling, which is related to examining key controls corresponding to the financial statement assertions of interest to the auditor. For the examination of AirCon's revenue cycle, the two major assertions of interest are *occurrence* and *accuracy*. Once the relevant assertions have been determined, the auditor then specifies one or more controls that, if functioning, allow the client to achieve these assertions. The following is a summary of the assertions and controls that will be tested for AirCon. In addition, for each of these two assertions, the auditor has identified one control that will be tested.[2]

Assertion	Control
Occurrence	Sales invoices are supported by a valid shipping document[3]
Accuracy	Sales invoices are initialed by client personnel as evidence of verification of mathematical accuracy

Defining the Deviation Conditions

Once the objective of attribute sampling has been identified, the auditor must next define the deviation conditions and the population from which the sample is to be selected. The term **deviation (commonly** *referred to as* error, occurrence, *or* exception) *refers to instances in which the client and/or its personnel do* not *follow prescribed controls; in other words, when controls* are not functioning as intended. *Defining the deviation conditions at the outset is important because deviation conditions provide the auditor with evidence regarding the* operating effectiveness of the client's internal control.

AirCon's control policies indicate that client personnel write their initials in a preprinted "verified by" space on the invoice itself after mathematically verifying the accuracy of each sales invoice. For the control that a sales invoice must be supported by a shipping document, a deviation would be a situation in which a shipping document does not exist to support a sales invoice. The deviation conditions defined by the auditor are as follows:

Control	Example of Deviation
Sales invoices are mathematically verified by client personnel	Lack of employee initials on sales invoice or mathematically incorrect invoice
Sales invoices are supported by a valid shipping document	Instance in which a sales invoice is not accompanied by a shipping document

While defining deviation conditions seems to be relatively straightforward, it is important that the auditor consider the surrounding circumstances. For example, if AirCon makes sales to customers on its premises, it will have sales invoices that are not (and should not) be accompanied by a shipping document. Defining these occurrences as

[2] In practice, a larger number of controls would pertain to the occurrence and accuracy assertions. We limit the number of controls examined by the auditor to focus on the application of attribute sampling.
[3] Of course, the possibility exists that the shipping document was fraudulently prepared in an effort to boost sales. However, this possibility is beyond the scope of our discussion of attribute sampling.

deviation conditions would understate the operating effectiveness of the client's internal control. This potential issue can be avoided by defining the population more specifically (i.e., sales invoices representing sales that were shipped to customers).

Note that a deviation does not necessarily indicate that an error in processing a transaction has occurred. For example, an employee could have mathematically verified a sales invoice but forgotten to record her initials on the sales invoice. In addition, the invoice could be correctly calculated regardless of whether the invoice was verified. However, the failure of client employees to document their performance of key controls causes auditor concern and should be investigated.

Notice that the nature of deviations lends itself to *attribute sampling,* which is concerned with determining the extent to which some attribute (in this case, deviation condition) exists within the population. For example, if the auditor is looking for evidence of client employee initials or other evidence that a control procedure was performed, the answer can be only "yes" or "no." With this definition, the auditor can count the number of deviations and use the count when evaluating the evidence.

Defining the Population

The *population* is the set of all items about which a conclusion is desired. In attribute sampling, the population represents all potential applications of the control policy or procedure of interest. Population definition is important because audit conclusions can only be made about the population from which the sample was selected. For example, consider the following relationships between the sales invoice and shipping document in the revenue cycle:

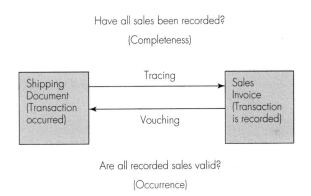

Notice that, by defining the population as sales invoices, the auditor is examining only transactions that have been recorded. As a result, this population cannot be used to provide evidence for the *completeness* objective. However, this population is appropriate if the auditor is interested in verifying that all recorded sales invoices represent valid transactions (as evidenced by the presence of shipping documents), which corresponds to the *occurrence* objective.

Conversely, if the population is defined as all shipping documents, the auditor is (presumably) examining only transactions that have occurred (*occurrence*), but tracing the shipping document to the corresponding sales invoices provides evidence with respect to *completeness.* In summary, the definition of the population is directly related to the very first step in the attribute sampling process (determining the objective of sampling).

Recall that the auditor is examining the following controls:

- Extensions and footings on sales invoices are mathematically accurate.
- Sales invoices are prepared only for items shipped to customers.

As a result, the population should be defined as all sales invoices prepared by AirCon during the period under audit.

A complicating factor in defining the population is the timing of the audit work. Tests of controls ideally should be applied to transactions throughout the entire period under audit because the auditor wants to reach a conclusion about control risk during the entire period. However, auditors often perform tests of controls at an interim date, which is any date prior to year end. One limitation of interim testing is that the entire population will not be available for examination on this date. If interim testing is done, the auditor must extend these tests to year-end transactions to ensure that the sample includes control policies and procedures applied throughout the entire year.

Somewhat related to interim testing is the need for the auditor to determine the **physical representation of the population.** The physical representation is the frame of reference the auditor uses in selecting the sample, also referred to as the "source" of the sample. That is, the auditor will select the sample from the physical representation. Some possible physical representations for selecting a sample of sales invoices include these:

- A journal list of recorded sales invoices.
- Copies of sales invoices contained in a file.
- A computerized list of sales invoices.

The primary concerns about the physical representation are that it is complete and corresponds with the actual population. For example, if the journal list used by the auditor to select sales invoices does not include invoices for the month of December, the auditor will not be able to select a random sample from the year. The auditor should exhibit appropriate levels of professional skepticism and take specific steps to ensure that the physical representation provides the opportunity to select the sample from the complete population. For example, a sales journal can be footed and agreed to the general ledger, or software controls can be examined to ensure all sales in the general ledger came from the sales journal.

AirCon Company has a computerized list of all sales invoices prepared during the year. It can be sorted by date, customer, or dollar amount. The auditor will use it to select the sample.

The first three steps in the sampling process for AirCon Company are summarized here.

Summary: Comprehensive Example of Steps in the Sampling Process for AirCon Company

1. The auditor's objective in sampling is to evaluate the operating effectiveness of controls related to the occurrence and accuracy assertions.

2. The auditor defined deviation conditions as (1) lack of employee initials on sales invoices or mathematical error on a sales invoice (accuracy) and (2) a sales invoice that is not accompanied by a shipping document (occurrence).

3. The auditor defined the population as a computerized list of all sales invoices prepared during the year.

Review Checkpoints

F.1 Define *attribute sampling.* In what stage of the audit would it be used?

F.2 How do the financial statement assertions relate to the objectives of attribute sampling?

F.3 Define *deviation condition.* Why are deviation conditions so important in an attribute sampling application?

F.4 Why is appropriately defining the population of interest so important in an attribute sampling application?

ATTRIBUTE SAMPLING: PERFORMING

LEARNING
OBJECTIVE

2. Understand how
various factors
influence the size of
an attribute sample.

The next three steps in attribute sampling relate to performing critical procedures necessary to gather evidence. These steps include determining sample size, selecting the sample, and measuring sample items.

Determining Sample Size: Factors to Consider

The *sample size* represents the number of items that the auditor examines. Four main factors influence the sample size in an attribute sampling application:

- Sampling risk (risk of assessing control risk too low).
- Tolerable deviation rate.
- Expected deviation rate.
- Population size.

Sampling Risk

Recall that sampling risk is the risk that the decision made based on the sample differs from the decision that would have been made had the entire population been examined. Module E summarized two types of sampling risks for attribute sampling applications: the **risk of assessing control risk too high** and the **risk of assessing control risk too low** (sometimes referred to as the *risk of underreliance* and the *risk of overreliance,* respectively). Exhibit F.2 summarizes some of the key characteristics of these risks.

As shown in Exhibit F.2, the risk of assessing control risk too low occurs when the auditor's sample evidence suggests that the control is functioning effectively (the adjusted sample deviation rate is less than the tolerable deviation rate) when the true (but unknown) state of the population is that the control is not functioning effectively (population deviation rate is higher than the tolerable deviation rate). Recall from Module E that because the risk of assessing control risk too low results in the auditor's failing to reduce audit risk to acceptable levels (an effectiveness loss), controlling exposure to this risk is of primary importance. Although the risk of assessing control risk too high is also a form of sampling risk, this risk will actually result in the auditor's achieving a lower level of audit risk than planned. Therefore, in an attribute sampling plan, the auditor will control only the exposure to the risk of assessing control risk too low in determining the appropriate sample size.

How does the auditor assess the acceptable level of the risk of assessing control risk too low? Generally, this risk depends on the planned level of control risk (which reflects the degree of reliance that the auditor wishes to place on the client's internal control). Recall that *control risk* is the risk that the client's internal control fails to prevent or detect material misstatements in an assertion related to an account balance or class of transactions. As the planned level of control risk is lower, it becomes quite important for the auditor to reduce the exposure to the risk of assessing control risk too low.

EXHIBIT F.2 Sampling Risks Associated with Attribute Sampling

Sampling Risk	Sample Results	Unknown State of the Population	Loss
Risk of assessing control risk too high (risk of underreliance)	Adjusted sample deviation rate > Tolerable deviation rate *Conclusion: Control is not functioning*	Population deviation rate < Tolerable deviation rate *Conclusion: Control is functioning*	Efficiency loss because additional substantive procedures will be performed
Risk of assessing control risk too low (risk of overreliance)	Adjusted sample deviation rate < Tolerable deviation rate *Conclusion:* Control is functioning	Population deviation rate > Tolerable deviation rate *Conclusion:* Control is not functioning	Effectiveness loss because an insufficient level of substantive procedures will be performed

EXHIBIT F.3

Effect of Control Risk Assessments on Risk of Assessing Control Risk Too Low and Tolerable Deviation Rates

Control Risk (Qualitative)	Control Risk (Quantitative)	RACTL	TDR
Low	0.10–0.30	5%	3%–7%
Moderate	0.40–0.60	5%–10%	6%–12%
Slightly below maximum	0.70–0.90	10%	11%–20%
Maximum	1.00	Not applicable	Not applicable

Exhibit F.3 illustrates one possible method of relating the planned level of control risk to the risk of assessing control risk too low (RACTL) and tolerable deviation rates (TDR) (we discuss tolerable deviation rates in the following subsection). Although the numerical relationships in Exhibit F.3 are not strictly observed in practice, they illustrate that lower planned levels of control risk are associated with lower levels of RACTL.[4]

Assume that the auditor has decided to assess control risk at low levels (0.30) for the occurrence objective and moderate levels (0.50) for the accuracy objective. Based on the relationships in Exhibit F.3, assume that these assessments of control risk are translated into 5 percent and 10 percent risks of assessing control risk too low for the occurrence and accuracy objectives, respectively.[5]

Tolerable Deviation Rate

The **tolerable deviation rate (TDR)** is the maximum rate of deviations permissible by the auditor without modifying the planned reliance on an internal control policy or procedure. In determining the tolerable rate, the auditor should consider (a) the planned assessed level of control risk and (b) the degree of assurance desired by the audit evidence in the sample (AU 350.4). If the auditor wishes to assess control risk at low levels, it seems reasonable to hold the client's internal control to a higher standard (that is, use a lower TDR). In contrast, if control risk is high, the auditor can use a higher TDR before reducing the reliance on internal control. Also, if the audit team requires a high degree of assurance from the test because related accounts are highly material and/or because they are not performing additional tests of controls, it again makes sense to have a lower TDR.

Exhibit F.3 illustrates how TDRs can be related to control risk assessments. Although control risk is not always assessed numerically in practice, note that lower levels of control risk are associated with lower TDRs (and vice versa). Using Exhibit F.3, if the auditor established a low acceptable control risk (between 0.10 and 0.30), the corresponding TDR would range from 3 to 7 percent. Notice that the auditor could attempt to refine the TDR even more by identifying a very low level of control risk (say 0.10) and assessing a specific TDR associated with that level (say 3 percent). A direct assessment of this type may not always be done in practice, but Exhibit F.3 illustrates that the TDR is a continuous measure and is directly related to the planned level of control risk. Note, however, that the TDR is a judgment made by the auditor based on the level of control risk.

As noted in the preceding subsection, AirCon Company's control risk was assessed at a low level (0.30) for the occurrence objective and a moderate level (0.50) for the accuracy objective. Using the matrix in Exhibit F.3, assume that the auditor translated these assessments into tolerable deviation rates of 6 percent and 10 percent for the occurrence and accuracy objectives, respectively.

[4] A white paper authored by nine large accounting firms (the Big Four plus BDO Seidman LLP, Crowe Chizek and Company LLC, Grant Thornton LLP, Harbinger PLC, and McGladrey & Pullen LLP) noted that to achieve a high level of assurance that controls are operating effectively (lower levels of control risk), auditors should not assess the risk of assessing control risk too low or the tolerable deviation rate at levels above 10 percent. See "A Framework for Evaluating Control Exceptions and Deficiencies," December 20, 2004.

[5] Exhibit F.3 reflects the common practice of selecting one of two levels of the risk of assessing control risk too low (5 percent and 10 percent).

Expected Deviation Rate

Auditors usually know or suspect that some level of exceptions or deviations occurs in the client's internal control policies or procedures; this rate is referred to as the **expected deviation rate.** The concept of reasonable assurance suggests that the client's internal control policies and procedures will not function perfectly (i.e., a zero deviation rate). Thus, some level of deviations is typically observed and is incorporated into the determination of sample size.

How is the expected deviation rate determined? If the client represents a recurring engagement, the auditor will have some knowledge of deviation rates from prior engagements. These rates could need to be adjusted if changes in the client's controls have occurred since the prior audit, but previous years' rates serve as a reasonable starting point. For example, if the observed deviation rate from prior audits was 4 percent, but the auditor is aware of improvement in controls, the current-year deviation rate could be estimated at a lower level (say 3 percent). If, on the other hand, the engagement is a first-year engagement, the auditor may use a small sample (referred to as a *pilot sample*) to estimate the deviation rate.

In establishing the expected deviation rate, the auditor should consider the relationship between this rate and the tolerable deviation rate. Simply stated, for tests of controls (and attribute sampling) to be used, the expected deviation rate must be less than the tolerable deviation rate. For example, in the AirCon example, the auditor assessed the TDR for the occurrence objective at 6 percent; in this instance, it makes little sense to invest the time to perform tests of controls if the expected deviation rate is higher than 6 percent. If so, the auditor would likely choose to reduce reliance on internal control and conduct more extensive substantive procedures.

As noted in Module E, the *precision* (or **allowance for sampling risk**) is the proximity of a sample estimate to the maximum deviation rate at a given confidence level. For planning purposes, the difference between the tolerable deviation rate and the expected deviation rate can be viewed as a form of planning precision. Considering the joint effects of the tolerable deviation rate and the expected deviation rate, as the difference between the two is lower (which could reflect either a higher expected deviation rate, a lower tolerable deviation rate, or both), the auditor's sample estimate therefore needs to be more precise, which requires a larger sample size. This is so because if the sample deviation rate (assuming that it approximates the expected deviation rate) is anticipated to be very close to the tolerable deviation rate, the auditor has very little "room for error" in making the decision.

Based on his previous experience in examining the operating effectiveness of these controls for AirCon Company, the auditor assessed the expected deviation rate at 2 percent and 3.5 percent for the occurrence and accuracy objectives, respectively.

Population Size

Common sense probably tells you that samples should be larger for larger populations (a *direct relationship*). Strictly speaking, your common sense is accurate; clearly, the sample size for a population of 10 items would be smaller than for a population of 1,000 items. However, once a population reaches a certain size, any increase has a minimal effect on sample size. As a result, unless the population size is very small (which is not common for most attribute sampling applications), the auditor does not consider population size in determining sample size to a great extent.

To illustrate, the AICPA's *Audit Sampling Guide* provides the following sample sizes for different populations for the same level of the risk of assessing control risk too low, expected deviation rate, and tolerable deviation rate:

Population Size	Sample Size
500	87
1,000	90
5,000	93
10,000	93

The preceding illustrates that, once the population exceeds 500 items, the effect of population size on sample size is relatively limited. Because AirCon processes more than 20,000 sales invoices per year, the population is of sufficient size not to influence the auditor's sample size.

Summary

Exhibit F.4 summarizes the general relationships between the factors discussed in this section and sample size.

EXHIBIT F.4 Factors Affecting Sample Size

Factor	How Determined	Effect on Sample Size
Sampling risk	Based on the auditor's judgment concerning acceptable level of control risk (typically controlled at low levels)	*Inverse* (as acceptable sampling risk increases, sample size decreases)
Tolerable deviation rate	Based on level of control risk (as level of control risk is lower, tolerable deviation rate is lower)	*Inverse* (as acceptable tolerable deviation rate increases, sample size decreases)
Expected deviation rate	Based on prior audits (for recurring engagements) or a pilot sample of controls (for first-year engagements)	*Direct* (as expected deviation rate increases, sample size increases)
Population size	Based on number of applications of control policy or procedure to transactions	*Direct* (as population size increases, sample size increases)

Determining Sample Size: Using AICPA Sampling Tables

LEARNING OBJECTIVE

3. Determine the sample size for an attribute sampling application.

How does the auditor use the preceding factors in determining sample size? The AICPA has developed sampling tables that specifically incorporate (1) the risk of assessing control risk too low, (2) the expected deviation rate, and (3) the tolerable deviation rate. In practice, computer programs are frequently used to determine sample size; these programs follow the logic of the statistical formulas that are used to construct the AICPA sampling tables. These tables are used as follows:

1. Based on the risk of assessing control risk too low, select the appropriate sample size table. Tables for a 5 percent and 10 percent risk of assessing control risk too low are reproduced as Exhibits F.5 and F.6, respectively.
2. Identify the row of the table corresponding to the expected deviation rate for the control being examined.
3. Identify the column of the table representing the assessed tolerable deviation rate for the control being examined.
4. Determine the sample size by identifying the junction of the row from step 2 and the column from step 3.

Exhibit F.7 summarizes important assessments made by the auditor for AirCon's two controls. These assessments relate to the risk of assessing control risk too low (RACTL), tolerable deviation rate (TDR), and expected deviation rate (EDR). (Recall that the population size of 20,000 was sufficiently large so it did not influence the auditor's sample size.)

Referring to the sample size table in Exhibit F.5 (5 percent risk of assessing control risk too low) and reading the sample size at the intersection of the 2 percent Expected Deviation Rate row and the 6 percent Tolerable Deviation Rate column reveals a sample size related to the occurrence objective of 127 items. Using the sample size table in Exhibit F.6 (10 percent risk of assessing control risk too low) and reading the sample size at the intersection of the 3.5 percent Expected Deviation Rate row and the 10 percent Tolerable

EXHIBIT F.5 **Sample Size Table for 5 Percent Risk of Assessing Control Risk Too Low**

Expected Deviation Rate	Tolerable Deviation Rate										
	2%	3%	4%	5%	6%	7%	8%	9%	10%	15%	20%
0.00%	149	99	74	59	49	42	36	32	29	19	14
0.25	236	157	117	93	78	66	58	51	46	30	22
0.50	*	157	117	93	78	66	58	51	46	30	22
0.75	*	208	117	93	78	66	58	51	46	30	22
1.00	*	*	156	93	78	66	58	51	46	30	22
1.25	*	*	156	124	78	66	58	51	46	30	22
1.50	*	*	192	124	103	66	58	51	46	30	22
1.75	*	*	227	153	103	88	77	51	46	30	22
2.00	*	*	*	181	127	88	77	68	46	30	22
2.25	*	*	*	208	127	88	77	68	61	30	22
2.50	*	*	*	*	150	109	77	68	61	30	22
2.75	*	*	*	*	173	109	95	68	61	30	22
3.00	*	*	*	*	195	129	95	84	61	30	22
3.25	*	*	*	*	*	148	112	84	61	30	22
3.50	*	*	*	*	*	167	112	84	76	40	22
3.75	*	*	*	*	*	185	129	100	76	40	22
4.00	*	*	*	*	*	*	146	100	89	40	22
5.00	*	*	*	*	*	*	*	158	116	40	30
6.00	*	*	*	*	*	*	*	*	179	50	30
7.00	*	*	*	*	*	*	*	*	*	68	37

*Sample size is too large to be cost effective for most audit applications.

Source: American Institute of Certified Public Accountants, "Audit Sampling," *Audit and Accounting Guide* (New York: AICPA, 2001).

Note: This table assumes a large population.

EXHIBIT F.6 **Sample Size Table for 10 Percent Risk of Assessing Control Risk Too Low**

Expected Deviation Rate	Tolerable Deviation Rate										
	2%	3%	4%	5%	6%	7%	8%	9%	10%	15%	20%
0.00%	114	76	57	45	38	32	28	25	22	15	11
0.25	194	129	96	77	64	55	48	42	38	25	18
0.50	194	129	96	77	64	55	48	42	38	25	18
0.75	265	129	96	77	64	55	48	42	38	25	18
1.00	*	176	96	77	64	55	48	42	38	25	18
1.25	*	221	132	77	64	55	48	42	38	25	18
1.50	*	*	132	105	64	55	48	42	38	25	18
1.75	*	*	166	105	88	55	48	42	38	25	18
2.00	*	*	198	132	88	75	48	42	38	25	18
2.25	*	*	*	132	88	75	65	42	38	25	18
2.50	*	*	*	158	110	75	65	58	38	25	18
2.75	*	*	*	209	132	94	65	58	52	25	18
3.00	*	*	*	*	132	94	65	58	52	25	18
3.25	*	*	*	*	153	113	82	58	52	25	18
3.50	*	*	*	*	194	113	82	73	52	25	18
3.75	*	*	*	*	*	131	98	73	52	25	18
4.00	*	*	*	*	*	149	98	73	65	25	18
5.00	*	*	*	*	*	*	160	115	78	34	18
6.00	*	*	*	*	*	*	*	182	116	43	25
7.00	*	*	*	*	*	*	*	*	199	52	25

*Sample size is too large to be cost effective for most audit applications.

Source: American Institute of Certified Public Accountants, "Audit Sampling," *Audit and Accounting Guide* (New York: AICPA, 2001).

Note: This table assumes a large population.

EXHIBIT F.7

Assessments of Sampling Risk, Tolerable Deviation Rate, and Expected Deviation Rate for AirCon Company

Control	RACTL	TDR	EDR
Occurrence: Sales invoices are prepared only for items shipped to customers	5.0%	6.0%	2.0%
Accuracy: Extensions and footings on sales invoices are mathematically verified.	10.0	10.0	3.5

Deviation Rate column reveals a sample size for the test of controls related to the accuracy objective of 52 items.[6]

In reviewing Exhibit F.5, you can see how the various factors affect sample size. For example, reading across the 2 percent Expected Deviation Rate row, you see that if the tolerable deviation rate for the occurrence control were reduced from 6 percent to 5 percent, the necessary sample size would increase from 127 items to 181 items. This increase is consistent with the *inverse relationship* between the tolerable deviation rate and sample size noted in Exhibit F.4:

Tolerable Deviation Rate

	5%	6%	7%	8%
2%	181	127	88	77

Decrease in tolerable deviation rate results in larger sample size

Examining the 6 percent Tolerable Deviation Rate column in Exhibit F.5, you can see how various levels of the expected deviation rate affect sample sizes. Note that, if the expected deviation rate were lowered from 2 percent to 1 percent, the sample size for the occurrence objective would decrease from 127 items to 78 items, consistent with the *direct relationship* between the expected deviation rate and sample size noted in Exhibit F.4.[7]

Expected Deviation Rate	Tolerable Deviation Rate = 6%
0%	49
1%	78
2%	127
3%	195

Decrease in expected deviation rate results in smaller sample size

Finally, comparing the cell entries in Exhibits F.5 and F.6 illustrates the *inverse relationship* between the risk of assessing control risk too low and sample size. For the occurrence control, the sample size for a risk of assessing control risk too low of 5 percent is 127. If the risk of assessing control risk too low was increased to 10 percent, but the expected deviation rate and tolerable deviation rate were held constant at 2 percent and 6 percent, respectively, the sample size would decrease to 88 items (see Exhibit F.6).

Exhibit F.8 is a sample of audit documentation prepared for the tests of controls performed for AirCon Company. At this point, you should focus on the first six columns of this exhibit, which summarize the control being examined (column 1), level of control

[6] Exhibit F.7 illustrates different risks of assessing control risk too low, tolerable deviation rates, and expected deviation rates for the two controls examined for AirCon Company. We do so primarily to show how these factors affect sample size. In practice, the cost of identifying and selecting sample items in attribute sampling is often far greater than the cost of measuring and evaluating these items. As a result, when selecting a single document to evaluate more than one control, the auditor may use the largest of the sample sizes and examine all controls related to the document selected.

[7] Note that the sample size does not necessarily increase with each incremental increase in the expected deviation rate. For example, using a 6 percent tolerable deviation rate and a 5 percent acceptable risk of assessing control risk too low, the sample size is 78 for expected deviation rates ranging from 0.25 percent to 1.25 percent. However, the sample size increases to 103 when the expected deviation rate increases to 1.50 percent.

EXHIBIT F.8 Sample Audit Documentation for AirCon Company Tests of Controls

Control Examined	Control Risk	RACTL	TDR	EDR	*n* (A)	Devs	ULDR	Conclusion
Occurrence: Sales invoices are prepared only for items shipped to customers	Low (0.30)	5.0%	6.0%	2.0%	127	2	5.0%	Can rely on internal control as planned because ULDR < TDR
Valuation: Extensions and footings on sales invoices are mathematically accurate	Moderate (0.50)	10.0	10.0	3.5	52	4	15.4	(B) Cannot rely on internal control as planned because ULDR > TDR

RACTL = Risk of assessing control risk too low
TDR = Tolerable deviation rate
EDR = Expected deviation rate
n = Sample size
Devs = Number of deviations observed
ULDR = Upper limit deviation rate, using RACTL, *n,* and Devs

(A) = Items selected based on a systematic selection method with random starts of 200, 865, 4,629, 13,942, and 18,569 and a sampling interval of 667.

(B) = Based on sample results, assessed control risk as slightly less than maximum (0.80).

risk (column 2), risk of assessing control risk too low (column 3), tolerable deviation rate (column 4), expected deviation rate (column 5), and sample size (column 6).

The fourth step in the sampling process (determining the sample size) for the AirCon Company example is summarized here.

Summary: Comprehensive Example: AirCon Company

4. Based on the acceptable risk of assessing control risk too low, expected deviation rate, and tolerable deviation rate, the auditor determined sample sizes of 127 (for the occurrence control) and 52 (for the accuracy control).

Review Checkpoints

F.5 Define the terms (a) *sampling risk,* (b) *tolerable deviation rate,* and (c) *expected deviation rate.* How are these factors assessed or determined by the auditor?

F.6 What two types of sampling risks could an auditor encounter when performing attribute sampling?

F.7 In attribute sampling, why is the risk of assessing control risk too low more important than the risk of assessing control risk too high?

F.8 What is the relationship between sample size and (a) sampling risk, (b) tolerable deviation rate, and (c) expected deviation rate?

F.9 Describe the general procedure used by the auditor to determine sample size using AICPA sampling tables.

Selecting the Sample

LEARNING OBJECTIVE

4. Identify various methods of selecting an attribute sample.

The auditor's basic goal in selecting a sample is to increase the likelihood that it is representative of the population. For example, if the auditor is examining a sample of sales invoices, this sample should include sales invoices that

- Have been prepared throughout the year.
- Represent both large and small dollar amounts.
- Have been prepared by different individuals involved in the invoice preparation process.
- Represent different customers and/or geographic areas.

For example, considering the first item, if sales invoices for only the month of November are examined, differences in the persons, processes, or other factors involved in the preparation or processing of sales invoices in the month of November can result in a nonrepresentative sample.

The auditor will then select the sample from the population; recall that, if the auditor wants to use statistical sampling, either random selection or systematic selection is appropriate. Assume that the auditor uses random selection and selects the sample of invoices for examination. Tickmark (A) in Exhibit F.8 provides a starting point for selecting the sample of sales invoices. AirCon's auditor used a Computer Assisted Audit Technique (CAAT) on the sales invoice file that totaled the invoices for agreement to the general ledger. It also scanned the file for gaps and duplicate numbers. Finally, the program printed a listing of 150 randomly selected invoices (some extra numbers were printed to replace any possible voids.) The auditors examined the first 52 invoices selected for *valuation* and *occurrence* and the next 75 for *occurrence* only.

AUDITING INSIGHT Danger in Systematic Selection

Assume that a company has a stable payroll of 50 hourly employees paid weekly throughout the year (that is, no employees were hired or terminated during the year). With 52 pay periods, 2,600 payroll transactions are processed each year (52 pay periods × 50 employees). Based on the acceptable risk of assessing control risk too low, tolerable deviation rate, and expected deviation rate, the auditor determined a sample size of 104 payroll transactions and used a systematic selection method to select a sample of 104 paychecks for tests of controls.

Based on the population size and sample size, the sampling interval is 25 (2,600 ÷ 104). A random starting point was selected

(Moe Howard's payroll transaction) and every 25th entry thereafter was selected. The auditor selected 52 payroll entries for Moe Howard and 52 entries for Lucy Fine.

What made this sample nonrepresentative? A sample size of 104 results in auditing two transactions per week (104 (52 weeks). The fact that the population of employees (50) was evenly divisible by the sampling interval (25 items) coincidentally resulted in the same employees' records being repeatedly selected for examination.

Summary: Comprehensive Example: AirCon Company

5. Using a random number CAAT and a starting point of 667, the auditor selected 150 invoices, of which 127 were examined.

Measuring Sample Items

Once the auditors have determined the sample size (step 4) and selected the sample items (step 5), they are now ready to measure the sample items. When measuring the sample items in an attribute sampling application, the auditor determines whether the control has been appropriately performed. It is important that the auditor not perform the control but examine some form of evidence that client personnel performed the control. If there is no evidence of the control being performed, the item will be classified as a deviation. The auditor examines evidence on the operating effectiveness of important controls by performing *tests of controls*.

Although measuring sample items is typically straightforward, one issue that could arise relates to missing items. For example, when evaluating a control related to a sales invoice that cannot be located, the auditor would classify this particular item as a deviation. The fact that the document is missing could indeed reflect the fact that a control was not applied in the intended manner and the related document has been intentionally destroyed or removed from the physical representation of the population.

EXHIBIT F.9 Tests of Controls for AirCon Company

Objective	Control	Test of Control
Occurrence: Sales invoices are prepared only for items shipped to customers	Existence of shipping document for all sales invoices	Check for existence of shipping document accompanying sales invoices
Accuracy: Extensions and footings on sales invoices are mathematically accurate	Initials of client employee indicating mathematical verification	Examine invoices for evidence of client employee initials or recalculation of a sample of invoices

Measuring sample items is the step in the sampling process when nonsampling risk can occur. Recall that *nonsampling risk* is the risk that the auditor's sample provides an incorrect conclusion for reasons other than the representativeness of the sample. For example, the auditor could make an unintentional error in evaluating evidence (such as classifying a deviation as a nondeviation or *vice versa*).

The tests of controls performed for AirCon Company by the auditor are shown in Exhibit F.9.

As shown in the seventh column of Exhibit F.8, a total of two deviations for the occurrence control and four deviations for the accuracy control were noted.

Summary: Comprehensive Example: AirCon Company

6. Two deviations for the occurrence control and four deviations for the accuracy control were identified.

Review Checkpoints

F.10 What are some important considerations for the auditor when selecting sample items?

F.11 What are *tests of controls?* What is the auditor's goal in performing them in an attribute sampling application?

F.12 When performing tests of controls, how would the auditor classify a situation when encountering a missing item?

ATTRIBUTE SAMPLING: EVALUATING

LEARNING OBJECTIVE

5. Evaluate the results of an attribute sampling application by determining the upper limit deviation rate.

Calculating the Upper Limit Deviation Rate

To this point, the auditor has planned the sample (by identifying the objective of sampling, defining a deviation condition, and defining the population) and performed the basics of the sampling plan (by determining the sample size, selecting the sample, and measuring the sample items). As noted in the preceding section, the auditor's tests of controls revealed two deviations for the occurrence control and four deviations for the accuracy control.

Based on this information, the auditor can calculate a **sample deviation rate,** which represents the rate of deviations from key controls noted by the auditor in his or her sample. The sample deviation rate is calculated by dividing the number of deviations noted in the sample by the sample size. Thus, the sample deviation rates for the occurrence and

accuracy controls were 1.6 percent (2 deviations (127 invoices) and 7.7 percent (4 deviations (52 invoices), respectively. Because the tolerable deviation rates for these controls are 6 and 10 percent, respectively, the auditor's initial conclusion might be to rely on the controls as planned because the sample deviation rates are less than the tolerable deviation rates.

What is the fallacy with this approach? The auditor's sample might not represent the population. This problem can occur, for example, if the auditor selected sales invoices for which controls were functioning more effectively than for the population as a whole. If the sample is not representative, the sample deviation rate can significantly understate the true population deviation rate. Although auditors will never know the true population deviation rate with any certainty, they can use sampling tables to "adjust" the sample deviation rate to one that has a certain probability of equaling or exceeding the true deviation rate. Simply stated, this adjusted rate (the **upper limit deviation rate** or **ULDR**) provides a conservative estimate of the population deviation rate that allows the auditor to control exposure to sampling risk to acceptable levels.

The ULDR provides the following information:

- There is a (1 – *risk of assessing control risk too low*) probability that the true population deviation rate is less than or equal to the ULDR.
- There is a (*risk of assessing control risk too low*) probability that the true population deviation rate exceeds the ULDR.

Auditors can use formulas or tables to determine the ULDR from the sample deviation rate; in practice, computer programs that follow the logic of the formulas are used to determine it. Exhibits F.10 and F.11 allow the ULDR to be determined for an acceptable risk of assessing control risk too low of 5 percent and 10 percent, respectively. Like the sample size tables shown in Exhibits F.5 and F.6, the values in these tables are determined by using the appropriate parameters in relatively complex statistical formulas. Using Exhibits F.10 and F.11, the auditor would calculate the ULDR as follows:

1. Based on the acceptable risk of assessing control risk too low, select the appropriate evaluation table.
2. Identify the row representing the appropriate sample size.
3. Identify the column corresponding to the number of deviations found by the auditor.
4. The ULDR is the value found at the intersection of the row in step 2 and the column in step 3.

To illustrate the use of sample evaluation tables, consider the findings for the occurrence control for AirCon Company. Recall that the auditor examined a sample of 127 sales invoices for the potential occurrence of this control, found two deviations, and calculated a sample deviation rate of 1.6 percent. Using Exhibit F.10 (for a risk of assessing control risk too low of 5 percent), the auditor would locate the row corresponding to a sample size of 127 items and the column for two deviations. Note that Exhibit F.10 contains a row for sample sizes of 125 and 150 but not 127. In this instance, the auditor can do one of the following:

1. Select an additional 23 ite.ms for examination for a sample size of 150 (the next highest sample size in the sample evaluation table).
2. Evaluate the results of the sample using a smaller sample size of 125. This will provide a conservative (higher) measure of the ULDR because the same number of deviations will be attributed to a smaller number of sample items.
3. Interpolate the values in Exhibit F.10 and estimate a ULDR for a sample of 127 items.

Because the original sample of 127 is very close to the sample size row of 125, assume that the auditor evaluates the two deviations using a sample size of 125. Reading the value

EXHIBIT F.10 Sample Evaluation Table for 5 Percent Risk of Assessing Control Risk Too Low

Sample Size	Actual Number of Deviations Found										
	0	**1**	**2**	**3**	**4**	**5**	**6**	**7**	**8**	**9**	**10**
25	11.3	17.6	*	*	*	*	*	*	*	*	*
30	9.5	14.9	19.6	*	*	*	*	*	*	*	*
35	8.3	12.9	17.0	*	*	*	*	*	*	*	*
40	7.3	11.4	15.0	18.3	*	*	*	*	*	*	*
45	6.5	10.2	13.4	16.4	19.2	*	*	*	*	*	*
50	5.9	9.2	12.1	14.8	17.4	19.9	*	*	*	*	*
55	5.4	8.4	11.1	13.5	15.9	18.2	*	*	*	*	*
60	4.9	7.7	10.2	12.5	14.7	16.8	18.8	*	*	*	*
65	4.6	7.1	9.4	11.5	13.6	15.5	17.4	19.3	*	*	*
70	4.2	6.6	8.8	10.8	12.6	14.5	16.3	18.0	19.7	*	*
75	4.0	6.2	8.2	10.1	11.8	13.6	15.2	16.9	18.5	20.0	*
80	3.7	5.8	7.7	9.5	11.1	12.7	14.3	15.9	17.4	18.9	*
90	3.3	5.2	6.9	8.4	9.9	11.4	12.8	14.2	15.5	16.8	18.2
100	3.0	4.7	6.2	7.6	9.0	10.3	11.5	12.8	14.0	15.2	16.4
125	2.4	3.8	5.0	6.1	7.2	8.3	9.3	10.3	11.3	12.3	13.2
150	2.0	3.2	4.2	5.1	6.0	6.9	7.8	8.6	9.5	10.3	11.1
200	1.5	2.4	3.2	3.9	4.6	5.2	5.9	6.5	7.2	7.8	8.4

*ULDR exceeds 20 percent.

Source: American Institute of Certified Public Accountants, "Audit Sampling," *Audit and Accounting Guide* (New York: AICPA, 2001).
Note: This table presents ULDRs as percentages and assumes a large population.

EXHIBIT F.11 Sample Evaluation Table for 10 Percent Risk of Assessing Control Risk Too Low

Sample Size	Actual Number of Deviations Found										
	0	**1**	**2**	**3**	**4**	**5**	**6**	**7**	**8**	**9**	**10**
20	10.9	18.1	*	*	*	*	*	*	*	*	*
25	8.8	14.7	19.9	*	*	*	*	*	*	*	*
30	7.4	12.4	16.8	*	*	*	*	*	*	*	*
35	6.4	10.7	14.5	18.1	*	*	*	*	*	*	*
40	5.6	9.4	12.8	16.0	19.0	*	*	*	*	*	*
45	5.0	8.4	11.4	14.3	17.0	19.7	*	*	*	*	*
50	4.6	7.6	10.3	12.9	15.4	17.8	*	*	*	*	*
55	4.1	6.9	9.4	11.8	14.1	16.3	18.4	*	*	*	*
60	3.8	6.4	8.7	10.8	12.9	15.0	16.9	18.9	*	*	*
70	3.3	5.5	7.5	9.3	11.1	12.9	14.6	16.3	17.9	19.6	*
80	2.9	4.8	6.6	8.2	9.8	11.3	12.8	14.3	15.8	17.2	18.6
90	2.6	4.3	5.9	7.3	8.7	10.1	11.5	12.8	14.1	15.4	16.6
100	2.3	3.9	5.3	6.6	7.9	9.1	10.3	11.5	12.7	13.9	15.0
120	2.0	3.3	4.4	5.5	6.6	7.6	8.7	9.7	10.7	11.6	12.6
160	1.5	2.5	3.3	4.2	5.0	5.8	6.5	7.3	8.0	8.8	9.5
200	1.2	2.0	2.7	3.4	4.0	4.6	5.3	5.9	6.5	7.1	7.6

*ULDR exceeds 20 percent.

Source: American Institute of Certified Public Accountants, "Audit Sampling," *Audit and Accounting Guide* (New York: AICPA, 2001).
Note: This table presents ULDRs as percentages and assumes a large population.

in the table at the intersection of this row and column reveals a ULDR of 5.0 percent, as shown in the following excerpt from Exhibit F.10.

Sample Size	Actual Number of Deviations Found			
	0	1	2	3
125	2.4	3.8	5.0	6.1

The ULDR is comprised of the following components:

- A *sample deviation rate* of 1.6 percent (2 deviations ÷ 127 items = 1.6 percent).[8]
- An *allowance for sampling risk* of 3.4 percent (ULDR of 5.0 percent − *sample deviation rate* of 1.6 percent = 3.4 percent). The allowance for sampling risk represents the "adjustment" of the *sample deviation rate* for the acceptable risk of assessing control risk too low.

Now, let us turn to the results for the accuracy control. Using a risk of assessing control risk too low of 10 percent (Exhibit F.11), note that a row for a sample of 52 items is not shown. Again, since this sample size is close to the row for a sample size of 50, the 4 deviations would be evaluated using a sample size of 50. Reading the ULDR at the intersection of the sample size of 50 row and deviation of 4 column yields a ULDR of 15.4 percent. This ULDR is comprised of a sample deviation rate of 7.7 percent[9] and an allowance for sampling risk of 7.7 percent (15.4 percent − 7.7 percent = 7.7 percent). In this case, the ULDR of 15.4 percent exceeds the tolerable deviation rate of 10 percent.

Review Checkpoints

F.13 What is the sample deviation rate? How does the auditor calculate it?

F.14 What is the upper limit deviation rate? What information does the upper limit deviation rate provide to the auditor?

F.15 What factors influence the determination of the upper limit deviation rate?

F.16 Describe the general process used to determine the upper limit deviation rate using AICPA sampling tables.

F.17 What options are available to the auditor for determining the upper limit deviation rate if the auditor's sample size is not included in the AICPA sampling tables?

F.18 If the auditor examines a sample of 100 items, finds 6 deviations, and calculates an upper limit deviation rate of 8.3 percent, what is the allowance for sampling risk?

Making the Evaluation Decision

The prior subsection discussed the determination of the ULDRs for the occurrence and accuracy controls. Comparing the ULDRs for the two key controls to the tolerable deviation

[8] The fact that the auditor uses a sample size of 125 items to determine the ULDR does not affect the calculation of the sample deviation rate using the original sample size (127 items).

[9] The fact that the auditor uses a sample size of 50 items to determine the ULDR does not affect the calculation of the sample deviation rate using the original sample size of 52 items (4 deviations ÷ 52 items = 7.7 percent sample deviation rate).

rates (TDRs) for these controls (also shown in the sample documentation in Exhibit F.8) reveals the following:

Control Procedure	ULDR		TDR[1]	Conclusion
Occurrence: All sales invoices are supported by shipping documents	5.0%	<	6%	Control is operating effectively
Accuracy: Sales invoices are mathematically verified	15.4%	>	10%	Control is not operating effectively

[1] Recall the TDR was established early in the sampling process (see page •••).

The auditor's decision rule after calculating the ULDR can be summarized as follows:

1. If the ULDR ≤ the tolerable deviation rate:
 a. Rely on internal control as planned and maintain control risk at planned levels.
 b. Consider obtaining a reduction in the level of control risk.
2. If the ULDR > the tolerable deviation rate:
 a. Reduce reliance on internal control and increase control risk.
 b. Expand the sample size to achieve an observed ULDR less than the tolerable deviation rate.

How would the auditor proceed from this point? It appears that the control for the occurrence objective is functioning effectively. As a result, the auditor could decide to rely on internal control as planned and maintain the planned level of control risk as well as the planned level of detection risk.

For the accuracy objective, the auditor has one of two options. The first option is to reduce the planned degree of reliance on internal control, increase the planned level of control risk, and reduce the planned level of detection risk by performing more effective substantive procedures. Recall that the ULDR for the accuracy control is 15.4 percent; assume that a tolerable deviation rate of 16 percent would correspond to a control risk assessment of 0.80 (slightly below maximum) (see Exhibit F.3). Thus, without gathering any further evidence, the auditor could increase the assessment of control risk from 0.50 (moderate) to 0.80 (slightly below maximum) and correspondingly decrease the necessary level of detection risk. This decrease in the necessary level of detection risk would require the auditor to perform more effective substantive procedures. This option is reflected by tickmark (B) in Exhibit F.8.

Alternatively, the auditor could attempt to reduce the ULDR to a level below the tolerable deviation rate of 10 percent by examining an expanded sample of controls. In Exhibit F.11, read down the column for four deviations (the number found by the auditor) to find a ULDR that is less than 10 percent. Notice that if a total of 80 items is examined and a total of four deviations is noted, the ULDR is 9.8 percent. Therefore, one option available to the auditor is to examine an additional 28 items (80 items – original sample of 52 items). Consider, however, that the most likely result of examining 28 additional items is to find two more deviations (7.7% SDR × 28). This would result in an ULDR of 12.8, which still exceeds the TDR. (Why is the ULDR lower than the original 15.4? Increasing the sample size reduces the allowance for sampling risk.) Therefore, examining additional items is generally not an effective solution unless the ULDR is very close to the TDR.

Which option would the auditor select? This decision depends on the relative costs of increasing the tests of controls versus the costs associated with performing more extensive substantive procedures. If the cost of examining additional items is relatively low and the likelihood of observing no additional deviations is high, the auditor would likely decide to extend the sample of controls. However, if the cost of selecting and evaluating additional items is relatively high and the auditor is likely to encounter additional deviations, it could be more cost effective to perform more effective substantive procedures. Either approach will maintain audit risk at an acceptable level.

7. The auditor determined an upper limit deviation rate of 5.0 percent and 15.4 percent for the occurrence and accuracy controls, respectively. Based on a comparison of the upper limit deviation rate to the tolerable deviation rate, the auditor would

- Conclude that the occurrence control is functioning effectively and rely on internal control as planned.

- Conclude that the accuracy control is not functioning effectively and either (1) reduce reliance on internal control or (2) expand the sample to examine a larger number of items.

Exhibit F.12 provides a summary of the total costs that the auditor could incur under some alternative scenarios for testing the accuracy control. This illustration assumes that the cost to perform a test of control is $6 per item and the cost to perform a substantive procedure is $10 per item. The following should be evident from Exhibit F.12.

1. To support lower levels of control risk, the auditor must set a lower tolerable deviation rate and the sample results must support lower ULDRs.

2. Lower levels of control risk and lower tolerable deviation rates result in a larger sample for tests of controls.

3. Lower levels of control risk are associated with smaller samples for substantive procedures.

At this point, the auditor may choose to examine the additional 28 invoices and attempt to attain a moderate assessment of control risk. Doing so would result in an additional cost of performing tests of controls of $168 ($480 − $312) while providing a cost savings in the form of reduced substantive procedures of $190 ($1,360 − $1,170), assuming the auditor does not find additional errors.

One final issue in calculating the ULDR is the effect of the acceptable risk of assessing control risk too low on the ULDR. Conceptually, it would seem logical that lower levels of this risk would provide more conservative (i.e., higher) ULDRs. Examining Exhibit F.11, you should note that the ULDR for a sample size of 200 items, five deviations, and a 10 percent risk of assessing control risk too low is 4.6 percent. Compare this to the ULDR of 5.2 percent for a risk of assessing control risk too low of 5 percent (Exhibit F.10). Essentially, a higher acceptable risk of assessing control risk too low would increase the likelihood that the auditor can conclude to rely on internal control as planned.

Qualitative Evaluation of Deviations

The focus thus far has been on quantitative factors: sample sizes, numbers of deviations, tolerable deviation rates, and ULDRs. Regardless of the results of the attribute sampling application, the auditor should conduct a *qualitative evaluation* of deviations to determine their nature and cause. In some cases, deviations can truly represent an isolated incident on a specific transaction; in others, they can represent something far more serious.

EXHIBIT F.12
Alternative Audit Approaches for the Accuracy Control

Control Risk	TDR	Tests of Controls		Substantive Procedures		Total Cost
		n	Cost	*n*	Cost	
Moderate (0.50)	10%	80	$480	117	$1,170	$1,650
Slightly below maximum (0.80)	16	52	312	136	1,360	1,672

TDR = Tolerable deviation rate
n = Sample size

A qualitative evaluation of deviations attempts to answer questions such as these with regard to observed deviations:

- Do deviations represent a pervasive error made consistently on all transactions or an isolated mistake made on a specific transaction?
- Are deviations intentional or unintentional in nature?
- Do deviations represent a misunderstanding of instructions or careless attention to duties?
- Do deviations have implications with regard to the effectiveness of other controls (for example, information technology general controls or other COSO components)?

If any deviations appear to be pervasively occurring throughout the sample, to represent intentional actions on the part of client employees, to represent careless attention, or to have implications with respect to other controls, they have additional implications for the audit examination and should be discussed with the client and its audit committee. It is important that the auditor not accept client explanations too readily without corroboration or attempt to "explain away" serious deviations.

ATTRIBUTE SAMPLING: DOCUMENTING

As shown in the overview of the seven-step procedure for attribute sampling, the auditor is required to document various information related to the sampling procedure. Some of this information is shown in Exhibit F.8 and typically includes the following:

- Information on the objective of sampling, definition of deviation conditions, and definition of the population from which the sample was selected, including the physical representation (steps 1–3).
- The levels of the risk of assessing control risk too low, tolerable deviation rate, and expected deviation rate, as well as the rationale for these assessments (step 4).
- The sample size determined based on the factors discussed (step 4).
- Information on the selection of sample items and a list of items selected and examined by the auditor (step 5).
- Results of the tests of controls performed on each item selected (step 6).
- Information regarding the number of deviations and the upper limit deviation rate (step 7).
- The auditor's conclusion with respect to the operating effectiveness of the control and the implications of this effectiveness on the auditor's reliance on internal control and substantive procedures (step 7).

Review Checkpoints

F.19 What is the auditor's decision rule with respect to the relationship between the upper limit deviation rate and the tolerable deviation rate?

F.20 What options are available to the auditor if the upper limit deviation rate is less than the tolerable deviation rate?

F.21 What options are available to the auditor if the upper limit deviation rate is greater than the tolerable deviation rate?

F.22 What information is typically documented by the auditor in an attribute sampling application?

SEQUENTIAL SAMPLING[10]

LEARNING
OBJECTIVE

6. Define *sequential
sampling* and
discovery sampling
and identify when
these types of
sampling applications
could be used.

The AirCon Company example in this module used a *fixed sampling plan*, in which the auditor selected and evaluated a single sample. In some instances, auditors may use a *variable sampling plan* to provide flexibility and efficiency, particularly if they anticipate a relatively low deviation rate. To illustrate, assume that the tolerable deviation rate is 5 percent and the expected deviation rate is 0.5 percent. In this case, if the first 20 items selected by the auditor did not reveal any deviations, the fact that (1) the difference between the tolerable deviation rate and expected deviation rate is high and (2) the preliminary evidence regarding the operating effectiveness of the client's internal control appears to be favorable could allow the auditor to conclude that the control is functioning effectively. Alternatively, if two deviations are noted in the sample of 20 items, the evidence might not be sufficient and the auditor would need to gather additional evidence.

Sequential (or *stop-or-go*) **sampling** methods provide the auditor the opportunity to draw conclusions using a smaller sample than a traditional fixed sampling plan. Sequential sampling plans generally operate as follows:

1. Based on the acceptable risk of assessing control risk too low, tolerable deviation rate, and expected deviation rate, determine an initial sample size. This initial sample size is smaller than that determined using the AICPA sampling tables in a fixed sampling plan.

2. Based on the number of deviations noted, one of three courses of action may be taken:

 a. If the number of deviations is sufficiently low, conclude that the control is operating effectively; no additional items need be selected.

 b. If the number of deviations is sufficiently high, conclude that the control is not operating effectively and increase the level of control risk beyond the planned level.

 c. If the number of deviations does not permit a clear decision in (a) or (b), increase the sample size and repeat the preceding steps.

Following is an excerpt from a sequential sampling table. Assume that you have established an acceptable sampling risk (risk of assessing control risk too low) of 5 percent and a tolerable deviation rate of 5 percent. If you select a sample of 100 items and find zero or only one deviation, your sample results allow you to achieve a sampling risk of 0.56 percent and 3.71 percent, respectively, which is less than your acceptable sampling risk of 5 percent. In either case, you could conclude that the control is functioning effectively and would assess control risk at the planned level.

Sample Size	Number of Deviations	Achieved Sampling Risk at Tolerable Deviation Rate = 5%
100	0	0.56%
	1	3.71
	2	11.83
	3	25.78
120	2	5.75
150	2	1.71
	3	5.48

Alternatively, if your sample revealed two deviations, the level of sampling risk (11.83 percent) is not sufficient to support your assessment of control risk at the planned level. In this instance, you could consider increasing your sample size. In examining the excerpted

[10] Note: Sequential *sampling* discussed here is not to be confused with sequential *selection* discussed previously.

values for samples of 120 and 150 items, note that if you increase your sample size to 120, even if you found no additional deviations, the achieved level of sampling risk (5.75 percent) is still not sufficient to support your planned assessment of control risk. If the sample size is increased to 150, note that if you find no deviations in the additional 50 items (total deviations = 2), you could support your planned assessment of control risk; however, even a single deviation in the additional 50 items (for a total of three deviations) would not allow you to support your planned level of control risk.

Sequential sampling is used when the expected deviation rate is relatively low in relation to the tolerable deviation rate. Because decisions to expand the sample will be based on the results of items that have been selected, it is important that the auditor examine items in the order in which they were selected: numerical, alphabetical, or chronological. A significant advantage of this approach is that it could allow the auditor to more efficiently evaluate the operating effectiveness of controls in an attribute sampling plan. One disadvantage of this method is that the allowable rate of deviations in the sample is lower than that in a fixed sampling plan (i.e., sequential sampling is more conservative). In addition, the auditor should be careful in continuing to extend the sample under sequential sampling approaches if the preliminary sample evidence does not support the planned level of control risk because an extremely large number of items could ultimately be examined.

DISCOVERY SAMPLING

Discovery sampling is a form of attribute sampling that is used when deviations from controls are very critical yet are expected to occur at a relatively low rate. Discovery sampling should be used when a control is extremely important for the auditor's examination or when the auditor suspects the existence of fraud. One of the unique features of discovery sampling is that the auditor can evaluate the sufficiency of evidence in the event that no deviations are ultimately found in the sample. That is, the auditor can make the following type of statement:

> If the rate of deviations in the population is 0.5 percent, my sample provides a 99 percent chance of observing at least one deviation.

From an operational standpoint, discovery sampling allows the auditor to determine the appropriate sample size necessary to find at least one example of a deviation if such deviations exist within a population. To use discovery sampling, the auditor must specify the following:

- The maximum allowable probability of observing at least one occurrence, which is calculated as (1 – *risk of assessing control risk too low*).
- The *critical rate of occurrence*, which is similar to the tolerable deviation rate in an attribute sampling application. Ordinarily, this rate should be very low.

Exhibit F.13 is a table used with discovery sampling applications. It can be used to determine the appropriate sample size to provide the auditor with a quantitative measure of the sufficiency of the evidence. For example, assume that the auditor was concerned that AirCon Company was creating invoices for fictitious sales and wanted to verify that all sales invoices were accompanied by shipping documents. Of the 20,000 sales invoices, the auditor was interested in finding an example of this type of deviation if as few as 100 fictitious invoices were created. In this case, the critical rate of occurrence is 0.5 percent (100 ÷ 20,000). If the acceptable risk of assessing control risk too low is 5 percent, the auditor would use Exhibit F.13 as follows:

1. Read down the column for the *critical rate of occurrence* (0.5 percent) to find the *desired probability*. For a risk of assessing control risk too low of 5 percent, the desired probability would be 95 percent (100 percent – 5 percent).

EXHIBIT F.13
Discovery Sampling
Table

Sample Size	Critical Rate of Occurrence							
	0.1%	0.2%	0.3%	0.4%	0.5%	0.75%	1%	2%
50	5	10	14	18	22	31	40	64
60	6	11	17	21	26	36	45	79
70	7	13	19	25	30	41	51	76
80	8	15	21	28	33	45	55	80
90	9	17	24	30	36	49	60	84
100	10	18	26	33	40	53	64	87
120	11	21	30	38	45	60	70	91
140	13	25	35	43	51	65	76	94
160	15	28	38	48	55	70	80	96
200	18	33	45	56	64	78	87	98
240	22	39	52	62	70	84	91	99
300	26	46	60	70	78	90	95	99+
340	29	50	65	75	82	93	97	99+
400	34	56	71	81	87	95	98	99+
460	38	61	76	85	91	97	99	99+
500	40	64	79	87	92	98	99	99+
600	46	71	84	92	96	99	99+	99+
700	52	77	89	95	97	99+	99+	99+
800	57	81	92	96	98	99+	99+	99+
900	61	85	94	98	99	99+	99+	99+
1000	65	88	96	99	99	99+	99+	99+
1500	80	96	99	99+	99+	99+	99+	99+
2000	89	99	99+	99+	99+	99+	99+	99+

Note: This table provides the probability (in percentage terms) of observing at least one deviation in a sample for populations of between 5,000 and 10,000 items.

2. Once the desired probability is found, read across the row to determine the necessary sample size. In this case, note that a 95 percent probability is not shown in Exhibit F.13. The auditor would use a 96 percent probability and, based on this probability, select a sample size of 600.

3. If zero deviations are found, read across the sample size row to determine various probabilities associated with different critical rates of occurrence. For example, if a sample of 600 items was selected and no deviations were found, the probability that the rate of occurrence (deviation) in the sample is less than 0.1 percent is 46 percent; less than 0.3 percent is 84 percent; less than 0.5 percent is 96 percent; and less than 1 percent is more than 99 percent.

Exhibit F.13 clearly indicates that discovery sampling is associated with extremely large sample sizes. As a result, this form of sampling is typically used only when deviations from a given control are extremely critical (such as a form of fraud).

Review Checkpoints

F.23 What is *sequential sampling?* What are the advantages and disadvantages of sequential sampling?

F.24 Define *discovery sampling.* When is discovery sampling typically used?

NONSTATISTICAL ATTRIBUTE SAMPLING

LEARNING OBJECTIVE

7. Understand how to apply nonstatistical sampling to attribute testing.

As discussed in Module E, nonstatistical sampling is acceptable for use in auditing, and it is commonly used in practice. The objectives are exactly the same whether the auditor uses statistical or nonstatistical sampling. The population and the characteristics of interest also would be identical. It is a common misperception that sample sizes will be smaller using nonstatistical sampling compared to using statistical sampling, but *SAS 111* is clear that the sample sizes should be comparable. For example, the AICPA *Audit Sampling Guide* (¶ 3.49) provides an example of guidelines for sample sizes shown in Exhibit F. The sample sizes in Exhibit F.14 are based on a 10 percent risk of assessing control risk too low and an expected population deviation rate of 0 percent.

The next step in the sampling plan, selecting the sample, may be performed differently for nonstatistical sampling than for statistical sampling. As nonstatistical sampling does not make use of tables based on probabilities, the sample is not required to be selected randomly. Haphazard or block selection may be used as well as random or sequential selection. However, auditors must be aware that using methods where the probabilities of each item being selected are unknown exposes them to a greater risk of bias in the sample that might lead to an unrepresentative sample (sampling risk).

Step 6, measuring the sample items, also is performed exactly the same whether statistical or nonstatistical sampling is being used. It is step 7, evaluating sample results, where the primary difference between the two methods arises. Auditors first calculate the sample deviation rate. If the sample deviation rate is greater than the tolerable deviation rate, the auditor can conclude that the control is not working effectively and revise the planned detection risk. However, if the sample deviation rate is less than tolerable deviation rate, auditors cannot conclude that the control is operating effectively. They must use professional judgment to estimate the allowance for sampling risk to determine the likely deviation rate in the population. They may examine tables such as the ones in Exhibits F.10 and F.11 to guide their judgment, knowing that the tables cannot be strictly relied on in a nonstatistical setting.

For example, if the auditors of AirCon Company had decided to use nonstatistical sampling, they would still need to select a sample size comparable to the one they select using the statistical sampling tables. Say they decided on 120 items for the occurrence test and selected the sales invoices by going through the sales invoice files and haphazardly pulling 120 sales invoices. If they found two deviations as in the previous example, the sample deviation rate would be about 1.7 percent. This is considerably lower than the tolerable deviation rate of 6 percent and even lower than the expected deviation rate of 2 percent. Thus, the auditors might conclude that the control is operating effectively. If they examined 50 of the invoices for accuracy and again found four deviations, their sample deviation rate would be 8 percent. This is also below the tolerable deviation rate of 10 percent, but it is above the expected deviation rate of 3.5 percent. This situation is more problematical for the auditors. As the sample deviation rate is higher than the expected deviation rate, the auditors would likely reject the control and increase their substantive testing. They might refer to a table such as the one in Exhibit F.10, which also would lead them to reject the control. Finally, they might increase their sample size hoping they would not find more deviations. This last alternative is usually inefficient because the most likely deviation percent for the added sample items is the same as for the ones they had already examined. *Note:* If the auditors use a sample size from Exhibit F.14, which assumes zero deviations, and find one or more deviations, they will need to either increase the sample size or increase the level of control risk.

EXHIBIT F.14
Sample Sizes for Test of Controls Based on Attribute Sampling Tables

Planned Assessed Level of Control Risk	Sample Size
Slightly below the maximum	12–20
Moderate	20–35
Low	30–75

Review Checkpoints

F.25 In what steps of a sampling plan would the use of nonstatistical sampling differ from the use of statistical sampling?

F.26 How should an auditor using nonstatistical sampling for attribute testing evaluate the results of the test?

Summary

This module discusses attribute sampling, which the auditor uses to evaluate operating effectiveness of internal control. When performing attribute sampling, the auditor's primary objective is to assess the extent to which the client's internal control policies and procedures are functioning effectively. As with any sampling application, the auditor is exposed to sampling risk (the risk that the decision made based on the sample differs from the decision that would have been made if the entire population had been examined). The auditor controls this sampling risk (referred to as the *risk of assessing control risk too low* or the *risk of overreliance*) in determining the appropriate sample size and evaluating the sample results.

After the sample is selected, the auditor performs tests of controls to determine whether the control is functioning as intended. A sample deviation rate is determined by dividing the number of deviations by the sample size; this rate is adjusted to control for the acceptable exposure to the risk of assessing control risk too low to determine the upper limit deviation rate. The upper limit deviation rate is a measure that has a (1 – *risk of assessing control risk too high*) probability of equaling or exceeding the true deviation rate in the population.

Once calculated, the upper limit deviation rate (ULDR) is compared to the tolerable deviation rate. If the ULDR is less than the tolerable deviation rate, the auditor can rely on internal control as planned and accept the planned level of control risk. If the ULDR is greater than the tolerable deviation rate, the auditor can either increase the assessed level of control risk or expand the sample to attempt to provide a ULDR that is less than the tolerable deviation rate. Decisions regarding the assessed level of control risk should consider the costs of performing additional tests of controls versus the cost savings from reduced substantive procedures.

Auditors may use nonstatistical sampling for attribute testing. Most of the steps of the sampling plan are performed exactly the same way. Sample sizes should be comparable to those determined for statistical sampling. The sample may be selected using nonprobabalistic techniques such as haphazard or block sampling. Evaluating the results of the sample is solely based on professional judgment as there is no method to estimate the allowance for sampling risk.

Key Terms

allowance for sampling risk: The difference between the upper limit deviation rate and the sample deviation rate; "adjusts" the sample deviation rate to allow the auditor to control the exposure to the risk of assessing control risk too low, 705

attribute sampling: A form of sampling that is used to determine the extent to which some characteristic (attribute) exists within a population of interest; used by the auditor during tests of controls, 699

deviation (error, occurrence, or exception): A condition that refers to instances in which the client and/or its personnel do not follow prescribed controls, 700

discovery sampling: A form of attribute sampling that provides the auditor a specified probability of observing a deviation if deviations exist at a certain level within the population; used when deviations from controls are very critical but are expected to occur at a relatively low rate, 719

expected deviation rate: The rate of deviations anticipated by the auditor in the client's internal control policies or procedures; based on prior experience or a pilot sample, 705

physical representation of the population: Auditor's frame of reference for selecting a sample, 702

risk of assessing control risk too high (*risk of underreliance*): Risk that represents the likelihood that the auditors' sample will provide evidence that the client's controls are not functioning effectively when examining the population would indicate that they are functioning effectively, 703

risk of assessing control risk too low (*risk of overreliance*): Risk that represents the likelihood that the auditors' sample will provide evidence that the client's controls are functioning effectively when examining the population would indicate they are not functioning effectively, 703

sample deviation rate: The extent of deviations found in the auditor's sample; determined by dividing the number of deviations by the sample size, 711

sequential sampling: A sampling plan in which an initial sample is selected and the auditor (1) draws a final conclusion regarding the effectiveness of the control or (2) selects additional items before drawing a final conclusion regarding the effectiveness of the control; also referred to as *stop-or-go sampling*, 718

tolerable deviation rate (TDR): The maximum rate of deviations permissible by the auditor without modifying the planned reliance on an internal control policy or procedure, 704

upper limit deviation rate (ULDR): A measure that adjusts the sample deviation rate for the auditor's acceptable level of sampling risk; the deviation rate that has a (1 – *risk of assessing control risk too low*) probability of equaling or exceeding the true population deviation rate, 712

Multiple Choice Questions for Practice and Review

F.27 Which of the following major stages of the audit examination is most closely related to attribute sampling?

 a. Determining preliminary levels of materiality.

 b. Performing tests of controls.

 c. Performing substantive procedures.

 d. Searching for the possible occurrence of subsequent events.

F.28 Which of the following steps in attribute sampling is most closely related to identifying key controls corresponding to the relevant financial statement assertions?

 a. Determine the objective of sampling.

 b. Define the deviation condition.

 c. Define the population.

 d. Determine the sample size.

F.29 Which of the following factors has a *direct* relationship with sample size in an attribute sampling application?

	Tolerable Deviation Rate	Expected Deviation Rate
a.	Yes	Yes
b.	No	Yes
c.	Yes	No
d.	No	No

F.30 Which of the following sampling risks does the auditor control in an attribute sampling application (RACTL = risk of assessing control risk too low, RACTH = risk of assessing control risk too high)?

	RACTL	RACTH
a.	Yes	Yes
b.	No	Yes
c.	Yes	No
d.	No	No

F.31 Why is the auditor more concerned with controlling the exposure to the risk of assessing control risk too low than with the risk of assessing control risk too high?
 a. Only the risk of assessing control risk too low results in an incorrect audit decision.
 b. The risk of assessing control risk too high is not related to the auditor's study and evaluation of internal control.
 c. The risk of assessing control risk too low can ultimately result in the auditor's failing to reduce audit risk to acceptable levels.
 d. The risk of assessing control risk too high can be controlled by performing tests of controls during the interim period.

F.32 Which of the following would not result in the auditor's selecting a larger sample of controls for examination?
 a. A reduction in the risk of assessing control risk too low from 10 percent to 5 percent.
 b. An increase in the tolerable deviation rate from 3 percent to 6 percent.
 c. An increase in the expected deviation rate from 2 percent to 4 percent.
 d. All of the above would result in a larger sample of controls.

F.33 B. Cox, an audit manager, judged that his test of controls of the company's 50,000 purchase transactions should be based on a tolerable deviation rate of 6 percent, a risk of assessing control risk too low of 5 percent, and an expected deviation rate of 3 percent. Using AICPA sample size tables, the appropriate sample size in this situation would be
 a. 49.
 b. 78.
 c. 132.
 d. 195.

F.34 T. LaRussa, an audit manager, considered the control risk assessments listed in the left column of the following table in evaluating A. Cardinal's internal control over sales transactions. The sample sizes for the substantive procedures of the customer accounts receivable are shown to the right of each control risk. What risk of assessing control risk too low (RACTL) could be assigned for tests of controls at each control risk level?

Control Risk	Accounts Receivable Sample	RACTL
0.20	190	?
0.50	350	?
0.80	390	?
0.90	400	10%

 a. From top to bottom: 5%, 10%, 1%.
 b. From top to bottom: 10%, 1%, 5%.
 c. From top to bottom: 1%, 10%, 5%.
 d. From top to bottom: 1%, 5%, 10%.

F.35 Assume that D. Lee found 2 deviations in a sample of 90 transactions. Using AICPA sample evaluation tables, the upper limit deviation rate at a 5 percent risk of assessing control risk too low is
 a. 2.0%.
 b. 2.2%.
 c. 5.9%.
 d. 6.9%.

F.36 The interpretation of the upper limit deviation rate in an attribute sampling application is
 a. The estimated deviation rate in the population with probability equal to the risk of assessing control risk too low that the actual deviation rate is higher.
 b. The estimated deviation rate in the population with probability equal to the risk of assessing control risk too low that the actual deviation rate is lower.
 c. The estimated deviation rate in the population with certainty that the actual deviation rate is lower.
 d. The estimated deviation rate in the population with certainty that the actual deviation rate is higher.

F.37 If an auditor examined 100 transactions and found one deviation from an important control procedure, the audit conclusion could be that control risk can be assessed at the associated control risk level when

 a. The relevant tolerable deviation rate is 2 percent.

 b. The relevant tolerable deviation rate is 3 percent.

 c. The relevant tolerable deviation rate is 4 percent.

 d. More information about decision criteria is available.

F.38 If an auditor calculated an upper limit deviation rate of 5 percent when she had a tolerable deviation rate of 4 percent, both at the same risk of assessing control risk too low,

 a. Control risk should be assessed at the level associated with the 4 percent tolerable deviation rate.

 b. Control risk should be increased and substantive procedures should be adjusted accordingly.

 c. Control risk should be assessed at the maximum level (100 percent) because the company's performance failed the test.

 d. Control risk should be decreased and substantive procedures should be adjusted accordingly.

F.39 In which of the following circumstances would the auditor most likely use attribute sampling?

 a. Selecting customer accounts receivable for confirmation.

 b. Selecting inventory items for verification of physical quantities.

 c. Selecting purchase orders for indication of proper authorization.

 d. Selecting additions to property, plant, and equipment during the year.

F.40 Using AICPA sample evaluation tables, what is the conclusion from a statistical sample of internal controls when a sample of 125 documents indicates five deviations if the tolerable deviation rate is 5 percent, the expected deviation rate is 2 percent, and the allowance for sampling risk is 3 percent?

 a. Accept the evidence as support for assessing a low control risk because the tolerable rate less the allowance for sampling risk is less than the expected deviation rate.

 b. Use the evidence to assess a higher control risk than planned because the sample deviation rate plus the allowance for sampling risk exceeds the tolerable deviation rate.

 c. Use the evidence to assess a higher control risk than planned because the tolerable deviation rate plus the allowance for sampling risk exceeds the expected deviation rate.

 d. Accept the evidence as support for assessing a low control risk because the sample deviation rate plus the allowance for sampling risk exceeds the tolerable deviation rate.

F.41 An auditor designed a sample that would provide a 10 percent risk of assessing control risk too low that not more than 7 percent of sales invoices lacked credit approval. From previous audits, the auditor expected that 3 percent of the sample invoices lacked proper approval. From the sample of 90 invoices, 7 were found to lack credit approval. Using AICPA sample evaluation tables, the upper limit deviation rate was

 a. 3.3%.

 b. 4.5%.

 c. 7.8%.

 d. 12.8%.

F.42 Based on the information in Question F.41, the allowance for sampling risk was

 a. 2.2%.

 b. 5.0%.

 c. 7.8%.

 d. 10.0%.

F.43 If the _____ exceeds the _____, the auditor would decide to rely on internal control as planned and maintain control risk at planned levels.

 a. Upper limit deviation rate; tolerable deviation rate.

 b. Tolerable deviation rate; upper limit deviation rate.

 c. Expected deviation rate; tolerable deviation rate.

 d. Tolerable deviation rate; expected deviation rate.

F.44 If the sample evidence does not support the planned level of control risk, the auditor could

 a. Increase the assessed level of control risk.

 b. Perform additional substantive procedures, reducing the necessary level of detection risk.

 c. Expand the sample to achieve an observed upper limit deviation rate less than the tolerable deviation rate.

 d. All of the above are correct responses.

F.45 Which of the following best describes the method of determining the upper limit deviation rate?

 a. Expected deviation rate + Allowance for sampling risk.

 b. Risk of assessing control risk too high + Allowance for sampling risk.

 c. Sample deviation rate + Allowance for sampling risk.

 d. Tolerable deviation rate + Allowance for sampling risk.

F.46 Which of the following factors used to determine sample size is normally based on the extent to which the auditor expects to rely on the internal control being examined?

 a. Allowance for sampling risk.

 b. Expected deviation rate.

 c. Sample deviation rate.

 d. Tolerable deviation rate.

F.47 A type of sampling application in which a relatively small initial sample is examined and decisions regarding expanding that sample are based on the results of this initial sample is known as

 a. Attribute sampling.

 b. Discovery sampling.

 c. Sequential sampling.

 d. Statistical sampling.

F.48 Jerry Tim is examining an important internal control in his audit of Langly Company. In past audits, deviations from this control have been observed at a minimal rate (less than 0.1 percent); however, because the account balance affected by this control is highly susceptible to fraud, it is important that Jerry obtain a high level of assurance that deviations occur at no higher than a predetermined (low) rate. Which of the following sampling methods would Jerry most likely use in his evaluation of this control?

 a. Attribute sampling.

 b. Discovery sampling.

 c. Sequential sampling.

 d. Statistical sampling.

F.49 If the risk of assessing control risk too low is 10 percent, the expected deviation rate is 3 percent, the tolerable deviation rate is 6 percent, and the upper limit deviation rate is 6.5 percent, what would your conclusion be with respect to the operating effectiveness of the internal control being examined?

 a. You should choose to rely on the internal control as planned because the upper limit deviation rate is less than the risk of assessing control risk too low.

 b. You should choose to rely on the internal control as planned because the upper limit deviation rate is greater than the tolerable deviation rate.

 c. You should choose to reduce reliance on the internal control from planned levels because the upper limit deviation rate is less than the risk of assessing control risk too low.

 d. You should choose to reduce reliance on the internal control from planned levels because the upper limit deviation rate is greater than the tolerable deviation rate.

F.50 The primary benefit of using nonstatistical sampling is

 a. It generally results in a smaller sample size.

 b. It removes the need to consider allowance for sampling risk.

 c. It is simpler to use.

 d. All of the above are true.

Exercises, Problems, and Simulations

F.51 **Test of Controls Objectives and Deviations.** Read each control in the following list.

Required:

Identify (a) the objective of the auditor's test of controls and (b) one example of a deviation from the control.

1. The credit department supervisor reviews each customer's order and approves credit by making a notation on the order.

2. The billing department must receive written notice from the shipping department of actual shipment to a customer before a sale is recorded. The sales record date is supposed to be the shipment date.

3. Billing clerks carefully identify the correct catalog list prices for goods shipped and calculate and verify the amounts billed on invoices for the quantities of goods shipped.

4. Billing clerks review invoices for intercompany sales and mark each one with the code 9 so they will be posted to intercompany sales accounts.

F.52 **General Attribute Sampling.** Holyfield Frazier, a new staff accountant, is evaluating important controls over the revenue cycle and, more specifically, assessing the operating effectiveness of the control that all shipments made to customers by Top Rank, Inc., have been properly invoiced.

Required:

Comment on the following actions that Holyfield performed. You should evaluate each of the following actions independently of any other actions.

1. Holyfield decided to inspect documentary evidence that all shipments made by Top Rank have been invoiced by matching shipping documents with invoices. Accordingly, she has identified the population from which she intends to sample as all sales invoices. Top Rank has a computerized list of invoiced sales that she can use to select the appropriate sample.

2. Because Holyfield plans to place a high degree of reliance on this particular control, she assesses the risk of assessing control risk too low at 5 percent. In previous years, a 10 percent level was used, but consultation with the engagement manager (Mike Evander) and partner (Don Arum) indicate that a higher degree of reliance is planned in the current audit.

3. Holyfield assessed the expected deviation rate at 1 percent. While the deviation rate from prior audits has approximated 2 percent, Top Rank has made several improvements in its processing of sales invoices; as a result, she believes that a lower expected deviation rate is appropriate.

4. Based on the risk of assessing control risk too low (5 percent), the expected deviation rate (1 percent), and tolerable deviation rate (4 percent), Holyfield uses sampling tables to calculate a sample size of 156. She then increases the sample size to 175 because the population of sales invoices is extremely large (more than 30,000 sales invoices are processed per year).

5. Based on her tests of controls, Holyfield determined a sample deviation rate of 2 percent. Using this deviation rate, along with the appropriate risk of assessing control risk too low, she determined an allowance for sampling risk of 2.5 percent. Because the sum of these two (4.5 percent) is less than the risk of assessing control risk too low, Holyfield concluded that the control is operating effectively and decided to rely on this control as planned to reduce the scope of her substantive procedures.

F.53 **Examples of Deviations.** D. Beckham, CPA, is performing an attribute sampling application for Posh Company. In doing so, he is interested in determining whether quantities on sales invoices are verified by client personnel and agreed with those on the corresponding shipping documents. Per Posh Company's instructions, client personnel are supposed to place check marks next to the quantities on the sales invoices to identify that these quantities have been verified.

During his tests of controls, Beckham selected a total of 100 invoices for examination. Of these invoices, 95 had client initials clearly indicated on them. Beckham's examination of the remaining five invoices revealed the following:

1. On one invoice, check marks were not placed next to the quantities; however, the designation "OK" was written next to them.

2. One of the invoices selected for examination could not be located. Posh Company indicated that invoices occasionally are discarded when customers return the merchandise for credit.

3. No marks or identification was noted next to the quantities on one of the invoices; however, this invoice was marked "VOID."

4. A check mark was placed on an invoice; however, this check mark was not adjacent to any of the quantities on the invoice and could not easily be associated with specific quantities noted on the invoice.

5. One of the invoices contained 15 different types of items. However, only five check marks were placed on the invoice, all adjacent to items from the same location in the warehouse.

Required:

a. For each of the five invoices noted, indicate whether you believe the item represents a deviation. Please justify your treatment of the invoice.

b. What is one fallacy associated with assuming that the internal controls related to the 95 remaining invoices are functioning effectively?

F.54 **Examples of Deviations.** M. Perry, CPA, is conducting an audit of Parker, Inc. In so doing, Perry is performing a study of Parker's internal control and has identified a number of important controls related to purchases on which he intends to rely. These controls are as follows:

1. There is segregation of duties between the individual authorizing the purchase, the individual preparing the purchase order, and the individual receiving goods and services being purchased.

2. Verification of approval of purchases is evidenced by having the individuals performing the verification place their initials on the purchase order.

3. On receipt of goods or services, invoices from vendors should be "matched" to purchase orders. This matching is evidenced by a handwritten notation of the purchase order number on each invoice.

4. Mathematical verification of vendor invoices should be evidenced by having the individuals performing the verification place their initials on the invoice itself.

5. Payments should be made only for vendor invoices that have been matched to purchase orders and mathematically verified.

Required:

a. For each of the five controls, describe one test of control that Perry could perform to verify the operating effectiveness of the control.

b. For each of the five controls, provide an example of a deviation that Perry might identify.

c. Assume that Perry encountered the following situation(s) during his tests of controls. Discuss whether you believe these situations represent deviations from the controls.

1. For a sample purchase, Perry could readily determine that different individuals authorized the purchase and prepared the purchase order. However, because receiving personnel were on vacation, the individual authorizing the purchase initially received the goods and services being purchased. This is a "one-time" occurrence and happened only on the day when all receiving personnel were on vacation or otherwise absent from work.

2. For one purchase, the individual did not initial the purchase order to evidence verification; however, she signed it at the bottom.

3. One vendor invoice did not have handwritten notation of the purchase order number; however, the notation "OK, approved" was written.

4. For one purchase, a vendor invoice could not be located. As a result, a substitute invoice was identified and this invoice was properly verified by Parker's personnel.

5. Perry identified a single cash disbursement to a vendor that was related to five separate invoices; all five invoices were properly approved for payment. Parker commonly combines several invoices into a single check to save costs.

d. Once identified by Perry, how do deviations affect his conclusion with respect to the operating effectiveness of Parker's internal control?

F.55 **Examples of Deviations.** C. Jones, CPA, is verifying that all sales made by Hicks Company to customers on account are properly approved by credit personnel. Hicks has established the following control related to this objective:

On receipt of a purchase order, evaluate the customer's creditworthiness. If the customer's name is included on an approved customer list, issue a credit authorization and begin processing the sale.

Required:

a. Define the word *deviation*. Provide an example of a deviation from this control.

b. In what stages of an attribute sampling plan does the audit team consider deviations? How do deviations influence the attribute sampling process?

c. What test of control could Jones perform to detect deviations from this control?

d. In addition to their effect on Jones's ability to rely on this control, would the following matters raise additional concerns?

1. The deviations were inadvertent mistakes and omissions made over a period of time by a number of different employees.

2. The deviations were all related to the activities of a recently hired employee that occurred during his first month with Hicks Company and appeared to be inadvertent mistakes and omissions. Additional tests of controls revealed that no deviations were noted following this period.

3. The deviations were the result of intentional activity on the part of Hicks Company's employees to increase reported sales to meet targeted earnings levels.

F.56 **Timing of Test of Controls and Sample Selection.** Auditor Susan Hill was examining controls for the authorization of cash disbursements. She selected cash disbursement entries made throughout the year and vouched them to paid invoices and canceled checks bearing the initials and signatures of people authorized to approve the disbursements. She performed the work on September 30 when the company had issued checks numbered from 43921 to 52920. Because 9,000 checks had been issued in nine months, she reasoned that 3,000 more could be issued in the three months before the December 31 year end. About 12,000 checks had been issued last year. She wanted to take one sample of 100 disbursements for the entire year, so she selected 100 random numbers in the sequence 43921 to 55920. She audited the 80 checks in the sample that were issued before September 30, and she held the other 20 randomly selected check numbers for later use. She found no deviations in the sample of 80, a finding that, in the circumstances, would cause her to assign a low (20 percent) control risk to the probability that the system would permit improper charges to be recorded in expense and purchase/inventory accounts.

Required:

Prepare a memorandum to the audit manager (dated October 1) describing the audit team's options with respect to evaluating control performance for the period from October through December.

F.57 **Sample Selection.** Read each of the following cases.

Required:

Explain for each case how you could select a sample having the best chance of being representative of the population using (1) unrestricted random selection and (2) systematic random selection.

a. You need to select a sample of recorded cash disbursements. The client used two bank accounts for general disbursements. Account 1 was used during January–August and issued checks numbered 3633–6632. Account 2 was used during May–December and issued checks numbered 0001–6000.

b. You need to select a sample of purchase orders. The client issued prenumbered purchase orders in the sequence 9000–13999. You realize that if you select five-digit random numbers from a table and look for numbers in this sequence, 95 percent of the random numbers you scan will be discards because a table has 100,000 different five-digit random numbers. (The computer is down today!) How can you alter this sequence to reduce the number of discards?

c. You need to select a sample of perpetual inventory records so you can count the quantities while the stock clerks take the physical inventory. The perpetual records have been printed in a control list showing location, item description, and quantity. You have a copy of the list. It is 75 pages long, with 50 lines to a page (40 lines on the last page). Find an efficient way to select 100 lines for your test of the client's counting procedure.

F.58 **Sample Selection.** Janice, CPA, is verifying a sample of controls related to the approval of vouchers for payment. Her client, Fave Company, uses a prenumbered voucher system in which a voucher is prepared and approved for all receiving reports and the corresponding vendor's invoice. Based on the prior audit, Janice has verified that the first receiving report number for the year is 12794 and the final receiving report prepared this year is 38121.

Required:

Indicate how Janice could use (1) unrestricted random selection and (2) systematic random selection to select the sample for sample sizes of 50, 100, and 500.

F.59 **Sample Selection.** McNeal is studying and evaluating Branyon's internal controls related to the mathematical verification of sales invoices. In this verification, Branyon's control policies require that employees perform the following procedures:

- Verify that sales invoices are prepared only for items actually shipped to customers. This policy is evidenced by requiring employees to place a check mark next to quantities on the sales invoices.

- Verify that prices charged to customers are from approved price lists. This policy is evidenced by requiring employees to place a check mark next to prices on the sales invoice.

- Verify that extensions and footings on invoices are mathematically accurate. This policy is evidenced by requiring employees to initial the bottom of the invoice in a section marked "Mathematically verified by."

To verify the operating effectiveness of these policies, McNeal established an expected deviation rate of 3 percent, a tolerable deviation rate of 6 percent, and a risk of assessing control risk too low of 10 percent. Using these parameters, McNeal determined a necessary sample size of 132 invoices. McNeal is now ready to select invoices for examination and is considering the use of systematic selection.

Required:

a. McNeal wants to ensure that he selects a representative sample of sales invoices. What are some of the characteristics that he should consider to ensure that his sample is representative of the population of sales invoices?

b. What issues do the use of systematic selection introduce with respect to McNeal's ability to select a representative sample of sales invoices from the population?

c. Identify any issues associated with the use of systematic selection in the following independent circumstances.

1. Branyon does not maintain invoices in a computerized format but files invoices manually by date. McNeal has full access to the files containing the invoices.

2. Branyon does not maintain invoices in a computerized format but files them manually according to customer classification ("A" represents high-volume customers; "B," middle-volume customers; and "C," low-volume customers"). McNeal has full access to the files containing the invoices.

3. Branyon does not maintain invoices in a computerized format but files them manually by date. Because they are maintained off-site, McNeal does not have full access to the files; however, Branyon has offered to pull invoices selected by McNeal and make them available for his tests of controls.

4. Branyon maintains invoices in a computerized format arranged alphabetically by customer name. This file can be sorted by date, amount of sale, customer number, customer classification, and ZIP code. McNeal has full access to the computerized files.

F.60 **Sample Size Determination.** Jeri Phillips is examining the internal control of Cowboy Company. She has identified the mathematical verification of sales invoices as an important control and decided to test this control. Based on her discussion with Cowboy's management, Phillips determined that Cowboy Company's employees were required to indicate their compliance with this control by writing their initials in an appropriate place on the invoice copy.

Assume that Phillips established an acceptable risk of assessing control risk too low of 5 percent, an expected deviation rate of 3 percent, and a tolerable deviation rate of 9 percent.

Required:

 a. Using AICPA sample size tables, what is the appropriate sample size?

 b. Indicate how Phillips would assess the three parameters that are used to determine sample size (risk of assessing control risk too low, expected deviation rate, and tolerable deviation rate).

 c. Use the original parameters but now assume that Phillips is willing to increase her acceptable risk of assessing control risk too low to 10 percent. Using AICPA sample size tables, what is the new sample size that she would examine?

 d. Provide an explanation for the change in sample size noted in (*c*).

F.61 **Sample Size Determination.** Read each of the following independent sets of conditions.

Required:

Use AICPA sample size tables to identify the appropriate sample size for use in a statistical sampling application (RACTL = risk of assessing control risk too low, EDR = expected deviation rate, TDR = tolerable deviation rate). Based on comparing the sample sizes across different combinations of these factors, what is your conclusion regarding the relationship of each of these factors to sample size?

 a. RACTL = 5%, EDR = 0%, TDR = 7%.

 b. RACTL = 5%, EDR = 3%, TDR = 7%.

 c. RACTL = 5%, EDR = 3%, TDR = 6%.

 d. RACTL = 10%, EDR = 0%, TDR = 7%.

F.62 **Sample Size Determination.** Read each of the following independent sets of conditions.

Required:

Use AICPA sample size tables to identify the appropriate sample size for use in a statistical sampling application (RACTL = risk of assessing control risk too low, EDR = expected deviation rate, TDR = tolerable deviation rate). Based on comparing the sample sizes across different combinations of these factors, what is your conclusion regarding the relationship of each of these factors to sample size?

 a. RACTL = 5%, EDR = 1%, TDR = 4%.

 b. RACTL = 5%, EDR = 1.5%, TDR = 4%.

 c. RACTL = 5%, EDR = 1.5%, TDR = 6%.

 d. RACTL = 10%, EDR = 1.5%, TDR = 4%.

F.63 **Sample Size Determination.** For each of the following independent cases, use AICPA sample size tables to identify the missing value(s).

	Control			
	1	2	3	4
Risk of assessing control risk too low	5.0%	5.0%	10%	(d)
Expected deviation rate	1.25%	2.5%	(c)	1.25%
Tolerable deviation rate	7.0%	(b)	6.0%	6.0%
Sample size	(a)	68	153	78

F.64 **Sample Size Determination.** G. Cambridge, CPA, is performing attribute sampling to determine whether all purchases on account are properly approved by the client. Because the client typically makes over 2,000 purchases on account per year, Cambridge has decided to use sampling instead of examining the entire population of purchases. Based on Cambridge's past experience with this client, she anticipates a deviation rate of 1 percent.

Required:

 a. What factors should Cambridge consider in determining the necessary sample size? How would she determine the level of these factors?

 b. Once the appropriate factors have been determined, describe the process that Cambridge would use in determining the necessary sample size.

c. Assume that Cambridge established a risk of assessing control risk too low of 10 percent and a tolerable deviation rate of 6 percent. Using AICPA sample size tables, determine the appropriate sample size that she would use in evaluating the controls over approval of purchases on account.

d. How would the following changes impact (i) the factors used to determine sample size and (ii) the sample size examined by Cambridge? (Do not determine an exact sample size but indicate whether the sample size would be larger, smaller, or unchanged. Treat each of these changes in factors independently in providing your answer.)

 1. Because of increased sales and new lines of business, the number of purchases made by the client on account increased markedly from over 2,000 to nearly 5,000 during the current year.

 2. The client remediated some control deficiencies related to the purchasing function noted in Cambridge's prior audits. One of these control deficiencies related specifically to the approval of purchases made by the client.

 3. The client has had turnover in the purchasing function during the most recent year. This turnover resulted in a higher-than-normal number of deviations during the first few months of the new employees' tenure.

 4. Cambridge has decided that it would be cost beneficial to seek a reduction in control risk from moderate to low.

 5. Cambridge has decided that it is no longer efficient to test controls at current levels and increased control risk from moderate levels to high levels.

 6. Because some of its previous suppliers are no longer in business or no longer competitive with respect to price, the client has added a number of new vendors to its approved vendor listing.

e. What are the trade-offs Cambridge must make between increasing her reliance on internal control and maintaining the current level of reliance on internal control?

f. What factors should Cambridge consider in deciding whether to increase her reliance on internal control?

F.65 **Sample Results Evaluation.** Joan Plane is testing the effectiveness of an important control for Blackheart, Inc. Because she is placing a high level of reliance on this control, she has assessed a relatively low risk of assessing control risk too low (5 percent) and tolerable deviation rate (6 percent). Based on the acceptable risk of assessing control risk too low, expected deviation rate, and tolerable deviation rate, she determined a sample size of 60 items. Her tests of controls revealed three deviations.

Required:

a. Calculate the sample deviation rate.

b. Using AICPA sample evaluation tables, calculate the upper limit deviation rate and allowance for sampling risk.

c. Why does the upper limit deviation rate differ from the sample deviation rate?

d. What would Joan's conclusion be with respect to the operating effectiveness of the control? What options are available to her at this time?

e. Ignoring the effects on sample size, how would Joan's decision to accept a higher risk of assessing control risk too low (10 percent) affect her conclusions with respect to the operating effectiveness of the control?

F.66 **Sample Results Evaluation.** Read each of the following independent sets of conditions.

Required:

For each condition, use AICPA sample evaluation tables to identify the (1) sample deviation rate, (2) upper limit deviation rate (ULDR), and (3) allowance for sampling risk (n = sample size, d = deviations, RACTL = risk of assessing control risk too low). Based on comparing the ULDRs across different combinations of these factors, what is your conclusion regarding the relationship of each of these factors to the ULDR?

a. $n = 60$, d $= 4$, RACTL $= 5\%$.

b. $n = 60$, d $= 6$, RACTL $= 5\%$.

c. $n = 60$, d $= 6$, RACTL $= 10\%$.

F.67 **Sample Results Evaluation.** Read each of the following independent sets of conditions.

Required:

For each condition, use AICPA sample evaluation tables to identify the (1) sample deviation rate, (2) upper limit deviation rate (ULDR), and (3) allowance for sampling risk (n = sample size, d = deviations, RACTL = risk of assessing control risk too low). Based on comparing the ULDRs across different combinations of these factors, what is your conclusion regarding the relationship of each of these factors to the ULDR?

a. n = 100, d = 8, RACTL = 5%.

b. n = 100, d = 4, RACTL = 5%.

c. n = 100, d = 8, RACTL = 10%.

F.68 **Sample Results Evaluation.** For each of the following independent cases, use AICPA sample size and sample evaluation tables to identify the missing value(s).

	Control			
	1	**2**	**3**	**4**
Sample size	30	(d)	200	50
Number of deviations	2	4	(g)	2
Sample deviation rate	(a)	(e)	2.5%	(i)
Risk of assessing control risk too low	5.0%	5.0%	10.0%	(j)
Upper limit deviation rate	(b)	12.6%	(h)	(k)
Allowance for sampling risk	(c)	(f)	2.1%	8.1%

F.69 **Sample Results Evaluation.** Assume that you are working on the audit of a small company and are examining purchase invoices for the presence of a "received" stamp. The omission of the stamp is thus a deviation. The population is composed of approximately 4,000 invoices processed by the company during the current year.

You decide that a deviation rate in the population as high as 5 percent would not require any extended audit procedures. However, if the population deviation rate is greater than 5 percent, you would want to assess a higher control risk and do more audit work.

In each case, write the letter of the sample (A or B) that, in your judgment, provides the best evidence that the deviation rate in the population is 5 percent or lower (using a risk of assessing control risk too low of 5 percent). Assume that each sample is selected at random. Refer to AICPA sample evaluation tables if necessary.

	Case 1		Case 2		Case 3		Case 4		Case 5	
Sample	**A**	**B**	**A**	**B**	**A**	**B**	**A**	**B**	**A**	**B**
Number of invoices examined	75	200	150	25	200	100	100	125	200	150
Number of deviations	1	4	2	0	6	2	1	3	8	4
Sample deviation rate	1.3	2.0	1.3	0.0	3.0	2.0	1.0	2.4	4.0	2.7

F.70 **Sample Results Evaluation.** H. Jackson, CPA, is examining the operating effectiveness of the internal control of Town Mo, a large conglomerate in the music industry. As part of his evaluation, Jackson determined a necessary sample size of 93 items (based on a tolerable deviation rate of 5 percent, an expected deviation rate of 0.5 percent, and a risk of assessing control risk too low of 5 percent). After properly selecting the 93 items, Jackson found no deviations from the prescribed control procedures.

Required:

a. Based on Jackson's sample, determine the sample deviation rate and upper limit deviation rate. (Because the AICPA sample evaluation tables do not contain a row for a sample size of 93, round down and use a sample size of 90.)

b. Explain the difference between the upper limit deviation rate and the sample deviation rate observed in (*a*). How does this difference relate to the use of statistical sampling?

 c.　What would Jackson conclude with respect to the operating effectiveness of Town Mo's internal control?

 d.　If Jackson found three deviations in the sample, use AICPA sample evaluation tables to determine the sample deviation rate and upper limit deviation rate. What would Jackson conclude with respect to the operating effectiveness of Town Mo's internal control in this case?

 e.　Using AICPA sample evaluation tables, what is the maximum number of deviations that Jackson could identify without reducing his reliance on Town Mo's internal control?

 f.　Repeat (e) using a 10 percent risk of assessing control risk too low. What is the explanation for any differences between this number of deviations and that in (e)?

F.71　**Evaluating a Sampling Application.**　Tom Barton, an assistant accountant with a local CPA firm, was recently graduated from Other University. He studied statistical sampling for auditing in college and wants to impress his employers with his knowledge of modern auditing methods.

 He decided to select a random sample of payroll checks for the test of controls, using a tolerable rate of 5 percent and an acceptable risk of assessing control risk too low of 5 percent. The senior accountant told Tom that 2 percent of the checks audited last year had one or more errors in the calculation of net pay. Tom decided to audit 100 random checks. Because supervisory personnel had paychecks with larger amounts than production workers, he selected 60 of the supervisor checks and 40 checks of the others. He was very careful to see that the selections of 60 from the April payroll register and 40 from the August payroll register were random.

 The audit of this sample yielded two deviations, exactly the 2 percent rate experienced last year. The first was the deduction of federal income taxes based on two exemptions for a supervisory employee whose W-4 form showed four exemptions. The other was payment to a production employee at a rate for a job classification one grade lower than it should have been. The worker had been promoted the week before and Tom found that in the next payroll he was paid at the correct (higher) rate.

 When he evaluated this evidence, Tom decided that these two findings were really not control deviations at all. The withholding of too much tax did not affect the expense accounts and the proper rate was paid the production worker as soon as the clerk caught up with the change orders. Tom decided that having found zero deviations in a sample of 100, the upper limit deviation rate at 5 percent risk of assessing control risk too low was 3 percent, which easily satisfied his predetermined criterion.

 The senior accountant was impressed. Last year he had audited 15 checks from each month and Tom's work represented a significant time savings. The reviewing partner on the audit also was impressed because he had never thought that statistical sampling could be so efficient, and that was the reason he had never studied the method.

Required:

Identify and explain the mistakes made by Tom and the others.

F.72　**Comprehensive Attribute Sampling.**　Dodge, CPA, is performing an attribute sampling plan for her audit of Truck Company. In her audit of cash disbursements, she has identified the preparation of a voucher and marking it as "paid" prior to preparing and mailing a check to the vendor as an important control. Dodge defined any voucher that was not marked as "paid" as being a deviation.

 In performing her sampling application, she established the following parameters:

Risk of assessing control risk too low	5 percent
Expected deviation rate	2.75 percent
Tolerable deviation rate	7 percent

Required:

 a.　Identify what factors Dodge considered in establishing the risk of assessing control risk too low, expected deviation rate, and tolerable deviation rate.

 b.　Assume that Dodge wished to place additional reliance on this control. How would that affect the three parameters in (a)?

 c.　Based on the original parameters, use AICPA sample size tables to determine the appropriate sample size.

 d. If Dodge selected the sample size in (*c*) and found four deviations, what is the sample deviation rate?

 e. Using AICPA sample evaluation tables, what is the upper limit deviation rate? (*Note:* If the sample size cannot be directly located on the sample evaluation table, round down to the next highest sample size.) –

 f. What would Dodge's conclusion be with respect to the functioning of this control?

F.73 **Comprehensive Attribute Sampling.** Alicia Marblehead is conducting tests of controls on the control that quantities on Rock's receiving reports are appropriately verified. In so doing, she has inquired of Rock's receiving personnel, who told her that they place a mark near the quantities verified and sign the receiving report upon delivery. Alicia has decided to use nonstatistical sampling for this engagement. Based on the importance of this control and the deviation rate that has been observed in prior audits, Alicia has established the following parameters.

Risk of assessing control risk too low	5 percent
Expected deviation rate	1.5 percent
Tolerable deviation rate	4 percent

Based on the parameters Alicia has established, she decides to use a sample of 100 receiving reports.

Required:

 a. How would Alicia define a deviation condition?

 b. How would Alicia appropriately define the population? What steps should she take to ensure that it is complete?

 c. If Rock has a computerized list of all receiving reports, what are some options available to Alicia in selecting specific items for examination? What precautions should she take before undertaking the selection of items?

 d. For each of the following number of deviations, determine the sample deviation rate and indicate Alicia's decision with respect to the functioning of the control.

 1. 2 deviations.

 2. 4 deviations.

 3. 10 deviations.

F.74 **Nonstatistical Attribute Sampling.** M. Curtis is auditing the revenue cycle of Kentucky Distilleries and has elected to perform a nonstatistical test of controls. Kentucky Distilleries sells Old Horse Bourbon to wholesale distributors around the country. Because bourbon is strictly controlled, Curtis does not expect deviations to be present in the system. She has assessed control risk as low and selected a sample size of 50 sales (from Exhibit F.14). Curtis has defined a deviation as a recorded sale not being supported by a shipping document with a federal tax stamp.

Required:

 a. How does nonstatistical sampling differ from statistical sampling?

 b. Why would Curtis choose to perform nonstatistical sampling instead of statistical sampling?

 c. How should Curtis select her sample?

 d. What conclusion should Curtis draw if she finds one deviation?

F.75 **Audit Simulation: Comprehensive Attribute Sampling.** The firm of Buy, CPAs, is engaged to conduct the audit of City Circuit, a retailer of electronic and other high-technology products. Because of technological advances in City Circuit's inventory products, an important risk that it faces is that prices charged by suppliers reflect current industry prices (which tend to fluctuate relatively significantly, particularly as new technologies are introduced and as older technologies are discontinued). The nature of City Circuit's inventories is such that a small number of suppliers exist and each supplier has a similar pricing structure. This pricing structure is reflected in an electronic industry pricing guide, which is updated on a daily basis.

 You are a staff accountant with Buy and have been asked to identify a potential audit approach to address this risk. In the past, your firm has decided to place relatively limited

reliance on internal control policies related to City Circuit's purchasing function and has instead conducted relatively extensive substantive procedures related to its inventories. However, the new partner on the City Circuit engagement has successfully reduced substantive procedures on her other clients in the retail industry by performing more extensive tests of controls. Because of her previous experience in the industry as well as her successful use of this audit approach for other clients, she asks you to evaluate the possibility of using more extensive tests of controls in the audit of City Circuit.

The following controls are relevant to City Circuit's processing of vendor invoices:

- Similar to most retailers in the industry, City Circuit has a highly automated inventory monitoring and control system. Based on anticipated product life, current sales, and existing inventory levels, an automatic purchase order is generated when inventory levels reach predetermined thresholds.

- Once a purchase order has been generated, the store manager reviews it prior to transmitting it to the appropriate vendor. This review ensures that the vendor is from an approved list and that the proposed purchase is consistent with the store's objectives and near-term plans (for example, not purchasing a large number of desktop computers just prior to a major promotion for laptop computers).

- Upon receipt of the items, warehouse personnel prepare "blind" copies of a receiving report, noting the quantity of each item received.

- Purchasing personnel verify the vendors' invoices as follows: (1) compare the invoice to a purchase order by referencing the purchase order number on the vendor invoice, (2) compare quantities on the vendor invoice to quantities from the receiving report prepared by warehouse personnel, (3) compare prices on the invoice for reasonableness through reference to industry pricing data, and (4) mathematically verify the accuracy of the invoice.

These controls have been in place for a number of years and City Circuit has experienced relatively little turnover in its purchasing and related functions. You did not observe any remediation or major changes with respect to these controls or to City Circuit's control environment during the past year.

You reviewed the prior audit documentation, which was prepared by another staff accountant who has since left the firm. Based on your review, you prepared the following notes:

- The control policy tested by the staff accountant is the employee verification of the reasonableness of prices on the invoices by placing a check mark or other notation adjacent to the price on the invoice.

- Using an expected deviation rate of 1 percent, a tolerable deviation rate of 7 percent, and a risk of assessing control risk too low of 10 percent, a sample of 55 invoices was selected.

- Tests of controls revealed three misstatements; based on the sample size of 55 and a risk of assessing control risk too low of 10 percent, the upper limit deviation rate was 11.8 percent. Because this exceeded the tolerable deviation rate of 7 percent, you reduced reliance on the control policy and conducted more extensive substantive procedures.

Required:

a. Comment on the appropriateness of the work done in the prior audit with respect to testing this control policy.

b. Based on the results of tests of controls in the prior year, what are your initial thoughts regarding the viability of increasing your reliance on this control policy in the current audit?

c. How will your decision to increase the reliance on the control policy affect the sample size in the current audit? What specific factors will be affected by this decision?

d. Assume that you have established a risk of assessing control risk too low of 5 percent, a tolerable deviation rate of 6 percent, and an expected deviation rate of 1 percent. Using AICPA sample size tables, what is the necessary sample size in the current audit? Is this sample size consistent with your expectations compared to that examined in the prior year?

e. Using AICPA sample size tables, what factor(s) resulted in the increased sample size from the prior year? Can you determine the extent to which each factor contributed to this increase?

Note: Requirements (f)–(h) are unrelated to (a)–(e).

f. Refer to the AICPA sample evaluation tables. Assuming a sample size of 100 items, how many deviations would be permissible for you to rely on this control policy using a 5 percent risk of assessing control risk too low and a 6 percent tolerable deviation rate?

g. Repeat (*f*), assuming that you decided to reduce your reliance on internal control and establish a risk of assessing control risk too low of 10 percent.

h. What does a comparison of your results in (*f*) and (*g*) tell you about the effect of the risk of assessing control risk too low on the upper limit deviation rate?

F.76 **Audit Simulation: General Attribute Sampling.** You overheard the following dialogue between Joe Ashley (a staff assistant) and Monique Estrada (his supervisor).

Required:

Referring to appropriate professional standards, comment on each of these statements.

a. "It's unfortunate that generally accepted auditing standards don't allow us to use non-statistical sampling for this control. I just don't feel that the extra time and effort to use statistical sampling are worth the benefits."

b. "I'm not sure what level of control risk we should plan to use. We need to determine the amount of substantive procedures that we will conduct and then assess control risk accordingly."

c. "We really need to be careful to limit our exposure to the risk of assessing control risk too low. This risk could result in our failure to perform enough substantive procedures."

d. "Separation of duties is such an important control that we should use statistical sampling to evaluate the extent to which the custody, recording, and approval functions for purchases are performed by different individuals."

e. "Because we're really relying heavily on this control, it's important that it be operating very effectively. That's why I set the tolerable deviation rate at such a low level."

f. "We found six deviations out of the 120 items we examined. That's a 5 percent deviation rate. Because our tolerable deviation rate is 8 percent, it looks like we can rely on internal control as planned."

g. "A deviation is a deviation. Some of these problems were honest mistakes, but others looked like client employees intentionally ignored the controls. However, they all have the same effect on the upper limit deviation rate."

h. "Since our upper limit deviation rate is lower than the tolerable deviation rate, we don't have to do anything with the deviations we found."

F.77 **Audit Simulation: Comprehensive Attribute Sampling.** In the planning stages of the audit of CardBerry, John Mays is using the audit risk model to reduce his overall exposure to the likelihood of issuing an unqualified opinion on financial statements that are materially misstated. Based on firm policy, he has decided to reduce audit risk to a relatively low level (5 percent) and has assessed inherent risk at 100 percent. He is now in the process of assessing control risk and is inquiring of his supervisor about the use of attribute sampling.

Required:

Respond to each of the following, referring to the professional auditing literature when appropriate.

a. Define *control risk*. In what circumstances would John decide to assess control risk (1) at the maximum level and (2) at less than the maximum level?

b. Identify the three objectives of internal control and the five components of internal control. Which combination of objectives and components is most closely related to attribute sampling?

c. Define the two broad types of sampling risks associated with attribute sampling. What type of losses is John exposed to because of these sampling risks?

d. What four primary factors should John consider in planning a sample for a test of controls?

e. What is the tolerable deviation rate? What factors should John consider in assessing the tolerable deviation rate?

f. What factor should John consider in establishing the acceptable level of sampling risk? How does the level of sampling risk influence sample size?

g. How would John treat instances in which an item selected for examination could not be located?

h. Assume that John's sampling procedures support the assessment of control risk at moderate levels (0.50). What factors should he consider in deciding whether to seek a further reduction in control risk to low levels (say, 0.30)?

CPA REVIEW

F.78 **Kaplan CPA Exam Simulation: Factors Affecting Sample Size.**

Required:
Go to the text Web site at www.mhhe.com/louwers3e, click on the AUD: Abernathy and Chapman case and the "Sample Size" tab, and complete your answer.

CPA REVIEW

F.79 **Kaplan CPA Exam Simulation: Communications Regarding Sampling Terminology.**

Required:
Go to the text Web site at www.mhhe.com/louwers3e, click on the AUD: Hardi case and the "Communication" tab, and complete your answer.

F.80 **ACL Assignment.**

Required:
Go to the ACL link at www.mhhe.com/louwers3e, click on "ACL Assignments," and complete the assignment for Module F.

Variables Sampling

Professional Standards References

Compendium Section	Document Reference	Topic
AU 312	*SAS 107*	"Audit Risk and Materiality in Conducting an Audit"
AU 316	*SAS 99*	"Consideration of Fraud in a Financial Statement Audit"
	ISA 240	"The Auditor's Responsibility to Consider Fraud in an Audit of Financial Statements"
AU 319	*SAS 109*	"Understanding the Entity and Its Environment and Assessing the Risks of Material Misstatement"
	ISA 330	"The Auditor's Procedures in Response to Assessed Risks"
AU 326	*SAS 106*	"Audit Evidence"
	ISA 500	"Audit Evidence"
AU 333	*SAS 89*	"Audit Adjustments"
AU 339	*SAS 103*	"Audit Documentation"
	AS 3	"Audit Documentation"
	ISA 230	"Audit Documentation"
AU 350	*SAS 39*	"Audit Sampling"
	SAS 111	"Amendment to Statement on Auditing Standards No. 39, *Audit Sampling*"
	ISA 530	"Audit Sampling and Other Means of Testing"
AU 9350		"Interpretations: Audit Sampling"

USA Today has come out with a new survey—apparently, three out of every four people make up 75 percent of the population.

David Letterman, late-night talk-show host

Learning Objectives

Module G builds on the sampling overview presented in Module E and provides a comprehensive example of the use of variables sampling in the auditor's substantive procedures.

Your objectives are to be able to:

1. Define *variables sampling* and understand when it is used in the audit examination.

2. Understand the basic process underlying *dollar unit sampling* (DUS) and when to use DUS.

3. Identify the factors affecting the size of a DUS sample and calculate the sample size for a DUS application.

4. Evaluate the sample results for a DUS sample by calculating the projected misstatement, incremental allowance for sampling risk, and basic allowance for sampling risk.

5. Understand the basic process underlying *classical variables sampling* and the use of classical variables sampling in an audit examination.

6. Understand the basic process underlying nonstatistical sampling and the use of nonstatistical sampling in an audit examination.

INTRODUCTION

1. Define *variables sampling* and understand when it is used in the audit examination.

Module F illustrated the use of sampling in the auditor's study and evaluation of the client's internal control, or *attribute sampling*. This module focuses on the use of variables sampling. **Variables sampling** is used to examine a population when the auditor wants to estimate the amount (or value) of that population; in the audit examination, this represents the "true" balance of a particular account or class of transactions. The **true balance** is the amount at which the account should be recorded if no misstatements[1] exist. Thus, variables sampling is used during the substantive procedures stage of the audit.

The following seven-step procedure (originally introduced in Module E) serves as the basis for our illustration of variables sampling:

The auditor can use one of two approaches for variables sampling. **Dollar unit sampling (DUS)** provides an estimate of the amount of misstatement in the account balance or class of transactions. The distinguishing feature of DUS is that it tends to select larger dollar transactions or components within an account balance for examination. **Classical variables sampling** uses the laws of probability and the Central Limit Theorem to estimate either (1) the amount of misstatement in the account balance or class of transactions or (2) the "true" balance for an account balance or class of transactions. Classical variables sampling procedures provide a range of estimates with a specific probability of including the amount of misstatement or the "true" account balance.

Auditors use both DUS and classical variables sampling to determine the fairness of the client's financial statements. When using either of these variables sampling methods, auditors examine transactions or components of clients' account balances or class of transactions. Based on this sample of transactions or components and analytical procedures, auditors then assess the overall fairness of the account balance or class of transactions.

Review Checkpoints

G.1 Define *variables sampling*. In what stage of the audit examination is variables sampling used?

G.2 What are two approaches available to the auditor for variables sampling?

[1] In variables sampling terminology, the difference between recorded amounts and true balances is referred to as "error"; however, the term includes both unintentional misstatements (referred to by *SAS 99* [AU 316] as *errors*) and intentional misstatements (referred to by *SAS 99* [AU 316] as *fraud*).

SAMPLING IN SUBSTANTIVE PROCEDURES: DOLLAR UNIT SAMPLING

LEARNING OBJECTIVE

2. Understand the basic process underlying *dollar unit sampling* (DUS) and when to use DUS.

Dollar unit sampling (DUS) is one method of variables sampling the auditor uses in substantive procedures that selects individual dollars from an account balance for verification. Under DUS, items in the sample are selected based on their size; that is, each item in the sample has a probability of being selected that is proportional to its size. For example, a customer's account recorded at $30,000 is 10 times more likely to be selected than a customer's account recorded at $3,000. Other names frequently used include combined attributes-variables (CAV) sampling, cumulative monetary amount (CMA) sampling, and monetary-unit sampling (MUS).

The unique feature of DUS is its definition of the population as the number of dollars in an account balance or class of transactions. (Viewed another way, individual dollars within an account balance or class of transactions are identified as sampling units.) DUS uses attribute sampling principles with the attribute of interest being whether the individual dollar amount is stated properly or not. Thus, if a client's accounts receivable are recorded at $300,000, the population is defined as 300,000 one-dollar units. Under DUS, the auditor will randomly select individual dollars from the population for examination. When a dollar is selected in this fashion, the entire "logical unit" (transaction or component of the account balance) is selected for examination. This feature typically makes DUS samples efficient because a small number of transactions or components can be selected for examination yet account for a relatively large dollar amount.

The following are advantages associated with the use of DUS:

- DUS typically results in relatively smaller sample sizes (in terms of the number of transactions or components selected for examination) compared to classical variables sampling.
- DUS samples typically include transactions or components reflecting relatively large dollar amounts.
- DUS is more effective in identifying misstatements in accounts when overstatement is the primary concern (such as revenues and assets).
- DUS is generally simpler to use than classical variables sampling, which often requires complex calculations.

In contrast, the following are disadvantages associated with the use of DUS:

- DUS provides a more conservative (higher) estimate of misstatement in the account balance or class of transactions.
- DUS is not effective in identifying misstatements in accounts when understatement (such as liabilities and expenses) is the primary concern.
- Expanding a DUS sample is difficult when preliminary results indicate a decision that the account balance or class of transactions is materially misstated.
- DUS requires special considerations for logical units having a zero or negative balance. In some cases, logical units having these characteristics indicate employee fraud.

In summary, DUS is best used when the auditor expects to find few or no misstatements and when overstatement is of greatest concern. In contrast, when a relatively large number of misstatements is expected or when understatement is of greatest concern, DUS is less effective.

To illustrate the use of DUS, consider the auditor's examination of accounts receivable for Rice, Inc. Rice's accounts receivable have a recorded value of $300,000 and are comprised of 1,500 individual customer accounts. The auditor is examining the *existence* and *valuation and allocation* assertions and selects customer accounts for confirmation. This example illustrates how the auditor calculates sample size, selects sample items, and evaluates sample results through manual calculations. When the client maintains its records in computerized format, computer software is used to perform these tasks.

DUS: Planning

In the planning stages of DUS, the auditor determines the objective, defines the attribute of interest, and defines the population. The objective of any variables sampling application is to provide evidence regarding the fairness of the relevant assertions. These assertions determine the type of substantive procedures selected by the auditor, which ultimately determines the nature of items selected for examination. To verify the *existence* and *valuation and allocation* assertions, the auditor confirms accounts receivable and selects a sample of "items" for confirmation as shown:

Once the objective of sampling has been determined, the auditor defines the attribute of interest. In a variables sampling application, the auditor is interested in determining the proper amount at which the items *should be* recorded; this amount is often referred to as the **audited value,** which is simply the dollar amount at which the item would be recorded assuming that no mistakes in judgment or application of generally accepted accounting principles were made. In a DUS application, the attribute of interest is the difference between the recorded value and the audited value, or the amount of *error.*

The final step in the planning stage of DUS is to define the population of interest. As noted earlier, one of the most important distinctions of DUS is that the population is defined as all of the *individual dollars* within the account balance or class of transactions. Recall that Rice's accounts receivable are comprised of 1,500 individual customer accounts and are recorded at $300,000. As a result, for Rice, DUS defines the population as 300,000 individual dollars of accounts receivable.

As with attribute sampling, the auditor's objective is critical in defining the population of interest. For example, consider the difference between the *existence assertion* and the *completeness assertion.* For existence, the auditor is interested in determining whether a *recorded* customer account is *bona fide* (that is, whether the account exists). In this case, the population of interest is defined as recorded account balances. In contrast, when examining the completeness assertion, the auditor is interested in ensuring that all transactions that actually occurred were included in the customer account balances. Thus, the population of interest in this case is composed of transactions representing bona fide sales. These relationships are summarized as follows:

AUDITING INSIGHT Are These Transactions Too Small?

One reason that Ernst & Young may have failed to detect a massive fraud at HealthSouth (the nation's largest provider of diagnostic imaging, outpatient surgery, and rehabilitation services) is its definition of the population from which its team selected transactions. HealthSouth executives knew that Ernst & Young would not examine items less than $5,000; as a result, they decomposed large entries that reclassified expenses into assets into thousands of entries having amounts of less than $5,000.

Source: "Behind the Wave of Corporate Fraud: A Change in How Auditors Work," *The Wall Street Journal,* March 25, 2004, pp. A1, A14.

Review Checkpoints

G.3 Define *dollar unit sampling (DUS)*. What is the unique feature of it?

G.4 What are the advantages and disadvantages of using DUS? Under what conditions is it best used?

G.5 How are the substantive procedures performed by the auditor related to the objective of DUS?

G.6 What is the typical attribute of interest in a DUS application?

DUS: Determining Sample Size

LEARNING OBJECTIVE

3. Identify the factors affecting the size of a DUS sample and calculate the sample size for a DUS application.

The *sample size* represents the number of items that the auditor examines. In variables sampling, these items are transactions or components underlying the account balance or class of transactions being audited. Four main factors influence the sample size in a DUS application:

- Sampling risk (risk of incorrect acceptance).
- Tolerable error.
- Expected error.
- Population size.

Sampling Risk

Module E summarized two types of sampling risks for variables sampling applications: the **risk of incorrect acceptance** and the **risk of incorrect rejection.** The risk of incorrect acceptance is sometimes referred to as *beta risk* or *Type II error;* the risk of incorrect rejection is sometimes referred to as *alpha risk* or *Type I error.* Exhibit G.1 summarizes some of the key characteristics of these risks.

Because the risk of incorrect acceptance results in the auditor issuing an inappropriate opinion on financial statements that are materially misstated, controlling exposure to this risk is of primary importance. Therefore, under DUS, the auditor controls exposure to the risk of incorrect acceptance in determining the appropriate sample size. If auditors wish to take a smaller risk, they must increase their sample size.

How is the level of the risk of incorrect acceptance established? Recall the audit risk model introduced earlier in the text.

$$\text{Audit Risk (AR)} = \text{Risk of Material Misstatement (RMM)}^2 \times \text{Detection Risk (DR)}$$

EXHIBIT G.1 Sampling Risks Associated with Variables Sampling

Sampling Risk	Sample Results	Unknown State of the Population	Loss
Risk of incorrect acceptance	Upper error limit ≤Tolerable error *Conclusion:* Account is fairly stated	Actual misstatement > Tolerable error *Conclusion:* Account is not fairly stated	Effectiveness loss because the auditor will make an incorrect conclusion and issue an inappropriate opinion on the financial statements
Risk of incorrect rejection	Upper error limit > Tolerable error *Conclusion:* Account is not fairly stated	Actual misstatement ≤ Tolerable error *Conclusion:* Account is fairly stated	Efficiency loss because additional transactions or components will be examined*

*If examining the additional transactions or components does *not* eventually result in the auditor making a correct decision, an effectiveness loss also would be incurred for the risk of incorrect rejection. This loss would occur because the auditor is proposing an adjustment to financial statements that are not materially misstated. However, because of the need to provide compelling evidence to the client prior to initiating a financial statement adjustment, these instances are relatively rare in practice.

² *SAS 107* expresses the product of inherent risk and control risk as the *risk of material misstatement.* This standard notes that auditors may choose to make a combined assessment of the risk of material misstatement or separate assessments of inherent risk (IR) and control risk (CR).

This model can be slightly expanded to replace detection risk with the risks associated with the two major types of substantive procedures performed by the auditor: analytical procedures and tests of details. Because these two types of substantive procedures are considered independent, detection risk equals the joint probability of analytical procedures risk (AP) and tests of details risk (TD), resulting in the following expanded audit risk model:

$$AR = RMM \times AP \times TD$$

where

AR = Audit risk (the risk that a material misstatement occurs, is not detected by the client's internal control, and is not detected by the auditor's substantive procedures)

RMM = Risk of material misstatement (IR × CR)

AP = Analytical procedures risk (the risk that the auditor's analytical procedures fail to detect a material misstatement)

TD = Tests of details risk (the risk that the auditor's test of details procedures fail to detect a material misstatement)

Once the auditor has established AR, assessed IR based on the susceptibility of the account balance or class of transactions to misstatement, performed tests of controls to determine the appropriate level of CR, and assessed the effectiveness of analytical procedures to determine AP, the audit risk model can be algebraically manipulated to solve for TD:

$$TD = \frac{AR}{RMM \times AP}$$

TD represents the risk that the auditor's substantive tests of details fail to detect a material misstatement in an account balance or class of transactions. Were this risk to occur, the auditor would conclude that the account balance or class of transactions was fairly stated when, in fact, it was misstated. This risk is similar in both concept and effect to the *risk of incorrect acceptance*. Thus, the auditor establishes the level of the risk of incorrect acceptance *after* defining the remaining components of the audit risk model and "solving" the expanded audit risk model for TD. Exhibit G.2 is taken from *SAS 111* (¶ 11) as a guideline for determining the appropriate risk of incorrect acceptance for tests of details (TD) given the auditor's assessment of risk of material misstatement and analytical procedures risk.

EXHIBIT G.2 Allowable Risk of Incorrect Acceptance (TD) for Various Assessments of RMM and AP; for AR = .05

	TD			
	AP[2]			
RMM[1]	10%	30%	50%	100%
10%	*	*	*	50%
30%	*	55%	33%	16%
50%	*	33%	20%	10%
100%	50%	16%	10%	5%

[1]Auditor's subjective assessment of risk of material misstatement.
[2]Auditor's subjective assessment of risk that substantive analytical procedures and other relevant substantive procedures might fail to detect aggregate misstatements equal to tolerable misstatement.

*The allowable level of AR of 5 percent exceeds the product of RMM and AP, and, thus, the planned test of details may not be necessary unless specified by regulation or other standards (e.g., confirmation or inventory observation procedures).

Note: The table entries for TD are computed from the illustrated model: TD equals AR/(RMM × AP). For example, for RMM = .50, AP = .30, TD = .05/(.50 × .30) or .33 (equals 33%).

EXHIBIT G.3 Factors Influencing Sample Sizes for a Test of Details in Sample Planning

	Conditions Leading to		
Factor	**Smaller Sample Size**	**Larger Sample Size**	**Related Factor for Substantive Sample Planning**
a. Assessment of risk of material misstatement	Low assessed level of risk of material misstatement	High assessed level of risk of material misstatement	Allowable risk of incorrect acceptance
b. Assessment of risk for other substantive procedures related to the same assertion (including substantive analytical procedures and other relevant substantive procedures)	Low assessment of risk associated with other relevant substantive procedures	High assessment of risk associated with other relevant substantive procedures	Allowable risk of incorrect acceptance.
c. Measure of tolerable misstatement for a specific account	Larger measure of tolerable misstatement	Smaller measure of tolerable misstatement	Tolerable misstatement
d. Expected size and frequency	Smaller misstatements or lower frequency	Larger misstatements or higher frequency	Assessment of population of characteristics
e. Number of items in the population	Virtually no effect on sample size unless population is very small		
f. Choice between statistical and nonstatistical sampling	Ordinarily, sample sizes are comparable		

Exhibit G.3 *(SAS 111, Table 2)* illustrates the relationships between the various factors that affect sample size in variables sampling.

For the examination of Rice's accounts receivable, assume that the auditor controls audit risk (AR) to relatively low levels (0.05, or 5 percent). In addition, because of the susceptibility of accounts receivable to misstatement in the absence of internal control, assume that inherent risk (IR) is assessed at the maximum level (1.00, or 100 percent). Next, assume that the auditor's study and evaluation of internal control yielded a moderate assessment of control risk (0.50, or 50 percent). Finally, assume that the auditor decided not to employ extensive or highly effective analytical procedures; as a result, analytical procedures risk (AP) is assessed at the maximum level (1.00, or 100 percent). Using these assessments, the necessary level of the risk of incorrect acceptance is 10 percent, calculated as shown:

$$TD = \frac{AR}{RMM \times AP}$$

$$TD = \frac{0.05}{0.50 \times 1.00}$$

$$TD = 0.10, \text{ or } 10 \text{ percent}$$

How does the sample size vary with changes in the necessary level of the risk of incorrect acceptance? Logically, if the auditor wants to reduce exposure to sampling risk, the necessary sample size increases. Recall that sampling risk occurs when the sample selected by the auditor is not representative of the population from which it is drawn. As the sample size increases, the likelihood that the sample is representative of the population increases. Therefore, sample size varies inversely with sampling risk (in this instance, TD risk).

Tolerable Error

The level of **tolerable error** is the maximum amount by which the account balance or class of transactions can be misstated without the auditor insisting on an adjusting entry. Logically, as the amount of tolerable error decreases, the necessary sample size increases because a larger number of transactions or components could ultimately result in materially misstated financial statements. Therefore, tolerable error has an *inverse relationship* with sample size.

The auditor assesses tolerable error judgmentally after considering the recorded balance of the account or class of transactions as well as the relationship between the account balance or class of transactions with important financial statement subtotals (such as total assets, total sales, and net income). Auditors normally estimate tolerable error after calculating overall financial statement materiality and allocating that materiality among various account balances and classes of transactions. This is done so that, when the results of all audit procedures across various account balances and classes of transactions are aggregated, the overall level of financial statement materiality is maintained. In the audit of Rice's accounts receivable, assume that the auditor assessed tolerable error at $10,000 (or 3.33 percent of the recorded balance of $300,000). This is consistent with rules of thumb commonly used in practice such as assessing materiality at between 1 and 5 percent of asset balances.

Expected Error

The **expected error** is the amount of misstatement the auditor anticipates in the account balance or class of transactions. The auditor's estimate of expected error is ordinarily based on prior experience with the client, that is, the amount by which misstatements have been identified in specific accounts in prior audits. Unless the client has changed its method of processing and recording transactions, the auditor's experience in prior audits is ordinarily a good indicator of what to expect in the current year. If the engagement is a first-year engagement, the auditor can estimate the expected error based either on a small preliminary sample (referred to as a *pilot sample*) or on experience with other clients in the same industry.

Recall that DUS should be used when a small number of misstatements are expected. Therefore, if the expected error is large relative to the tolerable error, the auditor may consider another form of variables sampling such as classical variables sampling. For the audit of Rice's accounts receivable, the auditor estimates an expected error of $4,000. This estimate is based on the percentage of misstatements that have been observed in prior audits of Rice.

How does expected error affect sample size? It seems reasonable to surmise that, as the expected error increases (particularly in relation to tolerable error), the auditor increases the level of assurance provided by substantive procedures. To do so, a larger number of components or transactions would be examined (i.e., the necessary sample size increases). Therefore, expected error has a *direct relationship* with sample size.

As noted in Module E, the *precision* (or *allowance for sampling risk*) is the numeric distance from the estimated population value in which the true (but unknown) population value may lie with a given probability. For planning purposes, the difference between the tolerable error and the expected error can be viewed as a form of planning precision. Considering the joint effects of the tolerable error and expected error as the difference between the tolerable error and expected error is lower (which could reflect either a higher expected error, a lower tolerable error, or both), the auditor's sample estimate needs to be more precise, which requires a higher sample size.

Population Size

One of the unique characteristics of DUS is that the sampling unit is defined as a dollar in an account balance or class of transactions. Thus, Rice's accounts receivable amount of $300,000 is characterized as a population size of 300,000 one-dollar items. Logically, as

EXHIBIT G.4 Reliability Factors for Risk of Incorrect Acceptance

Number of Overstatement Errors	Risk of Incorrect Acceptance								
	1%	5%	10%	15%	20%	25%	30%	37%	50%
0	4.61	3.00	2.31	1.90	1.61	1.39	1.21	1.00	0.70
1	6.64	4.75	3.89	3.38	3.00	2.70	2.44	2.14	1.68
2	8.41	6.30	5.33	4.72	4.28	3.93	3.62	3.25	2.68
3	10.05	7.76	6.69	6.02	5.52	5.11	4.77	4.34	3.68
4	11.61	9.16	8.00	7.27	6.73	6.28	5.90	5.43	4.68
5	13.11	10.52	9.28	8.50	7.91	7.43	7.01	6.49	5.68
6	14.57	11.85	10.54	9.71	9.08	8.56	8.12	7.56	6.67
7	16.00	13.15	11.78	10.90	10.24	9.69	9.21	8.63	7.67
8	17.41	14.44	13.00	12.08	11.38	10.81	10.31	9.68	8.67
9	18.79	15.71	14.21	13.25	12.52	11.92	11.39	10.74	9.67
10	20.15	16.97	15.41	14.42	13.66	13.02	12.47	11.79	10.67

Source: American Institute of Certified Public Accountants, "Audit Sampling," *Audit and Accounting Guide* (New York: AICPA, 2001), p. 97.

EXHIBIT G.5 Expansion Factors for Risk of Incorrect Acceptance

	Risk of Incorrect Acceptance								
	1%	5%	10%	15%	20%	25%	30%	37%	50%
Factor	1.9	1.6	1.5	1.4	1.3	1.25	1.2	1.15	1.10

Source: American Institute of Certified Public Accountants, "Audit Sampling," *Audit and Accounting Guide* (New York: AICPA, 2001), p. 98.

the population size increases, the necessary sample size increases. This represents a *direct relationship* between population size and sample size.

Calculating Sample Size

In DUS, sample size is calculated using the following formula:

$$n = \frac{\text{Recorded balance} \times \text{Reliability Factor}}{\text{Tolerable Error} - (\text{Expected Error} \times \text{Expansion Factor})}$$

The *reliability factor* and *expansion factor* in the preceding formula allow the auditor to explicitly control exposure to the risk of incorrect acceptance. Exhibits G.4 and G.5 provide the reliability factors and expansion factors for various levels of the risk of incorrect acceptance. Determining the appropriate expansion factor is relatively straightforward; simply select the factor corresponding to the risk of incorrect acceptance. With respect to the reliability factor, the auditor should select the reliability factor associated with zero overstatement errors when determining sample size. As you will see later, reliability factors from Exhibit G.4 for more than zero overstatement errors are used in evaluating the sample results.

The sample size for Rice's accounts receivable is calculated as follows. From Exhibit G.4, the reliability factor for a risk of incorrect acceptance of 10 percent and zero overstatement errors is 2.31; from Exhibit G.5, the expansion factor corresponding to a risk of incorrect acceptance of 10 percent is 1.50.

$$n = \frac{\text{Recorded Balance} \times \text{Reliability Factor}}{\text{Tolerable Error} - (\text{Expected Error} \times \text{Expansion Factor})}$$

$$n = \frac{\$300,000 \times 2.31}{\$10,000 - (\$4,000 \times 1.50)} = 173.25 \text{ items, or } 174 \text{ items (round up)}$$

EXHIBIT G.6 **Comparison of Reliability and Expansion Factors for Different Risks of Incorrect Acceptance**

Factor	5%	10%	Explanation
Reliability factor (Exhibit G.4) (assuming zero overstatement errors)	3.00	2.31	Higher reliability factor in numerator of formula for lower risk of incorrect acceptance provides a larger numerator, resulting in a larger sample size
Expansion factor (Exhibit G.5)	1.60	1.50	Higher expansion factor in denominator of formula for lower risk of incorrect acceptance provides a smaller denominator, resulting in a larger sample size

At this point, 174 items would be selected for examination (sample size should always be rounded up). The method of selecting these items is discussed in the following subsection.

An examination of the preceding formula should make clear how the population size (recorded balance) (*direct relationship*), tolerable error (*inverse relationship*), and expected error (*direct relationship*) influence sample size through their effects on the size of the numerator and denominator. The influence of the risk of incorrect acceptance is less clear and is exhibited through the reliability and expansion factors. Comparing the reliability and expansion factors for 5 and 10 percent risks of incorrect acceptance illustrates the *inverse relationship* between the risk of incorrect acceptance and sample size, as summarized in Exhibit G.6.

Review Checkpoints

G.7 What are the two sampling risks associated with variables sampling? What types of losses are associated with each of these risks?

G.8 How does the auditor determine the acceptable level of the risk of incorrect acceptance? What is the relationship between this risk and sample size?

G.9 How does the auditor determine tolerable error? What is the relationship between tolerable error and sample size?

G.10 How does the auditor determine expected error? What is the relationship between expected error and sample size?

G.11 In a DUS application, how is the population size defined? What is the relationship between population size and sample size?

DUS: Selecting the Sample

When using DUS, the auditor normally selects the sample using a *systematic random selection* method. When a systematic method is used, the auditor determines a random starting point within the population, which represents the first item selected. The auditor then bypasses a fixed number of items in the population and selects the next item for examination. This process is continued until the number of sampling units equal to the necessary sample size has been selected.

One unique feature of using systematic random selection in DUS is that the sampling unit is defined as *an individual dollar within an account balance*. However, it is not reasonable for the auditor to examine only a dollar of a customer's account balance; the entire balance should be verified. Thus, the auditor examines the **logical unit** that contains the individual sampling unit that is selected for examination. In this case, the logical unit is the individual customer's account; however, it could be an item of inventory, an account payable to a specific vendor, or any other component of an account balance or class of transactions.

To select a DUS sample, the auditor calculates a **sampling interval** by dividing the recorded account balance by the necessary sample size. In the examination of Rice's accounts receivable, recall that its accounts receivable were recorded at $300,000 and that the auditor determined a necessary sample size of 174 items. The sampling interval is $1,724, as follows (the sampling interval should be rounded down to achieve the necessary sample size):

$$\text{Sampling Interval} = \frac{\text{Population Size (recorded balance)}}{\text{Sample Size}}$$

$$= \frac{\$300,000}{174}$$

$$= \$1,724 \text{ (rounded)}$$

Thus, the auditor will examine every 1,724th dollar of Rice's accounts receivable. Recall that the tolerable error for Rice's accounts receivable was assessed at $10,000. As a result, the auditor will examine every customer account that would be material to the financial statements taken as a whole. This is an explicit advantage of DUS because it results in larger dollar components of an account balance or class of transactions having a higher likelihood of selection. In contrast, if the auditor randomly selected 174 customer accounts (of the 1,500 individual accounts) for examination, no guarantee exists that the larger dollar accounts would be selected.

Exhibit G.7 illustrates the selection of the first few items from Rice's accounts receivable. (In practice, assuming that the client maintains its records in computerized form, the selection would be done using computer software.)

The following should be noted in reviewing Exhibit G.7:

- The Account column refers to individual customer accounts. Note that Rice's accounts receivable are comprised of 1,500 individual customer accounts.

- The balance in each account is listed in the Account Balance column. These are the logical units that the auditor will examine if a dollar within those balances is selected for examination.

EXHIBIT G.7
DUS Sample Selection of Customer Accounts for Rice, Inc.

Account	Account Balance	Cumulative Balance	Dollar Selected
1	$ 126	$ 126	
2	819	945	600
3	1,411	2,356	2,324
4	75	2,431	
5	92	2,523	
6	204	2,727	
7	3,817	6,544	4,048
		5,772	
8	315	6,859	
9	271	7,130	
10	1,000	8,130	7,496
11	448	8,578	
12	983	9,561	9,220
13	121	9,682	
14	406	10,088	
15	1,651	11,739	10,944
16	339	12,078	
*	*	*	
*	*	*	
1,500	$ 687	$300,000	

- The Cumulative Balance column is simply a running total of the account balances. Note that Rice's accounts receivable are recorded at $300,000.
- The Dollar Selected column reflects a random start of 600 and a sampling interval of 1,724. Each entry in this column is determined by adding the sampling interval to the preceding entry. These are the individual dollar units selected for examination.

If a dollar within an account balance is selected, the logical unit (i.e., customer account balance) is selected for examination. For example, using a random start of 600, the auditor would examine the 600th dollar of the population. In Exhibit G.7, note that Account 2 (recorded at $819) contains dollars 127 through 945. Because this account contains the 600th dollar, the auditor examines the entire account. As noted previously in this module, one of the limitations of DUS is that special considerations must be made to examine logical units with a zero or negative balance.

Two other important points can be observed in Exhibit G.7:

1. DUS tends to select larger dollar transactions or components for examination. Note that the use of DUS selected for examination the six largest dollar account balances shown in Exhibit G.7. While DUS will not always select the largest dollar transactions or components, it provides a relatively high probability that these components will be selected. (Any account larger than the sampling interval has a 100 percent chance of selection.)
2. Account 7, recorded at $3,817, was selected "twice." This phenomenon can occur in DUS when individual logical units (i.e., accounts) are larger than the sampling interval. In these cases, the auditor counts this account as two selections and continues. As a result, the actual number of logical units examined under DUS can be smaller than the determined sample size.

DUS: Measuring Sample Items

Once the sample items have been selected, the auditor performs the appropriate substantive procedure and measures the sample items. In the examination of Rice's accounts receivable, the auditor sends a confirmation to the customers whose accounts were selected for examination and performs any additional follow-up procedures to verify discrepancies noted by the customers or perform alternative procedures for confirmations not returned by customers. After all procedures were performed, the auditor noted three misstatements, which are summarized in Exhibit G.8.[3]

The *audited value* is the amount at which the logical unit would have been recorded, assuming no misstatements or misapplications of generally accepted accounting principles. The **tainting percentage** represents the percentage by which the account is misstated. It is determined by dividing the difference between the recorded balance and the audited value by the recorded balance.

Note that the actual misstatement detected in Rice's accounts receivable is $2,125. This amount is less than the tolerable error of $10,000, but the auditor has not considered misstatements that could exist within the accounts that have not been examined. Projecting these misstatements across the population is the final step of DUS (evaluating sample results).

EXHIBIT G.8
Misstatements Noted in Examination of Rice, Inc.'s Accounts Receivable

Account	Recorded Balance	Audited Value	Difference	Tainting Percentage
10	$1,000	$ 900	$ 100	10%
598	3,840	1,920	1,920	50
1139	525	420	105	20
			$2,125	

[3] The misstatements shown in Exhibit G.8 include only overstatements (i.e., situations in which the recorded balance exceeds the audited value). While DUS is most useful in detecting overstatement errors, it can be extended to include understatement errors. We discuss treatment of understatements later in the module.

Measuring sample items is the point at which *nonsampling risk* can be encountered. Recall that nonsampling risk is the probability that an inappropriate conclusion is reached for reasons other than the representativeness of the sample. For example, the auditor could fail to note exceptions indicated by Rice's customers on their accounts receivable confirmations or could perform inappropriate substantive procedures that fail to detect misstatements that exist in the sample accounts.

Review Checkpoints

G.12 Describe the process used to select a DUS sample. Why does this process tend to select larger dollar components or transactions for examination?

G.13 What is the *sampling interval?* How is it calculated?

G.14 How does the auditor proceed if one logical unit contains two separate dollar selections?

G.15 What is the *audited value* of a transaction or component of an account balance or class of transactions?

G.16 What is the *tainting percentage?* How is it calculated?

DUS: Evaluating Sample Results

LEARNING OBJECTIVE

4. Evaluate the sample results for a DUS sample by calculating the projected misstatement, incremental allowance for sampling risk, and basic allowance for sampling risk.

At this point, the auditor has performed the following major steps in the audit of Rice's accounts receivable:

1. Made the following preliminary assessments prior to beginning the sampling process:

 a. Determined that Rice's accounts receivable were recorded at $300,000 and were comprised of 1,500 individual customer accounts.

 b. Assessed the exposure to audit risk at 5 percent, inherent risk at 100 percent, control risk at 50 percent, and analytical procedures risk at 100 percent.

 c. Assessed expected error at $4,000 and tolerable error at $10,000.

 d. Based on the assessments of audit risk, inherent risk, control risk, and analytical procedures risk, determined a risk of incorrect acceptance of 10 percent.

2. Using assessments of expected error, tolerable error, population size, and the risk of incorrect acceptance, determined a sample size of 174 items.

3. Based on the sample size of 174 items and the population size of $300,000, calculated a sampling interval of $1,724 ($300,000 ÷ 174).

4. Using systematic random selection, identified 174 dollar units and examined the related logical unit (customer account balance) through accounts receivable confirmation and follow-up procedures.

5. Through the substantive procedures performed in step 4, identified three misstatements totaling $2,125 (see Exhibit G.8).

As with all statistical sampling applications, the auditor must now adjust the detected misstatements to control for exposure to the risk of incorrect acceptance. This process requires the auditor to calculate a conservative estimate of the total misstatement composed of three separate components: projected misstatement, incremental allowance for sampling risk, and basic allowance for sampling risk.

Projected Misstatement

The **projected misstatement** assumes that the entire sampling interval contains the same percentage of misstatement as the item examined by the auditor. Recall that in DUS, the auditor selects individual dollars and examines the logical unit (in this case, the customer account balance) containing that unit. Note that, if the logical unit is less than the sampling interval, some portion of that interval remains unexamined by the

EXHIBIT G.9
Calculation of
Projected Misstatement
for Rice, Inc.'s
Accounts Receivable

Account	Difference	Tainting Percentage		Sampling Interval		Projected Misstatement
10	$ 100	10%	×	$1,724	=	$ 172.40
598	1,920	50	×	N/A	=	1,920.00
1139	105	20	×	1,724	=	344.80
	$2,125				=	$2,437.20

auditor. Therefore, one reasonable approach is to assume that the remainder of the sampling interval contains the same percentage of misstatement as the item the auditor examined.

From Exhibit G.8, you can see that the auditor detected three misstatements. Exhibit G.9 illustrates how these misstatements are projected to the sampling interval from which they were drawn.

While the calculations in Exhibit G.9 are straightforward, note that the misstatement related to account 598 is not projected to the sampling interval in the same manner as the other two misstatements. Why? Recall from Exhibit G.8 that this account has a recorded balance of $3,840 and an audited value of $1,920. Because the recorded balance is larger than the sampling interval, there is no need to project the misstatement to the sampling interval. As a result, the projected misstatement for this particular account would equal the actual misstatement detected by the auditor.

Incremental Allowance for Sampling Risk

The calculation of the projected misstatement in Exhibit G.9 assumes that the remainder of the sampling interval is misstated to the same extent (based on the tainting percentage) as the item examined by the auditor. Of course, the remainder of the interval could be misstated to a greater extent, lesser extent, or same extent as the item examined. To control exposure to sampling risk, the auditor calculates an adjustment to the projected misstatement that uses the reliability factors shown in Exhibit G.3. This adjustment is referred to as the **incremental allowance for sampling risk** and is calculated as follows:

1. For all projected misstatements where the recorded value is less than the sampling interval, rank the projected misstatements in descending order based on the dollar amount.

2. For each misstatement in step 1, determine the incremental reliability factor associated with the discovery of the misstatement. For example, recall that zero overstatement errors were assumed in calculating the sample size for Rice's accounts receivable. The reliability factor associated with zero overstatement errors and a 10 percent risk of incorrect acceptance from Exhibit G.3 is 2.31; for one overstatement error, the factor is 3.89. As a result, the *incremental reliability factor* for the discovery of the first overstatement error is 1.58 (3.89 − 2.31). The incremental reliability factor for the second overstatement error is 1.44 (5.33 − 3.89).

3. For each misstatement in steps 1 and 2, multiply the projected misstatement by the incremental reliability factor minus 1.00 (subtracting 1.00 accounts for the fact that the misstatement has already been projected over the sampling interval when determining the projected misstatement).[4] For projected misstatements where the recorded value is greater than or equal to the sampling interval, no incremental allowance for sampling risk needs to be determined because the projected misstatement exceeds the sampling interval.

[4] Alternatively, the auditor could multiply the projected misstatement by the incremental reliability factor and subtract the projected misstatement from this same amount. This calculation yields the same result as that illustrated in Exhibit G.10.

EXHIBIT G.10
Calculation of
Incremental Allowance
for Sampling Risk for
Rice, Inc.'s Accounts
Receivable

Account	Projected Misstatement		Incremental Reliability Factor		Allowance for Sampling Risk
1139	$344.80	×	0.58 (1.58 − 1.00)	=	$199.98
10	172.40	×	0.44 (1.44 − 1.00)	=	75.86
Incremental allowance for sampling risk					$275.84

The calculation of the incremental allowance for sampling risk for Rice's accounts receivable is shown in Exhibit G.10. The incremental allowance for sampling risk attempts to control for the possibility that the misstatements detected in items examined by the auditor were not representative of the misstatements in the remainder of the sampling interval that was not examined by the auditor.

Basic Allowance for Sampling Risk

Both the projected misstatement and the incremental allowance for sampling risk apply to sampling intervals in which the auditor's substantive procedures revealed a misstatement. However, what about those sampling intervals in which no misstatement was discovered? For example, assume that the auditor examined customer account 627 (recorded at $200) and found no misstatement. Is it reasonable to conclude that the entire sampling interval of $1,724 represented by account 627 contained no misstatements? To respond to this matter, the auditor calculates a **basic allowance for sampling risk** in an that attempt to provide a statistical measure of the misstatement that could be included in sampling intervals in which the auditor did not detect a misstatement.

While the philosophy behind the calculation of the basic allowance for sampling risk is somewhat technical, the calculation is relatively straightforward. To calculate the basic allowance for sampling risk, multiply the sampling interval by the reliability factor for the risk of incorrect acceptance. The reliability factor corresponding to zero overstatement errors is selected because these sampling intervals did not contain an overstatement error. The basic allowance for sampling risk for Rice's accounts receivable is calculated as follows:

$$\text{Basic Allowance for Sampling Risk} = \text{Sampling Interval} \times \text{Reliability Factor}$$
$$= \$1,724 \times 2.31$$
$$= \$3,982.44$$

Note that the basic allowance for sampling risk would be calculated in all instances even when the auditor detected no misstatements.

Upper Error Limit

The **upper error limit** is the sum of the three components discussed in this subsection: the projected misstatement, the incremental allowance for sampling risk, and the basic allowance for sampling risk. The upper error limit is the amount that has a (1 − *risk of incorrect acceptance*) probability of equaling or exceeding the true amount of misstatement in the population. Stated another way, there is a (*risk of incorrect acceptance*) probability that the true amount of misstatement in the population exceeds the upper error limit.

How do auditors use the upper error limit? They compare this measure to the amount of tolerable error, as follows:

Upper error limit ≤ Tolerable error ⟶ Accept account balance as fairly recorded

Upper error limit > Tolerable error ⟶ Conclude that account balance is not fairly recorded*

*As noted previously in this module, the auditor ordinarily chooses to perform additional substantive procedures prior to recommending that the client adjust the account balance.

Calculating the upper error limit for Rice, Inc.'s accounts receivable, we find

Projected misstatement	$2,437.20
Incremental allowance for sampling risk	275.84
Basic allowance for sampling risk	3,982.44
Upper error limit	$6,695.48

The upper error limit comprises

- Actual misstatements detected totaling $2,125.
- An additional projection of those misstatements to the sampling interval of $312.20 (projected misstatement of $2,437.20 – actual misstatements of $2,125.00).
- A total allowance for sampling risk of $4,258.28 (incremental allowance for sampling risk of $275.84 + basic allowance for sampling risk of $3,982.44).

Based on the upper error limit, the auditor would conclude that the true misstatement in accounts receivable has a 90 percent chance (1 minus the risk of incorrect acceptance of 10 percent) of being less than or equal to $6,695.48. Conversely, the true misstatement in accounts receivable has a 10 percent chance (risk of incorrect acceptance of 10 percent) of being more than $6,695.48.

Because the tolerable error for accounts receivable is $10,000, the audit team would accept the account balance as fairly stated. In so doing, they have controlled the risk of incorrect acceptance to a level of 10 percent. The audit team ordinarily accumulates the three known misstatements and recommends that the client adjust the financial statements to reflect these misstatements. The audit team also will investigate the causes of all the errors to ensure they do not represent a lack of controls or pattern of fraud. Despite the fact that the account balance is not materially misstated, generally accepted auditing standards require auditors to accumulate these misstatements and communicate them to those charged with governance and include them in the management representation letter.

What would have occurred if the upper error limit had exceeded $10,000? For example, assume that the upper error limit was calculated as $14,500. In this situation, the audit team would conclude that the true misstatement in the population had a 90 percent chance of being less than or equal to $14,500, which does not allow them to conclude that the account balance is fairly stated. In this instance, one of two options exists:

1. The audit team could increase the sample size and examine additional items. These additional items would effectively reduce the sampling interval used, reducing the projected misstatement, incremental allowance for sampling risk, and basic allowance for sampling risk. If enough additional items are examined and no misstatements are detected, the recalculated upper error limit could fall below the tolerable error of $10,000. If so, the auditor could conclude that the financial statements were not materially misstated.

2. The audit team could recommend adjustment to the recorded balance of the client's accounts receivable. With an upper error limit of $14,500, an adjustment of $4,500 would result in a revised upper error limit of $10,000 ($14,500 – $4,500). This revised upper error limit allows the auditor to conclude that the account balance is fairly stated at a risk of incorrect acceptance of 10 percent.

In any event, the audit team would likely recommend that the client review all similar accounts to ensure that they did not contain the same type of misstatement as that found in the sampling procedures. Most clients will voluntarily review their accounts in this manner if they suspect misstatements.

Exhibit G.11 summarizes the important components of the upper error limit.

Understatements

As we stated before, DUS is used primarily to detect overstatements. However, in practice there are often instances where an understatement would be detected along with the overstatements. One common method for including understatements in the evaluation of

EXHIBIT G.11
Summary of Components of Upper Error Limit

1. Assume the entire sampling interval is misstated to the same extent as logical unit selected (includes actual misstatements identified). ⟶ Projected misstatement

2. Consider the possibility that sampling intervals in which misstatements were identified are misstated to a greater extent than the logical unit selected. ⟶ Incremental allowance for sampling risk

3. Assume some misstatement in sampling intervals in which logical unit was not misstated. ⟶ Basic allowance for sampling risk

EXHIBIT G.12
Calculation of Projected Misstatement for Rice, Inc.'s Accounts Receivable Understatement

Account	Difference	Tainting Percentage		Sampling Interval		Projected Misstatement
573	$500	50%	×	$1,724	=	$862.00

results of a DUS sample is to simply subtract the projected understatement caused by the detected error from the upper error limit calculated based on overstatements found and the basic allowance for sampling risk. Thus, if Rice, Inc.'s auditors found that, in addition to the errors discussed above, account 573 also was understated by $500, they would project the understatement error as shown in Exhibit G.12.

The net upper error limit would then be the upper error limit calculated previously ($6,695.48.) less the projected understatement of $862.00, or $6195.48. This is a conservative estimate of the upper error limit because it does not consider an allowance for sampling risk for the understatement.[5]

Qualitative Evaluation of Errors

The preceding discussion focuses on calculating the upper error limit and comparing this upper error limit to the tolerable error. However, it is important that the auditor also consider the nature of the misstatements discovered during the DUS process. Very specifically, any misstatements that indicate fraudulent activity on the part of the client (for example, an intentional overstatement of a customer's account or the creation of a fictitious account) have additional implications for the audit examination and should be discussed with the client and those charged with governance.

Review Checkpoints

G.17 Identify the three components of the upper error limit. How is each component calculated?

G.18 Why are misstatements in logical units that are larger than the sampling interval not projected over the sampling interval?

G.19 What is the *upper error limit?* What information does it provide the auditor?

G.20 What options are available to the auditor if the upper error limit exceeds the tolerable error?

[5] If the auditor added an allowance for sampling risk for the understatement, the risk of incorrect acceptance would be somewhat higher than 10 percent. D. M. Roberts, *Statistical Auditing* (New York: AICPA, 1978).

CLASSICAL VARIABLES SAMPLING

5. Understand the basic process underlying *classical variables sampling* and the use of classical variables sampling in an audit examination.

When performing substantive procedures, an alternative approach to DUS is classical variables sampling. Classical variables sampling methods use normal distribution theory and the Central Limit Theorem to provide an estimated range of either the recorded balance of the account balance or class of transactions or the misstatement in the account balance or class of transactions. The Central Limit Theorem indicates that, because larger sample sizes provide a sampling distribution that more closely reflects a normal distribution, larger sample sizes will yield a lower level of sampling risk. The auditor then uses these estimates to determine whether the account balance or class of transactions is fairly stated.

Classical variables sampling methods are typically employed less frequently in practice than DUS methods. This section briefly illustrates one form of classical variables sampling, **mean-per-unit estimation.** As with the DUS example in the preceding section, we illustrate the manual calculations necessary to determine sample size and evaluate sample results. However, if the client maintains its records in computerized form, the auditor typically uses computer software to perform these tasks.

Classical Variables Sampling: Planning

In the planning stages of classical variables sampling, the auditor determines the objective of sampling, defines the attribute of interest, and defines the population as in DUS. We continue to use the basic information from the examination of Rice, Inc.'s accounts receivable introduced in the previous section. Recall that Rice's accounts receivable are comprised of 1,500 individual customer accounts and are recorded at $300,000. Also recall that the auditor is interested in evaluating the existence and valuation and allocation assertions and that the following assessments or judgments have been made prior to selecting individual customer accounts for confirmation:

- Overall exposure to audit risk = 5 percent.
- Inherent risk for the assertions = 100 percent.
- Control risk related to the assertions = 50 percent.
- Analytical procedures risk related to the assertions = 100 percent.
- Risk of incorrect acceptance = 10 percent (based on preceding risks).
- Expected error = $4,000.
- Tolerable error = $10,000.

One issue that arises under classical variables sampling is whether certain items should be included in the population to be sampled. For example, suppose that Rice's five largest customer balances totaled $120,000 and that all of these balances were larger than the $10,000 tolerable error. Also assume that no other customer had a balance larger than $2,000. What should the auditor do? Obviously, he would like to examine the five large balances separately because they comprise 40 percent ($120,000 ÷ $300,000) of the recorded balance of accounts receivable and each of these items is an *individually significant item* (that is, each item exceeds the tolerable error). The auditor would then sample from among the remaining 1,495 accounts, none of which is individually significant.

When using classical variables sampling, the auditor can reduce the variability of the population and ensure the selection of individually significant items by subdividing the population into different (more homogenous) groups based on account size. This process of subdivision is known as **stratification.** It is useful because it permits the auditor to reduce the necessary sample size in a classical variables sampling application. It accomplishes this by reducing the variability within each stratum. Stratification also allows auditors to give more attention to high-dollar items. In the preceding scenario, the auditor could break the population into two subgroups, or **strata:** the five large-dollar accounts and the remaining 1,495 customer accounts.

Classical Variables Sampling: Determining Sample Size

The formula for calculating sample size using mean-per-unit estimation is

$$n = \left(\frac{N \times [R(IR) + R(IA)] \times SD}{TE - EE} \right)^2$$

where

n = Sample size

N = Population size (number of accounts)

$R(IR)$ = Reliability factor for the risk of incorrect rejection

$R(IA)$ = Reliability factor for the risk of incorrect acceptance

SD = Standard deviation

TE = Tolerable error

EE = Expected error

The remainder of this section focuses on the two new factors that are considered in classical variables sampling but not DUS: the risk of incorrect rejection and standard deviation. Discussion of the determination of the remaining factors and their effects on sample size can be found in the section on DUS contained in this module.

Risk of Incorrect Rejection

Unlike DUS, classical variables sampling explicitly considers the risks of both incorrect acceptance and incorrect rejection in determining sample size. The risk of incorrect rejection is the probability that the auditor will conclude that the account balance is materially misstated when, in fact, it is fairly stated. As with any sampling risk, lower levels of the risk of incorrect rejection would result in an increase in the necessary sample size. That is, the risk of incorrect rejection has an *inverse relationship* with sample size, similar to that for the risk of incorrect acceptance shown in Exhibit G.2.

Remember that the risk of incorrect rejection results in an efficiency loss to the auditor because prior to proposing an adjustment to the financial statements, the auditor would ordinarily expand the sample to include additional components or transactions. The key question of interest to the auditor in assessing the level of exposure to the risk of incorrect rejection is related to the *efficiency loss* that this risk causes; that is, what is the cost to the auditor of expanding the sample? In some cases, the auditor can quickly and inexpensively select additional items; if so, it would be more cost efficient to examine a smaller initial sample and subsequently select additional items if necessary. This smaller initial sample would be achieved by assessing a higher level of the risk of incorrect rejection.

In contrast, if the cost of expanding the sample is relatively high, the auditor would be concerned about it and would ordinarily choose to assess a lower level of the risk of incorrect rejection. This lower risk would, in turn, result in an increased initial sample size.

How are sampling risks incorporated in the determination of sample size? Exhibit G.13 is a list of reliability factors for various levels of the risk of incorrect rejection and the risk

EXHIBIT G.13
Reliability Factors for Different Levels of Sampling Risk in Classical Variables Sampling

Level of Risk	Risk of Incorrect Rejection	Risk of Incorrect Acceptance
0.01	2.58	2.33
0.05	1.96	1.65
0.10	1.65	1.28
0.15	1.44	1.04
0.20	1.28	0.84

of incorrect acceptance that can be used in classical variables sampling. While the determination of these factors is beyond the scope of the text, they represent various areas of observations that fall within a certain number of standard deviations in a normally distributed population.

For Rice, after considering the costs of selecting and confirming additional accounts receivable balances, assume that the auditor assesses the risk of incorrect rejection at 15 percent. (Recall that the risk of incorrect acceptance has been established at 10 percent.)

Standard Deviation

The **standard deviation** represents the variability of the population being examined; it is the average of the squared differences between each item in the population and the population mean. When the population is more variable (i.e., the items composing the population differ more widely with respect to dollar amount), the standard deviation increases. When the standard deviation of dollar amounts is larger, it is more difficult for the auditor to select a representative sample. To do so, the necessary sample size is increased. Thus, the standard deviation has a *direct relationship* with sample size. That is, as the standard deviation increases, the sample size increases.

How can the auditor estimate the standard deviation? In using mean-per-unit estimation, the auditor is interested in knowing the standard deviation of audited values of customer accounts. As with expected error, the auditor can either rely on experience from prior audits or use a small subsample (pilot sample) in the current year. Assume that the sample standard deviation for Rice's accounts receivable is $31 (the standard deviation is easily calculated by using computer software; its calculation is beyond the scope of this text).

Recall that, if the population is highly variable, the auditor can use stratification to reduce the variability of the population. By examining individually significant items and selecting a sample from a stratum of the population with lower variability, the auditor can reduce the necessary sample size.

Calculating Sample Size

At this point, the sample size can be determined as follows:

$$n = \left(\frac{N \times [\text{R(IR)} + \text{R(IA)}] \times \text{SD}}{\text{TE} - \text{EE}} \right)^2$$

$$= \left(\frac{1{,}500 \times (1.44 + 1.28) \times \$31}{\$10{,}000 - \$4{,}000} \right)^2$$

$$= 444.37, \text{ or } 445 \text{ accounts}$$

N (the number of accounts) can be readily determined from the client's records; in this case, Rice's accounts receivable were comprised of 1,500 customer accounts. The factors for R(IR) and R(IA) correspond to a risk of incorrect rejection of 15 percent and risk of incorrect acceptance of 10 percent and are drawn from Exhibit G.13. Based on prior audits, the standard deviation was estimated as $31. Tolerable error was determined based on the recorded account balance and overall financial statement materiality and was established at $10,000. Finally, the auditor judgmentally established the expected error of $4,000 based on prior audits.

Using the preceding formula, if the auditor decided to examine the five individually significant customer account balances and reduce the variability of the remainder of the population from $31 to $26, the sample size for the nonsignificant items would be 311 accounts.[6] Including the five individually significant items, the total sample would be 316. This provides an example of how using stratification can result in a more efficient sample for the auditor.

[6] The sample size formula would be modified by replacing the 1,500 customer accounts with 1,495 and the $31 sample standard deviation with $26.

Review Checkpoints

G.21 Define *classical variables sampling*. How does it provide the auditor evidence as to the fairness of an account balance or class of transactions?

G.22 What is *stratification?* What are the benefits to the auditor of stratifying the sample?

G.23 What is the *standard deviation?* How does it affect the necessary sample size?

G.24 Identify differences between the determination of sample size under classical variables sampling and DUS.

Classical Variables Sampling: Selecting the Sample

One of the basic tenets of statistical sampling methods is that each sampling unit has an equal probability of selection. The sample of Rice's customer accounts could be selected in either of the following ways:

1. Identify 445 random numbers and select the corresponding customer accounts for confirmation (unrestricted random selection).
2. Randomly select a starting point (or a number of starting points) in the population and select every *n*th customer account thereafter for confirmation (systematic random selection).

One very important difference between sample selection under classical variables sampling and DUS is the definition of the sampling unit. Classical variables sampling defines the sampling unit as a logical unit, or customer account balance. As a result, the auditor will select 445 of Rice's 1,500 customer account balances for examination. In contrast, DUS defines the *sampling unit* as an individual dollar of accounts receivable and selects individual dollars for examination. Unlike DUS, classical variables sampling does not ensure that the largest dollar account balances are selected for examination. A one dollar account has an equal probability of being selected as a one million dollar account!

Classical Variables Sampling: Measuring Sample Items

Once the sample size has been determined and the sample has been selected, the auditor measures the sample items. In the audit of accounts receivable, measuring sample items requires the auditor to determine the audited value of the customers' accounts receivable. This will be done using standard accounts receivable confirmation procedures as well as additional procedures necessary to follow up on any discrepancies revealed by the confirmation procedures. The procedures performed in measuring sample items for Rice's accounts receivable under classical variables sampling are identical to those performed under DUS. In addition, as under DUS, this stage could expose the auditor to nonsampling risk if the substantive procedures fail to detect misstatements that exist in sample customer accounts.

Assume that the auditor's examination of the 445 customer accounts receivable revealed a total audited value of $86,775. Therefore, the mean audited value per unit is $195 ($86,775 ÷ 445). In addition, the standard deviation of the audited values is $25.

Classical Variables Sampling: Evaluating Sample Results

Evaluating sample results requires the auditor to determine an overall estimate of the audited balance (based on the mean audited value per unit) and construct an interval of sample estimates that controls the exposure to the risk of incorrect acceptance (10 percent) and risk of incorrect rejection (15 percent). This interval is referred to as the **precision interval**. Once it has been constructed, the auditor's decision rule is as follows:

- Accept the account balance as fairly stated if the distance between the recorded balance and the furthest limit of the precision interval is less than the tolerable error.
- Reject the account balance as fairly stated if the distance between the recorded balance and the furthest limit of the precision interval is greater than the tolerable error.

The first step in the construction of the precision interval is to determine the overall estimate of the audited balance. If the mean audited value of the sample of customer accounts is $195, the auditor's best estimate of the audited balance of the entire account is determined by multiplying $195 by the number of accounts in the population (1,500), or $292,500.

Next the auditor determines the appropriate level of precision. *Precision* represents the closeness of the sample estimate of the account balance to the true value; the determination of precision allows the auditor to construct a precision interval that controls exposure to sampling risk to acceptable levels. The auditor calculates precision using the following formula:

$$\text{Precision} = N \times \text{R(IA)} \times (\text{SD} \div \sqrt{n})$$

where

$$n = \text{Sample size}$$
$$N = \text{Population size (number of accounts)}$$
$$\text{R(IA)} = \text{Reliability factor for the risk of incorrect acceptance}$$
$$\text{SD} = \text{Standard deviation (for items selected for examination)}$$

Recall from the calculation of sample size that the population size is 1,500 customer accounts, the reliability factor for the risk of incorrect acceptance is 1.28, and the sample size is 445. Also, after measuring the sample items, recall that the standard deviation of audited values is $25. The precision is calculated as $2,275:

$$\begin{aligned}
\text{Precision} &= N \times \text{R(IA)} \times (\text{SD} \div \sqrt{n}) \\
&= 1,500 \times 1.28 \times (\$25 \div \sqrt{445}) \\
&= \$2,275
\end{aligned}$$

Once the precision has been calculated, the precision interval can be determined by adding and subtracting it from the sample estimate. The relationship between the sample estimate, precision, and the recorded balance is shown as

The significance of the precision interval is that it has a (1 − *risk of incorrect acceptance*) probability of including the true balance; conversely, the true balance has a (*risk of incorrect acceptance*) probability of falling outside the precision interval. The difference between the recorded balance and the farthest precision estimate ($300,000 − $290,225 = $9,745) is compared to the tolerable error ($10,000). In this case, the population can be accepted as fairly stated. If the precision interval were $3,000, then the lower interval would be $199,500, the distance from the recorded balance would be $10,500, and the population would be rejected, with the auditor's conclusion that the account balance is materially misstated.

As under DUS, the auditor can choose one of two courses of action when the sample evidence suggests that the account balance is materially misstated:

1. The auditor could increase the sample size and examine additional items. If the same percentage of errors is found, the precision would be smaller and the lower precision interval would be higher. Thus, the auditor would be more likely to accept the balance as fairly stated (i.e., the distance from the recorded balance would be more likely to be less than the tolerable error).

2. The auditor could recommend adjustment of the client's accounts receivable. In the rejected case above, the auditor would recommend an adjustment of at least $500 so that the difference between the new recorded balance ($299,500) and the farthest precision estimate would be the tolerable error, $10,000. Often clients would likely investigate all the accounts to determine the exact amount of adjustment required.

Other Approaches to Classical Variables Sampling

This subsection illustrated one approach to classical variables sampling (mean-per-unit estimation). Two other approaches are available to the auditor. **Difference estimation** is used to calculate an average difference between audited values and book values; the audited balance is then estimated by adjusting the recorded account balance by this average difference. **Ratio estimation** determines the ratio of audited values to recorded values and estimates the audited balance by multiplying the recorded balance by this ratio.

Difference estimation and ratio estimation normally provide smaller sample sizes than mean-per-unit estimation because the standard deviations of differences or ratios are typically smaller than the standard deviations associated with mean values. However, these methods require reliable measures of the book value. As a result, mean-per-unit estimation is most frequently employed when a reliable measure of the book value is not available such as following a fraud.

In either case, once the audited balance has been estimated, the auditor proceeds in a similar fashion as with mean-per-unit estimation. The auditor constructs a precision interval around the estimate of the error and identifies whether this precision interval falls within the tolerable error. If so, the account balance is accepted as fairly stated and the auditor has limited the exposure to the risk of incorrect acceptance to acceptable levels. If not, the auditor rejects the account balance as fairly stated and either gathers additional evidence or proposes an adjustment to the account balance.

Because these methods are very similar to mean-per-unit estimation and because DUS methods are used more extensively in practice, further discussion of difference estimation and ratio estimation is beyond the scope of this text.

DUS VERSUS CLASSICAL VARIABLES SAMPLING

This module has discussed two major approaches to variables sampling: DUS and classical variables sampling. These methods differ primarily with respect to determining the necessary sample size, selecting sample items, and evaluating sample results.

When should each be used? Recall that the distinguishing feature of DUS is that it defines the sampling unit as an individual dollar within an account balance or class of transactions. As a result, this method has a tendency to identify large-dollar items for examination. This is a primary benefit associated with the use of DUS. In contrast, classical variables sampling defines the sampling unit as a logical unit (i.e., customer account balance) and will not necessary select large-dollar items for examination.

Compared to classical variables sampling, DUS is most appropriate in these circumstances:

1. Overstatements are of more concern to the auditor (such as the audit of assets and revenues because DUS automatically selects items with larger recorded balances for examination.

2. It is difficult or impractical to estimate the standard deviation because DUS does not use the standard deviation in determining a sample size or evaluating sample results.

3. Zero or few misstatements are anticipated.

4. The population is relatively heterogeneous with respect to the dollar amount of components and a number of relatively large-dollar items exist (i.e., a high level of variation

exists). For example, DUS automatically selects items that are larger than the sampling interval.

In contrast, classical variables sampling should be used when understatements are of concern, the standard deviation can be estimated, misstatements are anticipated, and the population is relatively homogenous with respect to the dollar amount of components.

Review Checkpoints

G.25 How does sample selection under classical variables sampling differ from sample selection under DUS?

G.26 Define *precision* and the *precision interval.* What factors are used to determine the level of precision?

G.27 What is the auditor's decision rule when comparing the recorded balance to the precision interval?

G.28 When selecting a variables sampling approach, when should the auditor use DUS and classical variables sampling?

NONSTATISTICAL SAMPLING

LEARNING OBJECTIVE

6. Understand the basic process underlying nonstatistical sampling and the use of nonstatistical sampling in an audit examination.

To this point, the discussion has focused on statistical sampling methods. The primary advantage of these methods is that they explicitly measure and control the auditor's exposure to sampling risk in determining the sample size and evaluating the sample results. However, it is important to note that generally accepted auditing standards do not require the use of statistical sampling methods. In many cases, it is easier and more efficient to use **nonstatistical sampling methods.**

To illustrate the use of nonstatistical sampling for Rice's accounts receivable, recall that its accounts receivable are comprised of 1,500 individual customer accounts and are recorded at $300,000. Also recall that the auditor is interested in evaluating the *existence* and *valuation and allocation* assertions and that the following assessments or judgments have been made prior to selecting individual customer accounts for confirmation:

- Overall exposure to audit risk = 5 percent.
- Inherent risk for the assertions = 100 percent.
- Control risk related to the assertions = 50 percent.
- Risk of material misstatement = 50 percent ($1.00 \times .50$).
- Analytical procedures risk related to the assertions = 100 percent.
- Risk of incorrect acceptance = 10 percent (based on preceding risks).
- Expected error = $4,000.
- Tolerable error = $10,000.

To determine the sample size under nonstatistical sampling, the AICPA's *Auditing Sampling Guide* provides an assurance factor that reflects the necessary level of assurance required from the auditor's substantive procedures. The assurance required from the auditor's substantive procedures, in turn, depends on the assessments of risk of material misstatement and analytical procedures risk. Exhibit G.14 summarizes the assurance factors for various levels of these risks; note that these factors are based on qualitative rather than quantitative assessments. If the assessment of inherent and control risk is judged to be

EXHIBIT G.14
Assurance Factors for Nonstatistical Sampling

	Risk That Other Substantive Procedures Will Fail to Detect a Misstatement			
Assessment of RMM	Maximum	Slightly Below Maximum	Moderate	Low
Maximum	3.0	2.7	2.3	2.0
Slightly below maximum	2.7	2.4	2.1	1.6
Moderate	2.3	2.1	1.6	1.2
Low	2.0	1.6	1.2	1.0

"moderate" and the risk that other substantive procedures (e.g., analytical procedures) will fail to detect a material misstatement is "maximum," the assurance factor for Rice is 2.3.

The sample size would be calculated as follows:

$$\text{Sample Size} = \frac{\text{Recorded Balance}}{\text{Tolerable Error}} \times \text{Assurance Factor}$$

$$= \frac{\$300,00}{\$10,000} \times 2.3$$

$$= 69 \text{ items}$$

This equation considers three factors in determining the sample size in a nonstatistical sampling application: (1) the recorded balance, (2) the tolerable error, and (3) the risk of incorrect acceptance (by considering risk of material misstatement and analytical procedures risk). These factors have the same relationship with sample size as under either DUS or classical variables sampling. The primary difference is that the auditor has not statistically controlled the exposure to sampling risk.

The auditor then selects a sample of 69 items (account balances) for examination. Under nonstatistical sampling, the auditor can use a *nonprobabilistic selection technique* (such as block selection or haphazard selection); recall that statistical sampling requires the use of probabilistic selection techniques in which all items have an equal probability of being selected. However, the auditor should still make efforts to obtain a representative sample. Once the 69 items are selected, they are measured. If the 69 items had a recorded balance of $10,000 and an audited balance of $9,900, the auditor could estimate the audited balance as follows:

$$\frac{\text{Audited Value of Sample}}{\text{Recorded Balance of Sample}} \times \frac{\text{Recorded Balance}}{\text{of Population}} = \frac{\$9,900}{\$10,000} \times \$300,000 = \$297,000$$

The difference between the recorded balance ($300,000) and the audited balance ($297,000) is $3,000. Because the tolerable error is $10,000, the auditor would conclude that the account balance is fairly stated. One limitation is that, in this particular case, the auditor did not statistically control and is unable to identify the exposure to the risk of incorrect acceptance.

Alternatively, the auditor could choose to evaluate the results by projecting the misstatement to the population based on the number of items examined. For example, the 69 items had a total overstatement of $100, or $1.45 per item ($100 ÷ 69 items). Multiplying this $1.45 per item by the number of items in the population (1,500) yields a projected misstatement of $2,175, which is less than the tolerable error of $10,000. This approach is used when the auditor believes misstatements are related to the number of items instead of their relative size. For example, the client may have omitted a $1.45 shipping charge from each of its sales; if so, it would be logical to assume that each item was misstated by a similar dollar amount.

VARIABLES SAMPLING: DOCUMENTING

As the overview of the seven-step procedure for variables sampling shows, the auditor is required to document various information related to the sampling procedure. The information that would be documented depends on the type of sampling application (DUS, classical variables sampling, or nonstatistical sampling) but generally includes the following:

- Information on the objective of sampling, definition of the characteristic of interest, and definition of the population from which the sample was selected (steps 1–3).
- The parameters used to determine the sample size, which could include sampling risks, tolerable error, expected error, standard deviation of mean values, population size, assessment of inherent risk and control risk, and risk that other substantive procedures will fail to detect a misstatement. In addition to the levels of these factors, the auditor also should document the rationale for these assessments (step 4).
- The sample size determined based on the factors discussed (step 4).
- Information on the selection of sample items and a list of items selected and examined by the auditor (step 5).
- Results of the substantive procedures performed on each item selected (step 6) and the determination of the upper error limit (DUS), precision interval (classical variables sampling), or estimated audited balance (nonstatistical sampling) (step 7).
- The auditor's conclusion with respect to the fairness of the account balance and the effect of this conclusion on the opinion on the financial statements.

Review Checkpoints

G.29 How does nonstatistical sampling differ from statistical sampling?

G.30 What factors affect the size of a sample in a nonstatistical sampling application?

G.31 What information related to variables sampling applications does the auditor typically document?

Summary

This module discusses variables sampling, which the auditor uses in performing substantive procedures. When performing variables sampling, the auditor has the primary objective to determine whether an account balance or class of transactions is fairly stated. As with any sampling application, the auditor is exposed to sampling risk (the risk that the decision made based on the sample differs from the decision that would have been made if the entire population were examined). The auditor controls this sampling risk (referred to as the *risk of incorrect acceptance*) in determining the appropriate sample size and evaluating the sample results. Two primary types of variables sampling plans are dollar unit sampling (DUS) and classical variables sampling.

When using DUS, the auditor calculates an upper error limit. The upper error limit has a (1 – *risk of incorrect acceptance*) probability of equaling or exceeding the true amount of misstatement in the population. If the upper error limit is less than the tolerable error, the auditor would conclude that the account balance is fairly stated; in contrast, if the upper error limit exceeds the tolerable error, the auditor would either propose an adjustment to the account balance or class of transactions or expand the sample. DUS is unique in defining the sampling unit as an individual dollar in an account balance or class of transactions. As a result, DUS tends to select larger dollar components for examination.

Classical variables sampling uses normal distribution theory and the Central Limit Theorem to provide a range of either the recorded balance of the account balance or class of transactions or the misstatement in the account balance or class of transactions. Under mean-per-unit estimation, the auditor identifies a precision interval that has a (1 – *risk of incorrect acceptance*) probability of including the true account balance. If the difference between the recorded account balance and the furthest range of the precision interval falls within the tolerable error, the auditor will conclude that the account balance is fairly stated. Conversely, if the difference between the recorded account balance and the furthest range of the precision interval is greater than the tolerable error, the auditor will conclude that the account balance is materially misstated and would either propose an adjustment to the client or expand the sample.

Key Terms

audited value: The amount at which an account balance or component should be recorded, assuming no departures from generally accepted accounting principles, 742

basic allowance for sampling risk: A component of the upper error limit determined by multiplying the sampling interval by the reliability factor corresponding to the appropriate risk of incorrect acceptance; its calculation acknowledges that sampling intervals can contain some level of misstatement despite the fact that the logical unit drawn from that sampling interval was not misstated, 753

classical variables sampling: A variables sampling method that uses the laws of probability and the Central Limit Theorem to estimate either the amount of misstatement or the "true" balance of an account balance or class of transactions, 740

difference estimation: A classical variables sampling method that bases its calculation of the estimated balance on differences between audited values and recorded values of components of the account balance or class of transactions, 761

dollar unit sampling (DUS): A variables sampling method in which the population is viewed as being composed of individual dollars within an account balance or class of transactions; effective in ensuring that large dollar components are selected for examination, 740

expected error: The amount of misstatement the auditor anticipates in the account balance or class of transactions, 746

incremental allowance for sampling risk: A component of the upper error limit determined by adjusting the projected misstatement for the change in reliability factors resulting from detecting the misstatement; its calculation acknowledges that the sampling interval can be misstated to a greater extent than the logical unit drawn from that sampling interval, 752

logical unit: The component of an account balance or class of transactions containing an individual dollar selected under DUS; can include customer account balances, items of inventory, and accounts payable to specific vendors, 748

mean-per-unit estimation: A classical variables sampling method that bases its calculation of the estimated balance on the average audited values of components of the account balance or class of transactions, 756

nonstatistical sampling methods: Sampling methods that do not attempt to control the auditor's acceptable exposure to sampling risk in determining sample size or evaluating sample results, 762

precision interval: Used in classical variables sampling, an interval of sample estimates that controls the auditor's exposure to the risk of incorrect acceptance and risk of incorrect rejection, 759

projected misstatement: A component of the upper error limit determined by multiplying the sampling interval by the tainting percentage; its calculation assumes that the entire sampling interval is misstated to the same extent as the logical unit drawn from that sampling interval, 751

ratio estimation: A classical variables sampling method that bases its calculation of the estimated balance on the ratio of audited values to recorded values of components of the account balance or class of transactions, 761

risk of incorrect acceptance: The likelihood that the auditor will conclude that the client's account balance is fairly stated when, in fact, it is materially misstated, 743

risk of incorrect rejection: The likelihood that the auditor will conclude that the client's account balance is materially misstated when, in fact, it is fairly stated, 743

sampling interval: Used in DUS to represent the frequency with which sampling units are selected; determined by dividing the recorded amount of the population (account balance) by the sample size, 749

standard deviation: A measure of the variability of the population calculated by summing the squared differences between each item in the population and the population mean, 758

strata: See *stratification*, 756

stratification: Subdividing a population into more homogenous subgroups (or *strata*); reduces the necessary sample size in a classical variables sampling application, 756

tainting percentage: Represents the percentage by which a logical unit is misstated; determined by dividing the amount of the misstatement by the recorded balance, 750

tolerable error: The maximum amount by which the account balance or class of transactions can be misstated without influencing the decisions of third-party users; also known as *materiality*, 746

true balance: The amount at which the client's account balance should be recorded if no misstatements or departures from GAAP existed, 740

upper error limit: The amount that has a $(1 - risk\ of\ incorrect\ acceptance)$ probability of equaling or exceeding the true amount of misstatement in the population, 753

variables sampling: A form of sampling used to examine a population to estimate the amount or value of that population that the auditor uses during substantive procedures, 740

Multiple Choice Questions for Practice and Review

G.32 Which of the following major stages of the audit examination is most closely related to variables sampling?

a. Determining preliminary levels of materiality.

b. Performing tests of controls procedures.

c. Performing substantive procedures.

d. Searching for the possible occurrence of subsequent events.

G.33 Which of the following types of variables sampling plans has a tendency to select larger-dollar items for examination?

a. Difference estimation.

b. Mean-per-unit estimation.

c. Dollar unit sampling.

d. Ratio estimation.

G.34 Variables sampling methods can be used to estimate

	Amount of Misstatement	True Account Balance
a.	Yes	Yes
b.	Yes	No
c.	No	Yes
d.	No	No

G.35 When the audit risk is 0.015, inherent risk is 0.50, control risk is 0.30 (RMM = 0.15), and analytical procedures risk is 0.50, the risk of incorrect acceptance is

a. 0.02.

b. 0.20.

c. 0.50.

d. 2.00.

G.36 When making a decision about the dollar amount in an account balance based on a sample, the auditor considers the risk of incorrect acceptance more serious than the risk of incorrect rejection because

a. The incorrect rejection decision impairs the efficiency of the audit.

b. The auditor will do additional work and discover the error of the incorrect decision.

c. The incorrect acceptance decision impairs the effectiveness of the audit.

d. Sufficient appropriate audit evidence will not have been obtained.

G.37 The unique feature of dollar unit sampling is that

 a. Sampling units are not chosen at random.

 b. A dollar unit selected in a sample is not replaced before the sample selection is completed.

 c. Auditors need not worry about the risk of incorrect acceptance decision error.

 d. The population is defined as the number of dollar units in an account balance or class of transactions.

G.38 When determining sample size under dollar unit sampling, an auditor does not need to make a judgment or estimate of

 a. Audit risk.

 b. Tolerable error.

 c. Expected error.

 d. Standard deviation of error.

G.39 Which of the following statements is correct about dollar unit sampling?

 a. The risk of incorrect acceptance must be specified.

 b. Smaller logical units have a higher probability of selection in the sample than larger units.

 c. Each logical unit in the population has an equally likely chance of being selected in the sample.

 d. The projected misstatement cannot be calculated when one or more misstatements are discovered.

G.40 One of the primary advantages of dollar unit sampling is the fact that

 a. It is an effective method of sampling for evidence of understatement in asset accounts.

 b. The sample selection automatically achieves high-dollar selection and stratification.

 c. The sample selection provides for including a representative number of small-dollar components.

 d. Expanding the sample for additional evidence is very easy.

G.41 Which of the following would not cause the auditor to select a larger sample of items under a dollar unit sampling application?

 a. A reduction in the risk of incorrect acceptance from 10 percent to 5 percent.

 b. An increase in the tolerable error from $30,000 to $60,000.

 c. An increase in the expected error from $20,000 to $40,000.

 d. All of the above would result in selecting a larger sample.

G.42 Assume that an account with a recorded balance of $5,000 has an audited balance of $3,000. Using DUS, if the sampling interval is $1,500, the projected misstatement would be

 a. $600.

 b. $900.

 c. $2,000.

 d. $3,000.

G.43 If the _____ is less than the _____, the auditor would conclude that the account balance is fairly stated.

 a. Projected misstatement; tolerable error.

 b. Tolerable error; projected misstatement.

 c. Upper error limit; tolerable error.

 d. Tolerable error; upper error limit.

G.44 If the upper error limit is calculated at $17,800 and the tolerable error is $15,000, what is the minimum amount of adjustment necessary for the auditor to issue an unqualified opinion on the client's financial statements?

 a. $0.

 b. $2,800.

 c. $15,000.

 d. $17,800.

G.45 Alice Rathermel audited LoHo Company's inventory using sampling. She examined 120 items from an inventory compilation list and discovered net overstatement of $480. The audited items had a book (recorded) value of $48,000. There were 1,200 inventory items listed and the total inventory book amount was $490,000. Which *two* of these calculations are correct using mean-per-unit estimation?

a. Actual misstatement of $480.

b. Actual misstatement of $10,000.

c. Projected misstatement of $10,000.

d. Projected misstatement of $480,000.

G.46 To determine the sample size for a classical variables sampling application, an auditor should consider the tolerable error, risk of incorrect acceptance, risk of incorrect rejection, population size, population variability, and

a. Expected error in the account.

b. Overall materiality for the financial statements taken as a whole.

c. Risk of assessing control risk too low.

d. Risk of assessing control risk too high.

G.47 Which of the following components is *not* used in determining the upper error limit?

a. Basic allowance for sampling risk.

b. Incremental allowance for sampling risk.

c. Projected misstatement.

d. Tolerable error.

G.48 The projected misstatement is determined by multiplying the sampling interval by the

a. Expansion factor.

b. Incremental reliability factor.

c. Reliability factor.

d. Tainting percentage.

G.49 Which of the following steps involved with determining the upper error limit is ordinarily performed *earliest*?

a. Multiply the sampling interval by the tainting percentage.

b. Determine the audited amount of the item and compare it to the recorded amount.

c. Calculate the basic allowance for sampling risk.

d. Calculate the incremental allowance for sampling risk.

G.50 A component of an account balance has a recorded balance of $10,000 and an audited balance of $8,000. Using DUS, if the sampling interval is $20,000, the projected misstatement would be

a. $2,000.

b. $4,000.

c. $5,000.

d. $10,000.

G.51 Which of the following statements is *not* true with respect to the calculation of the upper error limit?

a. The tainting percentage is determined based on the difference between the recorded balance and the audited balance.

b. A separate incremental allowance for sampling risk is calculated for each misstatement discovered by the auditor.

c. If no misstatements are detected, the basic allowance for sampling risk equals zero.

d. The projected misstatement is determined by multiplying the sampling interval by the tainting percentage.

G.52 Which of the following courses of action would an auditor most likely follow in planning a sample of cash disbursements if the auditor is aware of several unusually large cash disbursements?

a. Increase the sample size to reduce the effect of the unusually large disbursements.

b. Continue to draw new samples until all unusually large disbursements appear in the sample.

c. Set the tolerable deviation rate at a lower level than originally planned.

d. Stratify the cash disbursements population so that the unusually large disbursements are selected.

(AICPA adapted)

Exercises, Problems, and Simulations

G.53 **Dollar Unit Sampling (DUS) and Classical Variables Sampling.** Read each of the following independent situations.

Required:

Indicate the advantages and disadvantages of DUS and classical variables sampling in each.

1. You are selecting a sample of customer accounts receivable balances for confirmation. The population is to be selected from a list of customer accounts receivable, the total of which exceeds $4 million. This list comprises 4,000 individual customer accounts that are relatively similar in dollar amount with balances ranging from $800 to $8,000. In past years, you have identified a moderate level of misstatement in the client's accounts receivable, although the level of misstatement was always less than the tolerable error.

2. You are selecting a sample of accounts payable balances for confirmation with vendors. The population is a list of accounts payable to vendors; at year end, the total (unaudited) accounts payable balance is $800,000. Amounts owed by the client to 200 separate vendors are included in this balance. Because the client has two major suppliers, a disproportionate amount of this balance ($500,000) is concentrated in these two accounts.

3. You are selecting a sample of customer accounts receivable balances for confirmation. The population is a list of customer accounts receivable; at year end, total accounts receivable are $2.5 million. Compared to most of your clients, the number of customer accounts included in this balance is relatively small and the balances range from $1,000 to $525,000.

G.54 **Sample Selection: Dollar Unit Sampling (DUS).** E. Washburn is examining the accounts receivable of Anaheim Company and has decided to use DUS to select a sample of customer accounts for confirmation. Anaheim's accounts receivable totaled $3.5 million and comprised 3,000 different customer accounts ranging in amount from $200 to $125,000. Based on the characteristics of the population and acceptable risk of incorrect acceptance, tolerable error, and expected error, Washburn determined a sample size of 20 accounts.

Required:

a. Without making any calculations, briefly describe how Washburn would select a sample of customer accounts from the population of accounts receivable.

b. If Washburn selected a random starting point of 172600, what are the first four dollars that would be selected? How would Washburn proceed to evaluate these dollars?

c. What would Washburn do if two of the dollars selected are contained within the same logical unit?

d. Anaheim maintains its accounts receivable balances in a computerized file that has the following information: (1) customer number, (2) customer name, (3) total account balance, and (4) account status (current versus past due). For each of these elements, comment on any procedures that Washburn should perform before selecting the sample if the population were arranged based on these elements (for example, arranged numerically by customer number, alphabetically by customer name).

G.55 **Sample Selection: Dollar Unit Sampling (DUS).** You have been assigned the task of selecting a DUS sample from Whitney Company's detailed inventory records as of September 30. Whitney's controller gave you a list of the 23 different inventory items and their recorded book amounts. The senior accountant told you to select a sample of 10 dollar units and the logical units that contain them.

Required:

Prepare audit documentation showing a systematic selection of 10 dollar units and the related logical units. Arrange the items in their numerical identification number order and take a random starting place at the 1,210th dollar.

ID	Amount	ID	Amount	ID	Amount	ID	Amount
1	$1,750	7	$1,255	13	$ 937	19	$2,577
2	1,492	8	3,761	14	5,938	20	1,126
3	994	9	1,956	15	2,001	21	565
4	629	10	1,393	16	222	22	2,319
5	2,272	11	884	17	1,738	23	1,681
6	1,163	12	729	18	1,228		

G.56 **Sample Size Determination: Dollar Unit Sampling (DUS).** The recorded accounts receivable balance for Warner Company was $500,000.

Required:

For each of the following independent sets of conditions, determine the appropriate sample size for the examination of Warner's accounts receivable in DUS. Based on the differences in your calculations, identify the general relationship between different factors and sample size. (RIA = risk of incorrect acceptance, TE = tolerable error, EE = expected error).

a. RIA = 5 percent, TE = $50,000, EE = $10,000.

b. RIA = 5 percent, TE = $50,000, EE = $25,000.

c. RIA = 10 percent, TE = $50,000, EE = $10,000.

d. RIA = 1 percent, TE = $50,000, EE = $25,000.

e. RIA = 10 percent, TE = $100,000, EE = $10,000

G.57 **Sample Size and Sampling Interval Determination: Dollar Unit Sampling (DUS).** R. Simmons is conducting the audit of Ace, Inc., and is using DUS to select a sample of inventory items for examination. The recorded balance in Ace's inventory account was $1,200,000. In carrying out his sampling plan, Simmons has established a risk of incorrect acceptance of 5 percent, a tolerable error of $100,000, and an expected error of $20,000.

Required:

a. What parameters would Simmons consider in determining the sample size for Ace's inventory?

b. How would Simmons identify or establish each of these parameters?

c. Determine the necessary sample size for the audit of Ace's inventory.

d. Based on the sample size determined in (*c*), what is the appropriate sampling interval?

e. Briefly describe how Simmons would select his sample from a computerized inventory list that Ace maintained.

G.58 **Sample Size and Sampling Interval Determination: Dollar Unit Sampling (DUS).** Paul is considering the use of DUS in his examination of Stanley's accounts receivable, which were recorded at $300,000. Using the audit risk model, Paul has identified a necessary risk of incorrect acceptance of 10 percent. In addition, he has established a tolerable error of $25,000 and an expected error of $10,000.

Required:

a. Determine the necessary sample size for the audit of Stanley's accounts receivable.

b. Based on the sample size determined in (*a*), what is the appropriate sampling interval?

c. Briefly describe how Paul would select the sample from a computerized customer list that Stanley maintained.

d. How would each of the following changes in Paul's sampling plan impact the sample size and sampling interval? For each change, use the original parameters noted in the problem background. (Verify your answer by calculating the sample size associated with each change.)

1. A reduction in the necessary level of the risk of incorrect acceptance to 5 percent.

2. An increase in the expected error to $15,000.

3. A decrease in the tolerable error to $20,000.

G.59 **Sample Size and Sampling Interval Determination: Dollar Unit Sampling (DUS).** B. Drake is conducting an audit of Newman and is using DUS to select a sample of customer accounts receivable for confirmation. Newman's accounts receivable are recorded at $10 million and comprise 2,000 customer accounts. Drake has established the following parameters for his investigation:

• Risk of incorrect acceptance = 5 percent.

• Tolerable error = $250,000.

• Expected error = $50,000.

Required:

 a. Determine the sample size and sampling interval that Drake used in the audit of Newman's accounts receivable.

 b. Based on the calculations in (*a*), briefly describe how Drake would select customer accounts from the population of accounts receivable balances for confirmation.

 c. Holding all other factors constant, determine the sample size and sampling interval assuming each of the following independent changes in Drake's sampling parameters:

 1. Because of improvements in Newman's internal control policies related to accounts receivable processing from prior years, Drake believes that a risk of incorrect acceptance of 10 percent is now acceptable in the current engagement.

 2. Because of the closeness of certain ratios to key debt covenants (particularly the current and quick ratios, which are highly influenced by accounts receivable), Drake believes that the tolerable error should be decreased from $250,000 (2.5 percent of the account balance) to $150,000 (1.5 percent of the account balance).

 3. Because of unusual circumstances in the prior year, some errors occurred in sales transaction processing that resulted in misstatements in accounts receivable. These errors are not anticipated to occur during the upcoming year. As a result, Drake believes that expected error can be decreased from $50,000 to $35,000.

 d. How do the changes noted in (*c*) illustrate the relationship between sample size and various factors?

 e. Describe the relationship between the sample size and sampling interval. Provide a brief explanation as to the nature of this relationship.

G.60 Sample Size Relationships: Dollar Unit Sampling (DUS). For each of the following cases, provide the missing information.

Recorded balance	$1,500,000	$190,000	(C)
Sample size	115	(B)	124
Sampling interval	(A)	4,222	18,000

G.61 Sample Size Relationships: Dollar Unit Sampling (DUS). N. Frehley is examining the accounts receivable of Kiss Company and is considering the use of DUS. Kiss's accounts receivable are recorded at $400,000. Based on the necessary level of risk, Frehley has established a risk of incorrect acceptance of 5 percent. In addition, based on prior audits, Frehley estimates misstatements of $10,000. Finally, based on the overall level of financial statement materiality, Frehley has established tolerable error at $17,500.

Required:

 a. Determine the necessary sample size for Frehley's examination of Kiss Company's accounts receivable.

 b. Assume that Frehley was interested in trying to reduce the necessary sample size. What are some options available in this regard?

 c. Based on a discussion with his senior manager, Frehley knows that increasing the level of the risk of incorrect acceptance will reduce sample size. For the same level of expected error, tolerable error, and population size, determine the sample size for a risk of incorrect acceptance of 10 percent.

G.62 Projected Misstatement Calculation: Dollar Unit Sampling (DUS). For each of the following independent misstatements, identify the missing value.

	1	2	3	4
Recorded balance	$15,000	$30,000	(E)	$12,000
Audited balance	$12,000	(C)	$6,000	(G)
Tainting percentage	(A)	5%	25%	(H)
Sampling interval	$50,000	(D)	$25,000	$48,000
Projected misstatement	(B)	$5,000	(F)	$24,000

G.63 **Upper Error Limit Calculation: Dollar Unit Sampling (DUS).** J. Thomas is using DUS to examine a client's accounts receivable balance. By using a sample size of 100 items and a sampling interval of $12,300, the following misstatements were identified:

Item	Recorded Balance	Audited Balance
1	$15,000	$12,500
2	10,000	4,000
3	3,000	2,000

Required:

 a. Calculate the upper error limit assuming a risk of incorrect acceptance of (1) 1 percent and (2) 5 percent.

 b. Based on your calculations in (*a*), comment on the relationship between the risk of incorrect acceptance and the upper error limit.

G.64 **Upper Error Limit Calculation: Dollar Unit Sampling (DUS).** C. Allister is performing a DUS application in the audit of Bird Company's accounts receivable. Based on the acceptable level of the risk of incorrect acceptance of 5 percent and a tolerable error of $120,000, Allister has calculated a sample size of 75 items and a sampling interval of $25,000. After examining the sample items, the following misstatements were identified:

Item	Recorded Balance	Audited Balance
1	$35,000	$28,000
2	10,000	8,000
3	6,000	3,000

Required:

 a. Calculate the upper error limit for Bird Company's accounts receivable.

 b. Provide a brief description of the meaning of the upper error limit calculated in (*a*).

 c. What would Allister's conclusion be with respect to the fairness of Bird's accounts receivable balance?

G.65 **Upper Error Limit Calculation: Dollar Unit Sampling (DUS).** The auditors mailed positive confirmations on 60 customers' accounts receivable balances. The company's accounts receivable balance comprised 2,356 customer accounts with a total recorded balance of $19.6 million and the sampling interval was $280,000. The auditors received four positive confirmation returns reporting exceptions. Upon follow-up, they found the following:

 • *Account 2333*. Recorded amount $8,345. The account was overstated by $1,669 because the client made an arithmetic mistake recording a credit memo. The company issued only 86 credit memos during the year. The auditors examined all of them for the same arithmetic mistake and found no similar misstatements.

 • *Account 363*. Recorded amount $7,460. The account was overstated by $1,865 because the company sold merchandise to a customer with payment due in six months plus 15 percent interest. The billing clerk made a mistake and recorded the sales price and the unearned interest as the sale and receivable amount. Inquiries revealed that the company always sold on "payment due immediately" terms but had made an exception for this customer. Numerous sales transactions had been audited in the sales control audit work and none had shown the extended terms allowed to Account 363.

 • *Account 1216*. Recorded amount $19,450. The account was overstated by $1,945 because an accounting clerk had deliberately misfooted several invoices to create extra charges to a business that competed with his brother's business unrelated to the company. The accounting clerk had forged the initials of the supervisor who normally reviewed invoices for accuracy. This clerk was a temporary employee. The auditors examined all invoices for this and other customers processed by this clerk and found no similar misstatements.

 • *Account 2003*. Recorded amount $9,700. The account was overstated by $1,455 because of a fictitious sale submitted by a salesperson, apparently part of an effort to boost third-quarter sales and commissions. The auditors learned that the salesperson was employed

from August 20 through October 30 before being dismissed as a result of customer complaints. They examined all other unpaid balances attributed to this salesperson and found no other fictitious sales.

Required:

a. Decide which, if any, of the account misstatements should be considered monetary misstatements and included in the calculation of the upper error limit using dollar unit sampling.

b. Calculate the upper error limit and decide whether the evidence from these misstatements indicates that the accounts receivable balance is or is not materially misstated. (The tolerable error for the accounts receivable was $1 million and the auditors had already decided on a risk of incorrect acceptance of 5 percent.)

G.66 **Upper Error Limit Calculations: Dollar Unit Sampling (DUS).** Assume that P. Fran has calculated a sampling interval for Tide, Inc.'s inventory of $10,000 and has conducted an examination of a sample of inventory balances. Fran has identified the following three misstatements:

Item No.	Recorded Balance	Audited Balance
X-21	$3,000	$1,200
Z-24	550	440
AA-02	6,000	1,500

Required:

Calculate the upper error limit for the following levels of the risk of incorrect acceptance. In general, what relationship do you observe between the risk of incorrect acceptance and the upper error limit?

a. 1 percent.

b. 5 percent.

c. 10 percent.

G.67 **Upper Error Limit Calculations: Dollar Unit Sampling (DUS).** Clyde Billy is conducting the audit of Hoops, Inc., and is examining Hoops's inventory balances. Billy plans to select a sample of inventory items for examination and will verify quantities and perform price tests to ascertain that the items are properly recorded according to generally accepted accounting principles.

Billy determined a sampling interval of $100,000 and, using systematic random selection techniques, has identified the following misstatements:

Item No.	Recorded Balance	Audited Balance
10-865	$ 12,600	$ 8,400
20-954	110,000	95,000
30-781	55,000	44,000
40-269	80,000	60,000

Required:

a. Using a 5 percent risk of incorrect acceptance, calculate the upper error limit.

b. Provide a brief description of the meaning of the upper error limit, using the information calculated in (*a*).

c. Reperform (*a*) using a risk of incorrect acceptance of (1) 1 percent and (2) 10 percent.

d. What relationship do you observe between the acceptable level of the risk of incorrect acceptance and the upper error limit? Provide a brief explanation about what causes this relationship.

e. Based on the levels of the upper error limit determined in this example, what are the advantages and disadvantages of establishing lower and higher acceptable levels of the risk of incorrect acceptance?

G.68 **Audit Simulation: Dollar Unit Sampling (DUS).** Zachary Mayo is a new staff accountant participating on his first audit engagement. He has been assigned to the Foley Company

engagement and is examining Foley's accounts receivable. Foley maintains a computerized ledger of its accounts receivable balances, which are recorded at $5 million and comprise 5,560 individual customer accounts.

Zachary established the following parameters for use in this year's audit. In so doing, he relied extensively on parameters established in prior audits:

- Expected error is established at $100,000, which is the average amount of misstatement identified in the past five audits. During the past year, Foley has experienced a great deal of turnover among its sales processing personnel and has made some relatively large sales that present some unusual revenue recognition issues. In addition, accounts receivable have increased by almost 15 percent from the prior year.

- The tolerable error is 10 percent of the ending accounts receivable balance, or $500,000 ($5 million × 0.10). Compared to prior years, Foley's financial condition has slightly deteriorated. Its current and quick ratios, while still above levels necessary to satisfy its debt covenants, have deteriorated.

- The risk of incorrect acceptance is 10 percent, which is the same as that used in the prior year. In evaluating the components of the audit risk model, some of the issues related to the turnover among sales processing personnel as well as the more limited use of analytical procedures during the current audit represent important differences from prior years.

Zachary sent positive confirmations. His work identified the following differences between audited balances and recorded balances.

Customer	Recorded Balance	Audited Balance
R. Gerer	$15,000	$10,000
D. Wings	25,000	20,000
L. Goss	60,000	30,000
K. David	120,000	90,000

Unfortunately, Zachary resigned from the firm shortly after identifying these differences. The only documentation you were able to locate was information related to (1) the levels of expected error, tolerable error, and risk of incorrect acceptance that were used in the Foley audit and (2) the four confirmations returned by customers who indicated differences between their records and Foley's recorded balances.

Required:

a. Zachary decided to use DUS primarily because it had been used in prior audits of Foley. Based on the nature of this sampling application, was the use of DUS appropriate?

b. Based on the parameters established by Zachary, determine the sample size and sampling interval he used in the sampling application.

c. Describe the sample selection process used by Zachary. Are you able to replicate or otherwise determine which customer balances he confirmed?

d. Based on the four overstatements identified by Zachary, calculate the upper error limit. Based on this upper error limit, what general statement can be made with respect to the extent of misstatement in the account balance?

e. What is your initial decision with respect to the fairness of Foley's accounts receivable balance?

f. Review each of the parameters established by Zachary (expected error, tolerable error, and risk of incorrect acceptance). Do any differences in the current engagement raise questions with respect to the level of these parameters?

g. What are the potential effect(s) of the changes in parameters noted in (*f*) on the sampling application?

G.69 **Audit Simulation: Dollar Unit Sampling (DUS).** Clint Walker was examining the accounts receivable of Country Music, Inc. Its accounts receivable were recorded at $1,500,000. Based on past audits, Walker established tolerable error at 10 percent of the recorded account balance and anticipated a very small level of misstatement in Country Music's accounts receivable ($50,000). In his previous assessments of audit risk, risk of material misstatement, and analytical procedures risk, Walker had established a necessary risk of incorrect acceptance of 10 percent.

Required:

a. Calculate the sampling interval and sample size that Walker would use in the audit of Country Music.

b. Reperform the calculations in (*a*) if Walker had established a risk of incorrect acceptance of (1) 5 percent and (2) 20 percent. Based on your calculations, describe the relationship between the necessary level of the risk of incorrect acceptance and the sample size and sampling interval.

c. *Note: Requirement (c) is unrelated to requirements (a) and (b).* If Walker detected the following four overstatements, determine the projected misstatement.

Recorded Balance	Audited Balance	Sampling Interval
$ 3,500	$ 1,750	$ 8,000
1,000	200	8,000
12,000	10,000	8,000
5,000	4,000	8,000

d. Based on the results in (*c*) and using a 10 percent risk of incorrect acceptance, calculate the upper error limit.

e. Reperform the calculation in (*d*) using a risk of incorrect acceptance of (1) 5 percent and (2) 20 percent. Based on your calculation, describe the relationship between the necessary level of the risk of incorrect acceptance and the upper error limit.

f. Using a risk of incorrect acceptance of (1) 5 percent, (2) 10 percent, and (3) 20 percent, what would Walker's conclusion be with respect to Country Music's accounts receivable? How do different levels of the risk of incorrect acceptance influence the likelihood of concluding that the account balance is fairly stated?

G.70 **Audit Simulation: Dollar Unit Sampling (DUS) with Understated Account.** D. Mays is auditing the accounts receivable of Channel Company. Channel's accounts receivable were recorded at $2,000,000 and comprised more than 1,500 customer accounts. However, Channel's 10 largest customers' balances comprised a high percentage of the recorded accounts receivable (over $500,000, or 25 percent). As a result, Mays is considering the use of DUS.

Based on prior audits and other judgments, Mays has established the following parameters:

Risk of incorrect acceptance	5%
Tolerable error	$120,000
Expected error	$20,000

Required:

a. Briefly identify what factors Mays should consider in determining sample size and how these factors would be assessed.

b. Calculate the necessary sample size and sampling interval used by Mays in the audit of Channel Company.

c. Given the information in (*b*), describe how Mays would select the sample from Channel's computerized accounts receivable ledger.

d. *Note: Requirement (d) is unrelated to requirements (b) and (c).* If Mays detected the following three overstatements, determine the projected misstatement.

Recorded Balance	Audited Balance	Sampling Interval
$45,000	$40,000	$13,000
8,000	6,000	13,000
12,000	9,000	13,000
10,000	12,000	13,000

e. Based on the results in (*d*) and a 5 percent risk of incorrect acceptance, calculate the upper error limit.

f. Based on the calculation in (*e*), what would Mays's conclusion be with respect to Channel Company's accounts receivable?

G.71 **Sample Size Determination: Classical Variables Sampling.** The recorded inventory balance for Faulk Company was $1,000,000 and comprised 2,500 customer accounts. For each of the following independent sets of conditions, determine the appropriate sample size for the audit of Faulk's inventory using classical variables sampling (mean-per-unit estimation). Based on the differences in your calculations, identify the general relationship between different factors and sample size. (RIA = risk of incorrect acceptance, RIR = risk of incorrect rejection, TE = tolerable error, EE = expected error, SD = standard deviation)

a. RIA = 5 percent, RIR = 5 percent, TE = $50,000, EE = $20,000, SD = $40.

b. RIA = 10 percent, RIR = 5 percent, TE = $50,000, EE = $20,000, SD = $40.

c. RIA = 10 percent, RIR = 10 percent, TE = $50,000, EE = $20,000, SD = $40.

d. RIA = 5 percent, RIR = 5 percent, TE = $30,000, EE = $20,000, SD = $40.

e. RIA = 5 percent, RIR = 5 percent, TE = $50,000, EE = $10,000, SD = $40.

f. RIA = 5 percent, RIR = 5 percent, TE = $50,000, EE = $10,000, SD = $30.

G.72 **Sample Size Determination: Classical Variables Sampling.** S. Solomon, CPA, is auditing the accounts receivable of Warner Company and is using mean-per-unit estimation. Accounts receivable were recorded at $2,000,000 and comprised 1,250 individual customer accounts. Solomon established the following parameters for the audit of accounts receivable:

- Using firm policy, tolerable error for accounts receivable is established at 6 percent of the recorded account balance.

- Based on prior audits of Warner's accounts receivable, the standard deviation of audited balances is estimated to be $100.

- Based on prior audits of Warner's accounts receivable, Solomon estimates that accounts receivable will be misstated by 4 percent of the recorded account balance.

Solomon is now establishing the acceptable levels of the risk of incorrect acceptance and the risk of incorrect rejection for the audit of Warner Company's accounts receivable.

Required:

a. What factors should Solomon consider in establishing acceptable levels of the risk of incorrect acceptance and the risk of incorrect rejection?

b. What are the advantages and disadvantages to Solomon of establishing lower levels of the risk of incorrect acceptance and the risk of incorrect rejection?

c. If Solomon establishes levels of the risk of incorrect acceptance and the risk of incorrect rejection of 5 percent, what is the resultant sample size?

d. Determine the sample size for each of the following combinations of risk of incorrect acceptance and risk of incorrect rejection:

1. Risk of incorrect acceptance of 5 percent, risk of incorrect rejection of 10 percent.

2. Risk of incorrect acceptance of 10 percent, risk of incorrect rejection of 5 percent.

3. Risk of incorrect acceptance of 10 percent, risk of incorrect rejection of 10 percent.

e. Based on the sample sizes you calculated in (*c*) and (*d*), how do the levels of sampling risks affect sample size?

G.73 **Evaluating Results: Classical Variables Sampling.** K. Berry is using mean-per-unit estimation in her audit of Leonard's inventory balances. Leonard's inventory is recorded at $240,000 and comprises 1,200 different items. Berry determined a sample size of 120 items and performed the appropriate substantive procedures. Based on this sample, she determined the following:

Average audited value (per item)	$204
Standard deviation of audited values	$22

A summary of some additional parameters estimated by Berry follow:

Tolerable error	$17,500
Expected error	$7,500
Risk of incorrect acceptance	5%
Risk of incorrect rejection	10%

Required:

a. What is Berry's estimate of the audited value of Leonard's inventory?

b. Calculate the precision and precision interval for Leonard's inventory. Provide a brief description of the meaning of the precision interval.

c. What is Berry's conclusion with respect to Leonard's inventory balance?

d. Using a risk of incorrect acceptance of (1) 1 percent and (2) 10 percent, calculate the precision and the precision interval for Leonard's inventory.

e. Based on your answers to (*b*) and (*d*), how does the risk of incorrect acceptance affect the precision interval and conclusions about the fairness of the account balance?

G.74 **Evaluating Sample Results: Classical Variables Sampling.** You are auditing Hernandez, Inc.'s accounts receivable balance using classical variables sampling. Hernandez's accounts receivable were comprised of 2,500 customer accounts and were recorded at $3.5 million.

Using a risk of incorrect acceptance and a risk of incorrect rejection of 5 percent, you selected a sample of 200 accounts for examination and confirmed the accounts with the customers. The total recorded balance of these 200 accounts was $1,000,000; based on your confirmations as well as an investigation of differences reported by customers, you determined an audited balance of $900,000.

Required:

a. What is the sample estimate of Hernandez's accounts receivable balance using (1) mean-per-unit estimation, (2) difference estimation, and (3) ratio estimation?

b. Why do the different methods of estimation in (*a*) result in such large differences in the sample estimate?

c. In what circumstances should each of the different methods of classical variables estimation be used?

d. If you calculate a sample estimate of $3,000,000 and precision of $750,000, form a precision interval for Hernandez's accounts receivable. Briefly describe the meaning of the precision interval as well as your conclusion with respect to Hernandez's accounts receivable balance.

G.75 **Audit Simulation: Classical Variables Sampling.** J. Howe is examining Met Company's accounts receivable balance and has decided to use mean-per-unit estimation. Met's accounts receivable were recorded at $650,000 and comprised 2,000 individual customer accounts. Howe established tolerable error at 5 percent of the recorded balance. Based on his prior experience with Met, Howe assessed expected error at $22,500 and estimated a standard deviation of the mean audited value of $30.

Required:

a. Using the preceding parameters, identify the appropriate sample size for the following combinations of risk of incorrect acceptance (RIA) and risk of incorrect rejection (RIR):

 1. RIA = 1 percent, RIR = 5 percent.
 2. RIA = 1 percent, RIR = 10 percent.
 3. RIA = 5 percent, RIR = 10 percent.

b. What factors would Howe consider in establishing the risk of incorrect acceptance and the risk of incorrect rejection?

c. Based on the results in (*a*), how do the risk of incorrect acceptance and the risk of incorrect rejection influence the determination of sample size?

d. If Howe had determined an audited value of $330 per account, determine the precision interval for each of the following combinations of the risk of incorrect acceptance (RIA)

and risk of incorrect rejection (RIR) (assume a standard deviation of $30). In each of these cases, what is Howe's conclusion with respect to Met's accounts receivable?

1. RIA = 1 percent, RIR = 5 percent.
2. RIA = 1 percent, RIR = 10 percent.
3. RIA = 5 percent, RIR = 10 percent.

e. Based on the results in (*d*), how do the risk of incorrect acceptance and risk of incorrect rejection influence the precision interval and evaluation of results?

G.76 **Audit Simulation: Classical Variables Sampling.** W. Wallace designed a classical variables sampling application to examine the accounts receivable for Rasheed, Inc. After considering several possibilities, Wallace decided to use mean-per-unit estimation. The following parameters are noted through a review of Wallace's audit documentation:

Recorded balance of accounts receivable	$800,000
Number of customer accounts included in accounts receivable balance	2,000
Risk of incorrect acceptance	5 percent
Risk of incorrect rejection	20 percent
Tolerable error	$50,000
Expected error	$10,000
Standard deviation of mean audited value	$52

Required:

a. Describe how Wallace would identify each of these parameters.

b. What is the appropriate sample size for this application?

c. Assume that Wallace is considering an increase in the necessary level of the risk of incorrect acceptance to 10 percent. How would this increase affect the sample size?

d. Using a 5 percent risk of incorrect acceptance, assume that Wallace determined a $380 average audited value per item and a $50 standard deviation of audited values. Construct the precision interval for Rasheed's accounts receivable.

e. Based on the precision interval in (*d*), provide Wallace's conclusion with respect to Rasheed's accounts receivable.

f. Repeat (*d*) and (*e*) assuming that the average audited value per item is $405. Why does Wallace's conclusion differ from that reached in (*e*)?

G.77 **Sample Size Determination: Nonstatistical Sampling.** M. Cordero is considering the use of nonstatistical sampling in her examination of Lubbock Company's accounts receivable. Lubbock's accounts receivable were recorded at $3 million.

Required:

a. For each of the following combinations of factors, determine the appropriate sample size (TE = tolerable error, IR/CR = assessment of inherent and control risk, OS = risk that other substantive procedures will fail to detect a misstatement).

1. TE = $60,000, IR/CR = Slightly below maximum, OS = Slightly below maximum.
2. TE = $60,000, IR/CR = Maximum, OS = Slightly below maximum.
3. TE = $60,000, IR/CR = Slightly below maximum, OS = Low.
4. TE = $30,000, IR/CR = Slightly below maximum, OS = Slightly below maximum.

b. Based on your calculations in (*a*), describe the relationship between each of these factors and sample size.

G.78 **Nonstatistical Sampling.** F. Gunny is using nonstatistical sampling in the examination of Highway Company's accounts receivable, which were recorded at $350,000. Gunny has established the following parameters for the sampling application:

Tolerable error	$15,000
Assessment of risk of material misstatement	Moderate
Risk that other substantive procedures will fail to detect a misstatement	Slightly below maximum

Required:

 a. Determine the necessary sample size for Gunny's examination of Highway's accounts receivable.

 b. If the items selected by Gunny had an aggregate recorded balance of $50,000 and an aggregate audited balance of $45,000, calculate the estimated audited balance.

 c. What would Gunny conclude with respect to the fairness of Highway's accounts receivable?

G.79 **Nonstatistical Sampling.** M. Brown is planning the substantive procedures for the audit of Longhorn Company's inventory, which had a recorded (unaudited) balance of $6.5 million. In prior audits, Brown used dollar unit sampling but is now considering the use of nonstatistical sampling. He has established the following parameters for the sampling application:

Tolerable error	$250,000
Assessment of risk of material misstatement	Slightly below maximum
Risk that other substantive procedures will fail to detect a misstatement	Maximum

Required:

 a. Compared to dollar unit sampling, what are the advantages and disadvantages to Brown of using nonstatistical sampling in this year's audit of Longhorn's inventory?

 b. Compare the factors used by Brown in determining sample size under dollar unit sampling to those that would be used in nonstatistical sampling.

 c. Using nonstatistical sampling, determine the necessary sample size for Brown's examination of Longhorn's inventory.

 d. Assume that Brown had the option to perform more extensive analytical procedures and, in so doing, could reduce the risk that other substantive procedures will fail to detect a misstatement from "maximum" levels to "moderate" levels. What is the impact of this decision on the necessary sample size?

 e. What factors would Brown consider in deciding whether to perform more extensive analytical procedures?

 f. If the items selected by Brown had an aggregate audited balance of $970,000 and an aggregate recorded balance of $1 million, what would he conclude with respect to the fairness of Longhorn's inventory?

G.80 **Mistakes in a Dollar Unit Sampling (DUS) Application.** This is a CPA examination essay question that contains some very subtle mistaken statements about statistical audit sampling. You will need to be very careful to notice them.

 Mead, CPA, was engaged to audit Jiffy Company's financial statements for the year ended August 31. Mead applied sampling procedures.

Required:

Describe each incorrect assumption, statement, and inappropriate application of sampling in Mead's procedures in the following.

For the current year, Mead decided to use dollar unit sampling (DUS) to select accounts receivable for confirmation because DUS uses each account in the population as a separate sampling unit. Mead expected to discover many overstatements but presumed that the DUS sample still would be smaller than the corresponding size for classical variables sampling.

Mead reasoned that the DUS sample would automatically result in a stratified sample because each account would have an equal chance of being selected for confirmation. Additionally, the selection of negative (credit) balances would be facilitated without special considerations.

Mead computed the sample size using the risk of incorrect acceptance, the total recorded book amount of the receivables, and the number of misstated accounts allowed. Mead divided the total recorded book amount of the receivables by the sample size to determine the sampling interval and then calculated the standard deviation of the dollar amounts of the accounts selected for evaluation of the receivables.

Mead's calculated sample size was 60 and the sampling interval was determined to be $10,000. However, only 58 different accounts were selected because two accounts were so large that the sampling interval caused each of them to be selected twice. Mead proceeded to send confirmation requests to 55 of the 58 customers. Three accounts originally selected for the sample each had insignificant recorded balances under $20. Mead ignored these three small accounts and substituted the three largest accounts that had not been selected by the random selection procedure. Each of these accounts had balances in excess of $7,000, so Mead sent confirmation requests to these customers.

The confirmation process revealed two differences. One account with an audited amount of $3,000 had been recorded at $4,000. Mead projected this to be a $1,000 misstatement. Another account with an audited amount of $2,000 had been recorded at $1,900. Mead did not count the $100 difference because the purpose of the procedure was to detect overstatements.

In evaluating the sample results, Mead decided that the accounts receivable balance was not overstated because the projected misstatement was less than the allowance for sampling risk.

(AICPA adapted)

G.81 **Sampling Application Evaluation: Variables Sampling.** The law firm of Spade & Associates hired D. Sayers to review the audit work that Hammer & Wimsey, CPAs, completed last year for Golden Sound and Records Company. Specifically, the attorneys engaged Sayers to determine whether the audit of Golden Sound's inventory of sound equipment and CDs conformed to generally accepted auditing standards. After Golden Sound declared bankruptcy three months ago (eight months after the latest audited financial statements were issued), stockholders sued Golden Sound alleging distribution of misleading financial statements, and Hammer & Wimsey hired Spade & Associates to prepare a defense in case Hammer & Wimsey were included later in the lawsuit. The latest year was the first time Golden Sound had been audited.

Golden Sound's business had grown rapidly. The company had 40 stores two years ago, opened 36 more last year, and added 23 more (for a total of 99) during the year of the inventory audit in question. The records showed the growth of the inventory:

	June 30		
	Two Years Ago	**Last Year**	**Audited Year**
Sound equipment	$5,800,000	$10,000,000	$12,200,000
CDs	2,200,000	6,800,000	9,000,000
Total inventory	$8,000,000	$16,800,000	$21,200,000
Number of stores	40	76	99
Average equipment	$145,000	$131,579	$123,232
Average CDs	$55,000	$89,474	$90,909

Sayers reviewed the Hammer & Wimsey audit documentation and wrote this summary:

In April of the year under audit, Bobby Earl (Hammer & Wimsey audit manager on the Golden Sound engagement) met with Golden Sound's managers and discussed the program for taking the physical inventory as of June 30. Mikki LaTouche (Golden Sound's chief financial officer) suggested that the auditors' inventory observation be conducted at the big-city stores in the area where Golden Sound had started business. According to LaTouche, "These stores are well stocked with a representative selection of all types of equipment and musical releases available across all the stores. The store managers are well acquainted with the inventory and can conduct an accurate counting with experienced store employees. The newer stores carry less stock, and the managers are relatively new to their jobs. You'll get a more accurate inventory-taking observation in the older stores."

Earl agreed and noted in the conference memorandum in the audit documentation that the prospect of sending auditors to distant stores in the Midwestern and Southeastern states (where Golden Sound had established new stores in the past year or so) would be very costly in terms of auditors' time and travel expenses. Together, LaTouche and Earl

selected eight of the stores in the Western Region. Earl supervised experienced audit teams as they observed the inventory taking at these eight stores. The auditors observed that the Golden Sound store managers gave good instructions to the inventory takers and that the count records were in good order. Test counts showed only minor mistakes, which the managers promptly and courteously corrected.

Everyone was interested in making an accurate count because Golden Sound had no reliable perpetual inventory records, and the financial statement figure for inventory was determined by this physical inventory taking. In fact, Earl wrote in the internal control communication to the board of directors and in the management letter addressed to the CFO the observation that Golden Sound needed to establish reliable inventory records for physical control and profit enhancement. The auditors determined the following inventory amounts in the eight stores. Using the total inventory of $1,712,700 in these stores, Earl divided by eight to find the average per store, then multiplied by 99, and projected the total inventory in the amount of $21,194,663. Because this figure was only $5,337 less than the book value of inventory in the general ledger, Earl and the reviewing partner did not perform further work and incorporated the $21,200,000 inventory in the financial statements, along with a standard unqualified auditor's report.

Store Location	Inventory
Los Angeles 1	$ 238,300
Los Angeles 3	212,500
San Diego 2	206,800
San Diego 4	195,400
Las Vegas 1	223,200
Sacramento	211,900
San Francisco 1	240,000
Phoenix	184,600
Total audit observation	$1,712,700

Required:

Complete Sayers' engagement by evaluating the Hammer & Wimsey conduct of the inventory portion of the Golden Sound audit. Specify to which of the 10 generally accepted auditing standards Hammer & Wimsey did not conform.

G.82 **Dollar Unit and Classical Variables Sampling.** Indicate whether each of the following characteristics applies to dollar unit sampling (DUS), classical variables sampling (CVS), both DUS and CVS (both), or neither DUS nor CVS (neither).

a. May be used in conjunction with substantive procedures.

b. Tends to select higher dollar items for examination.

c. Is more effective in identifying overstatements.

d. Incorporates assessments of tolerable error in determining sample size.

e. Incorporates assessments of the population variability in determining sample size.

f. Controls the auditor's exposure to the risk of incorrect rejection and the risk of incorrect acceptance.

g. Requires the auditor to project discovered misstatements to the population.

h. Can expose the auditor to nonsampling risk.

i. May be used in conjunction with the study and evaluation of internal control.

j. Is more appropriate for use when a larger number of misstatements are anticipated.

G.83 **Audit Simulation: Dollar Unit Sampling.** G. Costanza, CPA, is auditing the accounts receivable of Vandalay Industries and is considering the use of dollar unit sampling (DUS) techniques. Costanza has a number of questions regarding the use of DUS and has asked you to provide him responses using the professional auditing literature and citations to specific sections of the literature.

Required:

a. Under generally accepted auditing standards, can Costanza use nonstatistical sampling in the examination of Vandalay's accounts receivable?

b. What are the advantages to using statistical sampling in the audit examination?

c. What are the risks associated with sampling and to what type of losses do they expose Costanza?

d. How does Costanza establish the appropriate level of the risk of incorrect acceptance?

e. Is Costanza permitted to specify that certain items be examined or do all items need to be randomly selected?

f. How can Costanza increase the likelihood that the items in the sample are representative of the population?

g. Other than the dollar amount of the misstatements, are any other factors important for Costanza to consider with respect to the misstatements?

G.84 **ACL Assignment**

Required:

Go to the ACL link at www.mhhe.com/louwers3e, click on "ACL Assignments" and complete the assignment for Module G.

G.85 **Mini-Case: Sampling.**

Required:

Refer to the mini-case "Unhealthy Accounting at HealthSouth" shown on page 833 and respond to Question 6.

Information Systems Auditing

Professional Standards References

Compendium Section	Document Reference	Topic
Various*	AS 5	"An Audit of Internal Control over Financial Reporting That Is Integrated with an Audit of Financial Statements"
AU 311	SAS 108	"Planning and Supervision"
	ISA 300	"Planning an Audit of Financial Statements"
AU 314	SAS 109	"Understanding the Entity and Its Environment and Assessing the Risks of Material Misstatement"
	ISA 315	"Understanding the Entity and Its Environment and Assessing the Risks of Material Misstatement"
AU 316	SAS 99	"Consideration of Fraud in a Financial Statement Audit"
	ISA 240	"The Auditor's Responsibility to Consider Fraud in an Audit of Financial Statements"
AU 318	SAS 110	"Performing Audit Procedures in Response to Assessed Risks and Evaluating the Audit Evidence Obtained"
	ISA 330	"The Auditor's Procedures in Response to Assessed Risks"
AU 322	SAS 65	"Auditor's Consideration of the Internal Audit Function in an Audit of Financial Statements"
	ISA 610	"Considering the Work of Internal Auditing"
AU 324	SAS 70	"Service Organizations"
AU 326	SAS 106	"Audit Evidence"
	ISA 500	"Audit Evidence"
	ISA 501	"Audit Evidence—Additional Considerations for Specific Items"
AU 339	SAS 103	"Audit Documentation"
	AS 3	"Audit Documentation"
	ISA 230	"Audit Documentation"

*AS 5 amends AU 230, AU 310, AU 312, AU 313, AU 315, AU 316, AU 319, AU 322, AU 325, AU 328, AU 332, AU 333, AU 341, AU 342, AU 380, AU 508, AU 530, AU 543, AU 560, AU 561, AU 711, AU 722, *AS 3,* and *AS 4.*

> To err is human, but to really foul things up you need a computer.
>
> *Paul Ehrlich, Technology Commentator*

Learning Objectives

Given its extensive use by clients, auditors must consider clients' computer technology during all stages of the audit engagement. A textbook cannot describe fully all complexities of computerized processing of business transactions, so this module assumes that you have had a course in computer concepts and general computerized processing. The focus of this module is the examination of the client's computerized information system and its related computer controls. The module is subdivided into three parts. The first part reviews the basic elements of a computerized information system

and the related controls. The second part describes the procedures information system auditors perform to ensure that the client's computer controls are operating effectively. The module concludes with a discussion of computer fraud and the controls that can be used to prevent it.

Your objectives are to be able to:

1. List and describe the general and application controls in a computerized information system.

2. Explain the difference between auditing around the computer and auditing through the computer.

3. List several techniques auditors can use to perform tests of controls in a computerized information system.

4. Describe the characteristics and control issues associated with end-user and other computing environments.

5. Define and describe *computer fraud* and the controls that can be used to prevent it.

INTRODUCTION

It has been a rough few years for the **Federal National Mortgage Association,** or **Fannie Mae,** as it is popularly known. On December 6, 2006, the government-sponsored mortgage giant made its first periodic filing with the Securities and Exchange Commission since June 30, 2004. Why? Fannie Mae's audit committee and board of directors determined in December 2004 that previous financial statements were not prepared in conformity with GAAP and needed to be restated. After almost two years, Fannie Mae reported the net impact of its restatement: a decrease in retained earnings as of June 30, 2004, of $6.3 *billion*. During this time, Fannie Mae dismissed its chief executive officer, chief financial officer, and accounting firm (replacing **KPMG** with **Deloitte & Touche**). Its stock price fell from a high of $80.82 in the first quarter of 2004 to a low of $46.30 in the third quarter of 2006.

Why did these problems occur? An examination of Deloitte & Touche's report on Fannie Mae's internal control over financial reporting provides a clue. This report identified eight material weaknesses in internal control over financial reporting. Two of these relate to Fannie Mae's information technology applications:[1]

- Application of Accounting Principles Generally Accepted in the United States of America: [Fannie Mae] did not maintain effective internal control relating to its process and information technology applications for determining, monitoring, disseminating, implementing, and updating accounting policies that complied with accounting principles generally accepted in the United States of America.

- Information Technology Applications and Infrastructure: [Fannie Mae] did not maintain effective internal control related to information technology applications and infrastructure, including access controls, change management controls, and controls over end-user computing including spreadsheets.

Ultimately, this restatement was judged to be the result of a "flawed" system of accounting for the costs associated with loans and securities acquired by Fannie Mae from lenders. One particularly troubling problem was a $1.2 billion error in Fannie Mae's investment accounts that resulted from incorrect formulae in spreadsheet cells used to calculate the market value of these investments.[2] In the year 2006 alone, Fannie Mae anticipates spending over $1 billion for the development of new computerized information systems to address these and other problems.[3]

[1] *Fannie Mae 2004 10-K* (filed with the Securities and Exchange Commission on December 6, 2006).
[2] "Fannie Mae Corrects Mistakes in Results," *The New York Times,* October 30, 2003.
[3] "Fannie Battles an Ex-Manager over Accounting," *The Wall Street Journal,* December 7, 2006, p. C1; "Fannie Mae Moves toward Resolution with Restatement," *The Wall Street Journal,* December 7, 2006, p. A4.

AUDITING INSIGHT Does Anybody Understand It?

The importance and challenges of auditing in a computerized processing environment can be illustrated by early findings related to the assessment of internal control over financial reporting required by Sarbanes-Oxley. Almost all of the entities reporting material weaknesses or internal control deficiencies have found computerized processing to be a major source of the weaknesses. Additional conclusions of this survey of chief financial officers include

- Accounting regulators have not done a sufficient job in detailing entities' responsibilities with respect to computer controls to satisfy section 404 requirements.

- Auditors do not have a sufficient understanding of computerized processing issues to render an appropriate opinion on computer controls.

- Only 26 percent of respondents indicated it would be "easy" to remediate computerized processing control issues noted in the section 404 audit.

Source: "Sarbox Surprises," *CFO.com*, June 22, 2005.

In Chapter 4, we discussed the impact that client use of computerized processing has on the audit examination. As noted previously, the client's use of the computer *does not* affect the objective of an audit, the need for auditors to study and evaluate the client's internal control, or the need for auditors to gather appropriate evidence on which to support their opinion. The primary impact of computerized processing is the need for auditors to obtain an understanding of and test the operating effectiveness of controls that are unique to these environments. In this module, we identify the elements of a computerized information system and the controls operating within these systems. Then, we discuss methods used by auditors to test the operating effectiveness of these controls.

As shown the Auditing Insight "PCAOB Inspections and Computer Controls," evaluating the operating effectiveness of controls in a computerized processing environment poses challenges to auditors. These matters were identified by the PCAOB in its annual inspections in 2006 for audits conducted by the Big Four firms (Deloitte & Touche, Ernst & Young, KPMG, and PricewaterhouseCoopers).

AUDITING INSIGHT PCAOB Inspections and Computer Controls

- The firm chose not to test the operating effectiveness of information technology controls, despite the fact that the client's business is technology intensive and processes large volumes of customer data.

- The firm's audit documentation indicated that the results of the test of information technology general controls did not support a conclusion that the client's information processing was reliable. However, the firm did not perform additional procedures to address this finding nor modify its audit strategy.

Source: 2005 PCAOB Inspection of Deloitte & Touche, November 30, 2006; 2005 PCAOB Inspection of Ernst & Young, January 11, 2007; 2005 PCAOB Inspection of KPMG, January 11, 2007; and 2005 PCAOB Inspection of PricewaterhouseCoopers, December 14, 2006. All reports can be found on the PCAOB's Web site www.pcaob.org/Inspections/Public_Reports/index.aspx.

CONTROLS IN A COMPUTERIZED INFORMATION SYSTEM

LEARNING OBJECTIVE

1. List and describe the general and application controls in a comujterized information system.

Famous Cambridge mathematician and computer scientist Douglas Hartree is quoted as having said (around 1951) that the world market for computers was three. In his opinion, "no one else would ever need machines of their own, or would be able to afford to buy them."[4] Time has proven him to be mistaken: Today, entities use thousands of different

[4] *American Scientist* 58 (1970), pp 43–53.

computerized information systems, and rarely are two alike. No matter what technology is used for preparing financial statements, auditors should have enough familiarity with computers, computerized processing of transactions, and computer controls to be able to complete the audit of simple systems and to work with information system auditors on more complex ones.

In Chapter 5, we discussed the importance of internal control and the framework established for internal control by the Treadway Commission's Committee of Sponsoring Organizations (or COSO). While intended to be applicable to all environments, COSO does not focus on the role of information technology in an entity nor the issues related to internal control from the use of information technology (IT). In 1996, the Information Systems Audit and Control Association (ISACA) and the Information Technology Governance Institute (ITGI) created **Control Objectives for Information and Related Technology** (known as **COBIT**), which represents a set of best practices for IT management. COBIT has achieved general acceptance as the internal control framework for IT. COBIT's basic principle is

> To provide the information the enterprise requires to achieve its objectives, the enterprise needs to invest in and manage and control IT resources using a structured set of processes to provide the services that deliver the required enterprise information.[5]

An overview of the COBIT principle in the most recent release[6] is shown below. This principle acknowledges that investments in IT are based on the entity's basic business requirements (linkage 1); these investments are then utilized by IT processes (linkage 2) that produce information (including financial statements) (linkage 3), which correspond to and meet the business requirements identified in the initial step (linkage 4).

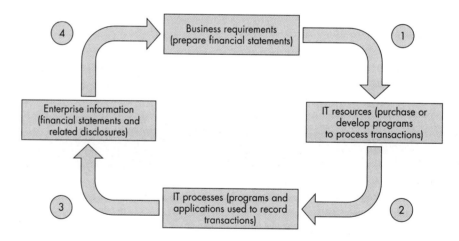

The COBIT framework consists of four domains, which include 34 high-level objectives. These domains are briefly described below; the objectives are summarized in Exhibit H.1.

1. *Plan and Organize.* Summarizes how information and technology can be used within an entity to best achieve its goals and objectives (related to both financial reporting and other general objectives). This domain focuses on the organization and infrastructure of IT within the entity.

2. *Acquire and Implement.* Once the entity's goals are identified (under "Plan and Organize"), this domain focuses on identifying the related IT requirements, acquiring the necessary technology, and implementing the technology within the entity's business processes. In addition to implementation, this domain considers appropriate maintenance to increase the useful life of technology.

[5] IT Governance Institute, *COBIT 4.1,* 2007, p. 10.
[6] IT Governance Institute, *COBIT 4.1,* 2007, p. 10 (Figure 5).

EXHIBIT H.1
**Domains and
High-Level Controls
under COBIT**

Plan and Organize

Define a strategic IT plan and direction
Define the information architecture
Determine technological direction
Define the IT processes, organization,
and relationships
Manage the IT investment
Communicate management aims
and direction
Manage IT human resources
Manage quality
Assess and manage IT risks
Manage projects

Delivery and Support

Deliver and manage service levels
Manage third-party services
Manage performance and capacity
Ensure continuous service
Ensure systems security
Identify and allocate costs
Educate and train users

Manage service desk and incidents
Manage the configuration
Manage problems
Manage data
Manage the physical environment
Manage operations

Acquire and Implement

Identify automated solutions
Acquire and maintain application software
Acquire and maintain technology
infrastructure
Enable operation and use
Procure IT resources
Manage changes
Install and accredit solutions and changes

Monitor and Evaluate

Monitor and evaluate IT processes
Monitor and evaluate internal control
Ensure regulatory compliance
Provide IT governance

3. *Delivery and Support.* Once the IT has been acquired and implemented (under "Acquire and Implement"), this domain focuses on the actual execution of applications within the IT system. That is, what actions are taken by the entity to ensure that programs and applications are functioning in the intended manner?

4. *Monitor and Evaluate.* This domain considers whether the IT system continues to meet the entity's objectives. An important element of this evaluation is whether appropriate controls are implemented to comply with applicable regulatory requirements.

While COSO and COBIT are intended for different audiences and purposes, some parallels can be drawn between these two frameworks in terms of common elements. For example, many of the high-level controls in the "Plan and Organize," "Acquire and Implement," and "Delivery and Support" domains are indicative of an effective control environment; in this case, these control environment factors are related to the role of IT within the organization. Further, objectives within the "Plan and Organize" domain correspond to the risk assessment (e.g., assess and manage IT risks) and information and communication (communicate management aims and direction) elements of COSO. The final two components of COSO are embedded in the "Monitor and Evaluate" domain (control procedures and monitoring).

COBIT notes that the entity's internal control affects IT at three levels:

1. At the *executive management level,* the overall strategy with respect to the deployment of IT is established and communicated throughout the entity. This level represents the control environment component of internal control.

2. At the *business process level,* automated controls are implemented with respect to processing information (including transactions) occurring within that process. These controls are commonly referred to as *information technology application controls.*

3. At the *support level,* IT services are provided throughout the organization (e.g., networks, databases, and storage). Controls related to these activities (which affect all business processes) are commonly referred to as *information technology general controls.*

A detailed discussion of COBIT is beyond the scope of this module, which is concerned with providing an overview of how the use of computerized processing by entities

affects the auditors' examination. While COBIT was originally prepared to assist management in ensuring that IT enhances the entity's objectives, the "best practices" nature of this framework provides auditors with an understanding of important characteristics of effective internal control in IT environments. While aspects of this module will touch on a number of the high-level objectives shown in Exhibit H.1, our focus will be on the internal controls commonly implemented in a computerized processing environment, which is represented by the second objective in the "Monitor and Evaluate" domain.

In addition to control environment factors, COBIT identifies two categories of controls operating within a computerized information system: general controls and application controls. **Information technology general controls (ITGC)** apply to all applications of a computerized system (for example, the processing of transactions across various cycles); the five categories of general controls are hardware controls, program development, program changes, computer operations, and access to programs and data. **Information technology application controls (ITAC),** on the other hand, are controls that are applied to specific business activities within a computerized information system to achieve financial reporting objectives. Thus, ITAC relate to specific types of transactions and operating cycles (for example, processing of transactions within the revenue cycle). It is important to note that, while similar ITAC can be implemented for various cycles, these controls operate at the transaction (and not overall) level. While ITAC are application-specific, ITGC can be thought of in the same light as the control environment in that, if the general controls are weak, the application controls cannot be relied on; ITGC have a pervasive effect on the objectives of internal control over financial reporting through their effect on the accurate processing of transactions.

In today's environment, almost all entities use computerized information systems in processing transactions (in fact, it would be difficult to find an entity of any reasonable size that did not). As a result, auditors must gain an understanding and test the operating effectiveness of ITGC and ITAC.

Review Checkpoints

H.1 What do financial statement auditors need to know about computerized information processing systems? Why?

H.2 What is COBIT? What is the basic principle of COBIT?

H.3 Identify and provide a brief description of the four domains of COBIT.

H.4 What is the primary difference between ITGC and ITAC?

Information Technology General Controls (ITGC)

Hardware Controls

Hardware refers to the physical equipment or devices that constitute a computer. These include the central processing unit (CPU), optical readers, tape drives, disk devices, printers, terminals, and other equipment. Modern computer equipment is very reliable. Machine malfunctions that go undetected are relatively rare. You are not expected to be a computer systems engineer, but you should be familiar with some of the hardware controls so you can converse knowledgeably with information systems personnel.

Hardware controls provide reasonable assurance that data are not altered or modified as they are transmitted within the system. The most important hardware control now incorporated in all computers is a **parity check** that ensures that the coding of data internal to the computer does not change when it is moved from one internal storage location to another. An additional hardware control commonly found is an **echo check,** which involves

a magnetic read after each writing to "echo" back to the sending location and compare results. Many computers also contain dual circuitry to perform arithmetic operations twice. Auditors (and management) cannot do much about the absence of such controls but should be concerned primarily with operator procedures when such errors occur. Modern computers are largely self-diagnostic. Therefore, written procedures should exist for all computer malfunctions, and all malfunctions as well as their causes and resolutions should be recorded.

Another important control related to computer hardware is *preventive maintenance* on the related equipment. Auditors should determine whether regular maintenance is scheduled and whether the schedule is followed and documented. Maintenance frequently is under contract with the computer vendor. In such cases, auditors should review the contract as well as the record of regular maintenance work. Other general evidence on hardware reliability may be obtained from a review of operating reports and downtime logs.

Program Development

The objectives of *controls over program development* are to provide reasonable assurance that (1) acquisition or development of programs and software is properly authorized, is conducted in accordance with entity policies, and supports the entity's financial reporting requirements; (2) appropriate users participate in the software acquisition or program development process; (3) programs and software are tested and validated prior to being placed into operation; and (4) all software and programs have appropriate documentation.

Program development controls include system programs (e.g, operating systems such as Windows Vista, Unix, and Linux) as well as more complex application systems (e.g., enterprise resource planning programs (ERPs) such as SAP/R3 and PeopleSoft). ERPs integrate information processing across functional areas (such as accounting, shipping, and purchasing). The primary benefit of ERPs is that they allow the contemporaneous capture of economic transactions and updating of client information databases on a real-time basis. This automation has both benefits and costs. Contemporaneous updating can increase internal control over completeness by reducing the likelihood that a transaction could be unrecorded (e.g., recording and billing a shipment). On the other hand, ERPs are often characterized by a lack of separation of duties.

ERP implementations are costly and fail more times than they succeed. After an investment of over \$130 million, **Allied Waste Industries Inc.** decided to pull the plug on its SAP/R3 software installation, claiming that it was too expensive and too complicated to use.[7] In addition, because of the interdependent nature of ERPs (i.e., each of the "modules" is linked across functional areas), breakdowns in one module could cause the entire system to collapse. A breakdown in **Hershey's** ERP system during the highly profitable Halloween season left unshipped candy sitting in their warehouses, causing millions of dollars in lost sales.

An important program development control is the entity's use of the **systems development life cycle** (SDLC) process to plan, develop, and implement new computerized information systems (or databases). As shown in Exhibit H.2, the SDLC begins with the identification of system requirements (basically, what do we need the system to do?). The feasibility analysis stage examines whether the entity should purchase the system "off the shelf" (i.e., from a commercial vendor), develop the system internally, or modify an "off the shelf" system for internal use. The answer depends on entity resources and expertise. Once a decision is made that a new system is feasible, system specifications are developed. Programmers next write programs to accomplish those specifications and then design procedures. On conversion from the old system to the new one, training employees to use the new system is critical. On successful implementation, the system must continue to be monitored to ensure that problems do not arise. As problems arise (e.g., due to capacity constraints), the cycle begins anew: is there a better system to meet the entity's needs?

[7] J. Bailey, "Trash Haulers Are Taking Fancy Software to the Dump," *The Wall Street Journal*, June 9, 1999, p. B4.

EXHIBIT H.2
Systems Development Life Cycle

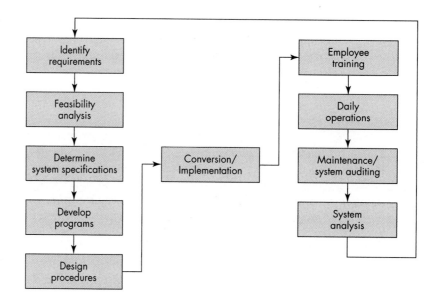

An effective SDLC will include the following important controls as part of its process:

- Ensuring that software acquisition and program development efforts are consistent with the entity's needs and objectives.
- Following established entity policies and procedures for acquiring or developing software or programs.
- Involving users in the design of programs, selection of prepackaged software and programs, and testing of programs.
- Testing and validating new programs and developing proper implementation and "back out" plans (plans to cancel the results of processing in the event of an error or program failure) prior to placing the programs into operation.
- Ensuring that data are converted completely and accurately for use in the new systems.
- Ensuring that consistent processes are followed and the most recent version of programs are implemented.
- Considering application controls that should be incorporated within the system to facilitate the accurate processing of data and transactions.
- Periodically reviewing entity policies and procedures for acquiring and developing software or programs for continued appropriateness and modifying these policies and procedures, as necessary.

In addition to the use of the SDLC noted above, it is important that appropriate documentation exist for each of the entity's programs. *Documentation* describes the system and its controls in relation to input, information processing, output, report processing, logic, and operator instructions. Documentation is the means of communicating the essential elements of the computerized information system to both current and potential users. The following purposes are served by computer system documentation:

- Provide for management review of proposed application systems.
- Provide explanatory materials for users.
- Instruct new personnel by providing background on previous application systems and serve as a guideline for developing new applications.
- Provide the information necessary for answering inquiries about the operation of a computer application.
- Serve as one source of information for an evaluation of controls.
- Provide operating instructions.

- Simplify program revision by providing details of processing logic.
- Supply basic information for planning and implementing audit software or other auditing techniques.[8]

In evaluating controls over documentation, auditors review the documentation to (1) gain an understanding of the system and determine whether the documentation is adequate to support the proper use of the programs and (2) determine whether standards are followed by client personnel. Of utmost importance in this area of the review is whether the client has established *systems development and documentation standards*. Unless written standards exist, it is difficult to determine whether the program development controls and the documentation are adequate. The **systems development and documentation standards manual** prepared by management should contain standards that ensure (1) proper user involvement in the systems design and modification process, (2) review of the specifications of the system, (3) approval by user management and information processing management, and (4) identification of controls and auditability. The *controls section* of the entity's documentation provides auditors with an overview of the controls involved in processing transactions in a particular application and identifies how the general controls are implemented within that application.

AUDITING INSIGHT Document, Document, Document

An interesting example of the importance of documentation was in the audit of **Thornburg Mortgage**, a Santa Fe, New Mexico–based financial institution. Thornburg had installed an up-to-date virus protection program in its computerized information systems;

however, their auditors reported an internal control deficiency because of the lack of documentation supporting this installation.

Source: "Solving the Audit Gap," *CFO.com*, October 2, 2006.

Program Changes

The objectives of *controls over program changes* parallel those related to program development in the preceding subsection. These controls are implemented by the entity to provide reasonable assurance that requests for modifications to existing programs (1) are properly authorized, conducted in accordance with entity policies, and support the entity's financial reporting requirements; (2) involve appropriate users in the program modification process; (3) are tested and validated prior to being placed into operation; and (4) have been appropriately documented. Like program development controls, the use of an SDLC (and the analogous controls related to the use of an SDLC) is an important consideration when modifying existing programs. It is also important that the entity prepare appropriate documentation with respect to the program modifications.

In addition to the controls included within the SDLC, two other important controls for program changes relate to "emergency" change requests and the migration of new programs into operations. In some cases, modifications to existing programs need to occur outside of the SDLC process. If so, it is important that appropriate documentation exist to support the "emergency" nature of the program modifications. In addition, these modifications should be subject to standard approval procedures after they have been made. In addition, when programs have been modified, they should only be migrated (or moved) into operation by appropriate individuals.

[8] Gordon B. Davis, Donald L. Adams, and Carol A. Schaller, *Auditing and EDP*, 4th ed. (New York: AICPA, 1991).

AUDITING INSIGHT Hershey's Harrowing Halloween

In 1999, Hershey Foods was facing a potential "Y2K" problem involving program coding that used only two-year digits (e.g., 99 for 1999) instead of four, therefore causing problems for date-related procedures. If not corrected, inventory software on January 1, 2000, could indicate that candy had been on the warehouse shelves for 100 years.

To address the problem and update their old systems, Hershey undertook an ambitious enterprise resource planning (ERP) system upgrade. In September 1999, facing implementation delays due to software integration complexities and an immoveable December 31, 1999, implementation deadline, Hershey decided to switch from its old system to its new system with a flip of a switch ("the cold turkey approach"), rather than the originally planned module-by-module approach. Unfortunately, the implementation "didn't take." Customer Halloween candy orders fell through the cracks. Candy inventory was "lost," remaining unaccounted for in their warehouses. The consequence was an estimated $150 million in lost sales. Hershey learned from its mistakes and recently successfully upgraded its inventory planning and distribution systems without a hitch.

Source: "Hershey's Sweet Victory," *Baseline*, December 2002 (www.baselinemag.com).

Computer Operations

Controls over computer operations are concerned with providing reasonable assurance that the processing of transactions through the computerized information system is in accordance with the entity's objectives and that actions are taken to facilitate the backup and recovery of important data when the need arises.

In a computerized information system, transactions can be processed using either *batch* or *real-time* (also known as *online* or *interactive*) processing methods. **Batch processing** is characterized by grouping similar transactions to be processed in a group (or batch) at the same time, using the same program. Simple batch processing systems deal with one component of an entity at a time such as payroll or billing. For example, all payroll records are run at one time with the input in the form of a batch of time cards or electronic file containing employees' identification numbers and hours worked. In contrast, **real-time processing** involves processing transactions as they occur without delay. For example, your long-distance telephone call is entered automatically into the telephone company's revenue and receivable accounts; therefore, accounting records are automatically updated as soon as the transactions occur. At the end of each billing period, your telephone bill is produced from the accounting information.

Complex computerized information systems are said to be *transaction driven* (or *event driven*) because the individual transaction triggers the processing activity and updates all relevant files; online systems have this characteristic. In contrast, a batch system could be said to be *program driven* because a specific program must be loaded into the computer to process all transactions that fit the program and its related files.

In practice, auditors often encounter combinations of simple batch systems and advanced systems. For example, terminals and workstations are commonly used for transaction data entry, and this hardware is always used in advanced systems. However, the same hardware also is used in a hybrid system to collect transaction data for batch update. Computer terminals may be used only for inquiry about the status of balances (e.g., perpetual inventory updated periodically by batch) instead of being used to enter transactions and update records. An entity can have some parts of its computerized information system involved in immediately updating processing (e.g., sale order entry) and parts batch processed (e.g., payroll that has a natural periodic cycle).

Several important controls over computer operations and the processing of transactions include policies and procedures related to

- Information processing operations such as job scheduling, monitoring, and responding to any incidents that occur during operations.
- Methods of resolving failures in a real-time processing environment as these failures occur.

- Methods of ensuring that failures in a batch processing environment are resolved on a timely basis and do not affect or unnecessarily delay the processing of other transactions within that batch.
- Appropriate separation of duties related to the computer operations function.

Because of important characteristics of computer operations, separation of additional duties beyond those in a manual processing environment is recommended. The duties associated with these and other important roles are defined as follows:

- *Systems analysts* analyze requirements for information, evaluate the existing system, and design new or improved computerized information systems. They also outline the system, prepare specifications that guide the programmers, and prepare documentation of the application system. Finally, they often acquire suitable commercial software.
- *Programmers* prepare flowcharts and code the logic of the computer programs required by the overall computerized information system designed by the systems analyst. They also often prepare program documentation.
- *Computer operators* operate the computer for each accounting application system according to written operating procedures found in the computer operation instructions.
- *Data conversion operators* prepare data for machine processing by converting manual data into machine-readable form or directly entering transactions into the system using remote terminals.
- *Librarians* maintain control over (1) system and program documentation and (2) data files and programs used in processing transactions. The librarian function or librarian software should control access to systems documentation and access to program and data files by using a checkout log (a record of entry and use) or a password to record the use by authorized persons. Someone who possesses both documentation and data files has enough information to alter data and programs for nefarious purposes.
- The *control group* receives input from user departments, logs the input and transfers it to data conversion, reviews documentation sequence numbers, reviews and processes error messages, monitors actual processing, compares control totals to computer output, and distributes output.

Separation of the duties performed by systems analysts, programmers, and computer operators is an important ITGC. The general idea is that anyone who designs a computerized information system should not do the technical programming work, and anyone who performs either of these tasks should not be the computer operator when "live" data are processed. Persons performing each function should not have access to each other's work, and only the computer operators should have access to the equipment. Computer systems are susceptible to manipulative handling, and the lack of separation of duties along the lines described should be considered a serious weakness in general control.

In addition to controls related to the processing of transactions, computer operations controls involve ensuring the use of the appropriate file within a given application and providing for the backup and recovery of important data. **Backup** is a retention system for files, programs, and documentation so master files can be reconstructed in case of accidental loss and processing can continue at another site if the computer center is lost to fire, flood, or other disaster. Thus, backup files must be stored at an off-site location, away from the main computer as part of a larger business continuity plan. Business continuity planning (often referred to as *disaster recovery planning*) encompasses more than data recovery. Plans must be made to accommodate lost equipment and, in the worst case, lost personnel. Some of the more important security and retention control techniques and procedures relating to data are explained next.

- *External labels* are paper labels on the outside of a file (e.g., portable disk packs or magnetic tapes). The label identifies the contents such as Accounts Receivable Master File so the probability of using the file inappropriately (e.g., in the payroll run) is minimized.

- *Header and trailer labels* are special internal records on magnetic tapes and disks. They are magnetic records on the tape or disk, but, instead of containing data, they hold label information similar to the external file label. Therefore, the header and trailer labels are sometimes called *internal labels*. Their function is to prevent using the wrong file during processing. The header label contains the name of the file and relevant identification codes. The trailer label gives a signal that the end of the file has been reached. Sometimes trailer labels are designed to contain accumulated control totals to serve as a check on loss of data during operation; for example, the number of accounts and the total balance of an accounts receivable file.

- *File security* is enhanced by many physical devices such as storage in fireproof vaults, backup in remote locations, and files sorted in computer-readable, printed, or microfilm form. In the majority of cases, the exposure to risk of loss warrants insurance on program and data files.

- *File retention practices* are related closely to file security. In general, retention provides the first line of defense against relatively minor loss while security generally consists of all measures taken to safeguard files against total loss. The entity should establish policies with respect to the length of time files and data are retained.

In essence, the problem is how to reconstruct records and files once they have been damaged. One of the most popular methods is the *grandfather-father-son process*. This involves retaining backup files such as the current transaction file and the prior master file, from which the current master file can be reconstructed. Exhibit H.3 illustrates the file retention plan. Particularly important files can be retained to the great-grandfather generation if it is considered necessary. Disk files are more difficult to reconstruct than tape files because the process of updating old records with new information is "destructive." The old or superseded data on a record are removed (destroyed) when new data are entered in the same place on a disk. One reconstruction method is to have a disk file "dumped" onto tape periodically (each day or each week). This file copy, along with the related transaction file also retained, can serve as the father to the current disk file (son). It is important that these file restoration processes are periodically tested to ensure they will be effective, if needed.

EXHIBIT H.3
Grandfather-Father-Son File Retention

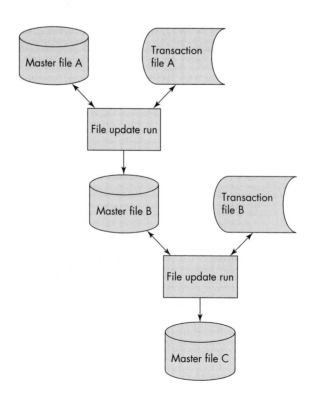

Access to Programs and Data

Controls over access to programs and data provide reasonable assurance that access to programs and data is only granted to authorized users. The proliferation of computer "hackers" has resulted in increased attention paid to access controls by organizations. Many of the computer frauds listed later in this module were the result of individuals both within and outside an entity obtaining unauthorized access to that entity's data.

The most common form of control related to access is the use of passwords. You are required to enter passwords to access your university's computer network, your bank account from an automated teller machine, and many other information services. The entity should establish an information security policy and identify various levels of access for each employee, based on the requirements for their position and job responsibilities. Once established, employee access should be restricted based on passwords. Important characteristics of passwords is that they should be of sufficient length (number of characters); include letters, numbers, and (in some instances) symbols; and be modified periodically (every six months is common). Establishing passwords in this manner will reduce the likelihood of an employee's password being hacked (or "guessed") by others.

In addition to passwords, physical security controls over terminals and input devices (such as locked doors and the use of badges or swipe cards to access certain locations) also are used. However, with the increasing ability of employees to access systems remotely (i.e., off site), physical security controls are becoming less effective in restricting access to programs and data.

Other common controls to restrict access to programs and data include

- Establishing time limits where user sessions automatically "time out" after a predetermined period of time (**automatic terminal logoff**).
- Periodically reviewing and confirming the access rights granted to employees.
- Ensuring that modifications in the level of access permitted to individual users has been properly authorized and is consistent with these changes in these individuals' responsibilities.
- Ensuring that access to programs and data is removed for recently terminated employees on a timely basis.
- Monitoring user activity to ensure that only authorized users are accessing programs and data.
- Promptly reporting and communicating observed security breaches.

AUDITING INSIGHT — New Developments in ITGC

The Institute of Internal Auditors recently issued guidance for auditors assessing ITGC. Referred to as the *Guide to the Assessment of IT General Controls Based on Risk* (or GAIT), this report was prepared with input from **General Motors**, **Intel**, and **Microsoft**. The four basic principles of *GAIT* are

1. When identifying risks and related ITGC, entities should use a top-down, risk-based approach.
2. When scoping risks related to ITGC, only those controls that could "reasonably" and likely lead to the risk of a material error should be considered.
3. To identify risks, entities should evaluate all levels of their technology systems, including programming codes and databases.
4. Risk mitigation should be based on the impact a failing control could have on the objectives of an entity's IT systems, not the risk of failure to an ITGC itself.

Source: Institute of Internal Auditors, *The GAIT Methodology*, January 2007.

Summary

ITGC are *pervasive* and the effectiveness of application controls (both manual and automated) relies on the effectiveness of ITGC. As a result, the effectiveness of ITGC is an important consideration for auditors in their assessment of control risk (and the risk of material misstatement) in a computerized information system environment. Simply stated, if ITGC are not designed or operating effectively, it is not likely that a great degree of reliance can be placed on the client's internal control and the assessment of control risk (and risk of material misstatement) will likely be relatively high, requiring more effective substantive tests.

Exhibit H.4 summarizes the ITGC in each of the areas of a client's computerized processing environment. For each of the ITGC, the most closely-related domain of COBIT also is provided.

EXHIBIT H.4 Information Technology General Controls

Category (COBIT domain)	Examples	Objective(s)
Hardware controls (No applicable domain)	• Parity check • Echo check • Preventative maintenance	Prevent or detect erroneous transmission of data as they move through the computerized information system
Program development (Acquire and Implement)	• Use of systems development life cycle (SDLC) for authorization, user involvement, and testing and validation of new programs • Appropriate documentation for new programs	Programs developed and software acquired by the entity are consistent with the entity's objectives
Program change (Acquire and Implement)	• Use of systems development life cycle (SDLC) for authorization, user involvement, and testing and validation of modifications to existing programs • Appropriate documentation to support "emergency" changes to existing programs • Implementation of program changes performed by appropriate personnel • Appropriate documentation for modifications to existing programs	Modifications to existing programs are authorized and are consistent with the entity's objectives
Computer operations (Delivery and Support)	• Separation of incompatible functions of systems analysts, systems programmers, and computer operators • Procedures for resolving transaction processing failures • Use of external and header and trailer labels to identify files and programs • Policies and procedures for periodic backup of programs and data and the ability to reconstruct programs and data	• Transactions are processed in accordance with the entity's objectives • Appropriate files and records are used in processing transactions • Programs and data are protected from loss
Access to programs and data (Delivery and Support)	• Use of passwords and appropriate characteristics of passwords • Physical security over terminals and input devices • Use of time limits and automatic "time out" of sessions • Periodic review of user access rights • Removal of access rights for terminated employees on a timely basis • Monitoring of activity and immediate communication of any security breaches	Access to programs and data is restricted to authorized users

Review Checkpoints

H.5 List the five major categories of ITGC and identify the objectives of these controls.

H.6 What do financial statement auditors need to know about computer hardware controls?

H.7 What is the SDLC? What type of controls does the use of the SDLC include with respect to program development and changes?

H.8 Describe the typical duties of computer personnel. Which duties should be separated within the computer department?

H.9 Why are ITGC so important in the auditors' evaluation of internal control and assessment of control risk and the risk of material misstatement?

Information Technology Application Controls (ITAC)

Information technology application controls (ITAC) "include computerized steps within the application software and related manual procedures to control the processing of various types of transactions."[9] ITAC are specific to each cycle (e.g., revenue and collection, acquisition and expenditure) and refer to a client's activities designed to ensure the proper recording of transactions and to prevent or detect errors and frauds for transactions within these cycles. ITAC fall within the "Monitor and Evaluate" domain of COBIT, as this domain is primarily concerned with the implementation of controls to meet the entity's objectives. These controls are organized under three categories: input controls, processing controls, and output controls.

Input Control Procedures

Input controls are designed to provide reasonable assurance that data received for processing by the computer department have been properly authorized and accurately entered or converted for processing. These controls also provide the opportunity for entity personnel to correct and resubmit data initially rejected as erroneous. The following controls are particularly important:

- *Authorization and approval controls.* Only properly authorized and approved input should be accepted for processing by the computer center. In a computerized environment, control procedures can have characteristics that differ from manual control procedures designed to accomplish the same control objectives. In a manual system, authorization usually is a clerical (noncomputer) procedure involving a person's signature or stamp on a source document such as a customer's order or invoice. However, some authorizations can be general (e.g., a management policy of automatic approval for sales under $1,000). In a computerized environment, some authorizations can be computer controlled (e.g., automatic production of a purchase order when an inventory item reaches a predetermined reorder point) or accomplished by utilizing a *digitized signature,* an approved encrypted password that releases a transaction by assigning a special code to it. The electronic signature provides access to programs that permit initiating a specific type of transaction or changing master files. In such a case, although the control objective is identical in the manual and computerized information systems, the methods used to achieve the objective and the visible evidence of conformity with authorized activities differ considerably, and the audit approach can be significantly different.

- *Check digits.* Numbers often are used in computerized information systems in lieu of customer names, vendor names, and so forth. One common type of number validation procedure is the calculation of a *check digit,* which is an extra number, precisely

[9] COSO Internal Control—Integrated Framework, p. 48.

calculated, that is tagged onto the end of a basic identification number such as an employee number. The basic code with its check digit sometimes is called a *self-checking number*. An electronic device can be installed on a data input device or the calculation can be programmed. The device or the program calculates the correct check digit and compares it to the one on the input data. When the digits do not match, an error message is indicated on the device or printed out on an input error report. Check digits are used only on identification numbers (not quantity or value fields) to detect coding errors or keying errors such as the transposition of digits (e.g., coding 387 as 837).

- *Record counts.* Counts of records are tallies of the number of transaction documents submitted for data conversion. The known number submitted can be compared to the count of records produced by the data-conversion device (e.g., the number of sales transactions or count of records). Differences between the manual counts of transactions and the number of transactions processed indicate that transactions may not have been input (if the manual count exceeds the processed count) or may have been input more than once (if the processed count exceeds the manual count). Record counts are used as batch control totals during processing and at the output stage (see subsequent discussion) whenever the comparison of a known count can be made with a computer-generated count.

- *Batch totals.* These totals are used in the same way as record counts except that the batch total is the sum of some important quantity or amount (e.g., the total sales dollars in a batch of invoices). These totals allow input errors to be detected prior to submission for processing and ensure that all transactions are entered once, and only once.

- *Hash totals.* These totals are similar to batch financial totals except that the hash total is not meaningful for accounting records (e.g., the sum of all the invoice numbers). Like batch totals, these totals allow input errors to be detected prior to submission for processing and ensure that all transactions are entered once, and only once.

- *Valid character tests.* These tests are used to check input data fields to see whether they contain numbers when they are supposed to have numbers or letters when they are supposed to have letters.

- *Valid sign tests.* Sign tests check data fields for appropriate positive or negative signs.

- *Missing data tests.* These edit tests check data fields to see whether any are blank when they must contain data for the record entry to be correct.

- *Sequence tests.* These test the input data for numerical sequence of documents when sequence is important for processing, as in batch processing. This validation routine also can check for missing documents in a prenumbered series.

- *Limit and reasonableness tests.* These tests are computerized checks to see whether data values exceed or fall below some predetermined limit. For example, a payroll application can have a limit test to flag or reject any weekly payroll time record of 50 or more hours. The limit tests are a computerized version of scanning: the general audit procedure of reviewing data for indication of anything unusual that might turn out to be an error.

- *Error correction and resubmission procedures.* Errors should be subject to special controls. Usually, the computer department itself is responsible only for correcting its own errors (data conversion errors, for example). Other error types such as those due to improper coding should be referred to and handled by the user departments. It is a good idea to have a control group log the contents of error reports in order to monitor the nature, disposition, and proper correction of rejected data. Unless properly supervised and monitored, the error-correction process itself can become a source of data input errors.

Processing Control Procedures

Processing controls are designed to provide reasonable assurance that data processing has been performed accurately, without any omission or duplicate processing of transactions. Many processing controls are the same as the input controls, but they are used in the

actual processing phases rather than at the time input is verified. Important processing controls include the following:

- *Run-to-run totals.* Movement of data from one department to another or one processing program to another should be controlled. One useful control is the run-to-run total. *Run-to-run* refers to sequential processing operations—runs—on the same data. These totals can be record counts, batch totals, and/or hash totals obtained at the end of one processing run. The totals are distributed to the next run and compared to corresponding totals produced at the end of the second run.
- *Control total reports.* Control totals—record counts, batch totals, hash totals, and run-to-run totals—should be calculated during processing operations and summarized in a report. Entity personnel (normally, the control group) should have the responsibility for comparing and/or reconciling these totals to input totals or totals from earlier processing runs. Loss or duplication of data thus can be detected. For example, the total of the balances in the accounts receivable master file from the last update run plus the total of the credit sales from the current update transactions should equal the total of the balances at the end of the current processing.
- *File and operator controls.* External and internal labels ensure that the proper files are used in applications. The systems software should produce a log to identify instructions entered by the operator and to make a record of time and use statistics for application runs. Supervisory personnel should review these logs on a periodic basis.
- *Limit and reasonableness tests.* These tests should be programmed to ensure that illogical conditions do not occur (for example, depreciating an asset below zero or calculating a negative inventory quantity). These conditions and others that are considered important should generate error reports for supervisory review. Other logic and validation checks also can be used during processing.

Output Control Procedures

Output controls represent the final check on the accuracy of the results of computerized processing. These controls also should be designed to provide reasonable assurance that only authorized persons receive output (or other type of reports generated by the computerized information system) or have access to files produced by the system. Typical output controls are the following:

- *Control total reports.* Control totals produced as output should be compared and/or reconciled to input and run-to-run control totals produced during transaction processing. An independent data control group should be responsible for reviewing of output control totals and investigating differences.
- *Master file changes.* During computerized processing, permanent information stored in master files is often updated or modified; these files should be viewed as "outputs" of the computerized processing. Any changes should be properly authorized by the entity and reported in detail to the user department from which the request for change originated because an error can be pervasive. For example, changing selling prices incorrectly can cause all sales to be billed at incorrect levels. Entity personnel should compare computer-generated change reports to original source documents for assurance that the changes to master file data are authorized and properly made.
- *Output distribution.* Systems output should be distributed only to persons authorized to receive the output. A distribution list should be maintained and used to deliver report copies. The number of copies produced should be restricted to the number needed.

Exhibit H.5 summarizes the ITAC discussed in the preceding section. Note that some of these controls (record counts, batch totals, hash totals, and limit and reasonableness tests) may be used as both input controls and processing controls.

EXHIBIT H.5　Information Technology Application Controls

	Input of Individual Transactions and Data Is Accurate	All Transactions Are Entered	Transactions Entered Only Once	Processing of Transactions Is Accurate	Other
Input authorization					Ensures input is approved and authorized
Check digits	X				
Record counts		X	X	X	
Batch totals	X	X	X	X	
Hash totals	X	X	X	X	
Valid character tests	X				
Valid sign tests	X				
Missing data tests	X				
Sequence tests		X			
Limit and reasonableness tests	X			X	
Error correction and resubmission	X				
Run-to-run totals				X	
Control total reports				X	
File and operator controls					Ensures proper files are used in applications
Master file changes				X	Ensures changes to master file data are authorized
Output distribution					Ensures output is distributed only to authorized users

AUDITING INSIGHT　　Always Lower Prices

Customers at **Meijer, Inc.** (a retailer of groceries and general merchandise in the midwestern United States) received an unexpected windfall when all items sold by the chain were mistakenly discounted by 50 percent in the company's master price file; the discount was only supposed to apply to Oriental rugs.

Source: "Meijer Glitch Led to Discount," *Chicago Tribune*, May 24, 2007.

Review Checkpoints

H.10　What is the objective of input controls?

H.11　Briefly describe record counts, batch totals, and hash totals. What types of errors in input would each of these controls likely identify?

H.12　What is the objective of processing controls? List and briefly describe different processing controls.

H.13　What is the objective of output controls? List and briefly describe different output controls.

APPROACHES TO CONTROL RISK ASSESSMENT IN A COMPUTERIZED ENVIRONMENT

LEARNING OBJECTIVE

2. Explain the difference between auditing around the computer and auditing through the computer.

According to generally accepted auditing standards (and, more recently, the Sarbanes-Oxley Act of 2002), the client's management is required to establish and maintain internal control. The policies and procedures included as elements of a computerized information system are part of that responsibility. As part of assessing the risk of material misstatement, the audit team's responsibility is to assess control risk in the system and, if appropriate, evaluate the design and operating effectiveness of the related controls. Management can meet its responsibility and assist auditors in the following ways: (1) ensure that documentation of the system is complete and up to date, (2) maintain a system of transaction processing that includes an audit trail, and (3) make computer resources and knowledgeable personnel available to auditors to help them understand and audit the system.

When a client uses computerized processing, control risk assessment involves the following steps. Note that these steps are the same as those used in a manual processing environment; they will involve different types of computer controls (ITGC and ITAC) as well as different methods of testing those controls.

- Identify specific control objectives based on the types of misstatements that can occur in significant accounting applications.
- Identify the points in the flow of transactions where specific types of misstatements could occur.
- Identify specific control procedures (such as the ITGC and ITAC described in the preceding section) designed to prevent or detect these misstatements.
- Evaluate the design of control procedures to determine whether the design suggests a low control risk and whether tests of controls might be cost-effective.
- Perform tests of the operating effectiveness of control procedures designed to prevent or detect misstatements (assuming it is cost-effective to do so).

Once control risk is assessed, auditors consider the inherent risk related to the account balance or class of transactions and assess the risk of material misstatement.

Identifying specific control objectives in a computerized information system is no different than doing so in a manual data processing system. However, the process of identifying the points in the flow of transactions where misstatements could occur is different in a computerized information system in comparison to a manual system, as many additional steps and sources of potential misstatement are introduced. For example, in a computerized information processing system, source data must be prepared and converted into computer-readable format, which is not necessary in a manual processing system; obviously, data entry errors may be introduced by this data conversion. Exhibit H.6 illustrates the following additional points of misstatement in a computerized processing environment:

1. Preparation of source data for input.
2. Manual summary of data (preparation of batch totals and hash totals).
3. Conversion of source data into computer-readable form.
4. Use of incorrect input files in processing.
5. Transfer of information from one computer program to another.
6. Use of incorrect computer files in processing transactions (e.g., customer credit reports).
7. Inappropriate initiation of transactions by the computer.
8. Creation of output files and update of master files.
9. Changes to master files outside the normal flow of transactions within each cycle through file maintenance procedures.
10. Production of output reports or files.
11. Correction of errors identified by control procedures.

EXHIBIT H.6 **Computerized Processing: Points of Vulnerability to Misstatement Errors**

Once the audit team has identified the points where a misstatement could occur, specific control objectives are identified that can be related to such points. For example, one possible misstatement could involve billing customers with incorrect prices because an inappropriate inventory price file was used in the application. One way to state a control objective relating to this type of misstatement is "Appropriate price information should be used during the billing process."

When points where misstatements could occur in the flow of transactions have been identified, auditors should focus on specific control procedures implemented by the client to prevent or detect such misstatements. Control procedures should be considered in terms of specific control objectives. For example, for the objective of using appropriate price information, one control procedure might be "The billing application program should identify the correct price file by matching the file name in the program to the name in the data file." This process is illustrated below; please note that this is no different from the process followed by auditors in a manual processing environment, but it recognizes that different types of misstatements are introduced through the computerized processing of transactions (as seen in Exhibit H.6).

Potential Source of Misstatement	Control Objective	Control Procedure
Use of inappropriate inventory price file to prepare invoices	Appropriate price information should be used during the billing process	The billing program should identify the correct price by matching the file name in the program to the name in the data file

EXHIBIT H.7
Example of Auditing around the Computer

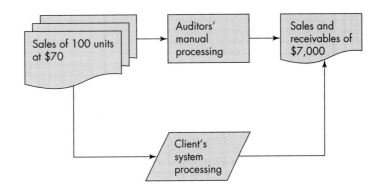

Auditing around the Computer

Auditors can use several methods to evaluate a client's computer controls. For example, auditors can conduct audits by **auditing around the computer**. Exhibit H.7 is an example of auditing around the computer. Auditors select a sample of source documents and verify the correspondence of the input (100 units sold at $70 per unit) with the output (sales and receivables of $7,000) (see the top row of Exhibit H.7). The client's computerized information system processes the transactions, but auditors treat it as a "black box," ensuring the accurate processing of transactions. No attempt is made to evaluate the existence of controls. When significant computer controls have not been implemented and the client essentially uses the computer to calculate amounts, auditing around the computer may be appropriate. However, auditors are still required to obtain an understanding of the controls and cannot ignore them; they will just not test the operating effectiveness of these controls. In addition, for audits of public entities, the requirements of *AS 5* would not permit auditors to issue opinions on the operating effectiveness of internal control if this approach were used.

Nothing is inherently wrong with auditing around the computer if auditors are satisfied with the control system and are able to gather sufficient evidence. However, in some complex and integrated systems where the input for one process is the computer output from another process, auditors may be unable to find a starting point that lies "outside" of the computerized information system.

Auditing through the Computer

In contrast, auditors can **audit through the computer.** When auditing through the computer, auditors evaluate the client's hardware and software to determine the reliability of operations that cannot be viewed by the human eye and test the operating effectiveness of the related computer controls. *Auditing through the computer* is common in practice because many computerized information systems have significant controls implemented within the related programs; indeed, it is normally cost-effective for clients to implement these controls to ensure the accurate processing of transactions. In cases such as this, ignoring the computer controls results in auditors not evaluating important features of the client's internal control.

For simple batch systems, adequate evidence of control performance frequently exists in the printed output and logs (thus, *auditing around the computer* is possible). For example, input error reports usually contain examples of each type of error the edit routines are designed to detect. A sample of each type of error can be traced to the error log maintained by the computer control group and to evidence of correction and resubmission. Likewise, printed documentation of compliance with authorized procedures required for execution of transactions or for changes to master files can exist. However, external auditors occasionally must use the computer as an audit tool to test the controls with the application programs of even simple systems. (Internal auditors more frequently use these techniques.)

Review Checkpoints

H.14 What are the major steps in auditors' assessment of control risk in a computerized processing environment?

H.15 List points in the processing of transactions at which misstatements may be introduced because of the use of computerized processing.

H.16 What is the difference between auditing "through the computer" and auditing "around the computer"?

TECHNIQUES FOR TESTING CONTROLS IN A COMPUTERIZED ENVIRONMENT

LEARNING OBJECTIVE

3. List several techniques auditors can use to perform tests of controls in a computerized information system.

When auditing through the computer, it will be necessary for auditors to evaluate the operating effectiveness of controls involved in the computerized processing of transactions. The tools and techniques for doing so can be classified as those that use (1) real (or "live") data, (2) simulated (or "dummy") data, (3) historical data following actual processing of those data, and (4) program analysis techniques.

Techniques Using Real or "Live" Data

One option for testing the effectiveness of the client's computer controls is through the use of real ("live") data and evaluating the controls as these transactions are being processed in the usual fashion by the client. In most cases, the techniques listed require that special audit modules be designed and coded into programs at the time of development. These *audit hooks* allow auditors to select specific transactions of interest before or during processing and save them for subsequent audit testing and follow-up. (Program modules created solely for audit or maintenance purposes are called **audit hooks.** The same concepts used for fraudulent purposes are called **trap doors.**) These techniques also enable internal auditors to continuously monitor the client's information processing system.

Tagging Transactions

Auditors "tag" selected transactions with an indicator at input. A computer trail of all processing steps of these transactions in the application system can be printed out or stored in computer files for subsequent evaluation by auditors.

Audit Files (Embedded Audit Modules)

Auditor-selected transactions are written to or embedded in a special file for later verification. Two methods can be employed. **Systems control audit review file (SCARF)** is a method in which auditors build into the processing programs special limits, reasonableness, or other audit tests. These tests produce reports of transactions selected according to auditors' criteria and the reports are delivered directly to auditors for review and follow-up. The SCARF procedure is especially attractive to internal auditors. A **sample audit review file (SARF)** technique is similar to SCARF except that instead of programming auditors' test criteria, a random sampling selection scheme is programmed. Auditors can review the report of sample transactions after each production run. The SARF method is efficient for producing representative samples of transactions processed over a period by the computer.

Snapshot

A "picture" of the main memory of transactions and database elements is taken before and after computerized processing operations have been performed. The picture is then printed for the auditors' use. For example, auditors can save the contents of an accounts receivable balance before and after a sales transaction is posted. Using these balances, along with the sales transaction, auditors can verify whether the update processing was correct.

Monitoring Systems Activity

Elements of hardware and software are available to analyze activity within a computer; a frequent use of these elements is to determine computer efficiency. However, these elements can be applied for auditing purposes to monitor the individuals who access the system, the various applications and operations accessed, and the time these applications and operations are accessed. For example, a record of passwords used to enter accounting transactions can be captured and compared to the list of persons authorized to enter these transactions. Similarly, a sign of hacking is the access of computer programs at times other than during normal operating periods.

Extended Records

Special programs provide an audit trail of an individual transaction by accumulating the results of all application programs that contributed to the processing of the transaction. The accumulated results are stored either as additional fields of the transaction record or as a separate audit file. For example, the snapshot example of accounts receivable balances before and after update processing could be added to the sales transaction, making an extended transaction record. Thus, auditors can follow the flow of a transaction without reviewing several files at various times and stages of processing.

Techniques Using Simulated or Dummy Data

Auditors often use two methods to test computer controls using fictional data: (1) the *test data* approach and (2) the *integrated test facility (ITF)* approach. Under each of these methods, auditors compare the results obtained from manual processing of simulated data and transactions with the results obtained from processing these same data and transactions through the client's computerized information system. In addition, auditors also will create "erroneous" transactions that allow them to test the operating effectiveness of the client's input controls (for example, using invalid account numbers or using two transactions having the same document or control number).

One important issue in processing data through the client's computerized information system is that the system or program used by auditors in these tests is the same as that actually used by the client in processing transactions (i.e., the client has not created an "alternative" program that differs from its actual program). Auditors can make this determination by requesting the program from the librarian on a surprise basis or requesting access to the program immediately following processing by the client.

Test Data

The basic concept of *test data* is that once a computer has been programmed to handle transactions in a certain logical way, it will faithfully handle every transaction exactly the same way. Therefore, the audit team need prepare only a limited number of simulated transactions (some with "errors" and some without) to determine whether each control operates as described in the program documentation.

A set of **test data** contains a sample of one of each possible combination of data fields that can be processed through the real system. Because transactions are processed identically, only one of each type of error needs to be included in the test data. The purpose of using test data is to determine whether computer controls operate effectively in preventing or detecting misstatements in the input or processing of transactions. Test transactions can consist of abstractions from real transactions and simulated transactions generated by auditors.[10] Auditors must prepare a worksheet listing each transaction and the predicted output based on the program documentation. Then these test transactions must be converted to the normal machine-sensed input form, and arrangements must be made to process the transactions with the actual program used for real transactions.

[10] This could be an oversimplification because computerized information systems can have multiple controls that create thousands of error combinations and possible test transactions. Computerized test data generators are available to help auditors overcome the magnitude of the test data creation task.

EXHIBIT H.8
Testing Controls with
Test Data

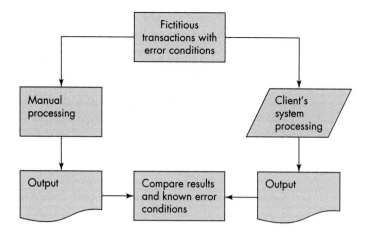

Auditors must be very familiar with the nature of the business and the logic of the programs to anticipate all data combinations that could exist as transaction input or that could be process-generated. Auditors must be able to assign degrees of audit importance to each type of error-checking control method. They must ensure that the test data are not commingled with real transactions and change the actual master files.

Test data are processed at a single point in time with the client program that is supposed to have been used in processing transactions during the period under audit. After the analysis of test output, the audit manager still must make an inference about processing throughout the entire period. To do so, he or she must be satisfied by a review of documentation that any program changes have been authorized and correctly made. Some auditors occasionally perform test data procedures on an irregular surprise basis during the year.

Exhibit H.8 above illustrates the test data approach. Auditors create source document input that contains one or more error conditions, in this case a shipment of fewer units than the customer ordered. Auditors know the desired outcome: an error message that the quantity shipped and the quantity billed do not match, perhaps with an accounting entry to charge the customer for the shipped quantity. If this result does not appear from the processing of the test data, auditors can conclude that the processing control over accurate sales recording contains a deficiency (weakness). Auditors are testing the controls embedded in the computer program and they are using the actual processing program for the test.

Integrated Test Facility

The use of an **integrated test facility (ITF)** is a technique commonly used by clients' program maintenance personnel, although auditors also can use the approach. This "minicompany" approach involves creating a dummy department or branch complete with records of employees, customers, vendors, receivables, payables, and other accounts. This overcomes one limitation of the test data approach (the fact that simulated data might accidentally be commingled with actual data). The ITF has master file records (or database records) carefully coded (such as "99") and included among the real master file records. Simulated transactions (test data) are inserted along with real transactions and the same application program(s) operates on both the test data and the real transactions. Because auditors know what the ITF output should be, the actual results of processing (output reports, error reports) can be reviewed to determine whether the application program is functioning properly.

A great deal of care is required when ITF is used because the fictitious master file records, the transactions, and the account outputs are placed in the actual information processing system and in the business records. The account amounts and other output data must be reversed or adjusted out of the financial statements. Also, care must be taken not to damage or misstate any of the real master file records and account balances.

Techniques Using Historical Data

The primary technique used to test computer controls using actual historic client data is called **parallel simulation** (also known as *controlled reprocessing* and *comparison program*

EXHIBIT H.9
System Concept of
Parallel Simulation

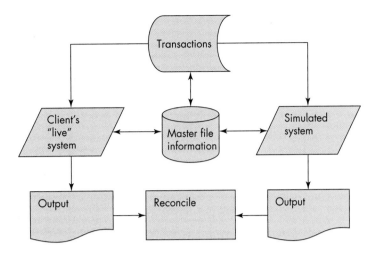

utilization). When using parallel simulation, the audit team prepares a computer program designed to process client data properly. The result of auditors' processing of real client data is compared with the result of the real data processed by the actual client program. In a sense, parallel simulation is a form of auditing around the computer with the use of computerized processing techniques. The concept of parallel simulation is illustrated in Exhibit H.9.

In conducting parallel simulation, auditors can have client personnel prepare special programs or prepare their own special programs. The first option requires close supervision and testing to ensure that the client's personnel have prepared the audit program correctly. The second option requires significant programming expertise of the audit staff or close liaison with expert independent programmers.

While one disadvantage of using auditor-prepared programs to conduct parallel simulations is the time, effort, and expertise necessary to prepare these programs, computer-assisted audit techniques (CAATs) make the parallel simulation option easier. CAATs (such as IDEA and ACL) were initially discussed in Chapter 4; these audit software programs consist of numerous prepackaged subroutines that can perform most tasks needed in auditing and business applications. Auditors' programming task consists of writing simple instructions that call up one or more of the subroutines. Thus, auditors do not need to write complete, complex programs and the expertise to use most CAATs software can be acquired through brief training.

Using the CAATs program capabilities, auditors can construct a system of information processing that will accept the same input as the real program, use the same files, and attempt to produce the same results. This simulated system contains all controls auditors believe to be appropriate, and, in this respect, the thought process is quite similar to the logic that goes into preparing test data. The simulated-system output then is compared to the real-system output for correspondence or difference, and at this point the audit evidence is similar to the evidence obtained by using test data with the real program: Conclusions can be reached about the error-detection capabilities of the real system.

Another way to create a parallel system is to conduct a thorough technical audit of the computer controls in the client's actual program and then keep a copy of it secure in the

AUDITING INSIGHT Parallel Simulation

A parallel simulation of a client's sales invoice and accounts receivable processing system revealed that invoices that showed no bill of lading or shipment reference were processed and charged to customers with a corresponding credit to sales. Further audit of the exceptions showed that the real-information processing program did not contain a missing-data test and did not provide error messages for lack of shipping references. This finding led to (1) a more extensive test of the sales invoice population with comparison to shipping documents and (2) a more extensive audit of accounts receivable for customers who were charged for such sales.

auditors' files. Actual client data later can be processed using this audited copy of the client's program (e.g., later in the year under audit or in the following-year audit). The goal is to determine whether output from the program that the client actually used in processing data produces satisfactory accounting output when compared to the output from the auditors' controlled copy of the program. This approach is often called **controlled reprocessing;** it is a version of parallel simulation.

The first audit application of parallel simulation may be costly, although it probably will be more efficient than auditing without the computer or utilizing test data. Real economies are realized, however, in subsequent audits of the same client.

When using any form of parallel simulation, the audit team must take care to determine that the real transactions selected for processing are "representative." Thus, some exercise in random selection and identification of important transactions could be required in conjunction with parallel processing.

Program Analysis Techniques

Computer technicians use numerous software packages for program documentation, debugging, and analysis. These tools also can be used for audit purposes in certain situations. Programs exist to take the source code and produce flowcharts or decision tables that can be used to understand the logic of an application program. **Cross-reference computer programs** provide a printed list of every occurrence of each name used in an application program or a list of every file used in an application system. Auditors can use these lists to follow the flow of transactions and identify significant data files. Auditors can use program analysis software to identify potential trapdoors created for fraudulent use.

The advanced computerized information system audit tools and techniques discussed in this section are summarized in Exhibit H.10. These tools and techniques may be used to test computer controls, perform substantive procedures, verify program logic, and determine the accuracy of data processing.

Review Checkpoints

H.17 Name some control techniques using live data that clients can embed in computerized information systems.

H.18 What is the difference between the test data technique and the integrated test facility technique?

H.19 "The use of the integrated test facility technique to test the client's application control procedures is unprofessional. We don't enter fake transactions into a client's manual system. Why should we do it in their computerized information system?" Evaluate this position and question posed by an audit partner.

H.20 What is the difference between the computerized tests of controls of test data and parallel simulation?

H.21 What is *controlled reprocessing?*

END-USER COMPUTING AND OTHER ENVIRONMENTS

LEARNING OBJECTIVE

4. Describe the characteristics and control issues associated with end-user and other computing environments.

As the storage and computation capacities of personal computers (PCs) surpass those of older mainframe computers, more and more of the day-to-day program development activities have become the responsibility of those individuals ("end-users") who use the programs in the entity's daily operations. Because of their proliferation, these personal computer environments should not be neglected in the assessment of control risk (and risk of material misstatement). Because the control objectives do not change, the computer controls illustrated and the audit techniques discussed in this module are still relevant but may have to be tailored to the PC or local area network (LAN) installation. The following explanations are designed to assist you in appreciating the issues involved

EXHIBIT H.10 Advanced Computerized Information System Audit Tools and Techniques

Technique	Description	Advantages	Disadvantages
Techniques Using Real Data			
Tagging transactions	Identifies ("tags") transactions at input and provides a computer trail of all processing steps to auditors.	• Auditors can select a wide range of transactions • Allows all processing steps to be evaluated	Requires special programming
Audit files (embedded audit modules)	Writes or embeds auditor-selected transactions to a special file for later verification	• Logs specified transactions for audit review • Can use either auditor-determined criteria for selection (SCARF) or randomly selected transactions (SARF)	• Requires special programming • Subject to manipulation by client
Snapshot	Obtains a record (or "snapshot") of transactions and database elements prior to and following computerized processing	Aids auditors' understanding of flow-of-transaction processing	Requires special programming
Monitoring system activity	Uses hardware and software to monitor and analyze activity within the system	Shows actual activity within the system such as access	Requires auditors' knowledge to interpret
Extended records	Provides an audit trail of transactions by accumulating the results of all processing	Provides complete account history and programs involved with processing a transaction	Requires special programming
Techniques Using Simulated Data			
Test data	Processes simulated transactions through the client's computerized information system and compares those results to predetermined results	Efficient, since it requires only one of each type of condition to be tested	• Separate processing may not correspond to programs actually used by client • Test data have the potential to be commingled with live data
Integrated test facility	Processes simulated transactions related to a fictitious department or branch created by auditors	• Since "minicompany" data are processed along with live data, programs are more likely to be those actually used by client • Separate "minicompany" isolates transactions tested by auditors from other transactions processed by the client	Data entered and processed as part of the "minicompany" must be reversed or adjusted out of the financial statements
Techniques Using Historical Data			
Parallel simulation (controlled reprocessing)	Processes actual transactions through programs designed to replicate appropriate processing by the client's computerized information system	Permits comparison with actual processing without entering simulated data into client systems CAATs can provide a cost-effective means of conducting parallel simulations	Can be expensive to develop programs if CAATs cannot be used
Program Analysis Techniques			
Program analysis techniques	Use software packages and programs to identify opportunities for fraudulent use of data	Give better understanding of application and provide assurance computer controls are functioning	• Can be expensive since they require auditors' knowledge of programming • Relatively limited usefulness

with assessing control risk in an end-user computing environment comprised of PCs or LANs.

Major Characteristics of End-User Computing Environments

PCs can be elements of a LAN or stand-alone systems involved in the client's information processing. In these environments, the overall control environment, and not the computer technology, is the most important consideration for auditors. The following are important elements in computerized processing in an end-user computing environment:

- *Terminals.* Terminals are used for transaction data entry, inquiry, and other interactive functions.
- *Software packages.* Purchased software packages, rather than internally-developed application software, are used extensively.
- *Storage.* Portable devices (such as compact disks (CDs) and Universal Serial Bus (USB) "thumb" or "key" drives) are used extensively for file storage.
- *Documentation.* Available system, program, operation, and user documentation can be limited or nonexistent.

These and other characteristics of end-user computing environments result in the following control issues:

1. *Lack of separation of duties.* Within the accounting function, individuals may be in position to initiate and authorize source documents, enter data, operate the computer, and distribute output reports. Within the computer function, small entities may fail to separate the functions of programming and operations. This lack of separation of duties arises because of a lack of resources and not the client's indifference with respect to internal control.
2. *Lack of physical security.* Computers and files often are located in end-user departments and not in a separate, secured area. As a result, access to computer terminals as well as programs and data files may not be properly restricted.
3. *Lack of documentation and testing.* Because users often modify or adapt existing programs for their own use, end-user computing environments are often characterized by a lack of appropriate documentation and testing.
4. *Limited computer knowledge.* The extensive reliance on packaged software and utility programs may result in personnel having limited computer knowledge.

End-User Computing Control Considerations

Most of the control problems noted above result from the lack of separation of duties and computer controls. It follows that most of the auditors' control considerations and techniques are designed to overcome these deficiencies. Auditors should consider the entire control system, including manual controls, and look for compensating control strengths that could offset apparent weaknesses.

Computer Operations Controls

An end-user computing environment is similar to the one-person bookkeeping department because a small number of individuals (in some cases, only one individual) perform the systems analysis, systems design, and programming operations. The main controls involve limiting the concentration of functions (to the extent possible) and establishing proper supervision over individuals performing these functions. With respect to separation of duties, important compensating controls that ensure accurate processing include (1) comparison of manual control totals with totals from computer output and (2) careful inspection of output for accuracy. In addition, some of the following operations controls may be useful in this regard:

- Joint operation by two or more individuals.
- Rotation of assigned duties among individuals.

- Comparisons of computer-use time to averages or norms and investigation of excess usage.
- Proper supervision of computer operations.
- Required vacations for all individuals.

Access to Programs and Data and Input Controls

In end-user computing environments, the most important controls are those over online data entry (accounting transactions).

- *Restrictions on access to input devices.* Common controls used to restrict access to input devices include (1) locking terminals; (2) requiring the use of passwords to access files, initiate changes, and access programs; and (3) using *automatic terminal logoff,* where the link between the computer and the system is terminated after a specified period of time.
- *Standard screens and computer prompting.* Computers can be programmed to produce a standard screen format when a particular function is accessed. The operator must complete all blanks as prompted by the computer, thus ensuring that complete transactions are entered before they are submitted for processing.
- *Online editing and sight verification.* The input edit and validation controls discussed previously can be programmed to occur at the time of input. In some installations, the data on the screen are not released until they have been sight-verified and the operator signals the computer to accept the entire screen. This control allows input errors to be detected prior to submission of the related data for processing.

AUDITING INSIGHT Problems with Data

One important control consideration in an end-user computing environment is when laptop computers are extensively used. The use of laptops introduces issues because of the potential for theft and the loss of significant data if the machine itself is stolen or lost. Some examples of significant data losses incurred during 2006 include

- **Boeing** lost the names, Social Security numbers, and salary data for 382,000 of its employees.

- **Ernst & Young** lost the credit information for 243,000 of **Hotels.com's** workers.
- **Starbucks** lost the Social Security numbers of 60,000 of their current and former employees.

Source: "The Biggest Lost-Laptop Incidents of 2006," *Fortune,* January 22, 2007, p. 36.

Processing Controls

Processing can be controlled by artificially creating the files equivalent to the grandfather-father-son retention concept found in batch systems. Important control procedures to ensure the appropriate processing of data include the following:

- *Transaction logs.* Transaction entry through the terminal should be captured automatically in a computerized log. The transaction logs (for each terminal or each class of terminals) should be summarized into the equivalent of batch totals (record counts, batch totals, or hash totals).
- *Control totals.* Master files should contain records that accumulate the number of records and batch totals. The update processing should automatically change these control records.
- *Comparing input to output.* The summary of daily transactions and the master file control totals from the computer should be compared to manual control totals maintained by the accounting department. If these comparisons are not feasible, techniques similar to auditors' analytical procedures can be employed to test the results for reasonableness.

- *Audit trail.* The transaction logs and periodic dumps of master files should provide an audit trail and means for recovery. In addition, some computer installations have systems software that can provide a log of all files accessed and all jobs processed.

Systems Development and Modification Controls

The control objectives and procedures in end-user computing environments are no different than those on more complex mainframe systems, even though the two environments are different. Many application programs are purchased from computer manufacturers or software vendors not completely familiar with online control techniques. Purchased programs should be reviewed carefully and tested before implementation.

The programming languages most frequently used in PCs are easily learned and programming ability can develop within the user group. Most PCs have "menu-type" instructions that are simple to use without technical training. Further, the programming is in an interpretative language, which means that it remains in the computer program library in source code form that is easy to change. Development standards and modification authorization become even more important than in more complex mainframe systems. Basically, end-users are doing the programming (e.g., creating complex spreadsheets). Should the end-user leave the entity, inadequate documentation of the changes to the application would prevent a replacement employee from being able to easily use the program. Another concern is the lack of adequate testing of program modifications to determine whether the modifications process transactions in the intended manner. Program documentation standards and procedures manuals can be the best solution, but some additional control over end-user changes to proprietary programs can be implemented by requiring passwords to restrict access to programs to only authorized employees.

AUDITING INSIGHT · Spreadsheet and Data Controls

One important consideration in an end-user computing environment is the ability to protect access to data in spreadsheets and other financial databases, especially when these spreadsheets are shared by multiple users. Enhanced password and data encryption features are becoming an important control when spreadsheets are used by various individuals within the entity. Microsoft Excel has developed Excel Services to enable spreadsheet sharing among users; Tom Rizzo, director of **SharePoint Technology,** notes that "the functions offered in Excel Services, particularly being able to lock down and hide data for specific groups of users, are highly flexible and can be personalized for individual sets of users."

The importance of spreadsheets is perhaps best illustrated by a $1.2 billion error in **Fannie Mae's** investment accounts that resulted from incorrect formulae in cells that calculated the market value of these investments.

Sources: "How to Put Your Spreadsheet in Lockdown," *CFO.com,* November 14, 2006; "Fannie Mae Corrects Mistakes in Results," *New York Times,* October 30, 2003.

Service Organizations

Because of a relative lack of expertise and a cost–benefit analysis, organizations (referred to as *user organizations*) may outsource specialized data processing to other organizations (referred to as *service organizations*). In such cases, specialized transactions (payroll is a common example) are processed in a computerized environment that is remotely located from the user organization's premises. As a result, the various computer controls discussed throughout this module are not easily accessible to auditors.

In cases such as this, the user organization's auditors obtain a report from the service organization's audit; because *SAS 70* covers the content of these reports, they are frequently referred to as *SAS 70* reports. It is important to note that the user organization's auditors must still evaluate controls that are related to the service organization's computerized processing of transactions. However, this evaluation considers the procedures performed and results obtained by the service organization's auditors. The reports on controls over processing at service organizations are discussed in detail in Module A.

Review Checkpoints

H.22 Which important duties are generally not separated in end-user computing environments?

H.23 What are the major characteristics and control problems in end-user computing environments?

H.24 What control procedures can be used to achieve control over computer operations in an end-user computing environment?

H.25 What control procedures can be used to achieve control over computerized processing in an end-user computing environment?

COMPUTER ABUSE AND COMPUTER FRAUD

LEARNING OBJECTIVE

5. Define and describe *computer fraud* and the controls that can be used to prevent it.

As technology has advanced, so have the number and type of crimes that can be committed with computers. Just as criminals use the Internet to commit "cybercrimes" in many forms (such as computer viruses, hackers, "cybertheft," "spamming," "phishing," "evil twins," credit scams, and pyramid and Ponzi schemes), corporate wrong-doers use computers to perform their scheme. Computer experts generally agree that an ingenious programmer can commit theft or misappropriation of assets that is difficult, if not impossible, to detect. Having said this, the box "Computer Frauds" gives a list of frauds committed with the assistance of computers that were detected.

Computer Frauds

Entity Type	Estimated Loss ($ millions)	Description of Fraud Committed
Armed guard entity	$ 21	An employee took advantage of an interbranch settlement account. The employee perpetrated the fraud, left for lunch one day, and never returned.
National bank	10	An employee obtained wire transfer codes and transferred the money to a Swiss bank account. The employee was caught after bragging to the wrong person.
World's largest dairy farm	17	An owner used a computer program that reduced sales data on an item-to-item basis.
National bank	69	An employee used four wire transfers to steal money.
Insurance entity	200	More than 64,000 insurance policy records that did not exist were added to the entity's master file.
National bank	6	Over an 11-year period, a vice president of information systems authorized the entity's information processing system to make payments to a fictitious shell entity that he owned. The individual amounts were not large enough to be noticed but were enough to allow the perpetrator to enjoy a lavish lifestyle.
Silicon Valley software entity	5	A recently fired employee used a modem to enter the entity's computerized information system and copied several million dollars of computer secrets. The employee then sold them to foreign competitors.

Source: L. Broom, T. Louwers, F. Messina, and K. Reynolds, "Technology as Pandora's Box," *Oil, Gas, & Energy Quarterly* 49 (September 2000), pp. 125–32.

How were the perpetrators caught? Despite their complexity, computer frauds usually produce an unsupported debit balance in some asset account. For example, someone might manipulate the computer to cause purchased goods to be routed to his or her own warehouse. In this case, the business inventory balances probably would be overstated. One bank employee caused checking account service charges to be credited to his own account instead of to the appropriate revenue account. In this case, the service charge revenue account would be less than the sum of charges to the checking account customers. Thorough auditing of accounting output records could detect computer-assisted frauds such as these.

Computer fraud is a matter of concern for entities, investors, and auditors. Experts in the field have coined two definitions related to computer chicanery: *Computer abuse* is the broad definition, but *computer fraud* is probably the term used more often. Both terms involve the use of computer technology by a perpetrator to achieve a gain at the expense of a victim.

Computer abuse and fraud include such diverse acts as intentional damage or destruction of a computer, use of the computer to assist in a fraud, and use of the mystique of computers to promote business. Perpetrators of the Equity Funding financial fraud used a computer to print thousands of fictitious records and documents that otherwise would have occupied the time of hundreds of clerks. Some services (such as "computerized" dating services) have promoted business on the promise of using computers when they are not actually used.

AUDITING INSIGHT Attention Shoppers

TJX Cos., a retail giant that owns **T.J. Maxx** and **Marshall's,** experienced a security breach when customer information was stolen from a computer network from an "unauthorized intruder." Hackers are believed to have used a radio antenna and laptop computer to decode data streaming through the air between hand-held price-checking devices, cash registers, and store computers. Subsequent evaluations concluded that TJX's network had less security than many home computer networks; one person familiar with the situation noted that "[i]t was as easy as breaking into a house through a side door that was wide open."

What are the total damages? As many as 200 million credit cards may have been compromised from four years of transactions. It may cost banks as much as $300 million to replace cards;

TJX's costs may exceed $1 billion over five years for consultants, security upgrades, attorney fees, and marketing programs designed to reassure customers. While unprecedented in potential magnitude, TJX is not unique in having its customers' information compromised. Other recent breaches of credit- and debit-card data in recent years include **B.J.'s Wholesale Club, Inc.** (40,000 cards), **DWS Retail Ventures, Inc.** (1.4 million cards), **CardSystems, Inc.** (40 million cards), and **Dollar Tree Stores, Inc.** (800 cards).

Sources: "Giant Retailer Reveals Customer Data Breach," *The Wall Street Journal*, January 18, 2007, pp. D1, D6; "How Credit-Card Data Went out Wireless Door," *The Wall Street Journal*, May 4, 2007, pp. A1, A12.

In a business environment, auditors and managers are concerned with acts of computer theft, embezzlement, or other misappropriation of the client's assets and the introduction of material misstatements in the client's financial statements. To perpetrate computer frauds, persons must have access to one or more of the following:

- The computer itself (or, in a LAN, a terminal connected to the computer network).
- Data files.
- Computer programs.
- System information.
- Time and opportunity to convert assets to personal use.

Computer financial frauds range from the crude to the complex and they hit financial institutions with alarming frequency. Moreover, computer financial frauds are frustratingly difficult to detect in the ordinary course of business. The AICPA conducted a study of computer frauds in the banking and insurance industry and found that customer complaints were the leading clues to discovery of fraud; routine audits were credited with discovery of 18 percent. Auditors have some success in detecting computer fraud, but they are not infallible detectives.

AUDITING INSIGHT Are Business Partners an IT Threat?

A recent survey by a global information security services firm (**Cybertrust**), found that nearly 75 percent of the respondents indicated their business partners (vendors and customers) increased the level of information security risk to their entities. Some of the most prevalent risks cited by respondents were network intrusions (68 percent), data theft (34 percent), virus infections (49 percent), and computer fraud (43 percent).

In addition to these findings, 32 percent of the surveyed entities reported a security incident with a business partner within the last year and 13 percent indicated they terminated a relationship with a business partner because of concerns regarding information security.

Source: "Are Your Business Partners an IT Threat?" *CFO.com*, October 16, 2006.

Preventive, Detective, and Damage-Limiting Controls

Entities can implement control procedures designed to prevent and detect computer frauds and to limit the extent of damage from them. Prevention controls avert errors and frauds entering the system. Detection controls are designed to discover frauds should they get past the prevention controls. Damage-limiting controls are designed to limit the damage if a fraud does occur. For example, transaction limit amounts restrict the amount of an individual fraudulent transaction to a preset tolerable amount. Some example prevention, detection, and damage limitation controls are presented in Exhibit H.11.

EXHIBIT H.11 Protecting the Computer from Fraud (Selected Controls)

	Objective of Control		
	Prevention	**Detection**	**Damage-Limiting**
Administrative Controls			
Security checks on personnel	X		
Separation of duties	X		
Access and execution log records (properly reviewed)		X	
Program testing after modification		X	
Rotation of computer duties		X	X
Transaction limit amounts			X
Physical Controls			
Inconspicuous location	X		
Controlled access	X		
Computer room guard (after hours)	X	X	
Computer room entry log record	X	X	
Preprinted limits on documents (e.g., checks)			X
Data backup storage			X
Technical Controls			
Data encryption	X		
Access control software and passwords	X		
Transaction logging reports		X	
Control totals (batch and hash totals)	X	X	
Program source comparisons (comparing versions of programs)		X	
Range checks on permitted transaction amounts			X
Reasonableness checks on permitted transaction amounts			X

As shown in Exhibit H.11, controls can be classified in three different levels: (1) administrative, (2) physical, and (3) technical. The administrative level refers to general controls that affect the management of an entity's computer resources. These controls are similar in nature to the entity's control environment and relate to the individuals employed by the entity and limitations or limits on the nature and scope of activities they perform.

The physical controls affect the computer equipment and related documents. The "inconspicuous location" control simply refers to placing PCs, terminals, and information processing centers in places out of the way of casual traffic. Of course, the equipment used daily must be available in employees' workplaces, but access must be controlled to prevent unauthorized persons from simply sitting down and invading the system and its data files.

Technical controls include some matters of electronic wizardry. Data encryption techniques convert information to scrambled form or code so it looks like garbled nonsense when transmitted or retrieved from a file. In recent years, industrial spying has increased. Businesses should assume that public and private intelligence services intercept and analyze data submitted by wire and airwaves (e.g., satellite transmission) for the purpose of commercial advantage. Unscrupulous industrial spies can try to break into an entity's computerized information system and elaborate password software will be necessary to thwart them. (Hackers have been known to program telephones to call random numbers to find a computerized information system and then try millions of random passwords to try to get in!) The "programmed range and reasonableness checks" refer to computer monitoring of transaction processing to try to detect potentially erroneous or fraudulent transactions. These are the equivalent of the low-tech imprint you may have seen on some negotiable checks (for example, "Not negotiable if over $500").

Computer Forensics

Computer forensics is one of the fastest growing areas of fraud investigation. The Federal Bureau of Investigation (FBI) defines *computer forensics* as "the science of acquiring, preserving, retrieving, and presenting data that has been processed electronically and stored on computer media."[11] In other words, computer hard drives are used as storage media; evidence can be retrieved even when the data have been deleted. Computer forensics has proven useful in tracking terrorists, prosecuting child pornographers, and even in impeaching a president. Compromising e-mails between President Bill Clinton and Monica Lewinsky and Congressman Mark Foley and one of his pages, although deleted, were recovered by computer forensic specialists. More recently, the FBI has successfully tracked several widespread computer viruses back to their creators.

Review Checkpoints

H.26 What are the five things a person must use to commit a computer fraud?

H.27 List physical controls that protect computerized information systems from fraud.

H.28 List technical controls that protect computerized information systems from fraud.

H.29 List administrative controls that protect computerized information systems from fraud.

H.30 How can an entity limit damages as a result of computer fraud?

[11] M. G. Noblett, M. M. Pollitt, and L. A. Presley, "Recovering and Examining Forensic Evidence," *Forensic Science Communications* 2 (October 2000).

Summary

Auditors should have enough familiarity with computers, computerized transaction processing, and computer controls to be able to audit simple systems and to work with information system auditors on more complex computerized information systems. This module provides insight into elements of a computerized information system, its related controls, and the methods used to evaluate the operating effectiveness of these controls.

The examination of client computer controls can take different forms. Auditors can audit "around" the computer as if computerized processing did not exist except as a very fast and accurate manual accounting processor. Alternatively, with enough computer expertise, auditors can audit "through" the computer to test its control features. Tests of computer controls described in the module include live data techniques (audit hooks, tagging transactions, SCARF, SARF, snapshot, monitoring of systems activity, and extended records), historical data techniques (parallel processing and generalized software applications), simulated data processing (test data and integrated test facility), and program analysis techniques (computer program flowcharting and cross-reference programs).

The ultimate goal of the tests of computer controls is to reach a conclusion about the operating effectiveness of control procedures in a computerized system. This conclusion allows auditors to assess the control risk (and risk of material misstatement) and determine the nature, timing, and extent of further substantive procedures for auditing the related account balances. This control risk assessment decision is crucial, particularly in computerized information systems, because subsequent work can be performed using data files that are produced by the computerized information system.

Not all businesses use large-scale systems, so this module includes an end-user (PC and LAN) environment orientation to information processing systems. Auditors must be aware of the typical control problems associated with such installations, as well as concerns when end-users develop their own applications. The module concludes with a section on computer fraud and computer forensics. While computer financial frauds range from the crude to the complex, computer financial frauds are frustratingly difficult to detect in the ordinary course of business. Computer forensics provides a tool to help auditors in their efforts to detect computer fraud and abuse.

Key Terms

audit hooks: Computer program modules used for audit or maintenance purposes, 804
auditing around the computer: Approach to auditing in a computerized processing environment in which auditors reconcile input to processing results without evaluating computer controls, 803
auditing through the computer: Auditors' actual evaluation of the client's hardware and software to determine the reliability of operations that cannot be viewed by the human eye, 803
automatic terminal logoff: A control that limits unauthorized computer access by automatically terminating the link between the PC and the LAN after a specified period of time, 795
backup: A retention system for files, programs, and documentation so master files can be reconstructed in case of accidental loss and processing can continue at another site if the computer center is lost to fire, flood, or other disaster, 793
batch processing: A method of processing transactions in which similar transactions are collected and periodically processed together through the same computer program, 792
Control Objectives for Information and Related Technology (COBIT): A set of best practices for information technology management; its objective is to provide the entity with information it needs to achieve its objectives with respect to the delivery of required information, 786
controlled reprocessing: See *parallel simulation*, 808
cross-reference computer programs: Programs that provide printed lists of every occurrence of each name used in an application program or of every file used in an application system, 808
echo check: A magnetic read after each magnetic write "echoing" back to the sending location and comparing results, 788

information technology application controls (ITAC): Computerized steps within the application software and related manual procedures to control the processing of various types of transactions. Major categories of ITAC are input controls, processing controls, and output controls, 788

information technology general controls (ITGC): Controls that apply to all application systems and help ensure their continued proper operations. Major categories of ITGC are hardware controls, program development controls, program change controls, computer operations controls, and access to programs and data controls, 788

integrated test facility (ITF): A technique used to test computer controls by creating a dummy department or branch complete with records of employees, customers, vendors, receivables, payables, and other accounts, 806

parallel simulation (or *controlled reprocessing* or *comparison program utilization*): Reprocessing live data to test program controls, 806

parity check: Electronic function that ensures that the coding of data internal to the computer does not change when it is moved from one internal storage location to another, 788

real-time processing: A method of processing transactions that does so on an individual basis as the transaction occurs, 792

sample audit review file (SARF): A random sampling selection scheme programmed into the data processing programs to produce representative samples of transactions processed over a period of time by the computer, 804

systems control audit review file (SCARF): Method in which auditors build into the data processing programs special limit, reasonableness, or other audit tests, 804

systems development and documentation standards manual: Computer documentation containing standards that ensure (1) proper user involvement in the systems design and modification process, (2) review of the specifications of the system, (3) approval by user management and data processing management, and (4) controls and auditability, 791

systems development life cycle: Process used to plan, develop, and implement new computerized information systems, 789

test data: Auditor-produced transactions used to audit computer controls with simulated data, 805

trap doors: Unauthorized computer program modules used for fraudulent purposes, 804

Multiple Choice Questions for Practice and Review

H.31 In a computerized information system, automated equipment controls or hardware controls are designed to
 a. Arrange data in a logical sequential manner for processing purposes.
 b. Correct errors in the computer programs.
 c. Monitor and detect errors in source documents.
 d. Detect and control errors arising from use of equipment.

H.32 A good example of application (user) computer software is
 a. Payroll processing program.
 b. Operating system program.
 c. Data management system software.
 d. Utility program.

H.33 Which of the following would lessen internal control in a computerized information system?
 a. The computer librarian maintains custody of computer program instructions and detailed lists.
 b. Computer operators have access to operator instructions and detailed program lists.
 c. The control group is solely responsible for the distribution of all computer output.
 d. Computer programmers write and debug programs that perform routines designed by the systems analyst.

H.34 Which of the following is true with respect to fraud risk factors in a computerized environment?
 a. Employees are more intelligent in a computerized environment.
 b. Auditors cannot audit the computerized information system during the year.
 c. Larger dollar amounts are involved in a computerized environment.
 d. Employees have greater access to information systems and computer resources in a computerized environment.

H.35 A procedural control used in the management of a computer center to minimize the possibility of data or program file destruction through operator error includes

 a. Control totals.

 b. Record counts.

 c. Limit checks.

 d. External labels.

H.36 Auditors would most likely use computer-assisted audit techniques (CAATs) to

 a. Make copies of client data files for controlled reprocessing.

 b. Construct a parallel simulation to test the client's computer controls.

 c. Perform tests of a client's hardware controls.

 d. Test the operative effectiveness of a client's password access control.

H.37 Which of the following client computerized information systems generally can be audited without examining or directly testing the computer programs of the system?

 a. A system that performs relatively uncomplicated processes and produces detailed output.

 b. A system that affects a number of master files and produces a limited output.

 c. A system that updates a few master files and produces no other printed output than final balances.

 d. A system that performs relatively complicated processing and produces very little detailed output.

H.38 The client's computerized exception reporting system helps auditors conduct a more efficient audit because it

 a. Condenses data significantly.

 b. Highlights abnormal conditions.

 c. Decreases the necessary level of tests of computer controls.

 d. Is an efficient computer input control.

H.39 Auditors will use the test data method to gain certain assurances with respect to

 a. Input data.

 b. Machine capacity.

 c. Control procedures contained within the program.

 d. Information technology general controls.

H.40 Assume auditors estimate that 10,000 cash disbursement checks were issued during the accounting period. If a computer application control that performs a limit check for each check request is to be subjected to the auditors' test data approach, the sample should include

 a. Approximately 1,000 test items.

 b. A number of test items determined by auditors to be sufficient under the circumstances.

 c. A number of test items under the circumstances.

 d. One transaction.

H.41 When auditing a computerized information processing system, which of the following is *not* true of the test data approach?

 a. The client's computer programs process test data under the auditors' control.

 b. The test data must consist of all possible valid and invalid conditions.

 c. The test data need consist only of those valid and invalid conditions in which auditors are interested.

 d. Only one transaction of each type need be tested.

H.42 Auditors cannot test the reliable operation of computer control procedures by

 a. Submission at several different times of test data for processing on the computer program the client uses for actual transaction processing.

 b. Manual comparison of detailed transactions that the internal auditors used to test a program to the program's actual error messages.

 c. Programming of a model transaction processing system and processing actual client transactions for comparison to the output produced by the client's program.

 d. Manual reperformance of actual transaction processing with comparison of results to the actual system output.

H.43 Auditors can obtain evidence of the proper functioning of password access control to a computerized information system by

 a. Writing a computer program that simulates the logic of a good password control system.

 b. Selecting a random sample of the client's completed transactions to check the existence of proper authorization.

 (c.) Attempting to sign onto the computerized information system with a false password.

 d. Obtaining representations from the client's computer personnel that the password control prevents unauthorized entry.

H.44 Control procedures within the computerized information system could leave no visible evidence indicating that the procedures were performed. In such instances, auditors should test these computer controls by

 a. Making corroborative inquiries.

 b. Observing the separation of duties of personnel.

 (c.) Reviewing transactions submitted for processing and comparing them to related output.

 d. Reviewing the run manual.

H.45 Which of the following statements most likely represents a disadvantage for an entity that performs its accounting using personal computers?

 a. It is usually difficult to detect arithmetic errors.

 (b.) Unauthorized persons find it easy to access the computer and alter the data files.

 c. Transactions are coded for account classifications before they are processed on the computer.

 d. Random errors in report printing are rare in packaged software systems.

H.46 Computerized processing performed <u>concurrently</u> with a particular activity so that results are available soon enough to influence a decision being made is referred to as

 a. Batch processing.

 (b.) Real-time processing.

 c. Integrated data processing.

 d. Random access processing.

H.47 Which of the following is *not* a characteristic of a batch processing system?

 a. The collection of like transactions that are sorted and processed sequentially against a master file.

 b. The keyboard input of transactions, followed by machine processing.

 c. The production of numerous printouts.

 (d.) The posting of a transaction, as it occurs, to several files, without intermediate printouts.

H.48 A customer intended to order 100 units of product Z96014 but incorrectly ordered product Z96015, which is not an actual product. Which of the following controls most likely would detect this error?

 (a.) Check digit verification.

 b. Record count.

 c. Hash total.

 d. Redundant data check.

H.49 Which of the following application controls would offer reasonable assurance that inventory data were completely and accurately entered?

 a. Sequence checking.

 (b.) Batch totals.

 c. Limit tests.

 d. Check digits.

H.50 Which of the following persons is responsible for controlling access to systems documentation and access to program and data files?

 a. Programmers.

 b. Data conversion operators.

 (c.) Librarians.

 d. Computer operators.

Exercises, Problems, and Simulations

H.51 **Auditing "around" versus Auditing "through" Computers.** Auditors may audit around or through computers in the examination of financial statements of clients who use computers to process accounting data.

Required:
- a. Describe the auditing approach referred to as *auditing around the computer*.
- b. Under what conditions do auditors decide to *audit through the computer* instead of *around* the computer?
- c. In auditing "through" the computer, auditors can use *test data*.
 - 1 What is the test data approach to testing computer controls?
 - 2 Why do auditors use the test data approach?
- d. How can auditors be satisfied that the client is actually using the computer program tested to process its accounting data?

<div align="right">(AICPA adapted)</div>

H.52 **Computer Internal Control Questionnaire Evaluation.** Assume that, when conducting procedures to obtain an understanding of Denton Seed Company's internal controls, you checked "No" to the following internal control questionnaire items:
- Does access to online files require specific passwords to be entered to identify and validate the terminal user?
- Does the user establish control totals prior to submitting data for processing? (Order entry application subsystem.)
- Are input control totals reconciled to output control totals? (Order entry application subsystem.)

Required:
Describe the errors and frauds that could occur due to the weaknesses indicated by the lack of computer controls.

H.53 **Batch versus Real-Time Processing.** In a computerized processing environment, transactions may be processed using either batch or real-time processing.

Required:
- a. Distinguish between batch and real-time processing. When is each method more likely to be used by the entity?
- b. Assume that input controls have been implemented to detect errors in entering numbers corresponding to customer accounts. How does the use of batch and real-time processing influence the ability of employees to make corrections to these account numbers if input errors have been made?

H.54 **File Retention and Backup.** You have audited the financial statements of Solt Manufacturing Company for several years and are making preliminary plans for the audit for the year ended June 30. This year, however, Solt has installed and used a computerized information system for processing a portion of its accounting data.

The following output computer files are produced in the daily processing runs:
1. Cash disbursements sequenced by check number.
2. Outstanding payable balances (alphabetized).
3. Purchase journals arranged by (i) account charged and (ii) vendor.

Solt's records as described are maintained in electronic format. All files are stored in a restricted area within the computer room. A grandfather-father-son policy is followed in retaining and safeguarding the files.

Vouchers (with supporting invoices, receiving reports, and purchase order copies) are filed by vendor code. Another purchase order copy and the checks are filed numerically.

Required:
- a. Explain the grandfather-father-son policy. Describe how files could be reconstructed when this policy is used.
- b. Discuss whether Solt's policies for retaining and safeguarding the files provide adequate protection against losses of data.

<div align="right">(AICPA adapted)</div>

H.55 **Separation of Duties and General Control Procedures.** You are engaged to examine the financial statements of Horizon Incorporated, which has its own computer installation. During the preliminary understanding phase, you found that Horizon lacked proper separation of the programming and operating functions. As a result, you intensified the evaluation of the internal control surrounding the computer and concluded that the existing compensating general controls provided reasonable assurance that the objectives of internal control were being met.

Required:

 a. In a properly functioning computerized environment, how is the separation of the programming and operating functions achieved?

 b. What are the compensating general controls that you most likely found?

<div align="right">(AICPA adapted)</div>

H.56 **Computer Frauds and Missing Control Procedures.** The following are brief stories of actual employee thefts and embezzlements perpetrated using computers.

Required:

What type of control procedure that might have prevented or detected the fraud was missing or inoperative?

 a. An accounts payable terminal operator at a subsidiary entity fabricated false invoices from a fictitious vendor and entered them in the parent entity's central accounts payable/cash disbursement system. Five checks totaling $155,000 were issued to the "vendor."

 b. A bank provided custodial and record-keeping services for several mutual funds. A proof-and-control department employee substituted his own name and account number for those of the actual purchasers of some shares. He used the computerized recordkeeping and correction system to conceal and shift balances from his name and account to names and accounts of the real investors when he needed to avoid detection because of missing amounts in the investors' accounts.

 c. The university computerized information system was entered. Vandals changed many students' first name to Susan, student telephone numbers were changed to the number of the university president, grade point averages were modified, and some academic files were deleted completely.

 d. A computer operator at a state-run horse race betting agency set the computer clock back three minutes. After the race had been won, he quickly telephoned bets to his girlfriend, an input clerk at the agency, gave her the winning horse and the bet amount, and won every time!

H.57 **Information Technology General Controls.** For each of the following examples of information technology general controls, classify the control based on appropriate category (hardware controls, controls over program development controls, controls over program changes, controls over computer operations, and controls over access to programs and data). In addition, for each, provide the objective of the control and one example of how auditors might test the operating effectiveness of the control.

 a. The entity schedules periodic, preventative maintenance on computer equipment.

 b. The entity requires the use of passwords and requires these passwords to be modified every three months.

 c. Proper documentation exists for "emergency" change requests for programs.

 d. Important files, programs, and documentation are backed up and stored in a safe, off-site location.

 e. The entity involves users in the design of programs and selection of prepackaged software.

 f. The entity resolves failures for transactions processed in a real-time environment on a timely basis.

 g. All program development activities are consistent with the entity's needs and objectives.

 h. All modifications to existing programs are properly documented.

 i. The functions of systems analyst, computer programmer, and computer operator are performed by different individuals.

 j. The entity monitors which individuals access various programs and cross-checks this use against an authorized user listing.

 k. Echo checks and parity checks are incorporated ("built in") to the computer hardware by the manufacturer.

H.58 **Information Technology Application Controls: Input Controls.** In its computerized information system over payroll transactions, Brady Company enters the following data from its employees' attendance records (# corresponds to a numeric field; A corresponds to an alphabetic field):

- Employee number (###-##-####, the employees' social security number).
- Entity division (AA##, an alphanumeric field containing two letters corresponding to the location of the employee and two numbers corresponding to that employees' supervisor).
- Hours worked (###.##, a weekly total of hours worked in 0.25-hour increments).

After data entry, these data are processed against the information maintained in that employee's master file record. The records are accessed based on employee number. If the employee is an hourly employee, the hours worked are multiplied by the pay rate; if a salaried employee, the hours worked are checked against a range of acceptable hours. After the gross pay is determined, information in the master file record is used to calculate income tax, FICA, and other withholdings from that employee's pay.

Required:

Provide an example of how Brady Company might incorporate each of the following input controls to verify the accuracy of input of employee attendance record information.

a. Check digit.

b. Record counts.

c. Batch totals.

d. Hash totals.

e. Valid character tests.

f. Valid sign tests.

g. Limit or reasonableness tests.

h. Error correction and resubmission procedures.

H.59 **Audit Simulation: Identify Computer Control Weaknesses.** Ajax, Inc., an audit client, recently installed a new computerized information system to process the shipping, billing, and accounts receivable records more efficiently. During interim work, an assistant completed the review of the computerized information system and the internal controls. The assistant determined the following information concerning the new computerized information system and the processing and control of shipping notices and customer invoices.

Each major computerized function (i.e., shipping, billing, accounts receivable) is permanently assigned to a specific computer operator who is responsible for making program changes, running the program, and reconciling the computer log. Responsibility for custody and control over the various databases and system documentation is randomly rotated among the computer operators on a monthly basis to prevent any one person from access to the database and documentation at all times. Each computer programmer and computer operator has access to the computer room via a magnetic card and a digital code that is different for each card. The systems analyst and the supervisor of computer operators do not have access to the computer room.

The computer system documentation consists of the following items: program lists, error lists, logs, and database dictionaries. To increase efficiency, batch totals (both batch totals and hash totals) and processing controls are not used in the system.

Ajax ships its products directly from two warehouses that forward shipping notices to general accounting. There, the billing clerk enters the price of the item and accounts for the numerical sequence of the shipping notices. The billing clerk also prepares daily adding machine tapes of the units shipped and the sales amounts. Shipping notices and adding machine tapes that are forwarded to the computer department for processing the computer output consist of the following:

1. A three-copy invoice that is forwarded to the billing clerk.

2. A daily sales register showing the aggregate totals of units shipped and sales amounts that the computer operator compares to the adding machine tapes.

The billing clerk mails two copies of each invoice to the customer and retains the third copy in an open invoice file that serves as a detail accounts receivable record.

Required:

 a. Prepare a list of weaknesses in internal control (manual and computerized); for each weakness, describe one or more ways to address it.

 b. Suggest how Ajax's computerized processing over shipping and billing could be improved through the use of remote terminals to enter shipping notices. Describe appropriate computer controls for such an online data entry system.

H.60 **Audit Simulation: Identify Control Weaknesses and Recommendations.** Georgia Beemster, CPA, is examining the financial statements of the Louisville Sales Corporation, which recently installed a computer. The following comments have been extracted from Beemster's notes on computer operations and the processing and control of shipping notices and customer invoices:

 To minimize inconvenience, Louisville made the conversion without changing its existing information processing system. The computer entity supervised the conversion and trained all computer department employees in systems design, operations, and programming.

 Each computer run is assigned to a specific employee who is responsible for making program changes, running the program, and answering questions. This procedure has the advantage of eliminating the need for records of computer operations because each employee is responsible for her or his own computer runs.

 At least one computer department employee remains in the computer room during office hours and only computer department employees have keys to the computer room.

 The computer entity furnished systems documentation consisting of a set of record formats and program lists. This documentation and the files are maintained in a corner of the computer department.

 The entity considered the desirability of computer controls but decided to retain the manual controls from its existing system.

 Entity products are shipped directly from public warehouses, which forward shipping notices to general accounting. There, a billing clerk enters the price of the items and accounts for the numerical sequence of shipping notices from each warehouse. The billing clerk also prepares daily adding machine tapes ("control tapes") of the units shipped and the unit prices.

 Shipping notices and control tapes are forwarded to the computer department for input and processing. Extension calculations are made on the computer. Output consists of invoices (in six copies) and a daily sales register. The daily sales register shows the aggregate totals of units shipped and unit prices, which the computer operator compares to the control tapes.

 All copies of the invoice are returned to the billing clerk. The clerk mails three copies to the customer, forwards one copy to the warehouse, maintains one copy in a numerical file, and retains one copy in an open invoice file that serves as a detailed accounts receivable record.

Required:

 Describe the weaknesses in the internal control over information and data flows and the procedures for processing shipping notices and customer invoices. Recommend some improvements in these control policies and procedures. Organize your answer sheet with two columns, one headed Weaknesses and the other headed Recommended Improvements.

 (AICPA adapted)

H.61 **Audit Simulation: Information Technology Application Controls.** The following provides a brief description of the computerized payroll system used by Merriman in its biweekly processing of payroll for its employees.

 1. Employee attendance (hours worked) is automatically recorded as they log in at the beginning and end of the workday.

 2. At the end of each payroll period (every two weeks), employees print and authorize their attendance records, submitting these records to their supervisor. These attendance records are prenumbered by the computer and are generated in chronological order based on when the employee submits his or her final attendance for that payroll period.

 3. Employee supervisors review the attendance records submitted by their employees and authorize these records. These records are then forwarded to data input personnel.

 4. Data conversion operators input the attendance record number, employee number, and hours worked from the attendance records that have been approved by the employee supervisors into a file to be used for computerized processing.

5. Once the entire batch of records has been accepted for processing, the computer program accesses the payroll master file data. Gross salary is then calculated as follows:

 a. For hourly wage employees, gross salary is determined by multiplying the hours worked from the transaction file by the wage rate contained within that employee's master file record.

 b. For salaried employees, the employee's gross salary is determined directly from the employee's master file record.

6. After the calculation of gross salary, information from the employee's payroll master file data, along with federal income tax and FICA withholding tables, is used to calculate deductions from that employee's pay.

7. A payroll register is generated, distributed, and reviewed for reasonableness and obvious processing errors.

8. Following the review of the payroll register, funds are transferred into the account designated by the employee (for those employees who have authorized electronic transfer of funds) or paychecks are prepared and held for employees.

Required:

For each of the above steps in Merriman's payroll processing, identify appropriate controls that either have been implemented or should be implemented by Merriman to ensure the authorized and accurate processing of payroll transactions.

H.62 **Flowchart Control Points.** Each number of the flowchart in Exhibit H.62.1 identifies a control point in the computerized payroll processing system. Make a list of the control points and, for each point, describe the type of internal control procedure that should be specified.

EXHIBIT H.62.1

H.63 **Audit Simulation: Internal Control Considerations in End-User Computing Environments.** Given the use of personal computers by many businesses, auditors must know about the potential internal control weaknesses inherent in such an environment. This knowledge is crucial if auditors are to make a proper assessment of the related control risk and to plan an effective and efficient audit approach.

Required:

In the following case study, assume that you are participating in the audit of Chicago Appliance Company and that the background information provided has been obtained during the planning phase. You have been asked to (1) consider the potential internal control weaknesses that exist in this end-user application and (2) assess how those internal control weaknesses could alter the audit plan for the current year.

BACKGROUND INFORMATION

Chicago Appliance is a wholesale distributor of electric appliances. The entity's sales in each of the last two years have been approximately $40 million. All accounting applications are handled at Chicago's corporate office.

Computerized information processing operations have historically centered on an onsite mainframe computer. The computer applications include accounts payable and cash disbursements, payroll, inventory, and general ledger. Accounts receivable and fixed asset records have been prepared manually in the past. Internal controls in all areas have been considered strong in the last few years.

During the past year, financial management decided to automate the processing of sales, accounts receivable, and fixed asset transactions and accounting. Management also concluded that purchasing a personal computer (PC) and related available software was more cost-effective than increasing the mainframe computer capacity and hiring a second computer operator. The controller and accounting clerks have been encouraged to find additional uses for the PC and to "experiment" with it when they are not too busy.

The accounts receivable clerk is enthusiastic about the PC but the fixed asset clerk seems somewhat apprehensive about it because he has no prior experience with computers. The accounts receivable clerk explained that the controller had purchased a "very easy-to-use" accounts receivable software application program for the PC, which enables her to input the daily information regarding billings and receipts quickly and easily. The controller has added some programming of his own to the software to give it better report-writing features.

During a recent demonstration, the accounts receivable clerk explained that the program required her to input only the customer's name and invoice amount in the case of billings or the customer's name and check amount in the case of receipts. The computer then automatically updates the respective customer's account balance. At the end of every month, the clerk prints and reconciles the accounts receivable trial balance to the general ledger balance and the controller reviews the reconciliation.

The fixed asset program also was purchased from an outside vendor. The controller indicated that the software package had just recently been put on the market and that it was programmed to compute tax depreciation based on recent changes in the federal tax laws. He also stated that, because of the fixed asset clerk's reluctance to use the computer, he had input all information from the fixed asset manual records. He indicated, however, that the fixed asset clerk would be responsible for the future processing related to the fixed asset files and for generating the month-end and year-end reports used to prepare the related accounting entries.

The various accounts receivable and fixed asset disks are all adequately labeled as to the type of program or data file. They are arranged in an organized manner in a disk holder located near the PC.

(Adapted from a case contributed by
PricewaterhouseCoopers to *The Auditor's Report.*)

H.64 **Test Data Transactions in a Payroll Processing Program.** Use the computer-based Electronic Workpapers on the textbook Web site to perform a test of the computerized payroll processing program.

The Electronic Workpapers contain a simple program that accepts payroll transaction input and calculates an individual's weekly gross and net pay. When you get to the proper place in the program, you will see places to input these data:

Employee identification (Social Security number).

Regular pay rate (round dollars, no cents).

Regular time (hours, 40 or fewer).

Overtime (hours over 40).

Gross earnings to date (gross pay prior to this payroll entry).

According to the client's description of the computer controls in the system:

1. The program checks for valid employee identification.
2. The regular pay rate is tested for reasonableness.
3. No more than 40 regular-time hours will be accepted by the system.
4. There is a limit on the number of overtime hours that will be paid.
5. Overtime is paid at the rate of 150 percent of the regular pay rate.
6. Social Security and Medicare taxes and federal income tax withholdings are calculated automatically according to applicable laws and regulations.

Applicable Laws and Regulations (Assume the following for this case)

The minimum wage is $7.25 per regular hour. Social Security tax is 6.2 percent on the first $97,500 of gross pay and Medicare tax is 1.45 percent of all pay. Federal income tax withholding is assumed to be 23 percent of gross pay.

Required:

The payroll calculation program contains control deficiencies. Your job is to identify and describe them. Follow the instructions in the Electronic Workpapers. Devise and enter test transactions of your own making. Write a memo to the audit partner identifying and describing the control failures in the payroll calculation program.

KAPLAN
CPA REVIEW

H.65 **Kaplan CPA Exam Simulation: The Effect of Computers on the Audit.**

Required:

Go to the Kaplan Web site at www.mhhe.com/louwers3e, click on AUD: Kerklaan Enterprises case and the "Research" tab, and complete the assigned task.

KAPLAN
CPA REVIEW

H.66 **Kaplan CPA Exam Simulation: Internal Control and Technology.**

Required:

Go to the Kaplan Web site at www.mhhe.com/louwers3e, click on AUD: Hardi Risk and Independence case and the "Audit and Technology" tab, and complete the assigned task.

Cases

Andersen: An Obstruction of Justice?

PROBLEM

Most students are familiar with Andersen as a CPA firm that failed to detect fraudulent financial activities in the audits of several companies including Sunbeam, Waste Management, Enron, and World-Com. While much has been written about the quality of these audits and how increasing the firm's revenues from both audit and nonaudit services may have supplanted audit quality as the main objective of Andersen as a firm, we should not lose sight of the facts that led to Andersen's demise and the findings that have occurred since Andersen ostensibly closed its doors as an audit and accounting firm.

In effect, Andersen had already received the maximum penalty even before the trial had begun. Once indicted, most of Andersen's clients had decided that an audit by a firm under indictment would be of little value, even if allowed by the SEC. During the shareholder proxy season in early 2002, company after company announced they would no longer retain Andersen as their auditor. Whether the firm was able to defend itself or not, the days of Andersen as a viable audit firm had come to an end.

ANDERSEN GOES TO TRIAL

In May 2002, Andersen LLP was tried for obstruction of justice in connection with the destruction of documents during a time period prior to a formal SEC investigation of Enron, one of Andersen's largest clients. The main witness for the prosecution was David Duncan, a former Andersen partner in charge of the Enron audit, who had already pleaded guilty to obstruction of justice. The guilt or innocence of Andersen hinged on the question of corporate direction. If David Duncan acted illegally on his own in an effort to save himself from consequences resulting from an SEC investigation of Enron, then Andersen as a firm would not likely be found guilty of obstructing justice. However, if David Duncan acted illegally on the direction of Andersen's management within the scope of his position in an attempt to save Andersen from the consequences of Enron, the firm as a whole can be held liable. Therefore, the questions to be answered are: (1) Were illegal acts committed and (2) Were they committed on behalf of David Duncan or on behalf of Andersen.

The Prosecution's Case

The chief prosecutor for the government was Samuel Bruell. The main points in Mr. Bruell's case were as follows:

- Top partners in Andersen's Chicago office had permitted Enron to use aggressive accounting practices that were very questionable given the nature of Enron's business.
- In late September through early October 2001, Andersen's legal department began creating a strategy designed to protect Andersen from regulators and litigants.
- A major part of the strategy was to invoke Andersen's document retention policy, which, according to prosecutors, was an obscure policy that was seldom read by its employees or followed on its audits. In addition, the policy was revised in 2000 by an Andersen partner who had been disciplined by the SEC for his involvement in the Waste Management audits. According to Mr. Bruell, management knew that involving the policy would lead to the destruction of "tons of papers and tens of thousands of computer files" that would be of interest to investigators.[1]

[1] Alexi Barrionuevo and Jonathan Weil, "High Noon: Andersen's Criminal Case Goes to the Jury," *The Wall Street Journal*, June 6, 2002, pp. C1, C20.

- The prosecution presented notes from an October 9 conversation between Nancy Temple, Andersen's legal council, and attorneys in Andersen's legal department. This conversation indicated that Ms. Temple believed an SEC investigation was imminent and that such an investigation could have devastating consequences for Andersen. Andersen was still operating under a court order signed in 2000 (due to a settlement of the Waste Management lawsuits) that could trigger a suspension of its license to audit publicly traded companies if it engaged in further securities law violations.

- David Duncan had admitted to destroying documents to keep them out of the investigation and that his actions were taken under direction and with the consent of Andersen management in Chicago.

- Finally, C. E. Andrews, an Andersen partner, in his testimony before Congress in January 2002 said that Mr. Duncan had given every appearance of destroying documents in anticipation of requests for documents from federal investigators.[2]

Andersen's Defense

Andersen's attorneys, led by Rusty Hardin, defended Andersen against all charges brought by the government.

- The government's case had fallen short of proving Andersen's guilt or even proving that a crime had occurred.

- Mr. Duncan had shredded documents prior to any formal investigation (Andersen was not subpoenaed until November 8, 2001) and the elimination of unnecessary documents was a normal audit procedure.

- It was clearly sound business practice to consult with the corporate attorneys with regard to potential litigation and the firm's rights and obligations with regards to that investigation. In fact, Mr. Duncan, at Ms. Temple's request, saved many documents that could have proved detrimental to Andersen.

- Mr. Hardin argued that David Duncan was innocent and that the government had overstated its case against Mr. Duncan in order to pressure him to cooperate with their investigation in exchange for a reduced sentence.

- While the prosecution focused on the part of the document retention policy that instructed auditors on the documents that could be destroyed, there were parts of the retention policy that indicated which documentation was required to be retained in the audit files.

THE CASE GOES TO THE JURY

While the prosecution and defense presentations were very contentious, possibly the most contentious part of the case focused on the instructions that Judge Melinda Harmon would give to the jury. The instructions hinged on the wording of the statute which makes it a crime to

> *knowingly* use intimidation or physical force, threaten, or *corruptly persuade* another person . . . with intent to . . . cause that person to withhold documents from or alter documents for use in an official proceeding (emphasis added).[3]

While both sides believed that the jury needed instructions that clarified the meaning of the statute in question, two issues were paramount in the argument concerning the instructions:

1. The phrase *knowingly . . . corruptly persuade* was discussed at length. The government contended that the word *knowingly* was not meant as a modifier of the term *corruptly persuade*. The jury was instructed that

> Even if the petitioner honestly and sincerely believed that the conduct was lawful, you may find the petitioner guilty.[4]

2. The government contended that the word *corruptly* needed to be defined for the jury. Prior rulings in the 5th district court (the same court district that was trying the Andersen case) had stated that corruptly was

> knowingly and *dishonestly,* with specific intent to *subvert or undermine* the integrity of the proceedings (emphasis added).[5]

[2] Ibid.

[3] 18 U.S.C. § 1512 (b)(2)(a) and (b).

[4] William H. Rehnquist, "Flawed Instructions Led to Andersen Verdict," *Chicago Daily Law Bulletin,* June 1 , 2005.

[5] Ibid.

The government insisted on excluding the word *dishonestly* and adding the word *impede* to the phrase "subvert and undermine." The instruction provided to the jury did not include the word *dishonestly* and included the phrase "subvert, undermine, or impede" government fact finding.

Having heard the testimony and been given these instructions, the jury convicted Andersen of obstruction of justice after deliberating for 10 days.

ROUND TWO

On May 31, 2005, in a unanimous decision, the Supreme Court of the United States overturned the Andersen conviction on the basis of flawed instructions to the jury. In writing the opinion, Chief Justice William Rehnquist cited the following arguments:

- Merely providing a person with information regarding a course of action cannot be construed as *persuading* another person . . . with *intent to* . . . *cause* that person to withhold documents.

- It is not necessarily *corrupt* in *persuading another person* . . . *with intent to* . . . *cause* that person to withhold documents. It may be proper for an attorney to persuade a client to withhold documents under attorney-client privilege from an investigation. In this circumstance, such persuasion would not be corrupt. Therefore, the withholding of documents from an investigation cannot by itself be presumed to be a *corrupt* action.

- Document retention polices are created to keep documents from being obtained by certain individuals and organizations, including the government. These policies are common in business and it is not wrongful for a manager to instruct employees to abide by such a policy.

- The term *knowingly* does modify the term *corrupt* both linguistically and per the intent of the statute. The jury instructions did not convey the requisite consciousness of wrongdoing that should be required for conviction.

- Substituting the term *impede* in place of *dishonestly* in the jury instructions removed the requirement that the action be with knowledge and forethought of wrongdoing. The term *impede* has a much broader concept. Anyone who innocently persuades another to withhold information might be considered to impede an investigation. Clearly, the term *corruptly* was included in the statute to exclude such innocent behavior from being consisted unlawful.

- A *knowingly corrupt persuader* cannot be someone who persuades others to shred documents under a document retention policy that was not enacted with regard to any particular proceeding in which those documents might be material. A series of events is not sufficient to indicate an intent to obstruct an investigation.

CONCLUSION

The headlines following the Supreme Court decision were telling:

"A Posthumous Victory," *USA Today,* June 1, 2005

"Arthur Andersen's Hollow Victory," *The Economist,* June 4, 2005

"Too Late for Andersen," *Legal Times,* June 6, 2005

"A Bittersweet Court Victory for Andersen," *Legal Times,* June 6, 2005

While Andersen had the verdict overturned because of faulty jury instructions, it is far from a vindication that what Andersen did was correct. In addition, such a decision comes much too late to provide anything but a moral victory to Andersen's former employees.

It is unlikely that the government will retry Andersen. First, there is little to gain in terms of either financial or other penalties. Andersen has already received the "death penalty" (and is no longer a viable entity), whether guilty or innocent. Second, should Andersen be retried, and should Andersen be found not guilty, the Department of Justice and the SEC would suffer severe blows to their reputation and receive a multitude of criticism from the business community. On the other hand, a retrial might be what the government needs to fend off criticism of being overzealous and overreaching in its prosecution of Andersen. But it does appear that the risks outweigh the rewards. Third, the government has received everything that it wanted with regards to Enron, WorldCom, and Andersen with the passage of the Sarbanes-Oxley Act. Most notably in terms of the Andersen case is a stricter document retention policy with more severe penalties.

It is interesting to note that many legal experts believe that the Department of Justice and the SEC took a vastly different attitude toward the 2005 tax-shelter problems of KPMG because of the lessons learned from the Andersen prosecution. Clearly, in the Andersen case there were no winners and the

elimination of another international CPA firm would further cause harm to innocent employees and create additional chaos in the business community.

Finally, in March 2007, a federal judge gave final approval to a $72.5 million settlement between Andersen and investors who sued the accounting firm over its role in Enron's collapse.[6] This finally puts to rest the case of Andersen and Enron, but the repercussions may live on indefinitely.

DISCUSSION QUESTIONS

1. Look up the term *corrupt* in the dictionary. What is the definition of *corrupt*? Was *corrupt* appropriately applied to the actions of Andersen?

2. The issues that overturned the Andersen verdict were based on faulty jury instructions and not on whether Andersen was in fact guilty or innocent. Based on the information in this case and other information you know, do you believe Andersen violated the law?

3. Do you believe that the Supreme Court's opinion overturning the lower court's decision was appropriate?

4. Should the SEC and the Department of Justice have tried Andersen as a firm or should they have targeted specific individuals that engaged in acts it believed to be unlawful?

5. While Andersen's conviction was overturned, do you believe that Andersen's employees acted in an ethical manner?

6. Comment upon the actions of David Duncan and Nancy Temple. Which of these parties do you feel is more responsible for the Andersen saga?

7. The class action lawsuit against Andersen also named the Canadian Imperial Bank of Commerce, J.P. Morgan Chase, Citigroup, Merrill Lynch, and Credit Suisse Group as co-defendants with Andersen. Why would the plaintiffs name so many entities in their lawsuit? Merrill Lynch and Credit Suisse have asked a U.S. appeals court to rule that the complaint should not have been certified as a class action suit. Why would these entities make such a claim?

[6] Jeff Feely, "Settlement Approved for Enron Investors," *Washington Post,* March 10, 2007.

Unhealthy Accounting at HealthSouth

PROBLEM

In 1996, key executives of HealthSouth, one of the nation's largest providers of health care services, began a massive fraud that eventually amounted to $2.7 billion[1] (a forensic review by PwC indicated the amount could be as high as $4.6 billion[2]).

HealthSouth was founded in 1984 by Richard Scrushy and co-workers at Lifemark, a Houston-based company that owned and managed hospitals.[3] They took HealthSouth public in 1986 and by 1996 the company had grown to a market value of $12 billion.[4] This massive fraud began in 1996 (although the government investigation team says that it may have started as early as 1986, but the team has not been able to prove it).[5]

According to the government's complaint, Scrushy, the chief executive officer, insisted that the company meet or exceed earnings expectations established by Wall Street analysts. Senior officers would present actual accounting earnings to Scrushy and, if they did not meet the forecasts, he reportedly told them to "fix it." Unknown to Scrushy (according to his testimony at trial), a team of senior accounting personnel, known as "the family," held "family meetings" to determine ways to increase accounting earnings. They would look for "holes" in the balance sheet to be filled. The fictitious accounting entries they used to plug those holes were referred to as "dirt." Methods included overestimating insurance reimbursements, overstating fixed assets, improperly capitalizing expenses, and overbooking reserve accounts.[6]

The "family" members started by manipulating contractual allowances through consolidating entry adjustments after the end of each quarter. The allowances accounted for the differences between what HealthSouth charged patients and the amounts the company could collect from the patients' health insurers. By lowering the allowances improperly, HealthSouth improved its net revenue and bottom-line earnings. To offset the contractual allowances, the company increased inventory, intangible assets, fixed assets, and even cash. The fictitious fixed asset line item at each facility was listed as "AP summary."[7] The company's CFO, William Owens, a former Ernst & Young senior manager and one of five CFOs who pled guilty to the fraud, also used the acquisition of Horizon/CMS to book $400 million worth of goodwill as part of the cover-up. He pulled the trick off with the help of two HealthSouth colleagues and a finance executive from Horizon.[8]

On paper, HealthSouth maintained impeccable corporate policies. It established a confidential whistle-blower hotline in 1997; developed a nonretaliation policy, which gave the compliance director direct access to the board; and established a centralized finance function. This centralized function seemed to be a particular advantage since other health care companies were falling apart because of problems in field offices. Reviewing these policies, it is not difficult to see why a massive fraud did not seem likely.[9]

Despite its appearances, actual corporate governance was quite different. Many decisions were made at the executive level, which limited checks and balances along the way. The audit committee met only once a year. The accounting systems in the field did not interface with the corporate enterprise-resource-planning software, making it necessary for results to be consolidated at the corporate level, where it was easy to "cook" the numbers.[10]

Scrushy, a former gas station attendant, fit the profile of the overbearing CEO who sets the wrong tone at the top. He reportedly managed by fear and intimidation. Scrushy installed security cameras throughout headquarters to watch employees. He allowed rank-and-file employees into his

[1] "Keeping Secrets: How Five CFOs Cooked the Books at HealthSouth," *CFO.com*, June 1, 2005.

[2] "HealthSouth Accounting Woes Grow to as Much as $4.6 Billion," *The Wall Street Journal*, January 21, 2004, p. B2.

[3] www.richardmscrushy.com/biography.aspx.

[4] "HealthSouth Faked Profits, SEC Charges—A $1.4 Billion Overstatement Cited as CEO Is Accused of Ordering 'Massive Accounting Fraud,'" *The Wall Street Journal*, March 20, 2003, p. C1.

[5] *Securities and Exchange Commission v. HealthSouth Corp. and Richard M. Scrushy*, Civ. Action No. CV-03-J-0615-S (N.D. Ala. filed March 19, 2003), Complaint for Injunctive and Other Relief.

[6] Ibid.

[7] Ibid.

[8] "Keeping Secrets: How Five CFOs Cooked the Books at HealthSouth," *CFO.com*, June 1, 2005.

[9] Ibid.

[10] "Questioning the Books: Audit Committee Met Only Once during 2001," *The Wall Street Journal*, March 21, 2003, p. A2.

executive suite only when he wanted to berate them.[11] According to the government's complaint, accounting personnel advised Scrushy in 1997 to abandon the fraud, but he refused, saying, "not until I sell my stock."[12] The five CFOs realized the error of their ways but most felt helpless to blow the whistle or even leave the company. One, Michael Martin, testified he tried to quit, but Scrushy reportedly said, "Martin, you can't quit. You'll be the fall guy."[13] However, when Treasurer Leif Murphy decided to leave the company because of the fraud, Martin punched him twice at his going-away party and wrote on his farewell card, "Eat [expletive] and die."[14]

AUDIT APPROACH

HealthSouth was the largest client of the Birmingham office of Ernst & Young (E&Y). The 2001 audit fee was $1.2 million and the firm billed an additional $2.5 million for other services. Many of HealthSouth's senior accounting staff had been E&Y employees.[15]

In hindsight, there had been red flags for the auditors to pursue. For example, from 1999 to 2001, net income rose nearly 500 percent while revenue grew only 5 percent.[16] The audit team also took no action when members learned that internal auditors were denied access to the corporate books. Finally, the team did not sufficiently investigate employee complaints.

The auditors were not oblivious to HealthSouth's risky profile. Jim Lamphron, a partner on the audit, said they focused on two risk factors: (1) "Company officials harboring a strong interest in seeing a rising stock price" and (2) "Management ranks dominated [by] those at the top." "Specifically, we were focusing on Richard Scrushy."[17] Despite E&Y's awareness of important fraud risks, the "family" was adept at the cover-up, making it difficult to detect certain aspects of the fraud. The SEC said that HealthSouth employees knew that E&Y questioned additions to fixed assets at any particular facility only if the additions exceeded a certain dollar threshold ($5,000), so the company avoided exceeding that dollar amount by spreading the adjustments below this materiality limit to various accounts and locations. When the auditors did question an accounting entry, HealthSouth officials created false documents to cover their tracks. When E&Y auditors asked for fixed assets ledgers for various facilities, accounting personnel would regenerate the ledgers, replacing the AP Summary line with the name of a specific fixed asset that did not exist at the facility.[18]

DISCOVERY

The fraud scheme began unraveling as a result of company whistle-blowers. One anonymous e-mail was sent to the auditors saying the company "fleeced shareholders" and listed four suspicious accounting practices. E&Y's review determined that the issues raised by the author of the e-mail "did not affect the presentation of HealthSouth's financial statements." Another e-mail, from Michael Vines and forwarded to audit partner Jim Lamphron, was passed onto CFO William Owens and George Strong, the audit committee chairman. Owens provided fake invoices for the questioned entries and dismissed the seriousness of this e-mail, indicating that Vines was just a disgruntled former employee.[19] (Vines had made frequent comments about the company's accounting on the employee electronic chat room and was regarded as something of a pest.)[20]

In October 1999, Diana Henze, assistant vice president of finance, noticed that earnings would jump with each iteration of quarter-end consolidations. She confronted Owens, who was controller at the time, and accused him of fraud. When she went to Kelly Cullison, corporate compliance officer, she was told the compliance officer "did not have access to the supporting documents" to determine whether or not the journal entries were legitimate. Henze brought the matter to her

[11] "Keeping Secrets."

[12] *SEC v. HealthSouth Corp.*, Civ. Action No. CV-03-J-0615-S, Complaint for Injunctive and Other Relief.

[13] "Keeping Secrets."

[14] "Former HealthSouth Executive Describes Deception and Abuse," *Bloomberg News*, February 18, 2005, p. E04.

[15] "Did Ernst Miss Key Fraud Risks at HealthSouth?" *The Wall Street Journal*, April 10, 2003, p. C1.

[16] "Missing the Red Flags," *BusinessWeek*, April 14, 2003, p. 72.

[17] "Scrushy Watch: The End Is Near. With Only a Handful of Witnesses Left, the Defense Needs a Lucky Break," www.birminghamweekly.com, December 1, 2005.

[18] *SEC v. HealthSouth Corp.*, Civ. Action No. CV-03-J-0615-S, Complaint for Injunctive and Other Relief.

[19] "Missed Signal: Accountant Tried in Vain to Expose HealthSouth Fraud—Ex-Employee Took His Case to Auditors, Then Web—But Convinced No One—What about the Others?" *The Wall Street Journal*, May 20, 2003, p. A1.

[20] "The Economy: Ernst & Young Got a Warning on HealthSouth," *The Wall Street Journal*, April 24, 2003, p. A2.

supervisor, cofounder Tony Tanner, who told her the entries were the result of reversing out a number of reserves and that the matter was closed.[21] Henze said that she was subsequently passed over for a promotion that would have given her more involvement with the books. When she asked why a less-qualified person got the job, Owens told her, "You have made it clear you won't do what we asked."[22]

William Owens finally went to the authorities when his wife threatened to divorce him because she thought (correctly) that he would end up in jail.[23] Owens agreed to wear a wire when meeting with Scrushy. Scrushy is on tape as saying, "You got accountants signing off on all this." In an impromptu meeting at a lake, Scrushy is recorded as telling Owens, "Just remember, I got eight kids. I got a bunch of babies at home. They need their daddy." Scrushy also told Owens, "If you want to go public with all this, get ready to get fired, and everyone goes down with you," according to the transcript of the recording Owens made of Scrushy.[24] Once Owens came forth, the investigation quickly uncovered the massive fraud as other employees cut deals with prosecutors.

Scrushy is a local hero in Birmingham with supporters in all corners. A lavish donor to local colleges, libraries, and medical centers, he was also a regular preacher at area churches. He even aired his own TV talk show each day before court and hosted his own Web site (www.richardm-scrushy.com/).[25] His defense attorneys sought to depict him as a detached leader and visionary rather than a micromanager with unchallenged influence. In the end, he was acquitted of all charges in what many see as a blow to enforcement of the Sarbanes-Oxley Act (Scrushy had certified statements on the 10-K dated August 14, 2002, under the Sarbanes-Oxley Act.).[26] Jurors said key witnesses were not credible and the prosecution failed to present substantial evidence linking the fraud to Scrushy. "The smoking gun wasn't pointing toward Mr. Scrushy."

Scrushy subsequently settled claims from the SEC by paying $81,000,000[27] and claims from the company for an undisclosed amount. Other claims are still outstanding.[28]

In October 2006 Scrushy was convicted for paying $500,000 to a campaign of former Alabama Governor Don Siegelman in exchange for a seat on a hospital regulatory board. He was sentenced in June 2007 to nearly seven years in prison.[29]

DISCUSSION QUESTIONS

1. What are several red flags that Ernst & Young either was or should have been aware of in the audit of HealthSouth?
2. What procedures can auditors perform to detect fraudulent entries made during the consolidation process?
3. How can auditors determine the true "tone at the top" of a company?
4. What is the appropriate response by auditors to information from "disgruntled" employees?
5. HealthSouth has sued Ernst & Young and Ernst & Young is also the target of a federal securities class action suit. What are Ernst & Young's likely defenses against HealthSouth? Against the class action suit?
6. HealthSouth concealed the fraud by keeping the fraudulent transactions below $5,000. What recommendation would you have to Ernst & Young to improve its sampling practices?

[21] "Executives on Trial: Witness Says HealthSouth Tried to Appease Street," *The Wall Street Journal*, February 23, 2005, p. C4.

[22] "Witness Lost Promotion after Asking Questions," *USA Today*, February 22, 2005, www.usatoday.com/money/industries/health/2005-02-22-scrushy-usat_x.htm.

[23] "Keeping Secrets."

[24] Ibid.

[25] Ibid.

[26] *SEC v. HealthSouth Corp.*, Civ. Action No. CV-03-J-0615-S, Complaint for Injunctive and Other Relief.

[27] "Scrushy Case Comes to Muted Settlement," *The Wall Street Journal*, April 24, 2007, p. A3.

[28] "HealthSouth Corp.: Scrushy Settles Claims Tied to Bonuses, Legal Bills," *The Wall Street Journal*, November 30, 2006, p. A14.

[29] "Business and Finance," *The Wall Street Journal*, June 29, 2007, p. A1.

KPMG: How Many Firms?

BACKGROUND

How many major accounting firms are needed to provide companies with enough choice? Because of their scale, expertise, and international presence, the world's largest corporations have traditionally relied on the largest accounting firms to conduct their audits. As late as 1988, the "Big Eight" firms (Arthur Andersen & Co., Arthur Young & Company, Coopers & Lybrand, Deloitte Haskins & Sells, Ernst & Whinney, KPMG, Price Waterhouse & Co., and Touche Ross & Co.) dominated the market for audit services. In 1989, mergers between Ernst & Whinney and Arthur Young (to form Ernst & Young) and Deloitte Haskins & Sells and Touche Ross (to form Deloitte & Touche) reduced choices to six providers. The merger of Price Waterhouse and Coopers & Lybrand in 1998 as PricewaterhouseCoopers limited them to five.

While a company's options with respect to the choice of an independent auditor were reduced by almost 50 percent, not until the Justice Department's dissolution of Arthur Andersen in 2002 were concerns raised about the lack of choices in the market for audit services and its impact on the competitiveness of the industry. (Arthur Andersen's verdict was overturned by the Supreme Court in 2005, but its partners and personnel had pursued other employment opportunities and it is unlikely that the firm will reemerge as a major international accounting firm under either its former or an alternative name.)

The gulf between the Big Four and the next tier of accounting firms can be best illustrated by comparing KPMG (the smallest of the Big Four, in terms of revenues) with Grant Thornton, the fifth largest accounting firm. In 2004, KPMG's revenues were $4.1 billion, compared to $635 million at Grant Thornton; in addition, the number of staff employed by these two firms was 18,300 versus 3,900, respectively.[1] Viewed from a consumer's standpoint, Big Four firms audited all but 12 of the Fortune 500 companies in 2004 and all but 13 of the Fortune 1000 companies in 2005.[2]

In addition to a smaller set of large accounting firms, public companies are further constrained by provisions of the Sarbanes-Oxley Act. In an effort to enhance auditor independence, Sarbanes-Oxley prohibits auditors from providing various types of nonaudit services to their audit clients. This prohibition was in response to the large shift of accounting firm revenues from primarily audit revenues to revenues for other services.[3] For example, in 1975, the percentage of total revenues from the then–Big Eight firms derived from audit services ranged from 62 percent (Touche Ross & Co.) to 76 percent (Price Waterhouse & Co.); in 2000, this same percentage ranged from 31 percent (Deloitte & Touche) to 45 percent (KPMG).[4]

As a result of Sarbanes-Oxley, public companies have engaged other Big Four firms for nonaudit services. As just one example, the Big Four are currently providing Wabtec Corp. with auditing (Ernst & Young), internal control testing (Deloitte & Touche), acquisitions advising (KPMG), and tax services (PricewaterhouseCoopers). If Wabtec decided to change auditors yet retain a Big Four firm, it would need to consider the effect of these services on the independence of its new auditor. A survey by J.D. Powers & Associates of the 400 companies with more than $1 billion in revenue revealed that 55 percent of these companies are using more than one Big Four firm to provide various types of services (including audit services).[5]

The bottom line is that two independent developments (a smaller number of international accounting firms and Sarbanes-Oxley's limitations on the nonaudit services that can be provided by a company's auditors) have significantly impacted companies' choices of auditors. Perhaps this dilemma can be best reflected by the recent experiences of two large organizations.

First, Intel Corp. recently considered proposals for its audit engagement from all four firms. Ernst & Young, who has audited Intel's financial statements for more than 30 years, was retained.

[1] "Grant Thornton Battles Its Image," *The Wall Street Journal,* June 9, 2005, p. C1.

[2] Ibid.; "BDO Seidman Faces Accounting's New World," *The Wall Street Journal,* September 27, 2005, pp. C1, C4.

[3] One particularly striking (and timely) example of this shift was Arthur Andersen's revenues derived from providing services to Enron. In the last year of the firm's audit of Enron, Arthur Andersen's audit revenues were $25 million, while revenues from other services provided to Enron were $27 million. These other services included business process and risk management consulting, tax compliance and consulting, due diligence procedures related to acquisitions or other activities, work performed in connection with registration statements, and various statutory or other audits (information drawn from Enron's March 27, 2001, proxy statement filed with the Securities and Exchange Commission).

[4] Stephen A. Zeff, "How the U.S. Accounting Profession Got Where It Is Today: Part II," *Accounting Horizons,* December 2003, p. 270.

[5] "Firms' Auditor Choices Dwindle," *The Wall Street Journal,* June 21, 2005, p. C1.

This decision was largely driven by the nonaudit service provided to Intel by the other Big Four firms. Cary Klafter, Intel's corporate secretary, noted that "[b]ecause there are only a limited number of large multinational audit firms that do the kind of work that we need, if we were to switch audit firms, all sorts of dominos would fall."[6]

Second, when Fannie Mae dismissed KPMG as its auditor in the wake of an accounting scandal, its choices for a successor were slim: Deloitte & Touche has been advising the federal government in its probe of Fannie Mae, Ernst & Young has been providing consulting services to Fannie Mae's audit committee responding to the probes related to the scandal, and PricewaterhouseCoopers audits Freddie Mac, a major competitor.[7]

Could something happen to limit companies' choices even further?

THE PROBLEM

KPMG recently disclosed that it was negotiating with the Department of Justice regarding "abusive" tax shelters sold to some of its clients between 1996 and 2002. KPMG received $124 million in tax consulting fees from promoting these shelters, which allowed individuals and corporations to improperly avoid over $1.4 billion in federal taxes.[8] E-mail messages obtained and released by the Internal Revenue Service indicated that KPMG officials were aware that the tax shelters were questionable.

As one example, a shelter referred to as bond-linked issue premium structures (BLIPS) created $5 billion in tax losses for investors. Under this shelter, clients would purchase foreign currency from offshore banks with funds borrowed from those same banks, only to sell the currency back to the same bank a few months later. These investments were presented to the Internal Revenue Service as seven-year investments.[9] Other shelters in question carried similar names such as FLIP, OPIS, and SOS.

As part of their ongoing negotiations, KPMG has admitted guilt on the part of some of its partners and has taken various internal actions to reduce the likelihood of further actions (such as terminating a number of partners in its tax services division, restructuring its management team, and discontinuing marketing of this type of tax service). On August 26, 2005, KPMG admitted to criminal tax fraud and agreed to a payment of $456 million in penalties (an average of $300,000 per KPMG partner); the government has agreed to deferred adjudication and will drop all charges after December 31, 2006.[10] Currently, eight former KPMG partners and one outside attorney have been indicted with conspiracy to defraud the U.S. government.

It appears that KPMG has avoided the fate of Arthur Andersen: dissolution. However, the KPMG case has raised numerous questions about the future of the accounting profession if the small number of international accounting firms should become even smaller. For example, the Securities and Exchange Commission discussed various actions to assist companies in changing auditors if KPMG was indicted, including allowing companies to seek waivers to the stricter independence rules on a case-by-case basis and allowing KPMG to continue to perform audits if it is indicted. An unidentified SEC official indicated that "[w]e have scenarios in place for any eventuality that could come out of this."[11] In addition, prior to the settlement, Deloitte & Touche, Ernst & Young, and PricewaterhouseCoopers reportedly requested that their partners not solicit current KPMG clients.[12]

EPILOGUE

On January 5, 2007, U.S. District Judge Loretta Preska agreed to dismiss criminal charges against KPMG. In its deferred prosecution agreement with the government, KPMG agreed to pay $456 million in fines, admit wrongdoing, and accept an outside monitor. On July 16, 2007, U.S. District Judge Lewis Kaplan dismissed indictments against 13 of 16 former KPMG partners because of

[6] Ibid.

[7] "Fannie Mae's Dismissal of KPMG Shows Dwindling Choices among Big Four," *The Wall Street Journal*, December 23, 2004, p. C1.

[8] "Grand July Investigating KPMG Tax Shelters," *CFO.com*, February 23, 2004, www.cfo.com//article.cfm/3012085.

[9] "Inside the KPMG Mess," *BusinessWeek*, September 12, 2005, pp. 46-47.

[10] Ibid.

[11] "SEC Weighs a 'Big Three' World," *The Wall Street Journal*, June 22, 2005, p. C1.

[12] "No Poaching from KPMG, Say Audit Firms," *CFO.com*, August 24, 2005, www.cfo.com//article.cfm/4315600.

violations of these individuals' rights to counsel. This violation occurred because prosecutors pressured KPMG not to pay for the partners' legal defense costs. Judge Kaplan ruled that the "government held the proverbial gun to its [KPMG's] head" and that prosecutors were "economical with the truth" in responding to allegations that they pressured KPMG regarding paying the legal costs of its ex-partners.[13] As of this writing, prosecutors were expected to appeal Judge Kaplan's ruling.

In the midst of this activity, federal prosecutors indicted four current and former partners of Ernst & Young on similar charges. The shelters designed and sold by these partners brought Ernst & Young $120 million in fees. Those familiar with the matter do not expect that the firm itself will face criminal charges in this matter.[14]

QUESTIONS

1. Do professional standards allow a company's auditor also to provide tax services and retain their independence?
2. How have provisions of the Sarbanes-Oxley Act limited a public company's choice of auditors?
3. What are some of the advantages and disadvantages of permitting auditors to provide nonaudit services (such as tax services) to clients?
4. What is the impact of a smaller number of major international accounting firms on public companies?

[13] "KPMG Case Turns Sour for U.S.," *The Wall Street Journal,* July 17, 2007, p. A3; "In KPMG Case, the Thorny Issue of Legal Fees," *The Wall Street Journal,* June 12, 2007, p. C5.

[14] "Tax-Shelter Indictments Leave a Cloud over Ernst," *The Wall Street Journal,* May 31, 2007, p. C1.

Something Went Sour at Parmalat[1]

PROBLEM

There was much confusion when Italian dairy food giant Parmalat defaulted on a $187 million bond payment in mid-November 2002. Default on a bond payment seemed difficult to believe with a Parmalat subsidiary in the Cayman Islands holding a $4.9 *billion* cash balance in a Bank of America account. The problem was that no such account existed.

Subsequent investigation revealed that, over a 15-year period, Parmalat's management falsified accounts and created assets to hide losses of $10 billion from Parmalat's Latin American operations. Other allegations charged that Parmalat's management had lied about repurchasing $3.6 billion in bonds, which they never did. By hiding losses and increasing assets on its balance sheet, Parmalat was able to continue to borrow enough money from investors and creditors to conceal and perpetuate the fraud.

AUDIT APPROACH

From 1990 to 1999, the Italian branch of Grant Thornton audited Parmalat. Under Italian law, however, Parmalat was forced to change auditors periodically and chose the Italian branch of Deloitte Touche Tohmatsu (Deloitte & Touche SpA) to be the company's new auditor in 2000. Grant Thornton, however, continued to audit Parmalat's off-shore subsidiaries located in the Cayman Islands.

Auditors first inquired about the Cayman Islands account in December, 2002, and received a letter on Bank of America letterhead in March, 2003, confirming the existence of the account. The letter, however, was a forgery, created in Parmalat's headquarters. Nevertheless, the $4.9 billion was listed on the subsidiary's balance sheet as of December 31, 2002, and consolidated into Parmalat's balance sheets dated December 31, 2002, and June 30, 2003.

The auditors missed several red flags. First, the size of the account should have been a red flag. It is very unusual for a large company to have so much cash in a bank account. In addition, between January 2000 and September 2003, Parmalat raised more than $5 billion in debt offerings. With so much cash available, why was Parmalat continuing to borrow money?

Second, the communication received from the Bank of America was in the form of a facsimile (see Exhibit 1), which raises two issues. First, a fax transmission is not subject to the same level of control as returning an original confirmation. Basically, a fax can be sent from almost anywhere and the originating phone number can be falsified by simply changing the phone number in the transmitting fax machine. A mailed confirmation, however, passes through the federal mail system and is postmarked with the originating zip code. Also, this particular fax was smudged, raising further suspicions. Forgers routinely "age" their "original" by repeatedly photocopying it to obscure any tell-tale photocopying lines. Given these circumstances, the auditors should have followed up directly with the bank.

Third, when such large balances comprise a significant portion of a company's balance sheet (in this case, 38 percent of Parmalat's assets were in the subsidiary's bank account), auditors should take additional care to obtain further corroboration. All told, the combination of a large bank account and a questionable form of confirmation should have provided Deloitte & Touche SpA sufficient warning to dig a little deeper.

DISCOVERY

Parmalat management also told Deloitte & Touche SpA that the company had a $617 million investment in an open-ended mutual fund that it could access at any time. The company, however, was unsuccessful in its attempts to retrieve the funds. Because no evidence was available to support management's claims, Deloitte & Touche SpA included a qualification in its audit review report highlighting the lack of evidence and alerted regulators of suspicions of a larger fraud.

Initial investigation revealed that massive amounts (estimates as high as $19 billion) of assets were missing or nonexistent. Parmalat and its subsidiaries filed for bankruptcy protection in Italy on December 27, 2003.

During the ongoing investigation, a Parmalat employee who disobeyed orders to destroy company documents turned over a number of incriminating floppy disks to investigators. With evidence mounting, Parmalat's founder and CEO Calisto Tanzi admitted to prosecutors that he was aware of

[1] G. Edmondson and L. Cohn, "How Parmalat Went Sour," *BusinessWeek Online,* January 12, 2004.

EXHIBIT 1

DEC 17 2003 16:01 FR BANK OF AMERICA 2019743539 TO 918467334872 P 01/1
17.DEC.2003 11:50 GRAN THORNTON SPA NR.201 P.3

Bank of America

New York Branch

Grant Thornton Spa
Largo Augusto, 7 March 6, 2003
20122 MILANO, ITALY

Re: Bonlat Financing Corporation
BANY Account No.: 6550-2-52252
BANY Securities Deposits No.: 6550-2-85419

Dear Sir/Madam

We have received your request for audit purposes dated December 20,2002. We confine our response to certain information concerning account balances and securities deposits from our records at this office.

1. As of the close of business on December 31,2002, our records indicate the following deposit balance(s):

Account Type	Account Name	Account Number	Account Balance
Demand Deposit	Bonlat Financing Corporation	6550-2-52252	USD $336,812,328.64 CR
AutoInvest Account	Bonlat Financing Corporation	N/A	N/A

2. As of the close of business on December 31,2002, our records indicate the following Securities Deposit balance(s):

Account Type	Account Name	Account Number	Account Balance
Securities Deposit	Bonlat Financing Corporation	6550-2-85419	EUR €2,811,000,000.00
Securities Deposit	Bonlat Financing Corporation	6550-2-85419	USD $949,000,000.00

3. As of the close of business on December 31,2002, our records indicate the following Letter of Credit balance:

Trade Finance	Customer Name	Reference Number	Outstanding
	N/A	N/A	N/A

This information is for your CONFIDENTIAL use and is furnished in reply to your inquiry. No responsibility is assumed by Bank of America or its officers to the accuracy or completeness of this information. No representation is made as to any other relationship the subject may have with other Bank of America offices.

Sincerely,

Agnes Belgrave

Bank of America
100 West 33rd Street, New York, NY 10001

the fraud. He also admitted to misappropriating Parmalat assets (over $1 billion, prosecutors believe) to cover losses in other family-owned companies. It is unlikely that investigators will ever know for certain what happened to the missing funds (whether they were used to cover operating losses, pay creditors, or illegally enrich management). Twenty other Parmalat executives, including Tanzi's son and brother, the company's former CFO, former board members, and even the company's lawyers, were indicted on charges including fraud, embezzlement, false accounting, and misleading investors. On June 28, 2005, a judge accepted plea bargains from eleven of those charged and sentenced them to prison ranging from 10 months to 2.5 years. Calisto Tanzi is currently in prison awaiting a trial scheduled to begin in January 2008. If convicted, Tanzi faces up to 15 more years in prison.

DISCUSSION QUESTIONS:

1. What steps does an auditor ordinarily take when confirming cash balances held on deposits with financial institutions?
2. What additional steps should the auditors have taken when they received the smudged fax copy printed on Bank of America letterhead?
3. What *red flags* did the auditors miss?
4. What steps should Deloitte & Touche SpA have taken with respect to Grant Thornton's audit of the Cayman Island subsidiaries?

To Indemnify or Not to Indemnify: That is the Question

More and more auditing firms are requiring "liability caps" (agreements to limit companies' abilities to sue their auditors for accounting problems found) be included in engagement letters. Understandably, the accounting firms prefer arbitration or mediation over potentially disastrous litigation. Clients have been agreeing to the indemnification clauses because they are afraid that they might lose their auditor if they don't.

SEC rules prohibit clients from indemnifying their auditors, so the actions have raised serious questions as to the agreements' enforceability. The SEC's concern is that such agreements impair auditing firm independence because they may result in reduced performance in reliance. In other words, because the firm is protected through the indemnification or limitation of liability provision, the firm doesn't have to do as good a job. Former SEC Chief Accountant Lynn Turner echoes this concern: "The auditors, rather than doing better audits, have chosen a course of action that will prohibit people from taking action to recoup their losses."

The firms don't see the provisions as a liability cap as much as a dispute resolution alternative. Robert Kueppers, deputy chief executive of Deloitte & Touche LLP's U.S. operations states: "I don't understand how they cap your liability. . . . The provisions are about setting up a mechanism to resolve disputes between auditors and clients and they don't interfere with auditor independence or investors' ability to sue auditors."

The AICPA's Professional Ethics Executive Committee (PEEC) is responsible for creating new ethics interpretations and rulings, for monitoring those standards, and making revisions as necessary. Their stand is that independence concerns "could be sufficiently mitigated provided the limitation of liability or indemnification agreement was contingent on the member's attest services being performed in compliance with professional standards." In other words, the liability cap (or other alternative dispute resolution) only works if the firm followed generally accepted auditing standards.

DISCUSSION QUESTIONS

1. Assume the role of the auditor. Why would you prefer alternative dispute resolution (e.g., arbitration, mediation) to the U.S. legal system?
2. Assume the role of the client company. How do you feel about liability caps for auditors?
3. Assume the role of an investor. How do you feel about liability caps for auditors?
4. Assume the role of the SEC. Why do liability caps impair independence?
5. Assume the role of the PEEC. What are your responsibilities to AICPA members? What are your responsibilities to the public?

Sources: "Audit-Engagement Provisions Raise Queries," *The Wall Street Journal,* March 6, 2006, p. C1; "Auditing 'Liability Caps' Face Fire," *The Wall Street Journal,* November 28, 2005, p. C3. "More Companies Are Disclosing Pacts With Auditors on Liability Caps," *The Wall Street Journal,* June 22, 2006, p. C4.

GE: How Much Are Auditors Paid?

The financial report accompanying this letter is historic in that it is our first one covered by Section 404 of The Sarbanes-Oxley Act of 2002 (SOX) . . . But what does it mean to you? Is it a "check-the-box" bureaucracy based on an overreaction to the market scandals of yesterday? None of us likes more regulation, but I actually think SOX 404 is helpful. It takes the process control discipline we use in our factories and applies it to our financial statements. Implementing SOX 404 cost GE $33 million in 2004. But we think it is a good investment.

Jeffrey R. Immelt, Chairman of the Board and Chief Executive Officer,
General Electric,
Letter to Shareholders from 2004 annual report

BACKGROUND

Since its required implementation in 2004, Section 404 of Sarbanes-Oxley has generated a great deal of controversy. Its requirement that auditors assess the operating effectiveness of their clients' internal controls over financial reporting and express opinions on both the effectiveness of their clients' internal controls over financial reporting and management's assessment of its internal control over financial reporting has imposed significant costs on accelerated filers.[1] Surveys conducted by the Financial Executives Institute (FEI) found that the average costs associated with Section 404 compliance were $4.4 million, $3.8 million, and $2.9 million in 2004, 2005, and 2006, respectively.[2] While these amounts pale in comparison to General Electric's costs ($33 million), they represent a significant expense for the affected companies.

The costs of Sarbanes-Oxley have been cited as having significant impact in the U.S. capital markets. For example, a higher dollar amount of initial public offerings (IPOs) have been made on overseas exchanges since the implementation of Section 404 (see Exhibit 1). Many companies cite the high costs of Sarbanes-Oxley compliance as a factor in their choice of stock market listing; in 2002 (prior to Sarbanes-Oxley), 9 of the top 20 IPOs were on U.S. stock exchanges, compared to only 3 of the top 20 IPOs in 2006.[3]

Among other reasons, the high costs of compliance with Section 404 resulted in the issuance of *Auditing Standard No. 5 (AS 5)*, which supersedes *Auditing Standard No. 2*. Major changes under *AS 5* include (1) eliminating the requirement for auditors to evaluate and opine on management's assessment of internal control over financial reporting; (2) encouraging auditors to adopt a "top-down, risk-based" approach, resulting in more efficient audits; and (3) expanding the potential use of others' work in the assessment of internal control over financial reporting. SEC Chairman Christopher Cox notes that, as a result of the passage of *AS 5*, "the unduly high costs of implementing Section 404 of the [Sarbanes-Oxley] act will come down" because companies "will be able to focus on the greatest risk of material misstatements in the financials."[4] Some estimate that this cost reduction could be as great as 10 percent.[5]

In addition to the provisions of Section 404 related to internal control over financial reporting, Sarbanes-Oxley reduced auditors' ability to provide nonaudit services to their clients. Section 201 prohibited two major types of services that had become a significant revenue source for accounting firms: (1) financial information systems design and implementation and (2) internal audit outsourcing. Not coincidentally, these were two areas in which Arthur Andersen provided extensive services to Enron prior to its failure. Further, Section 202 required that all nonaudit services (with

[1] Accelerated filers are those public entities filing a financial statement with the SEC that have market capitalizations of greater than $75 million. Initially, public entities with market capitalizations of less than $75 million were to be subject to the provisions of Section 404 in 2005 (one year following the effective date for accelerated filers). However, because of SEC-mandated delays, smaller entities have yet to implement Section 404.

[2] www.fei.org/eweb/Dynamicpage.aspx?webcode=adv_sox.

[3] "Business Wins Its Battle to Ease a Costly Sarbanes-Oxley Rule," *The Wall Street Journal*, November 10, 2006, p. A1.

[4] "Painful Memories: SEC Grilled on 404 Costs," *CFO.com*, June 12, 2007.

[5] "AS5 Could Trim Audit Bills by 10%," *CFO.com*, May 4, 2007.

EXHIBIT 1 Value of IPOs by Stock Exchange (in billions)

Source: "Business Wins Its Battle to Ease a Costly Sarbanes-Oxley Rule," *The Wall Street Journal,* November 10, 2006, p. A1. Reprinted by permission of The Wall Street Journal, Copyright © 2006 Dow Jones & Company, Inc. All Rights Reserved Worldwide. License number 1767270986868.

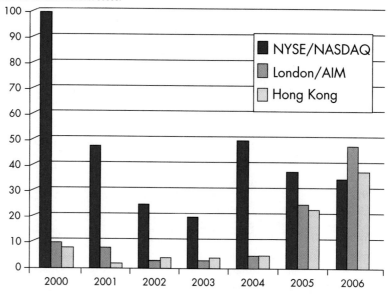

the exception of those less than 5 percent of the total revenues paid to the accounting firm) be approved by the entity's audit committee.

HOW DID SARBANES-OXLEY AFFECT ACCOUNTING FIRM REVENUES?

The above discussion suggests that Sarbanes-Oxley could have a significant (yet indeterminable) effect on accounting firm revenues. On one hand, the internal control requirements of Section 404 would presumably increase total revenues; however, the prohibition against providing financial information systems design and implementation and internal audit outsourcing services would likely reduce revenues. In addition, the requirement that all nonaudit services be approved by the entity's audit committee would presumably heighten these individuals' awareness of potential conflicts related to these services and reduce the likelihood that such services are approved (or reduce the dollar level at which they are approved).

Exhibit 2 summarizes fees paid by General Electric to its auditors (KPMG, LLP) for various years both preceding and following the issuance of Sarbanes-Oxley; Exhibit 3 provides similar information for the average of Fortune 100 and Fortune 500 companies during these same years.[6] "Audit fees" are identified based on SEC rules and include fees paid for the (1) audit of the annual financial statements, (2) review of quarterly financial statements, (3) audit of the effectiveness of

EXHIBIT 2 Fees Paid by General Electric to Auditors (in millions)

	2000	2002	2004	2006
Audit fees	$23.9	$38.7	$78.2	$85.8
Audit-related fees	15.5	23.3	15.5	20.6
Tax fees	13.8	21.2	8.9	9.0
Financial information systems fees	50.4	0.0	0.0	0.0
Other fees	0.0	6.1	0.0	0.0
Total fees	$103.6	$89.3	$102.6	$115.4

Source: Various General Electric proxy statements.

[6] The fees shown in Exhibits 2 and 3 reflect only those amounts paid to the entity's financial statement auditors. It is likely that services also are provided to these entities by other accounting firms who are not involved with the financial statement audit. However, these latter data are not publicly available.

EXHIBIT 3 Average Fees Paid by Fortune 100 (500) Companies to Auditors (in millions)

	2000		2002		2004		2006	
Audit fees	$7.1	($2.9)	$8.1	($3.5)	$16.3	($7.4)	$19.0	($8.4)
Audit-related fees	0.9	(0.5)	2.8	(1.1)	2.8	(1.2)	3.0	(1.2)
Tax fees	1.1	(0.3)	4.5	(1.6)	4.0	(1.5)	3.2	(1.2)
Financial information systems fees	3.9	(1.4)	1.0	(0.3)	0.0	(0.0)	0.0	(0.0)
Other fees	16.2	(5.9)	4.1	(1.8)	0.5	(0.2)	0.3	(0.1)
Total fees	$29.2	($11.0)	$20.5	($8.3)	$23.6	($10.3)	$25.5	($10.9)

Source: Data extracted from *Wharton Research Data Services*; Fortune 100 company data are shown outside parentheses; Fortune 500 company data are shown within parentheses.

internal control over financial reporting, (4) attestation of management's report on the effectiveness of internal control over financial reporting, and (5) other services provided in connection with statutory and regulatory filings and engagements. "Audit-related" fees include other fees that can be reasonably related to the above services as well as fees paid for due diligence and audit services on mergers and acquisitions and fees paid for audit services on employee benefit plans.

SEC-REQUIRED FEE DISCLOSURES

One additional phenomenon that may influence the fees reported by GE and the Fortune 100/500 companies in Exhibits 2 and 3 are the disclosure requirements implemented by the SEC. In November 2000, the SEC adopted requirements that registrants disclose the various types of fees paid to its financial statement auditors; under this initial guidance, audit fees included fees paid for the annual financial statement audit along with the fees paid for the reviews of quarterly financial statements. Beginning in 2003, the definition of "audit fees" was expanded by the SEC to include services that "generally only the independent accountant can reasonably provide, such as comfort letters, statutory audits, attest services, consents and assistance with and review of documents filed with the [SEC]."[7] Some argued that broadening the definition of audit fees would be misleading in terms of user perceptions of auditors' independence. Barbara Roper, director of investor protection for the Consumer Federation of America, noted that "[i]t's absolutely industry's water that's being carried here. It makes it look like their audit fees are bigger, their nonaudit fees are smaller, and it masks the conflict of interest."[8] Clearly, any comparison of fee breakdowns prior to and following Sarbanes-Oxley must take the SEC's revised definition of audit fees into consideration.

DISCUSSION QUESTIONS

1. From a conceptual standpoint, how do the requirements of Sarbanes-Oxley related to nonaudit services affect perceptions of the auditors' independence?

2. Assume your firm was auditing General Electric in 2000 and was recommending an adjustment to their financial statements that reduced net income. Based on the fees paid to your firm in 2000, what incentive(s) might your firm consider in insisting upon this adjustment? How are your firm's incentive(s) different in 2004 and 2006?

3. Compare General Electric's fees both prior to (2000 and 2002) and following (2004 and 2006) the implementation of Sarbanes-Oxley. Based on the trends in these fees and various components of these fees, comment on the effect of Sarbanes-Oxley on General Electric's fees.

4. Repeat Question (3) for the Fortune 100 and Fortune 500 companies. Are the trends for these companies similar to those for General Electric?

5. For General Electric, Fortune 100 companies, and Fortune 500 companies, can you identify the increased costs of Section 404 compliance cited in the press?

6. Based on the changes required by *AS 5*, how do you think fees paid to auditors will change in the future?

[7] Securities and Exchange Commission, "Strengthening the Commission's Requirements Regarding Auditor Independence," *Release No. 33-8183*, March 26, 2003.

[8] "Redefined by the SEC, 'Audit Fees' Get Murky," *The Wall Street Journal*, January 22, 2003.

Index

Audit Standards (PCAOB)

AS No.	Date Issued	Title
1	2004	References in Auditors' Reports to the Standards of the Public Company Accounting Oversight Board
3	2004	Audit Documentation
4	2005	Reporting on Whether a Previously Reported Material Weakness Continues to Exist
5	2007	An Audit of Internal Control over Financial Reporting That is Integrated with an Audit of Financial Statements

Government Auditing Standards (U.S. General Accounting Office)

2007 Governmental Auditing Standards (the "Yellow Book")

International Standards for the Professional Practice of Internal Auditing (IIA)

Title	Number
Attribute Standards	
Purpose, Authority, and Responsibility	1000
Independence and Objectivity	1100
Proficiency and Due Professional Care	1200
Quality Assurance and Improvement Program	1300
Performance Standards	
Managing the Internal Audit Activity	2000
Nature of Work	2100
Engagement Planning	2200
Performing the Engagement	2300
Communicating Results	2400
Monitoring Progress	2500
Resolution of Management's Acceptance of Risks	2600